ON COOKING

A TEXTBOOK OF
CULINARY FUNDAMENTALS

SARAH R. LABENSKY
ALAN M. HAUSE

PHOTOGRAPHS BY RICHARD EMBERY
DRAWINGS BY STACEY WINTERS QUATTRONE
EDITED BY STEVEN LABENSKY

PRENTICE HALL
ENGLEWOOD CLIFFS, NEW JERSEY 07632

Library of Congress Cataloging-in-Publication Data

Labensky, Sarah R.
  On Cooking: a textbook of culinary fundamentals / Sarah R.
  Labensky, Alan M. Hause.
      p. cm.
  Includes bibliographical references and index.
  ISBN 0-13-194515-7
  1. Cookery.   I. Hause, Alan M. II.   Title.
TX714.L29 1995   94-12053
641.5—dc20   CIP

Editorial/production supervision: Barbara Marttine
Interior design and electronic page layout: Laura C. Ierardi
Technical/production support: Julie Boddorf
Electronic art specialist: Rolando Corujo
Copyeditor: Nancy Velthaus
Proofreaders: Julie Boddorf/Kathryn Kasturas
Production coordinator: Ed O'Dougherty
Managing editors: Mary Carnis/Patrick Walsh
Creative director: Paula Maylahn
Cover design: Ruta Kysilewskyj
Cover photograph: Richard Embery
Acquisitions editor: Robin Baliszewski
Editorial assistant: Rose Mary Florio
Marketing manager: Ramona Sherman
Directors of production and manufacturing: Bruce Johnson/David W. Riccardi

Photo Credits:
Portrait of Fannie Farmer—courtesy of The Schlesinger Library, Radcliffe College
Portrait of Auguste Escoffier—courtesy of Musse de l'Art Culinaire, Villeneuve-Loubet (Village) France
Portraits of Alexis Soyer and Antonin Careme—courtesy of Barbara Wheaton
Drawing of the Reform Club's Kitchen—courtesy of the Reform Club, London, England

©1995 by Prentice-Hall, Inc.
A Simon & Schuster Company
Englewood Cliffs, New Jersey 07632

Printed in the United States of America
10 9 8 7 6 5 4 3 2

ISBN   0-13-194515-7

Prentice-Hall International (UK) Limited, *London*
Prentice-Hall of Australia Pty. Limited, *Sydney*
Prentice-Hall Canada Inc., *Toronto*
Prentice-Hall Hispanoamericana, S.A., *Mexico*
Prentice-Hall of India Private Limited, *New Delhi*
Prentice-Hall of Japan, Inc., *Tokyo*
Simon & Schuster Asia Pte. Ltd., *Singapore*
Editora Prentice-Hall do Brasil, Ltda., *Rio de Janeiro*

CONTENTS

PART 4
BAKING   737

PREFACE

Learning to cook is much more than simply learning to follow a recipe. Consequently, this is not a cookbook or a collection of recipes. It is a carefully designed text intended to teach you the fundamentals of the culinary arts and to prepare you for a rewarding career in the food service industry.

Many chapters have extensive illustrated sections identifying foods and equipment. Throughout the book we emphasize culinary principles, not recipes (although we include more than 550 of them). Whenever possible, we focus on the general procedure highlighting fundamental principles and skills whether it be for preparing a yeast bread or grilling a piece of fish. We discuss both the how and why of cooking. Only then are specific applications and sample recipes given.

Numerous hotel and restaurant chefs throughout the country have contributed recipes to this book, usually accompanied by photographs of the dishes as prepared in their kitchens. These recipes and illustrations allow you to explore the different techniques and presentation styles used by a range of professionals.

In order to provide you with a sense of the rich tradition of cookery, informative sidebars on food history, chef biographies and other topics are scattered throughout the book. Also included are several short essays written by prominent culinarians on topics ranging from tempering chocolate to tasting spicy foods.

We wish you much success in your culinary career and hope this text will continue to inform and inspire you long after graduation.

ACKNOWLEDGMENTS

This book would not have been possible without the assistance and support of many people. We are particularly indebted to Steve Labenksy for his countless hours with a sharp pencil, his comments and criticism and his constant support, as well as to our photographer, Richard Embery, for his professionalism and commitment to quality. Special thanks go to Kristy Riding, Tim Moore and the entire kitchen staff of Continental Catering for their support, without which this project would not have been possible. Thanks also to Leland Atkinson, Nancy Calomiris, Gaye Ingram, Lisa Kelly, Richard Martinez, Charlotte Morrissey, Ernst Reck, Chantal van de Brug and Stacey Winters Quattrone for their help. We are also grateful to the many chefs, restaurateurs, writers and culinary professionals who provided recipes and essays for this book.

The authors wish to thank the following companies for their generous donations of equipment and supplies: J.A. Henckels Zwillingswerk, Inc., All-Clad Metalcrafters, Inc. and Parrish's Cake Decorating Supplies, Inc. We also wish to thank Shamrock Foods Company, East Coast Seafood of Phoenix Inc.,

◆◆◆
A NOTE ON RECIPES

Recipes are important and useful as a means of standardizing food preparation and recording information. We include recipes that are primarily designed to reinforce and explain techniques and procedures presented in the text. Recipe yields are intentionally low in order to be less intimidating to beginning cooks and more useful in small schools and kitchens.

All ingredients are listed in both U.S. and metric measurements. The metric equivalents are rounded off to even, easily measured amounts. So, you should consider these ingredient lists as separate recipes or formulas; do not measure some ingredients according to the metric amounts and other ingredients according to the U.S. amount or the proportions will not be accurate and the intended result will not be achieved.

Throughout this book, unless otherwise noted, *mirepoix* refers to a preparation of 2 parts onion, 1 part celery and 1 part carrot by weight; *pepper* refers to ground black pepper, preferably freshly ground; *butter* refers to whole, unsalted butter, and *TT* means to taste.

Detailed procedures for standard techniques are presented in the text and generally are not repeated in each recipe. (For example, "deglaze the pan" or "monte au beurre.") No matter how detailed the written recipe, however, we must assume that you have certain knowledge, skills and judgement.

Variations appear at the end of selected recipes. These give you the opportunity to see how one set of techniques or procedures can be used to prepare different dishes with only minor modifications.

You should also reply upon the knowledge and skill of your instructor for guidance. While some skills and an understanding of theory can be acquired through reading and study, no book can substitute for repeated, hands-on preparation and observation.

KitchenAid Home Appliances, Taylor Environmental Instruments, Hobart Corporation, Williams-Sonoma, architect Michael Apostolos, and Randy Dougherty of ISF International.

Finally, we wish to thank everyone involved in this project at Prentice Hall and Paramount Publishing, including Barbara Marttine, Production Editor; Ramona Sherman, Marketing Manager; Laura Ierardi, Designer; Paula Maylahn, Creative Director; and Ruta Kysilewskjy, Advertising Art Director. As for our editor, Robin Baliszewski, this book could not have been completed without her patience, her persistence and her uncommonly good sense of humor.

The authors would also like to acknowledge the following reviewers for their comments and assistance—Richard W. Alford, University of Akron; Earl Arrowood, Bucks County Community College; Mike Artlip, Culinary School of Kendall College; Leland Atkinson; James Belch, Pennsylvania Institute of Culinary Arts; Lane Berrent, Pennsylvania Institute of Culinary Arts; Thom Boehm, Pennsylvania Institute of Culinary Arts; James Bressi, New England Culinary Institute; John D. Britto, San Joaquin Delta College; Walter Bronowitz CEE, Edmonds Community College; Mark Clink, Pennsylvania Institute of Culinary Arts; George Conte, New York Restaurant School; Noel Cullen, CMC, Boston University; Jeanne Curtis, Newbury College; William Day, Johnson & Wales University; Jim Douglas CEC: CCE, Everett Community College; Rolf Epprecht, Swiss Hospitality Institute; John Fitzpatrick; Maureen Garfolo, Pennsylvania Institute of Culinary Arts; George Geary; Jeff Graves, University of Houston/Conrad N. Hilton Hotel School; Bill Greathouse, Ivy Technical College; Kimberly Harris; Brenda Harsh, Pennsylvania Institute of Culinary Arts; Elizabeth S. Leite, Scottsdale Culinary Institute; Robert Lombardi, Spokane Community College; Deborah Lynch, Middlesex County College; Sylvia Marple M.S., R.D. , University of New Hampshire; Don McNicol, Madison Area Technical College; James Muth, Grand Rapids Community College; John Noe, Joliet Junior College; Philip H. Nudle CEC, Middlesex County College; Michael Piccinino, Shasta College; Marcia Rango; Ernst Reck; Christine Stamm, Johnson & Wales University; Clifford Steiner, New York Restaurant School; Cicely Stetson; Peter G. Tobin, Spokane Community College; and Susan Ward, Academy of Culinary Arts/Atlantic Community College.

PART ONE
PROFESSIONALISM

Chefs must be able to do more than properly prepare and present foods. They must understand traditions and factors influencing change. They are responsible for making sure that the food served is wholesome and safe to eat and that they and those around them work in a safe and efficient manner. Further, chefs must make sure that the foods they serve are nutritious or at least should offer his or her customers sufficient selection so they can construct a nutritious meal. And, finally, chefs are responsible for producing food in a cost-effective manner as well as accurately calculating, tracking and controlling the cost of food and labor in the kitchen.

Part I opens with a chapter on professionalism. It traces the history of chefs and restaurants, discusses the modern food service operation and factors influencing its development and explains what attributes a student chef must have to become a professional chef. The following chapters address food safety and sanitation, nutrition, menu planning and food costing.

CHAPTER 1 PROFESSIONALISM

"Cookery is become an art, a noble science; cooks are gentlemen."
—Robert Burton, British author, 1621

After studying this chapter you will be able to:

- discuss the development of the modern food service industry
- name key historical figures responsible for developing food service professionalism
- explain the organization of a classical kitchen brigade
- appreciate the role of the professional chef in modern food service operations
- understand the attributes a student chef needs to become a professional chef

*S*ubstitute *"professionals"* for *"gentlemen"* and Burton's words are as true today as they were almost four hundred years ago. Like the fine arts, great cookery requires taste and creativity, an appreciation of beauty and a mastery of technique. Like the sciences, successful cookery demands a certain level of knowledge and an understanding of basic principles. And, like the "gentlemen" of Burton's days, today's professional chefs must exercise sound judgment and be committed to achieving excellence in their endeavors.

This books helps implement Burton's philosophy. It describes foods and cooking equipment, explains culinary principles and cooking techniques and provides recipes utilizing these principles and techniques. This book cannot, however, provide taste, creativity, commitment and judgment. For these we rely upon you.

Chefs and Restaurants

Cooking—*(1) the transfer of energy from a heat source to a food; this energy alters the food's molecular structure, changing its texture, flavor, aroma and appearance; (2) the preparation of food for consumption.*

Cookery—*the art, practice or work of cooking.*

Professional cooking—*a system of cooking based upon a knowledge of and appreciation for ingredients and procedures.*

Cooks have produced food in quantity for as long as people have eaten together. For millennia, chefs have catered to the often elaborate dining needs of the wealthy and powerful, whether they be Asian, Native American, European or African. And for centuries, vendors in China, Europe and elsewhere have sold foods they prepared themselves or bought from others to the public.

But the history of the professional chef is of relatively recent origin. Its cast is mostly French and it is intertwined with the history of restaurants. For only with the development of restaurants during the late 18th and early 19th centuries were chefs expected to produce, efficiently and economically, different dishes at different times for different diners.

The 18th Century—Boulanger's Restaurant

The word "restaurant" is derived from the French word *restaurer* (to restore). Since the 16th century, the word "restorative" had been used to describe rich and highly flavored soups or stews capable of restoring lost strength. Restoratives, like all other cooked foods offered and purchased outside the home, were made by guild members. Each guild had a monopoly on preparing certain food items. For example, during the reign of Henri IV of France (1553–1610), there were separate guilds for *rotisseurs* (who cooked *la grosse viande*, the main cuts of meat), *patissiers* (who cooked poultry, pies and tarts), *tamisiers* (who baked breads), *vinaigriers* (who made sauces and some stews, including some restoratives), *traiteurs* (who made ragouts), and *porte-chapes* (caterers who organized feasts and celebrations).

The French claim that the first modern restaurant opened one day in 1765 when a Parisian tavernkeeper, a Monsieur Boulanger, hung a sign advertising the sale of his special restorative, a dish of sheep feet in white sauce. His establishment closed shortly thereafter as the result of lawsuit brought by a guild whose members claimed that Boulanger was infringing on their exclusive right to sell prepared dishes. Boulanger triumphed in court and later reopened.

Boulanger's establishment differed from the inns and taverns that had existed throughout Europe for centuries. These inns and taverns served foods prepared (usually off-premises) by the appropriate guild. The food—of which there was little choice—was offered by the keeper as incidental to the establishment's primary function: providing sleeping accommodations or drink. Customers were served family-style and ate at communal tables. Boulanger's contribution to the food service industry was to serve a variety of foods prepared on premises to customers whose primary interest was dining.

Several other restaurants opened in Paris during the succeeding decades, including the Grande Taverne de Londres in 1782. Its owner, Antoine Beauvilliers (1754–1817), was the former steward to the Comte de Provence, later King Louis XVIII of France. He advanced the development of the modern restaurant by offering his wealthy patrons a menu listing available dishes during fixed hours. Beauvilliers' impeccably trained wait staff served patrons at small, individual tables in an elegant setting.

The French Revolution (1789–1799) had a significant effect on the budding restaurant industry. Along with the aristocracy, guilds and their monopolies were generally abolished. The revolution also allowed the public access to the skills and creativity of the well-trained, sophisticated chefs who had worked in the aristocracy's private kitchens. Although many of the aristocracy's chefs either left the country or lost their jobs (and, some, their heads), a few opened restaurants catering to the growing urbanized middle class.

The Early 19th Century— *Carême and* Grande Cuisine

As the 19th century progressed, more restaurants opened, serving a greater selection of items and catering to a wider clientele. By mid-century, there were several large, grand restaurants in Paris serving elaborate meals, decidedly reminiscent of the *grande cuisine* (also known as *haute cuisine*) of the aristocracy. **Grande cuisine**, which arguably reached its peak of perfection in the hands of Antonin Carême, was characterized by meals consisting of dozens of courses of elaborately and intricately prepared, presented, garnished and sauced foods. Other restaurateurs blended the techniques and styles of *grande cuisine* with the simpler foods and tastes of the middle class (*cuisine bourgeoise*) to create a new cuisine simpler than *grande cuisine* but more than mere home cooking.

Grande cuisine—*the rich, intricate and elaborate cuisine of the 18th- and 19th-century French aristocracy and upper classes. It is based upon the rational identification, development and adoption of strict culinary principles. By emphasizing the how and why of cooking,* grande cuisine *was the first to distinguish itself from regional cuisines, which tend to emphasize the tradition of cooking.*

The Late 19th Century— *Escoffier and* Cuisine Classique

Following the lead set by the French in both culinary style and the restaurant business, restaurants opened in the United States and throughout Europe during the 19th century. Charles Ranhofer (1836–1899) was the first internationally renowned chef of an American restaurant, Delmonico's in New York City. In 1893 Ranhofer published his "franco-american" encyclopedia of cooking, *The Epicurean*, containing more than 3500 recipes.

Classic cuisine—*a late 19th- and early 20th-century refinement and simplification of French grande cuisine. Classic (or classical) cuisine relies upon the thorough exploration of culinary principles and techniques, and emphasizes the refined preparation and presentation of superb ingredients.*

♦♦♦

MARIE-ANTOINE (ANTONIN) CARÊME (1783–1833)

Carême, known as the "cook of kings and the king of cooks," was an acknowledged master of French *grande cuisine*. Abandoned on the streets of Paris as a child, he worked his way from cook's helper in a working-class restaurant to become one of the most prestigious chefs of his (or, arguably, any other) time. During his career he was chef to the famous French diplomat and gourmand Prince de Talleyrand, the Prince Regent of England (who became King George IV), Tsar Alexander I of Russia and Baron de Rothschild, among others.

His stated goal was to achieve "lightness," "grace," "order" and "perspicuity" in the preparation and presentation of food. As a *patissier*, he designed and prepared elaborate and elegant pastry and confectionery creations, many of which were based on architectural designs. (He wrote that "the fine arts are five in number, namely: painting, sculpture, poetry, music, architecture—the main branch of which is confectionery.") As a showman, he garnished his dishes with ornamental hatelets (skewers) threaded with colorful ingredients such as crayfish and intricately carved vegetables, and presented his creations on elaborate socles (bases). As a *saucier*, he standardized the use of roux as a thickening agent, perfected recipes and devised a system for sauce classification. As a *garde-manger*, Carême popularized cold cuisine, emphasizing molds and aspic dishes. As a culinary professional, he designed kitchen tools, equipment and uniforms.

As an author, he wrote and illustrated important texts on the culinary arts, including *Le Maitre d'hotel francais* (1822), describing the hundreds of dish-

Courtesy of Barbara Wheaton

es he personally created and cooked in the capitals of Europe; *Le Patissier royal parisian* (1825), containing fanciful designs for *les pieces montées*, the great decorative centerpieces that were the crowning glory of grand dinners; and his five-volume masterpiece on the state of his profession, *L'Art de la cuisine au XIXe siecle* (1833), the last two volumes of which were completed after his death by his associate Plumerey. Carême's writings almost

single-handedly refined and summarized five hundred years of culinary evolution. But his treatises were not mere cookbooks. Rather, he analyzed cooking, old and new, emphasizing procedure and order and covering every aspect of the art known as *grande cuisine*.

Carême died before the age of 50, burnt out, according to Laurent Tailhade, "by the flame of his genius and the coal of the spits." But this may have been the glory he sought, for he once wrote:

Imagine yourself in a large kitchen at the moment of a great dinner. … [S]ee twenty chefs coming, going, moving with speed in this cauldron of heat, look at the great mass of charcoal, a cubic meter for the cooking of entrees, and another mass on the ovens for the cooking of soups, sauces, ragouts, for frying and the water baths. Add to that a heap of burning wood in front of which four spits are turning, one which bears a sirloin weighing 45–50 pounds, the other fowl or game. In this furnace everyone moves with speed; not a sound is heard, only the chef has a right to speak, and at the sound of his voice, everyone obeys. Finally, the last straw; for about half an hour, all windows are closed so that the air does not cool the dishes as they are being served. This is the way we spend the best years of our lives. We must obey even when physical strength fails, but it is the burning charcoal that kills us. … [C]harcoal kills us but what does it matter? The shorter the life, the greater the glory.

One of the finest restaurants outside of France was the dining room at London's Savoy Hotel, opened in 1898 under the directions of Cesar Ritz (1850–1918) and Auguste Escoffier. Escoffier is generally credited with refining the *grande cuisine* of Carême to create *cuisine classique* or **classic cuisine**. By doing so, he brought French cuisine into the 20th century.

◆◆◆
AUGUSTE ESCOFFIER
(1846–1935)

Escoffier's brilliant culinary career began at the age of 13 in his uncle's restaurant and continued until his death at the age of 89. Called the "Emperor of the world's kitchens," he is perhaps best known for defining French cuisine and dining during *La Belle Epoque* (the "Gay Nineties").

Unlike Carême, Escoffier never worked in an aristocratic household. Rather, he exhibited his culinary skills in the dining rooms of the finest hotels in Europe, including the Place Vendôme in Paris and the Savoy and Carlton Hotels in London.

Escoffier did much to enhance the *grande cuisine* that arguably reached its perfection under Carême. Crediting Carême with providing the foundation for great—that is, French—cooking, Escoffier simplified the profusion of flavors, dishes and garnishes typifying Carême's work. He also streamlined some of Carême's overly elaborate and fussy procedures and classifications. For example, he reduced Carême's elaborate system of classify-

ing sauces into the five families of sauces still recognized today. Escoffier sought simplicity and aimed for the perfect balance of a few superb ingredients. Some consider his refinement of *grande cuisine* to have been so radical as to credit him

with the development of a new cuisine referred to as *cuisine classique* (classic or classical cuisine).

His many writings include *Le Livre des menus* (1912), in which, discussing the principles of a well-planned meal, he analogizes a great dinner to a symphony with contrasting movements that should be appropriate to the occasion, the guests, and the season, and *Ma cuisine* (1934), surveying *cuisine bourgeoisie*. But his most important contribution is a culinary treatise intended for the professional chef entitled *Le Guide culinaire* (1903). Still in use today, it is an astounding collection of more than five thousand classic cuisine recipes and garnishes. In it, Escoffier emphasizes technique and the thorough understanding of basic cookery principles and ingredients he considers to be the building blocks professional chefs should use to create great dishes.

Escoffier was honored as a Chevalier of the French Legion of Honour in 1920 for his work in enhancing the reputation of French cuisine.

The 20th Century—Point and Nouvelle Cuisine

This century has witnessed a trend toward lighter, more naturally flavored and more simply prepared foods. Fernand Point was a master practitioner of this movement. But this master's goal of simplicity and refinement was carried to even greater heights by a generation of chefs Point trained: principally, Paul Bocuse, Jean and Pierre Troisgros, Alain Chapel, Francois Bise and Louis

◆◆◆
FERNAND POINT
(1897–1955)

A massive man with a monumental personality, Point refined and modernized the classic cuisine of Escoffier. By doing so, he laid the foundations for *nouvelle cuisine*.

Point received his early training in some of the finest hotel-restaurant kitchens in Paris. In 1922 he and his family moved to Vienne, a city in southwest France near Lyon, and opened a restaurant. Two years later his father left the restaurant to Fernand, who renamed it *La*

Pyramide. During the succeeding years it became one of the culinary wonders of the world.

Point disdained dominating sauces and distracting accompaniments and garnishes. He believed that each dish should have a single dominant ingredient, flavor or theme; garnishes must be simple and match "like a tie to a suit." Procedure was of great importance. He devoted equal efforts to frying an egg and creat-

ing the marjolaine (a light almond and hazelnut spongecake filled with chocolate and praline buttercreams). His goal was to use the finest of raw ingredients to produce perfect food that looked elegant and simple. But simplicity was not easy to achieve. As he once said, " a bearnaise sauce is simply an egg yolk, a shallot, a little tarragon vinegar, and butter, but it takes years of practice for the result to be perfect."

Nouvelle cuisine—*literally, "new cooking," a mid-20th-century movement away from many classic cuisine principles and toward a lighter cuisine based on natural flavors and simpler preparations.*

Outhier. They, along with Michel Guérard and Roger Vergé, were the pioneers of **nouvelle cuisine** in the early 1970s.

Their culinary philosophy was principled on the rejection of overly rich, needlessly complicated dishes. These chefs emphasized healthful eating. The ingredients must be absolutely fresh and of the highest possible quality; the cooking methods should be simple and direct whenever possible. The accompaniments and garnishes must be light and must contribute to an overall harmony; the completed plates must be elegantly designed and decorated. Following these guidelines, some traditional cooking methods have been applied to untraditional ingredients, and ingredients have been combined in new and previously unorthodox fashions. For chefs with taste, skill, knowledge and judgment, this works.

INFLUENCES ON MODERN FOOD SERVICE OPERATIONS

From Monsieur Boulanger's humble establishment, a great industry has grown. Today there are more than 700,000 public dining facilities in the United States alone. The dramatic growth and diversification of the food service industry is due in part to the Industrial Revolution and the social and economic changes it wrought, including the introduction of new technologies, foods, concerns and consumers.

New Technologies

Technology has always had a profound effect on cooking. For example, the development of clay and, later, metal vessels that could contain liquids and withstand as well as conduct heat offered prehistoric cooks the opportunity to stew, make soups and porridge, pickle and brine foods and control fermentation. But it was not until the rapid technological advances fostered by the Industrial Revolution that anything approaching the modern kitchen was possible.

One of the most important advancements was the introduction of the cast iron stove. Prior to the 19th century, most cooking was done on spits or grills or in cauldrons or pots set on or in a wood- or coal-burning hearth. Hearthside cooking did not lend itself well to the simultaneous preparation of many items nor to items requiring constant and delicate attention. With the introduction of cast iron stoves during the 1800s (first wood- and coal-burning, then by mid-century, gas and, by the early 20th century, electric), cooks could more comfortably and safely approach the heat source and control its temperatures. They were also able to efficiently prepare and hold a multitude of smaller amounts of items requiring different cooking methods or ingredients for later use or service, a necessity at a restaurant simultaneously catering to different diners' demands.

Also of great importance were developments in food preservation and storage techniques. For thousands of years, food had been preserved by sun-drying, salting, smoking, pickling, sugar-curing or fermenting. Although useful, these procedures destroy or distort the appearance and flavor of most foods. By the early 19th century, preserving techniques that had minimal effect on appearance and flavor began to emerge. For example, by 1800 the Frenchman François Appert successfully "canned" foods by subjecting foods stored in sterilized glass jars to very high heat. An early mechanical refrigerator was developed by the mid-1800s; soon reliable iceboxes, refrigerators and, later, freezers were available. During the 20th century, freeze-drying, vacuum-packing and irradiation have become common preservation techniques.

While advancements were being made in preservation and storage techniques, developments in transportation technology were also underway. During the 19th century, steam-powered ships and railroads were able to bring foods quickly to market from distant suppliers. Indeed, by the 1870s, Chicago meatpackers were routinely supplying Europe with beef from the western plains. During the 20th century, temperature-controlled cargo ships, trains, trucks and airplanes all have been used as part of an integrated worldwide food transportation network.

Combined with dependable food preservation and storage techniques, improved transportation networks have freed chefs from seasonal and geographic limitations in their choice of foods and have expanded consumers' culinary horizons.

Engineering advancements also have facilitated or even eliminated much routine kitchen work. Since the start of the Industrial Revolution, chefs have come to rely increasingly on mechanical and motorized food processors, mixers and cutters as well as a wealth of sophisticated kitchen equipment such as high carbon stainless steel knife blades and convection steamers.

New Foods

Modern food preservation, storage, and transportation techniques have made both fresh and exotic foods regularly available to chefs and consumers. Many of these foods are themselves more wholesome as the result of progress in agriculture and animal husbandry.

Advancements in agriculture such as the switch from organic to chemical fertilizers and the introduction of pesticides and drought- or pest-resistant strains have resulted in increased yields of healthy crops. Traditional hybridization techniques and, more recently, genetic engineering have produced new or improved grains and, for better or for worse, fruits and vegetables that have a longer shelf life and are more amenable to mass-production handling, storage and transportation methods.

Likewise, advancements in animal husbandry and aquaculture have led to a more reliable supply of leaner, healthier meat, poultry and fish. Moreover, foods found traditionally only in the wild (for example game, wild rice and many mushrooms) are now being raised commercially and are routinely available.

Food preservation and processing techniques have also led to the development of prepackaged, prepared convenience foods, some of which are actually quite good. After careful thought and testing, today's chef can rely on some of these products. Doing so allows greater flexibility and more time to devote to other preparations.

New Concerns

Consumer concerns about nutrition and diet, particularly during the last decade or so, have fueled changes in the food service industry. Obviously, what we eat affects our health. Adequate amounts of certain nutrients promote good health by preventing deficiencies; good nutrition also helps prevent chronic diseases and increases longevity. Chefs should provide their customers with nutritious foods.

The public has long been concerned about food safety. Federal, state and local governments have helped promote food safety by inspecting and grading meats and poultry, regulating label contents for packaged foods and setting sanitation standards. All these standards, especially sanitation standards, affect the way foods are prepared, stored and served.

Concerns about nutrition and food safety have also resulted in renewed interest in organically grown fruits and vegetables and free-range-raised animals.

◆◆◆
CULINARY FRENCH

Perhaps one of the most enduring legacies of French chefs and culinarians is the common usage of many French words in today's professional kitchens. Some, like *canapé* and *bain marie*, are simply the name of a food item or piece of equipment of French origin. Others, such as *sauté*, are French verbs with no equally terse and descriptive English counterpart. Still others, for example, *julienne*, are not only used as nouns (julienne of carrot), but also as verbs (to julienne a carrot) and adjectives (julienned carrot). Often we forget the origins of these words and spell them without the original accent marks.

Here we list just a few of the more commonly encountered culinary French terms. As you study this book, note how many other words are of French origin.

Bain marie (bane mah-ree)—a hot-water bath for gently cooking foods or keeping cooked foods hot; the container holding the food in the hot water bath is also referred to as a bain marie.

Brunoise (broo-nwahz)—cube-shaped cuts (1/8 inch by 1/8 inch by 1/8 inch) of vegetables or other foods.

Canapé (kahn-ah-pay)—an hors d'oeuvre (another French term, meaning appetizer) usually composed of a small piece of bread or toast topped with a savory spread and garnish.

Chef (chehf)—literally, "leader" or "chief," the person in charge of a kitchen or department.

Demi-glace (de-me glass)—literally, "half-glaze," a mixture of brown stock and brown sauce reduced by half.

Ganache (gah-nasch)—a rich pastry or candy filling made with chocolate, heavy cream, and other flavorings.

Julienne (ju-lee-en)—noun: stick-shaped cuts (1/8 inch by 1/8 inch by 1 to 2 inches) of vegetables or other foods; verb: to cut food into the stick-shaped piece; adj.: stick-shaped.

Mayonnaise (may-o-nayz)—a basic cold emulsion sauce made of egg yolks and oil and seasoned with vinegar, mustard, and seasonings.

Mirepoix (meer-pwa)—a mixture of onions, carrots, and celery, used to flavor stocks, stews, and other dishes.

Mise en place (meez on plahs)—literally, "everything in place," the preparation and assembly of all ingredients and equipment needed before a dish can be cooked.

Purée (pur-ray)—noun: food that is processed by mashing, straining or fine chopping to achieve a smooth pulp; verb: to process food to achieve a smooth pulp.

Rondeau (ron-doe)—a shallow, wide, straight-sided pot with two loop handles.

Roux (roo)—a thickener for sauces made by cooking together equal parts of fat and flour.

Sachet (sa-shay)—or Sachet d'épices (sa-shay day pees), literally "bag of spices," aromatic ingredients such as bay leaf, thyme, cloves, peppercorns and parsley stems, tied in a cheesecloth bag and used to flavor stocks and other dishes.

Sauté (saw-tay)—to cook in an open pan in a small amount of fat at high temperature.

Sous-chef (sue chehf)—literally "under chef," the chef who is second in command of a kitchen.

Vinaigrette (vih-nay-greht)—a temporary emulsion of oil and vinegar seasoned with herbs, salt and pepper.

New Consumers

Demographic and social changes have contributed to the diversification of the food service industry by creating or identifying new consumer groups with their own desires or needs. By tailoring their menu, prices and décor accordingly, food service operations cater to consumers defined by age (baby boomers and seniors, in particular), type of household (singles, couples and families), income, education and geography.

During this century, especially in the decades following World War II, there has also been a rapid increase in the number and type of institutions providing food services. These include hospitals, schools, retirement centers, hotels and resorts (which may, in turn, have fine dining, coffee shop, banquet and room service facilities), factories and office complexes. Each of these institutions presents the professional chef with unique challenges, whether they be culinary, dietary or budgetary.

Through travel or exposure to the many books and magazines about food, consumers are becoming better educated and more sophisticated. Educated consumers provide a market for new foods and cuisines as well as an appreciation for a job well done.

Although some consumers may frequent a particular restaurant because its chef or owner is a celebrity or the restaurant is riding high on a crest of fad or fashion, most consumers choose a restaurant—whether it be a fast-food burger place or an elegant French restaurant—because it provides quality food at a cost they are willing to pay. To remain successful, then, the restaurant must carefully balance its commitment to quality with marketplace realities.

The Food Service Operation

To function efficiently, a food service operation must be well organized and staffed with appropriate personnel. This staff is sometimes called a **brigade**. Although a chef will be most familiar with the back of the house or kitchen brigade, he or she should also understand how the dining room or front of the house operates. Staffing any food service facility ultimately depends on the type and complexity of the menu. (Types and styles of menus are discussed in Chapter 4, Menu Planning and Food Costing.)

Escoffier is credited with developing the kitchen brigade system used in large restaurant kitchens. From the chaos and redundancy found in the private kitchens of the aristocracy, he created a distinct hierarchy of responsibilities and functions for commercial food service operations.

Brigade—*a system of staffing a kitchen so that each worker is assigned a set of specific tasks; these tasks are often related by cooking method, equipment or the type of foods being produced.*

The Classic Kitchen Brigade

At the top is the *chef du cuisine* or *chef*, who is responsible for all kitchen operations, developing menu items and setting the kitchen's tone and tempo.

His or her principal assistant is the *sous-chef* (the under chef or second chef), who is responsible for scheduling personnel and replacing the chef and station chefs as necessary. The *sous-chef* also often functions as the *aboyeur* (expediter or announcer), who accepts the orders from the dining room, relays them to the various station chefs and then reviews the dishes before service.

The *chefs de partie* (station chefs) produce the menu items and are under the direct supervision of the chef or *sous-chef*. Previously, whenever a cook needed an item, he or his assistants produced it; thus several cooks could be making the same sauce or basic preparation. Under Escoffier's system, each station chef is assigned a specific task based upon either cooking method and equipment or the category of items to be produced. They include:

◆ The *saucier* (sauté station chef), who holds one of the most demanding jobs in the kitchen, is responsible for all sautéed items and most sauces.

◆ The *poissonier* (fish station chef) is responsible for fish and shellfish items and their sauces. This position is occasionally combined with the sauce station.

◆ The *grillardin* (grill station chef) is responsible for all grilled items.

◆ The *friturier* (fry station chef) is responsible for all fried items.

◆ The *rotisseur* (roast station chef) is responsible for all roasted items and jus or other related sauces. The grill and fry stations are sometimes subsumed into the roast station.

◆ The *potager* (soup station chef) is responsible for soups and stocks.

◆ The *legumier* (vegetable station chef) is responsible for all vegetable and starch items.

◆ The *potager* and *legumier* functions are often combined into a single vegetable station whose chef is known as the *entremetier*. *Entremets* were the courses served after the roast and were usually composed of vegetables, fruits, fritters or sweet items (the sorbet served before the main course in some contemporary restaurants is a vestigial *entremet*).

◆ The *garde-manger* (pantry chef) is responsible for cold food preparations, including salads and salad dressings, cold appetizers, charcuterie items, pâtés, terrines and similar dishes. The *garde-manger* supervises:

> The *boucher* (butcher), who is responsible for butchering meats and poultry (fish and shellfish are usually fabricated by the fish station chef).

> Also under the *garde-manger*'s supervision are the chefs responsible for hors d'oeuvre and breakfast items.

◆ The *tournant*, also known as the roundsman or swing cook, works where needed.

◆ The *patissier* (pastry chef) is responsible for all baked items, including breads, pastries and desserts. Unlike the several station chefs, the *patissier* is not necessarily under the *sous-chef*'s direct supervision. The *patissier* supervises the following:

> The *boulanger* (bread baker), who makes the breads, rolls and baked dough containers used for other menu items (for example, *bouchées* and *feuilletés*).

> The *confiseur*, who makes candies and petits fours.

> The *glacier*, who makes all chilled and frozen desserts.

> The *decorateur*, who makes showpieces and special cakes.

◆ Depending upon the size and needs of any station or area, there are one or more *demi-chefs* (assistants) and *commis* (apprentices) who work with the station chef or pastry chef to learn the area.

The Modern Kitchen Brigade

Today most food service operations utilize a simplified version of Escoffier's kitchen brigade.

The **executive chef** coordinates kitchen activities and directs the kitchen staff's training and work efforts. Taking into consideration factors such as food costs, food availability and popularity as well as labor costs, kitchen skills and equipment, the executive chef plans menus and creates recipes. He or she sets and enforces nutrition, safety and sanitation standards and participates in (or at least observes) the preparation and presentation of menu items to ensure that quality standards are rigorously and consistently maintained. He or she is also responsible for purchasing food items and, often, equipment. In some food service operations, the executive chef may assist in designing the menu, dining room and kitchen. He or she also educates the dining room staff so they can correctly answer questions about the menu. He or she may also work with food purveyors to learn about new food items and products, as well as with equipment vendors, food stylists, restaurant consultants, public relations specialists, sanitation engineers, nutritionists and dietitians.

The executive chef is assisted by a **sous-chef** or **executive sous-chef**, who participates in, supervises and coordinates the preparation of menu items. His or her primary responsibility is to make sure that the food is pre-

---

◆◆◆
THE DINING ROOM

Like the back-of-the-house (i.e., kitchen) staff, the front-of-the-house (i.e., dining room) staff is also organized into a brigade. The dining room brigade is led by the **dining room manager** (French *maître d'hotel* or *maître d'*), who generally trains all service personnel, oversees wine selections and works with the chef to develop the menu. He or she organizes the seating chart and may also seat the guests. Working subordinate to him are:

The **wine steward** (French *chef de vin* or *sommelier*), who is responsible for the wine service, including purchasing wines, assisting guests in selecting wines and then serving the wine.

The **headwaiter** (French *chef de salle*), who is responsible for service throughout the dining room or a section of it. In smaller operations, his or her role may be assumed by the *maître d'* or a captain.

The **captains** (French *chefs d'étage*), who are responsible for explaining the menu to guests and taking their orders. They are also responsible for any tableside preparations.

The **front waiters** (French *chefs de rang*), who are responsible for assuring that the tables are set properly for each course, foods are delivered properly to the proper tables and the needs of the guests are met.

The **backwaiters** (French *demi-chefs de rang* or *commis de rang*, also known as dining room attendants or buspersons), who are responsible for clearing plates, refilling water glasses and other general tasks appropriate for new dining room workers.

Whether a restaurant uses this entire array of staff depends upon the nature and size of the restaurant and the type of service provided. With **American service** there is one waiter (also called a server) who takes the order and brings the food to the table. The table is then cleaned by a dining room attendant. With **French service** there are two waiters: a captain and a waiter. The captain takes the order, does the tableside cooking and brings the drinks, appetizers, entrees and desserts to the table. The waiter serves bread and water, clears each course, crumbs the table and serves the coffee. With **Russian service**, the entree, vegetables and potatoes are served from a platter onto a plate by the waiter. With **buffet service**, usually found in specialty restaurants and some institutional settings such as schools and correctional facilities, diners generally serve themselves or are served by workers assigned to specific areas of the buffet. Restaurants offering buffet service generally charge by the meal; if they charge by the dish they are known as cafeterias.

pared, portioned, garnished and presented according to the executive chef's standards. The sous-chef may be the cook principally responsible for producing menu items and supervising the kitchen.

Large hotels and conference centers with multiple dining facilities may have one or more **area chefs**, each responsible for a specific facility or function. There could be, for instance, a restaurant chef and a banquet chef. Area chefs usually report to the executive chef. Each area chef in turn has a brigade working under him or her.

Like Escoffier's station chefs, **cooks** (or section cooks) are responsible for preparing menu items according to recipe specifications. Making the most of time, talent, space and equipment, the chef assigns responsibilities to each of the line cooks. Depending upon the size and type of operation, the sauté, broiler, fry, soup and vegetable stations may be combined into one position, as may be the pantry, cold foods and salad stations.

The **pastry chef** is responsible for developing recipes for and preparing desserts, pastries, frozen desserts and breads. He or she is usually responsible for purchasing the food items used in the bake shop.

And, as in Escoffier's days, **assistants** and **apprentices** are assigned where needed in today's kitchens.

New styles of dining have created new positions since Escoffier's days. The most notable is the **short-order cook**, who is responsible for quickly preparing foods to order in smaller operations. He or she will work the broiler, deep fryer and griddle as well as make sandwiches and even some sautéed items.

Another is the **institutional cook**, who generally works with large quantities of prepackaged or prepared foods for a captive market such as a school, hospital or prison.

THE PROFESSIONAL CHEF

Although there is no one recipe for producing a good professional chef, we believe that with knowledge, skill, taste, judgment, dedication and pride a student chef will mature into a professional chef.

Knowledge

Chefs must be able to identify, purchase, utilize and prepare a wide variety of foods. They should be able to train and supervise a safe, skilled and efficient staff. To do all this successfully, chefs must possess a body of knowledge and understand and apply certain scientific and business principles. Schooling helps. A culinary program—whether at the secondary or post-secondary level—should, at a minimum, provide the student chef with a basic knowledge of foods, food styles and the methods used to prepare foods. Student chefs should also have an understanding of sanitation, nutrition and business procedures such as food costing.

This book is designed to help you learn these basics. Many chapters have extensive sections identifying foods and equipment. Throughout this book we emphasize culinary principles, not recipes. Whenever possible, whether it be preparing puff pastry or grilling a steak, we focus on the general procedure, highlighting fundamental principles and skills; we discuss both the how and why of cooking. Only then are specific applications and sample recipes given. We also want you to have a sense of the rich tradition of cookery, so informative sidebars on food history, chef biographies and other topics are scattered throughout the book.

In this way, we follow the trail blazed by Escoffier, who wrote in the introduction to *Le Guide culinaire* that his book is not intended to be a compendium of recipes slavishly followed, but rather his treatise should be a tool that leaves his colleagues "free to develop their own methods and follow their own inspiration; ... the art of cooking ... will evolve as a society evolves, ... only basic rules remain unalterable."

As with any profession, an education does not stop at graduation. The acquisition of knowledge continues after the student chef joins the ranks of the employed. He or she should take additional classes on unique or ethnic cuisines, nutrition, business management or specialized skills. He or she should regularly review some of the many periodicals and books devoted to cooking; he or she should travel and try new dishes to broaden his or her culinary horizons. He or she should also become involved in professional organizations in order to meet his peers and exchange ideas.

Skill

Schooling alone does not make a student a chef. Nothing but practical, hands-on experience will provide even the most academically gifted student with the skills needed to produce, consistently and efficiently, quality foods or to organize, train, motivate and supervise a staff.

Many food service operations recognize that new workers, even those who have graduated from culinary programs, need time and experience to develop and hone their skills. Therefore, many graduates start at entry-level positions. They should not be discouraged; advancement will come and the training pays off in the long run. Today culinary styles and fashions change frequently. What does not go out of fashion are well-trained, skilled and knowledgeable chefs. They can adapt.

Taste

No matter how knowledgeable or skilled the chef, he or she must be able to produce food that tastes great or the consumer will not return. He or she can only do so if he is confident about his own sense of taste.

Our total perception of taste is a complex combination of smell, taste, sight, sound and texture. All senses are involved in the enjoyment of eating; all must be considered in creating or preparing a dish. The chef should develop a taste memory by sampling foods, both familiar and unfamiliar. He or she should think about what he or she tastes, making notes and experimenting with flavor combinations and cooking methods. But he or she should not be inventive simply for the sake of invention. Rather, he or she must consider how the flavors, appearances, textures and aromas of various foods will interact to create a total taste experience.

Judgment

Selecting menu items, determining how much of what item to order, deciding whether and how to combine ingredients and approving finished items for service are all matters of judgment. Although knowledge and skill play a role in developing judgment, sound judgment comes only with experience.

Gastronomy—*the art and science of eating well.*

Gourmet—*a connoisseur of fine food and drink.*

Gourmand—*a connoisseur of fine food and drink, often to excess.*

Gourmet foods—*foods of the highest quality, perfectly prepared and beautifully presented.*

Dedication

Becoming a chef is hard work; so is being one. The work is often physically taxing, the hours are usually long and the pace is frequently hectic. Despite these pressures, the chef is expected to efficiently produce consistently fine foods that are properly prepared, seasoned, garnished and presented. To do so, the chef must be dedicated to the job.

The dedicated chef should never falter. The food service industry is competitive and dependent upon the continuing good will of an often fickle public. One bad dish or one off night can result in a disgruntled diner and lost business. The chef should always be mindful of the food prepared and the customer served.

The chef must also be dedicated to his or her staff. Virtually all food service operations rely on teamwork to get the job done well. Good teamwork requires dedication to a shared goal as well as a positive attitude.

Pride

Not only is it important that the job be well done, but the professional chef should have a sense of pride in doing it well. Pride should also extend to personal appearance and behavior in and around the kitchen. The professional chef should be well-groomed and in uniform when working.

The professional chef's uniform consists of comfortable shoes, trousers (either solid white, solid black, black-and-white checked or black-and-white striped), a white double-breasted jacket, an apron and a neckerchief usually knotted or tied cravat style. The uniform has certain utilitarian aspects: Checked trousers disguise stains; the double-breasted white jacket can be rebuttoned to hide dirt, and the double layer of fabric protects from scalds and burns; the neckerchief absorbs facial perspiration; and the apron protects the uniform and insulates the body. This uniform should be worn with pride. Shoes should be polished; trousers and jacket should be pressed.

The crowning element of your uniform is your toque. The toque is the tall white hat worn by chefs almost everywhere. Although the toque traces its origin to the monasteries of the 6th century, the style worn today was introduced at the end of the 19th century. Most chefs now wear a standard six- or nine-inch-high toque, but historically a cook's rank in the kitchen dictated the type of hat worn. Beginners wore flat-topped calottes; cooks with more advanced skills wore low toques and the master chefs wore high toques called *dodin-bouffants*. Culinary lore holds that the toque's pleats—101 in all—represent the 101 ways its wearer can successfully prepare eggs.

 ONCLUSION

The art and science of cookery form a noble profession with a rich history and long traditions. With knowledge, skill, taste, judgment, dedication and pride, the student chef can become part of this profession. In this book we provide you with the basic knowledge and describe the techniques at which you must become skilled. Dedicate yourself to learning this information and mastering your skills. Once you have done so, take pride in your accomplishments. Good luck.

QUESTIONS FOR DISCUSSION

1. Describe the kitchen brigade system. What is its significance in today's professional kitchens?
2. What are the roles of a chef, sous-chef and line cook in a modern kitchen?
3. Describe the differences in a meal prepared by Carême and one prepared by Point.
4. List and explain three technological advances affecting food preparation.
5. Discuss the societal changes that have contributed to diversification in the modern food service industry.

CHAPTER 2
FOOD SAFETY AND SANITATION

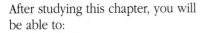
The United States Public Health Service identifies more than forty diseases that can be transmitted though food. Many can cause serious illness; some are even deadly. Providing consumers with safe food is the food handler's most important responsibility. Food handlers include anyone coming in contact with food or food preparation equipment. Unfortunately, food handlers are also the primary cause of food-related illnesses.

By understanding how food-borne illnesses are caused and what can be done to prevent them, you will be better able to protect your customers. This chapter is not meant to be a complete discussion of sanitation in food service operations. It should, however, alert you to practices that can result in food-borne illnesses.

Federal, state, county and municipal health, building and other codes are designed in part to ensure that food is handled in a safe and proper manner. Always consult your local health department for information and guidance. And always be conscious of what you can do to create and maintain a safe product and safe environment for your customers, your fellow employees and yourself.

Biological hazard—*a danger to the safety of food caused by disease-causing microorganisms such as bacteria, molds, yeasts, viruses or fungi.*

Chemical hazard—*a danger to the safety of food caused by chemical substances, especially cleaning agents, pesticides and toxic metals.*

Physical hazard—*a danger to the safety of food caused by particles such as glass chips, metal shavings, bits of wood or other foreign matter.*

Sanitation refers to the creation and maintenance of conditions that will prevent food contamination or food-borne illness. **Contamination** refers to the presence, generally unintentional, of harmful organisms or substances. Contaminants can be (1) biological, (2) chemical or (3) physical. When consumed in sufficient quantities, food-borne contaminants can cause illness or injury, long-lasting disease or even death.

Contamination occurs in two ways: direct contamination and cross-contamination. **Direct contamination** is the contamination of raw foods, or the plants or animals from which they come, in their natural setting or habitat. Chemical and biological contaminants such as bacteria and fungi are present in the air, soil and water. So, foods can be easily contaminated by general exposure to the environment: Grains can become contaminated by soil fumigants in the field and shellfish can become contaminated by ingesting toxic marine algae.

Chemicals and microorganisms generally cannot move on their own, however. They need to be transported, an event known as **cross-contamination**. The major cause of cross-contamination is people. Food handlers can transfer biological, chemical and physical contaminants to food while processing, preparing, cooking or serving it. It is therefore necessary to view sanitation as the correction of problems caused by direct contamination and the prevention of cross-contamination during processing and service.

DIRECT CONTAMINATION

Biological Contaminants

Biologically based food-borne illnesses can be caused by several **microorganisms**, primarily bacteria, parasites, viruses and fungi. By understanding how these organisms live and reproduce, you can better understand how to protect food from them.

> **Microorganism**—*single-celled organisms as well as tiny plants and animals that can only be seen through a microscope.*

Bacteria

Bacteria, which are single-celled microorganisms, are the leading cause of food-borne illnesses. See Figure 2.1. Most bacteria reproduce by binary fission: Their genetic material is first duplicated and the nucleus then splits, each new nucleus taking some of the cellular material with it. See Figure 2.2. Under favorable conditions each bacterium can divide every 15–30 minutes. Within 12 hours, one bacterium can become a colony of 72 billion bacteria, more than enough to cause serious illness.

Some rod-shaped bacteria are capable of forming spores. Spores are thick-walled structures used as protection against a hostile environment. The bacteria essentially hibernate within their spores where they can survive extreme conditions that would otherwise destroy them. When conditions become favorable, the bacteria return to a viable state. This is important in food sanitation because bacterial spores may not be destroyed by heating or sanitizing techniques.

Some bacteria are beneficial, such as those that aid in digesting food or decomposing garbage. Other bacteria spoil food, but without rendering it unfit for human consumption. These bacteria, called **putrefactives**, are not a sanitation concern. (Indeed, in some cultures, they are not even a culinary concern. Cultures differ on what constitutes "bad" meat, for example, and game is sometimes hung for a time to allow bacteria to grow.)

Rods

Coccus

Spirilla

FIGURE 2.1 *Bacteria can be classified by shape: Rods are short, tubular structures; coccus are discs, some of which form clusters; and spirilla are corkscrews.*

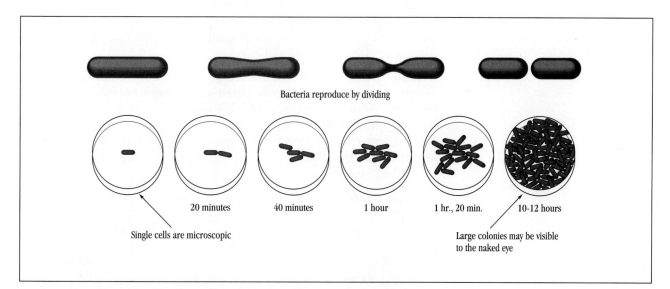

Bacteria reproduce by dividing

20 minutes 40 minutes 1 hour 1 hr., 20 min. 10-12 hours

Single cells are microscopic

Large colonies may be visible to the naked eye

FIGURE 2.2 *One bacterium divides into two; the two bacteria each divide, creating four; the four become 16 and so on. It takes only a very short time for one bacterium to produce millions more.*

Pathogen—*a living microorganism that can cause disease.*

The bacteria that are dangerous when consumed by humans are called **pathogenic**. These are the bacteria that must be destroyed or controlled in a food service operation.

Intoxications and Infections

Depending upon the particular microorganism, pathogenic bacteria can cause illnesses in humans in one of three ways: by intoxication, infection or toxin-mediated infection.

Botulism is a well-known example of an **intoxication**. Certain bacteria produce **toxins**, a byproduct of their life processes. You cannot smell, see or taste toxins. Ingesting these toxin-producing bacteria by themselves does not cause illness. But when their toxins are ingested, the toxins can literally poison the consumer. Proper food-handling techniques are critical in preventing an intoxication, because even if a food item is cooked to a sufficiently high temperature to kill all bacteria present, the toxins they leave behind are usually not destroyed.

The second type of bacterial illness is an **infection**. Salmonella is an especially well-known example. An infection occurs when live pathogenic bacteria are ingested. The bacteria then live in the consumer's intestinal tract. It is the living bacteria, not their waste products, that cause an illness. An infectant must be alive when eaten for it to do any harm. Fortunately, these bacteria can be destroyed by cooking foods to sufficiently high temperatures, usually 165°F (74°C) or higher.

The third type of bacterial illness has characteristics of both an intoxication and an infection, and is referred to as a **toxin-mediated infection**. Examples are Clostridium perfringens and Escherichia coli 0157:H7. When these living organisms are ingested they establish colonies in human or animal intestinal tracts where they then produce toxins. These bacteria are particularly dangerous for young children, the elderly or infirm.

Preventing Bacterial Intoxications and Infections

All bacteria, like other living things, need certain conditions in order to complete their life cycles. Like humans, they need food, a comfortable temperature, moisture, the proper pH, the proper atmosphere and time. The best way to prevent bacterial intoxications and infections is to attack the factors bacteria need to survive and multiply.

Food Bacteria need food for energy and growth. The foods on which bacteria thrive are referred to as **potentially hazardous foods**. Potentially hazardous foods include those high in protein such as meat, poultry, fish and shellfish. Dairy products, eggs, grains and some vegetables are also sufficiently high in protein to support bacterial growth. These foods and items containing these foods (for example, custard, hollandaise sauce and quiche) must be handled with great care.

Temperature Temperature is the most important factor in pathogenic bacteria's environment because it is the factor most easily controlled by food service workers. Most microorganisms are destroyed at high temperatures. Freezing slows, but does not stop, growth nor does it destroy bacteria.

Most of the bacteria that cause food-borne illnesses multiply rapidly at temperatures between 60°F and 120°F (16°C–49°C). Therefore, the broad range of temperatures between 40°F and 140°F (4–60°C) is referred to as the **temperature danger zone**. See Figure 2.3. By keeping foods out of the temperature danger zone you decrease the bacteria's ability to thrive and reproduce. (Regulations in some localities state that the "danger zone" begins at 45°F [7°C]. Here we use the broader range recommended by the United States Department of Agriculture—40°F–140°F—as this provides a slightly greater margin of safety.)

To control the growth of any bacteria that may be present, it is important to maintain the internal temperature of food at 140°F (60°C) or above or 40°F (4°C) or below. Simply stated: *Keep hot foods hot, keep cold foods cold.*

This is known as the **time-and-temperature principle**. Potentially hazardous foods should be heated or cooled quickly so that they are within the temperature danger zone as briefly as possible.

The high internal temperatures reached during cooking (165°F–212°F/74°C–100°C) kill most of the bacteria that can cause food-borne illnesses. When reheating foods it is important that the internal temperature reaches 165°F (74°C) or above to kill any bacteria that may have grown during storage. Once properly heated, hot foods must be held at temperatures of 140°F (60°C) or above. Foods that are to be displayed or served hot must be heated rapidly to reduce the time within the temperature danger zone. When heating or reheating foods:

+ Heat small quantities at a time.
+ Stir frequently.
+ Heat foods as close to service time as possible.
+ Use preheated ingredients whenever possible to prepare hot foods.
+ Never use a steam table for heating or reheating foods. Bring the food to an appropriate internal temperature (at least 165°F/74°C) before placing it in the steam table for holding.

Foods that are to be displayed, stored, or served cold must be cooled rapidly. When cooling foods:

+ Refrigerate semisolid foods at 40°F (4°C) or below in containers that are less than 2 inches deep. (Increased surface area decreases cooling time.)
+ Avoid crowding the refrigerator; allow air to circulate around foods.
+ Vent hot foods in an ice water bath as illustrated in Chapter 10, Stocks and Sauces.
+ Use prechilled ingredients, for example mayonnaise, to prepare cold foods.
+ Store cooked foods above raw foods to prevent cross-contamination.

Keep frozen foods frozen. Freezing at 0°F (–18°C) or below essentially stops bacterial growth but will not kill the bacteria. But do not place hot foods in a standard freezer. They will not cool more rapidly and the release of heat can raise the temperature of other foods in the freezer. Only a special blast freezer can be used for chilling hot items. If a special blast freezer is not available, cool hot foods as mentioned above before freezing them. When frozen foods are thawed, bacteria that are present will begin to grow. So:

+ Never thaw foods at room temperature.
+ Thaw foods gradually under refrigeration. Place them in a container to prevent cross-contamination from dripping or leaking liquids.
+ Thaw foods under running water at a temperature of 70°F (21°C) or cooler.
+ Thaw foods in a microwave *only* if the food will be prepared and served immediately.

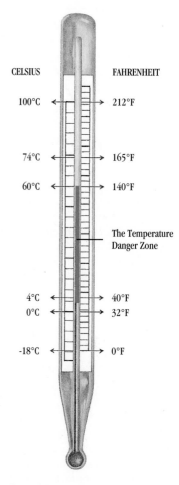

CELSIUS   FAHRENHEIT

100°C → 212°F

74°C → 165°F

60°C → 140°F

The Temperature Danger Zone

4°C → 40°F
0°C → 32°F

-18°C → 0°F

FIGURE 2.3

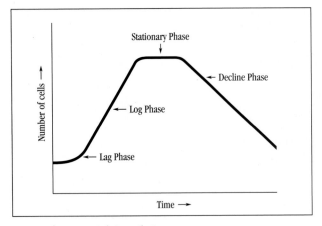

FIGURE 2.4 *Bacterial Growth Curve*

pH—*a measurement of the acid or alkaline content of a solution. Expressed on a scale of 0 to 14.0, 7.0 is considered neutral or balanced acid/alkaline; the lower the pH value, the more acidic the substance. The higher the pH value, the more alkaline the substance.*

TABLE 2.1	WATER ACTIVITY OF COMMON FOODS
0.0	
.1	
.2	
.3	
.4	
.5	dried pasta
.6	
.7	flour, dry milk
.75	jam, jelly, crisp cooked bacon
.8	
.85	MINIMUM FOR BACTERIAL GROWTH
.9	raw bacon
.95	soft cheese
.98	poultry and meat
1.0	distilled water

Time   When bacteria are moved from one place to another they require a period of time to adjust to new conditions. This resting period is known as the **lag phase**, when very little growth occurs. This phase may last from one to four hours. It is followed by the **log phase**, a period of accelerated growth, which lasts until the bacteria begin to crowd others within their colony, creating competition for food, space and moisture. This begins the **decline** or **negative growth phase**, during which bacteria die at an accelerated rate. See Figure 2.4.

Because of the lag phase, foods can be in the temperature danger zone for *very short periods* during preparation without an unacceptable increase in bacterial growth. Exposure to the temperature danger zone is cumulative, however, and should not exceed four hours total. The less time food is in the temperature danger zone, the less opportunity bacteria have to multiply.

Moisture   Bacteria need a certain amount of moisture, which is expressed as water activity or A_W. Water itself has an A_W of 1.0. Any food with an A_W of .85 or greater is considered potentially hazardous. See Table 2.1. Bacteria cannot flourish where the A_W is too low, usually below .85. This explains why dry foods such as flour, sugar or crackers are rarely subject to bacterial infestations. A low A_W only halts bacterial growth, however; it does not kill the microorganisms. When a dried food such as beans or rice is rehydrated, any bacteria present can flourish and the food may become potentially hazardous.

Acid/Alkaline Balance   Bacteria are affected by the **pH** of their environment. See Table 2.2. Although they can survive in a wider range, they prefer a neutral environment with a pH of 6.6 to 7.5. Growth is usually halted if the pH is 4.6 or less. So, acidic foods such as lemon juice, tomatoes and vinegar create an unfavorable environment for bacteria. The simple addition of an acidic ingredient (such as lemon juice or vinegar) should not, however, be relied upon to destroy bacteria or preserve foods. The amount of acidity appropriate from the standpoint of taste is not sufficient to ensure destruction of bacteria. The pH level of foods also varies depending on temperature, water content, the interaction with other ingredients and a host of additional factors.

Atmosphere   Bacteria need an appropriate atmosphere. Some bacteria, known as **aerobic**, thrive on oxygen, while others, known as **anaerobic**, cannot survive in the presence of oxygen. Others, known as **facultative**, can adapt and will survive with or without oxygen. Unfortunately, most pathogenic bacteria are facultative. See Table 2.3.

Canning, which creates an anaerobic atmosphere, destroys bacteria that need oxygen. But it also creates a favorable atmosphere for anaerobic and facultative bacteria. A complete vacuum need not be formed for anaerobic bacteria to thrive, however. A tight foil covering, a complete layer of fat, even a well-fitting lid can create an atmosphere sufficiently devoid of oxygen to permit growth of anaerobic bacteria.

TABLE 2.2   pH OF COMMON FOODS

	0	
	1.0	
A	2.0	limes, lemons
C	3.0	commercial mayonnaise
I	4.0	orange juice
D	4.6	bananas
	5.0	most vegetables (5.0 to 7.0)
	6.4	chicken and fresh meats
NEUTRAL	7.0	distilled water, fish
	8.0	crackers, hominy
A	8.5	baking soda in water
L	9.0	
K	10.0	
A	11.0	
L	12.0	household ammonia
I	13.0	
	14.0	

TABLE 2.3   CHARACTERISTICS OF BACTERIAL ILLNESSES

Common Name	Organism	Form	Common Source	Prevention
Staph	Staphylococcus aureus	Toxin	Starchy foods, cold meats, bakery items, custards, milk products, humans with infected wounds or sores	Wash hands and utensils before use; exclude unhealthy food handlers; avoid having foods at room temperature
Perfringens or CP	Clostridium perfringens	Cells and toxin	Reheated meats, sauces, stews, casseroles	Keep cooked foods at an internal temperature of 140°F (60°C) or higher; reheat leftovers to internal temperature of 165°F (74°C) or higher
Botulism	Clostridium botulinum	Toxin, cells, spores	Cooked foods held for an extended time at warm temperatures with limited oxygen, rice, potatoes, smoked fish, canned vegetables	Keep internal temperature of cooked foods above 140°F (60°C) or below 40°F (4°C); reheat leftovers thoroughly; discard swollen cans
Salmonella	Salmonella	Cells	Poultry, eggs, milk, meats, fecal contamination	Thoroughly cook all meat, poultry, fish and eggs; avoid cross-contamination with raw foods; maintain good personal hygiene
Strep	Streptococcus	Cells	Infected food workers	Do not allow employees to work if ill; protect foods from customers' coughs and sneezes
E. coli or 0157	Escherichia coli 0157:7 (enteropathogenic strains)	Cells and toxins	Any food, especially raw milk, raw vegetables, raw or rare beef, Humans	Thoroughly cook or reheat items
Listeriosis	Listeria monocytogenes	Cells	Milk products, Humans	Avoid raw milk and cheese made from unpasteurized milk

Parasites

Parasites are tiny multicelled organisms that depend on nutrients from a living host to complete their life cycle. Meat animals, fish, shellfish and humans can all play host to parasites. Several types of very small parasitic worms can enter an animal through contaminated feed, then settle in the host's intestinal tract or muscles, where they grow and reproduce. The ones most commonly found in foods are *trichinella spiralis* and *anisakis*.

Trichinosis is caused by eating undercooked game or pork infected with trichina larvae. Although trichinosis has been virtually eradicated by grain-feeding hogs and testing them before slaughter, some cases still occur each year. Traditionally it was thought that pork must be cooked to internal temperatures of 170°F (77°C) or higher to eradicate the larvae. This generally resulted in a dry, tough product. Scientists have now determined that trichina larvae are killed if held at 137°F (58°C) for 10 seconds. The United States Food and Drug Administration currently recommends cooking pork products to an internal temperature of 150°F (66°C). (All commercially packaged cured or smoked pork products must be heated to an internal temperature of 155°F [68°C] during processing.) The National Livestock and Meat Board continues to recommend cooking all pork products to 170°F (77°C), however.

Anisakiasis is another illness caused by parasitic roundworms. Anisakis worms reside in the organs of fish, especially bottom feeders or those taken from contaminated waters. Raw or undercooked fish are most often implicated in anisakiasis. Fish should be thoroughly cleaned immediately after being caught so that the parasites do not have an opportunity to spread. Thorough cooking to a minimum internal temperature of 140°F (60°C) is the only way to destroy the larvae, as they can survive even highly acidic marinades.

Viruses

Other biologically based food-borne illnesses such as hepatitis A and Norwalk virus are caused by viruses. Viruses are the smallest known form of life. They invade the living cells of a host, take over those cells' genetic material, and cause the cells to produce more viruses.

Viruses do not require a host to survive, however. They can survive—but not multiply—while lying on any food or food contact surface. Unlike bacteria, viruses can be present on any food, not just a potentially hazardous food. The food and food contact surface simply become a method of transportation between hosts.

Unlike bacteria, viruses are not affected by the water activity, pH or oxygen content of their environment. Some, however, can be destroyed by temperatures higher than 176°F (80°C). Basically, the only way to prevent food-borne viral illnesses is to prevent contamination in the first place.

Hepatitis A often enters the food supply through shellfish harvested from polluted waters. The virus is carried by humans, some of whom may never know they are infected, and is transmitted by poor personal hygiene and cross-contamination. The actual source of contamination may be hard to establish, though, because it sometimes takes months for symptoms to appear.

The Norwalk virus is spread almost entirely by poor personal hygiene among infected food handlers. The virus is found in human feces, contaminated water or vegetables fertilized by manure. The virus can be destroyed by high cooking temperatures but not by sanitizing solutions or freezing. In fact, Norwalk virus has even been found in ice cubes.

Foods most likely to transmit viral diseases are those that are not heated after handling. These include salads, sandwiches, milk, baked products, uncooked fish and shellfish and sliced meats. The best techniques for avoiding viral food-borne illnesses is to observe good personal hygiene habits, avoid cross-contamination, and use only foods obtained from reputable sources.

Fungi

Fungi are a large group of plants ranging from single-celled organisms to giant mushrooms. Fungi are everywhere: in the soil, air and water. Poisonous mushrooms, a type of fungus, can cause illness or death if consumed. The most common fungi, however, are molds and yeasts; they are the fungi of concern here.

Molds

Molds are algae-like fungi that form long filaments or strands. These filaments often extend into the air, appearing as cottony or velvety masses on food. Large colonies of mold are easily visible to the naked eye. Although many food molds are not dangerous, and some are even very beneficial, rare types known as mycotoxicoses do form toxins that have been linked to food-borne illnesses. For the most part, however, molds only affect food appearance and flavor. They cause discoloration, odors and off-flavors.

Unlike bacteria, molds can grow on almost any food at almost any temperature, moist or dry, acidic or alkaline. Mold cells can be destroyed by heating to 140°F (60°C) for 10 minutes. Their toxins are heat resistant, however, and are not destroyed by normal cooking methods. Therefore, foods that develop mold should be discarded and any container or storage area cleaned and sanitized.

Yeast

Yeast requires water and carbohydrates (sugar or starch) for survival. As the organism consumes carbohydrates it expels alcohol and carbon dioxide gas through a process known as **fermentation**. Fermentation is of great benefit in making bread and alcoholic beverages.

Although naturally occurring yeasts have not been proven to be harmful to humans, they can cause foods to spoil, developing off-flavors, odors and discoloration. Yeast is killed at temperatures of 136°F (58°C) or above.

Chemical Contaminants

The contamination of foods with a wide variety of chemicals is a very real and serious danger, one about which the public has shown a strong interest. Chemical contamination is usually inadvertent and invisible, making it extremely difficult to detect. The only way to avoid such hazards is for everyone working in a food service operation to follow proper procedures when handling foods or chemicals.

Chemical hazards include contamination with (1) the residual chemicals used in growing the food supply, (2) food service chemicals, and (3) toxic metals.

Residual Chemicals

Chemicals such as antibiotics, fertilizers, insecticides, and herbicides have brought about great progress in controlling plant, animal and human diseases, permitting greater food yields and stimulating animal growth. The benefits derived from these chemicals, however, must be contrasted with the adverse effects on humans when they are used indiscriminately or improperly.

The danger of these chemicals lies in the possible contamination of human foods, which occurs when chemical residues remain after the intended goal is achieved. Fruits and vegetables must be washed and peeled properly to reduce the risk of consuming residual chemicals.

Food Service Chemicals

A more common contamination problem involves the common chemicals found in most every food service operation. Cleaners, polishes, pesticides and abrasives are often poisonous to humans. Illness and even death can result from foods contaminated by such common items as bug spray, drain cleaner, oven cleaner or silver polish. These chemicals pose a hazard if used or stored near food supplies. Even improperly washing or rinsing dishes and utensils leaves a soap residue, which is then transmitted via food to anyone using the item.

To avoid food service chemical contamination, make sure all cleaning chemicals are clearly labeled and stored well away from food preparation and storage areas. Always use these products as directed by the manufacturer; never reuse a chemical container or package.

Toxic Metals

Another type of chemical contamination occurs when metals such as lead, mercury, copper, zinc and antimony are dispersed in food or water. For example:

+ Metals can accumulate in fish and shellfish living in polluted waters or in plants grown in soil contaminated by the metals.
+ Using an acid such as tomatoes or wine in a zinc (galvanized) or unlined copper container causes metal ions to be released into the food.
+ Antimony is used in bonding enamelware; it can be released into food when the enamel is chipped or cracked, so the use of enamelware is prohibited in food service facilities.
+ Lead enters the water supply from lead pipes and solder and is found in the glaze on some imported ceramic items.

Consuming any of these metals can cause poisoning.

To prevent metal contamination, use only approved food service equipment and utensils and re-tin copper cookware as needed. Never serve fish or shellfish that was illegally harvested or obtained from uninspected sources.

Physical Contaminants

Physical contaminants include foreign objects that find their way into foods by mistake. Examples include metal shavings created by a worn can opener, pieces of glass from a broken container, hair and dirt. Physical contaminants may be caused by intentional tampering, but they are most likely the result of poor safety and sanitation practices or a lack of training.

CROSS-CONTAMINATION

Generally, microorganisms and other contaminants cannot move by themselves. Rather, they are carried to foods and food contact surfaces by humans, rodents or insects. This transfer is referred to as cross-contamination.

Cross-contamination is the process by which one item, such as your fingers or a cutting board, becomes contaminated and then contaminates another food or tool. For example, a chef's knife and cutting board are used in butchering a potentially hazardous food such as a chicken. In this case, the chicken had been directly contaminated with salmonella at the hatchery. If the knife and board are not cleaned *and sanitized* properly, anything that touches them can also become contaminated. So, even though cooking the chicken to an appropriate internal temperature may destroy the salmonella in the chicken, the uncooked salad greens cut on the same cutting board or with the same knife can contain live bacteria.

Cross-contamination can occur with bacteria or other microorganisms, chemicals, dirt and debris. Side towels are an especially common source of cross-contamination. If a cook uses a side towel to wipe a spill off the floor, then uses that same towel to dry his hands after visiting the restroom, he has recontaminated his hands with whatever bacteria or dirt was on the floor. Cross-contamination also occurs when raw foods come in contact with cooked foods. Never store cooked food below raw food in a refrigerator, and never return cooked food to the container that held the raw food. Cross-contamination can also occur easily from smoking, drinking or eating, unless hands are properly washed after each of these activities.

Reducing Cross-Contamination

Cross-contamination can be reduced or even prevented by (1) personal cleanliness, (2) dish and equipment cleanliness and (3) pest management.

Personal Cleanliness

To produce clean, sanitary food, all food handlers must maintain high standards of personal cleanliness and hygiene. This begins with good grooming.

Humans provide the ideal environment for the growth of microorganisms. Everyone harbors bacteria in the nose and mouth. These bacteria are easily spread by sneezing or coughing, by not disposing of tissues properly and by not washing hands frequently and properly. Touching your body, then touching food or utensils, transfers bacteria. Human waste carries many dangerous microorganisms, so it is especially important to wash your hands thoroughly after visiting the restroom. An employee who is ill should not be allowed in the kitchen.

Current research shows that the human immunodeficiency virus (HIV), the causative agent of AIDS, is not spread by food. According to the United States Centers for Disease Control and Prevention, food service workers infected with HIV should not be restricted from work unless there is another infection or illness.

Here are several things you can do to decrease the risk of an illness being spread by poor personal hygiene:

◆ Wash your hands frequently and thoroughly.

◆ Keep your fingernails short, clean and neat. Do not bite your nails or wear nail polish.

◆ Keep any cut or wound antiseptically bandaged. An injured hand should also be covered with a disposable glove.

◆ Bathe daily, or more often if required.

◆ Keep your hair clean and restrained.

◆ Wear work clothes that are clean and neat. Avoid wearing jewelry or watches.

◆ Do not eat, drink, smoke or chew gum in food preparation areas.

Dish and Equipment Cleanliness

Clean—*to remove visible dirt and soil.*

Sanitize—*to reduce pathogenic organisms to safe levels.*

Sterilize—*to destroy all living microorganisms.*

The primary requirement for any food service facility is cleanability. But there is an important difference between clean and sanitary. **Clean** means that the item has no visible soil on it. **Sanitary** means that harmful substances are reduced to safe levels. Thus, something may be clean without being sanitary; the visible dirt can be removed, but disease-causing microorganisms can remain.

The cleaning of dishes, pots, pans and utensils in a food service operation involves both removing soil and sanitizing. Soil can be removed manually or by machine. Sanitizing can be accomplished with heat or chemical disinfectants.

Procedures for manually washing, rinsing and sanitizing dishes and equipment generally follow the three-compartment sink set-up shown in Figure 2.5. These procedures are:

1. Scrape and spray the item to remove soil.
2. Wash the item in the first sink compartment using an approved detergent. A brush or cloth may be used to remove any remaining soil.
3. Rinse the item in the second sink compartment using clear, hot water.
4. Sanitize the item in the third sink compartment by either:
    a. immersing it in 170°F (77°C) water for at least 30 seconds, or
    b. immersing it in an approved chemical sanitizing solution according to the manufacturer's directions.
5. Empty, clean and refill each sink compartment as necessary and check the water temperature regularly.

Food service items, dishes, silverware and utensils should always be allowed to air-dry, as towel-drying may recontaminate them.

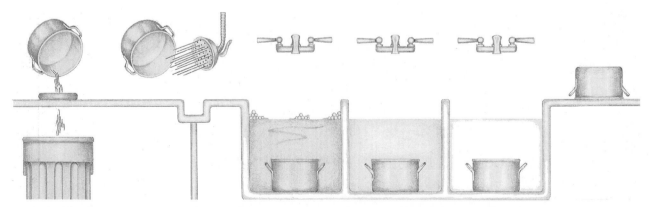

FIGURE 2.5   ***The Three-Compartment Sink***   *Procedure – scrape, spray, wash, rinse, sanitize and air-dry each item.*

Machine-washing dishes or utensils follows a similar procedure. The dish-washer should first scrape and prerinse items as needed, then load the items into dishwasher racks so that the spray of water will reach all surfaces. The machine cleans the items with a detergent, then sanitizes them with either a hot-water rinse (at least 180°F/82°C) or chemical disinfectant. When the machine cycle is complete, items should be inspected for residual soil, allowed to air-dry, and stored in a clean area.

Work tables and stationary equipment must also be cleaned and sanitized properly. Equipment and surfaces, including floors, walls and work tables, should be easily exposed for inspection and cleaning and should be con-structed so that soil can be removed effectively and efficiently with normal cleaning procedures. A thorough cleaning schedule should be implemented and closely monitored to prevent problems from developing.

The following points are important to the safety and cleanliness of any food service facility:

◆ Equipment should be disassembled for cleaning; any immersible pieces should be cleaned and sanitized like other items.

◆ All work tables or other food contact surfaces should be cleaned with deter-gent, then sanitized with a clean cloth dipped in a sanitizing solution. An acceptable sanitizing solution is made by combining one gallon (4 liters) of lukewarm water with one tablespoon (15 milliliters) of chlorine bleach. This solution must be replaced every two hours. Other chemical sanitizers should be prepared and used according to health department and manufac-turer's directions.

◆ Surfaces, especially work surfaces with which food may come in contact, should be smooth and free of cracks, crevices or seams in which soil and microorganisms can hide.

◆ Floors should be nonabsorbent and should not become slippery when wet.

◆ Walls and ceilings should be smooth and light-colored so that soil is easier to see.

◆ Light should be ample and well located throughout food preparation and storage areas. All light bulbs should be covered with a sleeve or globe to protect surroundings from shattered glass.

The design of a kitchen can also affect the sanitary habits of employees. Food preparation equipment should be arranged in such a way as to decrease the chances of cross-contamination. The work flow should eliminate crisscross-ing and backtracking. Employees should be able to reach storage, refrigeration and cleanup areas easily. Dish- and pot-washing areas and garbage facilities should be kept as far from food preparation and storage areas as possible. Cleaning supplies and other chemicals should be stored away from foods.

In most communities, the design of a food service facility is controlled in part by public health regulations. The local health and building codes should be consulted when planning any construction or remodeling, or when pur-chasing and installing new equipment.

Pest Management

Food can be contaminated by insects (e.g., roaches and flies) and rodents (e.g., mice and rats). These pests carry many harmful bacteria on their bodies, thus contaminating any surface with which they come in contact. An insect or rodent infestation is usually considered a serious health risk and should be dealt with immediately and thoroughly. Pests must be controlled by (1) building them out of the facility; (2) creating an environment in which they cannot find food, water or shelter; and (3) relying on professional extermination.

The best defense against pests is to prevent infestations in the first place by building them out. Any crack—no matter how small—in door frames, walls or window sills should be repaired immediately and all drains, pipes and vents should be well sealed. Inspect all deliveries thoroughly and reject any packages or containers found to contain evidence of pests.

Flies are the perfect method of transportation for bacteria because they feed and breed on human waste and garbage. Use screens or "fly fans" (also known as air curtains) to keep them out in the first place. Control of garbage is also essential because moist, warm, decaying organic material attracts flies and provides favorable conditions for eggs to hatch and larvae to grow.

Pest management also requires creating an inhospitable environment for pests. Store all food and supplies at least six inches off the floor and six inches away from walls. Rotate stock often to disrupt nesting places and breeding habits. Provide good ventilation in storerooms. Do not allow water to stand in drains, sinks or buckets, as cockroaches are attracted to moisture. Clean up spills and crumbs immediately and completely to reduce the food supply.

Despite your best efforts to build pests out and maintain proper housekeeping standards, it is still important to watch for the presence of pests. For example, cockroaches leave a strong, oily odor and feces that look like large grains of pepper. Cockroaches prefer to search for food and water in the dark, so seeing any cockroach on the move in the daylight is an indication of a large infestation.

Rodents (mice and rats) tend to hide during the day, so an infestation may be rather serious before any creature is actually seen. Rodent droppings, which are shiny black to brownish gray, may be evident, however. Rodent nests made from scraps of paper, hair or other soft materials may be spotted.

Should an infestation occur, consult a licensed pest control operator immediately. With early detection and proper treatment, infestations can be eliminated. Be very careful in attempting to use pesticides or insecticides yourself. These chemicals are toxic to humans as well as to pests. Great care must be used to prevent contaminating food or exposing workers or customers to the chemicals.

HACCP Systems

Now that you understand what contaminants are and how they can be destroyed or controlled, it is necessary to put this information into practice during day-to-day operations. Although local health departments inspect all food service facilities on a regular basis, continual self-inspection and control are essential for maintaining sanitary conditions.

Hazard Analysis Critical Control Points (HACCP) is proving to be an effective and efficient method for managing and maintaining sanitary conditions in all types of food service operations. Developed in 1971 for NASA to ensure food safety for astronauts, HACCP—and a similar system adopted by the National Restaurant Association known as Sanitary Assessment of the Food Environment/S.A.F.E.—is a rigorous system of self-inspection. It focuses on the *flow of food* through the food service facility, from the decision to include an item on the menu through service to the consumer.

TABLE 2.4   HACCP ANALYSIS—THE FLOW OF FOOD

Control Point	Hazard	Critical Action
Menu and recipes	Potentially hazardous foods; human hands involved in food preparation.	Plan physical work flow; train employees
Receiving	Contaminated or spoiled goods	Inspect and reject delivery if necessary
Storage	Cross-contamination to and from other foods; bacterial growth; spoilage	Maintain proper temperatures; rotate stock; discard if necessary
Preparation	Cross-contamination; bacterial growth	Wash hands and utensils; avoid temperature danger zone
Cooking	Bacterial survival; physical or chemical contamination	Cook to proper temperatures
Holding and service	Contamination; bacterial growth	Use clean equipment; maintain proper temperatures
Cooling leftovers	Bacterial survival and growth	Cool rapidly, cover and refrigerate
Reheating	Bacterial survival and growth	Heat rapidly to 165° F (74°C); maintain temperatures; do not mix old and new products

A HACCP critical control point is any step during the processing of a food when a mistake can result in the transmission, growth or survival of pathogenic bacteria. At each of these steps there is some hazard of contamination. The HACCP process begins by identifying the steps and evaluating the type and severity of hazard that can occur. It then identifies what actions can be taken to reduce or prevent each risk of hazard. See Table 2.4. The activities that present the highest risk of hazard should be monitored most closely. For example, a cook's failure to wash his hands before handling cooked food presents a greater risk of hazard than does a dirty floor. In other words, hazards must be prioritized and correction of critical concerns should take priority.

Whatever system is followed, however, all personnel must be constantly aware of and responsive to problems and potential problems associated with the safety of the food they are serving.

THE SAFE WORKER

Kitchens are filled with objects that can cut, burn, break, crush or sprain the human body. The best way to prevent work-related injuries is through proper training, adherence to good work habits and careful supervision.

The federal government enacted legislation designed to reduce hazards in the work area, thereby reducing accidents. The Occupational Safety and

Health Act (OSHA) covers a broad range of safety matters. Employers who fail to follow its rules can be severely fined. Unfortunately, human error is the leading cause of accidents, and no amount of legislation can protect someone who doesn't work in a safe manner.

Safe behavior on the job reflects pride, professionalism and consideration for fellow workers. The following list should alert you to conditions and activities aimed at preventing accidents and injuries:

◆ Clean up spills as soon as they occur.
◆ Learn to operate equipment properly; always use guards and safety devices.
◆ Wear clothing that fits properly; avoid wearing jewelry, which may get caught in equipment.
◆ Use knives and other equipment for their intended purpose only.
◆ Walk, do not run.
◆ Keep exits, aisles and stairs clear and unobstructed.
◆ Always assume a pot or pan is hot; handle with dry towels.
◆ Position pot and pan handles out of the aisles so they do not get bumped.
◆ Get help or use a cart when lifting or moving heavy objects.
◆ Avoid back injury by lifting with your leg muscles; stoop, don't bend, when lifting.
◆ Use a well-placed ladder or stool for climbing; do not use a chair, box, drawer or shelf.
◆ Keep breakable items away from food storage or production areas.
◆ Warn people when you must walk behind them, especially when carrying a hot pan.

Some accidents will inevitably occur, and it is important to act appropriately in the event of an injury or emergency. This may mean calling for help or providing first aid. Every food service operation should be equipped with a complete first-aid kit. Municipal regulations may specify the exact contents of the kit. Be sure that the kit is conveniently located and well stocked at all times.

The American Red Cross and local public health departments offer training in first aid, cardiopulmonary resuscitation (CPR), and the Heimlich Maneuver used for choking victims. All employees should be trained in basic emergency procedures. A list of emergency telephone numbers should be posted by each telephone.

CONCLUSION

All food service workers are responsible for supplying food that is safe to eat. Microorganisms that cause food-borne illnesses are found in all types of food; they can be destroyed or their growth can be severely limited by proper food handling procedures. By learning about food contaminants, how they are spread and how they can be prevented or controlled, you can help ensure customer safety. You are also responsible for your own physical safety as well as that of your customers and fellow workers. Maintaining sanitary and safe facilities and high standards of personal hygiene is a necessary part of this responsibility.

QUESTIONS FOR DISCUSSION

1. Foods can be contaminated in several ways. Explain the differences between biological, chemical and physical contamination. Give an example of each.
2. Under what conditions will bacteria thrive? Explain what you can do to alter these conditions.
3. What is the temperature danger zone? What is its significance in food preparation?
4. Explain how improper or inadequate pest management can lead to food-borne illnesses.
5. Define HACCP. How is this system used in a typical food service facility?

CHAPTER 3
NUTRITION

After studying this chapter you will be able to:

- identify categories of nutrients and explain their importance in a balanced diet
- explain the evolution of the USDA food pyramid and its significance in planning nutritious menus
- understand product nutrition labels
- explain the effect storage and preparation techniques have on various foods' nutritional values
- provide diners with nutritious foods

*S*ince the days of prehistoric hunters and gatherers, people have understood that some animals and plants are good to eat and others are not. For thousands of years, cultures worldwide have attributed medicinal or beneficial effects to certain foods, particularly plants, and have recognized that foods that would otherwise be fine to eat may be unhealthy if improperly prepared or stored.

But it was not until the past few decades that people have become increasingly concerned about understanding how all foods affect their health and what foods can and should be consumed in order to promote good health. These concerns comprise the study of nutrition.

This chapter cannot provide an in-depth study of the nutritional sciences. Rather, it sets forth basic information about nutrients, food additives, and ingredient substitutes and alternatives. It also provides guidelines for reading package labels and preparing nutritious meals. Detailed nutritional information about many specific foods is found throughout the book. Also found throughout the book are recipes for dishes particularly low in calories, fat or sodium; each recipe is accompanied by a chart of nutritional values. These recipes are marked with a 🍴.

Nutrition is the science that studies nutrients, the chemical substances found in food. Nutrients nourish the body by promoting growth, facilitating body functions and providing energy.

There are six categories of nutrients: carbohydrates, fats, proteins, vitamins, minerals and water. **Essential nutrients** are those that must be provided by food because the body does not produce them in sufficient quantities.

The six nutrients are classified as either macronutrients or micronutrients. Macronutrients—the ones needed in large quantities—include carbohydrates, fats, proteins and water. Micronutrients—the ones the body requires only in small amounts—are vitamins and minerals.

Our bodies depend upon the various nutrients for different purposes and require different amounts of each depending on our age, sex and health. In addition, some nutrients depend on one another for proper functioning. For example, calcium and vitamin D work together in the body: Vitamin D promotes the absorption of the calcium that the body utilizes for proper bone growth. Because foods differ with regard to their nutritional content, it is important to eat a variety of foods in order to achieve a proper nutritional balance.

Essential nutrients—*nutrients that must be provided by food because the body does not produce them in sufficient quantities.*

MACRONUTRIENTS

Three of the macronutrients (carbohydrates, fats and proteins) provide calories or energy. A **calorie** (abbreviated *kcal*) is a unit of energy measured by the amount of heat required to rise 1000 grams of water one degree Celsius. It is the way we describe the amount of energy in food. The number of calories in

Calorie—*the unit of energy measured by the amount of heat required to raise 1000 grams of water one degree Celsius; it is also written as* kilocalorie *or* kcal.

food is measured by a device called a calorimeter, which burns the food and analyzes the residue.

One gram of pure fat supplies 9 kcal; one gram of pure carbohydrate supplies 4 kcal, as does one gram of pure protein. Most foods are a combination of carbohydrates, proteins and fats; their kcal content may not be easily determined unless we know how much of each macronutrient the food contains.

Carbohydrates

Carbohydrates are formed from hydrogen, oxygen and carbon; they are classified as simple or complex. **Simple carbohydrates** are single chains of naturally occurring **sugars**. These include simple sugars, called monosaccharides (mono = single; saccharide = sugar unit), and double sugars, called disaccharides (di = double). **Complex carbohydrates** are long chains of polysaccharides (poly = many). Polysaccharides consist of thousands of glucose units linked together and arranged as a **starch** or **fiber**.

The body digests (or breaks down) these sugars and starches into glucose. Glucose, also known as blood sugar, is a very important source of energy for the body.

Fiber is not digested for energy. Indeed, little is absorbed for any purpose. Undigestible fiber is known as **dietary fiber**. It generally comes from the seeds and cell walls of fruits, vegetables and cereal grains. Because the body cannot digest dietary fiber, this fiber passes through the digestive system almost completely unchanged. This helps keep the digestive tract running smoothly. Fiber increases fecal bulk, which encourages proper elimination of waste products from the large intestines and helps avoid some forms of gastrointestinal distress.

Simple carbohydrates are found in the naturally occurring sugars in fruit, vegetables and milk as well as sweeteners such as honey, corn syrup and table sugar. Complex carbohydrates are found in vegetables, fruits and cereal grains such as wheat, barley and oats.

Vegetables and fruits vary with regard to the relative amounts of sugar, starch and dietary fiber they contain. Root vegetables such as beets or potatoes have a high starch content but low fiber content. Leafy and stalk vegetables—lettuce and celery, for example—have relatively small quantities of starch, but they do contain a great deal of fiber. Fruits also vary in carbohydrate values. Most are high in sugars. Some fruits, such as dates and figs, are high in starch but low in fiber. Fruits with a high water content, such as strawberries, are low in starch but high in fiber.

Fats

Fats, like carbohydrates, are composed of carbon, hydrogen and oxygen. The differences between carbohydrates and fats are the number and arrangement of the carbon, hydrogen and oxygen atoms. Fats are found in both animal and plant foods, although fruits contain very little fat.

Depending upon their molecular structure, the fats in foods can be classified as saturated, monounsaturated or polyunsaturated. Most foods contain a combination of the three, although one kind may predominate. If saturated fat is the most abundant kind (as in the fat surrounding muscle meats), we describe the food as being saturated even though it contains a mixture of all three fats.

Saturated fats are found mainly in animal products such as milk, eggs and meats as well as in tropical oils such as coconut and palm. Monounsaturated fats come primarily from plants and plant products such as avocados and olive oil. Polyunsaturated fats come from plants (soy, corn and safflower oils, for example) and fish.

Saturated fats such a butter, lard and other animal fats are usually solid at room temperature. Monounsaturated and polyunsaturated fats are usually liquid at room temperature. Liquid vegetable oils like rapeseed (canola) and olive are high in monounsaturated fat. Cottonseed, sunflower, corn and safflower oils are high in polyunsaturated fat. All oils, however, are a combination of the three kinds of fat.

Polyunsaturated fats can become saturated through a process known as hydrogenation in which pressurized hydrogen gas is used to solidify the fat. Stick margarine, for example, is made by hydrogenating vegetable oil.

The body has more difficulty breaking down saturated fats than it does monounsaturated and polyunsaturated fats. Research suggests that high-fat diets, especially diets high in saturated fat, may be linked to heart disease, obesity and certain forms of cancer. Saturated fats are also linked to high levels of blood cholesterol, which are associated with arteriosclerosis (hardening of the arteries). Although the liver can produce all the cholesterol the body needs, additional cholesterol is often provided in the diet. Dietary cholesterol is found only in foods of animal origin. Meats, poultry, fish, shellfish, eggs and dairy products are all sources of dietary cholesterol. Fruits, vegetables and grains are cholesterol free.

Fats in moderate amounts are necessary for proper body functioning. Some transport the fat-soluble vitamins A, D, E and K throughout the body. Without fat, the body could not absorb these vitamins. Fats are also an important energy source. Fats contain 9 calories per gram, more than twice as many as carbohydrates or proteins, which each contain 4 calories per gram. Therefore, fats are an efficient way for the body to store energy.

Proteins

Proteins differ from carbohydrates and fats in that they contain nitrogen as well as carbon, hydrogen and oxygen. Protein chains are composed of various combinations of the approximately two dozen different amino acids, nine of which are essential nutrients. The specific combination of amino acids gives each protein its unique characteristics and properties. Animal proteins such as milk, dairy products, eggs, meat, poultry and fish all supply significant amounts of the essential amino acids.

Proteins are necessary for manufacturing, maintaining and repairing body tissues. They are essential for the periodic replacement of the outer layer of skin as well as for blood clotting and scar tissue formation. Hair and nails, which provide a protective cover for the body, are composed of insoluble proteins.

Another important function of protein is regulating body processes. Proteins regulate the balance of water, acids and bases and move nutrients in and out of cells. Proteins contribute to the immune system by producing antibodies, which are necessary for combating diseases. Proteins also form the enzymes that act as catalysts for body functions and the hormones that help direct body processes.

Water

The human body is approximately 60% water. Water is necessary for transporting nutrients and waste throughout the body. It cushions the cells, lubricates the joints, maintains stable body temperatures and assists waste elimination. It also promotes functioning of the nervous system and muscles.

The main sources of water are beverages such as water itself and juice. Some foods such as tomatoes, oranges, watermelon and iceberg lettuce are particularly high in water, but all foods contain it. Water is also formed by the body when other nutrients are metabolized. The average adult should consume at least 8 to 10 glasses (64 fluid ounces or 2 liters) of water a day to ensure adequate intake.

MICRONUTRIENTS

Vitamins and minerals are micronutrients. They have no calories and are consumed in small quantities. Vitamins and minerals are essential nutrients because they must be provided through the diet; the body cannot manufacture them in quantities adequate to ensure good health.

Vitamins

Vitamins are vital dietary substances needed to regulate the **metabolism** and for normal growth and body functions. They are distinct from carbohydrates, proteins and fats and are not manufactured in the body; they must be supplied by food.

Metabolism—*all of the chemical reactions and physical processes that continually occur in living cells and organisms.*

There are 13 essential vitamins. Table 3.1 lists the most important vitamins, sets forth their principal functions in the human body and identifies foods containing high concentrations of these nutrients.

Vitamins are divided into two categories: fat soluble and water soluble. The fat-soluble vitamins are A, D, E and K. Excess supplies of these vitamins are stored in fatty tissue and the liver. Water-soluble vitamins are vitamin C and the B complexes, including thiamin (B1), riboflavin (B2), niacin (B3), cobalamin (B12), pyridoxine (B6), pantothenic acid, biotin and folacin. Water-soluble vitamins are not stored to the extent that fat-soluble vitamins are, and any excess is generally excreted in the urine. Because of these differences, deficiencies in water-soluble vitamins usually develop more rapidly.

Virtually all foods contain some vitamins. Many factors contribute to a particular food's vitamin concentration: an animal's feed; the manner by which the produce is harvested, stored or processed; even the type of soil, sunlight, rainfall and temperature have significant effects on vitamin content. For example, tomatoes have a higher concentration of vitamin C when picked ripe from the vine rather than picked green. Also, different varieties of fruits and vegetables have different vitamin contents. A Wegener apple, for example, has 19 mg of vitamin C while a Red Delicious has only 6 mg.

You can control vitamin concentration and retention through careful food preparation:

1. Try to prepare vegetables as close to service time as possible; vegetables cut long before service lose more vitamins than those cut immediately before cooking.

2. Whether a vegetable is boiled, steamed or microwaved also determines the amount of vitamins it retains. Because B complex and C vitamins are water soluble, they are easily leached (washed out) or destroyed by food processing and preparation techniques such as boiling. Steaming helps retain nutrients (when steaming, keep the water level below the vegetables). But microwave cooking is best because it cooks vegetables with minimal water.

3. Roasting and grilling meats, poultry, fish and shellfish preserve more vitamins than stewing and braising. The temperatures to which foods are cooked may affect vitamin retention as well.

4. Storage affects vitamin concentrations. For example, long exposure to air and incandescent light may destroy vitamin C. Using airtight containers prevents some of this loss.

Table 3.1 identifies some of the preparation and storage techniques that help retain the maximum amount of various vitamins.

TABLE 3.1 VITAMINS: THEIR FUNCTIONS, SOURCES AND TECHNIQUES FOR RETAINING MAXIMUM NUTRIENT CONTENT

Vitamin	Functions in the Human Body	Sources	Techniques for Nutrient Retention
Vitamin A	Keeps skin healthy; protects eyes; protects mouth and nose linings; helps resist infections	Deep yellow vegetables, leafy green vegetables, egg yolks, liver, whole milk, deep yellow fruits	Serve fruits and vegetables raw; store vegetables covered and refrigerated; steam vegetables; roast or broil meats
Vitamin E	Anti-oxidant; protects membranes and cell walls	Vegetable oils, whole grains, dark leafy vegetables, legumes, peanuts	Use whole-grain flours; store foods in airtight containers; avoid exposing the food to light
Vitamin C (Ascorbic acid)	Repairs connective tissues; helps resist infections; promotes healing	Citrus fruits, raw green vegetables, strawberries, cantaloupes, tomatoes, broccoli	Serve fruits and vegetables raw; steam or microwave vegetables
Vitamin B6	Promotes enzyme functions	Meats, whole grains, dark green vegetables, potatoes, liver	Serve vegetables raw; cook foods in a minimum amount of water and for shortest possible time; roast or broil meats and fish
Vitamin B12	Helps produce red blood cells; assists metabolism; helps prevent anemia	Animal foods only, particularly milk, eggs, poultry and fish	Roast or broil meats, poultry and fish
Vitamin D	Helps absorb calcium; regulates calcium and phosphorus in bones	Milk, butter, fish oils, cream, egg yolks (exposure to sunlight produces vitamin D)	Store milk in opaque containers away from light
Vitamin K	Assists proper blood coagulation	Liver, dark green leafy vegetables (bacteria in intestinal track also produce vitamin K)	Steam or microwave vegetables; do not overcook meats
Folic Acid	Helps metabolize amino acids; promotes cell formation; prevents anemia	Dark green leafy vegetables, meats, fish, poultry, eggs, whole-grain cereals	Serve vegetables raw; steam or microwave vegetables; store vegetables covered and refrigerated
Thiamin (Vitamin B1)	Promotes normal digestion; necessary for the nervous system; helps enzymes metabolize food	Meats, poultry, dry beans and peas, peanut butter, enriched and whole-grain pastas, breads, etc.	Use enriched or whole-grain pasta or rice; do not wash whole grains before cooking or rinse afterwards; steam or microwave vegetables; roast meats at moderate temperatures; cook meats only until done
Riboflavin (Vitamin B2)	Helps usage of oxygen; promotes good vision and smooth skin; helps enzyme functions	Milk, cheese, fish, poultry, enriched and whole-grain breads, dark green leafy vegetables	Store foods in opaque containers; roast or broil meats or poultry
Niacin	Promotes normal digestion; necessary for the nervous system; helps enzymes metabolize food	Meats, poultry, fish, dark green leafy vegetables, whole grain or enriched breads and cereals	Steam or microwave vegetables; roast or broil beef, veal, lamb and poultry (pork retains about the same amount of niacin regardless of cooking method)

Minerals

Minerals cannot be manufactured by the body. They are obtained by eating plants that have drawn minerals from the ground or the flesh of animals that have eaten such plants.

Minerals are considered micronutrients because only small quantities are needed. Minerals are a critical component in hard and soft tissues (e.g., the calcium, magnesium and phosphorus present in bones and teeth). Minerals also regulate certain necessary body functions. For example, nerve impulses are transmitted through an exchange of sodium and potassium ions in the nerve cells.

Minerals are divided into two categories: trace minerals and macrominerals. Trace minerals such as iron are needed in only very small amounts. Macrominerals such as calcium are needed in relatively larger quantities. Table 3.2 lists several of the most important minerals, sets forth their principal functions and identifies foods containing high concentrations of these nutrients.

As with vitamins, food processing and preparation can reduce a food's mineral content. Soaking or cooking in large amounts of water can leach out a food's content of water-soluble minerals. Processing or refining grains, such as the wheat used to make white bread, also removes minerals. Table 3.2 identifies preparation and storage techniques for retaining maximum mineral content.

TABLE 3.2 MINERALS: THEIR FUNCTIONS, SOURCES AND TECHNIQUES FOR RETAINING MAXIMUM NUTRIENT CONTENT

Mineral	Functions in the Human Body	Sources	Techniques for Nutrient Retention
Calcium (a macromineral)	Helps build bones and teeth; helps blood clot; promotes muscle and nerve functions	Dairy products	Cook foods in minimum amount of water and for shortest possible time
Iron (a trace mineral)	Combines with protein to form hemoglobin (the red substance in blood that carries oxygen); prevents anemia	Meats, poultry, fish, dark green leafy vegetables	Cook foods in minimum amount of water and for shortest possible time
Magnesium (a trace mineral)	Promotes electrical activity of nerve cells	Green leafy vegetables, whole grains, legumes, fish and shellfish	Cook foods in minimum amount of water and for shortest possible time
Zinc (a trace mineral)	Enhances healing; a component of many enzymes; helps cells use oxygen	Organ and muscle meats, whole grain breads and cereals, oysters, peanuts, legumes	Cook foods in minimum amount of water and for shortest possible time
Phosphorus (a macromineral)	Helps build bones and teeth; helps enzymes metabolize food	Milk, meats, fish, egg yolk, legumes, nuts	Roast or broil lamb, veal, pork and poultry (beef retains the same amount of phosphorus regardless of cooking method); cook foods in minimum amount of water and for shortest possible time
Potassium (a macromineral)	Maintains electrolyte and fluid balance; promotes normal body functions	Meats, poultry, fish, bananas, dried fruits, citrus fruits, broccoli, carrots, celery, potatoes, cantaloupes	Cook foods in minimum amount of water and for shortest possible time

---

The federal government plays an important role in the way various foodstuffs are grown, raised, slaughtered, processed, marketed, stored and transported. The principal actors are the Food and Drug Administration of the United States Department of Health and Human Services (FDA) and the United States Department of Agriculture (USDA).

The FDA's activities are directed toward protecting the nation's health against impure and unsafe foods, as well as drugs, cosmetics, medical devices and other things. It develops and administers programs addressing food safety. For example, the FDA must approve any new food additive before a manufacturer markets it to food producers and processors. To gain FDA approval, the manufacturer must prove to the FDA's satisfaction that the additive (1) is effective for the intended purpose, (2) can be detected and measured in the final product and (3) is safe. The FDA holds public hearings during which experts and consumers provide evidence and opinions before it decides to grant or deny approval. If it grants approval, the FDA issues regulations identifying the amount of the additive that can be used and the foods to which it can be added. The FDA also sets standards for labeling foods, including nutrition labels. Labeling regulations not only address the type of information that must be conveyed, but also the way it is presented.

The USDA's principal responsibility is to make sure that individual food items are safe, wholesome and accurately labeled. It attempts to meet these responsibilities through inspection and grading procedures. The USDA also provides consumer services. It conducts and publishes research on nutrition and assists those producing our food to do so efficiently and effectively.

Other federal agencies that have a role in the nation's health and food supply include the United States Centers for Disease Control and Prevention (CDC), which track illnesses, including those caused by food-borne pathogens; the National Institutes of Health (NIH), which do basic biological and nutritional research; and the Department of the Interior, which sets environmental and land-use standards.

INGREDIENT SUBSTITUTES AND ALTERNATIVES

More and more people are becoming aware that too much of certain foods can be detrimental to their health. Many are trying to cut down on foods high in salt, fat, added sugar and cholesterol. To a degree, people can accomplish their goals—and chefs can assist them—by turning to ingredient substitutes and alternatives where possible.

Here we use the term **ingredient substitute** to mean the replacement of one ingredient with another of presumably similar—although not necessarily identical—taste, texture, appearance and other characteristics. The substitute will be more nutritious, however. So, if someone is on a low-sodium diet, for example, he can avoid the sodium found in salt (sodium chloride) by substituting potassium chloride. Or, if he is avoiding fats, he can use nonfat sour cream in place of regular sour cream when baking quick breads. The differences in taste, texture, appearance and baking quality should be minimal.

We use the term **ingredient alternative** to mean the replacement of one ingredient with another of different taste, texture, appearance or other characteristic, but one which will not compromise—although it may change—the taste of the dish. As with the ingredient substitute, the ingredient alternative will be more nutritious. Lemon juice and herbs, for instance, can be used as flavoring alternatives to salt; a salsa of fresh vegetables can replace a cream-based sauce. The dishes will not taste the same, but they will still taste good.

Salt Substitutes and Alternatives

Minerals are essential to good health, but overdosing can be dangerous. A major concern in the American diet is excessive sodium (salt). The average American consumes 3000 to 7000 mg of sodium per day. Yet the necessary daily requirement according to the RDA (the Recommended Dietary

Allowance, discussed below) is 1100 to 3300 mg per day. Research has linked excessive amounts of sodium to hypertension (high blood pressure), heart and kidney diseases and strokes.

Chefs can contribute to a more healthful diet by decreasing the use of salt and other high-sodium products like soy sauce. Salt substitutes, which contain potassium chloride instead of sodium chloride, are available. "Lite" salt has a portion of the sodium content replaced by potassium but still contains some real salt for a truer flavor.

In addition, pepper, lemon, herbs, spices, fruits and vinegars can be used as salt alternatives.

Artificial Sweeteners

Saccharin, the oldest artificial sugar substitute, has been used for nearly a century. A petroleum derivative, it has no calories and tastes 300 times sweeter than sugar. Along with its sweetness, though, come health risks. Studies have shown that saccharin causes tumors in rats.

Aspartame (also known as Nutrasweet®) was developed as a substitute for saccharin. Approved by the FDA in 1981, aspartame is composed of aspartic acid and phenylalanine, both of which are naturally occurring amino acids. Unlike saccharin, aspartame does not have an aftertaste, but it is only 180 times sweeter than sugar. It is now widely used in soft drinks, frozen yogurt, candy and similar products. Aspartame breaks down when heated, however, so it cannot be used in baked products. According to the FDA, aspartame is a safe substitute for sugar, although it is a risk for those people with the rare disease phenylketonuria (PKU), who cannot metabolize the phenylalanine in aspartame.

Another sugar substitute is Acesulfame K (also known as Sunnette®), which the FDA approved in 1988. The body cannot metabolize Acesulfame K, so it passes through the digestive system unchanged. Like aspartame, it has no aftertaste. Acesulfame K is used in chewing gum, dry beverage mixes, instant coffee and tea, gelatins and nondairy creamers.

Fat Substitutes

Several types of fat substitutes are available; they are either synthetic or derived from naturally-occurring food substances. Two of the more recent products are Olestra® and Simplesse®.

Olestra® is made of sucrose and vegetable oil. The two are bonded together and the final product consists of molecules too large to be digested. Because it cannot be digested, Olestra® does not add any calories. Following FDA approval, Olestra® will be useful in cooking oils or shortening as well as in salted snacks.

Simplesse® is a popular fat substitute used in frozen desserts such as ice creams and yogurt. Simplesse®, made from egg whites or milk proteins, has a rich, creamy texture similar to fat.

Other Ingredient Substitutes and Alternatives

There are many other ingredient substitutes, some of which are identified in Table 3.3. Often ingredient substitutes and alternatives will have a dramatic impact on the nutritional values of a completed dish. For example, in Figures 3.1 A and B we list the ingredients for a traditional sausage and cheese omelet and

TABLE 3.3   INGREDIENT SUBSTITUTES

Instead of	Use
Bacon	Canadian bacon
Butter	Powdered butter granules plus liquid (either skim milk or water)
Chocolate	Cocoa (vegetable oil may be added as needed)
Cream cheese	Reduced fat or nonfat cream cheese
Emulsified salad dressing	Start with a base of reduced-fat or nonfat yogurt, sour cream or mayonnaise, then thin with skim milk
Light cream	Equal portions of 1% milk and skim evaporated milk
Mayonnaise	Reduced-fat mayonnaise (can be mixed with reduced-fat or nonfat sour cream)
Sour cream	Reduced-fat or nonfat sour cream; drained reduced fat or nonfat plain yogurt
Whipped cream	Whipped chilled evaporated skim milk

one made with ingredient substitutes. Similarly, in Figures 3.2 A and B we list the ingredients for a sheet pan of traditional fudge brownies and one made with ingredient substitutes. We also list the nutritional values for each of the four recipes. Note the differences, especially in the values for fat and cholesterol.

TRADITIONAL SAUSAGE AND CHEESE OMELET

Yield: 1 serving

Eggs, whole	3	3
Milk	3 Tbsp.	45 ml
Breakfast sausage, cooked	2 oz.	60 g
Cheddar cheese, grated	1 oz.	30 g
Salt	1/8 tsp.	1 ml
White pepper	1/8 tsp.	1 ml
Butter*	1 Tbsp.	15 ml

*The butter is used as the fat for cooking the omelet.

Nutritional values:

Calories	686	Protein	35 g
Calories from fat	76%	Vitamin A	1745 IU
Total fat	58 g	Vitamin C	0 mg
Saturated fat	26 g	Sodium	1342 mg
Cholesterol	740 mg		

FIGURE 3.1 A

OMELET WITH INGREDIENT SUBSTITUTES

Yield: 1 serving

Egg Beaters	6 oz.	180 ml
Turkey sausage, cooked and drained	2 oz.	60 g
Reduced-fat cheddar cheese, grated	1 oz.	30 g
Salt substitute	1/8 tsp.	1 ml
White pepper	1/8 tsp.	1 ml
Pan-release spray*		

*The omelet is cooked using pan-release spray instead of butter.

Nutritional values:

Calories	284	Protein	38 g
Calories from fat	41%	Vitamin A	170 IU
Total fat	13 g	Vitamin C	0 mg
Saturated fat	5 g	Sodium	780 mg
Cholesterol	61 mg		

FIGURE 3.1 B

TRADITIONAL FUDGE BROWNIES

Yield: one sheet pan

Unsweetened chocolate	2 lbs.	1 kg
Butter	2 lbs.	1 kg
Eggs	20	20
Sugar	5 lbs. 12 oz.	2.9 kg
Vanilla extract	2 oz.	60 ml
All-purpose flour	1 lb. 10 oz.	750 g
Pecan pieces	1 lb.	500 g

Nutritional values per two-inch square:

Calories	315	Protein	4 g
Calories from fat	49%	Vitamin A	367 IU
Total fat	17 g	Vitamin C	0 mg
Saturated fat	8 g	Sodium	92 mg
Cholesterol	65 mg		

The complete recipe is produced as Recipe 30.29.

FIGURE 3.2 A

BROWNIES MADE WITH INGREDIENT SUBSTITUTES

Yield: one sheet pan

Unsweetened chocolate	4 oz.	120 g
Cake flour	1 lb.	450 g
Cocoa powder	9 oz.	270 g
Salt substitute	2 tsp.	10 ml
Egg whites	12	12
Whole eggs	8	8
Granulated sugar	2 lbs. 2 oz.	1 kg
Corn syrup	2 lbs.	900 g
Unsweetened applesauce	1 1/2 pts.	670 ml
Canola oil	7 oz.	210 g
Vanilla extract	2 Tbsp.	30 ml

Nutritional values per two-inch square:

Calories	133	Protein	2 g
Calories from fat	24%	Vitamin A	30 IU
Total fat	3 g	Vitamin C	0 mg
Saturated fat	1 g	Sodium	38 mg
Cholesterol	18 mg		

The complete recipe is produced as Recipe 30.30.

FIGURE 3.2 B

Ingredient substitutes and, especially, ingredient alternatives will change the nutritional values of a dish; they may also change its taste, texture or appearance. Sometimes these changes will be acceptable; sometimes they will not. Because some ingredient substitutes and alternatives result in unsatisfactory flavors, textures or appearance, many recipes may not be suitable for substitution or alteration. Use your judgment.

ADDITIVES

Additives are substances added to many foods to prevent spoilage or improve appearance, texture, taste or nutritional value. Some food additives are incidental; some are intentional. Incidental food additives are those inadvertently or unintentionally added to foods during processing, such as pesticide residues on fruits and vegetables. Intentional food additives are those added to foods on purpose. These include the chemicals that ensure longer shelf life in baked goods and the food colorings used to make items more visually appealing.

Additives may be synthetic, synthetic materials copied from nature, or naturally occurring substances. For example, sugar substitutes used to sweeten beverages are synthetic substances, while the vitamin C and beta carotene used to preserve foods are substances copied from nature. Lecithin, an emulsifier, comes from natural sources. Although a chef will rarely use any of these additives directly, they will undoubtedly appear in many of the packaged or prepared products you may use.

PACKAGE LABELING

FDA Labeling Requirements

In an effort to provide chefs and consumers with greater information about the nutritional values of foods they purchase, the FDA sets standards for package labels. The FDA labeling requirements address (1) product identification, (2) product claims and (3) nutritional information.

Not all foods must be labeled according to FDA regulations, however. Common exceptions are (1) foods produced by small businesses, (2) foods produced and sold on site, including vending machine food, (3) foods shipped in bulk, (4) foods such as coffee, tea and some spices that have little or no nutritional value, (5) foods sold in packages with less than 12 square inches available for labeling, (6) foods sold for immediate consumption, (7) fresh fruits and vegetables and (8) raw poultry, meat and fish (USDA controls labeling practices for these items). The manufacturers, processors, distributors or retailers of these foods can voluntarily abide by the FDA labeling regulations if they wish.

Reading the Label

Product Identification

The FDA requires that products be clearly labeled with (1) the common name of the product, (2) the name and address of the manufacturer, packer or distributor, (3) the ingredients in descending order of predominance by weight and (4) the net contents by weight, measure or count. See Figure 3.3.

◆◆◆

BACK TO BASICS

Great strides in agriculture have been made during the past two centuries. Pesticides, fungicides and herbicides now eliminate or control pests that once would have devoured, ruined or choked crops. Chemical fertilizers increase yields of many of the world's staples. But not everyone has greeted these developments with open arms.

During the past few decades, scientific and medical investigators have documented, or at least suggested, health risks associated with certain synthetic pesticides, fertilizers and other products. These findings have led to a renewed interest in a back-to-the-basics approach to farming: organic farming. Specialty farms, orchards and even wineries now offer organically grown products (or, in the case of wineries, wines made from organically grown grapes). These products come with few, if any, intentional additives and should be free of any incidental additives. Proponents argue that these products are better for you and better for the health of the farm workers.

There are no federal guidelines identifying what can be called "organic." Approximately half of the states, however, have laws addressing the production of organically grown foods. These laws vary widely, but generally, most states require that products marketed as "organically grown" must have been grown in soil certified free of synthetic pesticides, fungicides, herbicides or fertilizers. Depending on the state, the land can be certified free of these products one to three years after their use has ceased.

Nutritional content claims.

The ingredient list in descending order by weight.

The net weight in U.S. and metric measures.

Health (diet-disease link) claim. (Back panel)

NET WT. 8.9 oz. (252 g)

Ingredients: Broccoli, carrots, green beans, water chestnuts, soybean oil, milk solids, modified cornstarch, salt, spices.

"While many factors affect heart disease, diets low in saturated fat and cholesterol may reduce the risk of this disease."

FIGURE 3.3 *Label Illustrating Product Identification and Product Claim Requirements*
Illustration Source: Food and Drug Administration 1993

Product Claims

The FDA requires that words such as "low fat" and "fat free" be used according to specific standards. The FDA has approved the following usages:

✦ *Free*—The food must contain no or only "physiologically inconsequential" amounts of fat, saturated fat, cholesterol, sodium, sugars or calories.

✦ *Low, Little, Few* and *Low Source of*—The food can be eaten frequently without exceeding dietary guidelines for fat, saturated fat, cholesterol, sodium or calories.

Specific usages include:

Low fat—The food has 3 grams or less of fat per serving.

Low saturated fat—The food has 1 gram or less of saturated fat per serving; not more than 15% of a serving's calories are from saturated fat.

Low sodium—The food has 140 mg or less of salt per serving.

Very low sodium—The food has 35 mg or less of salt per serving.

Low cholesterol—The food has 20 mg or less of cholesterol per serving.

Low calorie—The food has 40 calories or fewer per serving.

Reduced, less and *fewer*—The nutritionally-altered product must contain at least 25% fewer calories than the regular or reference (i.e., FDA standard) food product.

Light or *Lite*—The nutritionally altered product must contain at least one third or 50% less fat than the reference product. *Light in sodium* means that the nutritionally-altered product contains 50% or less sodium than the regular or reference product. *Light* may still be used to describe color, as in "light brown sugar."

+ *High*—The food must contain 20% or more of the daily value for a desirable nutrient per serving.

+ *More*—The food must contain at least 10% or more of the daily value for protein, vitamins, minerals, dietary fiber or potassium than the reference product.

+ *Good Source*—The food contains 10 to 19% of the daily value per serving for the specific nutrient such as calcium or dietary fiber.

+ *Lean*—The meat, poultry, game, fish or shellfish item contains less than 10 grams of fat, less than 4 grams of saturated fat and less than 95 mg cholesterol per serving and per 100 grams.

+ *Extra Lean*—The meat, poultry, game, fish or shellfish item contains less than 5 grams of fat, less than 2 grams of saturated fat and less than 95 mg cholesterol per serving and per 100 grams.

TABLE 3.4   DIET–DISEASE LINKS AND APPROVED HEALTH CLAIMS FOR LABELS

Food or Nutrient	Disease	Typical Foods	FDA-Approved Claim
Calcium	Osteoporosis	Low-fat and skim milks, yogurt, tofu, calcium-fortified citrus drinks, some calcium supplements	"Regular exercise and a healthy diet with enough calcium helps teen and young adult white and Asian women maintain good bone health and may reduce their high risk of osteoporosis later in life."
Sodium	Hypertension	Unsalted tuna, salmon, fruits and vegetables, low-fat milk and yogurt, cottage cheese, sherbet, cereal, flour and pasta (not egg pasta)	"Diets low in sodium may reduce the risk of high blood pressure, a disease associated with many factors."
Dietary fiber	Cancer	Fruits, vegetables, reduced-fat milk products, cereals, flours, sherbet	"Development of cancer depends on many factors. A diet low in total fat may reduce the risk of some cancers."
Dietary saturated fat and cholesterol	Coronary heart disease	Fruits, vegetables, skim and low-fat milks, cereals, whole-grain products, pasta (not egg pasta)	"While many factors affect heart disease, diets low in saturated fat and cholesterol may reduce the risk of this disease."
Fruits, vegetables and grain products that contain fiber	Cancer	Whole-grain breads and cereals, fruits and vegetables	"Low-fat diets rich in fiber-containing grain products, fruits, and vegetables may reduce the risk of some types of cancer, a disease associated with many factors."
Fruits, vegetables and grain products that contain fiber	Coronary heart disease	Fruits, vegetables and whole-grain breads and cereals	"Diets low in saturated fat and cholesterol and rich in fruits, vegetables, and grain products that contain some types of dietary fiber, particularly soluble fiber, may reduce the risk of heart disease, a disease associated with many factors."
Fruits and vegetables	Cancer	Fruits and vegetables	"Low-fat diets rich in fruits and vegetables (foods that are low in fat and may contain dietary fiber, vitamin A, or vitamin C) may reduce the risk of some types of cancer, a disease associated with many factors. Broccoli is high in vitamins A and C, and it is a good source of dietary fiber."

The FDA recognizes that there is a linkage between some foods or nutrients and certain diseases. It allows manufacturers and retailers (or their advertising agencies) to make certain specific claims regarding their products and these **diet–disease links**. See Table 3.4. For example, because the frozen mixed vegetables in Figure 3.3 are "low fat" and "cholesterol free," the manufacturer can make a specific claim about its product and the risk of heart disease.

Nutritional Information

The FDA requires that labels identify specific nutritional information including: (1) serving size, (2) total number of calories per serving, (3) number of calories from fat per serving, and (4) the percent of daily values for certain nutrients per serving. The labels must also include reference information such as the recommended daily values for certain nutrients and the number of calories per gram of fat, protein and carbohydrate. Products with limited label space do not have to include the reference information. Figure 3.4 reproduces a sample FDA nutritional label for the frozen mixed vegetables package illustrated in Figure 3.3.

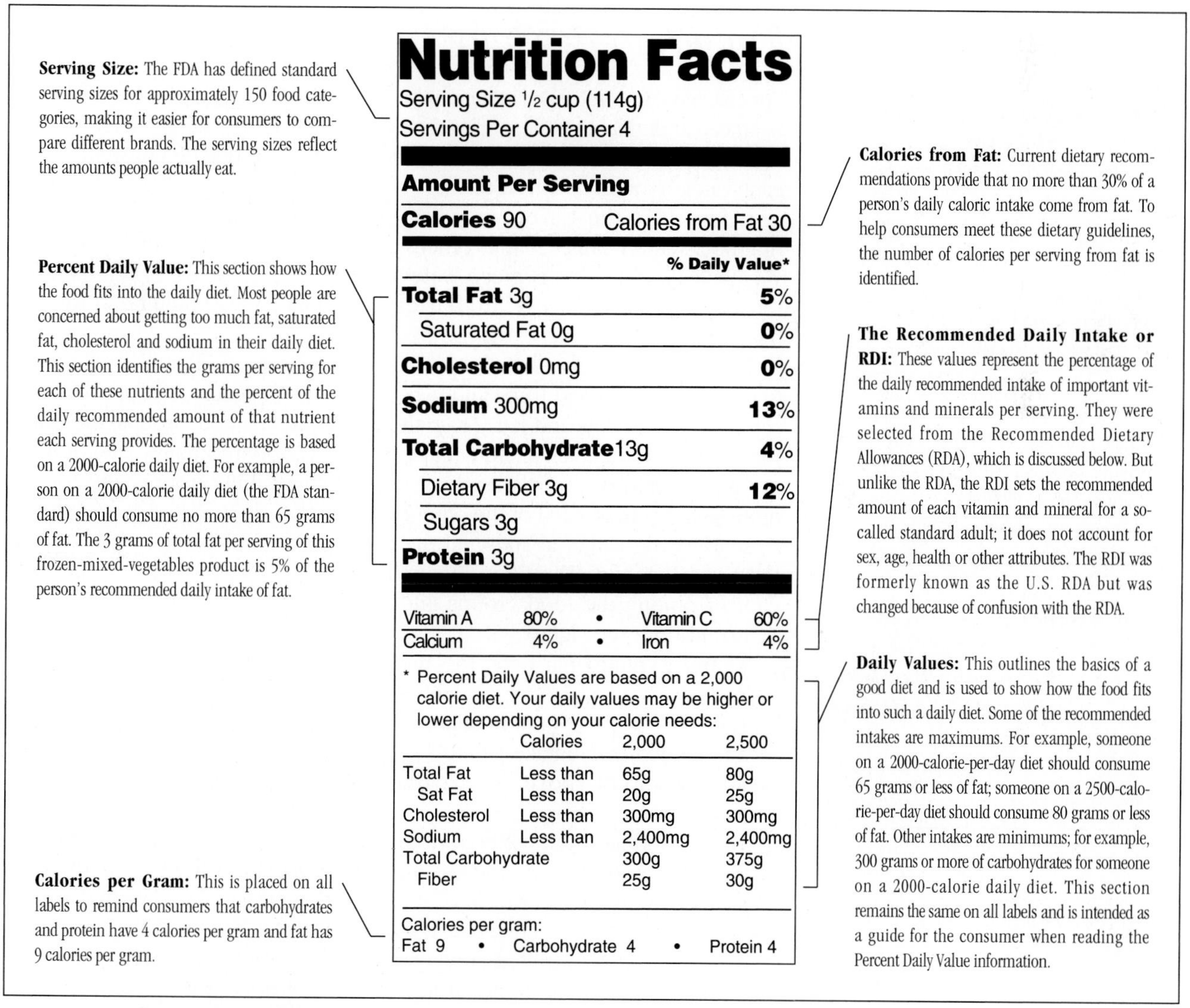

Serving Size: The FDA has defined standard serving sizes for approximately 150 food categories, making it easier for consumers to compare different brands. The serving sizes reflect the amounts people actually eat.

Percent Daily Value: This section shows how the food fits into the daily diet. Most people are concerned about getting too much fat, saturated fat, cholesterol and sodium in their daily diet. This section identifies the grams per serving for each of these nutrients and the percent of the daily recommended amount of that nutrient each serving provides. The percentage is based on a 2000-calorie daily diet. For example, a person on a 2000-calorie daily diet (the FDA standard) should consume no more than 65 grams of fat. The 3 grams of total fat per serving of this frozen-mixed-vegetables product is 5% of the person's recommended daily intake of fat.

Calories per Gram: This is placed on all labels to remind consumers that carbohydrates and protein have 4 calories per gram and fat has 9 calories per gram.

Calories from Fat: Current dietary recommendations provide that no more than 30% of a person's daily caloric intake come from fat. To help consumers meet these dietary guidelines, the number of calories per serving from fat is identified.

The Recommended Daily Intake or RDI: These values represent the percentage of the daily recommended intake of important vitamins and minerals per serving. They were selected from the Recommended Dietary Allowances (RDA), which is discussed below. But unlike the RDA, the RDI sets the recommended amount of each vitamin and mineral for a so-called standard adult; it does not account for sex, age, health or other attributes. The RDI was formerly known as the U.S. RDA but was changed because of confusion with the RDA.

Daily Values: This outlines the basics of a good diet and is used to show how the food fits into such a daily diet. Some of the recommended intakes are maximums. For example, someone on a 2000-calorie-per-day diet should consume 65 grams or less of fat; someone on a 2500-calorie-per-day diet should consume 80 grams or less of fat. Other intakes are minimums; for example, 300 grams or more of carbohydrates for someone on a 2000-calorie daily diet. This section remains the same on all labels and is intended as a guide for the consumer when reading the Percent Daily Value information.

Nutrition Facts

Serving Size ½ cup (114g)
Serving Per Container 4

Amount Per Serving

Calories 90   Calories from Fat 30

	% Daily Value*
Total Fat 3g	**5%**
Saturated Fat 0g	**0%**
Cholesterol 0mg	**0%**
Sodium 300mg	**13%**
Total Carbohydrate 13g	**4%**
Dietary Fiber 3g	**12%**
Sugars 3g	
Protein 3g	

Vitamin A	80%	Vitamin C	60%
Calcium	4%	Iron	4%

* Percent Daily Values are based on a 2,000 calorie diet. Your daily values may be higher or lower depending on your calorie needs:

		Calories	2,000	2,500
Total Fat	Less than		65g	80g
Sat Fat	Less than		20g	25g
Cholesterol	Less than		300mg	300mg
Sodium	Less than		2,400mg	2,400mg
Total Carbohydrate			300g	375g
Fiber			25g	30g

Calories per gram:
Fat 9 • Carbohydrate 4 • Protein 4

FIGURE 3.4 *Label Illustrating Nutritional Information Requirements*
Illustration Source: Food and Drug Administration 1993

THE RECOMMENDED DIETARY ALLOWANCE

The Recommended Dietary Allowance (RDA) is the standard for the daily intake of various nutrients. The RDA, first published in 1943 by the Food and Nutrition Board of the National Research Council, is revised about every five years. The Food and Nutrition Board also publishes the Nutritive Value of Foods which identifies serving sizes and nutrient information for a wide variety of foods.

The nutrients listed on the RDA table are protein; vitamins A, D, E, C, K; selenium; thiamin; riboflavin; niacin; B6; folacin; and B12 as well as the minerals calcium, phosphorus, magnesium, iron, zinc and iodine. The RDA table identifies nutrient allowances for both sexes and 15 age categories, including pregnant and lactating women. The tables are intended as guidelines for the intake of essential nutrients based upon the known needs of most healthy people.

The RDA assists chefs and dietitians, especially in schools, hospitals and other institutions, in developing nutritious meal plans.

THE FOOD PYRAMID

For many years, nutritionists and others have attempted to define a healthy, balanced diet. Most of these models divide foods into general categories and recommend that a certain number of servings or calories be consumed from each category for a balanced diet.

Before 1956 the USDA recognized seven food groups: (1) meats, eggs, dried peas and beans, (2) milk, cheese and ice cream, (3) potatoes and other vegetables and fruits, (4) green leafy and yellow vegetables, (5) citrus fruits, tomatoes and raw cabbage, (6) breads and flours and (7) butter and fortified margarine.

In 1956 the USDA reduced the seven groups to four: (1) milk and cheese, (2) meats and fish, (3) fruits and vegetables and (4) grains. An optional fifth category was sweets and fats. From these Four Basic Food Groups, the USDA recommended the average adult eat a total of 12 servings daily. Two or more servings should come from each of the meat and milk groups, and four or more servings from each of the other two groups.

In 1992 the USDA abandoned the Four Basic Food Groups and adopted the Food Pyramid. The Food Pyramid prioritizes and proportions the food choices among the food groups and gives a visual presentation of proper daily nutrition. See Figure 3.5.

As the pyramid narrows, the recommended number of daily servings decreases.

The base of the pyramid contains the bread, cereal, rice and pasta group; recommended daily intake is 6 to 11 servings. A serving consists of 1 slice of bread; 1/2 cup of cooked rice, pasta or cereal; or 1 ounce of ready-to-eat cereal.

The second tier from the bottom is divided into two unequal sections: vegetables and fruits. You should eat 3 to 5 servings from the vegetable group every day. A serving of vegetables consists of 1/2 cup of chopped raw or cooked vegetables or 1 cup of leafy raw vegetables. You should also eat 2 to 4 servings per day of fruit. A serving consists of 1 piece of fruit or melon, 3/4 cup of juice, 1/2 cup of canned fruit or 1/4 cup of dried fruit.

The third tier from the bottom is divided in half: the milk, yogurt and cheese group, and the meat, poultry, fish, shellfish, dry beans, eggs and nuts

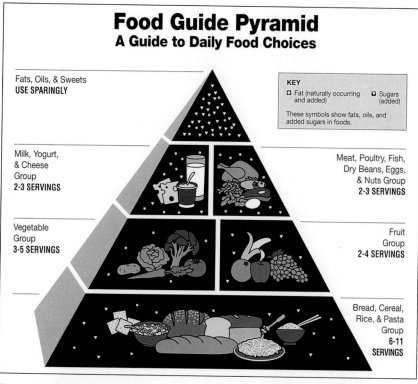

Food Guide Pyramid
A Guide to Daily Food Choices

Fats, Oils, & Sweets
USE SPARINGLY

KEY
◻ Fat (naturally occurring   ▾ Sugars
and added)   (added)

These symbols show fats, oils, and
added sugars in foods.

Milk, Yogurt,
& Cheese
Group
2-3 SERVINGS

Meat, Poultry, Fish,
Dry Beans, Eggs,
& Nuts Group
2-3 SERVINGS

Vegetable
Group
3-5 SERVINGS

Fruit
Group
2-4 SERVINGS

Bread, Cereal,
Rice, & Pasta
Group
**6-11
SERVINGS**

FIGURE 3.5   *The Food Pyramid*

group. You should have 2 to 3 servings from each group daily. A serving from the milk group consists of 1 cup of milk or yogurt, or 1-1/2 to 2 ounces of cheese. A serving from the meat group consists of 2-1/2 to 3 ounces of cooked lean meat, poultry, fish or shellfish; a 1/2 cup of cooked beans, 1 egg or 2 tablespoons of peanut butter counts as 1 ounce of meat.

Capping the pyramid is the fat, oil and sweets group; intake from this group should be limited. Small circles symbolizing fat and small triangles symbolizing sugar are scattered throughout the pyramid to show that some foods in these groups can add fats and sugar to the diet.

The Food Pyramid emphasizes that some foods are nutritionally better than others. It cautions against eating fats, while urging us to eat plenty of fruits, vegetables, grains, pasta and breads. These foods contain important nutrients such as vitamins, minerals, complex carbohydrates and dietary fiber.

NUTRITION AND THE CHEF

The Food Pyramid was designed to guide food consumption for a more healthful life. It presents a plan for a balanced diet. Chefs can use it to plan balanced menus as well. As the Food Pyramid suggests, chefs do not need to use only meat as the center of the plate presentation. It demands that a variety of breads, pasta and grains be included on the menu along with an interesting selection of vegetable dishes. And it cautions against the use of too much fat and sugar.

While not every food service operation can (or should) be devoted to "health food," to the extent appropriate you should offer healthful dining alternatives. Your ability to do so depends, of course, upon your facility. Chefs at hospitals, prisons and schools have much greater control over the foods their clientele consumes. Therefore, they have a far greater opportunity and responsibility to provide selections for a well-balanced diet. Chefs at most restaurants, however, do not have such captive audiences. But that does not mean that you can shirk your responsibilities.

You assist customers when you:

1. Use proper purchasing and storage techniques in order to preserve nutrients;
2. Offer a variety of foods from each tier of the Food Pyramid so that customers have a choice;
3. Offer entrees that emphasize plant instead of animal foods;
4. Offer dishes that are considerate of special dietary needs such as low fat or low salt;

♦♦♦

THE CUSTOMERS WHO COUNT

I have spent nineteen years of my professional life in the "fine dining" or "gourmet" field. As of the date of this publication, I will have completed my twentieth year in transition to what I now call a "Minimax" lifestyle.

Minimax is not the opposite of fine "gourmet dining." As a culinary philosophy it has its place about midway. *Minimax* is a constructed word that can be understood internationally. *Mini* refers to *minimum*, in this case to risks encountered by unwise or excessive consumption of food. *Max*, on the other hand, refers to *maximum* possible enhancement of food, using natural aromas, colors and textures rather than the classic western dependence on salts, fats and sugars.

Your future customers will be involved in a struggle when they read your menu. With their subjective right brains, they will be remembering former meals with enormous relish. With their objective left brains, they will apply what they know about fat, calories and sodium. Without some help they will either be confused, perplexed, rebellious or guilty.

Somehow then, you, who will make up the educated center of the restaurant business of the future, will have to address the needs of those who want to make changes and still celebrate a night out at a comforting restaurant.

My suggestion is that you devise recipes that avoid fat as a primary source of calories for *at least* two appetizers, two entrees and one dessert. I would simply describe these on the menu for what they contain and not call them "low-fat" or "diet" or, for that matter, by any special name (even Minimax!). I would then present a small, very attractive, folded menu card with a phrase such as "For Our Customers Who Count" on the outside, and then simply list the nutritional benefits from the low-fat specials in an attractive, easy-to-read manner.

If your management chooses to establish such a menu, it will be extremely important that you weigh each dish correctly and have it analyzed by an approved nutrition system such as NDS (from the University of Minnesota's Nutrition Coordinating Center, 2221 University Avenue SE, Suite 310, Minneapolis, MN 55414-3076; phone (612) 627-4862), or Heart Smart International (6617 N. Scottsdale Road, Scottsdale, AZ 85250; phone (800) 762-7819.)

The reason for accuracy is that some, if not most, of the "customers who count" do so for very critical reasons. To give someone an oversized portion of meat with a great sauce that far exceeds, say, 30% calories from fat is actually highly irresponsible and may even attract possible litigation in the future.

When you reduce fat in a classical dish, there will be a reduction in flavor, since "fat carries flavor." By drawing attention away from the taste change and enhancing the sense of smell (aroma), sight (color and presentation) and touch (texture), you can actually improve the finished dish.

I have found that the fusion idea has helped make this a reality. Fusion is simply merging seasonings from one culture with those from another. In this way it helps to see Northern European specialties that use abundant dairy products as "velvet memories," and North African and Asian seasonings as "future bright notes."

It is then possible to consider a modification to, say, sauce hollandaise by lowering the fat and adding a good Asian fish sauce to which shreds of mint and flecks of red pepper are added to spike interest with aroma, color and texture.

Whatever you choose to do, let met give you this last word of encouragement. Study hard, read the classics and see the future through them. If you've ever skipped smooth stones on flat water you'll know that the first bounce really matters. If your attitude to very rich classics is negative and condemning, then what you try to achieve will certainly fail to go the distance.

Therefore, don't condemn anyone's work. Aim to please today's customer with all the skills that our exciting profession has developed for thousands of years.

You have my very best wishes for a most successful career. Now go skip your stone … for your customers' sakes!

GRAHAM KERR, *author, chef and host of*
THE GALLOPING GOURMET
and GRAHAM KERR'S KITCHEN,
seen on PBS-TV and
The Discovery Channel

5. Use cooking procedures that preserve rather than destroy nutrients;
6. Use cooking procedures that minimize the use of added fat (e.g., stocks, sauces and soups can be cooled and the congealed fats removed; foods can be browned in the oven instead of being sautéed in hot fat);
7. Use equipment that minimizes the use of added fat (e.g., nonstick pans);
8. Train the wait staff to respond properly to nutritional questions diners may have about menu items, and
9. Use ingredient alternatives or substitutes where appropriate. If a dish does not lend itself to ingredient alternatives or substitutes, consider creating a new dish that replaces less nutritious traditional foods or preparations with more nutritious ones. For example, instead of serving a sauce made with butter, flour and cream, you can reduce an appropriately seasoned wine, stock or juice and then thicken it with fruit or vegetable purées or cornstarch.

Throughout this book are recipes marked with the symbol illustrated in Figure 3.6. This symbol indicates that the recipe is for a healthful dish. These dishes are generally low in calories, fat, saturated fat and/or sodium; if appropriate, they are also a good source of vitamins, protein, fiber or calcium. A table of nutritional values accompanies each recipe. These dishes are not necessarily dietetic. Rather, they should be consumed as part of a well-rounded, nutritious diet to meet the goals reflected in the Food Pyramid.

FIGURE 3.6 *The Symbol for a Healthful Recipe*

CONCLUSION

A basic understanding of and appreciation for nutrition are important for both the consumer and those who prepare the foods consumed.

What you serve is important. Carbohydrates, proteins, fats, water, vitamins and minerals, in varying amounts, are all necessary for good health. The Food Pyramid can guide selections to create and maintain a healthful diet.

How you prepare foods is also important. You should provide your customers with nutritious dishes. Remember that some cooking and storage techniques preserve nutrients; others do not. In addition, by substituting or modifying ingredients and preparation methods, many dishes can be made more nutritious.

QUESTIONS FOR DISCUSSION

1. Identify the six categories of nutrients and list two sources for each.
2. What are the differences between saturated fats and unsaturated fats? Identify two sources for each.
3. List four things you can do to reduce the loss of micronutrients when storing or preparing foods.
4. Describe the Food Pyramid. Explain how a chef can use it to plan well-balanced meals and how a consumer can use it to establish a healthful diet.
5. Create two menus for a traditional holiday dinner; one should be nutritionally well balanced and the other not. Explain your choices.

CHAPTER 4

MENU PLANNING

AND

FOOD COSTING

STANDARD RECIPE CARD FOR ITEM:				DATE:			DATE:			DATE:			DATE REVISED	
QUANTITY PRODUCED													RECIPE FILE NO.	
PORTION SIZE													RESTAURANT	
NO. OF PORTIONS PRODUCED													SALES PRICE	
INGREDIENTS	QTY/ WEIGHT	PURCH UNIT	UNIT COST	TOTAL		UNIT COST	TOTAL		UNIT COST	TOTAL		PREPARATION PROCEDURE		
TOTAL COST														
COST PER PORTION														
COST % PER PORTION														

FIGURE 4.1   *Standardized Recipe Form*

The form may also include information on costing and a photograph of the finished dish. Each form should be complete, consistent and simple to read and follow. The forms should be stored in a readily accessible place. Index cards, notebook binders or a computerized database may be used, depending on the size and complexity of the operation.

MEASUREMENTS AND CONVERSIONS

Measurement Formats

Accurate measurements are among the most important aspects of food production. Ingredients and portions must be measured correctly to ensure consistent product quality. In other words, the chef must be able to prepare a recipe the same way each time, and portion sizes must be at the same from one order to the next.

In a kitchen, measurements may be made in three ways: weight, volume and count.

Weight refers to the mass or heaviness of a substance. It is expressed in terms such as grams, ounces, pounds and tons. Weight may be used to measure liquid or dry ingredients (for example, 2 pounds of eggs for a bread recipe) and portions (for example, 4 ounces of sliced turkey for a sandwich). As weight is generally the most accurate form of measurement, portion scales or balance scales are commonly used in kitchens.

Volume refers to the space occupied by a substance. This is mathematically expressed as *height × width × length*. It is expressed in terms such as cups, quarts, gallons, teaspoons, fluid ounces, bushels and liters. Volume is most commonly used to measure liquids. It may also be used for dry ingredients when the amount is too small to be weighed accurately (for example, 1/4 teaspoon of salt). Although measuring by volume is somewhat less accurate than measuring by weight, volume measurements are generally quicker to do.

Frequently, mistakes are made in food preparation by chefs who assume wrongly that weight and volume are equal. Do not be fooled! One cup does not always equal 8 ounces. While it is true that one standard cup contains 8 *fluid* ounces, it is not true that the contents of that standard cup will *weigh* 8 ounces. For example, the weight of 1 cup of diced apples will vary depending on the size of the apple pieces. Errors are commonly made in the bakeshop by cooks who assume that 8 ounces of flour is the same as one cup of flour. In fact, one cup of flour weighs only about 4-1/2 ounces.

It is not unusual to see both weight and volume measurements used in a single recipe. When a recipe ingredient is expressed in weight, weigh it. When it is expressed as a volume, measure it. Like most rules, however, this one has exceptions. The weight and volume of water, butter, eggs and milk are, in each case, the same. For these ingredients you may use whichever measurement is most convenient.

Count refers to the number of individual items. Count is used in recipes (for example, 4 eggs) and in portion control (for example, 2 fish fillets or 1 ear of corn). Count is also commonly used in purchasing to indicate the size of the individual items. For example, a "96 count" case of lemons means that a 40-pound case contains 96 individual lemons; a "115 count" case means that the same 40-pound case contains 115 individual lemons. So, each lemon in the 96-count case is larger than those in the 115-count case. Shrimp is another item commonly sold by count. One pound of shrimp may contain from eight to several hundred shrimp, depending on the size of the individual pieces. When placing an order, the chef must specify the desired count. For example, when ordering one pound of 21–25-count shrimp the chef expects to receive not less than 21 nor more than 25 pieces.

Measurement Systems

The measurement formats of weight, volume and count are used in the imperial, U.S. and metric measurement systems. Because each of these systems is used in modern food service operations, you should be able to prepare recipes written in any of the three.

The **imperial system** is used in Great Britain, Canada and a few other countries. It uses pounds and ounces for weight, and pints and fluid ounces for volume.

The **U.S. system**, with which you are probably familiar, is the most difficult system to understand. It uses pounds for weight and cups for volume.

The **metric system** is the most commonly used system in the world. Developed in France during the late 18th century, it was intended to fill the need for a mathematically rational and uniform system of measurement. The

♦♦♦

FANNIE MERRITT FARMER
(1857–1915)

Fannie Farmer is more than the name on a cookbook. She was an early, vigorous and influential proponent of scientific cooking, nutrition and academic training for culinary professionals.

At the age of 30, Farmer enrolled in the Boston Cooking School. The school's curriculum was not designed to graduate chefs, but rather to produce cooking teachers. After graduating from the two-year course, Farmer stayed on, first as assistant principal and then as principal.

During her years there (and, indeed, for the rest of her career) she was obsessed with accurate measurements. She waged a campaign to eliminate measurements such as a "wine glass" of liquid, a "handful" of flour, a chunk of butter the "size of an egg" or a "heaping spoonful" of salt. For, as she once wrote, "correct measurements are absolutely necessary to insure the best results." Farmer also sought to replace the European system of measuring ingredients by weight with, for her, a more scientific measurement system based on volume and level measures (e.g., a level tablespoon). To a great degree, she succeeded.

Her writings reflect her concern for accurate measurements. Her first book, *The Boston Cooking School Cookbook* (1896), includes clearly written recipes with precise measurements. Later editions add recipe yields, oven temperatures and baking times.

After leaving the Boston Cooking School, she opened "Miss Farmer's School of Cookery." The curriculum listed 60 lessons divided into six courses. The first course covered the basics: laying a fire and using a gas stove; making breads, eggs, soups, potatoes and coffee. The second and third courses emphasized more advanced cooking. Pastry, desserts and salads were taught during the fourth course; presentation and service were taught during the fifth course. Quite progressively for the time, her sixth course taught cooking for nurses and emphasized nutrition and the dietary needs of the sick and elderly. (This may have reflected Farmer's personal interests, for she was partially disabled and in poor health from time to time.)

Farmer wrote other cookbooks, including *Food and Cookery for the Sick and Convalescent* (1904) and *A New Book of Cookery* (first published in 1912 and republished in several revised versions). Her writings never address the joys of cooking and eating; rather, they reflect a scientific approach to cooking and rely on clearly written, accurately measured recipes for good, solid food.

metric system is a decimal system in which the gram, liter and meter are the basic units of weight, volume and length, respectively. Larger or smaller units of weight, volume and length are formed by adding a prefix to the words *gram, liter* or *meter*. Some of the more commonly used prefixes in food service operations are deca- (10), kilo- (1000), deci- (1/10) and milli- (1/1000). Thus, a kilogram is 1000 grams; a decameter is 10 meters; a milliliter is 1/1000 of a liter. Because the metric system is based on multiples of 10, it is extremely easy to increase or decrease recipe amounts.

The most important thing for a chef to know about the metric system is that *you do not need to convert between the metric system and the U.S. system*

TABLE 4.1 COMMON ABBREVIATIONS AND CONVERSIONS

teaspoon	=	tsp.
tablespoon	=	Tbsp.
cup	=	c.
pint	=	pt.
quart	=	qt.
gram	=	g
milliliter	=	ml
liter	=	lt
ounce	=	oz.
fluid ounce	=	fl. oz.
pound	=	lb.
kilogram	=	kg
Dash	=	1/8 teaspoon
3 teaspoons	=	1 tablespoon
2 tablespoons	=	1 fl. oz.
4 tablespoons	=	1/4 cup (2 fl. oz.)
5-1/3 tablespoons	=	1/3 cup (2-2/3 fl. oz.)
16 tablespoons	=	1 cup (8 fl. oz.)
2 cups	=	1 pint (16 fl. oz.)
2 pints	=	1 quart (32 fl. oz.)
4 quarts	=	1 gallon (128 fl. oz.)
2 gallons	=	1 peck
4 pecks	=	1 bushel
1 gram	=	0.035 ounce (1/30 oz.)
1 ounce	=	28.35 grams
454 grams	=	1 pound
2.2 pounds	=	1 kilogram (1000 grams)
1 teaspoon	=	5 milliliters
1 tablespoon	=	15 milliliters
1 cup	=	.24 liters
1 gallon	=	3.80 liters

in recipe preparation. If a recipe is written in metric units, use metric measuring equipment; if it is written in U.S. units, use U.S. measuring equipment. Luckily, most modern measuring equipment is calibrated in both U.S. and metric increments. The need to convert amounts will arise only if the proper equipment is unavailable.

Converting Grams and Ounces

As you can see from Table 4.1, 1 ounce equals 28.35 grams. So, *to convert ounces to grams, multiply the number of ounces by 28* (rounded for convenience).

8 ounces × 28 = 224 grams

And *to convert grams to ounces, divide the number of grams by 28.*

224 ÷ 28 = 8 ounces.

To help you develop a framework for judging conversations, remember that:

◆ a kilogram is about 2.2 pounds
◆ a gram is about 1/30 ounce
◆ a pound is about 450 grams
◆ a liter is slightly more than a quart
◆ a centimeter is slightly less than 1/2 inch
◆ 0° Celcius is the freezing point of water (32° F)
◆ 100° Celcius is the boiling point of water (212° F)

These approximations are not a substitute for accurate conversions, however. Appendix II contains additional information on equivalents and metric conversions. There is no substitute for knowing this information. In fact, it should become second nature to you.

RECIPE CONVERSIONS

Yield—*the total amount of a product made from a specific recipe.*

Whether six servings or 60, every recipe is designed to produce or **yield** a specific amount of product. A recipe's yield may be expressed in *volume*, *weight* or *servings* (for example, 1 quart of sauce; 8 pounds of bread dough; 8 half-cup servings). If the expected yield does not meet your needs, you must convert (i.e., increase or decrease) the ingredient amounts. Recipe conversion is sometimes complicated by *portion size conversions.* For example, it may be necessary to convert a recipe that initially produces 24 8-ounce servings of soup into a recipe that produces 62 6-ounce servings.

It is just as easy to change yields by uneven amounts as it is to double or halve recipes. The mathematical principle is the same: *Each ingredient is multiplied by a* **conversion factor**. Do not take shortcuts by estimating recipe amounts or conversion factors. Inaccurate conversions lead to inedible foods, embarrassing shortages or wasteful excesses. Take the time to learn and apply proper conversion techniques.

Conversion factor (C.F.)—*the number used to increase or decrease ingredient quantities and recipe yields.*

Converting Total Yield

When portion size is unimportant or remains the same, recipe yield is converted by a simple two-step process:

STEP 1: Divide the desired (new) yield by the recipe (old) yield to obtain the conversion factor.

new yield ÷ old yield = conversion factor

STEP 2: Multiply each ingredient quantity by the conversion factor to obtain the new quantity.

old quantity × conversion factor = new quantity

Example 4.1

You need to convert a recipe for cauliflower soup. The present recipe yields 1-1/2 gallons. You only need to make 3/4 gallon.

First, determine the conversion factor:

.75 gallon ÷ 1.5 gallons = .50

The same conversion factor can be obtained after first converting the recipe amounts to fluid ounces:

96 fluid ounces ÷ 192 fluid ounces = .50

Second, the conversion factor (C.F.) is applied to each ingredient in the soup recipe:

CAULIFLOWER SOUP

	old quantity	×	C.F.	=	new quantity
Cauliflower, chopped	5 lb.	×	.5	=	2-1/2 lb.
Celery stalks	4	×	.5	=	2
Onion	1	×	.5	=	1/2
Chicken stock	2 qt.	×	.5	=	1 qt.
Heavy cream	3 pt.	×	.5	=	1-1/2 pt.

Converting Portion Size

A few additional steps are necessary to convert recipes when portion sizes must also be changed.

STEP 1: Determine the total yield of the existing recipe by multiplying the number of portions by the portion size.

original portions × original portion size = total (old) yield

STEP 2: Determine the total yield desired by multiplying the new number of portions by the new portion size.

desired portions × desired portion size = total (new) yield

STEP 3: Obtain the conversion factor as described above.

total (new) yield) ÷ total (old) yield = conversion factor

STEP 4: Multiply each ingredient quantity by the conversion factor.

old quantity × conversion factor = new quantity

Example 4.2

Returning to the cauliflower soup: The original recipe produced 1-1/2 gallons or 48 4-ounce servings. Now you need 72 6-ounce servings.

STEP 1: Total original yield is 48 × 4 = 192 ounces

STEP 2: Total desired yield is 72 × 6 = 432 ounces

STEP 3: Conversion factor is calculated by dividing total new yield by total old yield:

$$432 ÷ 192 = 2.25$$

STEP 4: Old ingredient quantities are multiplied by conversion factor to determine new quantities:

CAULIFLOWER SOUP

	old quantity	×	C.F.	=	new quantity
Cauliflower, chopped	5 lb.	×	2.25	=	11.25 lb.
Celery stalks	4	×	2.25	=	9
Onion	1	×	2.25	=	2.25
Chicken stock	2 qt.	×	2.25	=	4.5 qt.
Heavy cream	3 pt.	×	2.25	=	6.75 pt.

Additional Conversion Problems

When making very large recipe changes—for example, from 5 to 50 portions or 600 to 36 portions—you may encounter additional problems. The mathematical conversions described above do not take into account changes in equipment, evaporation rates, unforeseen recipe errors or cooking times. Chefs learn to use their judgment, knowledge of cooking principles and skills to compensate for these factors.

Equipment

When you change the size of a recipe, you must often change the equipment used as well. Problems arise, however, when the production techniques previously used no longer work with the new quantity of ingredients. For example, if you normally make a muffin recipe in small quantities by hand and you increase the recipe size, it may be necessary to prepare the batter in a mixer. But if mixing time remains the same, the batter may become overmixed, resulting in poor-quality muffins. Trying to prepare a small amount of product in equipment that is too large for the task can also affect its quality.

Evaporation

Equipment changes can also affect product quality because of changes in evaporation rates. Increasing a soup recipe may require substituting a tilt skillet for a saucepan. But because a tilt skillet provides more surface area for evaporation than does a saucepan, reduction time must be decreased to prevent overthickening the soup. The increased evaporation caused by an increased surface area may also alter the strength of the seasonings.

Recipe Errors

A recipe may contain errors in ingredients or techniques that are not obvious when it is prepared in small quantities. When increased, however, small mistakes often become big (and obvious) ones, and the final product suffers.

The only solution is to test recipes carefully and rely on your knowledge of cooking principles to compensate for unexpected problems.

Time

Do not multiply time specifications given in a recipe by the conversion factor used with the recipe's ingredients. All things being equal, *cooking time* will not change when recipe size changes. For example, a muffin requires the same amount of baking time whether you prepare one dozen or 14 dozen. Cooking time will be affected, however, by changes in evaporation rate or heat conduction caused by equipment changes. *Mixing time* may change when recipe size is changed. Different equipment may perform mixing tasks more or less efficiently than previously used equipment. Again, rely on experience and good judgment.

CALCULATING UNIT COSTS AND RECIPE COSTS

Unit Costs

Food service operations purchase most foods from suppliers in bulk or wholesale packages. For example, canned goods are purchased by the case; produce by the flat, case or lug; and flour and sugar by 25- or 50-pound bags. Even fish and meats are often purchased in large cuts, not individual serving-sized portions. The purchased amount is rarely used for a single recipe, however. It must be broken down into smaller units such as pounds, cups, quarts or ounces.

In order to allocate the proper ingredient costs to the recipe being prepared, it is necessary to convert **as-purchased costs or prices** to **unit costs or prices**. To find the unit cost (i.e., the cost of a particular unit, say a single egg) in a package containing multiple units (e.g., a 30-dozen case), divide the as-purchased cost (A.P. cost) of the package by the number of units in the package.

As-purchased (A.P.)—*the condition or cost of an item as it is purchased or received from the supplier.*

Unit cost—*the price paid to acquire one of the specified units.*

A.P. cost ÷ number of units = cost per unit

Example 4.3

A case of #10 cans contains six individual cans. If a case of tomato paste costs $23.50, then each can costs $3.92.

$$\$23.50 \div 6 = \$3.92$$

If your recipe uses less than the total can, you must continue dividing the cost of the can until you arrive at the appropriate unit amount. Continuing with the tomato paste example, if you need only 1 cup of tomato paste, divide the can price ($3.92) by the total number of cups contained in the can to arrive at the cost per cup (unit). The list of canned good sizes in Appendix II shows that a #10 can contains approximately 13 cups. Using the formula, each cup costs $0.30.

$$\$3.92 \div 13 = .30$$

The cost of one cup can be reduced even further if necessary. If the recipe uses only 2 tablespoons of tomato paste, divide the cost per cup by the number of tablespoons in a cup. As you can see, the final cost for 2 tablespoons of this tomato paste is $0.037.

$$.30 \div 16 = .018 \times 2 = \$0.037$$

RECIPE COSTING FORM

Menu Item _____ Date _____

Ingredient	Quantity	COST			TOTAL COST
		As Purchased	Yield %	Edible Portion	

TOTAL COST OF RECIPE $ _____

Total Yield _____   Size of Portion _____
                                              Cost per Portion _____

Food Cost Percentage _____   Selling Price _____

FIGURE 4.2   *Recipe Costing Form*

Recipe Costs

Total recipe cost—*the total cost of ingredients for a particular recipe; it does not reflect overhead, labor, fixed expenses or profit.*

With a typical recipe, you calculate the **total recipe cost** with the following two-step procedure:

STEP 1: Determine the cost for the given quantity of each recipe ingredient with the unit costing procedures described above.

STEP 2: Add all of the ingredient costs together to obtain the total recipe cost.

Cost per portion—*the amount of the total recipe cost divided by the number of portions produced from that recipe; the cost of one serving.*

The total recipe cost can then be broken down into the **cost per portion**, which is the most useful figure for food cost controls. To arrive at cost per portion, divide the total recipe cost by the total number of servings or portions produced by that recipe.

total recipe cost ÷ number of portions = cost per portion

The Recipe Costing Form shown in Figure 4.2 is useful for organizing recipe costing information. It provides space for listing each ingredient, the quantity of each ingredient needed, the cost of each unit and the total cost for the ingredient. Total yield, portion size and cost per portion are listed at the bottom of the form. Note that there is no space for recipe procedures, as these are irrelevant in recipe costing.

YIELD TESTS

Computing the cost of recipe ingredients is a simple matter if the foods are used the way they are received and there is no waste or trim. This is rarely the case, however. The amount of a food item **as purchased (A.P.)** and the amount of the **edible portion (E.P.)** of that same item may vary considerably, particularly with meats and fresh produce. In this context, **yield** is the usable or edible quantity remaining after processing the as-purchased quantity of the food item. That is, yield refers to the amount of usable lettuce after the case of iceberg is cleaned, or the amount of meat that is served after trimming. The **yield factor or percentage** is the ratio of the usable quantity to the purchased quantity. It is always less than 100% and may be calculated in dollars or weight/volume amounts.

Because purchase specifications and fabrication techniques vary from operation to operation, there are no precise, standard yield amounts. Each kitchen must determine its own yield factors. Yield tests must be conducted on A.P. items as they are received from purveyors. To be effective, several tests must be conducted and the results averaged to arrive at a specific operation's yield factor for that item.

The method of calculating yield varies depending on whether the item's trim is all waste (for example, vegetable peelings) or whether the trim creates usable or salable byproducts (for example, meat and poultry).

Raw Yield Tests Without Byproducts

The simplest yield test procedure is for items that have no usable or salable byproducts. These items include most produce as well as some fish and shellfish. Unless these items are ready to serve *as received* from the purveyor, trimming is required and all trim is waste. For example, one pound of apples may yield only 13 ounces of flesh after peeling and coring. If the recipe requires one pound of peeled, cored apples, the chef must start with slightly more than one pound of A.P. apples. In order to determine accurate costs for such items, the trim loss must be taken into account. Even seedless grapes do not have a 100% yield factor. The weight of stems and bad grapes must be calculated and deducted from the A.P. weight to determine the correct price per pound of servable fruit.

There are three steps for calculating yield when all trim is waste:

STEP 1: Calculate the total weight of the trim produced from the specified A.P. quantity. This is known as **trim loss**.

STEP 2: Subtract the trim loss from the A.P. weight to arrive at the total yield weight.

STEP 3: Divide the yield weight by the A.P. weight to determine the yield factor.

Example 4.4

Two pounds of fresh garlic generate 4-1/2 ounces of trim loss. Therefore, the yield weight is 27-1/2 ounces and the yield factor is 86%:

$$(2 \times 16 \text{ ounces}) = 32 \text{ ounces} - 4.5 \text{ ounces} = 27.5 \text{ ounces}$$

$$27.5 \div 32 = .859 = 86\%$$

Remember, subtract trim loss from A.P. weight, then divide yield weight by A.P. weight to arrive at the yield percentage. Note that the yield factor will always be some number less than 1, and the yield percentage will always be less than 100%.

Edible portion (E.P.)—*the amount of a food item available for consumption after trimming or fabrication.*

Yield—*the total amount of a food item created or remaining after trimming or fabrication.*

Yield factor or percentage—*the ratio of the edible portion to the amount purchased.*

Trim loss—*the amount of the product removed when preparing it for consumption.*

TABLE 4.2   COMMON PRODUCE YIELD FACTORS

Produce	Yield Factor (%)	Produce	Yield Factor (%)	Produce	Yield Factor (%)
Apples	75	Grapefruit	45	Pears	75
Apricots	94	Grapes	90	Pea pods	90
Artichokes	48	Kiwi	80	Peppers	82
Avocados	75	Leeks	50	Pineapple	50
Bananas	70	Lemons	45	Plums	75
Berries	95	Lettuce	75	Potatoes	80
Broccoli	70	Limes	45	Radishes	90
Cabbage	79	Melons	55	Rhubarb	85
Carrots	78	Mushrooms	90	Scallions	65
Cauliflower	55	Nectarines	86	Spinach	60
Celery	75	Okra	82	Squash, summer	90
Cherries	82	Onions	90	Squash, winter	70
Corn, cob	28	Oranges	60	Tomatoes	90
Cucumbers	95	Papayas	65	Turnips	75
Eggplant	85	Parsley	85	Watercress	90
Garlic	88	Peaches	75	Watermelon	45

Because each operation has its own standards for cleaning and trimming raw products, yield factors should be personalized. Lists of common yield factors are available, however, as an indication of industry norms. Some of these are included in Table 4.2.

Applying Yield Factors

Now that you understand what yield factors are and how to calculate them, we look at how they are used in costing recipes. First, yield factors are used for accurate recipe costing.

Example 4.5

Carrots cost $6.50 per 25-pound bag and have a yield factor of 78%. In other words, 22% of that 25-pound bag is waste. The price should be recalculated to account for that waste; that is, the A.P. (as purchased) unit cost must be converted to an E.P. (edible portion) unit cost. This is done by dividing A.P. cost by the yield percentage.

$$\text{A.P. Cost (\$)} \div \text{Yield Percentage} = \text{E.P. Cost (\$)}$$

$$.26/\text{pound } (6.50 \div 25) \div .78 = .33/\text{pound}$$

Thus, the carrots have an E.P. unit cost of $0.33 per pound (as compared with an A.P. price of $0.26 per pound). Note that E.P. cost is always greater than A.P. cost. When costing a recipe, you should use the $0.33-per-pound price as the accurate ingredient cost.

Second, yield factors are necessary for accurate purchasing. Most recipes list ingredients in E.P. quantities. Therefore, the chef must consider waste or trim amounts when ordering these items. If only the amounts listed in the recipe are ordered and then the item requires trimming, the number of portions (or recipe yield) will be less than the desired amount.

Example 4.6

A recipe requires 20 pounds of shredded cabbage. The yield factor for cabbage is 79%. Therefore, 20 pounds is 79% of the A.P. quantity. Divide the amount needed by the yield factor to determine the minimum A.P. quantity.

E.P. Quantity ÷ Yield Percentage = A.P. Quantity

20 pounds ÷ .79 = 25.3 pounds

It will take 25-1/3 pounds of cabbage to provide the 20 pounds of shredded cabbage. (This figure will be increased to an even amount for purchasing because yield factors are, at best, only an estimate.) Note that the A.P. figure must always be greater than the E.P. figure in this formula.

FOOD COST

Perhaps no other cost is emphasized as much by food service managers as **food cost**. Food cost refers to the cost of all foods used in the fabrication of menu items. This figure is also known as the **cost of goods sold** or **raw food cost** ("raw" is a bit misleading as food cost includes precooked and packaged foods as well as uncooked foods).

Food cost—*the cost of the materials that go directly into the production of the menu item.*

Food costs are calculated in two ways: (1) as a total cost of all foods used during a given time period, and (2) as a cost of one particular portion or menu item. Total cost is used as a general guideline for budgeting and menu planning. The portion or item cost is used to calculate menu prices; it helps the chef stay within cost limitations.

Cost of Goods Sold

The "goods" sold by a food service operation are, of course, the foods used in producing menu items. Before you can calculate cost of goods sold you must take a physical inventory of all foodstuffs on hand. **Inventory** should be taken periodically: at the end of each week, month, quarter or other accounting period. Taking inventory requires listing and counting all foods in the kitchen, storerooms and refrigerators. The quantities are then *extended*, that is, multiplied by the unit cost. The extended prices are then added to calculate the total inventory value.

Inventory—*the listing and counting of all foods in the kitchen, storerooms and refrigerators.*

Whether prepared foods or open containers are included in the inventory depends on the operation. Often small quantities of prepared foods or open containers are not inventoried on the theory that a certain amount of such items is always on hand, the value of which is minimal but fairly consistent from one accounting period to the next.

To properly calculate the cost of goods sold you must conduct an inventory at the beginning and end of the desired period and maintain records of all purchases during the period. The time period covered by this calculation could be any duration: week, month, quarter or year. After the total value of the inventory for both the beginning and the end of the period has been established, cost of goods sold is calculated as follows:

	Value of food inventory at beginning of period
PLUS	Food purchased during period
MINUS	Inventory at end of period
	Cost of food sold

Example 4.7

The total value of food in inventory on December 1 is $7600. The restaurant purchases $2300 worth of food during December and the inventory on January 1 is worth $5600. The cost of goods sold during the month of December is $4300 (in other words, the food produced during the month of December cost $4300):

$$(7600 + 2300) - 5600 = 4300$$

Once management knows the cost of goods sold, it can compare this figure with the dollar value of sales for the same period. This comparison gives management a good idea of how the business did for that period.

Food Cost Percentages

Food cost percentage—*the ratio of the cost of food served to the food sales dollars during a given period.*

The **food cost percentage** is the ratio of costs to sales. It shows what each dollar of sales costs. For example, a 35% food cost means that $0.35 of each dollar received went to pay for the foods the operation used. Food cost percentage is determined by dividing food cost by sales.

$$\text{food cost} \div \text{sales} = \text{food cost percentage}$$

Example 4.8

Refer back to Example 4.8 and assume that sales for December totaled $10,750. The food cost percentage for the month would be 40%:

$$4,300 \div 10,750 = .40 = 40\%$$

By itself a single food cost percentage is meaningless. To be useful, it should be compared with the food cost percentages for other months of the same year or the same month in previous years. It is also helpful to know the food cost percentages for other similarly situated food service operations.

Food cost percentages can also be calculated on individual menu items. If the food items in a sliced turkey sandwich cost $2.80 and the sandwich sells for $5.25, the food cost percentage is 53% (2.80 divided by 5.25). Many operations would find this unacceptably high. To reduce the percentage and increase gross profits, the operation must either increase the selling price or decrease the ingredient costs.

Changing menu price, raw food cost or portion size will change the food cost percentage. If the food cost percentage is too high, the gross profit will be insufficient to cover operating expenses. If the percentage is too low, customers may feel they are not getting their money's worth and take their business elsewhere. Setting an appropriate percentage requires sound judgment, knowledge of the competition and accurate cost information. Periodic evaluations are necessary to ensure that the desired objective is actually maintained.

ESTABLISHING MENU PRICES

After determining the cost of food items, you can calculate menu prices. A few of the many methods for setting menu prices are explained below. Some techniques are highly structured and closely related to food costs; others are unstructured and unrelated to actual food costs. As a practical matter, no one method is right for every operation and a combination of methods may provide the best pricing information.

Cost-Based Pricing

Food Cost Percentage Pricing

For this technique, you must first determine the food cost percentage desired for the particular facility. After calculating each item's raw food cost you determine the selling price with the following formula:

$$\text{cost per portion} \div \text{food cost percentage} = \text{selling price}$$

Example 4.9

If the raw food cost for one sandwich is $1.70 and the desired food cost percentage is 23%, the selling price must be at least $7.39:

$$1.70 \div .23 = 7.391$$

In this situation, 23% of the sales price for each item will go to cover the raw food cost for that item. The higher the food cost percentage, the lower the portion of the sales price available for labor, fixed expenses, overhead or profit. Determining the appropriate food cost percentage for the facility is critical to the successful use of this method.

Factor Pricing

A variation on food cost percentage pricing is factor pricing. First, you take the desired food cost percentage and divide it into 100 to arrive at a cost factor. The cost of each item is then multiplied by the cost factor to arrive at the menu price. Using the previous example, the factor is 4.35 (100 ÷ 23 = 4.35), and the menu price for a $1.70 item is $7.39 (1.70 × 4.35 = 7.39).

Both food cost percentage and factor pricings are fast and easy to use. But these methods are sometimes unreliable because they assume that other costs associated with preparing food stay the same for each menu item. These systems wrongly assume that the costs for labor, energy and overhead are the same for a rack of lamb entree and a seafood salad. These methods may be fine-tuned somewhat by adjusting the desired food cost percentage according to the type of food or menu category. Appetizers may be assigned a lower food cost percentage than, say, desserts or side dishes.

Prime Cost Pricing

The food service industry uses a figure known as **prime cost** to refer to the total of raw food cost plus direct labor. Direct labor is the labor actually required for an item's preparation. If, for example, food cost is $2.10 and direct labor is $1.50, then prime cost is $3.60. As with the food cost percentage example above, the prime cost percentage can be divided into the prime cost amount to determine menu price.

Prime cost—*the combination of food costs and direct labor.*

Example 4.10

The raw food cost for a rack of lamb is $7.50; it takes a cook a total of 9 minutes to clean and trim it for service. If that cook is paid $8.50 per hour, the direct labor cost is $1.27. (8.50 per hour = .14 per minute; .14 × 9 = $1.27).

The prime cost of the rack of lamb is $8.77 (7.50 + 1.27). A selling price is then determined by dividing prime cost by the desired prime cost percentage. If management decided that the desired prime cost percentage is 48 percent, then the rack of lamb should be priced at $18.27. (8.77 ÷ .48 = 18.27)

Perceived Value Pricing

This is a rather backwards way of setting prices based on what a customer will perceive as an appropriate price. First determine what the market price is for the same or similar item. Then calculate what you can serve for that price. Assume, for example,

1. the market price for a complete fried chicken dinner is $9.95,
2. the desired profit is 7% of sales,
3. overhead expenses are 27% of sales and
4. labor is approximately 23% of sales.

Subtract the total of these items (57%) from the $9.95 selling price and you find that your total food cost for the fried chicken dinner must not be more than $4.28. This technique requires a thorough knowledge of the market and good historical information on labor and overhead costs. With the necessary information, you can determine how much to spend on raw product for each menu item and still make the desired profit.

Noncost-Based Pricing

Noncost-based pricing techniques rely on nonmonetary factors to set menu prices. Traditional prices in the area for the same or similar items may affect an operation's ability to set prices. This is particularly true for special or loss-leader items such as 79-cent jumbo sodas or 99-cent breakfast specials.

While the competition's prices are an important consideration, you should not simply copy them. Your competition's costs are not your costs no matter how similar the final food items appear. If you must charge higher prices than your competition, seek out some way to differentiate your product or service.

Virtually all food service operations are seeking to charge the highest price possible without a loss of sales. The customer's perception of value is therefore critical. The menu can be used as a tool for educating customers. Descriptive language or an explanation of unique or special dishes can be included. Customers who understand the value of service, atmosphere, out-of-season foods and specialty products will tolerate higher prices for those items.

Psychological Impact of Pricing

Regardless of how you arrive at a menu price, you may wish to round the figure up or down for psychological impact. It is human nature to perceive some prices as higher or lower than they actually are. For example, using a 9 or 5 as the last digit in a price creates the impression of a discount; prices ending in a 9 or 5 appeal to price-conscious customers. Prices ending in a 0 are perceived as more expensive and higher quality and so are often used on fine-dining menus.

The number of digits in a price is also important: $9.95 seems much less expensive than $10.25. Likewise, the first numeral in a price affects perception. When changing menu prices, an increase from $5.95 to $6.45 is seen as greater than an increase from $6.25 to $6.75, although both are 50-cent increases.

Patrons do not like to see a large spread in menu prices. It may make them think something is wrong with one of the items or may cause confusion. For example, a lobster dinner for $14.50 may be a reasonable price, but it may be inappropriate on a menu where all other items are less than $6.00. In general, the highest price should not be more than double the lowest price within the same food category. If the least expensive appetizer is $4.00, then the most expensive appetizer should not exceed $8.00.

Establishing menu prices is one of the most difficult yet important things a chef or manager can do to affect the facility's success. No one method is best for all operations, so careful study of several approaches is recommended.

CONTROLLING FOOD COSTS

Many things affect food costs in any given operation; most can be controlled by the chef or manager. These controls do not require mathematical calculations or formulas, just basic management skills and a good dose of common sense. The following factors all have an impact on the operation's bottom line:

+ menu
+ purchasing/ordering
+ receiving
+ storing
+ issuing
+ kitchen procedures
    establishing standard portions
    waste
+ sales and service

Chefs tend to focus their control efforts in the area of kitchen preparation. While this may seem logical, it is not adequate. A good chef will be involved in all aspects of the operation to help prevent problems from arising or to correct those that may occur.

Menu

A profitable menu is based upon many variables including customer desires, physical space and equipment, ingredient availability, cost of goods sold, employee skills and competition. All management personnel, including the chef, should be consulted when planning the menu. Menu changes, while possibly desirable, must be executed with as much care as the original design.

Purchasing/Ordering

Purchasing techniques have a direct impact on cost controls. On the one hand, **parstock** must be adequate for efficient operations; on the other hand, too much inventory wastes space and resources and may spoil. Before any items are ordered, purchasing specifications should be established and communicated to potential purveyors. Specifications should precisely describe the item, including grade, quality, packaging and unit size. Each operation should design its own form to best meet its specific needs. A sample specification form is shown in Figure 4.3. This information can be used to obtain price quotes from several purveyors. Update these quotes periodically to ensure that you are getting the best value for your money.

Parstock (Par)—*the amount of stock necessary to cover operating needs between deliveries.*

Receiving

Whether goods are received by a full-time clerk, as they are in a large hotel, or by the chef or kitchen manager, certain standards should be

```
Menu Item:

Product:                                    Date:

Grade/Quality:

Weight/Size:                                NAMP/IMPS #:

Packaging:

Delivery conditions:

Comments:
```

FIGURE 4.3   *Specification Form*

observed. The person signing for merchandise should first confirm that the items were actually ordered. Second, determine whether the items listed on the invoice are the ones being delivered and that the price and quantity listed are accurate. Third, the items, especially meats and produce, should be checked for quality, freshness and weight. Established purchase specifications should be readily available.

Storing

Proper storage of foodstuffs is crucial in order to prevent spoilage, pilferage and waste. Stock must be rotated so that the older items are used first. Such a system for rotating stock is referred to as FIFO: First In, First Out. Storage areas should be well ventilated and lit to prevent infestation and mold.

Issuing

It may be necessary, particularly in larger operations, to limit storeroom access to specific personnel. Maintaining ongoing inventory records or par-stock sheets helps the ordering process. Controlling issuances eliminates waste caused by multiple opened containers and ensures proper stock rotation.

Kitchen Procedures: Establishing Standard Portions

Standardizing portions is essential to controlling food costs. Unless portion quantity is uniform, it will be impossible to compute portion costs accurately. Portion discrepancies can also confuse or mislead customers.

Actual portion sizes depend on the food service operation itself, the menu, the prices and the customers' desires. Some items are generally purchased preportioned for convenience (for example, steaks are sold in uniform cuts, baking potatoes are available in uniform sizes, butter comes in preportioned pats and bread comes sliced for service). Other items must be portioned by the establishment prior to service. Special equipment makes consistent portioning easy. There are machines to slice meats, cutting guides for cakes and pies and portion scales for weighing quantities. Standardized portion scoops and ladles are indispensable for serving vegetables, soups, stews, salads and similar foods. Many of these items are discussed and illustrated in Chapter 5, Tools and Equipment.

Once acceptable portion sizes are established, employees must be properly trained to present them. If each employee of a sandwich shop prepared sandwiches the way he or she would like to eat them, customers would probably never receive the same sandwich twice. Customers may become confused and decide not to risk a repeat visit. Obviously, carelessness in portioning can also drastically affect food cost.

Kitchen Procedures: Waste

The chef must also control waste from overproduction or failure to use leftovers. With an adequate sales history, the chef can accurately estimate the quantity of food to prepare for each week, day or meal. If the menu is designed properly, the chef can also use leftovers and trim from product fabrication. The less waste generated in food preparation, the lower the overall food cost will be.

Sales and Service

An improperly trained sales staff can undo even the most rigorous of food cost controls. Front-of-the-house personnel are, after all, ultimately responsible for the sales portion of the food cost equation. Proper training is once again critical. Prices charged must be accurate and complete. Poor service can lead to the need to serve for free ("comp") an excessive amount of food. Dropped or spilled foods do not generate revenues.

CONCLUSION

No food service operation can become successful on the chef's cooking ability alone. A well-designed, enticing and accurately priced menu is also necessary. By following a standardized recipe you should be able to repeatedly produce a known quality and quantity of food for your specific food service operation. Based upon the regularity with which you offer these foods, your menu can be classified as static, cycle, market or hybrid. You can offer your menu items either à la carte, semi à la carte or table d'hôte.

You must be able to understand and apply proper techniques for converting recipes, food costing, menu pricing and loss control. Although computers are useful and are becoming more common in kitchens, no machine can substitute for a chef's watchful eye and hands-on controls.

QUESTIONS FOR DISCUSSION

1. Describe the four types of menus. Can each type of menu offer foods à la carte, semi à la carte and/or table d'hôte? Explain your answer.
2. Discuss three factors in food preparation that affect successful recipe size changes.
3. Why is it important to calculate the portion cost of a recipe in professional food service operations? Why is the full recipe cost inadequate?

4. List several factors that might cause one operation's yield factor for lettuce to be higher than another operation's. Explain why standardized yield factor lists are unreliable.

5. How is food cost percentage calculated? How can this figure be used (or misused) to evaluate the success of an operation?

6. Discuss three psychological factors used in setting menu prices.

PART TWO
PREPARATION

Mise en place *is the essence of preparation. Although it means "everything in its place," the term connotes more than merely having all ingredients and tools on hand and being ready to begin preparing a dish. Rather, it suggests that the chef can identify, appreciate and understand how the necessary tools and equipment work, how the foods are cut and what the basic flavoring ingredients and staples are.*

To assist you in preparing to cook, Part II presents information about the tools and equipment routinely found in professional kitchens, then discusses how a professional kitchen is organized. There is a chapter on knife skills as well as chapters on kitchen staples (herbs and spices, condiments, oils, vinegars, nuts, coffee and tea) and eggs and dairy products (including milk, cream, cultured milk products and cheese).

Understanding this information is critical before successful cooking can begin.

CHAPTER 5

TOOLS AND EQUIPMENT

After studying this chapter you will be able to:

♦ recognize a variety of professional kitchen tools and equipment
♦ select and care for knives properly
♦ understand how a professional kitchen is organized

Having the proper tools and equipment for a particular task may mean the difference between a job well done and one done carelessly, incorrectly or even dangerously. This chapter introduces some of the tools and equipment typically used in a professional kitchen. Items are divided into categories according to their function: hand tools, knives, measuring and portioning devices, cookware, strainers and sieves, processing equipment, storage containers, heavy equipment and safety equipment.

A wide variety of specialized tools and equipment is available to today's chef. Breading machines, croissant shapers and doughnut glazers are designed to speed production by reducing handwork. Other devices—for instance, a duck press or a couscousière—are used only for unique tasks in preparing a few menu items. Much of this specialized equipment is quite expensive and found only in food manufacturing operations or specialized kitchens; a discussion of it is beyond the scope of this chapter. Brief descriptions of some of these specialized devices are, however, found in the Glossary. Baking pans and tools are discussed in Chapter 26, Principles of the Bakeshop.

This chapter is illustrated with generic drawings because manufacturers' designs differ. We end this chapter with a discussion of how a professional kitchen should be designed and organized.

Before using any equipment, study the operator's manual or have someone experienced with the particular item instruct you on proper procedures for its use and cleaning. And remember, always think safety.

STANDARDS FOR TOOLS AND EQUIPMENT

NSF International (NSF), previously known as the National Sanitation Foundation, promulgates consensus standards for the design, construction and installation of kitchen tools, cookware and equipment. Many states and municipalities require that food service operations use only NSF-certified equipment. Although NSF certification is voluntary, most manufacturers submit their designs to NSF for certification to show that they are suitable for use in professional food service operations. Certified equipment bears the NSF mark shown in Figure 5.1.

NSF standards reflect the following requirements:

1. Equipment must be easily cleaned.
2. All food contact surfaces must be nontoxic (under intended end use conditions), nonabsorbent, corrosion resistant and nonreactive.

FIGURE 5.1   *The NSF Mark*

3. All food contact surfaces must be smooth, that is, free of pits, cracks, crevices, ledges, rivet heads and bolts.

4. Internal corners and edges must be rounded and smooth; external corners and angles must be smooth and sealed.

5. Coating materials must be nontoxic and easily cleaned; coatings must resist chipping and cracking.

6. Waste and waste liquids must be easily removed.

SELECTING TOOLS AND EQUIPMENT

In general, only commercial food service tools and equipment should be used in a professional kitchen. Household tools and appliances not NSF certified may not withstand the rigors of a professional kitchen. Look for tools that are well constructed. For example, joints should be welded, not bonded with solder; handles should be comfortable, with rounded borders; plastic and rubber parts should be seamless.

Before purchasing or leasing any particular piece of equipment you should evaluate several factors:

1. Is this equipment necessary for producing menu items?

2. Will this equipment perform the job required in the space available?

3. Is this equipment the most economical for the operation's specific needs?

4. Is this equipment easy to clean, maintain and repair?

HAND TOOLS

Hand tools are designed to aid in cutting, shaping, moving or combining foods. They have few, if any, moving parts. Knives, discussed separately below, are the most important hand tools. Others are metal or rubber spatulas, spoons, whisks, tongs and specialized cutters. In addition to the items shown in Figure 5.2, many hand tools designed for specific tasks, such as pressing tortillas or pitting cherries, are available. Sturdiness, durability and safety are the watchwords when selecting hand tools. Choose tools that can withstand the heavy use of a professional kitchen and those that are easily cleaned.

KNIVES

Knives are the most important items in your tool kit. With a sharp knife, the skilled chef can accomplish a number of tasks more quickly and efficiently than any machine. Good-quality knives are expensive but will last for many years with proper care. Select easily sharpened, well-constructed knives that are comfortable and balanced in your hand. Knife construction and commonly used knives are discussed here; knife safety and care as well as cutting techniques are discussed in Chapter 6, Knife Skills.

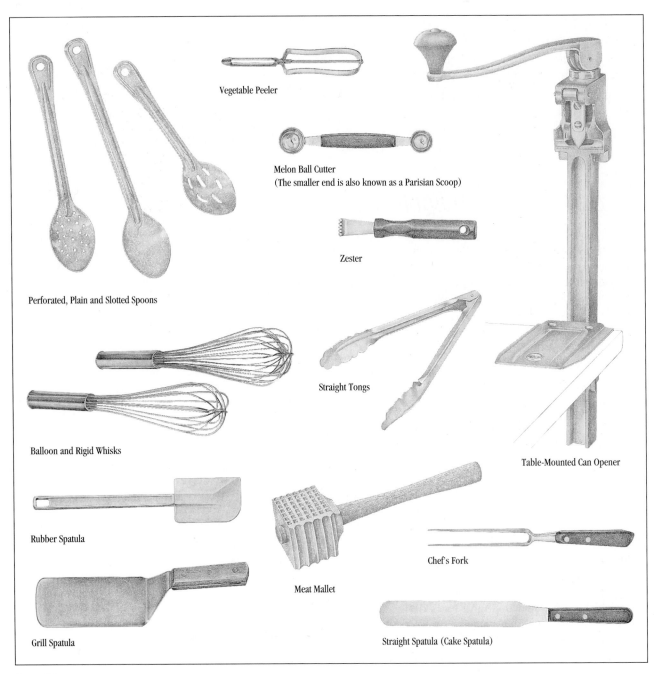

Vegetable Peeler

Melon Ball Cutter
(The smaller end is also known as a Parisian Scoop)

Zester

Perforated, Plain and Slotted Spoons

Straight Tongs

Balloon and Rigid Whisks

Table-Mounted Can Opener

Rubber Spatula

Chef's Fork

Meat Mallet

Grill Spatula

Straight Spatula (Cake Spatula)

FIGURE 5.2

Knife Construction

A good knife begins with a single piece of metal, stamped, cut or—best of all—forged and tempered into a blade of the desired shape. The metals generally used for knife blades are:

1. **Carbon steel**—An alloy of carbon and iron, it is traditionally used for blades because it is soft enough to be sharpened easily. It corrodes and discolors easily, however, especially when used with acidic foods.

2. **Stainless steel**—It will not rust, corrode or discolor and is extremely durable. But a stainless steel blade is much more difficult to sharpen than a

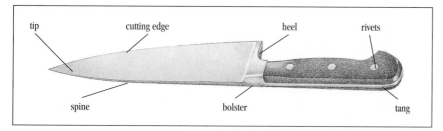

FIGURE 5.3

carbon steel one, although once an edge is established it lasts longer than the edge on a carbon steel blade.

3. **High carbon stainless steel**—An alloy combining the best features of carbon steel and stainless steel, it neither corrodes nor discolors and can be sharpened almost as easily as carbon steel. It is now the most frequently used metal for blades.

A portion of the blade, known as the tang, fits inside the handle. The best knives are constructed with a full tang running the length of the handle; they also have a bolster where the blade meets the handle (the bolster is part of the blade, not a separate collar). Less expensive knives may have a 3/4-length tang or a thin "rattail" tang. Neither provide as much support, durability or balance as a full tang.

Knife handles are often made of hard woods infused with plastic and riveted to the tang. Molded polypropylene handles are permanently bonded to a tang without seams or rivets. Any handle should be shaped for comfort and ground smooth to eliminate crevices where bacteria can grow.

Knife Shapes and Sharpening Equipment

You will collect many knives during your career, many with specialized functions not described here. This list includes only the most basic knives and sharpening equipment:

French or Chef's Knife

An all-purpose knife used for chopping, slicing and mincing. Its rigid 8- to 14-inch-long blade is wide at the heel and tapers to a point at the tip.

Utility Knife

An all-purpose knife used for cutting fruits and vegetables and carving poultry. Its rigid 6- to 8-inch-long blade is shaped like a chef's knife but narrower.

Boning Knife

A smaller knife with a thin blade used to separate meat from bone. The blade is usually 5 to 7 inches long and may be flexible or rigid.

Paring Knife

A short knife used for detail work or cutting fruits and vegetables. The rigid blade is from 2 to 4 inches long. A tournée or **bird's beak knife** is similar to a paring knife but with a curved blade; it is used for cutting curved surfaces or tournéeing vegetables.

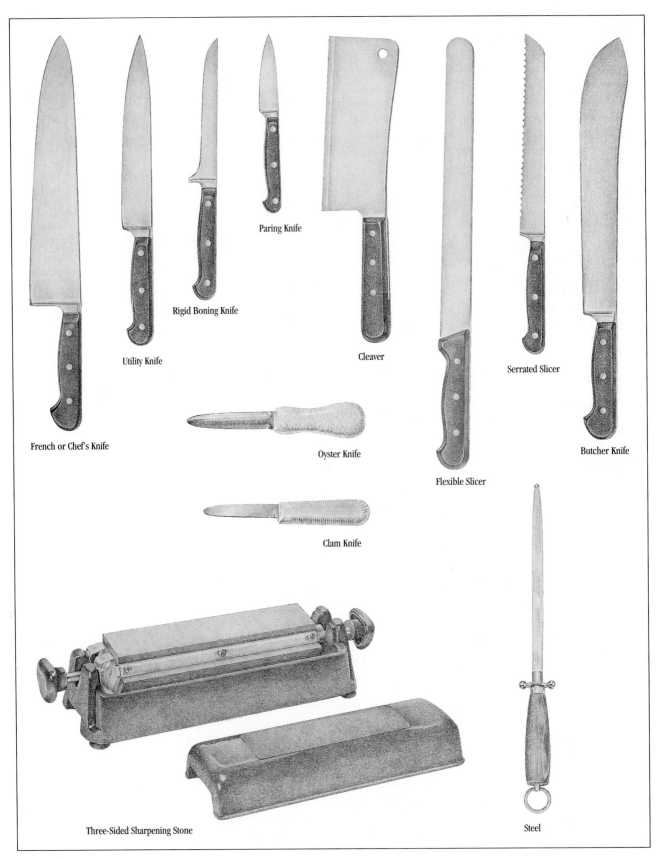

Paring Knife

Rigid Boning Knife

Utility Knife

Cleaver

Serrated Slicer

French or Chef's Knife

Oyster Knife

Butcher Knife

Flexible Slicer

Clam Knife

Three-Sided Sharpening Stone

Steel

 5.4

TOOLS AND EQUIPMENT **87**

Cleaver

The large, heavy rectangular blade is used for chopping or cutting through bones.

Slicer

A knife with a long, thin blade used primarily for slicing cooked meat. The tip may be round or pointed and the blade may be flexible or rigid. A similar knife with a serrated edge is used for slicing bread or pastry items.

Butcher Knife

Sometimes known as a **scimitar** because the rigid blade curves up in a 25-degree angle at the tip, it is used for fabricating raw meat and is available with 6- to 14-inch blades.

Oyster and Clam Knives

The short, rigid blades of these knives are used to open oyster and clam shells. The tips are blunt; only the clam knife has a sharp edge.

Sharpening Stone

Also known as a **whetstone**, it is used to put an edge on a dull blade.

Steel

It is used to hone or straighten a blade immediately after and between sharpenings.

MEASURING AND PORTIONING DEVICES

Recipe ingredients must be measured precisely, especially in the bakeshop, and foods should be measured when served to control portion size and cost. The devices used to measure and portion foods are, for the most part, hand tools designed to make food preparation and service easier and more precise. The accuracy they afford prevents the cost of mistakes made when accurate measurements are ignored.

Measurements may be based upon weight (e.g., grams, ounces, pounds) or volume (e.g., teaspoons, cups, gallons). Therefore it is necessary to have available several measuring devices, including liquid and dry measuring cups and a variety of scales. Thermometers and timers are also measuring devices and are discussed here. When purchasing measuring devices look for quality construction and accurate markings.

Scales

Scales are necessary to determine the weight of an ingredient or a portion of food (for example, the sliced meat for a sandwich). Portion scales use a spring mechanism, round dial and single flat tray. They are available calibrated in grams, ounces or pounds. Electronic scales also use a spring mechanism but provide digital readouts. They are often required by law where foods are priced for sale by weight. Balance scales (also known as baker's scales) use a two-tray and free-weights counterbalance system. A balance scale allows more weight to be measured at one time because it is not limited by spring capacity. Any scale must be properly used and maintained to provide an accurate reading.

TABLE 5.1   PORTION SCOOP CAPACITIES

Scoop Number	Volume		Approximate Weight*	
	U.S.	Metric	U.S.	Metric
6	2/3 c.	160 ml	5 oz.	160 g
8	1/2 c.	120 ml	4 oz.	120 g
10	3 fl. oz.	90 ml	3 to 3-1/2 oz.	85–100 g
12	1/3 c.	80 ml	2-1/2 to 3 oz.	75–85 g
16	1/4 c.	60 ml	2 oz.	60 g
20	1-1/2 fl. oz.	45 ml	1-3/4 oz.	50 g
24	1-1/3 fl. oz.	40 ml	1-1/3 oz.	40 g
30	1 fl. oz.	30 ml	1 oz.	30 g
40	0.8 fl. oz.	24 ml	0.8 oz.	23 g
60	1/2 fl. oz.	15 ml	1/2 oz.	15 g

*Weights are approximate because they vary by food.

Volume Measures

Ingredients may be measured by volume using measuring spoons and measuring cups. Measuring spoons sold as a set usually include 1/4-, 1/2-, 1-teaspoon and 1-tablespoon units (or the metric equivalent). Liquid measuring cups are available in capacities from 1 cup to 1 gallon. They have a lip or pour spout above the top line of measurement to prevent spills. Measuring cups for dry ingredients are usually sold in sets of 1/4-, 1/3-, 1/2-, and 1-cup units. They do not have pour spouts, so the top of the cup is level with the top measurement specified. Glass measuring cups are not recommended because they can break. Avoid using bent or dented measuring cups as the damage may distort the measurement capacity.

Ladles

Long-handled ladles are useful for portioning liquids such as stocks, sauces and soups. The capacity, in ounces, is stamped on the handle.

Portion Scoops

Portion scoops (also known as dishers) resemble ice cream scoops. They come in a range of standardized sizes and have a lever-operated blade for releasing their contents. Scoops are useful for portioning salads, vegetables, muffin batters or other soft foods. A number, stamped on either the handle or the release mechanism, indicates the number of level scoopfuls per quart. The higher the scoop number, the smaller the scoop's capacity.

Thermometers

Various types of thermometers are used in the kitchen.

Stem-type thermometers, including instant-read models, measure the temperature of a food. The thermometer is inserted into foods to obtain temperature readings between 0°F (–18°C) and 220°F (104°C). Temperatures are shown on either a dial noted by an arrow or a digital readout. An instant-read thermometer is a small stem-type model, designed to be carried in a pocket and used to provide quick temperature readings. An instant-read thermometer

---

♦♦♦
HOW TO CALIBRATE A STEM-TYPE THERMOMETER

All stem-type thermometers should be calibrated at least weekly as well as whenever they are dropped. To calibrate a stem-type thermometer, fill a glass with shaved ice, then add water. Place the thermometer in the ice slush and wait until the temperature reading stabilizes. Following the manufacturer's directions, adjust the thermometer's calibration nut until the temperature reads 32°F. Check the calibration by returning the thermometer to the slush. Then repeat the procedure, substituting boiling water for the ice slush, and calibrate the thermometer at 212°F.

should not be left in foods that are cooking because doing so damages the thermometer.

Candy and fat thermometers measure temperatures up to 400°F (204°C) using mercury in a column of glass. A back clip attaches to the pan, keeping the chef's hands free. Be careful not to subject glass thermometers to quick temperature changes or the glass may shatter.

Because proper temperatures must be maintained for holding and storing foods, oven and refrigerator thermometers are also useful. Select thermometers with easy-to-read dials or column divisions.

Timers

Portable kitchen timers are useful for any busy chef. Small digital timers can be carried in a pocket; some even time three functions at once. Select a timer with a loud alarm signal and long timing capability.

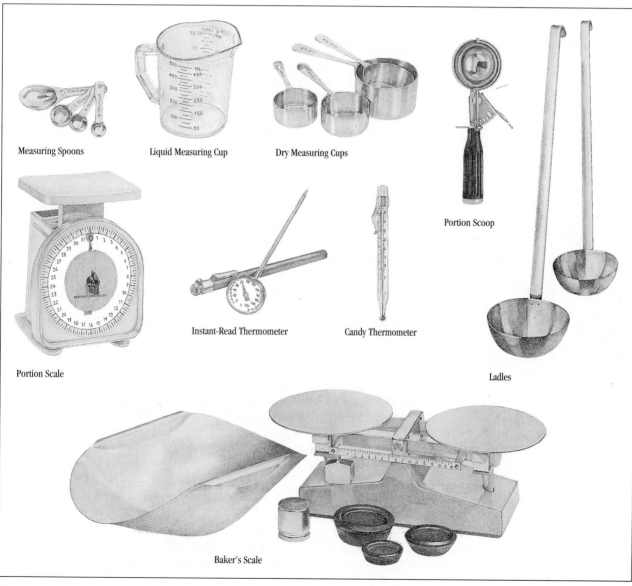

Measuring Spoons   Liquid Measuring Cup   Dry Measuring Cups   Portion Scoop

Portion Scale   Instant-Read Thermometer   Candy Thermometer   Ladles

Baker's Scale

FIGURE 5.5

COOKWARE

Cookware includes the sauté pans and stockpots used on the stove top as well as the roasting pans, hotel pans and specialty molds used inside the oven. Cookware should be selected for its size, shape, ability to conduct heat evenly and overall quality of construction.

Metals and Heat Conduction

Cookware that fails to distribute heat evenly may cause hot spots that burn foods. Because different metals conduct heat at different rates, and thicker layers of metal conduct heat more evenly than thinner ones, the most important considerations when choosing cookware are the type and thickness (known as the *gauge*) of the material used. No one cookware or material suits every process or need, however; always select the most appropriate material for the task at hand.

Copper

Copper is an excellent conductor: It heats rapidly and evenly and cools quickly. Indeed, unlined copper pots are unsurpassed for cooking sugar and fruit mixtures. But copper cookware is extremely expensive. It also requires a great deal of care and is often quite heavy. Moreover, because copper may react with some foods, copper cookware usually has a tin lining, which is soft and easily scratched. Because of these problems, copper is now often sandwiched between layers of stainless steel or aluminum in the bottom of pots and pans.

Aluminum

Aluminum is the metal used most commonly in commercial utensils. It is lightweight and, after copper, conducts heat best. Aluminum is a soft metal, though, so it should be treated with care to avoid dents. Do not use aluminum containers for storage or for cooking acidic foods because the metal reacts chemically with many foods. Light-colored foods, such as soups or sauces, may be discolored when cooked in aluminum, especially if stirred with a metal whisk or spoon.

Anodized aluminum has a hard, dark, corrosion-resistant surface that helps prevent sticking and discoloration.

Stainless Steel

Although stainless steel conducts and retains heat poorly, it is a hard, durable metal particularly useful for holding foods and for low-temperature cooking where hot spots and scorching are not problems. Stainless steel pots and pans are available with aluminum or copper bonded to the bottom or with an aluminum-layered core. Although expensive, such cookware combines the rapid, uniform heat conductivity of copper and aluminum with the strength, durability and nonreactivity of stainless steel. Stainless steel is also ideal for storage containers because it does not react with foods.

Cast Iron

Cast-iron cookware distributes heat evenly and holds high temperatures well. It is often used in griddles and large skillets. Although relatively inexpensive, cast iron is extremely heavy and brittle. It must be kept properly conditioned and dry to prevent rust and pitting.

Glass

Glass retains heat well but conducts it poorly. It does not react with foods. Tempered glass is suitable for microwave cooking provided it does not have any metal band or decoration. Commercial operations rarely use glass cookware because of the danger of breakage.

Ceramics

Ceramics, including earthenware, porcelain and stoneware, are used primarily for baking dishes, casseroles and baking stones because they conduct heat uniformly and retain temperatures well. Ceramics are nonreactive, inexpensive and generally suitable for use in a microwave oven (provided there is no metal in the glaze). Ceramics are easily chipped or cracked, however, and should not be used over a direct flame. Also, quick temperature changes may cause the cookware to crack or shatter.

Plastic

Plastic containers are frequently used in commercial kitchens for food storage or service, but they cannot be used for heating or cooking except in a microwave oven. Plastic microwave cookware is made of phenolic resin. It is easy to clean, relatively inexpensive and rigidly shaped, but its glasslike structure is brittle and it can crack or shatter.

Enamelware

Pans lined with enamel should not be used for cooking; in many areas, their use in commercial kitchens is prohibited by law. The enamel can chip or crack easily, providing good places for bacteria to grow. Also, the chemicals used to bond the enamel to the cookware can cause food poisoning if ingested.

◆◆◆

ROMAN POTS, SOUTHERN STILLS AND CRAFT FAIRS

Lead is poisonous. Ingesting it can cause severe gastrointestinal pains, anemia and central nervous system disorders including intelligence and memory deficits and behavioral changes.

The unwitting and dangerous consumption of lead is not limited to children eating peeling paint chips. Some historians suggest that the use of lead cookware and lead-lined storage vessels and water pipes may have caused pervasive lead poisoning among the elite of the Roman Empire and thus contributed to the Empire's decline. There is also ample evidence that from ancient times until just a few hundred years ago, wine was heated in lead vessels to sweeten it. This had a disastrous effect on the drinker and, for several centuries in countries throughout Europe, on the wine purveyor as well. The former could be poisoned and the latter could be punished by death for selling adulterated wine. More recently it was found that much of the moonshine whiskey produced in the American South contained lead in potentially toxic ranges. The source was determined to be the lead solder used in homemade stills, some of which even included old lead-containing car radiators as condensers.

Although commercially available cookware will not contain lead, be careful of imported pottery and those lovely hand-thrown pots found at craft fairs—there could be lead in the glaze.

Nonstick Coatings

Without affecting a metal's ability to conduct heat, a polymer (plastic) known as polytetrafluoroethylene (PTFE) and marketed under the trade-names Teflon® and Silverstone®, may be applied to many types of cookware. It provides a slippery, nonreactive finish that prevents food from sticking and allows the use of less fat in cooking. Cookware with nonstick coatings requires a great deal of care, however, as the coatings can scratch, chip and blister. Do not use metal spoons or spatulas in cookware with nonstick coatings.

Common Cookware

Pots

Pots are large round vessels with straight sides and two loop handles. Available in a range of sizes based on volume, they are used on the stove top for making stocks, soups or boiling or simmering foods, particularly where rapid evaporation is not desired. Flat or fitted lids are available.

Pans

Pans are round vessels with one long handle and straight or sloped sides. They are usually smaller and shallower than pots. Pans are available in a range of diameters and are used for general stove top cooking, especially sautéing, frying or reducing liquids rapidly.

Woks

Originally used to prepare Asian foods, woks are now found in many professional kitchens. Their round bottoms and curved sides diffuse heat and make it easy to toss or stir contents. Their large domed lids retain heat for steaming vegetables. Woks are useful for quickly sautéing strips of meat, simmering a whole fish or deep-frying appetizers. Stove top woks range in diameter from 12 to 30 inches; larger built-in gas or electric models are also available.

Hotel Pans

Hotel pans (also known as steam table pans) are rectangular stainless steel pans designed to hold food for service in steam tables. Hotel pans are also used for baking, roasting or poaching inside an oven. Perforated pans useful for draining, steaming or icing down foods are also available. The standard full-size pan is 12 by 20 inches, with pans one-half, one-third, one-sixth and other fractions of this size available. Hotel pan depth is standardized at 2 inches (referred to as a "200 pan"), 4, 6 and 8 inches.

Molds

Pâté molds are available in several shapes and sizes, and are usually made from tinned steel. Those with hinged sides, whether smooth or patterned, are more properly referred to as *pâté en croûte* molds. The hinged sides make it easier to remove the baked pâté. Terrine molds are traditionally lidded earthenware or enameled cast-iron containers used for baking ground meat mixtures. They may be round, oval or rectangular. Timbale molds are small (about 4 ounces) metal or ceramic containers used for molding aspic or baking individual portions of mousse, custard or vegetables. Their slightly flared sides allow the contents to release cleanly when inverted.

Stockpot with Spigot

Sauce Pot

Sautoir (Straight Sides)

Saucepan

Cast-Iron Skillet (Griswold)

Sauteuse (Sloped Sides)

Rondeau/Brazier

Wok

Pâté en Croûte Mold

Timbales

Hotel Pans

FIGURE 5.6

STRAINERS AND SIEVES

Strainers and sieves are used primarily to aerate and remove impurities from dry ingredients and drain or purée cooked foods. Strainers, colanders, drum sieves, china caps and chinois are nonmechanical devices with a stainless steel mesh or screen through which food passes. The size of the mesh or

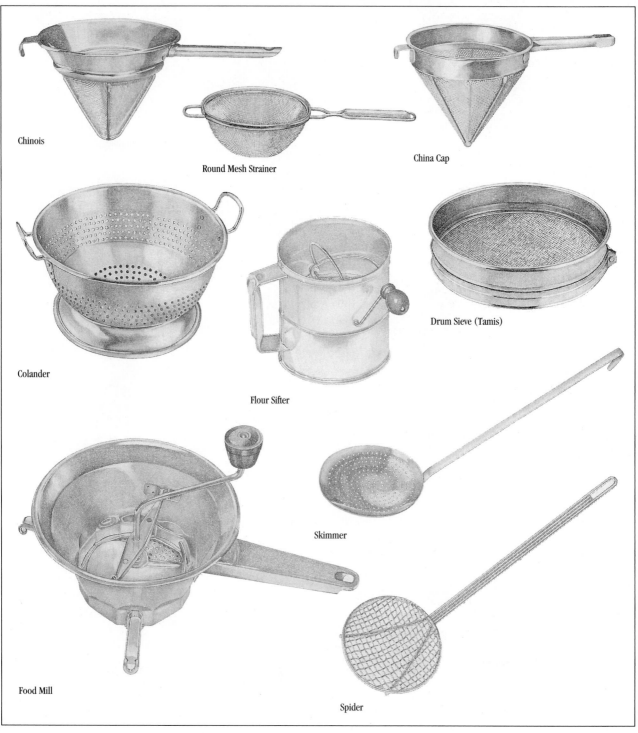

Chinois

Round Mesh Strainer

China Cap

Colander

Flour Sifter

Drum Sieve (Tamis)

Skimmer

Food Mill

Spider

FIGURE 5.7

screen varies from extremely fine to several millimeters wide; select the fineness best suited for the task at hand.

Chinois and China Cap

Both the chinois and china cap are cone-shaped metal strainers. The conical shape allows liquids to filter through small openings. A chinois is made from a very fine mesh, while a china cap has a perforated metal body. Both are used for straining stocks and sauces, with the chinois being particularly useful for consommé. A china cap can also be used with a pestle to purée soft foods.

Skimmer and Spider

Both the skimmer and spider are long-handled tools used to remove foods or impurities from liquids. The flat, perforated disk of a skimmer is used for skimming stocks or removing foods from soups or stocks. The spider has a finer mesh disk, which makes it better for retrieving items from hot fat. Wooden-handled spiders are available but are less sturdy and harder to clean than all-metal designs.

Cheesecloth

Cheesecloth is a loosely woven cotton gauze used for straining stocks and sauces and wrapping poultry or fish for poaching. Cheesecloth is also indispensable for making sachets. Always rinse cheesecloth thoroughly before use; this removes lint and prevents the cheesecloth from absorbing other liquids.

Food Mill

A food mill purées and strains food at the same time. Food is placed in the hopper and a hand-crank mechanism turns a blade in the hopper against a perforated disk, forcing the food through the disk. Most models have interchangeable disks with various-sized holes. Choose a mill that can be taken apart easily for cleaning.

Flour Sifter

A sifter is used for aerating, blending and removing impurities from dry ingredients such as flour, cocoa and leavening agents. The 8-cup hand-crank sifter shown in Figure 5.7 uses four curved rods to brush the contents through a curved mesh screen. The sifter should have a medium-fine screen and a comfortable handle.

PROCESSING EQUIPMENT

Processing equipment includes both electrical and nonelectrical devices used to chop, purée, slice, grind or mix foods. Before using any such equipment, be sure to review its operating procedures and ask for assistance if necessary. Always turn the equipment off and disconnect the power before disassembling, cleaning or moving the appliance. Any problems or malfunctions should be reported to your supervisor immediately. *Never place your hand into any machinery when the power is on. Processing equipment is powerful and can cause serious injury.*

Slicer

An electric slicer is used to cut meat, bread, cheese or raw vegetables into uniform slices. It has a circular blade that rotates at high speed. Food is placed in a carrier, then passed (manually or by an electric motor) against the blade.

Slice thickness is determined by the distance between the blade and the carrier. Because of the speed with which the blade rotates, foods can be cut into extremely thin slices very quickly. An electric slicer is convenient for preparing moderate to large quantities of food, but the time required to disassemble and clean the equipment makes it impractical when slicing only a few items.

Mandoline

A mandoline is a manually operated slicer made of stainless steel with adjustable slicing blades. It is also used to make julienne and waffle-cut slices. Its narrow, rectangular body sits on the work counter at a 45-degree angle. Foods are passed against a blade to obtain uniform slices. It is useful for slicing small quantities of fruits or vegetables when using a large electric slicer would be unwarranted. To avoid injury, always use a hand guard or steel glove when using a mandoline.

Food Chopper or Buffalo Chopper

This chopper is used to process moderate to large quantities of food to a uniform size, such as chopping onions or grinding bread for crumbs. The food is placed in a large bowl rotating beneath a hood where curved blades chop it. The size of the cut depends on how long the food is left in the machine. Buffalo choppers are available in floor or tabletop models. The motor can usually be fitted with a variety of other tools such as a meat grinder or a slicer/shredder, making it even more useful.

Food Processor

A food processor has a motor housing with a removable bowl and S-shaped blade. It is used, for example, to purée cooked foods, chop nuts, prepare compound butters and emulsify sauces. Special disks can be added that slice, shred or julienne foods. Bowl capacity and motor power vary; select a model large enough for your most common tasks.

Blender

Though similar in principle to a food processor, a blender has a tall, narrow food container and a four-pronged blade. Its design is better for processing liquids or liquefying foods quickly. A blender is used to prepare smooth drinks, purée soups and sauces, blend batters and chop ice. A **vertical cutter/mixer** (VCM) operates like a very large, powerful blender. A VCM is usually floor-mounted and has a capacity of 15 to 80 quarts.

Mixer

A vertical mixer is indispensable in the bakeshop and most kitchens. The U-shaped arms hold a metal mixing bowl in place; the selected mixing attachment fits onto the rotating head. The three common mixing attachments are the whip (used for whipping eggs or cream), the paddle (used for general mixing) and the dough hook (used for kneading bread). Most mixers have several operating speeds. Bench models range in capacity from 4.5 to 20 quarts, while floor mixers can as hold as much as 140 quarts. Some mixers can be fitted with shredder/slicers, meat grinders, juicers or power strainers, making the equipment more versatile.

Juicer

Two types of juicers are available: reamers and extractors. Reamers, also known as citrus juicers, remove juice from citrus fruits. They can be manual or electric. Manual models use a lever arm to squeeze the fruit with increased

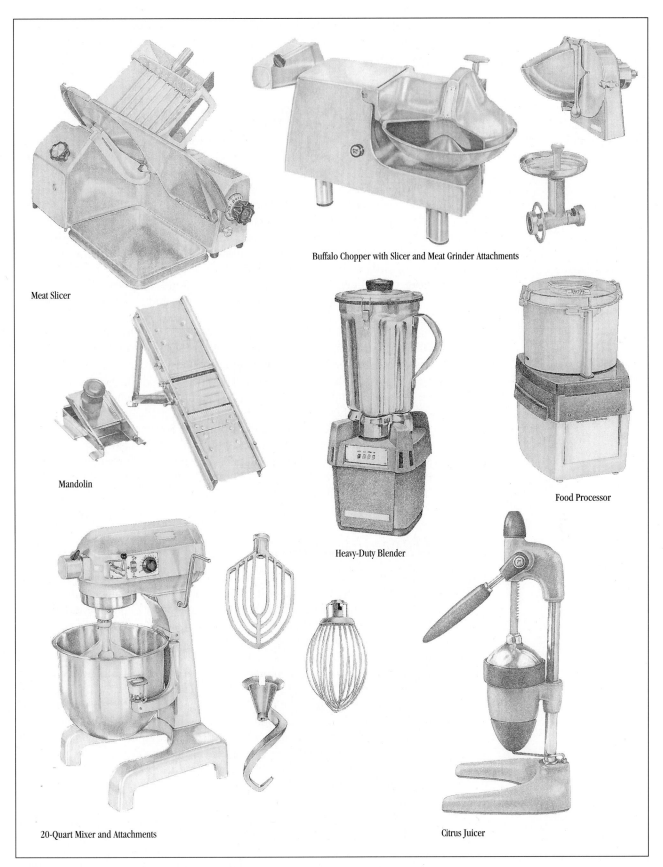

Meat Slicer

Buffalo Chopper with Slicer and Meat Grinder Attachments

Mandolin

Food Processor

Heavy-Duty Blender

20-Quart Mixer and Attachments

Citrus Juicer

FIGURE 5.8

pressure. They are most often used to prepare small to moderate amounts of juice for cooking or beverages. Juice extractors are electrical devices that create juice by liquefying raw fruits, vegetables and herbs. They use centrifugal force to filter out fiber and pulp.

STORAGE CONTAINERS

Proper storage containers are necessary for keeping leftovers and opened packages of food safe for consumption. Proper storage can also reduce the costs incurred by waste or spoilage.

While stainless steel pans such as hotel pans are suitable and useful for some items, the expense of stainless steel and the lack of air-tight lids makes these pans impractical for general storage purposes. Aluminum containers are not recommended because the metal can react with even mildly acidic items. Glass containers are generally not allowed in commercial kitchens because of the hazards of broken glass. The most useful storage containers are those made of high-density plastic (such as polyethylene and polypropylene).

Storage containers must have well-fitting lids and should be available in a variety of sizes, including some that are small enough to hold even minimal quantities of food without allowing too much exposure to oxygen. Round and square plastic containers are widely available. Flat, snap-on lids allow containers to be stacked for more efficient storage. Containers may be clear or opaque white, which helps protect light-sensitive foods. Larger containers may be fitted with handles and spigots, making them especially suited for storing stock. Some storage containers are marked with graduated measurements, so content quantity can be determined at a glance. See Figure 5.9.

Large quantities of dry ingredients, such as flour, sugar and rice, can be stored in rolling bins. The bins should be seamless with rounded corners for easy cleaning. They should have well-fitting but easy-to-open lids and should move easily on well-balanced casters.

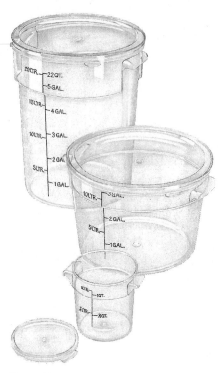

FIGURE 5.9

HEAVY EQUIPMENT

Heavy equipment includes the gas-, electric- or steam-operated appliances used for cooking, reheating or holding foods. Heavy equipment also includes dishwashers and refrigeration units. Heavy equipment should be installed in a fixed location determined by the kitchen's traffic flow and space limitations.

Heavy equipment may be purchased or leased new or used. Used equipment is most often purchased in an effort to save money. While the initial cost is generally less for used equipment, the buyer should also consider the lack of a manufacturer's warranty or dealership guarantee and how the equipment was maintained by the prior owner. Functional used equipment is satisfactory for back-of-the-house areas, but it is usually better to purchase new equipment if it will be visible to the customer. Leasing equipment may be appropriate for some operations. The cost of leasing is less than purchasing and, if something goes wrong with the equipment, the operator is generally not responsible for repairs or service charges.

Stove Tops

Stove tops or ranges are often the most important cooking equipment in the kitchen. They have one or more burners powered by gas or electricity. The burners may be open or covered with a cast-iron or steel plate. Open burners

FIGURE 5.10 *Gas burner and flat top range with dual ovens and an overhead broiler (salamander).*

supply quick, direct heat that is easy to regulate. A steel plate, known as a **flat top**, supplies even but less intense heat. Although it takes longer to heat than a burner, the flat top supports heavier weights and makes a larger area available for cooking. Many stoves include both flat tops and open burner arrangements.

Griddles are similar to flat tops except they are made of a thinner metal plate. Foods are usually cooked directly on the griddle's surface, not in pots or pans which can nick or scratch the surface. (A griddle is illustrated in Figure 5.11.) The surface should be properly cleaned and conditioned after each use. Griddles are popular for short-order and fast-food-type operations.

Ovens

An oven is an enclosed space where food is cooked by being surrounded with hot, dry air. Conventional ovens are often located beneath the stove top. They have a heating element located at the unit's bottom or floor, and pans are placed on wire racks inside the oven's cavity. See Figure 5.10. Conventional ovens may also be separate, free-standing units or decks stacked one on top of the other. In stack ovens, pans are placed directly on the deck or floor and not on wire racks.

Convection ovens use internal fans to circulate the hot air. This tends to cook foods more quickly and evenly. Convection ovens are almost always free-standing units, powered either by gas or electricity. Because convection ovens

Griddle

Deep Fryer

Stack Oven

Steam Kettle

Gas Grill

Overhead Broiler

Tilting Skillet

Convection Steamer

FIGURE 5.11

cook foods more quickly, temperatures may need to be reduced by 25 to 50 degrees F (10 to 20°C) from those recommended for conventional ovens.

Microwave Ovens

Microwave ovens are electrically powered ovens used to cook or reheat foods. They are available in a range of sizes and power settings. Microwave ovens will not brown foods unless fitted with special browning elements. Microwave cooking is discussed in more detail in Chapter 9, Principles of Cooking.

Broilers and Grills

Broilers and grills are generally used to prepare meats, fish and poultry. For a grill, the heat source is beneath the rack on which the food is placed. For a broiler, the heat source is above the food. Most broilers are gas powered; grills may be gas or electric or may burn wood or charcoal. A **salamander** is a small overhead broiler primarily used to finish or top-brown foods. See Figure 5.10. A **rotisserie** is similar to a broiler except that the food is placed on a revolving spit in front of the heat source. The unit may be open or enclosed like an oven; it is most often used for cooking poultry or meats.

Tilting Skillets

Tilting skillets are large, free-standing, flat-bottomed pans about 6 inches deep with an internal heating element below the pan's bottom. They are usually made of stainless steel with a cover, and have a hand-crank mechanism that turns or tilts the pan to pour out the contents. Tilting skillets can be used as stockpots, braziers, fry pans, griddles or steam tables, making them one of the most versatile of modern commercial appliances.

Steam Kettles

Steam kettles (also known as steam-jacketed kettles) are similar to stockpots except they are heated from the bottom and sides by steam circulating between layers of stainless steel. The steam may be generated internally or from an outside source. Because steam heats the kettle's sides, foods cook more quickly and evenly than they would in a pot sitting on the stove top. Steam kettles are most often used for making sauces, soups, custards or stock. Steam kettles are available in a range of sizes, from a 2-gallon tabletop model to a 100-gallon floor model. Some models have a tilting mechanism that allows the contents to be poured out; others have a spigot near the bottom through which liquids can be drained.

Steamers

Pressure and convection steamers are used to cook foods rapidly and evenly, using direct contact with steam. Pressure steamers heat water above the boiling point in sealed compartments; the high temperature and sealed compartment increase the internal pressure in a range of 4 to 15 pounds per square inch. The increased pressure and temperature cook the foods rapidly. Convection steamers generate steam in an internal boiler, then release it over the foods in a cooking chamber. Both types of steamer are ideal for cooking vegetables with a minimal loss of flavor or nutrients.

Deep Fryers

Deep fryers are only used to fry foods in hot fat. The fryers may be either gas or electric and should have thermostatic controls to maintain the fat at a preset temperature. Frying procedures are discussed in Chapter 21, Deep Frying.

Refrigerators

Proper refrigeration space is an essential component of any kitchen. Many foods must be stored at low temperatures to maintain quality and safety. Most commercial refrigeration is of two types: walk-in units and reach-in or upright units.

A walk-in is a large, room-sized box capable of holding hundreds of pounds of food on adjustable shelves. A separate freezer walk-in may be positioned nearby or even inside a refrigerated walk-in.

Reach-ins may be individual units or parts of a bank of units, each with shelves approximately the size of a full sheet pan. Reach-in refrigerators and freezers are usually located throughout the kitchen to provide quick access to foods. Small units may also be placed beneath the work counters. Freezers and refrigerators are available in a wide range of sizes and door designs to suit any operation.

Other forms of commercial refrigeration include chilled drawers located beneath a work area that are just large enough to accommodate a hotel pan, and display cases used to show foods to the customer.

Dishwashers

Mechanical dishwashers are available to wash, rinse and sanitize dishware, glassware, cookware and utensils. Small models clean one rack of items at a time, while larger models can handle several racks simultaneously on a conveyor belt system. Sanitation may be accomplished with either extremely hot water (180°F/82°C) or with chemicals automatically dispensed during the final rinse cycle. Any dishwashing area should be carefully organized for efficient use of equipment and employees and to prevent recontamination of clean items.

SAFETY EQUIPMENT

There are certain items that are critical to the well-being of a food service operation although they are not used in food preparation. These are safety devices, many of which are required by state or local law. Failing to include safety equipment in a kitchen or failing to maintain it properly endangers workers and customers.

Fire Extinguishers

Fire extinguishers are canisters of foam, dry chemicals (such as sodium bicarbonate or potassium bicarbonate) or pressurized water used to extinguish small fires. They must be placed within sight of and easily reached from the work areas in which fires are more likely to occur. Different classes of extinguishers use different chemicals to fight different types of fire. The appropriate class must be used for the specific fire. See Table 5.2. Fire extinguishers must be recharged and checked from time to time. Be sure they have not been discharged, tampered with or otherwise damaged.

TABLE 5.2	FIRE EXTINGUISHERS	
Class	Symbol	Use
Class A	▲	Fires involving wood, paper, cloth or plastic
Class B	■	Fires involving oil, grease or flammable chemicals
Class C	●	Fires involving electrical equipment or wiring

Combination extinguishers—AB, BC and ABC—are also available.

Ventilation Systems

Ventilation systems (also called ventilation hoods) are commonly installed over cooking equipment to remove vapors, heat and smoke. Some systems include fire extinguishing agents or sprinklers. A properly operating hood makes the kitchen more comfortable for the staff and reduces the danger of fire. The system should be designed, installed and inspected by professionals, then cleaned and maintained regularly.

First-Aid Kits

First-aid supplies should be stored in a clearly marked box, conspicuously located near food preparation areas. State and local laws may specify the kit's exact contents. Generally, they should include a first-aid manual, bandages, gauze dressings, adhesive tape, antiseptics, scissors, cold packs and other supplies. The kit should be checked regularly and items replaced as needed. In addition, cards with emergency telephone numbers should be placed inside the first-aid kit and near a telephone.

The Professional Kitchen

The kitchen is the heart of the food service operation. There, food and other items are received, stored, prepared and plated for service; dining room staff places orders, retrieves foods ready for service and returns dirty service items; dishes and other wares are cleaned and stored; and the chef conducts business. But commercial space is expensive, and most food service operators recognize that the greater number of customers served, the greater the revenues. Often this translates into a large dining area and small kitchen and storage facilities. Therefore, when designing a kitchen, it is important to use the space wisely so that each of its functions can be accomplished efficiently.

Regardless of the kitchen's size, its design begins with a consideration of the tasks to be performed. Analyzing the menu identifies these tasks. A restaurant featuring steaks and chops, for example, will need areas to fabricate and grill meats. If it relies on commercially prepared desserts and breads, it will not need a bakeshop but will still need space to hold and plate baked goods.

Once all food preparation tasks are identified, a work area for each particular task is designated. These work areas are called **work stations**. At a steak restaurant, an important work station is the broiler. If the restaurant serves fried foods, it will also need a fry station. The size and design of each work station is determined by the volume of food the operation intends to produce.

Usually work stations using the same or similar equipment for related tasks are grouped together into **work sections**. See Table 5.3. (Note that work stations correspond to the kitchen brigade system discussed in Chapter 1, Professionalism.) For example, in a typical full-service restaurant, there will be a single hot-foods

TABLE 5.3	WORK SECTIONS AND THEIR STATIONS
Sections	Stations
Hot-foods section	Broiler station
	Fry station
	Griddle station
	Sauté/sauce station
	Holding
Garde-manger section	Salad greens cleaning
	Salad preparation
	Cold foods preparation
	Sandwich station
	Showpiece preparation
Bakery section	Mixing station
	Dough holding and proofing
	Dough rolling and forming
	Baking and cooling
	Dessert preparation*
	Frozen dessert preparation*
	Plating desserts*
Banquet section	Steam cooking
	Dry heat cooking (roasting, broiling)
	Holding and plating
Short-order section	Griddle station
	Fry station
	Broiler station
Beverage section	Hot beverage station
	Cold beverage station
	Alcoholic beverage station

*These stations are sometimes found in the *garde-manger* section.

◆◆◆
ALEXIS SOYER
(1809–1858)

Alexis Soyer
Photo courtesy of Barbara Wheaton.

The father of the contemporary celebrity chef was Alexis Soyer, a Frenchman whose tragically short working life was spent mostly in London. He was a flamboyant, talented and egocentric showman. He was also a renowned chef, restaurateur, social activist, author, purveyor of prepared foods and inventor.

In 1831 Soyer left his thriving catering business and restaurant in Paris for London. (A scandal was rumored to be behind his sudden departure.) There he quickly established a reputation as a talented chef in the latest French fashion. By 1838 he was employed at a gentlemen's club called the Reform. Able to assist in planning the club's new kitchen facility, Soyer installed the most modern equipment: gas ovens with temperature controls, a steam-driven mechanical spit and a storage locker cooled by running water. From this modern kitchen he produced his signature dish: lamb chops Reform.

The Reform was founded by members of the Liberal Party, a political party interested in social reform. Their chef soon joined the party

"The Kitchen Department of the Reform Club" (1841). "To show them at one glance," wrote the *Spectator*, "the partition walls are cut away, and a bird's eye view is given of the several kitchens, larders, sculleries, and batterie de cuisine; the different functionaries are at their posts, and the accomplished chef, Monsieur Soyer, is in the act of pointing out to a favoured visitor the various contrivances suggested by his ingenuity and experience."

◆◆◆

ranks. He developed recipes for inexpensive, nutritious soups for the working class and in 1847 went to Ireland and opened soup kitchens to feed those who were starving as a result of the Potato Famine.

His most important writings reflect his interests in good food for the masses. The intended audience for *The Modern Housewife* (1849) was the middle class; the growing urban working class was the intended audience for his second book, *A Schilling Cookery for the People* (1855).

In 1851 Soyer opened his own lavishly decorated and expensively equipped restaurant called the Gastronomic Symposium of All Nations. It closed shortly thereafter, in part because of Soyer's debts, in part because he lost his operating license as a result of the rowdiness in the restaurant's American-style bar, at which customers were publicly served cocktails for the first time in London.

In addition to cooking and writing, Soyer created and marketed several prepared food items: Soyer's Sauce, Soyer's Nectar and Soyer's Relish. He was also fascinated with kitchen gadgets and invented several, including a sink stopper, jelly mold, egg cooker and coffeepot. The most notable, however, was a portable "Magic Stove" weighing less than 4 pounds, similar to a modern chafing dish. Soyer's final triumph was in the Crimean War (1854–1857). He developed army rations, reorganized field and hospital kitchens and introduced one of his last inventions, the campaign stove. Portable, efficient and requiring little fuel, it was used by the British army for the next 90 years.

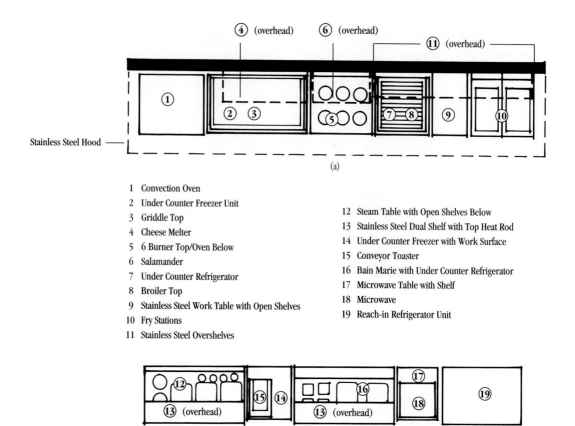

1 Convection Oven
2 Under Counter Freezer Unit
3 Griddle Top
4 Cheese Melter
5 6 Burner Top/Oven Below
6 Salamander
7 Under Counter Refrigerator
8 Broiler Top
9 Stainless Steel Work Table with Open Shelves
10 Fry Stations
11 Stainless Steel Overshelves

12 Steam Table with Open Shelves Below
13 Stainless Steel Dual Shelf with Top Heat Rod
14 Under Counter Freezer with Work Surface
15 Conveyor Toaster
16 Bain Marie with Under Counter Refrigerator
17 Microwave Table with Shelf
18 Microwave
19 Reach-in Refrigerator Unit

FIGURE 5.12 *Typical Hot-Foods Section Floor Plan*

section. It can consist of broiler, fry, griddle, sauté and sauce stations. Both advance preparation and last-minute cooking may be performed in the hot-foods section. The principal cooking equipment (a range, broiler, deep fryer, oven, griddle, etc.) will be arranged in a line under a ventilation hood. A typical plan for this hot-foods section is shown in Figure 5.12. Although each work station within the hot-foods section may be staffed by a different line cook, the proximity of the stations allows one line cook to cover more than one station if the kitchen is short-handed or when business is slow.

Merely considering the plan of the work station or section is not enough, however. When designing the work area, you must also consider the elevation. That is, a kitchen designer not only examines what equipment should be placed next to the other (for example, the range next to the deep fryer), but also what equipment and storage facilities can be placed beneath or on top of the other. For example, in a bakeshop, rolling storage carts for flour and sugar or an under-the-counter refrigerator for eggs and dairy products may be located beneath the work surface, while mixing bowls and dry ingredients are stored on shelves above. Figure 5.13 illustrates the elevation for the hot-foods section whose plan is shown in Figure 5.12. Ideally, each station should be designed so that the cook takes no more than three steps in any direction to perform all of his assigned station tasks.

In addition to the work sections where the menu items are produced, a typical restaurant kitchen includes areas dedicated to:

1. *Receiving and storing foods and other items.* There should be separate freezer, refrigerator and dry-goods storage facilities. Each should have

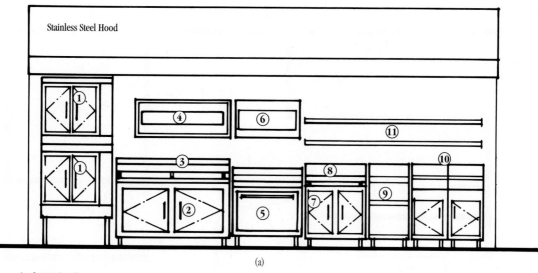

(a)

1 Convection Oven
2 Under Counter Freezer Unit
3 Griddle Top
4 Cheese Melter
5 6 Burner Top/Oven Below
6 Salamander
7 Under Counter Refrigerator
8 Broiler Top
9 Stainless Steel Work Table with Open Shelves
10 Fry Stations
11 Stainless Steel Overshelves

12 Steam Table with Open Shelves Below
13 Stainless Steel Dual Shelf with Top Heat Rod
14 Under Counter Freezer with Work Surface
15 Conveyor Toaster
16 Bain Marie with Under Counter Refrigerator
17 Microwave Table with Shelf
18 Microwave
19 Reach-in Refrigerator Unit

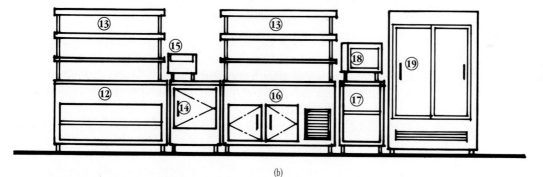

(b)

FIGURE 5.13 *Typical Hot-Foods Section Elevation*

proper temperature, humidity and light controls in order to properly and safely maintain the stored items. Depending upon the operation's size and the work stations' specific needs, there can be either a central storage area or each station or section can maintain its own storage facilities. Typically, however, there is a combination of central and section storage. For example, up to 100 pounds of flour and sugar can be stored in rolling bins under a work table in the bakeshop, while several hundreds of pounds more remain in a central dry goods area. Similarly, one box of salt can be stored near the hot line for immediate use, while the remainder of the case is stored in a central dry goods area. Additional storage space will be needed for cleaning and paper supplies, dishes and other service ware. *Never store cleaning supplies and other chemicals with foods.*

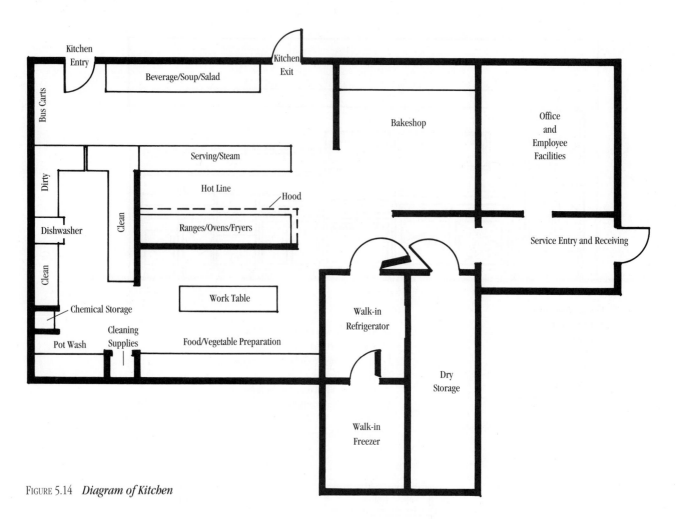

FIGURE 5.14   *Diagram of Kitchen*

2. *Washing dishes and other equipment.* These dish- and equipment-washing facilities should have their own sinks. Food-preparation and hand-washing sinks should be separate.

3. *Employee use.* Restrooms, locker facilities and an office are also found in most food service facilities.

The guiding principle behind a good kitchen design is to maximize the flow of goods and staff from one area to the next and within each area itself. Maximizing flow creates an efficient work environment and helps reduce preparation and service time.

Figure 5.14 shows the several sections of a professional kitchen. It includes an area for front-of-the-house staff to circulate, drop off orders, retrieve finished dishes and return dirty dishes. The design accounts for the flow of foods from receiving, to storage, to food preparation areas, to holding and service areas and then to the dining room as well as the flow of dirty dishes from the dining room back into the kitchen. The work sections are arranged to take advantage of shared equipment. For instance, by placing the bakeshop next to the hot-foods section, they can share ovens. The *garde-manger* and dessert sections, both of which rely on refrigerated foods, are conveniently located near the walk-in refrigerator and freezer area. The beverage station is located near the dining room entrance so that food servers do not have to walk through food preparation areas to fill beverage orders. The office is next to receiving so that the chef can easily check and receive orders. The central storage areas are easily accessible to the receiving area as well as to the food production areas, while the cleaning-supply storage is near the dishwashing area. In general, the design eliminates the need for staff from one work station or section to cross through another station or section.

Governmental building, health, fire and safety codes will dictate, to a degree, certain aspects of a professional kitchen's design. But to make the most of these spaces, the well-designed kitchen should reflect a sound understanding of the tasks to be performed and the equipment necessary to perform them.

CONCLUSION

There are hundreds of tools and pieces of equipment that can help you prepare, cook, store and present food. Every year, manufacturers offer new or improved items. Throughout your career you will use many of them. Select those that are well constructed, durable and best suited for the task at hand. Then use them in a safe and efficient manner.

The way in which equipment is arranged and stored in a kitchen is also important. Good kitchen design emphasizes the efficient flow of goods and staff from one work section to another as well as within each work section or station.

QUESTIONS FOR DISCUSSION

1. What is NSF International? What is its significance with regard to commercial kitchen equipment?
2. List the parts of a chef's knife and describe the knife's construction.
3. List six materials used to make commercial cookware and describe the advantages and disadvantages of each.
4. Describe six pieces of equipment that can be used to slice or chop foods.
5. List three classes of fire extinguishers. For each one, describe its designating symbol and identify the type or types of fire it should be used to extinguish.
6. Explain the relationship between work sections and work stations and the kitchen brigade system discussed in Chapter 1, Professionalism.

CHAPTER 6 KNIFE SKILLS

After studying this chapter you will be able to:

+ care for knives properly
+ use knives properly
+ cut foods into a variety of classic shapes

*E*very professional must become skilled in the use of certain tools. The professional chef is no exception. One of the most important tools the student chef must master is the knife. Good knife skills are critical to a chef's success because the knife is the most commonly used tool in the kitchen. Every chef spends countless hours slicing, dicing, mincing and chopping. Learning to perform these tasks safely and efficiently is an essential part of your training.

At first professional knives may feel large and awkward and the techniques discussed below may not seem all that efficient. But as you become familiar with knives and practice your knife skills, using knives correctly will become second nature.

Knives are identified in Chapter 5, Tools and Equipment. Here we show how they are used to cut vegetables. The techniques presented, however, can be used for most any food that holds its shape when cut. Knife skills for butchering and fabricating meat, poultry, fish and shellfish are discussed in Chapters 12, Principles of Meat Cookery, through 19, Fish and Shellfish.

A note about language: Many of the classic cuts are known by their French names: julienne, for example. Although these words are nouns and entered the English language as nouns (e.g., *a* julienne *of* carrot), they are also used as verbs (*to* julienne *a carrot*) and adjectives (julienned *carrots*).

USING YOUR KNIFE SAFELY

The first rule of knife safety is to *think about what you are doing.* Other basic rules of knife safety are:

1. Use the correct knife for the task at hand.
2. Always cut away from yourself.
3. Always cut on a cutting board. Do not cut on glass, marble or metal.
4. Keep knives sharp; a dull knife is more dangerous than a sharp one.
5. When carrying a knife, hold it point down, parallel to and close to your leg as you walk.
6. A falling knife has no handle. Do not attempt to catch a falling knife; step back and allow it to fall.
7. Never leave a knife in a sink of water; anyone reaching into the sink could be injured or the knife could be dented by pots or other utensils.

CARING FOR YOUR KNIFE

Knife Sharpening

A sharpening stone called a **whetstone** is used to put an edge on a dull knife blade. To use a whetstone, place the heel of the blade against the whetstone at a 20-degree angle. Keeping that angle, press down on the blade while pushing it away from you in one long arc, as if to slice off a thin piece of the stone. The entire length of the blade should come in contact with the stone during each sweep. Repeat the procedure on both sides of the blade until sufficiently sharp. With a triple-faced stone, such as that shown to the right, you progress from the coarsest to the finest surface. Any whetstone can be moistened with either water or mineral oil, but not both. Do not use vegetable oil on a whetstone as it will soon become rancid and gummy.

A **steel** does not sharpen a knife. Instead, it is used to hone or straighten the blade immediately after and between sharpenings. To use a steel, place the blade against the steel at a 20-degree angle. Then draw the blade along the entire length of the steel. Repeat the technique several times on each side of the blade.

A final note on knife care: Do not wash knives in commercial dishwashers. The heat and harsh chemicals can damage the edge and the handle. The blade can also be damaged if it knocks against cookware or utensils. In addition, the knife could injure an unsuspecting worker. Always wash and dry your knives by hand immediately after each use.

When sharpening a knife against a three-sided whetstone, go from the coarsest to the finest surface.

Honing a knife against a steel straightens the blade between sharpenings.

GRIPPING YOUR KNIFE

There are several different ways to grip a knife. Use the grip that is most comfortable for you or the one dictated by the job at hand. Whichever grip you use should be firm but not so tight that your hand becomes tired. Gripping styles are shown below.

The most common grip: Hold the handle with three fingers while gripping the blade between the thumb and index finger.

A variation on the most common grip: Grip the handle with four fingers and place the thumb on the front of the handle.

The underhand grip for a rigid boning knife: Grip the handle in a fist with four fingers and thumb. This grip allows you to use the knife tip to cut around joints and separate flesh from bone when boning meat and poultry.

CONTROLLING YOUR KNIFE

To safely produce even cuts, you must control (or guide) your knife with one hand and hold the item being cut with the other. Always allow the blade's sharp edge to do the cutting. Never force the blade through the item being cut. Smooth, even strokes should be used. Using a dull knife or excessive force with any knife produces, at best, poor results and, at worst, a significant safety risk. Cutting without using your hand as a guide may also be dangerous. Two safe cutting methods that produce good results are shown below.

Method A

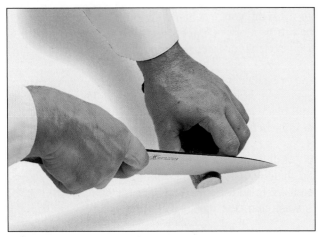

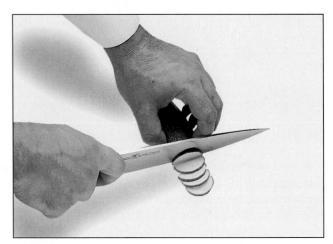

1. Keeping your fingertips curled back, grip the item being cut with three fingertips and your thumb. Hold the knife in the other hand. While keeping the knife's tip on the cutting board, lift the heel of the knife.

2. Using the second joint of your index finger as a guide, cut a slice using a smooth, even, downward stroke. Adjust the position of the guiding finger after each slice to produce slices of equal size. After a few cuts, slide your fingertips and thumb down the length of the item and continue slicing. For this slicing technique, the knife's tip acts as the fulcrum.

Method B

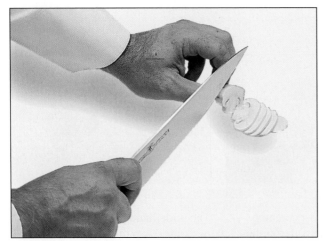

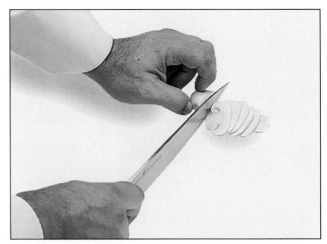

1. Grip the item as described above. Using the second joint of your index finger as a guide, lift the knife's tip and slice by drawing the knife slightly back toward you and down through the item, cutting the item to the desired thickness.

2. The motion of the knife should come almost entirely from the wrist, not the elbow. Allow the weight of the knife to do most of the work; very little downward pressure needs to be applied to the knife. For this slicing technique, your wrist should act as the fulcrum.

CUTTING WITH YOUR KNIFE

A knife is used to shape and reduce an item's size. Uniformity of size and shape ensures even cooking and enhances the appearance of the finished product. Items are shaped by slicing, chopping, dicing, mincing or other special cutting techniques.

Slicing

To slice is to cut an item into relatively broad, thin pieces. Slices may be either the finished cut or the first step in producing other cuts. Slicing is typically used to create three specialty cuts: the chiffonade, rondelle and diagonal.

A **chiffonade** is a preparation of finely sliced or shredded leafy vegetables used as a garnish or a base under cold presentations. As shown here, slicing spinach *en chiffonade* is a relatively simple process.

1. Wash and destem the leaves as necessary. Stack several leaves on top of each other and roll them tightly like a cigar.

2. Make fine slices across the leaves while holding the leaf roll tightly.

As seen below, **rondelles** or **rounds** are easily made disk-shaped slices of cylindrical vegetables or fruits.

Peel the item (if desired) and place it on a cutting board. Make even slices perpendicular to the item being cut.

Diagonals are elongated or oval-shaped slices of cylindrical vegetables or fruits. They are produced with a cut similar to that used to cut rondelles except that the knife is held at an angle to the item being cut.

Peel the item (if desired) and place it on a cutting board. Position the knife at the desired angle to the item being cut and slice it evenly.

Chopping

To chop is to cut an item into small pieces where uniformity of size and shape is neither necessary (for example, coarsely chopped onions for a *mirepoix* that will be removed from the stock before service) nor feasible (for example, parsley).

Coarse Chopping

Coarse chopping does not mean carelessly hacking up food. Rather, the procedure is identical to that used for slicing but without the emphasis on uniformity. Coarsely chopped pieces should measure approximately 3/4 inch × 3/4 inch × 3/4 inch (2 cm × 2 cm × 2 cm).

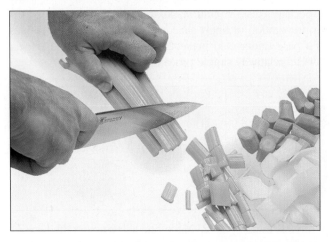

Grip the knife as for slicing. Hold the item being chopped with your other hand. It may not be necessary to use your finger as a guide because uniformity is not crucial.

Chopping Parsley and Similar Foods

Parsley can be cut very coarsely or very finely. As shown below, it is easy to chop parsley and similar foods properly regardless of the desired fineness.

1. Wash the parsley in cold water; drain well. Remove the parsley sprigs from the stems.

2. Grip the knife in one hand. With the other hand spread flat, hold the knife's tip on the cutting board. Keeping the knife's tip on the board, chop the parsley sprigs by rocking the curved blade of the knife up and down while moving the knife back and forth over the parsley.

3. Place the chopped parsley in a clean kitchen towel or a double layer of cheesecloth. Rinse it under cold water and squeeze out as much water as possible. The chopped parsley should be dry and fluffy.

Chopping Garlic

A daily chore in many food service facilities, peeling and chopping garlic is a simple job made easy with the procedure shown here.

1. Break the head of garlic into individual cloves with your hands. Lightly crush the cloves using the flat edge of a chef's knife or a mallet. They will break open and the peel can be separated easily from the garlic flesh.

2. With a flat hand, hold the knife's tip on the cutting board. Using a rocking motion, chop the garlic cloves to the desired size. Garlic is usually chopped very finely.

3. Garlic paste can be made by first finely chopping the garlic and then turning the knife on an angle and repeatedly dragging the edge of the knife along the cutting board, mashing the garlic.

Cutting Sticks and Dicing

To dice is to cut an item into cubes. Before an item can be diced, it must first be cut into certain-sized sticks. These techniques are most often used when uniformity of size and shape are important (for example, julienned carrots for a salad or brunoised vegetables for a garnish).

The dicing technique is typically used to create the classic cuts known as brunoise, small dice, medium dice, large dice and paysanne. Although most cooks have some notion of what size and shape "small diced" potatoes or julienne carrots may be, there are specific sizes and shapes for these cuts.

They are:

Julienne—a stick-shaped item with dimensions of 1/8 inch × 1/8 inch × 1 to 2 inches (3 mm × 3 mm × 2.5 to 5 cm). When used with potatoes, this cut is sometimes referred to as an *allumette*.

Batonnet—a stick-shaped item with dimensions of 1/4 inch × 1/4 inch × 2 to 2-1/2 inches (6 mm × 6 mm × 5 to 6 cm).

Brunoise—a cube-shaped item with dimensions of 1/8 inch × 1/8 inch × 1/8 inch (3 mm × 3 mm × 3 mm).

Small dice—a cube-shaped item with dimensions of 1/4 inch × 1/4 inch × 1/4 inch (6 mm × 6 mm × 6 mm).

Medium dice—a cube-shaped item with dimensions of 3/8 inch × 3/8 inch × 3/8 inch (9 mm × 9 mm × 9 mm).

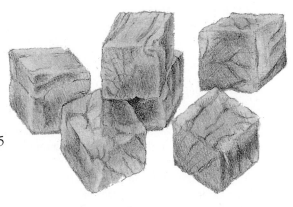

Large dice—a cube-shaped item with dimensions of 5/8 inch × 5/8 inch × 5/8 inch (1.5 cm × 1.5 cm × 1.5 cm).

Paysanne—a flat, square-shaped item with dimensions of 1/2 inch × 1/2 inch × 1/4 inch (1.2 cm × 1.2 cm × 6 mm).

Cutting Julienne and Batonnet

Both julienne and batonnet are matchstick-shaped cuts prepared using the same procedure as cutting sticks for dicing.

1. Peel the item (if desired) and square off the sides. Trim the item so that the slices cut from it will be the proper length. Cut even slices of the desired thickness, 1/8 inch (3 mm) for julienne or 1/4 inch (6 mm) for batonnet.

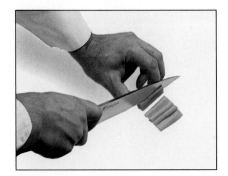

2. Stack the slices and cut them evenly into sticks (also referred to as "planks") that are the same thickness as the slices.

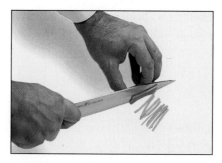

Cutting Brunoise and Small, Medium and Large Dice

Brunoise as well as small, medium and large dice are made by first cutting the item into sticks following the procedure for cutting julienne or batonnet, then making cuts perpendicular to the length of the sticks to produce small cubes. Making a 1/8-inch (3-mm) cut perpendicular to the length of a julienne produces a brunoise. Making a 1/4-inch (6-mm) cut perpendicular to the length of a batonnet produces a small dice. A 3/8-inch (9-mm) cut from a 3/8-inch (9-mm) stick produces a medium dice and a 5/8-inch (1.5-cm) cut from a 5/8-inch (1.5-cm) stick produces a large dice.

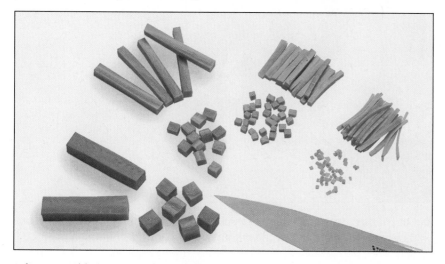

Julienne and batonnet sticks and the large, medium, small and brunoise dices cut from them.

Cutting Paysanne

Paysanne is a classic vegetable cut for garnishing soups and other dishes. It resembles a 1/2-inch dice that has been cut in half. It is produced by following the procedures for dicing, but in the final step the 1/2-inch × 1/2-inch (1.2-cm × 1.2-cm) sticks are cut into slices 1/4 inch (6 mm) thick.

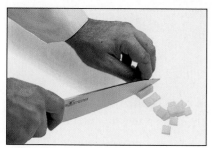

Cutting paysanne from a 1/2-inch × 1/2-inch (6-mm × 6-mm) stick.

Dicing an Onion

Onions are easily peeled and diced to any size desired using the procedure shown here.

1. Using a paring knife, remove the stem end. Trim the root end but leave it nearly intact (this helps prevent the onion from falling apart while dicing). Peel away the outer skin; be careful not to remove and waste too much onion.

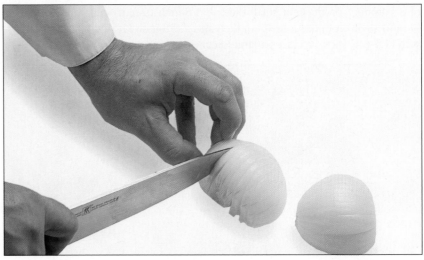

2. Cut the onion in half through the stem and root. Place the cut side down on the cutting board.

3. Cut parallel slices of the desired thickness vertically through the onion from the root toward the stem end without cutting completely through the root end.

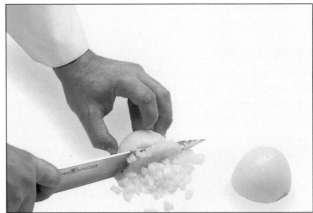

4. Make a single horizontal cut on a small onion or two horizontal cuts on a large onion through the width of the onion, again without cutting through the root end.

5. Turn the onion and cut slices perpendicular to the other slices to produce diced onion.

Mincing

To mince is to cut an item into very small pieces. The terms "finely chopped" and "minced" are often used interchangeably and are most often ~~referring~~ to garlic, shallots, herbs and other foods that do not have to be uni~~form~~ in shape.

Mincing Shallots

The procedure for mincing shallots is shown here.

1. Peel and dice the shallots, following the procedure for peeling and dicing an onion.

2. With a flat hand, hold the knife's tip on the cutting board. Using a rocking motion, mince the shallots with the heel of the knife.

Tourner

Tourner ("to turn" in French) is a cutting technique that results in a football-shaped finished product with seven equal sides and blunt ends. The size of the finished product may vary, the most common being 2 inches (5 cm) long.

This is a more complicated procedure than other cuts and takes considerable practice to produce good results.

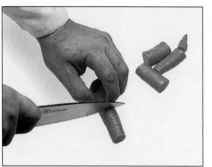 

1. Cut the item being "turned" into pieces 2 inches (5 cm) × 3/4 to 1 inch (2–2.5 cm). Each piece should have flat ends. (Potatoes, turnips and beets may be cut into as many as six or eight pieces; carrots can simply be cut into 2-inch lengths.) Peeling is optional because in most cases the item's entire surface area is trimmed away.

2. Holding the item between the thumb and forefinger, use a tourné knife or a paring knife to cut seven curved sides on the item, creating a flat-ended, foot-ball-shaped product.

Oblique or Roll Cut

Oblique or roll-cut items are small pieces with two angle-cut sides. It is a relatively simple cut most often used on carrots or parsnips.

Place the peeled item on a cutting board. Holding the knife at a 45-degree angle, make the first cut. Roll the item a half turn, keeping the knife at the same angle, and make another cut. The result is a wedge-shaped piece with two angled sides.

CONCLUSION

Although many slicing and dicing machines are available, none can ever completely replace a skilled chef with a sharp knife. As a student chef, becoming efficient with your knives should be a high priority. Possessing good knife skills allows you to produce more attractive products in a safe and efficient manner. You will use the classic cuts and techniques outlined in this chapter throughout your career. You should memorize the procedures and practice them often. And remember, a dull or carelessly handled knife is dangerous.

QUESTIONS FOR DISCUSSION

1. Explain the step-by-step procedures for sharpening a knife using a three-sided whetstone.
2. What is the purpose of steel?
3. Why is it necessary to cut vegetables into uniform shapes and sizes?
4. Describe the following cutting procedures: slicing, chopping and dicing.
5. Identify the dimensions of the following cuts: julienne, batonnet, brunoise, small dice, medium dice, large dice and paysanne.
6. Describe the procedure for making tournéed vegetables.

CHAPTER 7

KITCHEN STAPLES

After studying this chapter you will be able to:

◆ recognize and use a variety of herbs, spices, nuts, oils, vinegars and condiments
◆ prepare and serve good-quality coffees and teas

*ertain foods are used in almost all stations of the kitchen with such regularity that they have become known as **staples**. Included are many of the processed, packaged items we often take for granted: salt, pepper, flour, sugar, oil and flavorings. There is, however, no single list of staples. Each food service operation will have its own list depending on the menu and the cooking methods used.*

This chapter identifies and discusses selected herbs and spices, salt, nuts, oils, vinegars and condiments as well as two popular beverages, coffee and tea. We provide identifying characteristics for some of the more common staples and set forth standards of quality and usage. Other staples, such as flour and sugar, are covered in Chapter 26, Principles of the Bakeshop.

HERBS AND SPICES

Seasoning—*an item added to enhance the natural flavors of a food without dramatically changing its taste; salt and pepper are the most common seasonings.*

Flavoring—*an item that adds a new taste to a food and alters its natural flavors; flavorings include herbs, spices, vinegars and condiments. The terms* seasonings *and* flavorings *are often used interchangeably.*

Aromatic—*an item added to enhance the natural aromas of a food; aromatics include most flavorings, such as herbs and spices, as well as some vegetables.*

Condiment—*traditionally, any item added to a dish for flavor, including herbs, spices and vinegars; now also refers to cooked or prepared flavorings such as prepared mustards, relishes, bottled sauces and pickles.*

Herb—*any of a large group of aromatic plants whose leaves, stems or flowers are used as a flavoring; used either dried or fresh.*

Spice—*any of a large group of aromatic plants whose bark, roots, seeds, buds or berries are used as a flavoring; usually used in dried form, either whole or ground.*

Herbs and spices are the kitchen staples used as **flavorings**. **Herbs** refer to the large group of **aromatic** plants whose leaves, stems or flowers are used to add flavors to other foods. Most herbs are available fresh or dried. Because drying alters their flavors and aromas, fresh herbs are generally preferred and should be used if possible. **Spices** are strongly flavored or aromatic portions of plants used as flavorings, **condiments** or aromatics. Spices are the bark, roots, seeds, buds or berries of plants, most of which grow naturally only in tropical climates. Spices are almost always used in their dried form, rarely fresh, and can usually be purchased whole or ground. Some plants—dill, for example—can be used as both an herb (its leaves) and a spice (its seeds).

Herbs

Basil (Fr. *basilique*) is considered one of the great culinary herbs. It is available in a variety of "flavors"—cinnamon, garlic, lemon, even chocolate—but the most common is sweet basil. **Sweet basil** has light green, tender leaves and small white flowers. Its flavor is strong, warm and slightly peppery, with a hint of cloves. Basil is

Basil

used in Mediterranean cuisines and has a special affinity for garlic and tomatoes. When purchasing fresh basil, look for bright green leaves; avoid flower buds and wilted or rust-colored leaves. Dried sweet basil is readily available, but has a decidedly weaker flavor.

Opal basil is named for its vivid purple color. It has a tougher, crinkled leaf and a medium-strong flavor. Opal basil may be substituted for sweet basil in cooking and its appearance makes it a distinctive garnish.

Opal basil

Bay (Fr. *laurier*), also known as sweet laurel, is a small tree from Asia that produces tough, glossy leaves with a sweet balsamic aroma and peppery flavor. Bay symbolized wisdom and glory in ancient Rome; the leaves were used to form crowns or "laurels" worn by emperors and victorious athletes. In cooking, dried bay leaves are often preferred over the more bitter fresh leaves. Essential in French cuisine, bay leaves are part of the traditional bouquet garni and court bouillon. Whole dried leaves are usually added to a dish at the start of cooking, then removed when sufficient flavor has been extracted.

Bay leaves

Chervil

Chervil (Fr. *cerfeuil*), also known as sweet cicely, is native to Russia and the Middle East. Its lacy, fernlike leaves are similar to parsley and can be used as a garnish. Chervil's flavor is delicate, similar to parsley but with the distinctive aroma of anise. It should not be heated for long periods. Chervil is commonly used in French cuisine and is one of the traditional *fines herbes*.

Chives (Fr. *ciboulette*) are perhaps the most delicate and sophisticated members of the onion family. Their hollow, thin grass-green stems grow in clumps and produce round, pale purple flowers, which are used as a garnish. Chives may be purchased dried, quick-frozen or fresh. They have a mild onion flavor and bright green color. Chives complement eggs, poultry, potatoes, fish and shellfish. They should not be cooked for long periods or at high temperatures. Chives make an excellent garnish when snipped with scissors or carefully chopped and sprinkled over finished soups or sauces.

Chives

Garlic chives, also known as Chinese chives, actually belong to another plant species. They have flat, solid (not hollow) stems and a mild garlic flavor. They may be used in place of regular chives if their garlic flavor is desired.

Garlic chives

Cilantro is the green leafy portion of the plant that yields seeds known as coriander. The flavors of the two portions of this plant are very different and cannot be substituted for each other.

Cilantro, also known as Chinese parsley, is sharp and tangy with a strong aroma and an almost citrus flavor. It is widely used in Asian, Mexican and South American cuisines, especially in salads and sauces. It should not be subjected to heat and cilantro's flavor is completely destroyed by drying. Do not use yellow or discolored leaves or the tough stems.

Cilantro

Dill (Fr. *aneth*), a member of the parsley family, has tiny, aromatic, yellow flowers and feathery, delicate blue-green leaves. The leaves taste like parsley, but sharper, with a touch of anise. Dill seeds are flat, oval and brown, with a bitter flavor similar to caraway. Both the seeds and the leaves of the dill plant are used in cooking. Dill is commonly used in Scandinavian and Central European cuisines, particularly with fish and potatoes. Both leaves and seeds are used in pickling and sour dishes. Dill leaves are available fresh or dried but lose their aroma and flavor during cooking,

Dill

Epazote

Lemon grass

Marjoram

Oregano

so add them only after the dish is removed from the heat. Dill seeds are available whole or ground and are used in fish dishes, pickles and breads.

Epazote, also known as wormseed or stinkweed, grows wild throughout the Americas. It has a strong aroma similar to kerosene and a wild flavor. Fresh epazote is used in salads and as a flavoring in Mexican and Southwestern cuisines. It is often cooked with beans to reduce their gaseousness. Dried epazote is brewed to make a beverage.

Fine herbs (Fr. *fines herbes*) are a combination of parsley, tarragon, chervil and chives widely used in French cuisine. The mixture is available dried or you can create your own from fresh ingredients.

Lavender is an evergreen with thin leaves and tall stems bearing spikes of tiny purple flowers. Although lavender is known primarily for its aroma, which is widely used in perfumes, soaps and cosmetics, the flowers are also used as a flavoring, particularly in Middle Eastern and Provençal cuisines. These flowers have a sweet, lemony flavor and can be crystallized and used as a garnish. Lavender is also used in jams and preserves and to flavor teas and tisanes.

Lavender

Lemon grass, also known as citronella grass, is a tropical grass with the strong aroma and taste of lemon. It is similar to scallions in appearance but with a woody texture. Only the lower base and white leaf stalks are used. Available fresh or quick-frozen, lemon grass is widely used in Indonesian and Southeast Asian cuisines.

Marjoram (Fr. *marjolaine*), also known as sweet marjoram, is a flowering herb native to the Mediterranean and used since ancient times. Its flavor is similar to thyme but sweeter; it also has a stronger aroma. Marjoram is now used in many European cuisines. Although it is available fresh, marjoram is one of the few herbs whose flavor increases when dried. Wild marjoram is more commonly known as oregano.

Mint (Fr. *menthe*), a large family of herbs, includes many species and flavors (even chocolate). **Spearmint** is the most common garden and commercial variety. It has soft, bright green leaves and a tart aroma and flavor. Mint does not blend well with other herbs, so its use is confined to specific dishes, usually fruits or fatty meats such as lamb. Mint has an affinity for chocolate. It can also be brewed into a beverage or used as a garnish.

Spearmint

Peppermint has thin, stiff, pointed leaves and a sharper menthol flavor and aroma. Fresh peppermint is used less often in cooking or as a garnish than spearmint, but peppermint oil is a common flavoring in sweets and candies.

Peppermint

Oregano (Fr. *origan*), also known as wild marjoram, is a pungent, peppery herb used in Mediterranean cuisines, particularly Greek and Italian, as well as in Mexican cuisine. It is a classic complement to tomatoes. Oregano's thin, woody stalks bear clumps of tiny, dark green leaves, which are available dried and crushed.

Parsley (Fr. *persil*) is probably the best known and most widely used herb in the world. It grows in almost all climates and is available in many varieties, all of which are rich in vitamins and minerals. The most common type in the United States and Northern Europe is **curly parsley**. It has small curly leaves and a bright green color. Its flavor is tangy and clean. Other cuisines use a variety sometimes known as **Italian parsley**, which has flat leaves, a darker color and coarser flavor. Curly parsley is a ubiquitous garnish; both types can be used in virtually any food except sweets. Parsley stalks have a stronger flavor than the leaves and are part of the standard bouquet garni. Chopped parsley forms the basis of any fine herb blend.

Parsley

Italian Parsley

Rosemary (Fr. *romarin*) is an evergreen bush that grows wild in warm, dry climates worldwide. It has stiff, needlelike leaves; some varieties bear pale blue flowers. It is highly aromatic, with a slight odor of camphor or pine. Rosemary is best used fresh. When dried, it loses flavor and its leaves become very hard and unpleasant to chew. Whole rosemary stems may be added to a dish such as a stew and then removed when enough flavor has been imparted. They may also be added to a bouquet garni. Rosemary has a great affinity for roasted and grilled meats, especially lamb.

Rosemary

Sage (Fr. *sauge*) was used as a medicine for centuries before it entered the kitchen as a culinary herb. Culinary sage has narrow, fuzzy, gray-green leaves and blue flowers. Its flavor is strong and balsamic, with notes of camphor. Sage is used in poultry dishes, with fatty meats or brewed as a beverage. Sage's strong flavor does not blend well with other herbs. It dries well and is available in whole or chopped leaves or rubbed (coarsely ground).

Sage

Savory (Fr. *sariette*), also known as summer savory, has been used since ancient times. Its leaves are small and narrow and it has a sharp, bitter flavor, vaguely like thyme. It dries well and is used in bean dishes, sausages and herb mixtures.

Tarragon (Fr. *estragon*), another of the great culinary herbs, is native to Siberia. It is a bushy plant with long, narrow, dark green leaves and tiny gray flowers. Tarragon goes well with fish and tomatoes and is essential in many French dishes such as béarnaise sauce and fine herb blends. Its flavor is strong and diffuses quickly through foods. It is available dried, but drying may cause haylike flavors to develop.

Savory

Tarragon

Thyme (Fr. *thym*) has been popular since 3500 B.C., when Egyptians used it as a medicine and for embalming. Thyme is a small, bushy plant with woody stems, tiny green-gray leaves and purple flowers. Its flavor is strong but refined, with notes of sage. Thyme dries well and complements virtually all types of meat, poultry, fish, shellfish and vegetables. It is often included in a bouquet garni or added to stocks.

Thyme

Spices

Allspice

Anise Seeds

Capers

Allspice, also known as Jamaican pepper, is the dried berry of a tree that flourishes in Jamaica, and one of the few spices still grown exclusively in the New World. Allspice is available whole; in berries that look like large, rough, brown peppercorns; or ground. Ground allspice is not a mixture of spices, although it does taste like a blend of cinnamon, cloves and nutmeg. Allspice is now used throughout the world, in everything from cakes to curries, and is often included in peppercorn blends.

Anise (Fr. *anis*) is native to the eastern Mediterranean, where it was widely used by ancient civilizations. Today, it is grown commercially in warm climates throughout India, North Africa and southern Europe. The tiny, gray-green egg-shaped seeds have a distinctively strong, sweet flavor, similar to licorice and fennel. When anise seeds turn brown they are stale and should be discarded. Anise is used in pastries as well as fish, shellfish and vegetable dishes, and is commonly used in alcoholic beverages (e.g., Pernod and ouzo). The green leaves of the anise plant are occasionally used fresh as an herb or in salads.

Star anise, also known as Chinese anise, is the dried, star-shaped fruit of a Chinese magnolia tree. Although botanically unrelated, its flavor is similar to anise seeds but more bitter and pungent. It is an essential flavor in many Chinese dishes and one of the components of five-spice powder.

Capers (Fr. *capres*) come from a small bush that grows wild throughout the Mediterranean basin. Its unopened flower buds have been pickled and used as a condiment for thousands of years. Fresh capers are not used as the sharp, salty-sour flavor develops only after curing in strongly salted white vinegar. The finest capers are the smallest, known as *nonpareils*, which are produced in France's Provence region. Capers are used in a variety of sauces (tartare, remoulade) and are excellent with fish and game. Capers will keep for long periods if moistened by their original liquid. Do not add or substitute vinegar, however, as this causes the capers to spoil.

♦♦♦

A PINCH OF HISTORY

Spices have been used for many purposes for thousands of years. Egyptian papyri dating back to 2800 B.C. identify several spices native to the Middle and Far East that were used by the ruling and priestly classes for therapeutic, cosmetic, medicinal, ritualistic and culinary purposes.

By A.D. 300 the Romans were regularly importing spices for use as perfumes, medicines, preservatives and ingredients from China and India via long, difficult caravan journeys over sea and land. Spices were extremely expensive and unavailable to all but the wealthiest citizens.

After Rome fell in the second half of the 5th century A.D., much of the overland route through southern Europe became prey to bandits; and after Constantinople fell in 1453, the spice routes through the Middle East were controlled by the Ottoman Turks. Spice costs soared and economies based upon the spice trade, such as that of Venice, were at risk.

By then highly spiced food had become the norm, especially in wealthier households. So, in part to maintain their culinary norm, the Europeans set out to break the Ottoman Turk monopoly. These efforts led to Columbus' discovery of the Americas and Vasco de Gama's discovery of a sea route to India. Although the New World contained none of the spices for which Columbus was searching, it provided many previously unknown foods and flavorings that changed European tables forever, including chiles, vanilla, tomatoes, potatoes and chocolate.

Formation of the Dutch East India Company in 1602 marked the start of the Dutch colonial empire and made spices widely available to the growing European middle classes. The transplantation and cultivation of spice plants eventually weakened the once-powerful trading empires until, by the 19th century, no European country could monopolize trade. Prices fell dramatically.

Caraway is perhaps the world's oldest spice. Its use has been traced to the Stone Age and seeds have been found in ancient Egyptian tombs. The caraway plant grows wild in Europe and temperate regions of Asia. It produces a small, crescent-shaped brown seed with the peppery flavor of rye. Seeds may be purchased whole or ground. (The leaves have a mild, bland flavor and are rarely used in cooking.) Caraway is a very European flavor, used extensively in German and Austrian dishes, particularly breads, meats and cabbage. It is also used in liquors and cheeses.

Cardamom is one of the most expensive spices, second only to saffron in cost. Its seeds are encased in 1/4-inch-(6 millimeter) long light green or brown pods. Cardamom is highly aromatic. Its flavor, lemony with notes of camphor, is quite strong and is used in both sweet and savory dishes. Cardamom is widely used in Indian and Middle Eastern cuisines, where it is also used to flavor coffee. Scandinavians use cardamom to flavor breads and pastries. Ground cardamom loses its flavor rapidly and is easily adulterated, so it is best to purchase whole seeds and grind your own as needed.

Chiles, including paprika, chile peppers, bell peppers and cayenne, are members of the *capsicum* plant family. Although cultivated for thousands of years in the West Indies and Americas, capsicum peppers were unknown in the Old World prior to Spanish explorations during the 15th century. Capsicum peppers come in all shapes and sizes, with a wide range of flavors, from sweet to extremely hot. Some capsicums are used as a vegetable, while others are dried, ground and used as a spice. Fresh chiles and bell peppers are discussed in Chapter 22, Vegetables. Capsicums are botanically unrelated to *piper nigrum*, the black peppercorns discussed below.

Cayenne, sometimes simply labeled "red pepper," is ground from a blend of several particularly hot types of dried red chile peppers. Its flavor is extremely hot and pungent; it has a bright orange-red color and fine texture.

Paprika, also known as Hungarian pepper, is a bright red powder ground from particular varieties of red-ripened and dried chiles. The flavor ranges from sweet to pungent; the aroma is distinctive and strong. It is essential to many Spanish and eastern European dishes. Mild paprika is meant to be used in generous quantities and may be sprinkled on prepared foods as a garnish.

Chile powders are made from a wide variety of dried chile peppers, ranging from sweet and mild to extremely hot and pungent. The finest pure chile powders come from dried chiles that are simply roasted, ground and sieved. Commercial chilli powder, an American invention, is actually a combination of spices—oregano, cumin, garlic and other flavorings—intended for use in Mexican dishes. Each brand is different and should be sampled before using.

Crushed chiles, also known as chile flakes, are blended from dried, coarsely crushed chiles. They are quite hot and are used in sauces and meat dishes.

Cinnamon (Fr. *cannelle*) and its cousin **cassia** are among the oldest known spices: cinnamon's use is recorded in China as early as 2500 B.C.and the Far East still produces most of these products. Both cinnamon and cassia come from the bark of small evergreen trees, peeled from branches in thin layers and dried in the sun. High-quality cinnamon should be pale brown and thin, rolled up like paper into sticks known as quills. Cassia is coarser and has a stronger, less subtle flavor than cinnamon. Consequently, it is cheaper than true cinnamon. Cinnamon is usually purchased ground because it is difficult to grind. Cinnamon sticks are used when long cooking times can be allowed in order to extract the flavor (for example, in stews or curries). Cinnamons' flavor is most often associated with pastries and sweets, but has a great affinity for lamb and

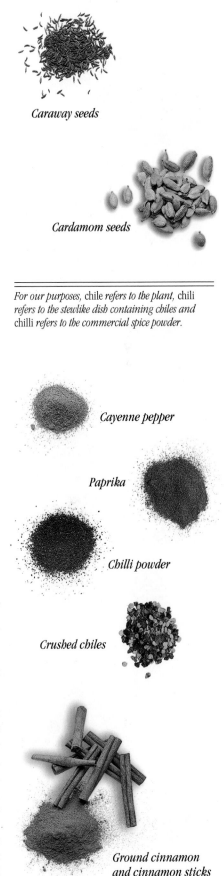

Caraway seeds

Cardamom seeds

For our purposes, chile *refers to the plant,* chili *refers to the stewlike dish containing chiles and* chilli *refers to the commercial spice powder.*

Cayenne pepper

Paprika

Chilli powder

Crushed chiles

Ground cinnamon and cinnamon sticks

Cloves

Coriander seeds

Cumin

Fennel

Fenugreek

Ginger root

Juniper berries

spicy dishes. Labeling laws do not require that packages distinguish between cassia and cinnamon, so most of what is sold as cinnamon in the United States is actually cassia, blended for consistent flavor and aroma.

Cloves (Fr. *girofles*) are the unopened buds of evergreen trees that flourish in muggy tropical regions. When dried, whole cloves have hard, sharp prongs that can be used to push them into other foods, such as onions or fruit, in order to provide flavor. Cloves are extremely pungent, with a sweet, astringent aroma. A small amount provides a great deal of flavor. Cloves are used in desserts and meat dishes, preserves and liquors. They may be purchased whole or ground.

Coriander seeds come from the cilantro plant. They are round and beige, with a distinctive sweet, spicy flavor and strong aroma. Unlike other plants in which the seeds and the leaves carry the same flavor and aroma, coriander and cilantro are distinct. Coriander seeds are available whole or ground and are frequently used in Indian cuisine and pickling mixtures.

Cumin is the seed of a small delicate plant of the parsley family that grows in North Africa and the Middle East. The small seeds are available whole or ground and look (but do not taste) like caraway seeds. Cumin has a powerful earthy flavor and tends to dominate any dish in which it is included. It is used in Indian, Middle Eastern and Mexican cuisines, in sausages and a few cheeses.

Fennel (Fr. *fenouil*) is a perennial plant with feathery leaves and tiny flowers long cultivated in India and China as a medicine and cure for witchcraft. Its seeds are greenish brown with prominent ridges and short, hairlike fibers. Their taste and aroma are similar to anise, though not as sweet. Whole seeds are widely used in Italian stews and sausages; Central European cuisines use fennel with fish, pork, pickles and vegetables. Ground seeds can also be used in breads, cakes and cookies. The same plant produces a bulbous stalk used as a vegetable.

Fenugreek (Fr. *fenugrec*), grown in Mediterranean countries since ancient times, is a small, beanlike plant with a tiny flower. The seeds, available whole or ground, are pebble-shaped and transfer their pale orange color to the foods with which they are cooked. Their flavor is bittersweet, like burnt sugar with a bitter aftertaste. Fenugreek is a staple in Indian cuisine, especially curries and chutneys.

Ginger (Fr. *gingembre*) is a well-known spice obtained from the root of a tall, flowering tropical plant. Fresh ginger root is known as a "hand" because it looks vaguely like a group of knobby fingers. It has grayish-tan skin and a pale yellow, fibrous interior. Fresh ginger should be plump and firm with smooth skin. It should keep for about a month under refrigeration. Its flavor is fiery but sweet, with notes of lemon and rosemary. Fresh ginger is widely available and is used in Indian and Asian cuisines. It has a special affinity for chicken, beef and curries. Ginger is also available peeled and pickled in vinegar, candied in sugar or preserved in alcohol or syrup. Dried, ground ginger is a fine yellow powder widely used in pastries. Its flavor is spicier and not as sweet as fresh ginger.

Juniper is an evergreen bush grown throughout the northern hemisphere. It produces round purple berries with a sweet flavor similar to pine. Juniper berries are used for flavoring gin and other alcoholic beverages, and are crushed and incorporated in game dishes, particularly venison and wild boar.

Mustard seeds (Fr. *moutarde*), available in black, brown and yellow, come from three different plants in the cabbage family. Mustard seeds are small, hard spheres with a bitter flavor. The seeds have no aroma, but their flavor is sharp and fiery hot. Yellow seeds have the mildest and black seeds the strongest flavor. All are sold whole and can be crushed for cooking. Mustard seeds are a standard component of pickling spices and are processed and blended for prepared mustards, which are discussed below. Ground or dry mustard is a bright yellow powder made from a blend of ground seeds, wheat flour and turmeric.

Mustard seeds

Ground mustard

Nutmeg (Fr. *muscade*) and **mace** come from the yellow plumlike fruit of a large tropical evergreen. These fruits are dried and opened to reveal the seed known as nutmeg. The seed is surrounded by a bright red lacy coating or aril; the aril is the spice mace. Whole nutmegs are oval and look rather like a piece of smooth wood. The flavor and aroma of nutmeg are strong and sweet, and a small quantity provides a great deal of flavor. Nutmeg should be grated directly into a dish as needed; once grated, flavor loss is rapid. Nutmeg is used in many European cuisines, mainly in pastries and sweets, but is also important in meat and savory dishes.

Mace is an expensive spice, with a flavor similar to nutmeg but more refined. It is almost always purchased ground and retains its flavor longer than other ground spices. Mace is used primarily in pastry items.

Mace (left) and whole and ground nutmeg (right)

Peppercorns (Fr. *poivre*) are the berries of a vine plant (*piper nigrum*) native to tropical Asia. Peppercorns should not be confused with the chile (capsicum) peppers discussed above. Peppercorns vary in size, color, pungency and flavor. Many of these differences are the result of variations in climate and growing conditions. Good-quality pepper is expensive and should be purchased whole and ground fresh in a peppermill as needed. Whole peppercorns will last indefinitely if kept dry. They should be stored well covered in a cool, dark place.

Black and **white peppercorns** are produced from the same plant, but are picked and processed differently. For black peppercorns, the berries are picked when green and simply dried whole in the sun. Black pepper has a warm, pungent flavor and aroma. Tellicherry peppercorns from the southwest coast of India are generally considered the finest black peppercorns in the world and are priced accordingly.

For white peppercorns, the berries are allowed to ripen until they turn red. The ripened berries are allowed to ferment, then the outer layer of skin is washed off. Nowadays, white pepper may be produced by mechanically removing the outer skin from black peppercorns. This is not true white pepper, and the resulting product should be labeled "decorticated." White pepper has less aroma than black pepper but is useful in white sauces or where the appearance of black speckles is undesirable.

Green peppercorns are unripened berries that are either freeze-dried or pickled in brine or vinegar. Pickled green peppercorns are soft, with a fresh, sour flavor similar to capers. They are excellent in spiced butters and sauces or with fish.

Pink peppercorns are actually the berries of a South American tree, not a vine pepper plant. Pink peppercorns are available dried or pickled in vinegar. Although attractive, their flavor is bitter and pinelike, with less spiciness than true pepper. Pink peppercorns are no longer available in some areas because of reported toxic side effects.

Black pepper (left) and white pepper (right)

Poppy seeds (Fr. *pavot*) are the ripened seeds of the opium poppy, which flourishes in the Middle East and India. (When ripe, the seeds do not contain any of the medicinal alkaloids found elsewhere in the plant.) The tiny blue-gray seeds are round and hard with a sweet, nutty flavor. Poppy seeds are used in pastries and breads.

Poppy seeds

Saffron

Sesame seeds

Turmeric

Saffron (Fr. *safran*) comes from the dried stigmas of the saffron crocus. Each flower bears only three threadlike stigmas, and each must be picked by hand. It takes about 250,000 flowers to produce one pound of saffron, making it the most expensive spice in the world. Beware of bargains; there is no such thing as cheap saffron. Luckily, a tiny pinch is enough to color and flavor a large quantity of food. Good saffron should be a brilliant orange color, not yellow, with a strong aroma and a bitter, honeylike taste. Saffron produces a yellow dye that diffuses through any warm liquid. Valencia or Spanish saffron is considered the finest. It is commonly used with fish and shellfish (a necessity for bouillabaisse) and rice dishes such as paella and risotto. When using saffron threads, first crush them gently, then soak them in some hot liquid from the recipe. Powdered saffron is less expensive but more easily adulterated. It may be added directly to the other ingredients when cooking.

Sesame seeds, also known as benne seeds, are native to India. They are small, flat ovals, with a creamy white color. Their taste is nutty and earthy, with a pronounced aroma when roasted or ground into a paste (known as tahini). Sesame seeds are the source of sesame oil, which has a mild, nutty flavor and does not go rancid easily. Sesame seeds are roasted and used in or as a garnish for breads and meat dishes. They are popular in Indian and Asian cuisines, with a black variety of seeds most popular as a Japanese condiment.

Turmeric, also known as Indian saffron, is produced from the roots of a flowering tropical plant related to ginger. Unlike ginger, fresh turmeric is not used in cooking. It is only available dried and usually ground. Turmeric is renowned for its vibrant yellow color and is used as a food coloring and dye. Turmeric's flavor is distinctive and strong; it should not be substituted for saffron. Turmeric is a traditional ingredient in Indian curries, to which it imparts color as well as flavor.

Spice Blends

Many countries and cuisines have created recognizable combinations of spice flavors that are found in a variety of dishes. Although many of these blends are available ready-prepared for convenience, most can be mixed by the chef as needed. A few of the more common spice blends are described here.

Chinese five-spice powder is a combination of equal parts finely ground Szechuan pepper, star anise, cloves, cinnamon and fennel seeds. This blend is widely used in Chinese and some Vietnamese foods and is excellent with pork and in pâtés.

Curry powder is a European invention that probably took its name from the Tamil word *kari*, meaning a sauce. Created by 19th-century Britons returning from colonial India, it was meant to be the complete spicing for a "curry" dish. There are as many different formulas for curry powder as there are manufacturers, some mild and sweet (Bombay or Chinese style), others hot and pungent (Madras style). Typical ingredients in curry powder are black pepper, cinnamon, cloves, coriander, cumin, ginger, mace and turmeric.

Pickling spice, as with other blends, varies by manufacturer. Most pickling spice blends are based on black peppercorns and red chiles, with some or all of the following added: allspice, cloves, ginger, mustard seeds, coriander seeds, bay leaves and dill. These blends are useful in making cucumber or vegetable pickles as well as in stews and soups.

Pickling spice

Quatre-épices, literally "four spices" in French, is a peppery mixture of black peppercorns with lesser amounts of nutmeg, cloves and dried ginger. Sometimes cinnamon or allspice is included. Quatre-épices is used in charcuterie and long-simmered stews.

KITCHEN STAPLES **135**

Using Herbs and Spices

Herbs and spices are a simple, inexpensive way to bring individuality and variety to foods. Their proper use leads to better-flavored and distinctively different dishes. They add neither fat nor sodium and virtually no calories to foods; most contain only 3 to 10 calories per teaspoon. Table 7.1 lists just a few uses for some of the more common herbs and spices.

TABLE 7.1 USES FOR SOME COMMON HERBS AND SPICES

Flavoring	Form	Suggested Uses
Allspice	Whole or ground	Fruits, relishes, braised meats
Anise	Whole or ground	Asian cuisines, pastries, breads, cheeses
Basil	Fresh or dried	Tomatoes, salads, eggs, fish, chicken, lamb, cheeses
Caraway	Whole or ground	Rye bread, cabbage, beans, pork, beef, veal
Chervil	Fresh or dried	Chicken, fish, eggs, salads, soups, vegetables
Chives	Fresh or dried	Eggs, fish, chicken, soups, potatoes, cheeses
Cilantro	Fresh leaves	Salsa, salads, Mexican cuisine, fish, shellfish, chicken
Cloves	Whole or ground	Marinades, baked goods, braised meats, pickles, fruits, beverages, stocks
Cumin	Whole or ground	Chili, sausages, stews, eggs
Dill	Fresh or dried leaves; whole seeds	Leaves or seeds in soups, salads, fish, shellfish, vegetables, breads; seeds in pickles, potatoes, vegetables
Fennel	Whole seeds	Sausages, stews, sauces, pickling, lamb, eggs
Ginger	Fresh root or powder	Asian, Caribbean and Indian cuisines, pastries, curries, stews, meats
Marjoram	Fresh or dried	Sausages, pâtés, meats, poultry, stews, green vegetables, tomatoes, game
Nutmeg	Ground	Curries, relishes, rice, eggs, beverages
Rosemary	Fresh or dried	Lamb, veal, beef, poultry, game, marinades, stews
Saffron	Threads or ground	Rice, breads, potatoes, soups, stews, chicken, fish, shellfish
Sage	Fresh or dried	Poultry, charcuterie, pork, stuffings, pasta, beans, tomatoes
Tarragon	Fresh or dried	Chicken, fish, eggs, salad dressings, sauces, tomatoes
Thyme	Fresh or dried	Fish, chicken, meats, stews, charcuterie, soups, tomatoes
Turmeric	Ground	Curries, relishes, rice, eggs, breads

Although the flavors and aromas of fresh herbs are generally preferred, dried herbs are widely used because they are readily available and convenient. Purchase only the amount of dried herbs that can be used within a short time. If stored in a closed container in a cool, dry place, dried herbs should last for two to three months.

Use less dried herbs than you would fresh herbs. The loss of moisture strengthens and concentrates the flavor in dried herbs. In general, you should use only one half to one third as much dried herb as fresh in any given recipe. For example, if a recipe calls for one *tablespoon* of fresh basil, you should substitute only one *teaspoon* of dried basil. You can usually add more later if necessary.

Spices are often available whole or ground. Once ground, they lose their flavors rapidly, however. Whole spices should keep their flavors for many months if stored in air-tight containers in a cool, dry place away from direct light. Stale spices lose their spicy aroma and develop a bitter or musty aftertaste. Discard them.

Because ground spices release their flavors quickly, they should be added to cooked dishes near the end of the cooking period. In uncooked dishes that call for ground spices (for example, salad dressings), the mixture should be allowed to stand for several hours to develop good flavor.

While some combinations are timeless—rosemary with lamb, dill with salmon, nutmeg with spinach, caraway with rye bread—less common pairings can be equally delicious and far more exciting. A chef must be willing and able to experiment with new flavors. But first you must be familiar with the distinctive flavor and aroma of the herb or spice. Then you can experiment, always bearing in mind the following guidelines:

◆ Flavorings should not hide the taste or aroma of the primary ingredient;

◆ Flavorings should be combined in balance, so as not to overwhelm the palate; and

◆ Flavorings should not be used to disguise poor quality or poorly prepared products.

Even when following a well-tested recipe, the quantity of flavorings may need to be adjusted because of changes in brands or the condition of the ingredients. A chef should strive to develop his or palate to recognize and correct subtle variances as necessary.

Bouquet Garni and Sachet

The *bouquet garni* and the *sachet* are used to introduce flavorings, seasonings and aromatics into stocks, sauces, soups and stews.

A bouquet garni, shown in Figure 7.1, is a selection of herbs (usually fresh) and vegetables tied into a bundle with twine. The twine makes it easy to remove the bouquet when sufficient flavor has been extracted. A standard bouquet garni consists of parsley stems, celery, thyme, leeks and carrots.

A sachet (also known as a *sachet d'épices*), shown in Figure 7.2, is made by tying seasonings together in cheesecloth. A standard sachet consists of peppercorns, bay leaves, parsley stems, thyme, cloves and, optionally, garlic. The exact quantity of these ingredients is determined by the amount of liquid the sachet is meant to flavor.

Bouquets garni and sachets are used to add flavors in such a way that the ingredients can be easily removed from a dish when the flavors have been extracted. A similar technique, although less commonly used, is an **onion**

FIGURE 7.1 *Bouquet garni*

FIGURE 7.2 *Sachet*

piquet. To prepare an onion piquet, peel the onion and trim off the root end. Attach one or two dried bay leaves to the onion using whole cloves as pins. The onion piquet is then simmered in milk or stock to extract flavors.

SALT

Salt (Fr. *sel*) is the most basic seasoning and its use is universal. It preserves foods, heightens their flavors and provides the distinctive taste of saltiness. The presence of salt can be tasted easily but not smelled. Temperature affects saltiness. The cooler a food, the saltier it tastes, so it is best to undersalt hot foods that will be chilled prior to service (chilled soups, for example).

Culinary or **table salt** is sodium chloride (NaCl), one of the minerals essential to human life. Salt contains no calories, proteins, fats or carbohydrates. It is available from several sources, each with its own flavor and degree of saltiness.

Rock salt, mined from underground deposits, is available in both edible and nonedible forms. It is used for home freezing.

Common kitchen or table salt is produced by pumping water through underground salt deposits, then bringing the brine to the surface to evaporate, leaving behind crystals. Chemicals are usually added to prevent table salt from absorbing moisture and thus keep it free-flowing. Iodized salt is commonly used in the United States. The iodine has no effect on the salt's flavor or use; it is simply added to provide an easily available source of iodine, an important nutrient, to a large number of people.

Sea salt is obtained, not surprisingly, by evaporating sea water and purifying the crystals left behind. Many chefs consider its flavor stronger or purer than mined salt.

Kosher salt has large, irregular crystals and is used in the "koshering" or curing of meats. It is purified rock salt that contains no iodine or additives. It can be substituted for common kitchen salt.

Because it is nonorganic, salt keeps indefinitely. It will, however, absorb moisture from the atmosphere, which prevents it from flowing properly. Salt is

◆◆◆

ABOUT FLAVORS

Flavor is to food what hue is to color. It is what timbre is to music. Flavor is adjective; food is noun. Each ingredient has its own particular character, which is altered by every other ingredient it encounters. A secret ingredient is one that mysteriously improves the flavor of a dish without calling attention to itself. It is either undetectable or extremely subtle, but its presence is crucial because the dish would not be nearly as good without it.

Primary flavors are those that are obvious, such as the flavors of chicken and tarragon in a chicken tarragon, shrimp and garlic in a shrimp scampi, or beef and red wine in a beef *à la Bourguignon*. Secret ingredients belong to the realm of secondary flavors. However obvious it is that you need tarragon to prepare a chicken tarragon, you would not achieve the most interesting result using *only* tarragon. Tarragon, in this case, needs secondary ingredients—a hint of celery seed and anise—to make it taste more like quintessential tarragon and at the same time more than tarragon. In

this way, primary flavors often depend on secret ingredients to make them more interesting and complex. Using only one herb or spice to achieve a certain taste usually results in a lackluster dish—each mouthful tastes the same. Whether they function in a primary or secondary way, flavors combine in only three different ways: They marry, oppose, or juxtapose.

When flavors marry, they combine to form one taste. Some secondary flavors marry with primary ones to create a new flavor greater than the sum of its parts, and often two flavors can do the job better than one. It may sound like an eccentric combination, but vanilla marries with the flavor of lobster, making it taste more like the essence of lobster than lobster does on its own. And when ginger and molasses marry, they create a flavor superior to either alone.

Opposite flavors can highlight or cancel each other; they can cut or balance each other. Sweet/sour, sweet/salty, sweet/hot, salty/sour, and salty/tart are all opposites. Salt and sugar

are so opposed, in fact, that when used in equal amounts they cancel each other entirely. Sweet relish helps to cancel the salty flavor of hot dogs. Chinese sauces usually contain some sugar to help balance the saltiness of soy sauce.

Because flavors are sensed on different parts of the tongue and palate, and because they are tasted at different times, we can juxtapose them, using flavors side by side or in layers. The layering of flavors makes the food we taste more interesting because each mouthful is different.

Knowing how to combine many flavors and aromas to achieve a simple and pure result (and knowing when not to combine flavors) will make you a better, more confident cook. Good cooks over the centuries have known these things intuitively—but they've had neither the huge variety of ingredients nor the knowledge of world cuisines that we have today.

from SECRET INGREDIENTS
by CHEF MICHAEL ROBERTS

---

a powerful preservative; its presence stops or greatly slows down the growth of many undesirable organisms. Salt is used to preserve meats, vegetables and fish. It is also used to develop desirable flavors in bacon, ham, cheeses and fish products as well as pickled vegetables.

NUTS

A **nut** (Fr. *noix*) is the edible single-seed kernel of a fruit surrounded by a hard shell. A hazelnut is an example of a true nut. The term is used more generally, however, to refer to any seed or fruit with an edible kernel in a hard shell. Walnuts and peanuts are examples of non-nut "nuts" (peanuts are legumes that grow underground; walnuts have two kernels). Nuts are a good source of protein and B vitamins but are high in fat. Their high fat content makes them especially susceptible to rancidity and odor absorption. Nuts should be stored in nonmetal, air-tight containers in a cool, dark place. Most nuts may be kept frozen for up to one year.

Nuts are used in foods to provide texture and flavor. They are often roasted in a low (275°F/135°C) oven before use to heighten their flavor. Allowing roasted nuts to cool to room temperature before grinding prevents them from releasing too much oil.

Almonds (Fr. *almande*) are the seeds of a plumlike fruit. Native to western India, the almond was first cultivated by the ancient Greeks. It is now a major commercial crop in California. Almonds are available whole,

Almonds

sliced, slivered or ground. Blanched almonds have had their brown, textured skins removed; natural almonds retain their skins. Unless the brown color of natural almond skin is undesirable, the two types can be used interchangeably in recipes. Almonds are frequently used in pastries and candies and are the main ingredient in marzipan.

Cashews, native to the Amazon, are now cultivated in India and east Africa. The cashew nut is actually the seed of a plant related to poison ivy. Because of toxins in the shell, cashews are always sold shelled. They are expensive and have a strong flavor. Cashews are used in some Asian cuisines and make a wonderful addition to cookies and candies.

Cashews

Chestnuts (Fr. *marrons*) are true nuts that must be cooked before using. Available steamed, dried, boiled or roasted, they are often sold as a canned purée, with or without added sugar. Candied or glazed chestnuts are also available. Most chestnuts are grown in Europe, primarily Italy, but new varieties are beginning to flourish in North America. Their distinctive flavor is found in many sweet dishes and pastries. Because of their high starch content, chestnuts are also used in soups and sauces and may be served as a side dish.

Chestnuts

Coconuts (Fr. *noix de coco*) are the seeds from one of the largest of all fruits. They grow on the tropical coconut palm tree. The nut is a dark brown oval, covered with coarse fibers. The shell is thick and hard; inside is a layer of white, moist flesh. The interior also contains a clear liquid known as coconut water. (This is not the same as coconut milk or coconut cream, both of which are prepared from the flesh.) Coconut has a mild aroma, a sweet, nutty flavor and a crunchy, chewy texture. Fresh coconuts are readily available but require some effort to use. Coconut flesh is available shredded or flaked, with or without added sugar. Coconut is most often used in pastries and candies and is also an important ingredient in Indian and Caribbean cuisines. A good fresh coconut should feel heavy; you should be able to hear the coconut water sloshing around inside. Avoid cracked, moist or moldy coconuts.

Coconuts

Hazelnuts (Fr. *noisette*) are true nuts that grow wild in the Northeast and Upper Midwest states. The cultivated form, known as a **filbert**, is native to temperate regions throughout the Northern Hemisphere. A bit larger than the hazelnut, it has a weaker flavor than its wild cousin. Both nuts look like smooth brown marbles. Filberts are more abundant, so are generally less expensive. Hazelnuts are often ground for use in cakes or pastries. Their distinctive flavor goes well with chocolate and coffee.

Hazelnuts

To remove the hazelnut's bitter skin, roast whole nuts in a 275°F (135°C) oven for 12 to 15 minutes. They should give off a good aroma and just begin to darken. While still hot, rub the nuts in a dry towel or against a mesh sifter to remove the skin.

Macadamias, although commercially significant in Hawaii, are actually native to Australia. This small round nut is creamy white with a sweet, rich taste and high fat content. Its shell is extremely hard and must be removed by machine, so the macadamia is always sold out of the shell. Its flavor blends well with fruits, coconut and white and dark chocolate.

Macadamias

Peanuts

Pecans

Pine Nuts

Peanuts (Fr. *arachide*), also known as groundnuts, are actually legumes that grow underground. The peanut is native to South America; it made its way into North America via Africa and the slave trade. Peanuts are a good source of protein and fat and became an important source of food and oil during World War II. They may be eaten raw or roasted and are available shelled or unshelled, with or without their thin red skins. Peanuts are used in Asian cuisines and are ubiquitous ground with a bit of oil into peanut butter.

Pecans (Fr. *noix de pacane*), native to the Mississippi River Valley, are perhaps the most popular nuts in America. Their flavor is rich and mapley and appears most often in breads, sweets and pastries. They are available whole in the shell or in various standard sizes and grades of pieces.

Pine nuts (Fr. *pignon*), also known as pinon nuts and pignole, are the seeds of several species of pine tree. The small, creamy white, teardrop-shaped nuts are commonly used in dishes from Spain, Italy and the American Southwest. They are rarely chopped or ground due to their small size, and will only need roasting if being used in a dish that will not receive further cooking. Pine nuts are used in breads, pastries and salads and are essential to classic pesto sauce.

Pistachios (Fr. *pistaches*) are native to central Asia, where they have been cultivated for over 3000 years. California now produces most of the pistachios marketed in this country. Pistachios are unique for the green color of their meat. When ripe, the shell opens naturally at one end, aptly referred to as "smiling," which makes shelling the nuts quite easy. Red pistachios are dyed, not natural. Pistachios are sold whole, shelled or unshelled, and are used in pastries and meat dishes, particularly pâtés.

Pistachios

TABLE 7.2   NUTRITIONAL VALUES OF COMMON NUTS

Per 1 Ounce (28 g) Serving	Calories	Protein (g)	Carbohydrates (g)	Total Fat (g)	Saturated Fat (g)	Sodium (mg)
Almonds, whole kernels	167	5.7	5.8	14.8	1.4	3
Cashews, dry roasted	163	4.4	9.3	13.2	2.6	4
Chestnuts, roasted and peeled	70	0.9	15.0	0.6	0.1	1
Filberts, blanched	191	3.6	4.5	19.1	1.4	1
Macadamias	199	2.4	3.9	20.9	3.1	1
Peanuts, raw	159	7.2	4.5	13.8	1.9	5
Pecans	190	2.2	5.2	19.2	1.5	trace
Walnuts, English	182	4.1	5.2	17.6	1.6	3

The Corinne T. Netzer Encyclopedia of Food Values 1992

Walnuts (Fr. *noix*), relatives of the pecan, are native to Asia, Europe and North America. The black walnut, native to Appalachia, has a dark brown meat and strong flavor. The English walnut, now grown primarily in California, has a milder flavor, is easier to shell and is less expensive. Walnuts are more popular than pecans outside the United States. They are used in baked goods and are pressed for oil.

English walnuts

Oils

Oils (Fr. *huile*) are a type of fat that remains liquid at room temperature. Cooking oils are refined from various seeds, plants and vegetables. (Other fats, such as butter and margarine, are discussed in Chapter 8, Eggs and Dairy Products; animal and solid fats are discussed in Chapter 26, Principles of the Bakeshop.)

When purchasing oils you should consider their use, **smoke point**, flavor and cost. Fats, including oils and **shortenings**, are manufactured for specific purposes such as deep-frying, cake-baking, salad dressings and sautéing. Most food service operations purchase different ones for each of these needs.

Fats break down at different temperatures. The temperature at which a given fat begins to break down and smoke is known as its smoke point. Choose fats with higher smoke points for high temperature cooking such as deep-frying and sautéing. If a fat with a low smoke point is used for high temperature cooking, it may break down, burn and impart undesirable flavors.

The flavor and cost of each oil must also be considered. For example, both corn oil and walnut oil may be used in a salad dressing. Their selection may depend on balancing cost (corn oil is less expensive) against flavor (walnut oil has a stronger, more distinctive flavor).

When fats spoil they are said to go **rancid**. Rancidity is a chemical change caused by exposure to air, light or heat. It results in objectionable flavors and odors. Different fats turn rancid at different rates, but all fats benefit from refrigerated storage away from moisture, light and air. (Some oils are packaged in colored glass containers because certain tints of green and yellow block the damaging light rays that can cause an oil to go rancid.) Oils may become thick and cloudy under refrigeration. This is not a cause for concern. The oils will return to their clear, liquid states at room temperature. Stored fats should also be covered to prevent the absorption of odors.

Vegetable Oils are extracted from a variety of plants, including corn, cottonseed, peanuts and soybeans, by pressure or chemical solvents. The oil is then refined and cleaned to remove unwanted colors, odors or flavors. Vegetable oils are virtually odorless and have a neutral flavor. Because they contain no animal products they are cholesterol-free. If a commercial product contains only one type of oil it is labeled "pure" (as in "pure corn oil"). Products labeled "vegetable oil" are blended from several sources. Products labeled "salad oil" are highly refined blends of vegetable oil.

Canola oil is processed from rapeseeds. Its popularity is growing rapidly because it contains no cholesterol and has a high percentage of monounsaturated fat. Canola oil is useful for frying and general cooking because it has no flavor and a high smoke point.

Canola oil

Smoke point—*the temperature at which a fat begins to break down and smoke.*

Shortening—*a fat, usually made from vegetable oils, that is solid at room temperature.*

Nut oils are extracted from a variety of nuts and are almost always packaged as a "pure" product, never blended. A nut oil should have the strong flavor and aroma of the nut from which it was processed. Popular examples are walnut and hazelnut oils. These oils are used to give flavor to salad dressings, marinades and other dishes. But heat diminishes their flavor, so nut oils are not recommended for frying or baking. Nut oils tend to go rancid quickly and therefore are usually packaged in small containers.

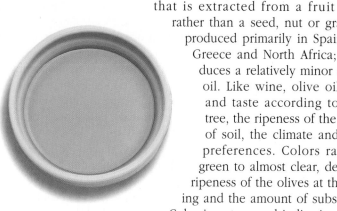

Hazelnut oil

Extra virgin olive oil

Olive oil is the only oil that is extracted from a fruit rather than a seed, nut or grain. Olive oil is produced primarily in Spain, Italy, France, Greece and North Africa; California produces a relatively minor amount of olive oil. Like wine, olive oils vary in color and taste according to the variety of tree, the ripeness of the olives, the type of soil, the climate and the producer's preferences. Colors range from dark green to almost clear, depending on the ripeness of the olives at the time of pressing and the amount of subsequent refining. Color is not a good indication of flavor, however. Flavor is ultimately a matter of personal preference. A stronger-flavored oil may be desired for some foods, while a milder oil is better for others. Good olive oil should be thicker than refined vegetable oils, but not so thick that it has a fatty texture.

The label designations—extra virgin, virgin and pure—refer to the acidity of the oil (a low acid content is preferable) and the extent of processing used to extract the oil. The first cold-pressing of the olives results in virgin oil. (The designation "virgin" is used only when the oil is 100% unadulterated olive oil, unheated and without any chemical processing.) Virgin oil may still vary in quality depending on its acidity level. Extra virgin oil is virgin oil with an acidity level of not more than 1%; virgin oil may have an acidity level of up to 3%. Pure olive oil is processed from the pulp left after the first pressing using heat and chemicals. Pure oil is lighter in flavor and less expensive than virgin oil.

Flavored oils, also known as **infused oils**, are an interesting and increasingly popular condiment. These oils may be used as a cooking medium or flavoring accent in marinades, dressings, sauces or other dishes. Flavors include basil and other herbs, garlic, citrus and spice. Flavored oils are generally prepared with olive oil for additional flavor or canola oil, both considered more healthful than other fats.

Top-quality commercially flavored oils are prepared by extracting aromatic oils from the flavoring ingredients and then emulsifying them with a high-grade oil; any impurities are then removed by placing the oil in a centrifuge. Using the aromatic oils of the flavoring ingredients yields a more intense flavor than merely steeping the same ingredients in the oil. Flavored oils should be stored as you would any other high-quality oil.

◆◆◆

THE OLIVE

Olives are the fruit of a tree native to the Mediterranean area. Green olives are those harvested unripened; black olives are fully ripened. The raw fruit is inedibly bitter and must be washed, soaked and pickled before eating. Green olives should have a smooth, tight skin. Ripe olives will be glossy but softer, with a slightly wrinkled skin. Many varieties and flavors are available, from the tiny black Niçoise to the large purplish Kalamata. Olives are packaged in a range of sizes, from medium (the smallest) to jumbo (the largest). (Colossal and super colossal olives are actually smaller than jumbos.) Pitted olives are also available. The cavity may be filled with strips of pimento, jalapeño pepper, almonds or other foods for flavor and appearance.

Olives are used as a finger food for snacks or hors d'oeuvres, or added to salads or pasta. They may even be cooked in breads, soups, sauces, stews or casseroles. A paste made of minced ripe olives, known as tapenade, is used as a dip or condiment.

TABLE 7.3	THE SMOKE POINT AND NUTRITIONAL VALUES OF COMMON FATS			
Per 1 Ounce (28 g) Serving	Smoke Point	Calories	Total Fat (g)	Saturated Fat (g)
Olive oil	437°F/225°C	251	28.4	3.8
Peanut oil	425°F/218°C	251	28.4	4.8
Lard*	370°F/188°C	230	25.6	10.0
Canola oil	425°F/218°C	251	28.4	2.0
Walnut oil	325–400°F/ 163–204°C	240	28.0	4.0
Butter, clarified*	400°F/204°C	248	28.2	17.6
Whole butter, unsalted*	260°F/127°C	200	22.8	14.2

The Corinne T. Netzer Encyclopedia of Food Values 1992

*discussed in Chapter 26

VINEGARS

Vinegar (Fr. *vinaigre*) is a thin, sour liquid used for thousands of years as a preservative, cooking ingredient, condiment and cleaning solution. Vinegar is obtained through the fermentation of wine or other alcoholic liquid. Bacteria attacks the alcohol in the solution, turning it into acetic acid. No alcohol will remain when the transformation is complete. The quality of vinegar depends upon the quality of the wine or other liquid on which it is based. Vinegar flavors are as varied as the liquids from which they are made.

Vinegars should be clear and clean looking, never cloudy or muddy. Commercial vinegars are pasteurized, so an unopened bottle should last indefinitely in a cool, dark place. Once opened, vinegars should last about three months if tightly capped. Any sediment that develops can be strained out; if mold develops, discard the vinegar.

Wine vinegars are as old as wine itself. They may be made from white or red wine, sherry or even champagne, and should bear the color and flavor hallmarks of the wine used. Wine vinegars are preferred in French and Mediterranean cuisines.

Malt vinegar is produced from malted barley. Its slightly sweet, mild flavor is used as a condiment, especially with fried foods.

Distilled vinegar, made from grain alcohol, is completely clear with a stronger vinegary flavor and higher acid content than other vinegars. It is preferred for pickling and preserving.

Cider vinegar is produced from unpasteurized apple juice or cider. It is pale brown in color with a mild acidity and fruity aroma. Cider vinegar is particularly popular in the United States.

Rice vinegar is a clear, slightly sweet product brewed from rice wine. Its flavor is clean and elegant, making it useful in a variety of dishes.

Flavored vinegars are simply traditional vinegars in which herbs, spices, fruits or other foods are steeped to infuse their flavors. They are easily produced from commercial wine or distilled vinegars, using any herb, spice or fruit desired. The use of flavored vinegars is extremely popular but definitely not new. Clove, raspberry and fennel vinegars were sold on the streets of Paris during the 13th century. Making fruit-flavored vinegars was also one of the responsibilities of American housewives during the 18th and 19th centuries.

Balsamic vinegar, Raspberry vinegar and Cider vinegar

Balsamic vinegar (It. *aceto Balsamico*) is newly popular in the United States, though it has been produced in Italy for over 800 years. To produce balsamic vinegar, red wine vinegar is aged in a succession of wooden barrels made from a variety of woods—oak, cherry, locust, ash, mulberry and juniper—for at least four, but sometimes up to 50 years. The resulting liquid is dark reddish-brown and sweet. Balsamic has a high acid level, but the sweetness covers the tart flavor, making it very mellow. True balsamic is extremely expensive because of the long aging process and the small quantities available. Most of the commercial products imported from Italy are now made by a quick carmelization and flavoring process. Balsamic is excellent as a condiment or seasoning and has a remarkable affinity for tomatoes and strawberries.

CONDIMENTS

Strictly speaking, a condiment is any food added to a dish for flavor, including herbs, spices and vinegars. Today, however, *condiments* more often refer to cooked or prepared flavorings, such as prepared mustards, relishes, bottled sauces and pickles. Several frequently used condiments are discussed here. These staples may be used to alter or enhance the flavor of a dish during cooking or added to a completed dish at the table by the consumer.

Yellow mustard

Dijon mustard

Whole-grain mustard

Brown mustard

Prepared mustard is a mixture of crushed mustard seeds, vinegar or wine and salt or spices. It can be flavored in many ways—with herbs, onions, peppers and even citrus zest. It can be a smooth paste or coarse and chunky, depending on how finely the seeds are ground and whether the skins are strained out. Prepared mustard gets its tangy taste from an essential oil that forms only when the seeds are crushed and mixed with water. Prepared mustard can be used as a condiment, particularly with meat and charcuterie items, or as a flavoring ingredient in sauces, stews and marinades.

Dijon mustard takes its name from a town and the surrounding region in France that produces about half of the world's mustard. French mustard labeled "Dijon" must, by law, be produced only in that region. Dijon and Dijon-style mustards are smooth with a rich, complex flavor.

English and Chinese mustards are made from mustard flour and cool water. They are extremely hot and powerful. American or "ballpark" mustard is mild and vinegary with a bright yellow color.

Mustard never really spoils, its flavor just fades away. Because of its high acid content, mustard does not turn rancid, but it will oxidize and develop a dark surface crust. Once opened, mustard should be kept well covered and refrigerated.

Soy sauce is a thin, dark brown liquid fermented from cooked soy beans, wheat and salt. Available in several flavors and strengths, it is ubiquitous in most Asian cuisines. Light soy sauce is thin, with a light brown color and a very salty flavor. Dark soy sauce is thicker and dark brown, with a sweet, less salty flavor. Necessary for preparing many Asian dishes, soy sauce is also used in marinades and sauces and as an all-purpose condiment. Other soy-based condiments include tamari, teriyaki sauce and fermented bean paste (miso).

Ketchup (also known as catsup or catchup) originally referred to any salty extract from fish, fruits or vegetables. Prepared tomato ketchup is really a sauce, created in America and used worldwide as a flavoring ingredient or condiment. It is bright red and thick, with a tangy, sweet-sour flavor. Ketchup can be stored either in the refrigerator or at room temperature; it should keep well for up to four months after opening. Ketchup does not turn rancid or develop mold but it will darken and lose flavor as it ages.

◆◆◆

Even the most sophisticated food service operation occasionally uses prepared condiments or flavorings. The products described here are widely used and available from grocery stores or wholesale purveyors. Some are brand-name items that have become almost synonymous with the product itself; others are available from several manufacturers.

Barbecue sauce—Like ketchup, commercial barbecue sauce is a mixture of tomatoes, vinegar and spices; it tends to be hotter and sweeter than ketchup, however. Commercial barbecue sauce is used primarily for marinating or basting meat, poultry or fish. A tremendous variety of barbecue sauces is available, with various flavors, textures and aromas. Sample several before selecting the most appropriate for your specific needs.

Fish sauce—Fish sauce is a thin, dark brown liquid made from anchovy extract and salt. It is the quintessential Thai seasoning, but is used throughout Southeast Asia. It is extremely salty with a powerful aroma. There is no substitute; only a small amount is necessary for most dishes.

Hoisin—Hoisin sauce is a dark, thick, salty-sweet sauce made from fermented soy beans, vinegar, garlic and caramel. It is used in Chinese dishes or served as a dipping sauce.

Old Bay® seasoning—Old Bay® is a dry spice blend containing celery salt, dry mustard, paprika and other flavorings. It is widely used in shellfish preparations, especially boiled shrimp and crab.

Oyster sauce—Oyster sauce is a thick, dark sauce made from oyster extract. It has a salty-sweet flavor and rich aroma. Oyster sauce is often used with stir-fried meats and poultry.

Pickapeppa® sauce—Pickapeppa® sauce is a dark, thick, sweet-hot blend of tomatoes, onions, sugar, vinegar, mango, raisins, tamarinds and spices. Produced in Jamaica, West Indies, it is used as a condiment for meat, game or fish and as a seasoning in sauces, soups and dressings.

Tabasco® sauce—Tabasco® sauce is a thin, bright red liquid blended from vinegar, chiles and salt. Its fiery flavor is widely used in sauces, soups and prepared dishes; it is a popular condiment for Mexican, southern and southwestern cuisines. Tabasco® sauce has been produced in Louisiana since 1868. Other "Louisiana-style" hot sauces (those containing only peppers, vinegar and salt) may be substituted.

Worcestershire sauce—Worcestershire sauce is a thin, dark brown liquid made from malt vinegar, tamarind, molasses and spices. It is used as a condiment for beef and as a seasoning in sauces, soups, stews and prepared dishes. Its flavor should be rich and full, but not salty.

COFFEES AND TEAS

Coffee and tea are the staples of most beverage menus. Despite their relatively low price a good cup of coffee or tea can be extremely important to a customer's impression of your food service operation. A cup of coffee is often either the very first or the very last item consumed by a customer. Tea, whether iced or hot, is often consumed throughout the meal. Consequently, it is important that you learn to prepare and serve these beverages properly.

Coffee

Coffee (Fr. *café*) begins as the fruit of a small tree growing in tropical and subtropical regions throughout the world. The fruit, referred to as a cherry, is bright red with translucent flesh surrounding two flat-sided seeds. These seeds are the coffee beans. When ripe, the cherries are harvested by hand, then cleaned, fermented and hulled, leaving the green coffee beans. The beans are then roasted, blended, ground and brewed. Note that any coffee bean can be roasted to any degree of darkness, ground to any degree of fineness and brewed by any number of methods.

Only two species of coffee bean are routinely used: *arabica* and *robusta*. Arabica beans are the most important commercially and the ones from which the finest coffees are produced. Robusta beans do not produce as flavorful a drink as arabica. Nevertheless, robusta beans are becoming increasingly significant commercially, due in part to the fact that robusta trees are heartier and more fertile than arabica trees.

The conditions in which the beans are grown have almost as much effect on the final product as subsequent roasting, grinding and brewing. Because coffee takes much of its flavor and character from the soil, sunlight and air, the beans' origin is critical to the product's final quality. Each valley and mountain produces coffee distinct from all others, so geographic names are used to identify the beans regardless of whether they are from arabica or robusta trees. Thus, purveyors may offer beans known as Columbian, Chanchamayo (from Peru), Kilimanjaro (from Tanzania), Blue Mountain (from Jamaica), Java, Sumatra or Kona (from Hawaii), to name a few.

While many so-called gourmet coffees are made from a single type of bean, nearly all coffee sold in the United States is a blend of various qualities and types of bean.

Roasting Coffee

Roasting releases and enhances the flavors in coffee. It also darkens the beans and brings natural oils to the surface. Traditionally, almost everyone roasted their own coffee beans because all coffee beans were sold green. Today, however, roasting is left to experts who possess the necessary equipment.

It is important to recognize and understand some of the standard descriptions used for various types of roasting. No single international organization controls the naming of roasted coffee, however, so a coffee roaster may refer to products by any name. The following descriptions are based on the most common terminology.

Green coffee beans

♦ **City Roast:** Also called American or brown roast, city roast is the most widely used coffee style in this country. City roast produces a beverage that may lack brilliance or be a bit flat, yet it is the roast most Americans assume they prefer because it is the roast most often used in grocery store blends.

♦ **Brazilian:** Somewhat darker than a city roast, Brazilian roast should begin to show a hint of dark-roast flavor. The beans should show a trace of oil. In this context, the word Brazilian has no relationship to coffee grown in Brazil.

♦ **Viennese:** Also called medium-dark roast, Viennese roast generally falls somewhere between a standard city roast and French roast.

♦ **French Roast:** French roast, also called New Orleans or dark roast, approaches espresso in flavor without sacrificing smoothness. The beans should be the color of semi-sweet chocolate, with apparent oiliness on the surface.

♦ **Espresso Roast:** Espresso roast, also called Italian roast, is the darkest of all. The beans are roasted until they are virtually burnt. The beans should be black with a shiny, oily surface.

City-roast beans

French-roast beans

Grinding Coffee

Unlike roasting, which is best left to the experts, the grinding of coffee beans is best left to the consumer or food service operation. Whole coffee beans stay fresh longer than ground coffee. Ground coffee kept in an airtight container away from heat and light will stay fresh for three or four days. Whole beans will stay fresh for a few weeks and may be kept frozen for several months, as long as they are dry and protected from other flavors. Frozen coffee beans do not need to be thawed before grinding and brewing. Do not refrigerate coffee.

The fineness of the grind depends entirely on the type of coffee maker being used. The grind determines the length of time it takes to achieve the optimum (19%) extraction from the beans. The proper grind is simply whatever grind allows this to happen in the time it takes a specific coffee maker to complete its brewing cycle. Follow the directions for your coffee maker or ask your specialty coffee purveyor for guidance.

Brewing Coffee

Coffee is brewed by one of two methods: decoction or infusion. **Decoction** means boiling a substance until its flavor is removed. Boiling is the oldest method of making coffee, but is no longer used except in preparing extremely strong Turkish coffee. **Infusion** refers to the extraction of flavors at temperatures below boiling. Infusion techniques include steeping (mixing hot water with ground coffee), filtering (slowly pouring hot water over ground coffee held in a disposable cloth or paper filter) and dripping (pouring hot water over ground coffee and allowing the liquid to run through a strainer). Percolating is undesirable as the continuous boiling ruins the coffee's flavor.

The secrets to brewing a good cup of coffee are knowing the exact proportion of coffee to water as well as the length of time to maintain contact between the two. The best results are nearly always achieved by using two level tablespoons of ground coffee per 3/4 measuring cup (6 ounces) of water. (A standard cup of coffee is three quarters the size of a standard measuring cup; one pound of coffee yields approximately 80 level tablespoons or enough for 40 "cups" of coffee.) An Approved Coffee Measure (ACM) was developed by the Coffee Brewing Institute to measure two level tablespoons accurately. ACM scoops are readily available and are often included with retail coffee packages.

Premeasured packages of ground coffee are generally used with commercial brewing equipment. These packages are available in a range of sizes for making single pots or large urns of coffee.

If stronger coffee is desired, use more coffee per cup of water, not a longer brewing time. For weaker coffee, prepare regular-strength coffee and dilute it with hot water. Never reuse coffee grounds.

Coffeepots and carafes should be cleaned well with hot water between each use; coffee makers should be disassembled and cleaned according to the manufacturer's directions. Unless properly cleaned, oils from coffee form an invisible film on the inside of the maker and pots, imparting a rancid or stale flavor to each subsequent batch.

Finally, coffee should be served as soon as it is brewed. Oxidation takes a toll on the aroma and taste, which soon become flat and eventually bitter. Coffee may be held for a short time on the coffeemaker's hot plate at temperatures of 185° to 190°F (85° to 88°C). A better holding method, however, is to immediately pour freshly brewed coffee into a thermal carafe. Never attempt to reheat cold coffee, as drastic temperature shifts destroy flavor.

Tasting Coffee

Coffee can be judged on four characteristics: aroma, acidity, body and flavor.

As a general rule, coffee will taste the way it smells. Some coffees, particularly Colombian, are more fragrant than others, however.

Acidity, also called wininess, refers to the tartness of the coffee. Acidity is a desirable characteristic that indicates snap, life or thinness. Kenyan and Guatemalan are examples of particularly acidic coffees.

Body refers to the feeling of heaviness or thickness that coffee provides on the palate. Sumatran is generally the heaviest, with Mexican and Venezuelan being the lightest.

◆◆◆

DON'T WRECK THE ENDING

Lots of time and thought are spent on selecting the wines to accompany the various savory courses of a meal, but too often at the sweet course the dessert wine finds itself up against its worst enemy: chocolate. A good sauterne, or a good quality dessert wine of almost any kind, works best with a fruit tart or with noncitrus sorbets accompanied by "dry cookie-like things," to use Richard Olney's phrase. Chocolate, whether in the form of pastry or confection, belongs with coffee, whose aromatic bitterness is a perfect foil for it.

RICHARD H. GRAFF
Chairman, CHALONE WINE GROUP

Flavor, of course, is the most ambiguous as well as the most important characteristic. Terms such as mellow, harsh, grassy or earthy are used to describe the rather subjective characteristic of flavor.

Serving Coffee

Coffee may be served unadorned, unsweetened and black (without milk or cream). The customer then adds the desired amount of sugar and milk. Other coffee beverages are made with specific additions and provide value-added menu alternatives. The most common ways of serving coffee are described here.

+ **Espresso:** Espresso (Sp. *café expreso*) refers to a unique brewing method in which hot water is forced through finely ground and packed coffee under high pressure. Properly made, it will be strong, rich and smooth, not bitter or acidic. Espresso is usually made with beans that have been roasted very dark, but any type of bean may be used. A single serving of espresso uses about 1/4 ounce (7 grams) of coffee to 1-1/2 ounces (45 milliliters) of water. Americans tend to prefer a larger portion, known as *espresso lungo*, made with 2 to 3 ounces (60–90 grams) of water.
+ **Espresso machiatto:** Espresso "marked" with a tiny portion of steamed milk.
+ **Cappuccino:** One third espresso, one third steamed milk and one third foamed milk; the total serving is still rather small, about 4 to 6 ounces (120–180 grams).
+ **Caffe latte:** One third espresso, two thirds steamed milk without foam; usually served in a tall glass.
+ **Café au lait:** the French version of the Italian *caffe latte*, café au lait (or *café creme*) is made with strong coffee instead of espresso and hot, not steamed, milk. It is traditionally served in a handleless bowl.
+ **Flavored coffees:** Dried, ground chicory root has long been added to coffee, particularly by the French who enjoy its bitter flavor. Toasted barley, dried figs and spices have also been used by various cultures for years. Coffees flavored with vanilla, chocolate, liquors, spices and nuts have recently become popular in the United States. These flavors are added to roasted coffee beans by tumbling the beans with special flavoring oils. The results are strongly aromatic flavors such as vanilla hazelnut, chocolate raspberry or maple walnut.

Decaffeinated Coffee

Caffeine is an alkaloid found in coffee beans (as well as in tea leaves and cocoa beans). It is a stimulant that can improve alertness or reduce fatigue. In excess, however, caffeine can cause some people to suffer palpitations or insomnia. Regular filtered coffee contains from 85 to 100 milligrams of caffeine per cup. Robusta beans contain more caffeine than the better-quality arabica beans. Decaffeinated coffee (with 97% or more of the caffeine removed) is designed to meet consumer desires for a caffeine-free product.

Other Uses

In addition to its use as a beverage, coffee is frequently an ingredient in mixed drinks such as Irish coffee (with whiskey and cream) or café brulot (with orange, cloves and brandy). Coffee is also used in stews, sauces and pan gravy. It may be added to breads, such as rye and pumpernickel, cakes, custards, ice creams, dessert sauces and frostings. The flavor of coffee has a strong affinity for chocolate, nuts and rum.

♦♦♦
A CUP OF COFFEE HISTORY

Some anthropologists suggest that coffee was initially consumed by central African warriors in the form of a paste made from mashed coffee beans and animal fat rolled into balls. Eaten before battle, the animal fat and bean protein provided nourishment; the caffeine provided a stimulant.

A hot coffee drink may first have been consumed sometime during the 9th century A.D. in Persia. Made by a decoction of ripe beans, the drink was probably very thick and acrid. Nevertheless, by the year 1000, the elite of the Arab world were regularly drinking a decoction of dried coffee beans. The beans were harvested in Abyssinia (Ethiopia) and brought to market by Egyptian merchants. Within a century or so, *kahwa* became immensely popular with members of all strata of Arab society. Coffeehouses opened throughout the Levant, catering to customers who sipped the thick, brown brew while discussing affairs of heart and state.

Although European travelers to the Ottoman Empire had tasted coffee, and a few Arab or Turkish merchants living in Marseilles offered their guests a chance to sample the rare drink, coffee did not become popular in Europe until the 17th century. Its popularity is due in great part to Suleiman Aga, the Grand Panjandrum of the Ottoman Empire. In 1669 he arrived at the court of King Louis XIV of France as ambassador, bringing with him many exotic treasures, including *caffe*. Offered at his opulent parties, *caffe* soon became the drink of choice for the French aristocracy.

Coffee became popular in Vienna as a fortune of war. By 1683 the Turks were at the gates of Vienna. A decisive battle was fought and the Turks fled, leaving behind stores of gold, equipment, supplies and a barely known provision—green coffee beans. One of the victorious leaders, Franz George Kolschitzky, recognized the treasure, took it as his own and soon opened the first coffeehouse in Vienna, The Blue Bottle.

Despite its growing popularity, coffee was exorbitantly expensive, in part, the result of the Sultan's monopoly on coffee beans. His agents, principally in Marseilles, controlled the sale of beans. But the monopoly was not to survive. By the end of the 17th century, the Dutch had stolen coffee plants from Arabia and began cultivating them in Java. By the early 18th century, the French had transported seedlings to the West Indies; from there coffee plantations spread throughout the New World.

Tea

Tea (Fr. *thé*) is the name given to the leaves of *Camellia sinensis*, a tree or shrub that grows at high altitudes in damp tropical regions. Although tea comes from only one species of plant, there are three general types of tea— black, green. and oolong. The differences among the three are the result of the manner in which the leaves are treated after picking.

Black tea is amber-brown and strongly flavored. Its color and flavor result from fermenting the leaves. Black tea leaves are named or graded by leaf size. Because larger leaves brew more slowly than smaller ones, teas are sorted by leaf size for efficient brewing. *Souchong* denotes large leaves, *pekoe* denotes medium-sized leaves and *orange pekoe* denotes the smallest whole leaves. (Note that *orange pekoe* does not refer to any type of orange flavor.) Broken tea, graded as either broken orange pekoe or broken pekoe, is smaller, resulting in a darker, stronger brew. Broken tea is most often used in tea bags. These grades apply to both Chinese and Indian black teas.

Green tea is yellowish-green in color with a bitter flavor. Leaves used for green tea are not fermented. Chinese green tea leaves are also graded according to leaf size and age. The finest green tea is Gunpowder, followed by Imperial and Hyson.

Fruit tea

Gunpowder

Darjeeling

TEA FLAVORS

The following descriptions apply to some of the teas frequently available through wholesalers or gourmet suppliers. Taste several different ones to find the best for your purposes. Remember that the same tea from different blenders or distributors may taste different, and that different flavors will be more or less appropriate for different times of the day. You may wish to offer your patrons a selection of flavors.

Assam—rich black tea with a reddish color from Northern India. It is valued by connoisseurs, especially for breakfast.

Ceylon—a full-flavored black tea with a golden color and delicate fragrance. Ideal for serving iced, it does not become cloudy when cold.

Darjeeling—the champagne of teas, it is a full-bodied, black tea with muscat flavor from the foothills of the Himalayas.

Earl Grey—a blend of black teas, usually including Darjeeling, flavored with oil of bergamot. A popular choice for afternoon tea.

English Breakfast—English blend of Indian and Sri Lankan black teas; it is full-bodied and robust, with a rich color.

Gunpowder—Green Chinese tea with a tightly curled leaf and gray-green color. It has a pungent flavor and a light straw color. It is often served after the evening meal.

Keemum—a mellow black Chinese tea with a strong aroma. It is less astringent than other teas and is delicious iced.

Lapsang Souchong—a large-leafed (souchong) tea from the Lapsang district of China. It has a distinctive tarry, smoky flavor and aroma, appropriate for afternoon tea or dinner.

Formosa Oolong—a unique and expensive large-leafed oolong tea with the flavor of ripe peaches. It is appropriate for breakfast or afternoon tea.

Tisanes—*herbal infusions that do not contain any "real" tea; examples include chamomile, ginseng and lemon balm. Tisanes are prepared in the same way as tea infusions.*

Oolong tea is partially fermented to combine the characteristics of black and green teas. Oolong is popular in China and Japan, often flavored with jasmine flowers. Oolong tea leaves are also graded by size and age.

As with coffee, tea takes much of its flavor from the geographic conditions in which it is grown. Teas are named for their place of origin, for example, Darjeeling, Ceylon (now Sri Lanka) or Assam. Many popular and commercially available teas are actually blends of leaves from various sources. Blended and unblended teas may also be flavored with oils, dried fruit, spices, flowers or herbs.

Brewing Tea

Tea may be brewed by the cup or the pot. In either case, it is important to use the following procedure.

1. Always begin with clean equipment and freshly drawn cold water. Water that has been sitting in a kettle or hot water tank contains less air and will taste flat or stale.
2. Warm the teapot by rinsing it out with hot water. This begins to relax the tea leaves and ensures that the water will stay hot when it comes in contact with the tea.
3. Place one teaspoon (5 millimeters) of loose tea or one tea bag per 3/4 cup (6 oz./180 grams) of water capacity in the warmed teapot.
4. As soon as the water comes to a boil, pour the appropriate amount over the tea. Do not allow the water to continue boiling as this removes the oxygen, leaving a flat taste. The water should be at a full boil when it comes in contact with the tea so that the tea leaves will uncurl and release their flavor.
5. Replace the lid of the teapot and allow the tea to infuse for 3 to 5 minutes. Time the brew. Color is not a reliable indication of brewing time: Tea leaves release color before flavor and different types of tea will be different colors when properly brewed.
6. Remove the tea bags or loose tea from the water when brewing is complete. This can be accomplished easily if the teapot is fitted with a removable leaf basket or if a tea bag or a perforated tea ball is used. Otherwise, decant the tea through a strainer into a second warmed teapot.
7. Serve immediately, accompanied with sugar, lemon, milk (not cream) and honey as desired. Dilute the tea with hot water if necessary.
8. Do not reuse tea leaves. One pound of tea yields 200 cups, making it the most inexpensive beverage after tap water.

For iced tea, prepare regular brewed tea using 50% more tea. Then pour into a pitcher or glass filled with ice. The stronger brew will hold its flavor better as the ice melts.

Serving Tea

Black and oolong tea may be served hot or cold, but green tea is best served hot. Black tea is served with milk or lemon and sugar; green and oolong tea are most often served plain. Adding milk to hot tea is a British preference (not normally followed in Europe or Asia) which reduces the astringency of the tea. Iced tea, an American invention, may be served plain or sweetened, and is often garnished with lemon, orange or fresh mint.

♦♦♦
A CUP OF TEA HISTORY

Some believe that the Chinese Emperor Shen Nung discovered tea drinking in 2737 B.C. Legend holds that the Emperor was boiling his drinking water beneath a tree when some leaves fell into the pot. Enchanted with the drink, he began to cultivate the plant. Whether myth or truth, it is known that a hot drink made from powdered dried tea leaves whipped into hot water was regularly consumed in China sometime after the 4th century. Later, decoctions of tea leaves (as well as rice, spices and nuts) became popular. But it was not until the Ming dynasty (A.D. 1368–1644) that infusions of tea leaves became commonplace.

By the 9th century, tea drinking had spread to Japan. In both Chinese and Japanese cultures, tea drinking developed into a ritual. For the Chinese, a cup of tea became the mirror of the soul. For the Japanese, it was the drink of immortality.

Tea was first transported from China to Europe by Dutch merchants during the early 1600s. By mid-century, it was introduced into England. In 1669 the East India Company was granted a charter by Queen Elizabeth I to import tea, a monopoly it held until 1833. To ensure a steady supply, the English surreptitiously procured plants from China and started plantations throughout the Indian subcontinent, as did the Dutch.

Tea drinking became fashionable in England, at least in court circles, through Charles II (raised in exile at The Hague in Holland, he reigned from 1660 until 1685) and his Portuguese wife, Catherine of Braganza. Queen Anne of England (reigned 1702–1714) introduced several concepts that eventually became part of the English tea custom. For example, she substituted tea for ale at breakfast and began using large silver pots instead of tiny china pots.

The social custom of afternoon tea began in the late 1700s, thanks to Anna, Duchess of Bedford. Historians attribute to her the late afternoon ritual of snacking on sandwiches and pastries accompanied by tea. She began the practice in order to quell her hunger pangs between breakfast and dinner (which was typically served at 9:30 or 10:00 P.M.).

Eventually two distinct types of teatime evolved. Low tea was aristocratic in origin and consisted of a snack of pastries and sandwiches, with tea, served in the late afternoon as a prelude to the evening meal. High tea was bourgeois in origin, consisting of leftovers from the typically large middle-class lunch, such as cold meats, bread and cheeses. High tea became a substitute for the evening meal.

CONCLUSION

Kitchen staples include fresh and dried herbs, spices, salt, nuts, oils, vinegars, condiments, coffees and teas. You must be able to recognize, purchase, store and use many of these staples.

The only way to determine which brand or type of staple is best for your particular needs is to taste, smell, sample and use a variety of those available. Cost, convenience and storage factors must also be considered. By maintaining a supply of seasonings, flavorings, condiments and other staples you will be able to create new dishes or enhance standard ones at a moment's notice.

QUESTIONS FOR DISCUSSION

1. What is a staple? Does every kitchen keep the same staples on hand? Explain your answer.

2. What are the differences between an herb and a spice? Give an example of a plant that is used as both an herb and a spice.

3. If a recipe calls for a fresh herb and you only have the herb dried, what do you do? Explain your answer.

4. What is the difference between a sachet and a bouquet garni? Identify the ingredients in a standard sachet and a standard bouquet garni.

5. How are condiments used by chefs and by customers?

6. Discuss the importance of using proper preparation and service techniques for coffee and tea. How can these beverages be used to improve or enhance your food service operation?

CHAPTER 8

EGGS AND DAIRY PRODUCTS

After studying this chapter you will be able to:

+ understand the composition of eggs
+ purchase and store eggs properly
+ identify, store and use a variety of milk-based products
+ identify, store and serve a variety of fine cheeses

Eggs and milk are unique in that they, along with seeds, are the only foods that are truly designed to support life: Eggs support chick embryos; milk supports calves. Thus they are among the most nutritious of foods. Eggs as well as milk and milk-based products (known collectively as dairy products) are also extremely versatile. They are used throughout the kitchen, either served alone or as ingredients in everything from soups and sauces to breads and pastries. High quality and freshness are critical for their proper use. Learn to select the finest products, whether they are eggs, whole milk, butter or brie, and handle them with care.

EGGS

Nature designed eggs as the food source for developing chicks. Eggs, particularly chicken eggs, are also an excellent food for humans because of their high protein content, low cost and ready availability. Quail eggs are also used in food service operations. Duck and goose eggs are too fatty to be useful, however

Eggs can be cooked in a variety of ways, some of which are described in Chapter 32, Breakfast and Brunch. Eggs are also incorporated into other dishes to provide texture, structure, flavor, moisture and nutrition.

Composition

The primary parts of an egg are the shell, yolk and albumen. See Figure 8.1.

The **shell**, composed of calcium carbonate, is the outermost covering of the egg. It prevents microbes from entering and moisture from escaping, and protects the egg during handling and transport. Shell color is determined by the breed of the hen; for chickens it can range from bright white to brown. Shell color has no effect on quality, flavor or nutrition.

The **yolk** is the yellow portion of the egg. It constitutes just over one third of the egg and contains three fourths of the calories, most of the minerals and

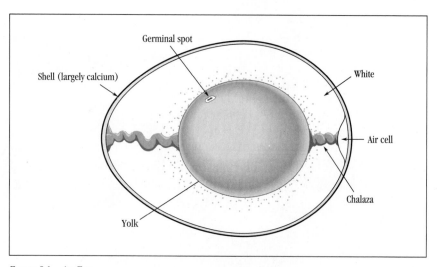

FIGURE 8.1 *An Egg*

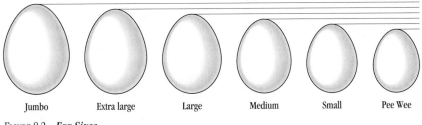

| Jumbo | Extra large | Large | Medium | Small | Pee Wee |

FIGURE 8.2 *Egg Sizes*

vitamins and all of the fat. The yolk also contains lecithin, the compound responsible for emulsification in products such as hollandaise sauce and mayonnaise. Egg yolk solidifies (coagulates) at temperatures between 149°F and 158°F (65°–70°C). Although the color of a yolk may vary depending on the hen's feed, color does not affect quality or nutritional content.

The **albumen** is the clear portion of the egg and is often referred to as the **egg white**. It constitutes about two thirds of the egg and contains more than half of the protein and riboflavin. Egg white coagulates, becoming firm and opaque, at temperatures between 144°F and 149°F (62–65°C).

An often misunderstood portion of the egg is the **chalazae cords**. These thick, twisted strands of egg white anchor the yolk in place. They are neither imperfections nor embryos. The more prominent the chalazae, the fresher the egg. Chalazae do not interfere with cooking or with whipping egg whites.

Eggs are sold in jumbo, extra large, large, medium, small and peewee sizes, as determined by weight per dozen. See Figure 8.2. Food service operations generally use large eggs.

Grading

Eggs are graded by the USDA or a state agency following USDA guidelines. The grade AA, A or B is given an egg based upon interior and exterior quality, not size. The qualities for each grade are described in Table 8.1. Grade has no effect on nutritional values.

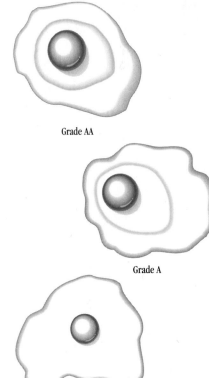

Grade AA

Grade A

Grade B

TABLE 8.1 EGG GRADES

	Grade AA	Grade A	Grade B
Spread*	Remains compact	Spreads slightly	Spreads over wide area
Albumen	Clear, thick and firm; prominent chalazae	Clear and reasonably firm; prominent chalazae	Clear; weak or watery
Yolk	Firm; centered; stands round and high; free from defects	Firm; stands fairly high; practically free from defects	Enlarged and flattened; may show slight defects
Shell	Clean; of normal shape; unbroken		Slight stains permissible; abnormal shape; unbroken
Use	Any use, especially frying, poaching and cooking in shell		Baking, scrambling, used in bulk egg products

*Spread refers to the appearance of the egg when first broken onto a flat surface.

Storage

Egg quality is quickly diminished by improper handling. Eggs should be stored at temperatures below 40°C (4°C) and at a relative humidity of 70–80%. Eggs will age more during one day at room temperature than they will during one week under proper refrigeration. As eggs age, the white becomes thinner and the yolk becomes flatter. While this will change the appearance of poached or fried eggs, age has little effect on nutrition or behavior during cooking procedures. Older eggs, however, should be used for hard-cooking, as the shells are easier to remove than on fresh eggs.

Cartons of fresh, uncooked eggs will keep for at least four to five weeks beyond the pack date if properly refrigerated. Hard-cooked eggs left in their shells and refrigerated should be used within one week.

Store eggs away from strongly flavored foods to reduce odor absorption. Rotate egg stock to maintain freshness. Do not use dirty, cracked or broken eggs as they may contain bacteria or other contaminants. Frozen eggs should be thawed in the refrigerator and used only in dishes that will be thoroughly cooked, such as baked products.

Sanitation

Eggs are a potentially hazardous food. Rich in protein, they are an excellent breeding ground for bacteria. Salmonella is of particular concern with eggs and egg products because this bacteria is commonly found in a chicken's intestinal tract. Although shells are cleaned at packing houses, some bacteria may remain. Therefore, to prevent contamination, it is best to avoid mixing a shell with the liquid egg.

Inadequately cooking or improperly storing eggs may lead to food-borne illnesses. USDA guidelines indicate that **pasteurization** is achieved when the whole egg stays at a temperature of 140°F (60°C) for 3.5 minutes. Hold egg dishes below 40°F (4°C) or above 145°F (63°C). Never leave an egg dish at room temperature for more than one hour, including preparation and service time. Never reuse a container after it has held raw eggs without thoroughly cleaning and sanitizing it.

Pasteurization—*the process of heating a liquid to a prescribed temperature for a specific period of time in order to destroy pathogenic bacteria.*

Whipped Egg Whites

Egg whites are often whipped into a foam that is then incorporated into cakes, custards, souffles, pancakes or other products. The air beaten into the egg foam gives products lightness and assists with leavening.

PROCEDURE FOR WHIPPING EGG WHITES

1. Use fresh egg whites that are completely free of egg yolk or other impurities. Warm the egg whites to room temperature before whipping; this causes a better foam to form.
2. Use a clean bowl and whisk. Even a tiny amount of fat can prevent the egg whites from foaming properly.
3. Whip the whites until very foamy, then add salt or cream of tartar as directed.
4. Continue whipping until soft peaks form, then gradually add granulated sugar as directed.
5. Whip until stiff peaks form. Properly whipped egg whites should be moist and shiny; over-whipping will make the egg whites appear dry and spongy or curdled.
6. Use the whipped egg whites immediately. If liquid begins to separate from the whipped egg whites discard them; they cannot be rewhipped successfully.

Egg whites whipped to soft peaks.

Egg whites whipped to stiff peaks.

Spongy, over-whipped egg whites.

Egg Products

Food service operations often want the convenience of buying eggs out of the shell in the exact form needed: whole eggs, yolks only or whites only. These processed items are called *egg products* and are subject to strict pasteurization standards and USDA inspections. Egg products can be frozen, refrigerated or dried. Precooked, preportioned and blended egg products are also available.

Egg Substitutes

Concerns about the cholesterol content of eggs have increased the popularity of egg substitutes. There are two general types of substitute. The first is a complete substitute made from soy or milk proteins. It should not be used in recipes where eggs are required for thickening. The second substitute contains real albumen, but the egg yolk has been replaced with vegetable or milk products. Egg substitutes have a different flavor than real eggs, but may be useful for persons on a restricted diet.

Nutrition

Eggs contain vitamins A, D, E, K and the B-complex vitamins. They are rich in minerals but also in cholesterol. The nutritional values of eggs as well as an egg substitute are listed in Table 8.2.

TABLE 8.2 NUTRITIONAL VALUES OF EGGS

	Calories	Protein (g)	Carbohydrates (g)	Total Fat (g)	Saturated Fat (g)	Cholesterol (mg)
Whole large egg, one approximately 1.75 ounces (53 g)	75	6.3	0.6	5	1.6	213
Yolk from one large egg	59	2.8	0.3	5	1.6	213
White from one large egg	16	3.5	0.3	0	0	0
Egg substitute (*Egg Beaters*), 1/4 cup (equivalent to one large egg)	25	5	1	0	0	0

The Corinne T. Netzer Encyclopedia of Food Values, 1992

DAIRY PRODUCTS

Dairy products include cow's milk and foods produced from cow's milk such as butter, yogurt, sour cream and cheese. The milk of other mammals, namely goats, sheep and buffaloes, is also made into cheeses that are used in commercial food service operations.

Milk

Milk is not only a popular beverage, it is also used in the preparation of many dishes. It provides texture, flavor, color and nutritional value for cooked or baked items. Indeed, milk is one of the most nutritious foods available, providing proteins, vitamins and minerals (particularly calcium). But milk is also highly perishable and an excellent bacterial breeding ground. Care must be exercised in the handling and storage of milk and other dairy products.

Whole milk—that is, milk as it comes from the cow—is composed primarily of water (about 88%). It contains approximately 3.25% milkfat and 8.25% other milk solids (proteins, milk sugar [lactose] and minerals).

Whole milk is graded A, B or C based upon standards recommended by the United States Public Health Service. Grades are assigned based on bacterial count, with Grade A products having the lowest count. Grades B and C, while still safe and wholesome, are rarely available for retail or commercial use. Fresh whole milk is not available raw, but must be processed as described below.

Processing Techniques

Pasteurization

By law, all Grade A milk must be pasteurized prior to retail sale. Pasteurization is the process of heating milk to a sufficiently high temperature for a sufficient length of time to destroy pathogenic bacteria. This typically requires holding milk at a temperature of 161°F (72°C) for 15 seconds. Pasteurization also destroys enzymes that cause spoilage thus increasing shelf life. Milk's nutritional value is not significantly affected by pasteurization.

Ultra-Pasteurization

Ultra-pasteurization is a process in which milk is heated to a very high temperature (275°F/135°C) for a very short time (2 to 4 seconds) in order to destroy virtually all bacteria. Ultra-pasteurization is most often used with whipping cream and individual creamers. Although the process may reduce cream's whipping properties, it extends its shelf life dramatically.

Ultra High Temperature Processing

UHT processing is a form of ultra-pasteurization in which milk is held at a temperature of 280° to 300°F (138°–150°C) for 2 to 6 seconds. It is then packed in sterile containers under sterile conditions and aseptically sealed to prevent bacteria from entering the container. UHT milk can be stored without refrigeration for at least three months if unopened. Although UHT milk can be stored unrefrigerated, it should be chilled before serving and stored like fresh milk once opened. UHT processing may give milk a slightly cooked taste but it has no significant effect on milk's nutritional value. Long available in Europe, it has been approved recently for sale in the United States.

Homogenization

Homogenization is a process in which the fat globules in whole milk are reduced in size and permanently dispersed throughout the liquid. This prevents the fat from clumping together and rising to the surface as a layer of cream. Although homogenization is not required, milk sold commercially is generally homogenized because it ensures a uniform consistency, a whiter color and a richer taste.

Certification

Certification is a method of controlling the quality of milk by controlling the condition of the animals from which milk is obtained. Certification is not a true processing technique; rather it requires frequent veterinary examinations of the cows and health department inspections of the dairy farm, the equipment and the employees who handle milk. Pasteurization has replaced the need for certification, but milk from certified herds is still available in a few areas.

Milkfat Removal

Whole milk can also be processed in a centrifuge to remove all or a portion of the milkfat, resulting in **lowfat milk** and **skim milk**.

Lowfat milk is whole milk from which sufficient milkfat has been removed to produce a liquid with .5% to 2.0% milkfat. (All lowfat milks must still contain approximately 8.25% milk solids.) Vitamin A is added to lowfat milk to replace that removed along with the milkfat. It will be labeled with either the fat content or the nonfat percentage. For example, milk containing 1% milkfat may be labeled "99% fat free" or "1% lowfat."

Skim milk, also referred to as **nonfat milk**, has had as much milkfat removed as possible. The fat content must be less than .5%. Skim milk must also contain at least 8.25% milk solids and be fortified with vitamin A.

Storage

Fluid milk should be kept refrigerated at or below 40°F (4°C). Its shelf life is reduced by half for every five-degree rise in temperature above 40°F (4°C). Keep milk containers closed to prevent absorption of odors and flavors. Freezing is not recommended.

Concentrated Milks

Concentrated or condensed milk products are produced by using a vacuum to remove all or part of the water from whole milk. The resulting products have a high concentration of milkfat and milk solids and an extended shelf life.

Evaporated milk is produced by removing approximately 60% of the water from whole, homogenized milk. Evaporated milk must contain at least 7.25% milkfat and 25.5% milk solids. The concentrated liquid is canned and heat-sterilized. This results in a cooked flavor and darker color. Evaporated skim milk, with a milkfat content of .5%, is also available. A can of evaporated milk requires no refrigeration until opened, although the can should be stored in a cool place. Evaporated milk can be reconstituted with an equal amount of water and used like whole milk for cooking or drinking.

Sweetened condensed milk is similar to evaporated milk in that 60% of the water has been removed. But unlike evaporated milk, sweetened condensed milk contains large amounts of sugar (40 to 45%). Sweetened condensed milk is also canned; the canning process darkens the color and adds a caramel flavor. Sweetened condensed milk cannot be substituted for whole milk or evaporated milk because of its sugar content. Its distinctive flavor is most often found in desserts and confections.

Dry milk powder is made by removing virtually all of the moisture from pasteurized milk. The moisture content must be less than 5% by weight. Dry whole milk contains between 26% and 40% milkfat. Nonfat milk powder is made from skim milk and must contain less than 1.5% milkfat by weight. Both types of dry milk are usually fortified with vitamins A and D.

The lack of moisture prevents the growth of microorganisms and allows dry whole and nonfat milk powders to be stored for extended periods without refrigeration. However, because of its high milkfat content, dried whole milk can turn rancid if not stored in a cool place. Either type of dry milk can be reconstituted with water and used like fresh milk. Milk powder may also be added to foods directly, with additional liquid included in the recipe. This procedure is typical in bread making and does not alter the function of the milk or the flavor in the finished product.

Cream

Cream is a rich, liquid milk product containing at least 18% fat. It must be pasteurized or ultra-pasteurized and may be homogenized. Cream has a slight yellow or ivory color and is more viscous than milk. It is used throughout the kitchen to give flavor and body to sauces, soups and desserts. Whipping cream, containing not less than 30% milkfat, can be whipped into a stiff foam and used in pastries and desserts. Cream is marketed in several forms with different fat contents, as described below.

Half-and-half is a mixture of whole milk and cream containing between 10% and 18% milkfat. It is often served with cereal or coffee, but does not contain enough fat to whip into a foam.

Light cream, coffee cream and **table cream** are all products with more than 18% but less than 30% milkfat. These products are often used in baked goods or soups as well as with coffee, fruit and cereal.

Light whipping cream or, simply, **whipping cream** contains between 30% and 36% milkfat. It is generally used for thickening and enriching sauces and making ice cream. It can be whipped into a foam and used as a dessert topping or folded into custards or mousses to add flavor and lightness.

Heavy whipping cream or, simply, **heavy cream** contains not less than 36% milkfat. It whips easily and holds its whipped texture longer than other creams. It must be pasteurized, but is rarely homogenized. Heavy cream is used throughout the kitchen in the same ways as light whipping cream.

Storage

Ultra-pasteurized cream will keep for six to eight weeks if refrigerated. Unwhipped cream should not be frozen. Whipped, sweetened cream can be frozen, tightly covered, for up to three months, then slowly thawed in the refrigerator. Keep cream away from strong odors and bright lights, as they can adversely affect its flavor.

Cultured Dairy Products

Cultured dairy products such as yogurt, buttermilk and sour cream are produced by adding specific bacterial cultures to fluid dairy products. The bacteria convert the milk sugar lactose into lactic acid, giving these products their body and tangy, unique flavors. The acid content also retards the growth of undesirable microorganisms; thus cultured products have been used for centuries to preserve milk.

Buttermilk originally referred to the liquid remaining after cream was churned into butter. Today buttermilk is produced by adding a culture

(*Streptococcus lactis*) to fresh, pasteurized skim or lowfat milk. This results in a tart milk with a thick texture. Buttermilk is most often used as a beverage or in baked goods.

Sour cream is produced by adding the same culture to pasteurized, homogenized light cream. The resulting product is a white, tangy gel used as a condiment or to give baked goods a distinctive flavor. Sour cream must have a milkfat content of not less than 18%.

Crème fraîche is a cultured cream popular in French cuisine. Although thinner and richer than sour cream, it has a similar tart, tangy flavor. It is used extensively in soups and sauces, especially with poultry, rabbit and lamb dishes. It is easily prepared from the following recipe.

♦♦♦

RECIPE 8.1
CRÈME FRAÎCHE

Yield: 1 pint (500 ml)

| Heavy cream | 16 oz. | 500 g |
| Buttermilk, with active cultures | 1 oz. | 30 g |

1. Heat the cream (preferably not ultra-pasteurized) to about 100°F (43°C).

2. Remove the cream from the heat and stir in the buttermilk.

3. Allow the mixture to stand in a warm place, loosely covered, until it thickens, approximately 12 to 36 hours.

4. Chill thoroughly before using. Crème fraîche will keep for up to 10 days in the refrigerator.

Yogurt is a thick, tart, custardlike product made from milk (either whole, lowfat or nonfat) cultured with *Lactobacillus bulgaricus* and *Streptococcus thermophilus*. Though touted as a health or diet food, yogurt contains the same amount of milkfat as the milk from which it is made. Yogurt may also contain a variety of sweeteners, flavorings and fruits. Yogurt is generally eaten as is, but may be used in baked products, salad dressings and frozen desserts. It is used in many Middle Eastern cuisines.

Storage

Cultured products should be kept refrigerated at 40°F (4°C) or below. Under proper conditions sour cream will last up to four weeks, yogurt up to three weeks and buttermilk up to two weeks. Freezing is not recommended for these products, but dishes prepared with cultured products generally can be frozen.

Butter

Butter is a fatty substance produced by agitating or churning cream. Its flavor is unequalled in sauces, breads and pastries. Butter contains at least 80% milkfat, not more than 16% water and 2–4% milk solids. It may or may not contain added salt. Butter is firm when chilled and soft at room temperature. It melts into a liquid at approximately 98°F (38°C) and reaches the smoke point at 260°F (127°C).

Government grading is not mandatory, but most processors submit their butters for testing. The USDA label on the package assures the buyer that the butter meets federal standards for the grade indicated:

+ USDA Grade AA—butter of superior quality, with a fresh, sweet flavor and aroma, a smooth, creamy texture and good spreadability.
+ USDA Grade A—butter of very good quality, with a pleasing flavor and fairly smooth texture.
+ USDA Grade B—butter of standard quality, made from sour cream; has an acceptable flavor but lacks the taste, texture and body of Grades AA and A. Grade B is most often used in the manufacturing of foods.

Salted butter is butter with up to 2.5% salt added. This not only changes the butter's flavor, it also extends its keeping qualities. When using salted butter in cooking or baking, the salt content must be considered in the total recipe.

Whipped butter is made by incorporating air into the butter. This increases its volume and spreadability, but also increases the speed with which the butter will become rancid. Because of the change in density, whipped butter should not be substituted in recipes calling for regular butter.

Storage

Butter should be well wrapped and stored at temperatures between 32° and 35°F (0°–2°C). Unsalted butter is best kept frozen until needed. If well wrapped, frozen butter will keep for up to nine months at a temperature of 0°F (–18°C).

Clarified Butter

Unsalted whole butter is approximately 80% fat, 15% water and 5% milk solids. Although whole butter can be used for cooking or sauce making, sometimes a more stable and consistent product will be achieved by using butter that has had the water and milk solids removed by a process called clarification.

PROCEDURE FOR CLARIFYING BUTTER

Skimming milk solids from the surface of melted butter.

Ladling the butterfat into a clean pan.

1. Slowly warm the butter in a saucepan over low heat without boiling or agitation. As the butter melts, the milk solids rise to the top as a foam and the water sinks to the bottom.
2. When the butter is completely melted, skim the milk solids from the top.
3. When all the milk solids have been removed, ladle the butterfat into a clean saucepan, being careful to leave the water in the bottom of the pan.
4. The clarified butter is now ready to use. One pound (454 grams) of whole butter will yield approximately 12 ounces (340 grams) of clarified butter (a yield of 75%).

Clarified butter will keep for extended periods in either the freezer or refrigerator.

Margarine

Margarine is not a dairy product but is included in this section because it is so frequently substituted for butter in cooking, baking and table service. Margarine is manufactured from animal or vegetable fats or a combination of such fats. Flavorings, colorings, emulsifiers, preservatives and vitamins are

---

♦♦♦

MARGARINE:
FROM LABORATORY BENCH TO DINNER TABLE

Margarine was invented by a French chemist in 1869 after Napoleon III offered a prize for the development of a synthetic edible fat. Originally produced from animal fat and milk, margarine is now made almost exclusively from vegetable fats.

In *On Food and Cooking, The Science and Lore of the Kitchen*, Harold McGee recounts the history of margarine. He explains that margarine caught on quickly in Europe and America, with large-scale production underway by 1880. But the American dairy industry and the U.S. government put up fierce resistance. First, margarine was defined as a harmful drug and its sale restricted. Then it was heavily taxed; stores had to be licensed to sell it and, like alcohol and tobacco, it was bootlegged. The U.S. government refused to purchase it for use by the armed forces. And, in an attempt to hold it to its true colors, some states did not allow margarine to be dyed yellow (animal fats and vegetable oils are much paler than butter); the dye was sold separately and mixed in by the consumer. World War II, which brought butter rationing, probably did the most to establish margarine's respectability. But it was not until 1967 that yellow margarine could be sold in Wisconsin.

Today Americans consume nearly three times as much margarine as butter. Both price and the concern about heart disease are responsible for this differential.

---

added, and the mixture is firmed or solidified by exposure to hydrogen gas at very high temperatures, a process known as hydrogenation. Generally, the firmer the margarine the greater the degree of hydrogenation and the longer its shelf life. Like butter, margarine is approximately 80% fat and 16% water. But even the finest margarine cannot match the flavor of butter.

Margarine packaged in tubs is softer and more spreadable than solid products and generally contains more water and air. Indeed, diet margarine is approximately 50% water. Because of their decreased density, these soft products should not be substituted for regular butter or margarine in cooking or baking.

Specially formulated and blended margarine is available for commercial use in making puff pastry, croissant doughs, frostings and the like.

Nutrition

Dairy products are naturally high in vitamins, minerals and protein. Often liquid products such as milk are fortified with additional vitamins and minerals. Their fat content varies depending upon the amount of milkfat left after processing. Specific nutritional values for selected dairy products are found in Table 8.3.

TABLE 8.3   NUTRITIONAL VALUES OF DAIRY PRODUCTS

Per 8-ounce (225 g) Serving	Calories	Protein (g)	Carbohydrates (g)	Total Fat (g)	Saturated Fat (g)	Cholesterol (mg)	Sodium (mg)
Whole milk (3.3% milk fat)	150	8	11	8.2	5.1	33	120
Nonfat milk	85	8.4	12	0.4	0.3	4	126
Buttermilk	100	8.1	12	2.2	1.3	9	257
Heavy whipping cream	821	5	6.6	88	55	326	89
Half and half	315	7.2	10.4	27.8	17.3	89	98
Sour cream	493	7.3	9.8	48.2	30	102	123

The Corinne T. Netzer Encyclopedia of Food Values, 1992

Natural Cheeses

Cheese (Fr. *fromage*; It. *fromaggio*) is one of the oldest and most widely used foods known to man. It is served alone or as a principal ingredient in or an accompaniment to countless dishes. Cheese is commonly used in commercial kitchens, appearing in everything from breakfast to snacks to desserts.

Literally hundreds of natural cheeses are produced worldwide. Although their shapes, ages and flavors vary according to local preferences and traditions, all natural cheeses are produced in the same basic fashion as has been used for centuries. Each starts with a mammal's milk; cows, goats and sheep are the most commonly used. The milk proteins (known as *casein*) are coagulated with the addition of an enzyme, usually rennet, which is found in calves' stomachs. As the milk coagulates, it separates into solid curds and liquid whey. After draining off the whey, either the curds are made into fresh cheese, such as ricotta or cottage cheese, or the curds are further processed by cutting, kneading and cooking. The resulting substance, known as "green cheese," is packed into molds to drain. Salt or special bacteria may be added to the molded cheeses, which are then allowed to age or ripen under controlled conditions to develop the desired texture, color and flavor.

Cheeses are a product of their environment, which is why most fine cheeses cannot be reproduced outside their native locale. The breed and feed of the milk animal, the wild spores and molds in the air and even the wind currents in a storage area can affect the manner in which a cheese develops. (Roquefort, for example, develops its distinctive flavor from aging in particular caves filled with crosscurrents of cool, moist air.)

Some cheeses develop a natural rind or surface because of the application of bacteria (bloomy rind) or by repeated washing with brine (washed rind). Most natural rinds may be eaten if desired. Other cheeses are coated with an inedible wax rind to prevent moisture loss. Fresh cheeses have no rind whatsoever.

Moisture and fat contents are good indicators of a cheese's texture and shelf life. The higher the moisture content, the softer the product and the more perishable it will be. Low-moisture cheeses may be used for grating and will keep for several weeks if properly stored. (Reduced water activity levels prohibit bacterial growth.) Fat content ranges from low fat (less than 20% fat) to double cream (at least 60% fat) and triple cream (at least 72% fat). Cheeses with a high fat content will be creamier and have a richer taste and texture than low-fat products.

Most cheeses contain high percentages of fat and protein. Cheese is also rich in calcium, phosphorus and vitamin A. As animal products, natural cheeses contain cholesterol. Today, many low-fat, even nonfat, processed cheeses are available. Sodium has also been reduced or eliminated from some modern products. See Table 8.4.

Cheese Varieties

Cheeses can be classified by country of origin, ripening method, fat content or texture. Here we classify fine cheeses by texture and have adopted five categories: fresh or unripened, soft, semi-soft, firm and hard. A separate section on goat's–milk cheeses is also included.

Fresh or Unripened Cheeses

Fresh cheeses are uncooked and unripened. Referred to as *fromage blanc* or *fromage frais* in French, they are generally mild and creamy with a tart tanginess. They should not taste acidic or bitter. Fresh cheeses have a moisture content of 40% to 80% and are highly perishable.

TABLE 8.4   NUTRITIONAL VALUES OF COMMON CHEESES

Per 1-ounce (28 g) Serving	Calories	Protein (g)	Carbohydrates (g)	Total Fat (g)	Saturated Fat (g)	Cholesterol (mg)	Sodium (mg)
Blue	100	6.1	0.7	8.2	5.3	21	396
Cheddar	114	7.1	0.4	9.4	6	30	176
Cottage, low fat	25	3.9	1	0.5	0.3	2	115
Feta	75	4	1.2	6	4.2	25	316
Goat's milk	132	2.7	12.1	8.4	5.4	n/a	170
Mozzarella, part skim	72	6.9	0.8	4.5	2.9	16	132
Swiss	110	8	1	8	5	25	20
Processed cheese (*Velveeta*)	100	6	3	7	4	20	410

The Corinne T. Netzer Encyclopedia of Food Values, 1992

Cream cheese is soft cow's milk cheese from the United States containing approximately 35% fat. It is available in various-sized solid white blocks or whipped and flavored. It is used throughout the kitchen in baking, dips, dressings and confections and is popular as a spread for bagels or toast.

Feta is a semi-soft Greek or Italian product made from sheep's and/or goat's milk. It is a white, flaky cheese that is pickled (but not ripened) and stored in brine water, giving it a shelf life of four to six weeks. Its flavor becomes sharper and saltier with age. Feta is good for snacks and salads and melts easily for sauces and fillings.

Feta

Mozzarella is a firm Italian cheese traditionally made with water buffalo's milk (today cow's milk is more common) and containing 40% to 45% fat. Mozzarella becomes elastic when melted and is well known as "pizza cheese." Fresh mozzarella is excellent in salads or topped simply with olive oil and herbs. It is a very mild white cheese best eaten within hours of production. Commercial mozzarella is rather bland and rubbery and is best reserved for cooking, for which it may be purchased already shredded.

Mozzarella

Ricotta is a soft Italian cheese, similar to American cottage cheese, made from the whey left when other cow's-milk cheeses are produced. It contains only 4% to 10% fat. It is white or ivory in color and fluffy, with a small grain and sweet flavor. Ricotta is an important ingredient in many pasta dishes and desserts.

Soft Cheeses

Soft cheeses are characterized by their thin skins and creamy centers. They are among the most delicious and popular of cheeses. They ripen quickly and are at their peak for only a few days, sometimes less. Moisture content ranges from 50% to 75%.

Bel paese is a 20th-century Italian creation made from cow's milk and containing approximately 50% fat. It is mild and creamy with a fruity flavor. The inside is yellowish and the outside is brown or gray. Bel paese is excellent for snacking and melts easily.

Brie

Brie is a rind-ripened French cheese made with cow's milk and containing about 60% fat. Brie is made in round, flat disks weighing 2 or 4 pounds; it is coated with a bloomy white rind. At the peak of ripeness it is creamy and rich, with a texture that oozes. Selecting a properly ripened brie is a matter of judgment and experience. Select a cheese that is bulging a bit inside its rind; there should be just the beginning of brown coloring on the rind. If underripe, brie will be bland with a hard, chalky core. Once the cheese is cut it will not ripen any further. If overripe, brie will have a brownish rind that may be gummy or sagging and will smell strongly of ammonia. The rind is edible, but trim it off if preferred. The classic after-dinner cheese, brie, is also used in soups, sauces and hors d'oeuvres.

Boursin is a triple-cream cow's-milk cheese from France containing approximately 75% fat. Boursin is usually flavored with peppers, herbs or garlic. It is rindless, with a smooth, creamy texture, and is packed in small, foil-wrapped cylinders. Boursin is a good breakfast cheese and a welcome addition to any cheese board. It is also a popular filling for baked chicken.

Camembert is a rind-ripened cheese from France containing approximately 45% fat. Bavaria also produces a Camembert, though of a somewhat lesser quality. Camembert is creamy, like brie, but milder. It is shaped in small round or oval disks and is coated with a white bloomy rind. Selecting a properly ripened Camembert is similar to selecting a brie, but Camembert will become overripe and ammoniated even more quickly than brie. Camembert is an excellent dessert or after-dinner cheese and goes particularly well with fruit.

Semisoft Cheeses

Semisoft cheeses include many mild, buttery cheeses with smooth, sliceable textures. Some semisoft cheeses are also known as monastery or Trappist cheeses because their development is traced to monasteries, some recipes having originated during the Middle Ages. The moisture content of semisoft cheeses ranges from 40% to 50%.

Doux de Montagne is a cow's milk cheese from France containing approximately 45% fat. Produced in the foothills of the Pyrenees, it is also referred to as **pain de Pyrenees**. Doux de Montagne is pale yellow with irregular holes and a mellow, sweet, nutty flavor. It is sometimes studded with green peppercorns, which provide a tangy flavor contrast. It is usually shaped in large spheres and coated with brown wax. Doux de Montagne is good before dinner and for snacking.

Fontina is a cow's-milk cheese from Italy's Piedmont region containing approximately 45% fat. The original, known as **fontina Val D'Aosta**, has a dark gold, crusty rind; the pale gold, dense interior has a few small holes. It is nutty and rich. The original must have a purple trademark stamped on the rind. Imitation fontinas (known as **fontal** or **fontinella**) are produced in Denmark, France, Sweden, the United States and other regions of Italy. They tend to be softer, with less depth of flavor, and may have a rubbery texture. Real fontina is a good after-dinner cheese; the imitations are often added to sauces, soups or sandwiches.

Doux de Montagne

Gorgonzola is a blue-veined cow's-milk cheese from Italy containing 48% fat. Gorgonzola has a white or ivory interior with bluish-green veins. It is creamier than Stilton or Roquefort, with a somewhat more pungent, spicy, earthy flavor. White gorgonzola has no veins but a similar flavor, while aged gorgonzola is drier and crumbly with a very strong, sharp flavor. The milder gorgonzolas are excellent with fresh peaches or pears or crumbled in a salad. Gorgonzola is also used in sauces and in the *torta con basilico*, a cakelike cheese loaf composed of layers of cheese, fresh basil and pine nuts.

Gorgonzola

Gouda is a Dutch cheese containing approximately 48% fat. Gouda is sold in various-sized wheels covered with red or yellow wax. The cheese is yellow with a few small holes and a mild, buttery flavor. Gouda may be sold soon after production or it may be aged for several months, resulting in a firmer, more flavorful cheese. Gouda is widely popular for snacking and in **fondue.**

Fondue—*a Swiss specialty made with melted cheese, wine and flavorings; eaten by dipping pieces of bread into the hot mixture with long forks.*

Havarti is a cow's-milk monastery-style cheese from Denmark containing 45% to 60% fat. Havarti is also known as **Danish Tilsit** or by the brand name **Dofino**. Pale yellow with many small, irregular holes, it is sold in small rounds, rectangular blocks or loaves. Havarti has a mild flavor and creamy texture. It is often flavored with dill, caraway seeds or peppers. Havarti is very popular for snacking and on sandwiches.

Port du Salut is a monastery cow's-milk product from France containing approximately 50% fat. Port du Salut (also known as Port Salut) is smooth, rich and savory. It is shaped in thick wheels with a dense, pale yellow interior and an edible, bright orange rind. The Danish version is known as **Esrom**. One of the best and most authentic Port du Saluts has the initials S.A.F.R. stamped on the rind. Lesser-quality brands may be bland and rubbery. It is popular for breakfast and snacking, especially with fruit.

Havarti

Roquefort is a blue-veined sheep's-milk cheese from France containing approximately 45% fat. One of the oldest cheeses, Roquefort is intensely pungent with a rich, salty flavor and strong aroma. It is a white paste with veins of blue mold and a thin natural rind shaped into thick, foil-wrapped cylinders. Roquefort is always aged for at least three months in the limestone caves of Mount Combalou. Since 1926 no producer outside this region can legally use the name Roquefort or even "Roquefort-style." Roquefort is an excellent choice for serving before or after dinner and is, of course, essential for Roquefort dressing.

Stilton is a blue-veined cow's-milk cheese from Great Britain containing 45% fat. Stilton is one of the oldest and grandest cheeses in the world. It has a white or pale yellow interior with evenly spaced blue veins. Stilton's distinctive flavor is pungent, rich and tangy, combining the best of blues and cheddars. It is aged in cool ripening rooms for four to six months to develop the blue veining; it is then sold in tall cylinders with a crusty, edible rind. Stilton should be wrapped in a cloth dampened with salt water and stored at cool temperatures, but not refrigerated. It is best served alone, with plain crackers, dried fruit or vintage port.

Stilton

Firm Cheeses

Firm cheeses are not hard or brittle. Some are close-textured and flaky, like cheddar; others are dense, holey cheeses like Swiss Emmenthaler. Most firm cheeses are actually imitators of these two classics. Their moisture content ranges from 30% to 40%.

Cheddars are produced in both North America and Great Britain. **American Cheddar** is a cow's-milk cheese made primarily in New York, Wisconsin, Vermont and Oregon, containing from 45% to 50% fat. The best cheddars are made from raw milk and aged for several months. (Raw milk may be used in the United States provided the cheese is then aged at least 60 days.) They have a dense, crumbly texture. Cheddars may be white or colored orange with vegetable dyes, depending on local preference. Flavors range from mild to very sharp, depending on the age of the cheese. **Colby** and **longhorn** are two well-known mild, soft-textured Wisconsin cheddars. Cheddars are sold in a variety of shapes and sizes, often coated with wax. Good-quality cheddars are welcome additions to any cheese board, while those of lesser quality are better reserved for cooking and sandwiches. **English Cheddar** is a variety of cow's-milk cheese produced in Great Britain containing approximately 45% fat. Perhaps the most imitated cheese in the world, true English cheddar is rarely seen in the United States because of import restrictions. It is a moist yet sliceable cheese, aged at least six months.

American Cheddar—Wisconsin Sharp, Vermont Cabot, Canadian Black Diamond

Emmenthaler (Swiss) is a cow's-milk cheese from Switzerland containing approximately 45% fat. Emmenthaler is the original Swiss cheese; it accounts for over half of Switzerland's cheese production. It is mellow, rich and nutty with a natural rind and a light yellow interior full of large holes. It is ripened in three stages with the aid of fermenting bacteria. The holes or "eyes" are caused by gases expanding inside the cheese during fermentation. Authentic Emmenthaler is sold in 200-pound wheels with the word "Switzerland" stamped on the rind like the spokes of a wheel. Emmenthaler, one of the basic fondue cheeses, is also popular for sandwiches, snacks and after dinner with fruit and nuts.

Emmenthaler (Swiss)

Gruyère is a cow's-milk cheese made near Fribourg in the Swiss Alps and containing approximately 45% to 50% fat. Gruyère is often imitated, as the name is not legally protected. True gruyère is moist and highly flavorful, with a sweet nuttiness similar to Emmenthaler. Gruyère is aged for up to 12 months and then sold in huge wheels. It should have small, well-spaced holes and a brown, wrinkled rind. Gruyère melts easily and is often used with meats and in sauces, but is also appropriate before or after dinner.

Gruyère

Jarlsberg is a Swiss-type cow's-milk cheese from Norway containing approximately 45% fat. Jarlsberg closely resembles Swiss Emmenthaler in both taste and appearance. It is mild with a delicate, sweet taste and large holes. Jarlsberg has a pale yellow interior; it is coated with yellow wax and sold in huge wheels. It has a long shelf life and is popular for sandwiches, snacks and in cooking.

Monterey Jack is a cheddarlike cow's-milk cheese from California containing 50% fat. It is very mild and rich, with a pale ivory interior. It is sold in wheels or loaves coated with dark wax. "Jack" is often flavored with peppers or herbs and is good for snacking, sandwiches and in Mexican dishes. Dry-aged Jack develops a tough, wrinkled brown rind and a rich, firm yellow interior. It has a nutty, sharp flavor and is dry enough for grating.

Provolone is a cow's-milk cheese from southern Italy containing approximately 45% fat. Provolone *dolce*, aged only two months, is mild, with a smooth texture. Provolone *piccante*, aged up to six months, is stronger and somewhat flaky or stringy. Smoked provolone is also popular, especially for snacking. Provolone is shaped in various ways, from huge salamis to plump spheres to tiny piglets shaped by hand. It is excellent in sandwiches and for cooking, and is often used for melting and in pizza and pasta dishes.

Hard Cheeses

Hard cheeses are not simply cheeses that have been allowed to dry out. Rather, they are carefully aged for extended periods of time and have a moisture content of about 30%. Hard cheeses are most often used for grating; the best flavor will come from cheeses grated as needed. Even the finest hard cheeses begin to lose their flavor within hours of grating. The most famous and popular of the hard cheeses are those from Italy, where they are known as *grana*. Hard cheeses can also be served as a table cheese or with a salad.

Asiago is a cow's-milk cheese from Italy containing approximately 30% fat. After only one year of aging, Asiago is sharp and nutty with a cheddarlike texture. If aged for two years or more, Asiago becomes dry, brittle and suitable for grating. Either version should be an even white to pale yellow in color with no dark spots, cracks or strong aromas. It is sold in small wheels and keeps for long periods if well wrapped. Asiago melts easily and is often used in cooking.

Asiago

Parmigiano-Reggiano (Parmesan) is a cow's-milk cheese made exclusively in the region near Parma, Italy, containing from 32% to 35% fat. Parmigiano-Reggiano is one of the world's oldest and most widely copied cheeses. Used primarily for grating and cooking, it is rich, spicy and sharp with a golden interior and a hard oily rind. It should not be overly salty or bitter. Reggiano, as it is known, is produced only from mid-April to mid-November. It is shaped into huge wheels of about 80 pounds (36 kilos) each, with the name stenciled repeatedly around the rind. Imitation Parmesan is produced in the United States, Argentina and elsewhere, but none can match the distinctive flavor of freshly grated Reggiano.

Pecorino Romano is a sheep's-milk cheese from central and southern Italy containing approximately 35% fat. Romano is very brittle and sharper than other grating cheeses, with a "sheepy" tang. Its light, grainy interior is whiter than Parmesan or Asiago. It is packed in large cylinders with a yellow rind. Romano is often substituted for, or combined with, Parmesan in cooking but it is also good eaten with olives, sausages and red wine.

Parmigiano-Reggiano (Parmesan)

Goat's-Milk Cheeses

Because of their increasing popularity, cheeses made from goat's milk deserve a few words of their own. Although goats give less milk than cows, their milk is higher in fat and protein and richer and more concentrated in flavor. Cheeses made with goat's milk have a sharp, tangy flavor. They may range in texture from very soft and fresh to very hard, depending on age.

Goat's Milk Cheeses

Chevre (French for "goat") refers to small, soft, creamy cheeses produced in a variety of shapes: cones, disks, pyramids or logs. Chevres are often coated with ash, herbs or seasonings. They are excellent for cooking and complement a wide variety of flavors. Unfortunately, they have a short shelf life, perhaps only two weeks. Cheese labeled *pur chevre* must be made with 100% goat's milk, while others may be a mixture of cow's and goat's milk.

The finest goat's-milk cheeses usually come from France. Preferred brands include Bucheron, exported from France in 5-pound (2-kilo) logs; Chevrotin, one of the mildest; and Montrachet, a tangy soft cheese from the Burgundy wine region. Spurred on by the increased popularity of chevre, a few American producers have developed excellent cheeses in a wide variety of shapes and styles.

Processed Cheeses

Pasteurized processed cheese is made from a combination of aged and green cheeses that are mixed with emulsifiers and flavorings, pasteurized and poured into molds to solidify. Manufacturers can thus produce cheeses with consistent textures and flavors. Processed cheeses are commonly used in food service operations because they are less expensive than natural cheeses. And, because they will not age or ripen, their shelf life is greatly extended. Nutritionally, processed cheeses generally contain less protein, calcium and vitamin A and more sodium than natural cheeses.

Processed cheese food contains less natural cheese (but at least 51% by weight) and more moisture than regular processed cheese. Often vegetable oils and milk solids are added, making cheese food soft and spreadable.

♦♦♦

AMERICAN CHEESE PRODUCTION

The first cheese factory in the United States was built in 1851 in Oneida County, New York. Herkimer County, which adjoins Oneida County, soon became the center of the American cheese industry and remained so for the next 50 years. During this time, the largest cheese market in the world was at Little Falls, New York, where farm-produced cheeses and cheeses from over 200 factories were sold. At the turn of the century, as New York's population increased, there was a corresponding increase in demand for fluid milk. Because dairymen could receive more money for fluid milk than for cheese, cheese production declined.

While New York still produces some outstanding cheddars, the bulk of the American cheese industry gradually moved westward, eventually settling in Wisconsin's rich farmlands. The United States is now the world's largest manufacturer of cheeses, producing nearly twice as much as its nearest competitor, France.

Imitation cheese is usually manufactured with dairy byproducts and soy products mixed with emulsifiers, colorings and flavoring agents and enzymes. Although considerably less expensive than natural cheese, imitation cheese tends to be dense and rubbery, with little flavor other than that of salt.

Serving Cheeses

Cheeses may be served at any time of day. In Northern Europe they are common for breakfast; in Great Britain they are a staple at lunch. Cheeses are widely used for sandwiches, snacks and cooking in America, and they are often served following the entree or instead of dessert at formal dinners.

The flavor and texture of natural cheeses are best at room temperature. So, except for fresh cheeses, all cheeses should be removed from the refrigerator 30 minutes to an hour before service to allow them to come to room temperature. Fresh cheeses, such as cottage and cream, should be eaten chilled.

Any selection of fine cheeses should include a variety of flavors and textures: from mild to sharp, from soft to creamy to firm. Use a variety of shapes and colors for visual appeal. Do not precut the cheeses as this only causes them to become dry. Provide an adequate supply of serving knives so that stronger-flavored cheeses will not combine with and overpower milder ones. Fine cheeses are best appreciated with plain bread and crackers, as salted or seasoned crackers can mask the cheese's flavor. Noncitrus fruits are also a nice accompaniment.

Storage

Most cheeses are best kept refrigerated, well wrapped to keep odors out and moisture in. Firm and hard cheeses can be kept for several weeks; fresh cheeses will spoil in 7 to 10 days because of their high moisture content. Some cheeses that have become hard or dry may still be grated for cooking or baking. Freezing is possible but not recommended because it changes the cheese's texture, making it mealy or tough.

Cheeseboard Set for Service

◆◆◆ CHEESE TERMINOLOGY

The following terms often appear on cheese labels and may help you identify or appreciate new or unfamiliar cheeses:

Affine—French term for a washed-rind cheese.

Bleu—French term for blue.

Brique or *briquette*—refers to a group of French brick-shaped cheeses.

Brosse—a French term for cheeses that are brushed during ripening.

Capra—Italian for goat's-milk cheese.

Carré—French term for square, flat cheeses.

Cendre—French term for cheeses ripened in ashes.

Coulant—French for "flowing," used to describe brie, Camembert and other cheeses when their interiors ooze or flow.

Ferme or *fermier*—French term for farm-produced cheeses.

Fromage à tartiner—French term for melting cheese, often applied to processed cheeses.

Kaas—Dutch for cheese.

Kase—German for cheese.

Lait cru—French term for raw milk.

Laiterie or *laitier*—French for dairy; appears on factory-made cheeses.

Mi chevre—a French product so labeled must contain at least 25% goat's milk.

Ost—Scandinavian term for cheese.

Pecorino—Italian term for all sheep's-milk cheeses.

Queso—Spanish term for cheese.

Rape—French term applied to cheeses that are suitable for grating.

Tome or *tomme*—term used by the French, Italians and Swiss to refer to mountain cheeses, particularly from the Pyrenees or Savoie regions.

Tyrophile—one who loves cheese.

Vaccino—Italian term for cow's-milk cheese.

◆◆◆

WINE AND CHEESE: CLASSIC COMBINATIONS

Some cheeses are delicious with beers or ales. Others are best with strong coffee or apple cider, and nothing accompanies a cheddar cheese sandwich as well as ice-cold milk. For most cheeses, however, the ultimate partner is wine. Wine and cheese bring out the best in each other. The proteins and fats in cheeses take the edge off harsh or acidic wines, while the tannins and acids in wines bring out the creamy richness of cheeses.

Because of their natural affinity, certain pairings are universal favorites: Stilton with port, Camembert with Bordeaux, Roquefort with Sauternes and English cheddar with Burgundy. Although taste preferences are an individual matter, cheese–wine marriages follow two schools of thought: Either pair likes or pair opposites.

Pairing like with like is simple: Cheeses are often best served with wines produced in the same region. For example, a white burgundy would be an excellent choice for cheeses from Burgundy such as Montrachet; and goat cheeses from the Rhone Valley go well with wines of that region. Hearty Italian wines such as Chianti, Barolo and Valpolicella are delicious with Italian cheese—gorgonzola, provolone, taleggio. And a dry, aged Monterey Jack is perhaps the perfect mate for California zinfandel.

Opposites do attract, however. Sweet wines such as Sauternes and Gewürztraminer go well with sharp, tangy blues, especially Roquefort. And light, sparkling wines such as Champagne or Spanish Cava are a nice compliment to rich, creamy cheeses like brie and Camembert.

CONCLUSION

Eggs and dairy products are versatile foods used throughout the kitchen. They may be served as is or incorporated into many dishes, including soups, sauces, entrees, breads and desserts. Fine natural cheeses are useful in prepared dishes but are most important for buffets, as the cheese course during a meal or whenever cheese is the primary ingredient or dominant flavor. Eggs and dairy products spoil easily and must be handled and stored properly.

QUESTIONS FOR DISCUSSION

1. Explain the criteria used in grading eggs. Why might you prefer to use eggs with lower grades?
2. What are the differences between egg products and egg substitutes?
3. What is milkfat and how is it used in classifying milk-based products?
4. If a recipe calls for whole milk and you only have dried milk, what do you do? Explain your answer?
5. What is clarified butter and when is it used? Describe the procedure for clarifying butter.
6. The texture and shelf life of cheese depend on what two factors?
7. Cheeses are categorized as fresh, soft, semisoft, firm and hard. Give two examples of each and explain how they are generally used.

PART THREE
COOKING

Learning to cook is not simply a matter of following recipes. You must understand and appreciate why and how chemical and physical reactions occur in foods, why foods respond to heat the way they do and which foods respond best to which cooking techniques. You must also be able to identify the foods being used.

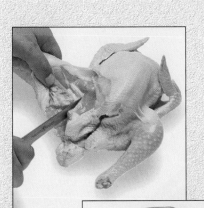

The following chapters present this information; each chapter is devoted to a specific category of food. A chapter on deep-frying is included in this section because the principles and techniques discussed there apply to a wide variety of foods. A chapter on the specialized subject of charcuterie is also included, as its study forms part of any well-rounded culinary education.

CHAPTER 9
PRINCIPLES OF COOKING

After studying this chapter you will be able to:

◆ understand how heat is transferred to foods through conduction, convection and radiation
◆ understand how heat affects foods
◆ understand the procedures for using various cooking methods

Cooking can be defined as the transfer of energy from a heat source to a food. This energy alters the food's molecular structure, changing its texture, flavor, aroma and appearance. But why is food cooked at all? The obvious answer is that cooking makes food taste better. Cooking also destroys undesirable microorganisms and makes foods easier to ingest and digest.

To cook foods successfully, you must first understand the ways in which heat is transferred: conduction, convection and radiation. You should also understand what the application of heat does to the proteins, sugars, starches, water and fats in foods.

Perhaps most importantly, you must understand the cooking methods used to transfer heat: broiling, grilling, roasting and baking, sautéing, pan-frying, deep-frying, poaching, simmering, boiling, steaming, braising and stewing. Each method is used for many types of food, so you will be applying one or more of them every time you cook. The cooking method you select gives the finished product a specific texture, appearance, aroma and flavor. A thorough understanding of the basic procedures involved in each cooking method helps you produce consistent, high-quality products.

This chapter discusses each of the cooking methods in general terms without applying them to any specific food. These methods will be discussed again in more detail as they are used in the following chapters.

HEAT TRANSFER

Heat is a type of energy. When a substance gets hot its molecules have absorbed energy, which causes the molecules to vibrate rapidly, expand and bounce off one another. As the molecules move they collide with nearby molecules, causing a transfer of heat energy. The faster the molecules within a substance move, the higher its temperature. This is true whether the substance is air, water, an aluminum pot or a sirloin steak.

Heat energy may be transferred *to* foods via conduction, convention or radiation. Heat then travels *through* foods by conduction. Only heat is transferred—cold is simply the absence of heat, so cold cannot be transferred from one substance to another.

Conduction

Conduction is the most straightforward means of heat transfer. It is simply the movement of heat from one item to another through direct contact. For example, when the flame of a gas burner touches the bottom of a sauté pan, heat is conducted to the pan. The metal of the pan then conducts heat to the surface of the food lying in that pan.

Some materials conduct heat better than others. Water is a better conductor of heat than air. This explains why a potato cooks much faster in boiling water than in an oven, and why you cannot place your hand in boiling water at a temperature of 212°F (100°C), but can place your hand, at least very briefly, into a 400°F (200°C) oven. Generally, metals are good conductors (as discussed in Chapter 5, Tools and Equipment, copper and aluminum are the best conductors), while liquids and gases are poor conductors.

Conduction is a relatively slow method of heat transfer because there must be physical contact to transfer energy from one molecule to adjacent molecules. Consider what happens when a metal spoon is placed in a pot of simmering soup. At first the spoon handle remains cool. Gradually, however, heat travels up the handle, making it warmer and warmer, until it becomes too hot to touch.

Conduction is important in all cooking methods because it is responsible for the movement of heat from the surface of a food to its interior. As the molecules near the food's exterior gather energy, they move more and more rapidly. As they move, they conduct heat to the molecules nearby, thus transferring heat *through* the food (from the exterior of the item to the interior).

In conventional heating methods (nonmicrowave) the heat source causes food molecules to react largely from the surface inward, so that layers of molecules heat in succession. This produces a range of temperatures within the food, which means that the outside can brown and form a crust long before the interior is noticeably warmer. That is why a steak can be fully cooked on the outside but still rare on the inside.

Convection

Convection refers to the transfer of heat through a fluid, which may be liquid or gas. Convection is actually a combination of conduction and a mixing in which molecules in a fluid (whether air, water or fat) move from a warmer area to a cooler one. There are two types of convection: natural and mechanical.

Natural convection occurs because of the tendency of warm liquids and gases to rise while cooler ones fall. This causes a constant natural circulation of heat. For example, when a pot of stock is placed over a gas burner, the molecules at the bottom of the pot are warmed. These molecules rise while cooler, heavier molecules sink. Upon reaching the pot's bottom, the cooler molecules are warmed and begin to rise. This ongoing cycle creates currents within the stock, and these currents distribute the heat throughout the stock.

Mechanical convection relies on fans or stirring to circulate heat more quickly and evenly. This explains why foods heat faster and more evenly when stirred. Convection ovens are equipped with fans to increase the circulation of air currents, thus speeding up the cooking process. But even conventional ovens (that is, not convection ovens) rely on the natural circulation patterns of heated air to transfer heat energy to items being baked or roasted.

Radiation

Unlike conduction and convection, **radiation** does not require physical contact between the heat source and the food being cooked. Instead, energy is transferred by waves of heat or light striking the food. Two kinds of radiant heat are used in the kitchen: infrared and microwave.

Infrared cooking uses an electric or ceramic element heated to such a high temperature that it gives off waves of radiant heat which cook the food. Radiant heat waves travel at the speed of light in any direction (unlike con-

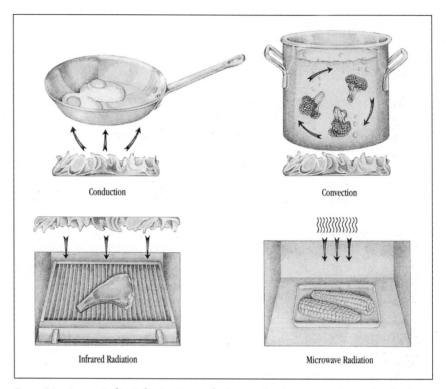

Conduction

Convection

Infrared Radiation

Microwave Radiation

FIGURE 9.1   *Arrows indicate heat patterns during conduction, convection and radiation.*

vection heat, which only rises) until they are absorbed by a food. Infrared cooking is commonly used with toasters and broilers. The glowing coals of a fire are another example of radiant heat.

Microwave cooking relies on radiation generated by a special oven to penetrate the food, where it agitates water molecules, creating friction and heat. This energy then spreads throughout the food by conduction (and by convection in liquids). Microwave cooking is much faster than other methods because energy penetrates the food up to a depth of several centimeters, setting all water molecules in motion at the same time. Heat is generated quickly and uniformly throughout the food. Microwave cooking does not brown foods, however, and often gives meats a dry, mushy texture, making microwave ovens an unacceptable replacement for traditional ovens.

Because microwave radiation only affects water molecules, a completely waterless material (such as a plate) will not get hot. Any warmth felt in a plate used when microwaving food results from heat being conducted from the food to the plate.

Microwave cooking requires the use of certain types of utensils, usually heat-resistant glass or microwavable plastic. Even heat-resistant glass can shatter and is not recommended for professional use, however. The aluminum and stainless steel utensils most common in professional kitchens cannot be used because metal deflects microwaves and this can damage the oven.

THE EFFECTS OF HEAT

Foods are composed of proteins, carbohydrates (starches and sugars), water and fats, plus small amounts of minerals and vitamins. Changes in shape, texture, color and flavor of foods may occur when heat is applied to each of these nutrients. By understanding these changes and learning to control them, you will be able to prepare foods with the characteristics desired. While volumes are written on these subjects, it is sufficient for you to know the following processes as you begin your study of cooking.

Proteins Coagulate

The proper term for the cooking of proteins is **coagulation**. Proteins are large, complex molecules found in every living cell, plant as well as animal. Coagulation refers to the irreversible transformation of proteins from a liquid or semiliquid state to a solid state. As proteins cook they lose moisture, shrink and become firm. Common examples of coagulation are the firming of meat fibers during cooking, egg whites changing from a clear liquid to a white solid when heated and the setting of the structure of wheat proteins (known as gluten) in bread during baking. Most proteins complete coagulation at 160 to 185°F (71 to 85°C).

Starches Gelatinize

Gelatinization is the proper term for the cooking of starches. Starches are complex carbohydrates present in plants and grains such as potatoes, wheat, rice and corn. When a mixture of starch and liquid is heated, remarkable changes occur. The starch granules absorb water, causing them to swell, soften and clarify slightly. The liquid visibly thickens because of the water being absorbed into the starch granules and the granules themselves swelling to occupy more space.

Gelatinization occurs gradually over a range of temperatures—150 to 212°F (66 to 100°C)—depending on the type of starch used. Starch gelatinization affects not only sauces or liquids to which starches are added for the express purpose of thickening, but also any mixture of starch and liquid that is heated. For example, the flour (a starch) in cake batter gelatinizes by absorbing the water from eggs, milk or other ingredients as the batter bakes. This causes part of the firming and drying associated with baked goods.

Sugars Caramelize

The process of cooking sugars is properly known as **caramelization**. Sugars are simple carbohydrates used by all plants and animals to store energy. As sugars cook they gradually turn brown and change flavor. Caramelized sugar is used in many sauces, candies and desserts. But caramelized sugar is also partly responsible for the flavor and color of bread crusts and the browning of meats and vegetables. In fact, it is the process of caramelization that is responsible for most flavors we associate with cooking.

Sucrose (common table sugar) begins to brown at about 338°F (170°C). The naturally occurring sugars in other foods such as maltose, lactose and fructose also caramelize, but at varying temperatures. Because high temperatures are required for browning (i.e., caramelizing), most foods will brown only on the outside and only through the application of dry heat. Because water cannot be heated above 212°F (100°C), foods cooked with moist-heat methods do not get hot enough to caramelize. Foods cooked with dry-heat methods, including those using fats, will reach the high temperatures at which browning occurs.

Water Evaporates

All foods contain some water. Some foods, especially eggs, milk and leafy vegetables, are almost entirely water. Even as much as 75% of raw meat is water. As the internal temperature of a food increases, water molecules move faster and faster until the water turns to a gas (steam) and vaporizes. This **evaporation** of water is responsible for the drying of foods during cooking.

Fats Melt

Fat is an energy source for the plant or animal in which it is stored. Fats are smooth, greasy substances that do not dissolve in water. Their texture varies from very firm to liquid. Oils are simply fats that remain liquid at room temperature. Fats **melt** when heated; that is, they gradually soften, then liquify. Fats will not evaporate. Most fats can be heated to very high temperatures without burning, so they can be used as a cooking medium to brown foods.

COOKING METHODS

Foods can be cooked in air, fat, water or steam. These are collectively known as cooking **media**. There are two general types of cooking **methods**: dry heat and moist heat.

Dry-heat cooking methods are those using air or fat. They are broiling, grilling, roasting and baking, sautéing, pan-frying and deep-frying. Foods cooked using dry-heat cooking methods have a rich flavor caused by browning.

Moist-heat cooking methods are those using water or steam. They are poaching, simmering, boiling and steaming. Moist-heat cooking methods are used to emphasize the natural flavors of food.

Other cooking methods employ a combination of dry- and moist-heat cooking methods. The two most significant of these **combination cooking methods** are braising and stewing.

TABLE 9.1   COOKING METHODS

Method	Medium	Equipment
Dry-Heat Cooking Methods		
Broiling	Air	Overhead broiler, salamander, rotisserie
Grilling	Air	Grill
Roasting	Air	Oven
Baking	Air	Oven
Sautéing	Fat	Stove
Pan-frying	Fat	Stove, tilt skillet
Deep-frying	Fat	Deep fryer
Moist-Heat Cooking Methods		
Poaching	Water or other liquid	Stove, oven, steam-jacketed kettle, tilt skillet
Simmering	Water or other liquid	Stove, steam-jacketed kettle, tilt skillet
Boiling	Water or other liquid	Stove, steam-jacketed kettle, tilt skillet
Steaming	Steam	Stove, convection steamer
Combination Cooking Methods		
Braising	Fat then liquid	Stove (and oven), tilt skillet
Stewing	Fat then liquid	Stove (and oven), tilt skillet

Each of these cooking methods can be applied to a wide variety of foods—meats, fish, vegetables and even pastries. Here, we discuss only the general characteristics of these cooking methods. Detailed procedures for applying these methods to specific foods are found in subsequent chapters.

Dry-Heat Cooking Methods

Cooking by dry heat is the process of applying heat either directly, by subjecting the food to the heat of a flame, or indirectly, by surrounding the food with heated air or heated fat.

Broiling

Broiling uses radiant heat from an overhead source to cook foods. The temperature at the heat source can be as high as 2000°F (1093°C). The food to be broiled is placed on a preheated metal grate. Radiant heat from overhead cooks the food, while the hot grate below marks it with attractive cross-hatch marks.

Delicate foods that may be damaged by being placed directly on a metal grate or foods on which cross-hatch marks are not desirable may be placed on a preheated heat-proof platter then placed under the broiler. Cooking will take place through indirect heat from the preheated platter as well as from the direct heat from the broiler's overhead heat source.

Grilling

Although similar to broiling, grilling uses a heat source located beneath the cooking surface. Grills may be electric or gas or they can burn wood or charcoal, which will add a smoky flavor to the food. Specific woods such as mesquite, hickory or vine clippings can be used to create special flavors. Grilled foods are often identified by crosshatch markings. The photos below show the correct procedure for positioning foods on the grill to create these markings.

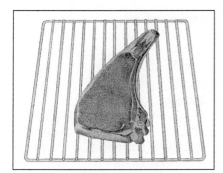 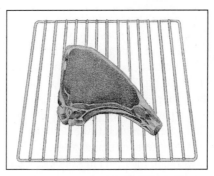 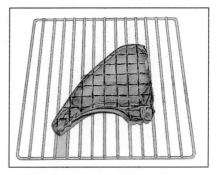

1. Decide which side of the grilled food will be presented face up to the customer. Place the food on the hot grill with this side facing down. If the item is oblong, place it at a 45-degree angle to the bars on the cooking grate. Cook long enough for the food to develop dark charred lines where it touches the grate.

2. Rotate the food 90 degrees and allow it to cook long enough for the grates to char it to the same extent as in step 1.

3. Turn the food over and finish cooking it. It is usually unnecessary to create the crosshatch markings on the reverse side, as this will not be seen by the customer.

Roasting and Baking

Roasting and baking are the processes of surrounding a food with dry, heated air in a closed environment. The term *roasting* is usually applied to meats and poultry, while *baking* is used when referring to fish, fruits, vegetables, starches, breads or pastry items. Heat is transferred by convection to the food's surface, and then penetrates the food by conduction. The surface dehydrates and the food browns from caramelization, completing the cooking process.

Sautéing

Sautéing is a dry-heat cooking method that uses conduction to transfer heat from a hot sauté pan to food with the aid of a small amount of fat. Heat then penetrates the food through conduction. High temperatures are used to sauté, and the foods are usually cut into small pieces to promote even cooking.

To sauté foods properly, begin by heating a sauté pan on the stove top, then add a small amount of fat. The fat should just cover the bottom of the pan. Heat the fat or oil to the point where it just begins to smoke. The food to be cooked should be as dry as possible when it is added to the pan to promote browning and to prevent excessive spattering. Place the food in the pan in a single layer. The heat should be adjusted so the food cooks thoroughly; it should not be so hot that the outside of the food burns before the inside is cooked. The food should be turned or tossed periodically to develop the proper color. Larger items should be turned using tongs without piercing the surface. Smaller items are often turned by using the sauteuse's sloped sides to flip them back on top of themselves. When tossing sautéed foods, keep the pan in contact with the heat source as much as possible to prevent it from cooling. Sautéing sometimes includes the preparation of a sauce directly in the pan after the main item has been removed.

Stir-frying is a variation of sautéing. A wok is used instead of a sauté pan; the curved sides and rounded bottom of the wok diffuse heat and facilitate tossing and stirring. Otherwise, stir-frying procedures are the same as those outlined for sautéing and will not be discussed separately here.

Pan-Frying

Pan-frying shares similarities with both sautéing and deep-frying. It is a dry-heat cooking method in which heat is transferred by conduction from the pan to the food, using a moderate amount of fat. Heat is also transferred to the food from the hot fat by convection. Foods to be pan-fried are usually coated in breading. This forms a seal that keeps the food moist and prevents the hot fat from penetrating the food causing it to become greasy.

To pan-fry foods properly, first heat the fat in a sauté pan. Use enough fat so that when the food to be cooked is added, the fat comes one third to one half way up the item being cooked. The fat should be at a temperature somewhat lower than that used in sautéing; it should not smoke but should be hot enough so that when the food is added it crackles and spatters from the rapid vaporization of moisture. If the temperature is too low, the food will absorb excessive amounts of fat; if it is too high, the food will burn on the outside before the interior is fully cooked. When the food is properly browned on one side, turn it without piercing it, using tongs. Always turn the food away from you to prevent being burned by any fat that may splash. When the food is fully cooked, remove it from the pan, drain it on absorbent paper and serve it immediately.

Deep-Frying

Deep-frying is a dry-heat cooking method that uses convection to transfer heat to food submerged in hot fat. Heat then penetrates the food, cooking the interior through conduction. Foods to be deep-fried are usually first coated in batter or breading. This preserves moisture and prevents the food from absorbing excessive quantities of fat. Deep-fried foods should cook thoroughly while developing an attractive deep golden-brown color. Foods to be deep-fried should be of a size and shape that allows them to float freely in the fat.

Today most deep-frying is done in specially designed commercial fryers. These fryers have built-in thermostats, making temperature control more precise. To deep-fry food, first heat the fat or oil to temperatures between 325° and 375°F (160–190°C). Slowly place the food in the fat, where it should float freely. Use tongs to turn it if necessary. When the food is done, remove it from the fat, drain it on absorbent paper and serve it immediately.

Moist-Heat Cooking Methods

Cooking with moist heat is the process of applying heat to food by submerging it directly into a hot liquid or by exposing it to steam.

Poaching

Poaching is a moist-heat cooking method that uses convection to transfer heat from a liquid to a food. For poaching, the food is submerged in a liquid held at temperatures between 160° and 180°F (71–82°C). The surface of the liquid should show only slight movement, but no bubbles.

The flavor of the poaching liquid strongly affects the ultimate flavor of the finished product, so stock, court bouillon or broth is generally used. Poaching is most often associated with foods that do not require lengthy cooking to tenderize them, such as eggs or fish.

To poach food, first bring the poaching liquid to a boil in a suitably shaped cooking vessel. Add the food to be poached by either placing it directly into the liquid or by lowering it into the liquid using a specially designed rack. Adjust the heat as necessary to maintain the desired temperature throughout the cooking process. Do not allow the liquid to reach a boil, as the agitation will cause meats to become tough and stringy and will destroy tender foods such as fresh fruit or fish. The liquid used to poach food is sometimes used to make an accompanying sauce.

Simmering

Simmering is another moist-heat cooking method that uses convection to transfer heat from a liquid to a food. For simmering, the food is submerged in a liquid held at temperatures between 185° and 205°F (85–96°C). Because simmering temperatures are slightly higher than those used for poaching, there should be more action on the liquid's surface, with a few air bubbles breaking through.

As with poaching, the liquid used for simmering has a great effect on the food's flavor. Be sure to use a well-flavored stock or broth and to add mirepoix, herbs and seasonings as needed. Simmered foods should be moist and very tender.

Boiling

Boiling is another moist-heat cooking method that uses the process of convection to transfer heat from a liquid to a food. Boiling uses large amounts of rapidly bubbling liquid to cook foods. The turbulent waters and the relatively high temperatures cook foods more quickly than do poaching or simmering. Few foods, however, are cooked by true boiling. Most "boiled" meats are actu-

TABLE 9.2   MOIST-HEAT COOKING METHODS

Method	Liquid's Temperature	Liquid's Condition	Uses
Poaching	160–180°F 71–82°C	Liquid moves slightly but no bubbles	Eggs, fish, fruits
Simmering	185–205°F 85–96°C	Small bubbles break through the liquid's surface	Meats, stews, chicken
Boiling	212°F 100°C	Large bubbles and rapid movement	Vegetables, pasta
Steaming	212°F or higher	Food is only in contact with the steam generated by a boiling liquid	Vegetables, fish, shellfish

ally simmered. Even "hard-boiled" eggs are really only simmered. Starches such as pasta and potatoes are among the only types of food that are truly boiled.

Under normal atmospheric pressure at sea level, water boils at 212°F (100°C). The addition of other ingredients or a change in atmospheric pressure can change the boiling point, however. As altitude increases, the boiling point decreases because of the drop in atmospheric pressure. For every 1000 feet above sea level, the boiling point of water drops 2°F (1°C). In the mile-high city of Denver, for example, water boils at 203°F (95°C). Because the boiling temperature is lower it will take longer to cook foods in Denver than in, for example, Miami.

The addition of alcohol also lowers the boiling point of water because alcohol boils at about 175°F (80°C). In contrast, the addition of salt, sugar or other substances raises the boiling point slightly. This means that foods cooked in salted water cook faster because the boiling point is one or two degrees higher than normal.

Steaming

Steaming is a moist-heat cooking method that uses the process of convection to transfer heat from the steam to the food being cooked. The food to be steamed is placed in a basket or rack above a boiling liquid. The food should not touch the liquid; it should be positioned so that the steam can circulate around it. A lid should be placed on the steaming pot to trap the steam and also create a slight pressure within the pot which speeds the cooking process. The liquid used to steam the food is sometimes used to make a sauce served with the item.

Another type of steaming uses a convection steamer. Convection steamers use pressurized steam to cook food very quickly in an enclosed chamber. Convection steamer cooking does not result in a flavored liquid that can be used to make a sauce.

Combination Cooking Methods

Some cooking methods employ both dry-heat and moist-heat cooking techniques. The two principal combination methods are braising and stewing. In both methods the first step is usually to brown the main item using dry heat. The second step is to complete cooking by simmering the food in a liquid. Combination methods are good for less tender but flavorful cuts of meat.

Braising

Braised foods benefit from the best qualities of both dry- and moist-heat cooking methods. Foods to be braised are usually large pieces that are first browned in a small amount of fat at high temperatures. As with sautéing, heat is transferred from the pan to the food mainly by the process of conduction. Vegetables and seasonings are added and enough sauce or liquid is added to come one third to one half way up the item being cooked. The pan is covered and the heat is reduced. The food is cooked at low heat, using a combination of simmering and steaming to transfer heat from the liquid (conduction) and the air (convection) to the food. This can be done on the stove top or in the oven. A long, slow cooking period helps tenderize the main item. Braised foods are usually served with a sauce made from the cooking liquid.

Stewing

Stewing also uses a combination of dry- and moist-heat cooking methods. Stewing is most often associated with smaller pieces of food that are first cooked either by browning them in a small amount of fat or oil, or by **blanching** them in a liquid. Cooking is then finished in a liquid or sauce. Stewed foods have enough liquid added to cover them completely and are simmered at a constant temperature until tender. Cooking time is generally shorter for stewing than for braising because the main items are smaller.

Blanch—*to very briefly and partially cook a food in boiling water or hot fat; used to assist preparation (for example, to loosen peels from vegetables), as part of a combination cooking method or to remove undesirable flavors.*

ONCLUSION

Cooking is the transfer of heat energy to foods by conduction, convection or radiation. Cooking changes the molecular structure of certain nutrients. When heat is applied, proteins coagulate, starches gelatinize, sugars caramelize, fats melt and water evaporates. Foods can be cooked using a variety of methods. Some use dry heat: broiling, grilling, roasting and baking, sautéing, pan-frying and deep-frying. Others use moist heat: poaching, simmering, boiling and steaming. Still others use a combination of the two: braising and stewing. The method used affects the texture, appearance and flavor of the cooked foods. You must understand these principles in order to ensure that foods are properly cooked.

QUESTIONS FOR DISCUSSION

1. Describe the differences between conduction and convection. Identify four cooking methods that rely on both conduction and convection to heat foods. Explain your choices.

2. Identify two cooking methods that rely on infrared heat. What is the principal difference between these methods?

3. At the same temperature, will a food cook faster in a convection oven or a conventional oven? Explain your answer.

4. Describe the process of caramelization and its significance in food preparation. Will a braised food have a caramelized surface? Explain your answer.

5. Describe the process of coagulation and its significance in food preparation. Will a pure fat coagulate if heated? Explain your answer.

6. Describe the process of gelatinization and its significance in food preparation. Will a pure fat gelatinize? Explain your answer.

CHAPTER 10
STOCKS AND SAUCES

After studying this chapter you will be able to:

♦ prepare a variety of stocks
♦ recognize and classify sauces
♦ use thickening agents properly
♦ prepare a variety of classic and modern sauces

stock is a flavored liquid; a good stock is the key to a great soup, sauce or braised dish. The French appropriately call a stock fond *("base"), as stocks are the basis for many classic and modern dishes.*

*A **sauce** is a thickened liquid used to flavor and enhance other foods. A good sauce adds flavor, moisture, richness and visual appeal. A sauce should complement food; it should never disguise it. A sauce can be hot or cold, sweet or savory, smooth or chunky.*

Although the thought of preparing stocks and sauces may be intimidating, the procedures are really quite simple. Carefully follow the basic procedures outlined in this chapter, use high-quality ingredients and, with practice and experience, you will soon be producing fine stocks and sauces.

This chapter addresses hot sauces as well as coulis, salsas and relishes. Cold sauces, generally based on mayonnaise, are discussed in Chapter 24, Salads and Salad Dressings; dessert sauces are discussed in Chapter 31, Custards, Creams, Frozen Desserts and Dessert Sauces.

STOCKS

There are several types of stocks. While they are all made from a combination of bones, vegetables, seasonings and liquids, each type uses specific procedures to give it distinctive characteristics.

A **white stock** is made by simmering chicken, veal or beef bones in water with vegetables and seasonings. The stock remains relatively colorless during the cooking process.

A **brown stock** is made from chicken, veal, beef or game bones and vegetables, all of which are caramelized before being simmered in water with seasonings. The stock has a rich, dark color.

Both a **fish stock** and a **fumet** are made by slowly cooking fish bones or crustacean shells and vegetables without coloring them, then adding water and seasonings and simmering for a short period of time. For a fumet, wine and lemon juice are also added. The resulting stock or fumet is a strongly flavored, relatively colorless liquid.

A **court bouillon** is made by simmering vegetables and seasonings in water and an acidic liquid such as vinegar or wine. It is used to poach fish or vegetables.

Ingredients

The basic ingredients of any stock are bones, a vegetable mixture known as a **mirepoix**, seasonings and water.

Bones

Bones are the most important ingredient for producing a good stock. Bones add flavor, richness and color. Traditionally, the kitchen or butcher shop saved the day's bones to make stock. But because many meats and poultry items are now purchased previously cut or portioned, food service operations often purchase bones specifically for stock making.

Different bones release their flavor at different rates. Even though the bones are cut into 3- to 4-inch (8 to 10 cm) pieces, a stock made entirely of beef and/or veal bones requires 6 to 8 hours of cooking time, while a stock made entirely from chicken bones requires only 5 to 6 hours.

Beef and Veal Bones

The best bones for beef and veal stock are from younger animals. They contain a higher percentage of **cartilage** and other **connective tissue** than do bones from more mature animals. Connective tissue has a high **collagen** content. Through the cooking process, the collagen is converted into **gelatin** and water. The gelatin adds richness and body to the finished stock.

The best beef and veal bones are back, neck and shank bones as they have a high collagen content. Beef and veal bones should be cut with a meat saw into small pieces, approximately 3 to 4 inches (8 to 10 cm) long, so that they can release as much flavor as possible while the stock cooks.

Chicken Bones

The best bones for chicken stock are from the neck and back. If a whole chicken carcass is used, it can be cut up for easier handling.

Fish Bones

The best bones for fish stock are from lean fish such as sole, flounder, whiting or turbot. Bones from fatty fish (e.g., salmon, tuna and swordfish) do not produce good stock because of their high fat content and distinctive flavors. The entire fish carcass can be used, but it should be cut up with a cleaver or heavy knife for easy handling and even extraction of flavors. After cutting, the pieces should be rinsed in cold water to remove blood, loose scales and other impurities.

Other Bones

Lamb, turkey, game and ham bones can also be used for white or brown stocks. While mixing bones is generally acceptable, be careful of blending strongly flavored bones, such as those from lamb or game, with beef, veal or chicken bones. The former's strong flavors may not be appropriate or desirable in the finished product.

Mirepoix

A mirepoix is a mixture of onions, carrots and celery added to a stock to enhance its flavor and aroma. Although chefs differ on the ratio of vegetables, generally a mixture of 50% onions, 25% carrots and 25% celery, by weight, is used. (Unless otherwise noted, any reference to mirepoix in this book refers to this ratio.) For a brown stock, onion skins may be used to add color. It is not necessary to peel the carrots or celery because flavor, not aesthetics, is important.

The size in which the mirepoix is chopped is determined by the stock's cooking time: The shorter the cooking time, the smaller the vegetables must be chopped to ensure that all possible flavor is extracted. For white or brown stocks made from beef or veal bones, the vegetables should be coarsely chopped into large, 1 to 2-inch (2-1/2 to 5-cm) pieces. For chicken and fish stocks, the vegetables should be more finely chopped into 1/2-inch (1-1/4-cm) pieces.

A white mirepoix is made by replacing the carrots in a standard mirepoix with parsnips and adding mushrooms and leeks. Some chefs prefer to use a

Connective tissue—*tissue found throughout an animal's body that binds together and supports other tissues such as muscles.*

Cartilage—*or gristle, a tough, elastic, whitish connective tissue that helps give structure to an animal's body.*

Collagen—*a protein found in nearly all connective tissue; it dissolves when cooked with moisture.*

Gelatin—*a tasteless, odorless and brittle mixture of proteins extracted from boiling bones, connective tissue and other animal parts; when dissolved in a hot liquid and then cooled, it forms a jellylike substance used as a thickener and stabilizer.*

FIGURE 10.1 *Mirepoix Ingredients*

white mirepoix when making a white stock, as it produces a lighter product. Sometimes parsnips, mushrooms and leeks are added to a standard mirepoix for additional flavors.

Seasonings

Principal stock seasonings are peppercorns, bay leaves, thyme, parsley stems, and optionally, garlic. These seasonings generally can be left whole. A stock is cooked long enough for all their flavors to be extracted so there is no reason to chop or grind them. Seasonings generally are added to the stock at the start of cooking. Some chefs do not add seasonings to beef or veal stock until mid-way through the cooking process, however, because of the extended cooking times. Seasonings can be added as a sachet d'épices or a bouquet garni.

Salt, an otherwise important seasoning, is not added to stock. Because a stock has a variety of uses, it is impossible for the chef to know how much salt to add when preparing it. If, for example, the stock was seasoned to taste with salt, the chef could not reduce it later; salt is not lost through reduction and the concentrated product would taste too salty. Similarly, seasoning the stock to taste with salt could prevent the chef from adding other ingredients that are high in salt when finishing a recipe. Unlike many seasonings whose flavors must be incorporated into a product through lengthy cooking periods, salt can be added at any time during the cooking process with the same effect.

Principles of Stock Making

The following principles apply to all stocks. You should follow them in order to achieve the highest-quality stock possible.

A. Start the Stock in Cold Water

The ingredients should always be covered with cold water. When bones are covered with cold water, blood and other impurities dissolve. As the water heats, the impurities coagulate and rise to the surface, where they can be removed easily by skimming. If the bones were covered with hot water, the impurities would coagulate more quickly and remain dispersed in the stock without rising to the top, making the stock cloudy.

If the water level falls below the bones during cooking, add water to cover them. No flavor can be extracted from bones not under water, and bones exposed to the air will darken and discolor a white stock.

B. Simmer the Stock Gently

The stock should be brought to a boil and then reduced to a simmer, a temperature of approximately 185°F (85°C). While simmering, the ingredients release their flavors into the liquid. If kept at a simmer, the liquid will remain clear as it reduces and a stock develops.

Never boil a stock for any length of time. Rapid boiling of a stock, even for a few minutes, causes impurities and fats to blend with the liquid, making it cloudy.

C. Skim the Stock Frequently

A stock should be skimmed often to remove the fat and impurities that rise to the surface during cooking. If they are not removed they may make the stock cloudy.

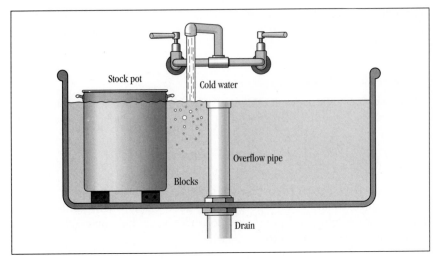

FIGURE 10.2 *Venting a Stockpot*

D. Strain the Stock Carefully

Once a stock finishes cooking, the liquid must be separated from the bones, vegetables and other solid ingredients. In order to keep the liquid clear, it is important not to disturb the solid ingredients when removing the liquid. This is easily accomplished if the stock is cooked in a steam kettle or stockpot with a spigot at the bottom.

If the stock is cooked in a standard stockpot, to strain it:

1. Skim as much fat and as many impurities from the surface as possible before removing the stockpot from the heat.
2. After removing the pot from the heat, carefully ladle the stock from the pot without stirring it.
3. Strain the stock through a china cap lined with several layers of cheescloth.

E. Cool the Stock Quickly

Most stocks are prepared in large quantities, cooled and held for later use. Great care must be taken when cooling a stock to prevent food-borne illnesses or souring. A stock can be cooled quickly and safely with the following procedure:

1. Keep the stock in a metal container. A plastic container insulates the stock and delays cooling.
2. Vent the stockpot in an empty sink by placing it on blocks or a rack. This allows water to circulate on all sides and below the pot when the sink is filled with water. See Figure 10.2 above.
3. Install an overflow pipe in the drain and fill the sink with cold water or a combination of cold water and ice. Make sure that the weight of the stockpot is adequate to keep it from tipping over.
4. Let cold water run into the sink and drain out the overflow pipe. Stir the stock frequently to facilitate even, quick cooling.

F. Store the Stock Properly

Once the stock is cooled, transfer it to a sanitized covered container (either plastic or metal) and store it in the refrigerator. As the stock chills, fat rises to

> Start the stock in cold water.
> Simmer the stock gently.
> Skim the stock frequently.
> Strain the stock carefully.
> Cool the stock quickly.
> Store the stock properly.
> Degrease the stock.

FIGURE 10.3 *Principles of Stock Making*

its surface and solidifies. If left intact, this layer of fat helps preserve the stock. Stocks can be stored for up to one week under refrigeration or frozen for several months.

G. Degrease the Stock

Degreasing a stock is simple: When a stock is refrigerated, fat rises to its surface, hardens and is easily lifted or scraped away before the stock is reheated.

White Stock

A white or neutral stock may be made from beef, veal or chicken bones. The finished stock should have a good flavor, good clarity, high gelatin content and little or no color. Veal bones are most often used, but any combination of beef, veal or chicken bones may be used.

Blanching Bones

Chefs disagree on whether the bones for a white stock should be blanched to remove impurities. Some chefs argue that blanching keeps the stock as clear and colorless as possible; others argue that blanching removes flavor.

PROCEDURE FOR BLANCHING BONES

If you choose to blanch the bones:

1. Wash the cut-up bones; place them in a stockpot and cover them with cold water.
2. Bring the water to a boil over high heat.
3. As soon as the water boils, skim the rising impurities. Drain the water from the bones and discard it.
4. Refill the pot with cold water and proceed with the stock recipe.

Degrease—*to remove fat from the surface of a liquid such as a stock or sauce by skimming, scraping or lifting congealed fat.*

FIGURE 10.4 *Lifting Fat from the Surface of a Cold Stock.*

◆◆◆

RECIPE 10.1

WHITE STOCK

Yield: 2 gal. (8 lt)

Bones: veal, chicken or beef	15 lb.	7 kg
Cold water	3 gal.	11 lt
Mirepoix	2 lb.	1 kg
Sachet:		
Bay leaves	2	2
Dried thyme	1/2 tsp.	2 ml
Peppercorns, crushed	1/2 tsp.	2 ml
Parsley stems	8	8

1. Cut the washed bones into pieces approximately 3–4 inches (8–10 cm) long.
2. Place the bones in a stockpot and cover them with cold water. If blanching, bring the water to a boil, skimming off the scum that rises to the surface. Drain off the water and the impurities. Then add the 3 gallons (11 liters) of cold water and bring to a boil. Reduce to a simmer.
3. If not blanching the bones, bring the cold water to a boil. Reduce to a simmer and skim the scum that forms.

4. Add the mirepoix and sachet to the simmering stock.
5. Continue simmering and skimming the stock for 6–8 hours. (If only chicken bones are used, simmer for 5–6 hours.)
6. Strain, cool and refrigerate.

Brown Stock

A brown stock is made from chicken, veal, beef or game bones. The finished stock should have a good flavor, rich dark brown color, good body and high gelatin content.

The primary differences between a brown stock and a white stock are that for a brown stock, the bones and mirepoix are caramelized before being simmered and a tomato product is added. These extra steps provide the finished stock with a rich dark color and a more intense flavor.

Caramelizing

Caramelization is the process of browning the sugars found on the surface of most foods. This gives the stock its characteristic flavor and color.

PROCEDURE FOR CARAMELIZING BONES

For caramelizing, do not wash or blanch the bones as this retards browning. To caramelize:

1. Place the cut-up bones in a roasting pan one layer deep. It is better to roast several pans of bones than to overfill one pan.
2. Roast the bones for approximately one hour in a hot oven (375°F/190°C). Stirring occasionally, brown the bones thoroughly but do not allow them to burn.
3. Transfer the roasted bones from the pan to the stockpot.

Deglazing the Pan

After the bones are caramelized, the excess fat should be removed and reserved for future use. The caramelized and coagulated proteins remaining in the roasting pan are very flavorful. To utilize them, you **deglaze** the pan.

Deglaze—*to swirl or stir a liquid (usually wine or stock) in a sauté pan or other pan to dissolve cooked food particles remaining on the bottom; the resulting mixture often becomes the base for a sauce.*

PROCEDURE FOR DEGLAZING THE PAN

1. Place the pan on the stove top over medium heat and add enough water to cover the bottom of the pan approximately 1/2 inch (12 mm) deep.
2. Stir and scrape the pan bottom to dissolve and remove all of the caramelized materials while the water heats.
3. Pour the deglazing liquid (also known as the deglazing liquor) over the bones in the stockpot.

PROCEDURE FOR CARAMELIZING MIREPOIX

1. Add a little of the reserved fat from the roasted bones to the roasting pan after it has been deglazed. (Or use a sautoir large enough to contain all of the mirepoix comfortably.)

Remouillage—*(French for "rewetting") a stock produced by reusing the bones left from making another stock. After draining the original stock from the stockpot, add fresh mirepoix, a new sachet and enough water to cover the bones and mirepoix and a second stock can be made. A remouillage is treated like the original stock; allow it to simmer for 4–5 hours before straining. A remouillage will not be as clear or as flavorful as the original stock, however. It is often used to make glazes or in place of water when making stocks.*

2. Sauté the mirepoix, browning all of the vegetables well and evenly without burning them.
3. Add the caramelized mirepoix to the stockpot.

Most any tomato product can be used in a brown stock: fresh tomatoes, canned whole tomatoes, crushed tomatoes, tomato purée or paste. If using a concentrated tomato product such as paste or purée, use approximately half the amount by weight of fresh or canned tomatoes. The tomato product should be added to the stockpot when the mirepoix is added.

◆◆◆

RECIPE 10.2
BROWN STOCK

Yield: 2 gal. (8 lt)

Bones: veal or beef, cut in 3–4 in. (8–10 cm) pieces	15 lb.	7 kg
Cold water	3 gal.	11 lt
Mirepoix	2 lb.	1 kg
Tomato paste	8 oz.	250 g
Sachet:		
Bay leaves	2	2
Dried thyme	1/2 tsp.	2 ml
Peppercorns, crushed	1/2 tsp.	2 ml
Garlic cloves, crushed	3	3
Parsley stems	12	12

1. Place the bones in a roasting pan, one layer deep, and brown in a 375°F (190°C) oven. Turn the bones occasionally to brown them evenly.
2. Remove the bones and place them in a stockpot. Pour off the fat from the roasting pan and reserve it.
3. Deglaze the roasting pan with part of the cold water.
4. Add the deglazing liquor and the rest of the cold water to the bones, covering them completely. Bring to a boil and reduce to a simmer.
5. Add a portion of the reserved fat to the roasting pan and sauté the mirepoix until evenly browned. Then add it to the simmering stock.

Caramelizing the bones.

Deglazing the pan with water.

Caramelizing the mirepoix.

Adding the proper amount of water.

6. Add the tomato paste and sachet to the stock and continue to simmer for 6–8 hours, skimming as necessary.

7. Strain, cool and refrigerate.

Fish Stock and Fish Fumet

A fish stock and fish fumet are similar and can be used interchangeably in most recipes. Both are clear with a pronounced fish flavor and very light body. A fumet, however, is more strongly flavored and aromatic.

The fish bones and crustacean shells used to make a fish stock or fumet should be washed but never blanched because blanching removes too much flavor. Because of the size and structure of fish bones and crustacean shells, stocks and fumets made from them require much less cooking time than even a chicken stock; 30 to 45 minutes is usually sufficient to extract full flavor. Mirepoix or other vegetables should be cut small so that all of their flavors can be extracted during the short cooking time.

The procedure for making a fish stock is very similar to that for making a white stock.

◆◆◆

RECIPE 10.3

FISH STOCK

Yield: 1 gal. (4 lt)

Fish bones or crustacean shells	10 lb.	4.5 kg
Water	5 qts.	5 lt
Mirepoix, small dice	1 lb.	450 g
Mushroom trimmings	8 oz.	250 g
Sachet:		
Bay leaves	2	2
Dried thyme	1/2 tsp.	2 ml
Peppercorns, crushed	1/4 tsp.	1 ml
Parsley stems	8	8

1. Combine all ingredients in a stockpot.

2. Bring to a simmer and skim impurities as necessary.

3. Simmer for 30 to 45 minutes.

4. Strain, cool and refrigerate.

Sweat—*to cook a food in a pan (usually covered), without browning, over low heat until the item softens and releases moisture; sweating allows the food to release its flavor more quickly when cooked with other foods.*

A fish stock is sometimes used to make fish fumet; if so, the resulting product is very strongly flavored. A fish fumet is also flavored with white wine and lemon juice. When making a fumet, **sweat** the bones and vegetables before adding the cooking liquid and seasonings.

◆◆◆

RECIPE 10.4
FISH FUMET

Yield: 2 gal. (8 lt)

Whole butter	2 oz.	60 g
Onion, small dice	1 lb.	500 g
Parsley stems	12	12
Fish bones	10 lb.	5 kg
Dry white wine	1-1/2 pt.	750 ml
Lemon juice	2 oz.	60 g
Cold water or fish stock	7 qt.	7 lt
Mushroom trimmings	2 oz.	60 g
Fresh thyme	1 sprig	1 sprig
Lemon slices	10	10

1. Melt the butter in a stockpot.
2. Add the onion, parsley stems and fish bones. Cover the pot and sweat the bones on low heat.
3. Sprinkle the bones with the white wine and lemon juice.
4. Add the cold water or fish stock, mushroom trimmings, thyme and lemon slices. Bring to a boil, reduce to a simmer and cook approximately 30 minutes, skimming frequently.
5. Strain, cool and refrigerate.

1. Sweating the onions, parsley stems and fish bones.

2. Adding cold water and seasonings.

Vegetable Stock

A good vegetable stock should be clear and light-colored. Because no animal products are used, it has no gelatin content. A vegetable stock can be used instead of a meat-based stock in most recipes. This substitution is useful when preparing vegetarian dishes or as a lighter, more healthful alternative when preparing sauces and soups. Although almost any combination of vegetables can be used for stock making, more variety is not always better. Sometimes a vegetable stock made with one or two vegetables that complement the finished dish particularly well will produce better results than a stock made with many vegetables.

===== ✦✦✦ =====

RECIPE 10.5

VEGETABLE STOCK

Yield: 1 gal. (4 lt)

Vegetable oil	2 oz.	60 g
Mirepoix, small dice	2 lb.	900 g
Leek, whites and greens, chopped	8 oz.	250 g
Garlic cloves, chopped	4	4
Fennel, small dice	4 oz.	120 g
Turnip, diced	2 oz.	60 g
Tomato, diced	2 oz.	60 g
White wine	8 oz.	250 g
Water	1 gal.	4 lt
Sachet:		
Bay leaf	1	1
Dried thyme	1/2 tsp.	2 ml
Peppercorns, crushed	1/4 tsp.	1 ml
Parsley stems	8	8

1. Heat the oil. Add the vegetables and sweat for 10 minutes.
2. Add the white wine, water and sachet.
3. Bring the mixture to a boil, reduce to a simmer and cook for 45 minutes.
4. Strain, cool and refrigerate.

Nutritional values per 4-ounce (120 gram) serving:

Calories	38	Protein	0 g
Calories from fat	44%	Vitamin A	2024 IU
Total fat	2 g	Vitamin C	4 mg
Saturated fat	0 g	Sodium	15 mg
Cholesterol	0 g		

===== ✦✦✦ =====

COMMERCIAL BASES

Commercially produced flavor (or convenience) bases are widely used in food service operations. They are powdered or dehydrated flavorings added to water to create stocks or, when used in smaller amounts, to enhance the flavor of sauces and soups. Although inferior to well-made stocks, flavor bases do reduce the labor involved in the production of stocks, sauces and soups. Used properly, they also ensure a consistent product. Because bases do not contain gelatin, stocks and sauces made from them do not benefit from reduction.

Bases vary greatly in quality and price. Sodium (salt) is the main ingredient in most bases. Better bases are made primarily of meat, poultry or fish extracts. To judge the quality of a flavor base, prepare it according to package directions and compare the flavor to that of a well-made stock. The flavor base can be improved by adding a mirepoix, standard sachet and a few appropriate bones to the mixture, then simmering for one or two hours. It can then be strained, stored and used like a regular stock.

Although convenience bases are widely used in the industry, it is important to remember that even the best base is a poor substitute for a well-made stock.

Court Bouillon

A court bouillon, while not actually a stock, is prepared in much the same manner as stocks so it is included here. A court bouillon (French for "short broth") is a flavored liquid, usually water and wine or vinegar, in which vegetables and seasonings have been simmered to impart their flavors and aromas.

Court bouillon is most commonly used to poach foods such as fish and shellfish. Recipes vary depending upon the foods to be poached. Although a court bouillon can be made in advance and refrigerated for later use, its simplicity lends itself to fresh preparation whenever needed.

◆◆◆

RECIPE 10.6
COURT BOUILLON

Yield: 1 gal. (4 lt)

Water	1 gal.	4 lt
Vinegar	6 oz.	180 g
Lemon juice	2 oz.	60 g
Salt	1/2 oz.	15 g
Mirepoix	1 lb. 8 oz.	650 g
Peppercorns, crushed	1 tsp.	5 ml
Bay leaves	4	4
Dried thyme	pinch	pinch
Parsley stems	1 bunch	1 bunch

1. Combine all ingredients and bring to a boil.
2. Reduce to a simmer and cook for 45 minutes.
3. Strain and use immediately or cool and refrigerate.

NOTE: This recipe can be used for poaching almost any fish, but it is particularly well suited to salmon, trout or shellfish. When poaching freshwater fish, replace the water and vinegar with equal parts white wine and water.

Glaze

A glaze is the dramatic reduction and concentration of a stock. One gallon (4 liters) of stock produces only 1–2 cups (2-1/2 to 5 deciliters) of glaze. *Glace de viande* is made from brown stock, reduced until it becomes dark and syrupy. *Glace de volaille* is made from chicken stock and *glace de poisson* from fish stock.

TABLE 10.1	TROUBLESHOOTING CHART FOR STOCKS	
Problem	Reason	Solution
Cloudy	Impurities	Start stock in cold water
	Stock boiled during cooking	Strain through layers of cheesecloth
Lack of flavor	Not cooked long enough	Increase cooking time
	Inadequate seasoning	Add more flavoring ingredients
	Improper ratio of bones to water	Add more bones
Lack of color	Improperly caramelized bones and mirepoix	Caramelize bones and mirepoix until darker
	Not cooked long enough	Cook longer
Lack of body	Wrong bones used	Use bones with a higher content of connective tissue
	Insufficient reduction	Cook longer
	Improper ratio of bones to water	Add more bones
Too salty	Commercial base used	Change base or make own stock; do not salt stock
	Salt added during cooking	

Glazes are added to soups or sauces to increase and intensify flavors. They are also used as a source of intense flavoring for several of the small sauces discussed below.

PROCEDURE FOR REDUCING A STOCK TO A GLAZE

1. Simmer the stock over very low heat. Be careful not to let it burn and skim it often.
2. As it reduces and the volume decreases, transfer the liquid into progressively smaller saucepans. Strain the liquid each time it is transferred into a smaller saucepan.
3. Strain it a final time, cool and refrigerate. A properly made glaze will keep for several months under refrigeration.

SAUCES

With a few exceptions, a sauce is a liquid plus thickening agent plus seasonings. Any chef can produce fine sauces by learning to:

1. Make good stocks;
2. Use thickening agents properly to achieve the desired texture, flavor and appearance; and
3. Use seasonings properly to achieve the desired flavors.

Classic hot sauces are divided into two groups: **mother** or **leading sauces** (Fr. *sauce mère*) and **small** or **compound sauces**. The five classic mother sauces are béchamel, velouté, espagnole (brown), tomato and hollandaise. Except for hollandaise, leading sauces are rarely served as is; more often they are used to create the many small sauces.

Not all sauces fall into the traditional classifications, however. Some sauces use purées of fruits or vegetables as their base; they are known as **coulis**. Others, such as **beurre blanc** (French for "white butter") and **beurre rouge** ("red butter"), are based on an acidic reduction in which whole butter is incorporated. **Flavored butters**, **salsas**, **relishes** and **pan gravy** are also used as sauces in modern food service operations.

Thickening Agents

Although there are exceptions, most sauces are thickened by the gelatinization of starches. As discussed in Chapter 9, Principles of Cooking, gelatinization is the process by which starch granules absorb moisture when placed in a liquid and heated. As the moisture is absorbed, the product thickens. Starches generally used to thicken sauces are flour, cornstarch and arrowroot. Gelatinization may sound easy, but it takes practice to produce a good sauce that

✦ is lump-free,
✦ has a good clean flavor that is not pasty or floury,
✦ has a consistency that will coat the back of a spoon (the French call this *nappé*), and
✦ will not separate or break when the sauce is held or reduced.

♦♦♦
A SAUCY HISTORY

The word "sauce" is derived from the Latin word *salus*, meaning "salted." This derivation is appropriate. For millennia, salt has been the basic condiment for enhancing and/or disguising the flavor of many foods. Over the centuries, sauces have also been used for these purposes.

Cooks of ancient Rome flavored many dishes with *garum*, a golden-colored sauce made from fermented fish entrails combined with brine, condiments, water and wine or vinegar. They also used a sauce referred to as a "single" made from oil, wine and brine. When boiled with herbs and saffron it became a "double" sauce. To this the Byzantines later added pepper, cloves, cinnamon, cardamom and coriander or spikenard (a fragrant ointment made from grains).

During the Middle Ages chefs (and their employers) were fond of either very spicy or sweet-and-sour sauces. A typical sauce for roasted meat consisted of powdered cinnamon, mustard, red wine and a sweetener such as honey. It was thickened, if at all, with bits of stale or grilled bread. Other sauces were based on verjuice, an acidic stock prepared from the juice of unripe grapes. To it were added other fruit juices, honey, flower petals and herbs or spices. Indeed, most medieval sauces were heavily spiced. Perhaps this was done to showcase the host's wealth, perhaps to hide the taste of salt-cured or less-than-fresh meats.

Guillaume Tirel (c. 1312–1395), who called himself **Taillevent**, was the master chef for Charles V of France. Around 1375 Taillevent wrote *Le Viandier*, the oldest-known French cookbook. The cooking style he describes relies heavily on pounding, puréeing and spicing most foods so that the finished dish bears little resemblance in shape, texture or taste to the original ingredients. Included in his methods

for what can only be described as ways of masking poor-quality ingredients are 17 sauces. Among them is a recipe for a *cameline* sauce. It is made from grilled bread soaked in wine; the wine-soaked bread is then drained, squeeze-dried and ground with cinnamon, ginger, pepper, cloves and nutmeg; this mixture is then diluted with vinegar. There is also a recipe for a sauce called *taillemaslée*, made of fried onions, verjuice, vinegar and mustard. (Appropriately, on his grave marker Taillevent is dressed as a sergeant-at-arms whose shield is decorated with three cooking pots.)

Recipes for some sauces of the Renaissance, such as *poivrade* or *Robert*, are recognizable today. Most sauces enjoyed in Renaissance-era Italy and France consisted of some combination of concentrated cooking juices, wines, herbs and spices (especially pepper), sometimes thickened with bread. Sweet, fruit-based sauces were also popular. Most importantly for the development of modern cuisine, however, was the growing use of sauces based on broths

thickened with cream, butter and egg yolks and flavored with herbs and spices.

Although he died in relative obscurity, many now consider **François Pierre de La Varenne** (1618–1678) to be one of the founding fathers of French cuisine. His treatises, especially *Le Cuisinier français* (1651), detail the early development, methods and manners of French cuisine. His analysis and recipes mark a departure from medieval cookery and a French cuisine heavily influenced by Italian traditions. His writings were uniquely modern in that he included recipes for new foods (especially fruits and vegetables native to the Americas or the Far East) and for indigenous foods (such as saltwater fish) that were gradually becoming more popular. La Varenne is credited with introducing roux as a thickening agent for sauces, especially velouté sauces. He emphasized the importance of properly prepared *fonds* and the reduction of cooking juices to concentrate flavors. He also popularized the use of bouquets garni to flavor stocks and sauces.

Sometime during the early 18th century, the chef to the French Duc de Levis-Mirepoix pioneered the use of onions, celery and carrots to enhance the flavor and aroma of stocks. The mixture, named for the chef's employer, soon became the standard way of enriching stocks. An enriched stock greatly improves the quality of the sauces derived from it.

During the early 19th century, **Antonin Carême** developed the modern system for classifying hundreds of sauces. It is unknown how many sauces Carême actually invented himself, but he wrote treatises containing the theories and recipes for many of the sauces still used today. Carême's extravagant lists of sauces were reduced and simplified by chefs later in the 19th century, most notably by **Auguste Escoffier**.

Roux

Roux is the principal means used to thicken sauces. It is a combination of equal parts, by weight, of flour and fat, cooked together to form a paste. Cooking the flour in fat coats the starch granules with the fat and prevents them from lumping together or forming lumps when introduced into a liquid.

In large production kitchens, large amounts of roux are prepared and held for use as needed. Smaller operations may make roux as required for each recipe.

There are three types of roux:

1. **White roux**—It is cooked only briefly and should be removed from the heat as soon as it develops a frothy, bubbly appearance. It is used in white sauces, such as béchamel, or in dishes where little or no color is desired.
2. **Blond roux**—Cooked slightly longer than white roux, blond roux should begin to take on a little color as the flour caramelizes. It is used in ivory-colored sauces, such as velouté, or where a richer flavor is desired.
3. **Brown roux**—It is cooked until it develops a darker color and a nutty aroma and flavor. Brown roux is used in brown sauces and dishes where a dark color is desired. It is important to remember that cooking a starch before adding a liquid breaks down the starch granules and prevents gelatinization from occurring. Therefore, because brown roux is cooked longer than white roux, more brown roux is required to thicken a given quantity of liquid.

FIGURE 10.5   *White, Blond and Brown Roux*

PROCEDURE FOR MAKING ROUX

Whether it will be white, blond or brown, the procedure for making roux is the same:

1. Using a heavy saucepan to prevent scorching, heat the clarified butter or other fat.
2. Add all of the flour and stir to form a paste. Although all-purpose flour can be used, it is better to use cake or pastry flour because they contain a higher percentage of starch. Do not use high gluten flour because of its greatly reduced starch content. (Flours are discussed in Chapter 26, Principles of the Bakeshop.)
3. Cook the paste over medium heat until the desired color is achieved. Stir the roux often to avoid burning. Burnt roux will not thicken a liquid; it will simply add dark specks and an undesirable flavor.

Cooking the roux.

The temperature and amount of roux being prepared determine the exact length of cooking time. Generally, however, a white roux needs to cook for only a few minutes, long enough to minimize the raw flour taste. Blond roux is cooked longer, until the paste begins to change to a slightly darker color. Brown roux requires a much longer cooking time to develop its characteristic color and aroma. A good roux will be stiff, not runny or pourable.

(a)

Cold stock

Hot roux

(b)

Hot stock

Cold roux

When thickening stock with roux, either:
a) add cold stock to hot roux
b) add cold roux to hot stock

TABLE 10.2		PROPORTIONS OF ROUX TO LIQUID				
Flour	+	Butter	=	Roux	+	Liquid	=	Sauce

Flour	+	Butter	=	Roux	+	Liquid	=	Sauce
6 oz./190 g	+	6 oz./190 g	=	12 oz./375 g	+	1 gal./4 lt	=	light
8 oz./250 g	+	8 oz./250g	=	1 lb./500 g	+	1 gal./4 lt	=	medium
12 oz./375 g	+	12 oz./375 g	=	24 oz./750 g	+	1 gal./4 lt	=	heavy

VARIABLES: The starch content of a flour determines its thickening power. Cake flour, being lowest in protein and highest in starch, has more thickening power than bread flour, which is high in protein and low in starch. In addition, a dark roux has less thickening power than a lighter one, so more will be needed to thicken an equal amount of liquid.

INCORPORATING ROUX INTO A LIQUID

There are two ways to incorporate roux into a liquid without causing lumps:

1. Cold stock can be added to the hot roux while stirring vigorously with a whisk.
2. Room-temperature roux can be added to a hot stock while stirring vigorously with a whisk.

When the roux and the liquid are completely incorporated and the sauce begins to boil, it is necessary to cook the sauce for a period of time to remove any raw flour taste that may remain. Most chefs feel a minimum of 20 minutes is necessary.

GUIDELINES FOR USING ROUX

1. Avoid using aluminum pots. The scraping action of the whisk will turn light sauces gray and will impart a metallic flavor.
2. Use sufficiently heavy pots to prevent sauces from scorching or burning during extended cooking times.
3. Avoid extreme temperatures. Roux should be no colder than room temperature so that the fat is not fully solidified. Extremely hot roux is dangerous and can spatter when combined with a liquid. Stocks should not be ice cold when combined with roux; the roux will become very cold and the solidified pieces may be very difficult to work out with a whisk.
4. Avoid overthickening. Roux does not begin to thicken a sauce until the sauce is almost at the boiling point; the thickening action continues for several minutes while the sauce simmers. If a sauce is to cook for a long time, it will also be thickened by reduction.

Cornstarch

Cornstarch, a very fine white powder, is a pure starch derived from corn. It is used widely as a thickening agent for hot and cold sauces and is especially popular in Asian cuisines for thickening sauces and soups. Liquids thickened with cornstarch have a glossy sheen that may or may not be desirable.

One unit of cornstarch thickens about twice as much liquid as an equal unit of flour. Sauces thickened with cornstarch are less stable than those thickened with roux because cornstarch can break down and lose its thickening power after prolonged heating. Products thickened with cornstarch should not be reheated.

Incorporating Cornstarch

Cornstarch must be mixed with a cool liquid before it is introduced into a hot one. The cool liquid separates the grains of starch and allows them to begin absorbing liquid without lumping. A solution of starch and cool liquid is called a **slurry**.

The starch slurry may be added to either a hot or cold liquid. If added to a hot liquid, it must be stirred continuously during incorporation. As opposed to a roux, the gelatinization of cornstarch begins almost immediately. Sauces thickened with cornstarch must be cooked gently until the raw starch flavor disappears, usually about five minutes.

Arrowroot

Arrowroot, derived from the roots of several tropical plants, is similar in texture, appearance and thickening power to cornstarch and is used in exactly the same manner. Although it is much more expensive, arrowroot does not break down as quickly as cornstarch and it produces a slightly clearer finished product.

Beurre Manié

Beurre manié is a combination of equal amounts, by weight, of flour and soft whole butter. The flour and butter are kneaded together until smooth. The mixture is then formed into pea-sized balls and whisked into a simmering sauce. Beurre manié is used for quick thickening at the end of the cooking process. The butter also adds shine and flavor to the sauce as it melts.

Liaison

Unlike the thickeners described above, a liaison does not thicken a sauce through gelatinization. A liaison is a mixture of egg yolks and heavy cream, which adds richness and smoothness with minimal thickening. Special care must be taken to prevent the yolks from coagulating when they are added to a hot liquid because this could curdle the sauce .

1. Adding hot liquid to the egg yolks and cream mixture.

PROCEDURE FOR USING A LIAISON

1. Whisk together one part egg yolk and three parts whipping cream. Combining the yolk with cream raises the temperature at which the yolk's proteins coagulate, making it easier to incorporate them into a sauce without lumping or curdling.
2. **Temper** the egg yolk mixture by slowly adding a small amount of the hot liquid while stirring continuously.
3. When enough of the hot liquid has been added to the egg yolk mixture to warm it thoroughly, begin adding the warmed egg yolk mixture to the remaining hot liquid. Be sure to stir the mixture carefully to prevent the yolk from overcooking or lumping. Plain egg yolks coagulate at temperatures between 149 and 158°F (65–70°C). Mixing them with cream raises the temperatures at which they coagulate to approximately 180–185°F (82–85°C). Temperatures over 185°F (85°C) will cause the yolks to curdle. Great care must be taken to hold the sauce above 140°F (60°C) for food safety and sanitation reasons, yet below 185°F (85°C) to prevent curdling.

2. Adding the tempered egg yolks and cream mixture to the hot liquid.

Tempering—*gradually raising the temperature of a cold liquid by slowly stirring in a hot liquid.*

Finishing Techniques

Reduction

As sauces cook, moisture is released in the form of steam. As steam escapes, the remaining ingredients concentrate, thickening the sauce and strengthening the flavors. This process, known as **reduction**, is commonly used to thicken sauces because no starches or other flavor-altering ingredients are needed. Sauces are often finished by allowing them to reduce until the desired consistency is reached.

Straining

Smoothness is important to the success of most sauces. They can be strained through either a china cap lined with several layers of cheesecloth or a fine mesh chinois. As discussed below, often vegetables, herbs, spices and other seasonings are added to a sauce for flavor. Straining removes these ingredients as well as any lumps of roux or thickener remaining in the sauce after the desired flavor and consistency have been reached.

Monter au Beurre

Monter au beurre is the process of swirling or whisking whole butter into a sauce to give it shine, flavor and richness. Compound or flavored butters, discussed below, can be used in place of whole butter to add specific flavors. Monter au beurre is widely used to enrich and finish small sauces.

Sauce Families

Leading or **mother sauces** are the foundation for the entire classic repertoire of hot sauces. The five leading sauces—béchamel, velouté, espagnole (also known as brown), tomato and hollandiase—can be seasoned and garnished to create a wide variety of small or compound sauces. The five leading sauces are distinguished principally by the liquids and thickeners used to create them.

    Small or **compound sauces** are grouped together into families based on their leading or mother sauce. Some small sauces have a variety of uses; others are traditional accompaniments for specific foods. A small sauce may be named for its ingredients, place of origin or creator. Although there are numerous classic small sauces, we have included only a few of the more popular ones following each of the leading sauce recipes.

TABLE 10.3	SAUCE FAMILIES	
Liquid	Thickener	Mother Sauce
Milk	Roux	Béchamel
White stock	Roux	Velouté
veal stock		Veal Velouté
chicken stock		Chicken Velouté
fish stock		Fish Velouté
Brown stock	Roux	Espagnole (Brown Sauce)
Tomato	Roux optional	Tomato sauce
Butter	Egg yolks	Hollandaise

The Béchamel Family

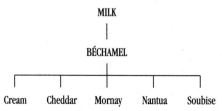

Named for its creator, Louis de Béchameil (1630–1703), steward to Louis XIV of

France, béchamel sauce is the easiest mother sauce to prepare. Traditionally it is made by adding heavy cream to a thick veal velouté. Although some chefs still believe a béchamel should contain veal stock, today the sauce is almost always made by thickening scalded milk with a white roux and adding seasonings. Often used for vegetable, egg and gratin dishes, béchamel has fallen into relative disfavor recently because of its rich, heavy nature. It is nevertheless important to understand its production and its place in traditional sauce making.

A properly made béchamel is rich, creamy and absolutely smooth with no hint of graininess. The flavors of the onion and clove used to season it should be apparent but not overwhelm the sauce's clean, milky taste. The sauce should be the color of heavy cream and have a deep luster. It should be thick enough to coat foods lightly but should not taste like the roux used to thicken it.

◆◆◆

RECIPE 10.7
BÉCHAMEL

Yield: 1 gal. (4 lt)

Onion piquet	1	1
Milk	1 gal.	4 lt
Flour	8 oz.	250 g
Clarified butter	8 oz.	250 g
Salt and white pepper	TT	TT
Nutmeg	TT	TT

1. Add the onion piquet to the milk in a heavy saucepan and simmer for 20 minutes.
2. In a separate pot, make a white roux with the flour and butter.
3. Remove the onion piquet from the milk. Gradually add the hot milk to the roux while stirring constantly with a whisk to prevent lumps. Bring to a boil.
4. Reduce the sauce to a simmer, add the seasonings and continue cooking for 30 minutes.
5. Strain the sauce through a china cap lined with cheesecloth. Melted butter can be carefully ladled over the surface of the sauce to prevent a skin from forming. Hold for service or cool in a water bath.

Small Béchamel Sauces

With a good béchamel, producing the small sauces in its family is quite simple. The quantities indicated below are for 1 quart (1 liter) of béchamel. The final step for each recipe is to season to taste with salt and pepper.

Cream Sauce Add to béchamel 8–12 ounces (250–360 grams) scalded cream and a few drops of lemon juice.

Cheddar Add to béchamel 8 ounces (250 grams) grated cheddar cheese, a dash of Worcestershire sauce and 1 tablespoon (15 milliliters) dry mustard.

Mornay Add to béchamel 4 ounces (120 grams) grated Gruyère cheese and 1 ounce (30 grams) grated parmesan cheese. Thin as desired with scalded cream. Remove the sauce from the heat and swirl in 2 ounces (60 grams) whole butter.

Nantua Add to béchamel 4 ounces (120 grams) heavy cream and 6 ounces (180 grams) crayfish butter (page 218). Add paprika to achieve the desired color. Garnish the finished sauce with diced crayfish meat.

Soubise (modern)   Sweat 1 pound (500 grams) diced onion in 1 ounce (30 grams) butter without browning. Add béchamel and simmer until the onions are fully cooked. Strain through a fine chinois.

The Velouté Family

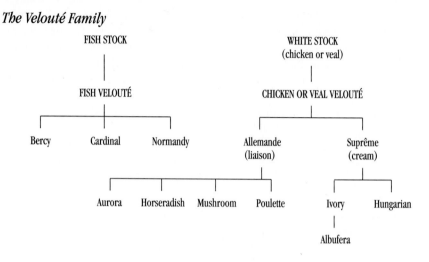

Velouté sauces are made by thickening a white stock or fish stock with roux. The white stock can be made from veal or chicken bones. A fish velouté sauce, made from fish stock, is used to create a few small sauces. A velouté sauce made from veal or chicken stock is usually used to make one of two intermediary sauces—allemande and suprême—from which many small sauces are derived. Allemande sauce is made by adding lemon juice and a liaison to either the veal or chicken velouté. (The stock used depends upon the dish with which the sauce will be served.) Suprême sauce is made by adding cream to a chicken velouté.

A properly made velouté should be rich, smooth and lump-free. If made from chicken or fish stock, it should taste of chicken or fish. A velouté made from veal stock should have a more neutral flavor. The sauce should be ivory-colored, with a deep luster. It should be thick enough to cling to foods without tasting like the roux used to thicken it.

◆◆◆

RECIPE 10.8

VELOUTÉ

Yield: 1 gal. (4 lt)

Clarified butter	8 oz.	250 g
Flour	8 oz.	250 g
Chicken, veal or fish stock	5 qt.	5 lt
Salt and white pepper	TT	TT

1. Melt the butter in a heavy saucepan. Add the flour and cook to make a blond roux.
2. Gradually add the stock to the roux, stirring constantly with a whisk to prevent lumps. Bring to a boil and reduce to a simmer. (Seasonings are optional; their use depends upon the seasonings in the stock and the sauce's intended use.)
3. Simmer and reduce to 1 gallon (4 liters), approximately 30 minutes.
4. Strain through a china cap lined with cheesecloth.
5. Melted butter may be carefully ladled over the surface of the sauce to prevent a skin from forming. Hold for service or cool in a water bath.

TABLE 10.4   VELOUTÉ SAUCES

Fish stock	+	Roux	=	Velouté				
Chicken stock	+	Roux	=	Velouté	+	Cream	=	Suprême
Chicken stock	+	Roux	=	Velouté	+	Liaison and lemon	=	Allemande
Veal stock	+	Roux	=	Velouté	+	Liaison and lemon	=	Allemande

Small Fish Velouté Sauces

A few small sauces can be made from fish velouté. The quantities given are for 1 quart (1 liter) fish velouté sauce. The final step for each recipe is to season to taste with salt and pepper.

Bercy   Sauté 2 ounces (60 grams) finely diced shallots in butter. Then add 8 ounces (250 grams) dry white wine and 8 ounces (250 grams) fish stock. Reduce this mixture by one third and add the fish velouté. Finish with butter and garnish with chopped parsley.

Cardinal   Add 8 ounces (250 grams) fish stock to 1 quart (1 liter) fish velouté. Reduce this mixture by half and add 1 pint (500 milliliters) heavy cream and a dash of cayenne pepper. Bring to a boil and swirl in 1-1/2 ounces (45 grams) lobster butter (page 218). Garnish with chopped lobster coral at service time.

Normandy   Add 4 ounces (120 grams) mushroom trimmings and 4 ounces (120 milliliters) fish stock to 1 quart (1 liter) fish velouté. Reduce by one third and finish with an egg yolk and cream liaison. Strain through a fine chinois.

◆◆◆

RECIPE 10.9

ALLEMANDE SAUCE

Yield: 1 gal. (4 lt)

Veal or chicken velouté sauce	1 gal.	4 lt
Egg yolks	8	8
Heavy cream	24 oz.	675 g
Lemon juice	1 oz.	30 g
Salt and white pepper	TT	TT

1. Bring the velouté to a simmer.
2. In a stainless steel bowl, whip the egg yolks with the cream to create a liaison. Ladle approximately one third of the hot velouté sauce into this mixture, while whisking, to temper the yolk and cream mixture.
3. When one third of the velouté has been incorporated into the now-warmed yolk and cream mixture, gradually add the liaison to the remaining velouté sauce while whisking continuously.
4. Reheat the sauce. Do not let it boil.
5. Add the lemon juice, salt and white pepper to taste.
6. Strain through a china cap lined with cheesecloth.

Small Allemande Sauces

Several small sauces are easily produced from an allemande sauce made with either a chicken or veal velouté. The quantities given are for 1 quart (1 liter) allemande. The final step for each recipe is to season to taste with salt and pepper.

Aurora Add to allemande 2 ounces (60 grams) tomato paste and finish with 1 ounce (30 grams) butter.

Horseradish Add to allemande 4 ounces (120 grams) heavy cream and 1 teaspoon (5 milliliters) dry mustard. Just before service add 2 ounces (60 grams) freshly grated horseradish. The horseradish should not be cooked with the sauce.

Mushroom Sauté 4 ounces (120 grams) sliced mushrooms in 1/2 ounce (15 grams) butter; add 2 teaspoons (10 milliliters) lemon juice. Then add the allemande to the mushrooms. Do not strain.

Poulette Sauté 8 ounces (250 grams) sliced mushrooms and 1/2 ounce (15 grams) diced shallots in 1 ounce (30 grams) butter. Add to the allemande; then add 2 ounces (60 grams) cream. Finish with lemon juice and 1 tablespoon (15 milliliters) chopped parsley.

◆◆◆

RECIPE 10.10

SUPRÊME SAUCE

Yield: 1 gal. (4 lt)

Chicken velouté sauce	1 gal.	4 lt
Mushroom trimmings	8 oz.	225 g
Heavy cream	1 qt.	1 lt
Salt and white pepper	TT	TT

1. Simmer the velouté sauce with the mushroom trimmings until reduced by one fourth.
2. Gradually whisk in the heavy cream and return to a simmer.
3. Adjust the seasonings.
4. Strain through a china cap lined with cheesecloth.

Small Suprême Sauces

The following small sauces are easily made from suprême sauce. The quantities given are for 1 quart (1 liter) suprême sauce. The final step for each recipe is to season to taste with salt and pepper.

Albufera Add to suprême 3 ounces (90 grams) glace de volaille and 2 ounces (60 grams) red pepper butter (page 219).

Hungarian Sweat 2 ounces (60 grams) diced onion in 1 tablespoon (15 milliliters) butter. Add 1 tablespoon (15 milliliters) paprika. Stir in the suprême sauce. Cook for 2–3 minutes, strain and finish with butter.

Ivory Add to suprême 3 ounces (90 grams) glace de volaille.

The Espagnole (Brown Sauce) Family

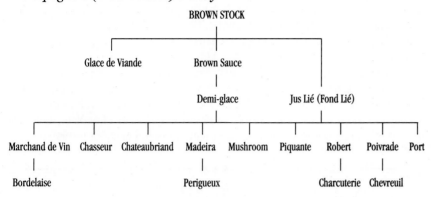

The mother sauce of the espagnole or brown sauce family is full-bodied and rich. It is made from brown stock to which brown roux, mirepoix and tomato purée are added. Most often this sauce is used to produce demi-glace. Brown stock is also used to make jus lié. Demi-glace and jus lié are usually used to create the small sauces of the espagnole family.

══════════════ ◆◆◆ ══════════════

RECIPE 10.11

ESPAGNOLE
(BROWN SAUCE)

Yield: 1 gal. (4 lt)

Mirepoix, medium dice	2 lb.	1 kg
Clarified butter	8 oz.	250 g
Flour	8 oz.	250 g
Brown stock	5 qt.	5 lt
Tomato purée	8 oz.	250 g
Sachet:		
Bay leaf	1	1
Dried thyme	1/2 tsp.	2 ml
Peppercorns, crushed	1/4 tsp.	1 ml
Parsley stems	8	8
Salt and pepper	TT	TT

1. Sauté the mirepoix in butter until well caramelized.
2. Add the flour and cook to make a brown roux.
3. Add the brown stock and tomato purée. Stir to break up any lumps of roux. Bring to a boil; reduce to a simmer.
4. Add the sachet.
5. Simmer for approximately 1-1/2 hours, allowing the sauce to reduce. Skim the surface as needed to remove impurities.
6. Strain the sauce through a china cap lined with several layers of cheesecloth. Adjust seasonings and cool in a water bath or hold for service.

Demi-Glace

Brown stock is used to make the espagnole or brown sauce described above. Espagnole sauce can then be made into demi-glace, which in turn is used to make the small sauces of the espagnole family. Demi-glace is half brown sauce, half brown stock, reduced by half. It is usually finished with a small amount of madeira or sherry wine. Because demi-glace creates a richer, more flavorful base, it produces finer small sauces than those made directly from a brown sauce.

A properly made demi-glace is rich, smooth and lump-free. Its prominent roasted flavor comes from the bones used for the brown stock. There should be no taste of roux. The caramelized bones and mirepoix as well as the tomato product contribute to its glossy dark brown, almost chocolate, color. It should be thick enough to cling to food without being pasty or heavy.

◆◆◆

RECIPE 10.12

DEMI-GLACE

Yield: 1 qt. (1 lt)

| Brown stock | 1 qt. | 1 lt |
| Brown sauce | 1 qt. | 1 lt |

1. Combine the stock and sauce in a saucepan over medium heat.
2. Simmer until the mixture is reduced by half (i.e., a yield of 1 quart or 1 liter).
3. Strain and cool in a water bath.

Jus Lié

Jus lié, also known as fond lié, is used like a demi-glace, especially to produce small sauces. Jus lié is lighter and easier to make than a demi-glace, however. It is made in one of two ways:

1. A rich brown stock is thickened with cornstarch or arrowroot and seasoned, or
2. A rich brown stock is simmered and reduced so that it thickens naturally due to concentrated amounts of gelatin and other proteins.

The starch-thickened method is a quick alternative to the long-simmering demi-glace. But because it is simply a brown stock thickened with cornstarch or arrowroot, it will only be as good as the stock with which it was begun. Sauces made from reduced stock usually have a better flavor but can be expensive to produce because of high food costs and lengthy reduction time.

A properly made jus lié is very rich and smooth. It shares many flavor characteristics with demi-glace. Its color should be dark brown and glossy from the concentrated gelatin content. Its consistency is somewhat lighter than demi-glace, but it should still cling lightly to foods.

Small Brown Sauces

Demi-glace and jus lié are used to produce many small sauces. The quantities given are for 1 quart (1 liter) demi-glace or jus lié. The final step for each recipe is to season to taste with salt and pepper.

Bordelaise   Combine 1 pint (250 milliliters) dry red wine, 2 ounces (60 grams) chopped shallots, 1 bay leaf, 1 sprig thyme and a pinch of black pepper in a saucepan. Reduce by three fourths, then add demi-glace and simmer for 15 minutes. Strain through a fine chinois. Finish with 2 ounces (60 grams) whole butter and garnish with sliced, poached beef marrow.

Chasseur (Hunter's Sauce) Sauté 4 ounces (120 grams) sliced mushrooms and 1 tablespoon (15 milliliters) diced shallots in butter. Add 8 ounces (250 grams) white wine and reduce by three fourths. Then add demi-glace and 6 ounces (170 grams) diced tomatoes; simmer for 5 minutes. Do not strain. Garnish with chopped parsley.

Chateaubriand Combine 1 pint (500 milliliters) dry white wine and 2 ounces (60 grams) diced shallots. Reduce the mixture by two thirds. Add demi-glace and reduce by half. Season to taste with lemon juice and cayenne pepper. Do not strain. Swirl in 4 ounces (120 grams) butter to finish and garnish with chopped fresh tarragon.

Chevreuil Prepare a poivrade sauce but add 6 ounces (170 grams) bacon or game trimmings to the mirepoix. Finish with 4 ounces (120 grams) red wine and a dash of cayenne pepper.

Madeira or Port Bring demi-glace to a boil, reduce slightly. Then add 4 ounces (120 milliliters) madeira wine or ruby red port.

Marchand de Vin Reduce 8 ounces (250 milliliters) dry red wine and 2 ounces (60 grams) diced shallots by two thirds. Then add demi-glace, simmer and strain.

Mushroom Blanch 8 ounces (250 grams) mushroom caps in 8 ounces (250 milliliters) boiling water seasoned with salt and lemon juice. Drain the mushrooms, saving the liquid. Reduce this liquid to 2 tablespoons (30 milliliters) and add it to the demi-glace. Just before service stir in 2 ounces (60 grams) butter and the mushroom caps.

Périgueux Add finely diced truffles to madeira sauce. *Périgourdine* sauce is the same, except that the truffles are cut into relatively thick slices.

Piquant Combine 1 ounce (30 grams) shallots, 4 ounces (120 grams) white wine and 4 ounces (120 grams) white wine vinegar. Reduce the mixture by two thirds. Then add demi-glace and simmer for 10 minutes. Add 2 ounces (60 grams) diced cornichons, 1 tablespoon (15 milliliters) fresh tarragon, 1 tablespoon (15 milliliters) fresh parsley and 1 tablespoon (15 milliliters) fresh chervil. Do not strain.

Poivrade Sweat 12 ounces (340 grams) mirepoix in 2 tablespoons (30 milliliters) oil. Add 1 bay leaf, a sprig of thyme and 4 parsley stems. Then add 1 pint (500 milliliters) vinegar and 4 ounces (120 milliliters) white wine. Reduce by half, add demi-glace and simmer for 40 minutes. Then add 20 crushed peppercorns and simmer for 5 more minutes. Strain through a fine chinois and finish with up to 2 ounces (60 grams) butter.

Robert Sauté 8 ounces (250 grams) chopped onion in 1 ounce (30 grams) butter. Add 8 ounces (250 milliliters) dry white wine and reduce by two thirds. Add demi-glace and simmer for 10 minutes. Strain and then add 2 teaspoons (10 milliliters) prepared Dijon mustard and 1 tablespoon (15 milliliters) sugar. If the finished Robert sauce is garnished with sliced sour pickles, preferably cornichons, it is known as *Charcuterie*.

◆◆◆
POIVRADE POUR GIBIER

Poivrade is also the name given a flavorful sauce traditionally made with game stock and seasoned with peppercorns. It is used for the wonderful *Sauce Grand Veneur*, one of the most complex small sauces in the classic repertoire. For *Grand Veneur*, game stock is flavored with demi-glace and finished with cream and currant jelly. The sweetness balances the strong flavor of the game meats.

The Tomato Sauce Family

Classic tomato sauce is made from tomatoes, vegetables, seasonings and white stock and thickened with a blond or brown roux. In today's kitchens, however, most tomato sauces are not thickened with roux. Rather, they are tomatoes, herbs, spices, vegetables and other flavoring ingredients simmered together and puréed.

A properly made tomato sauce is thick, rich and full-flavored. Its texture should be grainier than most other classic sauces, but it should still be smooth. The vegetables and other seasonings should add flavor, but none should be pronounced. Tomato sauce should not be bitter, acidic or overly sweet. It should be deep red and thick enough to cling to foods.

♦♦♦

RECIPE 10.13

TOMATO SAUCE

Yield: 1 gal. (4 lt)

Salt pork, small dice	4 oz.	120 g
Mirepoix	1 lb. 8 oz.	750 g
Tomato, fresh or canned	3 qt.	3 lt
Tomato purée	2 qt.	2 lt
Sachet:		
Dried thyme	1 tsp.	5 ml
Bay leaves	3	3
Garlic cloves	3	3
Parsley stems	10	10
Peppercorns, crushed	1/2 tsp.	3 ml
Salt	1-1/2 oz.	45 g
Sugar	3/4 oz.	20 g
White stock	3 qt.	3 lt
Pork bones	2 lb.	1 kg

1. Render the salt pork over medium heat.

2. Add the mirepoix and sauté, but do not brown.

3. Add the tomatoes and tomato purée, sachet, salt and sugar.

4. Add the white stock and bones.

5. Simmer slowly for 1/2–2 hours or until the desired consistency has been reached.

6. Remove the bones and sachet and pass the sauce through a food mill. Cool in a water bath and refrigerate.

Small Tomato Sauces

The following small sauces are made by adding the listed ingredients to 1 quart (1 liter) tomato sauce. The final step for each recipe is to season to taste with salt and pepper.

Creole   Sauté 6 ounces (170 grams) finely diced onion, 4 ounces (120 grams) thinly sliced celery and 1 teaspoon (5 milliliters) garlic in 1 ounce (30 milliliters) oil. Add tomato sauce, a bay leaf and a pinch of thyme; simmer for 15 minutes. Then add 4 ounces (120 grams) finely diced green pepper and a dash of hot pepper sauce; simmer for 15 minutes longer. Remove bay leaf.

Milanaise   Sauté 5 ounces (140 grams) sliced mushrooms in 1/2 ounce (15 grams) butter. Add tomato sauce and then stir in 5 ounces (140 grams) cooked ham (julienne cut) and 5 ounces (140 grams) cooked tongue (julienne cut). Bring to a simmer.

Spanish   Prepare creole sauce as directed, adding 4 ounces (120 grams) sliced mushrooms to the sautéed onions. Garnish with sliced black or green olives.

The Hollandaise Family

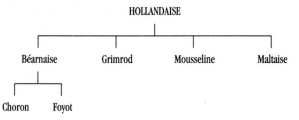

Hollandaise and the small sauces derived from it are **emulsified** sauces. Egg yolks, which contain large amounts of lecithin, a natural emulsifier, are used to emulsify warm butter and a small amount of water, lemon juice or vinegar. By vigorously whipping the egg yolks with the liquid, while slowly adding the warm butter, the lecithin coats the individual oil droplets and holds them in suspension in the liquid.

A properly made hollandaise is smooth, buttery, pale lemon-yellow-colored and very rich. It is lump-free and should not exhibit any signs of separation. The buttery flavor should dominate but not mask the flavors of the egg, lemon and vinegar. The sauce should be frothy and light, not heavy like a mayonnaise.

Emulsification—*the process by which generally unmixable liquids such as oil and water are forced into a uniform distribution.*

Temperatures and Sanitation Concerns

Temperatures play an important role in the proper production of a hollandaise sauce. As the egg yolks and liquid are whisked together, they are cooked over a bain marie until they thicken to the consistency of slightly whipped cream. Do not overheat this mixture, because even slightly cooked eggs lose their ability to emulsify. The clarified butter used to make the sauce should be warm but not so hot as to further cook the egg yolks. Although hollandaise sauce can be made from whole butter, a more stable and consistent product will be achieved by using butter that has had the water and milk solids removed through clarification. (Clarification is described in Chapter 8, Eggs and Dairy Products.)

Emulsified butter sauces are unique in that they must be held at the specific temperatures most conducive to bacterial growth: 40–140°F (4–60°C). If the sauce is heated above 150°F (65°C), the eggs will cook and the sauce will break and become grainy. If the sauce temperature falls below 45°F (7°C), the butter will solidify, making the sauce unusable. In order to minimize the risk of food-borne illnesses while maintaining the integrity of the sauce:

1. Always use clean, sanitized utensils.
2. Schedule sauce production as close to the time of service as possible. Never hold hollandaise-based sauces more than 1-1/2 hours.
3. Make small batches of sauce.
4. Never mix an old sauce with a new one.

With practice, classic hollandaise can be produced quickly and efficiently. Nevertheless, a recipe for blender hollandaise is included for those operations with a need for this technique.

◆◆◆

RECIPE 10.14

HOLLANDAISE

Yield: 1-1/2 qt. (1.5 lt)

White peppercorns, crushed	1/2 tsp.	2 ml
White wine vinegar	6 oz.	180 g
Water	4 oz.	120 g
Egg yolks	10	10
Lemon juice	2-1/2 oz.	75 g
Clarified butter, warm	1 qt.	1 lt
Salt and white pepper	TT	TT
Cayenne pepper	TT	TT

1. Combine the peppercorns, vinegar and water in a small saucepan and reduce by one half.
2. Place the egg yolks in a stainless steel bowl. Strain the vinegar and pepper reduction through a chinois, into the yolks.
3. Place the bowl over a double boiler, whipping the mixture continuously with a wire whip. As the yolks cook, the mixture will thicken. When the mixture is thick enough to leave a trail across the surface when the whip is drawn away, remove the bowl from the double boiler. Do not overcook the egg yolks.
4. Whip in 1 ounce (30 grams) lemon juice to stop the yolks from cooking.
5. Begin to add the warm clarified butter to the egg yolk mixture a drop at a time, while constantly whipping the mixture to form an emulsion. Once the emulsion is started, the butter may be added more quickly. Continue until all the butter is incorporated.
6. Whip in the remaining lemon juice. Adjust the seasonings with salt, white pepper and cayenne pepper.
7. Strain the sauce through cheesecloth if necessary and hold for service in a warm (not simmering) bain marie.

1. Combining the egg yolks with the vinegar and pepper reduction in a stainless steel bowl.

2. Whipping the mixture over a double boiler until it is thick enough to leave a trail when the whip is removed.

3. Using a kitchen towel and saucepot to firmly hold the bowl containing the yolks, add the butter slowly while whipping continuously.

4. Hollandaise at the proper consistency.

◆◆◆

RECIPE 10.15
HOLLANDAISE, BLENDER METHOD

Yield: 1 qt. (1 lt)

Egg yolks	9	9
Water, warm	3 oz.	90 g
Lemon juice	1 oz.	30 g
Cayenne pepper	TT	TT
Salt	1 tsp.	5 ml
White pepper	1/4 tsp.	1 ml
Tabasco sauce	TT	TT
Whole butter	24 oz.	750 ml

1. Place the egg yolks, water, lemon juice, cayenne pepper, salt, white pepper and Tabasco sauce in the bowl of the blender. Cover and blend on high speed for approximately 5 seconds.

2. Heat the butter to approximately 175°F (80°C). This allows the butter to cook the yolks as it is added to them.

3. Turn the blender on and immediately begin to add the butter in a steady stream. Incorporate all of the butter in 20–30 seconds. Adjust the seasonings.

4. If any lumps are present, strain the sauce through cheesecloth. Transfer the sauce to a stainless steel container and adjust the seasonings. Hold for service in a bain marie, remembering the sanitation precautions discussed above.

Procedure for Rescuing a Broken Hollandaise

Occasionally a hollandaise will break or separate and appear thin, grainy or even lumpy. A sauce breaks when the emulsion has not formed or the emulsified butter, eggs and liquid have separated. There are several reasons why this may happen: The temperature of the eggs or butter may have been too high or too low; the butter may have been added too quickly; the egg yolks may have been overcooked; too much butter may have been added or the sauce may not have been whipped vigorously enough.

Broken hollandaise can often be rescued and re-emulsified. To do so, you must first determine the cause of the problem.

Feel the bowl in which the sauce was prepared to determine if it is too hot or too cold. If the bowl is too hot, allow the sauce to cool. If it is too cold, reheat the sauce over a double boiler before attempting to rescue it.

For 1 quart (1 liter) of broken sauce, place 1 tablespoon (15 milliliters) of water in a clean stainless steel bowl and slowly beat in the broken sauce. If the problem seems to be that the eggs were overcooked or too much butter was added, add a yolk to the water before incorporating the broken sauce.

Small Hollandaise Sauces

The following small sauces are easily made by adding the listed ingredients to 1 quart (1 liter) of hollandaise. The final step for each recipe is to season to taste with salt and pepper. Béarnaise is presented here as a small sauce, although some chefs consider it a leading sauce.

Béarnaise Combine 2 ounces (60 grams) chopped shallots, 5 tablespoons (75 milliliters) chopped fresh tarragon, 3 tablespoons (45 milliliters) chopped fresh chervil and 1 teaspoon (5 milliliters) crushed peppercorns with 8 ounces (250 milliliters) white wine vinegar. Reduce to 2 ounces (60 milliliters). Add this reduction to the egg yolks and proceed with the hollandaise recipe. Strain the finished sauce and season to taste with salt and cayenne pepper. Garnish with additional chopped fresh tarragon.

Choron Combine 2 ounces (60 grams) tomato paste and 2 ounces (60 grams) heavy cream; add the mixture to a béarnaise.

Foyot Add to béarnaise 3 ounces (90 grams) melted glace de viande.

Grimrod Infuse a hollandaise sauce with saffron.

Maltaise Add to hollandaise 2 ounces (60 grams) orange juice and 2 teaspoons (10 milliliters) finely grated orange zest. Blood oranges are traditionally used for this sauce.

Mousseline (Chantilly sauce) Whip 8 ounces (250 grams) heavy cream until stiff. Fold it into the hollandaise just before service.

Beurre Blanc and Beurre Rouge

Beurre blanc and beurre rouge are emulsified butter sauces made without egg yolks. The small amounts of lecithin and other emulsifiers naturally found in butter are used to form an oil-in-water emulsion. Although similar to hollandaise in concept, they are not considered either classic leading or compound sauces. Beurre blancs are thinner and lighter than hollandaise and béarnaise. They should be smooth and slightly thicker than heavy cream.

Beurre blanc and beurre rouge are made from three main ingredients: shallots, white (Fr. *blanc*) wine or red (Fr. *rouge*) wine and whole butter (not clarified). The shallots and wine provide flavor, while the butter becomes the sauce. A good beurre blanc or beurre rouge is rich and buttery, with a neutral flavor that responds well to other seasonings and flavorings, thereby lending itself to the addition of herbs, spices and vegetable purées to complement the dish with which it is served. Its pale color changes depending upon the flavorings added. It should be light and airy yet still liquid, while thick enough to cling to food.

PROCEDURE FOR MAKING BEURRE BLANC OR BEURRE ROUGE

1. Use a nonaluminum pan to prevent discoloring the sauce. Do not use a thin-walled or nonstick pan, as heat is not evenly distributed in a thin-walled pan and a nonstick pan makes it difficult for an emulsion to set.
2. Over medium heat, reduce the wine, shallots and herbs or other seasonings, if used, until *au sec* (i.e., nearly dry). Some chefs add a small amount of heavy cream at this point and reduce the mixture. Although not necessary, the added cream helps stabilize the finished sauce.
3. Whisk in cold butter a small amount at a time. The butter should be well chilled, as this allows the butterfat, water and milk solids to be gradually incorporated into the sauce as the butter melts and the mixture is whisked.
4. When all of the butter is incorporated, strain and hold the sauce in a bain marie.

Temperature

Do not let the sauce become too hot. At 136°F (58°C) some of the emulsifying proteins begin to break down and release the butterfat they hold in emulsion.

Extended periods at temperatures over 136°F (58°C) will cause the sauce to separate. If the sauce separates, it can be corrected by cooling to approximately 110–120°F (43–49°C) and whisking to reincorporate the butterfat.

If the sauce is allowed to cool below 85°F (30°C), the butterfat will solidify. If the sauce is reheated it will separate into butterfat and water; whisking will not re-emulsify it. Cold beurre blanc can be used as a soft, flavored butter, however, simply by whisking it at room temperature until it smooths out to the consistency of mayonnaise.

◆◆◆

RECIPE 10.16

BEURRE BLANC

Yield: 1 qt. (1 lt)

White wine	1 oz.	30 g
White wine vinegar	4 oz.	120 g
Salt	1-1/2 tsp.	7 ml
White pepper	1/2 tsp.	2 ml
Shallots, minced	3 Tbsp.	45 ml
Whole butter, chilled	2 lb.	1 kg

1. Combine the white wine, white wine vinegar, salt, white pepper and shallots in a small saucepan. Reduce the mixture until approximately 2 tablespoons (30 milliliters) of liquid remain. If more than 2 tablespoons of liquid are allowed to remain the resulting sauce will be too thin. For a thicker sauce, reduce the mixture *au sec*.

2. Cut the butter into pieces approximately 1 ounce (30 grams) in weight. Over low heat, whisk in the butter a few pieces at a time, using the chilled butter to keep the sauce between 100° and 120°F (43–49°C).

3. Once all of the butter has been incorporated, remove the saucepan from the heat. Strain through a chinois and hold the sauce between 100° and 130°F (38–54°C) for service.

VARIATIONS: *Lemon-Dill*—Heat 2 tablespoons (30 milliliters) lemon juice and whisk it into the beurre blanc. Stir in 4 tablespoons (60 milliliters) chopped fresh dill.

Pink Peppercorn—Add 2 tablespoons (30 milliliters) coarsely crushed pink peppercorns to the shallot-wine reduction when making beurre rouge. Garnish the finished sauce with whole pink peppercorns.

1. Reducing the shallots and wine *au sec*.

2. Whisking in the cold butter a little at a time.

3. Straining the sauce.

Compound Butters

A compound butter is made by incorporating various seasonings into softened whole butter. These butters, also known as *beurres composés*, give flavor and color to small sauces or may be served as sauces in their own right. For example, a slice of maître d'hôtel butter (parsley butter) is often placed on a grilled steak or piece of fish at the time of service. The butter quickly melts, creating a sauce for the beef or fish.

Butter and flavoring ingredients can be combined with a blender, food processor or mixer. Using parchment paper or plastic wrap, the butter is then rolled into a cylinder, chilled and sliced as needed. Or it can be piped into rosettes and refrigerated until firm. Most compound butters will keep for two to three days in the refrigerator, or they can be frozen for longer storage.

1. Placing the butter on the plastic wrap.

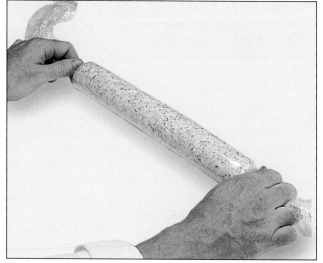

2. Rolling the butter in the plastic wrap to form a cylinder.

Recipes for Compound Butters

For each of the following butters, add the listed ingredients to 1 pound (500 grams) of softened, unsalted butter. The compound butter should then be seasoned with salt and pepper to taste.

Basil Butter   Mince 2 ounces (60 grams) basil, 2 ounces (60 grams) shallots and add to butter with 2 teaspoons (10 milliliters) lemon juice.

Herb Butter   Add to the butter up to 1 cup (250 milliliters) of mixed chopped fresh herbs such as parsley, dill, chives, tarragon or chervil.

Lobster or Crayfish Butter   Grind 8 ounces (250 grams) cooked lobster or crayfish meat, shells and/or coral with 1 pound (500 grams) butter. Place in a saucepan and clarify. Strain the butter through a fine chinois lined with cheesecloth. Refrigerate, then remove the butterfat when firm.

Maître d'Hôtel   Mix into the butter 4 tablespoons (60 milliliters) finely chopped parsley, 3 tablespoons (45 milliliters) lemon juice and a dash of white pepper.

Montpelier   Blanch 1 ounce (30 grams) parsley, 1 ounce (30 grams) chervil, 1 ounce (30 grams) watercress and 1 ounce (30 grams) tarragon in boiling water. Drain thoroughly. Mince two hard-boiled egg yolks, two garlic cloves and two gherkin pickles. Blend everything into the butter.

Red Pepper Purée 8 ounces (250 grams) roasted, peeled red bell peppers until liquid, then add to the butter.

Shallot Butter Blanch 8 ounces (250 grams) of peeled shallots in boiling water. Dry and finely dice them and mix with the butter.

Pan Gravy

Pan gravy is aptly named: It is made directly in the pan used to roast the poultry, beef, lamb or pork the gravy will accompany. Pan gravy is actually a sauce; it is a liquid thickened with a roux. Pan gravy gains additional flavors from the drippings left in the roasting pan and by utilizing a portion of the fat rendered during the roasting process to make the roux. This technique is used in Recipe 17.3, Roast Turkey with Giblet Gravy.

A properly made pan gravy should have all the characteristics of any brown sauce except that it has a meatier flavor as the result of the pan drippings.

PROCEDURE FOR MAKING PAN GRAVY

1. Remove the cooked meat or poultry from the roasting pan.
2. If mirepoix was not added during the roasting process, add it to the pan containing the drippings and fat.
3. Place the roasting pan on the stove top and clarify the fat by cooking off any remaining moisture.
4. Pour off the fat, reserving it to make the roux.
5. Deglaze the pan using an appropriate stock. The deglazing liquid may be transferred to a saucepan for easier handling or the gravy may be finished directly in the roasting pan.
6. Add enough stock or water to the deglazing liquid to yield the proper amount of finished gravy.
7. Determine the amount of roux needed to thicken the liquid and prepare it in a separate pan, using a portion of the reserved fat.
8. Add the roux to the liquid and bring the mixture to a simmer. Simmer until the mirepoix is well cooked, the flavor is extracted and the flour taste is cooked out.
9. Strain the gravy and adjust the seasonings.

Coulis

The term *coulis* most often refers to a sauce made from a purée of vegetables or fruit. A vegetable coulis can be served either as a hot or cold accompaniment to other vegetables, starches, meat, poultry, fish or shellfish. It is often made from a single vegetable base (popular examples include broccoli, tomatoes and sweet red peppers) cooked with flavoring ingredients such as onions, garlic, shallots, herbs and spices and then puréed. An appropriate liquid (stock, water or cream) may be added to thin the purée if necessary. Vegetable coulis are often prepared with very little fat and served as a healthy alternative to a heavier, classic sauce.

A fruit coulis, often made from fresh or frozen berries, is generally used as a dessert sauce. It is usually as simple as puréed fruit thinned to the desired consistency with sugar syrup.

Typically, both vegetable and fruit coulis have a texture similar to that of thin tomato sauce. But their textures can range from slightly grainy to almost lumpy, depending on their intended use. The flavor and color of a coulis should be that of the main ingredient. The flavors of herbs, spices and other flavoring ingredients should only complement and not dominate the coulis.

PROCEDURE FOR MAKING COULIS

Here, we include a procedure for making a vegetable coulis. Procedures for making fruit coulis are included as recipes in Chapter 31, Custards, Creams, Frozen Desserts and Dessert Sauces.

1. Cook the main ingredient and any additional flavoring ingredients with an appropriate liquid.
2. Purée the main ingredient and flavoring ingredients in a food mill, blender or food processor.
3. Combine the purée with the appropriate liquid and simmer to blend the flavors.
4. Thin and season the coulis as desired.

◆◆◆

RECIPE 10.17

RED PEPPER COULIS

Yield: 1 qt. (1 lt)

Vegetable oil	1 oz.	30 g
Garlic, chopped	2 tsp.	10 ml
Onion, small dice	3 oz.	90 g
Red bell pepper, medium dice	3 lb.	1.25 kg
White wine	8 oz.	250 g
Chicken stock	1 pt.	450 ml
Salt and pepper	TT	TT

1. Heat the oil and sauté the garlic and onion until translucent, without browning.
2. Add the red pepper and sauté until tender.
3. Deglaze the pan with the white wine.
4. Add the chicken stock, bring to a simmer and cook for 15 minutes. Season with salt and pepper.
5. Purée in a blender or food processor and strain through a china cap.
6. Adjust the consistency and seasonings and hold for service.

Nutritional values per 2-ounce (60 g) serving:

Calories	57	Protein	1 g
Calories from fat	32%	Vitamin A	4851 IU
Total fat	2 g	Vitamin C	162 mg
Saturated fat	0 g	Sodium	132 mg
Cholesterol	0 mg		

Salsa and Relish

Many people think of salsa (Spanish for sauce) as a chunky mixture of raw vegetables and chiles eaten with chips or ladled over Mexican food; they think of relish as a sweet green condiment spooned on a hot dog. But salsas and relishes—generally, cold chunky mixtures of herbs, spices, fruits and/or vegetables—can be used as sauces for many meat, poultry, fish and shellfish items. They can include ingredients such as oranges, pineapple, papaya, black beans, jicama, tomatillos and an array of vegetables.

Although not members of any classic sauce family, salsas and relishes are currently enjoying great popularity because of their intense fresh flavors, ease of preparation and low fat and calorie content. Salsas and relishes are often a riot of colors, textures and flavors, simultaneously cool and hot, spicy and sweet.

Chutney—*a sweet-and-sour condiment made of fruits and/or vegetables cooked in vinegar with sugar and spices until it has a consistency of jam. Some chutneys are reduced to a purée; others retain recognizable pieces of their ingredients.*

PROCEDURE FOR MAKING A SALSA OR RELISH

1. Cut or chop the ingredients.
2. Precook and chill items as directed in the recipe.
3. Toss all ingredients together and refrigerate, allowing the flavors to combine for at least 30 minutes before service.

◆◆◆

RECIPE 10.18

TOMATO SALSA (PICO DE GALLO)

Yield: 1 qt. (1 lt)

Tomatoes, seeded, small dice	5	5
Green onions, sliced	1 bunch	1 bunch
Garlic cloves, minced	3	3
Cilantro, chopped	1/2 bunch	1/2 bunch
Jalapeño peppers, chopped fine	3	3
Lemon juice	2 oz.	60 g
Cumin, ground	1/2 tsp.	2 ml
Salt and pepper	TT	TT

1. Combine all ingredients and gently toss. Adjust seasonings and refrigerate.

Nutritional values per 2 ounce (60 g) serving:

Calories	13	Protein	0 g
Calories from fat	0%	Vitamin A	338 IU
Total fat	0 g	Vitamin C	12 mg
Saturated fat	0 g	Sodium	232 mg
Cholesterol	0 mg		

TABLE 10.5   USING SAUCES

Sauce	Qualities	Small Sauce or Flavorings	Use
Béchamel	Smooth, rich and creamy; no graininess; cream-colored with rich sheen	Cream sauce Cheddar Mornay Nantua Soubise	Vegetables, pasta, eggs, fish Vegetables, pasta Fish, shellfish, poultry, vegetables Fish, shellfish Veal, pork, eggs

Velouté	Smooth and rich; ivory-colored; good flavor of the stock used; not pasty or heavy	Fish velouté
		  Bercy
		  Cardinal
		  Normandy
		Allemande (veal or chicken)
		  Aurora
		  Horseradish
		  Mushroom
		  Poulette
		Suprême (chicken)
		  Albufera
		  Hungarian
		  Ivory
			
			Poached fish
			Lobster, white fish, crab, eggs
			Delicate white fish, oysters
			
			Eggs, chicken, sweetbreads
			Roast beef, corned beef, baked ham
			Sautéed poultry, white meats
			Vegetables, sweetbreads
			
			Braised poultry, sweetbreads
			Eggs, chicken, chops, sweetbreads
			Eggs, braised poultry

Espagnole	Smooth and rich; dark brown color; good meat flavor	Bordelaise Chasseur Chateaubriand Chevreuil Madeira/Port Mushroom Périgueux/Périgourdine Piquant Poivrade Robert	Sautéed or grilled meats Sautéed or grilled meats and poultry Broiled meats Roasted meats and game Grilled or roasted meats and game, ham Sautéed or grilled meats and poultry Sautéed poultry, grilled meats and game, sweetbreads Pork Grilled or roasted meats, game Pork
Tomato	Thick and rich; slightly grainy; full-flavored	Tomato Creole Spanish Milanaise	Meats, poultry, vegetables, pasta and for making small sauces Fish, eggs, chicken Eggs, fish Pasta, grilled or sautéed poultry and white meats
Hollandaise	Smooth and rich; buttery flavor; light and slightly frothy; pale yellow color; no signs of separating	Béarnaise Choron Foyot Grimrod Mousseline Maltaise	Grilled or sautéed meats and fish Grilled meats and fish Grilled meats and fish Eggs, poached fish Poached fish, eggs, vegetables Poached fish
Beurre blanc and beurre rouge	Rich and buttery; thinner than hollandaise; light and airy; pale-colored	Wide variety of seasonings and flavorings may be used	Steamed, grilled or poached fish, chicken or vegetables
Compound butter	Flavor ingredients should be evenly distributed	Wide variety of seasonings and flavorings may be used	Grilled meats, poultry and fish; finishing sauces
Pan gravy	Smooth; deep rich color; meaty flavor	Made from pan drippings	Roasted meats and poultry
Coulis	Rich color; moderately thin, grainy texture; strongly flavored	Made with a wide variety of vegetables or fruits	Vegetables, grilled or poached meats, poultry and fish
Salsa and relish	Chunky; bright colors; not watery	Made with a wide variety of vegetables, fruits and seasonings	Meats, fish, vegetables and poultry; used as a sauce or condiment

USING SAUCES

Although many classic sauces were designed for or intended to be used with specific dishes, modern chefs often mix and match sauces with foods in unique or nontraditional ways. Nonclassic sauces, such as a beurre blanc, salsa or relish, may be prepared in a range of flavors using a wide variety of ingredients.

The uses shown in Table 10.5 for classic and nonclassic sauces are just suggestions. Most sauces can be used in many different dishes. It depends on your taste, creativity and judgment.

CONCLUSION

In *Le Guide culinaire*, Auguste Escoffier wrote "Indeed, stock is everything in cooking...without it, nothing can be done. If one's stock is good, what remains of the work is easy; if, on the other hand, it is bad or merely mediocre, it is quite hopeless to expect anything approaching a satisfactory result." Because stocks and the sauces made from them are still the basis for much of contemporary cuisine, Escoffier's words are as true today as when he wrote them.

Both the classic mother sauces and the small sauces derived from them as well as sauces such as beurre blanc and beurre rouge, coulis, salsas and relishes that are not based on classic recipes all share two goals: to complement the foods with which they are served and neither mask nor disguise poorly prepared foods. With practice and care (and the right ingredients), you will be able to make great sauces.

QUESTIONS FOR DISCUSSION

1. Why are the bones of younger animals preferred for making stocks?
2. Why should a stock made from beef or veal bones cook longer than a stock made from fish bones? What is the result if a stock does not cook long enough?
3. What can cause a stock to become cloudy? How can you prevent this from happening?
4. List three differences in the production of a white stock and a brown stock.
5. List the five classic mother sauces and explain how they are used to prepare small sauces.
6. Why is demi-glace preferred when making brown sauces? Is jus lié different from classic demi-glace? Can they be used interchangeably?
7. Why are temperatures important when making hollandaise sauce? What precautions must be taken when holding hollandaise for service?
8. Compare a beurre blanc and a hollandaise sauce. How are they similar? How are they different?
9. How are compound butters used in making sauces? What are the ingredients for a traditional maître d'hôtel butter?
10. What are the differences between a salsa, chutney and relish? Can these items be used in place of classic sauces? Explain your answer.

ADDITIONAL SAUCE RECIPES

RECIPE 10.19
MUSHROOM TARTS WITH GARLIC CREAM
NOTE: *This dish appears in the Chapter Opening photograph.*

CITRUS, LOS ANGELES, CA
Chef Michel Richard

Yield: 6 Servings

GARLIC CREAM

Garlic cloves, peeled	30	30
Heavy cream	1 pt.	500 ml
Salt and pepper	TT	TT

1. Place the garlic in a saucepan. Cover with 3 inches (8 cm) of cold water and bring to a boil. Drain and rinse with cold water. Repeat the process two more times. Then thinly slice the garlic and return it to the saucepan.
2. Add cream. Bring to a boil. Reduce the heat and simmer gently until reduced by half or to a thick, saucelike consistency, stirring occasionally.
3. Season with salt and pepper.

PUFF PASTRY

Puff pastry	8 oz.	225 g

1. Line a large baking sheet with parchment paper. Roll the pastry into a 10- × 9-inch (25 × 22.5 cm) rectangle on a lightly floured surface.
2. Cut into six 3- × 5-inch (7.5 × 12.5 cm) squares using a fluted pastry cutter. Transfer to a baking sheet and dock the dough with a fork.
3. Cover and refrigerate at least 1 hour before baking.
4. Bake at 350°F (180°C) until puffed, browned and baked through, approximately 30 minutes.

MUSHROOMS

Fresh shiitake mushrooms	1-1/2 to 2 lb.	750 to 1000 g
Olive oil	2 Tbsp.	30 ml
Salt and pepper	TT	TT

1. Trim the ends of the mushrooms. Heat a sauté pan over medium-high heat and film with oil. Add the mushrooms and cook until lightly brown and tender, approximately 5 minutes, stirring frequently.
2. Season with salt and pepper.
3. To serve the tart, slice each piece of puff pastry in half horizontally, using a serrated knife. Arrange on six plates.
4. Rewarm the garlic cream and mushrooms. Spoon cream onto the bottom of each piece of pastry. Overlap the mushrooms on top of cream, alternating light and dark pieces. Set the top pieces of pastry at an angle over the mushrooms so the filling is visible.
5. Serve with marchand de Vin (p. 211) and garnish with an herb sprig, if desired.

◆◆◆

RECIPE 10.20

DUXELLES SAUCE

Yield: 1-1/2 pt. (750 ml)

Mushrooms, chopped fine	8 oz.	250 g
Shallots, chopped fine	3 oz.	90 g
Clarified butter	1 oz.	30 g
Olive oil	1 oz.	30 g
Dry white wine	12 oz.	700 g
Demi-glace	1 pt.	500 ml
Heavy cream	2 oz.	60 g
Salt and pepper	TT	TT
Parsley, chopped fine	1 Tbsp.	15 ml

1. Sauté the mushrooms and the shallots in the butter and oil. The mushrooms will release their liquid and darken. Cook until completely dry.
2. Deglaze with the white wine and reduce by two thirds.
3. Add the demi-glace. Bring to a boil, then simmer for five minutes.
4. Stir in the cream. Adjust seasonings. Garnish with parsley.

◆◆◆

RECIPE 10.21

BARBECUE SAUCE

Yield: 1-1/2 qt. (1.5 lt)

Onion, small dice	8 oz.	250 g
Garlic, chopped	1 oz.	30 g
Vegetable oil	1 oz.	30 g
Red wine vinegar	6 oz.	180 g
Brown sugar	1 oz.	30 g
Honey	2 oz.	60 g
Beef stock	8 oz.	250 g
Ketchup	10 oz.	300 g
Dry mustard	1 oz.	30 g
Worcestershire sauce	2 Tbsp.	30 ml
Salt and pepper	TT	TT
Cayenne pepper	TT	TT

1. Sweat the onions and garlic in the oil until tender.
2. Combine the remaining ingredients and simmer for 30 minutes.

◆◆◆

RECIPE 10.22

MIGNONETTE SAUCE

Yield: 1 pt. (500 ml)

White pepper	2 tsp.	10 ml
Red wine vinegar	16 oz.	500 g
Shallots, minced	4 oz.	120 g
Salt	TT	TT

1. Combine all ingredients.

=== ◆◆◆ ===

RECIPE 10.23

FRESH TOMATO SAUCE
FOR PASTA

Yield: 2-1/2 qt. (2.5 lt)

Onion, small dice	8 oz.	250 g
Carrot, small dice	4 oz.	120 g
Garlic, minced	1 Tbsp.	15 ml
Olive oil	2 oz.	60 g
Tomato concasse	7 lb.	3.1 kg
Fresh oregano	1 Tbsp.	15 ml
Fresh thyme	2 tsp.	10 ml
Salt	1 tsp.	5 ml
Pepper	1/2 tsp.	2 ml
Fresh basil, chopped	1/2 oz.	15 g

1. Sweat the onion, carrot and garlic in the olive oil until tender.
2. Add the concasse and herbs. Simmer for approximately 1 hour or until the desired consistency is reached.
3. Pass the sauce through a food mill if a smooth consistency is desired. Do not purée if a chunkier sauce is desired.
4. Adjust seasonings and add the chopped basil.

Nutritional values per 4-oz. (120 g) serving:

Calories	87	Protein	2 g
Calories from fat	43%	Vitamin A	3090 IU
Total fat	4 g	Vitamin C	46 mg
Saturated fat	1 g	Sodium	165 mg
Cholesterol	0 mg		

=== ◆◆◆ ===

RECIPE 10.24

APPLE HORSERADISH SAUCE

Yield: 1 pt. (500 ml)

Granny Smith apples	4	4
Cider vinegar	2 oz.	60 g
Fresh horseradish, grated	2 oz.	60 g
Paprika	1 tsp.	5 ml
White wine	1 oz.	30 g

1. Grate the apples and moisten them with vinegar.
2. Add the horseradish and paprika.
3. Add wine to thin to the desired consistency.

◆◆◆

RECIPE 10.25

THAI MELON SALSA

Yield: 1 qt. (1 lt)

Assorted melons such as		
honeydew, cantaloupe, crenshaw	1 qt.	1 lt
Garlic, chopped	1 tsp.	5 ml
Brown sugar	2 Tbsp.	30 ml
Thai fish sauce	1 oz.	30 g
Serrano chiles, minced	1 Tbsp.	15 ml
Lime juice	2 oz.	60 g
Unsalted peanuts, roasted, chopped fine	4 Tbsp.	60 ml
Fresh mint	4 Tbsp.	60 ml

1. Cut the melons into small dice or shape into small balls using a parisienne scoop.
2. Combine remaining ingredients and toss with the melon pieces. Chill thoroughly. Serve with fish, shellfish or chicken.

Nutritional values per 2-oz. (60 g) serving:

Calories	46	Protein	1 g
Calories from fat	25%	Vitamin A	744 IU
Total fat	1 g	Vitamin C	17 mg
Saturated fat	0 g	Sodium	240 mg
Cholesterol	0 mg		

◆◆◆

RECIPE 10.26

STAR FRUIT CHUTNEY

Yield: 2 lb. (900 g)

Limes	3	3
Fresh ginger, julienne	4 oz.	120 g
Sugar	3 oz.	90 g
Apples, peeled, medium dice	2	2
Golden raisins	2 oz.	60 g
Dark raisins	2 oz.	60 g
Star fruit, peeled, medium dice	1-1/2 lb.	1.3 kg
Cider vinegar	1 Tbsp.	15 ml
Salt and pepper	TT	TT
Cayenne pepper	TT	TT

1. Zest 2 limes.
2. Squeeze the limes to make 4 ounces (120 grams) of juice.
3. Combine the lime juice, zest, ginger and sugar. Bring to a boil and simmer until the sugar is caramelized.
4. Add the apples and raisins; simmer until the apples are soft but not mushy.
5. Add the star fruit and bring back to a boil. Remove from heat. Add the vinegar. Season to taste with salt, pepper and cayenne pepper.

CHAPTER 11
SOUPS

*any classic soups are successfully prepared only if recipes are followed strictly. The successful preparation of other soups depends upon the mastery of specialized techniques. But where classic recipes need not be followed nor special techniques employed, perhaps no other area of the kitchen allows the chef to use his or her imagination and creativity as much as the soup station.*

The variety of ingredients, seasonings and garnishes that can be used for soups is virtually endless, provided you understand the basic procedures for making different kinds of soup. Great soups can be made using the finest and most expensive ingredients or leftovers from the previous evening's dinner service and trimmings from the day's production.

This chapter extends to soups the skills and knowledge learned in Chapter 10, Stocks and Sauces. In Chapter 10 we discussed making stocks, thickening liquids, using a liaison and skimming impurities, techniques that apply to soup making as well. Here we discuss techniques such as clarifying consommés and thickening soups with vegetable purées. This chapter also covers cream soups, cold soups and guidelines for garnishing and serving a variety of soups.

Most soups can be classified by cooking technique and appearance as either clear or thick.

Clear soups include **broths** made from meat, poultry, game, fish or vegetables as well as **consommés**, which are broths clarified to remove impurities.

Thick soups include cream soups and purée soups. The most common **cream soups** are those made from vegetables cooked in a liquid that is thickened with a starch and puréed; cream is then incorporated to add richness and flavor. **Purée soups** are generally made from starchy vegetables or legumes. After the main ingredient is simmered in a liquid, the mixture—or a portion of it—is puréed.

Some soups (notably **bisques** and **chowders** as well as **cold soups** such as gazpacho and fruit soup) are neither clear nor thick soups. Rather, they use special preparation methods or a combination of the methods mentioned above.

A soup's quality is determined by its flavor, appearance and texture. A good soup should be full flavored, with no off or sour tastes. Flavors from each of the soup's ingredients should blend and complement, with no one flavor overpowering another. Consommés should be crystal clear. The vegetables in vegetable soups should be brightly colored, not gray. Garnishes should be attractive and uniform in size and shape. The soup's texture should be very precise. If it is supposed to be smooth then it should be very smooth and lump-free. If the soft and crisp textures of certain ingredients are supposed to contrast, the soup should not be overcooked, as this causes all the ingredients to become mushy and soft.

Garnishing is an important consideration when preparing soups. When applied to soups, the word *garnish* has two meanings. The first is the one more typically associated with the word. It refers to foods added to the soup as decoration—for example, a broccoli floret floated on a bowl of cream of broccoli soup. The second refers to foods that may serve not only as decorations but also as critical components of the final product—for example, noodles in a bowl of chicken noodle soup. In this context, the noodles are not ingredients because they are not used to make the chicken soup. Rather they are added to chicken soup to create a different dish. These additional items are still referred to as garnishes, however.

CLEAR SOUPS

All clear soups start as broth. Broths may be served as finished items, used as the base for other soups or refined (clarified) into consommés.

Broths

The techniques for making stocks discussed in Chapter 10 are identical to those used for making broths. Like stocks, broths are prepared by simmering flavoring ingredients in a liquid for long periods of time. Broths and stocks differ, however, in two ways. First, broths are made with meat instead of just bones. Second, broths (often with a garnish) can be served as finished dishes, while stocks are generally used to prepare other items.

Broths are made from meat, poultry, fish or vegetables cooked in a liquid. An especially full-flavored broth results when a stock and not just water is used as the liquid. Cuts of meat from the shank, neck or shoulder result in more flavorful broths, as will the flesh of mature poultry. Proper temperature, skimming and straining help produce well-flavored, clear broths.

PROCEDURE FOR PREPARING BROTHS

1. Truss or cut the main ingredient.
2. Brown the meat; brown or sweat the mirepoix or vegetables as necessary.
3. Place the main ingredient and mirepoix or vegetables in an appropriate stockpot and add enough cold water or stock to cover. Add a bouquet garni or sachet d'epices if desired.
4. Bring the liquid slowly to a boil; reduce to a simmer and cook, skimming occasionally, until the main ingredient is tender and the flavor is fully developed.
5. Carefully strain the broth through a china cap lined with cheesecloth; try to disturb the flavoring ingredients as little as possible in order to preserve the broth's clarity.
6. Cool and store following the procedures for cooling stocks. Or bring to a boil, garnish as desired and hold for service.

◆◆◆

ESCOFFIER'S CLASSIFICATION OF SOUPS

In his 1903 culinary treatise *Le Guide culinaire*, Auguste Escoffier recognized many more categories of soups than we do today. They include:

Clear soups, which are always "clear consommés with a slight garnish in keeping with the nature of the consommé."

Purées, which are made from starchy vegetables and are thickened with rice, potato or soft bread crumbs.

Cullises, which use poultry, game or fish for a base and are thickened with rice, lentils, espagnole sauce or bread soaked in boiling salted water.

Bisques, which use shellfish cooked with a mirepoix as a base and are thickened with rice.

Veloutés, which use velouté sauce as a base and are finished with a liaison of egg yolks and cream.

Cream soups, which use béchamel sauce as a base and are finished with heavy cream.

Special soups, which are those that do not follow the procedures for veloutés or creams.

Vegetable soups, which are usually *paysanne* or peasant-type and "do not demand very great precision in the apportionment of the vegetables of which they are composed, but they need great care and attention, notwithstanding."

Foreign soups, "which have a foreign origin whose use, although it may not be general, is yet sufficiently common."

Because of changes in consumer health consciousness and kitchen operations, many of the distinctions between Escoffier's classic soups have now become blurred and, in some cases, eliminated. As discussed in this chapter, for example, clear consommés and vegetable soups are now made with stocks or broths; most cream soups use velouté as a base and are finished with milk or cream rather than a liaison. But not everything has changed: The procedures for making purées and bisques are essentially the same today as they were when Escoffier haunted the great kitchens of Europe.

◆◆◆

RECIPE 11.1
BEEF BROTH

Yield: 8 qt. (8 lt)

Beef shank, neck or shoulder cut in 2 in. (5 cm) thick pieces	12 lb.	5.5 kg
Vegetable oil	8 oz.	250 g
Cold water or stock	2 gal.	8 lt
Mirepoix	2 lb.	900 g
Turnip, medium dice	8 oz.	250 g
Leek, medium dice	8 oz.	250 g
Tomato, seeded and diced	8 oz.	250 g
Sachet:		
Bay leaf	1	1
Dried thyme	1/2 tsp.	2 ml
Peppercorns, crushed	1/2 tsp.	2 ml
Parsley stems	8	8
Garlic cloves, crushed	2	2
Salt	TT	TT

1. Brown the meat in 4 ounces (120 grams) of oil, then place it in a stockpot. Add the stock or water and bring to a simmer. Simmer gently for 2 hours, skimming the surface as necessary.

2. After the meat has simmered for 2 hours, caramelize the mirepoix in the remaining oil and add it to the liquid. Add the turnips, leeks, tomato and sachet.

3. Simmer until full flavor has developed, approximately 1 hour. Skim the surface as necessary.

4. Carefully strain the broth through cheesecloth and season to taste. Cool and refrigerate.

Broth-Based Soups

Broths are often used as bases for such familiar soups as vegetable, chicken noodle or beef barley.

Transforming a broth into a broth-based vegetable soup, for example, is quite simple. While a broth may be served with a vegetable (or meat) garnish, a broth-based vegetable soup is a soup in which the vegetables (and meats) are cooked directly in the broth, adding flavor, body and texture to the finished product. Any number of vegetables can be used to make a vegetable soup; it could be a single vegetable as in onion soup or a dozen different vegetables for a hearty minestrone. Making a mixed vegetable soup allows the chef to use his or her imagination and whatever produce may be on hand.

When making broth-based vegetable soups, each ingredient must be added at the proper time so that all ingredients are cooked when the soup is finished. The ingredients must cook long enough to add their flavors and soften sufficiently but not so long that they lose their identity and become too soft or mushy.

Because broth-based vegetable soups are made by simmering ingredients directly in the broth, they are generally not as clear as plain broths. But appearance is still important. So, when cutting ingredients for the soup, pay particular attention so that the pieces are uniform and visually appealing. Small dice, julienne, batonnet or paysanne cuts are recommended.

PROCEDURE FOR PREPARING BROTH-BASED VEGETABLE SOUPS

1. Sweat long-cooking vegetables in butter or fat.

2. Add the appropriate stock or broth and bring to a simmer.

3. Add seasonings such as bay leaves, dried thyme, crushed peppercorns, parsley stems and garlic, in a sachet, allowing enough time for the seasonings to fully flavor the soup.

4. Add additional ingredients according to their cooking times.

5. Simmer the soup to blend all the flavors.

6. If the soup is not going to be served immediately, cool and refrigerate it.

7. Just before service add any garnishes that were prepared separately or do not require cooking.

━━━━━ ◆◆◆ ━━━━━

RECIPE 11.2
HEARTY VEGETABLE BEEF SOUP

Yield: 5 qt. (5 lt)

Butter or beef fat	6 oz.	170 g
Mirepoix, small dice	3 lb.	1.5 kg
Turnip, small dice	8 oz.	250 g
Garlic cloves, chopped	2	2
Beef broth or beef stock	4 qt.	4 lt
Beef, small dice	1 lb.	450 g
Sachet:		
Bay leaf	1	1
Dried thyme	1/2 tsp.	2 ml
Peppercorns, crushed	1/2 tsp.	2 ml
Parsley stems	8	8
Tomato concasse	12 oz.	350 g
Corn kernels, fresh, frozen or canned	12 oz.	350 g
Salt and pepper	TT	TT

Tomato concasse—*peeled, seeded and diced tomato.*

1. In a soup pot, sweat the mirepoix and turnip in the butter or fat until tender.

2. Add the garlic and sauté lightly.

3. Add the beef broth or stock and the diced beef; bring to a simmer. Add the sachet. Skim or degrease as necessary.

4. Simmer until the beef and vegetables are tender, approximately 1 hour.

5. Add the tomato concasse and corn; simmer for 10 minutes. Season to taste with salt and pepper.

6. Cool and refrigerate or hold for service.

VARIATIONS: A wide variety of vegetables can be added or substituted in this recipe. If leeks, rutabagas, parsnips or cabbage are used, they should be sweated to bring out their flavors before the liquid is added. Potatoes, fresh beans, summer squash and other vegetables that cook more quickly should be added according to their cooking times. Rice, barley and pasta garnishes should be cooked separately and added just before service.

Consommés

A consommé is a stock or broth that has been clarified to remove impurities so that it is crystal clear. Traditionally, all clear broths were referred to as consommés; a clear broth further refined using the process described below was referred to as a double consommé. The term *double consommé* is still used occasionally to describe any strongly flavored consommé.

Well-prepared consommés should be rich in the flavor of the main ingredient. Beef and game consommés should be dark in color; consommés made from poultry should have a golden to light amber color. They should have substantial body as a result of their high gelatin content, and all consommés should be perfectly clear with no trace of fat.

Because a consommé is a refined broth, it is absolutely essential that the broth or stock used be of the highest quality. Although the clarification process adds some flavor to the consommé, the finished consommé will be only as good as the stock or broth from which it was made.

The Clarification Process

To make a consommé, you clarify a stock or broth. The stock or broth to be clarified must be cold and grease-free. To clarify, the cold degreased stock or broth is combined with a mixture known as a **clearmeat** or **clarification**. A clearmeat is a mixture of egg whites; ground meat, poultry or fish; mirepoix, herbs and spices; and an acidic product, usually tomatoes, lemon juice or wine. (An **onion brûlée** is also often added to help flavor and color the consommé.)

Onion brûlée—*literally, burnt onion, made by charring onion halves; used to flavor and color stocks and sauces.*

The stock or broth and clearmeat are then slowly brought to a simmer. As the albumen in the egg whites and meat begins to coagulate, it traps impurities suspended in the liquid. As coagulation continues, the albumen-containing items combine with the other clearmeat ingredients and rise to the liquid's surface, forming a **raft**. As the mixture simmers, the raft ingredients release their flavors, further enriching the consommé.

After simmering, the consommé is carefully strained through several layers of cheesecloth to remove any trace of impurities. It is then completely degreased, either by cooling and refrigerating, then removing the solidified fat or by carefully ladling the fat from the surface. The result is a rich, flavorful, crystal-clear consommé.

PROCEDURE FOR MAKING CONSOMMÉS

1. In a suitable stockpot (one with a spigot makes it much easier to strain the consommé when it is finished), combine the ground meat, lightly beaten egg white and other clearmeat ingredients.
2. Add the cold stock or broth and stir to combine with the clearmeat ingredients.
3. Over medium heat, slowly bring the mixture to a simmer, stirring occasionally.
4. As the raft forms, make a hole in its center so that the liquid can bubble through, cooking the raft completely and extracting as much flavor as possible from the raft ingredients.
5. Simmer the consommé until full flavor develops, approximately 1 to 1-1/2 hours.
6. Carefully strain the consommé through several layers of cheesecloth and degrease completely.

7. If the consommé will not be used immediately, it should be cooled and refrigerated, following the procedures for cooling stocks discussed in Chapter 10. When the consommé is completely cold, remove any remaining fat that solidified on its surface.

8. If, after reheating the consommé, small dots of fat appear on the surface, they can be removed by blotting with a small piece of paper towel.

1. Combining the ingredients for the clearmeat.

◆◆◆

RECIPE 11.3

BEEF CONSOMMÉ

Yield: 4 qt. (4 lt)

Egg whites	10	10
Ground beef, lean, preferably shank, neck or shoulder	2 lb.	1 kg
Mirepoix	1 lb.	450 g
Tomato, seeded and diced	12 oz.	340 g
Brown beef stock or broth, cold	5 qt.	5 lt
Onion brûlée	2	2
Sachet:		
Bay leaves	2	2
Dried thyme	1/2 tsp.	2 ml
Peppercorns, crushed	1/2 tsp.	2 ml
Parsley stems	8	8
Cloves, whole	2	2
Salt	TT	TT

1. Whip the egg whites until slightly frothy.
2. Combine the egg whites, beef, mirepoix and tomatoes in an appropriate stockpot.
3. Add the cold beef stock or broth; mix well and add the onion brûlée and sachet.
4. Bring the mixture to a simmer over moderate heat, stirring occasionally. Stop stirring when the raft begins to form.
5. Break a hole in the center of the raft to allow the consommé to bubble through.
6. Simmer until full flavor develops, approximately 1-1/2 hours.
7. Strain through several layers of cheesecloth, degrease and adjust the seasonings. Cool and refrigerate or hold for service.

NOTE: Guidelines for garnishing consommés as well as some classic garnishes are listed on page 245.

2. Making a hole in the raft to allow the liquid to bubble through.

3. Degreasing the consommé with a paper towel.

Correcting a Poorly Clarified Consommé

A clarification may fail for a variety of reasons. For example, if the consommé is allowed to boil or if it is stirred after the raft has formed, a cloudy consommé can result. If the consommé is insufficiently clear, a second clarification can be performed using the following procedure. This second clarification should be performed only once, however, and only if absolutely necessary,

4. The finished consommé.

because the eggs not only remove impurities but also some of the consommé's flavor and richness.

1. Thoroughly chill and degrease the consommé.
2. Lightly beat four egg whites per gallon (4 liters) of consommé and combine with the cold consommé.
3. Slowly bring the consommé to a simmer, stirring occasionally. Stop stirring when the egg whites begin to coagulate.
4. When the egg whites are completely coagulated, carefully strain the consommé.

THICK SOUPS

There are two kinds of thick soups: cream soups and purée soups. In general, cream soups are thickened with a roux or other starch, while purée soups rely on a purée of the main ingredient for thickening. But in certain ways the two soups are very similar: Some purée soups are finished with cream or partially thickened with a roux or other starch.

Cream Soups

Most cream soups are made by simmering the main flavoring ingredient (for example, broccoli for cream of broccoli soup) in a white stock or thin velouté sauce to which seasonings have been added. The mixture is then puréed and strained. After the consistency has been adjusted, the soup is finished by adding cream. In classic cuisine, thin béchamel sauce is often used as the base for cream soups and can be substituted for velouté in many cream soup recipes, if desired.

Both hard vegetables (e.g., celery and squash) and soft or leafy vegetables (e.g., spinach, corn, broccoli and asparagus) are used for cream soups. Hard vegetables are generally sweated in butter without browning before the liquid is added. Soft and leafy vegetables are generally added to the soup after the liquid is brought to a boil. Because cream soups are puréed, it is important to cook the flavoring ingredients until they are soft and can be passed through a food mill easily.

All cream soups are finished with milk or cream. Using milk thins the soup while adding richness; using the same amount of cream adds much more richness without the same thinning effect. Cold milk and cream curdle easily if added directly to a hot or acidic soup. But there are several steps that can be taken to prevent curdling:

1. Never add cold milk or cream to hot soup. Bring the milk or cream to a simmer before adding it to the soup. Or, temper the milk or cream by gradually adding some hot soup to it and then incorporating the warmed mixture into the rest of the soup.
2. If possible, add the milk or cream to the soup just before service.
3. Do not boil the soup after the milk or cream has been added.
4. The presence of roux or other starch helps prevent curdling. Therefore, béchamel or cream sauce is often used instead of milk or cream to finish cream soups.

(Recall from Chapter 10 that a béchamel sauce is made by thickening milk with a roux, and a cream sauce is made by adding cream to a béchamel sauce.)

PROCEDURE FOR MAKING CREAM SOUPS

1. In a soup pot, sweat hard vegetables such as squash, onions, carrots and celery in oil or butter without browning.

2. In order to thicken the soup:

  (a) add flour and cook to make a blond roux, then add the cooking liquid (i.e., the stock), or

  (b) add the stock to the vegetables, bring the stock to a simmer and add a blond roux that was prepared separately, or

  (c) add a thin velouté or béchamel sauce to the vegetables.

3. Bring to a boil and reduce to a simmer.

4. Add any soft vegetables such as broccoli or asparagus, and a sachet or bouquet garni as desired.

5. Simmer the soup, skimming occasionally, until the vegetables are very tender.

6. Purée the soup by passing it through a food mill, blender, food processor or vertical chopper mixer (VCM) and strain through a china cap. If the soup is too thick, adjust the consistency by adding boiling white stock.

7. Finish the soup by adding hot milk or cream or a thin béchamel or cream sauce. Adjust the seasonings and serve.

◆◆◆

RECIPE 11.4

CREAM OF BROCCOLI SOUP

Yield: 6 qt. (6 lt)

Whole butter	3 oz.	90 g
Onion, medium dice	12 oz.	340 g
Celery, medium dice	3 oz.	90 g
Broccoli, chopped	3 lb.	1.4 kg
Chicken velouté sauce, hot	4 qt.	4 lt
Chicken stock, hot	approx. 2 qt.	approx. 2 lt
Heavy cream, hot	24 oz.	700 g
Salt and white pepper	TT	TT
Broccoli florets	8 oz.	250 g

1. Sweat the onions, celery and broccoli in the butter, without browning, until they are nearly tender.

2. Add the velouté sauce. Bring to a simmer and cook until the vegetables are tender, approximately 15 minutes. Skim the surface periodically.

3. Purée the soup, then strain it through a fine china cap or chinois.

4. Return the soup to the stove and thin it to the correct consistency with the hot chicken stock.

5. Bring the soup to a simmer and add the hot cream. Season to taste with salt and white pepper.

6. Garnish with blanched broccoli florets just before service.

VARIATIONS: To make cream of asparagus, cauliflower, corn, pea or spinach soup, substitute an equal amount of the chosen vegetable for the broccoli. If using fresh spinach, precook the leaves slightly before proceeding with the recipe.

◆◆◆

CROUTONS

A crouton is simply a piece of bread that is toasted, sautéed or dried. Two types are often used.

The more familiar ones are small seasoned cubes of bread that are baked or toasted and sprinkled over soups or salads.

A more classic variety is made by sautéing slices of bread in clarified butter or olive oil until brown and crisp. The bread may be rough slices from a baguette or cut into shapes (such as hearts, diamonds or circles) from larger slices. Sautéed croutons have two advantages over the toasted variety: They stay crisp longer after coming in contact with moist foods, and they gain flavor from the butter or olive oil in which they are cooked. Sautéed croutons can be used to decorate the border of a serving dish, as a base for canapés, a garnish for soups, an accompaniment to spreads or caviar or as a base under some meat and game dishes.

Purée Soups

Purée soups are hearty soups made by cooking starchy vegetables or legumes in a stock or broth, then puréeing all or a portion of them to thicken the soup. Purée soups are similar to cream soups in that they both consist of a main ingredient that is first cooked in a liquid, then puréed. The primary difference is that unlike cream soups, which are thickened with starch, purée soups generally do not use additional starch for thickening. Rather, purée soups depend on the starch content of the main ingredient for thickening. Also, purée soups are generally coarser than cream soups and are typically not strained after puréeing. When finishing purée soups with cream, follow the guidelines discussed above for adding cream to cream soups.

Purée soups can be made with dried or fresh beans such as peas, lentils and navy beans, or with any number of vegetables including cauliflower, celery root, turnips and potatoes. Diced potatoes or rice are often used to help thicken vegetable purée soups.

PROCEDURE FOR MAKING PURÉE SOUPS

1. Sweat the mirepoix in butter without browning.
2. Add the cooking liquid.
3. Add the main ingredients and a sachet or bouquet garni.
4. Bring to a boil, reduce to a simmer and cook until all the ingredients are soft enough to purée easily. Remove and discard the sachet or bouquet garni.
5. Reserve a portion of the liquid to adjust the soup's consistency. Purée the rest of the soup by passing it through a food mill, food processor, blender or VCM.
6. Add enough of the reserved liquid to bring the soup to the correct consistency. If the soup is still too thick, add hot stock as needed.
7. Return the soup to a simmer and adjust the seasonings.
8. Add hot cream to the soup if desired.

◆◆◆

RECIPE 11.5

PURÉE OF SPLIT PEA SOUP

Yield: 4 qt. (4 lt)

Bacon, diced	3 oz.	90 g
Mirepoix, medium dice	1 lb.	450 g
Garlic cloves, chopped	2	2
Chicken stock	3 qt.	3 lt
Split peas, washed and sorted	1 lb.	450 g
Ham hocks or meaty ham bones	1-1/2 lb.	650 g
Sachet:		
Bay leaves	2	2
Dried thyme	1/2 tsp.	2 ml
Peppercorns, crushed	1/2 tsp.	2 ml
Salt and pepper	TT	TT
Croutons, sautéed in butter	as needed for garnish	

Render—*to melt and clarify fat.*

1. In a stockpot, **render** the bacon by cooking it slowly and allowing it to release its fat; sweat the mirepoix and garlic in the fat without browning them.

2. Add the chicken stock, peas, ham hocks or bones and sachet. Bring to a boil, reduce to a simmer and cook until the peas are soft, approximately 1 to 1-1/2 hours.

3. Remove the sachet and ham hocks or bones. Pass the soup through a food mill and return it to the stockpot.

4. Remove the meat from the hocks or bones. Cut the meat into a medium dice and add it to the soup.

5. Bring the soup to a simmer and, if necessary, adjust the consistency by adding hot chicken stock. Adjust the seasonings with salt and pepper and serve, garnished with croutons.

VARIATIONS: White beans, yellow peas, and other dried beans can be soaked overnight in water and used instead of split peas.

Adjusting the Consistency of Thick Soups

Cream and purée soups tend to thicken when made in advance and refrigerated. To dilute a portion being reheated, add a small amount of stock, broth, water or milk.

If the soup is too thin, additional roux, beurre manié or cornstarch mixed with cool stock can be used to thicken it. If additional starch is added to thicken the soup it should be used sparingly and the soup should be simmered a few minutes to cook out the starchy flavor. A liaison of egg yolks and heavy cream can be used to thicken cream soups when added richness is also desired. Remember, the soup must not boil after the liaison is added or it may curdle.

OTHER SOUPS

Several popular types of soup do not fit the descriptions of or follow the procedures for clear or thick soups. Soups such as bisques and chowders as well as many cold soups use special methods or a combination of the methods used for clear and thick soups.

Bisques

Traditional bisques are shellfish soups thickened with cooked rice. Today bisques are prepared using a combination of the cream and purée soup procedures. They are generally made from shrimp, lobster or crayfish and are thickened with a roux instead of rice for better stability and consistency.

Much of a bisque's flavor comes from crustacean shells, which are simmered in the cooking liquid, puréed (along with the mirepoix), returned to the cooking liquid and strained after further cooking. Puréeing the shells and returning them to the soup also adds the thickness and grainy texture associated with bisques.

Bisques are enriched with cream, following the procedures for cream soups, and can be finished with butter for additional richness. The garnish should be diced flesh from the appropriate shellfish.

PROCEDURE FOR MAKING BISQUES

1. Caramelize the mirepoix and main flavoring ingredient in fat.
2. Add a tomato product and deglaze with wine.

3. Add the cooking liquid (stock or velouté).

4. Incorporate roux if needed.

5. Simmer, skimming as needed.

6. Strain the soup, reserving the solids and liquid. Purée the solids in a food chopper or processor and return them to the liquid. Return to a simmer.

7. Strain the soup through a fine chinois or a china cap lined with cheesecloth.

8. Return the soup to a simmer and finish with hot cream.

To add even more richness to the bisque, monté au beurre with whole butter or a compound butter such as shrimp or lobster butter just before the soup is served. Also, if desired, add 3 ounces (90 milliliters) of sherry to each gallon (4 liters) of soup just before service.

◆◆◆

RECIPE 11.6

SHRIMP BISQUE

Yield: 4 qt. (4 lt)

Clarified butter	3 oz.	90 g
Mirepoix, small dice	1 lb.	450 g
Shrimp shells and/or lobster or crayfish shells and bodies	2 lb.	1 kg
Garlic cloves, chopped	2	2
Tomato paste	2 oz.	60 g
Brandy	4 oz.	120 g
White wine	12 oz.	350 g
Fish velouté (made with shrimp stock)	4 qt.	4 lt
Sachet:		
Bay leaf	1	1
Dried thyme	1/2 tsp.	2 ml
Peppercorns, crushed	1/2 tsp.	2 ml
Parsley stems	8	8
Heavy cream, hot	1 pt.	500 ml
Salt and white pepper	TT	TT
Cayenne pepper	TT	TT
Shrimp, peeled and deveined	1 lb.	450 g

1. Caramelize the mirepoix and shrimp shells in the butter.

2. Add the garlic and tomato paste and sauté lightly.

3. Add the brandy and flambé.

4. Add the white wine. Deglaze and reduce the liquid by half.

5. Add the velouté and sachet and simmer for approximately 1 hour, skimming occasionally.

6. Strain, discarding the sachet and reserving the liquid and solids. Purée the solids and return them to the liquid. Return to a simmer and cook for 10 minutes.

7. Strain the bisque through a fine chinois or china cap lined with cheesecloth.

8. Return the bisque to a simmer and add the hot cream.

9. Season to taste with salt, white pepper and cayenne pepper.

10. Cook the shrimp and slice or dice them as desired. Garnish each portion of soup with cooked shrimp.

Chowders

Although chowders are usually associated with the eastern United States where fish and clams are plentiful, they are of French origin. Undoubtedly the word *chowder* is derived from the Breton phrase *faire chaudière*, which means to make a fish stew in a caldron. The procedure was probably brought to Nova Scotia by French settlers and later introduced into New England.

Chowders are hearty soups with chunks of the main ingredients (including, virtually always, diced potatoes) and garnishes. With some exceptions (notably, Manhattan clam chowder), chowders contain milk or cream. Although there are thin chowders, most chowders are thickened with roux. The procedures for making chowders are similar to those for making cream soups except that chowders are not puréed and strained before the cream is added.

PROCEDURE FOR MAKING CHOWDERS

1. Render finely diced salt pork over medium heat.
2. Sweat mirepoix in the rendered pork.
3. Add flour to make a roux.
4. Add the liquid.
5. Add the seasoning and flavoring ingredients according to their cooking times.
6. Simmer, skimming as needed.
7. Add milk or cream.

◆◆◆

RECIPE 11.7

NEW ENGLAND STYLE CLAM CHOWDER

Yield: 3 qt. (3 lt)

Canned clams with juice*	2 qt.	2 lt
Water or fish stock	approx. 1-1/2 qt.	approx. 1.5 lt
Potato, small dice	1 lb. 4 oz.	600 g
Salt pork, small dice	8 oz.	250 g
Onion, small dice	1 lb.	500 g
Celery, small dice	8 oz.	250 g
Flour	4 oz.	120 g
Milk	1 qt.	1 lt
Heavy cream	8 oz.	250 g
Salt and pepper	TT	TT
Tabasco sauce	TT	TT
Worcestershire sauce	TT	TT
Fresh thyme	TT	TT

1. Drain the clams, reserving both the clams and their liquid. Add enough water or stock so that the total liquid equals 2 quarts (2 liters).
2. Simmer the potatoes in the clam liquid until nearly cooked through. Strain and reserve the potatoes and the liquid.
3. Render the salt pork without browning it. Add the onions and celery and sweat until tender.
4. Add the flour and cook to make a blond roux.
5. Add the clam liquid to the roux, whisking away any lumps.
6. Simmer for 30 minutes, skimming as necessary.

Continued

7. Bring the milk and cream to a boil and add to the soup.

8. Add the clams and potatoes and season to taste with salt, pepper, Tabasco, Worcestershire and thyme.

* If using fresh clams for the chowder, wash and steam approximately 1/2 bushel of chowder clams in a small amount of water to yield 1-1/4 quarts (1.25 liters) of clam meat. Chop the clams. Strain the liquid through several layers of cheese-cloth to remove any sand that may be present. Add enough water or stock so the total liquid is 2 quarts (2 liters). Continue with the recipe, starting at step 2.

Cold Soups

Cold soups can be as simple as a chilled version of a cream soup or as unique as a cold fruit soup blended with yogurt. Other than the fact that they are cold, cold soups are difficult to classify because many of them use unique or combination preparation methods. Regardless, they are divided here into two categories: cold soups that require cooking and those that do not.

Cooked Cold Soups

Many cold soups are simply a chilled version of a hot soup. For example, consommé madrilène and consommé portugaise are prepared hot and served cold. Vichyssoise, probably the most popular of all cold soups, is a cold version of purée of potato-leek soup. When serving a hot soup cold, there are several considerations:

1. If the soup is to be creamed, add the cream at the last minute. Although curdling is not as much of a problem as it is with hot soups, adding the cream at the last minute helps extend the soup's shelf life.

2. Cold soups should have a thinner consistency than hot soups. To achieve the proper consistency, use less starch if starch is used as the thickener, or use a higher ratio of liquid to main ingredient if the soup is thickened by puréeing. Consistency should be checked and adjusted at service time.

3. Cold dulls the sense of taste, so cold soups require more seasoning than hot ones. Taste the soup just before service and adjust the seasonings as needed.

4. Always serve cold soups as cold as possible.

◆◆◆

RECIPE 11.8

VICHYSSOISE (COLD POTATO-LEEK SOUP)

Yield: 4 qt. (4 lt)

Leek, white part only	2 lb.	1 kg
Whole butter	8 oz.	250 g
Potato, large dice	2 lb.	1 kg
Chicken stock	3-1/2 qt.	3-1/2 lt
Salt and white pepper	TT	TT
Heavy cream	24 oz.	700 g
Chives, snipped	as needed	as needed

1. Split the leeks lengthwise and wash well to remove all sand and grit. Slice them thinly.

2. Sweat the leeks in the butter without browning them.

3. Add the potatoes and chicken stock, season with salt and pepper and bring to a simmer.

4. Simmer until the leeks and potatoes are very tender, approximately 45 minutes.

5. Purée the soup in a food processor, blender or food mill; strain through a fine sieve.

6. Chill the soup well.

7. At service time, incorporate the heavy cream and adjust the seasonings. Serve in chilled bowls, garnished with snipped chives.

Many cooked cold soups use fruit juice (typically apple, grape or orange) as a base and are thickened with cornstarch or arrowroot as well as with puréed fruit. For additional flavor, wine is sometimes used in lieu of a portion of the fruit juice. Cinnamon, ginger and other spices that complement fruit are commonly added, as is lemon or lime juice, which adds acidity as well as flavor. Crème fraîche, yogurt or sour cream can be used as an ingredient or garnish to add richness.

◆◆◆

RECIPE 11.9
CHILLED CHERRY SOUP

Yield: 4 qt. (4 lt)

Cherries, pitted	5 lb.	2.25 kg
Apple juice	approx. 2 qt.	approx. 2 lt
Sachet:		
Cinnamon sticks	2	2
Cloves, whole	4	4
Honey	6 oz.	170 g
Cornstarch	1 oz.	30 g
Lemon juice	TT	TT
Dry champagne or sparkling wine	8 oz.	250 g
Crème fraîche	as needed for garnish	
Toasted almonds	as needed for garnish	

1. Combine the cherries, apple juice, sachet and honey. Bring to a simmer and cook for 30 minutes. Remove the sachet.

2. Dilute the cornstarch with a small amount of cold apple juice. Add it to the soup for thickening. Simmer the soup for 10 minutes to cook out the starchy taste.

3. Purée the soup in a food processor or blender and strain if desired.

4. Chill the soup thoroughly.

5. At service, adjust the seasoning with the lemon juice. Stir in the chilled champagne or sparkling wine and serve garnished with crème fraîche and toasted, slivered almonds.

Uncooked Cold Soups

Some cold soups are not cooked at all. Rather they rely only on puréed fruits or vegetables for thickness, body and flavor. Cold stock is sometimes used to adjust the soup's consistency. Dairy products such as cream, sour cream or crème fraîche are sometimes added to enrich and flavor the soup.

Because uncooked cold soups are never heated, enzymes and bacteria are not destroyed and the soup can spoil quickly. When preparing uncooked cold soups, always prepare small batches as close to service time as possible.

◆◆◆

RECIPE 11.10

Gazpacho

Yield: 4 qt. (4 lt)

Tomato, peeled and diced	2 lb. 8 oz.	1.2 kg
Onion, medium dice	8 oz.	250 g
Green pepper, medium dice	1	1
Red pepper, medium dice	1	1
Cucumber, peeled, seeded, medium dice	1 lb.	500 g
Garlic, minced	1 oz.	30 g
Red wine vinegar	2 oz.	60 g
Lemon juice	2 oz.	60 g
Olive oil	4 oz	120 g
Salt and pepper	TT	TT
Cayenne pepper	TT	TT
Fresh bread crumbs (optional)	3 oz.	90 g
Tomato juice	3 qt.	3 lt
White stock	as needed	as needed
Garnish:		
Tomato, peeled, seeded, small dice	8 oz	250 g
Red pepper, small dice	4 oz.	120 g
Green pepper, small dice	4 oz.	120 g
Yellow pepper, small dice	4 oz.	120 g
Cucumber, peeled, seeded, small dice	3 oz.	90 g
Green onion, sliced fine	2 oz.	60 g
Croutons	as needed	as needed

1. Combine and purée all ingredients except the tomato juice, stock and garnish in a VCM, food processor or blender.
2. Stir in the tomato juice.
3. Adjust the consistency with stock.
4. Stir in the vegetables, the garnishes and adjust the seasonings.
5. Serve in chilled cups or bowls garnished with croutons.

Garnishing Soups

Garnishes can range from a simple sprinkle of chopped parsley on a bowl of cream soup to tiny profiteroles stuffed with foie gras adorning a crystal-clear bowl of consommé. Some soups are so full of attractive, flavorful and colorful foods that are integral parts of the soup (for example, vegetables and chicken in chicken vegetable soup) that no additional garnishes (as either decoration or component) are necessary. In others, the garnish determines the type of soup. For example, a beef broth garnished with cooked barley and diced beef becomes beef barley soup.

Guidelines for Garnishing Soups

Although some soups (particularly consommés) have traditional garnishes, many soups depend on the chef's imagination and the kitchen's inventory for the finishing garnish. The only rules are:

1. The garnish should be attractive.
2. The meats and vegetables used should be neatly cut into an appropriate and uniform shape and size. This is particularly important when garnishing a clear soup such as a consommé, as the consommé's clarity highlights the precise (or imprecise) cuts.
3. The garnish's texture and flavor should complement the soup.
4. Starches and vegetables used as garnishes should be cooked separately, reheated and placed in the soup bowl before the hot soup is added. If they are cooked in the soup, they may cloud or thicken the soup or alter its flavor, texture and seasoning.
5. Garnishes should be cooked just until done; meat and poultry should be tender but not falling apart, vegetables should be firm but not mushy and pasta and rice should maintain their identity. These types of garnishes are usually held on the side and added to the hot soup at the last minute to prevent overcooking.

Garnishing Suggestions

✦ Clear soups—any combination of julienne cuts of the same meat, poultry, fish or vegetable that provides the dominant flavor in the stock or broth, vegetables (cut uniformly into any shape), pasta (flat, small tortellini or tiny ravioli), gnocchi, quenelles, barley, spaetzle, white or wild rice, croutons, crepes, tortillas, or won tons.

✦✦✦
CLASSIC CONSOMMÉS

Many classic consommés are known by their garnishes:

Consommé brunoise—blanched or sautéed brunoise of turnip, leek, celery and onion.

Consommé julienne—blanched or sautéed julienne of carrot, turnip, leek, celery, cabbage and onion.

Consommé paysanne—blanched or sautéed paysanne of leek, turnip, carrot, celery and potato.

Consommé bouquetière—assorted blanched vegetables.

Consommé royale—cooked custard cut into tiny shapes.

Angels' hair consommé—cooked angel hair (vermicelli) pasta.

Consommé with profiteroles—tiny profiteroles (pâte à choux rounds) stuffed with foie gras.

TABLE 11.1   SOUPS, THEIR THICKENING AGENTS AND FINISHES

Category	Type	Thickening Agent or Method	Finish
Clear soups	Broths	None	Assorted garnishes
	Consommés	None	Assorted garnishes
Thick soups	Cream soups	Roux and/or puréeing	Assorted garnishes, cream or béchamel sauce
	Purée soups	Puréeing	Assorted garnishes; cream is optional
Other soups	Bisques	Roux or rice and puréeing	Garnish of main ingredient, cream and/or butter
	Chowders	Roux	Cream
Cold soups	Cooked cold soups	Roux, arrowroot, cornstarch, puréeing, sour cream, yogurt	Assorted garnishes, cream, crème fraîche or sour cream
	Uncooked cold soups	Puréeing	Assorted garnishes, cream, crème fraîche or sour cream

+ Cream soups, hot or cold—toasted slivered almonds, sour cream or crème fraîche, croutons, grated cheese or puff pastry fleurons; cream vegetable soups are usually garnished with slices or florets of the main ingredient.
+ Purée soups—julienne cuts of poultry or ham, sliced sausage, croutons, grated cheese, bacon bits.
+ Any soup—finely chopped fresh herbs, snipped chives, edible flower blossoms or petals, parsley or watercress.

SOUP SERVICE

Preparing Soups in Advance

Most soups can be made ahead of time and reheated as needed for service. To preserve freshness and quality, small batches of soup should be heated as needed throughout the meal service.

Clear soups are quite easy to reheat because there is little danger of scorching. If garnishes are already added to a clear soup, care should be taken not to overcook the garnishes when reheating the soup. All traces of fat should be removed from a consommé's surface before reheating.

Thick soups present more of a challenge. To increase shelf life and reduce the risk of spoilage, cool and refrigerate a thick soup when it is still a base (that is, before it is finished with milk or cream). When needed, carefully reheat the soup base just before service using a heavy-gauge pot over low heat. Stir often to prevent scorching. Then finish the soup (following the guidelines noted above) with boiling milk or cream, a light béchamel sauce or a liaison and adjust the seasonings. Always taste the soup after reheating and adjust the seasonings as needed.

Temperatures

The rule is simple: Serve hot soup hot and cold soup cold. Hot clear soups should be served near boiling; 210°F (99°C) is ideal. Hot cream soups should be served at slightly lower temperatures; 190–200°F (90–93°C) is acceptable. Cold soups should be served at a temperature of 40°F (4°C) or below, and are sometimes presented in special serving pieces surrounded by ice.

CONCLUSION

Soup, often served as the first course, may determine the success or failure of an entire meal. Although a wide variety of ingredients can be used to make both clear and thick soups, including trimmings and leftovers, poor-quality ingredients make poor-quality soups. By using, adapting and combining the basic techniques described in this chapter with different ingredients, you can create an infinite number of new and appetizing hot or cold soups. But exercise good judgment when combining flavors and techniques; they should blend well and complement each other. Moreover, any garnishes that are added should contribute to the appearance and character of the finished soup. And remember, always serve hot soups hot and cold soups cold.

QUESTIONS FOR DISCUSSION

1. What are the differences between a stock and a broth?
2. What are the differences between a beef consommé and a beef-based broth? How are they similar?
3. What are the differences between a cream soup and a purée soup? How are they similar?
4. Create a recipe for veal consommé.
5. Discuss several techniques for serving soup. What can be done to ensure that soups are served at the correct temperature?
6. Explain how and why soups are garnished. Why is it sometimes said that the noodles in a chicken noodle soup are actually a garnish?

ADDITIONAL SOUP RECIPES

RECIPE 11.11

WILD MUSHROOM SOUP WITH FOIE GRAS

NOTE: *This dish appears in the Chapter Opening photograph.*

CHRISTOPHER'S AND CHRISTOPHER'S BISTRO, PHOENIX, AZ
Chef/Owner Christoper Gross

Yield: 8 servings

Port	6 oz.	180 g
Duck stock	2 qt.	2 lt
Chanterelles	4 oz.	120 g
White mushroom caps	4 oz.	120 g
Olive oil	1 Tbsp.	15 ml
Shallots, chopped fine	1 Tbsp.	15 ml
Fresh tarragon or chervil, chopped	3 Tbsp.	45 ml
Tomato concasse	4 oz.	120 g
Foie gras, sinew and veins trimmed	12 oz.	350 g
Fresh truffle (winter or summer)	1	1
White truffle oil	1 tsp.	5 ml

1. Reduce the port to 2 ounces (60 grams). Bring the stock to a boil and add the port and any mushroom stems or peels. Simmer 5 minutes; strain and reserve in a warm place.
2. Trim the stems from the chanterelles and sauté the caps with the white mushroom caps in the olive oil. Add the shallots and cook until they become soft and translucent.
3. Place the mushrooms, tomato concasse and tarragon or chervil in the bottom of eight shallow soup bowls.
4. Portion the foie gras into 8 slices and sear briefly in a very hot, dry pan.
5. Place a slice of the foie gras on top of the mushrooms in the center of each bowl.
6. Julienne the truffle and arrange a portion in each bowl.
7. Pour the hot soup into the bowls and add a drop of truffle oil to each bowl.

◆◆◆

RECIPE 11.12

WILD MUSHROOMS AND VEAL SOUP

Yield: 1 qt. (1 lt)

Garlic, minced	2 tsp.	10 ml
Olive oil	4 oz.	120 g
Assorted wild mushrooms, such as		
shiitake, oyster, cèpes and morels	8 oz.	250 g
Brown veal stock	24 oz.	700 g
Fresh parsley, minced	2 Tbsp.	30 ml
Fresh mint, minced	4 Tbsp.	60 ml
Salt and pepper	TT	TT
French bread croutons	as needed for garnish	
Fresh parsley, chopped fine	as needed for garnish	

1. Briefly sauté the garlic in the olive oil. Add the mushrooms and cook until tender and the liquid has evaporated.
2. Add the veal broth, parsley and mint; simmer for 15 minutes.
3. Place one crouton in each soup bowl. Ladle in the soup and garnish with finely chopped parsley.

◆◆◆

RECIPE 11.13

CHICKEN SOUP WITH MATZO BALLS

MATZO BALLS

Yield: 48 balls

Eggs	4	4
Water	2 oz.	60 g
Chicken fat or butter, softened	2 oz.	60 g
Matzo meal	4 oz.	120 g
Salt and white pepper	TT	TT

1. Beat the eggs with the water. Stir in the fat.
2. Add matzo meal, salt and pepper. The batter should be as thick as mashed potatoes.
3. Chill for at least 1 hour.
4. Bring 2 quarts of water to a gentle boil. Using a #70 portion scoop, shape the batter into balls. Carefully drop each ball into the hot water. Cover and simmer until fully cooked, approximately 30 minutes. Remove matzo balls from the water and serve in hot chicken soup.

RICH CHICKEN BROTH

Yield: 2 gal. (8 lt)

Chicken pieces	8–10 lb.	4–4.4 kg
Chicken stock	10 qt.	10 lt

Mirepoix	1 lb.	500 g
Sachet:		
Bay leaf	1	1
Dried thyme	1/2 tsp.	2 ml
Peppercorns, crushed	1/2 tsp.	2 ml
Parsley stems	10	10
Salt and pepper	TT	TT
Fresh Parsley, chopped	as needed for garnish	

1. Simmer the chicken in the stock for 2 hours, skimming as necessary.
2. Add the mirepoix and sachet. Simmer for another hour.
3. Strain and degrease the broth. Adjust seasonings.
4. Bring to a boil at service time. Portion into heated bowls, garnish with one or two matzo balls and chopped parsley.

═══════════ ◆◆◆ ═══════════

RECIPE 11.14
MOROCCAN HARIRA
(LAMB, CHICKEN AND LENTIL SOUP)

Yield: 4 qt. (4 lt)

Olive oil	5 oz.	140 g
Stewing lamb, cubed	2 lb. 8 oz.	1.2 kg
Chicken pieces	3–4 lb.	1.3–1.8 kg
Garlic cloves	5	5
Onion, chopped fine	2 lb.	1 kg
Chickpeas, canned	8 oz.	250 g
Chicken stock	5 qt.	5 lt
Turmeric	1-1/2 tsp.	7 ml
Ginger, ground	1-1/2 tsp.	7 ml
Coriander	1-1/2 tsp.	7 ml
Cinnamon	1-1/2 tsp.	7 ml
Tomatoes, canned, chopped	2 lb. 8 oz.	1.2 kg
Lentils, washed	9 oz.	250 g
Rice	4 oz.	120 g
Salt and pepper	TT	TT
Parsley, chopped	5 Tbsp.	75 ml
Whole eggs, beaten	5	5
Lemon juice	5 Tbsp.	75 ml

1. Heat the oil in a large, heavy sauté pan. Lightly brown the lamb, then transfer it to a large saucepot. Repeat for the chicken, garlic and onions.
2. Add the chickpeas, stock, spices, tomatoes and lentils. Cover and simmer for 40 minutes.
3. Add the rice and simmer 20 minutes longer.

Continued

4. Remove the chicken pieces from the soup. Skin them and remove the meat. Dice the meat and return it to the soup.

5. Adjust the seasonings, add the parsley and return to a simmer.

6. Immediately before service, whisk the eggs and lemon juice together. Then slowly pour them into the soup, stirring to create strands of egg throughout the soup.

7. Serve in heated bowls with lemon wedges and harissa on the side.

HARISSA

Yield: 6 Tbsp. (90 ml)

Dried chile peppers, crushed	1 Tbsp.	15 ml
Cayenne pepper	1 Tbsp.	15 ml
Cumin, ground	2 tsp.	10 ml
Caraway seeds	2 tsp.	10 ml
Garlic cloves	2	2
Olive oil	3 Tbsp.	45 ml
Salt	1 tsp.	5 ml

1. Grind the spices and garlic together in a mortar and pestle, blender or spice grinder.

2. Heat the oil. Stir in the spices and salt and cook over a low flame, stirring constantly, for 3 minutes.

◆◆◆

RECIPE 11.15

FRENCH ONION SOUP

Yield: 4 qt. (4 lt)

Yellow onion, thinly sliced	10 lb.	4.4 kg
Clarified butter	8 oz.	250 g
Beef stock	4 qt.	4 lt
Chicken stock	4 qt.	4 lt
Fresh thyme	1/2 oz.	14 g
Salt and pepper	TT	TT
Sherry	8 oz.	250 g
Toasted French bread slices	as needed for garnish	
Gruyère cheese, grated	as needed for garnish	

1. Sauté the onions in the butter over low heat. Carefully caramelize them thoroughly without burning.

2. Deglaze the pan with 8 ounces (250 grams) of the beef stock. Cook au sec. Repeat this process until the onions are a very dark, even brown.

3. Add the remaining beef stock, the chicken stock and thyme.

4. Bring to a simmer and cook 20 minutes to develop flavor. Adjust the seasonings and add the sherry.

5. Serve in warm bowls. Top each portion with a slice of toasted French bread and a thick layer of cheese. Place under the broiler or salamander until the cheese is melted and lightly browned.

♦♦♦

RECIPE 11.16

MINESTRONE

Minestrone is a rich vegetable soup of Italian heritage. Northern Italian versions are made with beef stock, butter, rice and ribbon-shaped pasta. Southern Italian versions, such as the one given here, contain tomatoes, garlic, olive oil and tubular-shaped pasta. The vegetables should be fresh and varied. Substitute or change those listed as necessary to reflect the season.

Yield: 2 gal. (8 lt)

Dry white beans	1 lb.	450 g
Olive oil	2 Tbsp.	30 ml
Onion, diced	10 oz.	300 g
Garlic cloves, minced	2	2
Celery, diced	1 lb.	450 g
Carrot, diced	12 oz.	340 g
Zucchini, diced	1 lb.	450 g
Green beans, cut in		
1/2-inch (1.25 cm) pieces	10 oz.	300 g
Cabbage, diced	1 lb.	450 g
Vegetable stock	5 qt.	5 lt
Tomato, concasse	1 lb.	450 g
Tomato paste, low-sodium	12 oz.	340 g
Fresh oregano, chopped	1 Tbsp.	15 ml
Fresh basil, chopped	2 Tbsp.	30 ml
Fresh chervil, chopped	1 Tbsp.	15 ml
Fresh parsley, chopped	2 Tbsp.	30 ml
Salt and pepper	TT	TT
Elbow macaroni, cooked	4 oz.	120 g
Parmesan cheese, grated	as needed for garnish (optional)	

1. Soak the beans in cold water overnight, then drain.
2. Cover the beans with water and simmer until tender, about 40 minutes.
3. Sauté the onions in the oil. Add garlic, celery and carrots and cook for three minutes.
4. Add the remaining vegetables, one type at a time, cooking each briefly.
5. Add the stock, tomatoes and tomato paste. Cover and simmer for 2-1/2–3 hours.
6. Stir in the chopped herbs and season to taste with salt and pepper.
7. Add the drained beans and cooked macaroni.
8. Bring the soup to a simmer and simmer 15 minutes. Serve in warm bowls, garnished with parmesan cheese.

Nutritional values per 6-ounce (180 grams) serving without cheese:

Calories	79	Protein	2 g	
Calories from fat	21%	Vitamin A	2764 IU	
Total fat	2 g	Vitamin C	14 mg	
Saturated fat	0 g	Sodium	923 mg	
Cholesterol	0 mg			

◆◆◆

RECIPE 11.17

SEAFOOD BOUILLABAISSE

GOTHAM BAR AND GRILL, NEW YORK, NY
Chef/Owner Alfred Portale

Yield: 8 Servings

Olive oil	as needed	as needed
Spanish onion, julienne	10 oz.	300 g
Fennel bulb, small dice, reserve tops for stock	1	1
Leek, julienne	3 oz.	90 g
Cayenne Pepper	TT	TT
Garlic, chopped	1 oz.	30 g
Fresh tomato, chopped	2 qt.	2 lt
Fresh thyme	8 sprigs	8 sprigs
Fish Stock (recipe follows)	3 qt.	3 lt
Saffron	1 pinch	1 pinch
Salt and white pepper	TT	TT
Lobsters, 1 lb. 8 oz. (680 g) each	2	2
Mussels	24	24
Littleneck clams, scrubbed	24	24
Large shrimp, peeled, reserve shells	6	6
Sea scallops	1 lb. 8 oz.	680 g
Squid	1 lb. 8 oz.	680 g
Pernod	6 oz.	170 g
New potatoes, small	16	16
Parsley, chopped	3 Tbsp.	45 ml
Rouille (recipe follows)		

1. In a pot large enough to hold all the shellfish comfortably, heat the olive oil. Add the onions, fennel, leeks and cayenne pepper; cook for 15 minutes over low heat. Add the garlic and continue cooking for one minute.
2. Add the tomatoes, thyme, 3 quarts (3 liters) of fish stock and saffron. Bring to a boil, reduce the heat and simmer until the stock is slightly reduced and intensely flavored. Adjust the seasonings.

3. While the soup is cooking, cook the lobsters in rapidly boiling salted water for 6 minutes. When cool enough to handle, shell them over a bowl to catch juices. Dice the meat and reserve.

4. To serve, bring the soup to a boil. Add the mussels and clams and cook for 2–3 minutes. Add the shrimp and scallops and cook until the mussels open.

5. Add the cooked lobster and reserved lobster juices. Add the squid. Heat thoroughly. Add the Pernod to taste.

6. Steam the potatoes, and arrange in the serving dish. Arrange the seafood over the potatoes.

7. Sprinkle the bouillabaisse with chopped parsley and serve with the rouille.

FISH STOCK

Yield: 3 qt. (3 lt)

Spanish onion, medium	1	1
Fennel top, chopped	1	1
Celery stalk	1	1
Tomatoes, large	3	3
Olive oil	as needed	as needed
Garlic cloves	10	10
Fish bones	3 lb.	1.3 kg
Shrimp shells	6	6
Fresh thyme	2 sprigs	2 sprigs
Orange peel	from 1 orange	from 1 orange
Coriander seed	1 Tbsp.	15 ml
White pepper, cracked	1 Tbsp.	15 ml
Bay leaves	2	2
Dry white wine	26 oz.	750 ml
Water	3 qt.	3 lt

1. Coarsely chop the vegetables and tomatoes. Heat the olive oil in a stock-pot. Add the onions, fennel tops, celery and tomatoes. Sauté for 15 minutes over low heat.

2. Add the garlic. Cook an additional 5 minutes.

3. Add the fish bones, shrimp shells, seasonings and white wine. Raise the heat and reduce the wine for 20 minutes.

4. Add 3 quarts (3 liters)of water. Simmer slowly for 45 minutes. Strain and reserve. This should be made one or two days in advance.

ROUILLE

White bread, crust removed	1 slice	1 slice
Heavy cream	2 oz.	60 g
Egg yolks	3	3
Garlic cloves, minced	6	6
Salt and white pepper	TT	TT
Olive oil	6 oz.	180 g
Cayenne pepper	TT	TT

1. In a bowl, soften the bread in the cream. Whisk in the egg yolks. Add the garlic, salt and white pepper.

2. Add the olive oil in a steady stream. Whisk constantly until the rouille is thick and fluffy. Season with cayenne pepper.

3. Serve in a separate bowl to drizzle over soup.

◆◆◆

RECIPE 11.18
CHEDDAR AND LEEK SOUP

Yield: 2 qt. (2 lt)

Whole butter	1 oz.	30 g
Mirepoix, chopped fine	8 oz.	250 g
Leek, chopped fine	8 oz.	250 g
Flour	2 oz.	60 g
Chicken stock	1-1/2 qt.	1-1/2 lt
Sachet:		
Bay leaf	1	1
Dried thyme	1/4 tsp.	1 ml
Peppercorns, crushed	1/4 tsp.	1 ml
Dry white wine or flat beer	4 oz.	120 g
Half-and-half	4 oz.	120 g
Cheddar cheese, grated	1 lb.	500 g
Salt	TT	TT
Cayenne pepper	TT	TT
Fresh parsley, chopped	as needed for garnish	
Croutons	as needed for garnish	

1. Sweat mirepoix and leeks in the butter until tender.
2. Stir in the flour and cook to make a blond roux.
3. Add stock and sachet and bring to a boil. Add wine (or beer), half-and-half and cheese. Simmer for 1 hour.
4. Strain; adjust seasonings with salt and cayenne pepper. Thin with additional warm half-and-half, if necessary.
5. Serve in warm bowls, garnished with parsley and croutons.

◆◆◆

RECIPE 11.19
SPELT SOUP

REX IL RISTORANTE, LOS ANGELES, CA
Executive Chef Odette Fada

Yield: 6 Servings

Extra-virgin olive oil	5 Tbsp.	75 ml
Mirepoix	10 oz.	300 g
Shallot, minced	1	1
Leek, small, chopped fine	1	1
Garlic cloves, minced	2	2
Bay leaves	2	2
Dried rosemary	1/2 tsp.	2 ml
Dried thyme	1 tsp.	5 ml
Spelt (whole, toasted wheat berries)	4 oz.	120 g
Vegetable stock	1-1/2 qt.	1-1/2 lt
Salt and pepper	TT	TT
Prosciutto	2 slices	2 slices
Spinach leaves	10	10

1. Sauté the mirepoix, shallot, leek, garlic and herbs in 3 tablespoons (45 milliliters) olive oil for 5 minutes.
2. Add the spelt and stock; simmer for 50 minutes. Remove the bay leaves.
3. Purée the soup, adding more stock to thin if necessary. Adjust seasonings.
4. Julienne the prosciutto. Cut the spinach in a chiffonade.
5. Serve the soup in hot bowls. Top each portion with some of the prosciutto and spinach and 1 teaspoon (5 milliliters) of olive oil.

◆◆◆

RECIPE 11.20

SOUTHWESTERN BLACK BEAN SOUP

Yield: 4 qt. (4 lt)

Dried black beans, soaked	1 lb.	500 g
Vegetable stock or water	5 qt.	5 lt
Sachet:		
Bay leaves	2	2
Dried thyme	1/2 tsp.	2 ml
Peppercorns, cracked	10	10
Canola oil	1 Tbsp.	15 ml
Onion, diced	4 oz.	120 g
Garlic cloves, minced	2	2
Anaheim chiles, diced	1 oz.	30 g
Jalapeño or Serrano chiles, minced	1 Tbsp.	15 ml
Cumin, ground	1 tsp.	5 ml
Coriander, ground	1 tsp.	5 ml
Dried oregano	1 tsp.	5 ml
Salt and pepper	TT	TT
Lime wedges	as needed for garnish	
Cilantro	as needed for garnish	

1. Combine the beans and stock or water and bring to a simmer. Add the sachet.
2. Sauté the onions, garlic and chiles in the oil. Add to the saucepot.
3. Stir in the cumin, coriander and oregano.
4. Simmer the soup, uncovered, approximately 2–3 hours. The beans should be very soft, just beginning to fall apart. Add additional water or stock if necessary.
5. Puree about half of the soup, then stir it back into the remaining soup. Season to taste with salt and black pepper.
6. Serve in warmed bowls garnished with lime wedges and chopped cilantro.

Nutritional Values per 6-ounce (180 gram) serving:

Calories	81	Protein	2 g
Calories from fat	31%	Vitamin A	302 IU
Total fat	3 g	Vitamin C	3 mg
Saturated fat	1 g	Sodium	1804 mg
Cholesterol	0 mg		

<hr>

♦♦♦

RECIPE 11.21

ROASTED CORN CHOWDER

Yield: 1 qt. (1 lt)

Corn, unshucked	10 ears	10 ears
Milk, warmed	3 pt.	1500 ml
Salt pork, small dice	4 oz.	120 g
Celery, small dice	5 oz.	150 g
Onion, small dice	10 oz.	300 g
Garlic cloves, minced	4	4
Flour	2 oz.	60 g
Cream, warmed	4 oz.	120 g
Worcestershire sauce	1 Tbsp.	15 ml
Fresh thyme	1 tsp.	5 ml
Nutmeg, ground	TT	TT
Salt and white pepper	TT	TT
Parsley, chopped fine	as needed for garnish	

1. Roast the ears of corn, in their husks, in a 400°F (200°C) oven for 45 minutes. Cool, shuck the corn and cut off the kernels. Purée half the corn kernels in a blender, adding a small amount of milk if necessary.
2. Render the salt pork. Add the celery, onions and garlic and sauté lightly.
3. Stir in the flour and cook to make a blond roux.
4. Add the remaining warm milk and bring to a simmer.
5. Add the puréed corn and the remaining corn kernels. Simmer 10 minutes.
6. Add the warm cream; adjust the seasonings with Worcestershire sauce, thyme, nutmeg, salt and white pepper.
7. Serve in warm bowls garnished with chopped parsley.

♦♦♦

RECIPE 11.22

CHICKEN AND SAUSAGE GUMBO

Gumbo, a thick, spicy stew, is traditional fare in the delta region of the American South. Gumbo is usually made with poultry, fish, shellfish or sausage and is thickened with dark roux. Okra or filé powder (ground sassafras leaves) may also be added for thickening. Filé powder is sometimes added at the time of service for additional flavor. Gumbo is traditionally served over white rice.

Yield: 3 qt. (3 lt)

Chicken pieces	3–4 lb.	1.3–1.8 kg
Flour	as needed	as needed
Onion powder	as needed	as needed
Salt	as needed	as needed
Cayenne pepper	as needed	as needed
Vegetable oil	8 oz.	250 g
Flour	4 oz.	120 g
Onion, medium dice	6 oz.	170 g
Celery, medium dice	3 oz.	90 g
Green bell pepper, medium dice	6 oz.	170 g

Garlic, minced	1 tsp.	5 ml
Okra, sliced and blanched	5 oz.	140 g
Chicken stock, hot	2 qt.	2 lt
Jalapeño pepper, minced	1 tsp.	5 ml
Dried thyme	1/2 tsp.	2 ml
Dried oregano	1 tsp.	5 ml
Tomato paste	4 oz.	120 g
Andouille sausage	8 oz.	250 g
Filé powder, optional	as needed	as needed
White rice, boiled	as needed	as needed

1. Dredge the chicken in flour seasoned with onion powder, salt and cayenne pepper.
2. Pan-fry in the oil until done; drain.
3. Degrease the pan, reserving 4 ounces (120 grams) of the oil.
4. Add the flour to the pan and cook to make a very dark brown roux.
5. Add the onions, celery, green pepper and garlic and sauté briefly. Add the okra.
6. Add the chicken stock. Stir in the jalapeños, thyme, oregano and tomato paste. Simmer uncovered for 30 minutes.
7. Bone the cooked chicken and cut the meat into 1/2-inch (1.2 cm) pieces.
8. Slice the sausage on a diagonal into thin pieces and sauté. Remove and drain.
9. Add the chicken and sausage pieces to the gumbo. Adjust seasoning and simmer 30 minutes.
10. If filé powder is used, stir 1–2 teaspoons (5–10 milliliters) into each portion at service time.
11. Serve ladled over bowls of white rice.

◆◆◆

RECIPE 11.23

FRESH PEACH AND YOGURT SOUP

Yield: 2 qt. (2 lt)

Fresh peaches	4 lb.	1.8 kg
Dry white wine	24 oz.	700 g
Honey	4 oz.	120 g
Lemon juice	2 oz.	60 g
Cinnamon, ground	1/4 tsp.	1 ml
Plain yogurt	8 oz.	225 g
Heavy cream	TT	TT
Pistachios, finely chopped	as needed for garnish	

1. Pit and coarsely chop the peaches without peeling. Place in a nonreactive saucepan. Add wine, honey and lemon juice. Cover and simmer for 30 minutes.
2. Purée the peach mixture in a blender. Strain and chill.
3. Stir in cinnamon, yogurt and heavy cream.
4. Chill thoroughly. Serve in chilled bowls, garnished with finely chopped pistachio nuts.

PRINCIPLES OF MEAT COOKERY

After studying this chapter you will be able to:

◆ understand the structure and composition of meats
◆ understand meat inspection and grading practices
◆ purchase meats appropriate for your needs
◆ store meats properly
◆ prepare meats for cooking
◆ apply various cooking methods to meats

*M*eats—*beef, veal, lamb and pork—often consume the largest portion of your food purchasing dollar. In this chapter we discuss how to protect your investment. You will learn how to determine the quality of meat, how to purchase meat in the form that best suits your needs and how to store it. We also discuss several of the dry-heat, moist-heat and combination cooking methods introduced in Chapter 9, Principles of Cooking, and how they can best be used so that a finished meat item is appealing to both the eye and palate. Although each of the cooking methods is illustrated with a single beef, veal, lamb or pork recipe, the analysis is intended to apply to all meats.*

In Chapters 13 through 16 you will learn about the specific cuts of beef, veal, lamb and pork typically used in food service operations, as well as some basic butchering procedures. Recipes using these cuts and applying the various cooking methods are included at the end of each of those chapters.

MUSCLE COMPOSITION

The carcasses of cattle, sheep, hogs and furred game animals consist mainly of edible lean muscular tissue, fat, connective tissue and bones. They are divided into large cuts called **primals**. Primal cuts are rarely cooked; rather, they are usually reduced to **subprimal cuts** which, in turn, can be cooked as is or used to produce **fabricated cuts**. For example, the beef primal known as a short loin can be divided into subprimals including the strip loin. The strip loin can be fabricated into other cuts including New York steaks. The primals, subprimals and fabricated cuts of beef, veal, lamb and pork are discussed in Chapters 13 through 16, respectively; game is discussed in Chapter 18.

Muscle tissue gives meat its characteristic appearance; the amount of connective tissue determines the meat's tenderness. Muscle tissue is approximately 72% water, 20% protein, 7% fat and 1% minerals. A single muscle is composed of many bundles of muscle cells or fibers held together by connective tissue. The thickness of the cells, the size of the cell bundles and the connective tissues holding them together form the grain of the meat and determine the meat's texture. When the fiber bundles are small, the meat has a fine grain and texture. Grain also refers to the direction in which the muscle fibers travel. When an animal fattens, some of the water and proteins in the lean muscle tissue are replaced with fat, which appears as **marbling**.

Connective tissue forms the walls of the long muscle cells and binds them into bundles. It surrounds the muscle as a membrane and also appears as the tendons and ligaments that attach the muscles to the bone. Most connective tissue is composed of either collagen or **elastin**. Collagen breaks down into gelatin and water when cooked using moist heat. Elastin, on the other hand, will not break down under normal cooking conditions. Because elastin remains stringy and tough, tendons and ligaments should be trimmed away before meat is cooked.

Primal cuts—*the primary divisions of muscle, bone and connective tissue produced by the initial butchering of the carcass.*

Subprimal cuts—*the basic cuts produced from each primal.*

Fabricated cuts—*individual portions cut from a subprimal.*

Marbling—*whitish streaks of inter- and intra-muscular fat.*

Subcutaneous fat—*the fat layer between the hide and muscles, also known as **exterior fat**.*

Elastin—*a protein found in connective tissues, particularly ligaments and tendons; it often appears as the white or silver covering on meats known as **silverskin**.*

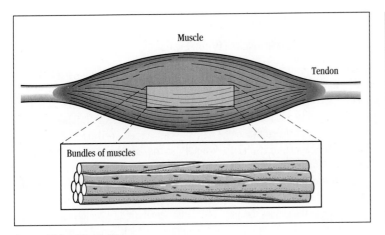

FIGURE 12.1   *Muscle Tissue*

FIGURE 12.2   *Crosscut of a Bundle of Muscle Fibers*

Connective tissue develops primarily in the frequently used muscles. Therefore, cuts of meat from the shoulder (also known as the chuck), which the animal uses constantly, tend to be tougher than those from the back (also known as the loin), which are used less frequently. As an animal ages, the collagen present within the muscles becomes more resistant to breaking down through moist heat cooking. Therefore, the meat of an older animal tends to be tougher than that of a younger one. Generally, the tougher the meat, the more flavorful it is.

Butcher—*to slaughter and dress or fabricate animals for consumption.*

Dress—*to trim or otherwise prepare an animal carcass for consumption.*

Fabricate—*to cut a larger portion of raw meat (for example, a primal or subprimal), poultry or fish into smaller portions.*

Carve—*to cut cooked meat or poultry into portions.*

NUTRITION

Although nutritional content of beef, veal, pork and lamb differs, generally, all are high in protein, saturated fats and cholesterol. See Table 12.1. Consumed in moderate quantities, however, meat can be part of a healthful diet.

TABLE 12.1   NUTRITIONAL VALUES OF MEATS

For 1 ounce (28 grams) Uncooked Lean Meat	Kcal	Protein (g)	Total Fat (g)	Saturated Fat (g)	Cholesterol (mg)	Sodium (mg)
Beef—brisket	94	4.6	8.2	3.4	22	18
Beef—T-bone steak	77	5.0	6.2	2.5	19	14
Beef—ground lean	75	5.0	5.9	2.4	21	20
Veal—chop	46	5.4	2.6	1.1	23	25
Veal—ground leg and shoulder	41	5.5	1.9	0.8	23	23
Lamb—leg	36	5.8	1.3	0.5	18	18
Lamb—chop	106	4.1	9.8	4.3	22	16
Pork—spareribs	81	4.9	6.7	2.7	22	21
Pork—shoulder (picnic)	40	5.6	1.8	0.6	18	23

The Encyclopedia of Food Values by Corrine T. Netzer, 1992.

INSPECTION AND GRADING OF MEATS

Inspection

FIGURE 12.3 *USDA Inspection Stamp for Whole Carcasses*

All meat produced for public consumption in the United States is subject to USDA inspection. Inspections ensure that products are processed under strict sanitary guidelines and are wholesome and fit for human consumption. Inspections do not indicate a meat's quality or tenderness, however. Whole carcasses of beef, pork, lamb and veal are labeled with a round stamp identifying the slaughterhouse. See Figure 12.3. The stamp shown in Figure 12.4 is used for fabricated or processed meats and is found either on the product or its packaging.

Grading

FIGURE 12.4 *USDA Inspection Stamp for Fabricated or Processed Meats*

USDA grading provides a voluntary, uniform system by which producers, distributors and consumers can measure differences in the quality of meats and make price/quality comparisons. There are two parts to this grading system: quality grades and yield grades.

Quality grades, established in 1927, are a guide to the eating qualities of meat: its tenderness, juiciness and flavor. Based on an animal's age and the meat's color, texture and degree of marbling, the USDA quality grades are:

◆ Beef—USDA Prime, Choice, Select, Standard, Commercial, Utility, Cutter and Canner
◆ Veal—USDA Prime, Choice, Good, Standard, Utility
◆ Lamb—USDA Prime, Choice, Good, Utility
◆ Pork—USDA No. 1, No. 2, No. 3, Utility

USDA Prime meats are produced in limited quantities for use in the finest restaurants, hotels and gourmet markets. They are well marbled and have thick coverings of firm fat.

USDA Choice meat is the most commonly used grade in quality food service operations and retail markets. Choice meat is well marbled (but with less fat than Prime) and will produce a tender and juicy product.

FIGURE 12.5 *Grade Stamp for USDA Prime*

FIGURE 12.6 *Grade Stamp for USDA Choice*

Although lacking the flavor and tenderness of the higher grades, beef graded USDA Select or USDA Standard, and lamb and veal graded USDA Good, are also used in food service operations and retail outlets.

The lower grades of beef, lamb and veal are usually used for processed, ground or manufactured items such as meat patties or canned meat products.

Yield grades, established in 1965, measure the amount of usable meat (as opposed to fat and bones) on a carcass and provide a uniform method of identifying cutability differences among carcasses. Yield grades apply only to beef and lamb and appear in a shield similar to that used for the quality grade stamp. The shields are numbered from 1 to 5, with number 1 representing the greatest yield and number 5 the smallest. Beef and lamb can be graded for either quality or yield or both.

Grading is a voluntary program. Many processors, purveyors and retailers (especially pork and veal producers) develop and use their own labeling systems to provide quality assurance information. These private systems do not necessarily apply the USDA's standards.

♦♦♦

A HISTORY OF MEAT SAFETY MEASURES

Ancient times: The biblical books of Exodus, Leviticus and Deuteronomy set forth strict instructions about the kinds of animals that should be eaten and how they should be slaughtered.

13–14th centuries: The first laws regarding meat hygiene were enacted in Florence (Italy). They required butchers to be licensed and to renew their licenses annually, prohibited misrepresentations, substitutions and unsanitary practices; and provided for inspections.

1706: New France (Canada) enacted the first meat inspection laws in North America. They required butchers to notify authorities when animals were to be slaughtered so that the meat could be inspected. Farmers were required to certify that animals destined for slaughter were healthy.

1880s: During this period of rising American meat exports, rumors circulated in Europe that American beef was diseased. Partially to allay these fears, Congress enacted laws providing for final product inspection upon the request of a buyer, seller or exporter.

1891 and 1895: United States meat inspection laws were strengthened. They did not, however, establish a national meat inspection system.

1906: Fueled in part by Upton Sinclair's novel *The Jungle*, in which he describes the horrendous working and sanitary conditions in Chicago slaughterhouses, public pressure persuaded Congress to pass the Comprehensive Meat Inspection Act. The Act strengthened requirements for sanitary conditions in packinghouses and required inspection of meat sold in interstate commerce.

1938: National legislation prohibited on-the-farm slaughter of animals and restricted commercial slaughter operations to packing plants.

1967: The Wholesome Meat Act enabled the USDA to regulate transporters, processors of meat byproducts, cold storage warehouses and animal food manufacturers. Hygiene requirements for imported meats were toughened and inspection of all animals before slaughter became mandatory.

1978: The Humane Methods of Slaughter Act amended previous laws to require that humane methods be used when slaughtering livestock.

Present: Meat inspection has been administered by the USDA's Food Safety and Inspection Service (FSIS) since 1981. The current deregulatory trend places heightened quality-control responsibility on the management of slaughter facilities. This reflects the belief that the wholesomeness of the final product is the responsibility of both industry and government.

═══ ◆◆◆ ═══

A TENDER HISTORY

In *Food in History*, Reay Tannahill suggests that prehistoric hunters developed weapons and stealth tactics in order to kill their quarry without alerting it to danger and provoking fright, fight or flight. She notes that muscle tissues from animals that die placidly contain glycogen. At death, glycogen breaks down into various substances including lactic acid, a natural preservative. Animals experiencing fright, fight or flight just before death, however, use up their glycogen. Tannahill theorizes that prehistoric hunters recognized and responded to what science much later confirmed: Meat from animals that die peacefully is sweeter and more tender.

Vacuum packaging—*a food preservation method in which fresh or cooked food is placed in an airtight container (usually plastic). Virtually all air is removed from the container through a vacuum process, and the container is then sealed.*

AGING MEATS

When animals are slaughtered their muscles are soft and flabby. Within 6 to 24 hours rigor mortis sets in, causing the muscles to contract and stiffen. Rigor mortis dissipates within 48 to 72 hours under refrigerated conditions. All meats should be allowed to rest, or age, long enough for rigor mortis to dissipate completely. Meats that have not been aged long enough for rigor mortis to dissipate, or that have been frozen during this period, are known as "green meats." They will be very tough and flavorless when cooked.

Typically, initial aging takes place while the meat is being transported from the slaughterhouse to the supplier or food service operation. Beef and lamb are sometimes aged for longer periods to increase their tenderness and flavor characteristics. Pork is not aged further because its high fat content turns rancid easily, and veal does not have enough fat to protect it during an extended aging period.

Wet Aging

Today, most pre-portioned or precut meats are packaged and shipped in vacuum-sealed plastic packages (sometimes known generically by the manufacturer's trade name, Cryovac®). Wet aging is the process of storing vacuum-packaged meats under refrigeration for up to six weeks. This allows natural enzymes and microorganisms time to break down connective tissue, which tenderizes and flavors the meat. As this chemical process takes place, the meat develops an unpleasant odor that is released when the package is opened and dissipates in a few minutes.

Dry Aging

Dry aging is the process of hanging fresh meats in an environment of controlled temperature, humidity and air flow for up to six weeks. This allows enzymes and microorganisms to break down connective tissues. Dry aging is actually the beginning of the natural decomposition process. Dry aged meats can lose from 5% to 20% of their weight through moisture evaporation. They can also develop mold, which adds flavor but must be trimmed off later. Moisture loss combined with additional trimming can substantially increase the cost of dry aged meats. Dry aged meats are generally available only through smaller distributors and specialty butchers.

PURCHASING AND STORING MEATS

Several factors determine the cuts of meat your food service operation should use:

1. Menu—The menu identifies the types of cooking methods used. If meats are to be broiled, grilled, roasted, sautéed or fried, more tender cuts should be used. If they are to be stewed or braised, flavorful cuts with more connective tissue can be used.

2. Menu price—Cost constraints may prevent an operation from using the best-quality meats available. Generally, the more tender the meat, the more expensive it is. But the most expensive cuts are not always the best choice for a particular cooking method. For example, a beef tenderloin is one of

the most expensive cuts of beef. Although excellent grilled, it will not necessarily produce a better braised dish than the fattier brisket.

3. Quality—Often, several cuts of meat can be used for a specific dish, so each food service operation should develop its own quality specifications.

Purchasing Meats

Once you have identified the cuts of meat your operation needs, you must determine the forms in which they will be bought. Meats are purchased in a variety of forms: as large as an entire carcass that must be further fabricated or as small as an individual cut (known as portion control or P.C.) ready to cook and serve. You should consider the following when deciding how to purchase meats:

1. Employee skills: Do your employees have the skills necessary to reduce large pieces of meat to the desired cuts?
2. Menu: Can you use the variety of bones, meat and trimmings that result from fabricating large cuts into individual portions?
3. Storage: Do you have ample refrigeration and freezer space so that you can be flexible in the way you purchase your meats?
4. Cost: Considering labor costs and trim usage, is it more economical to buy larger cuts of meat or P.C. units?

IMPS/NAMP

The USDA publishes Institutional Meat Purchasing Specifications (IMPS) describing products customarily purchased in the food service industry. IMPS identifications are illustrated and described in *The Meat Buyers Guide*, published by the National Association of Meat Purveyors (NAMP). The IMPS/NAMP system is a widely accepted and useful tool in preventing miscommunications between purchasers and purveyors. Meats are indexed by a numerical system: Beef cuts are designated by the 100 series, lamb by the 200 series, veal by the 300 series, pork by the 400 series, and portion cuts by the 1000 series. Commonly used cuts of beef, veal, lamb and pork and their IMPS numbers, as well as applicable cooking methods and serving suggestions, are discussed in Chapters 13 through 16.

Storing Meats

Meat products are highly perishable, so temperature control is the most important thing to remember when storing meats. Fresh meats should be stored at temperatures of 30–35°F (minus 1–+2°C). Vacuum-packed meats should be left in their packaging until they are needed. Under proper refrigeration, vacuum-packed meats with unbroken seals have a shelf life of three to four weeks. If the seal is broken, shelf life is reduced to only a few days. Meats that are not vacuum packed should be loosely wrapped or wrapped in air-permeable paper. Do not wrap meats tightly in plastic wrap, as this creates a good breeding ground for bacteria and will significantly shorten a meat's shelf life. Store meats on trays and away from other foods to prevent cross-contamination.

Meats freeze at about 28°F (minus 2°C). When freezing meats, the faster the better. Slow freezing produces large ice crystals that tend to rupture the muscle tissues, allowing water and nutrients to drip out when the meat is thawed. Most commercially packaged meats are frozen by blast freezing, which quickly cools by blasting minus 40°F (minus 40°C) air across the meat. Most food service facilities, however, use a slower and more conventional method known as still-air freezing. Still-air freezing is the common practice of placing meat in a standard freezer at about 0°F (minus 18°C) until it is frozen.

Freezer Burn—*the surface dehydration and discoloration of food that results from moisture loss at below-freezing temperatures.*

The ideal temperature for maintaining frozen meat is minus 50°F (minus 45°C). Frozen meat should not be maintained at any temperature warmer than 0°F (minus 18°C). Moisture- and vaporproof packaging will help prevent **freezer burn**. The length of frozen storage life varies with the species and type of meat. As a general rule, properly handled meats can be frozen for six months. Frozen meats should be thawed at refrigerator temperatures, not at room temperature or in warm water.

PREPARING MEATS

Certain procedures are often applied to meats before cooking to add flavor and/or moisture. These include marinating, barding and larding.

Marinating

Marinating is the process of soaking meat in a seasoned liquid to flavor and tenderize it. Marinades can be simple blends (herbs, seasonings and oil) or a complicated cooked recipe (red wine, fruit and other ingredients). Mild marinades should be used on more delicate meats, such as veal. Game and beef require strongly flavored marinades. In wine-based marinades, white wine is usually used for white meats and red wine for red meats. Not only does the wine add a distinctive flavor, the acids in it break down connective tissues and help tenderize the meat.

Veal and pork generally require less time to marinate than game, beef and lamb. Smaller pieces of meat take less time than larger pieces. When marinating, be sure to cover the meat completely and keep it refrigerated. Stir or turn the meat frequently to ensure that the marinate penetrates evenly.

Barding

Barding is the process of covering the surface of meat or poultry with thin slices of pork fatback and tying them in place with butcher's twine. Barded meat or poultry is usually roasted. As the item cooks, the fatback continuously bastes it, adding flavor and moisture. A drawback to barding is that the fatback prevents the meat or poultry from developing the crusty exterior associated with roasting.

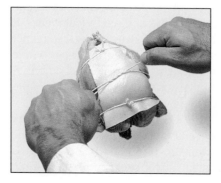

Barding a Pheasant

Larding

Larding is the process of inserting small strips of pork fat into meat with a larding needle. Larded meat is usually cooked by braising. During cooking, the added fat contributes moisture and flavor. Although once popular, larding is rarely used today because advances in selective breeding produce consistently tender, well-marbled meat.

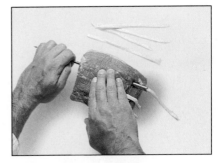

Larding Meat

APPLYING VARIOUS COOKING METHODS

In Chapter 9, Principles of Cooking, you learned the basic techniques for broiling, grilling, roasting, sautéing, pan-frying, poaching, simmering, braising and stewing. In Chapters 13 through 16 you will learn more about applying these cooking methods to beef, veal, lamb and pork. Here we apply these methods to meat cookery in general. Deep-frying is covered in Chapter 20, Deep-Frying.

Dry-Heat Cooking Methods

Dry-heat cooking methods subject food directly to the heat of a flame (broiling and grilling), hot air (roasting) or heated fat (sautéing and pan-frying). These cooking methods firm proteins without breaking down connective tissue. They are not recommended for tougher cuts or those high in connective tissue.

Broiling and Grilling

To serve a good-quality broiled or grilled product you must start with good-quality meat. The broiling or grilling process adds flavor; additional flavors are derived from seasonings. The broiler or grill should brown the meat, keeping the interior juicy. The grill should leave appetizing crosshatch marks on the meat's surface.

Selecting Meats to Broil or Grill

Only the most tender cuts should be broiled or grilled because direct heat does not tenderize. Fat adds flavor as the meat cooks, so the meat should be well marbled. Some external fat is also beneficial. Too much fat, however, will cause the broiler or grill to flare up, burning or discoloring the meat and adding objectionable flavors. Connective tissue toughens when meat is broiled or grilled. Trim away as much of it as possible.

Cooking Temperatures

Red meats should be cooked at sufficiently high temperatures to caramelize their surface, making them more attractive and flavorful. At the same time, the broiler or grill cannot be too hot or the meat's exterior will burn before the interior is cooked.

Because veal and pork are normally cooked to higher internal temperatures than beef and lamb, they should be cooked at slightly lower temperatures so their exteriors are not overcooked when their interiors are cooked properly. The exterior of white meats should be a deep golden color when finished.

Seasoning Meats to be Broiled or Grilled

Meats that have not been marinated should be well seasoned with salt and pepper just before being placed on the broiler or grill. If they are preseasoned

FIGURE 12.7 *Degrees of Doneness Meat cooked rare, medium rare, medium and medium well.*

and allowed to rest, the salt will dissolve and draw out moisture, making it difficult to brown the meat properly. Some chefs feel so strongly about this that they season broiled or grilled meats only after they are cooked. Pork and veal, which have a tendency to dry out when cooked, should be basted with seasoned butter or oil during cooking to help keep them moist. Meats can be glazed or basted with barbecue sauce as they cook.

Degrees of Doneness

Consumers request and expect meats to be properly cooked to specific degrees of doneness. It is your responsibility to understand and comply with these requests. Meats can be cooked very rare (or bleu), rare, medium rare, medium, medium well or well done. Figure 12.7 shows the proper color for these different degrees of doneness. This guide can be used for red meats cooked by any method.

Larger cuts of meat, such as a chateaubriand or thick chops, are often started on the broiler or grill to develop color and flavor and then finished in the oven to ensure complete, even cooking.

Determining Doneness

Broiling or grilling meat to the proper degree of doneness is an art. Larger pieces of meat will take longer to cook than smaller ones, but how quickly a piece of meat cooks is determined by many other factors: the temperature of the broiler or grill, the temperature of the piece of meat when placed on the broiler or grill, the type of meat and the thickness of the cut. Because of these variables, timing alone is not a useful tool in determining doneness.

The most reliable method of determining doneness is by pressing the piece of meat with a finger and gauging the amount of resistance it yields. Very rare (bleu) meat will offer almost no resistance and will feel almost the same as raw meat. Meat cooked rare will feel spongy and offer slight resistance to pressure. Meat cooked medium will feel slightly firm and springy to the touch. Meat cooked well done will feel quite firm and will spring back quickly when pressed. See Table 12.2.

Accompaniments to Broiled and Grilled Meats

Because a broiler or grill cannot be deglazed to form the base for a sauce, compound butters or sauces such as béarnaise are often served with broiled

TABLE 12.2	DETERMINING DONENESS	
Degree of Doneness	Color	Degree of Resistance
Very rare (bleu)	Very red and raw-looking center (the center is cool to the touch)	Almost no resistance
Rare	Large deep red center	Spongy; very slight resistance
Medium rare	Bright red center	Some resistance; slightly springy
Medium	Rosy pink to red center	Slightly firm; springy
Medium well	Very little pink at the center, almost brown throughout	Firm; springy
Well done	No red	Quite firm; springs back quickly when pressed

or grilled meats. Brown sauces such as bordelaise, chasseur, périgueux or brown mushroom sauce also complement many broiled or grilled items. Additional sauce suggestions are found in Table 10.5.

PROCEDURE FOR BROILING OR GRILLING MEATS

1. Heat the broiler or grill.
2. Use a wire brush to remove any charred or burnt particles that may be stuck to the broiler or grill grate. The grate can be wiped with a lightly oiled towel to remove any remaining particles and help season it.
3. Prepare the item to be broiled or grilled by trimming off excess fat and connective tissue and marinating or seasoning as desired. The meat may be brushed lightly with oil to help protect it and keep it from sticking to the grate.
4. Place the item in the broiler or on the grill. Following the example in Chapter 9, turn the meat to produce the attractive crosshatch marks associated with grilling. Use tongs to turn or flip the meat without piercing the surface in order to prevent valuable juices from escaping.
5. Cook the meat to the desired doneness while developing the proper surface color. To do so, adjust the position of the meat on the broiler or grill or adjust the distance between the grate and heat source.

1. Brushing the lamb chops with oil.

❖❖❖

RECIPE 12.1

GRILLED LAMB CHOPS WITH HERB BUTTER

Yield: 2 Servings

Lamb chops, loin or rib,		
approx. 1 in. (2.5 cm) thick	6	6
Salt and pepper	TT	TT
Oil	as needed	as needed
Herb butter	6 thin slices or 6 small rosettes	

1. Preheat the grill for 15 minutes.
2. Season the lamb chops with salt and pepper; brush with oil.
3. Place the lamb chops on the grill, turning as necessary to produce the proper crosshatching. Cook to the desired doneness.
4. Remove the lamb chops from the grill and place a slice or rosette of herb butter on each chop.
5. Serve immediately as the herb butter melts. The plate can be placed under the broiler for a few seconds to help melt the herb butter.

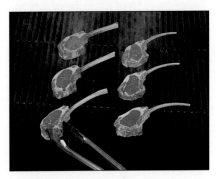

2. Placing the lamb chops on the grill.

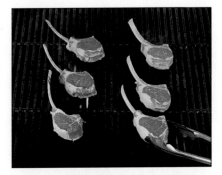

3. Rotating the lamb chops 90 degrees to create crosshatch marks.

Roasting

Properly roasted meats should be tender, juicy and evenly cooked to the appropriate degree of doneness. They should have a pleasant appearance when whole as well as when sliced and plated.

Selecting Meats to Roast

Because roasting is a dry-heat cooking method and will not tenderize the finished product, meats that are to be roasted should be tender and well marbled. They are usually cut from the rib, loin or leg sections.

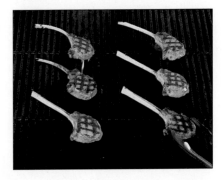

4. Turning the chops over to finish them on the other side.

TABLE 12.3

Degree of Doneness	Internal Temperature	Minutes per Pound*
Very rare	125–130°F 52–54°C	12–15
Rare	130–140°F 54–60°C	15–18
Medium	140–150°F 60–66°C	18–20
Well done	150–165°F 66–74°C	20–25

*Assumes meat was at room temperature before roasting and cooked at a constant 325°F (162°C).

FIGURE 12.8   *The Proper Placement of an Instant-Read Thermometer*

Cooking Temperatures

Small roasts such as a rack of lamb or a beef tenderloin should be cooked at high temperatures, 375–450°F (190–230°C), so that they develop good color during their short cooking times.

Traditionally, large roasts were started at high temperatures to sear the meat and seal in the juices; they were then finished at lower temperatures. Studies have shown, however, that roasts cooked at constant, low temperatures provide a better yield with less shrinkage than roasts that have been seared. Temperatures between 275° and 325°F (120–160°C) are ideal for large roasts. These temperatures will produce a large, evenly cooked pink center portion.

Seasoning Meats to be Roasted

Seasonings are especially important with smaller roasts and roasts with little or no fat covering. With these roasts, some of the seasonings penetrate the meat while the remainder help create the highly seasoned crust associated with a good roast. A large roast with heavy fat covering (for example, a steamship round or prime rib) does not benefit from being seasoned on the surface because the seasonings will not penetrate the fat layer, which is trimmed away before service.

When practical, a roast with excess fat should be trimmed, leaving just a thin fat layer so that the roast bastes itself while cooking. A lean roast can be barded or larded before cooking to add richness and moisture. Lamb legs are sometimes studded with garlic cloves by piercing the meat with a paring knife and then pressing slivers of raw garlic into the holes.

A roast is sometimes cooked on a bed of mirepoix, or mirepoix is added to the roasting pan as the roast cooks. The mirepoix raises the roast off the bottom of the roasting pan, preventing the bottom from overcooking. This mirepoix, however, does not add any flavor to the roast. Rather, it combines with the drippings to add flavor to the jus, sauce or gravy that is made with them.

Determining Doneness

The doneness of small roasts such as a rack of lamb is determined in much the same as with broiled or grilled meats. With experience, the chef develops a sense of timing as well as a feel for gauging the amount of resistance by touching the meat. These techniques, however, are not infallible, especially with large roasts.

Although timing is useful as a general guide for determining doneness, there are too many variables for it to be relied upon exclusively. With this caution in mind, Table 12.3 lists general cooking times for roasted meats.

The best way to determine the doneness of a large roast is to use an instant-read thermometer as shown in Figure 12.8. The thermometer is inserted into the center or thickest part of the roast and away from any bones. The proper finished temperatures for roasted meats are listed in Table 12.3.

Carryover Cooking and Resting

Cooking does not stop the moment a roast is removed from the oven. Through conduction, the heat applied to the outside of the roast continues to penetrate, cooking the center for several more minutes. Indeed, the internal temperature of a small roast can rise by as much as 5–10°F (3–6°C) after being removed from the oven. With a larger roast, such as a 50-pound steamship round, it can rise by as much as 20°F (11°C). Therefore, remove roasted meats before they reach the desired degree of doneness and allow carryover cooking to complete the cooking process. The temperatures listed in Table 12.3 are internal temperatures after allowing for carryover cooking.

As meat cooks, its juices flow toward the center. If the roast is carved immediately after it is removed from the oven, its juices would run from the meat, causing it to lose its color and become dry. Letting the meat rest before slicing allows the juices to redistribute themselves evenly throughout the roast, so the roast will retain more juices when carved. Small roasts, like a rack of lamb, need to rest only 5–10 minutes; larger roasts such as a steamship round of beef require as much as an hour.

Accompaniments to Roasted Meats

Roasts may be served with a sauce based on their natural juices (called *au jus*), as described in Recipe 12.2, Roast Prime Rib of Beef Au Jus, or with a pan gravy made with drippings from the roast. Additional sauce suggestions are found in Table 10.5.

PROCEDURE FOR ROASTING MEATS

1. Trim excess fat, tendons and silverskin from the meat. Leave only a thin fat covering, if possible, so the roast bastes itself as it cooks.
2. Season the roast as appropriate and place it in a roasting pan. The roast may be placed on a bed of mirepoix or on a rack.
3. Roast the meat, uncovered, at the desired temperature (the larger the roast, the lower the temperature), usually 275–425°F (135–220°C).
4. If a jus or pan gravy is desired and a mirepoix was not added at the start of cooking, it may be added 30–45 minutes before the roast is done, thus allowing it to caramelize while the roast finishes cooking.
5. Cook to the desired temperature.
6. Remove the roast from the oven, allowing carryover cooking to raise the internal temperature to the desired degree of doneness. Allow the roast to rest before slicing or carving it. As the roast rests, prepare the jus, sauce or pan gravy.

◆◆◆

RECIPE 12.2

ROAST PRIME RIB OF BEEF AU JUS

Yield: 18 8-oz. (250-g) boneless Servings

Oven-ready rib roast		
IMPS #109, approx. 16 lbs. (7.5 kg)	1	1
Salt and pepper	TT	TT
Garlic, chopped	TT	TT
Mirepoix	1 lb.	500 g
Brown stock	2 qt.	2 lt

1. Pull back the netting, fold back the fat cap and season the roast well with the salt, pepper and chopped garlic. Replace the fat cap and netting; place the roast in an appropriate-sized roasting pan. Roast at 300–325°F (160–165°C).
2. Add the mirepoix to the pan approximately 45 minutes before the roast is

Continued

finished cooking. Continue cooking until the internal temperature reaches 125°F (52°C), approximately 3–4 hours. Carryover cooking will raise the internal temperature of the roast to approximately 138°F (59°C).

3. Remove the roast from the pan and allow it to rest in a warm place for 30 minutes.

4. Drain the excess fat from the roasting pan, reserving the mirepoix and any drippings in the roasting pan.

5. Caramelize the mirepoix on the stove top; allow the liquids to evaporate, leaving only brown drippings in the pan.

6. Deglaze the pan with brown stock. Stir to loosen all the drippings.

7. Simmer the jus, reducing it slightly and allowing the mirepoix to release its flavor; season with salt and pepper if necessary.

8. Strain the jus through a china cap lined with cheesecloth. Skim any remaining fat from the surface with a ladle.

9. Remove the netting from the roast. Trim and slice the roast as described below and serve with approximately 1 to 2 ounces (30 to 60 milliliters) jus per person.

1. Draining off the excess fat.

2. Caramelizing the mirepoix.

3. Deglazing the pan with brown stock.

4. Simmering the jus, reducing it slightly and allowing the mirepoix to release its flavors.

5. Straining the jus through a china cap and cheesecloth.

Carving Roasts

All the efforts that went into selecting and cooking a perfect roast will be wasted if the roast is not carved properly. Roasts are always carved against the grain; carving it with the grain produces long stringy, tough slices. Cutting across the muscle fibers produces a more attractive and tender portion. Portions may be cut in a single thick slice, as with Roast Prime Rib of Beef, or in many thin slices. The photographs below illustrate several different carving procedures.

CARVING PRIME RIB

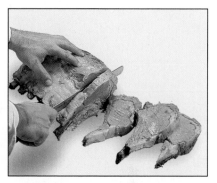

1. Removing the netting, cap fat and chine bones.

2. Trimming the excess fat from the eye muscle.

3. Slicing the rib in long, smooth strokes, the first cut (end cut) without a rib bone, the second cut with a rib bone, and so on.

CARVING PRIME RIB ON THE SLICER

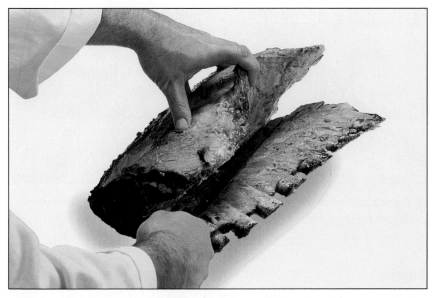

1. When producing large quantities of prime rib, it is often more practical to slice it on a slicing machine. Following the steps illustrated above, remove the netting, cap fat and chine bone; trim excess fat from the eye muscle. Then use a long slicer and completely remove the rib eye from the rib bones, being careful to stay as close as possible to the bones to avoid wasting any meat.

2. After placing the rib on the slicing machine, set the machine to the desired thickness. The blade will have to be adjusted often because a roast's thickness fluctuates.

CARVING A STEAMSHIP ROUND OF BEEF

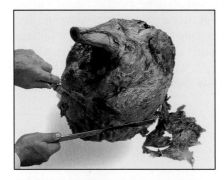

1. After setting the roast on the cutting board with the exposed femur bone (large end of the roast) down and the tibia (shank bone) or "handle" up, trim the excess exterior fat to expose the lean meat.

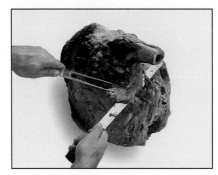

2. Begin slicing with a horizontal cut toward the shank bone, then make vertical cuts to release the slices of beef.

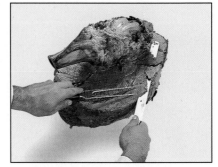

3. Keeping the exposed surface as level as possible. Continue carving, turning the roast as necessary to access all sides.

CARVING A LEG OF LAMB

1. Holding the shank bone firmly, cut toward the bone.

2. Cutting parallel to the shank bone to remove the slices.

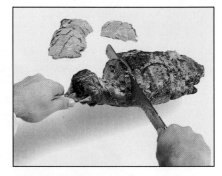

3. Rotating the leg as needed to access the meat on all sides.

Sautéing

Sautéing is a dry-heat cooking method in which heat is conducted by a small amount of fat. Sautéed meats should be tender (a reflection of the quality of the raw product), of good color (determined by proper cooking temperatures) and have a good overall flavor. Any accompanying sauce should be well seasoned and complement the meat without overpowering it.

Selecting Meats to Sauté

As with broiling, grilling and roasting, you should use tender meats of the highest quality in order to produce good results when sautéing. The cuts should be uniform in size and shape to promote even cooking.

Seasoning Meats to be Sautéed

The sauces that almost always accompany sautéed meats provide much of the seasoning. The meat, however, can be marinated or simply seasoned with salt and pepper. If marinated, the meat must be patted dry before cooking to ensure proper browning. Some meats are dusted with flour before cooking to seal in juices and promote even browning.

Determining Doneness

As with broiled and grilled meats, the doneness of sautéed meats is determined by touch and timing. Red meats should be well browned; veal and pork should be somewhat lighter.

Accompaniments to Sautéed Meats

Sauces served with sautéed meats are usually made directly in the sauté pan, utilizing the **fond**. They often incorporate a previously thickened sauce. Additional sauce suggestions for sautéed meats are found in Table 10.5.

> **Fond**—*(1) French for stock or base; (2) the concentrated juices, drippings and bits of food left in pans after foods are roasted or sautéed; it is used to flavor sauces made directly in the pans in which foods were cooked.*

PROCEDURE FOR SAUTÉING MEATS

1. Heat a sauté pan and add enough oil or clarified butter to just cover the bottom. The pan should be large enough to hold the meat in a single layer. A pan that is too large may cause the fat or meat to burn.
2. Cut the meat into **cutlets, scallops, émincés, medallions, mignonettes, noisettes, chops** or small even-sized pieces. Season the meat and dredge in flour if desired.
3. Add the meat to the sauté pan in a single layer. Do not crowd the pan.
4. Adjust the temperature so that the meat's exterior browns properly without burning and the interior cooks. The heat should be high enough to complete the cooking process before the meat begins to stew in its own juices.
5. Small items may be tossed using the sauté pan's sloped sides to flip them back on top of themselves. Do not toss the meat more than necessary, however. The pan should remain in contact with the heat source as much as possible to maintain proper temperatures. Larger items should be turned using tongs or a kitchen fork. Avoid burns by not splashing hot fat.
6. Larger items can be finished in an oven. Either place the sauté pan in the oven or transfer the meat to another pan. The latter procedure allows a sauce to be made in the original pan as the meat continues to cook.

> **Cutlet**—*a relatively thick, boneless slice of meat.*
>
> **Scallop**—*a thin, boneless slice of meat.*
>
> **Émincé**—*a small, thin, boneless piece of meat.*
>
> **Paillard**—*a scallop of meat pounded until thin, usually grilled.*
>
> **Medallion**—*a small, round, relatively thick slice of meat.*
>
> **Mignonette**—*a medallion.*
>
> **Noisette**—*a small, usually round, portion of meat cut from the rib.*
>
> **Chop**—*a cut of meat including part of the rib.*

PROCEDURE FOR MAKING SAUCE IN THE SAUTÉ PAN

1. If a sauce is to be made in the pan, hold the meat in a warm spot while preparing the sauce. When the meat is removed from the pan, leave a small amount of fat as well as the fond. If there is excessive fat, degrease the pan, leaving just enough to cover its bottom. Add ingredients such as garlic, shallots and mushrooms that will be used as garnishes and sauce flavorings; sauté them.

2. Deglaze the pan with wine or stock. Scrape the pan, loosening the fond and allowing it to dissolve in the liquid. Reduce the deglazing liquid by approximately three quarters.

3. Add jus lié or stock to the pan. Cook and reduce the sauce to the desired consistency.

4. Add any ingredients that do not require cooking such as herbs and spices. Adjust the seasonings with salt and pepper.

5. For service, the meat may be returned to the pan for a moment to reheat it and coat it with the finished sauce. The meat should remain in the sauce just long enough to reheat. Do not attempt to cook the meat in the sauce.

♦♦♦

RECIPE 12.3

SAUTÉED VEAL SCALLOPS WITH WHITE WINE LEMON SAUCE

Yield: 6 Servings

Veal scallops, 3 oz. (90 g) each	12	12
Clarified butter	2 oz.	60 g
Flour	4 oz.	120 g
Salt and pepper	TT	TT
Shallots, chopped	2 Tbsp.	30 ml
White wine	6 oz.	180 g
Lemon juice	2 oz.	60 g
Brown veal stock	4 oz.	120 g
Unsalted butter	2 oz.	60 g
Lemon wedges	12	12

1. Pound the scallops to a uniform thickness, as described in Chapter 14, Veal.

2. Heat a sauté pan and add the clarified butter.

3. Dredge the scallops in seasoned flour and add to the pan in a single layer. Sauté on each side for 1–2 minutes. As the first scallops are done, remove them to a warm platter and sauté the remaining scallops.

4. Add the chopped shallots to the pan and sauté.

5. Deglaze the pan with the white wine and lemon juice.

6. Add the brown veal stock and reduce by half.

7. Swirl in the butter (monte au beurre).

8. Adjust the seasonings with salt and pepper.

9. Serve 2 scallops per person with approximately 1 ounce (30 grams) of sauce. Garnish with lemon wedges.

1. Adding the veal scallops to the pan. Note the relationship of scallops to pan size.

2. Adding the chopped shallots to the pan and sautéing them.

3. Deglazing the pan with white wine and lemon juice.

4. Adding the brown veal stock and reducing by half.

5. Swirling in the butter and adjusting the seasonings.

Pan-Frying

Pan-frying uses more fat than sautéing to conduct heat. Pan-fried meats should be tender (a reflection of the quality of the raw product), of good color (determined by proper cooking temperatures) and with a good overall flavor. Meats to be pan-fried are usually breaded. In addition to providing flavor, breading seals the meat. The breading should be free from breaks, thus preventing the fat from coming into direct contact with the meat or collecting in a pocket formed between the meat and the breading. Pan-fried items should be golden in color and the breading should not be soggy.

Selecting Meats to Pan-Fry

As with other dry-heat cooking methods, tender meats of high quality should be used because the meat will not be tenderized by the cooking process. Meats that are pan-fried are often cut into cutlets or scallops.

Seasoning Meats to be Pan-Fried

Pan-fried meats are usually seasoned lightly with salt and pepper either by applying them directly to the meat or adding them to the flour and bread crumbs used in the breading procedure.

Determining Doneness

The most accurate way to determine the doneness of a pan-fried item is by timing. The touch method is difficult to use because of the large amounts of hot fat. It also may not be as accurate as with broiled or grilled meats because pan-fried meats are often quite thin.

Accompaniments to Pan-Fried Meats

Any sauce served with pan-fried meats is usually made separately because there is no fond created during the pan-frying process. Sauce suggestions are listed in Table 10.5.

PROCEDURE FOR PAN-FRYING MEATS

1. Slice and pound out the meat into scallops as described in Chapter 14, Veal.
2. Bread the meat using the standard breading procedure detailed in Chapter 20, Deep-Frying.
3. Heat a moderate amount of fat or oil in a heavy pan. The temperature

should be slightly lower than that used to sauté so that the breading will be nicely browned when the item is fully cooked.

4. Place the meat in the pan, being careful not to splash the hot fat. The fat should come one third to one half way up the side of the meat. Fry until brown. Turn and brown the other side. Ideally, pan-fried meats should be fully cooked when they are well browned on both sides.

5. Remove the meat from the pan; drain it on absorbent paper before serving.

♦♦♦

RECIPE 12.4

BREADED VEAL CUTLETS

Yield: 10 Servings

Veal cutlet, 4 oz. (120 g) each	10	10
Salt and pepper	TT	TT
Standard breading:	as needed	as needed
Flour		
Eggs		
Milk		
Bread crumbs		
Vegetable oil	as needed	as needed
Butter	6 oz.	180 g
Lemon wedges	20	20

1. Using a mallet, pound the cutlets to an even thickness, approximately 1/4 inch (6 millimeters).

2. Season the cutlets with salt and pepper.

3. Bread the cutlets using the standard breading procedure described in Chapter 20, Deep-Frying.

4. Heat a heavy pan to moderate heat; add approximately 1/4 inch (6 millimeters) of oil.

5. Add the cutlets in a single layer. Do not crowd the pan. Brown on one side, then the other. Total cooking time should be approximately 4 minutes.

6. Remove the cutlets and drain on absorbent paper.

7. Melt the butter in a small pan until it foams.

8. Place one cutlet on each plate and pour approximately 1/2 ounce (15 milliliters) butter over each portion. Garnish with lemon wedges.

1. Adding the breaded cutlets to the hot pan. Note the amount of oil in the pan.

2. Turning the cutlets to brown on the second side.

3. Melting the butter in a separate pan until it foams.

4. Pouring the butter over the cutlet.

Moist-Heat Cooking Methods

Moist-heat cooking methods subject food to heat and moisture. Moist heat is often, but not always, used to tenderize tougher cuts of meat through long, slow cooking. Simmering is the only moist-heat cooking method discussed here as it is the only one frequently used with meat.

Simmering

Simmering is usually associated with specific tougher cuts of meat that need to be tenderized through long, slow, moist cooking. Quality simmered meats have good flavor and texture. The flavor is determined by the cooking liquid; the texture is a result of proper cooking temperatures and time.

Selecting Meats to Simmer

Meats such as fresh or corned beef brisket, fresh or cured hams and tongue are often simmered. Beef briskets and tongues, pork butts and hams are often simmered whole.

Cooking Temperatures

Moist-heat cooking methods generally use lower temperatures than dry-heat cooking methods. Meats are normally simmered at temperatures between 180° and 200°F (82–85°C). In larger food service operations, meats such as hams and corned beef are cooked at temperatures as low as 150°F (66°C) for up to 12 hours. Although lower cooking temperatures result in less shrinkage and a more tender finished product, cooking times can be increased to the point that very low cooking temperatures may not be practical.

Seasoning Meats To Be Simmered

If the meat to be simmered was cured by either smoking (as with cured hams, ham hocks and smoked pork butt) or pickling (as with corned beef and pickled tongue), the cooking liquid will not be used to make a sauce and should not be seasoned. Indeed, simmering cured meats helps leach out some of the excess salt, making the finished dish more palatable.

Determining Doneness

Simmered meats are always cooked well done, which is determined by tenderness. The size and quality of the raw product determines the cooking time. Undercooked meats will be tough and chewy. Overcooked meats will be stringy and may even fall apart.

To test large cuts of meat for doneness, a kitchen fork should be easily inserted into the meat and the meat should slide off the fork. Smaller pieces of meat should be tender to the bite or easily cut with a table fork.

Accompaniments to Simmered Meats

Simmered meats are often served with boiled or steamed vegetables, as in the cases of corned beef and cabbage. Pickled meats are usually served with mustard or horseradish sauce on the side.

PROCEDURE FOR SIMMERING MEATS

1. Cut, trim or tie the meat according to the recipe.
2. Bring an adequate amount of liquid to a boil. There should be enough liquid to cover the meat completely. Too much liquid will leach off much of the meat's flavor; too little will leave a portion of the meat exposed, preventing it from cooking. Because the dish's final flavor is determined by the flavor of the liquid, use plenty of mirepoix, flavorings and seasonings.

3. When simmering smoked or cured items, start them in cold water. This helps draw off some of the strong pickled or smoked flavors.

4. Add the meat to the liquid.

5. Reduce the heat to the desired temperature and cook until the meat is tender. Do not allow the cooking liquid to boil. Boiling results in a tough or over-cooked and stringy product. If the simmered meat is to be served cold, a moister and juicier product can be achieved by removing the pot from the stove before the meat is fully cooked. The meat and the liquid can be cooled in a water bath like that for a stock, as described in Chapter 10, Stocks and Sauces. This allows the residual heat in the cooking liquid to finish cooking the meat.

1. Placing the corned beef and sachet in an appropriate pot and covering with stock.

2. Carving the beef and presenting it with the vegetable garnish.

◆◆◆

RECIPE 12.5

NEW ENGLAND BOILED DINNER

Yield: 12 6-oz (180-g) Servings

Corned beef brisket, 8 lb. (6.5 kg)	1	1
White stock	as needed	as needed
Sachet:		
Bay leaves	2	2
Dried thyme	1/2 tsp.	2 ml
Peppercorns, cracked	1/2 tsp.	2 ml
Parsley stems	10	10
Mustard seeds	1 Tbsp.	15 ml
Cinnamon sticks	2	2
Allspice berries	4	4
Baby red beets	24	24
Baby turnips	24	24
Baby carrots	24	24
Brussels sprouts	24	24
Pearl onions	24	24
Potatoes, Red Bliss	24	24

1. Place the beef in a pot and add enough stock to cover it. Add the sachet, bring to a boil and reduce to a simmer.

2. Simmer until the beef is tender, approximately 3 hours. Remove the beef and hold in a hotel pan in a small amount of the cooking liquid.

3. Peel or prepare the vegetables and potatoes as needed and cook separately in a portion of the cooking liquid.

4. Carve the beef and serve with 2 of each of the vegetables and horseradish sauce (page 208).

Combination Cooking Methods

Braising and stewing are referred to as combination cooking methods because both dry heat and moist heat are used to achieve the desired results.

Braising

Braised meats are first browned and then cooked in a liquid that serves as a sauce for the meat. A well-prepared braised dish has the rich flavor of the meat in the sauce and the moisture and flavor of the sauce in the meat. It should be almost fork tender but not falling apart. The meat should have an attractive color from the initial browning and final glazing.

Selecting Meats to Braise

Braising can be used for tender cuts (such as those from the loin or rib) or tougher cuts (such as those from the chuck or shank). Any meat to be braised should be well marbled with ample fat content to produce a moist finished product.

If tender cuts such as veal chops or pork chops are braised, the finished dish has a uniquely different flavor and texture than if they were cooked by a dry-heat method. Tender cuts require shorter cooking times than tougher cuts because lengthy cooking is not needed to break down connective tissue.

More often, braising is used with tougher cuts that are tenderized by the long, moist cooking process. Cuts from the chuck and shank are popular choices, as they are very flavorful and contain relatively large amounts of collagen, which adds richness to the finished product.

Large pieces of meat can be braised, then carved like a roast. Portion control cuts and diced meats can also be braised.

Cooking Temperatures

Braised meats are always browned before simmering. As a general rule, smaller cuts are floured before browning; larger cuts are not. Flouring seals the meat, promotes even browning and adds body to the sauce that accompanies the meat. Whether floured or not, the meat is browned in fat. After browning, white meats should be golden to amber in color; red meats should be dark brown. Do not brown the meat too quickly at too high a temperature, as it is important to develop a well-caramelized surface. The caramelized surface adds color and flavor to the final product.

The meat and the braising liquid are brought to a boil over direct heat. The temperature is then reduced below boiling and the pot is covered. Cooking can be finished in the oven or on the stove top. The oven provides gentle, even heat without the risk of scorching. If the braise is finished on the stove top, proper temperatures must be maintained carefully throughout the cooking process and great care must be taken to prevent scorching or burning. Lower temperatures and longer cooking times result in more even cooking and thorough penetration of the cooking liquid, providing a more flavorful final product.

Seasoning Meats to be Braised

The seasoning and overall flavor of a braised dish is largely a function of the quality of the cooking liquid and the mirepoix, herbs, spices and other ingredients that season the meat as it cooks. However, braised meats can be marinated before they are cooked to tenderize them and add flavor. The marinade is then sometimes incorporated into the braising liquid. Salt and pepper may be added to the flour if the meat is dredged before it is browned, or the meat may be seasoned directly (although the salt may draw out moisture and inhibit browning).

A standard sachet and a tomato product are usually added at the start of cooking. The tomato product adds flavor and color to the finished sauce as well as acid to tenderize the meat during the cooking process. Final seasoning should not take place until cooking is complete and the sauce will not be reduced further.

Finishing Braised Meats

Near the end of the cooking process, the lid may be removed from oven-braised meats. Finishing braised meats without a cover serves two purposes. First, the meat can be glazed by basting it often. (As the basting liquid evaporates, the meat is browned and a strongly flavored glaze is formed.) Second, removing the lid allows the cooking liquid to reduce, thickening it and concentrating its flavors for use as a sauce.

Determining Doneness

Braised meats are done when they are tender. A fork inserted into the meat should meet little resistance. Properly braised meats should remain intact and not fall apart when handled gently.

Braised meats that fall apart or are stringy are overcooked. If the finished product is tough, it was probably undercooked or cooked at too high a temperature. If the entire dish lacks flavor, the meat may not have been properly browned or the cooking liquid may have been poorly seasoned.

Accompaniments to Braised Meats

Large braised items are often served like roasts. They are carved against the grain in thin slices and served with their sauce. Vegetables can be cooked with the braised meat, cooked separately and added when the main items has finished cooking or added at service. If the vegetables are cooked with the main item they should be added at intervals based on their individual cooking times to prevent overcooking.

PROCEDURE FOR BRAISING MEATS

The liquid used for braising is usually thickened in one of three ways:

1. With a roux added at the start of the cooking process; the roux thickens the sauce as the meat cooks.
2. Prethickened before the meat is added.
3. Thickened after the meat is cooked either by puréeing the mirepoix or by using roux, arrowroot or cornstarch.

The procedure for braising meats includes variations for whichever thickening method is selected.

1. Heat a small amount of oil in a heavy pan.
2. Dredge the meat to be braised in seasoned flour, if desired, and add it to the oil.
3. Brown the meat well on all sides and remove from the pan.
4. Add a mirepoix to the pan and caramelize it well. If using roux, it should be added at this time.
5. Add the appropriate stock or sauce so that when the meat is returned to the pan the liquid comes approximately one third of the way up the side of the meat.
6. Add aromatics and seasonings.
7. Return the meat to the sauce. Tightly cover the pot and bring it to a simmer. Cook slowly either on the stove top or by placing the covered pot directly in an oven at 250–300°F (120–150°C).
8. Cook the item, basting or turning it often so that all sides of the meat benefit from the moisture and flavor of the sauce.
9. When the meat is done, remove it from the pan and hold it in a warm place while the sauce is finished.
10. The sauce may be reduced on the stove top to intensify its flavors. If the meat was braised in a stock, the stock may be thickened using a roux, arrowroot or cornstarch. Strain the sauce or, if desired, purée the mirepoix and other ingredients and return them to the sauce. Adjust the sauce's consistency as desired.

✦✦✦

RECIPE 12.6
Aunt Ruthie's Pot Roast

Yield: 12 6-oz. (180-g) meat and
4-oz. (120-g) sauce Servings

Vegetable oil	3 oz.	90 g
Beef brisket	6 lb.	2.7 kg
Onion, thinly sliced	3 lb.	1.4 kg
Garlic, minced	2 Tbsp.	30 ml
Brown veal stock	1 qt.	1 lt
Tomato sauce	1 pt.	450 ml
Brown sugar	4 oz.	120 g
Paprika	1 tsp.	5 ml
Dry mustard	2 tsp.	10 ml
Lemon juice	8 oz.	250 g
Tomato catsup	8 oz.	250 g
Red wine vinegar	8 oz.	250 g
Worcestershire sauce	2 oz.	60 g
Salt and pepper	TT	TT

3. Basting the brisket. Note the proper amount of cooking liquid.

1. Browning the brisket.

2. Sautéing the onions and garlic.

1. Heat the oil in a large skillet. Add the beef and brown thoroughly. Remove and reserve the brisket.
2. Add the onions and garlic to the pan; sauté.
3. Add the stock and tomato sauce to the pan.
4. Return the brisket to the pan, cover tightly and bring to a boil. Braise at 325°F (160°C) for 1-1/2 hours, basting or turning the brisket often.
5. Combine the remaining ingredients and add to the pan.
6. Continue cooking and basting the brisket until tender, approximately 1 hour.
7. Remove the brisket, degrease the sauce and adjust its consistency and seasonings. Do not strain the sauce.
8. Slice the brisket against the grain and serve with the sauce.

Stewing

Stewing, like braising, is a combination cooking method. In many ways the procedures for stewing are identical to those for braising, although stewing is usually associated with smaller or bite-sized pieces of meat.

There are two main types of stews: brown stews and white stews.

When making **brown stews**, the meat is first browned in fat; then a cooking liquid is added. The initial browning adds flavor and color to the finished product. The same characteristics apply to a good brown stew that apply to a good braised dish: It should be fork tender, have an attractive color and rich flavor.

There are two types of **white stews**: **fricassees**, in which the meat is first cooked in a small amount of fat without coloring, then combined with a cooking liquid; and **blanquettes**, in which the meat is first blanched, then rinsed and added to a cooking liquid. White stew should have the same flavor and texture characteristics as a brown stew, but should be white or ivory in color.

Selecting Meats to Stew

Stewing uses moist heat to tenderize meat just as braising does, therefore many of the same cuts can be used. Meats that are to be stewed should be trimmed of excess fat and connective tissue and cut into 1- to 2-inch (2.5- to 5-cm) cubes.

Cooking Temperatures

Meats for brown stews are first cooked at high temperatures over direct heat until well browned. Meats for fricassees are first sautéed at low temperatures so they do not develop color.

Once the cooking liquid has been added and the moist-heat cooking process has begun, do not allow the stew to boil. Stews benefit from low-temperature cooking. If practical, stews can be covered and finished in the oven.

Seasoning Meats To Be Stewed

Stews, like braised meats, get much of their flavor from their cooking liquid. A stew's seasoning and overall flavor is a direct result of the quality of the cooking liquid and the vegetables, herbs, spices and other ingredients added during cooking.

Determining Doneness

Stewed meats are done when they are fork tender. Test them by removing a piece of meat to a plate and cutting it with a fork. Any vegetables that are cooked with the meat should be added at the proper times so that they and the meat are completely cooked at the same time.

Accompaniments to Stewed Meats

Stews are often complete meals in themselves, containing meat, vegetables and potatoes in one dish. Stews that do not contain a starch are often served with pasta or rice.

PROCEDURE FOR STEWING MEATS—BROWN STEWS

Red meats, lamb or game are used in brown stews. The procedure for making a brown stew is very similar to braising.

1. Trim the meat of excess fat and silverskin and cut into 1- to 2-inch (2.5- to 5-cm) pieces.
2. Dredge the meat in flour if desired. Heat an appropriate-sized pan and add enough oil to cover the bottom. Cook the meat in the oil, browning it well on all sides. Onions and garlic can be added at this time and browned.
3. Add flour to the meat and fat and cook to make a brown roux.
4. Gradually add the liquid to the roux, stirring to prevent lumps. Bring the stew to a boil and reduce to a simmer.
5. Add a tomato product and a sachet or a bouquet garni. Cover and place in the oven or continue to simmer on the stove top until the meat is tender. Add other ingredients such as vegetables or potatoes at the proper time so that they will be done when the meat is tender.
6. When the meat is tender, remove the sachet or bouquet garni. The meat may be strained out and the sauce thickened with roux, cornstarch or arrowroot or reduced to concentrate its flavors.
7. If not added during the cooking process, vegetables and other garnishes may be cooked separately and added to the finished stew.

◆◆◆

RECIPE 12.7
BROWN BEEF STEW

Yield: 8 8-oz. (250-g) Servings

Oil	2 oz.	60 ml
Beef chuck or shank, trimmed and cut into 1-1/2-in. (3.5-cm) cubes	4 lb. 8 oz.	2 kg
Salt	2 tsp.	10 ml
Pepper	1/2 tsp.	2 ml
Onion, small dice	10 oz.	300 g
Garlic, chopped	1 tsp.	5 ml
Flour	1-1/2 oz.	45 g
Red wine	8 oz.	250 g
Brown stock	1 qt.	1 lt
Tomato purée	4 oz.	120 g
Sachet:		
Bay leaves	2	2
Dried thyme	1/2 tsp.	2 ml
Peppercorns, crushed	1/2 tsp.	2 ml
Parsley stems	10	10

1. Browning the beef.

2. Sautéing the garlic and onions until slightly browned.

3. Adding the flour and making a roux.

1. Heat a heavy pot until very hot and add the oil.

2. Season the beef and add it to the pot, browning it well on all sides. Do not overcrowd the pot. If necessary, cook the beef in several batches.

3. Add the onions and garlic and sauté until the onions are slightly browned.

4. Add the flour and stir to make a roux. Brown the roux lightly.

5. Add the red wine and brown stock slowly, stirring to prevent lumps.

6. Add the tomato purée and the sachet.

7. Bring to a simmer and cook until the beef is tender, approximately 1-1/2–2 hours.

8. Optional: Remove the cooked beef from the sauce and strain the sauce. Return the beef to the sauce.

9. Degrease the stew by skimming off the fat.

VARIATION: Vegetables such as turnips, carrots, celery and pearl onions can be cooked separately and added to the stew as garnish.

4. Adding the red wine and beef stock.

5. Adding the tomato purée and sachet.

6. Degreasing the stew.

PROCEDURE FOR STEWING MEATS—BRAISED WHITE STEWS (FRICASSEES)

The procedure for making fricassees is similar to the procedure for brown stews. The primary difference is that the meat is sautéed but not allowed to brown. The braised white stew (fricassee) procedure outlined below is the basis for Recipe 14.12, Veal Fricassee.

1. Trim meat of excess fat and silverskin and cut into 1- to 2-inch (2.5- to 5-cm) pieces.
2. Heat an appropriate-sized pan and add enough oil to cover the bottom. Add the meat (and often an onion) to the pan and cook without browning.
3. Sprinkle the meat (and onion) with flour and cook to make a blond roux.
4. Gradually add the liquid, stirring to prevent lumps. Bring the stew to a boil and reduce to a simmer.
5. Add a bouquet garni and seasonings. Cover the stew and place in the oven or continue to simmer on the stove top, being careful not to burn or scorch the stew.
6. Continue to cook until the meat is tender. If the sauce is too thin, remove the meat from the sauce and hold the meat in a warm place. Reduce the sauce to the proper consistency on the stove top or thicken it by adding a small amount of blond roux, cornstarch or arrowroot.

PROCEDURE FOR STEWING MEATS—SIMMERED WHITE STEWS (BLANQUETTES)

Unlike fricassees, blanquettes contain meat that was blanched, not sautéed. (Because the meat is cooked only by moist heat and never by dry heat, the blanquette cooking process is not a true combination cooking method; nevertheless, because of its striking similarities to stewing, it is included here.) The most common blanquette is made with veal and is known as blanquette de veau, but any white meat or lamb can be prepared in this manner using a variety of garnishes. The simmered white stew (blanquette) procedure outlined below is the basis for Recipe 15.14, Blanquette of Lamb.

1. Trim meat of excess fat and silverskin and cut into 1- to 2-inch (2.5- to 5-cm) pieces.
2. Blanch the cubed meat by placing the meat in an appropriate pot, covering with cool water, adding salt, and bringing it rapidly to a boil. Drain the water. Rinse the meat to remove any impurities.
3. Return the meat to the pot and add enough stock to cover. Add a bouquet garni, salt and pepper. Simmer until the meat is tender, approximately 1–1-1/2 hours.
4. Strain the meat from the stock. Discard the bouquet garni. Bring the stock to a boil, thicken it with a blond roux and simmer for 15 minutes.
5. Return the meat to the thickened stock. Add a liaison of cream and egg yolks to enrich and thicken the stew. Heat the stew to a simmer. Do not boil or the egg yolks will curdle.
6. If any vegetables are to be added they should be cooked separately and added to the thickened stock with the meat.
7. Adjust the seasoning with a few drops of lemon juice, nutmeg or salt and pepper as needed.

CONCLUSION

Because meat may account for the largest portion of your food-cost dollar, it should be purchased carefully, stored properly and fabricated appropriately. The various cuts and flavors of meat (beef, veal, lamb and pork) can be successfully broiled, grilled, roasted, sautéed, pan-fried, simmered, braised or stewed, provided you follow a few simple procedures and learn which cuts respond best to the various cooking methods.

QUESTIONS FOR DISCUSSION

1. Explain the difference between primals, subprimals and fabricated cuts of meat. Why is it important to be skilled in meat fabrication?

2. What is connective tissue composed of and where is it found? What happens to connective tissues at normal cooking temperatures?

3. Discuss the government's role in regulating the marketing and sale of meat.

4. At what temperature should fresh meat be stored? At what temperature should frozen meat be stored?

5. Would it be better to grill or braise a piece of meat that contains a great deal of connective tissue? Explain your answer.

6. List three ways to improve the cooking qualities of lean meats. What techniques can be used to compensate for the lack of fat?

7. Describe the similarities between sautéing meats and pan-frying them. Describe the differences.

8. Describe the similarities between braising meats and stewing them. Describe the differences.

CHAPTER 13
BEEF

eef is the meat of domesticated cattle. Most of the beef Americans eat comes from steers, which are male cattle castrated as calves and specifically raised for beef. Although Americans are consuming less beef today than we once did, we still consume far more beef than any other meat. The beef we are eating is leaner than that of years past, thanks to advances in animals husbandry and closer trimming of exterior fat.

PRIMAL AND SUBPRIMAL CUTS OF BEEF

After the steer is slaughtered it is cut into four pieces (called quarters) for easy handling. This is done by first splitting the carcass down the backbone into two bilateral halves. Each half is divided into the forequarter (the front portion) and hindquarter (the rear portion) by cutting along the natural curvature between the twelfth and thirteenth ribs. The quartered carcass is then further reduced into the primal cuts and the subprimal and fabricated cuts.

The primal cuts of beef are the chuck, brisket and shank, rib, short plate, short loin, sirloin, flank and round. Figure 13.1 shows the relationship between a steer's bone structure and the primal cuts. It is important to know the location of bones when cutting or working with meats. This makes meat fabrication and carving easier and aids in identifying cuts. Figure 13.2 shows the primal cuts of beef and their location on the carcass. An entire beef carcass can range in weight from 500 to more than 800 pounds (225–360 kg).

Forequarter

Chuck

The primal chuck is the animal's shoulder; it accounts for approximately 28% of carcass weight. It contains a portion of the backbone (which, in turn, consists of feather, finger and chine bones), five rib bones and portions of the blade and arm bones.

Because an animal constantly uses its shoulder muscles, chuck contains a high percentage of connective tissue and is quite tough. This tough cut of beef, however, is one of the most flavorful.

The primal chuck is used less frequently than other primal cuts in food service operations. If cooked whole, the chuck is difficult to cut or carve because of the large number of bones and relatively small muscle groups which travel in different directions.

The primal chuck produces several fabricated cuts: cross rib pot roast, chuck short ribs, cubed or tenderized steaks, stew meat and ground chuck. Because the meat is tough, the fabricated cuts usually benefit from moist-heat cooking or combination cooking methods such as stewing and braising.

Brisket and Shank

The brisket and shank are located beneath the primal chuck on the front half of the carcass. Together, they form a single primal that accounts for approximately 8% of the carcass weight. This primal consists of the steer's breast (the

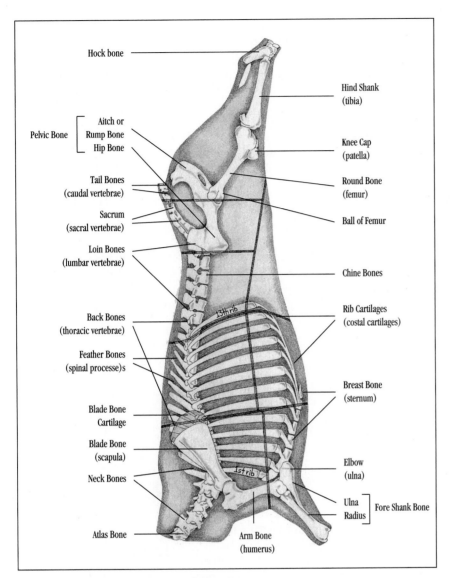

FIGURE 13.1 *The Skeletal Structure of a Steer*

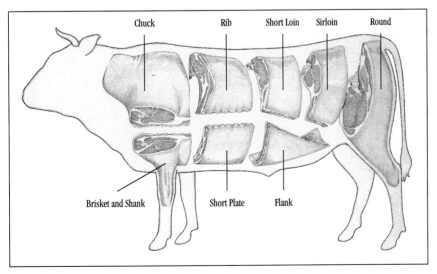

FIGURE 13.2 *The Primal Cuts of Beef*

brisket), which contains ribs and breast bone, and its arm (the foreshank), which contains only the shank bone.

The ribs and breast bone are always removed from the brisket before cooking. The boneless brisket is very tough and contains a substantial percentage of fat, both intermuscular and subcutaneous. It is well suited for moist-heat and combination cooking methods such as simmering or braising. It is often pickled or corned to produce corned beef brisket, or cured and peppered to make pastrami.

Beef foreshanks are very flavorful and high in collagen. Because collagen converts to gelatin when cooked using moist heat, foreshanks are excellent for making soups and stocks. Ground shank meat is often used to help clarify and flavor consommés because of its rich flavor and high collagen content.

Rib

The primal beef rib accounts for approximately 10% of carcass weight. It consists of ribs 6 through 12 as well as a portion of the backbone.

This primal is best known for yielding roast prime rib of beef. Prime rib is not named after the quality grade USDA Prime. Rather, its name reflects the fact that it constitutes the majority of the primal cut. The eye meat of the rib (the center muscle portion) is not a well-exercised muscle and therefore is quite tender. It also contains large amounts of marbling compared to the rest of the carcass and produces rich, full-flavored roasts and steaks. Although roasting the eye muscle on the rib bones produces a moister roast, the eye meat can be removed to produce a boneless rib eye roast or cut into rib eye steaks. The rib bones that are separated from the rib eye meat are quite meaty and flavorful and can be served as barbecued beef ribs. The ends of the rib bones that are trimmed off the primal rib to produce the rib roast are known as beef short ribs. They are meaty and are often served as braised beef short ribs.

Oven-ready Rib Roast

Beef Rib Eye Roll

Short Plate

The short plate is located directly below the primal rib on a side of beef; it accounts for only a small portion of the overall weight of the carcass, approximately 9%. The short plate contains rib bones and cartilage and produces the meaty plate short ribs and skirt steak.

Short ribs are meaty, yet high in connective tissue, and are best when braised. Skirt steak is often marinated and grilled as fajitas. Other, less meaty portions of the short plate are trimmed and ground.

Skirt Steak

Hindquarter

Short Loin

The short loin is the anterior (front) portion of the beef loin. It is located just behind the rib and becomes the first primal cut of the hindquarter when the side of beef is divided into a forequarter and hindquarter. It accounts for approximately 8% of carcass weight.

Porterhouse or T-bone Steaks

The short loin contains a single rib, the thirteenth, and a portion of the backbone. With careful butchering, this small primal can yield several subprimal and fabricated cuts, all of which are among the most tender, popular and expensive cuts of beef.

The loin eye muscle, a continuation of the rib eye muscle, runs along the top of the T-shaped bones that form the backbone. Beneath the loin eye muscle on the other side of the backbone is the tenderloin, the most tender cut of all.

When the short loin is cut in cross sections with the bone in, it produces—starting with the rib end of the short loin—club steaks (which do not contain any tenderloin), T-bone steaks (which contain only a small portion of tenderloin) and porterhouse steaks (which are cut from the sirloin end of the short loin and contain a large portion of tenderloin).

Strip Loin

The whole tenderloin also can be removed and cut into chateaubriand, filet mignon and tournedos. A portion of the tenderloin is located in the sirloin portion of the loin. When the entire beef loin is divided into the primal short loin and primal sirloin, the large end of the tenderloin (the butt tenderloin) is separated from the remainder of the tenderloin and remains in the sirloin; the smaller end of the tenderloin (the short tenderloin) remains in the short loin. If the tenderloin is to be kept whole, it must be removed before the short loin and sirloin are separated. The loin eye meat can be removed from the bones, producing a boneless strip loin, which is very tender and can be roasted or cut into boneless strip steaks.

Tenderloin

Sirloin

The sirloin is located in the hindquarter, between the short loin and the round. It accounts for approximately 7% of carcass weight and contains part of the backbone as well as a portion of the hip bone.

The sirloin produces bone-in or boneless roasts and steaks that are flavorful and tender. With the exception of the tenderloin portion, however, these subprimals and fabricated cuts are not as tender as those from the strip loin. Cuts from the sirloin are cooked using dry-heat methods such as broiling, grilling or roasting.

Top Sirloin Butt

Flank

The flank is located directly beneath the loin, posterior to (behind) the short plate. It accounts for approximately 6% of carcass weight. The flank contains no bones.

Although quite flavorful, it is tough meat with a good deal of fat and connective tissue. Flank meat is usually trimmed and ground, with the exception of the flank steak or London broil. The flank also contains a small piece of meat known as the hanging tenderloin. Although not actually part of the tenderloin, it is very tender and can be cooked using any method.

Flank Steak

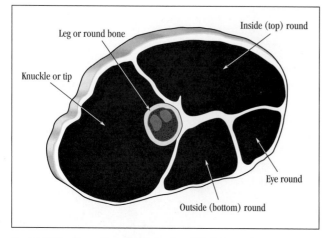

FIGURE 13.3 *Cross Cut of Muscles in a Whole Round*

Beef Round Rump and
Shank PartiallyRemoved
(Steamship Round)

Top (or Inside) Round

Round

The primal round is very large, weighing as much as 200 pounds (90 kg) and accounting for approximately 24% of carcass weight. It is the hind leg of the animal and contains the round, aitch, shank and tail bones.

Meat from the round is flavorful and fairly tender. The round yields a wide variety of subprimal and fabricated cuts: the top round, outside round, eye round (the outside round and the eye round together are called the bottom round), knuckle and shank. See Figure 13.3. Steaks cut from the round are tough, but because they have large muscles and limited intermuscular fat, the top round and knuckle make good roasts. The bottom round is best when braised. The hindshank is prepared in the same fashion as the foreshank.

Organ Meats

Several organ meats are used in food service operations. This group of products is known as **offal**. It includes the heart, kidney, tongue, tripe (stomach lining) and oxtail. Offal benefit from moist-heat cooking and are often used in soup, stew or braised dishes.

Offal— *also called variety meats, edible entrails (for example, the heart, kidneys, liver, sweetbreads and tongue) and extremities (for example, oxtail and pig's feet) of an animal.*

BUTCHERING PROCEDURES

Although many food service operations buy their beef previously cut and portioned, you still should be able to fabricate cuts of beef and perform basic butchering tasks.

PROCEDURE FOR CUTTING A NEW YORK STEAK FROM A BONELESS STRIP LOIN

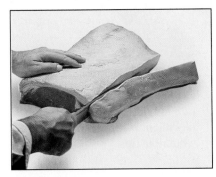

1. Square up the strip loin by trimming off the lip so it extends 1 to 2 inches (2.5 to 5 cm) from the eye muscle.

2. Turn the strip over and trim off any fat or connective tissue.

3. Turn the strip back over and trim the fat covering to a uniform thickness of 1/4 inch (6 mm).

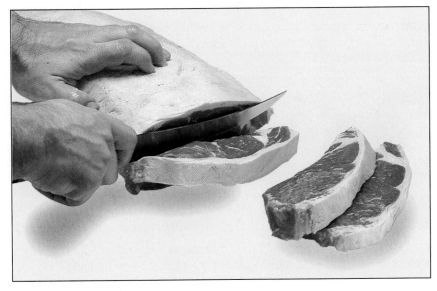

4. Cut the steaks to the thickness or weight desired.

5. The eye meat of steaks located on the sirloin end of the strip is divided by a strip of connective tissue. Steaks cut from this area are called vein steaks and are inferior to steaks cut from the rib end of the strip.

PROCEDURE FOR TRIMMING A FULL BEEF TENDERLOIN AND CUTTING IT INTO CHATEAUBRIAND, FILET MIGNON AND TENDER TIPS

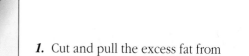

1. Cut and pull the excess fat from the entire tenderloin to expose the meat.

2. Remove the chain muscle from the side of the tenderloin. (Although it contains much connective tissue, the chain muscle may be trimmed and the meat used as tenderloin trimmings in various dishes.)

3. Trim away all the fat and silverskin. Do so by loosening a small piece of silverskin, then, holding the loosened silverskin tightly with one hand, cut it away in long strips, angling the knife up toward the silverskin slightly so that only the silverskin is removed and no meat is wasted.

4. Cut the tenderloin as desired into (left to right) tips, chateaubriand, filet mignon, tournedo tips, and tenderloin tips.

PROCEDURE FOR BUTTERFLYING MEATS

Many cuts of boneless meats such as tenderloin steaks and boneless pork chops can be butterflied to create a thinner cut that has a greater surface area and cooks more quickly.

1. Make the first cut nearly all the way through the meat, keeping it attached by leaving approximately 1/4 inch (6 mm) uncut.

2. Make a second cut, this time cutting all the way through, completely removing the steak from the tenderloin.

TABLE 13.1   USING COMMON CUTS OF BEEF

Primal	Subprimal or Fabricated Cut	IMPS	Cooking Methods	Serving Suggestions
Chuck	Chuck roll tied	116A	Combination (braise; stew)	Pot roast; beef stew
	Stew meat	135A	Combination (stew)	Beef stew
	Ground beef	136	Dry heat (broil or grill; roast)	Hamburgers; meatloaf
			Combination (braise; stew)	Chili con carne; beef stews
Brisket and Shank	Brisket	120	Moist heat (simmer)	Corned beef; New England boiled dinner
			Combination (braise)	Pot roast
	Shank	117	Combination (braise)	Shredded beef for tamales or hash
Rib	Oven ready rib roast	109	Dry heat (roast)	Roast prime rib
	Rib eye roll	112	Dry heat (roast)	Roast prime rib
Short Plate	Skirt steak	121D	Dry heat (broil or grill)	Steak; fajitas
	Short ribs	123A	Combination (braise)	Braised short ribs
Short Loin	Porterhouse or T-bone steaks	173, 174	Dry heat (broil or grill)	Steaks
	Strip loin	180	Dry heat (broil or grill; roast; sauté)	New York steak; minute steak entrecôtes bordelaise
	Tenderloin	189	Dry heat (broil or grill; roast)	Tournedos Rossini; beef Wellington
Flank	Flank steak	193	Dry heat (broil or grill)	London broil
			Combination (braise)	Braised stuffed flank steak
Round	Steamship round	160	Dry heat (roast)	Roast beef
	Top (inside) round	168	Dry heat (roast)	Roast beef
			Combination (braise)	Braised beef roulade

CONCLUSION

Antonin Carême once said that "beef is the soul of cooking." It is also the most popular meat consumed in the United States and undoubtedly will play an important role on almost any menu. Beef's assertive flavor stands up well to most any sauce and seasonings.

Prefabricated products are readily available. But preforming some basic fabrication procedures in your own kitchen saves money and allows you to cut the meat to your exact specifications. Each primal and subprimal cut has its own distinct characteristics. The primal rib, short loin and sirloin produce the most popular and most expensive cuts of beef. Once the beef is properly fabricated, choose the appropriate dry-heat, moist-heat or combination cooking method for that cut.

QUESTIONS FOR DISCUSSION

1. List each beef primal cut and describe its location on the carcass. For each primal cut, identify two subprimal or fabricated cuts taken from it.

2. Would it be better to use the chuck for grilling or stewing? Explain your answer.

3. Which fabricated cuts contain a portion of the tenderloin? What cooking methods are best suited for these cuts? Explain your answer.

4. Name four cuts that can be produced from a whole beef tenderloin. Describe a preparation procedure for each cut.

5. Most steaks are cut from the hindquarter. What popular steak is cut from the forequarter, and why is it tender when other cuts from the forequarter are relatively tough?

ADDITIONAL BEEF RECIPES

RECIPE 13.1

T-BONE STEAK

NOTE: *This dish appears in the Chapter Opening photograph.*

RUTH'S CHRIS STEAK HOUSE, PHOENIX, AZ

Yield: 1 Serving			Method: Broiling
T-bone steak, 24 oz. (700 g)	1	1	
Salt and pepper	TT	TT	
Whole butter, melted	1 oz.	30 g	
Parsley, chopped	as needed	as needed	

1. Season both sides of the steak with the salt and pepper.

2. Broil the steak to the desired degree of doneness and place on a very hot serving platter.

3. Ladle the melted butter over the steak and sprinkle with chopped parsley.

◆◆◆

RECIPE 13.2

MARINATED LONDON BROIL

Yield: 6 5-8 oz. (150- 250-g) Servings			Method: Grilling
Marinade:			
Olive oil	4 oz.	120 g	
Balsamic vinegar	4 oz.	120 g	
Fresh rosemary, chopped	2 Tbsp.	30 ml	
Garlic, minced	2 oz.	60 g	
Pepper	1 tsp.	5 ml	
Beef flank steak, 2–3 lb. (1 to 1-1/2 kg)	1	1	

1. Combine the marinade ingredients in a hotel pan.

2. Add the flank steak to the marinade and coat completely. Allow the meat to marinate for at least 4 hours.

3. Grill the steak rare to medium rare. If cooked further, the meat will become extremely tough.

4. Carve into 1/4-inch (6 millimeter) think slices, cutting diagonally across the grain.

◆◆◆

RECIPE 13.3

CHATEAUBRIAND

ANA WESTIN HOTEL, Washington D.C.
Chef Leland Atkinson

Yield: 2 Servings   **Method:** Roasting

Beef filet, cut from the "head" of the tenderloin, 16–24 ounces (500–750 grams)	1	1
Salt and pepper	TT	TT
Clarified butter	as needed	as needed

1. Tie the beef with butcher's twine and season with salt and pepper.
2. Sauté the beef in clarified butter until it is well browned.
3. Transfer the beef to a 450°F (230°C) oven and roast until done, approximately 10–12 minutes for rare (internal temperature of 125°F/52°C), or 15–18 minutes for medium (140°F/60°C).
4. Remove the beef from the oven and allow it to rest for at least 5 minutes before carving.
5. At service time, slice the beef evenly on a slight diagonal bias.

Chateaubriand is traditionally served with béarnaise sauce and a bouquetiére of vegetables.

◆◆◆

RECIPE 13.4

HOME-STYLE MEATLOAF

Yield: 16 8-oz. (250-g) Servings   **Method:** Baking

Onion, small dice	1 lb.	450 g
Celery, small dice	8 oz.	250 g
Garlic, chopped	2 Tbsp.	30 ml
Oil	2 oz.	60 g
Fresh bread crumbs	6 oz.	180 g
Tomato juice	12 oz.	350 g
Ground beef	4 lb.	1.8 kg
Ground pork	4 lb.	1.8 kg
Eggs, beaten	6	6
Salt	1 Tbsp.	15 ml
Pepper	1 tsp.	5 ml
Parsley, chopped	2 Tbsp.	30 ml

1. Sauté the onions, celery and garlic in the oil until tender. Remove from the heat and cool.
2. Combine all ingredients; mix well.
3. Form into loaves of the desired size and place in loaf pans.
4. Bake at 350°F (180°C) until the meatloaf reaches an internal temperature of 165°F (74°C), approximately 1 to 1-1/2 hours.
5. Allow the loaves to rest 15 minutes before slicing. Cut slices of the desired thickness and serve with a tomato or mushroom sauce.

◆◆◆

RECIPE 13.5

TOURNEDOS ROSSINI

Yield: 4 Servings		Method: Sautéing
Tournedos, 3 oz. (90 g) each	8	8
Clarified butter	as needed	as needed
Croutons	8	8
Foie gras, 1-oz. (30-g) slices	8	8
Truffle slices	8	8
Madeira	4 oz.	120 g
Demi-glace	8 oz.	225 g
Salt and pepper	TT	TT

1. Sauté the beef in clarified butter to the desired doneness. Place each tournedo on top of a crouton. Top each with a slice of foie gras, then a slice of truffle. Hold in a warm place.
2. Degrease the pan. Deglaze the pan with the madeira and add the demi-glace.
3. Reduce the sauce to the desired consistency and adjust the seasonings.
4. Warm the tournedos briefly under a broiler or in the oven. Pour the sauce around the tournedos. Garnish with watercress, sautéed asparagus and château potatoes.

◆◆◆

RECIPE 13.6

MINUTE STEAK DIJONAISE

Yield: 2 Servings		Method: Sautéing
Sirloin steak, trimmed, 6 oz. (170 g)	2	2
Dijon mustard	1 oz.	30 g
Onion, small dice	2 oz.	60 g
Clarified butter	1 oz.	30 g
Heavy cream	3 oz.	90 g
Whole butter	1 oz.	30 g
Salt and pepper	TT	TT

1. Pound the steaks to a 1/4-inch (6-millimeter) thickness.
2. Cover one side of each sirloin first with 1-1/2 teaspoons (8 milliliters) of the mustard and then half the onions, pressing the onions firmly into the steak.
3. Sauté the steaks in the clarified butter, presentation (onion) side down first. Remove and hold in a warm place.
4. Degrease the pan. Add the cream and reduce by half. Add the rest of the Dijon mustard.
5. Monte au beurre. Adjust the seasonings and serve the steaks with the sauce.

◆◆◆

RECIPE 13.7

BEEF STROGANOFF

Yield: 8 8-oz. (250-g) Servings		Method: Sautéing
Tenderloin tips, émincé	2 lb.	1 kg
Clarified butter	1-1/2 oz.	45 g
Onion, medium dice	4 oz.	120 g

Mushrooms, halved	1 lb.	450 g
Demi-glace	10 oz.	300 g
Heavy cream	10 oz.	300 g
Sour cream	8 oz.	250 g
Dijon mustard	1 Tbsp.	15 ml
Fresh dill, chopped	1 Tbsp.	15 ml
Fresh parsley, chopped	1 Tbsp.	15 ml
Salt and pepper	TT	TT
Egg noodles, cooked	24 oz.	700 g

1. Sauté the tenderloin tips in the butter, searing on all sides. Remove the meat and set aside.
2. Add the onion to the pan and sauté lightly. Add the mushrooms and sauté until dry.
3. Add the demi-glace. Bring to a boil, reduce to a simmer and cook 10 minutes.
4. Add the cream, sour cream, mustard and any meat juices that accumulated while holding the meat.
5. Return the meat to the sauce to reheat. Stir in the dill and parsley. Adjust the seasonings and serve over egg noodles.

◆◆◆

RECIPE 13.8
ENTRECÔTES BORDELAISE

Yield: 4 Servings   **Method:** Sautéing

Beef marrow	4 oz.	120 g
Entrecôtes, 14 oz. (400 g) each	2	2
Salt and pepper	TT	TT
Clarified butter	2 oz.	60 g
Shallots, chopped	2 Tbsp.	30 ml
Red wine	8 oz.	250 g
Demi-glace	12 oz.	340 g
Whole butter	1 oz.	30 g

1. Slice the marrow into rounds and poach in salt water for 3 minutes. Drain the marrow and set it aside.
2. Season the steaks and sauté them in the clarified butter to the desired doneness. Finish in the oven if desired. Remove to a platter and hold in a warm place.
3. Sauté the shallots in the same pan.
4. Deglaze the pan with the wine and reduce by half. Add the demi-glace; simmer for 5 minutes.
5. Monte au beurre.
6. Add the marrow to the sauce. Adjust the seasonings and serve the steaks with the sauce.

◆◆◆

RECIPE 13.9
PEPPER STEAK

Yield: 2 Servings   **Method:** Sautéing

Boneless strip steaks, approx. 8 oz. (250 g) each	2	2

Continued

Salt	TT	TT
Peppercorns, cracked	3 Tbsp.	45 ml
Clarified butter	1 oz.	30 g
Cognac	2 oz.	60 g
Heavy cream	4 oz.	120 g
Whole butter	2 oz.	60 g

1. Season the steaks with salt. Spread the peppercorns in a hotel pan and press the steaks into them, lightly coating each side.

2. Sauté the steaks in the clarified butter over high heat for 2 to 3 minutes on each side.

3. Remove the pan from the heat. Pour the cognac over the steaks, return the pan to the heat and flambé. When the flames subside, remove the steaks from the pan and keep them warm on a plate.

4. Add the cream to the pan. Bring to a boil and reduce for 2 minutes over high heat; monte au beurre. Pour this sauce over the steaks and serve immediately.

═══════════ ◆◆◆ ═══════════

RECIPE 13.10

SWISS STEAK

Yield: 10 Servings   **Method:** Braising

Beef bottom round steaks, 6 oz. (180 g) each	10	10
Flour	as needed	as needed
Salt and pepper	TT	TT
Oil	2 oz.	60 g
Onion, small dice	1 lb.	450 g
Garlic cloves, crushed	3	3
Celery	8 oz.	250 g
Flour	4 oz.	120 g
Brown stock	5 pt.	2.2 lt
Tomato purée	6 oz.	180 g
Sachet:		
Bay leaves	2	2
Dried thyme	1/2 tsp.	2 ml
Peppercorns, crushed	1/2 tsp.	2 ml
Parsley stems	8	8

1. Dredge the steaks in flour seasoned with salt and pepper.

2. Heat the oil in a braiser and brown the steaks well on both sides. Remove the steaks.

3. Add the onions, garlic and celery; sauté until tender.

4. Add the flour and cook to a brown roux.

5. Gradually add the brown stock, whisking until the sauce is thickened and smooth. Add the tomato purée and sachet.

6. Return the steaks to the braising pan, cover and cook in a 300°F (150°C) oven until tender, approximately 2 hours.

7. Remove the steaks from the sauce. Discard the sachet. Strain the sauce and adjust the seasonings. Serve the steaks with the sauce.

◆◆◆

RECIPE 13.11
BRAISED SHORT RIBS OF BEEF

Yield: 8 8-oz. (230-g) Servings   **Method:** Braising

Flour	4 oz.	120 g
Salt	1 Tbsp.	15 ml
Pepper	1 tsp.	5 ml
Dried rosemary	1/2 tsp.	2 ml
Short ribs of beef,		
cut in 2-in. (5 cm) portions	6 lbs.	2.7 kg
Vegetable oil	1 oz.	30 g
Onion, chopped	6 oz.	170 g
Celery, chopped	4 oz.	120 g
Brown beef stock	24 oz.	700 g
Roux	as needed	as needed
Salt and pepper	TT	TT

1. Combine the flour, salt, pepper and rosemary. Dredge the ribs in the seasoned flour.
2. Heat the oil and brown the ribs well in a heavy brazier. Remove and hold in a warm place.
3. Add the vegetables to the brazier and sauté lightly.
4. Return the ribs to the pan, add the stock and braise in an oven until done, approximately 2-1/2 hours.
5. Remove the ribs from the liquid and skim off the excess fat.
6. Bring the liquid to a boil on the stove top; thicken it with roux to the desired consistency and simmer 15 minutes. Strain the sauce and adjust the seasonings. Return the ribs to the sauce and simmer for 5 minutes.

◆◆◆

RECIPE 13.12
HUNGARIAN GOULASH

Yield: 10 8-oz. (250-g) Servings   **Method:** Stewing

Lard or vegetable oil	2 oz.	60 g
Onion, medium dice	2 lb.	900 g
Hungarian paprika	4 Tbsp.	60 ml
Garlic, chopped	1 Tbsp.	15 ml
Caraway seeds	1/2 tsp.	2 ml
Salt	TT	TT
Pepper	1/2 tsp.	2 ml
White stock	1 qt.	1 lt
Tomato paste	4 oz.	120 g
Beef stew meat,		
cut in 1-1/2-in. (4-cm) cubes	5 lb.	2.2 kg

1. Sauté the onions in the lard or oil, browning lightly.
2. Add the paprika, garlic, caraway seeds, salt and pepper; mix well.
3. Add the white stock and tomato paste. Bring to a boil, then reduce to a simmer.
4. Add the meat and braise until the meat is very tender, approximately 1-1/2 hours. Adjust the seasonings and serve.

◆◆◆

RECIPE 13.13
BEEF BOURGUIGNON

Yield: 10 8-oz. (250-g) Servings   **Method:** Stewing

Marinade:		
Garlic cloves, crushed	3	3
Onions, sliced	3	3
Carrots, sliced	2	2
Parsley stems	10	10
Bouquet garni:		
Carrot stick, 4 in. (10 cm)	1	1
Leek, split, 4-in. (10-cm) piece	1	1
Fresh thyme	1 sprig	1 sprig
Bay leaf	1	1
Peppercorns, crushed	10	10
Salt	TT	TT
Dry red wine, preferably Burgundy	26 oz.	750 ml
Beef chuck, cubed for stew	4 lb.	1.8 kg
Vegetable oil	2 oz.	60 g
Flour	2 Tbsp.	30 ml
Tomato paste	1 Tbsp.	15 ml
Tomatoes, quartered	4	4
Brown stock	1 pint	450 ml
Mushrooms, quartered	1 lb.	450 g
Unsalted butter	1-1/2 oz.	45 g
Pearl onions, boiled and peeled	30	30
Salt and pepper	TT	TT

1. Combine the garlic, onions, carrots, parsley, bouquet garni, peppercorns, salt and wine to make a marinade.
2. Marinate the meat several hours under refrigeration.
3. Remove and drain the meat. Reserve the marinade.
4. Dry the beef and sauté it in the oil until well browned. Do this in several batches if necessary.
5. Return all the meat to the pot. Sprinkle with flour and cook to make a blond roux.
6. Stir in the tomato paste and cook for 5 minutes.
7. Add the reserved marinade, tomatoes and brown stock. Cook in a 350°F (180°C) oven until the meat is tender, approximately 2-1/2 hours.
8. Remove the meat from the sauce. Strain the sauce through a china cap, pressing to extract all of the liquid. Discard the solids. Return the liquid and beef to the pot.
9. Sauté the mushrooms in the butter and add them to the meat and sauce. Add the onions and adjust the seasonings. Simmer for 10 minutes to blend the flavors.

◆◆◆

RECIPE 13.14
CHILI CON CARNE

Yield: 1 gal. (4 lt)   **Method:** Braising

Onion, medium dice	1 lb.	450 g
Vegetable oil	1 Tbsp.	15 ml

Garlic, chopped	1/2 oz.	15 g
Ground beef	2 lb. 8 oz.	1.2 kg
Tomato, crushed	2 lb.	1 kg
Tomato, diced	4 lb.	1.8 kg
Tomato paste	4 oz.	120 g
Brown stock	1 pt.	450 ml
Chili powder	1 oz.	30 g
Cumin	2 tsp.	10 ml
Bay leaves	4	4
Salt and pepper	TT	TT
Dry kidney beans, soaked and		
simmered in water until tender	12 oz.	350 g

1. Sauté the onions in the oil until tender. Add the garlic and sauté one minute.
2. Add the beef and brown, stirring occasionally. Drain off the excess fat.
3. Add the remaining ingredients, bring to a simmer, cover and cook for 1 hour.
4. Remove the bay leaves and adjust the seasonings.

◆◆◆

RECIPE 13.15

OXTAIL RAGOUT

Yield: 8 10-oz. (300-g) Servings   **Method:** Stewing

Oxtail pieces, 2 in. (5 cm)	4 lb.	1.8 kg
Flour	as needed	as needed
Salt and pepper	TT	TT
Oil	2 oz.	60 g
Mirepoix	1 lb.	450 g
Fatty prosciutto, small dice	4 oz.	120 g
Garlic cloves, crushed	4	4
Sachet:		
Bay leaf	1	1
Dried thyme	1/2 tsp.	2 ml
Peppercorns, crushed	1/2 tsp.	2 ml
Parsley stems	10	10
Tomato concasse	1 lb.	450 g
White wine	8 oz.	250 g
Lemon zest, julienne	1 tsp.	5 ml
Brown stock	2 qt.	2 lt

1. Trim the excess fat from the oxtail pieces and dredge them in flour seasoned with salt and pepper.
2. Brown the oxtail in the oil. Add the mirepoix, prosciutto and garlic; sauté until the vegetables are tender.
3. Add the sachet, tomato concasse, white wine, lemon zest and brown stock. Cover and bring to a simmer on the stove top or place in a 325°F (160°C) oven and cook until the oxtails are tender, approximately 2 hours.
4. Remove the oxtails from the sauce. Strain and degrease the sauce. Adjust the seasonings. Return the oxtails to the sauce.
5. Serve the ragout with buttered noodles; garnish with batonnet carrots and turnips that have been cooked separately.

CHAPTER 14
VEAL

*C*ows must calve before they begin to give milk. These calves are the basis of today's veal industry. Veal is the meat of calves under the age of nine months. Most veal comes from calves slaughtered when they are eight to sixteen weeks old, however. Veal is lighter in color than beef, has a more delicate flavor and is generally more tender. Young veal has a firm texture, light pink color and very little fat. As soon as a calf starts eating solid food, the iron in the food begins to turn the young animal's meat red. Meat from calves slaughtered when they are older than five months is called calf. It tends to be a deeper red, with some marbling and external fat.

Veal's low fat content makes it a popular meat, especially among those looking for an alternative to beef. Its delicate flavor is complemented by both classic and modern sauces.

After studying this chapter you will be able to:

♦ identify the primal, subprimal and fabricated cuts of veal
♦ perform basic butchering procedures
♦ apply appropriate cooking methods to several common cuts of veal

FORMULA-FED VEAL VERSUS FREE-RANGE VEAL

Most veal produced today is known as formula-fed veal. Formula-fed calves are fed only nutrient-rich liquids; they are tethered in pens only slightly larger than their bodies to restrict their movements. Preventing the calves from eating grasses and other foods containing iron keeps their flesh white; restricting movement keeps their muscles from toughening. In recent years controversy and allegations of cruelty have arisen concerning these methods.

An alternative to formula-fed veal is free-range veal. Free-range veal is produced from calves that are allowed to roam freely and eat grasses and other natural foods. Because they consume feed containing iron, their flesh is a reddish pink and has a substantially different flavor than meat from formula-fed calves of the same age.

Opinions differ on which has the better flavor. Some chefs prefer the consistently mild, sweet taste of formula-fed veal. Others prefer the more substantial flavor of free-range veal. The two are interchangeable in recipes. Cost, however, may be the ultimate deciding factor when determining which to use. Free-range veal is more expensive than formula-fed veal because of its limited production.

PRIMAL AND SUBPRIMAL CUTS OF VEAL

After slaughter, the calf carcass can be split down the backbone into two bilateral halves or, more typically, cut along the natural curvature between the eleventh and twelfth ribs into a foresaddle (front portion) and a hindsaddle (rear portion). The veal carcass yields five primal cuts: three from the foresaddle (the shoulder, foreshank and breast, and rib), and two from the hindsaddle (the loin and leg). The veal shoulder, rib and loin primals contain both bilateral portions; that is, a veal loin contains both sides of the animal's loin.

Figure 14.1 shows the relationship between the calf's bone structure and the primal cuts. As with all meats, it is important to know the location of bones when cutting or working with veal. This makes meat fabrication and carving easier and aids in identifying cuts. Figure 14.2 shows the primal cuts of veal and their location. A veal carcass weighs in a range of 60 to 245 pounds (27–110 kg).

Foresaddle

Shoulder

Similar to the beef shoulder or chuck, the veal shoulder accounts for 21% of carcass weight. It contains four rib bones (as opposed to five in the beef chuck) and portions of the backbone, blade and arm bones.

The backbone, blade and arm bones are sometimes removed and the meat roasted or stuffed and roasted. Although shoulder chops and steaks can be fabricated, they are inferior to the chops cut from more tender areas such as the loin or rib. Often the shoulder meat is ground or cubed for stew. Because of the relatively large amount of connective tissue it contains, meat from the shoulder is best braised or stewed.

Foreshank and Breast

The foreshank and breast are located beneath the shoulder and rib sections on the front half of the carcass. They are considered one primal cut. Combined,

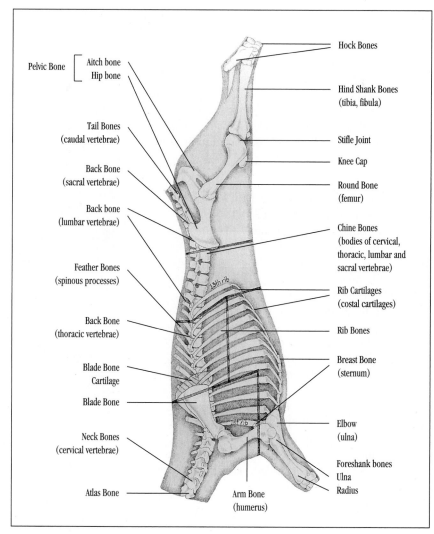

FIGURE 14.1   *The Skeletal Structure of a Calf*

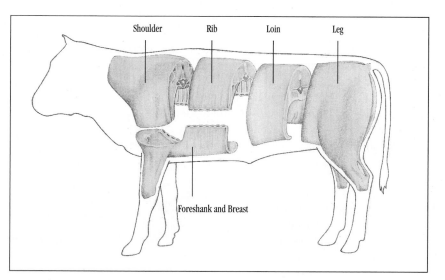

FIGURE 14.2   *The Primal Cuts of Veal*

they account for approximately 16% of carcass weight. This primal contains rib bones and rib cartilage, breast bones and shank bones. Because the calf is slaughtered young, many of the breast bones are cartilaginous rather than bony.

This cartilage, as well as the ample fat and connective tissue also present in the breast, breaks down during long moist cooking, thus making the flavorful breast a good choice for braising. Veal breast can also be cubed for stews such as veal fricassee and veal blanquette, rolled and stuffed, or trimmed and ground.

The foreshank is also very flavorful but tough. It can be braised whole or sliced perpendicular to the shank bone and braised to produce osso buco.

Rib

The double rib, also known as a veal hotel rack, is a very tender, relatively small cut accounting for approximately 9% of carcass weight. It is very popular and very expensive. The double rack consists of two racks, each with seven rib bones and a portion of the backbone.

Veal racks can be roasted either whole or split into two sides. Veal racks can be boned out; each side produces a veal rib eye and a small piece of tenderloin known as the short tenderloin, both of which make excellent roasts. More often, veal racks are trimmed and cut into chops, which can also be bone-in or boneless, to be grilled, sautéed or braised.

Veal Hotel Rack, Split

Hindsaddle

Loin

The veal loin is posterior to the primal rib, contains two ribs (numbers 12 and 13) and accounts for approximately 10% of carcass weight. The loin consists of the loin eye muscle on top of the rib bones and the tenderloin under them.

The veal loin eye is very tender and the tenderloin is, without a doubt, the most tender cut of veal. If the primal veal loin is separated from the primal leg before the tenderloin is removed, the tenderloin will be cut into two pieces. The small portion (short tenderloin) remains in the primal loin and the large portion (butt tenderloin) remains in the sirloin portion of the primal leg. The tenderloin is sometimes removed and cut into medallions. The veal loin is often cut into chops, bone-in or boneless. It is usually cooked using dry heat such as broiling, grilling, roasting or sautéing.

Veal Loin

Loin Chops

Boneless Strip Loin

Leg

The primal veal leg consists of both the sirloin and the leg. Together they account for approximately 42% of carcass weight. The primal leg is separated from the loin by a cut perpendicular to the backbone immediately anterior to the hip bone, and it contains portions of the backbone, tail bone, hip bone, aitch bone, round bone and hind shank.

Although it is tender enough to be roasted whole, the veal leg is typically fabricated into cutlets and scallops. To fabricate these cuts, the leg is first broken down into its major muscles: the top round, eye round, knuckle, sirloin, bottom round (which includes the sirloin) and butt tenderloin. Each of these muscles can be reduced to scallops by trimming all fat and visible connective tissue and slicing against the grain to the desired thickness. The scallops then should be pounded carefully to tenderize them further and to prevent them from curling when cooked.

The hindshank is somewhat meatier than the foreshank but both are prepared and cooked in the same manner.

Veal Leg

Because the veal carcass is small enough to be handled easily, it is sometimes purchased in forms larger than the primal cuts described above. Depending on employee skill, available equipment and storage space and an ability to utilize fully all the cuts and trimmings that fabricating meat produces, you may want to purchase veal in one of the following forms:

Top Round

- ✦ *Foresaddle:* The anterior portion of the carcass after it is severed from the hindsaddle by a cut following the natural curvature between the eleventh and twelfth ribs. It contains the primal shoulder, foreshank and breast, and rib.
- ✦ *Hindsaddle:* The posterior portion of the carcass after it is severed from the foresaddle. It contains the primal loin and leg.
- ✦ *Back:* The trimmed rib and loin sections in one piece. The back is particularly useful when producing large quantities of veal chops.
- ✦ *Veal side:* One bilateral half of the carcass, produced by cutting lengthwise thorough the backbone.

Hindshank Cut for Osso Buco

Organ Meats

Several calf organ meats are used in food service operations.

Sweetbreads

Sweetbreads are the thymus glands of veal and lamb. As an animal ages, its thymus gland shrinks; therefore sweetbreads are not available from older cattle or sheep. Veal sweetbreads are much more popular than lamb sweetbreads in this country. Good-quality sweetbreads should be plump and firm, with the exterior membrane intact. Delicately flavored and tender, they can be prepared by almost any cooking method.

Sweetbreads

Calves' Liver

Calves' liver is much more popular than beef liver because of its tenderness and mild flavor. Good quality calves' liver should be firm and moist, with a shiny appearance and without any off-odor. It is most often sliced and sautéed or broiled and served with a sauce.

Calves' Liver

Kidneys

Kidneys

Kidneys are more popular in other parts of the world than in the United States. Good-quality kidneys should be plump, firm and encased in a shiny membrane. Properly prepared kidneys have a rich flavor and firm texture; they are best prepared by moist-heat cooking methods and are sometimes used in stew or kidney pie.

BUTCHERING PROCEDURES

Many food service operations purchase veal in primal or other large cuts and fabricate it in-house to their own specifications. There are several important veal fabrication and butchering techniques you should master.

PROCEDURE FOR BONING A LEG OF VEAL

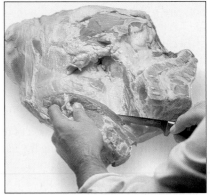

1. Remove the shank by cutting through the knee joint. Remove the excess fat and flank meat.

2. Remove the butt tenderloin from the inside of the pelvic bone.

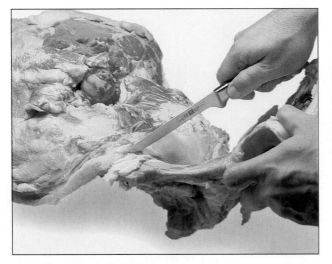

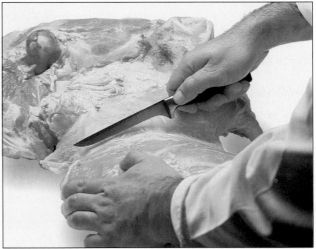

3. Remove the pelvic bone by carefully cutting around the bone, separating it from the meat. Continue until the bone is completely freed from the meat.

4. With the inside of the leg up, remove the top round by cutting along the natural seam.

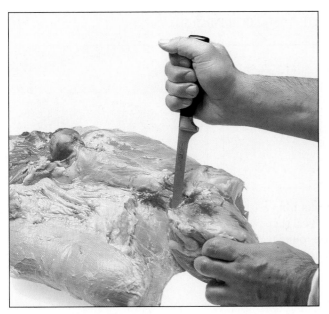

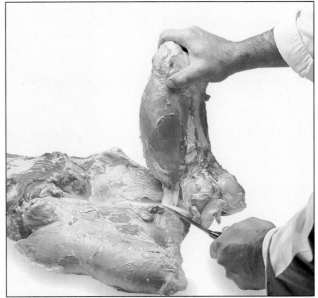

5. Remove the shank meat. (It is the round piece of meat lying between the eye round and the bone, on the shank end of the leg.)

6. Remove the round bone and the knuckle together by cutting around the bone and through the natural seams separating the knuckle from the other muscles. Separate the knuckle meat from the bone.

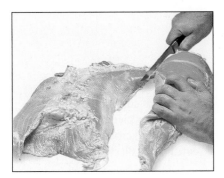

7. Remove the sirloin.

8. Remove the eye round from the bottom round.

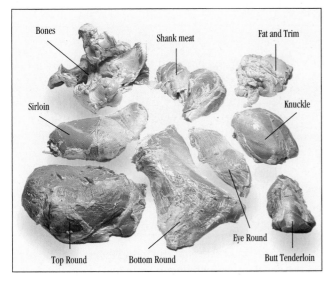

Bones

Shank meat

Fat and Trim

Sirloin

Knuckle

Top Round

Bottom Round

Eye Round

Butt Tenderloin

9. The completely boned-out veal leg, producing a top round, eye round, knuckle, shank meat, butt tenderloin, sirloin, bottom round bones and trimmings.

PROCEDURE FOR CUTTING AND POUNDING SCALLOPS

1. Veal scallops are cut from relatively large pieces of veal (here, a
portion of the top round). All fat
and silverskin must be trimmed.
Going against the grain, cut slices
approximately 1/4 inch (3 millimeter) thick; cut on the bias to
produce larger pieces.

2. Place the scallops between two
pieces of plastic wrap and pound
lightly to flatten and tenderize the
meat. Be careful not to tear or
pound holes in the meat.

PROCEDURE FOR CUTTING ÉMINCÉ

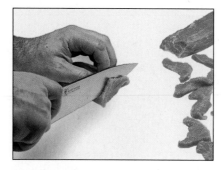

1. Émincé is cut from relatively
small, lean pieces of meat. Here
veal is cut across the grain into
small, thin slices.

PROCEDURE FOR BONING A VEAL LOIN
AND CUTTING IT INTO BONELESS VEAL CHOPS

1. Remove the tenderloin in a single piece from the
inside of the loin by following the vertebrae and cutting completely around the tenderloin.

2. From the backbone side, cut along the natural curve of
the backbone, separating the loin meat from the backbone.

3. Trim any excess fat from the loin, and trim the flank to create a 3-inch (7.5-centimeter) lip. Tightly roll up the loin with the flank on the outside.

4. Tie the loin, using the procedure described below, at 1-inch (2.5-centimeter) intervals. Cut between the pieces of twine for individual boneless loin chops.

PROCEDURE FOR TYING MEATS

Here we apply the tying procedure to a boneless veal loin; the same procedure can be used on any type of meat.

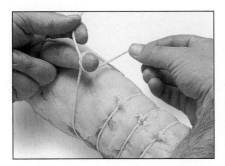

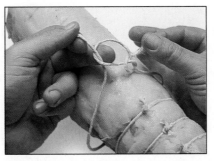

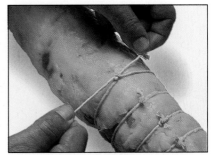

1. Cut a piece of string long enough to wrap completely around the loin. Holding one end between the thumb and forefinger, pass the other end around it and cross the strings. Loop the loose end of the string around your finger.

2. Wrap the string around itself and pass the loose end back through the hole.

3. Pull to tighten the knot. Adjust the string so it is snug against the meat.

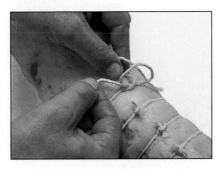

4. Loop one end of the string around your thumb and forefinger. Reach through with your thumb and forefinger and pull the other string back through the loop. Pull both strings to tighten the knot, thus preventing the first knot from loosening. Trim the ends of the strings.

5. Continue in this fashion until the entire loin is tied. The strings should be tied at even intervals, just snug enough to hold the shape of the loin; they should not dig into or cut the meat.

Procedure for Cleaning and Pressing Sweetbreads

Before fabrication, you should submerge the sweetbreads in cold water, cover and place them in the refrigerator overnight to soak out any blood. Then blanch them in a court bouillon for 20 minutes.

1. Remove the sweetbreads from the poaching liquid and allow them to cool.

2. Using your hands, pull off any sinew or membranes that may be present on the surface of the sweetbreads.

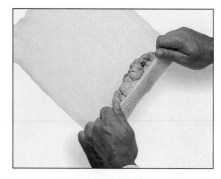

3. Wrap the sweetbreads in cheesecloth.

4. Tie the ends with butcher's twine.

5. Place the wrapped sweetbreads in a half hotel pan or similar container.

6. Place another half hotel pan on top of the sweetbreads; place a weight in the pan to press the sweetbreads. Pressing sweetbreads in this manner improves their texture.

PROCEDURE FOR CLEANING CALVES' LIVER

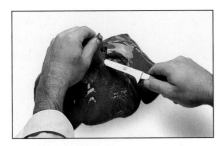

1. Trim the large sinew and outer membrane from the bottom of the liver.

2. Turn the liver over and peel the membrane off with your hands.

3. The liver can be cut into thick or thin slices as needed.

TABLE 14.1   USING COMMON CUTS OF VEAL

Primal	Subprimal or Fabricated Cut	IMPS	Cooking Methods	Serving Suggestions
Shoulder	Cubed veal	1395	Combination (stew)	Blanquette or fricassee
	Ground veal	1396	Dry heat (broil or grill) Combination (braise)	Veal patties Stuffing; meatballs
Foreshank and breast	Foreshank	312	Combination (braise)	Osso buco
	Breast	313	Combination (braise)	Stuffed veal breast
Rib	Hotel rack	306	Dry heat (broil or grill; roast)	Grilled veal chop; roast veal with porcini mushrooms
	Rib chops	1306	Dry heat (broil or grill) Combination (braise)	Grilled veal chop Braised veal chop with risotto
	Rib eye	307	Dry heat (broil or grill; roast) Combination (braise)	Broiled veal rib eye with chipotle sauce; roasted veal rib eye marchand de vin Braised rib eye
Loin	Veal loin	331	Dry heat (broil or grill; roast; sauté)	Roasted veal loin with wild mushrooms; Sautéed veal medallions with green peppercorn sauce;
	Loin chops	1332	Dry heat (broil or grill; sauté) Combination (braise)	Broiled or sautéed veal chops with mushroom sauce Braised veal chops lyonnaise
	Boneless strip loin	344	Dry heat (broil or grill; roast; sauté)	Roasted veal loin sauce poulette
	Veal tenderloin	346	Dry heat (broil or grill; roast; sauté)	Grilled tenderloin; roasted tenderloin; sautéed tenderloin with garlic and herbs
Leg	Leg	334	Dry heat (roast; sauté) Combination (stew)	Veal scallopini Blanquette
	Top round	349A	Dry heat (roast; sauté)	Veal marsala
	Bottom round	NA	Dry heat (sauté) Combination (braise)	Sautéed scallops with Calvados Stuffed veal scallops
	Hindshank	337	Moist heat (simmer) Combination (braise)	Veal broth Osso buco
Offal	Sweetbreads	715	Dry heat (pan-fry; sauté) Combination (braise)	Sautéed sweetbreads beurre noisette Braised sweetbreads madeira
	Calves' liver	704	Dry heat (broil or grill; sauté)	Broiled or sautéed calves' liver with onion and bacon
	Kidneys	NA	Combination (braise)	Kidney pie

PROCEDURE FOR CLEANING VEAL KIDNEYS

1. Split the kidneys lengthwise, exposing the fat and sinew.

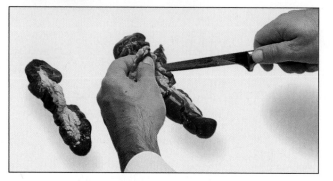

2. With a sharp knife, trim away the fat and sinew. The kidney is now ready for cooking.

*C*ONCLUSION

Although veal may not be as popular as beef or pork, it is versatile, easy to cook and adds variety to menus. Veal is much more delicately flavored than beef, with a finer texture and lighter color. Its flavor blends well with a variety of sauces and other ingredients without overpowering them. Veal can be cooked by almost any dry-heat, moist-heat or combination cooking method.

Veal quality varies greatly among purveyors. Purchase only from reputable companies to be sure you are receiving a consistently high quality product. Because veal carcasses are relatively small, they are sometimes purchased as primal cuts for your further fabrication.

*Q*UESTIONS FOR DISCUSSION

1. Compare and contrast the appearance and flavor of beef and veal.
2. What are the differences between milk-fed veal and free-range veal?
3. Describe two differences between a beef carcass and a veal carcass.
4. List each veal primal and describe its location on the carcass. For each primal, identify two subprimals or fabricated cuts taken from it.
5. Would it better to use a veal loin for grilling or braising? Explain your answer.
6. What are veal sweetbreads? Describe how sweetbreads should be prepared for cooking.

Additional Veal Recipes

Pan-Seared Veal Tenderloin with Maine Lobster and Braised Artichokes, Merlot-Thyme Pan Jus

Note: *This dish appears in the Chapter Opening photograph.*

ARIZONA BILTMORE HOTEL, Phoenix, AZ

Yield: 6 Servings   **Method:** Sautéing

Carrot, sliced	4 oz.	120 g
Onion, sliced	6 oz.	180 g
Garlic head, crushed	1	1
Fresh thyme	9 sprigs	9 sprigs
Bay leaves	2	2
Sea salt	TT	TT
White pepper	TT	TT
Sugar	1 Tbsp.	15 ml
Olive oil	3 Tbsp.	45 ml
Artichokes, small, trimmed, stem on	6	6
White wine	4 oz.	120 g
Chicken stock	1 pt.	450 ml
Carrots, small, tournéed	12	12
Rutabagas, small, tournéed	12	12
Turnips, small, tournéed	12	12
White potatoes, small, tournéed	12	12
Green asparagus tips, small	12	12
Unsalted butter	8 oz.	250 g
Veal medallions, 3 oz. (90 g) each	12	12
Garlic, chopped	1 tsp.	5 ml
Merlot	8 oz.	250 g
Brown veal stock	12 oz.	350 g
Lobster claws	6	6

1. Sauté the sliced carrots, onions and crushed garlic with 1 sprig of thyme, the bay leaves, salt, pepper and sugar in the olive oil. Add the artichokes and deglaze with the white wine. After 2 minutes, add the chicken stock; cover and simmer until tender.

2. Blanch the tournéed vegetables and asparagus tips. Then sauté them in a portion of the butter until tender.

3. In a separate pan, sauté the veal medallions in a portion of the butter. Season with salt and pepper and cook to the desired degree of doneness.

4. To make the sauce, sauté the chopped garlic in 1 tablespoon (15 milliliters) of the butter. Add the merlot and reduce by three quarters. Add the veal stock and 2 thyme sprigs. Monte au beurre with the remaining butter and adjust the seasonings.

5. Steam the lobster claws, remove the meat from the shells in one piece and keep warm.

6. To serve, place the whole artichoke in the top middle part of the plate. Place the tournéed vegetables inside the "trumpet" of the artichoke and the veal medallions crosswise over the stem of the artichoke. Stand the lobster claw between the two medallions. Finish with the sauce. Garnish each plate with a sprig of thyme.

◆◆◆

RECIPE 14.2

ROSEMARY-ROASTED VEAL CHOPS WITH PORCINI MUSHROOMS

THE FOUR SEASONS, New York, NY
Chef Christian Albin

Yield: 4 Servings   **Method:** Roasting

Veal chops, 12–14 oz. (350–400 g) each	4	4
Salt and pepper	TT	TT
Fresh rosemary	4 sprigs	4 sprigs
Flour	as needed	as needed
Paprika	TT	TT
Clarified butter	4 oz.	120 g
White wine	4 oz.	120 g
Brown veal stock	1 pt.	450 ml
Unsalted butter	2 oz.	60 g

1. Season the veal chops with salt and pepper. Press a rosemary sprig onto one side of each chop. Mix the flour and paprika and dredge the chops (both sides) in this mixture.

2. Heat the clarified butter in a sauté pan. Place the chops in the pan, rosemary side down. Roast in a preheated 375°F (190°C) oven for 7 minutes. Turn the chops carefully to keep the rosemary sprigs intact. Roast for 5–6 minutes more. Remove the chops and keep warm.

3. To make the sauce, degrease the pan and deglaze with the white wine. Add the veal stock and any juices that have accumulated under the chops. Simmer to reduce to 8 ounces (250 grams). Monte au beurre, strain and adjust the seasonings.

4. Serve the chops with grilled porcini mushrooms.

◆◆◆

RECIPE 14.3

VEAL KEBABS

Yield: 4 Servings   **Method**: Grilling

Onion	1	1
Green pepper	1	1
Boneless veal leg,		
cut in 1-in. (2.5-cm) cubes	2 lb.	1 kg
Marinade:		
Olive oil	4 oz.	120 g
White wine	2 oz.	60 g
Lemon juice	2 oz.	60 g
Assorted fresh herbs such as parsley,		
tarragon, sage and dill, chopped	2 Tbsp.	60 ml
Salt and pepper	TT	TT

1. Cut the onion and green pepper into 1-inch (2.5-centimeter) chunks.
2. Prepare the kebabs by threading the veal, onions and peppers onto each of four skewers, alternating the items.
3. Prepare the marinade by combining the oil, wine, lemon juice, herbs, salt and pepper.
4. Marinate the skewers, refrigerated, for 3 hours.
5. Drain the kebabs; season with salt and pepper and grill to the desired doneness.

◆◆◆

RECIPE 14.4

ROAST VEAL LOIN

Yield: 6-oz. (180-g) Servings   **Method**: Roasting

Boneless veal loin roast, 3 lb. (1.5 kg)	1	1
Salt and pepper	TT	TT
Onions, chopped medium	2	2
Carrots, chopped medium	2	2
Garlic cloves, chopped	4	4
Fresh thyme	3 sprigs	3 sprigs
Bay leaves	2	2
Jus lié	1 pt.	500 ml

1. Tie the veal loin roast with butcher's twine.
2. Season the meat with salt and pepper and place it in a roasting pan. Scatter the onions, carrots, garlic, thyme and bay leaves around it.
3. Roast at 425°F (220°C) for approximately 45 minutes.
4. Remove the meat from the roasting pan and cut away the twine. Hold in a warm place for service.
5. Deglaze the roasting pan with the jue lié. Strain the vegetables and liquid through a chinois into a small saucepan. Discard the solids.
6. Bring the sauce to a boil and skim as much fat as possible from the surface. Season with salt and pepper. Spoon a portion of the sauce over the veal; serve the remainder on the side.

◆◆◆

RECIPE 14.5

SAUTÉED VEAL SCALLOPS WITH CALVADOS

Yield: 6 Servings   **Method:** Sautéing

Mushrooms, sliced	12 oz.	340 g
Clarified butter	4 oz.	120 g
Golden Delicious apples	3	3
Veal scallops, pounded, 6 oz. (170 g) each	6	6
Salt and pepper	TT	TT
Shallots, minced	2	2
Calvados	2 oz.	60 g
Crème fraîche	8 oz.	250 g
Fresh parsley, chopped	1 Tbsp.	15 ml

1. Sauté the mushrooms in a portion of the clarified butter until dry. Remove and reserve.
2. Peel and core the apples. Cut each into 12 wedges.
3. Sauté the apple wedges in a portion of the clarified butter until slightly browned and tender. Remove and reserve.
4. Season the veal scallops with salt and pepper. Sauté in the remaining clarified butter. (This may be done in two or three batches.) Remove and reserve.
5. Add the shallots to the pan and sauté without browning.
6. Deglaze with the Calvados. Flambé the Calvados.
7. Add the sautéed mushrooms and crème fraîche. Bring to a boil and reduce until it thickens slightly.
8. Return the scallops to the pan to reheat. Serve each scallop with sauce, garnished with six apple slices and chopped parsley.

◆◆◆

RECIPE 14.6

SAUTÉED CALVES' LIVER WITH ONIONS

Yield: 10 Servings   **Method:** Sautéing

Onion, julienne	1 lb. 8 oz.	700 g
Clarified butter	3 oz.	90 g
Salt and pepper	TT	TT
White wine	8 oz.	250 g
Fresh parsley, chopped	1 Tbsp.	15 ml
Calves' liver, 6-oz. (180-g) slices	10	10
Flour	as needed	as needed

1. Sauté the onions in 1 ounce (30 grams) of butter until golden brown. Season with salt and pepper.
2. Add the white wine, cover and braise until the onions are tender, approximately 10 minutes. Stir in the chopped parsley.
3. Dredge the liver in flour seasoned with salt and pepper.
4. In a separate pan sauté the liver in the remaining clarified butter until done. The liver should be slightly pink in the middle.
5. Serve the liver with a portion of the onions and their cooking liquid.

◆◆◆

RECIPE 14.7

VEAL MARENGO

Yield: 6 10-oz. (300-g) Servings   **Method:** Braising

Lean boneless veal,		
cut in 2-in. (5-cm) cubes	2 lb. 8 oz.	1.1 g
Salt and pepper	TT	TT
Flour for dredging the veal	as needed	as needed
Vegetable oil	1-1/2 oz.	45 g
Clarified butter	3 oz.	90 g
Onion, sliced fine	12 oz.	350 g
Carrot, sliced fine	10 oz.	300 g
Garlic cloves, crushed	2	2
Tomato paste	1 oz.	30 g
Flour	2 Tbsp.	30 ml
Dry white wine	6 oz.	170 g
Brown veal stock	1 pt.	450 ml
Bouquet garni:		
Carrot stick, 4 in. (10 cm)	1	1
Leek, split, 4-in. (10-cm) piece	1	1
Fresh thyme	1 sprig	1 sprig
Bay leaf	1	1
Mushrooms, washed and quartered	8 oz.	250 g
Tomato, diced	1 lb.	500 g
Pearl onions, boiled and peeled	24	24

1. Season the veal cubes with salt and pepper and dredge in flour.
2. Sauté the veal in 1 ounce (30 grams) of oil and 1 ounce (30 grams) of butter, browning well on all sides. Remove the meat and set aside.
3. Add 1-1/2 ounces (45 grams) of butter and sauté the onions, carrots and garlic without coloring. Stir in the tomato paste and return the veal to the pan. Sprinkle with the 2 tablespoons (30 milliliters) flour and cook to make a blond roux.
4. Add the wine, stock and bouquet garni to the pan; bring to a boil. Cover and braise until the meat is tender, approximately 1-1/2 hours.
5. Sauté the mushrooms until dry in 1 tablespoon (15 milliliters) of oil and 1/2 ounce (15 grams) of butter without browning. Add the tomatoes to the pan and sauté over high heat for 3 minutes. Season with salt and pepper. Remove from the heat and reserve.
6. When the veal is tender, remove it from the pan with a slotted spoon and set aside. Strain the sauce.
7. Return the veal to the sauce along with the mushrooms, tomatoes and pearl onions. Bring to a boil and simmer for 5 minutes. Adjust the seasonings.

◆◆◆

RECIPE 14.8

GRILLED VEAL SWEETBREADS WITH WILD MUSHROOM RAGOUT AND RED WINE THYME SAUCE

VINCENT ON CAMELBACK, PHOENIX, AZ
Chef Vincent Guerithault

Yield: 6 Servings   **Method:** Grilling

Veal sweetbreads	2 lb.	1 kg
Water	1 gal.	4 lt
Lemons, cut in half	2	2
Bay leaves	4	4
Garlic cloves	5	5
Salt and pepper	TT	TT
Peppercorns	2 Tbsp.	30 ml
Olive oil	as needed	as needed

1. Soak the sweetbreads in water for 24 hours. Change the water at least every 8 hours.
2. Bring 1 gallon (4 lt) of fresh water to a boil with the lemons, bay leaves, garlic, salt and peppercorns. Add the sweetbreads. Simmer until the sweetbreads are firm yet slightly soft in the center, approximately 10 minutes.
3. Remove the sweetbreads; refresh in ice water and allow to cool.
4. Under running water, peel the membrane away from each sweetbread and discard. Place the sweetbreads between 2 hotel pans and press for at least 2 hours.
5. Divide the sweetbreads into 6 portions. Rub each with olive oil and season with salt and pepper.
6. Over a medium-hot grill, cook the sweetbreads for 3–4 minutes on each side.

WILD MUSHROOM RAGOUT

Oyster mushrooms	1 lb.	450 g
Olive oil	1 tsp.	5 ml
Unsalted butter	1 Tbsp.	15 ml
Garlic, chopped	1/2 tsp.	2 ml
Shallots, chopped	1 tsp.	5 ml
Brandy	1 Tbsp.	15 ml
Veal glaze	1 Tbsp.	15 ml
Heavy cream	4 oz.	120 g
Fresh thyme	1 tsp.	5 ml

1. Wash the mushrooms in cold water and pat dry.
2. Heat the olive oil in a sauté pan over medium-high heat. Add the mushrooms and cook for approximately 4 minutes. Add the butter, garlic and shallots and cook for an additional 3 minutes.
3. Add the brandy and ignite. When the flames die down, add the veal glaze and cream and simmer for 5 minutes. Remove from the heat and add the fresh thyme. Serve around the sweetbreads.

RED WINE THYME SAUCE

Red wine	8 oz.	250 g
Garlic, chopped	1 Tbsp.	15 ml
Shallots, chopped	2 oz.	60 g
Veal stock	1 qt.	1 lt
Fresh rosemary	1 sprig	1 sprig
Fresh thyme	1 sprig	1 sprig
Bay leaves	2	2
Unsalted butter	2 Tbsp.	30 ml

1. Reduce the red wine, garlic and shallots by one quarter.

2. Add the veal stock, rosemary, thyme and bay leaves and reduce by one quarter.

3. Remove from the heat and strain. Monte au beurre.

4. Serve with the grilled sweetbreads and mushroom ragout.

◆◆◆

RECIPE 14.9

OSSO BUCO

ANA WESTIN HOTEL, WASHINGTON, D.C.
Chef Leland Atkinson

Yield: 4 Servings   **Method:** Braising

Veal shank, cut in 1-in. (2.5-cm) pieces	8–12 pieces	8–12 pieces
Salt and pepper	TT	TT
Flour	4 oz.	120 g
Olive oil	as needed	as needed
Garlic clove, minced	1	1
Carrot, diced	4 oz.	120 g
Lemon zest, grated	1 Tbsp.	15 ml
White wine	8 oz.	250 g
Brown veal stock	1 qt.	1 lt
Tomato purée	2 Tbsp.	30 ml
Gremolada:		
Garlic clove, chopped fine	1	1
Lemon zest	1 Tbsp.	15 ml
Fresh Italian parsley, chopped	1 Tbsp.	15 ml

1. Season the veal with salt and pepper and dredge the pieces in flour. Sauté them in olive oil until brown on both sides.

2. Add the garlic and carrot and sauté briefly.

3. Add the lemon zest, wine, stock and tomato purée. Bring to a boil and reduce to a simmer. Braise on the stove top or in a 325°F (160°C) oven until the meat is tender but not falling from the bone, approximately 40–60 minutes.

4. Remove the cover and reduce the sauce until thick. Adjust the seasonings.

5. At service time, transfer the meat to a serving platter and ladle the sauce over it. Combine the gremolada ingredients and sprinkle over the meat and sauce.

◆◆◆

RECIPE 14.10
STUFFED BREAST OF VEAL

Yield: 12 8-oz. (250-g) Servings   **Method:** Braising

Stuffing:		
Onion, small dice	8 oz.	250 g
Garlic, chopped	2 tsp.	10 ml
Whole butter	1 oz.	30 g
Ground veal	1 lb.	450 g
Fresh bread crumbs	4 oz.	120 g
Nutmeg	TT	TT
Salt and pepper	TT	TT
Eggs, beaten	2	2
Mushrooms, sliced	1 lb.	450 g
Clarified butter	2 oz.	60 g
Spinach leaves, stemmed and washed	4 oz.	120 g
Veal breast, approx. 8 lb. (3.6 kg)	1	1
Mirepoix, large dice	1 lb.	450 g
White wine	8 oz.	250 g
Brown veal stock	3 pt.	1.5 lt
Garlic, chopped	1 tsp.	5 ml
Bouquet garni:		
Carrot stick, 4 in. (10 cm)	1	1
Leek, split, 4-in. (10-cm) piece	1	1
Fresh thyme	1 sprig	1 sprig
Bay leaf	2	2

1. To make the stuffing, sauté the onions and garlic in the butter until tender. Cool. Combine with the remaining stuffing ingredients and mix well.
2. Sauté the mushrooms in 1 ounce (30 grams) of the clarified butter and cool.
3. Blanch the spinach and cool.
4. Bone the veal breast. Reserve the bones.
5. Butterfly the veal breast and open it into a large rectangular shape.
6. Spread the stuffing over the breast; leave a 1-inch (2.5-centimeter) border around the edges.
7. Open the spinach leaves and carefully lay them on top of the stuffing. Sprinkle the mushrooms on top of the spinach leaves.
8. Roll the breast up in a cylindrical shape so the spinach leaves form a spiral in the center. Tie with butcher's twine.
9. Brown the breast in the remaining clarified butter.
10. Remove the breast and pour off all but 1 ounce (30 grams) of the grease. Add the mirepoix to the pan and sauté.
11. Add the reserved veal bones and place the veal breast on top of the bones.
12. Add the wine, stock, garlic and bouquet garni.
13. Cover and braise the breast until tender, approximately 2-1/2 hours.
14. Remove the breast from the pan and remove the twine. Skim any fat from the sauce.
15. Reduce the sauce and, if desired, thicken it slightly with a small amount of roux or beurre manié. Strain it through a fine chinois and adjust the seasonings.
16. Slice the veal breast and serve with the sauce.

◆◆◆

RECIPE 14.11

VEAL MARSALA

Yield: 6 Servings   **Method:** Sautéing

Veal scallops, pounded, 3 oz. (90 g) each	12	12
Salt and pepper	TT	TT
Flour	approx. 2 oz.	approx. 60 g
Clarified butter	2 oz.	60 g
Olive oil	2 oz.	60 g
Dry marsala	6 oz.	170 g
Brown veal stock	4 oz.	120 g
Whole butter	1-1/2 oz.	45 g

1. Season the scallops with salt and pepper. Dredge in flour and sauté the scallops in a mixture of the clarified butter and oil, a few at a time, until all are cooked.

2. Remove the scallops and set aside. Degrease the pan and deglaze with marsala. Add the stock and reduce until it begins to thicken.

3. Return the scallops to the sauce to reheat. Remove the scallops to plates or a serving platter.

4. Reduce the sauce until it becomes syrupy; adjust the seasonings. Monte au beurre and spoon the sauce over the veal.

◆◆◆

RECIPE 14.12

VEAL FRICASSEE

Yield: 16 8-oz. (250-g) Servings   **Method:** Stewing

Veal stew meat, cut in 2-in. (5-cm) cubes	8 lb.	3.5 kg
Salt and white pepper	TT	TT
Butter	6 oz.	180 g
Onion, small dice	12 oz.	350 g
Garlic, chopped	1 tsp.	5 ml
Flour	6 oz.	180 g
White wine	4 oz.	120 g
White stock	3 qt.	3 lt
Bouquet garni:		
Carrot stick, 4 in. (10 cm)	1	1
Leek, split, 4-in. (10-cm) piece	1	1
Fresh thyme	1 sprig	1 sprig
Bay leaf	1	1
Heavy cream, hot	1 pt.	450 ml

1. Season the veal with salt and pepper and sauté in the butter without browning, approximately 2 minutes.

2. Add the onions and garlic and sauté without coloring, approximately 2 minutes.

3. Add the flour and cook to make a blond roux, approximately 3 minutes.

4. Add the white wine and white stock, stir well to remove any lumps of roux and bring to a boil. Add the bouquet garni, cover and braise until the veal is tender, approximately 30 minutes.

5. Remove the veal from the sauce and reserve. Strain the sauce through a fine chinois and return it to the pan. Degrease the sauce.

6. Add the heavy cream to the sauce. Reduce slightly to thicken if necessary. Return the veal to the sauce and adjust the seasonings.

7. Serve the fricassee with rice pilaf.

CHAPTER 15
LAMB

After studying this chapter you will be able to:

+ identify the primal, subprimal and fabricated cuts of lamb
+ perform basic butchering procedures
+ apply appropriate cooking methods to several common cuts of lamb

*L*amb *is the meat of sheep slaughtered under the age of one year. Meat from sheep slaughtered after that age is called mutton. Spring lamb is young lamb that has not been fed grass or grains. Because lamb is slaughtered at an early age, it is quite tender and can be prepared by almost any cooking method.*

Lamb has a strong and distinctive flavor. It goes well with boldly flavored sauces and accompaniments.

PRIMAL AND SUBPRIMAL CUTS OF LAMB

After the young sheep is slaughtered, it is usually reduced to the primal cuts: shoulder, breast, rack, loin and leg. Like veal, these primals are crosscut sections and contain both bilateral halves (for example, the primal leg contains both hind legs). Lamb primals are not classified into a forequarter and hindquarter like beef, or a foresaddle and hindsaddle like veal.

Figure 15.1 shows the relationship between the lamb's bone structure and the primal cuts. As with all meats, it is important to know the location of bones when cutting or working with lamb. This makes meat fabrication and carving easier and aids in identifying cuts. Figure 15.2 shows the primal cuts of lamb and their location on the carcass. A lamb carcass generally weighs between 41 and 75 pounds (20–35 kg).

Shoulder

The primal lamb shoulder is a relatively large cut accounting for 36% of carcass weight. The lamb shoulder contains four rib bones and the arm, blade and neck bones as well as many small, tough muscles whose grains travel in different directions.

All these bones and muscle groups make it nearly impossible to cook and carve a whole shoulder. Although the shoulder may be cut into chops, or boned and then roasted or braised, with or without stuffing, it is more commonly diced for stew or ground for patties.

Breast

The primal lamb breast contains the breast and foreshank portions of the carcass. Together they account for approximately 17% of carcass weight and contain the rib, breast and shank bones. The primal breast is located beneath the primal rack and contains the rib tips, which are cut off to produce the rack. When separated from the rest of the breast, these small ribs are called Denver ribs and can be substituted for pork ribs where desired.

Although the breast is not used extensively in food service operations, it can be stuffed and braised, either bone-in or boneless. Lamb foreshanks are quite meaty and may be braised and served as an entree, used for broths, or ground.

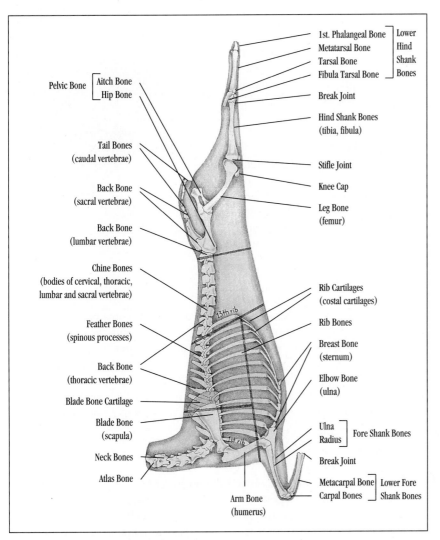

FIGURE 15.1 *The Skeletal Structure of a Lamb*

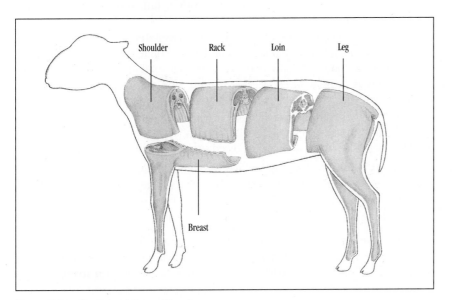

FIGURE 15.2 *The Primal Cuts of Lamb*

Frenched Lamb Rack

Rack

The primal lamb rack is also known as the hotel rack. It is located between the primal shoulder and loin. Containing eight ribs and portions of the backbone, it accounts for approximately 8% of carcass weight.

The rack is valued for its tender rib eye muscle. The hotel rack is usually split in half and trimmed so that each set of ribs can be easily cut into chops. The split racks can then be grilled, broiled or roasted as racks or cut into single or double rib chops before cooking.

Lamb Rack

French—*a method of trimming racks or individual chops of meat, especially lamb, in which the excess fat is cut away leaving the eye muscle intact; all meat and connective tissue is removed from the rib bone.*

Lamb Loin Trimmed

Loin

The loin is located between the primal rib and leg. It contains rib number 13 and portions of the backbone as well as the loin eye muscle, tenderloin and flank. It accounts for approximately 13% of carcass weight.

Except for the flank, the loin meat is very tender and is invariably cooked using a dry-heat method such as broiling, grilling or roasting. The loin may be boned to produce boneless roasts or chops or cut into chops with the bone in. The loin eye may be removed and cut into medallions or noisettes.

Leg

The primal leg is a large section accounting for approximately 34% of carcass weight. It is the posterior portion of the carcass, separated from the loin by a straight cut anterior to the hip bone cartilage. As with veal, the cut of meat that would be the sirloin on a beef carcass is separated from the lamb loin by this cut and becomes part of the primal leg. The lamb leg contains several bones: the backbone, tail, hip, aitch, round and shank bones.

The primal leg is rarely used as is. More often it is split into two legs and partially or fully boned. Lamb legs are quite tender—the sirloin end more so than the shank end—and are well suited to a variety of cooking methods. A bone-in leg is often roasted for buffet service or braised with vegetables or beans for a hearty dish. Steaks can also be cut from the bone-in leg, with the sirloin end producing the most tender cuts. A boneless leg can be tied and roasted, with or without stuffing, or trimmed and cut into scallops. The shank end can be diced for stew or ground for patties.

Lamb Leg

Because lamb carcasses are so easily handled, purveyors often sell them whole or cut in a variety of ways to better meet their customers' needs. As well as whole carcass, primal and fabricated cuts, lamb can be purchased in the following forms:

◆ *Foresaddle*: The anterior portion of the carcass after it is severed from the hindsaddle by a cut following the natural curvature between the twelfth and thirteenth ribs. It contains the primal shoulder, breast and foreshank and rack.

◆ *Hindsaddle*: The posterior portion of the carcass after it is severed from the foresaddle. It contains the primal loin and leg together with the kidneys.

Boned, Rolled and Tied Leg of Lamb

◆ *Back*: The trimmed rack and loin sections in one piece. The back is particularly useful when producing large quantities of lamb chops.

◆ *Bracelet*: The primal hotel rack with the connecting breast sections.

BUTCHERING PROCEDURES

Lamb is unique among the common meat animals in that it is small enough to be handled easily in its carcass form. Thus, food service operations sometimes purchase lamb whole and fabricate the desired cuts themselves. This is practical if the operation has the necessary employee skills, equipment and storage space, as well as a need for all the various cuts and trimmings butchering a whole carcass produces. A few important lamb fabrication and butchering techniques follow.

PROCEDURE FOR FRENCHING A RACK OF LAMB

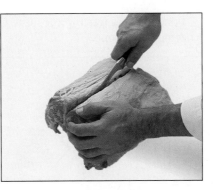

1. With a meat saw, trim the ribs to approximately 3 inches (7.5 centimeters), measuring from the rib eye on each side of the rack.

2. Turn the rack over and cut down both sides of the feather bones, completely separating the meat from the bone.

3. Turn the rack back over. Using a meat saw, cut between the ribs and the chine bone at a 45-degree angle, exposing the lean meat between the ribs and the vertebral junctures.

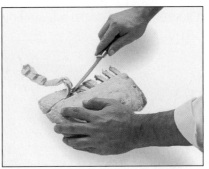

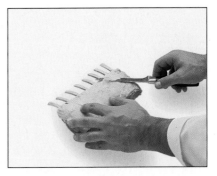

4. By pulling and cutting along the natural seam, remove the thick layers of fat and the meat between them from the rack's surface.

5. Make an even cut through the fat, perpendicular to the ribs, 1 inch (25 centimeters) from the rib eye. Trim away all meat and fat from the rib ends. The ribs should be completely clean.

6. Trim away the fat covering. Leave either a thin layer to protect the meat during cooking or trim the fat away completely to produce a very lean rack. The rack can also be cut into chops.

Procedure for Trimming and Boning a Lamb Leg for Roasting or Grilling

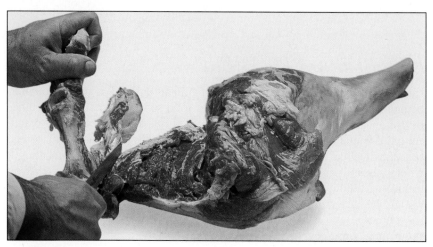

1. With the tip of the knife, trim around the pelvic bone; stay close to the bone to avoid wasting any meat. Cut the sinew inside the socket and remove the bone.

2. Trim away most of the exterior fat.

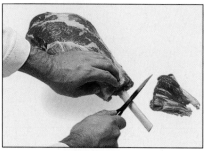

3. Cut off the shank portion completely and scrape the bone clean. This makes a handle to hold while carving the lamb.

4. Fold the flap of the sirloin over on top of the ball of the leg bone and tie with butcher's twine. This helps the leg cook evenly.

Procedure for Boning a Lamb Loin for Roasting

1. Start with a trimmed lamb loin (double). With the skin side up, trim the thin layer of connective tissue called the fell from the loin's surface.

2. Turn the loin over and trim the fat from around the tenderloins.

3. Starting in the middle of the backbone, cut between the tenderloin and the vertebrae, separating them but leaving the tenderloin attached to the flank. Continue until you reach the end of the vertebrae. Repeat on the other side.

4. Slide the knife under the vertebrae and rib and cut back all the way to the backbone, separating the eye muscle from the vertebrae.

5. Pull the backbone out with your hands, keeping the loins intact.

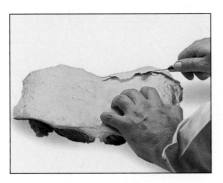

6. Turn the loins over and trim the surface fat to 1/4 inch (6 millimeters).

7. Roll the flank flaps under from each side.

8. Tie the roast with butcher's twine at even intervals.

PROCEDURE FOR CUTTING LAMB NOISETTES FROM A LOIN

1. Remove the loin eye muscle by cutting down along the backbone and along the vertebrae. Trim the eye muscle, leaving a thin layer of fat if desired.

2. Cut the eye meat into noisettes of the desired thickness.

TABLE 15.1   USING COMMON CUTS OF LAMB

Primal	Subprimal or Fabricated Cut	IMPS	Cooking Methods	Serving Suggestions
Shoulder	Shoulder lamb chop	1207	Dry heat (broil or grill)	Broiled or grilled lamb chops
	Diced lamb	1295	Combination (stew)	Lamb stew; lamb curry
	Ground lamb	1296	Dry heat (broil or grill; sauté)	Patties
Breast	Breast	209	Combination (braise)	Lamb breast stuffed with mushrooms
Hotel Rack	Lamb rack	204	Dry heat (broil or grill; roast; sauté)	Roast rack of lamb with garlic and rosemary
	Frenched lamb rack	204C	Dry heat (broil or grill; roast; sauté)	Broiled lamb with mustard and hazelnut crust
Loin	Lamb loin trimmed	232	Dry heat (broil or grill; roast; sauté)	Noisettes of lamb with roasted garlic sauce
	Loin chops	1232	Dry heat (broil or grill; sauté)	Broiled loin chops with herb butter
Leg	Lamb leg	233A	Dry heat (broil or grill; roast)	Kebabs; roast leg of lamb
	Boned rolled tied leg of lamb	233B	Dry heat (roast)	Roast leg of lamb

CONCLUSION

Even though lamb accounts for a small percentage of the meat consumed in this country, many people who do not prepare lamb at home will order it at a restaurant. Because lamb is slaughtered under the age of one year, its meat is tender and it can be prepared by almost any cooking method. Its strong, distinctive flavor allows you to offer bold, robust sauces and accompaniments that might mask the flavors of other meats.

QUESTIONS FOR DISCUSSION

1. Describe the basic differences between a lamb carcass and a beef carcass.
2. List each lamb primal and describe its location on the carcass. Identify two subprimals or fabricated cuts taken from each primal.
3. Which cooking methods are most appropriate for a breast of lamb? Explain your answer.
4. Describe the procedure for preparing a frenched rack of lamb from a primal hotel rack.
5. What is the best way to purchase lamb for a food service operation that cuts its own meat and uses large quantities of lamb chops? Explain your answer.

ADDITIONAL LAMB RECIPES

RECIPE 15.1

RACK OF LAMB WITH MUSTARD AND HAZELNUTS

NOTE: *This dish appears in the Chapter Opening photograph.*

CONTINENTAL CATERING, PHOENIX, AZ
Chef Alan Hause

Yield: 4 Servings   **Method:** Roasting

Lamb racks, frenched,		
2 lb. to 2 lb. 8 oz. (.9 to 1.1 kg) each	2	2
Salt and pepper	TT	TT
Olive oil	2 oz.	60 g
Dijon mustard	2 oz.	60 g
Fresh bread crumbs	1 oz.	30 g
Hazelnuts, chopped fine	2 oz.	60 g
Molasses	1 oz.	30 g

1. Season the racks with salt and pepper and brown well in the olive oil.
2. Spread the mustard over the surface of the racks.
3. Combine the bread crumbs, nuts and molasses and press this mixture into the mustard to form a crust.
4. Roast the racks at 375°F (190°C) until medium rare, approximately 30 minutes.
5. Allow the racks to rest 15 minutes. Carve into chops and serve with marchand de vin sauce made with lamb jus lié (Recipe 10.12), Polenta with Wild Rice (Recipe 23.15) and sautéed baby vegetables.

◆◆◆

RECIPE 15.2

SHISH KEBAB

Yield: 10 Servings   **Method:** Grilling or Broiling

Marinade:		
Onion, small dice	12 oz.	350 g
Garlic, chopped	1 oz.	30 g
Lemon juice	4 oz.	120 g
Salt	2 Tbsp.	30 ml
Pepper	1 tsp.	5 ml
Fresh oregano, chopped	2 tsp.	10 ml
Olive oil	8 oz.	250 g
Cumin, ground	2 tsp.	10 ml
Coriander, ground	1 Tbsp.	15 ml
Fresh mint, chopped	2 tsp.	10 ml
Lamb leg or shoulder, boneless, trimmed		
and cut in 2-in. (15-cm) cubes	5 lb.	2.2 kg

1. Combine the marinade ingredients and add the lamb. Marinate for 2 hours.
2. Place 3–4 cubes of lamb on each of ten skewers. Grill or broil to the desired doneness. Serve with rice pilaf.

◆◆◆

RECIPE 15.3
LAMB PATTIES WITH MINT

Yield: 6 Servings		**Method**: Grilling or Broiling
Ground lamb	1 lb. 12 oz.	800 g
Fresh bread crumbs	2 oz.	60 g
Egg, beaten	1	1
Onion, minced	3 oz.	90 g
Garlic cloves, crushed	2	2
Fresh mint, chopped	3 Tbsp.	45 ml
Salt and pepper	TT	TT

1. Place the lamb in a bowl and mix in the bread crumbs, egg, onion, garlic and mint. Add salt and pepper to taste and mix well. Form the mixture into 6 patties.
2. Grill or broil the patties until browned on both sides. Garnish with extra mint if desired.

◆◆◆

RECIPE 15.4
BROILED LAMB KIDNEYS

Yield: 10 Servings		**Method**: Broiling
Lamb kidneys	20	20
Bacon fat	2 oz.	60 g
Salt and pepper	TT	TT
Grain mustard	16 oz.	450 g

1. Split the lamb kidneys lengthwise; remove the fat and gristle.
2. Arrange the kidney halves on skewers, four halves per skewer.
3. Brush the kidneys with bacon fat, season with salt and pepper and broil, turning once halfway through cooking, until well browned but still pink in the center, approximately 6–8 minutes.
4. Serve four halves per portion with 1-1/2 ounces (45 grams) of grain mustard each.

◆◆◆

RECIPE 15.5
ROAST LEG OF LAMB WITH JALAPEÑO

VINCENT ON CAMELBACK, PHOENIX, AZ
Chef Vincent Guerithault

Yield: 12 Servings 5 to 6 oz. (150 to 180 g) each		**Method**: Roasting
Leg of lamb, 6–8 lb. (2.7–3.6 kg)	1	1
Jalapeño	6	6
Olive oil	1 Tbsp.	15 ml
Dixon (or Chimayo) chile powder	2 Tbsp.	30 ml
Salt and pepper	TT	TT
Garlic heads	12	12
Fresh thyme	1 sprig	1 sprig
Fresh rosemary	1 sprig	1 sprig

Water	8 oz.	250 g
Chicken glaze	2 oz.	60 g

1. Trim the leg, removing most of the fat; leave the bone intact.

2. Roast the jalapeños over an open flame. When they are blackened, remove the skin and cut each pepper in half. Make twelve slits in the lamb and slide one half jalapeño pepper into each slit.

3. Brush the lamb with olive oil and dust with the Dixon or Chimayo chile powder, salt and pepper.

4. Sauté the lamb over a high flame or grill, turning frequently.

5. When the lamb is golden in color, transfer it to a roasting pan. Surround the lamb with the garlic heads, thyme and rosemary. Roast at 400°F (200°C) for 45 minutes, turning the leg 3 or 4 times. When the lamb is done, remove it and the garlic from the pan and set aside.

6. To make the sauce, add the water and chicken glaze to the pan and bring to a boil. Simmer 5 minutes and strain.

7. Serve each lamb portion with one head of garlic. (Cut off the bottom of each garlic head before serving.) Top each serving with 1 tablespoon (15 milliliters) of sauce.

◆◆◆

RECIPE 15.6
STUFFED LEG OF LAMB

Yield: 12 Servings 5 to 6 oz. (150 to 180 g) each   **Method:** Roasting

Bacon, fine dice	3 oz.	90 g
Fennel, fine dice	1 bulb	1 bulb
Garlic cloves, chopped fine	2	2
Wild mushrooms such as shiitake, chanterelles or porcini, chopped	12 oz.	340 g
Parsley, chopped	2 Tbsp.	30 ml
Fresh thyme	1/2 tsp.	2 ml
Fresh rosemary	1/2 tsp.	2 ml
Salt and pepper	TT	TT
Dry white wine	8 oz.	250 ml
Fresh bread crumbs	3 oz.	90 g
Lamb leg 6–8 lb. (2.7–3.6 kg)	1	1
Mirepoix	1 lb.	500 g

1. To make the stuffing, sauté the bacon until crisp. Add the fennel and sauté lightly.

2. Add the garlic and sauté. Add the mushrooms, parsley, thyme, rosemary, salt and pepper and sauté an additional 2 minutes.

3. Deglaze with white wine and reduce by three quarters. Remove from the heat.

4. Stir in the bread crumbs.

5. Completely bone out the leg, following the natural seams in the meat. Cut off the shank meat for use in another recipe. Fill the cavity left by the bone with stuffing.

6. Season the lamb with salt and pepper. Close the leg around the stuffing and seal the opening by tying with butcher's twine.

7. Place the stuffed leg in a roasting pan on a bed of mirepoix.

8. Roast at 375°F (190°C) until medium rare, approximately 1 hour. Serve au jus or with a pan gravy.

◆◆◆

RECIPE 15.7

GRILLED RACK OF LAMB
WITH ROSEMARY AND SPICY BELL PEPPER JELLY

VINCENT ON CAMELBACK, PHOENIX, AZ
Chef Vincent Guerithault

Yield: 8 Servings

Method: Grilling

Red bell peppers	2	2
Yellow bell peppers	2	2
Red Serrano chiles	8	8
Sugar	8 oz.	250 g
Lamb racks, frenched, (9 oz. (270 g) each	4	4
Salt and pepper	TT	TT
Dried rosemary sprigs*	8	8

1. To make the pepper jelly, julienne the peppers and chiles. Mix with the sugar and refrigerate overnight.
2. At service time, cook the pepper mixture (along with the liquid formed while refrigerated) over low heat for approximately 10–15 minutes. Cool and keep the pepper jelly at room temperature.
3. Cut each lamb rack in half. Season with salt and pepper.
4. Grill the lamb over mesquite to the desired temperature.
5. Cut the racks into chops and plate the lamb and pepper jelly. Garnish each plate with a dried rosemary sprig and flame. When the rosemary flames, blow it out at once and serve immediately so that the essence of rosemary is fresh.

*To dry rosemary, place fresh rosemary sprigs in a 350°F (180°C) oven for approximately 10 minutes.

◆◆◆

RECIPE 15.8

ROAST RACK OF LAMB
WITH ROASTED GARLIC POTATOES
AND FENNEL ARTICHOKE RATATOUILLE

STOUFFER STANFORD COURT HOTEL, SAN FRANCISCO, CA
Chef Ercolino Crugnale

Yield: 10 Servings

Method: Roasting

Lamb racks, frenched, 9 oz. (270 g) each	10	10
Salt and pepper	TT	TT
Olive oil	as needed	as needed
Roasted Garlic Potatoes (recipe follows)	20 oz.	600 g
Fennel Artichoke Ratatouille (recipe follows)	1 qt.	1 lt
Lamb jus lié	1 pt.	450 ml

1. Season the lamb racks with salt and pepper; brush with olive oil.

2. Brown both sides in a hot sauté pan. Transfer to a 400°F (200°C) oven and roast to the desired degree of doneness, approximately 15 minutes.

3. Serve with Roasted Garlic Potatoes, Fennel Artichoke Ratatouille and lamb jus lié.

ROASTED GARLIC POTATOES

Yield: 2 lb. 8 oz. (1.1 kg)

Garlic heads, cloves separated	5	5
Olive oil	1 oz.	30 g
Idaho potatoes, peeled and cubed	1 lb. 8 oz.	700 g
Whole butter, softened	8 oz.	250 g
Heavy cream, warmed to 110°F (43°C)	8 oz.	250 g
Salt and white pepper	TT	TT

1. Rub the garlic cloves with the olive oil and bake in a 375°F (190°C) oven until tender, approximately 30 minutes.

2. Place the garlic cloves in a food mill fitted with the large plate; turn to separate the garlic purée from the skin. Reserve.

3. Bring 1 gallon (4 liters) of salted water to a boil. Add the potatoes and cook until tender, approximately 20 minutes. Drain well.

4. Push the potatoes through the large plate of the food mill.

5. Transfer the hot potatoes to a mixing bowl. Add the garlic purée, butter and half of the cream. Combine thoroughly, using the whip attachment of an electric mixer on low speed.

6. Create a smooth and creamy consistency by adding more cream if necessary. Adjust the seasonings and keep warm for service.

FENNEL ARTICHOKE RATATOUILLE

Yield: 2 qt. (2 lt)

Eggplant, peeled, small dice	3 c.	750 ml
Yellow zucchini, small dice	2 c.	500 ml
Green zucchini, small dice	1 c.	250 ml
Red onion, small dice	1 c.	250 ml
Fennel, small dice	3 c.	750 ml
Artichoke bottoms, fresh, small dice, then held in lemon water	2 c.	500 ml
Red bell pepper, small dice	1 c.	250 ml
Tomato, peeled, seeded, small dice	3 c.	750 ml
Garlic, minced	TT	TT
Olive oil	as needed	as needed
Fresh basil, chiffonade	1 c.	250 ml
Tomato paste	4 Tbsp.	60 ml
Salt and pepper	TT	TT

1. Sauté each of the vegetables separately in olive oil, adding garlic to taste. Cook each vegetable until just tender. After each vegetable is cooked, transfer it to a stainless steel bowl and cook the next. End with the tomatoes.

2. After all vegetables are cooked, toss them with the basil and tomato paste.

3. Adjust the seasonings. Spread the vegetable mixture on a parchment-lined sheet pan and cool.

4. At service time, heat a portion of the ratatouille in a sauté pan just until hot.

◆◆◆

RECIPE 15.9
HONEY-MUSTARD DENVER RIBS

Yield: 14 lb. (6.2 kg) **Method:** Roasting

Lamb ribs, trimmed	20 lb.	9 kg
Salt	4 oz.	120 g
Pepper	2 oz.	60 g
Honey	4 lb.	1.8 kg
Dijon-style mustard	3 lb.	1.4 kg
Lemon juice	1 pt.	450 ml

1. Rub the ribs with salt and pepper.
2. Place the ribs on a rack and roast at 375°F (190°C) for 30 minutes.
3. Combine the honey, mustard and lemon juice.
4. Baste the ribs generously with the honey-mustard mixture. Roast an additional 30 minutes, basting every 10 minutes.

◆◆◆

RECIPE 15.10
SAUTÉED LAMB LOIN
WITH STUFFED RÖSTI POTATOES AND CHERRY CONFIT

ANA WESTIN HOTEL, Washington, D.C.
Chef Leland Atkinson

Yield: 6 5-oz. (150-g) Servings **Method:** Sautéing

Idaho potatoes, large	2	2
Parmesan, grated	5 oz.	150 g
Salt and pepper	TT	TT
Clarified butter	as needed	as needed
Goat cheese	6 oz.	180 g
Fresh rosemary, chopped	1 tsp.	5 ml
Fresh chives, chopped	1 tsp.	5 ml
Lamb, eye of loin, trimmed, 2 lb. 4 oz. (1 kg)	1	1
Clarified butter	2 oz.	60 g
Port	4 oz.	120 g
Lamb jus lié	12 oz.	350 g
Whole butter	1 oz.	30 g
Cherry Confit (Recipe 25.13)	as needed	as needed

1. Peel and julienne the potatoes.
2. Combine the potatoes with the Parmesan, salt and pepper.
3. Heat the clarified butter in an 8-inch (20-centimeter) nonstick pan. Add the potato mixture and pack it tightly with the back of a spoon. Cook over moderate heat until the potatoes begin to brown.
4. Flip the rösti potatoes and place the pan in a 350°F (180°C) oven. Flipping once, cook until the potatoes are crisp and evenly browned on the outside and soft in the center, approximately 20 minutes on each side.
5. Transfer the rösti potatoes to a wire cooling rack to rest.

6. Slice the rösti horizontally into 2 round halves. Spread the bottom half with the room temperature goat cheese. Grind black pepper over the cheese, sprinkle the herbs evenly over the surface and carefully replace the top.

7. Season the lamb and sauté it in the 2 ounces (60 grams) of clarified butter, turning frequently, until the desired doneness is achieved, approximately 8–12 minutes.

8. Remove the lamb and allow it to rest before slicing.

9. Deglaze the pan with the port and add the lamb jus lié. Reduce by half and monte au beurre.

10. At service time, ladle the sauce onto 6 warm plates, slice the lamb and arrange over the sauce. Cut the rösti into wedges and arrange on the plate. Spoon cherry confit (Recipe 25.13) around the lamb and serve at once.

◆◆◆

RECIPE 15.11
CAROUSEL OF SONOMA LAMB

ARIZONA BILTMORE, PHOENIX, AZ
Executive Chef Peter Hoefler

Yield: 4 Servings

Method: Sautéing

Lamb loin, trimmed, approx. 1 lb. 8 oz. (700 g)	1	1
Salt and pepper	TT	TT
Unsalted butter	6 oz.	180 g
Fresh chanterelles	8 oz.	250 g
Shallots, chopped	1 tsp.	5 ml
Fresh basil, chopped	1 Tbsp.	15 ml
Fresh spinach	8 oz.	250 g
Garlic, chopped	1 Tbsp.	15 ml
Tomato concasse	8 oz.	250 g
Fresh thyme, chopped	1 tsp.	5 ml
Russet potatoes	2	2
Merlot	4 oz.	120 g
Lamb stock	1 pt.	450 ml
Fresh rosemary	4 sprigs	4 sprigs
Savory Hippen Masse (Recipe 35.1)	as needed	as needed
Fresh Italian parsley	as needed	as needed

1. Season the lamb with salt and pepper. Brown well in 1 ounce (30 grams) of butter and roast at 375°F (190°C) to medium rare, approximately 10 minutes.

2. In a separate pan, sauté the chanterelles and shallots in 1 tablespoon (15 milliliters) of butter, until tender. Add the basil, season with salt and pepper, remove from the pan and reserve.

3. Sauté the spinach with 1 teaspoon (5 milliliters) garlic in 1 tablespoon (15 milliliters) of butter. Season with salt and pepper, remove from the pan and reserve.

4. Sauté the tomato concasse in 1 tablespoon (15 milliliters) of butter with 1 teaspoon (5 milliliters) of garlic and the thyme and set aside.

5. Peel the potatoes and cut them into 16 1-1/2 inch (3.7 centimeter) diameter circles, approximately 1/4 inch (6 millimeters) thick. Trim one edge of each

Continued

slice so that the pieces will stand upright. Sauté the potatoes in 1 ounce (30 grams) of butter until brown and cooked and set aside.

6. Remove the lamb from the pan. Add 1 teaspoon (5 milliliters) garlic and sauté for 15 seconds. Deglaze the pan with the merlot and add the lamb stock. Reduce the sauce until slightly thickened. Strain the sauce and season to taste with salt and pepper. Monte au beurre with the remaining butter.

7. To serve, layer the spinach, chanterelles and tomatoes inside four, 4-inch (20-centimeter) ring molds positioned in the center of four plates. Remove the molds. Slice the lamb and arrange approximately 4 to 5 ounces (120 to 150 grams) of the slices in a spiral on top of each circle of vegetables. Insert the rosemary sprig and the hippen masse decoration in the center of the lamb spiral. Spoon 3 ounces (90 grams) of the sauce around the lamb and vegetables and arrange four potato slices on each plate.

◆◆◆

RECIPE 15.12

LAMB SHANK WITH PERSILLADE

Yield: 6 Servings   **Method:** Braising

Lamb shanks, trimmed,		
2 lb.–2 lb. 8 oz. (.9–1.1 kg) each	6	6
Salt and pepper	TT	TT
Olive oil	as needed	as needed
Shallots, minced	8 oz.	250 g
Carrot, chopped	8 oz.	250 g
Celery, chopped	8 oz.	250 g
Peppercorns, crushed	6	6
Fresh thyme	2 tsp.	10 ml
Garlic, chopped	2 tsp.	10 ml
Dry white wine	12 oz.	350 g
Lamb stock	1 qt.	1 lt
Demi-glace	1 pt.	450 ml
Dijon mustard	as needed	as needed
Persillade:		
Garlic, minced	1 tsp.	5 ml
Fresh parsley, chopped	1 oz.	30 g
Fresh bread crumbs	2 oz.	60 g
Butter, melted	2 oz.	60 g

1. Season the shanks with salt and pepper; brown in olive oil.

2. Remove the shanks and add the vegetables, peppercorns, thyme and garlic to the pan. Sauté until tender.

3. Place the shanks on top of the vegetables.

4. Add the wine, lamb stock and demi-glace.

5. Bring to a simmer, cover and braise in a 350°F (180°C) oven until tender, approximately 2 hours, adding more lamb stock if necessary.

6. Remove the shanks and hold for service.

7. Degrease the sauce and reduce to the desired consistency.

8. Strain the sauce and adjust the seasonings.

9. To make the persillade, combine all ingredients and toss together.

10. Warm the shanks thoroughly. Brush with mustard and sprinkle with the persillade. Brown under a broiler and serve with the sauce.

◆◆◆

RECIPE 15.13
IRISH LAMB STEW

Yield: 12 8-oz. (250-g) Servings   **Method:** Stewing

Lamb shoulder, 1-1/2-in. (4-cm) cubes	4 lb.	1.8 kg
White stock	3 pt.	1.5 lt
Sachet:		
Bay leaf	1	1
Dried thyme	1/2 tsp.	2 ml
Peppercorns, crushed	1/2 tsp.	2 ml
Parsley stems	10	10
Garlic cloves, crushed	4	4
Onion, sliced	1 lb.	450 g
Leek, sliced	8 oz.	225 g
Potato, peeled, large dice	1 lb. 8 oz.	700 g
Salt and white pepper	TT	TT
Carrots, tournéed or batonnet	20	20
Turnips, tournéed or batonnet	20	20
Potatoes, tournéed or batonnet	20	20
Pearl onions, peeled	20	20
Fresh parsley, chopped	1 Tbsp.	15 ml

1. Combine the lamb, stock, sachet, onions, leeks and potatoes. Season with salt and white pepper. Bring to a simmer and skim the surface. Simmer the stew on the stove or cover and cook in the oven at 350°F (180°C) until the lamb is tender, approximately 1 hour.

2. Degrease the stew; remove and discard the sachet.

3. Remove the pieces of potato and purée them in a food mill or ricer. Use the potato purée to thicken the stew to the desired consistency.

4. Simmer the stew for 10 minutes to blend the flavors.

5. Cook the tournéed or batonnet vegetables, potatoes and pearl onions separately. At service, heat the vegetable garnishes and add to each portion of stew.

6. Garnish with chopped parsley and serve.

◆◆◆

RECIPE 15.14
BLANQUETTE OF LAMB

Yield: 10 8-oz. (250-g) Servings   **Method:** Stewing

White beans, dried	1 lb.	500 g
Onion piquet	2	2
Bouquet Garni:	2	2
Carrot stick, 4 in. (10 cm)	1	1
Leek, split, 4-in. (10-cm) piece	1	1
Fresh thyme	1 sprig	1 sprig
Bay leaf	1	1
Lamb leg or shoulder, cut in 1-1/2-inch (4-cm) cubes	4 lb.	1.8 kg
White stock	1-1/2 qt.	1-1/2 lt

Continued

Sachet:		
Bay leaf	1	1
Dried thyme	1/2 tsp.	2 ml
Peppercorns, crushed	1/2 tsp.	2 ml
Parsley stems	10	10
Garlic cloves, crushed	4	4
Salt	TT	TT
Blond roux	2 oz.	60 g
Heavy cream	10 oz.	280 g
Dijon mustard	3 Tbsp.	45 ml
Egg yolks	4	4

1. Soak the beans in cold water for 12 hours. Drain, then add enough fresh water to cover the beans by 2–4 inches (5–10 centimeters).

2. Add one onion piquet and one bouquet garni and cook until the beans are tender, approximately 1-1/2 hours. Remove and discard the onion piquet and bouquet garni.

3. Blanch the lamb cubes in boiling salted water.

4. Place the blanched lamb in a pot. Add the stock and the second onion piquet, the second bouquet garni, the sachet and salt. Simmer until the meat is tender, approximately 1-1/2 hours.

5. Remove the meat from the liquid and reserve. Reduce the cooking liquid to 1 quart (1 liter). Incorporate the roux.

6. Combine the heavy cream, mustard and egg yolks and add to the reduced stock as a liaison.

7. Return the lamb to the sauce and adjust the seasonings. Heat the sauce and meat thoroughly but do not allow it to boil. Serve the blanquette with the cooked beans.

◆◆◆

RECIPE 15.15

LAMB NAVARIN

Yield: 10 10-oz. (300-g) Servings   **Method:** Stewing

Olive oil	3 Tbsp.	45 ml
Lean lamb shoulder, large dice	3 lb.	1.5 kg
Sugar	1 Tbsp.	15 ml
Salt and pepper	TT	TT
Flour	3 Tbsp.	45 ml
White stock	1 qt.	1 lt
White wine	4 oz.	120 g
Tomato concasse	8 oz.	250 g
Bouquet garni:		
Carrot stick, 4 in. (10 cm)	1	1
Leek, split, 4-in. (10-cm) piece	1	1
Fresh thyme	1 sprig	1 sprig
Bay leaf	1	1
Potato, peeled, medium dice	1 lb. 8 oz.	650 g
Carrot, medium dice	1 lb.	450 g
White turnip, peeled, medium dice	1 lb.	450 g
Pearl onions, peeled	12	12
Fresh green peas	6 oz.	170 g

1. In a braiser, brown the meat in the olive oil.
2. Sprinkle the meat with the sugar and season with salt and pepper.
3. Add the flour and cook to make a blond roux.
4. Add the stock and wine. Add the tomatoes and bouquet garni; bring to a boil. Cover and cook in the oven at 375°F (190°C) until the meat is almost tender, approximately 1 to 1-1/2 hours.
5. Remove the meat and hold in a warm place. Strain the sauce and skim off any excess fat.
6. Combine the sauce, meat, potatoes, carrots, turnips and onions. Cover and cook until the vegetables are almost tender, approximately 25 minutes.
7. Add the peas and cook for 10 minutes more.

◆◆◆

RECIPE 15.16
NOISETTES OF LAMB WITH GARLIC SAUCE

Yield: 4 Servings   **Method:** Sautéing

Lamb noisettes, 2–3 oz. (60–90 g) each	8	8
Salt and pepper	TT	TT
Fresh thyme	1 tsp.	5 ml
Garlic heads	3	3
Fresh rosemary	1 sprig	1 sprig
Olive oil	2 oz.	60 g
Red wine	4 oz.	120 g
Jus lié	1 pt.	450 ml

1. Season the noisettes with salt, pepper and thyme.
2. Break the garlic into cloves. Cook the cloves with the rosemary in 1 ounce (30 grams) of oil over low heat until they are very soft, approximately 10 minutes.
3. Deglaze with the wine. Add the jus lié; simmer and reduce by half.
4. Strain the sauce through a china cap, pushing to extract some of the garlic. Return the sauce to the saucepan and adjust the consistency and seasonings.
5. Sauté the noisettes to the desired degree of doneness in the remaining oil; serve with the sauce.

CHAPTER 16

PORK

After studying this chapter you will be able to:

+ identify the primal, subprimal and fabricated cuts of pork
+ perform basic butchering procedures
+ apply appropriate cooking methods to several common cuts of pork

ork is the meat of hogs usually butchered before they are one years old. With the exception of beef, Americans consume more pork than any other meat. The pork we eat is leaner and healthier than it once was because of advances in animal husbandry.

Since hogs are butchered at a young age their meat is generally very tender and has a delicate flavor. It is well suited to a variety of cooking methods. Over two thirds of the pork marketed in the United States is cured to produce products such as smoked hams and smoked bacon. Cured pork products are discussed in Chapter 21, Charcuterie.

PRIMAL AND SUBPRIMAL CUTS OF PORK

After a hog is slaughtered, it is generally split down the backbone, dividing the carcass into bilateral halves. Like the beef carcass, each side of the hog carcass is then further broken down into the primal cuts: shoulder, Boston butt, belly, loin and fresh ham.

Hogs are bred specifically to produce long loins: The loin contains the highest-quality meat and is the most expensive cut of pork. Pork is unique in that the ribs and loin are considered a single primal cut. They are not separated into two different primals as are the ribs and loin of beef, veal and lamb.

Figure 16.1 shows the relationship between the hog's bone structure and the primal cuts. As with all meats, it is important to know the location of bones when cutting or working with pork. This makes meat fabrication and carving easier and aids in identifying cuts. Figure 16.2 shows the primal cuts of pork and their location on the carcass. A hog carcass generally weighs in a range of 120 to 210 pounds (55–110 kg).

Shoulder

The primal shoulder, known as the picnic ham, is the lower portion of the hog's foreleg; it accounts for approximately 20% of carcass weight. The shoulder contains the arm and shank bones and has a relatively high ratio of bone to lean meat.

Because all pork comes from hogs slaughtered at a young age, the shoulder is tender enough to be cooked by any method. It is, however, one of the toughest cuts of pork. It is available smoked or fresh. The shoulder is fairly inexpensive and, when purchased fresh, it can be cut into shoulder butt steaks or boned and cut for chop suey or stew.

The foreshank is called the shoulder hock and is almost always smoked. Shoulder hocks are often simmered for long periods in soups, stews and braised dishes to add flavor and richness.

Boston Butt

The primal Boston butt is a square cut located just above the primal pork shoulder. It accounts for approximately 7% of carcass weight.

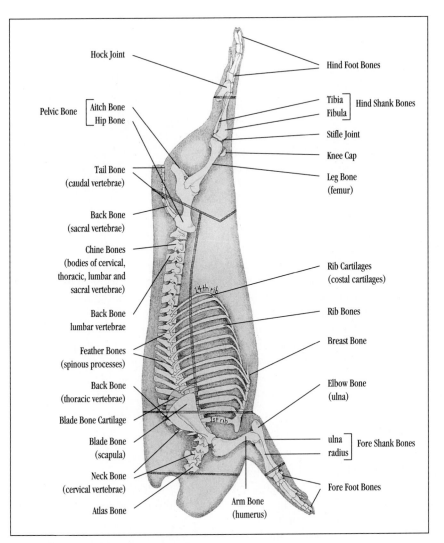

FIGURE 16.1   *The Skeletal Structure of a Hog*

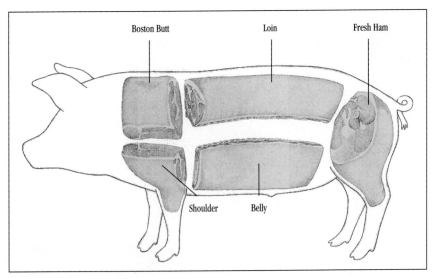

FIGURE 16.2   *The Primal Cuts of Pork*

The Boston butt is very meaty and tender, with a good percentage of fat to lean meat. Containing only a small portion of the blade bone, the Boston butt is a good choice when a recipe calls for a solid piece of lean pork. The fresh Boston butt is sometimes cut into steaks or chops to be broiled or sautéed. When the Boston butt is smoked it is usually boneless and called a cottage ham.

Boston Butt

Belly

The primal pork belly is located below the loin. Accounting for approximately 16% of carcass weight, it is very fatty with only streaks of lean meat. It contains the spareribs, which are always separated from the rest of the belly before cooking.

Pork Spareribs

Spareribs usually are sold fresh but can also be smoked. Typically they are simmered and then grilled or baked while being basted with a spicy barbecue sauce. The remainder of the pork belly is nearly always cured and smoked to produce bacon.

Loin

The loin is cut from directly behind the Boston butt and includes the entire rib section as well as the loin and a portion of the sirloin area. The primal loin accounts for approximately 20% of carcass weight. It contains a portion of the blade bone on the shoulder end, a portion of the hip bone on the ham end, all of the ribs and most of the backbone.

The primal pork loin is the only primal cut of pork not typically smoked or cured. Most of the loin is a single, very tender eye muscle. It is quite lean but contains enough intramuscular and subcutaneous fat to make it an excellent choice for a moist-heat cooking method such as braising. Or, it can be prepared with dry-heat cooking methods such as roasting or sautéing. The loin also contains the pork tenderloin, located on the inside of the rib bones on the sirloin end of the loin. The tenderloin is the most tender cut of

Pork Loin

Pork Tenderloin

Pork Backribs

Pork Loin Chops

pork; it is very versatile and can be trimmed, cut into medallions and sautéed or the whole tenderloin can be roasted or braised. The most popular cut from the loin is the pork chop. Chops can be cut from the entire loin, the choicest being center-cut chops from the primal loin after the blade bone and sirloin portions at the front and rear of the loin are removed. The pork loin can be purchased boneless or boned and tied as a roast. A boneless pork loin is smoked to produce Canadian bacon. The rib bones, when trimmed from the loin, can be served as barbecued pork back ribs.

Although not actually part of the primal loin, fatback is the thick layer of fat—sometimes more than an inch (2.5 centimeters) thick—between the skin and the lean eye muscle. It has a variety of uses in the kitchen, especially in the preparation of charcuterie items.

Fresh Ham

The primal fresh ham is the hog's hind leg. It is a rather large cut accounting for approximately 24% of carcass weight. The ham contains the aitch, leg and hind shank bones. Fresh ham, like the legs of other meat animals, contains large muscles with relatively small amounts of connective tissue.

Like many other cuts of pork, hams are often cured and smoked. But fresh hams also produce great roasts and can be prepared using almost any cooking method. When cured and smoked, hams are available in a variety of styles; they can be purchased bone-in, shankless or boneless, partially or fully cooked. Fully cooked hams are also available canned. There is a specific ham for nearly every use and desired degree of convenience. The shank portion of the ham is called the ham hock. It is used in the same manner as the shoulder hock.

Fresh ham

BUTCHERING PROCEDURES

Other than suckling pigs (which are very young, very small whole pigs used for roasting or barbecuing whole), pork products generally are not purchased in forms larger than the primal cuts described above. There are a few important pork fabrication and butchering techniques that you should master, however.

PROCEDURE FOR BONING A PORK LOIN

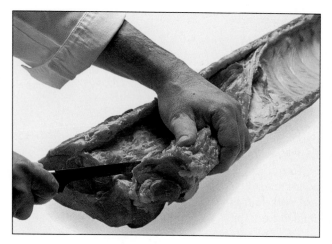

1. Starting on the sirloin end of a full pork loin, remove the tenderloin in one piece by making smooth cuts against the inside of the rib bones. Pull gently on the tenderloin as you cut.

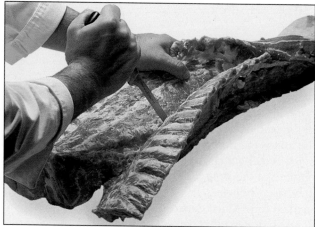

2. Turn the loin over and cut between the ribs and the eye meat. Continue separating the meat from the bones, following the contours of the bones, until the loin is completely separated from the bones.

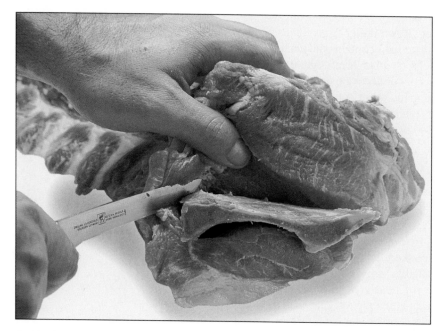

3. Trim around the blade bone on the shoulder end of the loin and remove it.

4. The fully boned loin will consist of (from left to right) the tenderloin, boneless loin and loin bones.

PROCEDURE FOR TYING A BONELESS PORK ROAST WITH THE HALF-HITCH METHOD

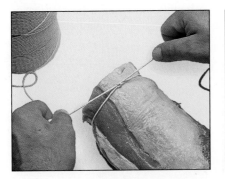

1. Wrap the loose end of the string around the pork loin and tie it with a double knot.

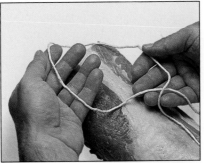

2. Make a loop and slide it down over the roast to approximately 1 inch (2.5 centimeters) from the first knot.

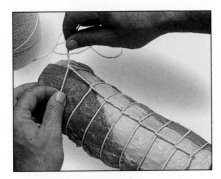

3. Make another loop and slide it down. Continue in this fashion until the whole roast has been tied.

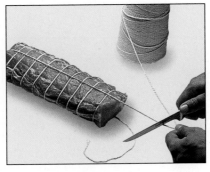

4. Turn the roast over and cut the string, leaving enough to wrap lengthwise around the roast to the original knot.

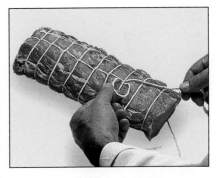

5. Wrap the string around the end of the roast, then around the string that formed the last loop. Continue in this fashion for the length of the roast, pulling the string tight after wrapping it around each loop.

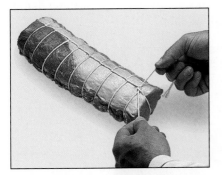

6. Turn the roast back over. Wrap the string around the front end of the roast and secure it to the first loop at the point where you tied the first knot.

7. The finished roast. Note the even intervals at which the strings are tied. They should be just snug enough to hold the shape of the roast; they should not dig in or cut the meat.

Procedure for Cutting a Chop from a Pork Loin

Center-cut pork chops can be cut from the center portion of a bone-in pork loin without the aid of a saw by using a boning knife and a heavy cleaver. Trim the excess fat from the loin, leaving a 1/4-inch (6-millimeter) layer to protect the meat during cooking.

1. Cut through the meat with the knife.

2. Use the cleaver to chop through the chine bone.

3. To produce a cleaner chop, trim the meat from the end of the rib bone. Then, with the boning knife, separate the loin meat from the chine bones and separate the chine bone from the rib with the cleaver.

Procedure for Cutting a Pocket in a Pork Chop

To make a pocket in a pork chop for stuffing, start with a thick chop or a double rib chop. Cut the pocket deep enough to hold ample stuffing, but be careful not to puncture either surface of the chop.

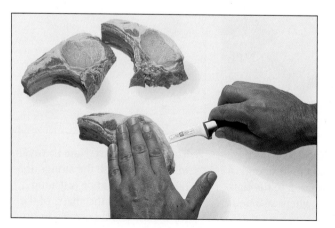

1. Use the tip of a boning knife to cut a pocket.

TABLE 16.1   USING COMMON CUTS OF PORK

Primal	Subprimal or Fabricated Cut	IMPS	Cooking Methods	Serving Suggestions
Shoulder	Picnic shoulder	405	Dry (baked)	Smoked picnic shoulder
Boston butt	Boston Butt	406	Dry heat (broil or grill; sauté) Moist heat (simmer)	Broiled Boston butt steaks Choucroute
Belly	Bacon	539	Dry heat (sauté) Moist heat (simmer) Combination (braise)	Breakfast meat Seasoning Seasoning
	Spare ribs	416A	Combination (steam then grill)	Barbecued spare ribs
Loin	Pork loin	410	Dry heat (roast) Combination (braise)	Roast pork Braised pork chops
	Pork tenderloin	415	Dry heat (broil or grill; sauté; roast)	Roast pork tenderloin
	Pork back ribs	422	Combination (steam then grill)	Barbecued back ribs
	Pork loin chops	1410	Dry heat (broil or grill) Combination (braise)	Broiled loin chop with mushroom sauce Braised loin chop with leeks and fennel
Fresh ham	Fresh Ham	401A	Dry heat (roast)	Roast pork with apricots and almonds

PROCEDURE FOR TRIMMING A PORK TENDERLOIN

As with a beef tenderloin, the pork tenderloin must be trimmed of all fat and silverskin. Follow the procedures outlined in Chapter 13, Beef, for trimming a beef tenderloin.

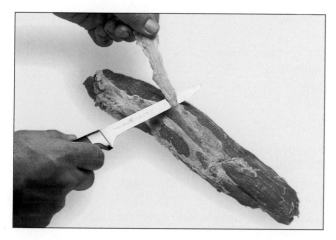

1. Use a boning knife to remove the silverskin from a pork tenderloin.

CONCLUSION

Pork can be enjoyed cured, processed or fresh. The mild flavor of fresh pork blends well with many different seasonings, making it a popular menu item. It is naturally tender and can be prepared by almost any dry-heat, moist-heat or combination cooking method. Properly fabricated and prepared, it can be a nutritious meat.

Questions for Discussion

1. List each pork primal and describe its location on the carcass. Identify two subprimals or fabricated cuts taken from each primal.

2. What is unique about the primal pork loin as compared to the beef or veal loin?

3. Are fatback and bacon taken from the same primal? How are they different?

4. What is the only primal cut of pork that is not typically smoked or cured? How is it best cooked? Explain your answer.

Additional Pork Recipes

RECIPE 16.1

Carolina Barbecued Ribs

Note: *This dish appears in the Chapter Opening photograph.*

Yield: 6 Servings, approx. 4 ribs each   **Method:** Baking

Salt and pepper	TT	TT
Crushed red pepper flakes	1 Tbsp.	30 ml
Pork backribs, 3–4 lb. (1.3–1.8 kg) slab	2	2
White vinegar	1 pt.	450 ml
Sauce:		
Onion, chopped coarse	5 oz.	150 g
Garlic cloves	3	3
Green bell pepper, chopped coarse	4 oz.	120 g
Plum tomatoes, canned	1 pt.	450 ml
Red Devil hot sauce	8 oz.	225 g
Brown sugar	10 oz.	300 g
Lemon juice	2 oz.	60 g

1. Combine the salt, pepper and red pepper flakes. Rub this mixture over both sides of the ribs, coating them well.

2. Place the ribs in a non-reactive pan and add the vinegar. Cover and refrigerate several hours or overnight.

3. Uncover the ribs, turn the presentation side down and bake in a 375°F (190°C) oven for 1-1/2 hours.

4. Remove the ribs from the liquid and place on a clean sheet pan, turning them so the presentation side is up. Increase the oven temperature to 400°F (200°C) and bake for an additional 30 minutes.

5. Prepare the sauce by puréeing the onion, garlic, green pepper and tomatoes in a food processor or blender. Pour this mixture into a non-reactive saucepan and add the remaining sauce ingredients.

6. Simmer the sauce over low heat until it thickens, approximately 15 to 20 minutes.

7. Brush the ribs with the sauce and serve additional sauce on the side. Serve with Creamy Cole Slaw, Recipe 24.33 and Baked Beans, Recipe 22.23.

◆◆◆

RECIPE 16.2

GRILLED MEDALLIONS OF PORK ON A CORNCAKE WITH BOURBONED APPLE BUTTER

ANA WESTIN HOTEL, WASHINGTON, D.C.
Chef Leland Atkinson

Yield: 4 Servings

Method: Grilling

Loin medallions, 3 oz. (90 g) each	8	8
Salt and pepper	TT	TT
Lemon juice	1 oz.	30 g
Garlic, minced	1 tsp.	5 ml
Jalapeño, minced	1 tsp.	5 ml
Corncakes (recipe follows)	4	4
Apple Butter (recipe follows)	as needed	as needed
Fresh cilantro	as needed	as needed

1. Season the pork with salt and pepper and marinate it in the lemon juice, garlic and jalepeño for 2–4 hours.

2. Grill the medallions until done, approximately 4–5 minutes per side.

3. Place the corncakes on four warm plates, top them with a dollop of warm Apple Butter and two pork medallions. Garnish with fresh cilantro and serve.

APPLE BUTTER

Yield: 24 oz. (700 g)

Onion, chopped fine	4 oz.	120 g
Sugar	2 oz.	60 g
Cider vinegar	1 oz.	30 g
Granny Smith apples, peeled and chopped coarse	3	3
Bourbon	6 oz.	180 g
Demi-glace	8 oz.	250 g
Cinnamon, ground	2 tsp.	10 ml
Cloves, ground	1 pinch	1 pinch
Whole butter	1 Tbsp.	15 ml
Salt and pepper	TT	TT

1. Combine the onion, sugar and vinegar; simmer for 5 minutes.

2. Add the apples, bourbon, demi-glace and spices. Simmer until the apples are completely tender.

3. Purée the mixture in a blender or food processor.

4. Strain and monte au beurre. Adjust the seasonings and keep warm for service.

CORNCAKES

Yield: 4 4-oz. (120-g) cakes

Green onion, sliced	2 Tbsp.	30 ml
Red bell pepper, small dice	2 Tbsp.	30 ml
Jalapeño, minced	1	1
Olive oil	1 oz.	30 g
Fresh corn kernels	8 oz.	250 g

Continued

Milk	3 oz.	90 g
Flour	2 oz.	60 g
Cornmeal	2 oz.	60 g
Eggs	2	2
Egg yolk	1	1
Fresh cilantro, chopped	1 tsp.	5 ml
Salt and pepper	TT	TT
Clarified butter	as needed	as needed

1. Sauté the onions, bell peppers and jalapeño in the olive oil. Drain and cool to room temperature.
2. In a food processor, blend the corn kernels with a little milk until the mixture is not quite smooth.
3. Remove the corn mixture to a bowl and stir in the remaining milk, the flour and cornmeal.
4. Beat the eggs with the yolk; add the pepper mixture to them. Add the cilantro and combine this mixture with the corn mixture. Season with salt and pepper.
5. Heat a portion of the clarified butter in a sauté pan or on a griddle. Add 4 ounces (120 grams) of the batter to form 5-inch (12-centimeter) pancakes; lightly brown them on each side.

◆ ◆ ◆

RECIPE 16.3

CHINESE BARBECUED SPARERIBS

Yield: approximately 24 ribs   **Method:** Roasting

Sparerib racks, 2 lb. 8 oz. (1.1 kg) each	2	2
Garlic cloves, crushed	2	2
Tomato catsup	2 Tbsp.	30 ml
Soy sauce	2 Tbsp.	30 ml
Hoisin sauce	2 Tbsp.	30 ml
Red wine	2 Tbsp.	30 ml
Fresh ginger, grated	1 Tbsp.	15 ml
Honey	1 Tbsp.	15 ml

1. Cut the spareribs into individual ribs and arrange them on a rack in a baking pan. Roast for 45 minutes at 300°F (150°C).
2. Combine the remaining ingredients into a sauce. Brush the spareribs lightly with the sauce. Roast for 30 minutes more.
3. Turn the spareribs and brush with more sauce. Roast until the ribs are well browned, approximately 30 minutes.

◆ ◆ ◆

RECIPE 16.4

PORK LOIN WITH PRUNES

Yield: 6 6-oz. (180-g) Servings   **Method:** Roasting

Boneless pork loin roast, 3 lb. (1.5 kg)	1	1
Salt and pepper	TT	TT
Prunes, pitted	1 lb. 8 oz.	750 g
Carrot, chopped coarse	3 oz.	90 g
Onion, chopped coarse	6 oz.	170 g
Vegetable oil	1 Tbsp.	15 ml
Clarified butter	1 Tbsp.	15 ml

Fresh rosemary	1 tsp.	5 ml
Fresh thyme	1 tsp.	5 ml
Bay leaf, crushed	1	1
Garlic cloves	2	2
Apple juice	8 oz.	250 g
White stock	8 oz.	250 g
Sugar	2 oz.	60 g
Vinegar	2 oz.	60 g

1. Trim and butterfly the pork loin; reserve the trimmings. (To butterfly the loin, slice it partway through the center and open it like a book, then flatten it into a rectangular shape.) Season with salt and pepper.

2. Reserve 12 prunes and arrange the remaining prunes along the length of the loin. Roll up the loin and tie with butcher's twine.

3. Brown the pork roll and pork trimmings, carrots and onions in the oil and butter.

4. Add the herbs and garlic and roast the pork on the bed of trimmings and vegetables at 350°F (170°C), basting frequently with the fat that accumulates in the pan, until done, approximately 45–60 minutes.

5. Poach the reserved prunes in the apple juice until plump; set aside.

6. Remove the roast from the pan and keep it warm. Degrease the pan and deglaze with white stock. Simmer for 15 minutes, then strain.

7. Combine the sugar and vinegar in a saucepan. Bring to a boil and cook without stirring until the mixture turns a caramel color. Immediately remove from the heat and add the juices from the roasting pan. When the sputtering stops, return the pan to the heat and skim any fat from the surface; keep the sauce warm over low heat.

8. Drain the prunes. Remove the twine from the roast. Slice and serve the meat with the sauce and prunes.

◆◆◆

RECIPE 16.5

Bourbon Baked Ham

Yield: 16 6-oz (180-g) Servings   **Method:** Roasting

Ham, fully cooked, bone in, 12–14 lb. (5.4–6.3 kg)	1	1
Brown sugar	6 oz.	170 g
Cloves, ground	1/2 tsp.	2 ml
Crushed pineapple, with juice	16 oz.	500 g
Bourbon	8 oz.	250 g
Orange marmalade	8 oz.	250 g

1. Peel the skin from the ham and trim the exterior fat to an even thickness of 1/4 inch (6 millimeters).

2. Combine the sugar and cloves and pat this mixture evenly over the top of the ham. Roast the coated ham at 350°F (170°C) for 30 minutes.

3. Combine the pineapple, bourbon and marmalade in a saucepan over medium heat. Do not allow the bourbon to flame.

4. Pour the sauce over the ham and cook until done, basting frequently, approximately 3 hours.

5. Remove the ham from the roasting pan. Keep it warm and allow it to rest 30 minutes before carving.

◆◆◆

RECIPE 16.6
GRILLED PORK TENDERLOIN WITH CASCABEL CHILE AND HONEY GLAZE

VINCENT ON CAMELBACK, PHOENIX, AZ
Chef Vincent Guerithault

Yield: 6 6-oz. (180-g) Servings   **Method:** Grilling

Pork tenderloins, approx. 14 oz. (400 g) each	3	3
Olive oil	1 Tbsp.	15 ml
Salt	1 tsp.	5 ml
Black pepper, coarsely ground	2 tsp.	10 ml
Cascabel Chile and Honey Glaze (recipe follows)		

1. Rub the tenderloins with oil and season with salt and pepper.
2. Grill the tenderloins on all sides, a total of approximately 5 minutes. Brush with the Cascabel Chile and Honey Glaze and cook an additional 2 minutes on each side.
3. Remove the pork from the grill and allow it to rest for 5 minutes before slicing.
4. Slice each tenderloin on the bias into 12 slices. Drizzle the remaining Cascabel Chile and Honey Glaze over the sliced pork.

CASCABEL CHILE AND HONEY GLAZE

Yield: 12 oz. (350 g)

Cascabel chiles (if not available, substitute 2 jalapeños)	4	4
Honey	8 oz.	250 g
Chicken stock	4 oz.	120 g
Tomato purée	3 Tbsp.	45 ml
Paprika	1 tsp.	5 ml
Cumin, ground	1 tsp.	5 ml

1. Soften the cascabel chiles by soaking them in warm water for approximately 2 hours.
2. Combine all ingredients in a sauce pan and simmer over medium heat for approximately 10 minutes.
3. Remove from the heat and purée in a blender.

◆◆◆

RECIPE 16.7
SAUTÉED PORK MEDALLIONS WITH RED PEPPER AND CITRUS

Yield: 8 Servings   **Method:** Sautéing

Pork loin, boneless, 3 lb. (1.4 kg)	1	1
Salt and pepper	TT	TT
Olive oil	6 oz.	180 g
Orange juice	6 oz.	180 g

Lemon juice	2 Tbsp.	30 ml
Green onion, sliced	4 oz.	120 g
Oranges	4	4
Flour	as needed	as needed
Red bell pepper, julienne	12 oz.	350 g
Grand Marnier	4 oz.	120 g
Demi-glace	1 pt.	450 ml

1. Season the pork with salt and pepper and marinate overnight in 4 ounces (120 grams) of the olive oil, 4 ounces (120 grams) of the orange juice, 1 tablespoon (15 milliliters) of the lemon juice and 2 ounces (60 grams) of the green onions.
2. Zest the oranges. Blanch and refresh the zest. Peel and section the oranges.
3. Cut the pork into 3-ounce (90-gram) medallions and pound lightly.
4. Dredge the medallions in flour seasoned with salt and pepper.
5. Sauté the medallions in the remaining olive oil until done, approximately 5 minutes. Remove from the pan and reserve.
6. Add the red peppers and remaining green onions to the pan and sauté lightly.
7. Remove the pan from the flame and deglaze with Grand Marnier.
8. Add the demi-glace, orange zest, and remaining orange and lemon juices. Adjust the seasonings.
9. Serve two medallions of pork per portion with sauce. Garnish with the orange sections.

◆◆◆

RECIPE 16.8

STUFFED PORK CHOPS

Yield: 10 Servings   **Method:** Braising

Thick-cut pork chops, approx. 8 oz. (250 g) each	10	10
Celery, small dice	4 oz.	120 g
Onion, small dice	6 oz.	170 g
Whole butter, melted	6 oz.	170 g
Fresh bread cubes, 1/2 in. (1.2 cm)	8 oz.	250 g
Parsley, chopped	1 Tbsp.	15 ml
Salt and pepper	TT	TT
White stock	approx. 8 oz.	approx. 250 g
Olive oil	2 oz.	60 g
Demi-glace	1 qt.	1 lt

1. Cut pockets in the chops.
2. Sauté the celery and onions in 2 ounces (60 grams) of butter until tender.
3. Combine the celery, onions and remaining butter with the bread cubes, parsley, salt and pepper. Add enough stock to moisten the dressing.
4. Stuff the mixture into each of the pork chops. Seal the pockets with toothpicks and tie with butcher's twine.
5. In a braiser, brown the stuffed chops well on each side in the olive oil.
6. Add the demi-glace. Bring to a simmer, cover and place in a 325°F (160°C) oven. Cook until tender, approximately 45 minutes.
7. Remove the chops from the pan. Degrease the sauce and reduce to the desired consistency. Strain the sauce and adjust the seasonings.

◆◆◆

RECIPE 16.9
CHOUCROUTE

Yield: 12 Servings, 4 oz. (120 g) sauerkraut,   **Method:** Braising
1 sausage and 7 oz. (200 g) pork

Bacon, medium dice	8 oz.	250 g
Onion, medium dice	12 oz.	340 g
Garlic, chopped fine	1-1/2 oz.	45 g
Granny Smith apples, medium dice	8 oz.	250 g
Sauerkraut	2 lb. 8 oz.	1 kg
Dry white wine	4 oz.	120 g
White wine vinegar	4 oz.	120 g
Chicken stock	1 pt.	500 ml
Sachet:		
Juniper berries	6	6
Bay leaves	3	3
Cloves	2	2
Caraway seeds	1 tsp.	5 ml
Boneless pork butt, 4 lb. (1.8 kg)	1	1
Smoked pork loin	2 lb.	1 kg
Red potatoes, peeled and quartered	3 lb.	1.4 kg
Bratwurst	12 links	12 links
Salt and pepper	TT	TT

1. Render the bacon.
2. Sauté the onions, garlic and apples in the bacon fat without browning.
3. Rinse the sauerkraut and squeeze out the liquid. Add the sauerkraut to the pan.
4. Stir in the wine, vinegar, stock and sachet.
5. Place the pork butt on the sauerkraut. Cover and braise in a 325°F (160°C) oven for 1 hour.
6. Add the smoked pork loin and potatoes and braise an additional 30 minutes.
7. Add the bratwurst and braise until all the meats are tender and the potatoes are done, approximately 30 minutes. Remove and discard the sachet. Season to taste with salt and pepper.
8. Carve the meats and serve with a portion of the sauerkraut and potatoes.

◆◆◆

RECIPE 16.10
CASSOULET

ANA WESTIN HOTEL, WASHINGTON, D.C.
Chef Leland Atkinson

Yield: 8 Servings, 8 oz. (250 g) pork stew,   **Method:** Stewing
1-1/2 oz. (45 g) sausage and
1 piece of duck each

White beans	1 lb.	450 g
White stock	2 qt.	2 lt
Smoked ham, large dice	8 oz.	250 g

Bouquet garni:		
Carrot stick, 4 in. (10 cm)	1	1
Leek, split, 4-in. (10-cm) piece	1	1
Fresh thyme	1 sprig	1 sprig
Bay leaf	1	1
Lamb or other sausage	1 lb.	450 g
Onion, medium dice	6 oz.	180 g
Garlic, chopped	1/2 oz.	15 g
Pork butt, cut in 2-in. (5 cm) cubes	1 lb. 8 oz.	700 g
Salt and pepper	TT	TT
Olive oil	1 oz.	30 g
Mirepoix	8 oz.	250 g
White wine	6 oz.	180 g
Tomato concasse	1 lb.	250 g
Demi-glace	1 pt.	450 ml
Brown stock	8 oz.	250 g
Sachet:		
Bay leaf	1	1
Dried thyme	1/2 tsp.	2 ml
Peppercorns, cracked	1/2 tsp.	2 ml
Parsley stems	8	8
Garlic cloves, crushed	2	2
Duck Confit (Recipe 20.16)	8 pieces	8 pieces

1. To make the bean stew, soak the white beans overnight in water. Drain and combine with the white stock, ham and bouquet garni. Bring to a simmer and cook for 30 minutes. Add the lamb sausage, onions and garlic; simmer until the beans are tender.

2. Remove and reserve the sausage.

3. Drain the beans, reserving both the beans and the cooking liquid. Reduce the cooking liquid by half and combine with the beans.

4. To make the meat stew, season the pork with salt and pepper and brown it in olive oil. Remove and reserve the meat.

5. Add the mirepoix to the pan and sauté. Deglaze with the white wine and add the tomato concasse, demi-glace, brown stock and sachet. Cover and simmer the pork until tender, approximately 45 minutes.

6. Remove the meat from the sauce and reserve. Discard the sachet. Reduce the sauce until thick; return the meat to the sauce.

7. To serve, scrape the excess fat from the duck confit. Place the duck in a roasting pan and roast at 350°F (180°C) until the meat is hot and the skin is crisp, approximately 20 minutes.

8. Place a portion of hot beans in a soup plate. Place a portion of the duck confit in the plate. Arrange a portion of the meat stew on top of the beans and around the duck.

9. Slice the lamb sausage and add it to the plate. Garnish with fresh herbs.

CHAPTER 17
POULTRY

After studying this chapter you will be able to:

◆ understand the structure and composition of poultry
◆ identify various kinds and classes of poultry
◆ understand poultry inspection and grading practices
◆ purchase poultry appropriate for your needs
◆ store poultry properly
◆ prepare poultry for cooking
◆ apply various cooking methods to poultry

*P*oultry *is the collective term for domesticated birds bred for eating. They include chickens, ducks, geese, guineas, pigeons and turkeys. (Game birds such as pheasant, quail and partridge are described in Chapter 18, Game.) Poultry is generally the least expensive and most versatile of all main dish foods. It can be cooked by almost any method and its mild flavor goes well with a wide variety of sauces and accompaniments.*

In this chapter we discuss the different kinds and classes of poultry and how to choose those that best suit your needs. You will learn how to store poultry properly to prevent food-borne illnesses and spoilage; how to butcher birds to produce the specific cuts you need and how to apply a variety of cooking methods properly.

Many of the cooking methods discussed here have been applied previously to meats. Although there are similarities with these methods, there are also many distinct differences. As you study this chapter, review the corresponding cooking methods for meats and note the similarities and differences.

MUSCLE COMPOSITION

The muscle tissue of poultry is similar to that of mammals in that it contains approximately 72% water, 20% protein, 7% fat and 1% minerals; it consists of bundles of muscle cells or fibers held together by connective tissue. Unlike red meat, poultry does not contain the intramuscular fat known as marbling. Instead, a bird stores fat in its skin, abdominal cavity and the fat pad near its tail. Poultry fat is softer and has a lower melting point than other animal fats. It is easily rendered during cooking.

As with red meats, poultry muscles that are used more often tend to be tougher than those used less frequently. Also, the muscles of an older bird

FREE-RANGE CHICKENS

Chicken has become increasingly popular in recent years, in part because it is inexpensive, versatile and considered healthier than meat. Indeed, more than 100 million chickens are processed weekly in this country. To meet an ever-increasing demand, chickens are raised indoors in huge chicken houses that may contain as many as 20,000 birds. They are fed a specially formulated mixture composed primarily of corn and soybean meal. Animal protein, vitamins, minerals and small amounts of antibiotics are added to produce quick-growing, healthy birds.

Many consumers feel that chickens raised this way do not have the flavor of chickens that

are allowed to move freely and forage for food. Some consumers are concerned about the residual effects of the vitamins, minerals and antibiotics added to the chicken feed. To meet the demand for chickens raised the "old-fashioned way," some farmers raise (and many fine establishments offer) free-range chickens.

Although the USDA has not standardized regulations for free-range chicken, generally the term *free-range* applies to birds that are allowed unlimited access to the area outside the chicken house. Often they are raised without antibiotics, fed a vegetarian diet (no animal fat or byproducts), processed without the use of preservatives

and raised under more humane growing methods than conventionally grown birds. Most free-range chickens are marketed at 9–10 weeks old and weigh 4-1/2 to 5 pounds (2 to 2-1/2 kilograms)—considerably more mature and heavier than conventional broilers. They are generally sold with heads and feet intact and are more expensive than conventionally raised chickens.

Many consumers (in both the dining room and the kitchen) feel that free-range chicken is superior in flavor and quality. Others find no perceptible differences. As a consumer you will have to decide whether any difference is worth the added expense.

tend to be tougher than those of a younger one. Because the majority of poultry is marketed at a young age, however, it is generally very tender.

The breast and wing flesh of chickens and turkeys is lighter in color than the flesh of their thighs and legs. This color difference is due to a higher concentration of the protein myoglobin in the thigh and leg muscles. Myoglobin is the protein that stores oxygen for the muscle tissues to use. More-active muscles require more myoglobin and tend to be darker than less-active ones. Because chickens and turkeys generally do not fly, their breast and wing muscles contain little myoglobin and are therefore a light color. Birds that do fly have only dark meat. Dark meat also contains more fat and connective tissue than light meat, and its cooking time is longer.

Skin color may vary from white to golden yellow, depending on what the bird was fed. Such color differences are not an indication of overall quality.

Rock Cornish Game Hen

IDENTIFYING POULTRY

The USDA recognizes six categories or **kinds** of poultry: chicken, duck, goose, guinea, pigeon and turkey. Each poultry kind is divided into **classes** based predominantly on the bird's age and tenderness. The sex of young birds is not significant for culinary purposes. It does matter, however, with older birds: Older male birds are tough and stringy and have less flavor than older female birds. Tables 17.1 through 17.6 list identifying characteristics and suggested cooking methods for each of the various kinds and classes of poultry.

Chicken Broiler/Fryer

Chicken

Chicken (Fr. *poulet*) is the most popular and widely eaten poultry in the world. It contains both light and dark meat and has relatively little fat. A young, tender chicken can be cooked by almost any method; an older bird is best stewed or braised. Chicken is extremely versatile and may be flavored, stuffed, basted or garnished with almost anything. Chicken is inexpensive and readily available, fresh or frozen, in a variety of forms.

Capon

TABLE 17.1   CHICKEN CLASSES

Class	Description	Age	Weight	Cooking Method
Game hen	Young or immature progeny of Cornish chickens or of a Cornish chicken and a White Rock chicken; very flavorful	5–6 weeks	2 lb. (1 kg) or less	Split and broil or grill; roast
Broiler/fryer	Young with soft, smooth-textured skin; relatively lean; flexible breastbone	13 weeks	3 lb. 8 oz. (1.5 kg) or less	Any cooking method; very versatile
Roaster	Young with tender meat and smooth-textured skin; breastbone is less flexible than broiler's	3–5 months	3 lb. 8 oz.–5 lb. (1.5–2 kg)	Any cooking method
Capon	Surgically castrated male; tender meat with soft, smooth-textured skin; bred for well-flavored meat; contains a high proportion of light to dark meat and a relatively high fat content	Under 8 months	6–10 lb. (2.5–4.5 kg)	Roast
Hen/stewing	Mature female; flavorful but less tender meat; nonflexible breastbone	Over 10 months	2 lb. 8 oz.–8 lb. (1–3.5 kg)	Stew or braise

TABLE 17.2   DUCK CLASSES

Class	Description	Age	Weight	Cooking Method
Broiler/fryer	Young bird with tender meat; a soft bill and windpipe	8 weeks or less	3 lb. 8 oz.–4 lb. (1.5–1.8 kg)	Roast at high temperature
Roaster	Young bird with tender meat; rich flavor; easily dented windpipe	16 weeks or less	4–6 lb. (1.8–2.5 kg)	Roast
Mature	Old bird with tough flesh; hard bill and windpipe	6 months or older	4–6 lb. (1.8–2.5 kg)	Braise

Roaster Duckling

Duck

The duck (Fr. *canard*) used most often in commercial food service operations is a roaster duckling. It contains only dark meat and large amounts of fat. In order to make the fatty skin palatable, it is important to render as much fat as possible. Duck has a high percentage of bone and fat to meat; for example, a four-pound duck will serve only two people, while a four-pound roasting chicken will serve four people.

Goose

A goose (Fr. *oie*) contains only dark meat and has very fatty skin. It is usually roasted at high temperatures to render the fat. Roasted goose is popular at holidays and is often served with an acidic fruit-based sauce to offset the fattiness.

Young Goose

TABLE 17.3   GOOSE CLASSES

Class	Description	Age	Weight	Cooking Method
Young	Rich, tender dark meat with large amounts of fat; easily dented windpipe	6 months or less	6–12 lb. (2.5–5.5 kg)	Roast at high temperature, accompany with acidic sauces
Mature	Tough flesh and hard windpipe	Over 6 months	10–16 lb. (4.5–7 kg)	Braise or stew

Young Guinea

Guinea

A guinea or guinea fowl (Fr. *pintade*) is the domesticated descendant of a game bird. It has both light and dark meat and a flavor similar to pheasant. Guinea is tender enough to sauté. Because it contains little fat, a guinea is usually barded prior to roasting. Guinea, which is relatively expensive, is not as popular here as it is in Europe.

TABLE 17.4 GUINEA CLASSES

Class	Description	Age	Weight	Cooking Method
Young	Tender meat; flexible breastbone	3 months	12 oz.–1 lb. 8 oz. (.3–.7 kilo)	Bard and roast; sauté
Mature	Tough flesh; hard breastbone	Over 3 months	1–2 lb. (.5–1 kg)	Braise or stew

TABLE 17.5 PIGEON CLASSES

Class	Description	Age	Weight	Cooking Method
Squab	Immature pigeon; very tender, dark flesh and a small amount of fat	4 weeks	12 oz.–1 lb. 8 oz. (.3–.7 kg)	Broil, roast or sauté
Pigeon	Mature bird; coarse skin and tough flesh	Over 4 weeks	1–2 lb. (.5–1 kg)	Braise or stew

Pigeon

The young pigeon (Fr. *pigeon*) used in commercial food service operations is referred to as squab. Its meat is dark, tender and well suited for broiling, sautéing or roasting. Squab has very little fat and benefits from barding.

Squab

Turkey

Turkey (Fr. *dinde*) is the second most popular poultry kind in the United States. It has both light and dark meat and a relatively small amount of fat. Younger turkey is economical and can be prepared in almost any manner.

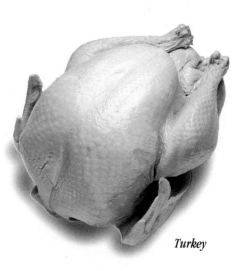

Turkey

TABLE 17.6 TURKEY CLASSES

Class	Description	Age	Weight	Cooking Method
Fryer/roaster	Immature bird of either sex (males are called toms); tender meat with smooth skin; flexible breastbone	16 weeks or less	4–9 lb. (2–4 kg)	Roast or cut into scallops and sauté or pan-fry
Young	Tender meat with smooth skin; less-flexible breastbone	8 months or less	8–22 lb. (3.5–10 kg)	Roast or stew
Yearling	Fully matured bird; reasonably tender meat and slightly coarse skin	15 months or less	10–30 lb. (4.5–13 kg)	Roast or stew
Mature	Older bird with coarse skin and tough flesh	15 months or older	10–30 lb. (4.5–13 kg)	Stew, ground or used in processed products

◆◆◆

A TURKEY BY ANY OTHER NAME ...

In *Food In History*, Reay Tannahill explains why we call a turkey a turkey and not a peru. Turkeys were known as *uexolotl* to 16th-century native Central Americans. They were first brought to Europe by returning Spanish explorers early in the 1500s. Turkish merchants visiting Seville, Spain, on their journeys to and from the eastern Mediterranean brought these exotic birds to England, where the English dubbed them "turkie-cocks." This was eventually shortened to "turkeys." The Turks called these birds "hindi," suggesting that they believed the birds originated in India (as opposed to the Indies). This was a belief shared by the French, who called the bird *coq d'Inde*, which was later corrupted to *dinde* or *dindon*. The Germans followed suit, calling the bird *indianische Henn* as did the Italians, who called it *galle d'India*. Meanwhile, in India, the bird was called a *peru*—which was a little closer to the geographical mark.

Livers, Gizzards, Hearts and Necks

Livers, gizzards, hearts and necks are commonly referred to as **giblets**. Although most poultry kinds are sold with giblets, chickens can be purchased with or without them, depending on your needs.

Giblets can be used in a variety of ways. Gizzards (a bird's second stomach), hearts and necks are most often used to make giblet gravy. Gizzards are sometimes trimmed and deep-fried; hearts are sometimes served sautéed and creamed. Necks are very flavorful and can be added to stocks for flavor and richness. Livers, hearts and gizzards are not added to stocks, however, because of their strong flavors.

Chicken livers are often used in pâtés, sautéed or broiled with onions and served as an entree.

Foie Gras

Foie gras is the enlarged liver of a duck or goose. Considered a delicacy since Roman times, it is now produced in many parts of the world, including the United States. Foie gras is produced by methodically fattening the birds by force-feeding them specially prepared corn while limiting their activity. Fresh foie gras consists of two lobes that must be separated, split and deveined. Good foie gras will be smooth, round and putty-colored. It should not be yellow or grainy. Goose foie gras is lighter in color and more delicate in flavor than that of duck. Duck foie gras has a deeper, winy flavor and is far more common than goose foie gras. Fresh foie gras can be grilled, roasted, sautéed or made into pâtés or terrines. No matter which cooking method is used, care must be taken not to overcook the liver. Foie gras is so high in fat that overcooking will result in the liver actually melting away. Most foie gras used in this country is pasteurized or canned.

Duck Foie Gras

Canned foie gras may consist of solid liver or small pieces of liver compacted to form a block. Canned foie gras mousse is also available. Truffles are a natural accompaniment to foie gras and are used in many canned preparations.

◆◆◆

FROGS

Frogs are amphibians that can be prepared like poultry or fish. Their texture and flavor are similar to those of chicken. Most of the frogs used in food service operations are farm-raised, so their meat is quite tender. Typically, only the legs are eaten. They are sold frozen, in pairs, attached by a small portion of backbone.

TABLE 17.7   NUTRITIONAL VALUES OF POULTRY

For 1 oz. (28 g) uncooked poultry with skin	Kcal	Protein (g)	Total fat (g)	Saturated fat (g)	Cholesterol (mg)	Sodium (mg)
Chicken, breast	49	5.9	2.6	0.8	18	18
Chicken, thigh	60	4.9	4.3	1.2	24	22
Duck	115	3.3	11.2	3.7	22	18
Goose	105	4.5	9.5	2.8	23	21
Squab	83	5.2	6.7	2.4	mq	mq
Turkey, breast	45	6.2	2.0	0.5	18	17
Turkey, leg	41	5.5	1.9	0.6	20	21

The Corinne T. Netzer Encyclopedia of Food Values 1992
mq = measurable quantity, but data is unavailable

NUTRITION

Poultry is an economical source of high-quality protein. Poultry's nutritional value is similar to other meats, except that chicken and turkey breast meat is lower in fat and higher in niacin than other lean meats. (Compare Table 12.1 with Table 17.7.) Generally, dark meat contains more niacin and riboflavin than white meat.

INSPECTION AND GRADING OF POULTRY

Inspection

All poultry produced for public consumption in the United States is subject to USDA inspection. Inspections ensure that products are processed under strict sanitary guidelines and are wholesome and fit for human consumption. Inspections do not indicate a product's quality or tenderness. The round inspection stamp illustrated in Figure 17.1 can be found either on a tag attached to the wing or included in the package labeling.

FIGURE 17.1   *USDA Inspection Stamp for Poultry*

Grading

Grading poultry is voluntary but virtually universal. Birds are graded according to their overall quality with the grade (USDA A, B or C) shown on a shield-shaped tag affixed to the bird or on a processed product's packaging. See Figure 17.2.

According to the USDA, Grade A poultry is free from deformities, with thick flesh and a well-developed fat layer; free of pinfeathers, cuts or tears and broken bones; the carcass is free from discoloration and, if it is frozen, free from defects that occur during handling or storage. Nearly all poultry used in wholesale and retail outlets is Grade A. Grade B and C birds are used primarily for processed poultry products.

Quality grades have no bearing on the product's tenderness or flavor. A bird's tenderness is usually indicated by its class (for example, a "young

FIGURE 17.2   *Grade Stamp for USDA Grade A Poultry*

turkey" is younger and more tender than a yearling). Its grade (USDA A, B or C) within each class is determined by its overall quality.

Purchasing and Storing Poultry

Purchasing Poultry

Poultry can be purchased in many forms: fresh or frozen, whole or cut up, bone-in or boneless, portion controlled (P.C.), individually quick frozen (IQF) or ground. Chicken and turkey are also widely used in prepared and convenience items and are available fully cooked and vacuum-wrapped or boned and canned. Although purchasing poultry in a ready-to-use form is convenient, it is not always necessary: Poultry products are easy to fabricate and portion. Whole fresh poultry is also less expensive than precut or frozen products.

As with meats, you should consider your menu, labor costs, storage facilities and employee skills when deciding whether to purchase whole fresh poultry or some other form.

Storing Poultry

Poultry is highly perishable and particularly susceptible to contamination by salmonella bacteria. It is critical that poultry be stored at the correct temperatures.

Fresh chickens and other small birds can be stored on ice or at 32–34°F (0–2°C) for up to two days; larger birds can be stored up to four days at these temperatures. Frozen poultry should be kept at 0°F (–18°C) or below (the colder the better) and can be held for up to six months. It should be thawed gradually under refrigeration, allowing two days for chickens and up to four days for larger birds. Never attempt to cook poultry that is still partially frozen: It will be impossible to cook the product evenly and the areas that were still frozen may not reach the temperatures necessary to destroy harmful bacteria. Never partially cook poultry one day and finish cooking it later: Bacteria are more likely to grow under such conditions.

Sanitation and Cross-Contamination

Review the information in Chapter 2, Food Safety and Sanitation, before butchering any poultry. Be sure that all work surfaces, cutting boards, knives, hands and other equipment used to prepare poultry products are clean and sanitary. Be careful that juices and trimmings from poultry do not come in contact with other foods. Anything coming in contact with raw poultry should be cleaned and sanitized before it comes in contact with any other food. Cooked foods should never be placed in containers that were used to hold the raw product. Kitchen towels that are used to handle poultry or clean up after butchering should be sanitized before being reused to prevent cross-contamination.

Butchering Procedures

Poultry is easier to butcher than meats and is often processed on-site. You should be able to perform the following commonly encountered procedures. Because the different kinds of poultry are similar in structure, these procedures apply to a variety of birds.

PROCEDURE FOR CUTTING A BIRD IN HALF

Often the first step in preparing poultry is to cut the bird in half. Broiler and fryer chickens are often split to make two portions. This procedure removes the backbone and breast bone (also known as the keel bone) for a neat finished product.

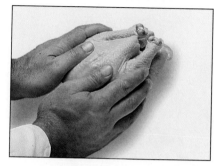

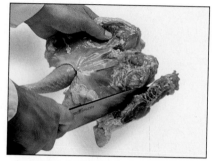

1. Square up the bird by placing it on its back and pressing on the legs and breast to create a more uniform appearance.

2. Place the bird on its breast and hold the tail tightly with the thumb and forefinger of one hand. Using a rigid boning knife and in a single swift movement, cut alongside the backbone from the bird's tail to head.

3. Lay the bird flat on the cutting board and remove the backbone by cutting through the ribs connecting it to the breast.

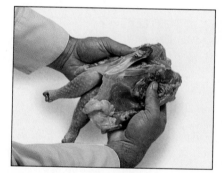

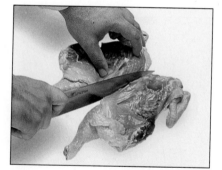

4. Bend the bird back, breaking the breast bone free.

5. Run your fingers along the bone to separate the breast meat from it; pull the bone completely free. Be sure to remove the flexible cartilage completely.

6. Cut through the skin to separate the bird into two halves. The halves are ready to be cooked; for a more attractive presentation, follow steps 7 and 8.

7. Trim off the wing tips and the ends of the leg bone.

8. Make a slit in the skin below the leg and tuck the leg bone into the slit.

PROCEDURE FOR CUTTING A BIRD INTO PIECES

This is one of the most common butchering procedures. It is also very simple once you understand the bird's structure and are able to find each of its joints.

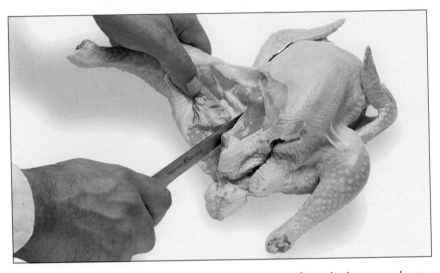

1. Remove the leg by pulling the leg and thigh away from the breast and cutting through the skin and flesh toward the thigh joint.

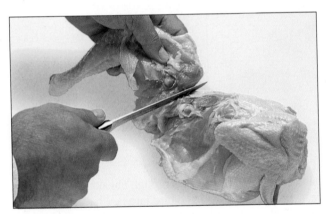

2. Cut down to the thigh joint, twist the leg to break the joint and cut the thigh and leg from the carcass. Be careful to trim around the oyster meat (the tender morsel of meat located next to the backbone); leave it attached to the thigh. Repeat with the other leg.

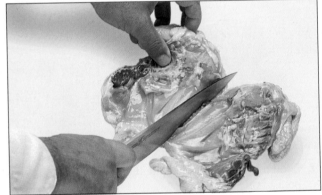

3. To split the breast, follow steps 2 through 6 for cutting a bird in half. Cut the breast into two halves.

4. The bird is now cut into four pieces.

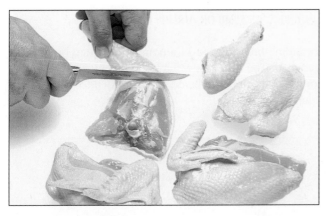 

5. To cut the bird into six pieces, separate the thigh from the leg by making a cut guided by the line of fat on the inside of the thigh and leg.

6. To cut the bird into eight pieces, separate the wing from the breast by cutting through the joint, or split the breast, leaving a portion of the breast meat attached to the wing.

PROCEDURE FOR PREPARING A BONELESS BREAST

A boneless chicken breast is one of the most versatile and popular poultry cuts. It can be broiled, grilled, baked, sautéed, pan-fried or poached. Boneless turkey breast can be roasted or sliced and sautéed as a substitute for veal. The skin can be removed or left intact.

 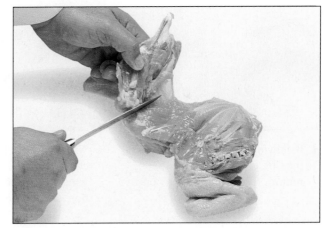

1. Remove the keel bone from the bone-in breast, following steps 4, 5 and 6 for cutting a bird in half.

2. With the chicken breast lying skin side down, separate the rib bones, wing and wishbone from the breast. Leave the two tender pieces of meat known as the tenderloins attached to the breast. Repeat the procedure on the other side, being sure to remove the small wishbone pieces from the front of the breast.

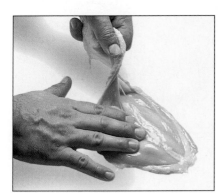

3. The skin may be left intact or removed to produce a skinless boneless breast.

PROCEDURE FOR PREPARING A SUPRÊME OR AIRLINE BREAST

A chicken suprême or airline breast is half of a boneless chicken breast with the first wing bone attached. The tip of the wing bone is removed, yielding a neat and attractive portion that can be prepared by a variety of cooking methods. The skin can be left on or removed.

1. Remove the legs from a chicken following steps 1 and 2 for cutting a bird into pieces. Place the bird on its back. Locate the wishbone, trim around it and remove it.

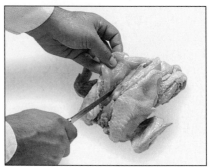

2. Cut along one side of the breast bone, separating the meat from the bone.

3. Following the natural curvature of the ribs, continue cutting to remove the meat from the bones.

4. When you reach the wing joint, cut through the joint, keeping the wing attached to the breast portion. Cut the breast free from the carcass.

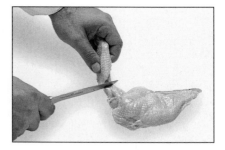

5. Make a cut on the back of the joint between the first and second wing bones.

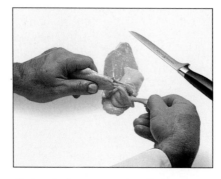

6. Break the joint and pull the meat and skin back to expose a clean bone. Trim the wing bone.

7. The suprême can be prepared skin-on or skinless.

PROCEDURE FOR BONING A CHICKEN LEG

Chicken breasts are usually more popular than legs and thighs. There are, however, uses for boneless, skinless leg and thigh meat; they can be stuffed or used for ballotines, for example.

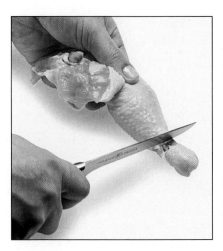

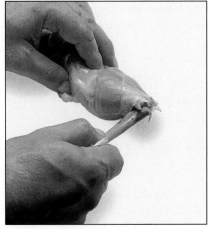

1. Carefully cut through the skin, meat and tendons at the base of the leg. Be sure to cut through completely to the bone.

2. Pull the skin off the leg with your hands, then break the joint between the leg and thigh. Twist and pull out the leg bone.

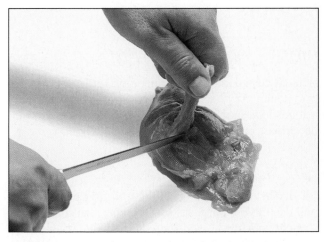

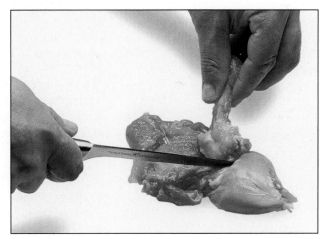

3. Working from the inside of the thigh, cut along both sides of the thigh bone, separating it from the meat.

4. Cut around the cartilage at the joint between the leg and thigh and remove the thigh bone and cartilage.

MARINATING POULTRY

Most poultry is quite mild in flavor, so a marinade is often used to add flavor and moisture, especially to poultry that will be broiled or grilled. Barbecued chicken is one of the simplest and best-known forms of marinated poultry. Poultry is often marinated in a mixture of white wine or lemon juice, oil, salt, pepper, herbs and spices, such as that given in Recipe 17.1.

◆◆◆

RECIPE 17.1
WHITE WINE MARINADE

Yield: 1 qt. (1 lt)

Garlic, minced	2 tsp.	10 ml
Onion, small dice	5 oz.	150 g
Dry white wine	24 oz.	750 g
Bay leaves	2	2
Dried thyme	2 tsp.	10 ml
White pepper	1 tsp.	5 ml
Salt	1 Tbsp.	15 ml
Lemon juice	1 oz.	30 g
Vegetable oil	4 oz.	120 g

1. Combine all ingredients.

Poultry absorbs flavors quickly, so if pieces are left too long in an acidic marinade they may take on undesirable flavors. Two hours is often sufficient, with smaller pieces requiring less time in the marinade than larger ones.

If the marinade contains oil, drain it well to avoid flare-up when the item is placed on the broiler or grill. Use a clean kitchen towel or a paper towel to wipe excess moisture from the poultry's surface so that it browns more easily. The marinade can be used to baste the item during cooking, but leftover marinade should not be served uncooked or reused because of the danger of bacterial contamination from the raw poultry.

APPLYING VARIOUS COOKING METHODS

The principles of cooking discussed in Chapter 9 and applied to meats in earlier chapters also apply to poultry. Dry-heat methods are appropriate for young, tender birds. Moist-heat methods should be used with older, less-tender products. In this section the various cooking methods are applied to poultry.

Dry-Heat Cooking Methods

Cooking poultry with dry-heat methods—broiling and grilling, roasting, sautéing, pan-frying and deep frying—presents some unique challenges. Large birds such as turkeys benefit from low-heat cooking but are better when served with the crispy skin gained through higher temperatures. Duck and goose skin contains a great deal of fat that must be rendered during the cooking process. Small birds such as squab must be cooked at sufficiently high temperatures to crisp their skins but can be easily overcooked. Boneless chicken breasts, particularly flavorful and popular when broiled or grilled, are easily overcooked and dried out because they do not contain bones to help retain moisture during cooking. Proper application of the following dry-heat cooking methods will help meet these challenges and ensure a good-quality finished product.

Broiling and Grilling

Broiled and grilled poultry should have a well-browned surface and can show crosshatched grill marks. It should be moist, tender and juicy throughout. It may be seasoned to enhance its natural flavors or marinated or basted with any number of butters or sauces.

Selecting Poultry to Broil or Grill

Smaller birds such as Cornish hens, chickens and squab are especially well suited for broiling or grilling. Whole birds should be split or cut into smaller pieces before cooking; their joints may be broken so they lie flat. Quail and other small birds can be skewered before being broiled to help them cook evenly and retain their shape. Be especially careful when cooking breast portions or boneless pieces: The direct heat of the broiler or grill can overcook the item very quickly.

Seasoning Poultry to be Broiled or Grilled

Poultry is fairly neutral in flavor and responds well to marinating. Poultry may also be basted periodically during the cooking process with flavored butter, oil or barbecue sauce. At the very least, broiled or grilled poultry should be well seasoned with salt and pepper just before cooking.

Determining Doneness

With the exception of duck breasts and squab, which are sometimes left pink, broiled or grilled poultry is always cooked well done. This makes the poultry particularly susceptible to becoming dry and tough because it contains little fat and is cooked at very high temperatures. Particular care must be taken to ensure that the item does not become overcooked.

Four methods are used to determine the doneness of broiled or grilled poultry:

1. *Touch*—When the item is done it will have a firm texture, resist pressure and spring back quickly when pressed with a finger.
2. *Temperature*—Use an instant read-thermometer to determine the item's internal temperature. This may be difficult, however, because of the item's size and the heat from the broiler or grill. Insert the thermometer in the thickest part of the item away from any bones. It should read 165–170°F (74–77°C) at the coolest point.
3. *Looseness of the joints*—When bone-in poultry is done, the leg will begin to move freely in its socket.
4. *Color of the juices*—Poultry is done when its juices run clear or show just a trace of pink. This degree of doneness is known in French as ***a point***.

Accompaniments to Broiled and Grilled Poultry

If the item was basted with an herb butter it can be served with additional butter; if the item was basted with barbecue sauce, it should be served with the same sauce. Be careful, however, that any marinade or sauce that came in contact with the raw poultry is not served unless it is cooked thoroughly to destroy harmful bacteria. Additional sauce suggestions are found in Table 10.5.

Broiled or grilled poultry is very versatile and goes well with almost any side dish. Seasoned and grilled vegetables are a natural accompaniment, and deep-fried potatoes are commonly served.

PROCEDURE FOR BROILING OR GRILLING POULTRY

As with meats, broiled or grilled poultry can be prepared by placing it directly on the grate. Poultry is also often broiled using a rotisserie.

1. Heat the broiler or grill.
2. Use a wire brush to remove any charred or burnt particles that may be stuck to the broiler or grill grate. The grate can be wiped with a lightly oiled towel to remove any remaining particles and help season it.
3. Prepare the item to be broiled or grilled by marinating or seasoning as desired; it may be brushed lightly with oil to keep it from sticking to the grate.

4. Place the item on the grate, presentation side (skin side) down. Following the example in Chapter 9, turn the item to produce the attractive cross-hatch marks associated with broiling or grilling. Baste the item often. Use tongs to turn or flip the item without piercing the surface so that valuable juices do not escape.

5. Develop the proper surface color while cooking the item until it is done *a point*. To do so, adjust the position of the item on the broiler or grill or adjust the distance between the grate and heat source. Large pieces and bone-in pieces that are difficult to cook completely on the broiler or grill can be finished in the oven.

A commonly used procedure to cook a large volume of poultry is to place the seasoned items in a broiler pan or other shallow pan and then place the pan directly under the broiler. Baste the items periodically, turning them once when they are halfway done. Items begun this way can be easily finished by transferring the entire pan to the oven.

◆◆◆

RECIPE 17.2

GRILLED SQUAB WITH BASIL BUTTER

Yield: 4 Servings

Squab, whole	4	4
Fresh basil leaves	16	16
White Wine Marinade (Recipe 17.1)	1 pt.	450 g
Salt and pepper	TT	TT
Basil butter	6 oz.	170 g

1. Remove the backbone and breast bone from each squab. The birds will lie flat and remain in one piece.
2. Make a slit below each leg and tuck the leg bone into the slit.
3. Carefully slide two basil leaves under the skin over each breast to cover the meat.
4. Marinate the squab in the white wine marinade for 1–2 hours.
5. Heat and prepare the grill.
6. Remove the squab from the marinade and pat dry.
7. Melt approximately 4 ounces (120 grams) of the basil butter, leaving enough for eight thin slices to be served with the finished dish.
8. Brush the squab with basil butter and place it skin side down on the grill. Grill the squab, turning once and basting periodically with the melted basil butter. Finish in the oven if necessary.
9. Serve the squab with a slice of basil butter melting over each breast.

1. Marinating the squab in white wine marinade.

2. Drying the squab.

3. Brushing the squab with the melted basil butter.

4. Grilling the squab.

5. Serving the squab with a slice of basil butter.

Roasting

Properly roasted (or baked) poultry is attractively browned on the surface and tender and juicy throughout. Proper cooking temperatures ensure a crisp exterior and juicy interior. Most roasted poultry is cooked until its juices run clear. Squab and duck breasts are an exception: They are often served medium rare or pink.

Selecting Poultry to Roast

Almost every kind of poultry is suitable for roasting, but younger birds produce a more tender finished product. Because of variations in fat content, different kinds of poultry require different roasting temperatures and procedures.

PROCEDURE FOR TRUSSING POULTRY

Trussing is tying a bird into a more compact shape with thread or butcher's twine. This allows the bird to cook more evenly, helps the bird retain moisture and improves the appearance of the finished product. There are many methods for trussing poultry, some of which require a special tool called a trussing needle. Here we show a simple method using butcher's twine.

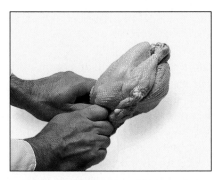

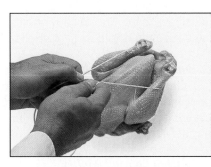

1. Square up the bird by pressing it firmly with both hands. Tuck the first joint of the wing behind the back or trim off the first and second joints as shown.

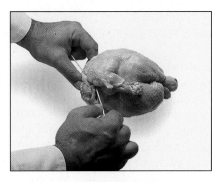

2. Cut a piece of butcher's twine approximately three times the bird's length. With the breast up and the neck toward you, pass the twine under the bird approximately one inch (2.5 centimeters) in front of the tail.

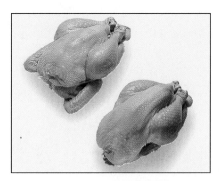

3. Bring the twine up around the legs and cross the ends, creating an X between the legs. Pass the ends of the twine below the legs.

4. Pull the ends of the twine tightly across the leg and thigh joint and across the wing if the first and second joint were trimmed off or just above the wings if they are intact.

5. Pull the string tight and tie it securely just above the neck.

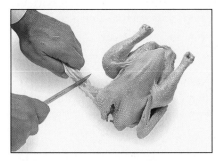

6. Two examples of properly trussed birds: one with the wings intact and one with the first and second wing joints removed.

Cooking Temperatures

Small birds such as squab and Cornish game hens should be roasted at the relatively high temperatures of 375–400°F (190–200°C). These temperatures help produce crisp, well-colored skins without overcooking the flesh. Chickens are best roasted at temperatures between 350 and 375°F (180–190°C). This temperature range allows the skin to crisp and the flesh to cook without causing the bird to stew in its own juices. Large birds such as capons and turkeys are started at high temperatures of 400–425°F (200–220°C) to brown the skin, then finished at lower temperatures of 275–325°F (135–160°C) to promote even cooking and produce a moister product. Ducks and geese, which are very high in fat, must be roasted at the high temperatures of 375–425°F (190–220°C) to render as much fat from the skin as possible. Duck and goose skin is often pricked before roasting so the rendered fat can escape, helping to create crispy skin.

Seasoning Poultry to be Roasted

Although the mild flavor of most poultry is enhanced by a wide variety of herbs and spices, roasted poultry is often only lightly seasoned with salt and pepper. Poultry that is roasted at high temperatures should never be seasoned with herbs on its surface because the high cooking temperatures will burn them. If herbs or additional spices are used they should be stuffed into the cavity. A mirepoix or a bouquet garni may also be added to the cavity for additional flavor. The cavities of dark-meated birds such as ducks and geese are often stuffed with fresh or dried fruits.

Barding Poultry to be Roasted

Guineas, squabs or any skinless birds without an adequate fat covering to protect them from drying out during roasting can be barded. Bard the bird by covering its entire surface with thin slices of fatback, securing them with butcher's twine. See page 266.

Basting Roasted Poultry

With the exception of fatty birds such as ducks and geese, all poultry items should be basted while they roast to help retain moisture. To baste a bird, spoon or ladle the fat that collects in the bottom of the roasting pan over the bird at 15-to-20-minute intervals. Lean birds that are not barded will not produce enough fat for basting and may be brushed with butter in the same manner.

Determining Doneness

Four methods are used to determine the doneness of roasted poultry. It is best to use a combination of these methods.

1. *Temperature*—Test the internal temperature of the bird with an instant-read thermometer. The thermometer should be inserted in the bird's thigh, which is the last part to become fully cooked. It should not touch the bone and should read 165–170°F (74–77°C) at the coolest point. This method works best with large birds such as capons and turkeys. Large birds are subject to some degree of carryover cooking. This is not as much of a concern with poultry as it is with meat because large birds are always cooked well done.

2. *Looseness of the joints*—The thigh and leg will begin to move freely in their sockets when the bird is done.

3. *Color of juices*—This method is used with birds that are not stuffed. Use a kitchen fork to tilt the bird, allowing some of the juices that have collected

TABLE 17.8   ROASTING TEMPERATURES AND TIMES

Poultry Kind or Class	Cooking Temperatures		Minutes
Capons	350–375°F	180–190°C	18–20 min. per lb.
Chickens	375–400°F	190–200°C	15–18 min. per lb.
Ducks and geese	375–425°F	190–220°C	12–15 min. per lb.
Game hens	375–400°F	190–200°C	45–60 min. total
Guineas	375–400°F	190–200°C	18–20 min. per lb.
Squab	400°F	200°C	30–40 min. total
Turkeys (large)	325°F	160°C	12–15 min. per lb.

in the cavity to run out. Clear juices indicate that the bird is done. If the juices are cloudy or pink, the bird is undercooked.

4. *Time*—Because there are so many variables, timing alone is less reliable than other methods. It is useful, however, for planning production when large quantities are roasted and as a general guideline when used with other methods. Table 17.8 gives some general timing guidelines for roasting several kinds of poultry.

Accompaniments to Roasted Poultry

The most common accompaniments to roasted poultry are bread stuffing and gravy. Large birds, such as capons and turkeys, produce adequate drippings for making sauce or pan gravy. Small birds, such as squab and Cornish game hens, are often stuffed with wild rice or other ingredients and served with a sauce that is made separately.

Ducks and geese are complemented by stuffings containing rice, fruits, berries and nuts. They are very fatty and if stuffed, they should be roasted on a rack or mirepoix bed to ensure that the fat that collects in the pan during roasting does not penetrate the cavity, making the stuffing greasy. Ducks and geese are often served with a citrus- or fruit-based sauce. Its high acid content complements these rich, fatty birds.

PROCEDURE FOR STUFFING POULTRY

Small birds such as Cornish game hens, small chickens and squab can be stuffed successfully. Stuffing larger birds, especially for volume production, is impractical and can be dangerous for the following reasons:

1. Stuffing is a good bacterial breeding ground and because it is difficult to control temperatures inside a stuffed bird, there is a risk of food-borne illness.
2. Stuffing poultry is labor intensive.
3. Stuffed poultry must be cooked longer to cook the stuffing properly; this may cause the meat to be overcooked, becoming dry and tough.

When stuffing any bird, use the following guidelines.

1. Always be aware of temperatures when mixing the raw ingredients. All ingredients should be cold when they are mixed together, and the mixture's temperature should never be allowed to rise above 45°F (7°C).
2. Stuff the bird as close to roasting time as possible.

3. The neck and main body cavities should be loosely stuffed. The stuffing will expand during cooking.
4. After the cavities are filled, their openings should be secured with skewers and butcher's twine or by trussing.
5. After cooking, remove the stuffing from the bird and store separately.

PROCEDURE FOR ROASTING POULTRY

1. Season, bard, stuff and/or truss the bird as desired.
2. Place the bird in a roasting pan. It may be placed on a rack or mirepoix bed to prevent scorching and promote even cooking.
3. Roast uncovered, basting every 15 minutes.
4. Allow the bird to rest before carving to allow even distribution of juices. As the bird rests, prepare the pan gravy or sauce.

♦♦♦

RECIPE 17.3

ROAST TURKEY WITH CHESTNUT DRESSING AND GIBLET GRAVY

Yield: 16 portions—4 oz. (120 g) turkey, 3 oz. (90 g) dressing, 4 oz. (120 ml) gravy.

Young turkey, 12–15 lb. (5.5–6.5 kg) with giblets	1	1
Salt and pepper	TT	TT
Mirepoix	20 oz.	600 g
Onion, small dice	8 oz.	225 g
Celery, small dice	6 oz.	180 g
Whole butter	4 oz.	120 g
Dried bread cubes	2 lb.	1 kg
Eggs, beaten	2	2
Fresh parsley, chopped	1 Tbsp.	15 ml
Chicken stock	2-1/4 qt.	2 lt
Chestnuts, cooked and peeled, chopped coarse	8 oz.	225 g
All-purpose flour	3 oz.	90 g

1. Placing the turkey in the roasting pan.

2. Adding the mirepoix to the roasting pan.

1. Remove the giblets from the turkey's cavity and set aside. Season the turkey inside and out with salt and pepper. Truss the turkey.
2. Place the turkey in a roasting pan. Roast at 400°F (200°C) for 30 minutes. Reduce the temperature to 325°F (160°C) and continue cooking the turkey to an internal temperature of 160°F (71°C), approximately 2-1/2 to 3 hours. Baste the turkey often during cooking. Approximately 45 minutes before the turkey is done, add the mirepoix to the roasting pan. If the turkey begins to overbrown, cover it loosely with aluminum foil.
3. To make the dressing, sauté the diced onion and celery in the butter until tender.
4. In a large bowl, toss together the bread cubes, salt, pepper, eggs, parsley,

sautéed onions and celery, 4 ounces (120 grams) of chicken stock and the chestnuts.

5. Place the dressing in a buttered hotel pan and cover with aluminum foil or buttered parchment paper. Bake at 350°F (180°C) until done, approximately 45 minutes.

6. As the turkey roasts, simmer the giblets (neck, heart and gizzard) in 1 quart (1 liter) of the chicken stock until tender, approximately 1-1/2 hours.

7. When the turkey is done, remove it from the roasting pan and set aside to rest. Degrease the roasting pan, reserving 3 ounces (90 grams) of the fat to make a roux.

8. Place the roasting pan on the stove top and brown the mirepoix.

9. Deglaze the pan with a small amount of chicken stock. Transfer the mirepoix and stock to a saucepot and add the remaining stock and the broth from the giblets. Bring to a simmer and degrease.

10. Make a blond roux with the reserved fat and the flour. Add the roux to the liquid, whisking well to prevent lumps. Simmer 15 minutes. Strain the gravy through a china cap lined with cheesecloth.

11. Remove the meat from the turkey neck. Trim the gizzard. Finely chop the neck meat, heart and gizzard and add to the gravy. Adjust the seasonings.

12. Carve the turkey and serve with a portion of chestnut dressing and giblet gravy.

3. Tossing the dressing ingredients together.

4. Browning the mirepoix.

5. Deglazing the roasting pan.

6. Transferring the mirepoix and stock to a saucepot.

7. Straining the gravy through a china cap and cheesecloth.

Carving Roasted Poultry

Poultry can be carved in the kitchen, at tableside or on a buffet in a variety of manners. The carving methods described below produce slices of both light and dark meat.

PROCEDURE FOR CARVING A TURKEY, CAPON OR OTHER LARGE BIRD

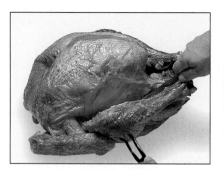

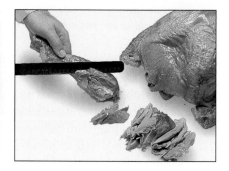

1. After roasting, allow the turkey to stand for 20 minutes so the juices can redistribute themselves. Holding the turkey firmly with a carving fork, pry a leg outward and locate the joint. Remove the leg and thigh in one piece by cutting through the joint with the tip of a knife.

2. Repeat the procedure on the other side. Once both legs and thighs have been removed, slice the meat from the thigh by holding the leg firmly with one hand and slicing parallel to the bone.

3. Separate the thigh from the leg bone by cutting through the joint. Slice the meat from the leg by cutting parallel to the bone.

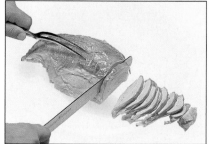

4. Cut along the backbone, following the natural curvature of the bones separating the breast meat from the ribs.

5. Remove an entire half breast and slice it on the cutting board as shown. Cut on an angle to produce larger slices.

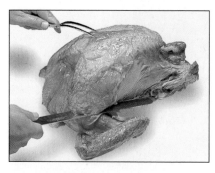

6. Alternatively, the breast can be carved on the bird. Make a horizontal cut just above the wing in toward the rib bones.

7. Slice the breast meat as shown.

Procedure for Carving a Chicken or Other Small Bird

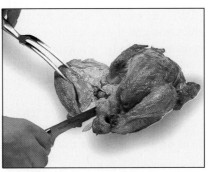

1. After allowing the chicken to rest for 15 minutes so the juices can redistribute themselves, cut through the skin between the leg and breast.

2. Use a kitchen fork to pry the leg and thigh away from the breast. Locate the thigh's ball joint and cut through it with the knife tip, separating it completely from the rest of the chicken. Be sure to cut around the delicate oyster meat, leaving it attached to the thigh.

3. With the knife tip, cut through the skin and meat on one side of the breast bone. Cut and pull the meat away from the bones with the knife.

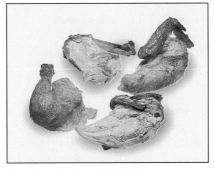

4. Cut through the wing joint, separating the breast and wing from the carcass. Repeat this procedure on the other side of the bird.

5. The chicken is now quartered.

6. To cut it into eight pieces, separate the wings from the breasts and the thighs from the legs.

Sautéing

Sautéed poultry should be tender and juicy, its flavor developed by proper browning. Additional flavors come from a sauce made by deglazing the pan, usually with wine, and adding garnishes, seasonings and liquids. Stir-frying is a popular method of sautéing poultry; boneless pieces are cut into strips and quickly cooked with assorted vegetables and seasonings.

Selecting Poultry to Sauté

Most poultry is quite tender and well suited for sautéing. Although small birds such as squab can be sautéed bone-in, large pieces and bone-in cuts from larger birds should not be sautéed. Boneless breasts, suprêmes, scallops and cutlets are the most common and practical cuts for sautéing. Because they are high in fat, boneless duck breasts (called *magrets*) can be sautéed without additional fat.

Cooking Temperatures

The sauté pan and the cooking fat must be hot before the poultry is added. The temperature at which the poultry is then sautéed is determined by its thickness and the desired color of the finished product. A thin, boneless slice requires relatively high temperatures so that its surface is browned before the center is overcooked. A thicker cut such as a suprême requires lower temperatures so that neither its surface nor the fond are burned before the item is fully cooked. Adjust the temperature throughout the cooking process to achieve the desired results, never letting the pan become too cool.

If the pan is overcrowded or otherwise allowed to cool, the poultry will cook in its own juices and absorb oil from the pan, resulting in a poor-quality product.

Seasoning Poultry to be Sautéed

Poultry has a delicate flavor that is enhanced by a wide variety of herbs, spices, condiments and marinades. Flavor combinations are limited only by your imagination. When poultry items are dusted with flour before sautéing, the seasonings may first be added to the flour.

Determining Doneness

Thin cuts of poultry cook very quickly, so timing is a useful tool; it is less useful with thicker cuts. Experienced cooks can tell the doneness of an item by judging the temperature of the sauté pan and the color of the item being cooked.

A more practical method is to press the item with your finger and judge the resistance. Very undercooked poultry will offer little resistance and feel mushy. Slightly underdone poultry will feel spongy and will not spring back when your finger is removed. Properly cooked poultry will feel firm to the touch and will spring back when your finger is removed. Overcooked poultry will feel very firm, almost hard, and will spring back quickly when your finger is removed.

Accompaniments to Sautéed Poultry

Sautéed poultry is usually served with a sauce made directly in the pan in which the item was cooked. The sauce uses the fond for added flavor. A wide variety of ingredients, including garlic, onions, shallots, mushrooms and tomatoes, are commonly added to the pan as well as wine and stock. Table 10.5 suggests several sauces for sautéed poultry.

Sautéed items are often served with a starch such as pasta, rice or potatoes.

PROCEDURE FOR SAUTÉING POULTRY

1. Heat a sauté pan and add enough fat or oil to just cover the bottom.
2. Add the poultry item, presentation side down, and cook until browned.
3. Turn the item, using tongs or by tossing the item back upon itself using the pan's sloped sides.
4. Larger items can be finished in an oven. Either place the sauté pan in the oven or transfer the poultry to another pan. The latter procedure allows a sauce to be made in the original pan as the poultry cooks in the oven. Hold smaller pieces that are thoroughly cooked in a warm place so that the pan can be used for making the sauce.

PROCEDURE FOR MAKING SAUCE IN THE SAUTÉ PAN

1. Pour off any excess fat or oil from the sauté pan, leaving enough to sauté the sauce ingredients.
2. Add ingredients such as garlic, shallots and mushrooms that will be used as garnishes and sauce flavorings; sauté them.

3. Deglaze the pan with wine, stock or other liquids. Scrape the pan, loosening the fond and allowing it to dissolve in the liquid. Reduce the liquid.

4. Add any ingredients that do not require long cooking times such as herbs and spices. Adjust the sauce's consistency and seasonings.

5. For service, the poultry can be returned to the pan for a moment to reheat and coat it with the sauce. The poultry should remain in the sauce just long enough to reheat. Do not attempt to cook the poultry in the sauce.

6. Serve the poultry with the accompanying sauce.

◆◆◆

RECIPE 17.4

CHICKEN SAUTÉ WITH ONIONS, GARLIC AND BASIL

Yield: 6 Servings

Chicken breasts, boneless, skinless, approx. 8 oz. (250 g) each	3	3
Salt and pepper	TT	TT
Flour	as needed	as needed
Clarified butter	1 oz.	30 g
Onion, small dice	2 oz.	60 g
Garlic cloves, chopped	6	6
Dry white wine	4 oz.	120 g
Lemon juice	1 Tbsp.	15 ml
Tomato concasse	6 oz.	180 g
Chicken stock	4 oz.	120 g
Fresh basil leaves, chiffonade	6	6

1. Sautéing the breasts in butter.

2. The fond left in the pan after sautéing the chicken.

1. Split the chicken breasts and remove the cartilage connecting the two halves.

2. Season the chicken with salt and pepper; dredge in flour.

3. Sauté the breasts in the butter, browning them and cooking *a point*. Hold in a warm place.

4. Add the onions and garlic to the fond and butter in the pan; sauté until the onions are translucent.

5. Deglaze the pan with the white wine and lemon juice.

6. Add the tomato concasse and chicken stock. Sauté to combine the flavors; reduce the sauce to the desired consistency.

7. Add the basil to the sauce and return the chicken breasts for reheating. Adjust the seasonings and serve 1/2 breast per portion with a portion of the sauce.

3. Sautéing the onions and garlic.

4. Deglazing the pan with white wine and lemon juice.

5. Adding the tomatoes and chicken stock and sautéing to combine the flavors.

6. Returning the chicken to the pan to reheat.

Pan-Frying

Pan-fried poultry should be juicy. Its coating or batter should be crispy, golden brown, not excessively oily and free from any breaks that allow fat to penetrate. Both the poultry and the coating should be well seasoned.

Selecting Poultry to Pan-Fry

The most common pan-fried poultry is fried chicken. Young tender birds cut into small pieces produce the best results. Other cuts commonly pan-fried are boneless portions such as chicken breasts and turkey scallops.

Cooking Temperatures

The fat should always be hot before the poultry is added. The temperature at which it is cooked is determined by the length of time required to cook it thoroughly. Pan-frying generally requires slightly lower temperatures than those used for sautéing. Within this range, thinner items require higher temperatures to produce good color in a relatively short time. Thicker items and those containing bones require lower cooking temperatures and longer cooking times.

Seasoning Poultry to be Pan-Fried

Pan-fried poultry is usually floured, breaded or battered before cooking. (Breadings and batters are discussed in Chapter 21, Deep-Frying). Typically, the seasonings are added to the flour, breading or batter before the poultry item is coated. Seasonings can be a blend of any number of dried herbs and spices. But often only salt and pepper are required because the poultry will be served with a sauce or other accompaniments for additional flavors.

Determining Doneness

Even the largest pan-fried items may be too small to be accurately tested with an instant-read thermometer, and using the touch method can be difficult and dangerous because of the amount of fat used in pan-frying. So, timing and experience are the best tools to determine doneness. Thin scallops cook very quickly, so it is relatively easy to judge their doneness. On the other hand, fried chicken can take as long as 30–45 minutes to cook, requiring skill and experience to determine doneness.

Accompaniments to Pan-Fried Poultry

Because pan-frying does not produce fond or drippings that can be used to make a sauce, pan-fried poultry is usually served with lemon wedges, a vegetable garnish or a separately made sauce. Fried chicken is an exception; it is sometimes served with a country gravy made by degreasing the pan, making a roux with a portion of the fat and adding milk and seasonings.

PROCEDURE FOR PAN-FRYING POULTRY

1. Heat enough fat in a heavy sauté pan to cover the item to be cooked one quarter to halfway up its side. The fat should be at approximately 325°F (160°C).
2. Add the floured, breaded or battered item to the hot fat, being careful not to splash. The fat must be hot enough to sizzle and bubble when the item is added.
3. Turn the item when the first side is the proper color; it should be half cooked at this point. Larger items may need to be turned more than once to brown them properly on all sides.
4. Remove the browned poultry from the pan and drain it on absorbent paper.

♦♦♦

RECIPE 17.5
PAN-FRIED CHICKEN WITH PAN GRAVY

Yield: 8 2-piece Servings

Frying chickens, 2 lb. 8 oz.–3 lb. each (1.1–1.4 kg), cut in 8 pieces	2	2
Salt and pepper	TT	TT
Garlic powder	2 tsp.	10 ml
Onion powder	2 tsp.	10 ml
Dried oregano	1 tsp.	5 ml
Dried basil	1 tsp.	5 ml
Flour	9-1/2 oz.	270 g
Buttermilk	8 oz.	250 g
Oil	as needed	as needed
Onion, small dice	4 oz.	120 g
Half-and-half or chicken stock	1-1/2 pt.	750 ml

1. Season the chicken with salt and pepper.
2. Add the herbs and spices to 8 ounces (250 grams) of the flour.
3. Dip the chicken pieces in the buttermilk.
4. Dredge the chicken in the seasoned flour.
5. Pan-fry the chicken in 1/4 to 1/3 inch (1 centimeter) oil until done, approximately 40 minutes, turning so it cooks evenly. Reduce the heat as necessary to prevent the chicken from becoming too dark. Or remove the chicken when well browned, drain it and finish cooking it in the oven.
6. To make the pan gravy, pour off all but 1-1/2 ounces (45 grams) of oil from the pan, carefully reserving the fond.
7. Add the diced onions and sauté until translucent.
8. Add 1-1/2 ounces (45 grams) of flour and cook to make a blond roux.
9. Whisk in the liquid and simmer approximately 15 minutes.
10. Strain through cheesecloth and adjust the seasonings.
11. Serve 1/4 chicken (2 pieces) per person with 4 ounces (120 milliliters) gravy.

1. Dipping the chicken pieces in the buttermilk.

2. Dredging the chicken in the flour mixture.

3. Adding the chicken to the oil. The bubbling fat indicates the proper cooking temperature.

4. Turning the chicken so it cooks evenly.

5. Sautéing the diced onions until translucent.

6. Adding the liquid to the roux.

Moist-Heat Cooking Methods

The moist-heat cooking methods most often used with poultry are poaching and simmering. Poaching is used to cook tender birds for short periods of time. Simmering is used to cook older, tougher birds for longer periods to tenderize them. Poaching and simmering are similar procedures, the principal differences being the temperature of the cooking liquid and the length of cooking time.

Poaching and Simmering

Poached or simmered poultry should be moist, tender and delicately flavored. Although cooked in water, overcooking will cause the poultry to be dry and tough. During cooking, some of the poultry's flavor is transferred to the cooking liquid, which can be used to make a sauce for the finished product.

Selecting Poultry to Poach or Simmer

Young birds are best suited for poaching; boneless chicken pieces are the most commonly used parts. Older, tougher birds are usually simmered. Duck and geese are rarely poached or simmered because of their high fat content.

Cooking Temperatures

For best results, poultry should be poached at low temperatures, between 160° and 175°F (70–80°C). Cooking poultry to the proper doneness at these temperatures produces a product that is moist and tender.

Simmering is done at slightly higher temperatures, between 185°F (85°C) and the boiling point. When simmering, do not allow the liquid to boil, as this may result in a dry, tough and stringy finished product.

Seasoning Poultry to be Poached or Simmered

When poaching poultry it is especially important to use a well-seasoned and highly flavored liquid in order to infuse as much flavor as possible into the item being cooked. Either strong stock with a sachet or a mixture of stock or water and white wine with a bouquet garni or onion piquet produces good results. The poultry should be completely covered with liquid so that it cooks evenly. However, if too much liquid is used and it is not strongly flavored, flavors may be leached out of the poultry, resulting in a bland finished product.

Poultry is often simmered in water instead of stock. A sachet and a generous mirepoix should be added to help flavor it. Typically, simmering birds results in a strong broth that may be used to complete the recipe or reserved for other uses.

Determining Doneness

Poached poultry, whether whole or boneless, is cooked just until done. An instant-read thermometer inserted in the thigh or thicker part of the bird should read 165°F (74°C). Any juices that run from the bird should be clear or show only a trace of pink.

Simmered poultry is usually cooked for longer periods to allow the moist heat to tenderize the meat. A chicken that weighs 3 pounds 8 ounces (1.5 kilograms), for example, may take 2-1/2 hours to cook.

Accompaniments to Poached and Simmered Poultry

Poached or simmered poultry can be served hot or cold. The meat from these birds can be served cold in salads, hot in casseroles or used in any dish that calls for cooked poultry.

Poached items are typically served with a flavored mayonnaise or a sauce made from the reduced poaching liquid, such as sauce suprême. Poultry is also often poached as a means of producing a low-calorie dish. If so, a vegetable coulis makes a good sauce or the poultry can be served with a portion of its cooking liquid and a vegetable garnish.

Simmered poultry to be served cold will be moister and more flavorful if it is cooled in its cooking liquid. To do so, remove the pot containing the bird and the cooking liquid from the heat when the bird is still slightly undercooked. Cool the meat and broth in a water bath following the procedures in Chapter 10, Stocks and Sauces. Once cooled, remove the meat and wipe off any congealed broth before proceeding with the recipe.

PROCEDURE FOR POACHING OR SIMMERING POULTRY

1. Cut or truss the item to be cooked as directed in the recipe.
2. Prepare the cooking liquid and bring it to a simmer. Submerge the poultry in the cooking liquid, or arrange the items to be poached in an appropriate pan and add the poaching liquid to the pan.
3. Poach or simmer the item to the desired doneness in the oven or on the stove top. Maintain the proper cooking temperature throughout the process.
4. Remove the item and hold it for service in a portion of the cooking liquid or, using an ice bath, cool the item in its cooking liquid.
5. The cooking liquid may be used to prepare an accompanying sauce or reserved for use in other dishes.

◆◆◆

RECIPE 17.6
POACHED BREAST OF CHICKEN WITH TARRAGON SAUCE

Yield: 8 Servings

Chicken breasts, boneless, skinless, approx. 8 oz. (250 g) each	4	4
Whole butter	1-1/2 oz.	45 g
Salt and white pepper	TT	TT
White wine	4 oz.	120 g
Chicken stock	1 pt.	450 ml
Bay leaf	1	1
Dried thyme	1/4 tsp.	1 ml
Dried tarragon	1 tsp.	5 ml
Flour	1 oz.	30 g
Heavy cream	4 oz.	120 g
Fresh tarragon sprigs	as needed	as needed

1. Trim any rib meat and fat from the breasts. Cut the breasts into two pieces, removing the strip of cartilage that joins the halves.
2. Select a pan that will just hold the breasts when they are placed close together. Rub the pan with approximately 1/2 ounce (15 grams) of butter.

Continued

3. Season the chicken breasts with salt and pepper and arrange them in the buttered pan, presentation side up.

4. Add the white wine, stock, bay leaf, thyme and dried tarragon.

5. Cut and butter a piece of parchment paper and cover the chicken breasts.

6. Bring the liquid to a simmer and reduce the temperature to poach the chicken.

7. Make a blond roux with 1 ounce (30 grams) of butter and 1 ounce (30 grams) of flour; set aside to cool.

8. When the breasts are done, remove them from the liquid. Thicken the liquid with the roux. Add the cream. Simmer and reduce to the desired consistency.

9. Strain the sauce through cheesecloth and adjust the seasonings.

10. Serve each half breast napped with approximately 2 fluid ounces (60 milliliters) of sauce; garnish each portion with a sprig of fresh tarragon.

1. Arranging the breasts in an appropriate pan.

2. Adding the white wine, chicken stock and seasonings to the pan.

3. Covering the breasts with a piece of buttered parchment paper.

4. Adding the cream to the thickened sauce.

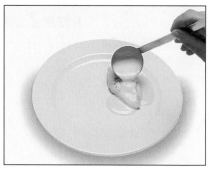

5. Plating the poached chicken breast.

Combination Cooking Methods

Braising and stewing use both dry and moist heat to produce a moist, flavorful product. The principal difference between braising and stewing when applied to meats is the size of the cut being cooked: Large cuts of meat are braised; smaller ones are stewed. Because most poultry is relatively small, this distinction does not readily apply in poultry cookery; therefore, the two cooking methods are discussed together here.

Braising and Stewing

Braised or stewed poultry should be moist and fork tender. The poultry is always served with the liquid in which it was cooked. Ducks and geese are braised or stewed in much the same way as red meats. Chicken cacciatore, coq au vin and chicken fricassee are examples of braised or stewed chicken dishes.

Selecting Poultry to Braise or Stew

Braising and stewing, being slow, moist cooking processes, are often thought of as means to tenderize tough meats. Although they can be used to tenderize older, tougher birds, these cooking methods are more often selected as a means to add moisture and flavor to poultry that is inherently tender, such as young ducks and chickens. Typically, the birds are disjointed and cooked bone-in, just until done, so that they retain their juiciness.

Cooking Temperatures

Some recipes, such as chicken cacciatore and coq au vin, require the main item to be thoroughly browned during the initial stages; others, such as chicken fricassee, do not. In either case, after the addition of the liquid it is important to maintain a slow simmer rather than a rapid boil. This can be done on the stove top or in the oven. Low temperatures control the cooking and produce a tender, juicy finished product.

Seasoning Poultry to be Braised or Stewed

Braised or stewed items obtain much of their flavor from the cooking liquid and other ingredients added during the cooking process. The main item and the cooking liquid should be well seasoned. If other seasonings such as an onion piquet, sachet, bouquet garni or dried herbs and spices are required, they should be added at the beginning of the cooking process rather than at the end. This allows the flavors to blend and penetrate the larger pieces of poultry. If the poultry is dredged in flour prior to browning, seasonings may be added directly to the flour. As with all dishes using combination cooking methods, the finished dish should have the flavor of the poultry in the sauce and the moisture and flavor of the sauce in the poultry.

Determining Doneness

Tenderness is the key to determining doneness. It can be determined by inserting a kitchen fork into the poultry. There should be little resistance and the poultry should freely fall off the fork. The pieces should retain their shape, however; if they fall apart they are overdone. Small boneless pieces can be tested by cutting into them with a fork.

Accompaniments to Braised or Stewed Poultry

All braises and stews are cooked in a liquid that results in a sauce or broth served as part of the finished dish. Rice, pasta or boiled potatoes are natural accompaniments to almost any braised or stewed dish, as are boiled vegetables.

PROCEDURE FOR BRAISING OR STEWING POULTRY

1. Sear the main item in butter or oil, developing color as desired.
2. Add vegetables and other ingredients as called for in the recipe and sauté.
3. Add flour or roux if used.
4. Add the appropriate liquid.

5. Cover and simmer on the stove top or in the oven until done.
6. Add seasonings and garnishes at the appropriate times during the cooking process.
7. Finish the dish by adding cream or a liaison to the sauce or by adjusting its consistency. Adjust the seasonings.
8. Serve a portion of the main item with the sauce and appropriate garnish.

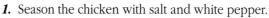

RECIPE 17.7

CHICKEN FRICASSEE

Yield: 8 2-piece Servings

Frying chickens, 2 lb. 8 oz.–3 lb. each (1.1–1.4 kg), cut into 8 pieces	2	2
Salt and white pepper	TT	TT
Clarified butter	3 oz.	90 g
Onion, medium dice	10 oz.	300 g
Flour	3 oz.	90 g
Dry white wine	8 oz.	250 g
Chicken stock	1 qt.	1 lt
Sachet:		
Bay leaf	1	1
Dry thyme	1/2 tsp.	2 ml
Peppercorns, cracked	1/2 tsp.	2 ml
Parsley stems	8	8
Garlic clove, crushed	1	1
Heavy cream	8 oz.	250 g
Nutmeg	TT	TT

1. Season the chicken with salt and white pepper.
2. Sauté the chicken in the butter without browning. Add the onions and continue to sauté until they are translucent.
3. Sprinkle the flour over the chicken and onions and stir to make a roux. Cook the roux for two minutes without browning.
4. Deglaze the pan with white wine. Add the chicken stock and sachet; season with salt. Cover the pot and simmer until done, approximately 30–45 minutes.

1. Sautéing the chicken and onions in butter.

2. Sprinkling the flour over the chicken.

3. Deglazing the pan with white wine.

4. Removing the chicken from the pot.

5. Straining the sauce through cheesecloth.

6. Returning the chicken to the sauce to reheat it for service.

5. Remove the chicken from the pot and hold in a warm place. Strain the sauce through cheesecloth and return it to a clean pan.

6. Add the cream and bring the sauce to a simmer. Add the nutmeg and adjust the seasonings. Return the chicken to the sauce to reheat it for service.

CONCLUSION

The renowned French gastronome and author Jean-Anthelme Brillat-Savarin (1755–1826) once observed that "poultry is for the cook what canvas is for the painter." He meant, of course, that poultry, including chicken, duck, goose, guinea, pigeon and turkey, are wonderfully versatile foods that can be cooked by almost any method and with almost any seasonings, and can be served with many accompaniments and garnishes.

QUESTIONS FOR DISCUSSION

1. List the six categories or kinds of poultry recognized by the USDA. How are these categories then divided into classes?
2. How should fresh poultry be stored? Discuss several procedures that should be followed carefully when working with poultry to prevent cross-contamination.
3. What is a suprême? Describe the step-by-step procedure for preparing a chicken suprême.
4. What is trussing? Why is this technique used with poultry?
5. Which poultry items are best suited for broiling or grilling? Explain your answer.
6. Describe the characteristics of properly roasted poultry. Which classes of poultry are recommended for roasting?
7. What is foie gras? Why must you be extremely careful when cooking foie gras?

ADDITIONAL POULTRY RECIPES

RECIPE 17.8
ROAST DUCK WITH RÖSTI POTATOES
NOTE: This dish appears in the Chapter Opening photograph.

THE FOUR SEASONS, NEW YORK, NY
Chef Christian Albin

Yield: 4 Servings   **Method:** Roasting

Ducks, 4-1/2 lb. (2 kg) each	2	2
Marinade:		
Fresh ginger, peeled and sliced thin	1 oz.	30 g
Garlic cloves, unpeeled and halved	2	2
Orange zest, julienne	1/2 orange	1/2 orange
Coriander seeds, crushed	2 tsp.	10 ml
Black peppercorns	1 1/2 tsp.	8 ml
Soy sauce	8 oz.	250 g
Honey	2 Tbsp.	30 ml
Jasmine tea leaves, loose	4 Tbsp.	60 ml
Szechuan pepper	1 Tbsp.	15 ml
Sugared Orange Zest and Orange		
Sauce (recipe follows)	as needed	as needed

1. Cut the wings off the ducks at the second joint and reserve. Remove the fat from the ducks' cavities.
2. Place the ducks on a rack in the refrigerator, breast sides up, a few inches apart. Air must circulate around the ducks so that the skin will dry. Leave the birds for 3 days.
3. Combine all of the marinade ingredients and refrigerate for 3 days, stirring daily.
4. Prick the duck skin with a knife point, except for the skin on the breast. Avoid touching or pressing on the breasts, as this will leave dark spots after roasting.
5. Place the ducks on a rack over a shallow pan. Strain the marinade and brush it liberally over the entire surface of both ducks. Spoon the remaining marinade into the ducks' cavities.
6. Let the ducks dry, breast side up, on the rack for 15 minutes. Scrape any marinade drippings from the pan into the cavities.
7. Adjust the oven racks so that one is at the lowest level and the other is directly above the first.
8. Place 3 quarts (3 liters) water in a roasting pan and add the tea leaves. Place the pan on the lower rack of a 350°F (180°C) oven.
9. Position the ducks on the higher oven rack directly over the roasting pan (the ducks should not be touching). Roast undisturbed for 1-1/2 hours.
10. Remove the ducks from the oven. Drain and reserve the juices that have accumulated in the cavity.
11. Sprinkle the ducks with the Szechuan pepper; allow them to rest, then carve.
12. To serve, spoon a layer of Orange Sauce over the bottom of a warmed serving platter.

13. Arrange a pair of drumsticks, wing bones and thighs at each end of the platter. Place the breast in the center and garnish with orange segments. Sprinkle with the Sugared Orange Zest. Serve the duck with rösti potatoes (Recipe 23.13) and the remaining sauce on the side.

SUGARED ORANGE ZEST AND ORANGE SAUCE

Yield: 12 oz. (350 g)

Oranges	2	2
Sugar	3 oz.	90 g
Sugar	as needed	as needed
Grand Marnier	2 Tbsp.	30 ml
Currant jelly	2 Tbsp.	30 ml
Basic Duck Sauce, hot (recipe follows)	12 oz.	350 g
Lightly salted butter	2 Tbsp.	30 ml
Kosher salt and black pepper	TT	TT

1. Remove the zest from the oranges and julienne. Blanch for 3 minutes in boiling water; drain.

2. Squeeze the oranges and boil the juice until reduced by one quarter.

3. Place 3 ounces (90 grams) of sugar and 8 ounces (250 grams) of water in a saucepan and bring to a boil. Add the julienned zest. Boil until the syrup begins to caramelize, turning light brown.

4. Have a bowl ready with a layer of granulated sugar. Remove the zest from the syrup and toss in the sugar until the zest is completely coated. Set the zest aside to cool.

5. Continue cooking the syrup until it becomes a dark caramel syrup. Stir in the Grand Marnier, currant jelly and reduced orange juice. Whisk until smooth.

6. Pour in the Basic Duck Sauce and whisk until smooth. Cook for a few minutes to thicken slightly. Monte au beurre and season with salt and pepper.

BASIC DUCK SAUCE

Yield: 1-1/2 pt. (700 ml)

Vegetable oil	1 Tbsp.	15 ml
Necks and wing tips from 2 ducks		
Celery, chopped	3 oz.	90 g
Carrot, chopped	3 oz.	90 g
Onion, chopped	6 oz.	180 g
Bay leaf	1	1
Mushrooms, large, halved	3	3
Garlic cloves	4	4
Black pepper, crushed	1 Tbsp.	15 ml
Whole cloves	6	6
Tomato purée	2 Tbsp.	30 ml
Flour	2 Tbsp.	30 ml
Dry red wine	8 oz.	250 g
Brown veal stock	2 pt.	900 ml
Cavity juices reserved from 2 roasted ducks		

1. Heat the oven to 400°F (200°C).

2. Heat the oil in a large sauté pan. Add the duck pieces and sauté until they are well caramelized. Place the pan in the oven and roast the duck pieces for 25 minutes at 350°F (180°C), stirring occasionally.

Continued

3. Add the celery, carrot, onion, bay leaf, mushrooms, garlic, pepper and cloves. Roast for 5 minutes.

4. Place the sauté pan on the stove top and add the tomato purée. Sprinkle the flour over the mixture and stir.

5. Add the red wine and brown stock. Stir; bring to a boil. Reduce the heat and simmer for 3 hours.

6. Stir in the cavity juices and cook for 10 minutes more.

7. Strain the sauce through a china cap into a saucepan. Press a ladle against the solids to remove as much liquid as possible.

8. Degrease the sauce and reduce until thick.

◆◆◆

RECIPE 17.9

ROAST CORNISH GAME HEN WITH WILD RICE STUFFING

Yield: 6 Servings   **Method:** Roasting

Whole butter, melted	6 oz.	180 g
Onion, fine dice	3 oz.	90 g
Mushrooms, chopped	6 oz.	180 g
Wild rice, cooked	1-1/2 c.	350 ml
Dried thyme, crushed	1/2 tsp.	2 ml
Dried marjoram, crushed	1/2 tsp.	2 ml
Salt and pepper	TT	TT
Rock Cornish game hens	6	6

1. Sauté the onions and mushrooms in 2 ounces (60 grams) of melted butter until tender. Cool.

2. Stir in the rice and herbs and season to taste with salt and pepper.

3. Stuff the cavity of each hen loosely with the rice mixture. Truss and place in a roasting pan.

4. Brush the hens with the remaining butter and season with salt and pepper. Roast at 400°F (200°C) for 15 minutes.

5. Reduce the oven temperature to 300°F (150°C) and roast until the juices run clear, approximately 30 minutes. Baste two or three times with melted butter.

6. Serve the hens with a pan gravy or a sauce made separately such as mushroom sauce.

◆◆◆

RECIPE 17.10

COQ AU VIN

Yield: 8 2-piece Servings   **Method:** Braising

Chickens, 2 lb. 8 oz.–3 lb. (1–1.4 kg)	2	2
Flour for dredging	as needed	as needed
Salt and pepper	TT	TT
Clarified butter	2 oz.	60 g
Brandy	4 oz.	120 g
Bouquet garni:		
Carrot stick, 4 in. (10 cm)	1	1
Leek, split, 4-in. (10-cm) piece	1	1
Fresh thyme	1 sprig	1 sprig
Bay leaf	1	1
Garlic cloves, peeled and crushed	6	6
Red wine	24 oz.	700 g

Chicken stock	8 oz.	250 g
Bacon **lardons**	4 oz.	120 g
Pearl onions, peeled	18	18
Mushrooms, medium, quartered	10	10
Beurre manie	as needed	as needed
Large triangular croutons	8	8

Lardon—*bacon cut into 1/4 inch × 1/4 inch × 2 inch (6 mm × 6 mm × 5 cm) strips; used to moisten braised dishes and stews.*

1. Cut each chicken into 8 pieces and dredge in flour seasoned with salt and pepper.
2. Heat the clarified butter in a braising pan; brown the chicken.
3. Add the brandy and ignite. When the flame dies, add the bouquet garni, garlic, red wine and chicken stock. Bring to a boil, then reduce to a simmer.
4. Cover the pan and simmer until the chicken is tender, approximately 40 minutes.
5. In a separate pan, sauté the bacon until the fat begins to render. Add the onions and sauté until they begin to brown. Cook the bacon and onions covered, over low heat, until the onions are tender. Add the mushroom caps and cook them until tender.
6. Remove the chicken from the pan and adjust the sauce's consistency with the beurre manie. Strain the sauce through a china cap and adjust the seasonings.
7. Spoon the bacon, onions and mushrooms onto a serving platter, place the chicken over them and ladle the sauce over the finished dish. Serve with triangular croutons.

◆◆◆

RECIPE 17.11

CHICKEN CACCIATORE

Yield: 8 2-piece Servings   **Method:** Braising

Frying chickens, 2 lb. 8 oz.–3 lb. each (1.1–1.4 kg)	2	2
Flour	2 oz.	60 g
Salt and pepper	TT	TT
Olive oil	2 oz.	60 g
Onion, medium dice	4 oz.	120 g
Garlic cloves, chopped	3	3
Mushrooms, sliced	8 oz.	250 g
Dried thyme	1/4 tsp.	1 ml
White wine	2 oz.	60 g
Brandy	1 oz.	30 g
Demi-glace	16 oz.	450 g
Tomato concasse	12 oz.	340 g

1. Cut each chicken into 8 pieces and dredge in flour seasoned with salt and pepper.
2. Heat the oil in a heavy braiser and brown the chicken well. Remove the chicken from the pan. Degrease the pan, leaving 1 tablespoon (15 milliliters) of fat.
3. Add the onions and garlic and sauté lightly. Add the mushrooms and thyme and continue sautéing until the mushrooms are tender.
4. Deglaze the pan with the white wine and brandy. Add the demi-glace and tomato concasse.
5. Return the chicken to the pan and season with salt and pepper. Cover and cook until the chicken is done, approximately 30 minutes.
6. Serve 2 pieces of chicken with a portion of sauce.

❖❖❖

RECIPE 17.12

CHICKEN WITH 40 CLOVES OF GARLIC

Yield: 4 2-piece Servings   **Method:** Braising

Chicken, 2 lb. 8 oz. (1.2 kg) cut in eight pieces	1	1
Dry white wine	26 oz.	750 g
Flour	as needed	as needed
Salt and pepper	TT	TT
Olive oil	2 Tbsp.	30 ml
Garlic cloves, unpeeled	40	40
Fresh thyme	4 sprigs	4 sprigs
Fresh rosemary	1 sprig	1 sprig
French bread croutons	8	8
Fresh parsley, chopped	as needed for garnish	

1. Marinate the chicken pieces in the white wine for 1–2 hours under refrigeration. Remove and pat dry.
2. Dredge the chicken in flour and season lightly with salt and pepper. Sauté the chicken in the olive oil.
3. Remove the chicken from the pan and sauté the garlic until it begins to brown. Place the chicken on top of the garlic in a single layer. Add the wine marinade and herbs and cover.
4. Braise in a 325°F (160°C) oven until tender, approximately 45 minutes.
5. Remove the chicken and garlic from the pan and reserve. Remove and discard the herbs. Place the pan on the stove top and reduce the wine until slightly thick. Season with salt and pepper.
6. Serve 2 pieces of chicken and several of the garlic cloves resting on 2 French bread croutons. Top with a portion of the sauce and garnish with chopped parsley.

Nutritional values for each 2-piece portion:

Calories	493	Protein	56 g
Calories from fat	46%	Vitamin A	2084 IU
Total fat	48 g	Vitamin C	16 mg
Saturated fat	13 g	Sodium	341 mg
Cholesterol	243 mg		

❖❖❖

RECIPE 17.13

GRILLED BREAST OF CHICKEN FLORENTINE WITH BRUDER BASIL CHEESE AND ROASTED GARLIC SAUCE

ANA WESTIN HOTEL, WASHINGTON, D.C.
Chef Leland Atkinson

Yield: 4 Servings   **Method:** Grilling

Marinade:		
Extra virgin olive oil	4 oz.	120 g
Garlic, chopped	1 Tbsp.	15 ml
Fresh basil, chopped	1 Tbsp.	15 ml

Fresh oregano, chopped	1 Tbsp.	15 ml
Lemon juice	2 Tbsp.	30 ml
Salt and pepper	TT	TT
Airline chicken breast, skinless	8	8
Bruder basil cheese (smoked havarti)	8 slices	8 slices
Fresh spinach, cleaned	4 bunches	4 bunches
Unsalted butter	1 oz.	30 g
Roasted Garlic Sauce (recipe follows)	as needed	as needed
Roasted Garlic Garnish		
(recipe follows)	as needed	as needed
Tomato concasse	2 oz.	60 g

1. Combine the marinade ingredients, add the chicken and marinate for 1 hour.
2. Remove the chicken from the marinade, drain well and pat dry. Grill the chicken until done, approximately 5–6 minutes on each side.
3. Place one slice of cheese over each breast and allow it to melt. Remove the chicken from the grill.
4. Sauté the spinach in butter, season and drain thoroughly. Divide the spinach evenly among 4 warm plates, mounding it in the center.
5. Spoon the Roasted Garlic Sauce around the spinach. Place 2 breasts on top and garnish with the Roasted Garlic Garnish and tomato concasse.

ROASTED GARLIC SAUCE

Yield: 12 oz.

Shallots, minced	4 Tbsp.	60 ml
Clarified butter	1 Tbsp.	15 ml
Madeira	4 oz.	120 g
Fresh thyme	1 sprig	1 sprig
Bay leaf	1	1
Garlic head, trimmed and roasted	1	1
Demi-glace	1 pt.	450 ml
Salt and pepper	TT	TT

1. Sauté the shallots lightly in the clarified butter until slightly caramelized.
2. Add the Madeira, thyme and bay leaf and reduce by one third.
3. Squeeze in the garlic, discarding the skins and root.
4. Add the demi-glace and reduce by one third.
5. Thicken slightly with roux if desired, adjust the seasonings and force through a fine strainer.

ROASTED GARLIC GARNISH

Yield: 4 Servings

Garlic heads	4	4
Whole butter	2 oz.	60 g
Salt and pepper	TT	TT
Chicken stock	8 oz.	250 g
Fresh thyme	1/2 bunch	1/2 bunch

1. Remove the tops from the garlic and trim the bottoms. Place the garlic in a shallow buttered baking dish. Season with salt and pepper; place a dollop of butter on top of each.
2. Add the chicken stock to the pan until it reaches halfway up the garlic. Lay the thyme over the garlic, cover and bake at 350°F (180°C) until tender, approximately 30 minutes. Uncover during the last 5 minutes of cooking to allow the garlic to brown slightly.

◆◆◆

RECIPE 17.14
CHICKEN STUFFED
WITH SPINACH AND RICOTTA CHEESE IN SAFFRON SAUCE

ANA WESTIN HOTEL, WASHINGTON, DC
Chef Leland Atkinson

Yield: 4 Servings   **Method:** Sautéing

Spinach, stemmed	1 lb.	450 g
Ricotta cheese	4 oz.	120 g
Egg whites, lightly beaten	2	2
Salt and pepper	TT	TT
Airline chicken breast		
skin on, 9 oz. (250 g) each	4	4
Clarified butter	2 Tbsp.	30 ml
White wine	1 pt.	450 ml
Saffron	1 pinch	1 pinch
Chicken velouté	8 oz.	250 g
Heavy cream, hot	2 oz.	60 g

1. Blanch, refresh and drain the spinach. Squeeze it tightly to remove as much moisture as possible, then chop it finely.
2. To make the stuffing, combine the cheese, egg whites and spinach in a mixing bowl; season to taste.
3. Place the chicken breasts on a cutting board, skin side down. Using a boning knife, carefully make a pocket that runs the length of each breast.
4. Put the stuffing in a pastry bag and pipe the stuffing into each pocket. Do not overfill the chicken breasts because the stuffing expands as it cooks.
5. Sauté the chicken in the clarified butter until well browned. Transfer the chicken to a sheet pan and finish in a 350°F (180°C) oven, approximately 10–12 minutes.
6. Deglaze the sauté pan with the white wine.
7. Add the saffron, bring to a boil and reduce by half.
8. Add the velouté and the cream. Adjust the seasonings and consistency; strain.
9. Ladle the sauce onto 4 warm plates. Slice and then arrange the chicken in the sauce; garnish as desired.

◆◆◆

RECIPE 17.15
ROMAN-STYLE FREE-RANGE CHICKEN

REX IL RISTORANTE, LOS ANGELES, CA
Executive Chef Odette Fada

Yield: 4 Servings   **Method:** Sautéing

Extra virgin olive oil	2 Tbsp.	30 ml
Free-range chicken breast halves, boneless	4	4
Salt	TT	TT
Vegetable or chicken broth	8 oz.	225 g
Garlic cloves, chopped fine	4	4
Anchovy fillets in oil, chopped fine	3	3
Fresh rosemary, chopped fine	TT	TT
White wine vinegar	2 Tbsp.	30 ml

1. Sauté the chicken breasts in the olive oil; skin side down. Season with salt.
2. Cook until the chicken begins to brown, then turn it and cook for an additional 2 minutes.
3. Add the broth and reduce by two-thirds, approximately 5 minutes.
4. Combine the garlic, anchovies, rosemary and vinegar.
5. When the chicken is done, add the vinegar mixture to the cooking liquid.
6. Remove the chicken from the heat, slice each breast in 6 pieces and arrange on a hot plate. Pour the sauce over the sliced chicken.

◆◆◆

RECIPE 17.16
SAUTÉED CHICKEN WITH KENTUCKY BOURBON

Yield: 1 Serving   **Method:** Sautéing

Chicken breast, boneless, skinless	1	1
Salt and pepper	TT	TT
Flour	as needed	as needed
Olive oil	as needed	as needed
Garlic, minced	1/2 tsp.	2 ml
Shallots, chopped	1 tsp.	5 ml
Spinach	1 oz.	30 g
Kentucky bourbon	1 Tbsp.	15 ml
Chicken stock	1 oz.	30 g
Heavy cream	2 oz.	60 g

1. Season the chicken breast with salt and pepper and dredge it in flour. Sauté in olive oil until done and remove from the pan.
2. Add the garlic and shallots to the pan and sauté until tender. Add the spinach and sauté until wilted.
3. Add the bourbon and flame. Then add the chicken stock and cream and reduce until slightly thickened.
4. Return the chicken to the sauce to reheat.
5. Pour the spinach and sauce on a plate and arrange the chicken on top.

◆◆◆

RECIPE 17.17
CHICKEN STUFFED WITH SPINACH AND CRAB IN LOBSTER BEURRE BLANC

ANA WESTIN HOTEL, WASHINGTON, DC
Chef Leland Atkinson

Yield: 4 Servings   **Method:** Roasting

Spinach	1 bunch	1 bunch
Lump crabmeat	8 oz.	250 g
Heavy béchamel	3 oz.	90 g
Parmesan cheese	1 oz.	30 g
Fresh tarragon, chopped	2 tsp.	10 ml
Chives, chopped	1 tsp.	5 ml
Egg yolk	1	1
Salt and white pepper	TT	TT
Cayenne pepper	TT	TT
Chicken breasts, boneless, skin on		
8 oz. (250 g) each	4	4
Unsalted butter	1 Tbsp.	15 ml
Lobster Beurre Blanc (recipe follows)	as needed	as needed

1. Lay the spinach leaves flat on a wire rack or perforated hotel pan. Steam them until they are just wilted, then chill.
2. Combine the crab, béchamel, cheese, herbs and egg yolk in a mixing bowl. Season to taste with salt, white pepper and cayenne pepper.
3. Lay the chicken breasts on a cutting board, skin side down, and remove the tenderloins. Cover the breasts with plastic wrap and lightly pound them with a mallet.
4. Lay the spinach over each chicken breast, one leaf thick, leaving 1/4 inch (6 millimeters) of meat uncovered around the edges.
5. Divide the crab mixture evenly among the breasts, placing it in a cylindrical mound down the center of each breast.
6. Roll each breast into a tight, fat cigar shape and place on a buttered sheet pan, seam side down.
7. Brush the tops with butter, season with salt and pepper and roast at 375°F (190°C) until they reach an internal temperature of 145°F (63°C), approximately 15–18 minutes.
8. At service time, pool the Lobster Beurre Blanc on each plate, slice the breasts and arrange on the sauce. Garnish as desired.

LOBSTER BEURRE BLANC

Yield: 10 oz.

Shallots, peeled and sliced	2 Tbsp.	30 ml
Clarified butter	1 Tbsp.	15 ml
Fresh tarragon	1 sprig	1 sprig
Bay leaf	1	1
White wine	8 oz.	250 g
Lobster stock	1 pt.	450 ml
Champagne vinegar	1 Tbsp.	15 ml
Lemon juice	2 tsp.	10 ml
Ginger, peeled, chopped coarse	2 Tbsp.	30 ml
Heavy cream, hot	6 oz.	180 g
Unsalted butter	4 oz.	120 g
Salt and white pepper	TT	TT

1. Sauté the shallots in clarified butter until lightly caramelized.

2. Add the tarragon, bay leaf, white wine, lobster stock, vinegar, lemon juice and ginger. Bring to a boil and reduce to approximately 8 ounces (250 grams).

3. Add the cream and reduce by half or until thick.

4. Monte au beurre, adjust the seasonings and strain. Hold in a warm place until service.

◆◆◆

RECIPE 17.18

BRAISED CHICKEN WITH APPLE CIDER AND CASHEW BUTTER

ANA WESTIN HOTEL, WASHINGTON, DC
Chef Leland Atkinson

Yield: 4 Servings   **Method:** Braising

Clarified butter	2-1/2 oz.	75 g
Shallots, minced	2 oz.	60 g
Calvados	12 oz.	375 g
Fresh thyme, chopped	2 tsp.	10 ml
Cashews	3 oz.	90 g
Honey	1 Tbsp.	15 ml
Unsalted butter	1 lb.	450 g
Salt and pepper	TT	TT
Chickens, 3 lb. 8 oz. (1.6 kg) each, quartered	2	2
Flour for dredging	as needed	as needed
Mirepoix	12 oz.	350 g
Garlic head, cut in half	1	1
Apple cider	1 pt.	450 ml
Cider vinegar	1 Tbsp.	15 ml
Chicken stock	3 pt.	1350 ml
Bay leaves	2	2
Fresh thyme	1 sprig	1 sprig
Blond roux	as needed	as needed

1. To make the cashew butter, lightly sauté the shallots in 1 tablespoon (15 milliliters) of the clarified butter. Add 4 ounces (120 grams) of the Calvados and the chopped thyme and reduce au sec. Remove from the heat and cool.

2. Place the cashews in a food processor and process to a medium-fine consistency. Add the cooled shallots, honey and unsalted butter. Season with salt and pepper and process well.

3. Season the chicken with salt and pepper and dredge in flour.

4. Brown the chicken evenly in the remaining clarified butter.

5. Remove the chicken. Add the mirepoix and garlic to the pan; sauté for 1 minute.

6. Add the remaining Calvados, cider and vinegar; reduce by half.

7. Return the chicken to the pan and add the chicken stock and herbs. Cover and braise until done, approximately 15 minutes. Remove the chicken from the pan. (The breasts and wings will cook more quickly and must be removed before the thigh and leg pieces.)

8. Reduce the stock by one half. Use the roux to thicken to a light sauce consistency.

9. Strain the sauce, monte au beurre with the cashew butter and season to taste with salt and pepper. Ladle the sauce over the chicken and serve at once.

◆◆◆

RECIPE 17.19
WARM DUCK BREAST SALAD WITH ASIAN SPICES AND HAZELNUT VINAIGRETTE

FETZER VINEYARDS, HOPLAND, CA
Culinary Director John Ash

Yield: 4 Servings   **Method:** Sautéing

Whole boneless duck breasts, 12 oz. (350 g) each	2	2
Marinade:		
Garlic, minced	1 tsp.	5 ml
Green onions, minced	2 Tbsp.	30 ml
Oyster sauce	2 tsp.	10 ml
Light soy sauce	1 tsp.	5 ml
Rice wine or dry sherry	1 tsp.	5 ml
Sugar	1 tsp.	5 ml
Five spice powder	1/2 tsp.	3 ml
Hazelnut Vinaigrette:		
Garlic, minced	1 Tbsp.	15 ml
Hazelnut oil	3 oz.	90 g
Walnut or light olive oil	3 oz.	90 g
Chives, minced	1 Tbsp.	15 ml
Balsamic vinegar	2 Tbsp.	30 ml
Light soy sauce	1 tsp.	5 ml
Sugar	1/4 tsp.	1 ml
Mixed baby greens	4–6 oz.	120–180 g
Hazelnuts, toasted, skinned and chopped coarse	2 oz.	60 g

1. Trim the excess fat from the duck breasts and separate the breasts into halves.
2. Combine the marinade ingredients. Thoroughly coat the duck with the marinade and marinate for at least 2 hours.
3. Combine the hazelnut vinaigrette ingredients at least 2 hours before service so that the flavors will develop.
4. Wipe the marinade from the breasts and sauté them, skin side down first, in a dry sauté pan until medium rare, approximately 2-1/2 minutes per side. Do not overcook.
5. Arrange a mixture of baby greens on 4 plates. Slice the breasts on the diagonal and arrange on the plates with the greens. Drizzle the hazelnut vinaigrette over the greens, sprinkle with hazelnuts and serve.

◆◆◆

RECIPE 17.20

Duck à L'Orange

ANA WESTIN HOTEL, Washington, DC
Chef Leland Atkinson

Yield: 4 Servings   **Method:** Roasting

Duckling, 5–6 lb. (2.2–2.8 kg)	1	1
Salt and pepper	TT	TT
Duck or chicken stock	8 oz.	250 g
Sugar	1 Tbsp.	15 ml
Champagne vinegar	1 Tbsp.	15 ml
Brandy	2 Tbsp.	30 ml
Orange juice	12 oz.	350 g
Lemon juice	from 1 lemon	from 1 lemon
Whole butter	1 tsp.	5 ml
Oranges, peeled and sectioned	4	4
Orange zest, julienne	4 Tbsp.	60 ml

1. Prick the duck with a fork and season well with salt and pepper.
2. Roast the duck at 400°F (200°C) for 15 minutes. Reduce the heat to 350°F (180°C) and cook until done, approximately 45–60 minutes. Remove the duck from the roasting pan and hold in a warm place.
3. Degrease the roasting pan. Place the pan on the stove top and deglaze with the stock.
4. Melt the sugar and vinegar together in a saucepan and lightly caramelize the mixture.
5. Remove the pan from the stove top and add the brandy.
6. Add the stock, pan drippings and juices and reduce until the sauce is slightly thickened, approximately 10 minutes. Monte au beurre. Strain and degrease the sauce.
7. Place the duck on a warm serving platter. Arrange the orange sections around it. Blanch the orange zest and sprinkle over the duck. Pour the sauce over the duck and serve additional sauce on the side.

◆◆◆

RECIPE 17.21

Roast Goose with Cabbage and Apples

Yield: 8 6-oz. (180-g) Servings   **Method:** Roasting

Goose, approx. 12 lb. (6 kg)	1	1
Salt and pepper	TT	TT
Caraway seeds	1 Tbsp.	15 ml
Onion, large dice	6 oz.	180 g
Carrot, large dice	3 oz.	90 g
Celery, large dice	3 oz.	90 g
Green cabbage, shredded	1 lb.	450 g
Potato, large dice	3 lb.	1.4 kg
Tart apple, cored and diced	1 lb.	450 g
Apple cider	1 qt.	1 lt

1. Remove the giblets from the goose; remove the fat from its cavity. Rinse the goose and pat dry. Sprinkle its interior and exterior with salt, pepper

Continued

and caraway seeds. Truss the goose and place breast side up on a rack in a roasting pan.

2. Roast in a 425°F (220°C) oven for 30 minutes. Prick the skin all over with a fork to release fat.

3. Reduce the oven temperature to 350°F (180°C) and continue roasting for another 45 minutes. Baste the bird occasionally with the fat accumulating in the pan.

4. Meanwhile, combine the vegetables and apple and season with salt and pepper.

5. After roasting for 1-1/4 hours, remove the goose from the pan and drain off all but 3 tablespoons (45 milliliters) of fat. Place the vegetable mixture in the roasting pan and toss to coat with the fat.

6. Place the goose on top of the vegetable mixture and pour the apple cider over all. Return to the oven and continue roasting until done, approximately 1-1/2 hours.

7. Remove the bird from the roasting pan and allow it to rest for 20–30 minutes before carving. Serve with the cooked vegetables.

◆◆◆

RECIPE 17.22

SQUAB SALAD WITH MELON

REX IL RISTORANTE, LOS ANGELES, CA
Executive Chef Odette Fada

Yield: 6 servings		Method: Sautéing
Squab	3	3
Salt and pepper	TT	TT
Extra virgin olive oil	as needed	as needed
Dry black currants	2 Tbsp.	30 ml
Tahitian squash, thin slices	18	18
Mâche lettuce, small bunches	6	6

1. Bone the squab breasts and remove the thighs and legs. Season with salt and pepper and sauté the breasts and thighs in olive oil until done, approximately 10–15 minutes.

2. Place the currants in a bowl and cover with hot water.

3. Cook the squash slices in boiling water for 40 seconds. Cut the slices in half and arrange them on each of 6 plates as fans opening toward the plate's border.

4. On the other side of each plate, arrange some mâche lettuce; season with salt and pepper.

5. Slice the breasts; arrange the meat with the legs on the squash. Keep the plates in a warm place.

6. Drain the currants and sauté in 2 tablespoons (30 milliliters) of olive oil. Sprinkle the currants around the plates and serve.

◆◆◆

RECIPE 17.23

TURKEY SCALLOPINE WITH CAPERS AND LEMON

Yield: 4 servings   **Method:** Sautéing

Turkey breast, cut into 1/8-in. (3-mm) scallopines, 3 oz. (90 g) each	8	8
Salt and white pepper	TT	TT
Flour	as needed	as needed
Clarified butter	2 oz.	60 g
Dry white wine	4 oz.	120 g
Fresh lemon juice	2 oz.	60 g
Capers	3 Tbsp.	45 ml

1. Gently pound each turkey slice with a meat mallet. Season with salt and pepper and dredge in flour.

2. Sauté the turkey in the clarified butter until golden brown. Remove and hold in a warm place.

3. Deglaze the pan with the wine, then add the lemon juice and capers. Return the turkey to the pan to coat with the sauce and reheat.

4. Serve 2 slices with a portion of the sauce.

◆◆◆

RECIPE 17.24

SAUTÉED CHICKEN LIVERS

Yield: 4 4-oz. (120-g) Appetizer Servings   **Method:** Sautéing

Chicken livers, trimmed	1 lb.	450 g
Salt and pepper	TT	TT
Flour	as needed	as needed
Vegetable oil	1 oz.	30 g
Shallots, minced	2 Tbsp.	60 g
Raspberry vinegar	4 oz.	120 g
Raspberry jam	2 Tbsp.	60 g
French bread croutons	4	4
Watercress	as needed for garnish	

1. Rinse the livers and pat dry. Season with salt and pepper and dredge in flour.

2. Sauté in the oil until just barely pink, approximately 3–4 minutes. Remove the livers from the pan and hold in a warm place.

3. Using the fat remaining in the pan, sauté the shallots until tender. Deglaze with the vinegar.

4. Add the jam. Simmer until thickened. Return the livers to the pan and toss to coat with the sauce.

5. Serve on warm plates with French bread croutons; garnish with watercress.

CHAPTER 18

GAME

After studying this chapter you will be able to:

+ identify a variety of game
+ understand game inspection practices
+ purchase game appropriate for your needs
+ store game properly
+ prepare game for cooking
+ apply various cooking methods to game

ame (Fr. gibier) are animals hunted for sport or food. Traditionally, game supplies depended upon the season and the hunter's success. But game's increasing popularity in food service operations has led to farm-raising techniques. As a result, pheasant, quail, deer, rabbit and other animals, although still considered game, are now ranch-raised and commercially available throughout the year.

The life of game creatures is reflected in their flesh's appearance, aroma, flavor and texture. Generally, game flesh has a dark color and strong but not unpleasant aroma. It has a robust flavor, less fat than other meats or poultry and is more compact, becoming quite tough in older animals.

Selecting the best cooking methods for game depends on the animal's age and the particular cut of flesh. Younger animals will, of course, be more tender than older ones. Flesh from the loin or less-used muscles will also be tender and therefore can be prepared with dry-heat cooking methods. Flesh from much-used muscles, such as the leg and shoulder, will be tougher and should be prepared with combination cooking methods. Less-tender cuts can also be used in sausages, pâtés and forcemeats as discussed in Chapter 20, Charcuterie.

IDENTIFYING GAME

Furred or Ground Game

Furred game includes large animals such as deer, moose, bear, wild boar and elk as well as smaller animals such as rabbit, squirrel, raccoon and opossum. Although each of these animals (and many others) are hunted for sport and food, only antelope, deer and rabbit are widely available to food service operations.

Large game animals are rarely sold whole or in primal portions. Instead, the meat is available precut into subprimals or portions. So, except for those that are used for rabbits, this chapter does not provide butchering techniques.

Antelope

The blackbuck antelope, about half the size of a large deer, is ranch-raised in this country. Although it has almost no body fat, the meat retains a high amount of moisture. The meat is fine-grained, with a flavor that is only slightly stronger than deer meat (venison). It should be butchered and cooked in a manner similar to venison.

Bison (American Buffalo)

Once found in huge herds roaming the plains states, bison or buffalo were hunted into near extinction during the 19th century. Buffalo now live on reser-

---

✦✦✦
MEAT OF THE FUTURE:
BEEFALO

Beefalo is produced by cross-breeding a bison with a domestic beef animal. To be a registered full-blooded beefalo, the animal has to be three-eighths bison and five-eighths domestic beef. The five-eighths domestic beef portion is not restricted to any breed; it is often a combination of two or more breeds such as Hereford, Angus or Charolais. In 1985 the USDA approved a special label for beefalo; it is labeled as either "Beef from Beefalo" or "Beefalo Beef."

Beefalo looks and tastes much like modern beef. The animal itself is hard to distinguish from any other beef animal. Beefalo meat is tender because the animals gain weight faster and go to market at younger ages. The meat is slightly sweeter in taste than beef.

Beefalo is lower in cholesterol than beef, fish or chicken and lower in calories and fat than beef. It offers a great alternative to beef for the diet- and health-conscious guest. The per-pound cost of beefalo may be slightly higher than beef cuts, but its low amount of interior and exterior fat gives it a higher yield with a price per usable pound comparable to beef.

Because of beefalo's finer fiber and low fat content, it cooks in one-third to one-half the time of beef and should be cooked to either rare or medium-rare.

JAMES J. MUTH, *MBA, CFBE*
Chef Instructor,
GRAND RAPIDS COMMUNITY COLLEGE

---

vations or ranches, where they are raised like beef cattle. Their meat is juicy, flavorful and may be prepared in the same manner as lean beef.

Deer

The deer family includes elk, moose, reindeer, red-tailed deer, white-tailed deer (Fr. *chevreuil*) and mule deer. Meat from any of these animals is known as venison (Fr. *venaisan*). Farm-raised venison, particularly from the Scottish red deer bred in New Zealand and the United States, is commercially available all year. Venison is typically dark red with a mild aroma. It is leaner than other meats, having almost no intramuscular fat or marbling.

The most popular commercial venison cuts are the loin, leg and rack. The loin is tender enough to roast, sauté or grill to medium rare. It can be left attached along the backbone to form a cut known as the saddle. The leg is often marinated in red wine and prepared with combination cooking methods. Other cuts can also be stewed or braised or used in sausages and pâtés. Butchering procedures for venison are similar to those for lamb discussed in Chapter 15.

Venison Saddle

Rabbit

Rabbits (Fr. *lapin*) are small burrowing animals that have long been raised for food. Rabbit has mild, lean and relatively tender flesh. Its taste and texture are similar to chicken. Ranch-raised rabbit is available all year, either whole or cut, fresh or frozen. The average weight of a whole dressed rabbit is 2 pounds 8 ounces to 3 pounds (1.2–1.4 kilograms). Young rabbit can be roasted, pan-fried, stewed or braised and is popular in rustic "country-style" dishes, especially casseroles and pâtés.

PROCEDURE FOR BUTCHERING RABBIT

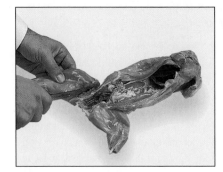

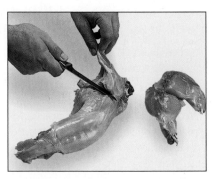

1. Place the rabbit on its back. Remove the hind legs by cutting close to the backbone and through the joint on each side. Each thigh and leg can be separated by cutting through the joint.

2. Remove the forelegs by cutting beneath the shoulder blades.

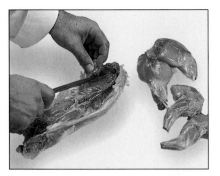

3. Cut through the breast bone and spread open the rib cage. Using a boning knife, separate the flesh from the rib bones and remove the bones.

4. Cut through the backbone to divide the loin into the desired number of pieces.

5. The cut-up rabbit: hind legs, thighs, loin in three pieces, forelegs.

TABLE 18.1   USING FURRED GAME

Animal	Commonly Purchased Cuts	Cooking Methods	Suggested Use
Antelope	Purchased and prepared in the same manner as deer.		
Bison	Purchased and prepared in the same manner as lean beef.		
Deer	Loin	Dry heat (roast; sauté; grill)	Sautéed medallions; whole roast loin; grilled steaks
	Leg	Combination (braise; stew)	Marinate and braise; pot roast with cranberries; chili; sausage; forcemeat
	Rack	Dry heat (roast; grill)	Grilled chops
Rabbit	Full carcass	Dry heat (sauté; pan-fry; roast; grill) Combination (braise; stew)	Pan-fried rabbit with cream gravy; Braised rabbit with mushrooms
Wild Boar	Loin	Dry heat (roast)	Roast loin with mustard crust
	Chops	Combination (braise)	Marinate and braise; stew with red wine and sour cream; sausage; forcemeat

---
♦♦♦

THE DARING DINER

While venison, boar and pheasant may seem unusual to many Americans, even rarer meats are available to the daring diner. Zebra, bear, wildebeest and other "big game" animals are sometimes available through exotic game purveyors based in major metropolitan areas. Most often the meat is grilled, roasted or stewed.

Reptiles, particularly rattlesnake, crocodile and alligator, are now also being raised on farms to meet increased demand. Reptiles may be braised, or sliced and deep-fried. They have a mild flavor with a texture similar to lobster.

Boar Saddle

Wild Boar

A close relative of the domesticated hog, wild boar (Fr. *sanglier*) is leaner, with a stronger flavor. Though plentiful in Europe and parts of America, wild boar is only available during autumn. A limited supply of farm-raised boar is available all year, however. Baby boar (under six months old) is considered a delicacy, but mature animals (one to two years old) have the best flavor. The meat is most often roasted, and may be used in sausages or terrines. Boar can often be substituted in recipes for venison or pork.

Feathered or Winged Game

Feathered game includes upland birds such as wild turkeys, pheasants, quails, doves and woodcocks; songbirds such as larks, and waterfowl such as wild geese and ducks. Wild birds cannot be sold in the United States. An ever-increasing number of these birds are being farm-raised to meet increased consumer demand, however.

Game birds are available whole or precut into pieces, fresh or frozen. Butchering techniques will not be shown in this chapter as they are the same as those for domesticated poultry discussed in Chapter 17.

Because game birds tend to have less fat than other poultry, they are often barded with fat and cooked to medium rare. If cooked well done they become dry and stringy.

Partridge

The Hungarian and chukar partridges (Fr. *perdrix*) of Europe were introduced to the United States and Canada during the 19th century. Now found principally in the prairie and western mountain states, partridges are widely raised on game preserves and farms, producing a good commercial supply.

Their flavor is less delicate than pheasant and the meat tends to be tougher. Partridge may be roasted or cut into pieces and sautéed or braised. Each bird weighs about 1 pound (450 grams) dressed.

Chukar Partridge

◆◆◆

FAISAN À LA SAINTE-ALLIANCE

Any dish prepared *à la sainte-alliance* evokes the festivities surrounding the 1815 signing of the Treaty of Paris, which ended the reign of Napoleon Bonaparte, forcing him into exile on Elba. *Faisan à la sainte-alliance* is a roast pheasant stuffed with woodcock and served on toast topped with woodcock purée. The renowned gastronome Brillat-Savarin gives the following recipe in his *Physiologie du Gout*, published in 1825:

When the pheasant has reached [its peak of ripeness], it is plucked, and not before, and it is larded carefully, with the freshest and firmest of material.... [T]he time has come to stuff it, and in the following manner:

Bone and draw a brace of woodcock, in such a way that you have one supply of the flesh, and another of the entrails.

Take the flesh and make a forcemeat of it by chopping it with some steamed beef marrow, a little scraped bacon, pepper, salt, fresh herbs, and enough fine truffles to make just the amount of stuffing needed to fill the pheasant.

Prepare a slice of bread that will be about two inches bigger on every side than the bird laid lengthwise. Then take the woodcock livers and entrails, and grind them in a mortar with two large truffles, an anchovy, a little finely minced bacon, and a sizeable lump of the best fresh butter.

Spread this paste evenly on the bread slice, and place it under the pheasant, already stuffed ... so that it will catch every drop of juice which will appear while the bird is roasting.

When the bird is done, serve it lying gracefully upon this crisp little couch; surround it with bitter oranges, and be assured of the fortunate outcome.

BRILLAT-SAVARIN,
THE PHYSIOLOGY OF TASTE,
translated and annotated by M. F. K. FISHER
(North Point Press, 1986),
pp. 374–75.

Pheasant

Pheasant

The most popular of game birds, the pheasant (Fr. *faisan*) was introduced into Europe from Asia during the Middle Ages. Its mild flavor is excellent for roasting, stewing or braising. The hen is smaller and more tender than the cock. Stock made from the carcass is often used for consommé or sauce.

Farm-raised birds are available fresh or frozen. A dressed bird weighs about 1 pound 8 ounces to 2 pounds 4 ounces (680 grams to 1 kilogram) and serves two people.

Quail

The quail (Fr. *caille*) is a migratory game bird related to the pheasant. The more popular European and Californian species are farm-raised and available all year.

Quail are rather small, with only about 1–2 ounces (30–60 grams) of breast meat each. Quail may be grilled (especially on skewers), roasted, broiled or sautéed and are often boned and served whole with a stuffing of forcemeat or rice. Because they are so lean, roasted quail benefit from barding.

Quail

NUTRITION

Even ranch-raised game animals live in the wild and are generally more active and less well fed than domesticated animals. This lifestyle produces animals whose meat has less fat than domesticated animals. Most game is also lower in cholesterol and has approximately one third fewer calories than beef. Game is also generally high in protein and minerals. Compare Table 18.2 with Tables 12.1 (Meats) and 17.7 (Poultry).

TABLE 18.2   NUTRITIONAL VALUES OF GAME

For 1 oz. (28 g) Uncooked Lean Meat	Kcal	Protein (g)	Total Fat (g)	Saturated Fat (g)	Cholesterol (mg)	Sodium (mg)
Beefalo	41	6.6	1.4	0.6	13	22
Bison (American buffalo)	31	6.1	0.5	0.2	18	15
Deer (venison)	34	6.5	0.7	0.3	24	15
Rabbit	39	5.7	1.6	0.5	16	12
Wild boar	35	6.1	1.0	0.3	mq	mq
Pheasant	51	6.4	2.6	0.8	mq	11
Quail	54	5.6	3.4	1.0	mq	15

mq = measurable quantity but data is unavailable The Corinne T.Netzer Encyclopedia of Food Values 1992

◆◆◆

WILD GAME— DELICIOUS, NUTRITIOUS AND AVAILABLE

Wild game is now widely available for use in restaurants and at home. The best of wild game provides a safe, delicious and nutritious dining experience.

In almost all states, our native game animals are protected from harvesting for commercial purposes. It is a violation of state wildlife laws to kill and sell the meat from native species such as the whitetail deer, mule deer, pronghorn antelope, etc. These laws were written when only native game was present in America. Since then, a growing number of non-native species of deer and antelope have been introduced to ranches in America and this has made it possible to harvest deer and antelope legally for meat production.

Oddly enough, however, meats such as antelope, venison, rabbit, and most other game meats are not subject to inspection under federal and most state meat inspection regulations. This is not because the authorities do not believe the meat should be inspected. When the meat inspection laws were written, these meats were not legally available and therefore were not included in the Federal Meat Act. County and city health codes, however, do require that any meat served to the public must be from "an approved source" which is interpreted as "inspected." Therefore, any game meat served in a restaurant should be certified as inspected by either state or federal meat inspection authorities.

Game meat is available from farmed (domesticated) deer and from free-ranging (ranched) deer and antelope. Most farmed deer are taken to a fixed conventional slaughterhouse where they are slaughtered and processed in the same way as cattle, sheep, and goats. Ranched deer can be properly harvested only by an elaborate procedure which involves taking a mobile slaughter facility and meat inspector to the field where the animals are killed by shooting them with a high powered rifle under the supervision of the meat inspector. The carcass is then processed inside the mobile facility to avoid any contamination of the meat. This field harvesting eliminates any stress which might occur in transport of farmed deer to the slaughterhouse.

Farmed deer tend to be relatively more uniform in size and flavor. Free-ranging deer and antelope produce meat of more complex flavor due to the variety of their diet. The difference is somewhat like the difference in cultivated mushrooms and wild mushrooms, or pen-raised chickens compared with free-range chickens. Meat from free-range animals is more expensive due to higher labor and inspection costs.

Meat from both deer and antelope can be legally labeled "venison." All venison is relatively lean when compared with conventional red meats and requires special attention when cooking to avoid drying out the meat and toughening it. Tender cuts should be cooked as little as possible (rare to medium rare) to retain the maximum amount of moisture. Quick sautéing, grilling or roasting to retain a medium rare center is most satisfactory for tender cuts such as the loin, tenderloin, and leg.

Braising is the most effective method for cooking the less tender cuts such as the shoulder, ribs and shanks. Beef broth or red wine are good liquids for braising. The toughest cut of meat will be very satisfactorily tenderized if braised for a sufficient period of time (which may be as long as two or three hours). When properly cooked, these cuts can surpass the more tender cuts in flavor.

MIKE HUGHES,
BROKEN ARROW RANCH, Ingram, Texas

INSPECTION OF GAME

The USDA and most states restrict the sale of wild game. Truly wild game can only be served by those who hunt and share their kill.

Domestic Game

As opposed to mandatory federal and state inspections for beef, veal, lamb, pork and poultry, farm- or ranch-raised game is only subject to voluntary inspections for wholesomeness. Generally, however, game is processed under the same federal inspection requirements as domesticated meats and poultry. State regulations vary and are constantly being expanded and improved in response to consumer demands. Also unlike meat and poultry from domesticated animals, game is not graded for quality.

Imported Game

The USDA and the FDA work together to ensure the wholesomeness of imported game. Only USDA-approved countries are permitted to export game to the United States. Upon arrival in this country, game shipments are subject to USDA spot inspections.

PURCHASING AND STORING GAME

Purchasing Game

Furred game meats are available fresh, usually in vacuum-sealed packaging, or frozen. Game birds are available cleaned and boned, fresh or frozen. Use the same criteria to determine the freshness of game as you would any other meat or poultry: The flesh should be firm, without slime or an off-odor.

Fresh game is sometimes **hung** before cooking to allow the meat to mature or age. During hanging, carbohydrates (glycogen) stored in muscle tissues are converted to lactic acid. This process tenderizes the flesh and strengthens its flavor. But hanging is not necessary, especially if you object to "gamy" flavors. Commercially sold game is generally fully aged and ready to use when delivered. It does not need nor will it benefit from hanging.

Storing Game

As with any fresh or frozen meat, game should be well wrapped and stored under refrigeration at temperatures below 40°F (4°C). Because the flesh is generally dry and lean, frozen game should be used within four months. Thaw frozen game slowly under refrigeration to prevent moisture loss.

MARINATING FURRED GAME

Tradition calls for marinating game, particularly furred game, in strong mixtures of red wine, herbs and spices. Commercially raised game does not necessarily have to be marinated. Modern animal husbandry techniques used at game ranches assure the cook of receiving meat from young, tender animals.

♦♦♦
HOW TO HANG GAME

The following information may be useful if you find yourself with a need to hang freshly killed game. Most game should be eviscerated (drawn or gutted) as soon as possible, then suspended by either the hind legs or the head in a dry, well-ventilated place. Because the fur or feathers help prevent bacterial contamination, they should be left intact during hanging; game should be skinned or plucked just before butchering. The length of time necessary for hanging depends on the species and age of the animal. Two days may be sufficient for a rabbit, while up to three weeks may be necessary for a deer or boar. Hanging is generally complete when the first whiff of odor is detected (although traditionalists prefer pheasant to be hung until extremely ripe).

Farm-raised game animals also have a naturally milder flavor than their truly wild cousins.

For those preferring the flavors imparted by traditional marinades, the following red wine marinade is included. After the meat is removed, the marinade may be added to the cooking liquid or reduced and used in a sauce. Do not serve uncooked marinade.

♦♦♦

RECIPE 18.1

RED-WINE GAME MARINADE

Yield: 1-1/2 qt. (1.5 lt)

Carrot, chopped fine	2 oz.	60 g
Onion, chopped fine	2 oz.	60 g
Garlic, minced	1 Tbsp.	15 ml
Dried thyme	1 tsp.	5 ml
Bay leaves	2	2
Juniper berries, whole	2 tsp.	10 ml
Peppercorns, whole	1 Tbsp.	15 ml
Sage, ground	1/2 tsp.	2 ml
Red wine	1 qt.	1 lt
Red wine vinegar	4 oz.	120 g

1. Combine all ingredients.
2. Place the meat in the marinade and marinate for the desired time. Tender, farm-raised game may need only 30 minutes; older, wild animals may need 1–2 days.

CONCLUSION

Game is becoming increasingly popular because of consumer desires for leaner, healthier meats. Only farm-raised game can be used in food service operations. Luckily, many popular game items are now farm-raised, government-inspected and readily available. Generally, game flesh has a dark color, strong but not unpleasant aroma and a robust flavor. You should butcher, prepare and cook game according to the comparable guidelines for other meats and poultry.

QUESTIONS FOR DISCUSSION

1. Explain the differences between truly wild game and ranch-raised game.
2. What is hanging? Is it necessary for modern food service operations to hang game?
3. Which cuts of furred game are best suited to dry-heat cooking methods? Which are best for combination cooking methods?
4. Can game birds be purchased whole? How are they fabricated?
5. What degree of doneness is best suited for game birds? Explain your answer.

ADDITIONAL GAME RECIPES

RECIPE 18.2

MARINATED LOIN OF VENISON ROASTED WITH MUSTARD, SERVED WITH CREAMY POLENTA WITH WILD MUSHROOMS

NOTE: *This dish appears in the Chapter Opening photograph.*

FETZER VINEYARDS, HOPLAND, CA
John Ash, Culinary Director

Yield: 8–10/6–8 oz. (180–250 g) Servings   **Method**: Roasting

Marinade:		
Carrots, medium	3	3
Yellow onion, large	1	1
Shallots, whole	3	3
Garlic cloves	3	3
Olive oil	2 Tbsp.	30 ml
Hearty red wine	40 oz.	1200 g
Red wine vinegar	4 oz.	120 g
Bay leaves	4	4
Parsley stalks	6	6
Juniper berries, whole	16	16
Sea salt	2 tsp.	10 ml
Peppercorns	12	12
Mustard coating:		
Garlic cloves	3	3
Green onion, chopped	2 oz.	60 g
Chardonnay	3 oz.	90 g
Fresh sage	1 tsp.	5 ml
Fresh thyme	1 tsp.	5 ml
Dijon mustard	1 c.	250 ml
Olive oil	2 oz.	60 g
Sea salt	1 tsp.	5 ml
Venison loin, 5 lb. (2.2 kg), well-trimmed	1	1

1. For the marinade, coarsely chop the vegetables and sauté in the oil until lightly browned.
2. Add the wine, vinegar and remaining marinade seasonings and bring to a boil.
3. Reduce the heat and simmer 10 minutes. Cool before using.
4. For the mustard coating, place all ingredients in a food processor or blender and quickly process until smooth. The mixture should be very thick. Cover and refrigerate.
5. In a nonreactive pan, pour the cooled marinade over the loin and marinate, covered, in the refrigerator for up to 24 hours. Turn occasionally.
6. Remove the meat from the marinade, pat dry and quickly sear the meat in a hot sauté pan or on the grill.

7. Place loin in a roasting pan and coat well with the mustard coating. Roast at 450°F (230°C) for 5 minutes; reduce heat to 375°F (190°C) and roast for an additional 10–15 minutes, until the meat is medium rare.

8. Serve on warm plates with Creamy Polenta with Wild Mushrooms.

CREAMY POLENTA WITH WILD MUSHROOMS

Yield: 8–10 Servings

Yellow onion, chopped coarse	12 oz.	340 g
White mushrooms, chopped coarse	4 oz.	120 g
Garlic, chopped fine	2 Tbsp.	30 ml
Dried porcini or cèpes mushrooms, rinsed, soaked in water and chopped coarse	2 oz.	60 g
Olive oil	5 oz.	150 g
Fresh basil, chopped fine	4 tsp.	20 ml
Fresh oregano, chopped fine	1 tsp.	5 ml
Chicken or vegetable stock	2 qt.	2 lt
Coarse polenta cornmeal	2 c.	450 ml
Salt and pepper	TT	TT
Heavy cream	1 pt.	450 ml
Aged Asiago or Fontina cheese, grated fine	4 oz.	120 g
Fresh wild mushrooms	8–10	8–10
Fresh basil sprigs	as needed for garnish	

1. Sauté the onion, white mushrooms, garlic and porcini in 4 ounces (120 grams) olive oil until lightly colored. Add the basil, oregano and stock; bring to a boil.

2. Slowly stir in the polenta. Simmer 10 minutes, stirring regularly. The polenta should be thick and creamy. Add more stock if necessary. Adjust the seasonings and keep warm.

3. Just before serving, add the cream and cheese and stir vigorously.

4. Sauté the fresh wild mushrooms in the remaining olive oil until tender. Spoon the polenta onto warm plates and garnish with the wild mushrooms and a sprig of fresh basil.

◆◆◆

RECIPE 18.3

BRAISED ANTELOPE IN SOUR CREAM

Yield: 8 Servings, 6–8 oz. (180–250 g) each　　　　**Method:** Braising

Salt pork	3 oz.	90 g
Bottom round of antelope, 4–5 lb. (2–2.5 kg)	1	1
Onion, small dice	12 oz.	350 g
Garlic cloves, sliced	2	2
Carrot, sliced	8 oz.	250 g
Red wine	24 oz.	700 g

Continued

Veal or game stock	3 pt.	1.5 lt
Bay leaves	2	2
Fresh rosemary, chopped	1 tsp.	5 ml
Fresh thyme	1/2 tsp.	2 ml
Juniper berries, crushed	10	10
Tomato paste	2 Tbsp.	30 ml
Clarified butter	2 Tbsp.	30 ml
Flour	2 Tbsp.	30 ml
Sour cream	1 pt.	500 ml
Salt and Pepper	TT	TT

1. Render the salt pork. Brown the meat well in the fat.
2. Add the onions, garlic and carrots; sauté until the vegetables are tender.
3. Add the red wine, stock, herbs, juniper berries and tomato paste. Braise in a 325°F (160°C) oven until the meat is tender, approximately 1-1/2 to 2 hours.
4. Remove the meat from the pan. If necessary, make a blond roux with the butter and flour and use to thicken the sauce. Bring to a simmer then strain the sauce.
5. Add the sour cream, heat thoroughly and season to taste with salt and pepper.

◆◆◆

RECIPE 18.4

SCALLOPINE OF VENISON WITH CHESTNUTS

Yield: 6 Servings   **Method:** Sautéing

Venison scallopine, cut from leg,		
2 oz. (60 g) each	12	12
Salt and pepper	TT	TT
Flour	as needed	as needed
Clarified butter	3 oz.	90 g
White wine	8 oz.	250 g
Heavy cream	8 oz.	250 g
Chestnut purée	3 oz.	90 g
Fresh dill, chopped	1 Tbsp.	15 ml

1. Pound the scallopine to a thickness of 1/4 inch (6 millimeters).
2. Season with salt and pepper; dredge in flour.
3. Sauté the scallopine in the clarified butter; remove to a warm platter.
4. Deglaze the pan with the wine. Add the cream and bring to a boil. Whisk in the chestnut purée. Thin with additional wine or cream if necessary.
5. Return the scallopine to the pan to reheat. Adjust the seasonings and add the chopped dill.
6. Serve 2 slices of venison per portion with 3 ounces (90 milliliters) sauce.

◆◆◆

RECIPE 18.5
VENISON MEDALLIONS GRAND VENEUR

Yield: 2 Servings   **Method:** Sautéing

Venison medallions, 3 oz. (90 g) each	4	4
Salt and pepper	TT	TT
Clarified butter	1 oz.	30 g
White wine	1 oz.	30 g
Poivrade sauce (pg 211)	6 oz.	180 g
Red currant jelly	2 tsp.	10 ml
Heavy cream	1 oz.	30 g

1. Season the medallions with salt and pepper and sauté in the clarified butter to the desired doneness. Remove and reserve.

2. Degrease the pan and deglaze with the white wine.

3. Add the poivrade sauce and bring to a simmer. Stir in the currant jelly, add the cream and adjust the seasonings.

4. Return the medallions to the sauce to reheat. Serve 2 medallions per person with a portion of the sauce.

◆◆◆

RECIPE 18.6
VENISON AND BLACK BEAN CHILI

Yield: 4 qt. (4 lt)   **Method:** Braising

Dried black beans	1 lb.	450 g
Water	2 qt.	2 lt
Peanut oil	3 oz.	90 g
Venison round, trimmed, medium dice	3 lb.	1.3 kg
Garlic cloves, minced	6	6
Onion, small dice	1 lb. 8 oz.	680 g
Jalapeños, seeded and chopped fine	3	3
Masa harina (corn flour)	2 oz.	60 g
Chilli powder	1 oz.	30 g
Cayenne pepper	1 tsp.	5 ml
Cumin, ground	3 Tbsp.	45 ml
Peeled tomatoes, canned	1 lb. 8 oz.	680 g
Veal stock	1 qt.	1 lt
Salt and pepper	TT	TT
Tabasco sauce	TT	TT

1. Soak the beans in water overnight. Drain and simmer in 2 quarts (2 lt) of water until tender, approximately 30–40 minutes.

2. Sauté the venison in the oil until brown. Remove and reserve.

3. Sauté the garlic, onions and jalapeño in the same pan until tender. Add the masa harina, chilli powder, cayenne and cumin. Cook 5 minutes.

4. Add the tomatoes, stock and reserved meat. Cover and braise on the stove top or in a 325°F (160°C) oven for 30–40 minutes.

5. Add the beans and cook an additional 15 minutes. Season to taste with salt, pepper and Tabasco sauce. Thin with additional stock if necessary.

♦♦♦

RECIPE 18.7
RABBIT RACK AND LOIN

STANFORD COURT HOTEL, San Francisco, CA
Chef Ercolino Crugnale

Yield: 4 Servings		Method: Sautéing
Rabbits	2	2
Pearl onions	12	12
Chicken or rabbit stock	10 oz.	300 g
Salt and pepper	TT	TT
Olive oil	1 oz.	30 g
Hazelnuts, skinned, cut in half	4 oz.	120 g
White wine	4 oz.	120 g
Pomegranate seeds	2 oz.	60 g
Turnip purée (recipe follows)	8 oz.	250 g
Taro root chips	4	4
Frisee	2 oz.	60 g
Japanese pear, peeled, julienne	1/2	1/2
Basic vinaigrette dressing	1 oz.	30 g

1. Separate the rabbit legs, racks and loins. Remove the eye muscle from the loins. Split the racks into two by cutting them along the backbone and trimming the rib ends so they extend 1/2 inch (1.2 centimeters) past the eye muscle. Use the legs in another recipe.

2. Peel the onions. Simmer them in 6 ounces (180 grams) of stock until tender, reducing the stock to a glaze as they cook. If the onions are not tender when the liquid is gone add a little more stock and continue cooking until they are done. Remove from the heat and reserve.

3. Season the rabbit racks and boneless loins with salt and pepper and sauté in olive oil until well browned and medium rare, approximately 3 minutes. Remove from the pan and reserve.

4. Add the onions and hazelnuts to the pan and sauté briefly. Add the white wine and 4 ounces (120 grams) of stock and reduce by one-third. Adjust the seasonings and add the pomegranate seeds.

5. Spoon 2 ounces (60 grams) of turnip purée on each plate and top with a taro chip. Place one piece of rabbit loin and one piece of rack on each chip.

6. Combine the frisee, pear and vinaigrette. Season and place one-fourth of the salad on each of the plates. Spoon the sauce around the plate and serve.

TURNIP PURÉE

Yield: 8 oz. (250 g)

Russet potato, peeled, large dice	2 oz.	60 g
Turnip, peeled, large dice	6 oz.	180 g
Garlic, chopped	1/2 tsp.	2 ml
Whole butter	1 oz.	30 g
Heavy cream	1-1/2 oz.	45 g
Salt and pepper	TT	TT

1. Cook the potatoes and turnips separately in salted water until tender. Drain and purée in a food mill.

2. Combine the garlic, butter and cream and bring to a boil. Add to the potato and turnip mixture and season with salt and pepper.

♦♦♦

RECIPE 18.8

GRILLED LOIN OF RABBIT WITH SPINACH, FENNEL AND WHITE BEANS

GOTHAM BAR AND GRILL, NEW YORK, NY
Chef/Owner Alfred Portale

Yield: 6 Servings   **Method:** Grilling

Rabbit saddles	6	6
Bacon slices	6	6
Lemon, sliced thin	1	1
Shallots, minced	1 Tbsp.	15 ml
Fresh sage	1 bunch	1 bunch
Fresh rosemary	3 sprigs	3 sprigs
Fresh thyme	3 sprigs	3 sprigs
Garlic cloves, sliced thin	2	2
White peppercorns, cracked	1 Tbsp.	15 ml
Olive oil	as needed	as needed
Baby fennel, steamed until tender	12 heads	12 heads
Fresh spinach, steamed	1 lb.	450 g
White Beans (recipe follows)	as needed	as needed
Rabbit Sauce (recipe follows)	as needed	as needed

1. Bone the saddles, removing the two loins and tenderloins.
2. Tightly wrap each loin and tenderloin together with half of a slice of bacon.
3. Place the rolled loins and tenderloins in a shallow container. Sprinkle with the lemon, shallots, herbs, garlic and cracked pepper and drizzle with olive oil; cover and refrigerate for 6–8 hours.
4. Bring the rabbit to room temperature. Remove from the marinade and grill over a medium fire until golden, approximately 6–8 minutes.
5. Cut each loin into medallions and arrange on the plates. Serve with fennel, spinach, White Beans and Rabbit Sauce.

WHITE BEANS

Yield: 2 lb. (.9 kg)

Dried Great Northern beans, soaked	8 oz.	250 g
Sachet:		
Onion, small	1	1
Carrot, 3-in. (8-cm.) piece	1	1
Celery, 2-in. (5-cm.) piece	1	1
Fresh thyme	1 sprig	1 sprig
Fresh rosemary	1 sprig	1 sprig
Black peppercorns	1 tsp.	5 ml
Garlic clove, minced	1	1
Parsley, chopped	1 Tbsp.	15 ml
Fresh rosemary	TT	TT
Fresh thyme	TT	TT
Whole butter, softened	4 oz.	120 g
Salt and white pepper	TT	TT
Heavy cream	2 oz.	60 g

Continued

1. Place the beans and the sachet in a large pot and cover with cold water. Bring to a simmer and cook until tender, approximately 45 minutes.
2. Cream together the garlic, parsley, rosemary, thyme and butter. Season with salt and white pepper.
3. Remove the sachet from the cooked beans and pour off all but 3–4 tablespoons (45–60 milliliters) of the cooking liquid. Return to the heat and swirl in the herb butter and cream. Keep warm.

RABBIT SAUCE

Yield: 1 pt. (450 ml)

Shallots, chopped	1 oz.	30 g
White peppercorns	1 Tbsp.	15 ml
Clarified butter	2 tsp.	10 ml
White wine	4 oz.	120 g
Brown stock, made from chicken and rabbit bones	24 oz.	700 g
Salt and white pepper	TT	TT
Whole butter	3 Tbsp.	45 ml

1. Sauté the shallots and peppercorns in the clarified butter over low heat until browned.
2. Add the white wine and reduce by one third. Add the stock and reduce by one third.
3. Season with salt and white pepper. Monte au beurre just before service.

◆◆◆

RECIPE 18.9

BRAISED RABBIT WITH CAVATELLI PASTA

FETZER VINEYARDS, HOPLAND, CA
John Ash, Culinary Director

Yield: 4 Servings		**Method:** Braising
Rabbit, 4 lb. (1.8 kg), cut into quarters	1	1
Salt and pepper	TT	TT
Olive oil	2 oz.	60 g
Chantrelle or shiitake mushrooms, stemmed and sliced	8 oz.	250 g
Yellow onion, sliced	6 oz.	170 g
Garlic, slivered	3 Tbsp.	45 ml
Carrot, small dice	3 oz.	90 g
Celery, sliced thin	3 oz.	90 g
Sun-dried tomatoes, sliced	1 pt.	500 ml
Zinfandel wine	1 pt.	500 ml
Tomato concassé	1 pt.	500 ml
Fresh thyme	1 tsp.	5 ml
Fresh sage, minced	1 tsp.	5 ml
Rabbit or chicken stock	1 qt.	1 lt
Parsley, chopped fine	4 Tbsp.	60 ml
Fresh basil, chopped	4 Tbsp.	60 ml
Cavatelli, cooked	24 oz.	700 g

Fresh basil sprigs	as needed for garnish
Asiago, Parmesan or	
Dry Jack cheese, shaved	as needed for garnish

1. Season the rabbit pieces with salt and pepper.
2. In a large saucepan, heat the oil and quickly brown the rabbit. Remove and reserve.
3. Add the mushrooms, onion, garlic, carrots and celery and sauté until very lightly browned.
4. Return the rabbit to the pan and add the sun-dried tomatoes, wine, tomatoes, thyme, sage and stock. Cover and simmer until the rabbit is tender and begins to pull away from the bones, approximately 45–50 minutes.
5. Remove the rabbit, separate the meat from the bones, discard the bones, and cut the meat into bite-sized pieces.
6. Strain the sauce, reserving the vegetables, and return the sauce to the saucepan. Bring to a boil and cook over high heat for 8–10 minutes to reduce and thicken slightly.
7. Adjust the seasonings. Add the reserved meat and vegetables and heat. Stir in the basil and parsley just before serving.
8. Toss the hot pasta with the rabbit sauce. Garnish with basil sprigs and cheese.

◆◆◆

RECIPE 18.10

MUSTARD-ROASTED LOIN OF BOAR WITH PAN GRAVY

Yield: 10 6-oz. (180-g) Servings   **Method:** Roasting

Crust:		
Flour	3 Tbsp.	45 ml
Brown sugar	2 Tbsp.	30 ml
Dry mustard	2 tsp.	10 ml
Dried thyme	2 tsp.	10 ml
Sage, rubbed	1 tsp.	5 ml
White wine	1 oz.	30 g
White wine vinegar	1 oz.	30 g
Boar loin, boneless, 4–6 lb. (2–2.7 kg)	1	1
Garlic cloves, sliced	3	3
Salt and pepper	TT	TT
Flour	2 oz.	60 g
Veal or game stock	1-1/2 qt.	1-1/2 lt

1. Combine the crust ingredients to make a paste.
2. Puncture the loin with a paring knife in several places and press a slice of garlic into each hole. Season the loin with salt and pepper.
3. Coat the loin with an even layer of the crust mixture. Roast at 450°F (230°C) for 10 minutes. Reduce the temperature to 325°F (160°C) and roast until done, approximately 1 hour.
4. Remove the roast from the roasting pan. Degrease the pan, leaving about 2 ounces (60 grams) of fat. Stir in 2 ounces (60 grams) of flour and cook to make a blond roux. Add the stock to make a pan gravy. Strain the gravy through a chinois and adjust the seasonings.
5. Carve the boar and serve with the sauce.

♦♦♦

RECIPE 18.11

GRILLED BUFFALO STEAK

Yield: 1 Serving   **Method:** Grilling

Buffalo strip loin steak, 8 oz. (250 g)	1	1
Salt and pepper	TT	TT
Oil	1 Tbsp.	15 ml

1. Season the steak well with salt and pepper.
2. Brush with oil and grill to the desired degree of doneness.
3. Serve the steak with a full-flavored sauce such as a bordelaise (pg 210) or poivrade sauce (pg 211).

Nutritional values without sauce:

Calories	368	Protein	49 g
Calories from fat	44%	Vitamin A	n/a
Total fat	18 g	Vitamin C	n/a
Saturated fat	2.6 g	Sodium	120 mg
Cholesterol	144 mg		

♦♦♦

RECIPE 18.12

BRAISED PARTRIDGE WITH RED CABBAGE

Yield: 4 Servings   **Method:** Braising

Bacon, medium dice	8 oz.	250 g
Partridges, halved	2	2
Salt and pepper	TT	TT
Onion, chopped coarse	6 oz.	180 g
Red cabbage, chopped	1 lb.	450 g
Red wine	8 oz.	250 g
Red wine vinegar	2 oz.	60 g

1. Cook the bacon until crisp. Remove the bacon from the pan and reserve. Pour off all but 4 ounces (120 grams) of fat. Reserve the excess fat.
2. Season the partridge halves with salt and pepper and brown in the pan with the bacon fat. Remove the partridge from the pan.
3. Add the onion to the pan and sauté until tender, approximately 5 minutes.
4. Stir in the cabbage. Season with salt and pepper. Add the wine and vinegar and bring to a simmer.
5. Place the partridges on top of the cabbage. Brush with the reserved bacon fat.
6. Cover and braise at 300°F (150°C) until done, approximately 1 hour.
7. Serve half of a partridge per person with a portion of the cabbage.

◆◆◆

RECIPE 18.13
ROAST PHEASANT WITH COGNAC AND APPLES

Yield: 2 Servings   **Method:** Roasting

Pheasant	1	1
Salt and pepper	TT	TT
Fatback	as needed	as needed
Mirepoix	12 oz.	350 g
Tart apples	2	2
Whole butter	1 oz.	30 g
Cognac	3 oz.	90 g
Crème fraîche	4 oz.	120 g

1. Season the pheasant with salt and pepper. Bard the body with fatback.

2. Roast on a bed of mirepoix at 350°F (170°C) until done, approximately 1-1/2 hours.

3. Peel, core and slice each apple into eight pieces. Sauté the apples in butter just until tender.

4. When the pheasant is done, remove it from the pan and reserve in a warm place. Deglaze the pan with the cognac, add the crème fraîche and bring to a simmer. Strain the sauce and adjust the seasonings.

5. Serve one half pheasant per person, accompanied by the sliced apples and sauce.

◆◆◆

RECIPE 18.14
STUFFED BREAST OF PHEASANT

Yield: 4 Servings   **Method:** Roasting

Stuffing:		
Prunes, chopped fine	4 oz.	120 g
Apple, chopped fine	4 oz.	120 g
Dried apricots, chopped fine	1 oz.	30 g
Walnuts, chopped fine	2 oz.	60 g
Onion, chopped fine	2 oz.	60 g
Salt	1/4 tsp.	1 ml
Pepper	1/4 tsp.	1 ml
Fresh thyme	1/2 tsp.	3 ml
Pheasant breast, boneless	4	4
Bacon, thin slices	8	8
Ivory sauce (pg. 208)	8 oz.	250 g

1. Combine the stuffing ingredients and set aside.

2. Separate each pheasant breast into two pieces. Pound each to a thickness of 1/4 inch (6 millimeters).

3. Place a portion of the stuffing in the center of four of the pieces of breast meat. Place a second piece of breast meat over the stuffing. Wrap each parcel tightly with two slices of bacon and tie with butcher's twine.

4. Bake at 325°F (160°C) until done, approximately 45 minutes.

5. Remove the twine, carve each bundle into slices and serve with 2 ounces (60 milliliters) of ivory sauce.

✦✦✦

RECIPE 18.15
GRILLED QUAIL
WITH POTATO GALETTE, ARTICHOKE WEDGES
AND BALSAMIC RASPBERRIES

STANFORD COURT HOTEL, SAN FRANCISCO, CA
Chef Ercolino Crugnale

Yield: 6 Servings   **Method:** Grilling

Bobwhite quail	6	6
Salt and pepper	TT	TT
Asparagus tips, 2 in. (5 cm) long, peeled and blanched	18 pieces	18 pieces
Artichoke Wedges (recipe follows)	18 pieces	18 pieces
Roma tomatoes, concasse	3	3
Cipolline onions, peeled and glazed with chicken stock and whole butter	12	12
Pure olive oil	3 oz.	90 g
Chicken stock	6 oz.	180 g
Dry white wine	6 oz.	180 g
Shallots, minced	2 Tbsp.	30 ml
Fresh tarragon, chopped	2 Tbsp.	30 ml
Fresh parsley, chopped	2 Tbsp.	30 ml
Potato Galette (recipe follows)	6 pieces	6 pieces
Mixed greens such as butter lettuce, yellow frisee and radicchio, torn into 1-in. (2.5-cm) pieces	1-1/2 c.	375 ml
Basic vinaigrette dressing	4 Tbsp.	60 ml
Balsamic Raspberries (recipe follows)		
Extra virgin olive oil	3 oz.	90 g

1. Season the quail with salt and pepper and grill on both sides until cooked just under medium.
2. Sauté the asparagus, artichoke wedges, tomatoes and onions in the pure olive oil.
3. Deglaze the pan with chicken stock and white wine. Add the shallots, tarragon and parsley. Season with salt and pepper.
4. To serve, place a potato galette on each plate. Arrange the vegetables around the potato.
5. Dress the mixed greens with the basic vinaigrette dressing and place a small amount in the center of each plate. Place the quail on greens.
6. Place raspberries around the plate; drizzle with extra virgin olive oil.

POTATO GALETTE

Yield: 6 Galettes

Clarified butter	as needed	as needed
Idaho potatoes, peeled and sliced thin on a mandoline	3	3
Salt and pepper	TT	TT

1. For each galette, completely line the bottom of a buttered 8-inch (20-cen-timeter) pan with potato slices, arranging the slices in a circular, overlapping pattern.
2. Season with salt and pepper and sauté until golden brown on each side. Hold at room temperature.

ARTICHOKE WEDGES

Yield: 20 Pieces

Olive oil	4 oz.	120 g
Artichoke bottoms, turned and cleaned, cut in quarters	5	5
Garlic, minced	2 Tbsp.	30 ml
Fresh thyme, chopped	1 Tbsp.	15 ml
Chicken stock	1 pt.	500 ml
Lemon juice	2 oz.	60 g
White wine	4 oz.	120 g
Salt and white pepper	TT	TT

1. Over high heat, sauté the artichokes in the olive oil for 2 minutes.
2. Add the garlic, thyme and 4 ounces (120 grams) chicken stock; reduce au sec.
3. Add the lemon juice, white wine and seasonings; reduce au sec.
4. Add another 6 ounces (170 grams) chicken stock, reduce au sec.
5. Add the remaining chicken stock; reduce au sec. The artichokes should be glazed, crisp and tender.

BALSAMIC RASPBERRIES

Yield: 1 qt.

Raspberries, ripe but firm	1 qt.	1 lt
Balsamic vinegar	6 oz.	170 g
Pepper	1 tsp.	5 ml

1. Gently combine all ingredients.
2. Let the raspberries macerate for 15 minutes.
3. Strain off the vinegar and reserve.

CHAPTER 19
FISH AND SHELLFISH

After studying this chapter you will be able to:

+ understand the structure and composition of fish and shellfish
+ identify a variety of fish and shellfish
+ purchase fish and shellfish appropriate for your needs
+ store fish and shellfish properly
+ prepare fish and shellfish for cooking
+ apply various cooking methods to fish and shellfish

ish are aquatic vertebrates with fins for swimming and gills for breathing. Of the more than thirty thousand species known, most live in the seas and oceans; freshwater species are far less numerous. Shellfish are aquatic invertebrates with shells or carapaces. They are found in both fresh and salt water.

Always an important food source, fish and shellfish have become increasingly popular in recent years, due in part to demands from health-conscious consumers. Because of increased demand and improved preservation and transportation techniques, good-quality fish and shellfish, once found only along seacoasts and lakes, are now readily available to almost every food service operation.

Many fish and shellfish species are very expensive; all are highly perishable. Because their cooking times are generally shorter and their flavors more delicate than meat or poultry, special attention must be given to fish and shellfish to prevent spoilage and to produce high-quality finished products.

In this chapter you will learn how to identify a large assortment of fish and shellfish as well as how to properly purchase and store them, fabricate or prepare them for cooking and cook them by a variety of dry-heat and moist-heat cooking methods. This chapter presents many of the cooking methods applied to meats and poultry in the previous chapters. Review the corresponding procedures for meats and poultry and note the similarities and differences.

Structure and Muscle Composition

The fish and shellfish used in food service operations can be divided into three categories: fish, mollusks and crustaceans.

Fish (Fr. *poisson*) include both fresh- and saltwater varieties. They have fins and an internal skeleton of bone and cartilage. Based upon shape and skeletal structure, fish can be divided into two groups: round fish and flatfish. **Round fish** swim in a vertical position and have eyes on both sides of their heads. Their bodies may be truly round, oval or compressed. **Flatfish** have asymmetrical, compressed bodies, swim in a horizontal position and have both eyes on top of their heads. Flatfish are bottom dwellers; most are found in deep ocean waters around the world. The skin on top of their bodies is dark, to camouflage them from predators, and can change color according to their surroundings. Their scales are small and their dorsal and anal fins run the length of their bodies.

Mollusks (Fr. *mollusque*) are shellfish characterized by soft, unsegmented bodies with no internal skeleton. Most mollusks have hard outer shells. Single-shelled mollusks such as abalone are known as **univalves**. Those with two shells, such as clams, oysters and mussels, are known as **bivalves**. Squid and octopus, which are known as **cephalopods**, do not have a hard outer shell. Rather, they have a single thin internal shell called a *pen* or *cuttlebone*.

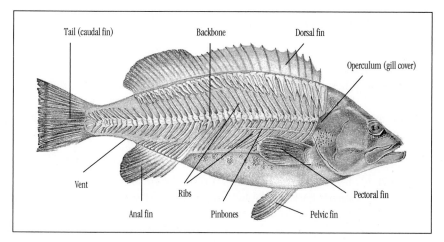

FIGURE 19.1 *Bone Structure of a Round Fish*

Crustaceans (Fr. *crustacé*) are also shellfish. They have a hard outer skeleton or shell and jointed appendages. Crustaceans include lobsters, crabs and shrimp.

The flesh of fish and shellfish consists primarily of water, protein, fat and minerals. Fish flesh is composed of short muscle fibers separated by delicate sheets of connective tissue. Fish, as well as most shellfish, are naturally tender, so the purpose of cooking is to firm proteins and enhance flavor. The absence of the oxygen-carrying protein myoglobin makes fish flesh very light or white in color. (The orange color of salmon and some trout comes from pigments found in their food.) Compared to meats, fish do not contain large amounts of intermuscular fat. But the amount of fat a fish does contain affects the way it responds to cooking. Fish containing a relatively large amount of fat, such as salmon and mackerel, are known as fatty or oily fish. Fish such as cod and haddock contain very little fat and are referred to as lean fish. Shellfish are also very lean.

SEAFOOD

Seafood means different things to different people. For some, the term applies just to shellfish or to shellfish and other small edible marine creatures. For others it is limited to saltwater shellfish or to saltwater shellfish and fish. For yet others, it refers to all fish and shellfish, both freshwater and saltwater. Because of the term's vagueness, it is not used here.

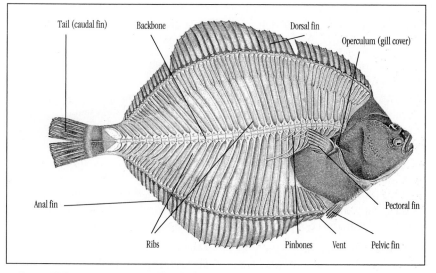

FIGURE 19.2 *Bone Structure of a Flatfish*

Identifying Fish and Shellfish

Identifying fish and shellfish properly can be difficult because of the vast number of similar-appearing fish and shellfish that are separate species within each family. Adding confusion are the various colloquial names given to the same fish or the same name given to different fish in different localities. Fish with an unappealing name may also be given a catchier name or the name of a similar but more popular item for marketing purposes. Moreover, some species are referred to by a foreign name, especially on menus.

The FDA publishes a list of approved market names for food fish in *The Fish List: FDA Guide to Acceptable Market Names for Food Fish Sold in Interstate Commerce* 1988, available from the U.S. Government Printing Office, Washington D.C. Deviations from this list are strongly discouraged but difficult to enforce. We attempt to list the most commonly used names for each item, whether they are zoologically accurate or not.

Fish

Round Fish

Bass (Fr. *bar*) commonly refers to a number of unrelated fish. The better-known freshwater bass varieties (largemouth, smallmouth, redeye and black) are actually members of the sunfish family. They are lean and delicate but, as game, not commercially available in the United States. The saltwater bass varieties (black sea bass and striped bass) are popular commercial items.

Black sea bass are sometimes referred to as rock sea bass. They have a lean, firm white flesh with a mild flavor and flaky texture. They usually weigh from 1-1/2 to 3 pounds (680–1360 grams) and are most prevalent in the Atlantic Ocean between New York and North Carolina. Black sea bass can be prepared by almost any cooking method and are often served whole in Chinese and Italian cuisines.

Black Sea Bass

Striped Bass

Aquafarming—*also known as aquaculture, is the business, science and practice of raising large quantities of fish and shellfish in tanks, ponds or ocean pens; used especially for catfish, trout, salmon, shrimp and other popular fish and shellfish.*

Striped bass, often erroneously referred to as rockfish, are ocean fish that depend on freshwater rivers to reproduce. True striped bass cannot be marketed because pollution and overfishing have damaged the supply. A hybrid of striped bass and either white bass or white perch is being **aquafarmed** for commercial use, however. It is this hybrid that food service operations receive as striped bass. Whole fish weigh from 1 to 5 pounds (450 grams to 2.2 kilograms). Striped bass have a rich, sweet flavor and firm texture. They can be steamed, baked, poached or broiled.

Catfish are scaleless freshwater fish common in southern lakes and rivers and now aquafarmed extensively. Aquafarm raising eliminates the "muddy" taste once associated with catfish and ensures a year-round supply. The flesh is pure white with a moderate fat content, a mild, sweet flavor and firm texture. Channel catfish are the most important commercially. They usually weigh from 1-1/2 to 5 pounds (650 grams to 2.2 kilograms). The smaller of these fish are known as **fiddlers**; they are often deep-fried and served whole. Catfish may be prepared by almost any cooking method, but are especially well suited to frying.

Catfish

The **cod** (Fr. *cabillaud*) family includes Atlantic and Pacific cod as well as pollock, haddock, whiting and hake. Cod have a mild, delicate flavor and lean, firm white flesh that flakes apart easily. Cod can be prepared by most

◆◆◆

SURIMI

Surimi is made from a highly processed fish paste colored, flavored and shaped to resemble shrimp, lobster, crab or other shellfish. Most surimi is based on Alaskan pollock, but some blends include varying amounts of real crab, shrimp or other items. Available chilled or frozen, surimi is already fully cooked and ready to add to salads, pasta, sauces or other dishes. Surami is very low in fat and relatively high in protein. Because of processing techniques, however, it has more sodium and fewer vitamins and minerals than the real fish or shellfish it replaces. Americans now consume over 100 million pounds of surimi each year and its popularity continues to grow. The FDA requires that all surimi products be labeled "imitation."

cooking methods, although grilling is not recommended because the flesh is too flaky.

Atlantic cod are the best-selling fish in America. They are available fresh, whole or drawn, or cut into fillets or steaks. They are also available frozen and are often used for pre-cooked or prebreaded sticks or portions. Smoked cod and salt cod are also available. While cod may reach 200 pounds (90 kilograms), most market cod weigh 10 pounds (4.4 kilograms) or less. **Scrod** is a marketing term for cod weighing less than 2-1/2 pounds (1.1 kilograms).

Atlantic Cod

Haddock, the second most commercially important fish, look like thin, small Atlantic cod and weigh about 2 to 5 pounds (900 grams to 2.3 kilograms). They have a stronger flavor and more delicate texture than Atlantic cod.

Pacific cod, also known as gray cod, are found in the northern Pacific Ocean and are not as abundant as their Atlantic cousins. Pacific cod are most often available frozen; they should be labeled "true cod" to distinguish them from rock cod and black cod, which are unrelated.

Pollock, also known as Boston bluefish or blue cod, are plentiful in the northern Atlantic and Pacific Oceans. Their flesh is gray-pink when raw, turning white when cooked. Pollock are often frozen at sea, then reprocessed into surimi. They can also be salted or smoked.

Pollock

Eels (Fr. *anguille*) are long, snakelike freshwater fish with dorsal and anal fins running the length of their bodies. (The conger eel is from a different family and has little culinary significance.) American and European eels are available live, whole, gutted or as fillets. Eels have a high fat content and firm flesh; they are sweet and mildly flavored. Their tough skin should be removed before cooking. Eels may be steamed, baked, fried or used in stews. Baby eels are a springtime delicacy, especially in Spain, where they are pan-fried in olive oil and garlic with hot red peppers. Smoked eels are also available.

Eel

The **grouper** family includes almost 400 varieties found in temperate waters worldwide. The more common Atlantic Ocean varieties are the yellowfin grouper, black grouper, red grouper and gag; the Pacific Ocean varieties are the sea bass (also known as jewfish and different from the black sea bass) and spotted cabrilla. Although some species can reach 800 pounds or more, most commercial varieties are sold in the 5 to 20-pound (2.2 to 8.8-kilogram) range. They have lean white flesh with a mild to sweet flavor and very firm texture. Their skin, which is tough and strongly flavored, is generally removed before cooking. Grouper fillets may be baked, deep-fried, broiled or grilled.

Grouper

Herring (Fr. *hareng*) are long, silvery-blue fish found in both the northern Atlantic and Pacific Oceans. Their strongly flavored flesh has a moderate to high fat content. Whole herring weigh up to 8 ounces (225 grams). Fresh herring may be butterflied or filleted and roasted, broiled or grilled. But because herring are very soft and tend to spoil quickly, they are rarely available fresh. More often, they are smoked (known as kippers) or cured in brine.

Sardines (Fr. *sardine*) are young, small herring with fatty, oily flesh that has a flaky texture. Sardines are usually sold canned, whole or as skinned and boned fillets, or fried or smoked and packed in oil or sauce. Sardines are used primarily for sandwiches and salads.

John Dory, also known as St. Peter's fish, have a distinctive round, black spot with a yellow halo on each side of the body. Their flesh is white, firm and finely flaked. They may be filleted and prepared like flounder and are a classic bouillabaisse ingredient.

John Dory

Mackerel

Mackerel (Fr. *maquereau*) of culinary importance include king and Spanish mackerel as well as tuna and wahoo, which are discussed separately below. The species known as Atlantic and Pacific mackerel are not generally used for food because of their small size and high fat content. Mackerel flesh has a high fat content, gray to pink coloring, a mild flavor and flaky texture. The flesh becomes firm and off-white when cooked. Mackerel are best broiled, grilled, smoked or baked.

Mahi-mahi is the more commonly used name for dolphin or dolphinfish; this Hawaiian name is used to distinguish them from the marine mammal of the same name. (Dolphins and porpoises are marine mammals.) Also known by their Spanish name, *dorado*, mahi-mahi are brilliantly colored fish found in tropical seas. Mahi-mahi weigh about 15 pounds (6.6 kilograms) and are sold whole or as fillets. Their flesh is off-white to pink, lean and firm with a sweet flavor. Dolphinfish can be broiled, grilled or baked. The meat may become dry when cooked, however, so sauce or marinade is recommended.

Mahi-Mahi

Monkfish are also known as angler fish, goosefish, rape and lotte. These extraordinarily ugly fish are rarely seen whole, for the large head is usually discarded before reaching market. Only the tail is edible; it is available in fillets, fresh or frozen. The scaleless skin must be removed. The flesh is lean, pearly white and very firm. Its texture and flavor have earned monkfish the nickname of "poor man's lobster." Monkfish absorb flavors easily and are baked, steamed, fried, grilled or broiled. They are also used for stews and soups.

Orange roughy are caught in the South Pacific off the coasts of New Zealand and Australia. They have bright orange skin and firm, pearly-white flesh with a low fat content and extremely bland flavor. Fresh-frozen fillets are widely available year round. Orange roughy are almost always marketed as skinless, boneless frozen fillets, averaging 6 to 8 ounces (140 to 225 grams) each. They can be broiled, steamed, grilled or prepared in the same manner as cod.

Red snapper is also known as the American or northern red snapper. Although there are many members of the snapper family, only one is the true red snapper. Red-skinned rockfish are often mislabeled as the more popular red snapper or Pacific snapper, a practice that is currently legal only in California. True red snapper has lean, pink flesh that becomes white when cooked; it is sweet-flavored and flaky. They are sold whole or as fillets with the skin left on for identification. Red snapper may reach 35 pounds, but most are marketed at only 4 to 6 pounds (1.8 to 2.7 kilograms) or as 1 to 3-pound (450 grams to 1.3 kilograms) fillets. Red snapper can be prepared using almost any cooking method. The head and bones are excellent for stock.

Red Snapper

Salmon (Fr. *saumon*) flourish in both the northern Atlantic and Pacific Oceans, returning to the freshwater rivers and streams of their birth to spawn. Salmon flesh gets its distinctive pink-red color from fat-soluble carotenoids found in the crustaceans on which they feed.

Atlantic salmon is the most important commercially, accounting for one quarter of all salmon produced worldwide. Extensive aquafarms in Norway, Canada and Scotland produce a steady supply of Atlantic salmon. For marketing purposes, the fish's point of origin is often added to the name (for example, Norwegian, Scottish or Shetland Atlantic salmon). Atlantic salmon have a rich pink color and moist flesh. Their average weight is from 4 to 12 pounds (1.8 to 5.4 kilograms). Wild Atlantic salmon are almost never available.

Atlantic Salmon

Chinook or **king salmon** from the Pacific are also highly desirable. They average from 5 to 30 pounds (2.2 to 13.2 kilograms) and have red-orange flesh with a high fat content and rich flavor. Like other salmon, their flesh separates into large flakes when cooked. Chinooks are often marketed by the name of the river from which they are harvested (for example, Columbia, Yukon or Copper Chinook salmon). They are distinguished by the black interior of their mouth.

Chinook or King Salmon

Coho or **silver** salmon have pinkish flesh and are available fresh or frozen, wild or from aquafarms. Wild coho average from 3 to 12 pounds (1.3 to 5.4 kilograms), while aquafarmed coho are much smaller, usually less than 1 pound (450 grams).

Other varieties, such as chum, sockeye, red, blueback and pink salmon, are usually canned but may be available fresh or frozen.

Salmon can be prepared by many cooking methods: broiling, grilling, poaching, steaming or baking. Frying is not recommended, however, because of their high fat content. Salmon fillets are often cured or smoked. **Gravlax** is salmon that has been cured for one to three days with salt, sugar and dill. **Lox** is salmon that is cured in a salted brine and then typically cold-smoked. **Nova** is used in the eastern U.S. to refer to a less-salty, cold-smoked salmon.

Mini Coho Salmon

Blacktip Shark

Sharks provide delicious eating, despite their less-than-appealing appearance and vicious reputation. Mako and blue sharks are the most desirable, with mako often being sold as swordfish. Sand shark, sharpnose, blacktip, angel and thresher are also available commercially. Most sharks have lean flesh with a mild flavor and firm texture. The flesh is white with tinges of pink or red when raw, turning off-white when cooked. Makos weigh from 30 to 250 pounds (13.5 to 112.5 kilograms); other species may reach as much as 1000 pounds (450 kilograms). All sharks have cartilaginous skeletons and no bones; therefore, they are not actually fish, but rather marine invertebrates. Sharks are usually cut into loins or wheels, then into steaks or cubes. They can be broiled, grilled, baked or fried. An ammonia smell indicates that the shark was not properly treated when caught. Do not buy or eat it.

Swordfish take their name from the long, swordlike bill extending from their upper jaw. These popular fish average about 250 pounds (112.5 kilograms). Their flesh is lean and sweet with a very firm, meatlike texture; it may be gray, pink or off-white when raw, becoming white when cooked. Swordfish are most often available cut into wheels or portioned into steaks perfect for grilling or broiling.

Swordfish Wheel

Tilapia is the name given to several species of freshwater, aquafarm-raised fish bred worldwide. They grow quickly in warm water, reaching about 3 pounds (1.3 kilograms); they are available whole or filleted, fresh or frozen. The flesh is similar to catfish—lean, white and sweet, with a firm texture. Tilapia are sometimes marketed as cherry snapper or sunshine snapper, even though they are not members of the snapper family.

Tilapia

Trout (Fr. *truite*) are members of the salmon family. Most of the freshwater trout commercially available are aquafarm-raised rainbow trout, although brown trout and brook trout are also being aquafarmed. Some trout species spend part of their lives at sea, returning to fresh water to spawn. On the West Coast, these are called salmon trout or steelhead. Trout have a low to moderate fat content, a flaky texture and a delicate flavor that can be easily overwhelmed by strong sauces. The flesh may be white, orange or pink. Trout are usually marketed at 8 to 10 ounces (225 to 280 grams) each, just right for an individual portion. Lake trout, sometimes known as char, are not aquafarmed and have little commercial value because of their extremely high fat content. Trout can be baked, panfried, smoked or steamed.

Red Mountain Trout

Rainbow Trout

Tuna (Fr. *thon*) varieties include the bluefin, yellowfin, bonito, bigeye and blackfin. Ahi is the popular market name for either yellowfin or bigeye tuna. All are members of the mackerel family and are found in tropical and subtropical waters around the world. Tuna are large fish, weighing up to several hundred pounds each. Bluefin, the finest and most desirable for sashimi, are becoming very scarce because of overfishing. Regular canned tuna is usually prepared from yellowfin or skipjack; canned white tuna is prepared from albacore, also known as longfin tuna. Pacific tuna that is frozen at sea to preserve its freshness is referred to as clipper fish. Any of these species may be found fresh or frozen, however. Tuna is usually cut into four boneless loins for market. The loins are then cut into steaks, cubes or chunks. The flesh has a low to moderate fat content (a higher fat content is preferred for sashimi) and a deep red color. The dark, reddish-brown muscle that runs along the lateral line is very fatty and can be removed. Tuna flesh turns light gray when cooked and is very firm, with a mild flavor. Tuna work well for grilling or broiling and may be marinated or brushed with seasoned oil during cooking. Tuna are often prepared medium rare to prevent dryness.

Yellowfin Tuna

Wahoo, also known as ono, are found throughout tropical and subtropical waters, but are particularly associated with Hawaii (*ono* even means "good to eat" in Hawaiian). They are actually a type of mackerel and are cooked like any other mackerel.

Wahoo

Whitefish species inhabit the freshwater lakes and streams of North America. Lake whitefish, the most important commercially, are related to salmon. They are marketed at up to 7 pounds (3.2 kilograms) and are available whole or filleted. The flesh is firm and white, with a moderate amount of fat and a sweet flavor. Whitefish may be baked, broiled, grilled or smoked and are often used in processed fish products.

Whitefish

♦♦♦
TRASH FISH

Ocean pout are considered a "trash fish," or fish that fishermen throw away because there is little or no consumer demand and therefore no market value.

Long ago, lobster were considered trash and good for nothing but chicken feed. More recently, monkfish was a trash fish in the U.S., and now we can't get enough. Obscure species are often trash fish until someone somewhere tastes them and realizes that they offer some incredible flavors and textures.

Searobins, dogfish, skate, and whiting are still considered trash fish in America, though they are gradually becoming more popular and will someday be readily available at fish markets.

from THE GREAT AMERICAN SEAFOOD COOKBOOK
by SUSAN HERRMANN LOOMIS

Flatfish

Flounder (Fr. *flet*) have lean, firm flesh that is pearly or pinkish-white with a sweet, mild flavor. Although they are easily boned, most are deheaded and gutted at sea and sold as fresh or frozen fillets. These fillets are very thin and can dry out or spoil easily, so extra care should be taken in handling, preparing and storing them. Recipes that preserve moisture work best with flounder; poaching, steaming or frying are recommended. Many types of flounder are marketed as sole, perhaps in an attempt to cash in on the popularity of true sole. The FDA permits this practice.

English sole are actually flounder caught off the West Coast of the United States. They are usually marketed simply as "fillet of sole." They are a plentiful species of fair to average quality.

Petrale sole, another West Coast flounder, are generally considered the finest of the domestic "soles." They are most often available as fillets, which tend to be thicker and firmer than other sole fillets.

English Sole

Petrale Sole

TABLE 19.1 FLOUNDER (ALSO KNOWN AS SOLE)

Atlantic Ocean	Pacific Ocean
blackback/winter flounder/lemon sole	arrowtooth
fluke/summer flounder	petrale sole
starry flounder	rex sole
yellowtail	English sole
windowpane flounder	rock sole
gray sole/witch flounder	sand sole
	yellowfin sole
	domestic Dover sole/Pacific flounder
	butter sole

Lemon Sole

Domestic Dover sole are also Pacific flounder. They are not as delicate or flavorful as other species of sole or flounder. Moreover, they are often afflicted with a parasite that causes the meat to have a slimy, gelatinous texture. Domestic Dover sole are not recommended if other sole or flounder are available.

Lemon sole are the most abundant and popular East Coast flounder. They are also known as blackback or winter flounder (during the winter they migrate close to shore from the deeper, colder waters). They average 2 pounds (900 grams) in weight.

Alaskan Halibut

Halibut are among the largest flatfish; they often weigh up to 300 pounds (135 kilograms). The FDA recognizes only two halibut species: Atlantic (eastern) and Pacific (northern, Alaskan, western) halibut. Both have lean, firm flesh that is snow-white with a sweet, mild flavor. California halibut, which are actually flounder, are similar in taste and texture but average only 12 pounds (5.4 kilograms) each. Halibut may be cut into boneless steaks or skewered on brochettes. The flesh, which dries out easily, can be poached, baked, grilled or broiled and is good with a variety of sauces.

Sole (Fr. *sole*) are probably the most flavorful and finely textured flatfish. Indeed, because of the connotations of quality associated with the name, "sole" is widely used for many species that are not members of the sole (*Soleidae*) family. Even though the FDA allows many species of flatfish to be called "sole" for marketing purposes, no true sole is commercially harvested in American waters. Any flatfish harvested in American waters and marketed as sole is actually flounder.

True Dover Sole

True **Dover sole**, a staple of classic cuisine, are a lean fish with pearly-white flesh and a delicate flavor that can stand up to a variety of sauces and seasonings. They are a member of the *Soleidae* family and come only from the waters off the coasts of England, Africa and Europe. They are imported into this country as fresh whole fish or fresh or frozen fillets.

Turbot are a Pacific flatfish of no great culinary distinction. In Europe, however, the species known as turbot (Fr. *turbot*) are large diamond-shaped fish highly prized for their delicate flavor and firm, white flesh. They are also marketed as brill.

Turbot

Mollusks

Univalves

Univalves are mollusks with a single shell in which the soft-bodied animal resides. They are actually marine snails with a single foot, used to attach the creature to fixed objects such as rocks.

Abalone have brownish-gray, ear-shaped shells. They are harvested in California, but California law does not permit canning abalone or shipping it out of state. Some frozen abalone is available from Mexico; canned abalone is imported from Japan. Abalone are lean with a sweet, delicate flavor similar to that of clams. They are too tough to eat unless tenderized with a mallet or rolling pin. They may then be eaten raw or prepared seviche-style. Great care must be taken when grilling or sautéing abalone as the meat becomes very tough when overcooked.

Conch are found in warm waters off the Florida Keys and in the Caribbean. The beautiful peachy-pink shell of the queen conch is prized by beachcombers. Conch meat is lean, smooth and very firm with a sweet-smoky flavor and chewy texture. It can be sliced and pounded to tenderize it, eaten raw with lime juice, or slow-cooked whole.

Bivalves

Bivalves are mollusks with two bilateral shells attached by a central hinge.

Clams (Fr. *clovisses*) are harvested along both the East and West Coasts, with Atlantic clams being more significant commercially. Atlantic Coast clams include hard-shell, soft-shell and surf clams. Clams are available all year, either live in the shell or fresh-shucked (meat removed from the shell). Canned clams, whether minced, chopped or whole, are also available.

Atlantic hard-shell clams or **quahogs** have hard, blue-gray shells. Their chewy meat is not as sweet as other clam meat. Quahogs have different names, depending upon their size. **Littlenecks** are generally under 2 inches (5 centimeters) across the shell and usually are served on the half shell or steamed. They are the most expensive clams. **Cherrystones** are generally under 3 inches (7.5 centimeters) across the shell and are sometimes eaten raw but are more often cooked. **Topnecks** are usually cooked and are often served as stuffed clams. **Chowders**, the largest quahogs, are always eaten cooked, especially minced for chowder or soup.

Soft-shell clams, also known as Ipswich, steamer and long-necked clams, have thin, brittle shells that do not completely close because of the clam's protruding black-tipped siphon. Their meat is tender and sweet. They are sometimes fried but are more often served steamed.

Surf clams are deep-water clams that reach sizes of 8 inches (20 centimeters) across. They are most often cut into strips for frying or are minced, chopped, processed and canned.

Pacific clams are generally too tough to eat raw. The most common is the **Manila clam**, which was introduced along the Pacific coast during the 1930s. Resembling a quahog with a ridged shell, it can be served steamed or on the half shell. **Geoducks** are the largest Pacific clam, sometimes weighing up to 10 pounds (4.5 kilograms) each. They look like huge soft-shell clams with a large, protruding siphon. Their tender, rich bodies and briny flavor are popular in Asian cuisines.

◆◆◆
SNAILS

Although snails (more politely known by their French name, *escargots*) are univalve land animals, they share many characteristics with their marine cousins. They can be poached in court bouillon or removed from their shells and boiled or baked briefly with a seasoned butter or sauce. They should be firm but tender; overcooking makes snails tough and chewy. The most popular varieties are the large white Burgundy snail and the small garden variety called *petit gris*. Fresh snails are available from snail ranches through speciality suppliers. The great majority of snails, however, are purchased canned; most canned snails are produced in France or Taiwan.

Littlenecks

Cherrystones

Topnecks

Soft-shell Clams

Manila Clams

Cockles

Greenshell Mussels

Cockles are small bivalves, about 1 inch (2.5 centimeters) long, with ridged shells. They are more popular in Europe than the United States and are sometimes used in dishes such as paella and fish soups or stews.

Mussels (Fr. *moule*) are found in waters worldwide. They are excellent steamed in wine or seasoned broth and can be fried or used in soups or pasta dishes.

Blue mussels are the most common edible mussel. They are found in the wild along the Atlantic Coast and are aquafarmed on both coasts. Their meat is plump and sweet with a firm, muscular texture. The orangish-yellow meat of cultivated mussels tends to be much larger than that of wild mussels and therefore worth the added cost. Blue mussels are sold live in the shell and average from 10 to 20 per pound. Although available all year, the best-quality blue mussels are harvested during the winter months.

Greenshell (or greenlip) **mussels** from New Zealand and Thailand are much larger than blue mussels, averaging 8–12 mussels per pound. Their shells are paler gray, with a distinctive bright-green edge.

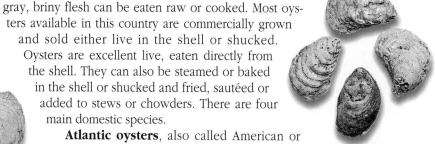

Blue Mussels

Oysters (Fr. *huître*) have a rough gray shell; their soft, gray, briny flesh can be eaten raw or cooked. Most oysters available in this country are commercially grown and sold either live in the shell or shucked. Oysters are excellent live, eaten directly from the shell. They can also be steamed or baked in the shell or shucked and fried, sautéed or added to stews or chowders. There are four main domestic species.

Atlantic oysters, also called American or Eastern oysters, have darker, flatter shells than other oysters.

Blue Point Oysters

Gulf Oysters

European flat oysters are often incorrectly called Belon (true Belon oysters live only in the Belon river of France); they are very round and flat and look like giant brownish-green Olympias.

Olympias are the only oysters native to the Pacific Coast; they are tiny (about the size of a 50-cent coin).

European Flat Oysters

Olympias

Pacific oysters, also called Japanese oysters, are aquafarmed along the Pacific Coast; they have curly, thick striated shells and silvery-gray to gold to almost-white meat.

Although it may seem like there are hundreds of oyster species on the market, there are only two that are commercially significant: the Atlantic oyster and the Pacific oyster. These two species yield dozens of different varieties, however, depending on their origin. For example, Atlantic oysters may be referred to as bluepoints, Chesapeake Bay, Florida Gulf, Long Island and so on, while Pacific oysters include Penn Cove Select, Westcott Bay, Hamma-hamma, Kumamoto and Portuguese, among others. An oyster's flavor reflects the minerals, nutrients and salts in its water and mud bed, so a Bristol from Maine and an Apalachicola from Florida will taste very different, even though they are the same Atlantic species.

Hamma-hamma Oysters

Scallops contain an edible white adductor muscle that holds together the fan-shaped shells. Because they die quickly, they are almost always shucked and cleaned on-board ship. The sea scallop and the bay scallop, both cold-water varieties, and the calico scallop, a warm-water variety, are the most important commercially. Sea scallops are the largest, with an average count of 20–30 per pound. Larger sea scallops are also available. Bay scallops average 70–90 per pound; calico scallops average 70–110 per pound. Fresh or frozen shucked, cleaned scallops are the most common market form, but live scallops in the shell and shucked scallops with roe attached (very popular in Europe) are also available. Scallops are sweet, with a tender texture. Raw scallops should be a translucent ivory color, nonsymmetrically round and should feel springy. They can be steamed, broiled, grilled, fried, sautéed or baked. When overcooked, however, scallops quickly become chewy and dry. Only extremely fresh scallops should be eaten raw.

Sea Scallops

Cephalopods

Cephalopods are marine mollusks with distinct heads, well-developed eyes, a number of arms that attach to the head near the mouth and a saclike fin-bearing mantle. They do not have an outer shell; instead, there is a thin internal shell called a *pen* or *cuttlebone*.

Octopus is generally quite tough and requires mechanical tenderization or long, moist-heat cooking to make it palatable. Most octopuses are imported from Portugal, though fresh ones are available on the East Coast during the winter. Octopus is sold by the pound, fresh or frozen, usually whole. Octopus skin is gray when raw, turning purple when cooked. The interior flesh is white, lean, firm and flavorful.

Squid, known by their Italian name, *calamari*, are becoming increasingly popular in this country. Similar to octopuses but much smaller, they are harvested along both American coasts and elsewhere around the world (the finest are the East Coast loligo or winter squid). They range in size from an average of 8–10 per pound to the giant South American squid that is sold as tenderized steaks. The squid's tentacles, mantle (body tube) and fins are edible. Squid meat is white to ivory in color, turning darker with age. It is moderately lean, slightly sweet, firm and tender, but it toughens quickly if overcooked. Squid are available either fresh, or frozen and packed in blocks.

Squid

Crustaceans

Crustaceans are found in both fresh and salt water. They have a hard outer shell and jointed appendages, and they breathe through gills.

Crayfish (Fr. *écrevisse*), generally called *crayfish* in the North and *crawfish* or *crawdad* in the South, are freshwater creatures that look like miniature lobsters. They are harvested from the wild or aquafarmed in Louisiana and the Pacific Northwest. They are from 3-1/2 to 7 inches (8 to 17.5 centimeters) in length when marketed and may be purchased live or precooked and frozen. The lean meat, found mostly in the tail, is sweet and tender. Crayfish can be boiled whole and served hot or cold. The tail meat can be deep-fried or used in soups, bisque or sauces. Crayfish are a staple of Cajun cuisine, often used in gumbo, étouffée and jambalaya. Whole crayfish become brilliant red when cooked and may be used as a garnish.

Crabs (Fr. *crabe*) are found along the North American coasts in great numbers and are shipped throughout the world in fresh, frozen and canned forms. Crab meat varies in flavor and texture and can be used in a range of prepared dishes, from chowders to curries to casseroles. Crabs purchased live should last up to five days; dead crabs should not be used.

King crabs are very large crabs (usually around 10 pounds or 4.4 kilograms) caught in the very cold waters of the North Pacific. Their meat is very sweet and snow-white. King crabs are always sold frozen, usually in the shell. In-shell forms include sections or clusters, legs and claws or split legs. The meat is also available in "fancy" packs of whole leg and body meat, or shredded and minced pieces.

Dungeness crabs are found along the West Coast. They weigh 1-1/2 to 4 pounds (680 grams to 1.8 kilograms), and have delicate, sweet meat. They are sold live, precooked and frozen, or as picked meat, usually in 5-pound (2.2-kilogram) vacuum-packed cans.

Dungeness Crab

Blue crabs are found along the entire eastern seaboard and account for approximately 50% of the total weight of all crab species harvested in the United States. Their meat is rich and sweet. Blue crabs are available as hard-shell or soft-shell. Hard-shell crabs are sold live, precooked and frozen, or as picked meat. Soft-shell crabs are those harvested within six hours after molting and are available live (generally only from May 15 to September 15) or frozen. They are often steamed and served whole. Soft-shells can be sautéed, fried, broiled or added to soups or stews. Blue crabs are sold by size, with an average diameter of 4–7 inches (10–18 centimeters).

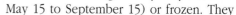

Blue Crab

Soft-Shell Crabs

Snow or **spider crabs** are an abundant species, most often used as a substitute for the scarcer and more expensive king crab. They are harvested from Alaskan waters and along the eastern coast of Canada. Snow crab is sold precooked, usually frozen. The meat can be used in soups, salads, omelettes or other prepared dishes. Legs are often served cold as an appetizer.

Stone crabs are generally available only as cooked claws, either fresh or frozen (the claws cannot be frozen raw because the meat sticks to the shell). In stone-crab fishery only the claw is harvested. After the claw is removed, the crab is returned to the water, where in about 18 months it regenerates a new claw. Claws average 2-1/2 to 5-1/2 ounces (75 to 155 grams) each. The meat is firm, with a sweet taste similar to lobster. Cracked claws are served hot or cold, usually with cocktail sauce, lemon butter or other accompaniments.

Lobsters have brown to blue-black outer shells and firm, white meat with a rich, sweet flavor. Lobster shells turn red when cooked. They are usually poached, steamed, simmered, baked or grilled, and can be served hot or cold. Picked meat can be used in prepared dishes, soups or sautés. Lobsters must be kept alive until just before cooking. Dead lobsters should not be eaten. The Maine, also known as American or clawed lobster, and the spiny lobster are the most commonly marketed species.

Maine lobsters have edible meat in both their tails and claws; they are considered superior in flavor to all other lobsters. They come from the cold

Maine Lobster

waters along the Northeast Coast and are most often sold live. Maine lobsters may be purchased by weight (i.e., 1-1/4 pound [525 grams], 1-1/2 pound [650 grams] or 2 pounds [900 grams] each), or as chix (i.e., less than one pound [450 grams]). Maine lobsters may also be purchased as culls (lobsters with only one claw) or bullets (lobsters with no claws). They are available frozen or as cooked, picked meat.

Figure 19.3 shows a cross section of a Maine lobster and identifies the stomach, tomalley (the olive-green liver) and coral (the roe). The stomach is not eaten; the tomalley and coral are very flavorful and are often used in the preparation of sauces and other items.

Spiny lobsters have very small claws and are valuable only for their meaty tails, which are notched with short spines. Nearly all spiny lobsters marketed in this country are sold as frozen tails, often identified as rock lobster. Harvested in many parts of the world, those found off Florida, Brazil and in the Caribbean are marketed as warm-water tails; those found off South Africa, Australia and New Zealand are called cold-water tails. Cold-water spiny tails are considered superior to their warm-water cousins.

Slipper lobster, lobsterette and **squat lobster** are all clawless species found in tropical, subtropical and temperate waters worldwide. Although popular in some countries, their flavor is inferior to both Maine and spiny lobsters. **Langoustine** are small North Atlantic lobsters.

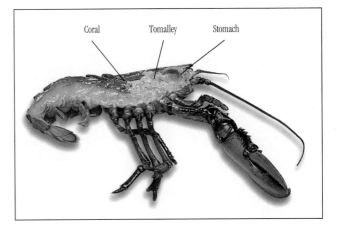

Coral   Tomalley   Stomach

FIGURE 19.3

Shrimp (Fr. *crevette*) are found worldwide and are widely popular. Gulf whites, pinks, browns and black tigers are just a few of the dozens of shrimp varieties used in food service operations. Although fresh, head-on shrimp are available, the most common form is raw, head-off (also called green headless) shrimp with the shell on. Most shrimp are deheaded and frozen at sea to preserve freshness. Shrimp are available in many forms: raw, peeled and deveined; cooked, peeled and deveined; individually quick frozen; as well as in a variety of processed, breaded or canned products. Shrimp are graded by size, which can range from 400 per pound (titi) to 8 per pound (extra-colossal), and are sold in counts per pound. For example, shrimp marketed as "21–26 count" means that there is an average of 21 to 26 shrimp per pound; shrimp marketed as "U-10" means that there are under 10 shrimp per pound.

Shrimp

Green Headless Shrimp

Prawn is often used interchangeably with the word *shrimp* in English-speaking countries. Although it is perhaps more accurate to refer to freshwater species as prawns and marine species as shrimp, in commercial practice prawn refers to any large shrimp. Equally confusing, *scampi* is the Italian name for the Dublin Bay prawn (which is actually a species of miniature lobster), but in this country *scampi* refers to shrimp sautéed in garlic butter.

NUTRITION

Fish and shellfish are low in calories, fat and sodium, and are high in vitamins A, B and D and protein. Fish and shellfish are also high in minerals, especially calcium (particularly in canned fish with edible bones), phosphorus, potassium and iron (especially mollusks). Fish are high in a group of polyunsaturated fatty acids called omega-3, which may help combat high blood cholesterol levels and aid in preventing some heart disease. Shellfish are not as high in cho-

TABLE 19.2   NUTRITIONAL VALUES OF FISH AND SHELLFISH

Per 1 oz. (28 g) Raw	Kcal	Protein (g)	Total Fat (g)	Saturated Fat (g)	Cholesterol (mg)	Sodium (mg)
Abalone	30	4.8	0.2	<0.1	24	85
Clam, mixed species	21	3.6	0.3	<0.1	10	16
Cod, Atlantic	23	5.0	0.2	<0.1	12	15
Crab, Alaska king	24	5.2	0.2	mq	12	237
Flatfish	26	5.3	0.3	0.1	14	23
Lobster	26	5.3	0.3	mq	27	mq
Oyster, eastern	20	20	0.7	0.2	16	32
Salmon	40	5.6	1.8	0.3	16	113
Sea bass	27	5.2	0.6	0.1	12	19
Shrimp, mixed species	30	5.7	0.5	0.1	43	42
Surimi	28	4.3	0.3	mq	9	41
Tuna, yellowfin	31	6.6	0.3	0.1	13	10
Whitefish	38	5.4	1.7	0.3	17	14

The Corinne T. Netzer Encyclopedia of Food Values 1992
mq = measurable quantity, but data is unavailable

lesterol as was once thought. Crustaceans are higher in cholesterol than mollusks, but both have considerably lower levels than red meat or eggs.

The cooking methods used for fish and shellfish also contribute to their healthfulness. The most commonly used cooking methods—broiling, grilling, poaching and steaming—add little or no fat.

INSPECTION AND GRADING OF FISH AND SHELLFISH

Inspection

Unlike mandatory meat and poultry inspections, fish and shellfish inspections are voluntary. They are performed in a fee-for-service program supervised by the United States Department of Commerce (USDC).

Type 1 inspection services cover plant, product and processing methods from the raw material to the final product. The "Packed Under Federal Inspection" (PUFI) mark or statement shown in Figure 19.4 can be used on product labels processed under Type 1 inspection services. It signifies that the product is safe and wholesome, properly labeled, has reasonably good flavor and odor, and was produced under inspection in an official establishment.

Type 2 inspection services are usually performed in a warehouse, processing plant or cold storage facility on specific product lots. See Figure 19.5. A lot inspection determines whether the product complies with purchase agreement criteria (usually defined in a spec sheet) such as condition, weight, labeling and packaging integrity.

Type 3 inspection services are for sanitation only. Fishing vessels or plants that meet the requirements are recognized as official establishments and are

FIGURE 19.4   *PUFI Mark and Statements*

included in the *USDC Approved List of Fish Establishments and Products*. The list is available to governmental and institutional purchasing agents as well as to retail and restaurant buyers.

Grading

Only fish processed under Type 1 inspection services are eligible for grading. Each type of fish has its own grading criteria, but because of the great variety of fish and shellfish, the USDC has been able to set grading criteria for only the most common types.

The grades assigned to fish are A, B or C. Grade A products are top quality and must have good flavor and odor and be practically free of physical blemishes or defects. The great majority of fresh and frozen fish and shellfish consumed in restaurants is Grade A. See Figure 19.6. Grade B indicates good quality; Grade C indicates fairly good quality. Grade B and C products are most often canned or processed.

PURCHASING AND STORING FISH AND SHELLFISH

Determining Freshness

Because fish and shellfish are highly perishable, an inspection stamp does not necessarily ensure top quality. A few hours at the wrong temperature or a couple of days in the refrigerator can turn high-quality fish or shellfish into garbage. It is important that you be able to determine for yourself the freshness and quality of the fish and shellfish you purchase or use. Freshness should be checked before purchasing and again just before cooking.

Freshness can be determined by:

1. *Smell*—By far the easiest way to determine freshness, fresh fish should have a slight sea smell or no odor at all. Any off-odors or ammonia odors are a sure sign of aged or improperly handled fish.

2. *Eyes*—The eyes should be clear and full. Sunken eyes mean the fish is drying out and is probably not fresh.

3. *Gills*—The gills should be intact and bright red. Brown gills are a sign of age.

4. *Texture*—Generally, the flesh of fresh fish should be firm. Mushy flesh or flesh that does not spring back when pressed with a finger is a sign of poor quality or age.

5. *Fins and scales*—Fins and scales should be moist and full without excessive drying on the outer edges. Dry fins or scales are a sign of age; damaged fins or scales may be a sign of mishandling.

6. *Appearance*—Fish cuts should be moist and glistening, without bruises or dark spots. Edges should not be brown or dry.

7. *Movement*—Shellfish should be purchased alive and should show movement. Lobsters and other crustaceans should be active. Clams, mussels and oysters that are partially opened should snap shut when tapped with a finger. (Exceptions are geoduck, razor and steamer clams whose siphons protrude, preventing the shell from closing completely.) Ones that do not close are dead and should not be used. Avoid mollusks with broken shells or heavy shells that might be filled with mud or sand.

FIGURE 19.5 *Product Inspection Stamps*

FIGURE 19.6 *Grade A Stamp*

Purchasing Fish and Shellfish

Fish are available from wholesalers in a variety of market forms:

+ **Whole** or **round**—as caught, intact.
+ **Drawn**—viscera (internal organs) is removed; most whole fish are purchased this way.
+ **Dressed**—viscera, gills, fins and scales are removed.
+ **Pan-dressed**—viscera and gills are removed; fish is scaled and fins and tail are trimmed. The head is usually removed, although small fish, such as trout, may be pan-dressed with the head still attached. Pan-dressed fish are then pan-fried.
+ **Butterflied**—a pan-dressed fish, boned and opened flat like a book. The two sides remain attached by the back or belly skin.

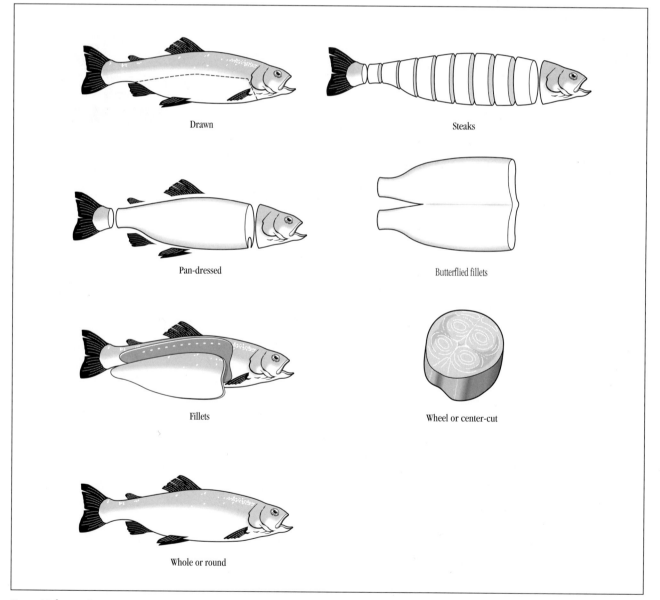

Drawn

Steaks

Pan-dressed

Butterflied fillets

Fillets

Wheel or center-cut

Whole or round

FIGURE 19.6   *Market Forms*

+ **Fillet**—the side of a fish removed intact, boneless or semi-boneless, with or without skin.
+ **Steak**—cross-section slice, with a small section of backbone attached; usually prepared from large round fish.
+ **Wheel** or **center-cut**—used for swordfish and sharks, which are cut into large boneless pieces from which steaks are then cut.

You should purchase fish in the market forms most practical for your operation. Although fish fabrication is a relatively simple chore requiring little specialized equipment, before you decide to cut your own fish you should consider

1. the food service operation's ability to utilize the bones and trim that cutting whole fish produces,
2. the employees' ability to fabricate fillets, steaks or portions as needed,
3. the storage facilities and
4. the product's intended use.

Most shellfish can be purchased live in the shell, shucked (the meat removed from the shell) or processed. Both live and shucked shellfish are usually purchased by counts (i.e., the number per volume). For example, standard live Eastern oysters are packed 200–250 (the count) per bushel (the unit of volume); standard Eastern oyster meats are packed 350 per gallon. Crustaceans are sometimes packed by size based on the number of pieces per pound; for example, crab legs or shrimp are often sold in counts per pound. Or, they are sold either by grades based on size (whole crabs) or by weight (lobsters).

Storing Fish and Shellfish

The most important concern when storing fish and shellfish is temperature. All fresh fish should be stored at temperatures between 30° and 34°F (-1 to 1°C). Fish stored in a refrigerator at 40°F (4°C) will have approximately half the shelf life of fish stored at 32°F (0°C).

Most fish are shipped on ice and should be stored on ice in the refrigerator as soon as possible after receipt. Whole fish should be layered directly in crushed or shaved ice in a perforated pan so that the melted ice water drains away. If crushed or shaved ice is not available, cubed ice may be used provided it is put in plastic bags and gently placed on top of the fish to prevent bruising and denting. Fabricated and portioned fish may be wrapped in moisture-proof packaging before icing to prevent the ice and water from damaging the exposed flesh. Fish stored on ice should be drained and re-iced daily.

Fresh scallops, fish fillets that are purchased in plastic trays, and oyster and clam meats should be set on or packed in ice. Do not let the scallops, fillets or meats come in direct contact with the ice.

Clams, mussels and oysters should be stored at 40°F (4°C), at high humidity and left in the boxes or net bags in which they were shipped. Under ideal conditions, shellfish can be kept alive for up to one week. Never store live shellfish in plastic bags and do not ice them.

If a saltwater tank is not available, live lobsters, crabs and other crustaceans should be kept in boxes with seaweed or damp newspaper to keep them moist. Most crustaceans circulate salt water over their gills; icing them or placing them in fresh water will kill them. Lobsters and crabs will live for several days under ideal conditions.

◆◆◆
HOW FRESH IS FROZEN FISH?

Fresh—the item is not and has never been frozen.

Chilled—now used by some in the industry to replace the more ambiguous "fresh"; indicates that the item was refrigerated, that is, held at 30 to 34°F (-1 to 1°C).

Flash-frozen—the item was quickly frozen on-board ship or at a processing plant within hours of being caught.

Fresh-frozen—the item was quick-frozen while still fresh but not as quickly as flash-frozen.

Frozen—the item was subjected to temperatures of 0°F (-18°C) or lower to preserve its inherent quality.

Glazed—a frozen product dipped in water; the ice forms a glaze that protects the item from freezer burn.

Fancy—code word for "previously frozen."

Like most frozen foods, frozen fish should be kept at temperatures of 0°F (-18°C) or colder. Colder temperatures greatly increase shelf life. Frozen fish should be thawed in the refrigerator; once thawed, they should be treated like fresh fish.

FABRICATING PROCEDURES

As discussed, fish and shellfish can be purchased in many forms. Here we demonstrate several procedures for cutting, cleaning and otherwise fabricating or preparing fish and shellfish for cooking and service.

PROCEDURE FOR SCALING FISH

This procedure is used to remove the scales from fish that will be cooked with the skin on.

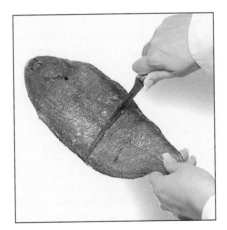

1. Place the fish on a work surface or in a large sink. Grip the fish by the tail and, working from the tail toward the head, scrape the scales off with a fish scaler or the back of a knife. Be careful not to damage the flesh by pushing too hard. Turn the fish over and remove the scales from the other side. Rinse the fish under cold water.

PROCEDURE FOR PAN-DRESSING FLATFISH

1. Scale the flatfish. Place the fish on a cutting board and remove the head by making a V-shaped cut around it with a chef's knife. Pull the head away and remove the viscera.

2. Rinse the fish under cold water, removing all traces of blood and viscera from the cavity.

3. Using a pair of kitchen shears, trim off the tail and all of the fins.

PROCEDURE FOR FILLETING ROUND FISH

Round fish produce two fillets, one from either side.

1. Using a chef's knife, cut down to the backbone just behind the gills. Do not remove the head.

2. Turn the knife toward the tail; using smooth strokes, cut from head to tail parallel to the backbone. The knife should bump against the backbone so that no flesh is wasted; you will feel the knife cutting through the small pin bones. Cut the fillet completely free from the bones. Repeat on the other side.

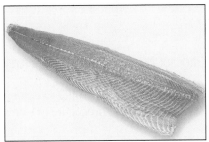

3. Trim the rib bones from the fillet with a flexible boning knife.

4. The finished fillet.

PROCEDURE FOR FILLETING FLATFISH

Flatfish produce four fillets: two large bilateral fillets from the top and two smaller bilateral fillets from the bottom. If the fish fillets are going to be cooked with the skin on, the fish should be scaled before cooking (it is easier to scale the fish before it is filleted). If the skin is going to be removed before cooking, it is not necessary to scale the fish.

1. With the dark side of the fish facing up, cut along the backbone from head to tail with the tip of a flexible boning knife.

2. Turn the knife and, using smooth strokes, cut between the flesh and the rib bones, keeping the flexible blade against the bone. Cut the fillet completely free from the fish. Remove the second fillet, following the same procedure.

3. Turn the fish over and remove the fillets from the bottom half of the fish, following the same procedure.

Procedure for Skinning Dover Sole

Dover sole is unique in that its skin can be pulled from the whole fish by following this procedure. The flesh of other small flatfish such as flounder, petrale sole and other types of domestic sole is more delicate; pulling the skin away from the whole fish could damage the flesh. These fish should be skinned after they are filleted.

1. Make a shallow cut in the flesh perpendicular to the length of the fish, just in front of the tail and with the knife angled toward the head of the fish. Using a clean towel, grip the skin and pull it toward the head of the fish. The skin should come off cleanly, in one piece, leaving the flesh intact.

Procedure for Skinning Fish Fillets

Here we use a salmon fillet to demonstrate the procedure for skinning fish fillets. Use the same procedure to skin all types of fish fillets.

1. Place the fillet on a cutting board with the skin side down. Starting at the tail, use a meat slicer or a chef's knife to cut between the flesh and skin. Angle the knife down toward the skin, grip the skin tightly with one hand and use a sawing motion to cut the skin cleanly away from the flesh.

Procedure for Pulling Pin Bones from a Salmon Fillet

Round fish fillets contain a row of intramuscular bones running the length of the fillet. Known as pin bones, they are usually cut out with a knife to produce boneless fillets. In the case of salmon, they can be removed with salmon tweezers or small needle-nose pliers.

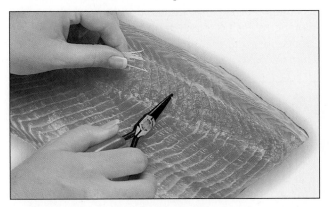

1. Place the fillet (either skinless or not) on the cutting board, skin side down. Starting at the front or head end of the fillet, use your fingertips to locate the bones and pull them out one by one with the pliers.

Procedure for Cutting Tranches

A **tranche** is a slice cut from fillets of large flat or round fish. Usually cut on an angle, tranches look large and increase plate coverage.

1. Place the fillet on the cutting board, skin side down. Using a slicer or chef's knife, cut slices of the desired weight. The tranche can be cut to the desired size by adjusting the angle of the knife. The greater the angle, the greater the surface area of the tranche.

Procedure for Cutting Steaks from Salmon and Similarly Sized Round Fish

Steaks are produced from salmon and similarly sized round fish by simply making crosscuts of the whole fish. First scale, gut and remove the fins from the fish. Then:

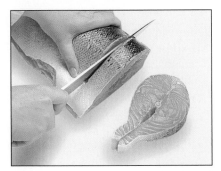

1. Using a chef's knife, cut through the fish, slicing steaks of the desired thickness. The steaks will contain some bones that are not necessarily removed.

PROCEDURE FOR PEELING AND DEVEINING SHRIMP

Peeling and deveining shrimp is a simple procedure done in most commercial kitchens. The tail portion of the shell is often left on the peeled shrimp to give it an attractive appearance or make it easier to eat. This procedure can be used on both cooked and uncooked shrimp.

1. Grip the shrimp's tail between your thumb and forefinger. Use your other thumb and forefinger to grip the legs and the edge of the shell.

2. Pull the legs and shell away from the flesh, leaving the tail and first joint of the shell in place if desired.

3. Place the shrimp on a cutting board and use a paring knife to make a shallow cut down the back of the shrimp, exposing the digestive tract or "vein."

4. Pull the vein out while rinsing the shrimp under cold water.

PROCEDURE FOR BUTTERFLYING SHRIMP

Butterflying raw shrimp improves their appearance and increases their surface area for even cooking. To butterfly shrimp, first peel them using the procedure outlined above, then:

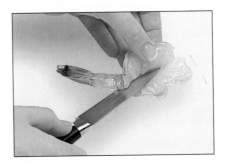

1. Instead of making a shallow cut to expose the vein, make a deeper cut that nearly slices the shrimp into two bilateral halves. Pull the vein out while rinsing the shrimp under cold water.

PROCEDURE FOR PREPARING LIVE LOBSTER FOR BROILING

A whole lobster can be cooked by plunging it into boiling water or court bouillon. If the lobster is to be broiled, it must be split lengthwise before cooking.

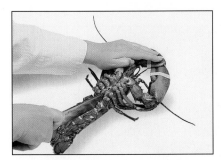

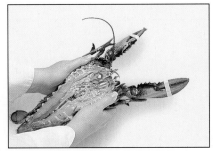

1. Place the live lobster on its back on a cutting board and pierce its head with the point of a chef's knife. Then, in one smooth stroke, bring the knife down and cut through the body and tail without splitting it completely in half.

2. Use your hands to crack the lobster's back so that it lies flat. Crack the claws with the back of a chef's knife.

3. Cut through the tail and curl each half of the tail to the side. Remove and discard the stomach. The tomalley (the olive-green liver) and, if present, the coral (the roe) may be removed and saved for a sauce or other preparation.

PROCEDURE FOR PREPARING LIVE LOBSTER FOR SAUTÉING

A whole lobster may also be cut into smaller pieces for sautéing or other preparations.

1. Using the point of a chef's knife, pierce the lobster's head.

2. Cut off the claws and arms.

3. Cut the tail into cross sections.

4. Split the head and thorax in half. The tomalley and coral (if present) may be removed and saved for further use. The head and legs may be added to the recipe for flavor, but there is very little meat in them and they are often discarded.

5. Crack the claws with a firm blow, using the back of a chef's knife.

PROCEDURE FOR REMOVING COOKED LOBSTER MEAT FROM THE SHELL

Many recipes call for cooked lobster meat. Cook the lobster by plunging it into a boiling court bouillon and simmering for 6–8 minutes per pound. Remove the lobster and allow it to cool until it can be easily handled. Then:

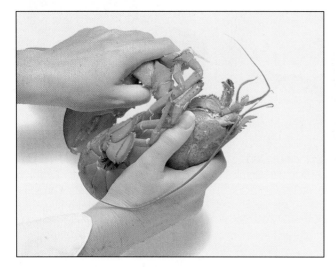

1. Pull the claws and large legs away from the body. Break the claw away from the leg. Split the legs with a chef's knife and remove the meat, using your fingers or a pick.

2. Carefully crack the claw with a mallet or the back of a chef's knife without damaging the meat. Pull out the claw meat in one piece.

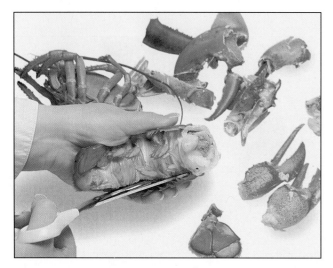

3. Pull the lobster's tail away from its body and use kitchen shears to trim away the soft membrane on the underside of the tail.

4. Pull the meat out of the shell in one piece.

PROCEDURE FOR OPENING CLAMS

Opening raw clams efficiently requires practice. Like all mollusks, clams should be cleaned under cold running water with a brush to remove all mud, silt and sand that may be stuck to their shells. A knife may be more easily inserted into a clam if the clam is washed and allowed to relax in the refrigerator at least an hour before it is opened.

1. Hold the clam firmly in a folded towel in the palm of your hand; the notch in the edge of the shell should be toward your thumb. With the fingers of the same hand, squeeze and pull the blade of the clam knife between the clamshells. Do not push on the knife handle with your other hand; you will not be able to control the knife if it slips and you can cut yourself.

2. Pull the knife between the shells until it cuts the muscle. Twist the knife to pry the shells apart. Slide the knife tip along the top shell and cut through the muscle. Twist the top shell, breaking it free at the hinge; discard it.

3. Use the knife tip to release the clam from the bottom shell.

PROCEDURE FOR OPENING OYSTERS

1. Clean the oyster by brushing it under running water.

2. Hold the cleaned oyster firmly in a folded towel in the palm of your hand. Insert the tip of an oyster knife in the hinge and use a twisting motion to pop the hinge apart. Do not use too much forward pressure on the knife; it can slip and you could stab yourself.

3. Slide the knife along the top of the shell to release the oyster from the shell. Discard the top shell.

4. Use the knife tip to release the oyster from the bottom shell.

PROCEDURE FOR CLEANING AND DEBEARDING MUSSELS

Mussels are not normally eaten raw. Before cooking, a clump of dark threads called the beard must be removed. Because this could kill the mussel, cleaning and debearding must be done as close to cooking time as possible.

1. Clean the mussel with a brush under cold running water to remove sand and grit.

2. Pull the beard away from the mussel with your fingers or a small pair of pliers.

APPLYING VARIOUS COOKING METHODS

Fish and shellfish can be prepared by the dry-heat cooking methods of broiling and grilling, roasting (baking), sautéing, pan-frying and deep-frying, as well as the moist-heat cooking methods of steaming, poaching and simmering. Other than deep-frying, which is discussed in Chapter 21, these cooking methods are discussed below.

Determining Doneness

Unlike most meats and poultry, nearly all fish and shellfish are inherently tender and should be cooked just until done. Indeed, overcooking is the most common mistake made when preparing fish and shellfish. The Canadian Department of Fisheries recommends that all fish be cooked 10 minutes for every inch (2.5 centimeters) of thickness, regardless of cooking method. Although this may be a good general policy, variables such as the type and form of fish and the exact cooking method used suggest that one or more of the following methods of determining doneness are more appropriate for professional food service operations.

1. *Translucent flesh becomes opaque*—The raw flesh of most fish and shellfish appears somewhat translucent. As the proteins coagulate during cooking, the flesh becomes opaque.
2. *Flesh becomes firm*—The flesh of most fish and shellfish firms as it cooks. Doneness can be tested by judging the resistance of the flesh when pressed with a finger. Raw or undercooked fish will be mushy and soft. As the fish cooks, the flesh offers more resistance and springs back quickly.
3. *Flesh separates from the bones easily*—The flesh of raw fish remains firmly attached to the bones. As the fish cooks, the flesh and bones separate easily.
4. *Flesh begins to flake*—Fish flesh consists of short muscle fibers separated by

thin connective tissue. As the fish cooks, the connective tissue breaks down and the groups of muscle fibers begin to flake, that is, separate from one another. Fish is done when the flesh *begins* to flake. If the flesh flakes easily the fish will be overdone and dry.

Remember, fish and shellfish are subject to carryover cooking. Because fish cooks quickly and at low temperatures, it is better to undercook the item and allow carryover cooking or residual heat to finish the cooking process.

Dry-Heat Cooking Methods

Dry-heat cooking methods are those that do not require additional moisture at any time during the cooking process. The dry-heat cooking methods used with fish and shellfish are broiling and grilling, roasting (usually referred to as baking when used with fish and shellfish), sautéing, pan-frying and deep-frying.

Broiling and Grilling

After brushing with oil or butter, fish can be grilled directly on the grate or placed on a heated platter under the broiler. Broiled or grilled fish should have a lightly charred surface and a slightly smoky flavor as a result of the intense radiant heat of the broiler or grill. The interior should be moist and juicy. Broiled or grilled shellfish meat should be moist and tender with only slight coloration from the grill or broiler.

Selecting Fish and Shellfish to Broil or Grill

Nearly all types of fish and shellfish can be successfully broiled or grilled. Salmon, trout, swordfish and other oily fish are especially well suited to grilling, as are lean fish such as bass and snapper. Fillets of lean flatfish with delicate textures, such as flounder and sole, are better broiled. They should be placed on a preheated broiling (sizzler) platter before being placed under the broiler.

Oysters and clams are often broiled on the half shell with flavored butters, bread crumbs or other garnishes and served sizzling hot. Squid can be stuffed, secured with a toothpick and broiled or grilled. Brushed with butter, split lobsters, king crabs and snow crabs are often broiled or grilled. Whole lobsters can be split and broiled or grilled, or their tails can be removed, split and cooked separately. Large crab legs can also be split and broiled or grilled. Shrimp and scallops are often broiled in flavored butters or grilled on skewers for easy handling.

Seasoning Fish and Shellfish to be Broiled or Grilled

All fish should be brushed lightly with butter or oil before being placed on the grill or under the broiler. The butter or oil prevents sticking and helps leaner fish retain moisture. For most fish, a simple seasoning of salt and pepper suffices. But most fish do respond well to marinades, especially those made with white wine and lemon juice. Because most fish are delicately flavored, they should be marinated for only a brief period of time. (Even marinated fish should be brushed with butter or oil before cooking.) Herbs should be avoided because they will burn from the intense heat of the broiler or grill.

Clams, oysters and other shellfish that are stuffed or cooked with butters, vegetables, bacon or other accompaniments or garnishes gain flavor from these ingredients. Be careful, however, not to overpower the delicate flavors of the shellfish with the addition of too many strong flavorings.

Accompaniments to Broiled and Grilled Fish and Shellfish

Broiled fish and shellfish are served with sauces made separately. Butter sauces such as a beurre blanc are popular, as the richness of the sauce complements the lean fish. Vegetable coulis are a good choice for a healthier, lower-fat accompaniment. Additional sauce suggestions are found in Table 10.5. If the item is cooked on a broiler platter with a seasoned butter, it is often served with that butter. Lemon wedges are the traditional accompaniment to any broiled or grilled fish.

Almost any side dish goes well with broiled or grilled fish or shellfish. Fried or boiled potatoes, pasta and rice are all good choices. Grilled vegetables are a natural choice.

PROCEDURE FOR BROILING OR GRILLING FISH AND SHELLFISH

All fish is delicate and must be carefully handled to achieve an attractive finished product. When broiling whole fish or fillets with their skin still on, score the skin by making several diagonal slashes approximately 1/4 inch (6 millimeters) deep at even intervals. This prevents the fish from curling during cooking, promotes even cooking and creates a more attractive finished product. Be especially careful not to overcook the item. It should be served as hot as possible as soon as it is removed from the broiler or grill.

1. Heat the broiler or grill.
2. Use a wire brush to remove any charred or burnt particles that may be stuck to the broiler or grill grate. The grate can be wiped with a lightly oiled towel to remove any remaining particles and help season it.
3. Prepare the item to be broiled or grilled. For example, cut the fish into steaks or tranches of even thickness; split the lobster; peel and/or skewer the shrimp. Season or marinate the item as desired. Brush the item with oil or butter.
4. Place the item under the broiler or on the grill presentation side down. If using a broiler, place the item directly on the grate or on a preheated broiler platter. Tender fish are usually broiled presentation side up on a broiler platter.
5. If practical, turn the item to produce the attractive crosshatch marks associated with grilling that are discussed in Chapter 9, Principles of Cooking. Items less than 1/2 inch (12 millimeters) thick cooked on a preheated broiler platter do not have to be turned over.
6. Cook the item to the desired doneness and serve immediately.

◆◆◆

RECIPE 19.1

BROILED BLACK SEA BASS WITH HERB BUTTER AND SAUTÉED LEEKS

Yield: 1 Serving

Black sea bass fillet, skin on, approx. 8 oz. (225 g)	1	1
Salt and pepper	TT	TT
Whole butter, melted	as needed	as needed
Leek, julienne	1	1
Lemon juice	2 tsp.	10 ml
Herb butter (pg. 218)	2 slices	2 slices

1. Score the skin of the bass with three diagonal cuts approximately 1/4 inch (6 millimeters) deep.

2. Season the bass fillet with salt and pepper and brush with melted butter.

3. Place the fillet on a preheated broiler platter, skin side up, and place under the broiler.

4. Blanch the julienned leeks in boiling water until nearly tender.

5. Drain the leeks and sauté them in 1 tablespoon (15 milliliters) of whole butter until tender. Add the lemon juice; season with salt and pepper.

6. Remove the fish from the broiler when done. Top with the herb butter and serve on a bed of sautéed leeks.

1. Scoring the skin of the fish.

2. Broiling the fish on a broiler platter.

3. Serving the fish on a bed of sautéed leeks.

Baking

The terms *baking* and *roasting* are used interchangeably when applied to fish and shellfish. One disadvantage of baking fish is that the short baking time does not allow the surface of the fish to carmalize. To help correct this problem, fish can be browned in a sauté pan with a small amount of oil to achieve the added flavor and appearance of a browned surface, and then finished in an oven.

Selecting Fish and Shellfish to Bake

Fatty fish produce the best baked fish. Fish fillets and steaks are the best market forms to bake, as they cook quickly and evenly and are easily portioned. Although lean fish can be baked, it tends to become dry, and must be basted often.

Seasoning Fish and Shellfish to be Baked

The most popular seasonings for baked fish are lemon, butter, salt and pepper. Fish can also be marinated before baking for added flavor. But baked fish usually depend on the accompanying sauce for much of their flavor.

Shellfish are often stuffed or mixed with other ingredients before baking. For example, raw oysters on the half shell can be topped with spinach, watercress and Pernod (oysters Rockefeller) and baked. Shrimp are often butterflied, stuffed and baked; lobsters are split, stuffed and baked. Many food service operations remove clams from their shells; mix them with bread crumbs, seasonings or other ingredients; refill the shells and bake the mixture.

Accompaniments to Baked Fish and Shellfish

Baked fish is often served with a flavorful sauce such as a creole sauce (pg 212) or a beurre blanc (pg 217). Additional sauce suggestions are found in

Table 10.5. Almost any type of rice, pasta or potato is a good accompaniment, as is any variety of sautéed vegetable.

PROCEDURE FOR BAKING FISH AND SHELLFISH

1. Portion the fish and arrange on a well-oiled or buttered pan, presentation side up.
2. Season as desired and brush the surface of the fish generously with melted butter; add garnishes or flavorings as desired or directed in the recipe.
3. Place the pan in a preheated oven at approximately 400°F (200°C).
4. Baste periodically during the cooking process (more often if the fish is lean). Remove from the oven when the fish is slightly underdone.

◆◆◆

RECIPE 19.2

BAKED RED SNAPPER WITH STAR FRUIT CHUTNEY

Yield: 4 Servings

Red snapper fillets, 8 oz. (250 g) each	4	4
Salt and white pepper	TT	TT
Whole butter, melted	2 oz.	60 g
Mint leaves, chopped	1 Tbsp.	15 ml
Garlic, minced	1 tsp.	5 ml
Tomato concasse	4 oz.	120 g
White wine	2 oz.	60 g
Lemon juice	2 oz.	60 g
Star Fruit Chutney (Recipe 10.29)	12 oz.	350 g

1. Place the snapper on a buttered baking pan. Season the fillets with salt and white pepper; brush with butter.
2. Top each portion with chopped mint and 1 ounce (30 grams) of tomato concasse.
3. Add the white wine and lemon juice to the pan.
4. Bake at 400°F (200°C), basting once halfway through the cooking process, until done, approximately 15 minutes.
5. Serve each portion on a bed of 3 ounces (90 grams) of star fruit chutney.

1. Brushing the fillets with butter.

2. Topping each portion with mint and tomato concasse.

3. The finished fish.

Sautéing

Sautéing is a very popular cooking method for fish and shellfish. It lightly caramelizes the food's surface, giving it additional flavor. Typically, other ingredients such as garlic, onions, vegetables, wine and lemon juice are added to the fond to make a sauce.

Selecting Fish and Shellfish to Sauté

Both oily and lean fish may be sautéed. Flatfish are sometimes dressed and sautéed whole, as are small round fish such as trout. Larger fish such as salmon can be cut into steaks or filleted and cut into tranches. The portions should be relatively uniform in size and thickness and fairly thin to promote even cooking. Although clams, mussels and oysters are not often sautéed, scallops and crustaceans are popular sauté items.

Cooking Temperatures

The sauté pan and cooking fat must be hot before the fish or shellfish are added. Do not add too much fish or shellfish to the pan at one time or the pan and fat will cool, letting the foods simmer in their own juices. Thin slices and small pieces of fish and shellfish require a short cooking time, so use high temperatures in order to caramelize their surfaces without overcooking. Large, thick pieces of fish or shellfish being cooked in the shell may require slightly lower cooking temperatures to ensure that they are cooked without over-browning their surfaces.

Seasoning Fish and Shellfish to be Sautéed

Many types of fish—especially sole, flounder and other delicate, lean fish fillets—are often dredged in flour before sautéing. Seasoned butter is used to sauté some items, such as scampi-style shrimp. These items derive their flavor from the butter; additional seasonings should not be necessary.

Accompaniments to Sautéed Fish and Shellfish

Sautéed fish and shellfish are nearly always served with a sauce made directly in the sauté pan. This sauce may be as simple as browned butter (beurre noisette) or a complicated sauce flavored with the fond. In some cases, seasoned butter is used to sauté the fish or shellfish and the butter is then served with the main item. See Table 10.5 for additional sauce suggestions.

Mildly flavored rice and pasta are good choices to serve with sautéed fish or shellfish.

PROCEDURE FOR SAUTÉING FISH AND SHELLFISH

1. Cut or portion the fish or shellfish.
2. Season the item and dredge in seasoned flour if desired.
3. Heat a suitable sauté pan over moderate heat; add enough oil or clarified butter to cover the bottom to a depth of about 1/8 inch (3 millimeters).
4. Add the fish or shellfish to the pan (fish should be placed presentation side down); cook until done, turning once halfway through the cooking process. Add other foods as called for in the recipe.
5. Remove the fish or shellfish. If a sauce is to be made in the sauté pan, follow the procedures discussed in Chapter 17, Poultry.

◆◆◆

RECIPE 19.3

SAUTÉED HALIBUT
WITH THREE-COLOR PEPPERS AND SPANISH OLIVES

Yield: 4 Servings

Halibut fillets, 6 oz. (170 g) each	4	4
Salt and pepper	TT	TT
Olive oil	2 oz.	60 g
Onion, sliced	3 oz.	90 g
Garlic, minced	2 tsp.	10 ml
Green bell pepper, julienned	3 oz.	90 g
Red bell pepper, julienned	3 oz.	90 g
Yellow bell pepper, julienned	3 oz.	90 g
Tomato concasse	8 oz.	250 g
Spanish olives, pitted and quartered	2 oz.	60 g
Fresh thyme, chopped	2 tsp.	10 ml
Lemon juice	2 oz.	60 g
Fish stock	2 oz.	60 g

1. Season the fillets with salt and pepper.
2. Heat a sauté pan and add the olive oil.
3. Sauté the halibut, turning once. Remove and reserve in a warm place.
4. Add the onions and garlic to the same pan and sauté for approximately 1 minute. Add the peppers and sauté for 1–2 minutes more.
5. Add the tomato concasse, olives and thyme; sauté briefly.
6. Add the lemon juice and deglaze the pan. Add the fish stock, simmer 2 minutes to blend the flavors and adjust the seasonings.
7. Return the fish to the pan to reheat. Serve each fish fillet on a bed of vegetables with sauce and an appropriate garnish.

1. Sautéing the halibut fillets.

2. Sautéing the onions, garlic and peppers.

3. Adding the fish stock.

4. Returning the fish to the pan to reheat.

Pan-Frying

Pan-frying is very similar to sautéing, but it uses more fat to cook the main item. Pan-fried fish is always coated with flour, batter or breading to help seal the surface and prevent the flesh from coming in direct contact with the cooking fat. Properly prepared pan-fried fish and shellfish should be moist and tender with a crisp surface. If battered or breaded, the coating should be intact with no breaks.

Selecting Fish and Shellfish to Pan-Fry

Both fatty and lean fish may be pan-fried. Trout and other small fish are ideal for pan-frying, as are portioned fillets of lean fish such as halibut. Pan-fried fish and shellfish should be uniform in size and relatively thin so they cook quickly and evenly.

Cooking Temperatures

The fat should always be hot before the fish or shellfish are added. Breaded or battered fish fillets cook very quickly, and the fat should be hot enough to brown the coating without overcooking the interior. Whole pan-fried fish take longer to cook and therefore require a slightly lower cooking temperature so the surface does not become too dark before the interior is cooked.

Seasoning Fish and Shellfish to be Pan-Fried

Although fish and shellfish can be marinated or seasoned directly, it is more common to season the flour, batter or breading that will coat them. Batters, for example, can contain cheese, and breadings can contain nuts and other ingredients to add different flavors to the fish or shellfish. Review the battering and breading procedures discussed in Chapter 21, Deep-Frying. Additional seasonings come from sauces and other accompaniments served with the pan-fried fish or shellfish.

Accompaniments to Pan-Fried Fish and Shellfish

Lemon wedges are the classic accompaniment to pan-fried fish and shellfish. Sauces that accompany pan-fried items are made separately. Mayonnaise-based sauces such as tartar sauce (Recipe 24.19) and rémoulade sauce are especially popular; rich wine-based sauces should be avoided. Vegetable coulis, such as tomato, also complement many pan-fried items. Additional sauce suggestions are found in Table 10.5.

PROCEDURE FOR PAN-FRYING FISH AND SHELLFISH

1. Heat enough clarified butter or oil in a heavy sauté pan so that it will come one third to half-way up the side of the item. The fat should be at a temperature between 325° and 350°F (160–180°C).
2. Add the floured, breaded or battered item to the pan, being careful not to splash the hot fat. Cook until done, turning once halfway through the cooking process.
3. Remove the food and drain on absorbent paper.
4. Serve it promptly with an appropriate sauce.

◆◆◆

RECIPE 19.4

BLUE CRAB CAKES WITH FRESH SALSA

Yield: 15 2-oz. (60-g) Cakes

Blue crab meat	1 lb.	450 g
Heavy cream	6 oz.	180 g
Red bell pepper, small dice	2 oz.	60 g

Continued

Green bell pepper, small dice	2 oz.	60 g
Clarified butter	as needed	as needed
Green onions, sliced	1 bunch	1 bunch
Fresh bread crumbs	6 oz.	180 g
Salt and pepper	TT	TT
Dijon mustard	1 Tbsp.	15 ml
Worcestershire sauce	TT	TT
Tabasco sauce	TT	TT
Egg, slightly beaten	1	1
Tomato Salsa (Recipe 10.18)	1 pt.	500 ml

1. Carefully pick through the crab meat, removing any pieces of shell. Keep the lumps of crab meat as large as possible.

2. Place the cream in a saucepan and bring to a boil. Reduce by approximately one half. Chill the cream well.

3. Sauté the red and green bell peppers in a small amount of clarified butter until tender.

4. Combine the crab meat, reduced cream, peppers, green onions and approximately 3 ounces (90 grams) of the bread crumbs along with the salt, pepper, Dijon mustard, Worcestershire sauce, Tabasco sauce and egg. Mix to combine all ingredients, trying to keep the lumps of crab meat intact.

5. Form the crab mixture into cakes of the desired size.

6. Place the remaining bread crumbs in an appropriately sized hotel pan. Place the crab cakes, a few at a time, in the hotel pan and cover with the bread crumbs. To help them adhere, press the crumbs lightly into the cakes.

7. Heat a sauté pan over moderate heat and add enough clarified butter to cover the bottom approximately 1/4 inch (1/2 centimeter) deep.

8. Add the crab cakes to the pan and cook until done, turning once when the first side is nicely browned. Remove and drain on absorbant paper.

9. Serve the crab cakes with fresh tomato salsa.

1. Mixing all ingredients for the crab cakes.

2. Forming the crab cakes.

3. Pan-frying the crab cakes.

Moist-Heat Cooking Methods

Fish and shellfish lend themselves well to moist-heat cooking methods, especially steaming, poaching and simmering. Steaming best preserves the food's natural flavors and cooks without adding fat. Poaching is also popular; especially for fish. Poached fish can be served hot or cold, whole or as steaks, fillets or portions. Boiling, which is actually simmering, is most often associated with crustaceans.

Steaming

Steaming is a very natural way to cook fish and shellfish without the addition of fats. Fish are steamed by suspending them over a small amount of boiling liquid in a covered pan. The steam trapped in the pan gently cooks the food while preserving its natural flavors and most nutrients. The liquid used to steam fish and shellfish can be water or a court bouillon with specific herbs, spices, aromatics or wine added to infuse the item with the desired flavors. Mussels and clams can be steamed by placing them directly in a pan, adding a small amount of wine or other liquid and covering them. Their shells will hold them above the liquid as they cook. Fish and shellfish can also be steamed by wrapping them in parchment paper together with herbs, vegetables, butters or sauces as accompaniments and baking them in a hot oven. This method of steaming is called **en papillote**.

Steamed fish and shellfish should be moist and tender. They should have clean and delicate flavors. Any accompaniments or sauces should complement the main item without masking its flavor. Fish and shellfish cooked en papillote should be served piping hot so the aromatic steam trapped by the paper escapes as the paper is cut open tableside.

Selecting Fish and Shellfish to Steam

Mollusks (e.g., clams and mussels), fatty fish (e.g., salmon and sea bass) and lean fish (e.g., sole) all produce good results when steamed. The portions should be of uniform thickness and no more than 1 inch (2.5 centimeters) thick to promote even cooking.

Seasoning Fish and Shellfish to be Steamed

Steamed fish and shellfish rely heavily on their natural flavors and often require very little seasoning. Nevertheless, salt, pepper, herbs and spices can be applied directly to the raw food before steaming. Flavored liquids used to steam fish and shellfish will contribute additional flavors. If the liquid is served with the fish or shellfish as a broth or used to make a sauce to accompany the item, it is especially important that the liquid be well seasoned. Lemons, limes and other fruits or vegetables can also be cooked with the fish or shellfish to add flavors. Clams and mussels often do not require additional salt as the liquor released when they open during cooking is sufficiently salty.

Accompaniments to Steamed Fish and Shellfish

Steamed fish and shellfish are popular partly because they are low in fat. In keeping with this perception, a low or nonfat sauce or a simple squeeze of lemon and steamed fresh vegetables are good accompaniments. If fat is not a concern, then an emulsified butter sauce such as beurre blanc (Recipe 10.16) or hollandaise (Recipe 10.15) may be a good choice. Table 10.5 lists several sauce suggestions.

Classic New England steamed clams are served with a portion of the steaming liquid; steamed mussels are served with a sauce that is created from the wine and other ingredients used to steam them.

PROCEDURE FOR STEAMING FISH AND SHELLFISH

1. Portion the fish to an appropriate size. Clean the shellfish.
2. Prepare the cooking liquid. Add seasoning and flavoring ingredients as desired and bring to a boil.

3. Place the fish or shellfish in the steamer on a rack or in a perforated pan and cover tightly.
4. Steam the fish or shellfish until done.
5. Serve the fish or shellfish immediately with the steaming liquid or an appropriate sauce.

◆◆◆

RECIPE 19.5

STEAMED SALMON
WITH LEMON AND OLIVE OIL

1. Placing the fish in the steamer.

2. Spooning the dressing over the fish.

Yield: 1 Serving

Lemon zest, blanched	1 Tbsp.	15 ml
Lemon juice	2 Tbsp.	30 ml
Salt and pepper	TT	TT
Virgin olive oil	2 Tbsp.	30 ml
White wine	8 oz.	250 g
Bay leaf	1	1
Leek, chopped	2 oz.	60 g
Fresh thyme	1 sprig	1 sprig
Peppercorns, cracked	1 tsp.	5 ml
Salmon tranche or steak, approx. 6 oz. (180)g	1	1

1. To make the dressing, combine the lemon zest, lemon juice, salt and pepper. Whisk in the olive oil.
2. Combine the wine, bay leaf, leeks, thyme and pepercorns in the bottom of a steamer.
3. Season the salmon with salt and pepper and place it in the steamer basket.
4. Cover the steamer and bring the liquid to a boil. Cook the fish until done, approximately 4–6 minutes.
5. Plate the salmon and spoon the dressing over it.

◆◆◆

RECIPE 19.6

RED SNAPPER EN PAPILLOTE

Yield: 6 Servings

Clarified butter	as needed	as needed
Leek, julienne	3 oz.	90 g
Fennel, julienne	4 oz.	120 g
Carrot, julienne	3 oz.	90 g
Celery, julienne	3 oz.	90 g
Red bell pepper, julienne	3 oz.	90 g
Red snapper fillets, skin on, 6 oz. (170 g) each	6	6
Salt and pepper	TT	TT
Basil Butter (pg 218)	9 oz.	270 g

1. Cut six heart-shaped pieces of parchment paper large enough to contain the fish and vegetables when folded in half.

2. Brush each piece of parchment paper with clarified butter.

3. Toss the vegetables together. Place one sixth of the vegetables on half of each piece of the buttered parchment paper.

4. Place one portion of red snapper on each portion of vegetables, skin side up; season with salt and pepper.

5. Top each portion of fish with 1-1/2 ounces (45 grams) of basil butter.

6. Fold each piece of paper over and crimp the edges to seal it.

7. Place the envelopes (papillotes) on sheet pans and bake in a preheated oven at 450°F (230°C) for 8–10 minutes.

8. When baked, the parchment paper should puff up and brown. Remove from the oven and serve immediately. The envelope should be carefully cut open tableside to allow the aromatic steam to escape.

1. Cutting heart-shaped pieces of parchment paper.

2. Placing the vegetables, red snapper and compound butter on the parchment paper.

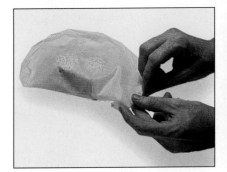

3. Crimping the edge of the parchment paper to seal it.

4. The finished papillotes.

Poaching

Poaching is a versatile and popular method for cooking fish. Shellfish are rarely poached, however. The exception is squid, which can be quickly poached and chilled for use in salads and other preparations.

There are two distinct poaching methods.

The first is the **submersion method**, in which the fish is completely covered with a liquid, usually a court bouillon, fish stock or fish fumet. It is cooked until just done. The poached fish is then served (either hot or cold) with a sauce sometimes made from a portion of the cooking liquid but more often made separately. Whole fish (wrapped in cheesecloth to preserve its shape during cooking), tranches and steaks can all be cooked by submersion poaching.

The second method, called **shallow poaching**, combines poaching and steaming to achieve the desired results. The main item, usually a fillet, tranche or steak, is placed on a bed of aromatic vegetables in enough liquid to come approximately halfway up its sides. The liquid, called a cuisson, is brought to a simmer on the stove top. The pan is then covered with a piece of buttered parchment paper or a lid, and cooking is completed either on the stove top or in the oven. Shallow-poached fish is usually served with a sauce made with the reduced cooking liquid. (Sometimes the main item is sautéed lightly before the cooking liquid is added. If so, the cooking method is more accurately braising, as both dry- and moist-heat cooking methods are used.)

Selecting Fish to Poach

Lean white fish such as turbot, bass and sole are excellent for poaching. Some fatty fish such as salmon and trout are also excellent choices.

Seasoning Fish to be Poached

Fish poached by either submersion or shallow poaching gain all of their seasonings from the liquid in which they are cooked and the sauce with which they are served. Therefore, it is very important to use a properly prepared court bouillon, fish fumet or a good-quality fish stock well seasoned with vegetables such as shallots, onions or carrots as well as ample herbs, spices and other seasonings. Many poached fish recipes call for wine. When using wine either in the cooking liquid or sauce, be sure to choose a wine of good quality. Most fish are very delicately flavored, and using poor-quality wine might ruin an otherwise excellent dish. Citrus, especially lemon, is always a popular seasoning; lemon juice or zest may be added to the poaching liquid, the sauce or the finished dish.

Accompaniments to Poached Fish

Poached fish cooked by submersion go well with rich sauces like hollandaise and beurre blanc. If fat is a concern, a better choice may be a vegetable coulis (for example, broccoli or red pepper). Cold poached fish are commonly served with mayonnaise-based sauces such as sauce vert or rémoulade. Shallow-poached fish are served with sauces such as a white wine sauce or beurre blanc made from a reduction of the liquids in which the fish were poached. See Table 10.5 for additional sauce suggestions.

Poached fish are often served with rice or pasta and steamed or boiled vegetables.

PROCEDURE FOR SUBMERSION POACHING

1. Prepare the cooking liquid. Whole fish should be started in a cold liquid; gradually increasing the liquid's temperature helps preserve the appearance of the fish. Portioned fish should be started in a simmering liquid to preserve their flavor and more accurately estimate cooking time.
2. Use a rack to lower the fish into the cooking liquid. Be sure the fish is completely submerged.
3. Poach the fish at 175–185°F (79–85°C) until done.

4. Remove the fish from the poaching liquid, moisten with a portion of the liquid and hold in a warm place for service. Or, remove the fish from the poaching liquid, cover it to prevent drying and allow it to cool, then refrigerate.

5. Serve the poached fish with an appropriate sauce.

——— ◆◆◆ ———

RECIPE 19.7

Whole Poached Salmon

Yield: 4 Servings

Salmon, drawn, 4–5 lb. (1.8–2.2 kg)	1	1
Court bouillon	as needed	as needed

1. Place the fish on a lightly oiled rack or screen and secure with butcher's twine.

2. Place the rack or screen in a pot and cover with cold court bouillon.

3. Bring the court bouillon to a simmer over moderate heat. Reduce the heat and poach the fish at 175–180°F (79–85°C) until done, approximately 30–45 minutes.

4. If the fish is to be served hot, remove it from the court bouillon, draining well, and serve immediately with an appropriate garnish. If it is to be served cold, remove it from the court bouillon, draining well, cool and refrigerate for several hours before decorating and garnishing as desired.

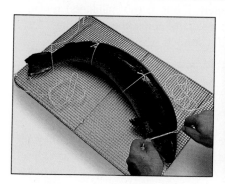

1. Arranging the whole fish on a rack.

2. Preparing the court bouillon.

3. Removing and draining the fish.

Procedure for Shallow Poaching

1. Butter a sauteuse and add aromatic vegetables as directed in the recipe.
2. Add the fish to the pan.
3. Add the cooking liquid to the pan.
4. Cover the pan with buttered parchment paper or a lid.
5. Bring the liquid to a simmer and cook the fish on the stove top or in the oven until done.
6. Remove the fish from the pan, moisten with a portion of the liquid and hold in a warm place for service.
7. Reduce the cuisson and finish the sauce as directed in the recipe.
8. Serve the poached fish with the sauce.

1. Arranging the sole on the bed of shallots and mushrooms.

2. Covering the fish with buttered parchment paper after the liquid is added.

3. Adding the velouté to the cuisson.

◆◆◆

RECIPE 19.8

FILLETS OF SOLE BONNE FEMME

Yield: 2 Servings

Sole fillets, approx. 2-1/2 oz. (75 g) each	4	4
Salt and pepper	TT	TT
Whole butter	2 tsp.	10 ml
Shallots, minced	1 tsp.	5 ml
Mushrooms, sliced	4 oz.	120 g
White wine	3 oz.	90 g
Fish stock	4 oz.	120 g
Fish velouté	4 oz.	120 g
Lemon juice	TT	TT
Parsley, chopped	1 tsp.	5 ml

1. Season the sole with salt and pepper.
2. Melt the butter in a sauté pan. Add the shallots and mushrooms and arrange the sole fillets over them. Add the wine and fish stock.
3. Bring the liquid to a simmer. Cover the fish with buttered parchment paper and cook on the stove top or in a 350°F (180°C) oven until done, approximately 5–8 minutes.
4. Remove the sole and reserve in a warm place.
5. Reduce the cuisson until approximately 1 ounce (30 milliliters) remains. Add the velouté. Add lemon juice to taste and adjust the seasonings. Serve the sauce with the fish, sprinkled with chopped parsley.

Simmering

"Boiled" lobster, crab and shrimp are not actually boiled; rather, they are cooked whole in their shells by simmering. Although they are not as delicate as some fish, these crustaceans can become tough and are easily overcooked if the cooking liquid is allowed to boil.

Selecting Shellfish to Simmer

Lobsters, crabs and shrimp are commonly cooked by simmering. Their hard shells protect their delicate flesh during the cooking process.

Seasoning Shellfish to be Simmered

The shellfish being simmered are not seasoned. Rather, they gain flavor by being cooked in a seasoned or flavored liquid, typically salted water or court bouillon. A sachet of pickling spice or Old Bay Seasoning is sometimes used for additional flavor.

Determining Doneness

Timing is the best method for determining the doneness of simmered shellfish. This varies depending on the size of the shellfish and how quickly the liquid returns to a simmer after the shellfish is added. Shrimp cook in as little as 3–5 minutes, crabs cook in 5–10 minutes and it can take as little as 6–8 minutes for a 1-pound (450-gram) lobster to cook and 15–20 minutes for a 2-1/2-pound (1.1- kilogram) lobster.

Accompaniments to Simmered Shellfish

The standard accompaniments to simmered shellfish are lemon wedges and melted butter. If the shellfish is being eaten cold, the traditional sauce is a tomato-based cocktail sauce. Nearly any type of vegetable or starch goes well with simmered shellfish, the most common being fresh corn on the cob and boiled potatoes.

Procedure for Simmering Shellfish

1. Bring court bouillon or water to a boil.
2. Add the shellfish to the liquid. Bring the liquid back to a boil and reduce to a simmer. (Whenever an item is added to boiling water, it lowers the water's temperature. The greater the amount of water, however, the faster it will return to a boil. So, to accelerate the time within which the water returns to a boil after the shellfish is added, use as much water as possible.)
3. Cook until done.
4. Remove the shellfish from the liquid and serve immediately. Or cool by dropping them in ice water if they are to be eaten cold.

◆◆◆

RECIPE 19.9

BOILED LOBSTER

Yield: 1 Serving

Lobster, 1 lb. 8 oz. (650 g)	1	1
Boiling salted water	4 gal.	16 lt
Lemon wedges	4	4
Whole butter, melted	2 oz.	60 g

1. Drop the lobster into the boiling water. Bring the water back to a boil, reduce to a simmer and cook the lobster until done, approximately 12 minutes.
2. Remove the lobster from the pot, drain and serve immediately with lemon wedges and melted butter on the side.
3. If the lobster is to be eaten cold, drop it in a sink of ice water to stop the cooking process. When cool enough to handle, remove the meat from the shell following the procedures discussed earlier.

Combination Cooking Methods

Combination cooking methods are used with meats, game and poultry in part to tenderize them. Because fish and shellfish are inherently tender, they do not necessarily benefit from such procedures. As noted above in the section on shallow poaching, fish can, on occasion, be lightly sautéed or browned and then poached. Although this procedure is a combination cooking method, it is used to enhance flavors and not to tenderize the product.

You may encounter fish or shellfish recipes with the word "braised" or "stew" in the title. Note, however, that these recipes rarely follow the traditional combination cooking methods discussed in this book.

CONCLUSION

In part because of consumers' increased health awareness, more and more food service operations are expanding their selections of fish and shellfish. Their task is aided by the tremendous variety of high-quality fish and shellfish now available. A variety of dry-heat and moist-heat cooking methods can be used with these products and a variety of sauces and accompaniments can be served with them. Regardless of how they are served, care and attention are required in order to select, store and avoid overcooking fish and shellfish.

QUESTIONS FOR DISCUSSION

1. Discuss six techniques for determining the freshness of fish and shellfish.
2. What are the physical differences between a flatfish and a roundfish? How do fabrication techniques vary for these fish?
3. List four market forms for fish and discuss several factors that may determine the form most appropriate for an operation to purchase.
4. List the three categories of mollusks and give an example of a commonly used food from each category.
5. Discuss four methods for determining the doneness of fish or shellfish. Why is it important not to overcook fish and shellfish?
6. Explain the differences between shallow poaching and submersion poaching. Why is poaching a commonly used method for preparing fish and shellfish?
7. Why are combination cooking methods rarely used with fish and shellfish? Why is boiling rarely used?

ADDITIONAL FISH AND SHELLFISH RECIPES

RECIPE 19.10

SHRIMP WITH BLOOD ORANGE SAUCE

NOTE: *This dish appears in the Chapter Opening photograph.*

TAVERN ON THE GREEN, NEW YORK, NY
Chef Marc Poidevin

Yield: 4 Servings   Method: Broiling or grilling

Sauce:

Blood-orange juice (fresh or frozen)	1 pt.	450 ml
Shallots, sliced	2 oz.	60 g
Fresh tarragon leaves	2 Tbsp.	30 ml
Fresh rosemary, chopped	1 Tbsp.	15 ml
Heavy cream	4 oz.	120 g
Whole butter	12 oz.	340 g
Kosher salt and white pepper	TT	TT
Orange	1	1
Sugar	1 Tbsp.	15 ml

U-15 shrimp	28	28
Basmati rice, cooked	1 lb.	450 g
Fresh chives, chopped	4 Tbsp.	60 ml
Fresh chervil	4 sprigs	4 sprigs

1. To make the sauce, combine the juice, shallots, tarragon and rosemary in a saucepan. Reduce by three quarters over high heat.

2. Add the cream and reduce by half. Add the butter a little at a time to make a beurre blanc. Strain through a chinois. Adjust the seasonings and keep warm.

3. Meanwhile, zest the orange and cut it julienne. Combine the zest with the sugar in a small saucepan with enough water to cover the mixture. Simmer, uncovered, until the water has evaporated. Set aside.

4. Peel and devein the shrimp, leaving the tails intact. Season with salt and pepper and grill on a preheated grill or broiler until done, approximately 4–5 minutes.

5. Place a 4-ounce (120-gram) serving of rice in the center of each of four individual plates. Ladle the sauce around the rice. Place one shrimp on top of the rice and arrange the other shrimp around it and on top of the sauce. Sprinkle with the orange zest and chives. Top with a sprig of chervil and serve.

═══ ◆◆◆ ═══

RECIPE 19.11
PANACHE OF SEAFOOD

STOUFFER STANFORD COURT HOTEL, San Francisco, CA
Chef Ercolino Crugnale

Yield: 1 Serving   **Method:** Sautéing

Scallop, U-10, halved	1	1
Shrimp, head on, large	1	1
Olive oil	1 oz.	30 g
Lobster claw meat, intact	1	1
Salt and pepper	TT	TT
Dry white wine	1 Tbsp.	15 ml
Chicken stock	1 Tbsp.	15 ml
Shallots, minced	1 tsp.	5 ml
Garlic, minced	1 tsp.	5 ml
Orange zest	2 tsp.	10 ml
Potato Basket (recipe follows)	1	1
Potato-Ginger Purée (recipe follows)	3 oz.	90 g
Frisée	1 oz.	30 g
Chives, 2-in. (5-cm) pieces	1 Tbsp.	15 ml
Iced Red Peppers (recipe follows)	2 Tbsp	30 ml
Basic vinaigrette dressing	1 tsp.	5 ml
Yellow Pepper Saffron Juice (recipe follows)	1 oz.	30 g
Herb Oil (recipe follows)	approx. 1 Tbsp.	15 ml

1. Sauté the scallop and shrimp in the olive oil until brown.

2. Add the lobster claw and season the shellfish with salt and pepper. Cook until the shellfish is just slightly undercooked.

Continued

3. Deglaze the pan with white wine. Add the chicken stock, shallots, garlic and orange zest; adjust the seasonings. Remove the shellfish from the pan.

4. Place the Potato Basket on a plate and fill with the Potato-Ginger Purée.

5. In a small bowl, combine the frisée, chives and Iced Red Peppers with the vinaigrette dressing. Place to the side of the potato basket.

6. Pour the Yellow Pepper Saffron juice on the plate.

7. Arrange the shellfish around the Potato Basket; drizzle the Herb Oil around the plate.

POTATO BASKETS

Yield: 10 Baskets

Idaho potatoes, large, peeled	10	10
Zucchini	10	10

1. Cut the potatoes on the wide cutter of a Japanese cutter. Wrap the potato slices around a zucchini and fasten with toothpicks.

2. Deep-fry until golden brown. Discard the zucchini.

POTATO-GINGER PURÉE

Yield: 2 lb. (1 kilogram)

Potato, peeled, 1-in. (2.5-cm) pieces	1 lb. 8 oz.	650 g
Heavy cream	4 oz.	120 g
Fresh ginger, grated	1 Tbsp.	15 ml
Whole butter	8 oz.	250 g
Salt and pepper	TT	TT

1. Boil the potatoes in salted water until tender. Drain and set aside.

2. While the potatoes cook, bring the cream to a boil, add the ginger and let steep for 15 minutes. Purée and strain through a fine chinois.

3. Purée the potatoes, add the butter and ginger cream. Season to taste with salt and pepper. Adjust the consistency with additional hot cream as needed.

ICED RED PEPPERS

Yield: 5 oz. (150 g)

Red bell peppers, cored and seeded	5 oz.	150 g

1. Cut the red peppers julienne.

2. Place in a container and add water and lots of ice. Store overnight if possible.

3. Drain and rinse well. Pat dry with a towel.

YELLOW PEPPER SAFFRON JUICE

Yield: 10 oz. (300 g)

Yellow pepper purée, strained	1 pt.	450 ml
Saffron threads	pinch	pinch
Shallots, minced	1-1/2 Tbsp.	45 ml
White wine	5 oz.	150 g
Salt	TT	TT
Tabasco sauce	TT	TT

1. Combine all ingredients and reduce by half.

2. Strain through a fine china cap. Adjust the seasonings. Serve chilled.

HERB OIL

Yield: 4 oz. (120 g)

Fresh parsley	2 oz.	60 g
Fresh tarragon	1 oz.	30 g
Fresh thyme	1 oz.	30 g
Olive oil	approx. 4 oz.	approx. 120 g

1. Blanch the herbs in hot water for 10 seconds. Cool and dry thoroughly.
2. Measure the volume of the herbs and put them in a blender. Add an equal volume of olive oil.
3. Purée and strain through a mesh strainer.

◆◆◆

RECIPE 19.12

RATATOUILLE CRUSTED SALMON

CITRUS, LOS ANGELES, CA
Chef Michel Richard

Yield: 4 Servings **Method:** Baking

Red bell pepper, roasted and peeled, brunoise	2 oz.	60 g
Yellow bell pepper, roasted and peeled, brunoise	2 oz.	60 g
Garlic, chopped	1/2 tsp.	3 ml
Olive oil	as needed	as needed
Zucchini, brunoise	4 oz.	120 g
Black olives	1 oz.	30 g
Scallops, 12–16 count	2	2
Salt and white pepper	TT	TT
Heavy cream	1 Tbsp.	15 ml
Salmon fillets, 5 oz. (140 g) each	4	4

1. Sauté the peppers and garlic in a small amount of olive oil until tender. Remove and spread in a pan to cool.
2. Sauté the zucchini in a small amount of olive oil until tender. Remove and spread in a pan to cool.
3. Remove the pits from the black olives and cut brunoise.
4. To make the scallop mousseline, process the scallops in the bowl of a chilled food processor. Season with salt and white pepper. With the motor running, add the cream and mix until incorporated.
5. Remove the mousseline to a bowl and stir in the sautéed vegetables and olives.
6. Place one fourth of the mixture between two sheets of plastic and roll out in a rectangle slightly larger than the surface of the salmon fillets.
7. Remove the top layer of plastic. Season the salmon fillets with salt and pepper. Turn the vegetable mixture over onto a salmon fillet and press so it adheres to the fish. Peel off the second layer of plastic. Repeat for each fillet.
8. Bake the salmon, ratatouille side up, at 350°F (180°C) until done, approximately 8–10 minutes. Serve with an appropriate sauce such as a red pepper coulis (Recipe 10.17).

◆◆◆

RECIPE 19.13

Sautéed Salmon with Asparagus and Morels

TAVERN ON THE GREEN, NEW YORK, NY
Chef Marc Poidevin

Yield: 6 Servings		**Method:** Sautéing
Sauce:		
Dry white wine	8 oz.	225 g
Fresh tarragon	2 sprigs	2 sprigs
Fresh rosemary	1 sprig	1 sprig
Fresh thyme	1 sprig	1 sprig
Shallots, sliced	3	3
Heavy cream	8 oz.	225 g
Unsalted butter	8 oz.	225 g
Lemon juice	2 oz.	60 g
Salt and pepper	TT	TT
Salmon fillets, center cut, 8 oz. (250 g) ea.	6	6
Olive oil	3 oz.	90 g
Fresh morels, cleaned and rinsed	1 lb.	450 g
Unsalted butter	3 Tbsp.	45 ml
Asparagus, jumbo spears, 1-1/2 -in. (4-cm) tips only, cooked	30	30

1. To make the sauce, combine the white wine, tarragon, rosemary, thyme and shallots in a small saucepan and reduce by two thirds.

2. Add the cream and reduce until thick, approximately 5–10 minutes. Stir in the butter, add the lemon juice and season with salt and pepper. Strain and reserve in a warm place for service.

3. Season the salmon with salt and pepper. Sauté the fish in olive oil until golden and cooked to the desired doneness.

4. In a separate pan, sauté the morels in 3 tablespoons (45 milliliters) of butter for 10 minutes. Season to taste with salt and pepper.

5. To assemble, place the salmon fillets on 6 individual plates, pour the sauce around them and arrange the morels and asparagus around the fillets.

♦ ♦ ♦

RECIPE 19.14

SALMON WITH LOBSTER-AND-CORN-STUFFED POTATO, GREEN PEA AND ROASTED PEPPER COMPOTE

STOUFFER STANFORD COURT HOTEL, SAN FRANCISCO, CA

Chef Ercolino Crugnale

Yield: 2 Servings **Method:** Grilling

Idaho potatoes, (120 ct.) lightly oiled, baked and hollowed	2	2
Whole butter	1 oz.	30 g
Salt and pepper	TT	TT
Lobster Stuffing:	6 Tbsp.	90 ml
Lobster meat, cut in large chunks, squeeze out any excess juice	10 oz.	280 g
Leek, small dice, blanched	2 oz.	60 g
Corn kernels, blanched	2 oz.	60 g
Fresh chives, minced	2 Tbsp.	30 ml
Fresh parsley, chopped	2 Tbsp.	30 ml
Fresh thyme, chopped	1 Tbsp.	15 ml
Boiled potatoes, puréed	12 oz.	350 g
Sour cream	4 oz.	120 g
Whole butter, softened	4 oz.	120 g
Salt	1 Tbsp.	15 ml
White pepper	1 tsp.	5 ml
Salmon fillets, 4 oz. (120 g) each, cut in diamond shape	2	2
Red cabbage, medium dice	3 Tbsp.	45 ml
English peas	3 Tbsp.	45 ml
Wax beans, trimmed to 1/2 inch (1.2 cm) and blanched	3 Tbsp.	45 ml
Pearl onions, simmered in seasoned chicken stock until tender	12	12
Roasted red peppers, medium dice	3 Tbsp.	45 ml
Chicken stock	2 oz.	60 g
White wine	1 oz.	30 g
Fresh lemon thyme, chopped	1/2 tsp.	2 ml
Fresh chives, minced	1/2 tsp.	2 ml
Lemon zest, grated	1 tsp.	5 ml
Red and yellow pear tomatoes, cut in half	4	4

1. Season the inside of the potatoes with 1 tablespoon (15 milliliters) whole butter, salt and pepper.

2. Combine all lobster stuffing ingredients. The stuffing should be chunky, not smooth.

3. Generously spoon the lobster stuffing into the potatoes. Bake the stuffed potatoes at 375° F (190° C) until warm and golden brown, approximately 10–12 minutes.

4. Season and grill the salmon. Keep warm.

5. To make the green pea and roasted pepper compote, sauté the red cabbage in 1 tablespoon (15 milliliters) whole butter for one minute. Add the remaining ingredients (except the tomatoes) and simmer for 3 minutes. Add the tomatoes and adjust the seasonings.

6. Pour a portion of the compote on each plate. Place a stuffed potato at the head of the plate and arrange the salmon on top of the compote.

$\blacklozenge \blacklozenge \blacklozenge$

RECIPE 19.15

CHILLED POACHED SALMON ROULADE WITH THAI NOODLE SALAD AND SOY MOLASSES VINAIGRETTE

ANA WESTIN HOTEL, WASHINGTON, D.C.
Chef Leland Atkinson

Yield: 5 Servings   **Method:** Poaching

Red bell pepper, julienne	6 oz.	180 g
Yellow bell pepper, julienne	6 oz.	180 g
Onion, julienne	5 oz.	150 g
Olive oil	1 oz.	30 g
Salmon fillet, skin off, pin bones removed, approx. 2 lb. (1 kg)	1	1
Salt and pepper	TT	TT
Fresh cilantro, chopped	2 bunches	2 bunches
Thai Noodle Salad (recipe follows)	as needed	as needed
Soy Molasses Vinaigrette (recipe follows)	as needed	as needed

1. Quickly sauté the peppers and onions in the olive oil; drain and cool.
2. Trim the fat and dark flesh from the skin side of the fillet. Carefully butterfly the fillet, cover it with plastic and pound gently.
3. Place the salmon, skin side up, on a rectangular piece of plastic wrap that extends at least 3 inches (7.5 centimeters) beyond each end of the fillet.
4. Season the fish with salt and pepper; sprinkle the cilantro over it. Distribute the cooled onions and peppers over the cilantro, leaving at least a 2-inch (5-centimeter) edge of salmon uncovered on all sides.
5. Roll the salmon and peppers into a tight pinwheel and firmly knot the ends of the plastic.
6. Tightly roll the fish in aluminum foil, twisting the ends to form a tight cylinder.
7. Poach or steam the fish until it reaches an internal temperature of 110°F (43°C). Remove from the poaching liquid and chill.
8. At service time, unwrap the chilled salmon and carefully slice it. Arrange the sliced salmon on plates with the Thai Noodle Salad. Pour 3 ounces (90 grams) of the Soy Molasses Vinaigrette around the salmon at the last moment.

THAI NOODLE SALAD

Yield: 5 Servings

Cellophane noodles	3.4 oz.	100 g
Fresh cilantro, chopped	2 bunches	2 bunches
Oyster sauce	2 Tbsp.	30 ml
Sesame oil	1 Tbsp.	15 ml
Garlic, minced	1/2 Tbsp.	8 ml
Soy sauce	2 Tbsp.	30 ml
Red pepper, crushed	1 pinch	1 pinch

1. Pour boiling water over the noodles and allow them to steep until they are al dente, approximately 5 minutes. Refresh in cold water. Drain well.
2. Toss the noodles with the other ingredients. Adjust the seasonings to taste.

SOY MOLASSES VINAIGRETTE

Yield: 1 pt. (450 ml)

Molasses	4 oz.	120 g
Rice vinegar	2 oz.	60 g
Soy sauce	8 oz.	250 g
Fresh ginger, chopped coarse	1 tsp.	5 ml
Olive oil	as needed	as needed

1. Combine the molasses, rice vinegar, soy sauce and fresh ginger in a saucepan. Bring to a boil and remove from the heat immediately. Allow the mixture to rest, undisturbed, for 1 hour.
2. Strain and chill the molasses mixture. Add the olive oil at service time.

◆◆◆

RECIPE 19.16

SALMON IN RICE PAPER
WITH A FRESH HERB MOSAIC
AND SOY BEURRE BLANC

ANA WESTIN HOTEL, WASHINGTON, D.C.
Chef Leland Atkinson

Yield: 4 Servings

Method: Sautéing

Salmon fillet portions, 6 oz. (180 g) each	4	4
Salt and pepper	TT	TT
Extra virgin olive oil	2 Tbsp.	30 ml
Rice vinegar	2 Tbsp.	30 ml
Rice paper circles, 8 in. (20 cm) in diameter	4	4
Fresh basil	4 leaves	4 leaves
Fresh dill	4 sprigs	4 sprigs
Fresh cilantro	4 leaves	4 leaves
Soy Beurre Blanc (recipe follows)	as needed	as needed

1. Season the skin side of the salmon with salt and pepper; drizzle the top with the olive oil and vinegar.
2. Soak the rice paper in warm water, one sheet at a time, for 30 seconds.
3. Transfer each paper to a work surface and let it stand until pliable.
4. Arrange a portion of the fresh herbs in a mosaic pattern in the center of the rice paper.
5. Place the salmon skin side down, centered over the mosaic.
6. Tightly fold in all four sides of the rice paper to enclose the fish.
7. Sauté the salmon, presentation side down first, in olive oil until the rice paper is golden brown. Use caution, as the rice paper browns quickly.
8. Transfer the fish to a 350°F (180°C) oven and cook for 2–3 minutes. Do not overcook.
9. Ladle the Soy Beurre Blanc onto four warm plates and center the fish on it.

Continued

SOY BEURRE BLANC

Yield: 12 oz. (350 g)

Shallots, chopped	1 oz.	30 g
Clarified butter	1 Tbsp.	15 ml
White wine	8 oz.	250 g
Fresh thyme	1 sprig	1 sprig
Bay leaf	1	1
Fresh ginger, peeled, chopped	1 oz.	30 g
Heavy cream	8 oz.	250 g
Champagne vinegar	1 tsp.	5 ml
Butter, room temperature	4 oz.	120 g
Soy sauce	2 tsp.	10 ml
Fresh lemon juice	1 Tbsp.	15 ml

1. Sweat the shallots in clarified butter.

2. Add the wine, thyme, bay leaf and ginger. Simmer slowly, reduce au sec.

3. Add the cream and reduce until slightly thick.

4. Add the vinegar and whisk in the room-temperature butter.

5. Add the soy sauce and fresh lemon juice and strain.

6. Hold the sauce warm and tightly covered until service.

◆◆◆

RECIPE 19.17

Red Snapper Veracruz

Yield: 4 Servings   **Method:** Sautéing

Red snapper fillets, skinless, 6 oz. (170 g) each	4	4
Salt and pepper	TT	TT
Flour	as needed	as needed
Olive oil	2 oz.	60 g
Onion, medium dice	6 oz.	180 g
Garlic cloves, minced	4	4
Lemon juice	1 oz.	30 g
Fish or chicken stock	8 oz.	250 g
Jalapeño, seeded, small dice	1	1
Tomato concasse	1 lb. 8 oz.	650 g
Pimento-stuffed green olives, quartered	20	20
Sugar	1 tsp.	5 ml
Cinnamon stick	1	1
Dried thyme	1/2 tsp.	2 ml
Dried marjoram	1/2 tsp	2 ml
Capers	2 Tbsp.	30 ml
Fresh cilantro	as needed for garnish	

1. Season the fillets with salt and pepper and dredge in flour. Sauté the fillets in olive oil until done. Remove and reserve in a warm place.

2. Add the onions and garlic to the pan and sauté until tender. Deglaze the pan with the lemon juice and add the stock, jalapeño, tomatoes, olives, sugar, cinnamon stick, thyme and marjoram.

3. Simmer 10 minutes. Remove the cinnamon stick and add the capers. Season to taste.
4. Return the fish to the pan to reheat. Serve on warm plates garnished with fresh cilantro.

VARIATIONS: Substitute bass or halibut fillets for the red snapper.

═══════ ◆◆◆ ═══════

RECIPE 19.18
PAN-FRIED TROUT
WITH TOASTED GARLIC

Yield: 1 Serving		Method: Pan-Frying
Trout, pan-dressed	1	1
Salt and pepper	TT	TT
Flour	as needed	as needed
Clarified butter	1 oz.	30 g
Whole butter	1 Tbsp.	15 ml
Garlic cloves, sliced thin	2	2
Lemon juice	1 oz.	30 g
Fresh parsley, chopped	1/2 tsp.	3 ml

1. Season the trout with salt and pepper; dredge in flour.
2. Pan-fry the trout in the clarified butter until lightly browned and cooked through. Remove and reserve.
3. Degrease the pan, add the whole butter and cook until it begins to brown.
4. Add the sliced garlic and sauté a few seconds until the garlic begins to brown.
5. Add the lemon juice and parsley and swirl to combine with the butter.
6. Top the fish with the sauce and serve.

═══════ ◆◆◆ ═══════

RECIPE 19.19
POACHED FISH STEAKS

Yield: 8 Servings		Method: Poaching
Court bouillon	as needed	as needed
Fish steaks (cod, salmon or turbot), 8 oz. (250 g) each	8	8

1. Bring the court bouillon to a boil.
2. Arrange the steaks on a rack and lower into the court bouillon.
3. Reduce the heat and poach the fish until done, approximately 5–10 minutes.
4. Remove the fish and drain well. Remove the skin or bones, if necessary. Serve with lemon wedges and an appropriate sauce, such as hollandaise, mousseline or beurre noisette.

♦♦♦

RECIPE 19.20
BRAISED EEL WITH RAISINS

Yield: 4 Servings   **Method:** Braising

Olive oil	2 oz.	60 g
Porcini mushrooms	8 oz.	250 g
Salt and pepper	TT	TT
Lemon juice	1 oz.	30 g
Whole butter	1 Tbsp.	15 ml
Eel, skinned, 2-in. (5-cm) pieces	2 lb.	1 kg
Mirepoix, small dice	1 lb.	450 g
Garlic, chopped	1 tsp.	5 ml
Flour	1 Tbsp.	15 ml
Red wine	8 oz.	250 g
Brandy	1 oz.	30 g
Brown stock	8 oz.	250 g
Bouquet garni:		
Carrot stick 4 in. (10 cm)	1	1
Leek, split, 4-in. (10-cm) piece	1	1
Fresh thyme	1 sprig	1 sprig
Bay leaf	1	1
Golden raisins	4 oz.	120 g

1. Sauté the mushrooms in half the oil. Season with salt and pepper and add the lemon juice. Remove and reserve in a warm place.
2. Add the remaining oil and the whole butter to the pan. Add the eel and sauté until browned. Remove and reserve the eel.
3. To make the sauce, add the mirepoix and garlic and sauté for 1 minute. Add the flour and cook to make a blond roux. Stir in the wine, brandy and brown stock. Add the bouquet garni and simmer for 30 minutes.
4. Plump the raisins in a small amount of warm water, then drain.
5. Strain the sauce though a chinois. Combine the sauce, mushrooms, raisins and eel and simmer to blend the flavors, approximately 15 minutes.

♦♦♦

RECIPE 19.21
SESAME SWORDFISH

Yield: 1 Serving   **Method:** Sautéing

Leek, julienne	4 oz.	120 g
Swordfish steak, 6 oz. (170 g)	1	1
Sesame oil	1 oz.	30 g
Sesame seeds	1 oz.	30 g
Fish stock	2 oz.	60 g
Tamari sauce	1 Tbsp.	30 ml

1. Deep-fry the leeks at 280°F (140°C) until golden brown. Drain well.
2. Brush both sides of the fish with sesame oil. Coat both sides of the fish with the sesame seeds, pressing to make a solid, even coating.
3. In a very hot pan, sauté the fish in the remaining oil. Turn the fish and finish cooking it in a 375°F (190°C) oven.

4. Remove the fish from the pan and hold on a warm plate. Deglaze the pan with the fish stock. Add the tamari sauce and heat thoroughly.

5. Place the fish on a bed of fried leeks, then pour the sauce over the fish and serve immediately.

VARIATIONS: Substitute a tuna or shark steak for the swordfish steak.

◆◆◆

RECIPE 19.22
PAN-SEARED SEA BASS WITH BEET VINAIGRETTE

STOUFFER STANFORD COURT HOTEL, SAN FRANCISCO, CA
Chef Ercolino Crugnale

Yield: 10 Servings   **Method:** Sautéing

Chilean sea bass, diamond-cut fillets,		
3 oz. (90 g) each	20	20
Salt and pepper	TT	TT
Olive oil	as needed	as needed
Shiitake mushrooms, sliced	10 oz.	300 g
Zucchini, julienne	10 oz.	300 g
Yellow squash, julienne	10 oz.	300 g
Red bell pepper, julienne	5 oz.	150 g
Chicken stock	10 oz.	300 g
Beet Vinaigrette (recipe follows)	3 oz.	90 g
Potato, peeled, julienne and deep-fried crisp	20 oz.	600 g

1. Season the fish on both sides. Sauté in olive oil until fully cooked.

2. Meanwhile, sauté the shiitake mushrooms in olive oil for 30 seconds. Add the zucchini, squash and red peppers.

3. Deglaze the pan with chicken stock and adjust the seasonings.

4. To serve, pool the Beet Vinaigrette onto warm plates. For an interesting effect, drizzle the sauce drop by drop into the middle of the plate from a height of 3 feet (1 meter), then pool the remaining sauce on the plate. Place the vegetables in the center with the fried potatoes on top. Arrange the fish on the vegetables.

BEET VINAIGRETTE

Yield: 1 qt. (1 lt)

Beet juice	3 pts.	1.5 lt
Fresh horseradish, grated	3 Tbsp.	45 ml
Shallots, minced	2 Tbsp.	30 ml
Garlic, minced	1 Tbsp.	15 ml
Fresh thyme	1 bunch	1 bunch
Black peppercorns	10	10
Apple cider vinegar	8 oz.	250 g
White wine	4 oz.	120 g
Poultry demi-glace	4 oz.	120 g
Cornstarch	2 Tbsp.	30 ml
Water	2 Tbsp.	30 ml
Salt	TT	TT

1. Combine the beet juice, horseradish, shallots, garlic, thyme and black peppercorns. Reduce to 1-1/2 pints (700 milliliters).

2. Add the vinegar, white wine and demi-glace; simmer 20 minutes.

3. Combine the cornstarch and water until smooth. Whisk into the sauce and bring to a boil. Strain through a fine-mesh china cap and season to taste.

◆◆◆

RECIPE 19.23
STEAMED BLACK BASS
WITH SANSHO PEPPER

THE FOUR SEASONS, NEW YORK, NY
Chef Christian Albin

Yield: 6 Servings   **Method:** Steaming

Black bass fillets, skin on,		
approx. 5 oz. (150 g) each	6	6
Leek, large, cut into strips	1	1
Sansho pepper and sea salt	TT	TT
Lime	1	1
Lemon	1	1
Olive oil	3 Tbsp.	45 ml
Pommeray mustard	1 tsp.	5 ml
Salt and pepper	TT	TT

1. Place the fish fillets, skin side up, and the leeks in a steamer basket. Season with sansho pepper and sea salt. Steam for approximately 5 minutes.
2. To make the vinaigrette, zest and juice the lime and lemon. Blanch the zests in water. Drain and mix the zests and juices with the olive oil and Pommeray mustard; season to taste with salt and pepper.
3. Plate the fish fillets and garnish with the leeks. Drizzle the vinaigrette over the fish and leeks.

◆◆◆

RECIPE 19.24
BAKED MONKFISH
WITH BACON

Yield: 8 Servings   **Method:** Baking

Bacon, thin slices	4	4
Monkfish fillets, 6 oz. (180 g) each	8	8
Whole butter, melted	as needed	as needed
Salt and pepper	TT	TT
Lemon juice	2 Tbsp.	30 ml

1. Partially cook the bacon on a sheet pan in a 350°F (180°C) oven for 5 minutes.
2. Cut each slice of bacon in half. Wrap each portion of fish with bacon and secure with a toothpick.
3. Butter a baking pan and place the fish in it. Season with salt and pepper.
4. Brush the fish with butter and sprinkle with lemon juice.
5. Bake the fish at 450°F (230°C) until done, approximately 12–15 minutes.
6. Serve the fish with an appropriate sauce such as tomato coulis or a tomato-based sauce such as Spanish or creole (Recipe 10.13).

◆◆◆

RECIPE 19.25

Sautéed Halibut with Citrus Beurre Blanc

VINCENT ON CAMELBACK, PHOENIX, AZ
Chef Vincent Guerithault

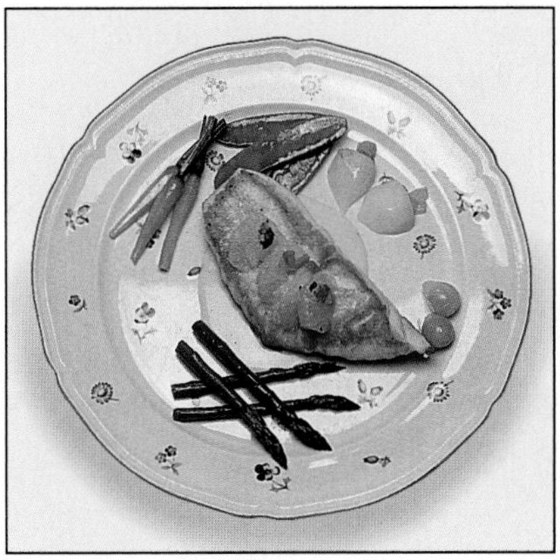

Yield: 4 Servings   **Method:** Sautéing

Halibut fillets, 8 oz. (225 g) each	4	4
Salt and pepper	TT	TT
Olive oil	1 Tbsp.	15 ml
Citrus Beurre Blanc (recipe follows)	as needed	as needed

1. Season the fillets with salt and pepper.
2. Sauté in olive oil for three minutes on each side. Serve in a pool of Citrus Beurre Blanc.

CITRUS BEURRE BLANC

Yield: 4 servings

Orange juice	8 oz.	225 g
Lime juice	1 Tbsp.	15 ml
Lemon juice	1 Tbsp.	15 ml
White wine	8 oz.	225 g
White wine vinegar	8 oz.	225 g
Shallots, chopped fine	1 Tbsp.	15 ml
Heavy cream	1 Tbsp.	15 ml
Unsalted butter	1 lb.	450 g
Salt and pepper	TT	TT
Orange rind, grated and blanced	1 Tbsp.	15 ml
Lime rind, grated and blanched	1 Tbsp.	15 ml
Lemon rind, grated and blanched	1 Tbsp.	15 ml

1. Combine the citrus juices, wine, vinegar and shallots and reduce au sec over moderate heat.
2. Whisk in the cream, then whisk in the butter 2 ounces (60 grams) at a time.
3. Strain the sauce, season with salt and pepper and stir in the citrus rinds. Keep hot for service.

✦✦✦

RECIPE 19.26
WALNUT SOLE

Yield: 4 Servings   **Method:** Sautéing

Flour	4 oz.	120 g
Egg wash	4 oz.	120 g
Walnuts, chopped fine	12 oz.	350 g
Sole fillets, 6 oz. (170 g) each	4	4
Whole butter	4 oz.	120 g

1. Prepare a standard breading station with the flour, egg wash and walnuts. (See Chapter 21, Deep-Frying.)
2. Bread the sole fillets, pressing the walnuts onto only one side of each fillet.
3. Sauté the fish in the butter, presentation (walnut-coated) side down. Turn and finish cooking in a 375°F (190° C) oven, approximately 5–8 minutes.
4. Serve with a citrus beurre blanc.

✦✦✦

RECIPE 19.27
PAUPIETTES OF SOLE WITH MOUSSELINE OF SHRIMP

Yield: 6 Servings   **Method:** Poaching

Shrimp meat	12 oz.	360 g
Egg white	1	1
Heavy cream	6 oz.	180 g
Salt and white pepper	TT	TT
Lemon sole fillets, skinless, 4 oz. (120 g) each	12	12
Whole butter	as needed	as needed
Shallots, chopped	2 oz.	60 g
Parsley stems, chopped	6	6
White vermouth	6 oz.	180 g
Shrimp stock	12 oz.	360 g
Beurre manié	approx. 1-1/2 oz.	approx. 45 g

1. Purée the raw shrimp meat in a food processor.
2. Add the egg white and pulse to incorporate.
3. Slowly add 2 ounces (60 milliliters) of the cream to the shrimp while pulsing the processor. Season the mousseline with salt and white pepper.
4. Place the sole fillets skin side up on a cutting board and flatten lightly with a mallet.
5. Spread each fillet with a portion of the mousseline. Roll up the fillets, starting with the thickest part and finishing with the tail portion.
6. Butter a sauteuse and sprinkle with the chopped shallots and parsley stems.
7. Place the sole paupiettes in the sauteuse and add the vermouth and shrimp stock.

8. Bring the liquid to a boil, cover with a piece of buttered parchment paper and place in a 350°F (180°C) oven. Poach until nearly done.

9. Remove the sole from the sauteuse and reserve in a warm place.

10. Return the sauteuse to the heat and reduce the cuisson slightly.

11. Thicken the cuisson to the desired consistency with the beurre manié.

12. Add the remaining cream, bring the sauce to a boil and strain through a fine chinois. Adjust the seasonings.

13. Serve two paupiettes per portion on a pool of sauce.

1. Flattening the fillets slightly with a mallet.

2. Spreading the fillets with the prepared mousseline.

3. Rolling the paupiettes.

◆◆◆

RECIPE 19.28

CHILLED SHELLFISH PLATTER

THE FOUR SEASONS, New York, NY
Chef Christian Albin

Yield: 2 Appetizer Servings **Method:** Simmering

Lobster, boiled	1	1
Oysters	4	4
Shrimp, U-10, boiled and peeled, tails intact	4	4
Crab meat, lump	3 oz.	90 g
Carrots	as needed	as needed
Celery	as needed	as needed
Scallions	2	2
Baby fennel, split and blanched	1	1
Red oak leaf lettuce	as needed	as needed

1. Remove the tail from the lobster. Remove the meat from the tail in one piece and cut it in half lengthwise.

2. Clean and open the oysters, leaving the oyster meat on the half-shell.

3. Mound crushed ice on a large serving platter. Position the lobster head and body in the center of the ice. Place the pieces of lobster tail around the lobster body. Arrange the remaining shellfish over the ice, using the carrots, celery, scallions, fennel and red oak leaf lettuce as garnish.

◆◆◆

RECIPE 19.29
PAELLA

ANA WESTIN HOTEL, WASHINGTON, D.C.
Chef Leland Atkinson

Yield: 4 Servings   **Method:** Steaming

Chicken thighs	4	4
Salt and pepper	TT	TT
Olive oil	2 oz.	60 g
Onion, medium dice	2 oz.	60 g
Garlic, chopped	1 Tbsp.	15 ml
Red bell pepper, medium dice	2 oz.	60 g
Green bell pepper, medium dice	2 oz.	60 g
Rice, long grain	12 oz.	350 g
Saffron	pinch	pinch
Chicken stock, well seasoned, hot	26 oz.	750 g
Chorizo, cooked, sliced	4 oz.	120 g
Clams, scrubbed	12	12
Cockels, scrubbed	12	12
Shrimp, 16–20 count	12	12
Lobster, cut up	1	1
Mussels, debearded and scrubbed	12	12

1. Season the chicken with salt and pepper. Pan-fry it in the olive oil, browning it well. Cook until done, approximately 20 minutes. Remove the chicken and reserve.
2. Add the onions, garlic and peppers to the pan and sauté until tender.
3. Add the rice and sauté until it turns translucent.
4. Add the saffron to the chicken stock. Stir the chicken stock into the rice and bring to a boil.
5. Add the sliced chorizo, clams and cockles to the pan. Cover and place in a 375°F (190°C) oven for 20 minutes.
6. Add the shrimp, lobster and cooked chicken to the pan. Cover and cook for an additional 15 minutes.
7. Add the mussels to the pan and cook until the shrimp and lobster are done, the chicken is hot and all the shellfish are opened, approximately 5 minutes.

◆◆◆

RECIPE 19.30
CLAMS CASINO

Yield: 36 clams   **Method:** Baking

Bacon, diced	4 slices	4 slices
Onion, minced	1 oz.	30 g
Red bell pepper, minced	1 oz.	30 g

Green bell pepper, minced	1 oz.	30 g
Whole butter	6 oz.	180 g
Lemon juice	1 Tbsp.	15 ml
Worcestershire sauce	2 tsp.	10 ml
Tabasco sauce	TT	TT
Clams, scrubbed	36	36
Fresh bread crumbs	2 oz.	60 g

1. Fry the bacon until well done. Drain the fat, reserving 2 tablespoons (30 milliliters).

2. Sauté the onions and peppers in the bacon fat until tender; remove from the heat and cool.

3. Combine 4 ounces (120 grams) of the butter, the lemon juice, Worcestershire sauce, Tabasco sauce, bacon pieces and sautéed vegetables and chill.

4. Open the clams, leaving the meat in the bottom shell. Top each clam with 1 teaspoon (5 milliliters) of the butter mixture.

5. Melt 2 ounces (60 grams) of butter in a sauté pan and toss the bread crumbs in the butter. Top each clam with a portion of the bread crumbs.

6. Bake at 400°F (200°C) until light brown and bubbling approximately 10 minutes. Serve immediately.

◆◆◆

RECIPE 19.31

STEAMED MUSSELS WITH LEEKS AND CARROTS

ANA WESTIN HOTEL, WASHINGTON, D.C.
Chef Leland Atkinson

Yield: 2 Servings   **Method:** Steaming

Mussels, debearded and scrubbed	2 lb.	900 g
Dry white wine	8 oz.	250 g
Garlic, chopped	1 oz.	30 g
Black pepper	1/2 tsp.	2 ml
Fresh thyme	4 sprigs	4 sprigs
Bay leaves	2	2
Leek, julienne	2 oz.	60 g
Carrot, julienne	2 oz.	60 g
Whole butter	4 oz.	120 g
Fresh parsley, chopped	1 Tbsp.	15 ml

1. Combine the mussels, wine, garlic, pepper, thyme, bay leaves, leeks and carrots in a large sautoir.

2. Cover the pan and bring to a boil. Steam until the mussels open.

3. Remove the mussels and arrange them in 2 large soup plates.

4. Reduce the cooking liquid by half, monte au beurre and pour the sauce over the mussels. The carrots and leeks should remain on top of the mussels as garnish.

5. Sprinkle with chopped parsley and serve with French bread.

✦✦✦

RECIPE 19.32
OYSTERS ROCKEFELLER

Yield: 36 Oysters **Method:** Baking

Unsalted butter	8 oz.	250 g
Fresh parsley, chopped	1 oz.	30 g
Celery, chopped	2 oz.	60 g
Fennel, chopped	2 oz.	60 g
Shallots, chopped	2 oz.	60 g
Garlic, chopped	1 tsp.	5 ml
Watercress, chopped	4 oz.	120 g
Pernod	2 oz.	60 g
Fresh bread crumbs	2 oz.	60 g
Salt and pepper	TT	TT
Oysters, on the half shell	36	36
Rock salt	as needed	as needed

1. Heat the butter in a sauté pan. Add the parsley, celery, fennel, shallots and garlic and cook for 5 minutes.
2. Add the watercress and cook for 1 minute.
3. Add the Pernod and bread crumbs; season with salt and pepper.
4. Transfer the mixture to a food processor and purée.
5. Top each oyster with approximately 2 teaspoons (10 milliliters) of the vegetable mixture; it should coat the oyster's entire surface.
6. Bake the oysters on a bed of rock salt at 450°F (230°C) until the mixture bubbles, approximately 6–7 minutes.

✦✦✦

RECIPE 19.33
FRIED OYSTERS
WITH HERBED CRÈME FRAÎCHE

Yield: 4 Appetizer Servings **Method:** Deep-Frying

Leeks, julienne	3	3
Oysters, scrubbed	24	24
Flour	4 oz.	120 g
Eggs	2	2
Egg yolks	2	2
Fresh bread crumbs	8 oz.	240 g
Sauce:		
Cornichons, chopped fine	1 Tbsp.	15 ml
Capers, chopped fine	2 Tbsp.	30 ml
Dijon mustard	1 tsp.	5 ml
Paprika	1/2 tsp.	2 ml
Parsley, minced	2 Tbsp.	30 ml
Crème fraîche	4 oz.	120 g

1. Deep-fry the leeks at 280°F (140°C) until golden brown. Drain and set aside.
2. Open the oysters. Strain and reserve the liquor.

3. Poach the oysters in the liquor for 30 seconds. Drain, reserving the liquid. Cool the liquid and oysters separately.

4. Set up a standard breading station with the flour, eggs, egg yolks and bread crumbs. (See Chapter 21, Deep-Frying.)

5. Bread the oysters, then deep-fry them at 375°F (190°C) until browned, approximately 1 minute.

6. Prepare the sauce by combining all remaining ingredients except the crème fraîche. Whip the crème fraîche until stiff. Fold in the cornichon mixture. Chill until service.

7. Serve the oysters on a nest of leeks with the sauce.

◆◆◆

RECIPE 19.34

STEAMED SCALLOPS
WITH GINGER, BASIL AND ORANGE

VINCENT ON CAMELBACK, PHOENIX, AZ
Chef Vincent Guerithault

Yield: 1 Serving

Method: Steaming

Oranges	2	2
Lime	1	1
Flour tortilla, 8-in. (20-cm)	1	1
Scallops, large	3	3
Ginger, grated	1 tsp.	5 ml
Carrot, julienne	2 oz.	60 g
Celery, julienne	1 oz.	30 g
Tomato, small dice	2 Tbsp.	30 ml
Fresh basil, chopped	1 Tbsp.	15 ml
Olive oil	1 Tbsp.	15 ml
Salt and pepper	TT	TT
White wine	8 oz.	250 g
Shallot, chopped	1 tsp.	5 ml

1. Zest the oranges and then cut them in 1/2-inch (1.2-centimeter) slices. Peel the lime and cut into 1/4-inch (6-millimeter) slices.

2. Line a small bamboo steamer with the flour tortilla.

3. Place the scallops on top of the tortilla. Add the orange zest, ginger, carrot, celery, tomato, basil, olive oil, two slices of lime and a dash of salt and pepper. Cover.

4. Place the white wine, chopped shallots, orange slices and remaining lime slices in the bottom of the steamer pan. Steam the scallops over the seasoned wine until done, approximately 5 minutes.

Nutritional values per serving:

Calories	470	Protein	25 g
Calories from fat	36%	Vitamin A	16216 Iu
Total fat	19 g	Vitamin C	19 mg
Saturated fat	3 g	Sodium	465 mg
Cholesterol	30 mg		

♦♦♦

RECIPE 19.35

SCALLOPS AND SHRIMP SAMBUCA

Yield: 1 9-oz. (270-g) Serving   **Method:** Sautéing

Fennel, julienne	1 oz.	30 g
Carrot, julienne	1 oz.	30 g
Celery, julienne	1 oz.	30 g
Shrimp, U-10, butterflied	3	3
Whole butter	1 Tbsp.	15 ml
Bay scallops	3 oz.	90 g
Salt and white pepper	TT	TT
Sambuca	1 oz.	30 g
Heavy cream	3 oz.	90 g
Puff pastry fleurons	2	2
Fresh dill	1 sprig	1 sprig

1. Blanch the fennel, carrots and celery. Refresh in cold water, drain and reserve.

2. Sauté the shrimp in the butter over high heat for 1 minute. Add the scallops and sauté for 30 more seconds. Season the shellfish with salt and pepper, remove and reserve in a warm place.

3. Deglaze the pan with Sambuca. Add the cream. Boil and reduce until the sauce thickens. Add the vegetables, scallops and shrimp to the pan and simmer until the shellfish is done, approximately 2 minutes. Adjust the seasonings.

4. Serve the vegetables and shellfish mounded on a warm plate, garnished with the fleurons and dill.

♦♦♦

RECIPE 19.36

GRILLED STUFFED SQUID

Yield: 6 Servings   **Method:** Grilling

Squid	12	12
Eggplant	8 oz.	250 g
Olive oil	2 Tbsp.	30 ml
Garlic, chopped	1 tsp.	5 ml
Fresh bread crumbs	1 oz.	30 g
Parmesan cheese, grated	1 oz.	30 g
Egg, beaten	1	1
Fresh oregano, chopped	1 tsp.	5 ml
Salt and pepper	TT	TT
Clarified butter	as needed	as needed

1. Separate the squid bodies and tentacles. Wash both and pat dry.

2. Slice the unpeeled eggplant 1/3 inch (1 centimeter) thick. Season the slices with salt and allow to drain for 30 minutes.

3. Pat the eggplant slices dry and brush with olive oil. Grill the slices over hot coals until browned and tender. Cool and cut the eggplant into small dice.

4. Sauté the garlic in the remaining oil. Add the tentacles and cook until done, approximately 3 minutes. Cool and chop the tentacles and combine with the eggplant, bread crumbs, Parmesan cheese, egg and oregano; season with salt and pepper.

5. Stuff each squid body with approximately 1 tablespoon (15 milliliters) of stuffing. Secure the open end with a toothpick.

6. Brush the squid with clarified butter and grill over hot coals for 10–12 minutes. Slice and serve two squid per portion.

◆◆◆

RECIPE 19.37
SPICY CALAMARI SALAD

THE BAMBOO CLUB, PHOENIX, AZ
Benny Chan, President

Yield: 4 6-oz (180-g) Servings   **Method:** Deep-Frying

Squid, cleaned and cut into rings	1 lb.	450 g
Marinade:		
Lemon juice	4 oz.	120 g
Red wine vinegar	1 pt.	450 ml
Garlic powder	1 Tbsp.	15 ml
Whole butter	1 Tbsp.	15 ml
Red bell pepper, sliced thin	3 oz.	90 g
Green bell pepper, sliced thin	3 oz.	90 g
Oyster mushrooms, sliced	12 oz.	350 g
Garlic, chopped	1 Tbsp.	15 ml
Oyster sauce	4 Tbsp.	60 ml
Chile pepper flakes	TT	TT
Flour	6 oz.	170 g
Baking powder	1-1/2 Tbsp.	22 ml
Cornstarch	1-1/2 Tbsp.	22 ml
Boston lettuce, torn into small pieces	8 oz.	250 g
Fresh cilantro or Italian parsley	as needed for garnish	

1. Marinate the squid in the lemon juice, vinegar and garlic powder for three days.

2. Sauté the peppers and mushrooms in the butter. Add the garlic, oyster sauce and chile peppers. Set aside.

3. Drain the squid, pressing out as much liquid as possible. Combine the flour, baking powder and cornstarch; toss with the squid until well coated.

4. Deep-fry the squid at 350°F (180°C) until crispy and golden brown. Drain and toss with the peppers and mushrooms. Serve on a bed of lettuce, garnished with cilantro or Italian parsley.

♦♦♦

RECIPE 19.38

CRAB MEAT FLAN
WITH RED PEPPER COULIS AND CHIVES

THE WHITE HOUSE, WASHINGTON, D.C.
Executive Sous Chef John Moeller

Yield: 6 Servings   **Method:** Baking

Lump crab meat	8 oz.	250 g
Fresh chives, chopped	1 bunch	1 bunch
Salt and white pepper	TT	TT
Eggs	5	5
Heavy cream	1 pt.	500 ml
Sherry	1 oz.	30 g
Whole butter, melted	as needed	as needed
Beurre Blanc (Recipe 10.16)	18 oz.	560 g
Red Pepper Coulis (Recipe 10.17)	3 oz.	90 g
Fresh chives	12 stems	12 stems
Caviar or lumpfish roe	as needed for garnish	

1. Clean the crab meat and toss with the chopped chives. Season with salt and white pepper.
2. Beat the eggs together lightly and add the cream. Add the sherry and the crab meat mixture. Adjust the seasonings.
3. Coat six ramekins with melted butter and fill with the flan mixture. Place the ramekins in a water bath and bake at 350° F (180° C) until set, approximately 45–50 minutes.
4. Pool the Beurre Blanc on six serving plates. Unmold the flans and place in the center of each plate. Decorate the plates with the Red Pepper Coulis and garnish with the chive stems and caviar.

♦♦♦

RECIPE 19.39

GRILLED LOBSTER WITH YELLOW HOT CHILES
AND CHIPOTLE PASTA WITH CHIPOTLE BEURRE BLANC

VINCENT ON CAMBELBACK, PHOENIX, AZ
Chef Vincent Guerithault

Yield: 4 Servings   **Method:** Grilling

Lobsters, 1 lb. (450 g) each	4	4
Olive oil	as needed	as needed
Yellow hot chile peppers, roasted, peeled and seeded	8	8
Shallots, peeled and chopped	2	2
Dry white wine	8 oz.	250 g
Heavy cream	4 oz.	120 g
Unsalted butter	1 tsp.	5 ml
Fresh basil, chopped	1 tsp.	5 ml
Fresh lemon	1/4	1/4

Salt and pepper	TT	TT
Chipotle Pasta (recipe follows)	as needed	as needed
Chipotle Beurre Blanc (recipe follows)	as needed	as needed

1. Cut each lobster in half lengthwise and remove the stomach, tomalley and coral.
2. Brush the meat with olive oil and grill over a very hot fire, meat side down, for approximately 7–8 minutes. Turn and grill for 5 minutes more. Crack the claws and set aside.
3. To make the sauce, combine 4 chopped yellow hot chiles, the shallots and the white wine. Bring to a boil and reduce au sec. Add the cream and simmer for approximately 8 minutes. Remove from the heat and monte au beurre. Strain, add the basil and the juice from 1/4 lemon and season to taste with salt and pepper.
4. Serve the sauce over the lobster and garnish with the remaining yellow chile peppers. Serve with Chipotle Pasta and Chipotle Beurre Blanc.

CHIPOTLE PASTA

Yield: 4 6-oz. (180-g) (cooked weight) Servings

All-purpose flour	10 oz.	300 g
Chipotle chile purée	2 Tbsp.	30 ml
Eggs, extra large	2	2
Olive oil	2 tsp.	10 ml
Salt	TT	TT
Fresh cilantro, chopped	as needed	as needed

1. Combine the flour with the chipotle purée in a food processor; add the eggs and mix.
2. Add the olive oil and salt, then process until the mixture forms a small ball around the blade. It may be necessary to add a few drops of water.
3. Run the dough through a pasta machine until the desired thinness, then cut. Hang the cut pasta on a rack to dry.
4. When ready to serve, cook the dried pasta in boiling salted water for approximately 15 seconds; drain. Add salt to taste and toss with Chipotle Beurre Blanc.
5. Garnish with chopped cilantro and serve hot.

CHIPOTLE BEURRE BLANC

Yield: 4 4-oz. (120-g) Servings

White wine	8 oz.	250 g
White wine vinegar	8 oz.	250 g
Shallots, chopped	1 Tbsp.	15 ml
Heavy cream	1 Tbsp.	15 ml
Unsalted butter, softened	1 lb.	450 g
Chipotle chile, pickled	1 Tbsp.	15 ml
Salt and pepper	TT	TT

1. Combine the wine, vinegar and shallots in a skillet and reduce au sec.
2. Whisk in the cream and slowly add the softened butter, 2 ounces (60 grams) at a time, whisking constantly.
3. Purée the chile and add it to the sauce. Season to taste with salt and pepper.

◆◆◆

RECIPE 19.40
LOBSTER À L'AMÉRICAINE

Yield: 4 4-5 oz. (120-130 g) Lobster   **Method:** Sautéing
and 4 oz. (120 g) Sauce Servings

Lobsters, 1 lb. 12 oz. (750 g) each	2	2
Clarified butter	2 oz.	60 g
Shallots, chopped	1 oz.	30 g
Garlic, chopped	1 tsp.	5 ml
Brandy	4 oz.	120 g
Dry white wine	8 oz.	250 g
Fish stock	16 oz.	450 g
Tomato concasse	8 oz.	250 g
Sachet:		
Bay leaf	1	1
Dry thyme	1/2 tsp.	2 ml
Peppercorns, cracked	1/2 tsp.	2 ml
Parsley stems	6	6
Cayenne	TT	TT
Heavy cream, hot	8 oz.	250 g
Whole butter, softened	2 oz.	60 g
Salt and pepper	TT	TT

1. Cut the lobster for sautéing. Reserve the tomalley and coral if present.
2. Heat the clarified butter and sauté the lobster pieces for 30 seconds.
3. Add the shallots and garlic to the pan and sauté for 30 seconds more.
4. Remove the pan from the stove and add the brandy. Return the pan to the flame, ignite the brandy and allow it to burn a few seconds. Add the white wine, fish stock, tomato concasse, sachet and cayenne.
5. Simmer for 5 minutes. Remove the lobster from the sauce. Remove the meat from the shells and reserve. Return the shells to the sauce.
6. Add the cream to the sauce. Bring to a boil and reduce by half.
7. Strain the sauce. Return to a simmer and thicken with beurre manié if needed.
8. Combine the whole butter with the reserved tomalley and coral and blend well. Monte au beurre with the tomalley and coral butter. Adjust the seasonings and serve the sauce over the lobster meat.

◆◆◆

RECIPE 19.41
LANGOUSTINE SALAD WITH ARTICHOKES

TAVERN ON THE GREEN, NEW YORK, NY
Chef Marc Poidevin

Yield: 6 Servings   **Method:** Sautéing

Artichoke bottoms	6 medium	6 medium
Lemon juice	1 Tbsp.	15 ml
Olive oil	3 Tbsp.	45 ml
Salt and pepper	TT	TT
Beefsteak tomato concasse	10 oz.	300 g
Dried thyme	1/2 tsp.	2 ml

Langoustines	30	30
Mesclun salad	1 lb.	450 g
Dressing:		
Balsamic vinegar	4 oz.	120 g
Extra virgin olive oil	8 oz.	250 g
Fresh basil	6 sprigs	6 sprigs

1. Cook the artichoke bottoms in water with lemon juice, 1 tablespoon (15 millimeters) of olive oil and salt until tender, approximately 20 minutes. Drain and set aside.

2. Cook the tomato concasse in 1 tablespoon (15 milliliters) of olive oil with the thyme for 10 minutes. Season to taste with salt and pepper and set aside.

3. Clean the langoustines; save six heads for decoration. Sauté the tails and six heads in 1 tablespoon (15 milliliters) of olive oil for 3–4 minutes. Set aside.

4. Place a layer of mesclun salad on six individual plates. Put an artichoke bottom in the center of each plate. Fill with tomatoes and hang five langoustines around the rim. Arrange the head on top of the center. Combine the vinegar and extra virgin olive oil and sprinkle it over the salad. Garnish with basil.

◆◆◆

RECIPE 19.42

FILET MIGNON
STUFFED WITH CRAYFISH

Yield: 4 Servings   **Method:** Simmering

Court bouillon	2 qt.	2 lt
Crayfish	36	36
Clarified butter	3 Tbsp.	45 ml
Shallots, chopped	1 Tbsp.	15 ml
Green onion, sliced	1 Tbsp.	15 ml
Garlic, minced	1 tsp.	5 ml
Fresh oregano, chopped	1 tsp.	5 ml
Fresh thyme, chopped	1 tsp.	5 ml
Salt and pepper	TT	TT
Cayenne pepper	TT	TT
Filet mignon steaks, 8 oz. (250 g) each	4	4
Red wine	6 oz.	180 g
Demi-glace	12 oz.	350 g
Whole butter	2 oz.	60 ml

1. Bring the court bouillon to a boil. Add the crayfish and cook until done, approximately 2–3 minutes. Remove and cool. Remove and peel the crayfish tails, reserving the shells from the tails and all of the juices, to yield approximately 3 ounces (90 grams) of meat. Reserve 4 large tails for garnish and coarsely chop the remaining meat.

2. Heat 1 ounce (30 grams) of the butter and sauté half the shallots, all of the green onions and the garlic for 30 seconds.

3. Add the chopped crayfish, oregano and thyme and season with salt, pepper and cayenne. Cool.

Continued

4. Cut a pocket in each of the steaks.

5. Season the steaks inside and out with salt and pepper. Stuff each filet with a portion of the crayfish mixture.

6. Sauté the remaining shallots in 1 tablespoon (15 milliliters) of clarified butter for 30 seconds. Add the red wine and reduce by half. Add the reserved crayfish shells and juice and bring to a boil. Add the demi-glace, bring to a boil and simmer for 5 minutes. Strain the sauce and adjust the seasonings. Return to the stove and monte au beurre.

7. Broil the steaks to the desired doneness and serve with the sauce. Garnish each steak with a large crayfish tail.

◆◆◆

RECIPE 19.43

SHRIMP WITH OLIVE OIL AND GARLIC

Yield: 4 Servings   **Method:** Sautéing

Garlic, chopped	4 Tbsp.	60 ml
Extra virgin olive oil	4 oz.	120 g
Shrimp, 26–30 count, in shell	2 lb. 8 oz.	1 kg
Coarse sea salt	1 Tbsp.	15 ml
Lemon juice	2 Tbsp.	30 ml

1. Sauté the garlic in the olive oil until translucent.

2. Add the shrimp and salt. Toss to coat the shrimp with the oil and cook just until the shrimp are pink, approximately 5 minutes. Add the lemon juice.

3. Arrange the shrimp on warm serving plates; top with the oil, garlic and lemon juice left in the pan. Serve immediately.

◆◆◆

RECIPE 19.44

SEVICHE

In a seviche, the fish and shellfish are "cooked" by the acids in the citrus juice. While a variety of fish or shellfish may be used, it is extremely important that the products be absolutely fresh. Use a nonreactive container such as stainless steel or plastic for mixing or storing the seviche. Aluminum and other metals may react with the acids in the lime juice, giving the food a metallic flavor.

Yield: 3 lb. (1.4 kg)

Raw scallops or shrimp	1 lb.	450 g
Raw firm white fish	1 lb.	450 g
Fresh lime juice	8 oz.	240 g
Serrano pepper, minced	4	4
Red onion, fine dice	6 oz.	170 g
Fresh cilantro, minced	4 Tbsp.	60 ml
Olive oil	2 Tbsp.	30 ml
Tomato concasse	8 oz.	250 g
Garlic, chopped	2 tsp.	10 ml
Salt and pepper	TT	TT

1. Chop the scallops or shrimp and fish coarsely but evenly. Place in a nonreactive container and add the lime juice. Cover and marinate in the refrigerator for four hours. The fish should turn opaque and become firm.

2. Toss in the remaining ingredients and season to taste with salt and pepper. Chill thoroughly and serve as a salad or with tortilla chips.

3. If the seviche is going to be held for more than 2 hours, drain the liquid and refrigerate separately. The reserved liquid can then be tossed with the other ingredients at service time.

Nutritional values per 4 oz. (120 g) serving:

Calories	117	Protein	16 g
Calories from fat	27%	Vitamin A	1919 IU
Total fat	4 g	Vitamin C	49 mg
Saturated fat	1 g	Sodium	114 mg
Cholesterol	89 mg		

CHAPTER 20
CHARCUTERIE

Traditionally, charcuterie was limited to the production of pork-based pâtés, terrines and galantines. Over the years, however, it has come to include similar products made with game, poultry, fish, shellfish and even vegetables. Many of these are discussed here.

Charcuterie is an art and science in itself. This chapter is not intended to be a complete guide to the charcutier's art. Instead, we focus on procedures for making common charcuterie items that can be prepared easily in most kitchens. We also discuss the preparation of sausages as well as curing methods, including salt curing, brining, and both cold and hot smoking. The chapter ends with information about several cured pork products.

FORCEMEATS AND THEIR USES

A **forcemeat** is a preparation made from uncooked ground meats, poultry, fish or shellfish, seasoned, then emulsified with fat. Forcemeats are the primary ingredient used to make pâtés, terrines, galantines and sausages.

The word *forcemeat* is derived from the French word *farce*, meaning stuffing. Depending on the preparation method, a forcemeat can be very smooth and velvety, well-textured and coarse, or anything in between. Regardless of its intended use, it has a glossy appearance when raw and will slice cleanly when cooked. A properly emulsified forcemeat provides a rich taste and a comforting texture on the palate.

Forcemeats are emulsified products. Emulsification is the process of binding two ingredients that ordinarily would not combine. (Emulsified sauces are discussed in Chapter 10, Stocks and Sauces; emulsified salad dressings are discussed in Chapter 24, Salads and Salad Dressings.) The proteins present in the meat, poultry, fish and shellfish combine easily with both fat and liquids. In forcemeats, these proteins act as a stabilizer that allows the fat and liquids, which ordinarily would not combine, to bind. When improperly emulsified forcemeats are cooked, they lose their fat, shrink and become dry and grainy. To ensure proper emulsification of a forcemeat:

1. the ratio of fat to other ingredients must be precise,
2. temperatures must be maintained below 40°F (4°C) and
3. the ingredients must be mixed properly.

Forcemeat Ingredients

Forcemeats are usually meat, poultry, fish or shellfish combined with binders, seasonings and sometimes garnishes. Selections from each of these basic categories are used to make an array of forcemeats. All ingredients must be of the finest quality and added in just the right proportions.

Meats

The **dominant meat** is the meat that gives the forcemeat its name and essential flavor. The dominant meat does not have to be beef, veal, lamb, pork or game. It can be poultry, fish or shellfish. When preparing meats, poultry or fish for forcemeat, it is important to trim all silverskin, gristle and small bones so that the meat will be more easily ground and will produce a smoother finished product.

Many forcemeats contain some pork. Pork adds moisture and smoothness to the forcemeat. Without it, poultry-based forcemeats tend to be rubbery, while venison and other game-based forcemeats tend to be dry. The traditional ratio is one part pork to two parts dominant meat.

Many forcemeats also contain some liver. Pork liver is commonly used, as is chicken liver. Liver contributes flavor as well as binding to the forcemeat. For a finer texture, grind the livers and then force them through a drum sieve before incorporating them into the forcemeat.

Fats

Here, **fat** refers to a separate ingredient, not the fat in the dominant meat or pork, both of which should be quite lean in order to ensure the correct ratio of fat to meat. Usually pork fatback or heavy cream is used to add moisture and richness to the forcemeat. Because fat carries flavor, it also promotes the proper infusion of flavors and smoke.

Binders

There are two principal types of binders: panadas and eggs.

A **panada** is something other than fat that is added to a forcemeat to enhance smoothness (especially in fish mousselines, which tend to be slightly grainy in texture), to aid emulsification (especially in vegetable terrines, where the protein levels are insufficient to bind on their own) or both (for example, in liver mousses). It should not make up more than 20% of the forcemeat's total weight. Usually a panada is nothing more than crustless white bread soaked in milk or, more traditionally, a heavy béchamel or rice.

Eggs or egg whites are used as a primary binding agent in some styles of forcemeat. If used in forcemeats that have a large ratio of liver or liquids, they also add texture.

Seasonings

Forcemeats are seasoned with salt, curing salt, marinades and various herbs and spices.

Salt not only adds flavor to a forcemeat but also aids in the emulsification of the meat and fat. As with other foods, a forcemeat that lacks salt will taste flat.

Curing salt is a mixture of salt and sodium nitrite. Sodium nitrite controls spoilage by inhibiting bacterial growth. Equally important, curing salt preserves the rosy pink colors of some forcemeats that might otherwise oxidize to an unappetizing gray. Although currently regarded as substantially safer than the previously used potassium nitrate (saltpeter), some studies suggest that sodium nitrite is a carcinogen. For a typical consumer, however, the amount of sodium nitrite consumed from cured meats should not pose a substantial health threat.

Traditionally, ingredients for forcemeats were marinated for long periods of time, sometimes days, before grinding. The trend today is for a shorter marinating times so that the true flavors of the main ingredients shine through. Both classic and contemporary marinades include herbs, citrus zest, spices and liquors, all of which lend flavor, character and nuance to the forcemeat.

Pâté spice is a mixture of several spices and herbs that can be premixed and used as needed.

◆◆◆

RECIPE 20.1
PATÉ SPICE

Yield: 7-2/3 oz. (220 g)

Cloves	1 oz.	30 g
Dried ginger	1 oz.	30 g
Nutmeg	1 oz.	30 g
Paprika	1 oz.	30 g
Dried basil	2/3 oz.	20 g
Black pepper	2/3 oz.	20 g
White pepper·	2/3 oz.	20 g
Bay leaf	1/3 oz.	10 g
Dried thyme	1 oz.	30 g
Dried marjoram	1/3 oz.	10 g

1. Grind all ingredients in a spice grinder. Pass through a sieve to remove any large pieces.

NOTE: This mixture can be used as is, or mix 1 ounce (30 grams) (or any amount desired) with 1 pound (450 grams) of salt. The salt and spice mixture can then be used to season forcemeats; 1/3 ounce (10 grams) per pound of forcemeat usually suffices for most pâtés.

A forcemeat's seasoning and texture can be tested by cooking a small portion before the entire forcemeat is cooked. (Unlike sauces, stews and other dishes, you cannot taste and adjust a forcemeat's flavoring during the cooking process.) A small portion of a hearty forcemeat can be sautéed; a small portion of a more delicate forcemeat should be poached for 3–5 minutes. When cooked, the forcemeat should hold its shape and be slightly firm but not rubbery. If it is too firm, add a little cream.

Garnishes

Forcemeat garnishes are meats, fat, vegetables or other foods added in limited quantities to provide contrasting flavors and textures and to improve appearance. The garnishes are usually diced, chopped or more coarsely ground than the dominant meat. Common garnishes include pistachio nuts, diced fatback, truffles or truffle peelings and diced ham or tongue.

Equipment for Preparing Forcemeats

To properly prepare forcemeats you should have a food chopper or food processor and a heavy-duty drum sieve with a metal band. You will also need a standard meat grinder or meat-grinding attachment with various-size grinding dies (see Figure 20.1).

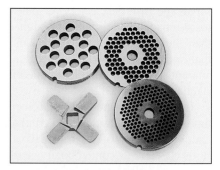

FIGURE 20.1 *A blade and assorted dies for a standard grinder.*

Preparing Forcemeats

The three common forcemeat preparations are **country-style**, **basic** and **mousseline**. Each can be produced easily in a typical food service operation. Other types of forcemeat preparations such as the emulsified mixture used to make hot dogs and bratwurst are not commonly encountered in food service operations and are not discussed here.

When preparing any forcemeat certain guidelines must be followed:

1. Forcemeat preparations include raw meats, liver, eggs and dairy products. If improperly handled, these potentially hazardous foods create a good environment for the growth of microorganisms. To avoid the risk of food-borne illness, temperatures must be carefully controlled and all cutting boards and food contact surfaces must be as sanitary as possible at all times.

2. To ensure a proper emulsification, the forcemeat must be kept cold—below 40°F (4°C)—at all times. Refrigerate all moist ingredients and keep forcemeats in progress in an ice bath. Chilling or freezing metal grinder and food processor parts helps keep the ingredients as cold as possible.

3. Cut all foods into convenient sizes that fit easily into grinder openings. Do not overstuff grinders or overfill food processors. When grinding items twice, always begin with a larger die, followed by a medium or small die. For exceptional smoothness, press the forcemeat through a sieve after grinding to remove any lumps or pieces of membrane.

Country-Style Forcemeats

A traditional country-style forcemeat is heavily seasoned with onions, garlic, pepper, juniper berries and bay leaves. It is the simplest of the forcemeats to prepare and yields the heartiest and most distinctive pâtés and sausages.

The dominant meat for a country-style forcemeat is usually ground once through the grinder's large die, then ground again through the medium die. This produces the characteristic coarse texture. As with most forcemeats, the dominant meat for a country-style forcemeat is usually marinated and seasoned prior to grinding and then mixed with some liver.

PROCEDURE FOR PREPARING A COUNTRY-STYLE FORCEMEAT

1. Chill all ingredients and equipment thoroughly. Throughout preparation they should remain at temperatures below 40°F (4°C).
2. Cut all meats into an appropriate size for grinding.
3. Marinate, under refrigeration, the dominant meat and pork with the desired herbs, spices and liquors.
4. If using liver, grind it and force it through a sieve.
5. Cut the fatback into an appropriate size and freeze.
6. Prepare an ice bath for the forcemeat. Then grind the dominant meat, pork and fat as directed in the recipe, usually once through the grinder's largest die and a second time through the medium die.
7. If using liver, eggs, panada or garnishes, fold them in by hand, remembering to keep the forcemeat over an ice bath at all times.
8. Cook a small portion of the forcemeat; adjust the seasonings and texture as appropriate.
9. Refrigerate the forcemeat until needed.

◆◆◆

RECIPE 20.2

COUNTRY-STYLE FORCEMEAT

Yield: 5 lb. (2.2 kg)

Lean pork, diced	2 lb.	900 g
Pâté spice	2 Tbsp.	30 ml
Salt	1 Tbsp.	15 ml
Pepper	TT	TT
Brandy	2 oz.	60 g
Pork liver, cleaned and diced	1 lb.	450 g
Fatback, diced	1 lb.	450 g
Onion, small dice	3 oz.	90 g
Garlic, minced	1 Tbsp.	15 ml
Fresh parsley, chopped	3 Tbsp.	45 ml
Eggs	6	6

1. Combine the diced pork with the pâté spice, salt, pepper and brandy; marinate under refrigeration for several hours.
2. Grind the liver and force it through a drum sieve. Reserve.
3. Grind the marinated pork and fatback through the grinder's large die.
4. Grind half the pork and fatback a second time through the medium die along with the onions, garlic and parsley.
5. Working over an ice bath, combine the coarse and medium ground pork with the liver and eggs.
6. Cook and taste a small portion of the forcemeat and adjust the seasonings as necessary.

The forcemeat is now ready to use as desired in the preparation of pâtés, terrines, galantines and sausages.

1. Marinating the meat with herbs and spices.

2. Forcing the ground liver through a sieve.

3. Grinding half the meat a second time.

4. Incorporating the liver and eggs into the ground mixture over an ice bath to keep the forcemeat cold.

Basic Forcemeats

Smoother and more refined than a country-style forcemeat, a basic forcemeat is probably the most versatile of all. It should be well seasoned, but the seasonings should not mask the dominant meat's flavor. Examples of basic forcemeats are most game pâtés and terrines as well as traditional pâtés en croûte.

A basic forcemeat is made by grinding the meat and fat separately—the meat twice and the fat once. The fat is then worked into the meat, either by hand or in a food processor or chopper. A quicker method involves grinding the fat and meat together and then blending them in a food processor. Whichever method is used, some recipes call for the incorporation of crushed ice to minimize friction, reduce temperature and add moisture.

PROCEDURE FOR PREPARING A BASIC FORCEMEAT

1. Chill all ingredients and equipment thoroughly. Throughout preparation they should remain at temperatures below 40°F (4°C).
2. Cut all meats into an appropriate size for grinding.
3. Marinate, under refrigeration, the dominant meat and pork with the desired herbs, spices and liquors.
4. If using liver, grind it and force it through a sieve.
5. Cut the fatback into an appropriate size and freeze.
6. Grind the meats twice, once through the grinder's large die and then through the medium die; hold on an ice bath.
7. Grind the chilled or frozen fat once through the medium die and add it to the meat mixture.
8. Work the fat into the meat over an ice bath or in a well-chilled food processor or chopping machine.
9. Over an ice bath, add any required eggs, panada and/or garnishes and work them into the mixture.
10. Cook a small portion of the forcemeat in stock or water; adjust the seasonings and texture as appropriate.
11. Refrigerate the forcemeat until needed.

An alternative method for preparing a basic forcemeat replaces steps 6 to 9 with the following procedures:

6A. Grind the meats and fats together twice.

7A. Place them in a food processor or chopper and blend until smooth.

8A. Add any required eggs or panada while the machine is running and blend them in with the meat and fat.

9A. Remove the forcemeat from the machine and, working over an ice bath, fold in any garnishes by hand.

Whichever method is used, a particularly warm kitchen or a lengthy running time in the food processor or chopping machine may necessitate the addition of small quantities of crushed ice to properly emulsify the forcemeat. Add the ice bit by bit while the machine is running.

=== ◆◆◆ ===

RECIPE 20.3
BASIC FORCEMEAT

Yield: 4 lb. 8 oz. (2 kg)

Veal, diced	1 lb. 8 oz.	650 g
Lean pork, diced	1 lb. 8 oz.	650 g
Brandy	2 oz.	60 g
Pâté spice	2 tsp.	10 ml
Salt	1-1/2 tsp.	7 ml
White pepper	TT	TT
Fatback, diced	1 lb. 8 oz.	650 g
Eggs	4	4
Ham, medium dice	4 oz.	120 g
Pistachio nuts	2 oz.	60 g
Black olives, chopped coarse	2 oz.	60 g

1. Combine the veal and pork with the brandy, pâté spice, salt and white pepper; marinate under refrigeration for several hours.

2. Grind the meats through the grinder's large die and again through the small die.

3. Grind the fatback through the grinder's small die.

4. Combine the meat and fat in the bowl of a food processor and blend until they are emulsified.

5. Work in the eggs until the forcemeat is smooth and well emulsified. Do not overprocess the forcemeat.

1. Grinding the meat through the chilled grinder.

2. Combining the fat with the meat in the food processor.

3. Adding the eggs to the meat.

4. Folding the garnishes into the forcemeat.

6. Fold in the ham, pistachio nuts and olives.

7. Cook a small portion of the forcemeat by poaching or sautéing it. Taste and adjust the seasonings as necessary.

The forcemeat is now ready to use as desired in the preparation of pâtés, terrines, galantines or sausages.

Mousseline Forcemeats

A properly made mousseline forcemeat is light, airy and delicately flavored. It is most often made with fish or shellfish but sometimes with veal, pork, feathered game or poultry. (A mousseline forcemeat is not the same as a mousse, which usually contains gelatin and is discussed below.)

A mousseline forcemeat is prepared by processing ground meats and cream in a food processor; often egg whites are added to lighten and enrich the mixture. The proportion of fish to eggs to cream is very important. Too many egg whites and the mousseline will be rubbery; too few and it may not bind together. If too much cream is added, the mousseline will be too soft or will fall apart during cooking.

A mousseline forcemeat can be served hot or cold. It can be used to make fish sausages and a variety of timbales and terrines. Or it can be used to make quenelles, which are discussed below. A shrimp mousseline is used with the Paupiettes of Sole, Recipe 19.27.

PROCEDURE FOR PREPARING A MOUSSELINE FORCEMEAT

1. Chill all ingredients and equipment thoroughly. Throughout preparation they should remain at temperatures below 40°F (4°C).

2. Cut all meats into an appropriate size for processing.

3. Grind the meat in a cold food processor until smooth. Do not overprocess.

4. Add eggs and pulse until just blended.

5. Add cream and seasonings in a steady stream while the machine is running. Stop the machine and scrape down the sides of the bowl once or twice during the processing. Do not run the machine any longer than necessary to achieve a smooth forcemeat.

6. If desired, pass the forcemeat through a drum sieve to remove any sinew or bits of bone.
7. Over an ice bath, fold in any garnishes by hand.
8. Poach a small amount of the mousseline in stock or water. Taste and adjust the seasonings and texture as necessary.
9. Refrigerate until ready for use.

$\diamond\diamond\diamond$

RECIPE 20.4
MOUSSELINE FORCEMEAT

Yield: 4 lb. (1.8 kg)

Fish, scallops, skinless chicken breast or lean veal	2 lb.	900 g
Egg whites	4	4
Salt	1 Tbsp.	15 ml
White pepper	TT	TT
Nutmeg	TT	TT
Cayenne pepper	TT	TT
Heavy cream	1 qt.	1 lt

1. Grind the dominant meat through a large die.
2. Process the meat in a food processor until smooth.
3. Add the egg whites one at a time and pulse the processor until they are incorporated.
4. Scrape down the sides of the processor's bowl and add the spices.
5. With the machine running, add the cream in a steady stream.
6. Scrape down the bowl again and process the mousseline until it is smooth and well mixed. Do not overprocess.
7. Remove the mousseline from the machine and hold in an ice bath. If additional smoothness is desired, force the mousseline through a drum sieve in small batches using a plastic scraper or rubber spatula.
8. Cook a small portion of the forcemeat. Taste and adjust the seasonings and texture as necessary.

The forcemeat is now ready to use as desired in the preparation of pâtés, terrines, galantines or sausages.

1. Processing the ground meat in a cold food processor just until smooth.

2. Adding the eggs and pulsing until blended.

3. Adding the cream in a steady stream while the machine runs.

4. Passing the forcemeat through a drum sieve to ensure a smooth finished product.

Quenelles

Quenelles are small dumpling-shaped portions of a mousseline forcemeat poached in an appropriately flavored stock. Quenelles are a traditional garnish for many soups and a popular appetizer usually accompanied by a tomato coulis or a fish velouté-based sauce such as sauce nantua. The technique used for making and poaching quenelles is also used for testing the seasoning and consistency of a mousseline forcemeat.

PROCEDURE FOR PREPARING QUENELLES

1. Prepare a mousseline forcemeat.
2. Bring an appropriately flavored poaching liquid to a simmer.
3. Use two spoons to form the forcemeat into oblong-shaped dumplings. For small quenelles use small spoons; for larger quenelles use larger spoons.
4. Poach the quenelles until done. Test by breaking one in half to check the center's doneness.
5. Small soup-garnish-sized quenelles can be chilled in ice water, drained and held for service. Reheat them in a small amount of stock before garnishing the soup.

Forming the quenelles using two spoons; poaching gently until done.

USING FORCEMEATS

Forcemeats are used as basic components in the preparation of other foods, including terrines, pâtés, galantines and sausages. Aspic jelly is also an important component of these products.

Terrines, Pâtés and Galantines

Traditionally, a **pâté** was a fine savory meat filling wrapped in pastry, baked and served hot or cold. A **terrine** was considered more basic, consisting of coarsely ground and highly seasoned meats baked in an earthenware mold and always served cold. (The mold is also called a terrine, derived from the French word *terre*, meaning earth.) Pâtés baked in pastry are called **pâtés en croûte**. Many types of pâté are baked in loaf-type pans, without a crust, which according to tradition would make them terrines. Today, the terms *pâté* and *terrine* are used almost interchangeably. **Galantines** are made from forcemeats of poultry, game or suckling pig wrapped in the skin of the bird or animal and poached in an appropriate stock.

◆◆◆

ASPIC JELLY

Aspic jelly is a savory jelly produced by increasing the gelatin content of a strong stock and then clarifying the stock following the process for preparing consommé discussed in Chapter 11, Soups. Brown stock produces an amber aspic jelly; white stock produces a light aspic jelly.

Although gelatin is a natural ingredient present in all good stocks, its concentration level is not normally high enough to produce a firm aspic jelly. Additional gelatin is usually added to the stock in order to assist gelling (setting). This can be done in two ways. The first is to produce a stock with an extremely high gelatin content by using gelatinous meats and bones such as calves' feet, pigs' ears and pork skin; the second is to add plain gelatin to a finished stock. An easier method of preparing aspic jelly is to add gelatin directly to a flavorful finished consommé.

Aspic jelly has many applications throughout the kitchen. In addition to adding flavor and shine, a coating of aspic jelly prevents displayed foods from drying out and inhibits the oxidation of sliced red meats. Aspic jelly is often lightly flavored with liquors such as madeira and cut into decorative garnishes for both plated presentations and buffet displays. It is also used to bind savory mousses, glaze slices of pâté and coat molded mousse. Aspic jelly is funneled into cooked pâtés en croûte to fill the gaps created when the forcemeat shrinks during the cooking process. Aspic jelly is also the basis of aspic molds or terrines (often simply called *aspics*), in which layers of cooked meats or vegetables are bound together and held in place by the aspic jelly. Many of these uses are discussed below.

The gelatin content of aspic jelly varies depending upon its intended use. Aspic jelly to be used only on a display can have a very high gelatin content for easier handling. Aspic jelly to be eaten should be fairly firm when cold, gelled at room temperature but tender enough to melt quickly in the mouth when eaten. To test the gelatin content of a liquid pour a teaspoon (5 milliliters) onto a plate and refrigerate the plate for a few minutes. If the liquid does not gel firmly, additional gelatin can be softened in a small amount of cool liquid then added to the hot liquid.

TABLE 20.1 GELATIN CONCENTRATIONS

Type of Gel	Amount of Gelatin per Gallon (4 lt) of Water	Typical Use
Soft	2 oz. (60 g)	Cubed aspic jelly for edible garnishes.
Firm	4 oz. (120 g)	Brushing slices of pâté or galantine; glazing edible centerpieces; molding terrines, aspics and brawns that will be sliced.
Very Firm	8 oz. + (225 g +)	Nonedible purposes such as coating nonedible centerpieces or trays for presentations.

Terrines, pâtés and galantines are often made with forcemeats layered with garnishes to produce a decorative or mosaic effect when sliced. A wide variety of foods can be used as garnishes including strips of ham, fatback or tongue; mushrooms or other vegetables; truffles and pistachio nuts. Garnishes should always be cooked before they are added to the pâté, terrine or galantine or they will shrink during cooking, creating air pockets.

Pâté Pans, Molds and Terrines

Pâté pans, molds and terrines come in a variety of shapes and sizes. Pâtés that are not baked in a crust can be prepared in standard metal loaf pans of any shape, although rectangular ones make portioning the cooked pâté much easier. For pâtés en croûte, the best pans are collapsible or hinged, thin-metaled ones. They make it easier to remove the pâté after baking. Collapsible and hinged pans come in various shapes and sizes from small plain rectangles to large intricately fluted ovals. Traditional earthenware molds and terrines as well as ones made from enamel, metal, glass or even plastic are available. Most terrines are rectangular or oval in shape. Several of these pans are illustrated in Chapter 5, Tools and Equipment.

Terrines

Terrines are forcemeats baked in a mold without a crust. The mold can be the traditional earthenware dish or some other appropriate metal, enamel or glass mold. Any type of forcemeat can be used to make a terrine. The terrine can be as simple as a baking dish filled with a forcemeat and baked until done. A more attractive terrine can be constructed by layering the forcemeat with garnishes to create a mosaic effect when sliced. A terrine can even be layered with different forcemeats; for example, a pink salmon mousseline may be layered with a white pike mousseline.

PROCEDURE FOR PREPARING A TERRINE

1. Prepare the desired forcemeat and garnishes and keep refrigerated until needed.
2. Line a mold with thin slices of fatback, blanched leafy vegetables or other appropriate liner. (Some chefs claim that the fatback keeps the terrine moist during cooking; most modern chefs do not agree but nevertheless use it for aesthetic purposes.) The lining should overlap slightly, completely covering the inside of the mold and extending over the edge of the mold by approximately 1 inch (2.5 centimeters). Alternatively, line the mold with plastic wrap.
3. Fill the terrine with the forcemeat and garnishes, being careful not to create air pockets. Tap the mold several times on a solid work surface to remove any air pockets.
4. Fold the liner or plastic wrap over the forcemeat and, if necessary, use additional pieces to completely cover its surface.
5. If desired, garnish the top of the terrine with herbs that were used in the preparation of the forcemeat.
6. Cover the terrine with its lid or aluminum foil and bake in a water bath in a 350°F (180°C) oven. Regulate the oven temperature so the water stays between 170° and 180°F (77–82°C).
7. Cook the terrine to an internal temperature of 150°F (66°C) for meat-based forcemeats or 140°F (60°C) for fish- or vegetable-based forcemeats.
8. Remove the terrine from the oven and allow it to cool slightly. If desired, pour off any fat and liquid from around the terrine and cover it with cool liquid aspic jelly.

Several types of terrines are not made from traditional forcemeats; many others are not made from forcemeats at all. But all are nonetheless called terrines because they are molded or cooked in the earthenware mold called a terrine. These include liver (and foie gras) terrines, vegetable terrines, brawns or aspic terrines, mousses, rillettes and confits.

Liver terrines are popular and easy to make. Puréed poultry, pork or veal livers are mixed with eggs and a panada of cream and flour, then baked in a fatback-lined terrine. Although most livers purée easily in a food processor, a smoother finished product is achieved if the livers are forced through a drum sieve after or in lieu of puréeing them in the processor.

Foie gras terrines are made with the fattened geese or duck livers called foie gras. Foie gras is unique, even among other poultry livers, in that it consists almost entirely of fat. (See Chapter 17.) It requires special attention during cooking; if it is cooked improperly or too long it turns into a puddle of very expensive fat.

Vegetable terrines can be made with a relatively low fat content and are becoming increasingly popular. Beautiful vegetable terrines are made by lining

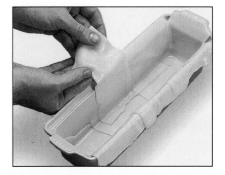

1. Lining a mold with thin slices of fatback.

2. Filling the terrine with the forcemeat and garnish.

3. Decorating the top of the terrine with herbs and placing the terrine in a water bath.

4. Slicing the finished terrine.

a terrine with a blanched leafy vegetable such as spinach, then alternating layers of two or three separately prepared vegetable fillings to create contrasting colors and flavors. A different style of vegetable terrine is made by suspending brightly colored vegetables in a mousseline forcemeat to create a mosaic pattern when sliced.

Brawns or **aspic terrines** are made by simmering gelatinous cuts of meat (most notably, pigs' feet and head, including the tongue) in a rich stock with wine and flavorings. The stock is enriched with gelatin and flavor from the meat, creating an unclarified aspic jelly. The meat is then pulled from the bone, diced and packed into the terrine mold. The stock is reduced to concentrate its gelatin content, strained through cheesecloth and poured over the meat in the terrine. After the terrine has set, it is removed from the mold and sliced for service. The finished product is a rustic and flavorful dish.

A more elegant-appearing brawn is made by lining a terrine mold with aspic jelly, arranging a layer of garnish (for example, sliced meats, vegetables or low-acid fruits) along the mold's bottom, adding aspic jelly to cover the garnish and repeating the procedure until the mold is full.

A **mousse** can be sweet or savory. Sweet mousses are described in Chapter 31, Custards, Creams, Frozen Desserts and Dessert Sauces. A savory mousse—which is not a mousseline forcemeat—is made from fully cooked meats, poultry, game, fish, shellfish or vegetables that are puréed and combined with a béchamel or other appropriate sauce, bound with gelatin and lightened with whipped cream. A mousse can be molded in a decorated, aspic-jelly-coated mold such as that described immediately below, or it can be formed in molds lined with plastic wrap, which is peeled off after the mousse is unmolded. A small mousse can be served as an individual portion; a larger molded mousse can be displayed on a buffet.

PROCEDURE FOR PREPARING AN ASPIC-JELLY-COATED CHILLED MOUSSE

A mold can be lined with aspic jelly, then decorated and filled with cold mousse. The aspic-jelly-coated mousse is then unmolded for an attractive presentation.

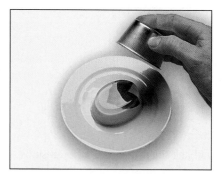

1. Set a metal mold in ice water and add 8 ounces (250 grams) of cool liquid aspic jelly. Swirl the mold so the aspic jelly adheres to all sides. Pour out the excess aspic jelly. Repeat as needed to achieve the desired thickness; 1/4 inch (6 millimeters) or less is usually sufficient.

2. Garnish the mold by dipping pieces of vegetable or other foods in the liquid aspic jelly and placing them carefully inside the aspic-jelly-coated mold. The mold can now be filled with a cold filling such as a mousse.

3. Refrigerate the mold until it is well chilled. Unmold the aspic by dipping the mold in warm water, then inverting and tapping the mold on a plate.

Rillettes and **confits** are actually preserved meats. Rillettes are prepared by seasoning and slow-cooking pork or fatty poultry such as duck or goose in generous amounts of their own fat until the meat falls off the bone. The warm meat is mashed and combined with a portion of the cooking fat. The mixture is then packed into a crock or terrine and rendered fat is strained over the top to seal it. Rillettes are eaten cold as a spread accompanied by bread or toast.

Confit is prepared in a similar manner except before cooking the meat or poultry is often lightly salt-cured to draw out some moisture. The confit is then cooked until very tender but not falling apart. Confits are generally served hot. Like rillettes, confits can be preserved by sealing them with a layer of strained rendered fat. Properly prepared and sealed rillettes and confits will keep for several weeks under refrigeration.

Although it is sometimes incorrectly called chicken liver pâté, **chopped chicken liver** is prepared in a similar fashion to a rillette. Chopped chicken liver, however, will not have the keeping qualities of traditional rillettes or confits because it is not normally sealed in a crock or terrine with rendered fat. It should be eaten within a day or two of its preparation.

Pâtés en Croûte

Considered by some to be the pinnacle of the charcutier's art, pâtés en croûte are forcemeats baked in a crust. The forcemeat can be country-style, basic or mousseline, but a basic forcemeat is most commonly used. Although pâtés en croûte can be baked without using a mold, a mold helps produce a more attractive finished product.

Pâté Dough (Pâte au Pâté)

The crust surrounding a baking forcemeat must be durable enough to hold in the juices produced as the pâté bakes and to withstand the long baking process. Unfortunately, some of the more durable crusts are tough and unpleasant to eat.

The goal is to achieve a balance so that the crust will hold the juices of the baking pâté and still be relatively pleasant to the palate. Some pâtés, especially more delicate ones such as fish mousselines, can be wrapped in brioche dough (Recipe 28.16).

◆◆◆

RECIPE 20.5
PÂTÉ DOUGH

Yield: 1 lb. 8 oz. (680 g)

All-purpose flour	1 lb.	450 g
Shortening	7 oz.	200 g
Salt	1-1/2 tsp.	7 ml
Water	5 oz.	150 ml
Egg	1	1

1. Place the flour in the bowl of a mixer. Add the shortening and mix on low speed until smooth.

2. Combine the salt, water and egg; add them to the flour and shortening mixture.

3. Knead until smooth and refrigerate. The dough will be easier to work with if allowed to rest for at least 1 hour.

PROCEDURE FOR ASSEMBLING AND BAKING PÂTÉS EN CROÛTE

After preparing a forcemeat and pastry dough, all that remains is to assemble and bake the pâté en croûte. The amount of pastry dough and forcemeat needed is determined by the size of the mold or pan chosen.

1. Prepare the pâté dough and the forcemeat, keeping the forcemeat refrigerated until needed.
2. Roll out the dough into a rectangular shape 1/8 inch (3 millimeters) thick.
3. Using the pâté mold as a pattern, determine how much dough is needed to line its inside; allow enough dough along each side of the mold's length to cover the top when folded over. Mark the dough. Cut the dough slightly larger than the marked lines. Cut a second rectangular piece of dough that is slightly larger than the top of the mold; it will be used as a lid.
4. Lightly butter the inside of the mold.
5. Lightly dust the large rectangle of dough with flour, fold it over and transfer it to the mold.
6. Use your thumbs and a dough ball made from dough trimmings to form the dough neatly into the corners of the mold. Continue until the dough is of even thickness on all sides and in the corners.
7. Trim the dough, leaving 3/4 inch (2 centimeters) on the ends and enough dough to cover the top along the sides.
8. Line the mold with thin slices of fatback or ham, allowing 3/4 inch (2 centimeters) extra around the top of the mold, or as directed in the recipe. This layer helps protect the pastry crust from coming in contact with the moist forcemeat, which would make it soggy.
9. Fill the lined mold with the forcemeat to 1/2 inch (1.2 centimeters) below the top of the mold, pressing it well into the corners to avoid air pockets. Layer and garnish as appropriate.
10. Fold the fatback or ham over the top of the forcemeat, using additional pieces if necessary to cover its entire surface. Fold the pastry over the forcemeat.
11. Brush the exposed surface of the pastry with egg wash; carefully cap with the top piece of dough. Press any overlapping dough down inside the sides of the mold with a small spatula.
12. Using round cutters, cut one or two holes in the top to allow steam to escape during cooking. Egg-wash the surface. Place a doughnut-shaped piece of dough around each of the holes. Egg-wash the decorations.

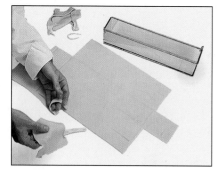

1. Cutting the dough into a large rectangle.

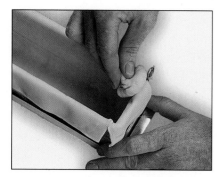

2. Pressing the dough into the mold with a floured dough ball and your thumbs.

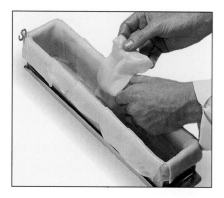

3. Lining the mold with thin slices of fatback.

4. Filling the lined mold with the forcemeat and garnish.

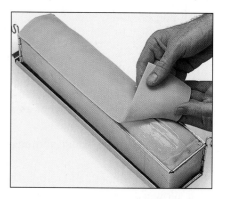

5. Using egg wash on the surface and placing the top on the pâté.

6. Inserting an aluminum chimney in one of the holes of the baked pâté and pouring aspic jelly into the hole.

7. Slicing the pâté with a thin-bladed knife.

13. Bake the pâté in a preheated 450°F (230°C) oven for 15 minutes. Then cover the surface of the pâté with aluminum foil. Reduce the heat to 350°F (180°C) and continue baking until the internal temperature reaches 150°F (66°C) for meat pâtés or 140°F (60°C) for fish and vegetable pâtés.

14. Allow the pâté to cool for at least 1 hour or overnight. Using a funnel, pour cool liquid aspic jelly through the holes to fill the space created when the pâté shrank during cooking. Allow the pâté en croûte to cool overnight before slicing.

PROCEDURE FOR GLAZING PÂTÉ SLICES WITH ASPIC JELLY

Slices of chilled terrines, pâtés en croûte or gallantines (discussed below) may be garnished and coated with aspic to preserve their color, prevent drying and create a more attractive presentation.

1. Stirring slowly to cool the clarified aspic jelly.

2. Brush or spoon the aspic jelly over slices of chilled pâté arranged on a cooling rack. Repeat the process until the coating reaches the desired thickness.

Galantines

A classic **galantine** is a boned chicken stuffed with a chicken-based force-meat to resemble its original shape and then poached. Today, galantines are still most often prepared from whole ducks or chickens, but they can also be made from game, veal, fish or shellfish. When appropriate, the forcemeat is stuffed in the skin, which has been removed in one piece, sometimes with flesh still attached. When the skin is not available, its use is inappropriate or in the case of fish and shellfish where there is no skin, the galantine is made by forming the forcemeat into a cylindrical shape and wrapping it in cheesecloth or plastic wrap and foil before poaching. Galantines are always served cold and are often displayed on buffets, sliced and glazed with aspic jelly.

A **ballottine** is similar to a galantine. It is made by removing the bones from a poultry leg, filling the cavity with an appropriate forcemeat and poaching or braising the leg with vegetables. Ballottines are often served hot with a sauce made from the cooking liquid.

PROCEDURE FOR PREPARING A POULTRY GALANTINE

1. Bone the chicken by cutting through the skin along the length of the backbone and then following the natural curvature of the carcass. Keep all the meat attached to the skin. Remove the legs and wings by cutting through the joints when you reach them; leave the legs and wings attached to the skin. Then cut off the wings. Bone the thighs and legs, leaving the skin and meat attached to the rest of the bird. Trim the skin to form a large rectangle.
2. Prepare a forcemeat using the meat from the skinned bird or any other appropriate meat. Reserve a portion of the meat as garnish if desired. Prepare any other garnishes. Refrigerate the forcemeat and garnishes until ready for use.
3. Spread out the skin and meat on plastic wrap or several layers of cheesecloth with the skin side down and the flesh up.
4. Remove the chicken tenderloins and pull the tendon out of each. Butterfly the breasts and tenderloins and cover the entire skin with a thin layer of meat.
5. Arrange the forcemeat and garnishes in a cylindrical shape across the center of the skin.
6. Using the plastic or cheesecloth to assist the process, tightly roll the skin around the forcemeat and garnishes to form a tight cylinder.

1. Butterflying the breasts and tenderloins and placing a thin layer of meat over the skin.

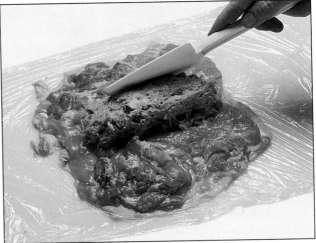

2. Arranging the forcemeat and garnishes in a cylindrical shape across the center of the skin.

3. Using the plastic wrap to roll the galantine into a tight cylinder.

4. Securing the galantine with heavy-duty aluminum foil.

5. Slicing the finished product.

7. Tie the ends of the cheesecloth with butcher's twine and secure the galantine at even intervals using strips of cheesecloth. If plastic wrap was used, wrap the galantine with heavy-duty aluminum foil.
8. Poach the galantine in a full-flavored stock to an internal temperature of 150°F (66°C) for meat-based forcemeats or 140°F (60°C) for fish- or vegetable-based forcemeats.
9. Cool the galantine in its cooking liquid until it can be handled. Remove the cheesecloth or plastic wrap and aluminum foil and rewrap the galantine in clean cheesecloth or plastic wrap. Refrigerate overnight before decorating or slicing.

Sausages

Sausages are forcemeats stuffed into casings. For centuries, sausages consisted of ground meat, usually pork, and seasonings. Today not only are sausages made from pork, but also from game, beef, veal, poultry, fish, shellfish and even vegetables.

There are three main types of sausages:

1. Fresh sausages include breakfast sausage links and Italian sausages. They are made with fresh ingredients that have not been cured or smoked.
2. Smoked and **cooked sausages** are made with raw meat products treated with chemicals, usually the preservative sodium nitrite. Examples are kielbasa, bologna and hot dogs.
3. Dried or **hard sausages** are made with cured meats, then air-dried under controlled conditions. Dry sausages may or may not be smoked or cooked. Dried or hard sausages include salami, pepperoni, Lebanon bologna and landjäger.

Smoked and cooked sausages and dry or hard sausages are rarely prepared in typical food service operations. They are produced by specialty shops and will not be discussed here. We do discuss the ingredients and procedures for a variety of fresh sausages that can be prepared in almost any kitchen.

Sausage Components

Sausage Meats
Sausage meats are forcemeats with particular characteristics and flavorings. Course Italian and lamb sausages, for example, are simply a country-style

forcemeat without liver and with different seasonings, stuffed into casings and formed into links. Hot dogs, bratwurst and other fine-textured sausages are variations of basic forcemeats stuffed into casings and formed into links.

Sausage Casings

Although sausage mixtures can be cooked without casings, most sausages are stuffed into casings before cooking. Two types of sausage casings are commonly used in food service operations:

1. **Natural casings** are portions of hog, sheep or cattle intestines. Their diameters are measured in millimeters and they come in several sizes depending upon the animal or portion of the intestine used. Hog casings are the most popular; sheep casings are considered the finest-quality small casings. Both hog and sheep casings are used to make hot dogs and many types of pork sausage. Beef casings are quite large and are used to make sausages such as ring bologna and Polish sausage. Most natural casings are purchased in salt packs. In order to rid them of salt and impurities, the casings must be carefully rinsed in warm water and allowed to soak in cool water for at least 1 hour or overnight before use.

2. **Collagen casings** are manufactured from collagen extracted from cattle hides. They are generally inferior to natural casings in taste and texture, but they do have advantages: Collagen casings do not require any washing or soaking prior to use and they are uniform in size.

Preparing Sausages

Equipment for Sausage Making

Sausage-stuffing machines are best if you engage in large-scale sausage production. Otherwise, all you need is a grinder with a sausage nozzle attachment such as the ones shown in Figure 20.2. Nozzles are available in several sizes to accommodate the various casing sizes.

FIGURE 20.2 *Sausage nozzles*

PROCEDURE FOR MAKING SAUSAGES

1. Prepare a forcemeat.
2. Thoroughly chill all parts of the sausage stuffer that will come in contact with the forcemeat.
3. Rinse and soak the casings if using natural ones. Cut the casings into 4–6-foot (1.2–1.8-meter) lengths.
4. Put the sausage in the sausage stuffer.
5. Slide the casing over the nozzle of the sausage stuffer. Tie the end in a knot and pierce with a skewer to prevent an air pocket.

1. Sliding the casing over the nozzle of the sausage stuffer.

2. Knotting and piercing the casing with a skewer.

3. Supporting and guiding the casing off the end of the nozzle as the sausage is extruded from the machine into the casing.

4. Twisting or tying the sausage into uniform links.

6. Support and guide the casing off the end of the nozzle as the sausage is extruded from the nozzle into the casing.

7. After all the sausage has been stuffed into the casing, twist or tie the sausage into uniform links of the desired size.

SALT-CURING, BRINING AND SMOKING

Curing, brining and smoking are ancient techniques for preserving food. Today, foods such as hams, corned beef and smoked salmon are salt-cured, brined or smoked primarily for flavor. Cured meats have a characteristic pink color caused by the reaction of sodium nitrite, which is added during processing, with the naturally occurring myoglobin protein in the meat.

Salt-Curing

Salt-curing is the process of surrounding a food with salt or a mixture of salt, sugar, nitrite-based curing salt, herbs and spices. Salt-curing dehydrates the food, inhibits bacterial growth and adds flavor. It is most often used with pork products and fish. Salt-curing is not a quick procedure—and the time involved adds money to production costs. For example, country-style hams are salt-cured. Proper curing requires approximately 1-1/2 days per pound of ham, which means 3 weeks for the average ham.

Some salt-cured hams such as Smithfield and prosciutto are not actually cooked. The curing process preserves the meat and makes it safe to consume raw.

Gravlax is a well-known salmon dish prepared by salt-curing salmon fillets with a mixture of salt, sugar, pepper and dill. A recipe for gravlax (Recipe 20.22) is included at the end of this chapter.

Brining

A brine is actually a very salty marinade. Most brines have approximately 20% salinity, which is equivalent to 1 pound (450 grams) of salt per gallon (4 liters) of water. As with dry-salt cures, brines can also contain sugar, nitrites, herbs and spices. Brining is sometimes called pickling.

Today, most cured meats are prepared in large production facilities where the brine is injected into the meat for rapid and uniform distribution. Commercially brined corned beef is cured by this process, as are most common hams. After brining, hams are further processed by smoking.

Smoking

There are two basic methods of smoking foods: cold smoking and hot smoking. The principal difference is that hot smoking actually cooks the food, cold smoking does not.

Both are done in a **smoker** specifically designed for this purpose. Smokers can be gas or electric; they vary greatly in size and operation. But they have several things in common. All consist of a chamber that holds the food being smoked, a means of burning wood to produce smoke and a heating element.

Different types of wood can be used to smoke food. Specific woods are selected to impart specific flavors. Hickory is often used for pork products; alder is excellent for smoked salmon. Maple, chestnut, juniper, mesquite and many other woods are also used. Resinous woods such as pine give food a bitter flavor and should be avoided.

Cold smoking is the process of exposing foods to smoke at temperatures of 50–85°F (10–29°C). Meat, poultry, game, fish, shellfish, cheese, nuts and even vegetables can be cold-smoked successfully. Most cold-smoked meats are generally salt-cured or brined first. Salt-curing or brining adds flavor, allows the nitrites (which give the ham, bacon and other smoked meats their distinctive pink color) to penetrate the flesh and, most importantly, extracts moisture from the food, allowing the smoke to penetrate more easily. Cold-smoked foods are actually still raw. Some, like smoked salmon (lox), are eaten without further cooking. Others, such as bacon and hams, must be cooked before eating.

Hot smoking is the process of exposing foods to smoke at temperatures of 200–250°F (93–121°C). As with cold smoking, a great variety of foods can be prepared by hot smoking. Meats, poultry, game, fish and shellfish that are hot-smoked also benefit from salt-curing or brining. Although most hot-smoked foods are fully cooked when removed from the smoker, many are used in other recipes that call for further cooking.

Pork Products

Preparing hams and curing and smoking pork products are a traditional part of charcuterie. Although most bacon and ham are now produced in large commercial facilities, the chef still works with these products and must be able to identify them properly.

Most **bacon** comes from a hog's fatty belly.

Common bacon is produced by brining and cold smoking trimmed pork belly. It is available in slab or sliced form. Sliced bacon is purchased by count (number of slices) per pound; thick-sliced bacon runs 10–14 slices per pound, while thin-sliced bacon may contain as many as 28–32 slices per pound.

Canadian bacon is produced from a boneless pork loin, trimmed so that only a thin layer of fat remains on its surface. It is then brined and smoked.

Pancetta is an Italian pork-belly bacon that is not smoked. It is salt-cured, peppered and often rolled into a cylinder

FIGURE 20.3 *Canadian Bacon, Sliced Bacon, and Pancetta*

shape. It can be sliced into rounds and fried; it is diced, rendered and combined with sauce to make fettuccine carbonara.

A **fresh ham** is a hog's hind leg; it is a primal cut. Many processed products produced from the primal fresh ham are also called ham.

Ham, in the United States, describes a variety of processed pork products, most of which come from the primal fresh ham. **Boneless** or **formed hams** are produced by separating a primal ham into its basic muscles, defatting the meat, curing it, stuffing the meat into various-sized and -shaped casings and cooking it. Boneless or formed hams are either smoked or chemical smoke flavoring is added during the curing process. The quality of boneless or formed hams varies greatly. The best hams are formed from only one or two large muscles, have low fat content and no added water other than that used during the curing process. Hams of lesser quality are formed from many small pieces of muscle and have a higher fat and water content. Many boneless or formed hams are listed in *The Meat Buyers Guide* and are indexed by the NAMP/IMPS system.

IMPS No. 501, Ham short shank, cured and smoked.

IMPS No. 510, Ham, boneless, skinless, cured and smoked, fully cooked.

Country ham is a specialty of the southeastern United States. Country hams are dry-cured, smoked and hung to air-dry for a period ranging from several weeks to more than a year. During drying, a mold develops on the ham rind that must be scrubbed off before the ham is cooked. It is best cooked by first soaking, then slow simmering. The most famous country hams are Virginia hams; those from Smithfield, Virginia, are considered the finest. Only hams produced in rural areas can be called country hams; others must be labeled country-style ham.

Prosciutto is Italian for ham. What we call prosciutto in this country is called **Parma** in Italy. Parma ham, produced near that Italian city, is made from hogs fed on the whey of cheese processed nearby. It is salt-cured and air-dried but not smoked. The curing process makes it safe and wholesome to consume raw. Several domestic varieties of prosciutto are produced, varying widely in quality. Imported prosciuttos are much larger than the domestic varieties because Italian hogs are larger when butchered.

Westphalian ham is dry-cured, brined and then smoked with beechwood. Authentic Westphalian hams are produced in the Westphalia region of Germany and are quite similar to prosciutto. They are sold bone-in or boneless. Their characteristic flavor is derived from the juniper berries used in the curing process and the beechwood used for smoking.

*C*ONCLUSION

The classic art of charcuterie is as popular today as ever. Consumers regularly enjoy high-quality pâtés, sausages, hams and other charcuterie products.

Although production procedures have changed as new technologies and equipment have developed, the basic principles remain the same: Terrines, pâtés and sausages can only be produced from high-quality forcemeats, and temperature control is fundamental to the proper production of forcemeats and other charcuterie products.

Armed with a basic knowledge of the procedures used for charcuterie, you can use your imagination and creativity to produce a variety of charcuterie products.

QUESTIONS FOR DISCUSSION

1. Explain why the art of charcuterie is relevant to the training of modern chefs.
2. Compare and contrast the three styles of forcemeat.
3. In what way is a terrine different from a pâté? How does a pâté differ from a pâté en croûte?
4. Describe the differences and the similarities between a ballottine and a galantine.
5. Describe the typical procedure for making sausages. Why is the selection of casings important?
6. Explain the difference between hot smoking and cold smoking. Describe a food typically prepared by each of these methods.

ADDITIONAL CHARCUTERIE RECIPES

RECIPE 20.6

SMOKED DUCK AND FOIE GRAS GALANTINE ON A PEAR GALETTE

NOTE: *This dish appears in the Chapter Opening photograph.*

ANA WESTIN HOTEL, WASHINGTON, D.C.
Chef Leland Atkinson

Yield: 1 Galantine

Duck breast, 10 oz. (300 g), boneless, skinless	1	1
Duck meat, lean	1 lb.	450 g
Pork butt, boneless, cubed	8 oz.	240 g
Pâté spice	2 tsp.	10 ml
Salt	1 Tbsp.	15 ml
Orange zest	1 Tbsp.	15 ml
Fresh thyme	1 tsp.	5 ml
Fresh ginger	1 tsp.	5 ml
Juniper berries, crushed	10	10

Port	4 oz.	120 g
Olive oil	1 oz.	30 g
Fatback, cubed	8 oz.	240 g
Foie gras pâté, diced	3 oz.	90 g
Ham, medium dice	2 oz.	60 g
Pistachio meats, chopped	2 oz.	60 g
Fatback, slab	as needed	as needed
Smoker marinade:		
Brown sugar	2 oz.	60 g
Garlic, chopped	1 tsp.	5 ml
Lemon juice	3 oz.	90 g
Walnut oil	6 oz.	180 g
Salt and pepper	TT	TT
Galette (per order)		
Pears	1	1
Clarified butter	1 tsp.	5 ml
Sugar	1/2 tsp.	3 ml
Italian parsley	as needed	as needed

1. Cut the duck breast into several long strips.
2. Marinate the duck breast, duck meat and pork in the pâté spice, salt, orange zest, ginger, thyme, juniper berries and port for 2 days.
3. Remove the strips of duck breast from the marinade and sauté in the olive oil to brown. Remove, drain and reserve.
4. Grind the remaining duck meat, pork butt, marinade ingredients and the cubed fatback in a chilled grinder, first through the large die then through the small die.
5. Place the ground meat in a stainless steel bowl over an ice bath. Fold in the foie gras, ham and pistachios.
6. Slice the fatback into thin sheets. Spread a piece of plastic wrap on the work surface and lay out the slices of fatback in a large rectangle with the edges overlapping slightly.
7. Place the forcemeat and duck breast strips along the length of the fatback rectangle so that when the galantine is rolled up the strips of duck will be arranged in the center. Use the plastic wrap to roll the galantine into a large cylinder.
8. Roll the cylinder in heavy-duty aluminum foil and poach until it reaches an internal temperature of 140°F (60°C). Remove and chill the galantine for at least 6 hours.
9. Combine the ingredients for the smoker marinade in a blender. Unwrap the galantine, brush it with the smoker marinade and chill for 1 hour. Place the galantine in a smoker and cold smoke for 2 hours. Remove and chill before slicing.
10. For each galette, core the pear and slice 1/8 inch (3 millimeters) thick. Add the clarified butter to a warm sauté pan and arrange the pears in the pan by overlapping the slices to form a circle. Sprinkle the pears with the sugar. Sauté the galette, using a spatula to carefully turn it over when browned on the first side.
11. Place a pear galette on a plate and place a slice of galantine directly in the center of the galette. Garnish with Italian parsley or as desired. May be accompanied by Cherry Confit (Recipe 25.13).

◆◆◆

RECIPE 20.7

LAMB SAUSAGE WITH TRICOLOR BEAN SALAD

NOTE: *This dish appears in the Chapter Opening photograph.*

ANA WESTIN HOTEL, WASHINGTON, D.C.
Chef Leland Atkinson

LAMB SAUSAGE

Yield: 12 4-oz. (120-g) Links

Lamb shoulder	3 lb.	1.5 kg
Salt	1 Tbsp.	15 ml
Garlic, chopped	2 tsp.	10 g
Paprika	1 Tbsp.	15 ml
Cayenne pepper	1/2 tsp.	2 ml
Black pepper	1/2 tsp.	2 ml
Cumin	1 Tbsp.	15 ml
Fresh cilantro, chopped	2 Tbsp.	30 ml
Tricolor Bean Salad (recipe follows)	as needed	as needed
Baby lettuces, assorted	12 heads	12 heads
Belgian endive	2 heads	2 heads
Olive oil	as needed	as needed
Red wine vinegar	as needed	as needed

1. Cut the meat in small cubes.
2. Combine the meat with the seasonings and herbs and refrigerate for 1 hour.
3. Grind the meat through a medium die directly into casings.
4. Grill or sauté the sausage links. Present the cooked links with a portion of the Tricolor Bean Salad garnished with baby greens and Belgian endive. Accent with drizzled olive oil and red wine vinegar.

TRICOLOR BEAN SALAD

Yield: 24 oz. (700 g)

Dijon mustard	2 Tbsp.	30 ml
Garlic, minced	1 tsp.	5 ml
Red onion, small dice	1 oz.	30 g
Jalapeños, seeded and minced	2	2
Red wine vinegar	2 Tbsp.	30 ml
Olive oil	3 Tbsp.	45 ml
Black beans, cooked	4 oz.	120 g
Black-eyed peas, cooked	4 oz.	120 g
Plum tomatoes, concasse	3	3
Fresh cilantro, chopped	1 bunch	1 bunch
Salt and pepper	TT	TT

1. Combine the mustard, garlic, onions, jalapeños and red wine vinegar in a mixing bowl.
2. Slowly whisk in the olive oil in a steady stream.
3. Add the beans, black-eyed peas, tomato concasse and cilantro and season with salt and pepper. Refrigerate 1 hour to allow the flavors to blend.

◆◆◆

RECIPE 20.8

VEGETABLE TERRINE IN BRIOCHE

NOTE: *This dish appears in the Chapter Opening photograph.*

ANA WESTIN HOTEL, WASHINGTON, D.C.
Chef Leland Atkinson

Yield: 1 12 in. x 4 in. x. 3 in.
(30 cm x 10 cm x 7.5 cm) Terrine

Chicken breast meat, lean	2 lb.	900 g
Egg whites	3	3
Heavy cream	4 oz.	120 g
Brandy	2 oz.	60 g
Salt and pepper	TT	TT
Carrot, medium dice	3 oz.	90 g
Broccoli florets	8 oz.	250 g
Shiitake mushrooms, trimmed	12–18	12–18
Olive oil	1 oz.	30 ml
Red bell pepper, medium dice	2 oz.	60 g
Leek, white part only, medium dice	2 oz.	60 g
Fresh chives, basil and parsley, chopped	4 Tbsp.	60 ml
Nutmeg	TT	TT
Brioche dough, rolled out to approximately 1/8 in. (3 mm), well chilled	1 lb.	450 g
Egg yolks, beaten	2	2
Eggs	2	2
Water	1 oz.	30 g
Madeira aspic	as needed	as needed

1. Dice or grind the chicken; place it in the bowl of a cold food processor and process.

2. Add the egg whites and then the cream and brandy in a steady stream while the motor is running.

3. Season the mousseline and poach a small amount to test for texture and seasonings.

4. Adjust the seasonings and transfer to a metal mixing bowl in an ice bath.

5. Separately blanch the carrots and broccoli; drain and blot dry on a paper towel.

6. Sauté the shiitakes in olive oil. Drain and chill. In the same pan, sauté the red peppers and leeks. Remove from the stove and add the herbs. Fold the carrots, peppers, leeks and herbs into the mousseline.

7. Line a buttered pâté mold with the chilled brioche, reserving the excess for the top and garnish.

8. Fill the mold one-fourth full with the mousseline. Layer the shiitakes over the mousseline, cover them with another layer of mousseline, followed by the dry broccoli. Repeat this process until the mold is filled, finishing with a layer of mousseline.

9. Fold the ends of the brioche over the filling and brush with beaten egg yolk.

10. Make a top from the remaining brioche and place it over the mold; cut a vent and insert a foil funnel into the vent.

11. Beat the eggs with the water to make an egg wash. Brush the exposed

Continued

brioche with the egg wash and bake at 425°F (220°C) until the internal
temperature reaches 125°F (52°C), approximately 35–40 minutes.

12. When cold, fill the pâté with madeira aspic, if needed.

✦✦✦

RECIPE 20.9

BASIC GAME FORCEMEAT

Yield: 4 lb. 8 oz. (2 kg)

Venison or antelope, cubed	1 lb. 8 oz.	675 g
Veal, cubed	1 lb. 8 oz.	675 g
Brandy	4 oz.	120 g
Salt and pepper	TT	TT
Dried thyme	1 tsp.	5 ml
Pork fatback, cubed	1 lb.	450 g
Eggs	3	3
Game stock, cold	1 pt.	450 ml
Fresh parsley, chopped	1 oz.	30 g
Green peppercorns	1/2 oz.	15 g

1. Combine the venison or antelope and veal with the brandy, salt, pepper and thyme; marinate for several hours or overnight.

2. Grind the marinated meat and marinade ingredients in a chilled meat grinder once through a large die and then once through a small die; refrigerate.

3. Grind the fatback once through the small die.

4. Emulsify the fat with the ground meats in the bowl of a cold food processor. This can be done in several batches. Place the forcemeat in a stainless steel bowl over an ice bath.

5. Add the eggs, stock, parsley and green peppercorns to the forcemeat in several batches; work them in by hand.

6. Additional garnishes may be added as desired. The forcemeat can be used to make a variety of pâtés or terrines.

✦✦✦

RECIPE 20.10

SALMON AND SEA BASS TERRINE
WITH SPINACH AND BASIL

Yield: 1 12 in. x 4 in. x. 3 in.
     (30 cm x 10 cm x 7.5 cm) Terrine

Salmon fillet, boneless, skinless	1 lb. 8 oz.	700 g
Egg whites	3	3
Salt and white pepper	TT	TT
Cayenne pepper	TT	TT
Heavy cream	24 oz.	700 g
Basil leaves	12	12
Truffle, brunoise (optional)	3/4 oz.	22 g
Spinach leaves, cleaned	6 oz.	180 g
Sea bass fillet	12 oz.	350 g

1. Grind the salmon through the large die of a well-chilled meat grinder.

2. Place the salmon in the bowl of a food processor and process until smooth.

3. Add the egg whites, one at a time, pulsing the processor to incorporate. Scrape down the bowl and season with salt, white pepper and cayenne pepper.

4. With the machine running, add the cream in a steady stream. Scrape down the bowl again and process the mousseline until it is smooth and well mixed.

5. Blanch the basil leaves and refresh. Chop them finely.

6. Remove the mousseline from the bowl of the processor. Fold in the basil leaves and truffles and refrigerate.

7. Blanch and refresh the spinach leaves.

8. Spread the spinach leaves on a piece of plastic wrap, completely covering a rectangle approximately the length and width of the terrine mold.

9. Cut the sea bass fillet into strips approximately 1 inch (2.5 centimeters) wide and place end to end on the spinach leaves. Season with salt and white pepper.

10. Use the plastic wrap to wrap the spinach leaves tightly around the fish fillets.

11. Butter a terrine and line it with plastic wrap.

12. Half-fill the lined terrine with salmon mousseline.

13. Carefully unwrap the spinach and sea bass fillets and place them down the center of the terrine. Fill the terrine with the remaining mousseline.

14. Tap the terrine mold firmly to remove any air pockets, then fold the plastic wrap over the top.

15. Cover and bake the terrine in a water bath at 300°F (150°C) to an internal temperature of 140°F (60°C), approximately 1-1/2 hours.

16. Cool the terrine well, unmold, slice or decorate and serve as desired.

◆◆◆

RECIPE 20.11

SWEETBREAD TERRINE

Yield: 1 12 in. x 4 in. x 3 in.
(30 cm x 10 cm x 7.5 cm) Terrine

Lean veal, cubed	2 lb.	1 kg
Pork butt, cubed	1 lb.	450 g
Pâté spice	1 Tbsp.	15 ml
Salt and pepper	TT	TT
Brandy	6 oz.	180 g
Fatback	1 lb.	450 g
Eggs	4	4
Sweetbreads	2 lb.	1 kg
Morels	4 oz.	120 g
Chanterelles	4 oz.	120 g
Shiitake mushrooms	4 oz.	120 g
Clarified butter	1 oz.	30 g
Fresh thyme, chopped	1 Tbsp.	15 ml
Rosemary	2 tsp.	10 ml
Fresh chives, chopped	2 Tbsp.	30 ml

Continued

1. Combine the veal and pork butt with the pâté spice, salt, pepper and brandy; marinate for several hours or overnight.

2. Dice and freeze the fatback.

3. Grind the veal, pork and marinade ingredients in a well-chilled grinder, once through the large die, then once through the medium die. Hold in an ice bath.

4. Grind the fatback once through the medium die; add to the ground meat mixture.

5. Place the meat mixture and fatback in a chilled food processor and process until emulsified.

6. Over an ice bath, incorporate the eggs into the forcemeat. Refrigerate the forcemeat while preparing the garnishes.

7. Blanch the sweetbreads. Remove the connective tissue and cut the sweetbreads into large dice.

8. Wash the mushrooms, sauté them in the butter; season with the thyme and rosemary. Chill them well.

9. Fold the sweetbreads, mushrooms and chives into the forcemeat and follow the procedures for preparing a terrine.

———— ◆◆◆ ————

RECIPE 20.12

LIVER TERRINE

Yield: 1 12 in. x 4 in. x 3 in.
(30 cm x 10 cm x 7.5 cm) Terrine

Pork liver	1 lb. 4 oz.	600 g
Fatback, diced	12 oz.	350 g
Onion, diced	6 oz.	180 g
Eggs	2	2
Salt	1 Tbsp.	15 ml
Green peppercorns	1/2 tsp.	2 ml
Allspice, ground	1/2 tsp.	2 ml
Cloves, ground	1/4 tsp.	1 ml
Ginger, ground	1/4 tsp.	1 ml
Cream sauce	8 oz.	250 g
Brown veal stock	6 oz.	180 g
Fatback, sliced	as needed	as needed

1. Trim and dice the liver.

2. Grind the liver and diced fatback through a grinder with a fine die.

3. Add the onion and pass the liver and fatback through the grinder again.

4. Beat together by hand the eggs, salt, green peppercorns, allspice, cloves and ginger.

5. Combine the cream sauce and brown veal stock, add the egg mixture and mix well.

6. Add the ground liver mixture and beat until smooth.

7. Line a terrine with slices of fatback. Fill the mold with the forcemeat and cover with the overhanging slices of fatback.

8. Cover the terrine with its lid or aluminum foil and bake in a water bath at

350° F (180° C) to an internal temperature of 150° F (66° C), approximately 1-1/2 hours.

9. Cool, unmold, slice and serve as desired.

═══════════════ ◆◆◆ ═══════════════

RECIPE 20.13

VEGETABLE TERRINE

Yield: 1 12 in. x 4 in. x 3 in.
(30 cm x 10 cm x 7.5 cm) Terrine

Carrots, batonnet	6 oz.	180 g
Green beans	4 oz.	120 g
Leeks, small, white part only	4 oz.	120 g
Shiitake mushrooms	6 oz.	180 g
Whole butter	1 oz.	30 g
Artichoke hearts, cooked and chilled	5	5
Red bell peppers, roasted and peeled, julienne	4 oz.	120 g
Gruyère cheese, shredded	6 oz.	180 g
Heavy cream	1-1/2 pt.	700 ml
Egg yolks	9	9
Nutmeg	TT	TT
Salt and pepper	TT	TT
Fresh chives, chopped	1 Tbsp.	15 ml
Granulated gelatin	1 Tbsp.	15 ml
Red Pepper Coulis (Recipe 10.17)	as needed	as needed

1. Boil the carrots in salted water until tender, approximately 3 minutes. Refresh and reserve.

2. Clean the green beans and boil in salted water until tender, approximately 5 minutes. Refresh and reserve.

3. Trim the roots from the leeks and boil in salted water until tender, approximately 3 minutes. Refresh and reserve.

4. Trim the stems from the shiitake mushrooms. Sauté the caps in butter until tender. Remove from the heat and set aside.

5. Line a terrine mold with plastic wrap, allowing the wrap to extend over the top of the mold.

6. Dry the vegetables well and arrange them in the terrine in loose layers, adding the gruyère cheese between each layer.

7. Whisk the cream and egg yolks together and season with nutmeg, salt and pepper. Stir in the chives.

8. Soften the gelatin in 2 ounces (60 grams) of cool water. Gently warm the softened gelatin, stirring until completely dissolved. Stir the gelatin into the cream mixture.

9. Pour the cream mixture over the layered vegetables. Tap the terrine firmly against the work surface to remove any air pockets. Fold the plastic wrap over the top of the terrine and cover with the lid. Cook the terrine in a water bath at 325° F (160° C) until the custard reaches 145° F (63° C), approximately 1-1/2 hours. Cool the terrine for several hours or overnight.

10. Unmold the terrine and portion into 1/2-inch (12-millimeter) slices. Serve with chilled Red Pepper Coulis.

✦✦✦

RECIPE 20.14

ROASTED RED PEPPER MOUSSE

Yield: 1-1/2 pt. (700 ml)

Onion, small dice	3 oz.	90 g
Garlic, chopped	1 tsp.	5 ml
Olive oil	1 oz.	30 g
Red bell pepper, roasted and peeled, small dice	10 oz.	300 g
Salt and pepper	TT	TT
Chicken stock	8 oz.	225 g
Granulated gelatin	1 Tbsp.	15 ml
Dry white wine	2 oz.	60 g
Heavy cream, whipped	6 oz.	180 g

1. Sauté the onions and garlic in the olive oil until tender, approximately 2 minutes.

2. Add the bell pepper, salt, pepper and chicken stock. Bring to a boil, reduce to a simmer and cook 5 minutes.

3. Soften the gelatin in the white wine, then add to the pepper mixture. Purée the pepper mixture in a blender or food processor and strain through a china cap.

4. Place the pepper purée over an ice bath. Stir until cool but do not allow the gelatin to set. Fold in the whipped cream. Pour the mousse into aspic-lined or well-oiled timbales or molds and refrigerate several hours or overnight.

5. Unmold the mousse and serve as desired.

VARIATIONS: Substitute yellow or green bell peppers for part or all of the red bell peppers.

Broccoli Mousse: Substitute 8 ounces (225 grams) of blanched, chopped broccoli for the red bell peppers.

✦✦✦

RECIPE 20.15

SALMON MOUSSE

Yield: 1 lb. 8 oz. (650 g)

Salmon, boneless, skinless	12 oz.	350 g
Fish velouté, warm	8 oz.	250 g
Heavy cream	8 oz.	250 g
Granulated gelatin	1-1/2 Tbsp.	23 ml
White wine	4 oz.	120 g
Salt and white pepper	TT	TT
Cayenne pepper	TT	TT

1. Steam the salmon and transfer it to the food processor while still warm. Add the warm velouté in a steady stream while the machine is running.

2. Whip the cream to soft peaks and reserve.

3. Add the gelatin to the wine and allow it to rest for 5 minutes. Heat the gelatin mixture to a simmer.

4. Transfer the salmon and velouté to a mixing bowl and stir in the gelatin mixture. Season with salt, pepper and cayenne.

5. When the mixture has cooled to near room temperature, fold in the whipped cream with a rubber spatula until just mixed.

6. The mousse is now ready to be formed into timbales, or molded into various shapes as desired.

========= ◆◆◆ =========

RECIPE 20.16

DUCK CONFIT

Yield: 4 Servings

Duck, 4 lb. (1.8 kg), cut into 4 pieces	1	1
Kosher salt	2 Tbsp.	30 ml
Black pepper, cracked	1 tsp.	5 ml
Bay leaves	4	4
Fresh thyme	6 sprigs	6 sprigs
Garlic cloves, crushed	6	6
Duck or goose fat, melted	2 lb.	900 g

1. Rub the duck with the salt. Place skin side down in a roasting pan just large enough to hold the pieces in one layer; season with the black pepper, crumbled bay leaves, thyme and garlic. Cover and refrigerate overnight.

2. Bake the duck at 325°F (160°C) until brown, approximately 15–20 minutes. Add enough melted duck or goose fat to cover the pieces completely.

3. Cover the pan and cook in a 300°F (150°C) oven until the duck is very tender, approximately 2 hours.

4. Remove the duck from the fat and place in a deep hotel pan. Ladle enough of the cooking fat over the pieces to cover them completely. Be careful not to add any of the cooking juices.

5. Cover the pan and refrigerate for 2 days to allow the flavors to mellow.

6. To serve, remove the duck from the fat and scrape off the excess fat. Bake at 350°F (180°C) until the skin is crisp and the meat is hot, approximately 30 minutes.

========= ◆◆◆ =========

RECIPE 20.17

CHOPPED CHICKEN LIVER

Yield: 20 oz. (600 g)

Chicken livers, trimmed	1 lb.	450 g
Chicken fat or butter	2 oz.	60 g
Kosher salt	TT	TT
Eggs, hard-cooked	2	2
Onion, small dice	6 oz.	170 g
Salt and pepper	TT	TT

1. Sauté the livers in the chicken fat or butter until lightly browned with a slightly pink interior. Season with kosher salt.

2. Chop the livers with a chef's knife, blending in the eggs and onions. Season to taste with salt and pepper.

3. The final product should be slightly coarse and peppery. Blend in additional chicken fat or butter if necessary to make the mixture hold together.

4. Pack into a serving bowl, cover well and chill for 24 hours. Serve with crackers, toast or matzos and sliced radishes.

◆◆◆

RECIPE 20.18

RABBIT PÂTÉ
EN CROÛTE

Yield: 1 3 in x 3.5 in. x 16 in.
(7.5 cm x 8.7 cm x 40 cm) Pâté

Rabbit meat, boneless, large dice	2 lb.	1 kg
Pork butt, large dice	1 lb.	450 g
Marinade:		
Pâté spice	1 Tbsp.	15 ml
Orange zest	2 Tbsp.	30 ml
Lime zest	1 Tbsp.	15 ml
Brandy	4 oz.	120 g
Fresh thyme	1 bunch	1 bunch
Juniper berries	6	6
Salt and pepper	TT	TT
Fatback, large dice	1 lb.	450 g
Eggs	4	4
Pistachios, chopped coarse	8 oz.	250 g
Ham, diced	6 oz.	180 g
Black olives, chopped coarse	2 oz.	60 g
Rabbit loins, browned lightly in oil	4	4
Rabbit livers, browned lightly in oil	6	6
Pâté dough	1 lb. 8 oz.	700 g

1. Combine the rabbit meat and pork butt with the marinade ingredients and marinate several hours or overnight.
2. Freeze the fatback.
3. Remove the thyme and juniper berries from the marinated meat mixture and grind the meat in a well-chilled grinder once through the large die, then through the medium die. Hold the mixture in an ice bath.
4. Grind the fatback through the medium die and add to the meat mixture.
5. Place the meat mixture and fat in a chilled food processor and process until emulsified.
6. Over an ice bath, incorporate the eggs into the forcemeat.
7. Fold the pistachios, ham and olives into the forcemeat.
8. Follow the procedure for preparing a pâté en croûte using the rabbit loins and livers as garnishes running the length of the pâté.

◆◆◆

RECIPE 20.19

TEX-MEX
TURKEY SAUSAGE

Yield: 4 lb. (1.8 kg)

Canola oil	4 Tbsp.	60 ml
Onion, chopped fine	12 oz.	340 g
Garlic, minced	1 Tbsp.	15 ml

Jalapeño, chopped	1 Tbsp.	15 ml
Turkey breast meat, trimmed of fat	2 lb.	1 kg
Veal, lean	8 oz.	250 g
White wine vinegar	2 oz.	60 g
Water	8 oz.	250 g
Fresh cilantro, chopped	4 oz.	120 g
White pepper	1 tsp.	5 ml
Chile powder	1 tsp.	5 ml
Cumin, ground	1/2 tsp.	2 ml
Salt	1 tsp.	5 ml

1. Heat the oil and sauté the onion, garlic and jalapeño until the onions are translucent; remove and chill well.
2. Grind the turkey and veal in a cold meat grinder, once through the large die and then through the medium die. Working over an ice bath, combine the meats, vinegar, water and seasonings. Add the sautéed vegetables.
3. Blend well, then cook a small portion to test the flavor and texture. Adjust the seasonings.
4. Stuff into casings or portion into 2-ounce (60-gram) patties and broil. Serve with papaya salsa.

Nutritional values per 2-ounce (60-gram) patty:

Calories	81	Protein	11 g
Calories from fat	36%	Vitamin A	175 IU
Total fat	3 g	Vitamin C	2 mg
Saturated fat	0 g	Sodium	138 mg
Cholesterol	31 mg		

◆◆◆

RECIPE 20.20

SPICY ITALIAN SAUSAGE

Yield: 5 lb. (2.2 kg)

Pork butt	5 lb.	2.2 kg
Salt	1-1/2 Tbsp.	23 ml
Black pepper	1-1/2 tsp	7 ml
Fennel seeds	1-1/2 tsp.	7 ml
Paprika	1 Tbsp.	15 ml
Red pepper, crushed	1-1/2 tsp.	7 ml
Coriander, ground	3/4 tsp.	4 ml
Cold water	5 oz.	150 g

1. Cut the meat into 2-inch (5-centimeter) cubes.
2. Combine the pork with the remaining ingredients except the water.
3. Grind the meat once through the coarse die of a well-chilled grinder.
4. Add the cold water and mix well.
5. Stuff the sausage into casings.

◆◆◆

RECIPE 20.21
CHORIZO

Yield: 7 lb. 8 oz. (3.4 kg)

Pork, lean	5 lb.	2.2 kg
Fatback	2 lb. 8 oz.	1.1 kg
Red pepper flakes	1 tsp.	5 ml
Garlic, chopped	1 oz.	30 g
Cumin	3 Tbsp.	45 ml
Cayenne pepper	2 Tbsp.	30 ml
Salt	4 tsp.	20 ml
Paprika	5 Tbsp.	75 ml
Red wine vinegar	3 oz.	90 g

1. Cut the pork and fatback in 1-inch (2.5-centimeter) pieces. Grind the pork once using a medium die. Grind half of the pork a second time together with the fatback through a fine die.
2. Combine all the ingredients in the bowl of a mixer using the paddle attachment. The sausage may be used in bulk or formed into links as desired.

◆◆◆

RECIPE 20.22
GRAVLAX

Yield: Approximately 5 lb. (2.2 kg)

Salmon, drawn, 10–12 lb.	1	1
Kosher salt	8 oz.	240 g
White peppercorns, cracked	1 oz.	30 g
Fresh dill, chopped	2 bunches	2 bunches
Sugar	8 oz.	250 g

1. Fillet the salmon, following the procedure discussed in Chapter 19, Fish and Shellfish. Remove the pin bones but leave the skin attached.
2. To make the salt cure, combine the salt, white peppercorns, dill and sugar.
3. Coat the salmon fillets with the salt cure and wrap each fillet separately in plastic wrap.
4. Place the fillets in a hotel pan and place another hotel pan on top. Place two #10 cans in the top hotel pan to weigh it down and press the fish.
5. Refrigerate the salmon 2–3 days.
6. Unwrap the gravlax, scrape off the salt cure and slice it very thin.

◆◆◆

RECIPE 20.23
SMOKED SALMON WITH TUNA

CHRISTOPHER'S AND **CHRISTOPHER'S BISTRO**, PHOENIX, AZ
Chef/Owner Christopher Gross

Yield: 4 Servings

Smoked salmon	8 oz.	225 g
Fresh tuna, cut into 4-oz. (120-g) squares	2	2
Salt and white pepper	TT	TT
Butter, melted	as needed	as needed
Fresh parsley, chopped fine	1 bunch	1 bunch
Fresh thyme, chopped fine	1 bunch	1 bunch
Fresh chervil, chopped fine	1 bunch	1 bunch
Fresh tarragon, chopped fine	1 bunch	1 bunch
Fresh basil leaves, chopped fine	5	5
Saffron	pinch	pinch
Crème fraîche	1 pt.	450 ml
Fresh dill	1 sprig	1 sprig
Fresh spinach	8 oz.	225 g
Caviar (Osetra)	1 oz.	30 g
Baby lettuces, assorted	4 heads	4 heads
Olive oil	2 Tbsp.	30 ml
Brioche	4 slices	4 slices

1. Thinly slice the salmon and arrange it in a single-layer circle on four plates. Leave a 1-inch (2.5-centimeter) border around the edge of each plate.
2. Season the tuna with salt and pepper and coat with a small amount of butter. Roll in an assortment of chopped herbs.
3. Sear the tuna in a hot sauté pan, keeping it rare. Refrigerate until ready to serve.
4. To make the yellow sauce, add a pinch of saffron to 6 ounces (180 grams) of the crème fraîche and simmer until the crème turns yellow, approximately 10 minutes. Strain the sauce, season with salt and white pepper and refrigerate.
5. To make the green sauce, add the dill to another 6 ounces (180 grams) of crème fraîche and simmer for 10 minutes. Place the spinach in a blender. Add the dilled crème fraîche and blend for several seconds. Strain, season with salt and white pepper and cool quickly to preserve the color.
6. Whip the remaining crème fraîche until stiff.
7. Cut the two squares of tuna in half diagonally, creating four triangles. Place a triangle of tuna in the center of each plate of salmon.
8. Form a small quenelle of whipped crème fraîche and place it at the edge of the salmon. Spoon caviar onto the crème fraîche.
9. Toss the baby greens with the olive oil and place a small mound next to the tuna.
10. Garnish the border of each plate with small dots of the yellow and green sauces.
11. Cut the slices of brioche into mushroom shapes and toast. Place one slice against each piece of tuna.

✦✦✦

RECIPE 20.24
THOUSAND-LAYER SMOKED SALMON TERRINE WITH CAVIAR SAUCE

CITRUS, LOS ANGELES, CA
Chef Michel Richard

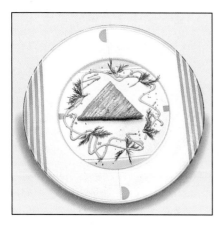

Yield: 12 Servings

Smoked salmon, sliced	3 lb.	1.4 kg
Salmon mousse:		
Smoked salmon slices or trimmings	8–9 oz.	225–250 g
Basil leaves	1 oz.	30 g
Chilled cream cheese,		
coarsely chopped	8 oz.	225 g
Unsalted butter, chilled,		
coarsely chopped	4 oz.	120 g
Tabasco sauce	TT	TT
Olive oil	2 oz.	60 g
Chicken stock, unsalted	3-1/2 oz.	100 g
Lemon juice, fresh	2 oz.	60 g
Unflavored gelatin	1/2 oz.	15 g
Flying fish roe, salmon roe		
or other caviar	2 Tbsp.	30 ml
Caviar Sauce (recipe follows)	as needed	as needed
Cucumber slices for garnish (optional)	as needed	as needed

1. Line three identical 12-x-17-inch (30-x-43-centimeter) baking sheets with parchment paper and cover completely with the smoked salmon slices, overlapping if necessary. Top each tray with parchment paper. Freeze for 30 minutes.

2. For the salmon mousse, process the smoked salmon trimmings and basil in a food processor until smooth. With the machine running, add the cream cheese and then the butter, several pieces at a time. Add the Tabasco and process until smooth. With the machine running, pour in the olive oil in a slow, thin stream.

3. Place the stock and lemon juice in a small pot and sprinkle the gelatin over the liquids. Stir over low heat until the gelatin is dissolved, then cool until tepid. With the food processor running, slowly pour the gelatin mixture into the mousse. Transfer to a bowl and stir in the roe.

4. To assemble the terrine, remove the top pieces of parchment paper from the trays of salmon. Spread one third of the mousse evenly over 1 tray, covering the salmon completely. Take the salmon layer from the second tray and invert it over the salmon on the first tray, paper side up, forming 2 layers. Rub and press the paper so that the 2 layers adhere. Remove the paper. Spread one third of the mousse over this second layer. Invert the third tray over the salmon layers, paper side up. Rub and press the paper so that the 3 layers adhere. Invert the tray onto a work surface and remove the tray. Rub the top layer of paper, pressing the salmon layers together.

5. Using a sharp knife and a ruler as a guide, divide the layers equally into five 12-inch (30-centimeter) strips, each just short of 3-1/2 inches (9 centimeters) wide. Remove the top paper. Invert 1 strip onto a cutting board or tray, paper side up. Remove the paper and cover completely with a thin

layer of the remaining salmon mousse. Repeat, stacking the remaining strips. Spread any remaining salmon mousse evenly over the top and sides of the terrine. Cover with plastic wrap. Place in the freezer until firm but not frozen, approximately 30 minutes.

6. Cut the terrine crosswise in half. Stack one half on top of the other. Smooth and square off the edges using a metal spatula dipped in hot water. Freeze until firm, approximately 1 hour, or refrigerate until well chilled, approximately 4 hours or overnight.

7. To serve, cut into 1/2-inch- (1.2-centimeter-) thick slices. If desired, cut each slice in half again, diagonally, forming 2 triangles. Transfer the slices to 12 plates. Let sit for 30 minutes. Ladle caviar sauce alongside. Garnish with cucumber slices and serve immediately.

CAVIAR SAUCE

Mayonnaise	1 pt.	450 ml
Chicken stock, unsalted	2 oz.	60 g
Lemon juice, fresh	TT	TT
Tabasco sauce	10 drops	10 drops
Flying fish roe, salmon roe or other caviar	6 oz.	180 g
Fresh chives, minced	1 oz.	30 g
Tomato paste or beet juice	2 Tbsp.	30 ml

1. Place the mayonnaise in a small bowl. Stir in the chicken stock, lemon juice, Tabasco sauce, roe and chives.

2. Mix in enough tomato paste or beet juice to tint the mayonnaise a slightly lighter shade than the salmon.

CHAPTER 21
DEEP-FRYING

After studying this chapter you will be able to:

◆ select and maintain the proper equipment and fats for deep-frying
◆ use breadings and batters
◆ prepare fritters and croquettes

*eep-frying has a bad reputation. Too many consumers think of deep-fried foods as greasy convenience items with thick breadings or batters masking the principal ingredient's inferior quality. But properly prepared deep-fried foods can be deliciously tender and juicy—and their contrasting crispy crusts and moist interiors add to eating enjoyment.*

Perhaps no other cooking method can be applied to such a wide variety of foods. Meats, poultry, fish and shellfish, vegetables, potatoes and other starches, fruits, pastries and even ice cream can be deep-fried successfully. That is why we devote a separate chapter to the process.

This versatile procedure is relatively simple provided a few basic guidelines are followed. This chapter explains those guidelines and provides recipes for breading and batters. Also included are illustrative recipes utilizing deep-frying techniques. Other recipes that use deep-frying are found in the various chapters on vegetables, fish, starches and quick breads.

Deep-frying is a dry-heat cooking method using fat as the cooking medium. Boiling and deep-frying are conceptually similar. For both cooking methods, food is placed in a liquid and heat is transferred from the hot liquid (water or fat, respectively) to the food being cooked through conduction (the transfer of heat by direct contact) and convection (the transfer of heat through the currents in a liquid or gas).

The principal difference between boiling and deep frying is the temperature of the cooking medium. The boiling point, 212°F (100°C), is the hottest temperature at which food can be cooked in water. At this temperature, most foods require a long cooking period and surface sugars cannot caramelize. With deep-frying, temperatures up to 400°F (200°C) are used. These high temperatures cook food more quickly and allow the food's surface to brown. Even though the food is cooked in a liquid, deep-frying is not a moist-heat cooking method because the liquid fat contains no moisture.

SELECTING EQUIPMENT FOR DEEP-FRYING

Unlike most kitchen equipment, a deep-fat fryer has only one purpose: to cook foods in a large amount of hot fat. Fryers are sized by the amount of fat they hold. Most commercial fryers range between 15 and 82 pounds. Fryers can be either gas or electric and are thermostatically controlled for temperatures between 200° and 400°F (90–200°C).

When choosing a fryer, look for a fry tank with curved, easy-to-clean sloping sides. Some fryers have a cold zone (an area of reduced temperature) at the bottom of the fry tank to trap particles. This prevents them from burning, creating off-flavors and shortening the life of the fryer fat.

Deep-fryers usually come with steel wire baskets to hold the food during cooking. Fryer baskets are usually lowered into the fat and raised manually, although some models have automatic basket mechanisms controlled by timers.

As with any piece of equipment, read the operator's manual or have an experienced colleague show you how to operate any deep-fryer before using or cleaning it.

The most important factor when choosing a deep-fryer is **recovery time**. Recovery time is the length of time it takes the fat to return to the desired cooking temperature after food is submerged in it. When food is submerged, heat is immediately transferred to the food from the fat. This heat transfer lowers the fat's temperature. The more food added at one time, the greater the drop in the fat's temperature. If the temperature drops too much or does not return quickly to the proper cooking temperature, the food may absorb excess fat and become greasy.

Deep-frying foods in a sauce pot on the stove top is discouraged because it is both difficult and dangerous. Recovery time is usually very slow and temperatures are difficult to control. Also the fat can spill easily, leading to injuries or creating a fire hazard.

SELECTING FATS FOR DEEP-FRYING

Many types of fats can be used for deep-frying. (In this chapter, the term *fat* applies to both solid fats and liquid oils.) Although animal fats, such as rendered beef fat, are sometimes used to impart their specific flavors to deep-fried foods, by far the most common fats used for deep-frying are vegetable oils such as soybean, safflower and canola oil.

Specially formulated deep-fat frying compounds are also available. These are usually composed of a vegetable oil or oils to which antifoaming agents, antioxidants and preservatives have been added. These additives increase usable life and raise smoke points.

A fat's **smoke point** is the temperature at which it visibly begins to smoke and chemically begins to break down. Animal fats generally have low smoke points of about 350°F (180°C), making them unsuitable for deep-frying. Vegetable oils generally have higher smoke points of about 475°F (250°C), thus providing the high temperatures desired for deep-frying. (See Chapter 7, Kitchen Staples, for a list of fat smoke points.)

Some frying fats are also hydrogenated. Hydrogenation is a chemical process that adds hydrogen to oils and turns a liquid oil into a solid (margarine is hydrogenated vegetable oil). Hydrogenated fats are more resistant to oxidation and chemical breakdown.

When fats break down, their chemical structure is altered; the triglyceride molecules that make up fat are converted into individual fatty acids. These acids add undesirable flavors to the fat and can ruin the flavor of the food being cooked. When a fat becomes very dark, foams excessively or adds off-flavors to foods, it has broken down and should be changed.

To choose the right fat, consider flavor, smoke point and resistance to chemical breakdown. High-quality frying fat should have a clean or natural flavor, a high smoke point and, when properly maintained, be resistant to chemical breakdown.

Maintaining Fryer Fat

Properly maintaining fryer fat greatly extends its useful life. To do so:

1. Store the fat in tightly sealed containers away from strong light; cover the fat in the fryer when not in use. Prolonged exposure to air and light turns fat rancid.

2. Skim and remove food particles from the fat's surface during frying. Food particles cause fat to break down; if they are not removed they will accumulate in the fryer and burn.

3. Do not salt food over the fat. Salt causes fat to break down chemically.

4. Prevent excessive water from coming into contact with the fat; pat-dry moist foods as much as possible before cooking and dry the fryer, baskets and utensils well after cleaning. Water, like salt, causes fat to break down.

5. Do not overheat the fat (turn the fryer down or off if not in use). High temperatures break down the fat.

6. Filter the fat each day or after each shift if the fryer is heavily used. Best results are obtained by using a filtering machine designed specifically for this purpose. Many large commercial fryers even have built-in filter systems. Less well equipped operations can simply pour the hot fat through a paper cone filter.

TABLE 21.1

Fryer fat can be damaged by:	Change fryer fat when it:
Salt	Becomes dark
Water	Smokes
Overheating	Foams
Food particles	Develops off-flavors
Oxygen	

PROCEDURES FOR DEEP-FRYING

The temperature of the fat is critical to successful deep-frying. The fat must be hot enough to quickly seal the surface of the food so it does not become excessively greasy, yet it should not be so hot that the food's surface burns before the interior is cooked.

Nearly all deep-fried foods are cooked at temperatures between 325° and 375°F (160–190°C). The fat's temperature can be adjusted within this range to allow the interior of thicker foods or frozen foods to cook before their surfaces become too dark.

Try not to fry delicately flavored foods in the same fat used for more strongly flavored ones. For example, do not deep-fry fruit fritters in the same fat used for catfish. If the fritters are fried in the catfish fat, they could develop an odd taste from the residual flavors left from the catfish.

Deep-Frying Methods

There are two distinct deep-frying methods for standard electric or gas fryers: the basket method and the swimming method. Which is used depends upon the food being fried.

The **basket method** of deep-frying uses a basket to hold foods that are breaded, individually quick frozen or otherwise do not tend to stick together during cooking. The basket is removed from the fryer and filled as much as two-thirds full of product. (Do not fill the basket while it is hanging over the fat as this allows unnecessary crumbs, salt and food particles to fall into the fat, shortening its life.) The filled basket is then submerged in the hot fat. When cooking is completed, the basket is used to remove the food from the fat.

Basket Method of Deep-Frying

A variation on this procedure is the **double-basket method**. This variation is necessitated by the fact that many fried foods float as they cook. This may produce undesirable results because the section of the food not submerged may not cook. To prevent this and to promote even cooking, a second basket is used to keep the foods submerged in the fat.

Most battered foods initially sink to the bottom when placed in hot fat, then rise to the top as they cook. Because they would stick to a basket, the **swimming method** of deep-frying is used for these foods. With the swimming method, battered foods are carefully dropped directly into the hot fat. (Baskets are not used.) They will rise to the top as they cook. When the surface that is in contact with the fat is properly browned, the food is turned over with a spider or a pair of tongs so that it can cook evenly on both sides. When done, the product is removed and drained, again using a spider or tongs.

Double-Basket Method of Deep-Frying

Draining and Holding Deep-Fried Foods

All deep-fried foods must be drained of excess oil before they are served. When removing foods from the deep-fryer, allow excess fat to drain into the fryer. Then transfer the foods to a hotel pan that is either lined with absorbent paper or fitted with a rack.

Deep-fried foods should be kept under a heat lamp. Steam tables do not keep deep-fried foods hot because very little of the crisp foods' surface actually touches the hot surface of the steam table's pan.

SELECTING FOODS FOR DEEP-FRYING

Only tender foods should be deep-fried. Deep-frying cooks foods at relatively high temperatures for short periods of time and does not have a tenderizing effect. Young tender poultry is ideal, as are most types of lean fish and shellfish. Fruits and vegetables can also be deep-fried. Probably the most popular deep-fried foods of all are potatoes, which are cooked in an endless variety of shapes and forms. (Several of the recipes found in Chapter 23, Potatoes, Grains and Pasta, require deep-frying.) Foods that are deep-fried together should be of the same size or thickness so they cook evenly. Slow-cooking vegetables such as broccoli, cauliflower and okra can be blanched first so they deep-fry more quickly.

Swimming Method of Deep-Frying

PREPARING FOODS FOR DEEP-FRYING

With some exceptions (french fries, for example), most foods to be deep-fried are first breaded or battered. Breading and batter coat the food, keeping it moist and preventing it from becoming excessively greasy during cooking.

Seasoning Foods to be Deep-Fried

Breaded and battered foods can be seasoned before the breading or batter is applied. Seasonings may also be added to the flour, bread crumbs or batter before the main item is coated.

Many types of deep-fried food are salted after they are removed from the fat. This should be done immediately after the food is removed from the fryer so the salt will cling more readily.

Breading Foods to be Deep-Fried

A breaded item is any food that is coated with bread crumbs, cracker meal, cornmeal or other dry meal to protect it during cooking. Breaded foods are generally cooked by deep-frying or pan-frying. The breading makes a solid coating that seals during cooking to prevent the fat from coming in direct contact with the food and making it greasy.

Standard Breading Procedure

Whether breading meats, poultry, fish, shellfish or vegetables, a three-step process is typically used. Called the **standard breading procedure**, it gives foods a relatively thick, crisp coating.

1. Pat the food dry and dredge it in seasoned flour. The flour adds seasoning to the food, helps seal it, and allows the egg wash to adhere.
2. Dip the floured food in an egg wash. The egg wash should contain whole eggs whisked together with approximately 1 tablespoon (15 milliliters) milk or water per egg. The egg wash will cause the crumbs or meal to completely coat the item and form a tight seal when the food is cooked.
3. Coat the food with bread crumbs, cracker crumbs or other dry meal. Shake off the excess crumbs and place the breaded item in a pan. As additional breaded items are added to the pan, align them in a single layer; do not stack them or the breadings will get soggy and the foods will stick together.

Figure 21.1 shows the proper setup for breading foods using the standard breading procedure.

The following procedure helps to bread foods more efficiently:

1. Assemble the mise en place as depicted in Figure 21.1.
2. With your left hand, place the food to be breaded in the flour and coat it evenly. With the same hand, remove the floured item, shake off the excess flour and place it in the egg wash.
3. With your right hand, remove the item from the egg wash and place it in the bread crumbs or meal.
4. With your left hand, cover the item with crumbs or meal and press lightly to make sure the item is completely and evenly coated. Shake off the excess crumbs or meal and place the breaded food in the empty pan for finished product.

The key is to use one hand for the liquid ingredients and the other hand for the dry ingredients. This prevents your fingers from becoming coated with layer after layer of breading.

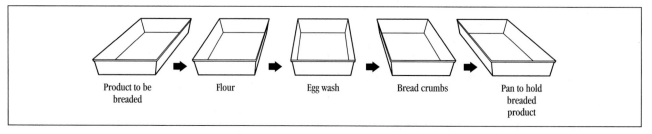

| Product to be breaded | Flour | Egg wash | Bread crumbs | Pan to hold breaded product |

Figure 21.1   *Setup for the Standard Breading Procedure*

◆◆◆

RECIPE 21.1
DEEP-FRIED CATFISH FILLETS WITH TARTAR SAUCE

Yield: 8 Servings

Catfish fillets, cut into uniform-size pieces	3 lb.	1.5 kg
Salt and pepper	TT	TT
Flour	as needed	as needed
Egg wash	as needed	as needed
White cornmeal	as needed	as needed
Tartar Sauce (Recipe 24.19)	12 oz.	360 ml

1. Season the fillets with salt and pepper.
2. Bread the fillets using the standard breading procedure (the white cornmeal is the final coating).
3. Using the basket method, deep-fry the fillets until done. Drain well and serve with the tartar sauce.

1. Flouring the seasoned fish fillets.

2. Passing the floured fillets through the egg wash.

3. Coating the fillets with white cornmeal.

4. Deep-frying the fillets using the basket method.

Croquettes

Croquettes are cooked meats, poultry, vegetables, fish or potatoes, usually bound with a heavy béchamel or velouté sauce and seasoned. They are then breaded and deep-fried.

◆◆◆

RECIPE 21.2

SALMON CROQUETTES

Yield: 12 Croquettes

Onion, small dice	2 oz.	60 g
Whole butter	3 oz.	90 g
Flour	3 oz.	90 g
Milk	8 oz.	250 g
Salmon, poached and flaked	1 lb.	450 g
Fresh dill, chopped	TT	TT
Salt and pepper	TT	TT
Lemon juice	1 Tbsp.	15 ml

1. Sauté the onion in the butter until translucent.
2. Add the flour and cook to make a white roux.
3. Add the milk to make a heavy béchamel sauce. Cook the sauce until very thick, approximately 5 minutes.
4. Remove the sauce from the heat and transfer it to a mixing bowl. Add the flaked salmon. Season the mixture with dill, salt, pepper and lemon juice and mix well.
5. Spread the mixture in a hotel pan, cover and refrigerate until cold.
6. Portion the mixture using a #20 portion scoop. Form each portion into a cone shape. Bread the croquettes using the standard breading procedure.
7. Using the basket method, deep-fry the breaded croquettes until done.

1. Portioning the croquette mixture with a portion scoop.

2. Forming the mixture into cone shapes.

3. Deep-frying the croquettes using the basket method.

Battering Foods to be Deep-Fried

Batters, like breading, coat the food being cooked, keeping it moist and preventing it from becoming excessively greasy.

Batters consist of a liquid such as water, milk or beer, combined with a starch such as flour or cornstarch. Many batters also contain a chemical leavening agent such as baking powder. Two common batters are beer batter, which uses the beer for leavening as well as for flavor, and tempura batter.

Procedure for Battering Foods

1. Pat the food dry and dredge in flour if desired.
2. Dip the item in the batter and place it directly in hot fat.

=== ◆◆◆ ===

RECIPE 21.3

Beer-Battered Onion Rings

Yield: 1 qt. (1 lt), enough for approx. 4 lb. (1.8 kg) rings

Flour	10 oz.	300 g
Baking powder	2 tsp.	10 ml
Salt	2 tsp.	10 ml
White pepper	1/4 tsp.	1 ml
Egg	1	1
Beer	1 pt.	450 ml
Flour, for dredging	as needed	as needed
Onions, whole	4 lb.	1.8 kg

1. Sift the dry ingredients together.
2. Beat the egg in a separate bowl. Add the beer to the beaten egg.
3. Add the egg-and-beer mixture to the dry ingredients; mix until smooth.
4. Peel the onions and cut in 1/2-inch-(2-centimeter-) thick slices.
5. Break the slices into rings and dredge in flour.
6. Dip the rings in the batter a few at a time and fry at 375°F (190°C) until done. Drain on absorbent paper, season with additional salt and white pepper and serve hot.

1. Dredging the onion rings in flour.

2. Dipping the floured rings in batter.

3. Frying the onion rings using the swimming method.

♦♦♦

RECIPE 21.4

TEMPURA SHRIMP AND VEGETABLES WITH DIPPING SAUCE

Yield: 1 qt. (1 lt), enough for 4 lb. (1.8 kg) vegetables or shrimp

Sweet potato	8 oz.	250 g
Dipping Sauce		
Mirin	2 oz.	60 g
Soy sauce	4 oz.	120 g
Rice wine vinegar	2 oz.	60 g
Lemon juice	1 Tbsp.	15 ml
Wasabi powder	1 tsp.	5 ml
Tempura Batter:		
Eggs	2	2
Sparkling water, cold	1 pt.	500 ml
Flour	10 oz.	300 g
Shrimp, 21–25 count, butterflied with tails on	2 lb.	1 kg
Mushrooms, small, whole	1 lb.	450 g
Zucchini, batonnet	8 oz.	250 g

1. Peel the sweet potato and cut in 1/4-inch-(6-millimeter-) thick slices. If the potato is large, cut each slice in half to make semicircles.
2. Combine all ingredients for the dipping sauce. Set aside.
3. To prepare the batter, beat the eggs and add the cold water.
4. Add the flour to the egg-and-water mixture and mix until the flour is incorporated. There should still be small lumps in the batter. Overmixing develops gluten, which is undesirable.
5. Dry the shrimp well. Holding them by the tail, dip them into the batter and drop them into the deep-fryer using the swimming method. Cook until done.
6. Drop the vegetables in the batter a few at a time. Remove them from the batter one at a time and drop into the deep-fryer using the swimming method. Cook until done.
7. Arrange the tempura shrimp and vegetables on a serving platter. Serve the dipping sauce on the side.

Fritters

Fritters contain diced or chopped fish, shellfish, vegetables or fruits bound together with a thick batter and deep-fried. The main ingredient is usually precooked. Fritters are spooned or dropped directly into the hot fat; they form a crust as they cook. Popular examples are clam fritters, corn fritters, artichoke fritters and apple fritters.

♦♦♦

RECIPE 21.5

APPLE FRITTERS

Yield: 100 2-in. (5-cm) Fritters

Eggs, separated	6	6
Milk	1 pt.	500 ml
Flour	1 lb.	450 g

Baking powder	1 Tbsp.	15 ml
Salt	1 tsp.	5 ml
Sugar	2 oz.	60 g
Cinnamon	1/2 tsp.	2 ml
Apples, peeled, cored, medium dice	1 lb. 8 oz.	700 g
Powdered sugar	as needed	as needed

1. Combine the egg yolks and milk.
2. Sift together the flour, baking powder, salt, sugar and cinnamon. Add the dry ingredients to the milk-and-egg mixture; mix until smooth.
3. Allow the batter to rest 1 hour.
4. Stir the apples into the batter.
5. Just before the fritters are to be cooked, whip the egg whites to soft peaks and fold into the batter.
6. Scoop the fritters into 350°F (180°C) deep fat, using the swimming method. Cook until done.
7. Dust with powdered sugar and serve hot.

1. Adding the dry ingredients to the liquids.

2. Folding the egg whites into the batter.

3. Dropping the fritters into the deep fat.

4. Dusting the fritters with powdered sugar.

DETERMINING DONENESS

It is difficult to determine the doneness of deep-fried foods, especially breaded or battered ones. The keen sense of timing that develops with experience is a useful tool. Otherwise:

1. Color is the most commonly used method for determining doneness. Most fried foods should be deep golden brown when done. But color can be deceiving. If the temperature of the fat is too high, the food's surface will darken quickly and appear done while the center remains raw. Also, fat becomes dark with use; dark fat prematurely darkens food, again allowing foods to appear done before they are. Similarly, foods with high sugar content darken quickly in hot fat.

2. Large items such as fried chicken can be removed from the fat and checked with an instant-read thermometer. The internal temperature should be 165–170°F (74–77°C).

3. Fish and shellfish cook quickly and are easily overcooked. If practical, remove a piece and cut it open to determine its doneness. Then rely on timing and color for the remaining batches.

4. Vegetables should be tender when their surfaces are the proper color.

5. Potatoes should be attractively browned and cooked to the desire crispness.

Generally, deep-fried foods must be completely cooked in the deep-fryer. It is possible, however, to finish some deep-fried foods (for example, fried chicken) in the oven after being browned in the fat. But there is a problem to doing so. As the food cooks in the oven, moisture is released that may cause the breading to become soggy on the bottom.

Conclusion

Deep-frying is a useful and versatile dry-heat cooking method. To produce high-quality deep-fried foods it is important to understand which foods respond well to deep-frying and how to prepare them for cooking. You must also understand how to prevent deep-fried food from becoming excessively greasy by properly coating them with batters or breadings and controlling cooking temperatures. Finally, you must understand how to determine doneness. By following the guidelines discussed in this chapter you will be able to consistently produce the desired results.

Questions for Discussion

1. What qualities should be considered when choosing a fat for deep-frying?
2. Name and describe two styles of deep-frying.
3. List three signs that fryer fat has broken down and should be replaced. What causes fryer fat to break down? What can you do to extend the life of fryer fat?
4. Explain the differences between breading and battering foods for deep-frying.
5. Describe the correct mise en place for the standard breading procedure.
6. Explain several similarities and differences between fritters and croquettes.

Additional Deep-Frying Recipe

RECIPE 21.6

Whole Sizzling Catfish with Ginger and Panzu Sauce

Note: *This dish appears in the Chapter Opening photograph.*

CHINOIS ON MAIN, Santa Monica, CA
Chef Wolfgang Puck

Yield: 4 Servings

Catfish, cleaned, 3 lb. (1.3 kg)	1	1
Salt and pepper	TT	TT
Fresh ginger, sliced and blanched	6 pieces	6 pieces
Peanut oil	as needed	as needed
Lemon juice	as needed	as needed
Panzu Sauce:		
Soy sauce	4 oz.	120 g
Mirin	4 oz.	120 g
Rice vinegar	4 oz.	120 g
Lemon juice	4 oz.	120 g
Fresh wood ear mushrooms	as needed for garnish	
Fresh cilantro	as needed for garnish	
Green onions	as needed for garnish	

1. Season the catfish with salt and pepper. Make three 2-inch (5-centimeter) incisions on each side of the fish and stuff each incision with blanched ginger.

2. Deep-fry the catfish in peanut oil, being careful to submerge the entire fish. Cook until golden-colored and crispy.

3. Squeeze fresh lemon juice over the top of the fish.

4. Make the sauce by combining the listed ingredients.

5. Serve the whole catfish on a platter garnished with wood ear mushrooms, cilantro and green onions. Serve the Panzu Sauce on the side.

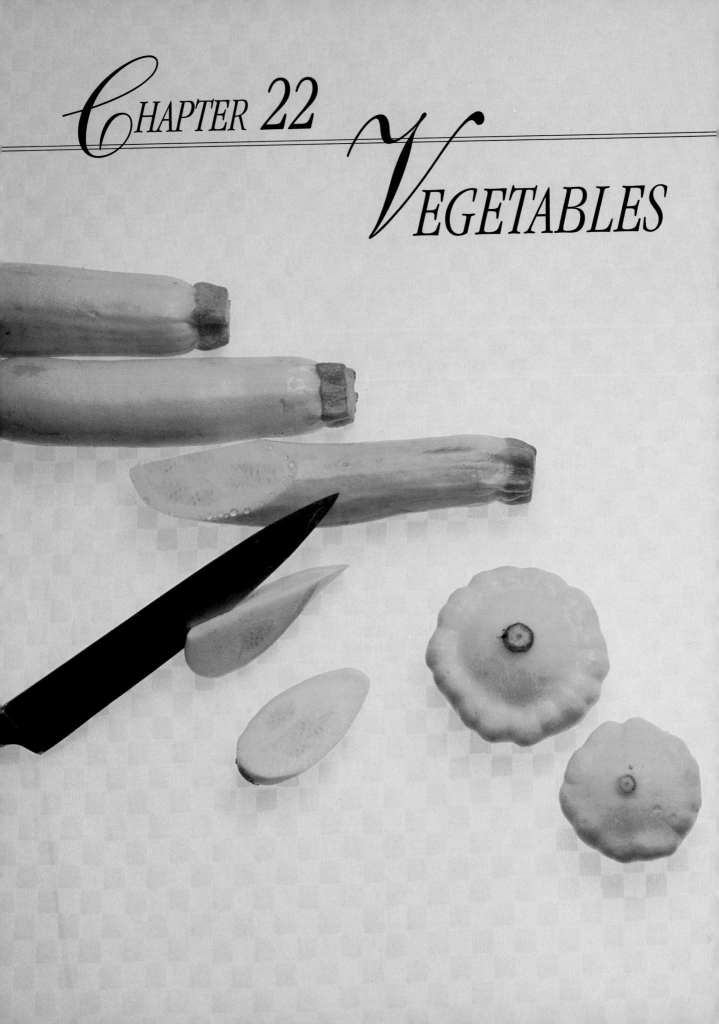

CHAPTER 22 VEGETABLES

After studying this chapter you will be able to:

+ identify a variety of vegetables
+ purchase vegetables appropriate for your needs
+ store vegetables properly
+ understand how vegetables are preserved
+ prepare vegetables for cooking or service
+ apply various cooking methods to vegetables

Long overcooked and underrated, vegetables are enjoying a welcome surge in popularity. Gone are the days when a chef included vegetables as an afterthought to the "meat and potatoes" of the meal. Now, properly prepared fresh vegetables are used to add flavor, color and variety to almost any meal. Many restaurants are featuring vegetarian entrees, an extensive selection of vegetable side dishes or an entire vegetarian menu. This trend reflects the demands of more knowledgeable and health-conscious consumers as well as the increased availability of high-quality fresh produce.

In this chapter we identify many of the vegetables typically used by food service operations. (Potatoes, although vegetables, are discussed in Chapter 23, Potatoes, Grains and Pasta, while salad greens are discussed in Chapter 24, Salads and Salad Dressings.) Here we also discuss how fresh and preserved vegetables are purchased, stored and prepared for service or cooking. Many of the cooking methods analyzed in Chapter 9, Principles of Cooking, are then applied to vegetables.

The term **vegetable** refers to any herbaceous plant that can be partially or wholly eaten. An herbaceous plant has little or no woody tissue. The portions we consume include the leaves, stems, roots, tubers, seeds and flowers. Vegetables contain more starch and less sugar than fruits. Therefore vegetables tend to be savory, not sweet. Also unlike fruits, vegetables are most often eaten cooked, not raw.

IDENTIFYING VEGETABLES

This book presents fruits and vegetables according to the ways most people view them and use them, rather than by rigid botanical classifications. Although produce such as tomatoes, peppers and eggplants are botanically fruits, they are prepared and served like vegetables and are included here under the category we call "fruit-vegetables." Potatoes, although botanically vegetables, are discussed with other starches in Chapter 23, Potatoes, Grains and Pasta.

We divide vegetables into nine categories based upon either botanical relationship or edible part. They are: cabbages, fruit-vegetables, gourds and squashes, greens, mushrooms and truffles, onions, pods and seeds, roots and tubers, and stalks. A vegetable may have several names, varying from region to region or on a purveyor's whim. The names given here follow generally accepted custom and usage.

Cabbages

The *Brassica* or cabbage family includes a wide range of vegetables used for their heads, flowers or leaves. They are generally quick-growing, cool-weather crops. Many are ancient plants with unknown origins. They are inexpensive, readily available and easy to prepare.

Bok Choy

Bok choy, also known as pok choy, is a white-stemmed variety of southern Chinese cabbage. The relatively tightly packed leaves are dark green, with long white ribs attached at a bulbous stem. The stalks are crisp and mild with a flavor similar to romaine lettuce. Although bok choy may be eaten raw, it is most often stir-fried or used in soups.

Choose heads with bright white stalks and dark green leaves; avoid those with brown, moist spots. Fresh bok choy is available all year. Jars of pickled and fermented bok choy (known as Korean kim chee) are also available.

Bok Choy

Broccoli

Broccoli, a type of flower, has a thick central stalk with grayish-green leaves topped with one or more heads of green florets. Broccoli may be eaten raw or steamed, microwaved or sautéed and served warm or cold. Broccoli stalks are extremely firm and benefit from blanching. Stems are often slow-cooked for soups. Generally, broccoli leaves are not eaten.

Choose firm stalks with compact clusters of tightly closed dark green florets. Avoid stalks with yellow flowers. Broccoli is available all year.

Broccoli

PROCEDURE FOR CUTTING BROCCOLI SPEARS

1. Cut off the thick, woody portion of the stalk, then cut the florets and stems into spears.

Brussels Sprouts

Brussels sprouts (Fr. *choux de Bruxelles*) were first cultivated around 1700. The plant produces numerous small heads arranged in neat rows along a thick stalk. The tender young sprouts are similar to baby cabbages and are usually steamed or roasted. Brussels sprouts have a strong, nutty flavor that blends well with game, ham, duck or rich meats.

Choose small, firm sprouts that are compact and heavy. The best size is 3/4 to 1-1/2 inches (2 to 4 centimeters) in diameter. They should be bright green and free of blemishes. Their peak season is from September through February.

Brussels Sprouts

Cauliflower

Cauliflower (Fr. *chou-fleur*) is the king of the cabbage family. Each stalk produces one flower or head surrounded by large green leaves. The head, composed of creamy white florets, can be cooked whole or cut into separate florets for steaming, blanching or stir-frying.

Cauliflower

Choose firm, compact heads. Any attached leaves should be bright green and crisp. A yellow color or spreading florets indicate that the vegetable is overly mature. Cauliflower is available all year, especially from the late fall through the spring.

PROCEDURE FOR CUTTING CAULIFLOWER FLORETS

1. Cut off the stem and leaves.   ***2.*** Cut the florets off the core.

Green and Red Cabbages

Cabbage (Fr. *chou*) has been a staple of northern European cuisine for centuries. The familiar green cabbages have large, firm, round heads with tightly packed pale green leaves. Flat and conical-shaped heads are also available. Red (or purple) cabbages are a different strain and may be tougher than green cabbages. Cabbage can be eaten raw (as in coleslaw) or used in soups or stews; it can be braised, steamed or stir-fried. The large, waxy leaves can also be steamed until soft, then wrapped around a filling of seasoned meat.

Choose firm heads without dried cores. Cabbages are available all year.

Kale

Kale has large ruffled, curly or bumpy leaves. Its rather bitter flavor goes well with rich meats such as game, pork or ham. Kale is typically boiled, stuffed or used in soups.

Choose leaves that are crisp, with a grayish-green color. Kale is available all year, with peak season during the winter months.

Ornamental or flowering kale, sometimes marketed as "savoy," is edible, but its pink, purple, yellow or white-and-green variegated leaves are best used for decoration and garnish.

Green and Red Cabbages

Kale

Ornamental Kale

Kohlrabi

Although it looks rather like a round root, kohlrabi is actually a bulbous stem vegetable created by cross-breeding cabbages and turnips. When purchased, both the leaves (which are attached directly to the bulbous stem) and roots are generally removed. Depending on the variety, the skin may be light green, purple or green with a hint of red. The interior flesh is white, with a sweet flavor similar to turnips. (Kohlrabies can be substituted for turnips in many recipes.) Younger plants are milder and more tender than large, mature ones. The outer skin must be removed from mature stems; young stems only need to be well scrubbed before cooking. Kohlrabi can be eaten raw, or it can be cooked (whole, sliced or diced) with moist-heat cooking methods such as boiling and steaming. The stems may also be hollowed out and stuffed with meat or vegetable mixtures.

Choose small, tender stems with fresh, green leaves. Peak season for kohlrabi is from June through September.

Kohlrabi

Napa Cabbage

Napa cabbage, also known as Chinese cabbage, is widely used in Asian cuisines. It has a stout, elongated head with relatively tightly packed, firm, pale green leaves. It is moister and more tender than common green and red cabbages, with a milder, more delicate flavor. Napa cabbage may be eaten raw but is particularly well suited for stir-frying or steaming.

Choose heads with crisp leaves that are free of blemishes. Napa cabbage is available fresh all year.

Napa Cabbage

Savoy

Savoy

Savoy cabbage has curly or ruffled leaves, often in variegated shades of green and purple. (The term "savoyed" is used to refer to any vegetable with bumpy, wavy or wrinkled leaves.) Savoy cabbage tends to be milder and more tender than regular cabbages and can be substituted for them, cooked or uncooked. Savoy leaves also make an attractive garnish.

Choose heads that are loose or tight, depending on the variety, with tender, unblemished leaves. Peak season is from August through the spring.

Fruit-Vegetables

Botanists classify avocados, eggplants, peppers and tomatoes as fruits because they develop from the ovary of flowering plants and contain one or more seeds. Chefs, however, prepare and serve them like vegetables; therefore they are discussed here.

Avocados

Avocados include several varieties of pear-shaped fruits with rich, high-fat flesh. This light golden-green flesh surrounds a large, inedible, oval-shaped seed (pit). Some varieties have smooth, green skin; others have pebbly, almost black skin. Avocados should be used at their peak of ripeness, a condition

Avocados

that lasts only briefly. Firm avocados lack the desired flavor and creamy texture. Ripe avocados should be soft to the touch but not mushy. Ripe Haas avocados have almost-black skins; the skins of the other varieties remain green when ripe. Firm avocados can be left at room temperature to ripen, then refrigerated for one or two days. Avocados are most often used raw to garnish salads, mashed or puréed for sauces, sliced for sandwiches or diced for omelets. Avocado halves are popular containers for chilled meat, fish, shellfish or poultry salads. Because avocado flesh turns brown very quickly once cut, dip avocado halves or slices in lemon juice and keep unused portions tightly covered with plastic wrap.

Choose avocados that are free of blemishes or moist spots. The flesh should be free of dark spots or streaks. Available all year, the peak season for Haas avocados is April through October; for Fuertes avocados it is November through April.

PROCEDURE FOR CUTTING AND PITTING AVOCADOS

1. Cut the avocado in half lengthwise. Separate the two halves with a twisting motion.

2. Insert a chef's knife into the pit and twist to remove.

3. Scoop the flesh out of the skin with a large spoon.

Eggplants

Two types of eggplants (Fr. *aubergine*) are commonly available: Asian and western. Asian varieties are either round or long and thin, with skin colors ranging from creamy white to deep purple. Western eggplants, which are more common in the United States, tend to be shaped like a plump pear with shiny lavender to purple-black skin. Both types have a dense, khaki-colored flesh with a rather bland flavor that absorbs other flavors well during cooking. Eggplants can be grilled, baked, steamed, fried or sautéed. They are commonly used in Mediterranean and East Indian cuisines (especially in vegetarian dishes), but also appear in European and North American dishes. The skin may be left intact or removed before or after cooking, as desired.

Western Eggplant

Sliced eggplants may be salted and left to drain for 30 minutes to remove moisture and bitterness before cooking.

Choose plump, heavy eggplants with a smooth, shiny skin that is not blemished or wrinkled. Asian varieties tend to be softer than western. Eggplants are available all year, with peak season during the late summer.

Asian Eggplants

Peppers

Members of the *Capsicum* family are native to the New World. When "discovered" by Christopher Columbus he called them "peppers" because of their sometimes fiery flavor. These peppers, which include sweet peppers and hot peppers (chiles), are unrelated to peppercorns, the East Indian (Asian) spice for which Columbus was actually searching. Interestingly, New World peppers were readily accepted in Indian and Asian cuisines, in which they are now considered staples.

Fresh peppers are found in a wide range of colors—green, red, yellow, orange, purple or white—as well as shapes, from tiny teardrops to cones to spheres. They have dense flesh and a hollow central cavity. The flesh is lined with placental ribs (the white internal veins), to which tiny white seeds are attached. A core of seeds is also attached to the stem end of each pepper.

Chile peppers get their heat from capsaicin, which is found not in the flesh or seeds, but in the placental ribs. Thus a pepper's heat can be greatly reduced by carefully removing the ribs and attached seeds. Generally, the smaller the chile, the hotter it is. The amount of heat varies from variety to variety, however, and even from one pepper to another depending on growing conditions. Hot, dry conditions result in hotter peppers than do cool, moist conditions. A pepper's heat can be measured by Scoville Heat Units, a subjective rating in which the sweet bell pepper usually rates 0 units, the jalapeño rates from 2500 to 5000 units, the tabasco rates from 30,000 to 50,000 units and the habanero rates a whopping 100,000 to 300,000 units.

When selecting peppers, choose those that are plump and brilliantly colored with smooth, unblemished skins. Avoid wrinkled, pitted or blistered peppers. A bright green stem indicates freshness.

Green Bell Pepper

Sweet Peppers

Common sweet peppers, known as bell peppers, are thick-walled fruits available in green, red, yellow, purple, orange and other colors. They are heart-shaped or boxy, with a short stem and crisp flesh. Their flavor is warm, sweet (red peppers tend to be the sweetest) and relatively mild. Raw bell peppers may be sliced or diced and used in salads or sandwiches. Bell peppers may also be stuffed and baked, grilled, fried, sautéed or puréed for soups, sauces or condiments. Green bell peppers are available all year; other colors are more readily available during the summer and fall.

*Red and Yellow
Bell Peppers*

PROCEDURE FOR CUTTING PEPPERS JULIENNE

1. Trim off the ends of the pepper; cut away the seeds and core.

2. Cut away the pale ribs, trimming the flesh to the desired thickness.

3. Slice the flesh in julienne.

Hot Peppers

Hot peppers, also known as chiles, are also members of the *Capsicum* family. Although a chile's most characteristic attribute is its pungency, each chile actually has a distinctive flavor, from mild and rich to spicy and sweet to fiery hot.

Chiles are commonly used in Asian, Indian, Mexican and Latin American cuisines. The larger (and milder) of the hot peppers, such as Anaheim and poblano, can be stuffed and baked or sautéed as a side dish. Most chiles, however, are used to add flavor and seasoning to sauces and other dishes. Fresh chiles are available all year and are also available canned in a variety of processed forms such as whole or diced roasted, pickled or marinated.

(clockwise from bottom left) Red and Green Serrano; Green and Red Jalapeño; Yellow Hot; Poblano; and Anaheim chiles.

PROCEDURE FOR CORING JALAPEÑOS

1. Cut the jalapeño in half lengthwise. Push the core and seeds out with your thumb. You can avoid burning your fingers by wearing rubber gloves when working with hot chiles.

Dried chiles are widely used in Mexican, Central American and southwestern cuisines. They may be ground to create a powdered spice called chilli or soaked in liquid, then puréed, for sauces or condiments. Drying radically alters the flavor of chiles, making them stronger and more pungent. Dried chiles are often called by names different from those of their fresh versions. For example, the fresh poblano becomes the dried ancho; the fresh jalapeño becomes the dried, smoked chipotle.

Choose dried chiles that are clean and unbroken, with some flexibility. Avoid any with white spots or a stale aroma.

PROCEDURE FOR ROASTING PEPPERS

1. Roast the pepper over an open flame until completely charred.

2. Remove the burnt skin and rinse under running water.

Tomatillos

Tomatillos, also known as Mexican or husk tomatoes, grow on small, weedy bushes. They are bright green, about the size of a small tomato, and are covered with a thin, papery husk. They have a tart, lemony flavor and crisp, moist flesh. Although an important ingredient in southwestern and northern Mexican cuisines, tomatillos may not be readily available in other areas. Tomatillos can be used raw in salads, puréed for salsa or cooked in soups, stews or vegetable dishes.

Choose tomatillos whose husks are split but still look fresh. The skin should be plump, shiny and slightly sticky. They are available all year, with peak season during the summer and fall.

Tomatillos

Tomatoes

Tomatoes (Fr. *tomate* or *pomme d'amour*; It. *pomodoro*) are available in a wide variety of colors and shapes. They vary from green (unripe) to golden yellow to ruby red; from tiny spheres (currant tomatoes) to huge, squat ovals (beefsteak). Some, such as the plum tomato, have lots of meaty flesh with only a few seeds; others, such as the slicing tomato, have lots of seeds and juice, but only a few meaty membranes. All tomatoes have a similar flavor, but the levels of sweetness and acidity vary depending on the species, growing conditions and ripeness at harvest.

(clockwise from lower right) Pear, Cherry, Plum and Beefsteak Tomatoes

THREE TREASURES OF THE NEW WORLD

In lieu of many spices, golden treasures and precious gems, early Spanish explorers returned to Spain with items of much greater significance: tomatoes, potatoes and corn. Unfortunately for those who financed the voyagers, the value of this produce was not immediately appreciated.

The Spanish and the Italians hailed the tomato (whose name comes from the Aztec name *tomatl*) as an aphrodisiac—perhaps because of its resemblance to the human heart—when it arrived from the New World during the 16th century. But even though tomatoes soon became part of Spanish and Italian cuisines, most other Europeans, New World colonists and, later, Americans considered tomatoes poisonous. (There is some truth to this notion: tomato vines and leaves contain tomatine, an alkaloid that can cause health problems.) Thus for many years and in many societies, only the adventurous ate tomatoes. Tomato historians consider September 26, 1820, a red-letter day marking the popular acceptance of the tomato. On that day, the then-well-known eccentric Colonel Robert Gibbon Johnson ate an entire bushel of toma-toes on the Salem, New Jersey, courthouse steps before a crowd of thousands—and lived. Tomatoes soon became one of the most popular of all vegetables.

Similarly, the potato, first delivered to Europe from its native Peru by Francisco Pizarro in the 16th century, did not win wide acceptance in haute cuisine until Antoine-Augustin Parmentier (1737–1813), a French army pharmacist, induced King Louis XVI of France (reign 1775–1793) to try one. He and his courtiers liked them so much they even began wearing potato blossom boutonnières. Parmentier was ultimately honored for his starchy contribution to French cuisine by having several potato dishes named for him. Indeed, the French still call potato soup *potage Parmentier* in his honor. Not only did Parmentier lobby for the acceptance of the potato as a food fit for a king, he also prophesied that the potato would make starvation impossible. Potatoes ultimately did become a staple of many diets. But, sadly, the converse of Parmentier's prophecy came true during the Irish Potato Famine of 1846–48, when a terrible blight destroyed the potato crop. Nearly 1.5 million people died and an equal number emigrated to the United States. They brought with them a cuisine that incorporated potatoes; thus an appreciation of the common potato was reintroduced to its native land.

When returning from his second voyage to the New World, Columbus took corn with him. Called *mahiz* or *maize* by West Indian natives, corn had been a staple of Central American diets for at least 5000 years. Although Europeans did not actively shun corn as they did tomatoes and potatoes, corn never really caught on in most of Europe. (As with another famous New World import, corn's origin was mistakenly attributed by the British, Dutch, Germans and Russians to Turkey. They called corn "Turkish wheat"; the Turks simply called it "foreign grain.") Grown for human consumption mostly in Italy, Spain and southwestern France, corn was and still is usually eaten ground and boiled as polenta. But despite an unenthusiastic European reception, corn's popularity quickly spread well beyond Europe: Within 50 years of Columbus's journey, corn was being cultivated in lands as distant from the New World as China, India and sub-Saharan Africa.

Because tomatoes are highly perishable, they are usually harvested when mature but still green (unripe), then shipped to wholesalers who ripen them in temperature- and humidity-controlled rooms. The effect on flavor and texture is unfortunate.

Tomatoes are used widely in salads, soups, sauces and baked dishes. They are most often eaten raw, but can be grilled, pickled, pan-fried, roasted or sautéed as a side dish.

Choose fresh tomatoes that are plump with a smooth, shiny skin. The color should be uniform and true for the variety. Tomatoes are available all year, with a summer peak season for most varieties. Many canned tomato products are also available (for example, purée, paste, sauce or stewed whole), as are dried tomatoes.

PROCEDURE FOR MAKING TOMATO CONCASSE

1. With a paring knife, mark an X on the bottom of the tomato just deep enough to penetrate the skin.

2. Blanch the tomato in boiling water for 20 seconds; refresh in ice water.

3. Using a paring knife, cut out the core and peel the tomato.

4. Cut the tomato in half horizontally and squeeze out the seeds and juice.

5. Chop or dice the tomato as desired for the recipe.

Gourds and Squashes

The *Cucurbitaceae* or gourd family includes almost 750 species; its members are found in warm regions worldwide. Gourds are characterized by large, complex root systems with quick-growing, trailing vines and large leaves. Their flowers are often attractive and edible. Although some members of the gourd family originated in Africa, chayotes and most squashes are native to the Americas.

Chayotes

The chayote, also known as merliton or vegetable pear, is a food staple throughout Central America. The vine bears slightly lumpy, pear-shaped fruits with a smooth, light green skin and a paler green flesh. There is a single white, edible seed in the center. Chayotes are starchy and very bland and are usually combined with more flavorful ingredients. They may be eaten raw, but their flavor and texture benefit from roasting, steaming, sautéing or grilling.

Chayotes

Choose chayotes that have well-colored skin with few ridges. Avoid those with very soft spots or bruises. Their peak season is the late fall and winter.

Cucumbers

Cucumbers can be divided into two categories: pickling and slicing. The two types are not interchangeable. Pickling cucumbers include the cornichon, dill and gherkin. They are recognizable by their sharp black or white spines and are quite bitter when raw. Slicing cucumbers include the burpless, the seedless English (or hothouse), the lemon (which is round and yellow) and the common green market cucumber. Most have relatively thin skins and may be marketed with a wax coating to prevent moisture loss and improve appearance. Waxed skins should be peeled. All cucumbers are valued for their refreshing cool taste and astringency. Slicing cucumbers are usually served raw, in salads or mixed with yogurt and dill or mint as a side dish, especially for spicy dishes. Pickling cucumbers are generally served pickled, without any further processing.

Choose cucumbers that are firm but not hard. Avoid those that are limp, yellowed or have soft spots. The common varieties are available all year, although peak season is from April through October.

(from left to right)
Pickling, Green and Hothouse Cucumbers

Squashes

Squashes are the fleshy fruits of a large number of plants in the gourd family. Many varieties are available in a range of colors, shapes and sizes. Squashes can be classified as winter or summer based on their peak season and skin type. All squashes have a center cavity filled with many seeds, although in winter varieties the cavity is more pronounced. Squash blossoms are also edible: They may be added to salads raw, dipped in batter and deep-fried or filled with cheese or meat and baked.

Choose squashes with unbroken skins and good color for the variety. Avoid any squash with soft, moist spots.

Acorn

Spaghetti

Banana

Butternut

Pumpkin

Winter Squashes

Winter squashes include the acorn, banana, butternut, Hubbard, pumpkin and spaghetti varieties. They have hard skins (shells) and seeds, neither of which are generally eaten. The flesh, which may be removed from the shell before or after cooking, tends to be sweeter and more strongly flavored than that of summer squash. Winter squashes should not be served raw; they can be baked, steamed or sautéed. Most winter squashes can also be puréed for soups or pie fillings. Their peak season is October through March.

Summer Squashes

Summer squashes include the pattypan, yellow crookneck and zucchini varieties. They have soft edible skins and seeds that are generally not removed before cooking. Most summer squashes may be eaten raw, but are also suitable for grilling, sautéing, steaming or baking. Although summer squashes are now available all year, their peak season is April through September.

Yellow Crookneck

Zucchini

Greens

The term *greens* refers to a variety of leafy green vegetables that may be served raw, but are usually cooked. Greens have long been used in the cuisines of India, Asia and the Mediterranean and are an important part of regional cuisine in the southern United States. Most have strong, spicy flavors. Mustard, sorrel, spinach, Swiss chard, dandelion and turnip greens fall into this category. The milder varieties of greens that are eaten almost always raw include the lettuces discussed in Chapter 24, Salads and Salad Dressings.

Greens have an extremely high water content, which means that cooking causes drastic shrinkage. As a general rule, allow 8 ounces (250 grams) per portion before cooking.

Choose young, tender greens with good color and no limpness. Avoid greens with dry-looking stems or yellow leaves. Most greens are available fresh all year, especially from November through June. The more popular greens are also available canned or frozen.

Mustard

Mustard, a member of the cabbage family, was brought to America by early European immigrants. Mustard has large, dark green leaves with frilly edges. It is known for its assertive, bitter flavor. Mustard greens can be served raw in salads or used as garnish. Or they can be cooked, often with white wine, vinegar and herbs.

Choose crisp, bright green leaves without discoloration.

Mustard

Sorrel

Sorrel is an abundant and rather ordinary wild member of the buckwheat family. Its tartness and sour flavor are used in soups and sauces and to accent other vegetables. It is particularly good with fatty fish or rich meats. Sorrel leaves naturally become the texture of a purée after only a few minutes of moist-heat cooking.

Choose leaves that are fully formed, with no yellow blemishes.

Sorrel

Spinach

Spinach (Fr. *épinard*) is a versatile green that grows rapidly in cool climates. It has smooth, bright green leaves attached to thin stems. Spinach may be eaten raw in salads, cooked by almost any moist-heat method, microwaved or sautéed. It can be used in stuffings, baked or creamed dishes, soups or stews. Spinach grows in sandy soil and must be rinsed repeatedly in cold water to remove all traces of grit from the leaves. It bruises easily and should be handled gently during washing. Stems and large mid-ribs should be removed.

Choose bunches with crisp, tender, deep green leaves; avoid yellow leaves or those with blemishes.

Spinach

Swiss Chard

Chard—the reference to "Swiss" is inexplicable—is a type of beet that does not produce a tuberous root. It is used for its wide, flat, dark green leaves. Chard can be steamed, sautéed or used in soups. Its tart, spinachlike flavor blends well with sweet ingredients such as fruit.

Choose leaves that are crisp, with some curliness or savoying. Ribs should be an unblemished white or red.

Turnip Greens

The leaves of the turnip root have a pleasantly bitter flavor, similar to peppery mustard greens. The dark green leaves are long, slender and deeply indented. Turnip greens are best eaten steamed, sautéed, baked or microwaved.

Swiss Chard

Turnip Greens

Black Trumpet

Clam Shell

Pom Pom Blanc

Mushrooms and Truffles

Mushrooms

Mushrooms (Fr. *champignon*; It. *funghi*) are members of a broad category of plants known as fungi. (Fungi have no seeds, stems or flowers; they reproduce through spores.) Mushrooms have a stalk with an umbrellalike top. Although not actually a vegetable, mushrooms are used and served in much the same manner as vegetables.

Several types of cultivated mushroom are available. They include the common (or white), shiitake, straw, enokidake (also called enoki) and cloud ear (also known as wood ear or Chinese black). Button mushrooms are the smallest, most immature form of the common mushroom.

Many wild mushrooms are gathered and sold by specialty purveyors. Because wild mushroom spores are spread around the world by air currents, the same item may be found in several areas, each with a different common name. Wild mushrooms have a stronger earthy or nutty flavor than cultivated mushrooms, and should generally be cooked before eating.

Mushrooms, whether cultivated or gathered from the wild, are available fresh, canned or dried. Because mushrooms are composed of up to 80% water, dried products are often the most economical, even though they may cost hundreds of dollars per pound. Dried mushrooms can be stored in a cool, dry place for months. When needed, they are rehydrated by soaking in warm water until soft, approximately 10–20 minutes.

Choose fresh mushrooms that are clean, without soft or moist spots or blemishes. Fresh cultivated mushrooms are generally available all year; fresh wild mushrooms are available seasonally, usually during the summer and fall. Cultivated mushrooms with exposed gills (the ridges on the underside of the umbrellalike top) are old and should be avoided. Fresh mushrooms can be refrigerated in an open container for up to five days. Normally, it is not necessary to peel mushrooms; if they are dirty, they should be quickly rinsed (not soaked) in cool water just before use.

Porcini (cèpe or cep)

Hen of the Woods

Morel

Shiitake

White

Oyster

Enokidake

Truffles

Truffles are actually tubers that grow near the roots of oak or beech trees. They can be cultivated only to the extent that oak groves are planted to encourage truffle growth. The two principal varieties are the Périgord (black) and the Piedmontese (white). Fresh truffles are gathered in the fall and are rarely marketed outside their locale. Truffles, especially white ones, have a strong aroma and flavor, requiring only a small amount to add their special flavor to soups, sauces, pasta and other items. Black truffles are often used as a garnish or to flavor pâtés, terrines or egg

Black Truffles

dishes. Because fresh imported truffles can cost several hundred dollars per pound, most kitchens purchase truffles canned, dried or processed.

Onions

Onions are strongly flavored, aromatic members of the lily family. Most have edible grasslike or tubular leaves. Almost every culture incorporates them into its cuisine as a vegetable and for flavoring.

Bulb Onions

Common or bulb onions (Fr. *oignons*) may be white, yellow (Bermuda or Spanish) or red (purple). Medium-sized yellow and white onions are the most strongly flavored. Larger onions tend to be sweeter and milder. Widely used as a flavoring ingredient, onions are indispensable in mirepoix. Onions are also prepared as a side dish by deep-frying, roasting, grilling, steaming or boiling.

Pearl onions are small, about 1/2 inch (1.25 centimeters) in diameter, with yellow or white skins. They have a mild flavor and can be grilled, boiled, roasted or sautéed whole as a side dish, or used in soups or stews.

Choose onions that are firm, dry and feel heavy. The outer skins should be dry and brittle. Avoid onions that have begun to sprout. They should be stored in a cool, dry, well-ventilated area. Do not refrigerate onions until they are cut. Onions are available all year.

Red Onion

Pearl Onion

Yellow Onion

Shallots

White Onions

Garlic

Garlic (Fr. *ail*; Sp. *ajo*) is also used in almost all of the world's cuisines. A head of garlic is composed of many small cloves. Each clove is wrapped in a thin husk or peel; the entire head is encased in several thin layers of papery husk. Of the 300 or so types of garlic known, only three are commercially significant. The most common is pure white, with a sharp flavor. A Mexican variety is pale pink and more strongly flavored. Elephant garlic is apple-sized and particularly mild. Although whole bulbs can be baked or roasted, garlic is most often separated into cloves, peeled, sliced, minced or crushed and used to flavor a wide variety of dishes. When using garlic remember that the more finely the cloves are crushed, the stronger the flavor will be. And, cooking reduces garlic's pungency; the longer it is cooked, the milder it becomes.

Choose firm, dry bulbs with tightly closed cloves and smooth skins. Avoid bulbs with green sprouts. Store fresh garlic in a cool, well-ventilated place; do not refrigerate. Fresh garlic is available all year. Jars of processed and pickled garlic products are also available.

Garlic

Leeks

Leeks (Fr. *poireaux*) look like large, overgrown scallions with a fat white tip and wide green leaves. Their flavor is sweeter and stronger than scallions, but milder than common bulb onions. Leeks must be carefully washed to remove the sandy soil that gets between the leaves. Leeks can be baked, braised or grilled as a side dish, or used to season stocks, soups or sauces.

Choose leeks that are firm, with stiff roots and stems. Avoid those with dry leaves, soft spots or browning. Leeks are available all year.

Leeks

Scallions

Scallions

Scallions, also known as green onions or bunch onions, are the immature green stalks of bulb onions. The leaves are bright green with either a long and slender or slightly bulbous white base. Green onions are used in stir-fries and as a flavoring in other dishes. The green tops can also be sliced in small rings and used as a garnish.

Choose scallions with bright green tops and clean white bulbs. Avoid those with limp or slimy leaves. Scallions are available all year, with a peak summer season.

Shallots

Shallots (Fr. *échalotes*) are shaped like small bulb onions with one flat side. When peeled, a shallot separates into multiple cloves, similar to garlic. They have a mild yet rich and complex flavor. Shallots are the basis of many classic sauces and meat preparations; they can also be sautéed or baked as a side dish.

Choose shallots that are plump and well shaped. Avoid those that appear dry or have sprouted. They should be stored in a cool, dry, unrefrigerated place. Shallots are available all year.

Pods and Seeds

Pod and seed vegetables include corn, legumes and okra. They are grouped together here because the parts consumed are all the seeds of their respective plants. In some cases only the seeds are eaten; in others, the pod containing the seeds is eaten as well. Seeds are generally higher in protein and carbohydrates (starch and fiber) than other vegetables.

Corn

Yellow and White Corn

Sweet corn (Fr. *maïs*; Sp. *maíz*) is actually a grain, a type of grass. Corn kernels, like peas, are plant seeds. (Dried corn products are discussed in Chapter 23, Potatoes, Grains and Pasta.) The kernels, which may be white or yellow, are attached to a woody, inedible cob. The cob is encased by strands of hairlike fibers called silks and covered in layers of thin leaves called husks. The silks and husks should be shucked prior to cooking, although the husks may be left on for roasting or grilling. Shucked ears can be grilled, boiled, microwaved or steamed. The kernels can be cut off the cob before or after cooking. Corn on the cob is available fresh or frozen; corn kernels are available canned or frozen.

Choose freshly picked ears with firm, small kernels. Avoid those with mold or decay at the tip of the cob or brownish silks. Summer is the peak season for fresh corn.

PROCEDURE FOR CUTTING KERNELS OFF EARS OF CORN

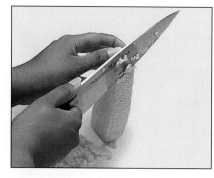

1. Hold the cob upright and use a chef's knife to slice off the kernels.

Legumes

Beans (Fr. *haricots*; It. *fagiolio*) and peas (Fr. *pois*) are members of the legume family, a large group of vegetables with double-seamed pods containing a single row of seeds. Of the hundreds of known varieties of beans, some are used for their edible pods, others for shelling fresh and some only for their dried seeds. Dried beans are actually several varieties of seeds or peas left in the pod until mature, then shelled and dried.

Fresh Beans

Beans used for their edible pods, commonly referred to as green beans, string beans, runner beans or snap beans, are picked when immature. Except for the stem, the entire pod can be eaten. This category includes the American green bean, the yellow wax bean and the French haricot vert, a long, slender pod with an intense flavor and tender texture. If there are any strings along the pod's seams, they should be pulled off before cooking. Beans may be left whole, cut lengthwise into thin slivers (referred to as French cut) or cut crosswise on the diagonal.

Shelling beans are those grown primarily for the edible seeds inside the pod. Common examples are flageolets, lima beans and fava (broad) beans. Their tough pods are not usually eaten.

All beans can be prepared by steaming, microwaving or sautéing. They can be added to soups or stews and they blend well with a variety of flavors, from coconut milk to garlic and olive oil. Cooked beans can be chilled and served as a salad or crudité.

Choose beans that have a bright color without brown or soft spots. Large pods may be tough or bitter. The peak season for fresh beans is from April through December. Most bean varieties are available frozen or canned, including pickled and seasoned products.

Green Beans

Haricots Verts

Dried Beans

Anthropologists report that for thousands of years cultures worldwide have preserved some members of the legume family by drying. Common dried beans include kidney beans, pinto beans, chickpeas, lentils, black beans, black-eyed peas and split green peas. Shape is the clearest distinction among these products: Beans are oval or kidney-shaped; lentils are small, flat disks; peas are round.

Beans and peas destined for drying are left on the vine until they are fully matured and just beginning to dry. They are then harvested, shelled and quickly dried with warm air currents. Some dried legumes are sold split, which means the skin is removed, causing the seed's two halves to separate.

Most dried beans need to be soaked in water before cooking. Soaking softens and rehydrates the beans, thus reducing cooking time. Lentils and split peas generally do not require soaking, however, and will cook faster than beans. After soaking, beans are most often simmered or baked in a liquid until soft and tender. One type may be substituted for another in most recipes, although variations in color, starch content and flavor should be considered.

Dried beans and peas are available in bulk or in poly-bags. They should be stored in a cool, dry place, but not refrigerated. Many of these beans are also available fully cooked, then canned or frozen. Some dried beans may be fermented or processed into flour, oil or bean curd.

Dried Black-eyed Peas

Lentils

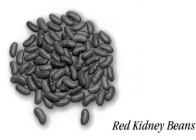

Red Kidney Beans

Pinto Beans

Great Northern Beans

PROCEDURE FOR SOAKING DRIED BEANS

1. Pick through the dried beans and remove any grit, pebbles or debris.
2. Place the beans in a bowl and cover with cold water; remove any skins or other items that float to the surface.
3. Drain the beans in a colander, then rinse under cold running water.
4. Return the beans to a bowl and cover with fresh cold water. Allow approximately 3 cups (750 milligrams) of water for each cup of beans.
5. Soak the beans in the cold water for the time specified in the recipe, usually several hours or overnight. Drain through a colander, discarding the water.

PROCEDURE FOR QUICK-SOAKING DRIED BEANS

The soaking procedure can be accelerated by the following technique:

1. Rinse and pick through the beans.
2. Place the beans in a saucepan and add enough cool water to cover them by 2 inches (5 centimeters).
3. Bring to a boil and simmer for 2 minutes.
4. Remove from the heat, cover and soak for 1 hour.
5. Drain and discard the soaking liquid. Proceed with the recipe.

Fresh Shelling Peas

Fresh Shelling Peas

Of the shelling peas that are prepared fresh, the most common are green garden peas (English peas) and the French petit pois. Because they lose flavor rapidly after harvest, most shelling peas are sold frozen or canned. Shelling peas have a delicate, sweet flavor best presented by simply steaming until tender but still al dente. Peas may also be braised with rich meats such as ham or used in soups. Cooked peas are attractive in salads or as garnish.

Choose small fresh pea pods that are plump and moist. Peak season is April and May.

Snow Peas

Edible Podded Peas

Snow peas, also known as Chinese pea pods, are a common variety of edible pea pod. They are very flat and have only a few very small green peas. Snow peas have a string along their seams which can be removed by holding the leafy stem and pulling from end to end. The pods can be eaten raw, lightly blanched or steamed, or stir-fried.

Another variety of edible pea pod is the sugar snap pea, a cross between the garden pea and snow pea, which was developed during the late 1970s. They are plump, juicy pods filled with small, tender peas. The entire pod is eaten; do not shell the peas before cooking.

Choose pea pods that are firm, bright green and crisp. Avoid those with brown spots or a shriveled appearance. Pea pods are available all year, with a peak season in March and April.

Okra

Okra

Okra, a common ingredient in African and Arab cuisines, was brought to the United States by slaves and French settlers. It is now integral to Creole, Cajun, southern and southwestern cuisines. Its mild flavor is similar to asparagus. Okra is not eaten raw; it is best pickled, boiled, steamed, or deep-fried. Okra develops a gelatinous texture when cooked for long periods, so it is used to

---

♦♦♦
TOFU

Tofu or bean curd (Fr. *fromage de soja*) is a staple of Japanese and Chinese cuisines and is gaining acceptance in American kitchens because of its high nutritional value, low cost and flavor adaptability. Tofu is made by processing soybeans into "milk," which is then coagulated (nowadays with calcium sulfate). The curds are then placed in a perforated mold lined with cloth and pressed with a weight to remove the liquid. The result is a soft, creamy-white substance similar to cheese. Tofu is easy to digest, very high in protein, with very little fat and sodium and no cholesterol.

Tofu is an ancient foodstuff, probably created in China during the 2nd century A.D. It was introduced to Japan by Buddhist priests during the 8th century and was "discovered" by Western travelers during the 17th century. Today Japanese tofu is said to be the finest, perhaps because of the superiority of the soybeans grown in the Yamato region, near the city of Kyoto. Japanese cuisine values the natural flavor and texture of tofu and uses it in a tremendous variety of ways. Chinese cuisine uses it as an additive, not as a principal ingredient.

Tofu may be eaten fresh; added to soup, broth or noodle dishes; tossed in cold salads; grilled; deep-fried or sautéed. Its flavor is bland, but it readily absorbs flavors from other ingredients.

Two types of tofu are widely available: cotton and silk. Cotton tofu is the most common. Its texture is firm, with an irregular surface caused by the weave of the cotton fabric in which it is wrapped for pressing. Silk tofu has a silky-smooth appearance and texture, and a somewhat more delicate flavor. Unlike cotton tofu, the water has not been pressed out of silk tofu. Consequently, silk tofu should not be cooked at high temperatures or for a long time, as it falls apart easily. The use of either type in most recipes is simply a matter of personal preference.

Fresh tofu is usually packaged in water. It should be refrigerated and kept in water until used. If the water is drained and changed daily, the tofu should last for one week.

---

thicken gumbos and stews. To avoid the slimy texture some find objectionable, do not wash okra until ready to cook, then trim the stem end only. Cook okra in stainless steel as other metals cause discoloration.

Choose small to medium pods (1 to 1/2–2 inches; 3.75 to 5 centimeters) that are deep green, without soft spots. Pale spears with stiff tips tend to be tough. Okra's peak season is from June through September. Frozen okra is widely available.

Roots and Tubers

Taproots (more commonly referred to as roots) are single roots that extend deep into the soil to supply the above-ground plant with nutrients. Tubers are fat underground stems. Most roots and tubers can be used interchangeably. All store well at cool temperatures, without refrigeration. Potatoes, the most popular tuber, are discussed in Chapter 23, Potatoes, Grains and Pasta.

Beets

Although records suggest that they were first eaten in ancient Greece, beets are most often associated with the colder northern climates, where they grow for most of the year. Beets can be boiled, then peeled and used in salads, soups or baked dishes.

Choose small to medium-sized beets that are firm, with smooth skins. Avoid those with hairy root tips, as they may be tough. Beets are available all year, with a peak season from March to October.

Beets

Carrots

Carrots

Carrots, (Fr. *carotte*) among the most versatile of vegetables, are large taproots. Although several kinds exist, the Imperator is the most common. It is long and pointed, with a medium to dark orange color. It has a mild, sweet flavor. Carrots can be cut into a variety of shapes and eaten raw, used for a mirepoix or prepared by moist-heat cooking methods, grilling, microwaving or roasting. They are also grated and used in baked goods, particularly cakes and muffins.

Choose firm carrots that are smooth and well shaped, with a bright orange color. If the tops are still attached, they should be fresh-looking and bright green. Carrots are available all year.

Celery Root

Celery root, also known as celeriac, is a large, round root, long popular in northern European cuisines. It is a different plant from stalk celery, and its stalks and leaves are not eaten. Celery root has a knobby brown exterior; a creamy white, crunchy flesh and a mild, celerylike flavor. Its thick outer skin must be peeled away; the flesh is then cut as desired. Often eaten raw, celery root can be baked, steamed or boiled. It is used in soups, stews or salads and goes well with game and rich meats. Raw celery root may be placed in acidulated water to prevent browning.

Choose small to medium-sized roots that are firm and relatively clean, with a pungent smell. Their peak season is October through April.

Celery Root

Jicama

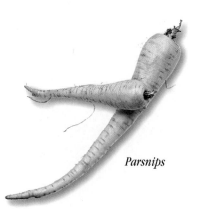

Jicama

Jicama is actually a legume that grows underground as a tuber. It is becoming increasingly popular because of its sweet, moist flavor; crisp texture; low calorie content and long shelf life. After its thick brown skin is cut away, the crisp, moist white flesh can be cut as desired. Jicama is often eaten raw in salads, with salsa or as a crudité. It is also used in stir-fried dishes.

Choose firm, well-shaped jicamas that are free of blemishes. Size is not an indication of quality or maturity. They are available all year, with a peak season from January through May.

Parsnips

Parsnips (Fr. *panais*) are taproots that look and taste like white carrots and have the texture of sweet potatoes. Parsnips should be 5 to 10 inches (12.5 to 25 centimeters) in length, with smooth skins and tapering tips. Parsnips, peeled like carrots, can be eaten raw or cooked by almost any method. When steamed until very soft, they can be mashed like potatoes.

Choose small to medium-sized parsnips that are firm, smooth and well shaped; avoid large, woody ones. Parsnips are available all year, with peak supplies from December through April.

Parsnips

Radishes

Radishes (Fr. *radis*) are used for their peppery flavor and crisp texture. Radishes are available in many colors, including white, black and all shades of red; most have a creamy to pure white interior. Asian radishes, known as daikons, produce roots 2 to 4 inches (5 to 10 centimeters) in diameter and 6 to 20 inches (15 to 20 centimeters) long. Radishes can be steamed or stir-fried, but most often are eaten raw, in salads or used as garnish. Radish leaves can be used in salads or cooked as greens.

Choose radishes that are firm, not limp. Their interior should be neither dry nor hollow. Radishes are available all year.

Red Radishes

Daikon

Rutabagas

Rutabagas are a root vegetable and a member of the cabbage family. Their skin is purple to yellow and they have yellow flesh with a distinctive starchy, cabbagelike flavor. Rutabagas and turnips are similar in flavor and texture when cooked and may be used interchangeably. Rutabaga leaves are not eaten. Rutabagas should be peeled with a vegetable peeler or chef's knife, then cut into quarters, slices or cubes. They are often baked, boiled and then puréed, or sliced and sautéed. They are especially flavorful when seasoned with caraway seeds, dill or lemon juice.

Choose small to medium-sized rutabagas that are smooth, firm and feel heavy. Their peak season is January through March.

Rutabagas

Turnips

Also a root vegetable from the cabbage family, turnips have white skin with a rosy-red or purple blush and white interior. Their flavor, similar to that of a radish, can be rather hot. Turnips should be peeled, then diced, sliced or julienned for cooking. They may be baked or cooked with moist-heat cooking methods, and are often puréed like potatoes.

Choose small to medium-sized turnips that have smooth skin and feel heavy. They should be firm, not rubbery or limp. Any attached leaves should be bright green and tender. Spring is their peak season.

Turnips

Stalks

Stalk vegetables are plant stems with a high percentage of **cellulose** fiber. These vegetables should be picked while still young and tender. Tough fibers should be trimmed before cooking.

> **Cellulose**—*A complex carbohydrate found in the cell wall of plants; it is indigestible by humans.*

Artichokes

Artichokes (Fr. *artichaut*) are the immature flowers of a thistle plant introduced to America by Italian and Spanish settlers. Young, tender globe artichokes can be cooked whole, but more mature plants need to have the fuzzy center (known as the choke) removed first. Whole artichokes can be simmered, steamed or microwaved; they are often served with lemon juice, garlic butter or hollandaise sauce. The heart may be cooked separately, then served in salads, puréed as a filling or served as a side dish. Artichoke hearts and bottoms are both available canned.

Artichokes

Choose fresh artichokes with tight, compact heads that feel heavy. Their color should be solid green to gray-green. Brown spots on the surface caused by frost are harmless. Artichoke's peak season is March through May.

PROCEDURE FOR PREPARING FRESH ARTICHOKES

1. Using kitchen shears or scissors, trim the barbs from the large outer leaves of the artichoke.

2. With a chef's knife, cut away the stem and the top of the artichoke. Steam or boil the artichoke as desired.

Asparagus

Asparagus (Fr. *asperges*), a member of the lily family, has bright green spears with a ruffle of tiny leaves at the tip. Larger spears tend to be tough and woody, but can be used in soups or for purée. Asparagus are eaten raw or steamed briefly, stir-fried, microwaved or grilled. Fresh spring asparagus is excellent with nothing more than lemon juice or clarified butter; asparagus with hollandaise sauce is a classic preparation.

Choose firm, plump spears with tightly closed tips and a bright green color running the full length of the spear. Asparagus should be stored, refrigerated at 40°F (4°C), upright in 1/2 inch (1.25 centimeter) of water or with the ends wrapped in moist paper toweling. They should not be washed until just before use. Canned and frozen asparagus are also available. Peak season is March through June.

A European variety of white asparagus is sometimes available fresh, or readily available canned. It has a milder flavor and soft, tender texture. It is produced by covering the stalks with soil as they grow; this prevents sunlight from reaching the plant and retards the development of chlorophyll.

Asparagus

Celery

Once a medicinal herb, stalk celery (Fr. *céleri*) is now a common sight in kitchens worldwide. Stalk celery is pale green with stringy curved stalks. Often eaten raw in salads or as a snack, it can be braised or steamed as a side dish. Celery is also a mirepoix component.

Choose stalks that are crisp, without any sign of dryness. Celery is available all year.

Celery

Fennel

Fennel (Fr. *fenouil*) is a Mediterranean favorite used for thousands of years as a vegetable (the bulb), an herb (the leaves) and a spice (the seeds). The bulb (often incorrectly referred to as sweet anise) has short, tight, overlapping celerylike stalks with feathery leaves. The flavor is similar to anise or licorice, becoming milder when cooked. Fennel bulbs may be eaten raw or grilled, steamed, sautéed, baked or microwaved.

Choose fairly large, bright white bulbs on which the cut edges appear fresh, without dryness or browning. The bulb should be compact, not spreading. Fresh fennel's peak season is September through May.

Fennel

Nopales

The pads of a prickly pear cactus can be prepared as a vegetable known as nopales. Cactus pads have a flavor similar to green bell peppers. Their texture tends to be rather gelatinous or mucilaginous, making them good for stews or sauces. To prepare fresh nopales, hold the pad with tongs and cut off the thorns and "eyes" with a sharp knife or vegetable peeler. Trim off the edge all the way around. Slice the pad into julienne strips or cubes. The pieces can be boiled or steamed and served hot, or chilled and added to salads. Nopales can also be sautéed with onions, peppers and seasonings for a side dish or added to southwestern-style casseroles.

Nopales

Some cultivated varieties have thin, thornless pads. Choose pads that are stiff and heavy without blemishes. They should not be dry or soggy. Fresh cactus pads are available all year, with peak season in the late spring. Canned and pickled nopales are also available.

Baby Vegetables

Many fine restaurants serve baby vegetables: tiny turnips, finger-length squash, miniature carrots and petite heads of cauliflower. First cultivated in Europe but now widely available throughout the United States, baby vegetables include both hybrids bred to be true miniatures as well as regular varieties that are picked before maturity. Baby vegetables are often marketed with blossoms or greens still attached. They tend to be easily bruised and are highly perishable. Many baby vegetables can be eaten raw, but they are usually left whole, then steamed or lightly sautéed and attractively presented as an accompaniment to meat, fish or poultry entrees.

Baby Yellow Squash with Blossoms

Baby Globe Carrots

Chiogghi Beets

Baby Zucchini with Blossoms

◆◆◆

ANCIENT PLANTS AND
ANCIENT WAYS VANISH

Since the days of Columbus, half of all native American crop varieties have become extinct. If this trend continues, several hundred more will become extinct in our lifetimes. Similarly, ancient farming practices have all but been abandoned. As late as the 1920s, the Tohono O'odham Indians of Arizona still used traditional methods to cultivate more than 10,000 acres without pumping groundwater. Today, only a few scattered floodwater fields remain.

When species disappear we lose an irreplaceable source of genetic diversity—a source of extraordinary genes that could someday improve modern hybrid crops. When native desert crops vanish, so does the ancient tradition of native agriculture, which has selected these crops over millennia to thrive in extreme temperatures, in alkaline soils without millions of gallons of precious water and without expensive, ecologically destructive chemicals.

Today, six highly bred species—wheat, rice, corn, sorghum, potatoes and cassava—supply most of the world's nutrition. As food crops become more and more homogeneous, they often lose their natural ability to tolerate pests, disease and drought. In the past, farmers grew thousands of food crop varieties. These traditional crop varieties contain a storehouse of genetic diversity that enables them to flourish in the most difficult environments. This broad spectrum of genetic variability is a cushion against natural predators and diseases. Wild chiles from the Sierra Madre, for example, are highly disease resistant. Their virus-tolerant genes have been bred into commercial varieties of bell pepper and jalapeños.

Native Seeds/SEARCH, one of the country's first regional seed banks, was founded to keep ancient desert plants and traditional farming methods from disappearing forever. Since 1983 we've ridden mules into remote areas and made more than 1200 collections of desert-adapted crops and wild relatives. We've gathered the seeds of chapalote (a brown popcorn), blue indigo (used for dyes), tepary (a heat- and drought-tolerant bean), teosinte (a wild relative of corn), wild chiles and other plants. These seeds are available to researchers, gardeners, farmers and seed banks. Seeds are offered free to Native Americans.

Each loss of biological and cultural diversity alters and damages the balance of life on earth, often in ways we do not understand. Each loss of leaf, stem and flower diminishes our earth's richness and beauty in ways we often don't appreciate until they're gone.

Dr. Gary Paul Nabhan
Native Seeds/SEARCH
Tucson, Arizona

TABLE 22.1   NUTRITIONAL VALUES OF SELECTED VEGETABLES

Per 4-oz. (112-g) serving, fresh, trimmed and prepared as noted	Kcal	Protein (g)	Carbohydrates (g)	Fiber (g)	Total Fat (g)	Vitamin A (I.U.)	Vitamin C (mg)	Calcium (mg)	Iron (mg)
Asparagus, boiled and drained	28	2.9	5	0.9 c	0.4	896	28.8	39.6	1
Broccoli, boiled and drained	32	3.4	5.7	2.9 d	0.4	1586	85	52	0.9
Cabbage, green, boiled and drained	24	1.1	5.4	0.7 c	0.3	96	27	37.5	0.4
Carrots, raw	48	1.2	11.6	3.6 d	0.4	32,404	11.2	30.4	0.6
Corn, boiled and drained	122	3.8	28.5	4.2 d	1.5	247	6.9	2.8	0.7
Mushrooms, white, raw	28	2.4	5.2	1.6 d	0.4	0	5.8	5.8	1.3
Onions, raw	44	1.2	9.6	2 d	0.3	0	6.7	21.3	0.2
Peppers, bell, green or red, raw	32	1.2	7.2	2 d	0.4	585	56.3	8.7	0.4
Pinto beans, boiled and drained	155	9.3	29.1	4.5 d	0.6	2.6	2.6	53.3	2.9
Snow peas, raw	48	3.2	8.4	2.8 d	0.4	42	17.2	12.4	0.6
Spinach, boiled and drained	26	3.4	4.3	2.5 d	0.3	7371	9	122	3.2
Tomatoes, raw	24	0.8	5.2	1.6 d	0.4	645	20.2	5	0.5
Zucchini, raw	16	1.2	3.2	0.4 d	0.3	100	2.7	4.5	0.1

Corinne T. Netzer Encyclopedia of Foods 1992

c = crude fiber (a designation given to a less-accurate measurement of fiber content)

d = dietary fiber (a designation given to a newer and more accurate measurement of fiber content)

NUTRITION

Most vegetables are more than 80% water; the remaining portions consist of carbohydrates (primarily starches) as well as small amounts of protein and fat. The relative lack of protein and fat makes most vegetables especially low in calories.

Much of a vegetable's physical structure is provided by generally indigestible substances such as cellulose and lignin, also known as fiber. This fiber produces the characteristic stringy, crisp or fibrous textures associated with vegetables.

Vegetables are also a good source of vitamins and minerals. Care must be taken during preparation to preserve their nutritional content, however. Once peeled or cut, vegetables lose nutrients to the air, or to any liquid in which they are allowed to soak. Vitamins are concentrated just under the skin, so peel vegetables thinly, if at all.

PURCHASING AND STORING FRESH VEGETABLES

Fresh vegetables should be selected according to seasonal availability. Using a vegetable at the peak of its season has several advantages: Price is at its lowest, selection is at its greatest and the vegetable's color, flavor and texture are at their best.

Grading

The USDA has a voluntary grading system for fresh vegetables traded on wholesale markets. The system is based on appearance, condition and other factors affecting waste or eating quality. Grades for all vegetables include, in descending order of quality, U.S. Extra Fancy, U.S. Fancy, U.S. Extra No. 1 and U.S. No. 1. There are also grades that apply only to specific vegetables, for example, U.S. No. 1 Boilers for onions.

Consumer or retail grading is currently required only for potatoes, carrots and onions. It uses alphabetical listings, with Grade A being the finest.

Purchasing

Fresh vegetables are sold by weight or count. They are packed in cartons referred to as cases, lugs, bushels, flats or crates. The weight or count packed in each of these containers varies depending on the size and type of vegetable as well as the packer. For example, celery is packed in 55-pound cartons containing 18–48 heads depending on the size of each head.

Some of the more common fresh vegetables (e.g., onions, carrots, celery and lettuces) can be purchased from wholesalers trimmed, cleaned and cut according to your specifications. Although the unit price will be higher for diced onions than for whole onions, for example, the savings in time, labor, yield loss and storage space can be substantial. Processed vegetables may suffer a loss of nutrients, moisture and flavor, however.

Ripening

Although vegetables do not ripen in the same manner as fruits, they do continue to breathe (respire) after harvesting. The faster the respiration rate, the faster the produce ages or decays. This decay results in wilted leaves and dry, tough or woody stems and stalks. Respiration rates vary according to the vegetable variety, its maturity at harvest and its storage conditions after harvest.

Ripening proceeds more rapidly in the presence of ethylene gas. Ethylene gas is emitted naturally by fruits and vegetables and can be used to encourage further ripening in some produce, especially fruit-vegetables such as tomatoes. Items harvested and shipped when mature but green (unripe) can be exposed to ethylene gas to induce color development (ripening) just before sale.

Storing

Some fresh vegetables are best stored at cool temperatures, between 40° and 60°F (4–16° C), ideally in a separate produce refrigerator. These include winter squash, potatoes, onions, shallots and garlic. If a produce refrigerator is not available, store these vegetables at room temperature in a dry area with good ventilation. Do not store them in a refrigerator set at conventional temperatures. Colder temperatures convert the starches in these vegetables to sugars, changing their texture and flavor.

Most other vegetables benefit from cold storage at temperatures between 34° and 40°F (2–4°C) with relatively high levels of humidity. Greens and other delicate vegetables should be stored away from apples, tomatoes, bananas and melons, as the latter give off a great deal of ethylene gas.

PURCHASING AND STORING PRESERVED VEGETABLES

Preservation techniques are designed to extend the shelf life of vegetables. These methods include irradiation, canning, freezing and drying. Except for drying, these techniques do not substantially change the vegetable's texture or flavor. Canning and freezing can also be used to preserve cooked vegetables.

Irradiated Vegetables

The irradiation process uses ionizing radiation (usually gamma rays of cobalt 60 or cesium 137) to sterilize foods. When foods are subjected to radiation, parasites, insects and bacteria are destroyed, ripening is slowed and sprouting is prevented. Irradiation works without a noticeable increase in temperature; consequently, the flavor and texture of fresh foods are not affected. Some nutrients, however, may be destroyed. Irradiated vegetables do not need to be sprayed with post-harvest pesticides and they have an extended shelf life.

The FDA classifies irradiation as a food additive. Although not yet approved for all foods, grains, fruits and vegetables may be treated with low-dose radiation. Irradiated foods must be labeled "Treated with radiation" or "Treated by irradiation." The symbol shown in Figure 22.1 may also be used.

Irradiated produce is purchased, stored and used like fresh produce.

FIGURE 22.1   *Irradiation Symbol*

Canned Vegetables

Canned vegetables are the backbone of menu planning for many food service operations. In commercial canning, raw vegetables are cleaned and placed in a sealed container, then subjected to high temperatures for a specific period of time. Heating destroys the microorganisms that cause spoilage, and the sealed environment created by the can eliminates oxidation and retards decomposition. But the heat required by the canning process also softens the texture of most vegetables and alters their nutritional content; many vitamins and minerals may be lost through the canning process. Green vegetables may also suffer color loss, becoming a drab olive hue.

Canned vegetables are graded by the USDA as U.S. Grade A or Fancy, U.S. Grade B or Extra-Select, and U.S. Grade C or Standard. U.S. Grade A vegetables must be top quality, tender and free of blemishes. U.S. Grade C vegetables may lack uniformity or flavor, but can be used in casseroles or soups if cost is a concern.

Combinations of vegetables as well as vegetables with seasonings and sauces are available canned. For example, corn kernels are available canned in water, in seasonings and sauces, combined with other vegetables or creamed. Canned vegetables are easy to serve because they are essentially fully cooked during the canning process.

Canned vegetables are purchased in cases of standard-sized cans (see Appendix II). Canned vegetables can be stored almost indefinitely at room temperature. Once a can is opened, any unused contents should be transferred to an appropriate storage container and refrigerated. Cans with bulges should be discarded immediately, without opening.

Frozen Vegetables

Frozen vegetables are almost as convenient to use as canned. However, they often require some cooking, and expensive freezer space is necessary if an inventory is to be maintained. Regardless, freezing is a highly effective method for preserving vegetables. It severely inhibits the growth of microorganisms that cause spoilage without destroying many nutrients. Generally, green vegetables retain their color, although the appearance and texture of most vegetables may be somewhat altered because of their high water content: Ice crystals form from the water in the cells and burst the cells' walls.

Some vegetables are available individually quick frozen (IQF). This method employs blasts of cold air, refrigerated plates, liquid nitrogen, liquid air or other techniques to chill the vegetables quickly. By speeding the freezing process, the formation of ice crystals can be greatly reduced.

Combinations of vegetables as well as vegetables with seasonings and sauces are available frozen. Some frozen vegetables are raw when frozen; others are blanched before freezing so final cooking time is reduced. Many others are fully cooked before freezing and only need to be thawed or heated for service. Frozen vegetables generally do not need to be thawed before being heated. Once thawed or cooked, they should be stored in the refrigerator and reheated in the same manner as fresh vegetables. Do not refreeze previously frozen vegetables.

Frozen vegetables are graded in the same manner as canned vegetables. They are usually packed in cases containing 1- to 2-pound (450 grams–1.8 kilograms) boxes or bags. All frozen vegetables should be sealed in moisture-proof wrapping and kept at a constant temperature of 0°F (–18°C) or below. Temperature fluctuations can draw moisture from the vegetables, causing poor texture and flavor loss. Adequate packaging also prevents freezer burn, an irreversible change in the color, texture and flavor of frozen foods.

Dried Vegetables

Except for beans, peas, peppers and tomatoes, few vegetables are commonly preserved by drying. Unlike other preservation methods, drying dramatically alters flavor, texture and appearance. The loss of moisture concentrates flavors and sugars and greatly extends shelf life.

APPLYING VARIOUS COOKING METHODS

Vegetables are cooked in order to break down their cellulose and gelatinize their starches. Cooking gives vegetables a pleasant flavor; creates a softer, more tender texture; and makes them more digestible. Ideally, most vegetables should be cooked as briefly as possible in order to preserve their flavor, nutrients and texture. Unfortunately, sometimes you must choose between emphasizing appearance and maintaining nutrition, because cooking methods that preserve color and texture often remove nutrients.

Acid/Alkali Reactions

The acid or alkaline content of the cooking liquid affects the texture and color of many vegetables. This is of greater concern with moist-heat cooking methods, but it is also a consideration with dry-heat cooking methods, as they often call for blanched or parboiled vegetables.

Texture

The acidity or alkalinity of the vegetable's cooking liquid influences the finished product's texture. If an acid such as lemon juice, vinegar or wine is added to the liquid for flavoring, the vegetable will resist softening and will require a longer cooking time. On the other hand, an alkaline cooking medium will quickly soften the vegetable's texture and may cause it to become mushy. Alkalinity also causes nutrient loss (especially thiamin) and may impart a bitter flavor. Alkalinity can be caused by tap water, detergent residue on utensils or the addition of baking soda (a base) to the cooking liquid. (You could add, for example, 1/8 teaspoon (.6 milliliter) of baking soda per cup (225 ml) of beans to speed the softening of dried beans.)

Color

The acidity or alkalinity of the liquid also affects the plant's pigments, causing both desirable and undesirable color changes. There are three principal pigment categories: chlorophyll, carotenoid and flavonoid. A plant's unique color is the

TABLE 22.2   ACID/ALKALI REACTIONS

Vegetable	Pigment Family	Effect of Acid on:		Effect of Alkali on*:		Cook Covered?
		Color	Texture	Color	Texture	
Spinach, Broccoli	chlorophyll	drab olive green	firm	bright green	mushy	no
Carrots, Rutabagas	carotenoid	no change	firm	no change	mushy	no difference
Cauliflower	flavonoid	white	firm	yellow	mushy	yes
Red Cabbage	flavonoid	red	firm	blue	mushy	yes

*Alkalinity always causes a loss of thiamin and other nutrients.

result of a combination of these pigments. Chlorophyll pigments predominate in green vegetables such as spinach, green beans and broccoli. Carotenoid pigments predominate in orange and yellow vegetables such as carrots, tomatoes, red peppers and winter squashes. Flavonoid pigments predominate in red, purple and white vegetables such as red cabbage, beets and cauliflower.

Initially, as vegetables are cooked, their original colors intensify. Exposure to heat makes pigments, especially chlorophyll, appear brighter. Exposure to acids and bases affects both chlorophyll and flavonoid pigments. Acids will gradually turn green vegetables an olive-drab color, while a slight alkalinity promotes chlorophyll retention. The opposite occurs with vegetables containing flavonoids: They retain desirable colors in a slightly acidic environment while losing colors in an alkaline one. (Carotenoid is not affected by either acidity or alkalinity.) Color changes alone do not affect flavor; but the altered appearance can make the product so visually unappealing as to become inedible.

Colors also change as the naturally occurring acids in vegetables are released during cooking. If the cooking pan is kept covered, the acids can concentrate, creating richer flavonoid pigments but destroying chlorophyll pigments.

Thus, if color is the *one and only* concern, vegetables with a high amount of chlorophyll should be cooked in an alkaline liquid, and vegetables with a high amount of flavonoids should be cooked in an acidic liquid. Just remember, the improvement in color usually comes at the expense of texture and nutrients.

Guidelines for Vegetable Cookery

The following general guidelines for vegetable cookery should be considered regardless of the cooking method used.

1. Vegetables should be carefully cut into uniform shapes and sizes to promote even cooking and provide an attractive finished product.

2. Cook vegetables for as short a time as possible to preserve texture, color and nutrients.

3. Cook vegetables as close to service time as possible. Holding vegetables in a steam table continues to cook them.

4. When necessary, vegetables may be blanched in advance, refreshed in ice water and refrigerated. They can then be reheated as needed.

5. White and red vegetables (those with flavonoid pigments) may be cooked with a small amount of acid such as lemon juice, vinegar or white wine to help retain their color.

6. When preparing an assortment of vegetables, cook each type separately, then combine them. Otherwise some items would be overcooked in the time required to properly cook others.

Determining Doneness

There are so many types of vegetables, with such varied responses to cooking, that no one standard for doneness is appropriate. Each item should be evaluated on a recipe-by-recipe basis. Generally, however, most cooked vegetables are done when they are just tender when pierced with a fork or the tip of a paring knife. Leafy vegetables should be wilted but still have a bright color.

You can avoid overcooking vegetables by remembering that some carryover cooking will occur through the residual heat contained in the foods. Always rely on objective tests—sight, feel, taste and aroma—rather than the clock.

◆◆◆
VEGETABLE SAUNA

"Sweating vegetables" in a little oil over low heat in a covered pot is, in effect, a vegetable sauna. All of the flavors of the vegetables emerge slowly in a juicy tangle, in a much more intense manner than if you simply added them just-cut to a stock. Like roasting garlic, it is a way to enlarge the natural flavors very dramatically.

—*from* CHINA MOON COOKBOOK
by BARBARA TROPP

Dry-Heat Cooking Methods

Broiling and Grilling

Broiling and grilling use high heat to cook vegetables quickly. This preserves their nutritional content and natural flavors. The radiant heat of the broiler or grill caramelizes the vegetables, creating a pleasant flavor that is not generally achieved when vegetables are cooked by other methods.

Selecting and Preparing Vegetables to Broil or Grill

Broiling is often used to cook soft vegetables such as tomatoes or items that might not rest easily on a grill rack. Broiling is also used to warm and brown items just before service. If necessary, the vegetables can be basted to prevent them from drying out under the broiler's direct heat. Sometimes a cooked vegetable is napped with sauce or clarified butter and placed briefly under the broiler as a finishing touch at service time.

A large range of vegetables can be grilled. Carrots, peppers, squashes, eggplants and similar vegetables should be cut into broad, thin slices. They can then be placed on the grill in the same manner as a portion of meat or fish to create attractive crosshatchings. (See Chapter 9, Principles of Cooking.) Smaller vegetables such as mushrooms, cherry tomatoes and pearl onions can be threaded onto skewers for easy handling.

Seasoning Vegetables to be Broiled or Grilled

Vegetables contain little fat and therefore benefit greatly from added fat when being broiled or grilled. The added fat can be a brushing of clarified butter or a marinade such as one made from olive oil and herbs. Some vegetables may be brushed with butter and coated with bread crumbs or parmesan cheese before broiling.

PROCEDURE FOR BROILING OR GRILLING VEGETABLES

1. Heat the grill or broiler.
2. Use a wire brush to remove any charred or burnt particles that may be stuck to the broiler or grill grate. The grate may be wiped with a lightly oiled towel to remove any remaining particles and help season it.
3. Prepare the vegetables to be broiled or grilled by cutting them into appropriate shapes and sizes, then seasoning, marinating or otherwise preparing them as desired or directed in the recipe.
4. Place the vegetables on the broiler grate, broiler platter or grill grate and cook to the desired doneness while developing the proper surface color.

◆◆◆

RECIPE 22.1

GRILLED VEGETABLE SKEWERS

Yield: 12 Skewers

Marinade:

Rice wine vinegar	4 oz.	120 g
Vegetable oil	8 oz.	250 g
Garlic, chopped	1 oz.	30 g
Dried thyme	2 tsp.	10 ml
Salt	1 Tbsp.	15 ml
Pepper	1/2 tsp.	2 ml

Zucchini	6 oz.	180 g
Yellow squash	6 oz.	180 g
Broccoli florets, large	12	12
Cauliflower florets, large	12	12
Onion, large dice	24 pieces	24 pieces
Red bell pepper, large dice	12 pieces	12 pieces
Mushroom caps, medium	12	12

1. Combine all ingredients for the marinade and set aside.

2. Cut the zucchini and yellow squash into 1/2-inch- (1.2-centimeter-) thick semicircles.

3. Blanch and refresh the zucchini, yellow squash, broccoli florets, cauliflower florets, onions and red bell pepper as discussed below (Moist-Heat Cooking Methods).

4. Drain the vegetables well and combine them with the marinade. Add the mushroom caps to the marinade. Marinate the vegetables for 30–45 minutes, remove and drain well.

5. Skewer the vegetables by alternating them on 6-inch (10-centimeter) bamboo skewers.

6. Place the vegetable skewers on a hot grill and cook until done, turning as needed. The vegetables should brown and char lightly during cooking. Serve hot.

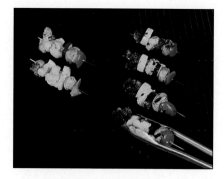

1. Grilling skewers of marinated vegetables.

Roasting and Baking

The terms *roasting* and *baking* are used interchangeably when referring to vegetables. Roasting or baking is used to bring out the natural sweetness of many vegetables while preserving their nutritional values. The procedures are basically the same as those for roasting meats.

Selecting and Preparing Vegetables to Roast or Bake

Hearty vegetables such as winter squash and eggplant are especially well suited for roasting or baking. Vegetables such as onions, carrots and turnips are sometimes cooked alongside roasting meats or poultry. The vegetables add flavor to the finished roast and accompanying sauce, and the fats and juices released from the cooking roast add flavor to the vegetables.

Vegetables can be baked whole or cut into uniform-size pieces. Squash, for example, is usually cut into large pieces. Vegetables may be peeled or left unpeeled, depending on the desired finished product.

Seasoning Vegetables to be Roasted or Baked

Vegetables may be seasoned with salt and pepper and rubbed with butter or oil before baking, or they may be seasoned afterward with a wide variety of herbs and spices. Some vegetables, such as winter squashes and sweet potatoes, may be seasoned with brown sugar or honey as well.

PROCEDURE FOR ROASTING OR BAKING VEGETABLES

1. Wash the vegetables. Peel, cut and prepare them as desired or directed in the recipe.

2. Season the vegetables and rub with oil or butter if desired.

3. Place the vegetables in a baking dish and bake in a preheated oven until done.

♦♦♦

RECIPE 22.2
BAKED BUTTERNUT SQUASH

Yield: 4 4-oz. (120-g) Servings

Butternut squash, medium dice	1 lb.	450 g
Salt and pepper	TT	TT
Cinnamon	1/4 tsp.	1 ml
Cardamom, ground	1/8 tsp.	1/2 ml
Brown sugar	2 Tbsp.	30 ml
Lemon juice	2 Tbsp.	30 ml
Whole butter, melted	2 oz.	60 g

1. Place the squash in a buttered pan. Season with salt, pepper, cinnamon, cardamom and brown sugar.
2. Drizzle the lemon juice and butter over the top of the squash.
3. Bake, uncovered, in a 350°F (180°C) oven until tender, approximately 50 minutes.

Sautéing

Sautéed vegetables should be brightly colored and slightly crisp when done and show little moisture loss. When sautéing vegetables, all preparation must be complete before cooking begins because timing is important and cooking progresses rapidly. Have all vegetables, herbs, spices, seasonings and sauces ready before you begin.

Selecting and Preparing Vegetables to Sauté

A wide variety of vegetables can be sautéed. Whatever vegetables are used, they should be cut into uniform-size pieces to ensure even cooking.

Quick-cooking vegetables such as summer squashes, onions, greens, stalks, fruit-vegetables and mushrooms can be sautéed without any preparation except washing and cutting. Other vegetables such as Brussels sprouts, green beans, winter squashes, broccoli, cauliflower and most root vegetables are usually first blanched or otherwise partially cooked by baking, steaming or simmering. They are then sautéed to reheat and finish. Carrots, squash and other vegetables are sometimes finished by sautéing in butter and then adding a small amount of honey or maple syrup to glaze them. Some cooked vegetables are reheated by simply sautéing them in a small amount of stock or sauce.

Seasoning Vegetables to be Sautéed

Sautéed vegetables can be seasoned with a great variety of herbs and spices. Seasonings should be added toward the end of the cooking process after all other ingredients have been incorporated in order to accurately evaluate the flavor of the finished dish.

Because sautéing vegetables uses slightly lower temperatures than sautéing meats and poultry, usually whole butter can be used in place of clarified butter. For additional flavors, fats such as bacon fat, olive oil, nut oils or sesame oil can be used in lieu of butter.

PROCEDURE FOR SAUTÉING VEGETABLES

1. Wash and cut the vegetables into uniform shapes and sizes.

2. Heat a sauté pan and add enough fat to just cover the bottom. The pan should be large enough to hold the vegetables without overcrowding.

3. When preparing an assortment of vegetables, add the ingredients according to their cooking times (first add the vegetables that take the longest to cook). Plan carefully so that all vegetables will be done at the same time. Do not overcrowd the pan; maintain high enough heat so the vegetables do not cook in their own juices.

4. Toss the vegetables using the sloped sides of the sauté pan or wok to flip them back on top of themselves. Do not toss more than necessary. The pan should remain in contact with the heat source as much as possible to maintain proper temperatures.

5. Add any sauces or vegetables with high water content, such as tomatoes, last.

6. Season the vegetables as desired with herbs or spices, or add ingredients for a glaze.

◆◆◆

RECIPE 22.3

Stir-Fried Asparagus with Shiitake Mushrooms

Yield: 1 lb. (450 g)

Asparagus	1 lb.	450 g
Shiitake mushrooms, fresh	6 oz.	180 g
Vegetable oil	1 Tbsp.	15 ml
Sesame oil	1 Tbsp.	15 ml
Garlic, chopped	2 tsp.	10 ml
Oyster sauce	4 oz.	120 g
Crushed red chiles, optional	TT	TT

1. Wash the asparagus, trim the ends and slice on the bias into 1- to 2-inch (2.5–5-centimeter) pieces.

2. Wash the mushrooms, trim off the stems and slice the caps into 1/2-inch- (1.2-centimeter-) thick slices.

3. Heat the oils in a wok or sauté pan.

4. Add the garlic and stir-fry for a few seconds.

5. Add the mushrooms and asparagus and stir-fry for 1 minute.

6. Add the oyster sauce and crushed red chiles (if used) and continue to stir-fry until the asparagus is nearly tender, approximately 3 minutes.

1. Stir-frying mushrooms and asparagus.

Pan-Frying and Deep-Frying

Pan-frying is not as popular as other techniques for cooking vegetables. Green tomatoes, however, are sometimes seasoned, floured and pan-fried; eggplant slices are seasoned, floured, pan-fried and used for eggplant parmesan. When pan-frying vegetables, follow the procedures outlined in Chapter 9, Principles of Cooking.

Deep-frying is a popular method of preparing vegetables such as potatoes, squashes and mushrooms. They can be served as hors d'oeuvre, appetizers or accompaniments to a main dish. Starchy vegetables may be deep-fried plain. Most other vegetables are first breaded or battered. Vegetables can also be grated or chopped and incorporated into fritters or croquettes. Any deep-fried item should have a crisp, golden exterior with a tender, nongreasy center. See Chapter 21, Deep-Frying, for additional information.

Moist-Heat Cooking Methods

Blanching and Parboiling

Blanching and parboiling are variations on boiling; the difference between them is the length of cooking time. Blanched and parboiled vegetables are often finished by other cooking methods such as sautéing.

Blanching is the partial cooking of foods in a large amount of boiling water for a very short period of time, usually only a few seconds. Besides preparing vegetables for further cooking, blanching is used to remove strong or bitter flavors, soften firm foods, set colors or loosen skins for peeling. Kale, chard, snow peas and tomatoes are examples of vegetables that are sometimes blanched for purposes other than preparation for further cooking.

Parboiling is the same as blanching, but the cooking time is longer, usually several minutes. Parboiling is used to soften vegetables and shorten final cooking times. Parboiling is commonly used for preparing root vegetables, cauliflower, broccoli and winter squashes.

Boiling

Vegetables are often boiled. Boiled vegetables can be served as is, or they can be further prepared by quickly sautéing with other ingredients, puréeing or mashing. Boiled vegetables are also chilled, then used in salads.

Starchy root vegetables are generally not boiled but rather simmered slowly so that the heat penetrates to their interiors and cooks them evenly. Green vegetables should be boiled quickly in a large amount of water in order to retain their color and flavor.

Refreshing

Unless the boiled, blanched or parboiled vegetables will be eaten immediately, they must be quickly chilled in ice water after they are removed from the cooking liquid. This prevents further cooking and preserves (sets) their colors. This process is known as **refreshing** or **shocking** the vegetables. The vegetables are removed from the ice water as soon as they are cold. Never soak or hold the vegetables in the water longer than necessary or valuable nutrients and flavor will be leached away.

PROCEDURE FOR REFRESHING VEGETABLES

1. Blanch, parboil or boil the vegetables to the desired doneness.

2. Remove the vegetables from the cooking liquid and submerge them in ice water just until they are cold.

Selecting and Preparing Vegetables to Boil

Nearly any type of vegetable can be boiled. Carrots, cabbages, green beans, turnips and red beets are just a few of the most common ones. Vegetables can be large or small, but they should be uniform in size to ensure even cooking. Some vegetables are cooked whole and only require washing before boiling. Others must be washed, peeled and trimmed or cut into smaller or more manageable sizes.

Seasoning Vegetables to be Boiled

Often vegetables are boiled in nothing more than salted water. Lemon juice, citrus zest, wine and other acidic ingredients are sometimes added to white and red vegetables; if so, they should be added to the liquid before the vegetables. Herbs and spices in a sachet or a bouquet garni are often used to add flavor to boiled vegetables and should be added according to the recipe.

After boiling, vegetables are sometimes finished with herbs, spices, butter, cream or sauces.

PROCEDURE FOR BOILING VEGETABLES

1. Wash, peel, trim and cut the vegetables into uniform shapes and sizes.
2. Bring an adequate amount of water, stock, court bouillon or other liquid to a boil. The liquid should cover the vegetables and they should be able to move around freely without overcrowding.
3. Add seasonings if desired or directed in the recipe.
4. Add the vegetables to the boiling liquid. If more than one vegetable is to be cooked and they have different cooking times, they should be cooked separately to ensure that all are cooked to the proper doneness. The pot may be covered if cooking white, red or yellow vegetables. Do not cover the pot when boiling green vegetables.
5. Cook the vegetables to the desired doneness.
6. Remove the vegetables from the water with a slotted spoon or a spider or drain through a colander.
7. Refresh the vegetables in ice water, drain and refrigerate until needed, or finish the hot boiled vegetables as desired and serve immediately.

◆◆◆

RECIPE 22.4

BRUSSELS SPROUTS IN PECAN BUTTER

Yield: 6 3-oz. (90-g) Servings

Brussels sprouts	1 lb.	450 g
Whole butter	2 oz.	60 g
Pecans, chopped	4 oz.	120 g
Salt and pepper	TT	TT

1. Trim the Brussels sprouts and mark an X in the bottom of each with a paring knife to promote even cooking.
2. Boil the sprouts in salted water until tender, approximately 10 minutes.
3. Drain and hold the sprouts in a warm place.

Continued

1. Marking an X in the bottom of each Brussels sprout.

2. Boiling the Brussels sprouts in the appropriate amount of water.

3. Tossing the Brussels sprouts with the butter.

Beurre noisette—*(Fr.) whole butter heated until it turns light brown and gives off a nutty aroma.*

4. Heat the butter in a sauté pan until it turns nut brown; this is called **beurre noisette**. Add the pecans and toss to brown them.
5. Add the Brussels sprouts and toss to reheat and blend flavors. Adjust the seasonings and serve.

PROCEDURE FOR COOKING DRIED BEANS

Dried beans are best rehydrated by soaking as discussed above and then cooking in a boiling (actually simmering) liquid. After rehydration and cooking, the beans can be served or further cooked in baked, sautéed or puréed dishes.

1. After soaking, place the drained beans in a heavy saucepan and cover with cold water or stock. Allow approximately three times as much liquid as there are beans. Add flavoring ingredients as directed in the recipe, but do not add acids or salt until the beans have reached the desired tenderness. Acids and salt cause the exterior of beans to toughen and resist any further efforts at tenderizing.
2. Slowly bring the liquid to a boil. Boil uncovered for 10 minutes or as directed in the recipe. Use a ladle to remove any scum that rises to the surface.
3. Cover and reduce the heat. Allow the mixture to simmer until the beans are tender. Whole beans generally require 1 to 2-1/2 hours, lentils 20–35 minutes and split peas 30–60 minutes. Add additional hot liquid if necessary. Do not stir the beans during cooking.
4. Drain the cooked beans through a colander.

◆◆◆

RECIPE 22.5

CHICKPEAS
WITH OLIVE OIL AND LEMON

Yield: 3 lb. (1.3 kg)

Chickpeas, dried	1 lb.	450 g
Chicken stock	3 pt.	1.5 lt
Onion, medium dice	10 oz.	300 g

Bouquet garni:		
Carrot stick, 4 in. (10 cm)	1	1
Leek, split, 4-in. (10-cm) piece	1	1
Fresh thyme	1 sprig	1 sprig
Bay leaves	2	2
Salt	1 tsp.	5 ml
Lemon juice	2 oz.	60 g
Olive oil	4 oz.	120 g
Garlic, minced	1 oz.	30 g
Fresh oregano, chopped	1 tsp.	5 ml
Lemon zest, grated	2 Tbsp.	30 ml
Pepper	TT	TT

1. Soak the chickpeas in water for 4 hours or overnight.

2. Drain the chickpeas and combine with the chicken stock, onion and bouquet garni. Simmer, uncovered, until the chickpeas are tender, approximately 2-1/2 hours. Add the salt to the chickpeas; cook for 5 minutes.

3. Combine the lemon juice, olive oil, garlic, oregano and lemon zest to make a dressing.

4. Remove the peas from the heat; drain. Combine with the dressing and season to taste with pepper. Serve the peas hot or refrigerate and serve cold.

Steaming

Vegetables can be steamed in a convection steamer or by suspending them over boiling liquid on a rack set over a wok, saucepan or hotel pan. Vegetables can also be pan-steamed by cooking them in a covered pan with a small amount of liquid. Although the food will be touching the cooking liquid, most of the cooking is done by steam because only a small portion of the food is submerged in the liquid. Steamed vegetables can be eaten plain, partially cooked and sautéed lightly to finish, incorporated into casseroles or puréed. If they are not served immediately, they must be refreshed and refrigerated until used.

Properly steamed vegetables should be moist and tender. They generally retain their shape better than boiled vegetables. Vegetables cook very rapidly in steam and overcooking is a common mistake.

Selecting and Preparing Vegetables to Steam

Nearly any vegetable that can be boiled can also be steamed successfully. All vegetables should be washed, peeled and trimmed if appropriate and cut into uniform-size pieces. Pan-steaming is appropriate for vegetables that are small or cut into fairly small pieces such as peas and beans or broccoli and cauliflower florets.

Seasoning Vegetables to be Steamed

Steaming produces vegetables with clean, natural flavors. Foods cooked in convection steamers can be seasoned with herbs and spices; but convection steamers use water to produce steam and the foods being cooked do not gain flavor from the cooking liquid. Vegetables steamed over liquids or pan-steamed in small amounts of liquids can be flavored by using stocks or court bouillon as the cooking liquid. Herbs, spices and aromatic vegetables can be added to any liquid for additional flavor.

PROCEDURE FOR STEAMING VEGETABLES

1. Wash, peel, trim and cut the vegetables into uniform shapes and sizes.
2. If a convection steamer is not being used, prepare a steaming liquid and bring it to a boil in a covered pan or double boiler.
3. Place the vegetables in a perforated pan in a single layer; do not crowd the pan. Place the pan over the boiling liquid, or add the vegetables to the liquid.
4. Cover the pan and cook to the desired doneness.
5. Remove the vegetables from the steamer and serve, or refresh and refrigerate until needed.

◆◆◆

RECIPE 22.6

BROCCOLI ALMONDINE

Yield: 6 Servings

Broccoli, fresh	2 lb.	1 kg
Salt and pepper	TT	TT
Whole butter	2 oz.	60 g
Almonds, sliced	1 oz.	30 g
Garlic clove, minced	1	1
Lemon juice	2 oz.	60 g

1. Cut the broccoli into uniform spears. Rinse and sprinkle lightly with salt and pepper.
2. Place the broccoli in a single layer in a perforated hotel pan and cook in a convection steamer until tender but slightly crisp, approximately 3 minutes.
3. Melt the butter in a sauté pan. Add the almonds and garlic and cook just until the nuts are lightly browned.
4. Arrange the broccoli on plates for service and sprinkle with the lemon juice. Drizzle the almonds and butter over the broccoli and serve immediately.

1. Placing the broccoli spears in a perforated pan.

2. Drizzling the browned almonds and butter over the broccoli.

Combination Cooking Methods

Braising and Stewing

Braised and stewed vegetables are cooked slowly in a small amount of liquid. The liquid, including any given off by the vegetables, is reduced to a light sauce, becoming part of the finished product. Generally, a braised dish is prepared with only one vegetable; a stew is a mixture of several vegetables. The main ingredients are sometimes browned in fat before the liquid is added in order to enhance flavor and color.

Both braises and stews can be exceptionally flavorful because they are served with all of their cooking liquid. (Boiled vegetables lose some of their flavor to the cooking liquid.) Braised and stewed vegetables generally can be held hot for service longer than vegetables prepared by other cooking methods.

Selecting and Preparing Vegetables to Braise or Stew

Various lettuces, especially romaine and Boston, are often braised. Cabbages, Belgium endive, leeks and many other vegetables are also commonly braised. Stews may contain a wide variety of vegetables such as summer squashes, eggplant, onions, peppers, tomatoes, carrots, celery and garlic. Leafy green vegetables and winter squashes are less commonly braised or stewed.

The vegetables should be washed and peeled or trimmed if appropriate. Vegetables to be braised may be left whole, cut into uniform pieces or shredded, as desired. Lettuces are usually cut into halves or quarters; cabbage is usually shredded.

Seasoning Vegetables to be Braised or Stewed

Both braises and stews usually include flavoring ingredients such as garlic, herbs, bacon or mirepoix. The liquid may consist of water, wine, stock or tomato juice. Vegetables can even be braised in butter and sugar or honey to create a glazed dish.

Both braises and stews can be seasoned with a variety of herbs and spices. Add the seasonings before covering the pot to finish the cooking process. Strongly flavored vegetables such as celery root and turnips are usually parboiled first in order to reduce their strong presence.

PROCEDURE FOR BRAISING AND STEWING VEGETABLES

1. Wash, peel, trim and cut the vegetables.
2. Sauté or sweat the flavoring ingredients in fat to release their flavors. Or, sauté or sweat the main ingredients in fat.
3. For a braise, add the main ingredient in a single layer. For a stew, add the ingredients according to their cooking times or as directed in the recipe.
4. Add the cooking liquid; it should partially cover the vegetables. Bring the liquid to a boil, reduce to a simmer, cover and cook in the oven or on the stove top until done.
5. If desired, remove the main ingredients from the pan and reduce the sauce or thicken it with beurre manié, cornstarch or arrowroot. Then return the main ingredients to the sauce.

◆◆◆

RECIPE 22.7

BRAISED CELERY WITH BASIL

Yield: 12 Servings

Celery	3 heads	3 heads
Onion, small dice	8 oz.	250 g
Garlic, minced	2 tsp.	10 ml
Whole butter	2 oz.	60 g
Olive oil	1 oz.	30 g

Continued

Fresh thyme	1 tsp.	5 ml
Fresh basil, chiffonade	20 leaves	20 leaves
Dry white wine	8 oz.	250 g
Chicken stock	1 pt.	500 ml
Salt and pepper	TT	TT

1. Trim the outer ribs from the celery heads, leaving only the tender hearts. Trim the heads to 6-inch (15-centimeter) lengths. Trim the root slightly, leaving each head together. Cut each head lengthwise into quarters.
2. Sauté the onions and garlic in the butter and olive oil, without coloring, until tender. Add the celery quarters to the pan and sauté, turning occasionally.
3. Add the thyme, basil, wine and chicken stock. Bring to a boil, reduce to a simmer, cover and braise in the oven at 350°F (180°C) until tender, approximately 1 hour.
4. Remove the celery and reserve. Reduce the cooking liquid on the stove top until it thickens. Adjust the liquid's seasonings and return the celery to the pan to reheat. Serve the celery with a portion of the sauce.

1. Trimming and cutting the celery.

2. Adding the liquid to the celery.

3. Reducing the sauce.

Microwaving

Fresh vegetables are among the few foods that can be consistently well prepared in a microwave oven. Often microwave cooking can be accomplished without any additional liquid, thus preserving nutrients. With microwaving, colors and flavors stay true and textures remain crisp.

Microwave cooking is actually a form of steaming. As explained in Chapter 9, Principles of Cooking, microwaves agitate water molecules, thus creating steam. The water may be the moisture found naturally in the food or may be added specifically to create the steam.

Cooking time depends on the type of microwave oven as well as on the freshness, moisture content, maturity and quantity of vegetables being prepared.

Selecting and Preparing Vegetables to Microwave

Any vegetable that can be steamed successfully can be microwaved with good results. Because typical microwave ovens are relatively small, they are impractical for producing large quantities of food. They are most useful for reheating small portions of vegetables that have been blanched or partially cooked using another cooking method.

Seasoning Vegetables to be Microwaved

Microwaving, like steaming, brings out the natural flavors of food and produces a clean, unadulterated flavor. Herbs and spices can be added to the vegetables before they are microwaved. Or, after microwaving, the vegetables can be tossed with butter, herbs and spices or combined with a sauce.

PROCEDURE FOR MICROWAVING VEGETABLES

1. Wash, peel, trim and cut the vegetables into uniform shapes and sizes.
2. Place the vegetables in a steamer designed for microwave use or arrange the vegetables on a microwavable dish. Cover the vegetables with the lid or plastic wrap. If using plastic wrap, it should be punctured to allow some steam to escape during cooking.
3. Cook the vegetables to the desired doneness, allowing for some carryover cooking. Or, reheat the previously cooked vegetables until hot. Stir or turn the vegetables as necessary to promote even cooking.
4. Serve the vegetables or refresh and refrigerate until needed.

Puréeing

Puréeing is a technique often used with vegetables. Cooked vegetable purées can be served as is, or they can be used as an ingredient in other preparations such as pumpkin pie, mashed potatoes or vegetable soufflés. Purées can also be bound with eggs, seasoned and used to make vegetable timbales and terrines.

Puréed vegetables are generally first cooked by baking, boiling, steaming or microwaving. White, red and yellow vegetables should be cooked until quite soft. They are more easily puréed when hot or warm; this also helps ensure a smooth finished purée. For most preparations, green vegetables must be refreshed after cooking and puréed while cold or they will overcook and become discolored.

Seasoning Vegetables to be Puréed

Vegetables for purées can be seasoned before they are puréed following the guidelines for the cooking procedure used. They can also be seasoned after they are puréed with a wide variety of ingredients such as herbs or spices, cheese, honey or brown sugar.

Finishing Puréed Vegetables

Purées can be finished with stocks, sauces, butter or cream to add richness and flavor. First purée the main ingredient, then add additional liquids to obtain the desired consistency.

PROCEDURE FOR PURÉEING VEGETABLES

1. Cook the vegetables. White, red and yellow vegetables should be cooked until very soft. Green vegetables should be cooked until tender but not overcooked to the point of being discolored.
2. Purée the vegetables in a VCM, food processor or blender or by passing them through a food mill.
3. Season or finish the puréed vegetables as desired or directed in the recipe, or use them in another recipe.

♦♦♦

RECIPE 22.8
PARSNIP PURÉE

Yield: 2 qt. (2 lt)

Parsnips	4 lb.	1.8 kg
Russet potatoes	1 lb. 8 oz.	650 g
Heavy cream, hot	8 oz.	250 g
Whole butter, melted	4 oz.	120 g
Salt and white pepper	TT	TT

1. Peel the parsnips and potatoes and cut into large pieces of approximately the same size.
2. Boil the parsnips and potatoes separately in salted water until tender.
3. Drain the parsnips and potatoes well. Purée them together through a food mill.
4. Add the cream and butter and mix to combine. Adjust the consistency by adding cream as desired. Season the mixture with salt and white pepper and serve hot.

CONCLUSION

Vegetables are an essential part of the human diet. They provide the body with vitamins, minerals and fiber and appeal to the appetite with taste, color and texture. Increasing market availability of fresh, high-quality vegetables as well as new hybrids gives you an ever-increasing variety of vegetables from which to choose. Vegetables are a relatively inexpensive food that can be prepared in limitless ways. They can be served as an entire meal or as an accompaniment to or part of a wide variety of other dishes. And when cooking vegetables, remember what James Beard (1903–1985), the great American food consultant, culinary educator and writer once said: "No vegetable exists which is not better slightly undercooked."

QUESTIONS FOR DISCUSSION

1. Explain how season affects the price, quality and availability of vegetables.
2. List and describe three processing techniques commonly used to extend the shelf life of vegetables.
3. What special concerns exist regarding the storage of fresh vegetables? Explain why some vegetables should not be refrigerated.
4. Why is it important to cut vegetables into a uniform size before cooking?
5. Discuss several techniques used for determining the doneness of vegetables. Is carryover cooking a concern when preparing vegetables? Explain your answer.
6. Discuss the role of acid in a cooking liquid used for preparing vegetables. Which vegetables, if any, benefit from an acidic cooking environment?
7. Describe the necessary mise en place and procedure for refreshing vegetables.

ADDITIONAL VEGETABLE RECIPES

RECIPE 22.9

SUMMER VEGETABLES WITH TARRAGON AIOLI

NOTE: *This dish appears in the Chapter Opening photograph.*

GREENS, SAN FRANCISCO, CA
Executive Chef Annie Somerville

Yield: 6 Servings   **Method:** Boiling

Baby artichokes	6	6
Carrots	8 oz.	250 g
Yellow or green zucchini	1 lb.	500 g
Sunburst squash	1 lb.	500 g
Blue lake green beans	8 oz.	250 g
Yellow wax beans	8 oz.	250 g
Broccoli florets	1 lb.	500 g
Cauliflower florets	1 lb.	500 g
Red radishes	1 bunch	1 bunch
Cherry tomatoes	1/2 pt.	250 ml
Niçoise or Gaeta olives	8 oz.	250 g
Tarragon Aioli (recipe follows)	8 oz.	250 g

1. Trim the artichokes. Steam or boil them until tender; refresh.
2. Cut the carrots, zucchini and squash as desired. Snip the ends from the beans. Parboil the vegetables (except the radishes, tomatoes and olives), one variety at a time, in salted water until nearly tender but still crisp. Refresh each and drain well.
3. Wash the radishes. Trim the root end but leave the green tops attached.
4. Wash the cherry tomatoes and remove the stems.
5. Loosely arrange the vegetables on a platter, leaving room for the aioli unless it is to be served separately in a small bowl.

TARRAGON AIOLI

Yield: 1/2 pt. (250 ml)

Egg yolk, large	1	1
Fresh lemon juice	1 Tbsp.	15 ml
Light olive oil	8 oz.	250 g
Garlic clove, chopped	1	1
Champagne vinegar	1 tsp.	5 ml
Fresh tarragon, chopped	2 tsp.	10 ml
Salt	TT	TT

1. Whisk the yolk and 1/2 teaspoon (3 milliliters) of lemon juice together until smooth.
2. Whisk in the oil, very slowly at first, until the aioli begins to emulsify. Add a few drops of lemon juice as necessary to thin the sauce. Continue until all the oil and lemon juice have been incorporated.
3. Season with the garlic, vinegar, tarragon and salt. If the aioli is too thick, thin it with a little warm water.

◆◆◆

RECIPE 22.10

SPINACH AU GRATIN

RUTH'S CHRIS STEAK HOUSE, PHOENIX, AZ

Yield: 8 8-oz. Servings (250 g)   **Method:** Boiling

Clarified butter	1 oz.	30 g
Flour	1 oz.	30 g
Half-and-half	1 pt.	450 ml
Frozen chopped spinach, thawed	2 lb. 8 oz.	2.4 kg
Salt and pepper	TT	TT
Cheddar cheese, shredded	1 lb. 8 oz.	700 g

1. Heat the butter in a saucepan. Add the flour and cook to make a blond roux.

2. Add the half-and-half, whisking to remove any lumps of roux. Bring to a simmer and cook for 15 minutes.

3. Drop the spinach into boiling salted water and cook for 2 minutes. Remove from the heat and drain well.

4. Combine the hot spinach with the cream sauce and adjust the seasonings.

5. Fill eight 10-ounce gratin dishes with the creamed spinach. Top each with 3 ounces (90 grams) shredded cheddar cheese and place under the broiler until the cheese is melted and browned and the spinach is very hot. Serve immediately.

◆◆◆

RECIPE 22.11

BROILED TOMATO

NOTE: This dish appears in the Beef Chapter Opening photograph.

RUTH'S CHRIS STEAK HOUSE, PHOENIX, AZ

Yield: 1 Serving   **Method:** Broiling

Tomato, large	1	1
Sugar	2 tsp.	10 ml
Whole butter, melted	1 oz.	30 g
Fresh parsley, chopped	1 Tbsp.	15 ml

1. Core and halve the tomato.

2. Sprinkle sugar on top of each half. Place on a broiler platter and broil until tender.

3. Drizzle with butter and garnish with parsley.

◆◆◆

RECIPE 22.12

GRILLED PORTOBELLO CAPS

Yield: 3 4-oz. (120-g) Servings   **Method:** Grilling

Portobello mushroom caps	1 lb.	500 g
Olive oil	1 Tbsp.	15 ml
Garlic, chopped	1 tsp.	5 ml

| Salt and pepper | TT | TT |
| Fresh thyme | 1 tsp. | 5 ml |

1. Wipe the mushroom caps clean with a damp towel.
2. Combine the olive oil and garlic and brush the mixture on the mushroom caps.
3. Season the mushrooms with salt, pepper and thyme.
4. Grill or broil the mushrooms until tender, approximately 8 minutes, depending on the size of the caps.

♦♦♦

RECIPE 22.13
DUXELLES

Yield: 12 oz. (350 g) **Method:** Sautéing

Mushrooms	1 lb.	500 g
Whole butter	1 Tbsp.	15 ml
Shallots, minced	2 Tbsp.	30 ml
Garlic, chopped	1 tsp.	5 ml
Salt and pepper	TT	TT
Fresh parsley, chopped	1 Tbsp.	15 ml

1. Chop the mushrooms very finely.
2. Sauté the shallots and garlic in butter until tender. Add the mushrooms and sauté until dry.
3. Season with salt and pepper and add the parsley. Cool.
4. Use the duxelles as a stuffing for vegetables or as a flavoring ingredient in other recipes.

♦♦♦

RECIPE 22.14
STIR-FRIED SNOW PEAS WITH DRIED SHRIMP

Yield: 6 3-oz. (90-g) Servings **Method:** Sautéing

Dried shrimp	1 oz.	30 g
Snow peas	1 lb.	500 g
Garlic, chopped	2 tsp.	10 ml
Vegetable oil	2 oz.	60 g
Sesame oil	1 tsp.	5 ml
Water chestnuts, sliced	4 oz.	120 g
Salt	TT	TT

1. Soak the dried shrimp in hot water for 15 minutes. Drain well.
2. Snap the snow peas and remove the strings.
3. Blanch the snow peas and refresh.
4. Stir-fry the garlic and shrimp in the vegetable and sesame oils for 10 seconds. Add the water chestnuts.
5. Add the snow peas and stir-fry until tender, approximately 1 minute. Season to taste with salt.

♦♦♦

RECIPE 22.15
GLAZED PEARL ONIONS

Yield: 1 lb. (450 g)   **Method:** Boiling

Pearl onions, peeled	1 lb.	500 g
Whole butter	1-1/2 oz.	45 g
Sugar	1 Tbsp.	15 ml
Salt and pepper	TT	TT

1. Place the onions, butter and sugar in a sauté pan and add enough water to barely cover.
2. Boil the onions, allowing the water to evaporate. As the water evaporates, the butter-and-sugar mixture will begin to coat the onions. When the water is nearly gone, test the doneness of the onions. If they are still firm, add a small amount of water and continue to boil until the onions are tender.
3. Sauté the onions in the butter-and-sugar mixture until they are glazed.

VARIATIONS: Vegetables such as carrots, turnips, zucchini and other squashes can also be glazed with this procedure. They should be cut into appropriate shapes such as a tourné and be large enough so they glaze properly without overcooking. When preparing a mix of glazed vegetables, cook each type separately because each has a different cooking time.

♦♦♦

RECIPE 22.16
HARVARD BEETS

Yield: 8 4-oz. (120-g) Servings   **Method:** Boiling

Sugar	4 oz.	120 g
Cornstarch	2 tsp.	10 ml
Red wine vinegar	2 oz.	60 g
Salt and pepper	TT	TT
Whole butter	1 oz.	30 g
Beets, boiled, peeled, medium dice	2 lb.	1 kg

1. Combine the sugar, cornstarch, vinegar, salt and pepper in a heavy saucepan. Whisk until the cornstarch and sugar dissolve.
2. Bring to a boil, then cook, stirring constantly, until the mixture is thick and clear.
3. Add the butter and the beets, tossing gently. Serve warm.

♦♦♦

RECIPE 22.17
MAPLE-GLAZED CARROTS

Yield: 16 4-oz. (120-g) Servings   **Method:** Sautéing

Carrots	4 lb.	1.8 kg
Whole butter	4 oz.	120 g
Salt and pepper	TT	TT

| Maple syrup | 4 oz. | 120 g |
| Fresh parsley, chopped | 2 Tbsp. | 30 ml |

1. Peel the carrots and cut into a shape such as oblique, tourné or rondelle.
2. Parboil the carrots in salt water and refresh. The carrots should be very firm.
3. Sauté the carrots in butter until nearly tender.
4. Season with salt and pepper and add the maple syrup. Garnish with the parsley.

= ◆◆◆ =

RECIPE 22.18

CREAMED CORN WITH BASIL

Yield: 10 4-oz. (120-g) Servings **Method:** Sautéing

Corn	12 ears	12 ears
Whole butter	2 oz.	60 g
Onion, small dice	4 oz.	120 g
Heavy cream	8 oz.	250 g
Basil leaves, chopped	2 Tbsp.	30 ml
Salt and white pepper	TT	TT

1. Cut the kernels from the ears.
2. Sauté the onions in the butter without browning.
3. Add the corn and sauté until hot.
4. Add the cream. Bring to a boil and reduce slightly. Add the basil and season with salt and white pepper.

= ◆◆◆ =

RECIPE 22.19

RATATOUILLE

Yield: 16 4-oz. (120-g) Servings **Method:** Sautéing

Onion, medium dice	12 oz.	360 g
Garlic, chopped	1 Tbsp.	15 ml
Olive oil	4 oz.	120 g
Green bell pepper, medium dice	6 oz.	180 g
Red bell pepper, medium dice	6 oz.	180 g
Eggplant, medium dice	12 oz.	360 g
Zucchini, medium dice	8 oz.	250 g
Tomato concasse	24 oz.	620 g
Fresh basil, chiffonade	1 oz.	30 g
Salt	1 oz.	30 g
Pepper	TT	TT

1. Sauté the onion and garlic in the olive oil.
2. Add the peppers, eggplant and zucchini and sauté until tender, approximately 10 minutes.
3. Add the tomatoes, fresh basil and seasonings. Sauté for 5 minutes. Adjust the seasonings.

◆◆◆

RECIPE 22.20

GARLIC TIMBALES

Yield: 8 2-oz. (60-ml) Timbales   **Method:** Baking

Garlic cloves, peeled	10	10
Milk	3 oz.	90 g
Heavy cream	8 oz.	250 g
Eggs	2	2
Dried thyme	1 tsp.	5 ml
Salt and pepper	TT	TT

1. Butter 8 small ramekins or timbales.
2. Place the garlic in a small saucepan, add enough water to cover and bring to a boil. Drain. Repeat this blanching procedure two more times.
3. Place the garlic in a blender with the milk and blend. Add the cream, eggs and thyme; blend until smooth. Season with salt and pepper.
4. Divide the custard among the timbales and place in a water bath. Bake for 30–45 minutes at 325°F (160°C).
5. Run a paring knife around the rim and unmold onto the serving plate.

VARIATIONS: Broccoli or cauliflower timbales. Place 1 ounce (30 grams) of blanched broccoli or cauliflower in each buttered timbale before adding the garlic custard mixture.

◆◆◆

RECIPE 22.21

ARTICHOKES STUFFED WITH ITALIAN SAUSAGE

Yield: 8 Servings   **Method:** Braising

Artichokes	8	8
Bulk sausage meat	1 lb.	500 g
Onion, chopped fine	1 lb.	500 g
Garlic, chopped fine	2 Tbsp.	30 ml
Cumin, ground	1 tsp.	5 ml
Fresh cilantro, chopped	4 oz.	120 g
Fresh thyme	2 tsp.	10 ml
Fresh bread crumbs	4 oz.	120 g
Tabasco sauce	TT	TT
Salt and pepper	TT	TT
Olive oil	2 oz.	60 g
Chicken stock	1 qt.	1 lt

1. Trim the stem and barbs from the artichokes. Using a tablespoon, scoop out the choke from the center of each artichoke.
2. Cook the sausage meat, breaking it up into small pieces. Pour off the fat. Add the onions and garlic and sauté until tender.
3. Add the cumin, cilantro, thyme and bread crumbs. Season with Tabasco sauce, salt and pepper.
4. Stuff the artichokes with the sausage mixture.
5. Place the artichokes in a braising pan and drizzle with olive oil. Add the chicken stock.
6. Bring the stock to a boil. Cover and braise until the artichokes are tender, approximately 1 hour.

◆◆◆

RECIPE 22.22

MIXED BEAN SALAD

Yield: 12 3-oz. (90-g) Servings   **Method:** Boiling

Green beans, cut in 1/2-in. (1.2-cm) pieces	4 oz.	120 g
White wine vinegar	2 oz.	60 g
Olive oil	3 oz.	90 g
Lemon juice	1 Tbsp.	15 ml
Lemon peel, grated	1 tsp.	5 ml
Garlic cloves, crushed	2	2
White wine	1 Tbsp.	15 ml
Dried red chile, chopped fine	1	1
Red kidney beans, soaked and cooked	8 oz.	250 g
Chickpeas, soaked and cooked	8 oz.	250 g
Lima or cannellini beans, soaked and cooked	8 oz.	250 g
Green onions, chopped	1 bunch	1 bunch
Salt and pepper	TT	TT

1. Steam the green beans until done but still crisp, approximately 3–4 minutes.

2. To make the dressing, combine the white wine vinegar, olive oil, lemon juice, lemon peel, garlic, white wine and chile.

3. Mix together all the drained beans and peas and pour the dressing over them. Add the green onions, season with salt and pepper and toss to combine. Marinate several hours before serving.

◆◆◆

RECIPE 22.23

BAKED BEANS

NOTE: This dish appears in the Pork Chapter Opening photograph.

Yield: 1-1/2 qt. (1.5 lt)   **Method:** Baking

Great Northern beans, soaked	1 lb.	450 g
Onion, small dice	4 oz.	120 g
Anaheim chile, small dice	1 oz.	30 g
Molasses	3 oz.	90 g
Brown sugar	3 oz.	90 g
Catsup	8 oz.	250 g
Prepared mustard	2 Tbsp.	30 ml
Cider vinegar	1 Tbsp.	15 ml
Worcestershire sauce	2 Tbsp.	30 ml
Tabasco sauce	TT	TT
Salt and pepper	TT	TT

1. Simmer the beans in water until almost tender, approximately 45 minutes. Drain well.

2. Combine the remaining ingredients, blending well.

3. Add the sauce to the beans, tossing to coat thoroughly. Adjust the seasonings.

4. Place the beans in a hotel pan or a 2-quart (2-liter) baking dish. Cover and bake in a 350°F (180°C) oven until the beans are completely tender, approximately 30–40 minutes.

◆◆◆

RECIPE 22.24
FENNEL AND MUSHROOMS À LA GRECQUE

Yield: 18 3-oz. (90-g) Servings   **Method:** Boiling

Mushrooms, small	1 lb.	500 g
Pearl onions, peeled	4 oz.	120 g
Olive oil	2 oz.	60 g
White wine	4 oz.	120 g
White stock	1 pt.	500 ml
Tomato concasse	12 oz.	360 g
Tomato paste	1 oz.	30 g
Lemon juice	1 oz.	30 g
Coriander, ground	1 tsp.	5 ml
Bouquet garni:		
Carrot stick, 4 in. (10 cm)	1	1
Leek, split, 4-in. (10-cm) piece	1	1
Fresh thyme	1 sprig	1 sprig
Bay leaf	2	2
Salt and pepper	TT	TT
Fennel, batonnet	1 lb.	500 g

1. Wash the mushrooms and trim the stems.
2. Sauté the onions in the olive oil, browning lightly. Add the white wine, stock, tomato concasse, tomato paste, lemon juice, coriander and bouquet garni. Season to taste with salt and pepper and bring to a boil.
3. Add the fennel and mushrooms and simmer for 15 minutes.
4. Remove from the heat and allow to cool to room temperature. Remove the bouquet garni. Adjust the seasonings and refrigerate. Serve chilled.

◆◆◆

RECIPE 22.25
SORREL SAUCE

Yield: 1 qt. (1 lt)   **Method:** Puréeing

Shallots, chopped coarsely	1 Tbsp.	15 ml
Whole butter	1 oz.	30 g
White wine	8 oz.	250 g
Heavy cream	1 pt.	500 g
Sorrel, stemmed	8 oz.	250 g
Spinach, stemmed	8 oz.	250 g
Salt and white pepper	TT	TT
Lemon juice	1 oz.	30 ml

1. Sauté the shallots in the butter until tender.
2. Add the white wine and reduce by half.
3. Add the cream and reduce until it begins to thicken.
4. Add the sorrel and spinach leaves to the cream and cook just until the leaves are wilted.
5. Purée the sauce in a blender or food processor and season with salt, pepper and lemon juice. Serve the sauce with egg, chicken, veal or rich fish dishes.

◆◆◆

RECIPE 22.26

SWISS CHARD WITH LEMON AND PINE NUTS

Yield: 8 3-oz. (90-g) Servings   **Method:** Simmering

Swiss chard, trimmed, stems and leaves separated	2 lb.	1 kg
Water	1 pt.	500 g
Lemon juice	2 oz.	60 g
Extra virgin olive oil	2 oz.	60 g
Salt and pepper	TT	TT
Pine nuts, toasted and chopped	2 oz.	60 g

1. Cut the chard into 1 to 2-inch (2.5 to 5-centimeter) strips on a diagonal.
2. Combine the chard, water and 1 ounce (30 grams) lemon juice in a nonreactive pan. Simmer until tender, stirring frequently, approximately 10–15 minutes.
3. Drain. Toss with the remaining lemon juice and the olive oil. Season with salt and pepper and arrange on plates. Garnish with the pine nuts.

◆◆◆

RECIPE 22.27

BRAISED RED CABBAGE WITH APPLES AND WINE

Yield: 16 4-oz. (120-g) Servings   **Method:** Braising

Red cabbage	3 lb.	1.4 kg
Bacon, medium dice	12 oz.	360 g
Onions, medium dice	8 oz.	250 g
Salt and pepper	TT	TT
Red wine	8 oz.	250 g
White stock	8 oz.	250 g
Cinnamon sticks	2	2
Apples, tart, cored and diced	12 oz.	360 g
Brown sugar	1 oz.	30 g
Cider vinegar	2 oz.	60 g

1. Shred the cabbage.
2. Render the bacon. Add the onions and sweat in the bacon fat until tender.
3. Add the cabbage and sauté for 5 minutes. Season with salt and pepper. Add the wine, stock and cinnamon sticks. Cover and braise until the cabbage is almost tender, approximately 20 minutes.
4. Add the apples, brown sugar and vinegar and mix well.
5. Cover and braise until the apples are tender, approximately 5 minutes.

◆◆◆

RECIPE 22.28

BRAISED ROMAINE LETTUCE

Yield: 12 Servings   **Method:** Braising

Romaine lettuce	3 heads	3 heads
Onions, small dice	8 oz.	250 g
Celery, small dice	8 oz.	250 g
Carrots, small dice	8 oz.	250 g
Bacon ends and pieces, small dice	8 oz.	250 g
Brown stock	24 oz.	700 g
Salt and pepper	TT	TT

1. Trim the lettuce heads. Blanch them in salted boiling water and refresh.
2. Combine the onions, celery, carrots, bacon pieces and brown stock in a sauce pot and simmer for 10 minutes.
3. Quarter the heads of romaine and trim off most of the core, leaving just enough to hold the leaves together.
4. Pour the brown stock mixture into a hotel pan and arrange the lettuce portions in the pan. Season with salt and pepper.
5. Cover the pan and braise in a 350°F (180°C) oven for approximately 1 hour. Serve each portion with vegetables, bacon and a portion of the cooking liquid.

◆◆◆

RECIPE 22.29

CUCUMBER-YOGURT SALAD

Yield: 1 qt. (1 lt)

Plain yogurt	1 lb.	500 g
Cucumber, peeled and grated	12 oz.	360 g
Cumin	1 tsp.	5 ml
Salt and pepper	TT	TT
Sugar	1/2 oz.	15 g
Lime juice	1/2 oz.	15 g
Fresh cilantro, chopped	2 Tbsp.	30 ml
Jalapeño, minced	1 tsp.	5 ml
Paprika	as needed	as needed

1. Stir together all ingredients except the paprika. Chill for several hours before service.
2. Dust the top lightly with paprika at the time of service.

Nutritional values per 4 oz. (120 g) serving:

Calories	51	Protein	2 g
Calories from fat	35%	Vitamin A	125 IU
Total fat	2 g	Vitamin C	3 mg
Saturated fat	1 g	Sodium	34 mg
Cholesterol	7 mg		

◆◆◆

TOMATILLO SALSA

Yield: 2 qt. (2 lt)

Tomatillos	5 lb.	2 kg
Water	8 oz.	250 g
Jalapeños	3	3
Salt	1 Tbsp.	15 ml
Pepper	1/2 tsp.	2 ml
Garlic	2 Tbsp.	30 ml
Onions, chopped	4 oz.	120 g
Cilantro, chopped	2 oz.	60 g

1. Remove the husks from the tomatillos.
2. Combine the tomatillos with the water, jalapeños, salt, pepper, garlic and onions. Bring to a boil and simmer until tender, approximately 20 minutes.
3. Chop all ingredients in a food chopper or purée them in a blender for a smoother sauce.
4. Add the cilantro and adjust the seasonings. The sauce may be served warm or cold.

Nutritional values per 2 oz. (60 g) serving:

Calories	24	Protein	1 g
Calories from fat	7%	Vitamin A	316 IU
Total fat	0 g	Vitamin C	18 mg
Saturated fat	0 g	Sodium	291 mg
Cholesterol	0 mg		

CHAPTER 23
POTATOES, GRAINS AND PASTA

After studying this chapter you will be able to:

+ identify a variety of potatoes
+ apply various cooking methods to potatoes
+ identify a variety of grains
+ apply various cooking methods to grains
+ identify pasta products
+ make fresh pasta
+ cook pasta

otatoes, grains (corn, rice, wheat and others) and pastas are collectively known as starches. *Some of these foods are vegetables; others are grasses. Pastas, of course, are prepared products made from grains. Starches are, for the most part, staple foods: foods that define a cuisine and give it substance. All are high in starchy carbohydrates, low in fat and commonly used as part of a well-balanced meal.*

Today's chefs are rediscovering traditional and ethnic dishes that rely on grains seldom used in typical American food service operations. Pasta, made from a variety of grains in numerous shapes and flavors and accompanied by countless sauces and garnishes, now regularly appears on many menus alongside the ubiquitous potato prepared in many classic and modern manners.

POTATOES

Potatoes (Fr. *pommes de terre*) are one of the few vegetables native to the New World, probably originating in the South American Andes. Botanically, potatoes are succulent, nonwoody annual plants. The portion we consume is the tuber, the swollen fleshy part of the underground stem. Potatoes are hardy and easy to grow, making them inexpensive and widely available.

Identifying Potatoes

Discussed below are some of the more commonly used types of potatoes. Other varieties are regularly being developed or rediscovered and tested in the marketplace.

Choose potatoes that are heavy and very firm with clean skin and few eyes. Avoid those with many eyes, sprouts, green streaks, soft spots, cracks or cut edges. Most varieties are available all year.

Purple Potatoes

Purple (or blue) potatoes have a deep purple skin. The flesh is bright purple, becoming lighter when cooked. They are mealy, with a flavor and texture similar to russets. The most common varieties are All Blue and Caribe, which were also quite popular in the mid-19th century.

Purple Potatoes

Red Potatoes

Red Potatoes

Red potatoes have a thin red skin and crisp, white, waxy flesh, best suited to boiling or steaming. They do not have the dry, mealy texture successful baking requires. **New potatoes** are small, immature red potatoes usually marketed during the early summer. When ordering red-skinned new potatoes, size A is larger than size B.

Russet Potatoes

Russet potatoes, commonly referred to as Idaho potatoes, are the standard baking potato. They are long with rough, reddish-brown skin and mealy flesh.

Russets are excellent baked and are the best potatoes for frying. They tend to fall apart when boiled. They are marketed in several size categories and should be purchased in the size most appropriate for their intended use.

Russet Potatoes

White Potatoes

White potatoes are available in round or long varieties. They have a thin, tender skin with a tender, waxy yellow or white flesh. The smaller ones are sometimes marketed as new potatoes (not to be confused with new red potatoes). Round white potatoes are also referred to as chef or all-purpose potatoes. Yukon Gold and White Rose are common varieties. Finnish Yellow (or Yellow Finn) is an increasingly popular variety; it has a golden skin, creamy flesh and buttery flavor. White potatoes are usually cooked with moist heat or used for sautéing.

White Potatoes

Sweet Potatoes

Sweet potatoes are from a different botanical family than ordinary potatoes, although they are also tubers that originated in the New World. Two types are commonly available. One has yellow flesh and a dry, mealy texture; it is known as a boniato, white or Cuban sweet potato. The other has a darker orange, moister flesh and is high in sugar; it is known as a red sweet potato. Both types have thick skins ranging in color from light tan to brownish red. (Sometimes dark-skinned sweet potatoes are erroneously labeled *yams*.) Sweet potatoes should be chosen according to the desired degree of sweetness. They are best suited for boiling, baking and puréeing, although the less sweet varieties can be deep-fried. The cooked flesh can also be used in breads, pies and puddings. Sweet potatoes are available canned, often in a spiced or sugary sauce.

Sweet Potatoes

Yams

Yams are a third type of tuber, botanically different from both sweet and common potatoes. Yams are less sweet than sweet potatoes, but they can be used interchangeably. The flesh of yams ranges from creamy white to deep red. Yams are Asian in origin and are now found in Africa, South America and the southern United States.

Nutrition

Potatoes contain a high percentage of easily digested complex carbohydrates and little or no fat. They are also a good source of many minerals and some vitamins.

TABLE 23.1   NUTRITIONAL VALUES OF SELECTED POTATOES

Per 4 oz. (112 g), baked in skin	Kcal	Protein (g)	Carbohydrates (g)	Fiber (g)	Total Fat (g)	Niacin (g)	Phosphorous (mg)	Potassium (mg)
Russet	124	2.6	28.6	0.7	0.1	1.9	64.8	475.5
Sweet potato	93	1.6	21.7	2.4	<0.1	mq	mq	mq
Yam	132	1.7	31.2	mq	0.2	0.4	33	455

The Corinne T. Netzer Encyclopedia of Food Values 1992
mq = measurable quantity, but data is unavailable

Purchasing and Storing Potatoes

Mealy Versus Waxy

One of the most important considerations in selecting potatoes is choosing between the mealy and waxy varieties. You should understand the differences and purchase the type best suited to your needs.

Mealy potatoes (also known as starchy potatoes) have a high starch content and thick skin. They are best for baking and are often ordered from suppliers simply as "bakers." Their low sugar content also allows them to be deep-fried long enough to fully cook the interior without burning the exterior. Mealy potatoes tend to fall apart when boiled, making them a good choice for whipped or puréed potatoes.

Waxy potatoes have a low starch content and thin skin. They are best for boiling. They will not develop the desired fluffy texture when baked. They tend to become limp and soggy when deep-fried because of their high moisture content.

TABLE 23.2	COMPARISON OF MEALY AND WAXY POTATOES						
	Content of:			Best to:			
	Starch	Moisture	Sugar	Bake	Boil	Sauté	Deep-fry
Mealy: russet, white rose, purple	high	low	low	✓			✓
Waxy: red, new (red), Finnish yellow	low	high	high		✓	✓	

Grading

Like other vegetables, potatoes are subject to the voluntary USDA grading system. Although U.S. Fancy is the highest grade, most potatoes sold on the wholesale market are U.S. No. 1. Potatoes sold on the retail market can also be graded as either U.S. Grade A or U.S. Grade B.

Purchasing

Potatoes are usually packed in 50-pound cartons. Counts vary depending on average potato size. For example, in a 100-count carton, each potato would weigh an average of 8 ounces. Eighty-, 90- and 100-count cartons are the most common. Generally, larger-sized potatoes (i.e., smaller counts) are more expensive. Size does not affect quality, however, and selection should be based on intended use.

Storing

Temperatures between 50° and 65°F (10–18°C) are best for storing potatoes. Do not store potatoes in the refrigerator. At temperatures below 40°F (4°C) potato starch turns to sugar, making the cooked product too sweet and increasing the risk that the potato will turn gray or streaky when cooked. Potatoes with a high sugar content also burn more easily when fried.

Potatoes should be stored in a dark room, as light promotes chlorophyll production, turning them green and bitter. Any green patches indicate the possible presence of solanine, a toxin harmful if eaten in large amounts, and should be peeled away. Solanine is also present in the eyes and sprouts and they, too, should be removed and discarded before cooking.

Under proper conditions, fresh potatoes should last for two months. Do not wash potatoes until ready to use, as washing promotes spoilage.

Applying Various Cooking Methods

Potatoes have a relatively neutral flavor, making them a perfect accompaniment to many savory dishes. They can be prepared with almost any dry- or moist-heat cooking method: baking, sautéing, pan-frying, deep-frying, boiling or steaming. They can be combined with other ingredients in braises and stews. Potatoes are used in soups (vichyssoise), dumplings (gnocchi), breads, pancakes (latkes), puddings, salads and even vodka.

Many potato dishes, both classic and modern, employ more than one cooking method. For example, lorette potatoes require boiling and deep-frying; hash browns require parboiling, then sautéing. Even french fries are best when first blanched in hot oil.

Determining Doneness

Most potatoes are considered done when they are soft and tender or offer little resistance when pierced with a knife tip. Fried potatoes should have a crisp, golden-brown surface; the interior should be moist and tender.

Roasting and Baking

Potatoes are often roasted with meat or poultry, becoming coated with the fat and drippings released from the main item as it cooks. Either mealy or waxy potatoes, peeled or unpeeled, can be roasted successfully.

Mealy potatoes such as russets are ideal for baking. The skin is left intact, although it may be pierced with a fork to allow steam to escape. A true baked potato should not be wrapped in foil or cooked in a microwave; this changes the cooking method to steaming and prevents a crisp skin from forming. A properly baked potato should be white and fluffy, not yellowish or soggy. Once baked, potatoes can be eaten plain (or with butter, sour cream and other garnishes) or used in other recipes.

PROCEDURE FOR BAKING POTATOES

1. Scrub the potatoes well.
2. Using a fork, pierce the potato skins.
3. Rub the potatoes with oil and salt if desired. Do not wrap them in foil.
4. Bake the potatoes until done. A paring knife should penetrate them easily.

◆◆◆

RECIPE 23.1
BAKED POTATOES

Yield: 8 Servings

Russet potatoes	8	8
Vegetable oil	3 Tbsp.	45 ml
Kosher salt	3 Tbsp.	45 ml

1. Scrub the potatoes well, but do not peel. Pierce the skin of each potato to allow steam to escape.
2. Rub the potatoes with the oil, then sprinkle with kosher salt.
3. Place the potato on a rack over a sheet pan. Bake in a 400°F (200°C) oven until done, approximately 1 hour. The potatoes should yield to gentle pressure and a paring knife inserted in the thickest part should meet little resistance.
4. Hold uncovered in a warm spot and serve within 1 hour.

Baking en Casserole

Many classic potato dishes require baking either raw or parboiled potatoes with sauce, cheese, meat or other seasonings in a baking dish or casserole. Well-known examples include scalloped potatoes, which are baked in béchamel sauce, and au gratin, which are topped with cheese and baked. These dishes usually develop a crisp, brown crust, which is part of their appeal.

The casserole should hold its shape when cut; the potatoes should be tender and the sauce should be smooth, not grainy.

Potato casseroles can be fully baked, then held loosely covered in a steam table for service. Portions can be reheated or browned briefly under a broiler or salamander at service time.

PROCEDURE FOR BAKING POTATOES EN CASSEROLE

1. Prepare the potatoes by washing, peeling, slicing or partially cooking as desired or as directed in the recipe.
2. Add the potatoes to the baking pan in layers, alternating with the sauce, cream, cheese or other ingredients. Or combine the potatoes with the other ingredients and place in a buttered baking pan.
3. Bake the potatoes until done.

◆◆◆

RECIPE 23.2
GRATIN DAUPHINOISE

Yield: 4–5 lb. (1.8 – 2.2 kg)

Potatoes	3 lb.	1.3 kg
Whole butter	as needed	as needed
Salt and white pepper	TT	TT
Nutmeg	1/4 tsp.	2 ml

Gruyère cheese, grated	8 oz.	250 g
Half-and-half	24 oz.	700 ml
Egg yolks	3	3

1. Peel the potatoes and cut into very thin slices.
2. Place a single layer of potatoes in a well-buttered, full-size hotel pan.
3. Season with salt, pepper and a small amount of nutmeg. Sprinkle on a thin layer of cheese.
4. Add another layer of potatoes and cheese and repeat until all the potatoes and about three quarters of the cheese are used.
5. Heat the half-and-half to a simmer. Whisk the egg yolks together in a bowl, then gradually add the hot half-and-half.
6. Pour the cream-and-egg mixture over the potatoes. Top with the remaining cheese.
7. Bake uncovered at 350°F (180°C) until the potatoes are tender and golden brown, approximately 50–60 minutes.

Sautéing and Pan-Frying

Waxy potatoes, such as red- and white-skinned varieties, are best for sautéing or pan-frying. Often they are first parboiled or even fully cooked—a convenient way to use leftover boiled potatoes. They are then cooked in fat following the general procedures for sautéing and pan-frying discussed in Chapter 9, Principles of Cooking.

The fat can be clarified butter, oil, bacon fat or lard, depending on the desired flavor of the finished dish. The fat must be hot before the potatoes are added so that they will develop a crust without absorbing too much fat. Sautéed potatoes should have a crisp, well-browned crust and tender interior. They should be neither soggy nor greasy.

Potatoes can be sautéed or pan-fried by two methods: tossing and still-frying. The **tossing method** is used to cook relatively small pieces of potatoes in a small amount of fat. The potatoes are tossed using the pan's sloped sides so that they brown evenly on all sides. The **still-frying method** is used to create a disc-shaped potato product. The shredded or sliced potatoes are added to the pan, usually covering its bottom, and allowed to cook without stirring or flipping until they are well browned on the first side. The entire mass is then turned and cooked on the second side. When the potatoes are done, they can be cut into wedges for service.

PROCEDURE FOR SAUTÉING AND PAN-FRYING POTATOES

1. Wash, trim, peel, cut and/or cook the potatoes as desired or as directed in the recipe.
2. Heat the pan, add the fat and heat the fat. Add the potatoes to the hot fat. Do not overcrowd the pan. Use enough fat to prevent the potatoes from sticking to the pan. Depending on the recipe, use either the tossing method or still-frying method.
3. Add garnishes, seasonings and other ingredients as desired or as directed in the recipe.
4. Cook the potatoes until done.

More Than a French Fry

Thanks to the genius of Carême, Escoffier and others, few vegetables have as extensive a classic repertoire as potatoes. Some of these dishes begin with the duchesse potatoes mixture; in this regard, duchesse potatoes can be considered the mother of many classic potato preparations. For example,

Duchesse + Tomato concasse = *Marquis*

Duchesse + Chopped truffles + Almond coating + Deep-frying = *Berny*

Duchesse + Pâte à choux = *Dauphine*

Dauphine + Grated Parmesan + Piped shape + Deep-frying = *Lorette*

Duchesse + Shaping + Breading + Deep-frying = *Croquettes*

Other classic potato preparations not based on duchesse potatoes include:

Anna—thin slices are arranged in several circular layers in a round pan coated with clarified butter; additional butter is brushed on and the potatoes are baked until crisp, then cut into wedges for service.

Boulangère—onions and potatoes are sautéed in butter, then transferred to a baking pan or added to a partially cooked roast in a roasting pan; stock is added and the potatoes are cooked uncovered until done.

Chateau—tournéed potatoes are sautéed in clarified butter until golden and soft.

Parisienne—small spheres are cut from raw, peeled potatoes with a parisienne scoop; they are seasoned and sautéed in clarified butter, then tossed with a meat glaze and garnished with chopped parsley.

Rösti—potatoes are shredded, seasoned and pan-fried in the shape of a pie, then cut into wedges for service.

◆◆◆

RECIPE 23.3

Lyonnaise Potatoes

Yield: 8 4-oz. (120-g) Servings

Potatoes, waxy variety	2 lb.	1 kg
Onion, julienne	8 oz.	250 g
Clarified butter	4 oz.	120 g
Salt and pepper	TT	TT

1. Partially cook the potatoes by baking, boiling or steaming. Allow to cool.
2. Peel and cut the potatoes into 1/4-inch- (1/2-centimeter-) thick slices.
3. Sauté the onions in half the butter until tender. Remove the onions from the pan with a slotted spoon and set aside.
4. Add the remaining butter to the pan. Add the potatoes and sauté, tossing as needed, until well browned on all sides.
5. Return the onions to the pan and sauté to combine the flavors. Season to taste with salt and pepper.

Deep-Frying

Potato chips and french fries (Fr. *pomme frites*) are extremely popular in a variety of shapes, sizes and seasonings. While a wide range of shapes, sizes and preseasoned frozen products are available, fresh fried potatoes can be a delicious, economical menu item.

Top-quality russet potatoes are recommended for deep-frying. The peel may be removed or left attached. If peeled, the potatoes should be soaked in clear, cold water until ready to cut and cook. This keeps them crisp and white by leaching some of the starch that might otherwise make the potatoes gummy or cause smaller cuts to stick together when cooked.

Deep-fried potatoes are usually blanched in oil ranging in temperature from 250° to 300°F (120–150°C) until tender and translucent. They are then drained and held for service, at which time they are finished in hotter oil, usually at a temperature between 350° and 375°F (180–190°C).

Deep-frying is also used to finish cooking several classic potato dishes such as croquettes and dauphine, in which fully cooked potatoes are puréed, seasoned, shaped and fried.

Deep-fried potatoes should be drained on absorbent paper briefly and served immediately.

In general, the procedures for deep-frying found in Chapter 21 also apply here. Specific recipes for several types of deep-fried potatoes are given at the end of this chapter.

Boiling

Waxy potatoes are best for all moist-heat cooking methods. Boiled potatoes (which are actually simmered) may be served as is or used in multistep preparations such as purées, salads, soups and baked casseroles. Potatoes are usually boiled in water, although stock may be used or milk added for flavor. Always begin cooking potatoes in cold liquid to ensure even cooking. Unlike other vegetables, potatoes should not be refreshed in cold water; it makes them soggy.

PROCEDURE FOR BOILING POTATOES

1. Wash, peel or trim the potatoes as desired.

2. Cut the potatoes into uniform-size pieces. The pieces should not be too small or they will absorb a large amount of water as they cook, making the final product soggy.

3. Add the potatoes to enough cool liquid to cover them by several inches. Bring to a boil, reduce to a simmer and cook until done. If a slightly firm finished product is desired, remove and drain the potatoes when they are slightly underdone and allow carryover cooking to finish cooking them.

4. Drain the potatoes in a colander and serve or use for further preparation.

◆◆◆

RECIPE 23.4

DUCHESSE POTATOES

Yield: 2 lb. (1 kg)

Potatoes, peeled and quartered	2 lb.	1 kg
Butter	1 oz.	30 g
Nutmeg	TT	TT
Salt and pepper	TT	TT
Eggs	1	1
Egg yolks	2	2

1. Boil the potatoes in salted water until tender. Drain and immediately turn out onto a sheet pan to allow the moisture to evaporate.

2. While still warm, press the potatoes through a ricer or food mill, or grind through a grinder's medium die. Blend in the butter and season to taste with nutmeg, salt and pepper.

3. Mix in the eggs and egg yolks, blending well.

4. Place the duchesse mixture in a piping bag fitted with a large star tip. Pipe single portion-sized spirals onto a parchment-lined sheet pan. Brush with clarified butter and bake at 375°F (190°C) until the edges are golden brown, approximately 8–10 minutes. Serve immediately.

USAGE: Duchesse potatoes are often used to decorate platters used for buffets, tableside preparations or to present chateaubriand. To create borders and garnishes, the standard mixture for duchesse potatoes is forced through a piping bag while still very hot and relatively soft.

1. Passing boiled potatoes through a food mill.

2. Piping duchesse potatoes.

3. The finished potatoes.

GRAINS

Botanically, grains are grasses that bear edible seeds. Corn, rice and wheat are the most significant. Both the fruit (i.e., the seed or kernel) and the plant are called a grain.

Most grain kernels are protected by a **hull** or husk. All kernels are composed of three distinct parts: the **bran**, **endosperm** and **germ**. The bran is the tough outer layer covering the endosperm. Bran is a good source of fiber and B vitamins. The endosperm is the largest part of the kernel and is a source of protein and carbohydrates (starch). It is the part used primarily in milled products such as flour. The germ is the smallest portion of the grain and is the only part that contains fat. It is also rich in thiamin. The bran, endosperm and germ can be separated by milling.

Identifying Grains

This section presents information on corn, rice and wheat as well as several minor grains that are nutritionally significant and gaining popularity.

Some products are available in a stone-ground form. This means that the grains were ground with a stone mill rather than by the steel blades typically used for **cracking**, **grinding**, **hulling** and **pearling**. Stone grinders are gentler and more precise, so they are less likely to overgrind the grain. Stone-ground products will always be labeled as such and are usually more expensive than steel-ground ones.

Corn

Corn (Sp. *maíz*; It. *granturco*) is the only grain that is also eaten fresh as a vegetable. (Fresh corn is discussed in Chapter 22, Vegetables.) Its use as a dried grain dates back several thousand years in Central America and long preceded its use as a vegetable.

Cracking—*a milling process in which grains are broken open.*

Grinding—*a milling process in which grains are reduced to a powder; the powder can be of differing degrees of fineness or coarseness.*

Hulling—*a milling process in which the hull is removed from grains.*

Pearling—*a milling process in which all or part of the hull, bran and germ are removed from grains.*

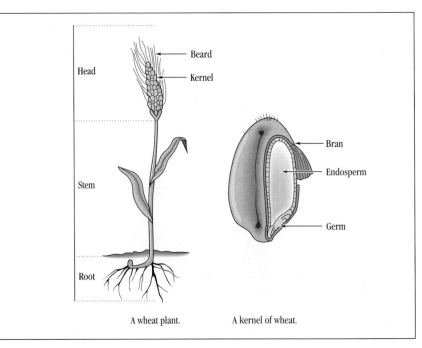

A wheat plant.   A kernel of wheat.

FIGURE 23.1

Cornmeal

Cornmeal is made by drying and grinding a special type of corn known as *dent*, which may be yellow, white or blue. Cornmeal is most often used in breads, as a coating for fried foods or cooked as polenta or mush. Products made with cornmeal have a gritty texture and a sweet but starchy flavor.

Cornmeal

Hominy

Hominy, also known as posole or samp, is dried corn that has been soaked in hydrated lime or lye. This causes the kernels to swell, loosening the hulls. The hulls and germs are removed and the kernels dried. These white or yellow kernels resemble popcorn, but with a soft, chewy texture and smoky-sour flavor. Hominy is available dried or cooked and canned. It may be served as a side dish or used in stews or soups. **Masa harina**, a finely ground flour made from hominy, is used for making breads, tortillas, tamales and other Mexican and southwestern dishes.

Hominy

Grits

Grits are traditionally made by grinding dried hominy. These tiny white granules may be used in baked dishes but are most often served as a hot breakfast cereal, usually topped with butter or cheese. Quick-cooking and instant grits are available.

Rice

Rice (Fr. *riz*; It. *riso*; Sp. *arroz*) is the starchy seed of a semiaquatic grass. Probably originating on the Indian subcontinent or in Southeast Asia, rice is used as a staple by more than half of the world's population.

Rice can be incorporated into almost any cuisine, from Asian to Spanish to classic French. Its flavor adapts to the foods and seasonings with which the rice is cooked or served. Its texture adds an appealing chewiness to meat and poultry dishes, salads, breads and puddings. Rice is not limited to a side dish, but may be used in stews or curries, for stuffing vegetables or game birds, in puddings, salads, beverages (such as *horchata*) and breads.

Rice is divided into three types based on seed size: **long-grain, medium-grain** and **short-grain**. Long-grain rice is the most versatile and popular worldwide. The grains remain firm, fluffy and separate when cooked. (Long-grain rice can, however, become sticky if overcooked or stirred frequently during cooking.) Short-grain rice has more starch and becomes quite tender and sticky when cooked. Italian risotto, Japanese sushi and Spanish paella are all traditionally made with short-grain rice. The appearance and starch content of medium-grain rice falls somewhere in between. Medium-grain rice becomes sticky when cool, so it is best eaten freshly made and piping hot.

Long-grain, medium-grain and short-grain rice are available in different processed forms. All rice is originally brown. The grains can be left whole, with the bran attached, for **brown rice**. Or they can be pearled for the more familiar polished **white rice**. Both brown rice and white rice can be processed into Converted rice and instant rice.

Converted rice is parboiled to remove the surface starch. This procedure also forces nutrients from the bran into the grain's endosperm. Therefore, converted rice retains more nutrients than regular milled white rice, although the flavor is the same. Converted rice is neither precooked nor instant; in fact, it cooks more slowly than regular milled white rice.

Instant or **quick-cooking rice** is widely available and useful if time is a concern. Instant rice is created by fully cooking then flash-freezing milled rice. Unfortunately, this processing removes some of the nutrients and flavor.

Converted Rice

Arborio Rice

Basmati Rice

Wild Rice

Wild Pecan Rice

Arborio Rice

Arborio is a round, short-grain rice used primarily in Italian dishes such as risotto. It is very sticky, with a white color and mild flavor.

Basmati Rice

Basmati is one of the finest long-grain rices in the world. It grows in the Himalayan foothills and is preferred in Indian cuisine. It is highly aromatic, with a sweet, delicate flavor and a creamy yellow color. Basmati rice is usually aged to improve its aromatic qualities and should be washed well before cooking.

Brown Rice

Brown rice is the whole natural grain of rice. Only the husk has been removed. Brown rice has a nutty flavor; its chewy texture is caused by the high-fiber bran. Brown rice absorbs more water and takes longer to cook than white rice.

Brown Rice

Wild Rice

Wild rice is prepared in the same manner as traditional rice, although it is actually the seed of an unrelated reedlike aquatic plant. Wild rice has long, slender grains with a dark brown to black color. It has a nuttier flavor and chewier texture than traditional rice. Three grades are available: giant (the best quality, with very long grains); fancy (a medium-sized grain, suitable for most purposes); and select (a short grain, suitable for soups, pancakes or baked goods). Cultivated in California, Idaho and Washington, it is generally served with game, used as a stuffing for poultry or combined with regular rice for a side dish. Wild rice is expensive, but small quantities are usually sufficient.

Wild Pecan Rice

Wild pecan rice is neither wild nor made with pecans. It is a unique long-grain rice grown only in the bayou country of southern Louisiana. Wild pecan rice has a nutty flavor and exceptionally rich aroma.

Guidelines for Cooking Rice

Rice may be rinsed before cooking to remove dirt and debris, but doing so also removes some nutrients. It is not necessary to rinse most American-grown rice as it is generally clean and free of insects. Rice may also be soaked before cooking. Soaking softens the grains, removes some starch and speeds cooking.

TABLE 23.3   GUIDELINES FOR COOKING RICE

Type of Rice	Ratio Rice: Water (by Volume)	Preparation	Cooking Time (simmering)	Yield from 1 Cup Raw Rice
Arborio	1 : 2.5–3	Do not rinse or soak	15–20 min.	2.5–3 c.
Basmati	1 : 1.75	Rinse well; soak	15 min.	3 c.
Brown, long-grain	1 : 2.5	Do not rinse; can soak	45–50 min.	3–4 c.
Converted	1 : 2.5	Do not rinse	20–25 min.	3–4 c.
White, long-grain (regular milled)	1 : 2	Do not rinse	15 min.	3 c.
Wild	1 : 3	Rinse	35–60 min., depending on grade	3–4 c.

The standard ratio for cooking rice is 2 parts liquid to 1 part rice. The actual ratio varies, however, depending on the type of rice. Guidelines for cooking rice are found in Table 23.3.

Once cooked, rice is highly perishable. Because of its neutral pH and high protein content, cooked rice is a potentially hazardous food. To avoid the risk of food-borne illnesses, be sure to store cooked rice out of the temperature danger zone.

Wheat

Wheat (Fr.: *blé*) is most often milled into the wide range of flours discussed in Chapter 26, Principles of the Bakeshop. But wheat and products derived from it are also used as starchy side dishes or ingredients in soups, salads, ground meat dishes and breads. These products include cracked wheat, bulgur and couscous. When cooked they are slightly chewy with a mild flavor. All should be fluffy; none should be soggy or sticky.

Wheat germ and *wheat bran* are widely available and highly touted for their nutritional values. Bran and germ are not generally used plain, but may be added to bread or other cooked dishes.

Cracked Wheat

Cracked wheat is the whole wheat kernel (known as a **berry**) broken into varying degrees of coarseness. It is not precooked, and the kernel's white interior should be visible. The bran and germ are still intact, so cracked wheat has a great deal of fiber but a short shelf life. Whole wheat berries must be soaked for several hours before cooking. Cracked wheat can be fully cooked by long, gentle simmering.

Bulgur

Bulgur is a wheat berry that has had the bran removed; it is then steam-cooked, dried and ground into varying degrees of coarseness. Bulgur has a nutlike flavor and texture; it is a uniform golden-brown color (uncooked cracked wheat is not) and requires less cooking time than cracked wheat. Generally, cracked wheat and bulgur cannot be substituted for one another in recipes.

Bulgur only needs to be soaked in water, then drained, for use in salads, or briefly cooked when used in stews or pilafs. Bulgur is good with grilled meats and as an alternative to rice in stuffings and other dishes. The fine grind is most often used in packaged mixes such as tabouli; the medium grind is most often available in bulk.

Bulgur

Couscous

Couscous

Couscous is made by removing the bran and germ from **durum wheat** berries. The endosperm is then steamed, pressed to form tiny pellets and dried. Couscous is available in varying degrees of coarseness; medium-fine is the most popular. Couscous is prepared by steaming over water or stock in a pot called a couscousier. Couscous, traditionally served with North African stews, can be used or served like rice.

Durum wheat—*a species of very hard wheat with a particularly high amount of protein; it is milled into* **semolina***, which is used for making pasta.*

Other Grains

Barley

Barley is one of the oldest culinary grains, used by humans since prehistoric times. Barley is extremely hardy, growing in climates from the tropics to the near-Arctic. Although much of the barley crop is used to make beer or

Barley

feed animals, some does find its way into soups, stews and stuffings. The most common type is pearled to produce a small, round white nugget of endosperm. It has a sweet, earthy flavor similar to oats, and goes well with onions, garlic and strong herbs. Barley's texture ranges from chewy to soft, depending on the amount of water in which it is cooked. Its starchiness can be used to thicken soups or stews.

Buckwheat/Kasha

Buckwheat is not a type of wheat; it is not even a grain. Rather, it is the fruit of a plant distantly related to rhubarb. Buckwheat is included here, how- ever, because it is prepared and served in the same manner as grains.

The whole buckwheat kernel is known as a **groat**. The product most often sold as buckwheat is actually kasha, which is a hulled, roasted buckwheat groat. Kasha is reddish brown with a strong, nutty, almost scorched flavor. It is available whole or ground to varying degrees of coarseness. Whole kasha remains in separate grains after cooking; the finer grinds become rather sticky. Kasha can be served as a side dish, usually combined with pasta or vegeta- bles, or it can be chilled and used in salads.

Raw buckwheat groats are ground into flour typically used in pasta, blini and other pancakes. Buckwheat flour contains no gluten-forming proteins and it tends to remain grainy, with a sandy texture. Therefore, it should not be substituted for all of the white or whole wheat flour in breads or baked goods.

Buckwheat/Kasha

Oats

Oats

After rice, oats are probably the most widely accepted whole-grain product in the American diet. Oats are consumed daily as a hot breakfast cereal (oat- meal) and are used in breads, muffins, cookies and other baked goods.

An oat groat is the whole oat kernel with only the husk removed. It con- tains both the bran and germ. *Steel-cut oats*, sometimes known as Irish oats, are groats that are toasted then cut into small pieces with steel blades. *Rolled oats*, marketed as "old-fashioned oats," are groats that have been steamed, then rolled into flat flakes. *Quick-cooking oats* are simply rolled oats cut into smaller pieces to reduce cooking time. *Instant oats* are partially cooked and dried before rolling so they only need to be rehydrated in boiling water. Several flavored versions are also marketed as breakfast cereal. Rolled oats and quick-cooking oats can be used interchangeably, but instant oats should not be substituted in most recipes.

Oat bran is the outer covering of a hulled oat. It is available as a separate product, although rolled and cut oats do contain some oat bran.

The term *oatmeal* is commonly used to refer to both processed groats and the cooked porridge made from them. The processed groats known as oat- meal are a gray-white color with a starchy texture and sweet flavor. They cook into the soft, thick porridge with a robust flavor called oatmeal.

Nutrition

Grains are an excellent source of vitamins, minerals, proteins and fiber. The amount of milling or refining and the method of preparation affects their nutritional values, however. Unrefined and less-refined grains are excellent sources of dietary fiber. Rice is also quite nutritious: It is low in sodium and calories and contains all the essential amino acids. Some grains, especially white rice and oats, are usually enriched with calcium, iron and B vitamins.

TABLE 23.4 NUTRITIONAL VALUES OF SELECTED GRAINS

Per 4 oz. (112 g), cooked	Kcal	Protein (g)	Carbohydrates (g)	Fiber (g)	Total Fat (g)	Niacin (g)	Phosphorous (mg)	Potassium (mg)
Barley, pearled	139	2.6	32	0.3	0.5	1.6	42.5	72.5
Bulgur	94	3.5	21.1	0.4	0.3	0.9	36.5	62
Grits	68	1.6	14.7	0.1	0.2	0.8	15	27
Kasha	104	3.8	22.6	0.6	0.7	1.2	80	95
Oats	45	3.6	13	0.4	1	0.2	89	66
Rice, brown, long-grain	126	2.9	26	1.9	1	1.5	81	42
Rice, Converted	90	1.5	21.1	mq	0.7	mq	mq	mq
Rice, white, long-grain	146	3.1	31.6	0.1	0.3	1.5	47	40
Wheat germ (toasted)	432	33.2	56.4	14.8	12	6.4	1280	1076

The Corinne T Netzer Encyclopedia of Food Values 1992

mq = measurable quantity, but data is unavailable

Purchasing and Storing Grains

Purchasing

When buying grains, look for fresh, plump ones with a bright, even color. Fresh grains should not be shriveled or crumbly; there should be no sour or musty odors.

Grains are sold by weight. They come in bags or boxes ranging from 1 to 100 pounds. Ten-, 25- and 50-pound units are usually available.

Storing

All grains should be stored in air-tight containers placed in a dark, cool, dry place. Air-tight containers prevent dust and insects from entering. Air-tight containers and darkness also reduce nutrient loss caused by oxidation or light. Coolness inhibits insect infestation; dryness prevents mold.

Vacuum-sealed packages will last for extended periods. Whole grains, which contain the oily germ, should be refrigerated to prevent rancidity.

Applying Various Cooking Methods

Three basic cooking methods are used to prepare grains: simmering, risotto and pilaf. Unlike simmered grains, those cooked by either the risotto or pilaf method are first coated with hot fat. The primary distinction between the pilaf and risotto methods is the manner in which the liquid is then added to the grains. When grains are used in puddings, breads, stuffings and baked casseroles, they are almost always first fully cooked by one of these methods.

Determining Doneness

Most grains should be cooked until tender, although some recipes do require a chewier or more al dente product. Doneness can usually be determined by cooking time and the amount of liquid remaining in the pan. Some grains, such as wild rice, are fully cooked when they puff open.

In general, grains will be fully cooked when almost all of the cooking liquid is absorbed. This is indicated by the appearance of tunnel-like holes between the grains. Grains can be cooked until almost all of the liquid is absorbed, then removed from the heat and left to stand, covered, for 5–10 minutes. This allows the cooked grains to absorb the remaining moisture without burning.

Simmering

The most commonly used method for preparing grains is simmering. To do so, simply stir the grains into a measured amount of boiling salted water in a saucepan on the stove top. When the liquid returns to a boil, lower the heat, cover, and simmer until the liquid is absorbed and the grains are tender. The grains are not stirred during cooking.

The grains can be flavored by using stock as the cooking liquid. Herbs and spices can also be added.

PROCEDURE FOR SIMMERING GRAINS

1. Bring the cooking liquid to a boil.
2. Stir in the grains. Add herbs or spices as desired or as directed in the recipe.
3. Return the mixture to a boil, cover and reduce to a simmer.
4. Simmer the grains until tender and most of the liquid is absorbed.
5. Remove the grains from the heat.
6. Drain if appropriate or keep covered and allow the excess moisture to evaporate, approximately 5 minutes. Fluff the grains with a fork before service.

◆◆◆

RECIPE 23.5

BASIC SIMMERED RICE

Yield: 3 c. (750 ml)

Water	1 pt.	500 ml
Salt	1/2 tsp.	2 ml
White rice	1 c.	250 ml

1. Bring the water and salt to a boil in a heavy saucepan. Slowly add the rice.
2. Cover the pan and reduce the heat so that the liquid simmers gently. Cook until the rice is tender and the water is absorbed, approximately 15–20 minutes.
3. Remove from the heat and transfer to a hotel pan. Do not cover. Allow any excess moisture to evaporate for approximately 5 minutes.
4. Fluff the rice and serve, or refrigerate for use in another recipe.

Risotto Method

Risotto is a classic Northern Italian rice dish in which the grains remain firm but merge with the cooking liquid to become a creamy, almost puddinglike dish. True risotto is made with a short-grain starchy rice such as Arborio, but the risotto method can also be used to cook other grains such as barley and oats.

The grains are not rinsed before cooking, as this removes the starches needed to achieve the desired consistency. The grains are coated, but not cooked, in a hot fat such as butter or oil. A hot liquid is then gradually added to the grains so that the mixture is kept at a constant simmer. The cooking liquid should be a rich, flavorful stock. Unlike simmering and the pilaf method, the risotto method requires frequent, sometimes constant, stirring.

When finished, the grains should be creamy and tender, but still al dente in the center. Grated cheese, heavy cream, cooked meat, poultry, fish, shellfish, herbs and vegetables can be added to create a flavorful side dish or a complete meal.

PROCEDURE FOR PREPARING GRAINS BY THE RISOTTO METHOD

1. Bring the cooking liquid to a simmer.
2. Heat the fat in a heavy saucepan over moderate heat. Add any onions, garlic or other flavoring ingredients and sauté for 1–2 minutes without browning.
3. Add the grains to the saucepan. Stir well to make sure the grains are well coated with fat. Do not allow the grains to brown.
4. Add any wine and cook until it is fully absorbed.
5. Begin to add the simmering stock 4 ounces (120 milliliters) at a time, stirring frequently. Wait until each portion of cooking liquid is almost fully absorbed before adding the next.
6. Test for doneness after the grains have cooked for approximately 18–20 minutes.
7. Remove the saucepan from the heat and stir in any butter, grated cheese, herbs or other flavoring ingredients as directed. Serve immediately.

1. Sautéing the rice and onions in butter.

❖❖❖

RECIPE 23.6

RISOTTO MILANESE

Yield: 24 4-oz. (120-g) Servings

Chicken stock	2-1/2 qt.	2.5 lt
Whole butter	4 oz.	120 g
Onions, minced	5 oz.	150 g
Arborio rice	1 lb. 8 oz.	700 g
Dry white wine	8 oz.	250 ml
Saffron threads, crushed	1/2 tsp.	2 ml
Parmesan cheese, grated	4 oz.	120 g

2. Adding the stock gradually while stirring frequently.

1. Bring the chicken stock to a simmer.
2. Heat 3 ounces (90 grams) of the butter in a large, heavy saucepan. Add the onion and sauté without browning until translucent.
3. Add the rice to the onion and butter. Stir well to coat the grains with butter but do not allow the rice to brown. Add the wine and stir until it is completely absorbed.
4. Add the saffron. Add the simmering stock, 4 ounces (120 milliliters) at a time, stirring frequently. Wait until the stock is absorbed before adding the next 4-ounce (120-milliliter) portion.
5. After approximately 18–20 minutes all of the stock should be incorporated and the rice should be tender. Remove from the heat and stir in the remaining 1 ounce (30 grams) of butter and the grated cheese. Serve immediately.

Continued

3. Stirring in the butter and grated cheese.

VARIATIONS: Risotto with Radicchio (*al Radicchio*)—Omit the saffron and Parmesan. Just before the risotto is fully cooked, stir in 4 ounces (120 milliliters) heavy cream and 3 ounces (90 grams) finely chopped radicchio leaves.

Risotto with Four Cheeses (*al Quattro Formaggi*)—Omit the saffron. When the risotto is fully cooked, remove from the heat and stir in 2 ounces (60 grams) each of grated Parmesan, gorgonzola, fontina and mozzarella cheeses. Garnish with toasted pine nuts and chopped parsley.

Risotto with Smoked Salmon (*al Salmone Affumicato*)—Omit the butter, saffron and Parmesan. Sauté the onion in 3 ounces (90 milliliters) of corn or safflower oil instead of butter. When the risotto is fully cooked, remove from the heat and stir in 8 ounces (240 milliliters) half-and-half, 3 ounces (90 milliliters) fresh lemon juice and 8–10 ounces (240–300 grams) good-quality smoked salmon. Garnish with chopped fresh parsley and dill. Serve with lemon wedges.

Pilaf Method

With the pilaf method, the raw grains are lightly sautéed in oil or butter, usually with onions or seasonings for additional flavor. Hot liquid, often a stock, is then added. The pan is covered and the mixture left to simmer until the liquid is absorbed.

PROCEDURE FOR PREPARING GRAINS BY THE PILAF METHOD

1. Bring the cooking liquid (either water or stock) to a boil.
2. Heat the fat in a heavy saucepan over moderate heat. Add any onions, garlic or other flavorings and sauté for 1–2 minutes without browning.
3. Add the grains to the saucepan. Stir well to make sure the grains are well coated with fat. Do not allow the grains to brown.
4. All at once, add the hot cooking liquid to the sautéed grains.
5. Return the liquid to a boil, reduce to a simmer and cover.
6. Allow the mixture to simmer, either in the oven or on the stove top, until the liquid is absorbed.

◆◆◆

RECIPE 23.7

BULGUR PILAF

Yield: 8 4-oz. (120-g) Servings

Whole butter	2 oz.	60 g
Onions, fine dice	4 oz.	120 g
Bulgur	10 oz.	300 g
Bay leaf	1	1
Chicken stock, hot	1 qt.	1 lt
Salt and pepper	TT	TT

1. Melt the butter in a large, heavy saucepan over moderate heat. Add the onions and cook until translucent.
2. Add the bulgur and bay leaf. Sauté until the grains are well coated with butter.
3. Add the hot stock and season to taste with salt and pepper. Reduce the heat until the liquid barely simmers.

1. Sautéing the bulgur in butter.

2. Adding the hot stock to the bulgur.

4. Cover and continue cooking until all of the liquid is absorbed and the grains are tender, approximately 18–20 minutes.

5. Fluff with a fork and adjust the seasonings before service.

VARIATION: Barley pilaf—Substitute 2 cups of pearled barley for the bulgur. Cooking time may increase by 10–15 minutes.

3. Fluffing the finished bulgur.

PASTA

Pasta is made from an unleavened dough of liquid mixed with flour. The liquid is usually egg and/or water. The flour can be from almost any grain: wheat, buckwheat, rice or a combination of grains. The dough can be colored and flavored with puréed vegetables, herbs or other ingredients and it can be cut or **extruded** into a wide variety of shapes and sizes.

Pasta can be cooked fresh while the dough is still moist and pliable, or the dough can be allowed to dry completely before cooking. Pasta can be filled or sauced in an endless variety of ways. It can stand alone or be used in salads, desserts, soups or casseroles.

Pasta is widely used in the cuisines of Asia, North America and Europe. In Italy, pasta dishes are usually served as a separate course, referred to as the *minestre*; in other European countries, Asia and the United States, pasta dishes may be served as an appetizer, entree or side dish.

Extrusion—*the process of forcing pasta dough through perforated plates to create various shapes; pasta dough that is not extruded must be rolled and cut.*

Identifying Pastas

The better-known pastas are based on the Italian tradition of kneading wheat flour with water and eggs to form a smooth, resilient dough. This dough is rolled very thin and cut into various shapes before being boiled in water or dried for longer storage.

Macaroni—*any dried pasta made with wheat flour and water; only in America does the term refer to elbow-shaped tubes.*

◆◆◆
THE MACARONI MYTH

The popular myth holds that noodles were first invented in China and discovered there by the Venetian explorer Marco Polo during the 13th century. He introduced the food to Italy and from there the rest of Europe. While there is little doubt that the Chinese were making noodles by the 1st century A.D., it is now equally clear that they were not alone.

Middle Eastern and Italian cooks were preparing macaroni long before Marco Polo's adventures. A clear reference to boiled noodles appears in the *Jerusalem Talmud* of the 5th century A.D. There, rabbis debate whether noodles violate Jewish dietary laws (they do, but only during Passover). Tenth-century Arabic writings refer to dried noodles purchased from

vendors. Literary references establish that dishes called lasagna, macaroni and ravioli were all well known (and costly) in Italy by the mid-13th century.

Pasta's current popularity dates from the 18th century, when mass production by machine began in Naples, Italy. English gentlemen on their Grand Tours of the Continent developed a fondness for pasta; the word *macaroni* became a synonym for a dandy or a vain young man. Macaroni arrived in America with English colonists, who preferred it with cream sauce and cheese or in a sweet custard. Domestic factories soon opened, and by the Civil War (1861–1865) macaroni was available to the working class. Pasta became a staple of the

American middle-class diet following the wave of Italian immigrants in the late 19th century.

During the 1980s pasta became ubiquitous. Restaurants began serving it in ways previously unimagined. Corner grocery stores and local supermarkets began offering at least a dozen different shapes, often fresh and sometimes flavored. Dedicated cooks began to make pasta from scratch, though they sometimes tossed it with bottled sauce. Many also became interested in Asian noodles. Chinese, Japanese, Korean and Thai restaurants expanded their menu offerings to include traditional noodle dishes eagerly ordered by curious consumers. Pasta's popularity continues to grow as chefs discover the versatility of this inexpensive, nutritious food.

Commercially prepared dried pasta products are usually made with semolina flour. Semolina flour, ground from hard durum wheat and available from specialty purveyors, has a rich cream color and produces a very smooth, durable dough. Semolina dough requires a great deal of kneading, however, and bread flour is an acceptable substitute when preparing fresh pasta by hand.

Asian pasta, generally known as noodles, is made from wheat, rice, bean or buckwheat flour. It is available fresh or dried from commercial purveyors and at specialty markets.

Italian-Style Pasta

Although all Italian-style pasta is made from the same type of dough, the finest commercial pastas are those made with pure semolina flour, which gives the dough a rich, yellow color. Gray or streaked dough probably contains softer flours. Dried pasta should be very hard and break with a clean snap. The surface should be lightly pitted or dull. (A smooth or glossy surface will not hold or absorb sauces as well.)

Dried pasta, both domestic and imported, is available in a wide range of flavors and shapes. In addition to the traditional white (plain), green (spinach) and red (tomato) pastas, manufacturers are now offering such unusual flavor combinations as lemon–peppercorn, whole wheat–basil, jalapeño–black bean and carrot–ginger. Small pieces of herbs or other flavorings are often visible in these products.

There are hundreds of recognized shapes of pasta, but only two or three dozen are generally available in the United States. When experimenting with unusual flavors and shapes, be sure to consider the taste and appearance of the final dish after the sauce and any garnishes are added.

Italian-style pasta can be divided into three groups based on the shape of the final product: ribbons, tubes and shapes. There is no consistent English nomenclature for these pastas; the Italian names are recognized and applied virtually worldwide. (A specific shape or size may be given different names in different regions of Italy, however. These distinctions are beyond the scope of this text.)

Ribbons

Pasta dough can be rolled very thin and cut into strips or ribbons of various widths. All ribbon shapes work well with tomato, fish and shellfish sauces. Thicker ribbons, such as spaghetti and fettuccine, are preferred with cream or cheese sauces. Sheets of fresh pasta dough can be filled and shaped to create ravioli, cappelletti and tortellini. Filled pasta is usually served with a light cream- or tomato-based sauce that complements the filling's flavors.

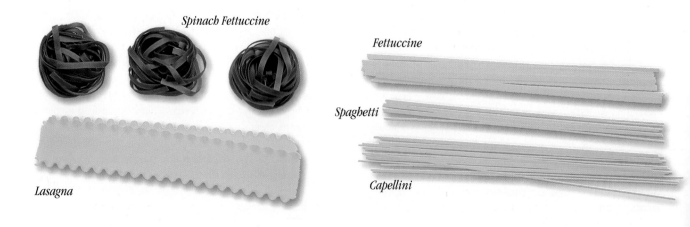

Spinach Fettuccine

Fettuccine

Spaghetti

Lasagna

Capellini

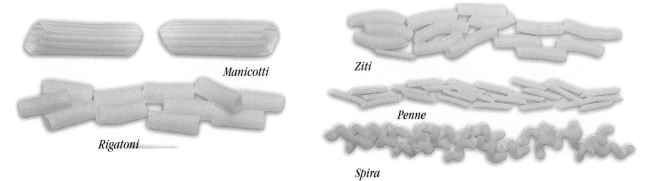

Manicotti

Ziti

Rigatoni

Penne

Spira

Tubes

Cylindrical forms or tubes are made by extrusion. The hollow tubes can be curved or straight, fluted or smooth. Tubes are preferred for meat and vegetable sauces and are often used in baked casseroles.

Shapes

The extrusion process can also be used to shape pasta dough into forms. The curves and textures produced provide nooks and crevices that hold sauces well. Shaped pastas, such as conchiglie, farfalle and fusilli, are preferred with meat sauces and oil-based sauces such as pesto. Larger shaped pastas can be cooked, then stuffed with meat or cheese fillings and baked or served as a casserole.

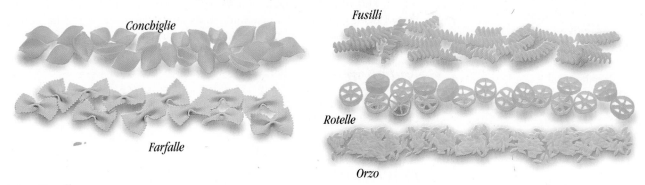

Conchiglie

Fusilli

Farfalle

Rotelle

Orzo

Asian Noodles

Asian noodles are not cut into the same wealth of shapes and sizes as Italian-style pasta, nor are they flavored or colored with vegetable purées, herbs or other ingredients.

Virtually all Asian noodles are ribbons—some thin, some thick—folded into bundles and packaged. Differences arise because of the flours used for the dough.

Most dried Asian noodles benefit by soaking in hot water for several minutes before further preparation. The water softens the noddle strands; the bundles separate, and the noodles cook more evenly.

Wheat Noodles

Wheat noodles, also known as egg noodles, are the most popular and widely available of the Asian noodles. They are thin, flat noodles with a springy texture; they are available fresh or dried. Dried egg noodles can be deep-fried after boiling to create crisp golden noodles (chow mein) used primarily as a garnish.

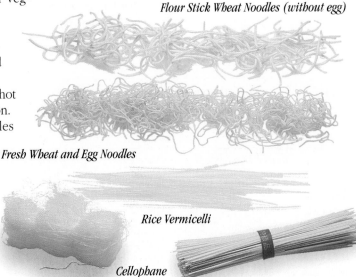

Flour Stick Wheat Noodles (without egg)

Fresh Wheat and Egg Noodles

Rice Vermicelli

Cellophane Noodles

Japanese Wheat Somen

♦♦♦

DUMPLINGS

A **dumpling** is a small mound of dough cooked by steaming or simmering in a flavorful liquid. Dumplings are found in many cuisines: Italian gnocchi, Jewish matzo balls, German spaetzle, Chinese wontons and Polish pierogi. Dumplings can be sweet or savory, plain or filled.

Plain or **drop dumplings** are made with a breadlike dough, often leavened with yeast or chemical leavening agents. They should be light and tender, but firm enough to hold their shape when cooked. Drop dumplings may be served with stews or broths, or coated with butter or sauce as an appetizer or side dish. Recipes for gnocchi and spaetzle are included at the end of this chapter. A recipe for matzo balls is included in Chapter 11, Soups.

Filled dumplings are made by wrapping noodle dough around seasoned meat, vegetables, cheese or fruit. These parcels are then steamed, fried or baked and served as a snack food, appetizer or side dish. A recipe for deep-fried wontons is included in Chapter 33, Hors d'Oeuvres and Appetizers.

Japanese wheat noodles, know as somen (if thick) and udon (if thin), may be round, square or flat. They are eaten in broth or with a dipping sauce.

Rice Noodles

Rice noodles are dried thin noodles made with rice flour. They should be soaked in hot water before cooking and rinsed in cool running water after boiling to remove excess starch and prevent sticking. Rice noodles are often served in soups or sautéed.

Rice vermicelli, which has very fine strands, can be fried in hot oil without presoaking. In only a few seconds the strands will turn white, puff up and become crunchy. Mounds of crunchy rice noodles can be used as a base for sautéed dishes or for presenting hors d'oeuvres.

Bean Starch Noodles

Bean starch noodles are also known as spring rain noodles, bean threads, bean noodles or cellophane noodles. They are thin, transparent noodles made from mung beans. Dried bean noodles can be fried in the same manner as rice vermicelli. Otherwise, they must be soaked in hot water before using in soups, stir-fries or braised dishes.

Buckwheat Noodles

Buckwheat flour is used in the noodles of Northern Japan and the Tokyo region, known as soba noodles. Soba noodles are available fresh or dried and do not need soaking before cooking. They are traditionally served in broth or with a dipping sauce, but may be substituted for Italian-style pasta if desired.

Nutrition

Pastas are very low in fat and are an excellent source of vitamins, minerals, proteins and carbohydrates. Also, the processed products are sometimes enriched with additional nutrients.

Purchasing and Storing Pasta Products

Pasta products are purchased by weight, either fresh or dried. Tubes and shapes are not generally available fresh. Dried products, by far the most common, are available in boxes or bags, usually in 1-, 10- and 20-pound units. They can be stored in a cool, dry place for several months. Fresh pasta can be stored in an airtight wrapping in the refrigerator for a few days or in the freezer for a few weeks.

TABLE 23.5   NUTRITIONAL VALUES OF SELECTED PASTA

Per 4 oz. (112 g), cooked	Kcal	Protein (g)	Carbohydrates (g)	Fiber (g)	Total Fat (g)	Niacin (g)	Phosphorous (mg)	Potassium (mg)
Noodle, Japanese soba (buckwheat)	113	5.8	24.4	mq	0.1	0.6	29	40
Pasta, wheat, dried	186	9.2	35.9	0.3	0.2	1.2	38	22
Pasta, wheat, spinach and egg, fresh	147	5.7	28.4	mq	1.10	1.2	65	42

The Corinne T. Netzer Encyclopedia of Food Values 1992
mq = measurable quantity, but data is unavailable

Preparing Fresh Pasta

Making Fresh Pasta

Fresh pasta is easy to make, requiring almost no special equipment and only a few staples. The basic form is the **sfoglia**, a thin, flat sheet of dough that is cut into ribbons, circles or squares.

Although pasta dough can be kneaded by hand, stretched and rolled with a rolling pin and cut with a chef's knife, pasta machines make these tasks easier. Pasta machines are either electric or manual. Some electric models mix and knead the dough, then extrude it through a cutting disk. An extrusion machine is most practical in a food service operation regularly serving large quantities of pasta. The pasta machine more often encountered is operated manually with a hand crank. It has two rollers that knead, press and push the dough into a thin, uniform sheet. Adjacent cutting rollers slice the thin dough into various widths for fettuccine, spaghetti, capellini or the like.

◆◆◆

RECIPE 23.8

BASIC PASTA DOUGH

Yield: 4 lb. (1.8 kg)

Eggs	15	15
Olive oil	1 oz.	30 ml
Salt	1 Tbsp.	15 ml
Bread flour*	2 lb. 8 oz.	1.1 kg

1. Place the eggs, oil and salt in a large mixer bowl. Use the paddle attachment to combine.
2. Add one third of the flour and stir until the mixture begins to form a soft dough. Remove the paddle attachment and attach the dough hook.
3. Gradually add more flour until the dough is dry and cannot absorb any more flour.
4. Remove the dough from the mixer, wrap it well with plastic wrap and set it aside at room temperature for 20–30 minutes.
5. After the dough has rested, roll it into flat sheets by hand or with a pasta machine. Work with only a small portion at a time, keeping the remainder well covered to prevent it from drying out.
6. While the sheets of dough are pliable, cut them into the desired width with a chef's knife or pasta machine. Sheets can also be used for making ravioli, as illustrated below.

VARIATIONS: Garlic-Herb—Roast 1 head of garlic. Peel and purée the cloves and add to the eggs. Add up to 2 ounces (60 grams) of finely chopped assorted fresh herbs just before mixing is complete.

Spinach—Add 8 ounces (250 grams) of cooked, puréed and well-drained spinach to the eggs. Increase the amount of flour slightly if necessary.

Tomato—Add 4 ounces (120 grams) of tomato paste to the eggs; omit the salt. Increase the amount of flour slightly if necessary.

*Semolina flour can be substituted in this recipe, although it makes a tougher dough that is more difficult to work with.

1. Adding flour to the mixing bowl and using the paddle until the mixture forms a soft dough.

2. The finished dough.

Procedure for Rolling and Cutting Pasta Dough

1. Work with a small portion of the dough. Leave the rest covered with plastic wrap to prevent it from drying out.
2. Flatten the dough with the heel of your hand.
3. Set the pasta machine rollers to their widest setting. Insert the dough and turn the handle with one hand while supporting the dough with the other hand. Pass the entire piece of dough through the rollers.
4. Dust the dough with flour, fold it in thirds and pass it through the pasta machine again.
5. Repeat the folding and rolling procedure until the dough is smooth. This may require 4–6 passes.
6. Tighten the rollers one or two marks, then pass the dough through the machine. Without folding it in thirds, pass the dough through the machine repeatedly, tightening the rollers one or two marks each time.
7. When the dough is thin enough to see your hand through, but not so thin that it begins to tear, it is ready to use or cut into ribbons. This sheet is the *sfoglia*.
8. To cut the sfoglia into ribbons, gently feed a manageable length of dough through the desired cutting blades.
9. Lay out the pasta in a single layer on a sheet pan dusted with flour to dry. Layers of pasta ribbons can be separated with parchment paper.

1. Passing the entire piece of dough through the pasta machine.

2. Folding the dough in thirds.

3. Passing the dough through the pasta machine to achieve the desired thickness.

4. Using the pasta machine to cut the pasta into the desired width.

Filling Pasta

Sheets of raw pasta dough can be filled or folded to create ravioli (squares), tortellini (round "hats" with a brim of dough), lunettes (circles of dough folded into half-moons), agnolotti (squares of dough folded into rectangles) and other shapes. The filled pieces of dough are then cooked in boiling water using the procedure for cooking pasta ribbons discussed below. The filling can include almost anything—cheese, herbs, vegetables, fish, shellfish, meat or poultry. It can be uncooked or precooked. But any meat filling should be fully cooked before the pasta is assembled, as the time it takes for the dough to cook may not be sufficient to cook the filling.

Cannelloni is a different type of filled pasta: a large square of cooked dough is wrapped around a meat or cheese filling and baked. Popular lasagna dishes are similar. Lasagna pasta, which consists of wide, flat sheets, are cooked then layered with cheese, tomato sauce and meat or vegetables as desired. The finished casserole is baked and cut into portions.

Some of the larger, commercially prepared pasta shapes such as large shells (conchigloni or rigate) or large tubes (manicotti) can be partially cooked in boiling water, then filled, sauced and baked as a casserole.

Asian noodle dough is also made into filled items such as dumplings, wontons, egg rolls (made with egg noodle dough) and spring rolls (made with rice paper). These items are usually steamed, pan-fried or deep-fried.

When making filled pasta, consider the flavors and textures of the filling, dough and sauce. Each should complement the others. Combinations can range from traditional unflavored semolina pasta with herb and ricotta filling in a tomato sauce to an elegant escargot in garlic-and-herb pasta served with a beurre blanc to pork, ginger, soy and scallions in Asian egg noodle dough served with a soy-based dipping sauce.

PROCEDURE FOR MAKING RAVIOLI

1. Prepare a basic pasta dough of the desired flavor.
2. Prepare and chill the desired filling.
3. Roll out two thin sheets of dough between the rollers of a pasta machine. Gently lay the dough flat on the work surface.
4. Using a piping bag or a small portion scoop, place small mounds of filling on one of the dough pieces. Space the fillings evenly, allowing approximately 2 inches (5 centimeters) between each mound.
5. Brush the exposed areas of dough with water.
6. Gently place the second sheet of dough over the mounds and press firmly around each mound to remove air pockets and seal the dough.
7. Cut between the mounds with a chef's knife, pastry wheel or circular cutter.

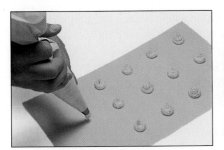

1. Piping the filling onto the dough.

2. Pressing around the mounds of filling to seal the dough and remove any air pockets.

3. Cutting around the mounds with a circular cutter.

Cooking Method

Determining Doneness

Italian-style pastas are properly cooked when they are al dente, firm but tender. Cooking times vary depending on the shape and quantity of pasta, the amount of water used, the hardness of the water and even the altitude. Fresh pasta cooks rapidly, sometimes in seconds. Noodles and dried pasta may require several minutes.

Although package or recipe directions offer some guidance, the only way to accurately test doneness is to bite into a piece. When the pasta is slightly firmer than desired, remove it from the stove and drain. It will continue to cook through residual heat.

Unlike Italian pasta, Asian noodles are not served al dente. Rather, they are either boiled until very soft or stir-fried until very crisp.

Boiling

All Italian-style pasta and most Asian noodles are cooked by just one method: boiling. The secret to boiling pasta successfully is to use ample water. Allow 1 gallon (4 liters) of water for each pound (450 grams) of pasta.

Use a saucepan or stockpot large enough to allow the pasta to move freely in the boiling water, otherwise the starch released by the dough will make the pasta gummy and sticky. The water should be brought to a rapid boil, then all the pasta should be added at once.

Salt should be added to the water. Pasta absorbs water and salt during cooking. Adding salt to the pasta after it is cooked will not provide the same seasoning effect.

Chefs disagree on whether to add oil to the cooking water. Purists argue against adding oil, on the theory that it makes the dough absorb water unevenly. Others think oil should be added to reduce surface foam. Another theory is that oil keeps the pasta from sticking, although this only works when added to cooked, drained pasta.

Asian noodles may be prepared by boiling until fully cooked, or they may be parboiled then stir-fried with other ingredients to finish cooking.

PROCEDURE FOR COOKING PASTA TO ORDER

1. Bring the appropriate amount of water to a boil over high heat.
2. Add oil to the water if desired.
3. Add the pasta and salt to the rapidly boiling water.
4. Stir the pasta to prevent it from sticking together. Bring the water back to a boil and cook until the pasta is done.
5. When the pasta is properly cooked, immediately drain it through a colander. A small amount of oil may be gently tossed into the pasta if desired to prevent it from sticking together.
6. Serve hot pasta immediately, or refresh in cold water for use in salads or other dishes. (Do not rinse pasta that is to be served hot.)

PROCEDURE FOR COOKING DRIED PASTA IN ADVANCE

Fresh pasta is so delicate and cooks so rapidly (sometimes in as little as 15 seconds) that it should be cooked to order. Dried pasta, however, can be cooked in advance for quantity service.

1. Follow the above directions for cooking pasta, but stop the cooking process when the pasta is about two-thirds done.
2. Drain the pasta, rinse it lightly and toss it in a small amount of oil.
3. Divide the pasta into appropriate-sized portions. Individual portions can be wrapped in plastic or laid on a sheet pan and covered. Refrigerate until needed.
4. When needed, place a portion in a china cap and immerse in boiling water to reheat. Drain, add sauce and serve immediately.

Accompaniments to Pasta

Pasta is widely accepted by consumers and easily incorporated in a variety of cuisines—from Italian and Chinese to Thai and spa. It is used in broths; as a bed for stews, fish, shellfish or meat; or tossed with sauce. Today's creative chefs are constantly developing nontraditional but delicious ways of serving pasta.

TABLE 23.6   COMBINING SAUCES, PASTA AND GARNISHES

Sauce	Pasta Shape	Garnish
Ragu	Ribbons, tubes, shapes, filled	Grated cheese
Seafood	Ribbons (fettuccine and capellini)	Fish or shellfish
Vegetable	Ribbons, tubes, filled	Meatballs, sausage, grated cheese
Cream	Thick ribbons (spaghetti and fettuccine), filled	Ham, peas, sausage, mushrooms, smoked salmon, nuts, grated cheese
Garlic-oil	Ribbons, shapes, filled	Grated cheese (if uncooked or cold), herbs
Uncooked	Ribbons, shapes	Cubed or grated cheese, fresh vegetables, herbs

Pasta and Broths

Small shapes can be cooked in the broth with which they are served, or cooked separately, then added to the hot liquid at service time. Soups such as cappelletti in brodo and chicken noodle are examples of these techniques.

Pasta Sauces

There are hundreds of Italian pasta sauces as well as sauces for Italian-style pasta, but most can be divided into six categories: ragus, seafood sauces, vegetable sauces, cream sauces, garlic-oil sauces and uncooked sauces. Recipes for a selection of pasta sauces are included at the end of this chapter.

Although there are no firm rules governing the combinations of sauces and pasta, Table 23.6 offers some of the more common combinations.

✦✦✦
PASTA SAUCES

Ragus are braised dishes used as a sauce. Usually, several flavoring ingredients and meat or poultry are browned, then a liquid and often a tomato product are added. The liquid can be a combination of stock, wine, water, milk or cream.

Seafood sauces can be white or red. White seafood sauces are most often made with white wine or stock and rarely use cream. They are often flavored with herbs. Red seafood sauces are tomato-based. Traditionally, these sauces are not garnished with cheese.

Vegetable sauces often use tomatoes as the base and a stock as the liquid. Mirepoix, garlic and red pepper flakes are commonly used for flavorings. Vegetable sauces include the traditional tomato sauce as well as primavera.

Cream sauces are based on milk or cream and are sometimes thickened with roux. Cheese is often included for flavor and richness.

Garlic-oil sauces (It. *aglio-olio*) consist mainly of garlic and oil; often herbs are added. Garlic-oil sauces can be hot or cold, cooked or uncooked. Pesto is a well-known example of an uncooked, cold garlic-oil sauce.

Uncooked sauces include a variety of dressings such as fresh tomatoes, basil and olive oil; or olive oil, lemon juice, parsley, basil and hot red pepper flakes. Other flavoring ingredients include capers, anchovies, garlic and olives as well as fresh herbs, fresh vegetables, flavored oils and cubed cheeses.

CONCLUSION

Most meals would seem incomplete without a starch. The most popular starches are potatoes, grains (especially rice) and pasta. All are low in fat and a good source of energy. Most can be prepared with several dry- and moist-heat cooking methods. Starches can be sauced, seasoned or flavored in limitless ways.

QUESTIONS FOR DISCUSSION

1. Explain the differences between mealy and waxy potatoes. Give two examples of each.
2. Describe the two methods of sautéing or pan-frying potatoes.
3. Explain why duchesse potatoes are regarded as the "mother" of many classic potato dishes. Name and describe two such dishes.
4. All grains are composed of three parts. Name and describe each of these parts.
5. Describe and compare the three general cooking methods used to prepare grains.
6. Name the three categories of Italian-style pasta shapes and give an example of each.
7. Why is it necessary to use ample water when cooking pasta? Should pasta be cooked in salted water? Should oil be added to the cooking water? Explain your answers.
8. Discuss the differences between cooking fresh pasta and cooking dried, factory-produced pasta.

ADDITIONAL STARCH RECIPES

RECIPE 23.9
VEGETABLE CANNELLONI

NOTE: *This dish appears in the Chapter Opening photograph.*

STOUFFER STANFORD COURT HOTEL, SAN FRANCISCO, CA
Executive Chef Ercolino Crugnale

Yield: 1 Serving

Pasta square of striped beet and saffron fettucine, 5 in. × 5 in. (12.5 cm × 12.5 cm), blanched	1	1
Braised Fennel and Cipolline Onions (recipe follows)	3 oz.	90 g
Thyme-scented Celery Broth (recipe follows)	2 oz.	60 g
Asparagus spears, peeled and blanched	6	6
Black truffles, shaved thin	2 Tbsp.	30 ml

1. Warm the pasta in boiling water; remove and dry.

2. Heat the Braised Fennel and Cipolline Onions and fill one side of the pasta square. Roll up the pasta to form the cannelloni.

3. Place the cannelloni on a dinner plate and ladle the Thyme-scented Celery Broth around it. Garnish with the warm asparagus and truffle shavings.

BRAISED FENNEL AND CIPOLLINE ONIONS

Yield: 3 lb. (1.6 kg)

Whole butter	8 oz.	250 g
Cipolline onions, sliced thin	12 oz.	360 g
Chicken stock	1 pt.	500 ml
Madeira	8 oz.	250 g
Yellow bell peppers, julienne	1 lb.	500 g
Fennel, sliced thin	20 oz.	600 g
Garlic, minced	2 Tbsp.	30 ml
Fresh parsley, chopped	3 Tbsp.	45 ml

1. Heat the butter over medium heat.

2. Add the onions and caramelize well. Deglaze with the chicken stock and add the madeira.

3. Add the peppers, fennel and garlic. Cover and sweat until tender. Add additional stock or Madeira if necessary.

4. Remove from the heat and add the parsley.

5. Spread on a sheet pan and cool.

THYME-SCENTED CELERY BROTH

Yield: 1 qt. (1 lt)

Celery juice	1 qt.	1 lt
Tomato juice	1 pt.	500 ml
Fresh thyme, chopped	1/2 oz.	15 g
Whole butter	6 oz.	180 g
Salt	TT	TT
Tabasco sauce	TT	TT

1. Combine the celery juice, tomato juice and thyme. Bring to simmer and reduce to 1-1/2 pints (750 milliliters).

2. Whisk in the butter and adjust the seasonings with salt and Tabasco sauce.

3. Strain through a chinois.

❖❖❖

RECIPE 23.10

GRILLED POTATO SALAD

GREENS RESTAURANT, SAN FRANCISCO, CA
Executive Chef Annie Somerville

Yield: 4 Servings	**Method:** Baking/Grilling	
New potatoes	2 lb.	1 kg
Light olive oil	as needed	as needed
Salt and pepper	TT	TT
Cherry tomatoes, sweet one hundreds or pear cherry tomatoes	4 oz.	120 g
Frisée or salad greens (optional)	4 oz.	120 g

Continued

Red and yellow bell peppers, roasted, seeded and cut into strips	1 lb.	500 g
Basil Vinaigrette (recipe follows)		
Champagne vinegar	as needed	as needed
Niçoise or Gaeta olives	12	12

1. Toss the potatoes with the olive oil in a baking dish; sprinkle with a few pinches of salt and pepper.
2. Cover the potatoes and place in a 400°F (200°C) oven. Cook until tender, approximately 35–40 minutes. Set aside to cool.
3. Cut the cooled potatoes in half or quarters if they are large. Thread onto skewers for grilling. (Skewers are not necessary if the grill grating is close together.) Grill the potatoes cut side down until they are golden and crisp with defined grill marks.
4. Cut the tomatoes in half or leave whole if small.
5. Prepare, wash and spin-dry the salad greens.
6. To assemble the salad, slide the grilled potatoes from the skewers and toss with the peppers, cherry tomatoes and vinaigrette. Adjust the seasoning, if necessary, with a splash of champagne vinegar and salt and pepper.
7. Loosely arrange the greens on plates or a platter, spoon the potatoes and other vegetables over the greens and garnish with the olives.

BASIL VINAIGRETTE

Yield: 4 oz. (120 g)

Champagne vinegar	1 oz.	30 g
Extra virgin olive oil	3 oz.	90 g
Fresh basil leaves	1/2 c.	250 ml
Salt	1/2 tsp.	3 ml
Garlic clove, chopped	1	1

1. Combine the ingredients in a blender or food processor until smooth.

◆◆◆

RECIPE 23.11

CANDIED SWEET POTATOES

Yield: 6 4-oz. (120-g) Servings　　　　　　　　　**Method:** Baking

Sweet potatoes	2 lb.	1 kg
Brown sugar	5 oz.	150 g
Water	2 oz.	60 g
Whole butter	2 oz.	60 g
Vanilla extract	1 tsp.	5 ml

1. Wash the sweet potatoes and cut as necessary to promote even cooking.
2. Bake the sweet potatoes on a sheet pan at 350°F (180°C) until cooked but still firm, approximately 30 minutes.
3. Combine the brown sugar, water and butter and bring to a boil. Add the vanilla and remove from the heat.
4. Peel the potatoes and slice or cut as desired. Arrange the potatoes in a baking dish and pour the sugar mixture over them.
5. Sprinkle the potatoes with additional brown sugar if desired and bake for 20 minutes, basting occasionally with the sugar mixture.

◆◆◆

RECIPE 23.12
POTATO PANCAKES

Yield: 12 2-1/2 oz. (75 g) Pancakes

Method: Pan-frying

Potatoes, all purpose	2 lb.	1 kg
Eggs, beaten	2	2
Onion, minced	6 oz.	180 g
Flour	2 oz.	60 g
Baking powder	1 Tbsp.	15 ml
Nutmeg	1 tsp.	5 ml
Salt and pepper	TT	TT
Vegetable oil	4 oz.	120 ml

1. Peel and coarsely grate the potatoes.

2. Transfer the grated potatoes to a bowl and add the beaten eggs, onion, flour and baking powder. Season with nutmeg, salt and pepper. Blend well.

3. Heat the oil. Add the potato mixture to the oil in uniform-size pancakes. Pan-fry the pancakes until tender, turning once when well browned on the first side. Remove from the pan and drain well.

◆◆◆

RECIPE 23.13
RÖSTI POTATOES

THE FOUR SEASONS, NEW YORK, NY
Chef Christian Albin

Yield: 6 Servings

Method: Pan-frying

Boiling potatoes, large	4	4
Bacon fat	2 oz.	60 g
Lard	2 oz.	60 g
Kosher salt and pepper	TT	TT
Whole butter	1 oz.	30 g

1. Partially cook the potatoes in salted water until almost done.

2. Drain and cool the potatoes, then peel and coarsely grate them.

3. Heat the bacon fat and lard in a heavy, shallow 10-inch (25-centimeter) skillet with sloping sides until quite hot. Spread half the potatoes over the bottom of the pan; sprinkle with salt and pepper. Cover with the remaining potatoes and cook over medium-high heat until the bottom turns brown and crusty, approximately 10 minutes.

4. Turn the potatoes in one piece. This is easiest to do by placing a large plate over the pan and turning both together so that the potatoes fall onto the plate. Slip the turned-over potatoes off the plate back into the pan, browned side up. Cook until the bottom is browned.

5. Before serving, smooth the edges of the potatoes with a spatula. Sprinkle with salt and brush the edge of the pan with whole butter. It will melt and run into the potatoes.

VARIATION: Cheddar Cheese Rösti Potatoes—Make two thin potatoes cakes. Top one with a layer of 7 ounces (210 grams) sour cream, 2 ounces (60 grams) cubed sharp cheddar cheese and 2 tablespoons (30 milliliters) chopped chives. Top with the other cake. Dot with 1 tablespoon (15 milliliters) whole butter and bake in a 400°F (200°C) oven for 15 minutes.

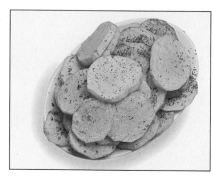

Cottage fries.

Shoestring potatoes.

French fries.

Steak fries.

◆◆◆

RECIPE 23.14

COTTAGE FRIES, SHOESTRING POTATOES, FRENCH FRIES, STEAK FRIES

RUTH'S CHRIS STEAK HOUSE, PHOENIX, AZ

Method: Deep-frying

Idaho potatoes, 70 count	as needed
Hot fat	as needed
Parsley, chopped	as needed for garnish

1. Cut each potato into the desired shape:

   Cottage fries—circles 1/4-inch (60-millimeters) thick

   Shoestring potatoes—long juliennes (allumettes)

   French fries—sticks 3/8 inch × 3/8 inch × 3 inches (1 centimeter × 1 centimeter × 7 centimeters)

   Steak fries—four large wedges

2. Deep-fry in 250°F (120°C) fat until lightly brown, approximately 2–3 minutes. Remove and drain. Season to taste with salt and pepper.

3. For service, deep-fry the partially cooked potatoes in 350°F (180°C) fat until golden in color and done.

4. Garnish with parsley if desired.

◆◆◆

RECIPE 23.15

POLENTA

Yield: 1 lb. 12 oz. (800 g)

Method: Simmering

Shallots, chopped	2 tsp.	10 ml
Whole butter	as needed	as needed
Milk, white stock or water	2 lb.	950 g
Cornmeal, yellow or white	6 oz.	180 g
Salt and pepper	TT	TT

1. Sauté the shallots in 1 tablespoon (15 milliliters) of butter for 30 seconds. Add the liquid and bring to a boil.

2. Slowly add the cornmeal while stirring constantly to prevent lumps, then simmer for 30 minutes.

3. Scrape the polenta into a buttered nonaluminum dish; spread to an even thickness with a spatula that has been dipped in water. Refrigerate the polenta until well chilled.

4. To serve, unmold the polenta and cut into shapes following the procedure discussed in Chapter 35, Presentation. Sauté or grill the polenta for service, or sprinkle with grated Parmesan cheese and heat under a broiler or salamander.

VARIATIONS: Wild Mushroom Polenta—Sauté 6 ounces (180 grams) cleaned, sliced wild mushrooms such as shiitake, chanterelles or morels in 1 tablespoon (15 milliliters) whole butter with 1 tablespoon (15 milliliters) chopped shallots until dry. Add to the polenta after it has simmered; stir to incorporate.

Wild Rice Polenta—Add 4 ounces (120 grams) cooked wild rice to the polenta after it has simmered; stir to incorporate.

◆◆◆

RECIPE 23.16

GRITS AND CHEDDAR SOUFFLÉ

Yield: 8 Servings   **Method:** Simmering/Baking

Grits	1-1/2 c.	350 ml
Water	1-1/2 pt.	700 ml
Milk	1-1/2 pt.	700 ml
Unsalted butter	4 oz.	120 g
Salt	TT	TT
Sharp cheddar cheese, grated	8 oz.	225 g
Tabasco sauce	1/2 tsp.	2 ml
Eggs, separated	6	6
Sugar	2 tsp.	10 ml

1. Combine the grits, water, milk, butter and salt in a heavy saucepan. Bring to a simmer and cook, stirring constantly, until thick, approximately 5–10 minutes.
2. Remove from the heat and stir in 6 ounces (180 grams) of the cheese and the Tabasco sauce.
3. Whisk the egg yolks together, then stir them into the grits mixture.
4. Whip the egg whites to soft peaks, add the sugar and whip to stiff peaks. Fold the egg whites into the grits mixture.
5. Pour the soufflé into a well-buttered 2-quart casserole or soufflé dish. Top with the remaining 2 ounces (60 grams) of cheese. Bake at 350°F (180°C) until set and browned, approximately 30 minutes. Serve immediately.

◆◆◆

RECIPE 23.17

BROWN RICE PILAF WITH PINE NUTS

Yield: 10 3-oz. (90-g) Servings   **Method:** Pilaf

Saffron threads	1/2 tsp.	2 ml
Chicken stock, hot	1 pt.	500 ml
Sesame oil	1 Tbsp.	15 ml
Vegetable oil	1 Tbsp.	15 ml
Pine nuts	2 oz.	60 g
Onion, medium dice	6 oz.	180 g
Red bell pepper, medium dice	6 oz.	180 g
Garlic, chopped	2 tsp.	10 ml
Brown rice	1 c.	250 ml
Salt	1 tsp.	10 ml
Pepper	TT	TT
Currants, dry	2 oz.	60 ml

1. Steep the saffron threads in the hot stock for 5 minutes.
2. Heat the oils and sauté the pine nuts until lightly browned.
3. Add the onion, red pepper and garlic and sauté without browning.
4. Add the rice and stir to coat the rice with the oil.
5. Add the salt and stock to the rice. Season with pepper, bring to a boil, reduce the heat and cover. Cook on the stove top or in the oven until done, approximately 30 minutes.
6. Stir in the currants, cover and allow them to soften for 5 minutes.

♦♦♦

RECIPE 23.18

WILD RICE AND CRANBERRY STUFFING

Yield: 5 pints (2.5 lt)   **Method:** Simmering

Dried morels	1 oz.	30 g
Wild rice	12 oz.	340 g
Onion, minced	8 oz.	225 g
Butter or chicken fat	2 oz.	60 g
Chicken stock, hot	approx. 1 qt.	approx. 1 lt
Dried cranberries	6 oz.	180 g
Salt and pepper	TT	TT
Fresh parsley, chopped fine	4 Tbsp.	60 ml

1. Soak the dried morels overnight in lightly salted water. Drain, reserving the liquid. Rinse well, drain again and chop coarsely.
2. Rinse the wild rice well in cold water.
3. Sauté the onion in the butter or chicken fat until tender. Add the mushrooms and wild rice.
4. Strain the reserved liquid from the mushrooms through several layers of cheesecloth to remove all sand and grit. Add enough chicken stock so that the liquid totals 3 pints (1.5 liters). Add the stock mixture and cranberries to the rice. Cover and simmer until the rice is dry and fluffy, approximately 45 minutes.
5. Season to taste with salt and pepper and stir in the parsley. This rice may be served as a side dish or used for stuffing duck or game hens.

♦♦♦

RECIPE 23.19

TABOULI (BULGUR WHEAT) SALAD

Yield: 15 3-oz. (90-g) Servings

Bulgur	10 oz.	300 g
Onions, brunoise	8 oz.	250 g
Green onions, sliced	2 oz.	60 g
Fresh parsley, chopped	6 oz.	180 g
Fresh mint, chopped	2 oz.	60 g
Olive oil	8 oz.	250 g
Lemon juice	8 oz.	250 g
Tomato, concasse	1 lb.	500 g
Salt and pepper	TT	TT
Pine nuts, toasted	4 oz.	120 g

1. Place the bulgur in a bowl and cover with cold water. Soak the bulgur until tender, approximately 2 hours.
2. Drain the bulgur and squeeze out all of the excess water.
3. Add the onions, green onions, parsley, mint, olive oil and lemon juice. Mix well.
4. Add the tomatoes; mix to combine. Season with salt and pepper.
5. Garnish with the toasted pine nuts.

✦✦✦

RECIPE 23.20
KASHA VARNISHKES WITH WILD MUSHROOMS

Yield: 4 lb. (1.8 kg) **Method:** Pilaf

Onion, medium dice	8 oz.	250 g
Kasha	2 c.	450 ml
Chicken fat or clarified butter	4 oz.	120 g
Mushrooms—shiitake, morels, white or a combination, sliced	4 oz.	120 g
Garlic, chopped	1 Tbsp.	15 ml
Chicken stock	1 qt.	1 lt
Salt and pepper	TT	TT
Bow tie pasta (farfalle)	10 oz.	300 g

1. Sauté the onions and kasha in 2 ounces (60 grams) of the fat or butter.
2. Add the mushrooms and garlic and stir in the stock. Season with salt and pepper. Bring to a boil, reduce to a simmer and cover. Cook until done, approximately 10–12 minutes.
3. Cook the bow tie pasta; refresh and drain.
4. Sauté the pasta in the remaining fat or butter.
5. Combine the kasha and pasta. Adjust the seasonings and serve.

✦✦✦

RECIPE 23.21
FETTUCCINE CON PESTO ALLA TRAPANESE

REX IL RISTORANTE, LOS ANGELES, CA
Executive Chef Odette Fada

Yield: 4 8-oz (250-g) Servings

Fresh fettuccine	1 lb.	500 g
Salt	TT	TT
Fresh basil leaves	1/2 oz.	15 g
Garlic cloves, chopped fine	4	4
Bread crumbs	2 Tbsp.	30 ml
Almonds, chopped	1 oz.	30 g
Extra virgin olive oil	approx. 3 oz.	approx. 90 g
Roma tomatoes, peeled, seeded and julienned	8 oz.	250 g

1. Boil the pasta in salted water until almost done.
2. Lightly sauté the basil, garlic, bread crumbs and almonds in the oil.
3. Add the tomatoes and sauté to blend the flavors.
4. Drain the pasta, add it to the pan and sauté for a minute over a low flame.
5. Add more olive oil and salt as needed.

♦♦♦

RECIPE 23.22
GOAT-CHEESE RAVIOLI IN HERBED CREAM SAUCE

Yield: 72 2-in. (5-cm) Ravioli
and 1-1/2 pt. (1.5 lt) Sauce

Fresh goat cheese	11 oz.	330 g
Cream cheese	8 oz.	250 g
Fresh basil, chopped fine	3 Tbsp.	45 ml
Fresh thyme, chopped fine	2 tsp.	10 ml
Fresh parsley, chopped	3 Tbsp.	45 ml
Pepper	TT	TT
Pasta, fresh	2 lb.	1 kg
Heavy cream	1 qt.	1 lt
Parmesan cheese, grated	2 oz.	60 ml
Salt	TT	TT

1. To make the cheese filling, combine the goat and cream cheeses with 2 tablespoons (30 milliliters) basil, 1 teaspoon (5 milliliters) thyme and the parsley; season to taste with pepper.
2. Make ravioli using the cheese mixture and pasta.
3. To make the sauce, combine the cream with the remaining herbs and bring to a boil. Reduce by one third and add the Parmesan cheese. Season with salt and pepper.
4. Boil the ravioli until done. Drain, toss gently with the sauce and serve.

♦♦♦

RECIPE 23.23
FETTUCCINE ALFREDO

Yield: 4 6-oz. (180-g) Servings

Fresh fettuccine	8 oz.	250 g
Whole butter	2 oz.	60 g
Heavy cream	12 oz.	350 g
Parmesan cheese, grated	2 oz.	60 g
Salt and white pepper	TT	TT

1. Boil the pasta, keeping it slightly undercooked. Refresh and drain.
2. To make the sauce, combine the butter, cream and cheese in a sauté pan. Bring to a boil and reduce slightly.
3. Add the pasta to the pan and boil the sauce and pasta until the sauce is thick and the pasta is cooked. Adjust the seasonings and serve.

♦♦♦

RECIPE 23.24
PASTA WITH SHRIMP AND SCALLOPS

Yield: 20 8-oz. (250-g) Servings

Onion, small dice	6 oz.	180 g
Garlic, chopped	1 Tbsp.	15 ml

Olive oil	2 oz.	60 g
Whole butter	2 oz.	60 g
Mushrooms, sliced	8 oz.	250 g
Salt and pepper	TT	TT
White wine	4 oz.	120 g
Tomato, concasse	8 oz.	250 g
Shrimp, peeled and deveined	1 lb.	500 g
Bay scallops	1 lb.	500 g
Mussels or clams, steamed and shucked, including 8 oz. (250 g) of their cooking liquid	2 lb.	1 kg
Fresh parsley, chopped	2 oz.	60 g
Spaghetti	2 lb.	1 kg

1. Sauté the onions and garlic in the oil and butter until tender. Add the mushrooms, season with salt and pepper and sauté.
2. Add the white wine. Boil and reduce by half.
3. Add the tomatoes and simmer for 2 minutes.
4. Add the shrimp and scallops and simmer for 2 minutes.
5. Add the mussels or clams, their cooking liquid and the chopped parsley.
6. Boil the spaghetti. Drain the spaghetti and toss it with the shellfish and sauce, adjust the seasonings and serve.

◆◆◆

RECIPE 23.25

BOLOGNESE SAUCE

Yield: 1 qt. (1 lt)

Mirepoix, fine dice	8 oz.	250 g
Olive oil	2 oz.	60 g
Whole butter	1 oz.	30 g
Ground beef	1 lb.	500 g
White wine	8 oz.	250 g
Milk	6 oz.	180 g
Nutmeg	TT	TT
Tomato, concasse	2 lb.	1 kg
White stock	approx. 8 oz.	approx. 250 g
Salt and pepper	TT	TT

1. Sauté the mirepoix in the olive oil and butter until tender. Add the beef and cook until no pink remains. Drain fat if necessary.
2. Add the wine. Cook and reduce the wine until nearly dry.
3. Add the milk and season with nutmeg. Cook and reduce the milk until nearly dry.
4. Add the tomatoes and 8 ounces. (250 grams) of stock; season with salt and pepper. Simmer for 3–4 hours, adding stock as needed to prevent scorching. Adjust the seasonings.

◆◆◆

RECIPE 23.26
TOMATO VINAIGRETTE

Yield: 4 8-oz. (250-g) Servings

Vinaigrette:		
Tomato, concasse	8 oz.	250 g
Fresh basil, thyme or marjoram	1 oz.	30 g
Balsamic vinegar	3 oz.	90 g
Shallots, minced	2 Tbsp.	30 ml
Olive oil	8 oz.	250 g
Salt and pepper	TT	TT
Pasta, cooked	1 lb.	500 g

1. Combine all vinaigrette ingredients. Season to taste with salt and pepper. Set aside for 20–30 minutes to allow the flavors to blend.
2. Toss the sauce with 1 pound (500 grams) warm or cold cooked pasta such as spaghetti or fettuccine. Adjust the seasonings. Serve immediately or refrigerate and serve chilled.

◆◆◆

RECIPE 23.27
PESTO SAUCE

Yield: 1-1/2 pt. (750 ml)

Olive oil	12 oz.	360 g
Pine nuts	3 oz.	90 g
Fresh basil leaves	6 oz.	180 g
Garlic, chopped	1 Tbsp.	15 ml
Parmesan cheese, grated	4 oz.	120 g
Romano cheese, grated	4 oz.	120 g
Salt and pepper	TT	TT

1. Place one third of the olive oil in a blender or food processor and add all the remaining ingredients.
2. Blend or process until smooth. Add the remaining olive oil and blend a few seconds to incorporate.

VARIATION: Walnut Pesto—Substitute walnuts for pine nuts in the above recipe.

◆◆◆

RECIPE 23.28
CAPPELLETTI IN BRODO

Yield: 10 1-pt. (450-ml) Servings
with 12 cappelletti each

Filling:		
Pork loin, roasted	6 oz.	180 g
Mortadella	4 oz.	120 g
Ricotta cheese	6 oz.	180 g
Parmesan cheese, finely grated	6 oz.	180 g
Egg	1	1
Nutmeg	TT	TT

Basic Pasta Dough (Recipe 23.8)	1 lb. 8 oz.	750 g
Beef Broth (Recipe 11.1)	5 qt.	5 lt
Parmesan cheese, shredded	8 oz.	250 g
Fresh parsley, chopped fine	3 Tbsp.	45 ml

1. To prepare the cappelletti filling, place the meats and cheeses in a food processor fitted with the metal blade. Process until finely ground. Add the egg and season lightly with nutmeg. Process until blended but not smoothly puréed.

2. Work with one quarter of the pasta dough at a time, keeping the rest covered to prevent it from drying out. Roll out a portion of the dough until it is very thin. Cut the dough into 2-inch (5-centimeter) squares using a fluted pasta wheel.

3. Place 1 teaspoon (5 milliliters) of filling in the center of each square. Fold the dough over the filling to form a rectangle, pinching the edges together to seal. Bring the ends of each rectangle together, overlapping them and pressing to seal.

4. Place the finished cappelletti on a paper-lined sheet pan. Leave them uncovered and turn them over once or twice so that they dry evenly. Continue working until all of the filling is used. The cappelletti may be cooked immediately or refrigerated for later use.

5. Heat the beef broth to a gentle boil. Drop the cappelletti in and cook until tender, approximately 3–5 minutes.

6. Portion the broth and cappelletti into warmed soup bowls and garnish with the shredded Parmesan and parsley.

◆◆◆

RECIPE 23.29

SOBA NOODLES IN BROTH

Yield: 6 1-pt. (450-ml) Servings

Soba noodles	1 lb.	500 g
Dashi* or chicken broth	1-1/2 qt.	1-1/2 lt
Soy sauce	3 Tbsp.	45 ml
Mirin	1 Tbsp.	15 ml
Sugar	1 Tbsp.	15 ml
Green onions, chopped	4 Tbsp.	60 ml
White sesame seeds	1 Tbsp.	15 ml

1. Boil the noodles in salted water until tender. Drain, rinse in hot water and drain again. Set aside.

2. Heat the dashi or chicken broth with the soy sauce, mirin and sugar. Add the noodles to the hot broth, simmering just until thoroughly reheated.

3. Portion into warmed bowls and top with the green onions and sesame seeds.

*Dashi is a stock made with dried bonito flakes and dried kelp. It is used extensively in Japanese cuisine and is available as an instant powder or a concentrate.

◆ ◆ ◆

RECIPE 23.30
MACARONI AND CHEESE

Yield: 24 8-oz. (250-g) Servings

Cheese sauce (page 205)	2 qt.	2 lt
Worcestershire sauce	TT	TT
Tabasco sauce	TT	TT
Elbow macaroni, boiled and refreshed	2 lb.	1 kg
Cheddar cheese	2 lb.	1 kg
Whole butter	8 oz.	250 g
Bread crumbs	1 oz.	30 g

1. Season the cheese sauce with Worcestershire and Tabasco.
2. Mix the macaroni with the cheese sauce and the cheese.
3. Pour into a buttered full-size hotel pan. Sprinkle with bread crumbs.
4. Bake uncovered at 350°F (180°C) until hot, approximately 30 minutes.

VARIATIONS: Macaroni and cheese with ham and tomato—Stir 2 pounds (1 kilogram) each diced cooked ham and tomato concasse into the macaroni and cheese before pouring it into the hotel pan.

◆ ◆ ◆

RECIPE 23.31
BAKED ZITI WITH FRESH TOMATO SAUCE

Yield: 30 Servings

Eggs	6	6
Ricotta cheese	4 lb.	1.8 kg
Fresh thyme	2 Tbsp.	30 ml
Fresh oregano	2 Tbsp.	30 ml
Fresh basil	2 Tbsp.	30 ml
Salt and pepper	TT	TT
Italian sausage links	3 lb.	1.4 kg
Ziti, cooked, refreshed and drained	4 lb.	1.8 kg
Parmesan cheese, grated	8 oz.	250 g
Fresh Tomato Sauce (Recipe 10.23)	3 qt.	3 lt
Mozzarella cheese, shredded	2 lb.	1 kg

1. Combine the eggs, ricotta cheese, thyme, oregano, basil, salt and pepper. Mix well and reserve.
2. Place the sausage links in a 2-inch-deep (5-centimeter) full-sized hotel pan; cook in a 350°F (180°C) oven for 20 minutes. Remove and cool. Drain the sausage. Slice the links into rounds and reserve.
3. Place the ziti in the hotel pan that was used to cook the sausage. Top with an even coating of the cheese mixture, sausage slices and Parmesan cheese.
4. Pour the tomato sauce over the top layer and stir slightly to distribute the sauce.
5. Bake at 375°F (190°C) for 1 hour. Sprinkle the mozzarella evenly over the pasta and return to the oven for 10 minutes. Serve.
6. Ziti may also be prepared in individual casseroles. Decrease baking time as necessary.

===== ◆◆◆ =====

RECIPE 23.32

Spinach and Ricotta Lasagna with Bolognese Sauce

Yield: 28 8-oz. (250-g) Servings

Fresh spinach pasta dough, rolled into sheets	2 lb.	1 kg
Spinach, stemmed	2 lb.	1 kg
Whole butter	2 oz.	60 g
Ricotta cheese	1 lb.	500 g
Parmesan cheese, grated	6 oz.	180 g
Eggs	2	2
Salt and pepper	TT	TT
Bolognese sauce (Recipe 23.25)	3 qt.	3 lt
Béchamel sauce (Recipe 10.7)	1 qt.	1 lt

1. Cut the pasta dough into 4-inch (10-centimeter) strips. Boil in salted water until done and drain well.
2. Sauté the spinach in the butter. Drain well and cool.
3. Combine the spinach with the ricotta cheese, 4 ounces (120 grams) of the Parmesan cheese and eggs. Season to taste with salt and pepper.
4. Ladle a small amount of the Bolognese sauce in to the bottom of a standard full-size hotel pan. Cover the sauce with a layer of cooked pasta. Spread a thin layer of the spinach-and-cheese mixture on the pasta. Ladle a portion of the Béchamel sauce over the spinach and spread in a thin even layer. Ladle a portion of the Bolognese sauce over the Béchamel sauce and spread in an even layer.
5. Add another layer of pasta and repeat the process until all of the ingredients are used, finishing with a layer of Béchamel sauce. Sprinkle the remaining Parmesan cheese on top and bake covered at 350°F (180°C) until heated through, approximately 40 minutes. Uncover the lasagna for the last 15 minutes so it browns.

===== ◆◆◆ =====

RECIPE 23.33

Chilled Chinese Noodle Salad

Yield: 8 4-oz. (120-g) Servings

Dressing:		
Dark soy sauce	2 Tbsp.	30 ml
White vinegar	2 Tbsp.	30 ml
Salt	1 tsp.	5 ml
Sugar	1 Tbsp.	15 ml
Peanut oil	1 Tbsp.	15 ml
Sesame oil	1 Tbsp.	15 ml
Orange zest	1 tsp.	5 ml
Red chile flakes	1/2 tsp.	2 ml
Chinese egg noodles, fresh	8 oz.	250 g
Bean sprouts, blanched	8 oz.	250 g

Continued

Carrot, finely shredded	6 oz.	180 g
Daikon, finely shredded	3 oz.	90 g
Green onion, sliced	2 oz.	60 g
Black sesame seeds	1 Tbsp.	15 ml
Fresh cilantro leaves	as needed	as needed

1. Combine the dressing ingredients and whisk thoroughly.
2. Cook the egg noodles in rapidly boiling salted water until tender, approximately 2 minutes. Drain and refresh; drain again.
3. Toss the noodles with the bean sprouts, carrots, daikon, green onion and sesame seeds. Add the dressing and toss gently until the noodles and vegetables are thoroughly coated.
4. Chill well. Serve mounds of this noodle salad as an appetizer or an accompaniment for grilled fish or chicken. Garnish with cilantro.

◆◆◆

RECIPE 23.34

GNOCCHI

Yield: 2 lb. 4 oz. (1 kg)

Milk	1 qt.	1 lt
Whole butter	2 oz.	60 g
Salt	2 tsp.	10 ml
Semolina	5 oz.	150 g
Egg yolks	2	2
Parmesan cheese, grated	approx. 6 oz.	approx. 180 g

1. Combine the milk, butter and salt and bring to a boil.
2. Add the semolina in a steady stream while stirring constantly.
3. Cook the mixture over low heat for 15 minutes. The mixture will be thick—be careful not to scorch it.
4. Remove the mixture from the heat and stir in the egg yolks and 4 ounces. (120 grams) of Parmesan cheese.
5. Form the mixture into quenelles, using two spoons, and arrange them in a buttered baking dish. Alternatively, spread the mixture in a pan with a spatula to the thickness of 1/2 inch (12 millimeters) and refrigerate until firm. Cut the desired shapes from the mixture and place them in a buttered baking dish.
6. Sprinkle the gnocchi with Parmesan cheese and place under the salamander or broiler or bake in a hot oven until hot and lightly browned on top.

◆◆◆

RECIPE 23.35

SPAETZLE

Yield: 30 3-oz. (90-g) Servings

Eggs	12	12
Water	1 qt.	1 lt
Flour	3 lb.	1.4 kg
Salt	2 tsp.	10 ml
Nutmeg	1/2 tsp.	2 ml

| Whole butter | 8 oz. | 250 g |
| Fresh parsley, chopped | as needed | as needed |

1. Whisk the eggs to blend. Add the water, flour, salt and nutmeg. Mix until well blended; do not overmix.
2. Place the batter in a colander suspended over a large pot of boiling water. Work the batter through the colander's holes using a plastic bowl scraper or rubber spatula. The batter should drop into the boiling water.
3. Cook the dumplings in the boiling water for approximately 3–4 minutes. Remove them with a skimmer and refresh.
4. For service, sauté the dumplings lightly in butter, just until hot. Garnish with chopped parsley.

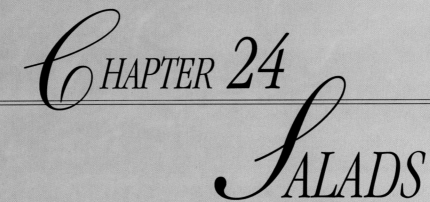

CHAPTER 24
SALADS
AND
SALAD DRESSINGS

This chapter discusses all types of salads: the small plate of crisp iceberg lettuce with tomato wedges, cucumber slices and ranch dressing; the dinner plate of sautéed duck breast fanned across bright red grilled radicchio and toothy green arugula, sprayed with a vinaigrette dressing; the scoop of shredded chicken, mango chutney and seasonings, bound with mayonnaise; and the bowl of artichokes and mushrooms marinated in olive oil and lemon juice.

Each of these dishes fits the definition of a salad: a single food or a mix of different foods accompanied or bound by a dressing. A salad can contain meat, grains, fruits, nuts or cheese and absolutely no lettuce. It can be an appetizer, a second course served after the appetizer, an entree (especially at lunch) a course following the entree in the European manner or even dessert.

The color, texture and flavor of each salad ingredient should complement those of the others, and the dressing should complement all of the ingredients. Harmony is critical to a salad's success—no matter what type of salad is being prepared.

This chapter opens with a section identifying greens commonly used in salads. A discussion of salad dressings follows. Finally, techniques for preparing green salads (both tossed and composed), bound salads, vegetable salads and fruit salads are discussed.

SALAD GREENS

Identifying Salad Greens

Salad greens are not necessarily green: Some are red, yellow, white or brown. They are all, however, leafy vegetables. Many are members of the lettuce or chicory families.

Lettuce

Lettuce (Fr. *laitue*; It. *lattuga*) has been consumed for nearly as long as people have kept records of what they and others ate. Archaeologists found that Persian royalty were served lettuce at their banquets more than 2500 years ago. Now grown and served worldwide, lettuces are members of the genus *Lactuca*. The most common types of lettuce are butterhead, crisp head, leaf and romaine.

Boston

Boston and bibb are two of the most popular butterhead lettuces. Their soft, pliable, pale green leaves have a buttery texture and flavor. Boston is larger and paler than bibb. Both Boston and bibb lettuce leaves form cups when separated from the heads; these cups make convenient bases for holding other foods on cold plates.

Boston

Iceberg

Iceberg lettuce is the most common of all lettuce varieties in the United States; it outsells all other varieties combined. Its tightly packed spherical head is comprised of crisp, pale green leaves with a very mild flavor. Iceberg lettuce remains crisp for a relatively long period of time after being cut or prepared. Select heads that are firm but not hard and leaves that are free of burnt or rusty tips.

Iceberg

Leaf

Leaf lettuce grows in bunches. It has separate, ruffle-edged leaves branching from a stalk. Because it does not grow into a firm head, it is easily damaged during harvest and transport. Both red and green leaf lettuce have bright colors, mild flavors and tender leaves. Good-quality leaf lettuce should have nicely shaped leaves free of bruises, breaks or brown spots.

Red and Green Leaf Lettuces

Romaine

Romaine lettuce, also known as cos, is a loosely packed head lettuce with elongated leaves and thick midribs. Its outer leaves are dark green and although they look coarse, they are crisp, tender and tasty without being bitter. The core leaves are paler and more tender but still crisp. Romaine has enough flavor to stand up to strongly flavored dressings such as the garlic and Parmesan cheese used in a Caesar salad. A good-quality head of romaine has dark green outer leaves that are free of blemishes or yellowing.

Baby Lettuces

Innovative chefs are always looking for new and different foods to add a twist or flair to their dishes. This has led to the popularity of baby lettuces and other specialty greens. Baby greens have similar but more subtle flavors than their mature versions. They are often less bitter and are always more tender and delicate. Because of their size and variety, they are perfect for composed salads. **Mesclun** is a mixture of several kinds of baby lettuce.

Romaine

Brune d'Hiver

Lola Rosa

Red Sails

Baby Green Bibb

Baby Red Bibb

Baby Red Oak Leaf

Pirate

Baby Red Romaine

Belgian Endive

Curly Endive

Escarole

Radicchio

Arugula

Dandelion

Chicory

Chicories come in a variety of colors, shapes and sizes; most are slightly bitter. Chicories are quite hearty and can also be cooked, usually grilled or braised.

Belgian Endive

Belgian endive grows in small, tight heads with pointed leaves. It is actually the shoot of a chicory root. The small sturdy leaves are white at the base with yellow fringes and tips. (A purple-tipped variety is sometimes available.) Whole leaves can be separated, trimmed and filled with soft butters, cheeses or spreads and served as an hors d'oeuvre. Or they can be used for composed salads. The leaves, cut or whole, can also be added to cold salads. Heads of Belgian endive are often braised or grilled and served with meat or poultry. As the name suggests, Belgian endive is imported from Belgium.

Curly Endive

In this country, curly endive is often called by its family name, chicory, or its French name, frisée. The dark green outer leaves are pointed, sturdy and slightly bitter. The yellow inner leaves are more tender and less bitter. Curly endive has a strong flavor that goes well with strong cheeses, game and citrus. It is often mixed with other greens to add texture and flavor.

Escarole

Escarole, sometimes called broadleaf endive, has thick leaves and a slightly bitter flavor. It has green outer leaves and pale green or yellow center leaves. Escarole is very sturdy and is often mixed with other greens for added texture. Its strong flavor stands up to full-flavored dressings and is a good accompaniment to grilled meats and poultry.

Radicchio

Radicchio resembles a small red cabbage. It retains its bright reddish color when cooked and is popular braised or grilled and served as a vegetable side dish. Because of its attractive color, radicchio is popular in cold salads, but it has a very bitter flavor and should be used sparingly and mixed with other greens in a tossed salad. The leaves form cups when separated and can be used to hold other ingredients when preparing composed salads. Radicchio is quite expensive and availability is sometimes limited.

Other Salad Greens and Ingredients

Leafy vegetables besides lettuce and chicory, as well as other ingredients, are used to add texture, flavor and color to salads. A partial listing follows.

Arugula

Arugula, also known as rocket, is a member of the cabbage family. Available as individual leaves, they are similar to dandelion leaves in size and shape. The best are 2 to 4 inches (5 to 10 centimeters) long. Arugula has a very strong, spicy, peppery flavor—so strong, in fact, that it is rarely served by itself. It is best when used to add zip to salads by combining it with other greens.

Dandelion

Dandelion grows as a weed throughout most of the United States. It has long, thin, toothed leaves with a prominent midrib. When purchasing dandelion for salads, look for small leaves. They are more tender and less bitter. Older, tougher leaves can be cooked and served as a vegetable.

Mâche

Mâche or lamb's lettuce is very tender and very delicately flavored. Its small, cuplike pale to dark green leaves have a slightly nutty flavor. Because its flavor is so delicate, mâche should only be combined with other delicately flavored greens such as Boston or bibb lettuce and dressed sparingly with a light vinaigrette dressing.

Mâche

Sorrel

Sorrel, sometimes called sourgrass, has leaves similar to spinach in color and shape. Sorrel has a very tart, lemony flavor that goes well with fish and shellfish. It should be used sparingly and combined with other greens in a salad. Sorrel can also be made into soups, sauces and purées.

Sorrel

Spinach

Like sorrel, spinach can be cooked or used as a salad green. As a salad green, it is popularly served wilted and tossed with a hot bacon dressing. Spinach is deep green with a rich flavor and tender texture. Good-quality spinach should be fairly crisp. Avoid wilted or yellowed bunches.

Sprouts

Sprouts are not salad greens but are often used as such in salads and sandwiches. Sprouts are very young alfalfa, daikon or mustard plants. Alfalfa sprouts are very mild and sweet. Daikon and mustard sprouts are quite peppery.

Sprouts

Spinach

Watercress

Watercress has tiny, dime-sized leaves and substantial stems. It has a peppery flavor and adds spice to a salad. Good-quality fresh watercress is dark green with no yellowing. To preserve its freshness, watercress must be kept very cold and moist. It is normally packed topped with ice. Individual leaves are plucked from the stems and rinsed just before service.

Watercress

Edible Flowers

Many specialty produce growers offer edible, pesticide-free blossoms. They are used for salads and as garnishes wherever a splash of color would be appreciated. Some flowers such as nasturtiums, calendulas and pansies are grown and picked specifically for eating. Others, such as yellow cucumber flowers and squash blossoms, are byproducts of the vegetable industry.

Nasturtiums

Squash blossoms and other very large flowers should be cut in julienne strips before being added to salads. Pick petals from large and medium-sized flowers. Smaller whole flowers can be tossed in a salad or used as a garnish when composing a salad. Very small flowers or petals can be sprinkled on top of a salad so they are not hidden by the greens.

Calendulas

Pansies

Fresh Herbs

Basil, thyme, tarragon, oregano, dill, cilantro, marjoram, mint, sage, savory and even rosemary are used to add interesting flavors to otherwise ordinary salads. Because many herbs have strong flavors, use them sparingly so the delicate flavors of the greens are not overpowered. Leafy herbs such as basil and sage can be cut chiffonade. Other herbs can be picked into sprigs or chopped before being tossed with the salad greens. Flowering herbs such as chive blos-

♦♦♦
FLOWER SAFETY

Many flowers and blossoms are toxic, especially those grown from bulbs. Even flowers that would otherwise be edible may contain pesticides that can be harmful if ingested. Use only flowers grown specifically for use as food; purchase edible flowers only from reputable purveyors.

TABLE 24.1   NUTRITIONAL VALUES OF SELECTED SALAD GREENS AND DRESSINGS

Salad greens per 4-oz. (112-g) serving, trimmed; Salad dressings per 1-oz. (28-g) serving	Kcal	Protein (g)	Carbohydrates (g)	Fiber (g)	Total Fat (g)	Vitamin A (I.U.)	Vitamin C (mg)	Calcium (mg)	Iron (mg)
Belgian endive	20	1.6	3.6	1.2	0.4	2052	8	52	0.8
Boston lettuce	16	1.6	2.8	1.2	0.4	816	6.7	mq	0.2
Chicory greens	28	2	5.2	0.8	0.4	14,400	88	360	3.2
Dandelion greens	52	3.2	10.4	2	0.8	mq	mq	mq	mq
Iceberg lettuce	16	1.2	2.4	1.2	0.4	383	5.8	23	0.6
Romaine lettuce	20	2	2.8	2	0.4	2912	28	40	1.2
Blue cheese dressing	143	1.4	2.1	<0.1	14.8	32	<1	12	tr
Mayonnaise	110	0.3	6.8	0	9.5	32	0	2	tr
Vinaigrette	67	<0.1	2.3	mq	6.5	0	0	0	0

The Corinne T. Netzer Encyclopedia of Food Values 1992

mq = measurable quantity, but data is unavailable   tr = trace amounts

soms are used like other edible flowers to add color, flavor and aroma. Refer to Chapter 7, Kitchen Staples, for more information on herbs.

Nutrition

Salad greens are an especially healthful food. Greens contain virtually no fat and few calories and are high in vitamins A and C, iron and fiber. But when garnished with meat and cheese and tossed with a dressing (many of which are oil-based), fat and calories are added. In an attempt to maintain the healthful nature of greens, low-fat or fat-free dressings should be available to customers.

Purchasing and Storing Salad Greens

Purchasing

Lettuces are grown in nearly every part of the United States; nearly all types are available year-round. Principal salad greens such as spinach are available all year; many of the specialty greens are seasonal.

Lettuce is generally packed in cases of 24 heads with varying weights. Other salad greens are packed in trays or boxes of various sizes and weights.

Because salad greens are simply washed and eaten, it is extremely important that they be as fresh and blemish-free as possible. Try to purchase salad greens daily. All greens should be fresh-looking, with no yellowing. Heads should be heavy, with little or no damage to the outer leaves.

Many types of salad greens are available precut and prewashed. These greens are often vacuum-packed to increase shelf life, although delicate greens are sometimes loosely packaged in 5–10-pound (2–5-kilo) boxes. Precut and prewashed greens are relatively expensive, but can reduce labor costs dramatically.

Storing

Although some types of salad greens are hearty enough to keep for a week or more under proper conditions, all salad greens are highly perishable.

Generally, softer-leaved varieties such as Boston and bibb tend to perish more quickly than the crisper-leaved varieties such as iceberg and romaine.

Greens should be stored in their original protective cartons in a specifically designated refrigerator. Ideally, greens should be stored at temperatures between 34° and 38°F (1–3°C) (most other vegetables should be stored at warmer temperatures of 40–50°F [4–10°C]). Greens should not be stored with tomatoes, apples or other fruits that emit ethylene gas, which causes greens to wilt and accelerates spoilage.

Do not wash greens until you need them, as excess water causes them to deteriorate quickly.

Preparing Salad Greens

Unless salad greens are purchased precut and prewashed, they will need to undergo some preparation before service, principally tearing, cutting, washing and drying.

Tearing and Cutting

Some chefs want all salad greens torn by hand. Delicate greens such as butterhead and baby lettuces look nicer and it is less likely they will be bruised if hand-torn. But often it is not practical to hand-tear all greens. It is perfectly acceptable to cut hardy greens with a knife.

PROCEDURE FOR CUTTING ROMAINE LETTUCE

1. To cut romaine lettuce, trim the outer leaves and damaged tips with a chef's knife and split the head lengthwise.

2. Make one or two cuts along the length of the head, leaving the root intact, then cut across the width of the head.

Alternative method:

1A. Trim the outer leaves and damaged tips with a chef's knife. Pull the leaves from the core and cut the rib out of each leaf. The leaf can then be cut to the desired size.

PROCEDURE FOR CORING ICEBERG LETTUCE

1. Loosen the core by gripping the head and smacking the core on the cutting board. (Do not use too much force or you may bruise the lettuce.)

2. Remove the core and cut the lettuce as desired.

PROCEDURE FOR REMOVING THE MIDRIB FROM SPINACH

1. Fold the leaf in half and pull off the stem and midrib. Only the tender leaf should remain.

Washing

All lettuce and other salad greens should be washed before use. Even though they may look clean, greens may harbor hidden insects, sand, soil and pesticides. All greens should be washed after they are torn or cut. Whole heads can be washed by repeatedly dipping them in cold water and allowing them to drain. But washing whole heads is not recommended: It will not remove anything trapped near the head's center, and water trapped in the leaves can accelerate spoilage.

PROCEDURE FOR WASHING SALAD GREENS

1. Fill a sink with very cold water. Place the cut or torn greens in the water.

2. Gently stir the water and greens with your hands and remove the greens. Do not allow the greens to soak. Using fresh water each time, repeat the procedure until no grit can be detected on the bottom of the sink after the greens are removed.

Drying

Salad greens should be dried after washing. Wet greens do not stay as crisp as thoroughly dried ones. Also, wet greens tend to repel oil-based dressings and dilute their flavors. Greens may be dried by draining them well in a colander and blotting them with absorbent cloth or paper towels, or, preferably, they can be dried in a salad spinner, which uses centrifugal force to remove the water.

PROCEDURE FOR DRYING GREENS

1. After washing the greens, place them in the basket of a salad spinner and spin for approximately 30 seconds.

SALAD DRESSINGS

A dressing is a sauce for a salad. Just as sauces for hot foods should complement rather than mask the flavor of the principal food, the sauce (dressing) for a salad should complement rather than mask the flavors of the other ingredients. Although a great many ingredients can be used to make salad dressings, most are based on either a mixture of oil and vinegar, called a vinaigrette, or a mayonnaise or other emulsified product.

Vinaigrette-style dressings can be made without oil; creamy dressings similar to mayonnaise-based dressings can be made with sour cream, yogurt or buttermilk instead of mayonnaise. Nevertheless, for all practical purposes these dressings are still prepared like vinaigrettes and mayonnaise-based dressings and they are treated that way here.

Vinaigrette Dressings

The simple vinaigrette, also known as **basic French dressing**, is a temporary emulsion of oil and vinegar seasoned with salt and pepper. The standard ratio is three parts oil to one part vinegar. The ratio can vary, however. When using strongly flavored oils, less than three parts oil to one part vinegar generally suffices. In some recipes, all or part of the vinegar is replaced with citrus juice, in which case it may take more than one part vinegar and citrus juice to three parts oil to achieve the proper acidity level. The best way to determine the correct ratio of oil to vinegar is to taste the dressing, preferably on the food it will dress.

Oils and vinegars have unique flavors that can be mixed and matched to achieve the correct balance for a particular salad. Olive oil goes well with red wine vinegar; nut oils go well with balsamic or sherry vinegars. Neutral-flavored oils such as canola, corn or safflower can be mixed with a flavored vinegar.

Oil and vinegar repel each other and will separate almost immediately when mixed. They should be whisked together immediately before use.

Oils

Many types of oil can be used to make salad dressings. Light, neutral-flavored oils such as canola, corn, cottonseed, soybean and safflower are relatively low priced and used extensively for this purpose. Other oils can be used to add flavor. Olive oil is very popular; both mild-flavored pure olive oil and full-flavored extra virgin olive oil are used. Nut oils such as hazelnut and walnut are expensive but they add unique and interesting flavors. Infused oils are also popular.

Vinegars

Many different vinegars can be used to make salad dressings. Red wine vinegar is the most common because it is inexpensive and its flavor blends well with many foods. But other vinegars such as cider, balsamic and white wine are also used. Fruit-flavored vinegars (particularly raspberry) are extremely popular and widely available, so are herb- and garlic-flavored ones.

Flavored vinegars are easy to make. Fruit, herbs or garlic are added to a wine vinegar (either red or white) and left for several days for the flavors to blend. The vinegar is then strained off and used as desired.

Acidic juices such as lemon, orange and lime are sometimes substituted for all or part of the vinegar in a salad dressing.

Other Flavoring Ingredients

Herbs, spices, shallots, garlic, mustard and sugar are only a few of the many flavoring ingredients used to enhance a vinaigrette dressing. Items such as herbs, shallots and garlic should be minced or chopped before being added to the dressing. If dried herbs are used, the dressing should rest for at least 1 hour to allow the flavors to develop. Other ingredients may be added at any time.

PROCEDURE FOR PREPARING A VINAIGRETTE

1. Choose an oil and vinegar that complement each other as well as the foods they will dress.

2. Combine the vinegar, seasonings and any other flavorings in a bowl.

3. Whisk in the oil.

4. Allow the finished dressing to rest a few hours at room temperature before using so that the flavors can blend.

5. Rewhisk immediately before use.

◆◆◆

RECIPE 24.1

BASIC VINAIGRETTE DRESSING

Yield: 1 qt. (1 lt)

Wine vinegar	8 oz.	250 ml
Salt and pepper	TT	TT
Salad oil	24 oz.	750 ml

1. Combine all ingredients and mix well. Store at room temperature.

VARIATIONS: Dijon vinaigrette—Add 4 ounces (120 grams) Dijon-style mustard to the vinegar and proceed with the recipe.

Herbed vinaigrette—Add 2 tablespoons (30 milliliters) of fresh herbs or 1 tablespoon (15 milliliters) dried herbs such as basil, tarragon, thyme, marjoram or chives to the vinaigrette.

Mayonnaise

Although most food service operations buy commercially made mayonnaise, every chef should know how it is made to more fully understand how to use it and why it reacts the way it does when used. Knowing how to make mayonnaise also allows you to create a mayonnaise with the exact flavorings you want.

Mayonnaise is an **emulsified sauce**. An emulsified sauce is formed when two liquids that would not ordinarily form a stable mixture are forced together and held in suspension. To make mayonnaise, oil is whisked together with a very small amount of vinegar (it is the water in the vinegar that does not normally mix with oil). As the oil and vinegar are whisked together, the oil breaks into microscopic droplets that are separated from each other by a thin barrier of vinegar. If left alone, the droplets would quickly regroup, forming a large puddle of oil and a small puddle of vinegar. To prevent the oil droplets from regrouping, an emulsifier is added. For mayonnaise, the emulsifier is lecithin, a protein found in egg yolks. (The acid in the vinegar also helps form the emulsion.) Lecithin has the unique ability to combine with both oil and water. It surrounds the oil droplets, preventing them from coming in contact with each other and regrouping.

The balance of vinegar, oil, lecithin and agitation (whipping) is crucial to achieve a proper emulsion. The higher the proportion of oil to vinegar, the thicker the sauce will be. The higher the proportion of vinegar to oil, the thinner the sauce will be. (For example, the emulsified vinaigrette dressing discussed on page 673 is a thin emulsion.)

There is a limit to how much oil each egg yolk can emulsify, however. One yolk contains enough lecithin to emulsify approximately 7 ounces (200 milliliters) of oil. If more than that amount of oil per egg yolk is added, the sauce will break; that is, the oil and vinegar will separate and the mayonnaise will become very thin.

Ingredients

A neutral-flavored vegetable oil is most often used for a standard mayonnaise. Other oils are used to contribute their special flavors. For example, olive oil is used to make a special mayonnaise called *aioli*.

Wine vinegar is used for a standard mayonnaise. Flavored vinegars such as tarragon vinegar are often used to create unique flavors.

Seasonings vary according to the intended use but typically include dry mustard, salt, pepper and lemon juice.

PROCEDURE FOR PREPARING MAYONNAISE

1. Gather all ingredients and hold at room temperature. Room-temperature ingredients emulsify more easily than cold ones.
2. By hand or in an electric mixer or food processor, whip the egg yolks on high speed until frothy.
3. Add the seasonings to the yolks and whip to combine. Salt and other seasonings will dissolve or blend more easily when added at this point rather than if added to the finished mayonnaise.
4. Add a small amount of the liquid from the recipe and whip to combine.
5. With the mixer on high or whisking vigorously by hand, begin to add the oil very slowly until an emulsion forms.
6. After the emulsion forms, the oil can be added a little more quickly but still in a slow, steady stream. The mayonnaise can now be whipped at a slightly slower speed.
7. The mayonnaise will become very thick as more oil is added. A small amount of liquid can be added if it becomes too thick. Alternate between oil and liquid two or three times until all the oil is added and the correct consistency is reached. *Important:* A large egg yolk has the ability to emulsify up to 7 ounces (200 milliliters) of oil; adding more oil may cause the mayonnaise to break.
8. Taste the mayonnaise and adjust the seasonings. Refrigerate immediately.

❖❖❖

RECIPE 24.2

MAYONNAISE

Yield: 1 qt. (1 lt)

Egg yolks	4	4
Salt	1 tsp.	5 ml
White pepper	TT	TT
Dry mustard	1 tsp.	5 ml
Wine vinegar	3 Tbsp.	45 ml
Salad oil	28 oz.	840 g
Lemon juice	TT	TT

1. Place the egg yolks in the bowl of a mixer and whip on high speed until frothy.

2. Add the dry ingredients and half the vinegar to the yolks; whisk to combine.

3. Begin to add the oil a drop at a time until the mixture begins to thicken and an emulsion beings to form.

4. Add the remaining oil in a slow steady stream, thinning the mayonnaise occasionally by adding a little vinegar. Continue until all oil and vinegar have been incorporated.

5. Adjust the seasonings and add lemon juice to taste.

6. Refrigerate until needed.

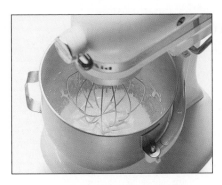

1. Whipping the egg yolks until frothy.

2. Adding the oil very slowly, allowing the emulsion to form.

3. The finished mayonnaise.

Mayonnaise-Based Dressings

Mayonnaise-based salad dressings are salad dressings that use mayonnaise as a base, with other ingredients added for flavor, color and texture. These ingredients include dairy products (especially buttermilk and sour cream), vinegar, fruit juice, vegetables (either puréed or minced), tomato paste, garlic, onions, herbs, spices, condiments, capers, anchovies and boiled eggs. Recipes for several mayonnaise-based salad dressings are at the end of this chapter.

Emulsified Vinaigrette Dressings

An emulsified vinaigrette is a standard vinaigrette dressing emulsified with whole eggs. An emulsified vinaigrette dressing is thinner and lighter than a mayonnaise-based dressing and heavier than a basic vinaigrette. Its taste is similar to a basic vinaigrette, but it will not separate and it clings to greens quite easily.

PROCEDURE FOR PREPARING AN EMULSIFIED VINAIGRETTE DRESSING

1. Gather all ingredients and hold at room temperature. Room-temperature ingredients emulsify more easily than cold ones.

2. Whip the eggs until frothy.

3. Add the dry ingredients and any flavorings such as garlic, shallots and herbs.

4. Add a small amount of the liquid from the recipe and whip to incorporate the ingredients.

♦♦♦

CONVENIENCE PRODUCTS

A great many prepared and dry-mix salad dressings are available. Although they vary greatly in quality, they can be very economical; they reduce labor costs and sometimes food costs. Some of these products use stabilizers, artificial flavorings and colors; nearly all contain preservatives. When considering the advantages of prepared or dry-mix salad dressings, always keep quality in mind.

5. With the mixer on high or whisking vigorously by hand, begin adding the oil very slowly until the emulsion forms.

6. After the emulsion is formed, the oil can be added a little more quickly, but still in a slow, steady stream.

7. Alternate between oil and liquid two or three times until all the oil is added. The dressing should be much thinner than mayonnaise. If it is too thick it can be thinned with a little water, vinegar or lemon juice. Determine which to use by first tasting the dressing.

♦♦♦

RECIPE 24.3

EMULSIFIED VINAIGRETTE DRESSING

Yield: 1 qt. (1 lt)

Eggs, whole	2	2
Salt	1 Tbsp.	15 ml
White pepper	1/2 tsp.	2 ml
Paprika	1 Tbsp.	15 ml
Dry mustard	1 Tbsp.	15 ml
Sugar	1 Tbsp.	15 ml
Herbes de Provence	1 Tbsp.	15 ml
Cayenne pepper	TT	TT
Wine vinegar or cider vinegar	4 oz.	120 g
Salad oil	24 oz.	720 g
Lemon juice	3 oz.	90 g

1. Place the eggs in the bowl of a mixer and whip at high speed until frothy.

2. Add the dry ingredients and approximately 1 ounce (30 grams) of vinegar to the eggs; whip to combine.

3. While whipping at high speed, begin adding the oil very slowly until a emulsion forms.

4. Add the remaining oil in a slow, steady stream. Occasionally thin the dressing by adding a little vinegar and lemon juice. Continue until all of the oil, vinegar and lemon juice have been incorporated.

5. Adjust the flavor and consistency.

6. Refrigerate until needed.

1. Whipping the whole eggs.

2. Adding the oil drop by drop to establish the emulsion.

3. The finished emulsified vinaigrette dressing.

PREPARATION METHODS

There are two types of **green salads**: tossed and composed. The more informal **tossed salad** is prepared by placing the greens, garnishes and dressing in a large bowl and tossing to combine. A **composed salad** usually has a more elegant look. It is prepared by arranging each of the ingredients on plates in an artistic fashion.

Other types of salads include **bound salads**, which are cooked meats, poultry, fish, shellfish, pasta or potatoes bound with a dressing, **vegetable salads** and **fruit salads**.

Green Salads

Tossed

Tossed salads are made from leafy vegetables such as lettuce, spinach, watercress, arugula or dandelion greens. They may consist only of greens and dressing or they can be garnished with fruits, vegetables, nuts or cheese. They can be dressed with many different types of dressings, from a light oil and vinegar to a hearty hot bacon. It is important that salad dressings be added at the last possible moment before service. Acidic dressings cause most greens to wilt and become soggy.

Matching Dressings and Salad Greens

There is a simple rule to follow when choosing dressings for salads: The more delicate the texture and flavor of the greens or other ingredients, the lighter and more subtle the dressing should be. Vinaigrette-based dressings are much lighter than mayonnaise-based or similar dressings and should be used with butterhead lettuces, mâche or other delicate greens. Crisp head lettuce like iceberg and hardy lettuce like romaine can stand up to heavier, mayonnaise-based or similar dressings.

TABLE 24.2	MATCHING DRESSINGS AND SALAD GREENS
Dressing	Greens
Vinaigrette dressing made with vegetable oil and red wine vinegar	Any greens: iceberg, romaine, leaf lettuce, butterhead lettuce, escarole, curly endive, Belgian endive, radicchio, baby lettuces, sorrel, arugula, dandelion
Vinaigrette dressing made with a nut oil and balsamic vinegar	Delicate greens: butterhead lettuce, bibb lettuce, Belgian endive, radicchio, baby lettuces, arugula, mâche, watercress
Emulsified vinaigrette dressing	Any greens: romaine, leaf lettuce, butterhead lettuce, escarole, curly endive, Belgian endive, radicchio, baby lettuces, sorrel, arugula, watercress
Mayonnaise-based dressing such as blue cheese or green goddess	Hardy greens: iceberg, romaine, leaf lettuce, escarole, curly endive, sorrel, dandelion

Salad Garnishes

It is impossible to make a complete list of the garnishes that can be combined with salad greens for a tossed salad. A partial list includes:

+ Vegetables—nearly any vegetable—raw, blanched or fully cooked—cut into appropriate sizes and uniform shapes.
+ Fruits—citrus segments, apples or pears; dried fruits such as raisins, currants or apricots.
+ Meats, poultry, fish and shellfish—cooked meats and poultry sliced or diced neatly and uniformly; poached, grilled or cured fish, diced or flaked; small, whole cooked shellfish such as shrimp and scallops; lobster or crab sliced, diced or chopped.
+ Cheeses—grated hard cheeses such as Parmesan, Romano or Asiago; semi-hard cheese such as cheddar and Swiss, cut julienne or shredded.
+ Nuts—nearly any are appropriate, roasted, candied or smoked.
+ Croutons—assorted breads, seasoned in various ways and toasted.

PROCEDURE FOR MAKING TOSSED SALADS

1. Select greens with various colors, textures and flavors.
2. Carefully cut or tear, wash and dry the greens.
3. Prepare the garnishes as directed or desired.
4. Prepare the dressing.
5. Combine the greens, garnishes and dressing by tossing them together. Or toss the greens and garnishes and, using a spray bottle, spray the greens with the dressing.

◆◆◆

RECIPE 24.4

MESCLUN SALAD
WITH RASPBERRY VINAIGRETTE

Yield: 6 Servings

Baby lettuces, assorted	approx. 8 heads	approx. 8 heads
Mâche	4 oz.	120 g
Fresh herbs	2 Tbsp.	30 ml.
Edible flowers	approx. 12	approx. 12
Raspberry Vinaigrette (Recipe 24.9)	4 oz.	120 g

1. Trim, wash and dry the baby lettuces and mâche.
2. Pick the fresh herbs from their stems. If using leafy herbs such as basil, they may be cut chiffonade or left as whole leaves.
3. If desired, pick the petals from the edible flowers. Small flowers may be left whole.
4. Place the lettuces and mâche in a bowl and add the herbs. Ladle the dressing over them and toss gently, using two spoons.
5. Transfer the salads to cold plates. Some of the larger leaves may be used as liners if desired.
6. Garnish each salad with flowers or flower petals.

1. A simple mesclun salad.

Composed

Composed green salads usually use a green as a base and are built by artistically arranging other ingredients on the plate. There are usually four components: the base, body, garnish and dressing.

The **base** is usually a layer of salad greens that line the plate on which the salad will be served. Depending upon the desired effect, the leaves can be cup-shaped or flat.

The **body** is the main ingredient. It can be lettuce or other greens, or another salad made from cooked or blended ingredients, such as chicken salad or fruit.

The **garnish** is added to the salad for color, texture and flavor. It can be as substantial as a grilled, sliced duck breast or as simple as a sprinkling of chopped herbs; it can be warm or cold. The choice is unlimited but whatever is used should always complement and balance the flavor of the body.

The salad **dressing** should complement rather than mask the other flavors in the salad. If the body already contains a dressing, such as a bound salad, additional dressing may not be necessary.

Composed green salads are usually dressed by ladling the dressing over the salad after it is plated. Alternatively, the individual ingredients can be dressed before they are arranged on the plate. A third method that may be limited by the intricacy of the salad but will save precious time during a busy period is to prepare individual salads on a sheet pan. Then, just before service, mist them with dressing using a spray bottle designated for this purpose, then transfer them to chilled plates using a spatula. This is illustrated below.

1. Misting salads while on a sheet pan and transferring to chilled plates for service.

Procedure for Making Composed Salads

1. Gather all ingredients for the salad and wash, trim, cut, cook, chill or otherwise prepare them as necessary or as called for in the recipe.

2. Arrange all ingredients artistically on the plates, dressing each ingredient as desired or as directed in the recipe.

3. At service time, heat or cook any items that are being served hot and add them to the salad.

◆◆◆

RECIPE 24.5
SALAD NIÇOISE

Yield: 6 Servings

Ingredient	US	Metric
Red wine vinegar	4 oz.	120 g
Salt and pepper	TT	TT
Virgin olive oil	12 oz.	360 g
Basil leaves, chiffonade	12	12
Chicory	1 head	1 head
Tomatoes	6	6
Cucumbers	1 lb. 8 oz.	680 g
Green beans	12 oz.	340 g
Eggs, hard-boiled	6	6
Artichokes	6	6
Romaine lettuce, large leaves, washed	12	12
Green bell peppers, batonnet	2	2
Tuna, fresh, grilled and chilled	1 lb. 8 oz.	680 g
Niçoise olives	4 oz.	120 g

1. Lining a cold salad plate with a base of lettuce leaves.

2. Arranging the remaining ingredients for the salad.

1. Make a vinaigrette dressing using the red wine vinegar, salt, pepper, olive oil and basil leaves.

2. Wash and dry the chicory.

3. Core and cut each tomato into 8 wedges.

4. Peel and slice the cucumbers.

5. Trim and cook the green beans al dente.

6. Peel the eggs and cut into wedges.

7. Cook the artichokes. Trim the outer leaves from each artichoke leaving only the heart. Remove the choke from the heart and cut each heart into quarters.

8. Line each cold plate with two romaine lettuce leaves, then arrange the remaining ingredients artistically. Use the contrasting shapes, colors and textures to create an attractive presentation.

9. At service, whisk the dressing to combine the ingredients and pour approximately 2-1/2 ounces (75 milliliters) over each salad.

Bound Salads

The creative chef can prepare a wide variety of salads by combining cooked meats, poultry, fish, shellfish, potatoes, pasta, grains and/or legumes with a dressing and garnishes. Although the combinations vary greatly, these salads are grouped together here because their ingredients are all bound. That is, each salad consists of one or more ingredients held together in a cohesive mass. The binding agent can be either a vinaigrette or mayonnaise-based or similar dressing. The ingredients should be evenly distributed throughout, and the degree of cohesiveness can range from tightly packed to flaky and easily separated.

The foods that can be used to produce bound salads are so varied that it is impossible to list them all. Generalizing preparation techniques is also very difficult. There are as many ways to prepare a bound salad as there are ingredients, dressings and garnishes.

Bound salads can be used as the body of a composed salad (for instance, a serving of egg salad on a bed of greens). Some are used in sandwiches but not ordinarily as side dishes—for example, tuna or chicken salad. Some are served as side dishes but not in sandwiches, for example, potato or pasta salad. Follow specific recipes and traditional uses for each salad until you are confident enough in your skills to let your imagination take over.

Guidelines for Making Bound Salads

1. Preparing a salad from cooked foods is a good opportunity to use left-overs, but be sure they are fresh and of good quality. The finished salad can only be as good as each of its ingredients.

2. When making a bound salad, choose ingredients whose flavors blend well and complement each other.

3. Choose ingredients for color; a few colorful ingredients will turn a plain salad into a spectacular one.

4. To improve appearance, cut all ingredients the same size and shape. If the main ingredient is diced, then dice the other ingredients. Avoid combining diced, sliced and julienned foods in the same salad.

5. All ingredients should be cut into pieces that are small enough to be eaten easily with a fork.

6. Be sure all meats, poultry, fish and shellfish are fully cooked before using them. Undercooked foods can cause food-borne illness and spoilage.

7. Always chill cooked ingredients well before using them. Warm ingredients promote bacterial growth, especially in mayonnaise-based salads.

8. Always use dressings sparingly. They should enhance the flavors of the other salad ingredients, not mask them.

━━━━━━━ ◆◆◆ ━━━━━━━

RECIPE 24.6

CHUTNEY CHICKEN SALAD

Yield: 8 lb. (3.6 kg)

Chicken meat, cooked	5 lb.	2.2 kg
Celery, small dice	8 oz.	250 g
Green onion, sliced	3 oz.	90 g
Mango chutney	12 oz.	340 g
Mayonnaise	1 lb.	500 g
Seedless grapes	12 oz.	340 g

1. Remove any bones, skin and fat from the chicken and cut the meat into large dice.

2. Combine the chicken meat, celery, green onions, mango chutney and mayonnaise in a bowl; mix well.

3. Cut the grapes in half. Add them to the chicken mixture and toss gently to combine.

Vegetable Salads

Vegetable salads are made from cooked or raw vegetables or a combination of both. They can be served on buffets, as an appetizer or salad course. As with other salads, vegetable salads must successfully combine color, texture and flavor. Some vegetable salads such as coleslaw and carrot-raisin salad are made with mayonnaise. Most, however, are made by either marinating the vegetables or combining them in a vinaigrette dressing.

Almost any vegetable can be successfully marinated. The amount of time depends on the vegetables and the marinade, but several hours to overnight is usually sufficient for flavors to blend. Soft vegetables such as mushrooms, zucchini and cucumbers can be added directly to a cold marinade. Hard vegetables such as carrots and cauliflower should be blanched in salted water, refreshed, drained and then added to a cold marinade. Carrots, artichokes, mushrooms, cauliflower, zucchini, pearl onions and the like are sometimes simmered quickly in a marinade flavored with lemon juice and olive oil, and then served cold. This style is called *à la grecque*.

Many marinated salads will last several days under proper refrigeration. As the salads age in the marinade they will change in appearance and texture. This may or may not be desirable. For example, mushrooms and artichokes become more flavorful, while green vegetables are discolored by the acids in the marinade. If marinated salads are prepared in advance, check their appearance as well as their seasonings carefully at service time.

PROCEDURE FOR PREPARING VEGETABLE SALADS

1. Gather and wash all vegetables.
2. Trim, cut, shred or otherwise prepare the vegetables as desired or as directed in the recipe.
3. Blanch or cook the vegetables if necessary.
4. Combine the vegetables with the marinade or dressing. Adjust the seasonings.

♦♦♦

RECIPE 24.7

TOMATO AND ASPARAGUS SALAD WITH FRESH MOZZARELLA

Yield: 6 Servings

Asparagus	2 lb.	1 kg
Vinaigrette Dressing (Recipe 24.1)	1 pt.	450 ml
Tomatoes	6	6
Leaf lettuce	1 head	1 head
Fresh mozzarella	12 oz.	340 g
Basil leaves	12	12

1. Trim and blanch the asparagus in salted water. Refresh, drain and marinate in 8 ounces (250 grams) of the vinaigrette dressing for approximately 15 minutes.
2. Remove the core and cut each tomato into six wedges.
3. Clean the lettuce and separate the leaves.
4. Slice the mozzarella into 18 slices.
5. Cut the basil leaves chiffonade.
6. Arrange the tomatoes, cheese and asparagus on plates using the lettuce as a base. Pour on the remaining dressing and garnish with the basil.

Fruit Salads

There are so many different fruits with beautiful bright colors and sweet delicious flavors that preparing fruit salads is easy work. Fruit salads are a refreshing addition to buffets and can be served as the first course of a lunch or dinner. A more elaborate fruit salad can be served as a light lunch.

Always prepare fruit salads as close to service time as possible. The flesh of many types of fruit becomes soft and translucent if cut long before service. Other fruits turn brown in a matter of minutes after cutting. Refer to Chapter 25, Fruits, for more information on this browning reaction and for information on specific fruits. Fruit salad recipes are found at the end of that chapter.

If a fruit salad is dressed at all, the dressing is usually sweet and made with honey or yogurt mixed with fruit juices or purées. Alternatively, Grand Marnier, crème de menthe or other liqueurs sprinkled over the salad can serve as a dressing. Fruit salads can be tossed or composed. Either should offer the consumer a pleasing blend of colors, shapes, sizes, flavors and textures.

Conclusion

A salad can be a small part of a meal or the entire meal. There are many styles of salads, and a seemingly endless variety of foods can be used to prepare them. Salads are extremely popular, especially with those interested in lighter dining alternatives. You can tempt these diners by determining the appropriate style of the salads and skillfully combining the main ingredients and dressing to achieve a delicious and appealing balance of colors, textures and flavors.

Questions for Discussion

1. Name several factors that will cause salad greens to wilt or deteriorate.
2. Describe the proper procedure for washing and drying lettuce.
3. Explain the difference between a vinaigrette and an emulsified vinaigrette dressing.
4. Describe the procedure for making mayonnaise. How can the flavor of a mayonnaise be altered?
5. Explain what happens to the ingredients when an emulsion "breaks." How can it sometimes be repaired?
6. Describe a typical bound salad. How does a bound salad differ from a dressed salad?
7. List five ways salads can be presented or offered on a menu.

Additional Salad Recipes

RECIPE 24.8

Seafood Salad

Note: *This dish appears in the Chapter Opening photograph.*

GOTHAM BAR AND GRILL, NEW YORK, NY
Chef/Owner Alfred Portale

Yield: 4 Servings

Lobster, 1 lb. 8 oz. (680 g)	1	1
Court bouillon	4 qt.	4 lt
Sea scallops	4 oz.	120 g
Squid, cleaned	3 oz.	90 g
Mussels, debearded	12	12
Avocado	1	1
Frisée	1 head	1 head
Baby red oak	1 head	1 head
Shallot, finely minced	2 Tbsp.	30 ml
Fresh basil, chopped	1 Tbsp.	15 ml
Fresh chives, finely minced	1 Tbsp.	15 ml
Fresh Italian parsley, chopped	1 Tbsp.	15 ml
Lemon Vinaigrette (recipe follows)	as needed	as needed
Salt and white pepper	TT	TT

1. Boil the lobster in the court bouillon, then chill it. Remove the meat from the shell; dice it.
2. Poach the sea scallops and squid in the same court bouillon. Cool and thinly slice each of them.
3. Steam the mussels in a portion of the court bouillon. Chill and remove the meat from the shells.
4. Peel, pit, quarter and thinly slice the ripe avocado.
5. Wash and dry the greens.
6. Toss the shellfish with the shallots, herbs and a portion of the vinaigrette. Dress the lettuces and avocado.
7. Season all with salt and white pepper. Arrange the lettuces, shellfish and fanned avocado on four plates.

LEMON VINAIGRETTE

Yield: 14 oz. (400 g)

Dijon-style mustard	1 tsp.	5 ml
Salt and white pepper	TT	TT
Red wine vinegar	1 oz.	30 g
Extra virgin olive oil	10 oz.	300 g
Lemon juice	2 oz.	60 g
Cayenne pepper	pinch	pinch

1. Whisk together the mustard, salt, white pepper and red wine vinegar. Slowly whisk in the olive oil.
2. Adjust the acidity with the lemon juice and add a pinch of cayenne.

◆◆◆

RECIPE 24.9
RASPBERRY VINAIGRETTE

Yield: 2 qt. (2 lt)

Red wine vinegar	8 oz.	250 g
Rice wine vinegar	8 oz.	250 g
Lemon juice	3 Tbsp.	45 ml
Dried thyme	1 Tbsp.	15 ml
Salt	1 Tbsp.	15 ml
Pepper	1 Tbsp.	15 ml
Garlic, minced	1 Tbsp.	15 ml
Honey	4 oz.	120 g
Raspberry preserves, without seeds	8 oz.	250 g
Olive oil	12 oz.	350 g
Salad oil	1 pt.	450 g

1. Whisk together the vinegars, lemon juice, thyme, salt, pepper and garlic.
2. Slowly whisk in the honey and raspberry preserves.
3. Whisk in the oils slowly, emulsifying the dressing.

◆◆◆

RECIPE 24.10
FAT-FREE
RASPBERRY VINAIGRETTE

Yield: 1 pt. (450 ml)

Raspberry vinegar	4 oz.	120 g
Fructose*	1 Tbsp.	15 ml
Garlic, minced	1 tsp.	5 ml
Worcestershire sauce	2 tsp.	10 ml
Dijon-style mustard	1 Tbsp.	15 ml
Lemon juice	2 oz.	30 g
Water	8 oz.	250 g
Salt and pepper	TT	TT

1. Whisk all ingredients together.

Nutritional values per 1-ounce (30-gram) serving:

Calories	8	Protein	0 g
Calories from fat	7 %	Vitamin A	1 Iu
Total fat	< 1 g	Vitamin C	2 mg
Saturated fat	0 g	Sodium	25 mg
Cholesterol	0 mg		

*Fructose is a naturally occurring simple sugar; it is readily available as a white granulated powder.

=== ◆◆◆ ===

RECIPE 24.11

THREE-PEPPERCORN CRANBERRY VINAIGRETTE

Yield: 1 qt. (1 lt)

White peppercorns	2 oz.	60 g
Red wine vinegar	2 oz.	60 g
Water	6 oz.	180 g
Sugar	7 oz.	220 g
Lemon juice	2 Tbsp.	30 ml
Cranberries	12 oz.	350 g
Orange zest	1 Tbsp.	15 ml
Green peppercorns	4 Tbsp.	60 ml
Pink peppercorns	4 Tbsp.	60 ml
Raspberry vinegar	6 oz.	180 g
Walnut oil	4 oz.	120 g
Salt and black pepper	TT	TT

1. Combine the white peppercorns and red wine vinegar with 2 ounces (60 grams) of water and bring to a simmer. Simmer 5 minutes, then transfer to a small container and allow to rest for at least one day.
2. Combine the sugar, remaining water and lemon juice. Cook until the sugar is completely dissolved and the mixture reaches a full boil.
3. Add the cranberries and orange zest and simmer 5 minutes.
4. Add the white peppercorn mixture, the green and pink peppercorns and simmer 1 minute. Remove from the heat and cool.
5. Add the rasberry vinegar and oil. Purée briefly in a blender or food processor. Season with salt and black pepper.

=== ◆◆◆ ===

RECIPE 24.12

RED ONION VINAIGRETTE

Yield: 1 pt. (450 g)

Walnut oil	8 oz.	250 g
Champagne vinegar	4 oz.	120 g
Sugar	1 Tbsp.	15 ml
Salt and pepper	TT	TT
Red onions, sliced thin	8 oz.	250 g

1. Whisk together the oil, vinegar, sugar, salt and pepper.
2. Blanch the onions for a few seconds in boiling water. Drain thoroughly.
3. Add the onions to the oil mixture and allow the dressing to rest for several hours so that the flavors blend.

=== ◆◆◆ ===

RECIPE 24.13

CAESAR DRESSING

Yield: 2 qt. (2 lt)

Garlic, chopped	1 Tbsp.	15 ml
Eggs	2	2
Parmesan cheese, grated	4 oz.	120 g
Balsamic vinegar	2 oz.	60 g

Red wine vinegar	2 oz.	60 g
Whole-grain mustard	1 Tbsp.	15 ml
Dijon-style mustard	1 Tbsp.	15 ml
Anchovy fillets	1 oz.	30 g
Salt	1 Tbsp.	15 ml
Pepper	1 tsp.	5 ml
Vegetable oil	12 oz.	340 g
Olive oil	12 oz.	340 g

1. Combine the garlic, eggs, cheese, vinegars, mustards, anchovies, salt and pepper in the bowl of a food processor and process until smooth, approximately 1 minute.
2. With the machine running slowly, begin adding the oils to form an emulsion.
3. Continue until all of the oil is incorporated.

❖❖❖

RECIPE 24.14

SAUCE GRIBICHE

Yield: 1 qt. (1 lt)

Hard-cooked egg yolks	4	4
Salt and pepper	TT	TT
Dijon-style mustard	1 Tbsp.	15 ml
Olive oil	1-1/2 pt.	700 ml
White wine vinegar	3 oz.	90 g
Cornichons, chopped	1 oz.	30 g
Capers, chopped	1 Tbsp.	15 ml
Fresh mixed herbs such as parsley, chervil, tarragon or chives, chopped	1 oz.	30 g

1. Blend the egg yolks with the salt, pepper and mustard.
2. Very slowly, as if for mayonnaise, whisk in the olive oil. Add a few drops of vinegar occasionally to thin the sauce.
3. Add the cornichons, capers and herbs; mix well. Adjust the seasonings and acidity with the remaining vinegar.

❖❖❖

RECIPE 24.15

THOUSAND ISLAND DRESSING

Yield: 1 qt. (1 lt)

Red wine vinegar	1 Tbsp.	15 ml
Sugar	1 Tbsp.	15 ml
Mayonnaise	1 pt.	450 ml
Ketchup	8 oz.	250 g
Sweet pickle relish	6 oz.	180 g
Hard-cooked eggs, chopped	4	4
Fresh parsley, chopped	2 Tbsp.	30 ml
Green onions, chopped	1 bunch	1 bunch
Salt and pepper	TT	TT
Worcestershire sauce	TT	TT

1. Combine the vinegar and sugar; stir to dissolve the sugar.
2. Add the remaining ingredients and mix well.
3. Adjust the seasonings with the salt, pepper and Worcestershire sauce.

◆◆◆

RECIPE 24.16
GREEN GODDESS DRESSING

Yield: 1 qt. (1 lt)

Fresh parsley	1 oz.	30 g
Mayonnaise	1 pt.	450 ml
Sour cream	12 oz.	340 g
Garlic, chopped	1 Tbsp.	15 ml
Anchovy fillets, minced	1 oz.	30 g
Fresh chives, chopped	1 oz.	30 g
Fresh tarragon, chopped	1 Tbsp.	15 ml
Lemon juice	1 oz.	30 g
Red wine vinegar	1 oz.	30 g
Salt and white pepper	TT	TT
Worcestershire sauce	TT	TT

1. Rinse and chop the parsley but do not dry it or you will remove some of the chlorophyll.

2. Combine all ingredients and mix well. Season to taste with salt, white pepper and Worcestershire sauce.

◆◆◆

RECIPE 24.17
ROQUEFORT DRESSING

Yield: 1 qt. (1 lt)

Mayonnaise	8 oz.	250 g
Red wine vinegar	1 oz.	30 g
Sour cream	8 oz.	250 g
Buttermilk	4 oz.	120 g
Garlic, chopped	1 tsp.	5 ml
Worcestershire sauce	1 tsp.	5 ml
Tabasco sauce	TT	TT
Pepper	TT	TT
Roquefort cheese, crumbled	12 oz.	340 g

1. Combine all ingredients except the Roquefort cheese; mix well.

2. Add the crumbled Roquefort cheese and combine.

◆◆◆

RECIPE 24.18
LOW-FAT BLUE CHEESE DRESSING

Yield: 1 qt. (1 lt)

Nonfat yogurt	20 oz.	560 g
Low-fat buttermilk	6 oz.	170 g
Blue cheese, crumbled	4 oz.	120 g
White pepper	1/4 tsp.	1 ml
Worcestershire sauce	TT	TT

Dry mustard	1 tsp.	5 ml
Tabasco sauce	TT	TT

1. Combine all ingredients in the bowl of a mixer or food processor. Process until smooth.

Nutritional values per 1-ounce (30-gram) serving:

Calories	25	Protein	2 g
Calories from fat	41 %	Vitamin A	29 Iu
Total fat	1 g	Vitamin C	0 mg
Saturated fat	1 g	Sodium	69 mg
Cholesterol	3 mg		

◆◆◆

RECIPE 24.19
TARTAR SAUCE

Yield: 1 pt. (500 ml)

Mayonnaise	1 pt.	500 ml
Capers, chopped	2 oz.	60 g
Sweet pickle relish	3 oz.	90 g
Onion, minced	2 Tbsp.	30 ml
Fresh parsley, minced	2 Tbsp.	30 ml
Lemon juice	1 Tbsp.	15 ml
Salt	TT	TT
Worcestershire sauce	TT	TT
Tabasco sauce	TT	TT

1. Stir all of the ingredients together until well blended. Chill thoroughly before serving.

◆◆◆

RECIPE 24.20
GARLIC CROUTONS FOR SALADS

Yield: 1 lb. 4 oz. (550 g)

Whole butter	6 oz.	180 g
Garlic, chopped	1 Tbsp.	15 ml
French or sourdough bread cubes	1 lb. 8 oz.	700 g
Parmesan cheese, grated	1 oz.	30 g
Dried basil	2 tsp.	10 ml
Dried oregano	2 tsp.	10 ml

1. Melt the butter in a small saucepan and add the garlic. Cook the garlic in the butter for 5 minutes.
2. Place the bread in a bowl, add the Parmesan cheese and herbs.
3. Pour the garlic butter over the bread cubes and immediately toss to combine.
4. Spread the bread cubes on a sheet pan in a single layer and bake at 350°F (180°C). Stir the croutons occasionally and cook until dry and lightly browned, approximately 15 minutes.

◆◆◆

RECIPE 24.21

WILTED SPINACH SALAD WITH ROASTED PEPPERS

GREENS RESTAURANT, SAN FRANCISCO, CA
Executive Chef Annie Somerville

Yield: 2 Large or 4 Small Servings

Red or yellow bell pepper, medium	1	1
Extra virgin olive oil	3 oz.	90 g
Salt and pepper	TT	TT
Red onion, sliced thin	2 oz.	60 g
Baguette, thin slices for croutons	12	12
Spinach	1 lb.	450 g
Frisée or escarole	1 head	1 head
Balsamic vinegar	3 Tbsp.	45 ml
Garlic clove, chopped fine	1	1
Niçoise or Gaeta olives, pitted	10	10
Parmesan cheese, grated	1 oz.	30 g

1. Roast, peel and cut the pepper into 1/4-inch (6-millimeter) strips. Toss the pepper strips with 1/2 tablespoon (8 milliliters) of olive oil and a few pinches of salt and pepper. Set aside to marinate.

2. Cover the onion slices with cold water to leach the strong onion flavor. Set aside.

3. Place the baguette slices on a baking sheet and brush them lightly with olive oil. Toast in a 375°F (190°C) oven until crisp and lightly browned, approximately 5 minutes.

4. Stem, wash and dry the spinach. Trim the stem end of the frisée or escarole and discard the tough outer leaves. Wash and dry.

5. Drain the onions. In a large bowl, combine the vinegar, garlic, 1/2 teaspoon (2 milliliters) salt and a few pinches of pepper. Add the greens, onions, peppers and olives.

6. Heat the remaining olive oil in a small pan until it is very hot and just below the smoking point. Immediately pour it over the salad and toss with a pair of metal tongs to coat and wilt the leaves. Sprinkle on the Parmesan cheese.

7. Add the croutons and serve immediately.

◆◆◆

RECIPE 24.22

WHITE ASPARAGUS MOUSSE WITH GARDEN-FRESH LETTUCES

ARIZONA BILTMORE, PHOENIX, AZ
Executive Chef Peter Hoefler

Yield: 10 Servings

White asparagus	8 oz.	250 g
Sugar	1 oz.	30 g
Béchamel sauce	3 oz.	90 g
Gelatin powder, added to		
1 oz. (30 g) cool water	1/2 oz.	15 g

Heavy cream	12 oz.	340 g
Sea salt and white pepper	TT	TT
Cayenne pepper	TT	TT
Lemon juice	1 Tbsp.	15 ml
Worcestershire sauce	TT	TT
Mâche	5 small bunches	5 small bunches
Frisée	5 small bunches	5 small bunches
Radicchio	5 small heads	5 small heads
Green oak leaf	5 small bunches	5 small bunches
Chervil sprigs	1/4 c.	60 ml
Chives, sliced	1/4 c.	60 ml
Fresh Italian parsley, leaves	1/4 c.	60 ml
Fresh dill sprigs	1/4 c.	60 ml
Basic vinaigrette	as needed	as needed
Crayfish, steamed	as needed for garnish	

1. Peel the asparagus. Depending on the stalk's toughness, trim approximately 1 inch (2.5 centimeters) from the end. Cook in boiling salted water with the sugar. Remove the asparagus when tender.

2. Combine the hot asparagus in a food processor with the béchamel. Add the softened gelatin and purée until smooth.

3. Pass through a sieve and cool slightly.

4. Whip the cream until stiff. Combine one third of the cream with the asparagus mixture. Season with salt, the peppers, lemon juice and Worcestershire sauce. Fold in the remaining cream. Refrigerate for 6 hours or overnight.

5. Dress the lettuces and herbs with the basic vinaigrette dressing and arrange on plates.

6. Form quenelles of asparagus mousse and place two on each lettuce-lined plate.

7. Garnish as desired with the steamed crayfish.

◆◆◆

RECIPE 24.23

ROSACE OF WARM SCALLOPS WITH NEW POTATO SALAD AND BLACK TRUFFLES

TAVERN ON THE GREEN, NEW YORK, NY
Chef Marc Poidevin

Yield: 6 Servings

Dressing:		
Sherry vinegar	4 oz.	120 g
Extra virgin olive oil	8 oz.	250 g
Truffle juice	1 Tbsp.	15 ml
Coarse salt and pepper	TT	TT
Salad:		
New potatoes, medium	6	6
Sea scallops, jumbo		
(about 4 oz./120 g each)	6	6
Olive oil	1 oz.	30 g
Black truffles	3 oz.	90 g

Continued

Red onion, sliced	2 oz.	60 g
Fresh chervil sprigs	as needed	as needed
Fresh chives, chopped	as needed	as needed

1. To make the dressing, combine the vinegar with the olive oil and truffle juice. Season to taste with salt and pepper.
2. Steam the potatoes until tender but still firm. Set aside.
3. Sauté the scallops in the olive oil until done. Set aside.
4. When the potatoes and scallops have cooled to room temperature, cut them into 1/4-inch (6-millimeter) slices.
5. Slice the truffles very thin.
6. Arrange the potatoes, scallops and truffles in circles on six individual plates. The items should overlap. Sprinkle with the red onion slices and the dressing. Garnish with the chervil and chives.

◆◆◆

RECIPE 24.24

SALAD OF AHI TUNA SEARED WITH LAVENDER AND PEPPER WITH WHOLE-GRAIN MUSTARD SAUCE

FETZER VINEYARDS, Hopland, CA
Culinary Director John Ash

Yield: 8 Servings, 3 oz. (90 g) tuna
and 1 oz. (30 g) greens each

Lavender-pepper coating:		
Coarse sea salt	1-1/2 tsp.	7 ml
Whole black peppercorns	2 tsp.	10 ml
Whole fennel seeds	2 tsp.	10 ml
White peppercorns	1 tsp.	5 ml
Dried lavender flowers	1-1/2 tsp.	7 ml
Ahi tuna, a solid 3-in.- (7.5-cm) -square piece, well trimmed	1 lb. 8 oz.	700 g
Olive oil	3 Tbsp.	45 ml
Mustard sauce:		
Whole-grain mustard	2 oz.	60 g
Olive oil	1 oz.	30 g
Mustard seeds, toasted	1 tsp.	5 ml
Rice wine vinegar	1 tsp.	5 ml
Sugar or honey	1 tsp.	5 ml
Baby greens	8 oz.	250 g

1. Using a mortar and pestle or a rolling pin, crush the ingredients for the lavender-pepper coating.
2. Lightly oil the tuna with 2 teaspoons (10 milliliters) of olive oil; coat lightly and evenly with the lavender-pepper mixture. Heat the remaining oil in a skillet to just smoking and quickly sear the tuna on all sides. This should not take more than 2 minutes. Immediately chill the seared tuna.
3. Mix the ingredients for the mustard sauce. Set aside.
4. To serve, thinly slice the tuna into 3 or 4 medallions per serving. Arrange on a chilled plate with baby greens and a small dollop of the mustard sauce.

✦✦✦

RECIPE 24.25
VINE-RIPENED TOMATO SALAD

GREENS RESTAURANT, SAN FRANCISCO, CA
Executive Chef Annie Somerville

Yield: 4 Servings

Vine-ripened tomatoes	1 lb.	450 g
Cherry tomatoes	1/2 pt.	250 ml
Mixed baby greens	4 heads	4 heads
Salt and pepper	TT	TT
Cucumber, sliced on bias	1	1
Extra virgin olive oil	3 Tbsp.	45 ml
Red wine vinegar	2 Tbsp.	30 ml

1. Core the vine-ripened tomatoes and cut into wedges or thick slices. Pluck the stems from the cherry tomatoes; leave whole if small or cut in half if large.
2. Wash the mixed baby greens and dry. Spread the greens on plates or a serving platter and arrange the vine-ripened tomatoes over them. Sprinkle the tomatoes with salt and pepper.
3. Garnish the tomatoes with cucumber slices.
4. Drizzle on the olive oil; follow with a light drizzle of vinegar.
5. Sprinkle the cherry tomatoes over the salad.

✦✦✦

RECIPE 24.26
COBB SALAD

Yield: 8 Entree Servings

Romaine lettuce	8 oz.	250 g
Green leaf lettuce	4 oz.	120 g
Watercress	4 oz.	120 g
Avocados	4	4
Bacon slices	16	16
Roquefort cheese, crumbled	1 lb.	450 g
Turkey breast, roasted, julienne	1 lb.	450 g
Tomato, concasse	1 lb.	450 g
Eggs, hard-cooked, chopped	4	4
Dijon mustard vinaigrette	24 oz.	700 ml

1. Tear, wash and dry the lettuces. Pick over and wash the watercress.
2. Pit, peel and cut the avocados into wedges.
3. Dice the bacon and cook in a sauté pan until crisp. Remove and drain well.
4. Toss the salad greens together and arrange each of the garnishes on top in an artistic fashion.
5. Prepare a simple vinaigrette dressing using Dijon mustard; serve on the side.

♦♦♦

RECIPE 24.27

GREEK SALAD

Yield: 3 lb. 8 oz. (1.6 kg)

Extra virgin olive oil	4 oz.	120 g
Lemon juice	2 oz.	60 g
Red wine vinegar	2 oz.	60 g
Garlic, minced	1 tsp.	10 ml
Fresh oregano, chopped	1 Tbsp.	30 ml
Cucumber	2	2
Feta cheese	12 oz.	350 g
Olives, kalamata or other Greek variety	1 lb.	450 g
Fresh parsley, chopped	1 oz.	30 g
Green onions, sliced	1 bunch	1 bunch
Pepper	TT	TT
Romaine lettuce	1 head	1 head
Anchovy fillets	8	8
Tomatoes, cut into 6 wedges	3	3

1. To make the dressing, whisk together the olive oil, lemon juice, vinegar, garlic and oregano.
2. Peel the cucumber and slice in half lengthwise. Remove the seeds and cut into batonnet.
3. Dice or crumble the feta cheese into small pieces.
4. Combine the olives, cucumbers, chopped parsley and green onions in a bowl and add the dressing. Toss to combine and season to taste with pepper.
5. Line plates or a platter with the romaine lettuce leaves. Add the olive-cucumber mixture and sprinkle on the feta cheese. Garnish as desired with the anchovies and tomato wedges.

♦♦♦

RECIPE 24.28

WARM LAMB SALAD
WITH BOURBON VINAIGRETTE

Yield: 4 Servings

Lamb loin, eye only	1	1
Salt and pepper	TT	TT
Olive oil	1 Tbsp.	15 ml
New potatoes	8	8
Green onions	4	4
Radicchio	2 heads	2 heads
Garlic cloves, chopped	2	2
Fresh rosemary, chopped	1/2 tsp.	2 ml
Whole butter	2 oz.	60 g
Bourbon	4 oz.	120 g
Balsamic vinegar	2 oz.	60 g
Mustard seeds	1 tsp.	5 ml
Orange supremes	24	24

1. Cut the lamb loin into 4 portions and tie each piece so it retains its shape during cooking.

2. Season the lamb with salt and pepper. Sauté it in the olive oil. Transfer to a 350°F (180°C) oven and finish to medium rare.

3. Steam the new potatoes until tender but still firm.

4. Cut the green onions on the bias.

5. Separate the radicchio leaves from the heads.

6. To make the dressing, sauté the garlic and rosemary in the butter without browning. Whisk in the bourbon, vinegar and mustard seeds, season with salt and pepper and keep hot.

7. Remove the twine and slice each portion of lamb into 6 slices. Slice the potatoes to the same thickness as the lamb.

8. Using the radicchio as the base, arrange the sliced potatoes, lamb and orange supremes on the plate. Sprinkle with the green onions. Drizzle the dressing over all the ingredients.

◆◆◆

RECIPE 24.29

ASIAN CHICKEN SALAD

Yield: 3 lb. (1.4 kg)

Rice vinegar	6 oz.	180 g
Soy sauce, reduced sodium	4 oz.	120 g
Sugar	2 Tbsp.	30 ml
Fresh ginger, minced	3 Tbsp.	45 ml
White pepper	1 tsp.	5 ml
Chicken breast, boneless, skinless	1 lb. 8 oz.	680 g
Sesame oil	1 oz.	30 g
Snow peas	4 oz.	120 g
Carrot, julienne	4 oz.	120 g
Celery, julienne	4 oz.	120 g
Jicama, julienne	4 oz.	120 g
Fresh cilantro leaves	2 Tbsp.	30 ml

1. Combine the vinegar, soy sauce, sugar, ginger and white pepper. Set aside.

2. Cut the chicken breast into strips approximately 1/2 × 1/2 × 3 inches (1.2 × 1.2 × 8 centimeters). Stir-fry the chicken in the sesame oil until done. Remove, cool and refrigerate.

3. Blanch the vegetables in salted water. Refresh and drain well.

4. Combine the chicken with the vegetables and the dressing; add the cilantro. Toss and serve.

Nutritional values per 4-ounce (120-gram) serving:

Calories	109	Protein	15g
Calories from fat	26%	Vitamin A	2714 IU
Total fat	3 g	Vitamin C	8 mg
Saturated fat	1 g	Sodium	577 mg
Cholesterol	33 mg		

RECIPE 24.30

NEW POTATO SALAD WITH MUSTARD AND DILL

Yield: 5 lb. (2.2 kg)

New potatoes	4 lb.	1.8 kg
Mayonnaise	4 oz.	120 g
Sour cream	4 oz.	120 g
Garlic, chopped	1-1/2 tsp.	7 ml
Salt	TT	TT
Black pepper	1-1/2 tsp.	7 ml
Fresh dill, chopped	2 Tbsp.	30 ml
Dijon-style mustard	2 Tbsp.	30 ml
Green bell pepper, julienne	1	1
Red bell pepper, julienne	1	1
Red onion, julienne	6 oz.	180 g
Celery, julienne	4 oz.	120 g

1. Boil the potatoes in salted water until done but still firm. Chill well and cut into quarters.
2. Combine the mayonnaise, sour cream, garlic, salt, pepper, dill and Dijon-style mustard; mix well.
3. Combine all ingredients and adjust the seasonings with salt and pepper.

RECIPE 24.31

POTATO SALAD

Yield: 6 lb. 8 oz. (3 kg)

Potatoes, chef	4 lb.	1.8 kg
Eggs, hard-cooked	6	6
Celery, medium dice	8 oz.	250 g
Green onions, sliced	1 bunch	1 bunch
Radishes, chopped coarse	6 oz.	180 g
Mayonnaise	1 lb.	450 g
Dijon-style mustard	2 oz.	60 g
Fresh parsley, chopped	1 oz.	30 g
Salt and pepper	TT	TT

1. Boil the potatoes in salted water until nearly cooked. Drain the potatoes, spread them on a sheet pan and refrigerate until cold.
2. Peel and cut the cold potatoes into large dice.
3. Peel and chop the eggs.
4. Combine all ingredients and adjust the seasonings with salt and pepper.

RECIPE 24.32

CREAMY COLESLAW

NOTE: *This dish appears in the Pork Chapter Opening photograph.*

Yield: 2 lb. (1 kg)

Mayonnaise	8 oz.	250 g
Sour cream or crème fraîche	4 oz.	120 g
Sugar	1 oz.	30 g
Cider vinegar	1 oz.	30 g
Garlic clove, minced	1	1
Green cabbage, shredded	1 lb.	450 g
Red cabbage, shredded	8 oz.	250 g
Carrot, shredded	4 oz.	120 g
Salt and white pepper	TT	TT

1. Combine the mayonnaise, sour cream or crème fraîche, sugar, vinegar and garlic in a bowl; whisk together.
2. Add the shredded cabbages and carrots to the dressing and mix well. Season to taste with salt and pepper.

RECIPE 24.33

COUSCOUS SALAD

Yield: 3 lb. (1.4 kg)

Couscous	6 oz.	180 g
Red bell pepper, medium dice	1	1
Green bell pepper, medium dice	1	1
Green onions, sliced on the bias	1 bunch	1 bunch
Cucumbers, peeled, seeded, medium dice	6 oz.	180 g
Black olives, pitted	4 oz.	120 g
Red onion, julienne	6 oz.	180 g
Dressing:		
Orange juice concentrate	3 oz.	90 g
Water	2 oz.	60 g
Rice vinegar	2 oz.	60 g
Garlic, chopped	1 tsp.	5 ml
Salt	1 tsp.	5 ml
Pepper	1 tsp.	5 ml
Fresh oregano, chopped	2 tsp.	10 ml
Salad oil	3 oz.	90 ml
Honey	1 oz.	30 g
Fresh thyme, chopped	2 tsp.	10 ml

1. Steam the couscous until tender; set aside to cool.
2. Combine the couscous with the vegetables.
3. Whisk together all dressing ingredients.
4. Combine the salad ingredients with the dressing. Chill thoroughly before serving.

CHAPTER 25 FRUITS

After studying this chapter you will be able to:

◆ identify a variety of fruits
◆ purchase fruits appropriate for your needs
◆ store fruits properly
◆ understand how fruits are preserved
◆ prepare fruits for cooking or service
◆ apply various cooking methods to fruits

otanically, a fruit is an organ that develops from the ovary of a flowering plant and contains one or more seeds. Culinarily, a fruit is the perfect snack food; the basis of a dessert, colorful sauce or soup; or an accompaniment to meat, fish, shellfish or poultry. No food group offers a greater variety of colors, flavors and textures than fruit.

This chapter identifies many of the fruits typically used by food service operations. It then addresses general considerations in purchasing fresh and preserved fruits. A discussion follows about some of the cooking methods presented in Chapter 9, Principles of Cooking, as they apply to fruits. Recipes in which a fruit is the primary ingredient are presented at the chapter's end.

IDENTIFYING FRUITS

This book presents fruits according to the ways most people view them and use them, rather than by rigid botanical classifications. Fruits are divided here into eight categories: berries, citrus, exotics, grapes, melons, pomes, stone fruits and tropicals, according to either their shape, seed structure or natural habitat. Botanically, tomatoes, beans, eggplant, capsicum peppers and other produce are fruits. But in ordinary thinking they are not; they are vegetables and are discussed in Chapter 22, Vegetables.

A fruit may have several names, varying from region to region or on a purveyor's whim. Botanists are also constantly reclassifying items to fit new findings. The names given here follow generally accepted custom and usage.

Berries

Berries are small, juicy fruits that grow on vines and bushes worldwide. Berries are characterized by thin skins and many tiny seeds that are often so small they go unnoticed. Some of the fruits classified here as berries do not fit the botanical definition (for example, raspberries and strawberries), while fruits that are berries botanically (for example, bananas and grapes) are classified elsewhere.

Berries may be eaten plain or used in everything from beer to bread, soup to sorbet. They make especially fine jams and compotes.

Berries must be fully **ripened** on the vine, as they will not ripen further after harvesting. Select berries that are plump and fully colored. Avoid juice-stained containers and berries with whitish-gray or black spots of mold. All berries should be refrigerated and used promptly. Do not wash berries until you are ready to use them, as washing removes some of their aroma and softens them.

Blackberries

Blackberries are similar to raspberries, but are larger and shinier, with a deep purple to black color. Thorny blackberry vines are readily found in the wild; commercial production is limited. Peak season is mid-June through August. Loganberries, ollalie berries and boysenberries are blackberry hybrids.

HYBRIDS AND VARIETIES

Several varieties of fruits are extremely responsive to selective breeding and crossbreeding and have been toyed with by botanists and growers since at least the time of ancient Rome. Two distinct products are recognized: hybrids and varieties. **Hybrids** result from crossbreeding fruits from different species that are genetically unalike. The result is a unique product. Citrus is particularly responsive to hybridization. **Varieties** result from breeding fruits of the same species that have different qualities or characteristics. Breeding two varieties of apples, for example, produces a third variety with the best qualities of both parents.

Ripe — *fully grown and developed; the fruit's flavor, texture and appearance are at their peak and the fruit is ready to use as food.*

Blackberries

Blueberries

Blueberries (Fr. *myrtilles*) are small and firm, with a true blue to almost black skin and a juicy, light gray-blue interior. Cultivated berries (high-bush varieties) tend to be larger than wild (low-bush) ones. Blueberries are native to North America and are grown commercially from Maine to Oregon and along the Atlantic seaboard. Peak season is short, from mid-June to mid-August.

Cranberries

Cranberries, another native North American food, are tart, firm fruit with a mottled red skin. They grow on low vines in cultivated bogs (swamps) throughout Massachusetts, Wisconsin and New Jersey. Rarely eaten raw, they are made into sauce or relish or are used in breads, pies or pastries. Cranberries are readily available frozen or made into a jelly-type sauce and canned. Although color does not indicate ripeness, cranberries should be picked over before cooking to remove those that are soft or bruised. Peak harvesting season is from Labor Day through October, leading to the association of cranberries with Thanksgiving dinner.

Currants

Currants are tiny, tart fruits that grow on shrubs in grapelike clusters. The most common are a beautiful, almost translucent red, but black and golden (or white) varieties also exist. All varieties are used for jams, jellies and sauces, and black currants are made into a liqueur, crème de cassis. Although rarely grown in the United States, currants are very popular and widely available in Europe, with a peak season during the late summer. (The dried fruits called currants are not produced from these berries; they are a special variety of dried grapes.)

Raspberries

Raspberries (Fr. *framboises*) are perhaps the most delicate of all fruits. They have a tart flavor and velvety texture. Red raspberries are the most common, with black, purple and golden berries available in some markets. When ripe, the berry pulls away easily from its white core, leaving the characteristic hollow center. Because they can be easily crushed and are susceptible to mold, most of the raspberries grown are marketed frozen. They grow on thorny vines in cool climates from Washington State to western New York and are imported from New Zealand and South America. The peak domestic season is from late May through November.

Strawberries

Strawberries (Fr. *fraises*) are brilliant red, heart-shaped fruits that grow on vines. Actually a perennial herb, the berry's flesh is covered by tiny black seeds called achenes, which are the plant's true fruits. Select berries with a good red color and intact green leafy hull. (The hulls can be easily removed with a paring knife.) Avoid berries with soft or brown spots. Huge berries may be lovely to look at but they often have hollow centers and little flavor or juice. Although available to some extent all year, fresh California strawberries are at their peak from April through June.

The tiny wild or Alpine berries, known by their French name *fraises des bois*, have a particularly intense flavor and aroma. They are not widely available in the United States.

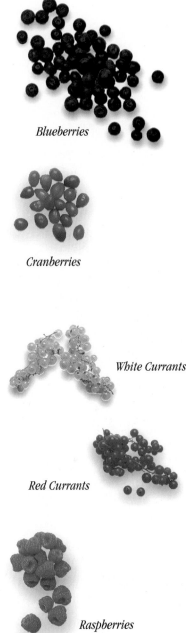

Blueberries

Cranberries

White Currants

Red Currants

Raspberries

Strawberries

Citrus (genus Citrus)

Citrus fruits include lemons, limes, grapefruits, tangerines, kumquats, oranges and several hybrids. They are characterized by a thick rind, most of which is a bitter white pith (albedo) with a thin exterior layer of colored skin known as the zest. Their flesh is segmented and juicy. Citrus fruits are acidic, with a strong aroma; their flavors vary from bitter to tart to sweet.

Citrus fruits grow on trees and shrubs in tropical and subtropical climates worldwide. All citrus fruits are fully ripened on the tree and will not ripen further after harvesting. They should be refrigerated for longest storage.

Select fruits that feel heavy and have thin, smooth skins. Avoid those with large blemishes or moist spots.

White Grapefruits

Kumquats

Lemons

Limes

Valencia Oranges

Grapefruits

Grapefruits (Fr. *pamplemousse*) are large and round with a yellow skin, thick rind and tart flesh. They are an 18th-century hybrid of the orange and pummelo (a large, coarse fruit used mostly in Middle and Far Eastern cuisines). Two varieties of grapefruit are widely available all year: white-fleshed and pink- or ruby-fleshed. White grapefruits produce the finest juice, although pink grapefruits are sweeter. Fresh grapefruits are best eaten raw or topped with brown sugar and lightly broiled. Grapefruit segments are available canned in syrup.

Ruby Grapefruits

Kumquats

Kumquats are very small, oval-shaped, orange-colored fruits with a soft, sweet skin and slightly bitter flesh. They can be eaten whole, either raw or preserved in syrup, and may be used in jams and preserves.

Lemons

The most commonly used citrus fruits, lemons (Fr. *citrons*), are oval-shaped, bright yellow fruits available all year. Their strongly acidic flavor makes them unpleasant to eat raw but perfect for flavoring desserts and confections. Lemon juice is also widely used in sauces, especially for fish, shellfish and poultry. Lemon zest is candied or used as garnish.

Limes

Limes (Fr. *limons*) are small fruits with thin skins ranging from yellow-green to dark green. Limes are too tart to eat raw and are often substituted for lemons in prepared dishes. They are also juiced or used in cocktails, curries or desserts. Lime zest can be grated and used to give color and flavor to a variety of dishes. Limes are available all year, with a peak season during the summer.

Oranges

Oranges are round fruits with a juicy, orange-colored flesh and a thin, orange skin. They can be either sweet or bitter.

Valencia oranges and navel oranges (a seedless variety) are the most popular sweet oranges. They can be juiced for beverages or sauces and the flesh may be eaten raw, added to salads, cooked in desserts or used as a garnish. The zest may be grated or julienned for sauces or garnish. Sweet oranges are available all year, with peak season from December to April. Blood oranges are also sweet but are small, with a rough, reddish skin. Their flesh is streaked with a blood-red color. Blood oranges are available primarily during the winter months and are eaten raw, juiced or used in salads or sauces. When selecting sweet oranges, look for fruits that feel plump and heavy, with unblemished skin. The color of the skin depends on weather conditions; a green rind does not affect the flavor of the flesh.

Bitter oranges include the Seville and bergamot. They are used primarily for the essential oils found in their zest. Oil of bergamot gives Earl Gray tea its distinctive flavor; oil of Seville is essential to curaçao, Grand Marnier and orange flower water. Seville oranges are also used in marmalades and sauces for meats and poultry.

Tangerines

Tangerines, sometimes referred to as mandarins, are small and dark orange. Their rind is loose and easily removed to reveal sweet, juicy, aromatic segments. Tangerines are most often eaten fresh and uncooked, but are available canned as mandarin oranges.

Tangelos are a hybrid of tangerines and grapefruits. They are the size of a medium orange; they have a bulbous stem end and few to no seeds.

Navel Oranges

Blood Oranges

Tangerines

PROCEDURE FOR SEGMENTING CITRUS FRUITS

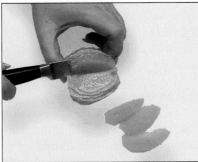

1. Citrus segments, known as *supremes*, are made by first carefully cutting off the entire peel (including the bitter white pith) in even slices.

2. Individual segments are then removed by gently cutting alongside each membrane.

PROCEDURE FOR ZESTING CITRUS FRUITS

1. A five-hole zester is used to remove paper-thin strips of the colored rind.

Procedure for Cutting Citrus Peels

1. Large strips of citrus zest may be used as a garnish or to flavor soups or sauces.

Exotics

Improved transportation has led to the increasing availability (although sporadic in some areas) of exotic or unusual fresh fruits such as figs, persimmons, pomegranates, prickly pears, rhubarb and star fruits. Other exotic fruits, such as breadfruit, lychee, guava, feijoa and loquat, are still only available on a limited basis from specialty purveyors and are not discussed here.

Figs

Figs (Fr. *figues*) are the fruit of ficus trees. They are small, soft, pear-shaped fruits with an intensely sweet flavor and rich, moist texture made crunchy by a multitude of tiny seeds. Fresh figs can be sliced and served in salads or with cured meats such as prosciutto. They can also be baked, poached or used in jams, preserves or compotes.

Dark-skinned figs, known as Mission figs, are a variety planted at Pacific Coast missions during the 18th century. They have a thin skin and small seeds and are available fresh, canned or dried. The white-skinned figs grown commercially include the White Adriatic, used principally for drying and baking, and the all-purpose Kadota. The most important domestic variety, however, is the Calimyrna. These large figs have a rich yellow color and large nutty seeds. Fresh Calimyrna figs are the finest for eating out of hand; they are also available dried.

For the best flavor, figs should be fully ripened on the tree. Unfortunately, fully ripened figs are very delicate and difficult to transport. Most figs are in season from June through October; fresh Calimyrna figs are only available during June.

Persimmons

Persimmons

Persimmons, sometimes referred to as kaki or Sharon fruits, are a bright orange, acorn-shaped fruit with a glossy skin and a large papery blossom. The flesh is bright orange and jellylike, with a mild but rich flavor similar to honey and plums. Persimmons should be peeled before use; any seeds should be discarded. Select bright orange fruits and refrigerate only after they are completely ripe. When ripe, persimmons will be very soft and the skin will have an almost translucent appearance.

Ripe persimmons are delicious eaten raw; halved and topped with cream or soft cheese; or peeled, sliced and added to fruit salads. Persimmon bread, muffins, cakes and pies are also popular. Underripe persimmons are almost inedible, however. They are strongly tannic with a chalky or cottony texture.

Persimmons are tree fruits grown in subtropical areas worldwide, although the Asian varieties—now grown in California—are the most common. Fresh persimmons are available from October through January.

Pomegranates

An ancient fruit native to Persia (now Iran), pomegranates have long been a subject of poetry and a symbol of fertility. Pomegranates are round, about the size of a large orange, with a pronounced calyx. The skin forms a hard shell with a pinkish-red color. The interior is filled with hundreds of small, red seeds (which are, botanically, the actual fruits) surrounded by juicy red pulp. An inedible yellow membrane separates the seeds into compartments. Pomegranates are sweet-sour and the seeds are pleasantly crunchy. The bright red seeds make an attractive garnish. Pomegranate juice is a popular beverage in Mediterranean cuisines and grenadine syrup is made from concentrated pomegranate juice.

Pomegranates

Select heavy fruits that are not rock-hard, cracked or heavily bruised. Whole pomegranates can be refrigerated for several weeks. Pomegranates are available from September through December, with peak season in October.

Prickly Pears

Prickly pear fruits, also known as cactus pears and barbary figs, are actually the berries of several varieties of cactus. They are barrel- or pear-shaped, about the size of a large egg. Their thick, firm skin is green or purple with small sharp pins and nearly invisible stinging fibers. Their flesh is spongy, sweet and a brilliant pink-red, dotted with small black seeds. Prickly pears have the aroma of watermelon and the flavor of sugar-water.

Prickly Pears

Once peeled, prickly pears can be diced and eaten raw, or they can be puréed for making jams, sauces, custards or sorbets, to which they give a vivid pink color. Prickly pears are especially common in Mexican and southwestern cuisines.

Select fruits that are full-colored, heavy and tender, but not too soft. Avoid those with mushy or bruised spots. Ripe prickly pears can be refrigerated for a week or more. Prickly pears are grown in Mexico and several southwestern states and are available from September through December.

PROCEDURE FOR PEELING PRICKLY PEARS

1. To avoid being stung by a prickly pear, hold it steady with a fork, then use a knife to cut off both ends.

2. Cut a lengthwise slit through the skin. Slip the tip of the knife into the cut and peel away the skin by holding it down while rolling the fruit away.

Rhubarb

Rhubarb

Although botanically a vegetable, rhubarb is most often prepared as a fruit. It is a perennial plant that grows well in temperate and cold climates. Only the pinkish-red stems are edible; the leaves contain high amounts of oxalic acid, which is toxic.

Rhubarb stems are extremely acidic, requiring large amounts of sugar to create the desired sweet-sour taste. Cinnamon, ginger, orange and strawberry are particularly compatible with rhubarb. It is excellent for pies, cobblers, preserves or stewing. Young, tender stalks of rhubarb do not need to be peeled. When cooked, rhubarb becomes very soft and turns a beautiful light pink color.

Fresh rhubarb is sold as whole stalks, with the leaves removed. Select crisp, unblemished stalks. Peak season is during the early spring, from February through May. Frozen rhubarb pieces are readily available and are excellent for pies, tarts or jams.

Star Fruits

Star fruits, also known as carambola, are oval, up to 5 inches (12.5 centimeters) long, with five prominent ribs or wings running their length. A cross-section cut is shaped like a star. The edible skin is a waxy orange-yellow; it covers a dry, paler yellow flesh. Its flavor is similar to plums, sweet but bland. Star fruits do not need to be peeled or seeded. They are most often sliced and added to fruit salad or used as a garnish. Unripe fruits can be cooked in stews or chutneys.

Star Fruit

Color and aroma are the best indicators of ripeness. The fruits should be a deep golden-yellow and there should be brown along the edge of the ribs. The aroma should be full and floral. Green fruits can be kept at room temperature to ripen, then refrigerated for up to two weeks. Star fruits are cultivated in Hawaii, Florida and California, though some are still imported from the Caribbean. Fresh fruits are available from August to February.

Grapes *(*Vitis vinifera*)*

Grapes are the single largest fruit crop in the world, due, of course, to their use in wine making. This section, however, discusses only table grapes, those grown for eating. Grapes are berries that grow on vines in large clusters. California is the world's largest producer, with more than a dozen varieties grown for table use. Grapes are classified by color as white (which are actually green) or black (which are actually red). White grapes are generally blander than black ones, with a thinner skin and firmer flesh.

The grape's color and most of its flavor are found in the skin. Grapes are usually eaten raw, either alone or in fruit salads. They are also used as a garnish or accompaniment to desserts and cheeses. Dried grapes are known as raisins (usually made from Thompson Seedless or muscat grapes), currants (made from Black Corinth grapes and labeled as Zante currants) or sultanas (made from sultana grapes).

Grapes are available all year because the many varieties have different harvesting schedules. Look for firm, unblemished fruits that are firmly attached to the stem. A surface bloom or dusty appearance is caused by yeasts and indicates recent harvesting. Wrinkled grapes or those with brown spots around the stem are past their prime. All grapes should be rinsed and drained prior to use.

◆◆◆

GRAPES INTO WINE

Virtually all the fine wine made in the world comes from varieties of a single grape species, *Vitis vinifera*. Although a European species, it is also grown in the United States, South Africa, South America, the Middle East, Australia and wherever fine wine is made. The variety of grapes used in any given wine determines the wine's character, and most wine-producing countries carefully regulate the growing areas and production of grapes.

American wines are known by their varietal names, whereas European wines are generally known by the vineyard's location. The major varietals of wine grapes and the wines in which they are used are listed below.

Grape Varietal	Wine
Pinot Noir	red Burgundy and champagne
Chardonnay	white Burgundy, Chablis and champagne
Syrah	Côte Rotie and Hermitage
Cabernet Sauvignon	Bordeaux and red Graves
Sauvignon Blanc	Sauterne, white Graves, fumé blanc and Sancerre
Merlot	Saint-Emilion and for blending with Cabernet Sauvignon
Zinfandel	red and white zinfandel (California claims a virtually monopoly)
Chenin Blanc	Vouvray

Red Flame Grapes

Red Flame Grapes

Red Flame grapes are a seedless California hybrid, second only in importance to the Thompson Seedless. Red Flame grapes are large and round with a slightly tart flavor and variegated red color.

Thompson Seedless Grapes

The most commercially important table grapes are a variety known as Thompson Seedless, which are pale green with a crisp texture and sweet flavor. Peak season is from June to November. Many are dried in the hot desert sun of California's San Joaquin Valley to produce dark raisins. For golden raisins, Thompson Seedless grapes are treated with sulfur dioxide to prevent browning, then dried mechanically.

Of the table grapes containing seeds, the most important varieties are the Concord, Ribier and Emperor. They range from light red to deep black in color, and all three are in season during the autumn. Concord grapes, one of the few grape varieties native to the New World, are especially important for making juices and jellies.

Thompson Seedless Grapes

Melons

Like pumpkins and cucumbers, melons are members of the gourd family (*Cucurbitaceae*). The dozens of melon varieties can be divided into two general types: sweet (or dessert) melons and watermelons. Sweet melons have a tan, green or yellow netted or farrowed rind and dense, fragrant flesh. Watermelon has a thick, dark green rind surrounding crisp, watery flesh.

Melons are almost 90% water, so cooking destroys their texture, quickly turning the flesh to mush. Most are served simply sliced, perhaps with a bit of lemon

Cantaloupes

or lime juice. Melons also blend well in fruit salads or with rich, cured meats such as prosciutto. Melons may be puréed and made into soups or sorbets.

Melons should be vine-ripened. A ripe melon should yield slightly and spring back when pressed at the blossom end (opposite the stem). It should also give off a strong aroma. Avoid melons that are very soft or feel damp at the stem end. Ripe melons may be stored in the refrigerator, although the flavor will be better at room temperature. Slightly underripe melons can be stored at room temperature to allow flavor and aroma to develop.

Cantaloupes

American cantaloupes, which are actually muskmelons, are sweet melons with a thick, yellow-green netted rind, a sweet, moist, orange flesh and a strong aroma. (European cantaloupes, which are not generally available in this country, are more craggy and furrowed in appearance.) As with all sweet melons, the many small seeds are found in a central cavity. Cantaloupes are excellent for eating alone and are especially good with ham or rich meats.

Avoid cantaloupes with the pronounced yellow color or moldy aroma that indicates overripeness. Mexican imports ensure a year-round supply, although their peak season is summer.

Casaba Melons

Casaba Melons

Casaba melons are a teardrop-shaped sweet melon. They have a coarse, yellow skin and a thick, ridged rind; their flesh is creamy white to yellow. Casaba melons are used like cantaloupes. Casaba melons do not have an aroma, so selection must be based on a deep skin color and the absence of dark or moist patches. Peak season is during September and October.

Crenshaw Melons

Crenshaw Melons

Crenshaw (or cranshaw) melons have a mottled, green-yellow ridged rind and orange-pink flesh. Crenshaws are large and pear-shaped, with a strong aroma. The flesh has a rich, spicy flavor and may be used like cantaloupe. Crenshaws are available from July through October, with peak season during August and September.

Honeydew Melons

Honeydew melons are large oval melons with a smooth rind that ranges from white to pale green. Although the flesh is generally pale green, with a mild, sweet flavor, pink- or gold-fleshed honeydews are also available.

Gold Honeydews

Green Honeydews

Like casaba melons, honeydew melons have no aroma. They are available almost all year, with peak season from June through October.

Santa Claus Melons

Santa Claus or Christmas melons are large, elongated melons with a green-and-yellow-striped, smooth rind. The flesh is creamy white or yellow and tastes like casaba. They are a winter variety, with peak availability during December, which explains the name.

Watermelons

Watermelons are large (up to 30 pounds or 13.5 kilograms) round or oval-shaped melons with a thick rind. The skin may be solid green, green-striped or mottled with white. The flesh is crisp and extremely juicy with small, hard, black seeds throughout. Seedless hybrids are available, although they are relatively expensive. Most watermelons have pink to red flesh, although golden-fleshed varieties are becoming more common.

Watermelons are of a different genus from the sweet melons described above. They are native to tropical Africa and are now grown commercially in Texas and several southern states.

Santa Claus Melons

Red Seedless Watermelon

Gold Watermelon

Pomes *(family* Rosaceae*)*

Pomes are tree fruits with thin skin and firm flesh surrounding a central core containing many small seeds called pips or carpels. Pomes include apples, pears and quince.

Apples

Apples (Fr. *pommes*), perhaps the most common and commonly appreciated of all fruits, grow on trees in temperate zones worldwide. They are popular because of their convenience, taste, variety and availability.

Rome   *Red Delicious*

Granny Smith   *Golden Delicious*

McIntosh

Apples can be eaten raw out of hand, or they can be used in a wide variety of cooked or baked dishes. They are equally useful in breads, desserts or vegetable dishes and go well with game, pork and poultry. Classic dishes prepared with apples are often referred to as *à la Normande*. Apple juice (cider) produces alcoholic and nonalcoholic beverages and cider vinegar.

Of the hundreds of known apple varieties, only 20 or so are commercially significant in the United States. Several varieties and their characteristics are noted in Table 25.1. Most have a moist, creamy white flesh with a thin skin of yellow, green or red. They range in flavor from very sweet to very tart, with an equally broad range of textures, from firm and crisp to soft and mealy.

In Europe, apples are divided into distinct cooking and eating varieties. Cooking varieties are those that disintegrate to a purée when cooked. American varieties are less rigidly classified. Nevertheless, not all apples are appropriate for all types of cooking. Those that retain their shape better during cooking are the best choices where slices or appearance are important. Varieties with a higher malic acid content break down easily, making them more appropriate for applesauce or juicing. Either type may be eaten out of hand, depending on personal preference.

Although not native to North America, apples are now grown commercially in 35 states, with Washington and New York leading in production. Apples are harvested when still sightly underripe, then stored in a controlled atmosphere (temperature and oxygen are greatly reduced) for extended periods until ready for sale. Modern storage techniques make fresh apples available all year, although peak season is during the autumn.

When selecting apples, look for smooth, unbroken skins and firm fruits, without soft spots or bruises. Badly bruised or rotting apples should be discarded immediately. They emit quantities of ethylene gas that speed spoilage of nearby fruits. (Remember the saying about "one bad apple spoils the barrel.") Store apples chilled for up to six weeks. Apple peels (the skin) may be eaten or removed as desired, but in either case, apples should be washed just prior to use to remove pesticides and any wax that was applied to improve appearance. Apple slices may be frozen (often with sugar or citric acid added to slow spoilage) or dried.

TABLE 25.1   APPLE VARIETIES

Variety	Skin Color	Flavor	Texture	Peak Season	Use
Golden Delicious	Glossy, greenish-gold	Sweet	Semifirm	Sept.– Oct.	In tarts; with cheese; in salads
Granny Smith	Bright green	Tart	Firm and crisp	Oct.– Nov.	Eating; in tarts
Jonathan	Brilliant red	Tart to acidic	Tender	Sept.– Oct.	Eating; all-purpose
McIntosh	Red with green background	Tart to acidic	Soft	Fall	Applesauce; in closed pies
Pippin (Newton)	Greenish-yellow	Tart	Semifirm	Fall	In pies; eating; baking
Red Delicious	Deep red	Sweet but bland	Soft to mealy	Sept.– Oct.	Eating
Rome	Red	Sweet-tart	Firm	Oct.– Nov.	Baking; pies; sauces
Winesap	Dark red with yellow streaks	Tangy	Crisp	Oct.– Nov.	Cider; all-purpose

PROCEDURE FOR CORING APPLES

1. Remove the core from a whole apple with an apple corer by inserting the corer from the stem end and pushing out the cylinder containing the core and seeds.

2. Alternatively, first cut an apple into quarters, then use a paring knife to cut away the core and seeds.

Pears

Pears (Fr. *poires*) are an ancient tree fruit grown in temperate areas throughout the world. Most of the pears marketed in this country are grown in California, Washington and Oregon.

Although literally thousands of pear varieties have been identified, only a dozen or so are commercially significant. Several varieties and their characteristics are noted in Table 25.2. Pear varieties vary widely in size, color and flavor. They are most often eaten out of hand, but can be baked or poached. Pears are delicious with cheese, especially blue cheeses, and can be used in fruit salads, compotes or preserves.

Asian pears, also known as Chinese pears or apple-pears, are of a different species than common pears. They have the moist, sweet flavor of a pear and the round shape and crisp texture of an apple. They are becoming increasingly popular in this country, particularly those known as Twentieth Century or Nijisseiki.

Anjou

Red d'Anjou

Bartlett

Bosc

Asian Pears

TABLE 25.2 PEAR VARIETIES

Variety	Appearance	Flavor	Texture	Peak Season	Use
Anjou (Beurre d'Anjou)	Greenish-yellow skin; egg-shaped with short neck; red variety also available	Sweet and juicy	Firm, keeps well	Oct.– May	Eating; poaching; baking
Bartlett (Williams)	Thin yellow skin; bell-shaped; red variety also available	Very sweet, buttery, juicy	Tender	Aug.– Dec.	Eating; canning; in salads
Bosc	Golden-brown skin; long, tapered neck	Buttery	Dry, holds its shape well	Sept.– May	Poaching; baking
Comice	Yellow-green skin; large and chubby	Sweet, juicy	Smooth	Oct.– Feb.	Eating
Seckel	Tiny; brown to yellow skin	Spicy	Very firm, grainy	Aug.– Dec.	Poaching; pickling

When selecting pears, look for fruits with smooth, unbroken skin and an intact stem. Pears will not ripen properly on the tree, so they are picked while still firm and should be allowed to soften before use. Underripe pears may be left at room temperature to ripen. A properly ripened pear should have a good fragrance and yield to gentle pressure at the stem end. Pears can be prepared or stored in the same way as apples.

Quince

Quince

Common quince (Fr. *coing*) resemble large, lumpy yellow pears. Their flesh is hard, with many pips or seeds, and they have a wonderful fragrance. Too astringent to eat raw, quince develop a sweet flavor and pink color when cooked with sugar. Quince are used in meat stews, jellies, marmalades and pies. They have a high **pectin** content and may be added to other fruit jams or preserves to encourage gelling.

Fresh quince, usually imported from South America or southeast Europe, are available from October through January. Select firm fruits with a good yellow color. Small blemishes may be cut away before cooking. Quince will keep for up to a month under refrigeration.

Pectin—*a carbohydrate obtained from certain fruits; used to thicken jams and jellies.*

Stone Fruits (genus Prunus)

Stone fruits, also known as drupes, include apricots, cherries, nectarines, peaches and plums. They are characterized by a thin skin, soft flesh and one woody stone or pit. Although most originated in China, the shrubs and trees producing stone fruits are now grown in temperate climates worldwide.

The domestic varieties of stone fruits are in season from late spring through summer. They tend to be fragile fruits, easily bruised, difficult to transport and with a short shelf life. Do not wash them until ready to use, as moisture can cause deterioration. Avoid ingesting the pits—most contain toxic acids. Stone fruits are excellent dried and are often used to make liqueurs or brandies.

Apricots

Apricots

Apricots (Fr. *abricots*) are small, round stone fruits with a velvety skin that varies in color from deep yellow to vivid orange. Their juicy orange flesh surrounds a dark, almond-shaped pit. Apricots can be eaten out of hand, poached, stewed, baked or candied. They are often used in fruit compotes or savory sauces for meat or poultry, and are also popular in quick breads, fruit tarts or puréed for dessert sauces, jams, custards or mousses.

Apricots enjoy a short season, peaking during June and July, and do not travel well. Select apricots that are well shaped, plump and fairly firm. Avoid ones that are greenish-yellow or mushy. Fresh apricots will last for several days under refrigeration, but the flavor is best at room temperature. If fresh fruits are unavailable, canned apricots are usually an acceptable substitute. Dried apricots and apricot juice (known as nectar) are readily available.

Cherries

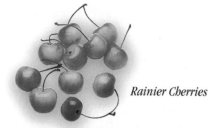

Rainier Cherries

From the northern states, particularly Washington, Oregon, Michigan and New York, come the two most important types of cherry: the sweet cherry and the sour (or tart) cherry.

Sweet cherries (Fr. *cerises*) are round to heart-shaped, about 1 inch (2.5 centimeters) in diameter, with skin that ranges in color from yellow to deep red to nearly black. The flesh, which is sweet and juicy, may vary from yellow to dark red. The most common and popular sweet cherries are the dark red Bings. Yellow-red Royal Ann and Rainier cherries are also available in some areas.

Sweet cherries are often marketed fresh, made into maraschino cherries or candied for use in baked goods. Fresh sweet cherries have a very short season, peaking during June and July. Cherries will not ripen further after harvesting. Select fruits that are firm and plump with a green stem still attached. There should not be any brown spots around the stem. A dry or brown stem indicates that the cherry is less than fresh. Once the stem is removed, the cherry will deteriorate rapidly. Store fresh cherries in the refrigerator and do not wash them until ready to use.

Sour cherries are light to dark red in color and are so acidic they are rarely eaten uncooked. The most common sour cherries are the Montmorency and Morello. Most sour cherries are canned or frozen, or cooked with sugar and starch (usually cornstarch or tapioca) and sold as prepared pastry and pie fillings.

Both sweet and sour varieties are available dried.

Bing Cherries

Procedure for Pitting Cherries

1. Remove the stem and place the cherry in the pitter with the indentation facing up. Squeeze the handles together to force out the pit.

Peaches and Nectarines

Peaches (Fr. *pêches*) are moderate-sized, round fruits with juicy, sweet flesh. Nectarines are a variety of peach, the main difference between the two being their skin. Peaches have a thin skin covered with fuzz, while nectarines have a thin, smooth skin. The flesh of either fruit ranges from white to pale orange. Although their flavors are somewhat different, they may be substituted for each other in most recipes.

Peaches and nectarines are excellent for eating out of hand or in dessert tarts or pastries. They are also used in jams, chutneys, preserves and savory relishes, having a particular affinity for Asian and Indian dishes. Although the skin is edible, peaches are generally peeled before being used. (Peaches are easily peeled if blanched first.)

Peaches and nectarines are either freestones or clingstones. With freestones, the flesh separates easily from the stone; freestone fruits are commonly eaten out of hand. The flesh of clingstones adheres firmly to the stone; they hold their shape better when cooked and are the type most often canned.

Select fruits with a good aroma, an overall creamy, yellow or yellow-orange color and an unwrinkled skin free of blemishes. Red patches are not an indication of ripeness; a green skin indicates that the fruit was picked too early and it will not ripen further. Peaches and nectarines will soften but do not become sweeter after harvesting.

Peaches

Nectarines

The United States, especially California, is the world's largest producer of peaches and nectarines. Peak season is through the summer months, with July and August producing the best crop. South American peaches are sometimes available from January to May. Canned and frozen peaches are readily available.

Plums

Plums (Fr. *prunes*) are round to oval-shaped fruits that grow on trees or bushes. Dozens of plum varieties are known, although only a few are commercially significant. Plums vary in size from very small to 3 inches (7.5 centimeters) in diameter. Their thin skin can be green, red, yellow or various shades of blue-purple.

Plums are excellent for eating out of hand. Plums can also be used in pies, cobblers or tarts, or be baked or poached; they are often used in jams or preserves, and fresh slices can be used in salads or compotes.

Santa Rosa Plums

Fresh plums are widely available from June through October, with a peak season in August and September. When selecting plums, look for plump, smooth fruits with unblemished skin. Generally, they should yield to gentle pressure, although the green and yellow varieties remain quite firm. Avoid plums with moist, brown spots near the stem. Plums may be left at room temperature to ripen, then stored in the refrigerator. Prunes, discussed below, are produced by drying special plum varieties, usually the French Agen.

Damson Plums

Tropicals

Tropical fruits are native to the world's hot, tropical or subtropical regions. Most are now readily available throughout the United States thanks to rapid transportation and distribution methods. All can be eaten fresh, without cooking. Their flavors complement each other and go well with rich or spicy meat, fish and poultry dishes.

Bananas

Common yellow bananas (Fr. *bananes*) are actually the berries of a large tropical herb. Grown in bunches called hands, they are about 7–9 inches (17.5–22.5 centimeters) long, with a sticky, soft, sweet flesh. Their inedible yellow skin is easily removed.

Properly ripened bananas are excellent eaten out of hand or used in salads. Lightly bruised or overripe fruits are best used for breads or muffins. Bananas blend well with other tropical fruits and citrus. Their unique flavor is also complemented by curry, cinnamon, ginger, honey and chocolate.

Common Yellow Bananas

Fresh bananas are available all year. Bananas are always harvested when still green, because the texture and flavor will be adversely affected if the fruits are allowed to turn yellow on the tree. Unripe bananas are hard, dry and starchy. Because bananas ripen after harvesting, it is acceptable to purchase green bananas if there is sufficient time for final ripening before use. Bananas should be left at room temperature to ripen. A properly ripened banana has a yellow peel with brown flecks. The tip should not have any remaining green coloring. As bananas continue to age, the peel darkens and the starches turn to sugar, giving the fruits a sweeter flavor. Avoid bananas that have large brown bruises or a gray cast (a sign of cold damage).

Plantains

Plantains, also referred to as cooking bananas, are larger but not as sweet as common bananas. They are frequently cooked as a starchy vegetable in tropical cuisines.

Dates

Dates are the fruit of the date palm tree, which has been cultivated since ancient times. Dates are about 1–2 inches (2.5–5 centimeters) long, with a paper-thin skin and a single grooved seed in the center. Most are golden to dark brown when ripe.

Medjool

Although dates appear to be dried, they are actually fresh fruits. They have a sticky-sweet, almost candied texture and rich flavor. Dates provide flavor and moisture for breads, muffins, cookies and tarts. They can also be served with fresh or dried fruits, or stuffed with meat or cheese as an appetizer.

Pitted dates are readily available in several packaged forms: whole, chopped or extruded (for use in baking). Whole unpitted dates are available in bulk. Date juice is also available for use as a natural sweetener, especially in baked goods. Although packaged or processed dates are available all year, peak season for fresh domestic dates is from October through December. When selecting dates, look for those that are plump, glossy and moist.

Kiwis

Kiwis, sometimes known as kiwifruits or Chinese gooseberries, are small oval fruits, about the size of a large egg, with a thin, fuzzy brown skin. The flesh is bright green with a white core surrounded by hundreds of tiny black seeds.

Kiwis

Kiwis are sweet, but somewhat bland. They are best used raw, peeled and eaten out of hand or sliced for fruit salads or garnish. Although kiwis are not recommended for cooking because heat causes them to fall apart, they are a perfect addition to glazed fruit tarts and can be puréed for sorbets, mousses or Bavarians. Kiwis contain an enzyme similar to that in fresh pineapple or papaya, which has a tenderizing effect on meat and prevents gelling.

◆◆◆

FRIEDA AND THE KIWIFRUIT

How did a fuzzy brown unknown become a media darling and a hugely viable crop? The answer is thanks to Frieda Caplan. In 1962 Frieda, founder of Frieda's Inc., launched her historical worldwide promotion of kiwifruit. Acting on a suggestion that Chinese gooseberries, then grown only in New Zealand, might sell better under the name kiwifruit (the kiwi is the national bird of New Zealand), Frieda unleashed a produce giant. This story of the kiwifruit is studied throughout the world as one of the great successes in food marketing.

In 1980, after 18 years of Frieda's continual, creative, aggressive and expensive marketing, the kiwifruit became a North American star when nouvelle cuisine chefs prominently featured it in their mixes of strawberry, banana, melon and pineapples. Since that time, the question asked most commonly of Frieda's Inc. is "What will be the next kiwifruit?"

The answer is that there will never be another kiwifruit. When the kiwifruit was accepted into the world's fruit vernacular, there was an unconditional paradigm shift. Today, new specialty produce does not have to go through the rigorous acceptance process inflicted on the kiwifruit. There can never be another kiwifruit because the marketing climate and consumer palate have shifted in a wonderful, irreversible way. Now when a new fruit like red bananas or yellow seedless watermelon comes onto the market, the consuming public does not react with fear and say "Bananas are supposed to be yellow" or "It really isn't watermelon if there aren't any seeds and it's not red." They respond with positive open minds (much the same as Frieda did when she purchased her first flat of kiwifruit in 1962) and a new-found knowledge that new foods will bring quality and variety, not discord, to their diets.

—KAREN CAPLAN
Frieda's eldest daughter and president of FRIEDA'S, INC.

Mangoes

Mangoes

Mangoes are oval or kidney-shaped fruits that normally weigh between 6 ounces and 1 pound (180–500 grams). Their skin is smooth and thin but tough, varying in color from yellow to orange-red, with patches of green, red or purple. As mangoes ripen, the green disappears. The juicy, bright orange flesh clings to a large, flat pit.

A mango's unique flavor is spicy-sweet, with an acidic tang. Mangoes can be puréed for use in drinks or sauces, or the flesh can be sliced or cubed for use in salads, pickles, chutneys or desserts. Mangoes go well with spicy foods such as curry and with barbecued meats.

Although Florida produces some mangoes, most of those available in this country are from Mexico. Peak season is from May through August. Select fruits with good color that are firm and free of blemishes. Ripe mangoes should have a good aroma, and should not be too soft or shriveled. Allow mangoes to ripen completely at room temperature, then refrigerate for up to one week.

PROCEDURE FOR PITTING AND CUTTING MANGOES

1. Cut along each side of the pit to remove two sections.

2. Each section can then be cubed using the "hedgehog" technique: Make crosswise cuts through the flesh, just to the skin; press up on the skin side of the section, exposing the cubes.

3. The mango may be served like this, or the cubes can be cut off to use in salads or other dishes.

Regular Papayas

Papain—*an enzyme found in papayas that breaks down proteins; used as the primary ingredient in many commercial meat tenderizers.*

Papayas

Papayas, also known as pawpaws, are greenish-yellow fruits shaped rather like large pears and weighing 1–2 pounds (500–1000 grams). When halved, they resemble a melon. The flesh is golden to reddish-pink; its center cavity is filled with round, silver-black seeds resembling caviar. Ripe papayas can be eaten raw, with only a squirt of lemon or lime juice. They can also be puréed for sweet or spicy sauces, chilled soups or sorbets.

Papayas contain **papain**, which breaks down proteins, and therefore papayas are an excellent meat tenderizer. Meats can be marinated with papaya juice or slices before cooking. Papain, however, makes fresh papayas unsuitable for use in gelatins because it inhibits gelling. Unripe (green) papayas are often used in pickles or chutneys, and can be baked or stewed with meat or poultry.

Papaya seeds are edible, with a peppery flavor and slight crunch. They are occasionally used to garnish fruit salads or add flavor to fruit salsas and compotes.

Papayas are grown in tropical and subtropical areas worldwide. Although available year round, peak season is from April through June. Select papayas that are plump, with a smooth, unblemished skin. Color is a better determinant of ripeness than is softness: The greater the proportion of yellow to green skin color, the riper the fruit. Papayas may be held at room temperature until completely ripe, then refrigerated for up to one week.

Red Papayas

Passion Fruits

Passion fruits (It. *granadillas*) have a firm, almost shell-like purple skin with orange-yellow pulp surrounding large, black, edible seeds. They are about the size and shape of large hen eggs, with a sweet, rich and unmistakable citrusy flavor. The pulp is used in custards, sauces and ice creams.

Select heavy fruits with dark, shriveled skin and a strong aroma. Allow them to ripen at room temperature, if necessary, then refrigerate. Passion fruits are in season only during February and March. Bottles or frozen packs of purée are readily available, however, and provide a strong, true flavor.

Passion Fruits

Pineapples

Pineapples (Fr. *ananas*) are the fruit of a shrub with sharp spear-shaped leaves. Each fruit is covered with rough, brown eyes, giving it the appearance of a pine cone. The pale yellow flesh, which is sweet and very juicy, surrounds a cylindrical woody core that is edible but too tough for most uses. Most pineapples weigh approximately 2 pounds (1 kilogram), but dwarf varieties are also available.

Pineapples are excellent eaten raw, alone or in salads. Slices can be baked or grilled to accompany pork or ham. The cuisines of Southeast Asia incorporate pineapple into various curries, soups and stews. Pineapple juice is a popular beverage, often used in punch or cocktails. Canned or cooked pineapple can be added to gelatin mixtures, but avoid using fresh pineapple, as an enzyme (bromelin) found in fresh pineapple breaks down gelatin.

Pineapples do not ripen after harvesting. They must be left on the stem until completely ripe, at which time they are extremely perishable. The vast majority of pineapples come from Hawaii. Fresh pineapples are available all year, with peak supplies in March through June. Select heavy fruits with a strong, sweet aroma and rich color. Avoid those with dried leaves or soft spots. Pineapples should be used as soon as possible after purchase. Pineapples are also available canned in slices, cubes or crushed, dried or candied.

Pineapples

Procedure for Trimming and Slicing Pineapples

1. Slice off the leaves and stem end. Stand the fruit upright and cut the peel off in vertical strips.

2. Cut the peeled fruit in quarters, then cut away the woody core.

3. The flesh can then be cut as desired.

Nutrition

Most fruits are quite nutritious. They have a high water content (usually 75% to 95%) and low protein and fat contents, all of which makes them low in calories. They are also an excellent source of fiber, and the sugar content of ripe fruits is a good source of energy. Some fruits, such as citrus, melons and strawberries, contain large amounts of vitamin C (which may be destroyed, however, by cooking or processing). Deep yellow and green fruits, such as apricots, mangoes and kiwis, are high in vitamin A; bananas, raisins and figs are a good source of potassium.

Purchasing Fresh Fruits

Fresh fruits have not been subjected to any processing (such as canning, freezing or drying). Fresh fruits may be ripe or unripe, depending on their condition when harvested or the conditions under which they have been stored. In order to use fresh fruits to their best advantage, it is important to make careful purchasing decisions. The size of each piece of fruit, its grade or quality, its ripeness on delivery and its nutritional content may affect your ability to use the fruit in an appropriate and cost-effective manner.

TABLE 25.3 NUTRITIONAL VALUES OF SELECTED FRUITS

Per serving, fresh, raw and/or as noted	Kcal	Protein (g)	Carbohydrates (g)	Fiber (g)	Total Fat (g)	Vitamin A (I.U.)	Vitamin C (mg)	Phosphorous (mg)	Potassium (mg)
Apple, 1 medium 2-3/4″ diameter, unpeeled	81	0.3	21.1	3	0.5	74	8	10	159
Banana, peeled 4 oz. (112 g)	104	1.2	26.4	2	0.4	59.4	6.4	14.2	290
Cantaloupe, 1/2 of 5″ diameter melon, approx. 7 oz. (210 g) of flesh	94	2.3	22.3	2.1	0.7	8608	113	45	825
Cherries, Bing, 10 medium, approx. 2.6 oz. (73 g)	49	0.8	11.3	1	0.7	146	5	13	152
Figs, 10 dried, approx. 6.6 oz. (185 g)	477	5.7	122.2	17.4	2.2	248	2	128	1332
Grapes, Thompson Seedless, 20, approx. 3.5 oz. (98 g)	72	0.6	17.8	0.8	0.6	72	10	12	186
Orange, navel, 1/2 medium, approx. 3.6 oz. (101 g)	35.6	0.8	8.9	0.3	<0.1	128	40	13.5	125
Pineapple, trimmed, 4 oz. (112 g)	56	0.4	14	1.2	0.4	25	17	8.5	125
Raisins, seedless, 4 oz. (112 g)	340	3.6	89.6	6	0.4	8	4	108	852
Strawberries, trimmed, 4 oz. (112 g)	36	0.8	8	2.5	0.4	28.7	60	19.8	175

The Corinne T. Netzer Encyclopedia of Food Values 1992

Grading

Fresh fruits traded on the wholesale market may be graded under the USDA's voluntary program. The grades, based on size and uniformity of shape, color and texture as well as the absence of defects, are: U.S. Fancy, U.S. No. 1, U.S. No. 2 and U.S. No. 3. Most fruits purchased for food service operations are U.S. Fancy. Fruits with lower grades are suitable for processing into sauces, jams, jellies or preserves.

Ripening

Several important changes take place in a fruit as it ripens. The fruit reaches its full size; its pulp or flesh becomes soft and tender; its color changes. In addition, the fruit's acid content declines, making it less tart, and its starch content converts into the sugars fructose and glucose that provide the fruit's sweetness, flavor and aroma.

Unfortunately, these changes do not stop when the fruit reaches its peak of ripeness. Rather, they continue, deteriorating the fruit's texture and flavor and eventually causing spoilage.

Depending upon the species, fresh fruits can be purchased either fully ripened or unripened. Figs and pineapples, for example, ripen only on the plant and are harvested at or just before their peak of ripeness then rushed to market. They should not be purchased unripened as they will never attain full flavor or texture after harvesting. On the other hand, some fruits, including bananas and pears, continue to ripen after harvesting and can be purchased unripened.

With most harvested fruits, the ripening time as well as the time during which the fruits remain at their peak of ripeness can be manipulated. For instance, ripening can be delayed by chilling. Chilling slows down the fruit's respiration rate (fruits, like animals, consume oxygen and expel carbon dioxide). The slower the respiration rate, the slower the conversion of starch to sugar. For quicker ripening, fruit can be stored at room temperature.

Ripening is also effected by ethylene gas, a colorless, odorless hydrocarbon gas. Ethylene gas is naturally emitted by ripening fruits and can be used to encourage further ripening in most fruits. Apples, tomatoes, melons and bananas give off the most ethylene and should be stored away from delicate fruits and vegetables, especially greens. Fruits that are picked and shipped unripened can be exposed to ethylene gas to induce ripening just before sale. Conversely, if you want to extend the life of ripe fruits a day or two, isolate them from other fruits and keep them well chilled.

Fresh fruits will not ripen further once they are cooked or processed. The cooking or processing method applied, however, may soften the fruits or add flavor.

Purchasing

Fresh fruits are sold by weight or by count. They are packed in containers referred to as crates, bushels, cartons, cases, lugs or flats. The weight or count packed in each of these containers varies depending on the type of fruit, the purveyor and the state in which the fruits were packed. For example, Texas citrus is packed in cartons equal to 7/10 of a bushel; Florida citrus is packed in cartons equal to 4/5 of a bushel. Sometimes fruit size must be specified when ordering. A 30-pound case of lemons, for example, may contain 96, 112 or 144 individual lemons, depending on their size.

Some fresh fruits, especially melons, pineapples, peaches and berries, are available trimmed, cleaned, peeled or cut. Sugar and preservatives are sometimes added. They are sold in bulk containers, sometimes packed in water. These items offer a consistent product with a significant reduction in labor costs. The purchase price may be greater than that for fresh fruits and flavor, freshness and nutritional qualities may suffer somewhat from the processing.

Purchasing and Storing Preserved Fruits

Preserving techniques are designed to extend the shelf life of fruits in essentially fresh form. These methods include irradiation, acidulation, canning, freezing and drying. Except for drying, these techniques do not substantially change the fruits' texture or flavor. Canning and freezing can also be used to preserve cooked fruits.

Preserves such as jellies and jams are cooked products and are discussed later in this chapter.

Irradiated Fruits

As described in Chapter 22, Vegetables, some fruits can be subjected to ionizing radiation to destroy parasites, insects and bacteria. The treatment also slows ripening without a noticeable effect on the fruits' flavor and texture. Irradiated fruits must be labeled "treated with radiation," "treated by irradiation" or with the symbol shown in Figure 22.1.

Acidulation

Apples, pears, bananas, peaches and other fruits turn brown when cut. Although this browning is commonly attributed to exposure to oxygen, it is actually caused by the reaction of enzymes.

Enzymatic browning can be retarded by immersing cut fruits in an acidic solution such as lemon or orange juice. This simple technique is sometimes referred to as **acidulation**. Soaking fruits in water or lemon juice and water (called acidulated water) is not recommended. Unless a sufficient amount of salt or sugar is added to the water, the fruits will just become mushy. But if enough salt or sugar is added, the flavor will be affected.

Canned Fruits

Almost any type of fruit can be canned successfully; pineapple and peaches are the largest sellers. In commercial canning, raw fruits are cleaned and placed in a sealed container, then subjected to high temperatures for a specific amount of time. Heating destroys the microorganisms that cause spoilage, and the sealed environment created by the can eliminates oxidation and retards decomposition. But the heat required by the canning process also softens the texture of most fruits. Canning has little or no effect on vitamins A, B, C and D because oxygen is not present during the heating process. Canning also has no practical effect on proteins, fats or carbohydrates.

In *solid pack* cans, little or no water is added. The only liquid is from the fruits' natural moisture. *Water pack* cans have water or fruit juice added, which must be taken into account when determining costs. *Syrup pack* fruits have a sugar syrup—light, medium or heavy—added. The syrup should also be taken into account when determining food costs, and the additional sweetness should be considered when using syrup-packed fruits. Cooked fruit products such as pie fillings are also available canned.

Canned fruits are purchased in cases of standard-size cans (see Appendix II). Canned fruits can be stored almost indefinitely at room temperature. Once a can is opened, any unused contents should be transferred to an appropriate storage container and refrigerated. Cans with bulges should be discarded immediately, without opening.

Frozen Fruits

Freezing is a highly effective method for preserving fruits. It severely inhibits the growth of microorganisms that cause fruits to spoil. Freezing does not destroy nutrients, although the appearance or texture of most fruits can be affected because of their high water content. This occurs when ice crystals formed from the water in the cells burst the cells' walls.

Many fruits, especially berries and apple and pear slices, are now individually quick frozen (IQF). This method employs blasts of cold air, refrigerated plates, liquid nitrogen, liquid air or other techniques to chill the produce quickly. By speeding the freezing process, the formation of ice crystals can be greatly reduced.

Fruits can be trimmed and sliced before freezing and are also available frozen in sugar syrup, which adds flavor and prevents browning. Berries are frozen whole, while stone fruits are usually peeled, pitted and sliced. Fruit purées are also available frozen.

Frozen fruits are graded as U.S. Grade A (Fancy), U.S. Grade B (Choice or Extra Standard), or U.S. Grade C (Standard). The "U.S." indicates that a government inspector has graded the product, but packers may use grade names without an actual inspection if the contents meet the standards of the grade indicated.

IQF fruits can be purchased in bulk by the case. All frozen fruits should be sealed in moistureproof wrapping and kept at a constant temperature of 0°F (–18°C) or below. Temperature fluctuations can cause freezer burn.

Dried Fruits

Drying is the oldest-known technique for preserving fruits, having been used for 5000 years. When ripe fruits are dried they lose most of their moisture. This concentrates their flavors and sugars and dramatically extends shelf life. Although most fruits can be dried, plums (prunes), grapes (raisins, sultanas and currants), apricots and figs are the fruits most commonly dried. The drying method can be as simple as leaving ripe fruits in the sun to dry naturally or the more cost-efficient technique of passing fruits through a compartment of hot, dry air to quickly extract moisture.

Dried fruits actually retain from 16% to 25% residual moisture, which leaves them moist and soft. They are often treated with sulfur dioxide to prevent browning (oxidation) and to extend shelf life.

Dried fruits may be eaten out of hand; added to cereals or salads; baked in muffins, breads, pies or tarts; stewed for chutneys or compotes; or used as a stuffing for roasted meats or poultry. Before use, dried fruits may be softened by soaking them for a short time in a hot liquid such as water, wine, rum, brandy or other liquor. Some dried fruits should be simmered in a small amount of water before use.

Store dried fruits in air-tight containers to prevent further moisture loss; keep in a dry, cool area away from sunlight. Dried fruits may mold if exposed to both air and high humidity.

Golden Raisins

Currants

Apricots

Apples

Persimmons

Pears

Kiwis

JUICING

Fruit juice is used as a beverage, alone or mixed with other ingredients, and as the liquid ingredient in other preparations. Juice can be extracted from fruits (and some vegetables) in two ways: pressure and blending.

Pressure is used to extract juice from fruits such as citrus that have a high water content. Pressure is applied by hand-squeezing or with a manual or electric reamer. All reamers work on the same principle: A ribbed cone is pressed against the fruit to break down its flesh and release the juice. Always strain juices to remove seeds, pulp or fibrous pieces.

A blender or an electric juice extractor can be used to liquify less juicy fruits and vegetables such as apples, carrots, tomatoes, beets and cabbage. The extractor pulverizes the fruit or vegetable, then separates and strains the liquid from the pulp with centrifugal action.

Interesting and delicious beverages can be made by combining the juice of one or more fruits or vegetables: Pineapple with orange, apple with cranberry, strawberry with tangerine and papaya with orange. Color should be considered when creating mixed-juice beverages, however. Some combinations can cause rather odd color changes. Although yellow and orange juices are not a problem, those containing red and blue flavonoid pigments (such as Concord grapes, cherries, strawberries, raspberries and blueberries) can create some unappetizing colors. Adding an acid such as lemon juice helps retain the correct red/blue hues.

Juice—*the liquid extracted from any fruit or vegetable.*

Nectar—*the diluted, sweetened juice of peaches, apricots, guavas, black currants or other fruits, the juice of which would be too thick or too tart to drink straight.*

Cider—*mildly fermented apple juice, although nonalcoholic apple juice may also be labeled cider.*

Applying Various Cooking Methods

Although most fruits are edible raw and typically served that way, some fruits can also be cooked. Commonly used cooking methods are broiling and grilling, baking, sautéing, deep-frying, poaching, simmering and preserving.

When cooking fruits, proper care and attention are critical. Even minimal cooking can render fruits overly soft or mushy. To combat this irreversible process, sugar can be added. When fruits are cooked with sugar, the sugar will be absorbed slowly into the cells, firming the fruits. Acids (notably lemon juice) also help fruits retain their structure. (Alkalis, such as baking soda, cause the cells to break down more quickly, reducing the fruits to mush.)

Determining Doneness

There are so many different fruits with such varied responses to cooking that no one standard for doneness is appropriate. Each item should be evaluated on a recipe-by-recipe basis. Generally, however, most cooked fruits are done when they are just tender when pierced with a fork or the tip of a paring knife. Simmered fruits, such a compotes, should be softer, cooked just to the point of disintegration.

You can avoid overcooking fruits by remembering that some carryover cooking will occur through the residual heat contained in the foods. Always rely on objective tests—sight, feel, taste and aroma—rather than the clock.

Dry-Heat Cooking Methods

Broiling and Grilling

Fruits are usually broiled or grilled just long enough to caramelize sugars. But cooking must be done quickly in order to avoid breaking down the fruits' structure. Good fruits to broil or grill are pineapples, apples, grapefruits, bananas, persimmons and peaches. The fruits may be cut into slices, chunks or halves as appropriate. A coating of sugar, honey or liqueur adds flavor, as do lemon juice, cinnamon and ginger.

When broiling fruits, use an oiled sheet pan or broiling platter. When grilling fruits, use a clean grill grate or thread the pieces onto skewers. Only thick fruit slices will need to be turned or rotated to heat fully. Broiled or grilled fruits can be served alone, as an accompaniment to meat, fish or poultry or as topping for ice creams or custards.

PROCEDURE FOR BROILING OR GRILLING FRUITS

1. Select ripe fruits and peel, core or slice as necessary.
2. Top with sugar or honey to add flavor and aid caramelization.
3. Place the fruits on the broiler platter, sheet pan or grill grate.
4. Broil or grill at high temperatures, turning as necessary to heat the fruits thoroughly but quickly.

♦♦♦

RECIPE 25.1

BROILED GRAPEFRUIT

Yield: 8 Servings

Ruby grapefruits	4	4
Sweet sherry	2 Tbsp.	30 ml
Brown sugar	4 Tbsp.	60 ml

1. Cut each grapefruit in half (perpendicular to the segments), then section with a sharp knife, carefully removing any visible seeds.
2. Sprinkle the grapefruit halves with the sherry and sugar.
3. Arrange on a baking sheet and place under a preheated broiler. Cook briefly, only until well heated and the sugar caramelizes. Serve immediately.

Baking

After washing, peeling, coring or pitting, most pomes, stone fruits and tropicals can be baked to create hot, flavorful desserts. Fruits with sturdy skins, particularly apples and pears, are excellent for baking alone as their skin (peel) holds in moisture and flavor. They can also be used as edible containers by filling the cavity left by coring with a variety of sweet or savory mixtures.

Combinations of fruits can also be baked successfully. Try mixing fruits for a balance of sweetness and tartness (for example, strawberries with rhubarb, apples with plums).

Several baked desserts are simply fruits (fresh, frozen or canned) topped with a crust (and called a *cobbler*), strudel (and called a *crumple* or *crisp*) or batter (and called a *buckle*). (See Recipe 29.17 Blackberry Cobbler.) Fruits, sometimes poached first, can also be baked in a wrapper of puff pastry, flaky dough or phyllo dough to produce an elegant dessert.

PROCEDURE FOR BAKING FRUITS

1. Select ripe but firm fruits and peel, core, pit or slice as necessary.
2. Add sugar or any flavorings.

3. Wrap the fruits in pastry dough if desired or directed in the recipe.

4. Place the fruits in a baking dish and bake uncovered in a moderate oven until tender or properly browned.

═══════════ ◆◆◆ ═══════════

RECIPE 25.2

BAKED APPLES

Yield: 8 Servings

Apples, Red or Golden Delicious	8	8
Raisins	6 oz.	170 g
Orange zest	1-1/2 Tbsp.	20 g
Brown sugar	4 oz.	120 g

1. Rinse and core each apple. The peels should be scored or partially removed to allow the pulp to expand without bursting the skin during baking.

2. Plump the raisins by soaking them in boiling water for 10 minutes. Drain the raisins thoroughly.

3. Combine the raisins, orange zest and brown sugar. Fill the cavity of each apple with this mixture.

4. Stand the apples in a shallow baking dish. Add enough water to measure about 1/2 inch (1.25 centimeters) deep.

5. Bake the apples at 375°F (190°C) for 15 minutes. Reduce the temperature to 300°F (150°C) and continue baking until the apples are tender but still hold their shape, approximately 1 hour. Occasionally baste the apples with liquid from the baking dish.

Sautéing

Fruits develop a rich, syrupy flavor when sautéd briefly in butter, sugar and, if desired, spices or liqueur. Cherries, bananas, apples, pears and pineapples are good choices. They should be peeled, cored and seeded as necessary and cut into uniform-size pieces before sautéing.

For dessert, fruits are sautéed with sugar to create a caramelized glaze or syrup. The fruits and syrup can be used to fill crêpes or to top spongecakes or ice creams. Liquor may be added and the mixture flamed (flambéed) in front of diners, as with Bananas Foster (Recipe 25.14).

For savory mixtures, onions, shallots or garlic are often added.

In both sweet and savory fruit sautés, the fat used should be the most appropriate for the finished product. Butter and bacon fat are typical choices.

PROCEDURE FOR SAUTÉING FRUITS

1. Peel, pit and core the fruits as necessary and cut into uniform-size pieces.

2. Melt the fat in a hot sauté pan.

3. Add the fruit pieces and any flavoring ingredients. Do not crowd the pan, as this will cause the fruit to stew in its own juices.

4. Cook quickly over high heat.

◆◆◆

RECIPE 25.3
SAVORY FRUIT
FOR ROAST PORK

Yield: 1 pt. (500 ml)

Onion, fine dice	6 oz.	170 g
Butter or bacon fat	1 oz.	30 g
Apricots	3	3
Apples (tart) or peaches, peeled	3	3
Granulated sugar	4 oz.	120 g
Hot paprika	TT	TT
Salt and white pepper	TT	TT

1. Sweat the onions in the butter or bacon fat without browning.
2. Slice the apricots and apples into thin, even pieces. Add the apples to the onions and cook for 1–2 minutes. Add the apricots.
3. Sprinkle the sugar over the fruits and cook, uncovered, over medium heat until tender. Season with paprika, salt and white pepper.
4. Serve warm as an accompaniment to roast pork.

Deep-Frying

Few fruits are suitable for deep-frying. Apples, bananas, pears, pineapples and firm peaches mixed in or coated with batter, however, produce fine results. These fruits should be peeled, cored, seeded and cut into evenly sized slices or chunks. They may also need to be dried with paper towels so that the batter or coating can adhere. The procedures for deep-frying are found in Chapter 21, Deep-Frying.

Moist-Heat Cooking Methods

Poaching

One of the more popular cooking methods for fruits is poaching. Poaching softens and tenderizes fruits and infuses them with additional flavors such as spices or wine. Poached fruits can be served hot or cold and used in tarts, pastries or as an accompaniment to meat or poultry dishes.

The poaching liquid can be water, wine, liquor or sugar syrup. (As noted above, sugar helps fruits keep their shape, although it takes longer to tenderize fruits poached in sugar syrup.) The low poaching temperature (185°F/85°C) allows fruits to soften gradually. The agitation created at higher temperatures would damage them.

Cooked fruits should be allowed to cool in the flavored poaching liquid or syrup. Most poaching liquids can be used repeatedly. If they contain sufficient sugar, they can be reduced to a sauce or glaze to accompany the poached fruits.

Procedure for Poaching Fruits

1. Peel, core and slice the fruits as necessary.
2. In a sufficiently deep, nonreactive saucepan, combine the poaching liquid (usually water or wine) with sugar, spices, citrus zest and other ingredients as desired or as directed in the recipe.
3. Submerge the fruits in the liquid. Place a circle of parchment paper over the fruits to help them stay submerged.
4. Place the saucepan on the stove top over a medium-high flame; bring to a boil.
5. As soon as the liquid boils, reduce the temperature. Simmer gently.
6. Poach until the fruits are tender enough for the tip of a small knife to be easily inserted. Cooking time depends on the type of fruit used, its ripeness and the cooking liquid.
7. Remove the saucepan from the stove top and allow the liquid and fruits to cool.
8. Remove the fruits from the liquid and then refrigerate. The liquid can be returned to the stove top and reduced until thick enough to use as a sauce or glaze or refrigerated for further use.

◆◆◆

RECIPE 25.4

PEARS POACHED IN RED WINE

NOTE: *This dish appears in the Chapter Opening photograph.*

SCOTTSDALE COMMUNITY COLLEGE, Scottsdale, AZ
Pastry Chef Sarah Labensky

Yield: 8 Servings

Ripe pears, Anjou or Bartlett	8	8
Zinfandel wine	52 oz.	1500 ml
Whole peppercorns	8–10	8–10
Vanilla bean	1	1
Granulated sugar	12 oz.	340 g
Fresh basil, chopped	1 oz.	30 g
Zest of one orange		

1. Peel and core the pears, leaving the stems intact.
2. Combine the remaining ingredients in a large nonreactive saucepan. Arrange the pears in the liquid in a single layer.
3. Place the pears on the stove top over a medium-high flame. Bring to just below a boil, then immediately reduce the heat and allow the liquid to simmer gently. Cover with a round of parchment paper if necessary to keep the pears submerged.
4. Continue poaching the pears until tender, approximately 1 to 1-1/2 hours. Remove the saucepan from the stove and allow the pears to cool in the liquid.
5. Remove the pears from the poaching liquid and return the liquid to the stove top. Reduce until the liquid is thick enough to coat the back of a spoon, then strain.
6. Serve the pears chilled or at room temperature in a pool of the reduced wine syrup.

Simmering

Simmering techniques are used to make stewed fruits and compotes. Fresh, frozen, canned and dried fruits can be simmered or stewed. As with any moist-heat cooking method, simmering softens and tenderizes fruits. The liquid used may be water, wine or the juices naturally found in the fruits. Sugar, honey and spices may be added as desired. Stewed or simmered fruits can be served hot or cold, as a first course, a dessert or an accompaniment to meat or poultry dishes.

PROCEDURE FOR SIMMERING FRUITS

1. Peel, core, pit and slice the fruits as necessary.
2. Bring the fruits and cooking liquid, if used, to a simmer. Cook until the fruit is tender.
3. Add sugar or other sweeteners as desired or as directed in the recipe.

◆◆◆

RECIPE 25.5

DRIED FRUIT COMPOTE

Yield: 2 lb. (1 kg)

Dried apricots	5 oz.	150 g
Prunes, pitted	5 oz.	150 g
Dried pears or apples	5 oz.	150 g
Dried peaches	5 oz.	150 g
Hot water	24 oz.	720 g
Cinnamon stick	1	1
Light corn syrup	12 oz.	340 g
Cointreau	2 oz.	60 g

1. Coarsely chop the fruits. Place the pieces in a nonreactive saucepan and add the water and cinnamon stick.
2. Bring the mixture to a simmer, cover and cook until tender, approximately 12–15 minutes.
3. Add the corn syrup and Cointreau. Simmer uncovered until thoroughly heated. Serve warm or refrigerate for longer storage.

Preserving

Concentrate—*also known as a fruit paste or compound, is a reduced fruit purée, without a gel structure, used as a flavoring.*

Jam—*a fruit gel made from fruit pulp and sugar.*

Jelly—*a fruit gel made from fruit juice and sugar.*

Marmalade—*a citrus jelly that also contains unpeeled slices of citrus fruit.*

Preserve—*a fruit gel that contains large pieces or whole fruits.*

Fresh fruits can be preserved with sugar if the fruit and sugar mixture is concentrated by evaporation to the point that microbial spoilage cannot occur. The added sugar also retards the growth of, but does not destroy, microorganisms.

Pectin, a substance present in varying amounts in all fruits, can cause cooked fruits to form a semisolid mass known as a **gel**. Fruits that are visually unattractive but otherwise of high quality can be made into gels, which are more commonly known as **jams**, **jellies**, **marmalades** and **preserves**.

The essential ingredients of a fruit gel are fruit, pectin, acid (usually lemon juice) and sugar. They must be carefully combined in the correct ratio for the gel to form. For fruits with a low pectin content (such as strawberries) to form gels, pectin must be added, either by adding a fruit with a high pectin content (for example, apples or quinces) or by adding packaged pectin.

PROCEDURE FOR MAKING FRUIT PRESERVES

1. Clean, peel, core, pit and cut the fruits as necessary.
2. Firm fruits should be simmered in water or juice until tender.
3. Add sugar and other flavorings to the fruits as desired or as directed in the recipe.
4. Simmer until the mixture thickens.

◆◆◆

RECIPE 25.6

QUINCE JAM

Yield: 1 qt. (1 lt)

Water	1 qt.	1 lt
Lemon juice	1 oz.	30 g
Fresh quince	3 lb.	1.3 kg
Granulated sugar	12 oz.	340 g
Vanilla bean	1/2	1/2

1. Combine the water and 1/2 ounce (15 grams) of lemon juice in a large, nonreactive saucepan.
2. Peel, quarter and core the quince. Cut each quarter into small cubes and add to the water.
3. Bring the water to a boil, reduce the heat, cover and simmer until the quince is tender, approximately 30 minutes.
4. Remove about half the quince with a slotted spoon and set aside. Purée the remaining quince and the cooking liquid.
5. Return the purée and the quince pieces to the saucepan and bring to a simmer. Add the remaining 1/2 ounce (15 grams) of lemon juice, the sugar and vanilla bean.
6. Simmer uncovered, stirring frequently, until the jam holds its shape, approximately 15 minutes. Remove from the heat and cool over an ice bath.

CONCLUSION

Fruits, whether fresh, frozen, canned or dried, are one of the most versatile and popular of foods. Fruits can be used uncooked or incorporated into a soup, salad, bread, meat dish or dessert. When selecting fresh fruits it is important to consider seasonal availability, storage conditions and ripeness. When using them, it is important that they be at their peak of ripeness for the best flavor, texture, aroma and appearance.

QUESTIONS FOR DISCUSSION

1. Define ripeness and explain why ripe fruits are most desirable. How does the ripening process affect the availability of some fruits?
2. Describe the proper storage conditions for most fruits. Which fruits emit ethylene gas and why is this a consideration when storing fruits?

3. Explain why some apple varieties are preferred for cooking, while other varieties are preferred for eating. Which variety is generally preferred for making applesauce?

4. Which types of fruits are best for dry-heat cooking methods? Explain your answer. Why is sugar usually added when cooking any type of fruit?

5. List and describe three ways to prepare fruits for extended storage.

Additional Fruit Recipes

RECIPE 25.7
Tropical Fruit with Passion Fruit Purée

CAMPTON PLACE RESTAURANT, KEMPINSKI HOTELS, San Francisco, CA
Executive Chef Jan Birnbaum

Yield: 6 Servings

Mangoes	2	2
Papayas	2	2
Brazilian red bananas	2	2
Fresh coconut	1	1
Lime	1	1
Cherimoya (optional)	1	1
Guavas	2	2
Pineapple, medium, trimmed	1/3	1/3
Passion fruit	12	12
Sugar	4 oz.	120 g
Honey	6 oz.	180 g

1. Trim, peel and slice or cut all of the fruit, except the passion fruit, into interesting shapes. Hold in the refrigerator for service.

2. Cut the passion fruit in half and scoop out the seeds and membrane into a nonreactive saucepan. Add any fleshy trimmings from the mango, papaya, guava and pineapple. Add the sugar and honey and cook to a sauce consistency. Strain and cool.

3. Ladle 1-1/2 ounces (45 grams) of the sauce onto a cold plate or bowl. Arrange the sliced fruit attractively on the sauce.

◆◆◆

RECIPE 25.8
Figs with Berries and Honey Mousse

GREENS RESTAURANT, San Francisco, CA
Executive Chef Annie Somerville

Yield: 4 Servings

Raspberries or blackberries	1 pt.	450 ml
Fresh figs such as Black Mission, Kadota or Calmyrna	1 pt.	450 ml
Honey	6 oz.	170 g
Egg yolks	4	4

| Salt | TT | TT |
| Heavy cream | 1 pt. | 450 g |

1. Pick through the berries, but do not rinse them because water will dilute their flavor.
2. Rinse the figs and cut them in half, leaving the stem attached.
3. To make the mousse, whisk the honey, yolks and salt together in a bowl over a pan of barely simmering water. Whisk the mixture continuously for 8 minutes. After 5 minutes, the mousse will begin to thicken and the texture will become creamy. Whisk vigorously until the mousse leaves thick ribbons on its surface when poured over itself. Set aside to cool. The texture of the cooled mousse will be stiff and sticky.
4. Whisk 2 tablespoons (30 milliliters) of cream into the mousse, working it until it loosens.
5. Whip the remaining cream until it is firm, fold it into the mousse until it is just incorporated, then whisk the two together. The texture will be light and creamy.
6. Loosely arrange the figs on a platter, sprinkle with the berries and serve with the mousse.

◆◆◆

RECIPE 25.9

PINEAPPLE PAPAYA SALSA

Yield: 2 qt. (2 lt)

Tomatoes	3	3
Pineapple, fresh	1	1
Papaya, fresh	1	1
Green onions, sliced	1 bunch	1 bunch
Fresh cilantro, chopped	1 bunch	1 bunch
Jalapeños, seeded, minced	2	2
Lemon juice	3 Tbsp.	45 ml
Garlic, chopped	1 tsp.	5 ml
Salt	2 tsp.	10 ml

1. Core and dice the tomatoes.
2. Peel and dice the pineapple.
3. Peel, seed and dice the papaya.
4. Combine all ingredients and chill well.

Nutritional values per 2-ounce (60-gram) portion:

Calories	43	Protein	1 g
Calories from fat	7 %	Vitamin A	474 Iu
Total fat	< 1 g	Vitamin C	28 mg
Saturated fat	0 g	Sodium	150 mg
Cholesterol	0 g		

◆◆◆

RECIPE 25.10

TROPICAL FRUIT SALAD WITH YOGURT DRESSING

Yield: 4 Small Salads

Mango, cut into 1/2-in. (12-mm) cubes	6 oz.	170 g
Pineapple, cut into 1/2-in. (12-mm) cubes	6 oz.	170 g
Papaya, cut into 1/2-in. (12-mm) cubes	4 oz.	120 g
Grapefruit segments	16	16
Pineapple or grapefruit juice	2 oz.	60 g
Plain, nonfat yogurt	4 oz.	120 g
Honey	2 Tbsp.	30 ml
Fresh lime juice	1 Tbsp.	15 ml
Butterhead lettuce, large leaves, separated and cleaned	4	4
Kiwi, peeled and sliced	1	1
Poppy seeds	1 tsp.	5 ml

1. Mix the mango, pineapple, papaya and grapefruit together with the pineapple or grapefruit juice.
2. To make the dressing, whisk the yogurt, honey and lime juice together.
3. Line the plates with the butterhead lettuce. Arrange the kiwi slices and the fruit salad over the lettuce.
4. Drizzle the dressing over the fruits and top with poppy seeds.

Nutritional values per serving:

Calories	187	Protein	5 g
Calories from fat	6 %	Vitamin A	3623 IU
Total fat	1 g	Vitamin C	109 mg
Saturated fat	0 g	Sodium	34 mg
Cholesterol	1 mg		

◆◆◆

RECIPE 25.11

GRATIN OF FRESH BERRIES WITH CRÈME FRAÎCHE

Yield: 1 Serving

Assorted fresh berries, such as raspberries, blueberries and blackberries	4 oz.	120 g
Crème fraîche	2 oz.	60 g
Orange liqueur	1 tsp.	5 ml
Brown sugar	1 Tbsp.	15 ml

1. Arrange the berries in an even layer in a shallow, heatproof serving dish.

2. Stir the crème fraîche and orange liqueur together. Spoon this mixture over the berries.

3. Sprinkle the brown sugar over the creme. Place under a broiler or salamander just until the sugar melts. Serve immediately.

◆◆◆

RECIPE 25.12
GRILLED FRUIT KEBABS

Yield: 8 Skewers

Cantaloupe	6 oz.	170 g
Honeydew melon	6 oz.	170 g
Pineapple	6 oz.	170 g
Strawberries	8	8
Brown sugar	2 oz.	60 g
Lime juice	4 oz.	120 g
Cinnamon, ground	1/4 tsp.	1 ml

1. Remove the rind and cut the melons and pineapple into 1-inch (2.5-centimeter) cubes. Hull the strawberries and leave whole.

2. To make the sugar glaze, combine the sugar, lime juice and cinnamon, stirring until the sugar dissolves.

3. Heat the grill and clean the grate thoroughly.

4. Thread the fruits onto kebab skewers, alternating colors for an attractive appearance.

5. Brush the fruits with the sugar glaze. Grill, rotating the skewers frequently to develop an evenly light brown surface.

6. Serve immediately as an appetizer, a garnish for ice cream or an accompaniment to rich meats such as pork or lamb.

◆◆◆

RECIPE 25.13
CHERRY CONFIT

Yield: 4 oz. (120 g)

Red onion, small dice	2 Tbsp.	30 ml
Whole butter	2 tsp.	10 ml
Dried cherries	3 oz.	90 g
Brandy	1 Tbsp.	15 ml
Port	1 Tbsp.	15 ml
Sherry vinegar	1/2 tsp.	3 ml

1. Sauté the onions in butter without coloring.

2. Add the cherries. Add the brandy and flambé.

3. Add the port and sherry vinegar; cook until almost dry. Serve warm or at room temperature with charcuterie items, or grilled or roasted meats.

✦✦✦

RECIPE 25.14

BANANAS FOSTER

Bananas Foster is an American classic, created in New Orleans during the 1950s and named for a local celebrity. It is usually prepared for customers tableside, using a portable burner known as a réchaud.

Yield: 1 Serving

Banana, medium	1	1
Unsalted butter	1/2 oz.	15 g
Brown sugar	1/2 oz.	15 g
Fresh orange juice	1 oz.	30 g
Dark rum	1/2 oz.	15 g
Brandy or crème de banana	1/2 oz.	15 g
Cinnamon	TT	TT
Vanilla ice cream	1 portion	1 portion

1. Peel the banana and cut in half lengthwise. Cut each half into three chunks and set aside.
2. Melt the butter in a sauté pan. Add the brown sugar and stir until the sugar melts.
3. Add the bananas and stir to coat them completely with the sauce. Cook until tender, approximately 1–2 minutes.
4. Stir in the orange juice. Add the rum and brandy, then flame the mixture. Sprinkle the cinnamon onto the bananas.
5. When the flames die, spoon the bananas and sauce over the ice cream and serve immediately.

✦✦✦

RECIPE 25.15

BANANA FRITTERS

Yield: 40 Fritters

Egg, beaten	1	1
Milk	8 oz.	250 g
Unsalted butter, melted	2 oz.	60 g
Vanilla extract	1 tsp.	5 ml
Orange zest, finely grated	2 Tbsp.	30 ml
Orange juice	2 oz.	60 g
Ripe banana, large	1	1
Pastry flour, sifted	12 oz.	340 g
Granulated sugar	4 oz.	120 g
Baking powder	1 Tbsp.	15 ml
Salt	1/2 tsp.	2 ml
Confectioner's sugar	as needed for garnish	

1. Whisk together the egg, milk, butter and vanilla. Add the orange zest and juice.
2. Peel and dice the banana and add to the egg mixture.
3. Sift together the flour, sugar, baking powder and salt. Gently stir in the banana-egg mixture to form a thick batter.

4. Heat deep-fryer oil to 350°F (180°C). Fry 1-tablespoon (15-milliliter) portions of the batter until the fritters are brown and crisp, approximately 5 minutes.

5. Drain on paper towels, dust with confectioner's sugar and serve hot.

◆◆◆

RECIPE 25.16

LEMON CURD

Yield: 1-1/2 qt. (1.5 lt)

Whole eggs	12	12
Egg yolks	4	4
Granulated sugar	2 lb.	900 g
Unsalted butter, cubed	1 lb.	450 g
Lemon zest	from 8 lemons	from 8 lemons
Fresh lemon juice	12 oz.	340 g

1. Whisk everything together in a large bowl.

2. Place the bowl over a pan of simmering water and cook, stirring frequently, until very thick, approximately 20–25 minutes.

3. Strain, cover and chill completely. Serve with scones or use as a filling for tartlets or layer cakes.

◆◆◆

RECIPE 25.17

BRAISED RHUBARB

Yield: 10 lb. (4.5 kg)

Tart green apples, peeled and cubed	2 lb. 8 oz.	1.1 kg
Rhubarb, IQF pieces	7 lb.	3.2 kg
Unsalted butter	4 oz.	120 g
Sweet white wine	8 oz.	250 g
Brown sugar	14 oz.	400 g
Vanilla extract	2 tsp.	10 ml
Cinnamon	1 Tbsp.	15 ml
Nutmeg	1/4 tsp.	1 ml
Orange juice	2 oz.	60 g
Salt	1/2 tsp.	2 ml

1. Sauté the apples and rhubarb in the butter until they begin to soften.

2. Add the wine and reduce by half. Add the remaining ingredients. Simmer until the rhubarb is very tender.

3. Serve at room temperature in prebaked pastry cups, topped with crème chantilly or serve warm over ice cream.

◆◆◆

RECIPE 25.18

BERRY COMPOTE

Yield: 1 pt. (450 ml)

Berries, fresh or frozen	1 pt.	500 ml
Granulated sugar	4 oz.	120 g
Oranges, juice and zest	2	2
Honey	3 oz.	90 g
Cinnamon stick	1	1
Brandy	3 Tbsp.	45 ml

1. Select an assortment of fresh or frozen berries—strawberries, blueberries, raspberries, blackberries and cherries can be used, depending on availability.
2. Place the fruits and sugar in a nonreactive saucepan. Add the juice of two oranges. Bring to a simmer over low heat; cook until the fruits are soft but still intact.
3. Strain the mixture, saving both the fruits and the liquid. Return the liquid to the saucepan. Add the finely grated zest from one orange, the honey, cinnamon and brandy.
4. Bring to a boil and reduce until the mixture thickens enough to coat the back of a spoon. Remove from the heat and cool to room temperature.
5. Gently stir the reserved fruits into the sauce, cover and chill.

◆◆◆

RECIPE 25.19

APPLESAUCE

Yield: 1 qt. (1 lt)

McIntosh apples	4 lb.	1.8 g
Granulated sugar	5 oz.	150 g
Lemon juice	1 Tbsp.	15 ml
Cinnamon sticks	2	2

1. Peel, core and quarter the apples. Place in a saucepan with just enough cold water to cover the bottom of the pan. Add the cinnamon sticks.
2. Bring to a simmer, cover and cook until the apples are tender, approximately 15 minutes.
3. Add the sugar and lemon juice. Simmer 10 minutes more.
4. Remove the cinnamon stick and press the apples through a food mill.

◆◆◆

RECIPE 25.20

FRESH CRANBERRY-ORANGE SAUCE

Yield: 3 qt. (3 lt)

Granulated sugar	1 lb.	450 g
Orange juice	4 oz.	120 g
Water	8 oz.	225 g
Fresh or frozen cranberries	1 lb. 8 oz.	700 g
Cinnamon stick	1	1
Orange liqueur	2 oz.	60 g

Orange zest, finely grated	2 Tbsp.	30 ml
Orange segments	20	20

1. Combine the sugar, juice and water in a nonreactive saucepan; bring to a boil.
2. Add the cranberries and cinnamon stick and simmer uncovered until the berries begin to burst, approximately 15 minutes. Skim off any foam that rises to the surface.
3. Add the orange liqueur and zest and simmer for another 5 minutes.
4. Remove from the heat and remove the cinnamon stick. Add the orange segments. Cool and refrigerate.

◆◆◆

RECIPE 25.21

MANGO CHUTNEY

Yield: 1-1/2 qt. (1-1/2 lt)

Mango, peeled and diced	2 lb.	900 g
Onion, fine dice	4 oz.	120 g
Garlic cloves, minced	2	2
Cider vinegar	8 oz.	250 g
Dark brown sugar	8 oz.	250 g
Golden raisins	2-1/2 oz.	75 g
Crystallized ginger	4 oz.	120 g
Salt	1/2 tsp.	2 ml
Cinnamon sticks	2	2
Red pepper flakes	1/2 tsp.	2 ml
Mustard seeds	1/2 tsp.	2 ml
Fresh ginger	1 tsp.	5 ml
Lime juice	1 oz.	30 g

1. Combine the mango, onion, garlic, vinegar and sugar in a large, heavy saucepan. Cook until the sugar dissolves.
2. Stir in the raisins, crystallized ginger, salt and spices. Simmer until the onions and raisins are very soft, approximately 45 minutes. Skim foam from the surface as necessary.
3. Stir in the lime juice and adjust the seasonings.
4. Remove from the heat and cool uncovered. The chutney will thicken somewhat as it cools but should be thinner than fruit preserves.

◆◆◆

RECIPE 25.22

SWEET ORANGE MARMALADE

Yield: 1-1/4 qt. (1-1/4 lt)

Lemon	1	1
Valencia oranges	4	4
Water	as needed	as needed
Granulated sugar	as needed	as needed

1. Cut the lemon and oranges in half lengthwise, then slice very thinly. Remove all seeds. Measure the volume of the fruits and then place them in

Continued

a nonreactive pan. Add 12 ounces (360 grams) of cold water for each cup of fruit and allow to soak several hours or overnight.

2. Place the fruits and water in a heavy saucepan and bring to a boil over medium-high heat. Allow to boil gently for 2 hours. Skin foam from the surface as necessary.

3. Remeasure the volume of fruit and liquid. Add 6 ounces (180 grams) of sugar for each cup of the boiled fruit and liquid. Return to the stove and boil until the temperature reaches 218°F (103°C), approximately 30 minutes. Remove from heat and cool uncovered.

PART FOUR
BAKING

Like cooking, learning to bake
fresh breads and to prepare both
classic and contemporary pastries
and desserts is not simply a mat-
ter of following written directions. You must understand the baking process as well as fundamental
techniques and procedures.

In order to provide you with a
thorough introduction to the skills
needed in a bakeshop, we focus on
preparing the types of breads and
desserts usually found in a small
retail shop or restaurant. Because this book is
not designed for large wholesale or commercial
bakeries, mixes, stabilizers and
mechanical preparation and shaping
skills are not included.

Part IV begins with a chapter on preparation
and ingredients, then presents chapters on quick
breads and yeast breads. We then shift to desserts
with chapters on pies, pastries and cookies
(including classic doughs such as puff pastry
and éclair paste), cakes and frostings (including
brownies), and creams, custards, frozen desserts and dessert sauces. Many of
the recipes found at the end of these chapters are assembled using components
from one or more other chapters.

Throughout this portion of the book, you will see the word formula used in
place of recipe. This is standard terminology in the industry.

CHAPTER 26

PRINCIPLES OF THE BAKESHOP

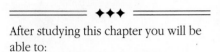

After studying this chapter you will be able to:

◆ recognize and select ingredients used in a bakeshop
◆ control the development of gluten
◆ cook sugar correctly
◆ understand the baking process
◆ recognize many of the specialized tools and equipment used in the bakeshop

lour, sugar, eggs, milk, butter, flavorings—with this simple list of ingredients you can produce an extremely wide variety of goods, from breads to sauces to pastries. But to produce consistently good brioche, Bavarians, biscuits or the like, you must pay careful attention to the character and quantity of each ingredient, the way the ingredients are combined and how heat is applied to them. Unlike a cut of meat that can be grilled, roasted, sautéed or braised and still be the same cut of meat, bakeshop products depend on careful, precise preparation for their very identity.

Accurate measurements are critical in the bakeshop. It is equally important to follow bakeshop formulas carefully and completely. Unlike the rest of the kitchen, mistakes in the bakeshop often cannot be discovered until the product is finished, by which time it is too late to correct them. For example, if you omit the salt when preparing a stew, the mistake can be corrected by adding salt at service time. If you omit the salt from a loaf of bread, however, the mistake cannot be corrected after the bread has baked—its texture and flavor will suffer as a result. It is more important to follow a written formula, measure ingredients precisely and combine them accurately in the bakeshop than anywhere else in the kitchen.

INGREDIENTS

While substituting ingredients may have little or no effect on some dishes (you can use carrots instead of turnips in a stew, for instance), this is not the case with baked goods. Different flours, fats, liquids and sweeteners function differently. Bread flour and cake flour are not the same, nor are shortening and butter. If you substitute one ingredient for another, the results will be different.

Understanding ingredients, why they function the way they do and how to adjust for their differences will make your baking experiences more successful and consistent. This chapter discusses flours, sugar and other sweeteners, fats, thickeners and flavorings such as chocolate, extracts and liquors. Eggs and dairy products, also common in baked goods, are discussed in Chapter 8, Eggs and Dairy Products.

Flours

Wheat Flour

The most frequently used—and therefore the most important—ingredient in the bakeshop is wheat flour (Fr. *farine*). Flour provides bulk and structure to baked goods.

Flour is produced by milling wheat kernels (berries). As discussed in Chapter 23, Potatoes, Grains and Pasta, a wheat kernel has an outer covering called bran. It is composed of several layers that protect the endosperm, which contains starches and proteins. The innermost part is the germ, which contains fat and serves as the wheat seed (see Figure 23.1). During milling, the kernels first pass through metal rollers to crack them, then the bran and germ are removed through repeated stages of sifting and separation. The remaining endosperm is then ground into flour. Flour derived from the portion of the endosperm closest to the germ is finer; flour derived from the portion of the endosperm nearer the bran is coarser and darker.

The character of the wheat determines the character of the flour. Wheats are classified as *soft* or *hard* depending on the kernel's hardness. The harder the wheat kernel, the higher its protein content. Soft wheat yields a soft flour with a low protein content. Soft flour, also called weak flour, is best for tender products such as cakes. Hard wheat yields a hard flour with a high protein content. Hard flour, also known as strong flour, is used for yeast breads.

Various types of flour are created by mixing or blending flours from different sources. **All-purpose flour**, a blend of hard and soft flours, is designed for use in a wide range of foods. It is also referred to throughout this book because it is readily available in quantities appropriate for small food service operations. Large bakeshops rarely use all-purpose flour; instead, they choose flours specifically milled and blended for industrial uses.

Aging and Bleaching

Any flour develops better baking qualities if allowed to rest for several weeks after milling. Freshly milled flour produces sticky doughs and products with less volume than those made with aged flour. While aging, flour turns white through a natural oxidation process referred to as bleaching.

Natural aging and bleaching are somewhat unpredictable, time-consuming processes, however, so chemicals are now used to do both. Potassium bromate or chlorine dioxide gas ages flour rapidly. Chlorine dioxide or other chemicals bleach flour by removing yellow pigments to obtain a uniform white color. Bleaching destroys small amounts of the flour's naturally occurring vitamin E, which is replaced in fortified or enriched products.

Composition of Flour

Flour is composed primarily of five nutrients: fat, minerals, moisture, starches and proteins. Fat and minerals each generally account for less than 1% of flour's content. The moisture content of flour is also relatively low—when packaged, it cannot exceed 15% under government standards. But its actual moisture content varies depending on climatic conditions and storage. In damp areas, flour absorbs moisture from the atmosphere.

Starches comprise 63% to 77% of flour, and are necessary for the absorption of moisture during baking. This process, known as **gelatinization**, occurs primarily at temperatures above 140°F (60°C). Starches also provide food for yeast during **fermentation**.

Flour proteins are important because of their gluten-forming potential. **Gluten** is the tough, rubbery substance created when wheat flour is mixed with water. Gluten strands are both plastic (i.e., they change shape under pressure) and elastic (they resume their original shape when that pressure is removed). Gluten is responsible for the volume, texture and appearance of baked goods. It provides structure and enables dough to retain the gases given off by leavening agents. Without gluten, there could be no raised breads: The gases created by yeast fermentation or chemical leaveners would simply escape if there were no network of gluten strands to trap them in the dough.

The higher a flour's protein content, the greater that flour's gluten-forming potential. The proteins responsible for gluten formation are *glutenin* and *gliadin*. Flour does not contain gluten; only a dough or batter can contain gluten. Gluten is produced when glutenin and gliadin are moistened and

TABLE 26.1   PROTEIN CONTENT OF FLOURS

Type of Flour	Percent Protein	Uses
Cake	7–9.5	Tender cakes
Pastry	7.5–12	Biscuits, pie crusts
All-Purpose	10–13	General baking
Bread	12–15	Yeast breads
Whole Wheat	13–14	Breads
High Gluten	41–42	To increase protein content of weaker flours for bread making

manipulated, as when they are stirred or kneaded. Generally, the longer a substance is mixed, the more gluten will develop. Products requiring a dough that can be kneaded and shaped, such as French rolls, require a flour with a higher protein content than products meant to be tender, such as cakes or muffins.

Table 26.1 lists the protein content and uses for several common flours. Remember that substitutions will result in a changed and probably less desirable product.

Specialty Flours

Whole Wheat

Whole wheat flour, also referred to as graham flour, is made by milling the entire wheat kernel, including the bran and germ. Whole wheat flour has a nutty, sweet flavor and brown, flecked color. Products made with whole wheat flour will be denser, with less volume than those made with white flour. Whole wheat flour has a reduced shelf life because fats in the germ can become rancid during storage.

Self-Rising

Self-rising flour is an all-purpose flour to which salt and a chemical leavener, usually baking powder, have been added. It is not recommended for professional use. Chemicals lose their leavening ability over time and may cause inconsistent results. Furthermore, different formulas call for different ratios of salt and leaveners; no commercial blend is appropriate for all purposes.

Nonwheat Flours

Nonwheat flours, also referred to as composite flours, are made from grains, seeds or beans. Corn, soybeans, rice, oats, buckwheat, potatoes and other items provide flours, but none of them contain the gluten-forming proteins of wheat flour. Composite flours are generally blended with a high-protein wheat flour for baking. Substituting a composite flour for wheat flour changes the flavor and texture of the product.

Rye flour is commonly used in bread baking. It is milled from the rye berry much like wheat flour is milled from the wheat berry. Rye flour comes in four grades or colors: white, medium, dark and pumpernickel. White rye flour is made from only the center of the rye berry. Medium and dark rye flours are made from the whole rye berry after the bran is removed. Pumpernickel is made by grinding the entire rye berry, including the bran. All rye flours have a warm, pungent flavor similar to caraway and a gray-brown color. Although

TABLE 26.2   NUTRITIONAL VALUES OF SELECTED FLOURS

Per 1-oz. (28-g) unit	Kcal	Protein (g)	Carbohydrates (g)	Fiber (g)	Total fat (g)
All-purpose flour	103	2.9	21.6	0.8	0.3
Bread flour	102	3.4	20.6	mq	0.5
Rye flour, dark	92	4	19.5	mq	0.8
Whole wheat flour	96	3.9	20.6	3.6	0.5

The Corinne T. Netzer Encyclopedia of Food Values 1992
mq = measurable quantity but data is unavailable

rye flour contains proteins, they will not form gluten, so a bread made with 100% rye flour will be dense and flat. Therefore, rye flour is usually blended with a high-protein wheat flour to produce a more acceptable product.

Nutrition

Flours are generally high in carbohydrates and low in fat. The grains from which they are milled are often rich in vitamins and minerals. Some of these nutrients, however, are lost during milling. In enriched flours, thiamin, riboflavin, niacin and iron are added at levels set by the government.

Purchasing and Storing

Most flours are purchased in 50- and 100-pound bags. They should be stored in a lit, ventilated room at temperatures no higher than 80°F (27°C). Flour can be stored in a refrigerator or freezer if necessary to prevent the onset of rancidity. Refrigeration may cause the flour to absorb moisture, however, which will limit the flour's ability to absorb additional moisture during actual use.

An open bag of flour should be transferred to a closed container to prevent contamination. Even unopened bags of flour should not be stored near items with strong odors, as flour readily absorbs odors.

Sugar and Sweeteners

Sugar (Fr. *sucre*) and other sweeteners serve several purposes in the bakeshop: They provide flavor and color, tenderize products by weakening gluten strands, provide food for yeasts, serve as a preservative and act as a creaming or foaming agent to assist with leavening.

Sugar

Sugars are carbohydrates. They are classified as either (1) single or simple sugars (monosaccharides) such as glucose and fructose, which occur naturally in honey and fruits, or (2) double or complex sugars (disaccharides) which may occur naturally, such as lactose in milk, or in refined sugars.

The sugar most often used in the kitchen is **sucrose**, a refined sugar obtained from both the large tropical grass called sugar cane (*saccharum officinarum*) and the root of the sugar beet (*beta vulgaris*). Sucrose is a disaccharide, composed of one molecule each of glucose and fructose. The chemical composition of beet and cane sugars is identical. The two products taste,

◆◆◆

SUGAR:
A SWEET AND SORDID PAST

Few foods have so murky an early history as sugar, now one of the most commonplace of foods. Neither botanists nor anthropologists know precisely where sugar cane first grew or when sugar was first extracted from it.

Nevertheless, there are records of a crude sugar being used as a sweetener in India over 2500 years ago. Sugar cane was being cultivated in the Middle East by the 6th century A.D. and spread from there to North Africa and Spain. Egyptians were manufacturing sugar commercially by the 10th century A.D.

Western Europeans first encountered sugar in the Middle East during the 12th-century Crusades. During the succeeding centuries, sugar remained a rare luxury in Europe. The small amounts available were traded by spice merchants and dispensed by apothecaries. At first sugar was used only as a medicine, a condiment or, occasionally, as a preservative. English cookbooks dating from the late 1300s illustrate an indiscriminate use of sugar as a condiment for meats, fish and vegetables. Like spices, sugar was used to mask the underlying flavor of foods past their prime.

When Columbus landed in the West Indies he found an environment perfectly suited for growing sugar cane, so he brought sugar cane cuttings to the New World on his second voyage in 1493. Huge sugar cane plantations soon flourished in the New World, built and worked by enslaved Africans and their descendants.

By the 18th century European and American middle classes were able to afford sugar by the pound. Sugar was now being used principally as a sweetener, particularly in connection with three other imports: coffee, tea and chocolate. Sugar, in fact, had become one of the principal components of a vast and complex trade network involving molasses from the West Indies, distilled rum from New England, finished goods from Europe and slaves from Africa.

Early sugars bore little resemblance to the white granulated substance we use today. Until vacuum pans and centrifuges were invented in the late 19th century, pure sugars were unobtainable. All contained varying amounts of molasses and other impurities. Most of the world's sugar was sold only in large, brown cones. The price of sugar depended on its whiteness and fineness, with the whitest sugar being the most costly.

After two centuries of prosperity, the sugar cane industry began to decline in the 19th century. Several factors contributed to this: abolition of slavery, discovery of alternative sweeteners and falling sugar prices.

If cane sugar was an ancient plant exploited in the New World, then beet sugar is a modern plant fully realized in the Old World. While the ability to refine a crude sweetener from root vegetables had been known for centuries, scientists and chefs mistakenly believed that sugar could be obtained only from plants grown in tropical heat. It was not until 1747 that a German chemist, Andreas Marggraf, proved otherwise. He isolated sucrose—the same substance produced from sugar cane—from white beets. His research, however, did not have a commercial application until cane sugar supplies were threatened. During the Napoleonic Wars, the British blockade of European ports cut off supplies of cane sugar. At Napoleon's urging, research into manufacturing beet sugar progressed. The first beet sugar factory was built in France in 1812. Soon France, Germany and Belgium were virtually self-sufficient in sugar production.

Consumers accepted this new sugar with few complaints; most were totally unaware of any difference. Today about 40% of the world's sugar is manufactured from beets, primarily in Russia, Germany and the United States.

look, smell and react the same. Sucrose is available in many forms: white granulated, light or dark brown granulated, molasses or powdered.

Sugar Manufacturing

Common **refined** or **table sugar** is produced from sugar cane or sugar beets. The first step in sugar production is to crush the cane or beet to extract the juice. This juice contains tannins, pigments, proteins and other undesirable components that must be removed through refinement. Refinement begins by dissolving the juice in water, then boiling it in large steam evaporators. The solution is then crystallized in heated vacuum pans. The uncrystallized liquid byproduct, known as **molasses**, is separated out in a centrifuge. The remaining crystallized product, known as **raw sugar**, contains many impurities; the USDA considers it unfit for direct use in food.

Raw sugar is washed with steam to remove some of the impurities. This yields a product known as **turbinado sugar**. Refining continues as the turbinado is heated, liquefied, centrifuged and filtered. Chemicals may be used to bleach and purify the liquid sugar. Finally, the clear liquid sugar is recrystallized in vacuum pans as **granulated white sugar**.

Pure sucrose is sold in granulated and powdered forms and is available in several grades. Because there are no government standards regulating grade labels, various manufacturers' products may differ slightly.

Turbinado Sugar

Turbinado sugar, sometimes called Demerara sugar, is the closest consumable product to raw sugar. It is partially refined, light brown in color, with coarse crystals and a caramel flavor. It is sometimes used in beverages and certain baked goods. Because of its high and variable moisture content, turbinado sugar is not recommended as a substitute for granulated or brown sugar.

Sanding Sugar

Sanding sugar has a large, coarse crystal structure that prevents it from dissolving easily. It is used almost exclusively for decorating cookies or pastries.

Regular Granulated Sugar

This is the all-purpose sugar used throughout the kitchen. The crystals are a fine, uniform size suitable for a variety of purposes.

Cube Sugar

Sugar cubes are formed by pressing moistened granulated sugar into molds and allowing it to dry. Cube sugar is most often used for beverage service.

Brown Sugar

Brown sugar is simply regular refined sugar with some of the molasses returned to it. Light brown sugar contains approximately 3.5% molasses; dark brown sugar contains about 6.5%. Molasses adds moisture and a distinctive flavor. Brown sugar can be substituted for refined sugar, measure for measure, in any formula where its flavor is desired. Because of the added moisture, brown sugar tends to lump, trapping air into pockets. It should be measured by weight or by packing it firmly into a cup to remove any air pockets. Always store brown sugar in an airtight container to prevent it from drying and hardening.

Clockwise from top left, Demerara sugar cubes, light brown sugar, powdered sugar, sugar cubes, brown sugar crystals, granulated sugar

Superfine or Castor Sugar

Superfine sugar is granulated sugar with a smaller-sized crystal. Also known as castor sugar, it can be produced by processing regular granulated sugar in a food processor for a few moments. Superfine sugar dissolves quickly in liquids and produces light and tender cakes.

Powdered or Confectioner's Sugar

Powdered sugar (Fr. *sucre en poudre*) is made by grinding granulated sugar crystals through varying degrees of fine screens. Powdered sugar cannot be made in a food processor. It is widely available in three degrees of fineness: 10X is the finest and most common; 6X and 4X are progressively coarser. Because of powdered sugar's tendency to lump, 3% cornstarch is added to absorb moisture. Powdered sugar is most often used in icings and glazes and for decorating baked products.

Liquid Sweeteners

Liquid sweeteners can be used to achieve the same benefits as sugar, except for leavening, in baked goods. Most of these liquids have a distinctive flavor as well as sweetness. Some liquid sweeteners are made from sugar cane; others are derived from other plants, grains or bees.

Corn Syrup

Corn syrup is produced by extracting starch from corn kernels and treating it with acid or an enzyme to develop a sweet syrup. This syrup is extremely thick or viscous and less sweet-tasting than honey or refined sugar. Its viscosity gives foods a thick, chewy texture. Corn syrup is available in light and dark forms; the dark syrup has caramel color and flavor added. Corn syrup is a **hygroscopic** (water-attracting) sweetener, which means it will attract water from the air on humid days and lose water through evaporation more slowly than granulated sugar. Thus, it keeps products moister and fresher longer.

Honey

Honey (Fr. *miel*) is a powerful sweetener composed of fructose and glucose. It is created by honey bees from nectar collected from flowers. Its flavor and color vary depending on the season, the type of flower the nectar came from and its age. Commercial honey is often a blend, prepared to be relatively neutral and consistent. Like corn syrup, honey is highly hygroscopic. Its distinctive flavor is found in several ethnic foods such as baklava and halvah, and beverages such as Drambuie and Benedictine.

Maple Syrup

Maple syrup is made from the sap of sugar maple trees. Sap is collected during the spring, then boiled to evaporate its water content, yielding a sweet brown syrup. One sugar maple tree produces about 12 gallons of sap each season; 30–40 gallons of sap will produce 1 gallon of syrup. Pure maple syrup must weigh not less than 11 pounds per gallon; it is graded according to color, flavor and sugar content. The more desirable products, Grades AA and A, have a light amber color and delicate flavor. Pure maple syrup is expensive, but it does add a distinct flavor to baked goods, frostings and, of course, pancakes and waffles.

Maple-flavored syrups, often served with pancakes, are usually corn syrups with artificial colorings and flavorings added.

Molasses

As mentioned earlier, molasses (Fr. *mélasse*) is the liquid byproduct of sugar refining. Edible molasses is only derived from cane sugar, as beet molasses has an unpleasant odor and bitter taste. *Unsulfured molasses* is not a true byproduct of sugar making. It is intentionally produced from pure cane syrup and is preferred because of its lighter color and milder flavor. *Sulfured molasses* is a byproduct and contains some of the sulfur dioxide used in secondary sugar processing. It is darker and has a strong, bitter flavor.

The final stage of sucrose refinement yields *blackstrap molasses*, which is somewhat popular in the American South. Blackstrap molasses is very dark and thick, with a strong, unique flavor that is unsuitable for most purposes.

Sorghum molasses is produced by cooking down the sweet sap of a brown corn plant, known as sorghum, which is grown for animal feed. The flavor and appearance of sorghum molasses are almost identical to unsulfured sugar cane molasses.

TABLE 26.3   NUTRITIONAL VALUES OF SELECTED SWEETENERS

Units as Noted	Kcal	Carbohydrates (g)	Sodium (mg)
Corn syrup, light, 2 Tbsp. (30 ml)	120	30	60
Honey, 2 Tbsp. (30 ml)	120	32	na
Molasses, unsulfured, 2 Tbsp. (30 ml)	140	34	56
Sugar, brown, light, 1 oz. (28 g)	106	27	1
Sugar, granulated, 1 oz. (28 g)	109	28	<1
Sugar, powdered, 1 oz. (28 g)	109	28	<1

The Corinne T. Netzer Encyclopedia of Food Values 1992

Nutrition

Sweeteners are carbohydrates. They are high in calories and contain no fiber, protein, fat, vitamin A or vitamin C. They contain only trace amounts of thiamin, riboflavin and niacin.

Cooking Sugar

Sugar can be incorporated into a prepared item in its dry form or first liquefied into a syrup. **Sugar syrups** (not to be confused with liquid sweeteners such as molasses) take two forms: **simple syrups**, which are mixtures of sugar and water, and **cooked syrups**, which are made of melted sugar cooked until it reaches a specific temperature. Be extremely careful when working with hot sugar syrup. Because sugar reaches very high temperatures it can cause severe burns.

Simple Sugar Syrups

Simple or stock syrups are solutions of sugar and water. They are used in the bakeshop to moisten cakes and to make sauces, fruit sorbets, buttercreams and candied fruits.

The syrup's density or concentration is dictated by its intended purpose. Cold water will dissolve up to double its weight in sugar; heating the solution forms denser, more concentrated syrups. A hydrometer, which measures specific gravity and shows degrees of concentration on the Baume scale, is the most accurate guide to density. See the photo to the right.

Simple syrups can be prepared without the aid of a hydrometer, however. To make a simple sugar syrup, specific amounts of water and sugar are combined in a saucepan and brought to a boil. Once the solution boils, it is important not to stir, as this may cause recrystallization or lumping. For successful simple sugar syrups, the following formulas must be followed precisely.

Using a Baume hydrometer.

+ Light syrup—Boil 2 parts water with 1 part sugar for 1 minute. This concentration would measure 17–20° on the Baume scale. A light syrup can be used for making sorbet or moistening spongecake.
+ Medium syrup—Boil 1 part sugar with 1-1/2 parts water for 1 minute. This concentration would measure 21–24° on the Baume scale. A medium syrup can be used for candying citrus peel.
+ Heavy syrup—Boil equal parts of water and sugar for 1 minute. This concentration would measure 28–30° on the Baume scale, and the solution should be at 220°F (104°C). Heavy syrup is a basic, all-purpose syrup kept on hand in many bakeshops.

Cooked Sugars

Caramel sauce, candy and other confections often need liquid sugar that will have a cooked caramel flavor or be firm when cool. For these purposes, sugar needs to be cooked to temperatures far higher than simple syrups. A small amount of water is generally added at the beginning to help the sugar dissolve evenly. As the mixture boils, the water evaporates, the solution's temperature rises and its density increases. The syrup's concentration depends on the amount of water remaining in the final solution: The less water, the harder the syrup will become when cool.

The sugar's temperature indicates its concentration. If there is a great deal of water present, the temperature will not rise much above 212°F (100°C). As water evaporates, however, the temperature will rise until it reaches 320°F (160°C), the point at which all water is evaporated. At temperatures above 320°F (160°C), the pure sugar begins to brown or caramelize (see the photo to the left). As sugar caramelizes, its sweetening power decreases dramatically. At approximately 375°F (190°C), sugar will burn, developing a bitter taste. If allowed to continue cooking, sugar will ignite.

Sugar solutions are unstable because of their molecular structure. They can recrystallize because of agitation or uneven heat distribution. Several steps should be taken to prevent recrystallization:

Caramelizing sugar.

1. Always use a heavy, clean saucepan, preferably copper.
2. Stir the solution to make sure all sugar crystals dissolve before it reaches a boil. Do not stir the solution after it begins boiling, however.
3. An interferent may be added when the solution begins to boil. Cream of tartar, vinegar, glucose (a monosaccharide) and lemon juice are known as **interferents** because they interfere with the formation of sugar crystals. Some formulas specify which interferent to use, although most are used in such small quantities that their taste cannot be detected.
4. Brush down the sides of the pan with cold water to wash off crystals that may be deposited there (see the photo below). These sugar crystals may seed the solution, causing more crystals (lumps) to form if not removed. Instead of using a brush to wash away crystals, you can cover the pan for a few moments as soon as the solution comes to a boil. Steam will condense on the cover and run down the sides of the pan, washing away the crystals.

Washing sugar crystals from the side of the pan.

The concentration of sugar syrup should be determined with a candy thermometer that measures very high temperatures. If a thermometer is not available, use the traditional but less accurate ice-water test: Spoon a few drops of the hot sugar into a bowl of very cold water. Check the hardness of the cooled sugar with your fingertips. Each stage of cooked sugar is named according to its firmness when cool—for example, soft ball or hard crack.

TABLE 26.4	STAGES OF COOKED SUGAR	
Stage	Temperature	Ice-Water Test
Thread	236°F (110°C)	Spins a 2-in. (5-cm) thread when dropped
Soft Ball	240°F (116°C)	Forms a soft ball
Firm Ball	246°F (119°C)	Forms a firm ball
Hard Ball	260°F (125°C)	Forms a hard, compact ball
Soft Crack	270°F (132°C)	Separates into a hard, but not brittle, thread
Hard Crack	300°F (149°C)	Separates into a hard, brittle sheet
Caramel	338°F (170°C)	Liquid turns brown

Soft Ball stage

Hard Ball stage

Hard Crack stage

Table 26.4 lists the various stages of cooked sugar and the temperature for each. Each stage is also identified by the ice-water test result. Note that even a few degrees makes a difference in the syrup's concentration.

Fats

Fat is the general term for butter, lard, shortening, oil and margarine. Fats provide flavor and color, add moisture and richness, assist with leavening, help extend a product's shelf life and shorten gluten strands.

The flavor and texture of a baked good depends on the type of fat used and the manner in which it is incorporated with other ingredients. In pastry doughs, solid fat shortens or tenderizes the gluten strands; in bread doughs, fat increases loaf volume and lightness; in cake batters, fat incorporates air bubbles and helps leaven the mixture. Fats should be selected based on their flavor, melting point and ability to form emulsions.

Most bakeshop ingredients combine completely with liquids; fats do not. Fats will not dissolve but will break down into smaller and smaller particles through mixing. With proper mixing, these fat particles are distributed, more or less evenly, throughout the other ingredients.

All-Purpose Shortening

Any fat is a shortening in baking because it shortens gluten strands and tenderizes the product. What is generally referred to as shortening, however, is a type of solid, white, generally tasteless fat, specially formulated for baking. Shortenings are made from animal fats and/or vegetable oils that are solidified through hydrogenation. These products are 100% fat with a relatively high melting point. Solid shortenings are ideal for greasing baking pans because they are tasteless and odorless.

Emulsified Shortening

Emulsifiers may be added to regular shortening to assist with moisture absorption and retention as well as leavening. Emulsified shortenings, also known as high-ratio shortenings, are used in the commercial production of cakes and frostings where the formula contains a large amount of sugar. If a formula calls for an emulsified shortening, use it. If you substitute any other fat, the product's texture suffers.

Lard

Lard (Fr. *saindoux*) is rendered pork fat. It is a solid white product of almost 100% pure fat; it contains only a small amount of water. Lard yields flaky, flavorful pastries, such as pie crusts, but is rarely used commercially because it turns rancid quickly.

Butter and Margarine

Butter is prized in the bakeshop for its flavor; however, it melts at a relatively low temperature of 93°F (33°C) and burns easily. Unsalted butter is preferred for baking because it tends to be fresher, and additional salt might interfere with product formulas. Margarine melts at a slightly higher temperature than butter, making it useful for some rolled-in doughs such as puff pastry or danish. For detailed information on butter and margarine see Chapter 8, Eggs and Dairy Products.

Oil

Unlike butter and other fats, oil blends thoroughly throughout a mixture. It therefore coats more of the proteins, and the gluten strands produced are much shorter, a desirable result in fine-textured products such as muffins or chiffon cakes. For baking, select a neutral-flavored oil unless the distinctive taste of olive oil is desired, as in some breads. Never substitute oil in a formula requiring a solid shortening. For detailed information on oil, see Chapter 7, Kitchen Staples.

Nutrition

Fats are high in calories and contain varying levels of saturated fats. Although they have no carbohydrates, a few fats such as butter have trace amounts of protein and minerals. Butter is also high in Vitamin A.

TABLE 26.5   NUTRITIONAL VALUES OF SELECTED FATS

Per 2 Tbsp. (30 ml)	Kcal	Total fat (g)	Saturated fat (g)	Cholesterol (mg)	Sodium (mg)
Butter, unsalted	200	22.8	14.2	62	2
Corn oil	240	27.2	3.4	0	0
Lard	230	25.6	10	24	0
Margarine	200	22	4	0	200
Margarine, diet	100	12	2	0	260
Shortening, all-purpose	226	25.6	6.4	0	0

The Corinne T. Netzer Encyclopedia of Food Values 1992

Thickeners

Starches are often used as thickening agents in bakeshop products. Cornstarch, arrowroot and flour can be used as thickeners for pastry creams, sauces, custards and fruit fillings. These thickeners are discussed in Chapter 10, Stocks and Sauces.

One of the most commonly used thickeners in the bakeshop is **gelatin**, a natural product derived from the animal protein collagen. It is available in two forms: granulated gelatin and sheet (also called leaf) gelatin. A two-step process is necessary to use either form: The gelatin must first be softened in a cold liquid, then dissolved in a hot liquid.

Granulated gelatin is available in bulk or in 1/4-ounce (7 grams or slightly less than 1 tablespoon) envelopes. One envelope is enough to set 1 pint (500 milliliters) of liquid. Granulated gelatin should be softened in a cool liquid for at least 5 minutes, then heated gently to dissolve. The initial softening in a cold liquid is necessary to separate the gelatin molecules so that they will not lump together when the hot liquid is added.

Sheet or leaf gelatin is available in 1-kilogram boxes, sometimes further packaged in 5- or 6-sheet envelopes. The sheets are produced in varying thicknesses and weights. They must be separated and soaked in ice water until very soft, at least 15 minutes. They are then removed from the water and stirred into a hot liquid until completely dissolved.

PROCEDURE FOR USING SHEET GELATIN

1. Gelatin sheets are submerged in ice water for several minutes to soften.

2. Softened gelatin sheets are then removed from the ice water and incorporated into a hot liquid.

Granulated and sheet gelatin can be substituted weight for weight in any formula. Sheet gelatin, though more expensive, is preferred for its lack of flavor and color. It also tends to dissolve more readily and evenly and has a longer shelf life than the granulated product.

Once incorporated into a product such as a Bavarian, gelatin can be frozen, or melted and reset once or twice without a loss of thickening ability. Because it scorches easily, gelatin and mixtures containing gelatin should not be allowed to boil.

Flavorings

Many spices and flavorings are used in the bakeshop. The most popular spices such as cinnamon, cloves, nutmeg and allspice are discussed in Chapter 7, Kitchen Staples. Here we discuss emulsions and extracts, vanilla, chocolate and alcoholic beverages.

Emulsions and Extracts

Emulsions and extracts are liquid flavoring agents derived from various oils.

Emulsions are flavoring oils mixed into water with the aid of emulsifiers. Lemon and orange are the most common emulsions. Emulsions are much stronger than extracts and should be used carefully and sparingly.

Extracts are mixtures of flavoring oils and ethyl alcohol. Vanilla, almond and lemon are frequently used extracts. An extract may be made with pure flavoring oils or with artificial flavors and colors. Contents are regulated by the FDA, and package labels must indicate any artificial ingredients.

Emulsions and extracts are highly volatile. They should be stored in sealed containers in a cool area away from direct light.

Vanilla

Vanilla (Fr. *vanille*) is the most frequently used flavoring in the bakeshop. It comes from the pod fruit, called a bean, of a vine in the orchid family. Vanilla beans are purchased whole, individually or by the pound. They should be soft and pliable, with a rich brown color and good aroma. The finest vanilla comes from Tahiti and Madagascar.

Scraping seeds from the interior of a vanilla bean.

To use a vanilla bean, cut it open lengthwise with a paring knife. Scrape out the moist seeds with the knife's tip and stir them into the mixture being flavored. The seeds do not dissolve and will remain visible as small black or brown flecks. After all the seeds have been removed, the bean can be stored in a covered container with sugar to create vanilla sugar.

Vanilla beans should be stored in an airtight container in a cool, dark place. During storage, the beans may develop a white coating. This is not mold, but rather crystals of vanilla flavor known as **vanillin**. It should not be removed.

Pure vanilla extract is an easy and less expensive way to give bakeshop products a true vanilla flavor. It is dark brown and aromatic, and comes in several strengths referred to as folds. Each fold requires the extract from 13.35 ounces of vanilla beans per gallon of liquid. A two-fold contains 26.7 ounces per gallon and a four-fold contains 40.5 ounces. Single or two-fold are the most commonly available; the stronger products are used only in manufacturing. By law, any product labeled vanilla extract must not contain artificial flavorings and must be at least 35% alcohol by volume.

Vanilla extract should be stored at room temperature in a closed, opaque container. It should not be frozen.

Artificial or imitation vanilla flavoring is made with synthetic vanillin. Artificial flavoring is available in a clear form, which is useful for white buttercreams where the dark brown color of pure vanilla extract would be undesirable. Although inexpensive, artificial vanilla is, at best, weaker and less aromatic than pure extract. It can also impart a chemical or bitter taste to foods.

Chocolate

Chocolate is one of the most—perhaps *the* most—popular flavoring for candies, cookies, cakes and pastries. Chocolate is also served as a beverage and is an ingredient in the traditional spicy Mexican molé sauce. Chocolate is available in a variety of forms and degrees of sweetness.

Chocolate Production

Chocolate (Fr. *chocolat*) begins as yellow fruit pods dangling from the trunk and main branches of the tropical cacao tree. Each pod contains about 40 almond-sized cocoa beans. After the pods ripen, the beans are placed in the sun for several days to dry and ferment. They are then cleaned, dried, cured and roasted to develop flavor and reduce bitterness. Next the beans are crushed to remove their shells, yielding the prized chocolate **nib**.

Nibs are shipped to manufacturers worldwide where they can be further roasted. They are crushed into a thick (nonalcoholic) paste known as **chocolate liquor** or **chocolate mass**. Chocolate mass contains about 53% fat, known as **cocoa butter**. The chocolate mass is further refined depending on the desired product. If **cocoa powder** is to be produced, virtually all of the cocoa butter is removed. A variety of other products are created by adding

---

♦♦♦

FROM CACAO TO CHOCOLATE CHIPS

To understand the history of chocolate a chef or chocoholic must first understand the fundamental difference between its original use as a beverage and its later transformation into a candy.

The cacao tree (called *theobroma cacao*, meaning "food of the gods") originated in the river valleys of South America and was carried into what is now Mexico by the Mayans before the 7th century A.D. It was cultivated by Mayans, Aztecs and Toltecs not only as a source of food but also as currency. Chocolate was consumed only as a treasured drink. Cacao beans were roasted, crushed to a paste and steeped in water, then thickened with corn flour to create a cold, bitter beverage. Sometimes honey, vanilla or spices, including chiles, were added. The Aztec emperor Montezuma was so enamored with the beverage that he reportedly consumed 50 cups at each meal.

Columbus brought cacao beans to Spain from his forth voyage to the New World in 1504. (The common term *cocoa* is actually a western European mispronunciation of the proper term *cacao*, caused by confusion with another New World delicacy, the coconut.) But almost 20 years passed before Spanish conquistadors, led by Cortez, understood the beans' value. With Montezuma's encouragement, Cortez and his soldiers slowly acquired a taste for the bitter beverage, spurred on by the intoxicating effects of caffeine.

Cortez's most important contribution to the history of chocolate was to take beans with him when he left Mexico. He planted them on the islands he passed on his return to Spain: Trinidad, Haiti and Fernando Po, from which the giant African cocoa industry grew. Through Cortez's far-sighted efforts, Spain controlled all

aspects of the cocoa trade until well into the 18th century.

The Spanish began drinking chocolate at home during the 16th century. It was usually mixed with two other expensive imports, sugar and vanilla, and frothed with a carved wooden swizzle stick known as a *molinet*. This thick, cold drink was made from tablets of crushed cocoa beans produced and sold by monks. The Spanish believed that cocoa cured all ills and supplied limitless stamina. In the early 17th century cocoa beverages, now served hot, crept into France via royal marriages.

Cocoa spread through the rest of Europe by different routes. The Dutch, who had poached on Spanish trade routes for many years, even-

Chocolate Chef, sculpted by Chef Rubin Foster, Arizona Biltmore, Phoenix, AZ.

tually realized the value of the unusual beans they found on Spanish ships. Holland soon became the most important cocoa port outside of Spain. From there, a love of cocoa spread to Germany, Scandinavia and Italy. In 1655 England acquired Jamaica and its own cocoa plantations.

Until the Industrial Revolution, cocoa was made by hand using mortar and pestle or stone-grinding disks to crush the cocoa nibs. By the 1700s cocoa factories had opened throughout Europe. James Baker opened the first cocoa factory in the United States in 1765.

Conrad van Houten, a Dutch chemist, patented "chocolate powder" in 1825. His work marked the beginning of a shift from drinking to eating chocolate. It also paved the way for everything we know as chocolate today. Van Houten developed a screw press that removed most of the cocoa butter from the bean, leaving a brown, flaky powder, essentially the same substance as modern cocoa powder.

Eventually it was discovered that the extra cocoa butter resulting from the production of cocoa powder could be added to ground beans to make the paste more malleable, smoother and more tolerant of added sugar. The English firm of Fry and Sons introduced the first eating chocolate in 1847. Their recipe was the same then as today: crushed cocoa beans, cocoa butter and sugar.

In 1876 Swiss chocolatier Daniel Peter invented solid milk chocolate using the new condensed milk created by baby food manufacturer Henri Nestlé. Pennsylvania cocoa manufacturer Milton Hershey introduced his milk chocolate bars in 1894, followed by Hershey's Kisses in 1907. Nestlé Foods introduced the chocolate chip, perfect for cookies, in 1939.

✦✦✦
MELTING CHOCOLATE

Two important rules for melting chocolate:

1. Chocolate must never exceed 120°F or there will be a loss of flavor.
2. Water—even a drop in the form of steam—must never touch the chocolate.

When a droplet of water enters melted chocolate, the chocolate becomes lumpy (a process called *seizing*). There must be a minimum of 1 tablespoon water per ounce of chocolate to keep this from happening.

If seizing does occur, the addition of fat such as vegetable shortening, clarified butter, or cocoa butter will somewhat restore the chocolate to a workable condition.

For melting chocolate, unlined copper is the traditional "chocolate pot" because it is so responsive to changes in temperature. Aluminum or heatproof glass also works well. Ideally, chocolate should be heated to 120°F, the point at which all the different fat fractions in the cocoa butter are melted.

When melting chocolate or cocoa butter, temperatures exceeding 120°F adversely affect the flavor. There are many acceptable methods for melting dark chocolate. If the heat source does not exceed 120°F it is fine to add the dark chocolate in large pieces and leave it to melt unmonitored. When the heat source is capable of bringing the chocolate over 120°F, however, the chocolate should be finely chopped or grated to ensure uniformity of melting. The chocolate must be carefully watched and stirred to avoid overheating. If using a double boiler, water in the lower container should not exceed 140°F and the upper container should not touch the water. The chocolate should be stirred constantly.

Milk and white chocolate must always be stirred frequently while melting because they contain milk solids which seed (lump) if left undisturbed.

Remove chocolate from the heat source when it reaches 115°F as the temperature may continue to rise, and stir vigorously to prevent overheating and to distribute the cocoa butter evenly.

Always melt chocolate uncovered as moisture could condense on the lid, drop back in the chocolate, and cause seizing.

—*from* THE CAKE BIBLE *by*
ROSE LEVY BERANBAUM

---

more cocoa butter, sugar, milk solids and flavorings to the chocolate mass. Most manufacturers of fine chocolates use the Swiss technique of **conching** to increase smoothness. Conching involves stirring large vats of blended chocolate with a heavy roller or paddle to smooth out sugar crystals and mellow the flavor, a process that may last from a few hours to three days.

Tasting Chocolates

There are two types of chocolate beans: a very hardy, abundant African variety used as a base bean, and a very flavorful, aromatic variety from Costa Rica used for flavor. Unlike wine or coffee, you cannot taste processed chocolate and tell which beans were used. All chocolates are blends, created by their manufacturer to be unique yet consistent.

Roasting greatly affects the final flavor of chocolate. Generally, German and Spanish manufacturers use a high (or strong) roast; Swiss and American makers use a low (or mild) roast.

Refining is also a matter of national taste. Swiss and German chocolate is the smoothest, followed by English chocolates. American chocolate is noticeably more grainy.

Chocolate quality is actually the product of several factors besides taste. All these factors should be evaluated when selecting chocolates.

1. Appearance—color should be even and glossy, without any discoloration.
2. Smell—should be chocolatey with no off-odors or staleness.
3. Break—should snap cleanly without crumbling.
4. Texture—should melt quickly and evenly on the tongue.

Unsweetened Chocolate

Unsweetened chocolate is pure hardened chocolate liquor without any added sugar or milk solids. It is frequently used in baking and is sometimes referred to as "baking chocolate." Unsweetened chocolate is approximately 53% cocoa butter and 47% cocoa solids. Its flavor is pure and chocolatey, but the absence of sugar makes it virtually inedible as is.

Bittersweet and Semisweet Chocolates

Both bittersweet and semisweet chocolates contain at least 35% chocolate liquor plus additional cocoa butter, sugar, flavorings and sometimes emulsifiers. Generally, semisweet chocolate will be sweeter than bittersweet chocolate, but there are no precise definitions so flavor and sweetness will vary from brand to brand. Both are excellent eating chocolates and can usually be substituted measure for measure in any formula.

Sweet Chocolate

Government standards require that sweet chocolate contain not less than 15% chocolate liquor and varying amounts of sugar, milk solids, flavorings and emulsifiers. As the name implies, sweet chocolate is sweeter, and thus less chocolatey, than semisweet chocolate.

Milk Chocolate

The favorite eating chocolate in the United States is milk chocolate. It contains sugar, vanilla, perhaps other flavorings and, of course, milk solids. The milk solids that make the chocolate milder and sweeter than other chocolates also make it less suitable for baking purposes. Do not substitute milk chocolate for dark chocolate in any product that must be baked, as the milk solids tend to burn. If melted slowly and carefully, milk chocolate can be used in glazes, mousses or candies.

Cocoa Powder

The brown powder left after the fat (cocoa butter) is removed from cocoa beans is known as cocoa powder. It does not contain any sweeteners or flavorings and is primarily used in baked goods. Alkalized or Dutch-processed cocoa powder has been treated with an alkaline solution, such as potassium carbonate, to raise the powder's pH from 5.5 to 7 or 8. Alkalized powder is darker and milder than nonalkalized powder and has a reduced tendency to lump. Either can be used in baked goods, however.

Cocoa Butter

Chocolate liquor is approximately 53% cocoa butter. Cocoa butter has long been prized for its resistance to rancidity and its use as a cosmetic. Cocoa butter has a very precise melting point, just below body temperature. Fine chocolatiers use high percentages of cocoa butter to give their chocolates melt-in-the-mouth quality.

Clockwise from lower left, semisweet chips, disks of chocolate liquor, block of bittersweet chocolate, block of milk chocolate, disks of white chocolate, alkalized cocoa powder.

White Chocolate

This ivory-colored substance is not the product of an albino cocoa bean. It is actually a confectionary product that does not contain any chocolate solids or liquor. (Thus it cannot be labeled "chocolate" in the United States.) The finest white chocolates contain cocoa butter, sugar, milk solids, vanilla or other flavors. Other products replace all or part of the cocoa butter with vegetable oils. These confectionary products will be less expensive than those containing pure cocoa butter, but their flavor and texture will be noticeably inferior. White chocolate melts at a lower temperature than dark chocolate and burns easily. It is excellent for eating and candy making, but is less-often used in baked goods.

Imitation Chocolate

A less-expensive product substituted in many prepared foods, imitation chocolate is made with vegetable oils instead of cocoa butter. The resulting product melts at a higher temperature. Products containing imitation chocolate should be labeled "chocolate flavored."

Nutrition

Chocolates are high in calories and fat. They contain minimal amounts of Vitamin A and trace amounts of other vitamins as well as some sodium, phosphorous, potassium and other minerals.

TABLE 26.6   NUTRITIONAL VALUES OF SELECTED CHOCOLATES

Per 1-oz. (28-g) unit	Kcal	Protein (g)	Carbohydrates (g)	Total fat (g)	Sodium (mg)
Chocolate, semisweet chips (Nestlé's)	150	2	18	8	0
Chocolate, unsweetened (Baker's)	140	3	9	15	0
Cocoa powder (Hershey's)	120	7	13	4	10
Milk chocolate (Hershey's)	150	2	27	12	55
White chocolate (Nestlé's)	160	2	15	10	25

The Corinne T. Netzer Encyclopedia of Food Values 1992

───────── ✦✦✦ ─────────

To Temper or Not to Temper

The number-one mystique that surrounds chocolate has to do with tempering. From the dessert maker and pastry chef's point of view, I take a radical position: I do not think it is necessary or practical to temper. But what are we talking about anyway?

Briefly, tempering is a process of slowly raising and lowering the temperature of melted chocolate, stirring constantly, until the complex fat crystals in the cocoa butter stabilize and "behave" in concert with each other. At a cool room temperature, chocolate that has been tempered will dry rapidly to a hard and shiny piece that breaks with a snap. It shrinks slightly as it dries, enabling it to release easily from a mold. A tempered chocolate piece keeps at room temperature for months without losing its luster or snap. Any bar of chocolate that you purchase to eat or to melt has been tempered. Once melted or exposed to heat, however, it loses its temper, though it can be retempered.

Chocolate that is melted but not tempered will dry slowly, at room temperature, to a soft, almost cakey texture. It will stick inside a mold. Untempered chocolate "blooms"—that is, it becomes dull and streaky, or it takes on a mottled appearance—unless it is refrigerated immediately.

Candy makers almost always temper the chocolate they use. But dessert chefs have little need to temper. There is no reason to temper the chocolate used in cake and torte batters, buttercreams, and most ganaches. The same is true for mousses, custards, and creams. Chocolate that will be stored in the refrigerator or consumed quickly need not be tempered. Chocolate glazes, properly handled, do not require tempering to remain shiny for the short life of the dessert.

—from Cocolat: Extraordinary Chocolate Desserts *by* Alice Medrich

───────────────────────────

Storing Chocolate

All chocolates should be stored at a cool, consistent temperature, away from strong odors and moisture. Dark chocolate, white chocolate and cocoa powder can be kept for up to one year without loss of flavor. Milk chocolate will not keep as well because it contains milk solids.

Chocolate may develop grayish-white spots during storage. This is called **bloom**; it results from the migration of cocoa butter crystals to the surface when temperatures change. Bloom will not affect the flavor or function of chocolate and will disappear when the chocolate is melted.

Alcoholic Beverages

Liquor—*an alcoholic beverage made by distilling grains, vegetables or other foods; includes rum, whiskey and vodka.*

Liqueur—*a strong, sweet, syrupy alcoholic beverage made by mixing or redistilling neutral spirits with fruits, flowers, herbs, spices or other flavorings; also known as a cordial.*

Wine—*an alcoholic beverage made from the fermented juice of grapes; may be sparkling (effervescent) or still (noneffervescent) or fortified with additional alcohol.*

Brandy—*an alcoholic beverage made from distilling the fermented mash of grapes or other fruits.*

Liquors, **liqueurs**, **wines** and **brandies** are frequently used flavorings in the bakeshop. Rum is a popular flavoring liquor because it blends well with other flavors such as chocolate and coffee. Liqueurs are selected for their specific flavors: for example, kirsch for cherry, amaretto for almond, kahlúa for coffee, crème de cassis for black current and crème de cacao for chocolate. They are used to either add or enhance flavors. Wine, both still and sparkling, is used as a flavoring (for example, in sabayon sauce) or as a cooking medium (for example, pears poached in red wine). Brandy, especially the classic orange-flavored Grand Marnier, is another common bakeshop flavoring. Brandy complements fruits and rounds off the flavor of custards and creams.

When selecting an alcoholic beverage for baking, make quality your first concern. Only high-quality products will enhance the flavor and aroma of your baked goods.

MIXING METHODS

An important step in the production of all baked goods is the mixing of ingredients. The techniques used to mix or combine ingredients affect the baked good's final volume, appearance and texture. There are several mixing methods: **beating**, **blending**, **creaming**, **cutting**, **folding**, **kneading**, **sifting**, **stirring** and **whipping**. These terms are used throughout this part of the text, especially in procedure discussions and formulas. Use the designated mixing method as well as the appropriate equipment or tool to ensure a good-quality finished product.

THE BAKING PROCESS

Baked goods are made from doughs and batters. A **dough** has a low water content. The water-protein complex known as gluten forms the continuous medium into which other ingredients are embedded. A dough is usually prepared by beating, blending, cutting or kneading and is often stiff enough to cut into various shapes.

A **batter** generally contains more fat, sugar and liquids than a dough. Gluten development is minimized and liquid forms the continuous medium in which other ingredients are disbursed. A batter bakes into softer, moister and more crumbly products. A batter is usually prepared by blending, creaming, stirring or whipping and is generally thin enough to pour.

The changes that occur in a dough or batter as it bakes seem mysterious and complex. A pourable liquid becomes a tender, light cake; a sticky mass becomes soft, chewy cookies; a soft, elastic dough becomes firm, crusty French bread. Yet the same physical changes that occur during baking cause all of these results. Namely, gases form and are trapped within the dough or batter; starches, proteins and sugars cook; fats melt; moisture evaporates and staling begins.

By learning to control these changes, you are also learning to control the final product. Control can be exerted in the selection of ingredients and method by which those ingredients are combined as well as the baking temperature and duration.

Gases Form

A baked good's final texture is determined by the amount of leavening or rise that occurs both before and during baking. This rise is caused by the gases present in the dough or batter. These gases are carbon dioxide, air and steam. Air and carbon dioxide are present in doughs and batters before they are heated. Other gases are formed when heat is applied. For example, steam is created as the moisture in a dough is heated; yeast and baking powder rapidly release additional carbon dioxide when placed in a hot oven. These gases then expand and leaven the product. Additional information on baking powder and baking soda is found in Chapter 27, Quick Breads; additional information on yeast is found in Chapter 28, Yeast Breads.

Beating—*vigorously agitating foods to incorporate air or develop gluten; use a spoon or electric mixer with its paddle attachment.*

Blending—*mixing two or more ingredients until evenly distributed; use a spoon, rubber spatula, whisk or electric mixer with its paddle attachment.*

Creaming—*vigorously combining fat and sugar while incorporating air; use an electric mixer with its paddle attachment on medium speed.*

Cutting—*incorporating solid fat into dry ingredients only until lumps of the desired size remain; use pastry cutters, fingers or an electric mixer with its paddle attachment.*

Folding—*very gently incorporating ingredients, such as dry ingredients with whipped eggs; use a rubber spatula.*

Kneading—*working a dough to develop gluten; use hands or an electric mixer with its dough hook. If done by hand, the dough must be vigorously and repeatedly folded and turned in a rhythmic pattern.*

Sifting—*passing one or more dry ingredients through a wire mesh to remove lumps, combine and aerate ingredients; use a rotary or drum sifter or mesh strainer.*

Stirring—*gently mixing ingredients until blended; use a spoon, whisk or rubber spatula.*

Whipping—*beating vigorously to incorporate air; use a whisk or an electric mixer with its whip attachment.*

Gases Are Trapped

The stretchable network of proteins created in a batter or dough either by egg proteins or gluten traps gases in the product. Without an appropriate network of proteins, the gases would just escape without causing the mixture to rise.

Starches Gelatinize

When starch granules reach a temperature of approximately 140°F (60°C), they absorb additional moisture—up to 10 times their own weight—and expand. This contributes to the baked good's structure.

Proteins Coagulate

Gluten and dairy and egg proteins begin to coagulate (solidify) when the dough or batter reaches a temperature of 160°F (71°C). This process provides most of the baked good's structure.

Proper baking temperatures are important for controlling the point at which proteins coagulate. If the temperature is too high, proteins will solidify before the gases in the product have expanded fully, resulting in a product with poor texture and volume. If the temperature is too low, gases will escape before the proteins coagulate, resulting in a product that may collapse.

Fats Melt

As fats melt, steam is released and fat droplets are dispersed throughout the product. These fat droplets coat the starch (flour) granules, thus moistening and tenderizing the product by keeping the gluten strands short. Shortenings melt at different temperatures. It is important to select a fat with the proper melting point for the product being prepared.

Water Evaporates

Throughout the baking process the water contained in the liquid ingredients will turn to steam and evaporate. This steam is a useful leavener. As steam is released, the dough or batter dries out, starting from the outside, resulting in the formation of a crust.

TABLE 26.7	LEAVENING AGENTS IN BAKED GOODS
Leavening Agent	Present in
Air	All products, especially those containing whipped eggs or creamed fat
Steam	All products when liquids evaporate or fats melt
Carbon Dioxide	Products containing baking soda, baking powder, baking ammonia or yeast

Sugars Caramelize

As sugars are heated above the boiling point they caramelize, adding flavor and causing the product to darken. Sugars are found in eggs, dairy products and other ingredients, not just in refined sugar and liquid sweeteners.

Carryover Baking

The physical changes in a baked good do not stop when it is removed from the oven. The residual heat contained in a product continues the baking process as the product cools. That is why a cookie or biscuit may seem a bit underbaked when removed from the oven; it will finish baking as it cools.

Staling

Staling is a change in a baked good's texture and aroma caused by both moisture loss and changes in the structure of the starch granules. Stale products have lost their fresh aroma and are firmer, drier and more crumbly than fresh goods.

Staling is not just a general loss of moisture into the atmosphere, it is also a change in the location and distribution of water molecules within the product. This process, known as **starch retrogradation**, occurs as starch molecules cool, becoming more dense and expelling moisture.

In breads, this moisture migrates from the interior to the drier crust, causing the crust to become tough and leathery. If the product is not well wrapped, moisture will escape completely into the surrounding air. In humid conditions, unwrapped bread crusts absorb moisture from the atmosphere, resulting in the same loss of crispness. The flavor and texture of breads can be revived by reheating them to approximately 140°F (60°C), the temperature at which starch gelatinization occurs. Usually, products can be reheated only once without causing additional quality loss.

The retrogradation process is temperature-dependent. It occurs most rapidly at temperatures of approximately 40°F (4°C). Therefore, baked products should not be refrigerated unless they contain perishable components such as cream fillings. It is better to store products frozen or at room temperature.

Products containing fats and sugars, which retain moisture, tend to stay fresh longer. Commercial bakeries usually add chemical emulsifiers or gums to retard staling, but these additives are not practical for small-scale production.

Bakeshop Tools and Equipment

As a beginning cook, you may find the tools of the bakeshop a bit complex. Indeed, the tools required for a professional patisserie are quite specialized. A well-rounded chef need not be concerned with possessing every gadget available, but should recognize and be familiar with most of the items shown in Figure 26.1. While many of these hand tools will make a task easier, most can be improvised by a creative chef. Several of the items shown, such as the springform pans, tartlet pans and petit four molds, are used for shaping or holding batters and doughs. The various spatulas are used for spreading icings or fillings. The piping tools and cake comb are used for decorating and finishing baked goods.

FIGURE 26.1 *Clockwise from center back, cake turntable, cake pans, flan ring, tartlet pans, cannoli forms, cake comb, offset spatulas, flat cake spatula, blade for slashing breads, flower nail, rectangular tartlet pans, piping bag and tips, metal spatula, dough cutter, rolling pin, springform pan, copper sugar pot (on cooling rack), nest of round cutters*

When purchasing tools and equipment, look for quality and durability. As your baking skills grow, so will your equipment selection.

Bakeshop ovens may be conventional, convection or steam injection models. Convection ovens can reduce cooking time, but the air currents may damage delicate products such as spongecake or puff pastry. Steam injection ovens use conventional heat flow but allow the baker to automatically add steam to the cooking chamber as needed to produce crisp-crusted breads. Although expensive, steam injection ovens are a necessity for commercial bakeries and most larger restaurant and hotel bakeshops. Baking instructions in the following chapters are based on the use of a conventional oven. If a convection oven is used instead, remember that the temperature and baking time may need to be reduced.

CONCLUSION

Of the many stations of the kitchen, the bakeshop often requires the most conscientious attention to detail. The correct use of flour, thickeners, sugar, fat, chocolate and other flavorings is essential. During preparation and baking, doughs and batters go through many physical changes. One of the most important is the development of gluten, the elastic network of wheat proteins created when doughs and batters are prepared, which gives baked goods body and structure. You should understand the changes baked goods undergo and learn to control or adjust them as needed.

QUESTIONS FOR DISCUSSION

1. What is gluten? How is it produced and why is it important in the preparation of baked goods?

2. Discuss four functions of sugar and other sweeteners in baked goods.

3. Describe several steps that can be taken to prevent crystals from forming in sugar solutions.

4. Describe the effect of fat on gluten strands. Why is fat an important ingredient in baked goods?

5. Explain the difference between chocolate liquor and semisweet chocolate. Can these two types of chocolate be used interchangeably in most recipes? Explain your answer.

6. List and describe the nine steps in the baking process.

7. Name several specialized hand tools or pans often used in the bakeshop.

8. What are the differences between a steam-injection oven, a convection oven and a conventional oven? Why might you select one type of oven over another?

CHAPTER 27

QUICK BREADS

*B*uttermilk biscuits, blueberry muffins, banana-nut bread and currant scones are all quick breads. Although the origin of the name may be a mystery, why they are so named is obvious: They are quick to make and quick to bake. With only a few basic ingredients and no yeast, almost any food service operation can provide its customers with fresh muffins, biscuits, scones and loaf breads.

The variety of ingredients is virtually limitless: cornmeal, whole wheat, fruits, nuts, spices and vegetables all yield popular products. And the use of these products is not limited to breakfast service; they are equally appropriate for lunch, snacks and buffets.

CHEMICAL LEAVENING AGENTS

Quick breads are made with chemical leavening agents, principally baking soda and baking powder. This sets them apart from breads that are made with yeast and require additional time for fermentation and proofing. Understanding how chemical leavening agents operate is essential to successful quick-bread production.

Chemical leavening agents release gases through chemical reactions between acids and bases contained in the formula. These gases form bubbles or air pockets throughout the dough or batter. As the product bakes, the dough or batter sets around these air pockets, thus giving the quick bread its rise and texture.

Baking Soda

Sodium bicarbonate ($NaHCO_3$) is more commonly known as household baking soda. Baking soda is an alkaline compound (a base), which releases carbon dioxide gas (CO_2) if both an acid and moisture are present. Heat is not necessary for this reaction to occur. Therefore, products made with baking soda must be baked at once, before the carbon dioxide has a chance to escape from the batter.

Acids commonly used with baking soda are buttermilk, sour cream, lemon juice, honey, molasses and fresh fruit. Generally, the amount of baking soda used in a formula is only the amount necessary to neutralize the acids present. If more leavening action is needed, baking powder, not more baking soda, should be used. Too much baking soda causes the product to taste soapy or bitter; it may also cause a yellow color and brown spots to develop.

Baking Powder

Baking powder is a mixture of sodium bicarbonate and one or more acids, generally cream of tartar ($KHC_4H_4O_6$) and/or sodium aluminum sulfate ($Na_2SO_4 \cdot Al_2[SO_4]_3$). Baking powder also contains a starch to prevent lumping and balance the chemical reactions. Because baking powder contains both the acid and the base necessary for the desired chemical reaction, the formula does not need to contain any acid. Only moisture is necessary to induce the release of gases.

There are two types of baking powder: single-acting and double-acting. An excess of either type produces undesirable flavors, textures and colors in baked products.

Single-acting baking powder requires only the presence of moisture to start releasing gas. This moisture is supplied by the eggs, milk, water or other liquids in the formula. As with baking soda, products using single-acting baking powder must be baked immediately.

Double-acting baking powder is more popular. With double-acting baking powder, there is a small release of gas upon contact with moisture and a second, stronger release of gas when heat is applied. Products made with double-acting baking powder need not be baked immediately, but can sit for a short time without loss of leavening ability. All formulas in this book rely on double-acting baking powder.

Both baking soda and baking powder are sometimes used in one formula. This is because baking soda can only release CO_2 to the extent that there is also an acid present in the formula. If the soda/acid reaction alone is insufficient to leaven the product, baking powder is needed for additional leavening.

Baking Ammonia

Baking ammonia (ammonia bicarbonate or ammonia carbonate) is also used as a leavening agent in some baked goods, primarily cookies and crackers. Baking ammonia releases ammonia and carbon dioxide very rapidly when heated. It is suitable for low-moisture products with large surface areas that are baked at high temperatures, such as crackers. Consequently, it is rarely used in quick breads.

Purchasing and Storing

Purchase chemical leaveners in the smallest unit appropriate for your operation. Although a large can of baking powder may cost less than several small ones, if not used promptly the contents of a larger container can deteriorate, causing waste or unusable baked goods.

Chemical leavening agents should always be kept tightly covered. Not only is there a risk of contamination if left open, but they can also absorb moisture from the air and lose their effectiveness. They should be stored in a cool place, as heat deteriorates them. A properly stored and unopened container of baking powder or baking soda has a shelf life of approximately one year.

MIXING METHODS

Quick breads are generally mixed by either the **biscuit method**, the **muffin method** or the **creaming method**.

Biscuit Method

The biscuit method is used for biscuits and scones and is very similar to the technique used to make flaky pie doughs. The goal is to create a baked good that is light, flaky and tender.

PROCEDURE FOR PREPARING PRODUCTS WITH THE BISCUIT METHOD

1. Measure all ingredients.
2. Sift the dry ingredients together.
3. Cut in the fat, which should be in a solid form.
4. Combine the liquid ingredients, including any eggs.
5. Add the liquid ingredients to the dry ingredients. Mix just until the ingredients are combined. Do not overmix, as this causes toughness and inhibits the product's rise.
6. Place the dough on the bench and knead it lightly 10 or 15 times (about 20–30 seconds). The dough should be soft and slightly elastic, but not sticky. Too much kneading toughens the biscuits.
7. The dough is now ready for makeup and baking.

MAKEUP OF BISCUIT METHOD PRODUCTS

1. Roll out the dough on a floured surface to a thickness of 1/2 to 3/4 inch (1.25 to 1.8 centimeters). Be careful to roll it evenly. Biscuits should double in height during baking.
2. Cut into the desired shapes. Cut straight down; do not twist the cutters, as this inhibits rise. Space cuts as close together as possible to minimize scraps.
3. Position the biscuits on a lightly greased or paper-lined sheet pan. If placed with sides nearly touching, the biscuits will rise higher and have softer sides. Place farther apart for crusty sides.
4. Scraps may be rerolled one time without overtoughening the product. To do so, press the dough together gently; do not knead.
5. Tops may be brushed with egg wash before baking or with melted butter after baking. Bake immediately in a hot oven.
6. Cool the finished products on a wire rack.

♦♦♦

BISCUITS AND SCONES: A GENEALOGY

Biscuit is a French word used to describe any dry, flat cake, whether sweet or savory. It was, perhaps, originally coined to describe twice-baked cakes (*bis* = twice + *cuit* = cooked). Crusader chronicles, for example, mention soldiers eating a "bread called 'bequis' because it is cooked twice" and still, today, the Reims biscuit is returned to the oven for further baking after it is removed from its tin.

Over the centuries the French began to use the term *biscuit* generically and appended modifiers to identify the particular type of dry, flat cake. For example, a *biscuit de guerre* was the very hard, barely risen product of flour and water used from the time of the Crusades to the era of Louis XIV as an army ration (*guerre* is French for war); *biscuit de Savoie* is a savory spongecake; *biscuit de pâtisserie* is a sweet biscuit.

To the British, a biscuit is what Americans call a cracker or cookie. Yet there appears to be no British quick bread quite comparable to the American biscuit—the closest relative would be the scone. But because a scone contains eggs and butter, it is much richer than a biscuit.

Elizabeth Alston, in *Biscuits and Scones*, proposes that the biscuit is an American variant of the scone. She theorizes that early British colonists in America brought with them traditional scone recipes. Unable to find or afford the necessary fresh butter and eggs, these practical bakers substituted lard and omitted the eggs. What they created, however, were not mock scones, but rather a new product, different from scones but still delicious. Alston further speculates that French cooks initially called the new American product "biscuit de something" and eventually dropped the "de something."

◆◆◆

RECIPE 27.1
COUNTRY BISCUITS

Yield: 36 Biscuits   **Method:** Biscuit

All-purpose flour	2 lb. 8 oz.	1 kg
Salt	3/4 oz.	21 g
Sugar	2 oz.	60 g
Baking powder	2 oz.	60 g
Unsalted butter, cold	14 oz.	400 g
Milk	1 lb. 8 oz.	680 g

1. Sift the dry ingredients together, making sure they are blended thoroughly.

2. Cut in the shortening. The mixture should look mealy; do not overmix.

3. Add the milk and stir, combining only until the mixture holds together.

4. Transfer the dough to a lightly floured work surface; knead until it forms one mass, approximately 5 or 6 kneadings.

5. Roll out the dough to a thickness of 1/2 inch (1.25 centimeters). Cut with a floured cutter and place the biscuits on a paper-lined sheet pan.

6. Bake at 425°F (220°C) for approximately 10–15 minutes. Tops should be light brown, sides almost white and interiors still moist. Internal heat will continue to cook the biscuits after they are removed from the oven.

7. Remove the biscuits to a wire rack to cool.

1. Sifting the dry ingredients together.

2. Cutting in the fat.

3. Kneading the dough.

4. Cutting the biscuits.

Muffin Method

Muffins are any small, cakelike baked good made in a muffin tin (pan). Batters for muffins and loaf quick breads are generally interchangeable. For example, banana muffin batter may be baked in a loaf pan by altering the baking time.

When preparing baked goods by the muffin method, the goal is to produce a tender product with an even shape and an even distribution of fruits, nuts or other ingredients. The most frequent problem with muffin-method products is overmixing. This causes toughness and may cause holes to form inside the baked product, a condition known as **tunneling**.

PROCEDURE FOR PREPARING PRODUCTS WITH THE MUFFIN METHOD

1. Measure all ingredients.
2. Sift the dry ingredients together.
3. Combine the liquid ingredients, including melted fat or oil. Melted butter or shortening may resolidify when combined with the other liquids; this is not a cause for concern.
4. Add the liquid ingredients to the dry ingredients and stir just until combined. Do not overmix. The batter will be lumpy.
5. The batter is now ready for makeup and baking.

MAKEUP OF MUFFIN METHOD PRODUCTS

1. Muffin pans and loaf pans should be greased with butter, shortening or a commercial pan grease. Paper liners may be used and will prevent sticking if the batter contains fruits or vegetables. Paper liners, however, inhibit rise.
2. A portion scoop is convenient for ensuring uniform-sized muffins. Be careful not to drip or spill batter onto the edge of the muffin cups; it will burn and cause sticking.
3. Allow muffins and loaf breads to cool for several minutes before attempting to remove them from the pan.
4. Cool the finished products on a wire rack.

◆◆◆

RECIPE 27.2

BLUEBERRY MUFFINS

Yield: 12 Muffins   **Method:** Muffin

All-purpose flour	8 oz.	250 g
Sugar	5 oz.	150 g
Baking powder	2 tsp.	10 ml
Salt	1/4 tsp.	1 ml
Egg	1	1
Milk	8 oz.	250 g
Unsalted butter, melted	2 oz.	60 g
Vanilla	1 tsp.	5 ml
Blueberries	6 oz.	170 g
Lemon zest	1 Tbsp.	15 ml

1. Sift the dry ingredients together.

2. Stir together the liquid ingredients, including the melted butter.
3. Stir the liquid mixture into the dry ingredients. Do not overmix. The batter should be lumpy.
4. Gently fold in the blueberries and lemon zest.
5. Portion into greased or paper-lined muffin cups and bake at 350°F (180°C) until light brown and set in the center, approximately 18 minutes.
6. Cool the muffins in the pan for several minutes before removing.

1. Combining the liquid ingredients.   *2.* Folding in the blueberries.   *3.* Portioning the batter.

Creaming Method

The creaming method is comparable to the mixing method used for many butter cakes. The final product will be cakelike, with a fine texture. There is less danger of overmixing with this method because the higher fat content shortens gluten strands and tenderizes the batter.

PROCEDURE FOR PREPARING PRODUCTS WITH THE CREAMING METHOD

1. Measure all ingredients.
2. Sift the dry ingredients together.
3. Combine softened fat and sugar in a mixer bowl. Cream until the color lightens and the mixture fluffs.
4. Add eggs gradually, mixing well.
5. Add the dry and liquid ingredients to the creamed fat alternately. In other words, a portion of the flour is added to the fat and incorporated, then a portion of the liquid is added and incorporated. These steps are repeated until all of the liquid and dry ingredients are incorporated. By adding the liquid and dry ingredients alternately you avoid overmixing the batter and prevent the butter and sugar mixture from curdling.
6. The batter is now ready for makeup and baking.

MAKEUP OF CREAMING METHOD PRODUCTS

Panning and baking procedures are the same as those for quick breads prepared with the muffin method.

♦♦♦

RECIPE 27.3
SOUR CREAM MUFFINS

Yield: 15 Muffins   **Method:** Creaming

Unsalted butter, room temperature	8 oz.	225 g
Sugar	8 oz.	225 g
Eggs	2	2
All-purpose flour	10 oz.	300 g
Baking powder	1 tsp.	5 ml
Baking soda	1 tsp.	5 ml
Salt	1 tsp.	5 ml
Sour cream	10 oz.	300 g
Vanilla	1 tsp.	5 ml

1. Cream the butter and sugar until light and fluffy. Add the eggs.
2. Sift the dry ingredients together.
3. Stir the dry ingredients and sour cream, alternately, into the butter mixture. Stir in the vanilla.
4. Portion and bake at 350°F (180°C) until light brown and set, approximately 20 minutes.
5. Allow the muffins to cool briefly in the pan before removing.

Streusel—*a crumbly mixture of fat, flour, sugar and, sometimes, nuts and spices used to top baked goods.*

VARIATIONS: Sour cream muffins can be topped with **streusel** or flavored with a wide variety of fruits or nuts by adding approximately 4–6 ounces (1 cup or 120–180 grams) fresh or frozen drained fruit to the batter. Blueberries, dried cherries, candied fruits, pecans and diced pears yield popular products. By adding 1/2 teaspoon (2 milliliters) each of cinnamon and nutmeg, basic spice muffins are produced.

1. Creaming the butter and sugar.

2. Adding the sour cream.

3. Topping the muffins with streusel.

♦♦♦

RECIPE 27.4
STREUSEL TOPPING

Yield: 3 lb. 8 oz. (1.5 kg)

All-purpose flour	8 oz.	225 g
Cinnamon	1/4 oz.	7 g

Salt	1 tsp.	5 ml
Brown sugar	8 oz.	225 g
Sugar	1 lb. 8 oz.	680 g
Whole butter, cold	1 lb. 4 oz.	560 g

1. Combine all dry ingredients. Cut in the butter until the mixture is coarse and crumbly.
2. Sprinkle on top of muffins or quick breads prior to baking. Streusel topping will keep for several weeks under refrigeration.

TABLE 27.1 TROUBLESHOOTING CHART

Problem	Cause	Solution
Soapy or bitter taste	Chemical leaveners not properly mixed into batter	Sift chemicals with dry ingredients
	Too much baking soda	Adjust formula
Elongated holes (tunneling)	Overmixing	Do not mix until smooth; mix only until moistened
Crust too thick	Too much sugar	Adjust formula
	Oven temperature too low	Adjust oven
Flat top with only a small peak in center	Oven temperature too low	Adjust oven
Cracked, uneven top	Oven temperature too high	Adjust oven
No rise; dense product	Old batter	Bake promptly
	Damaged leavening agents	Store new chemicals properly
	Overmixing	Do not overmix

CONCLUSION

First you must master the three mixing methods used in producing quick breads (muffin, biscuit and creaming) and understand the interaction between chemical leaveners and other ingredients. Then, with an imaginative use of flavoring ingredients, you can successfully produce a wide array of fresh-baked breads for almost any food service operation.

QUESTIONS FOR DISCUSSION

1. Name two chemical leavening agents and explain how they cause batters and doughs to rise.
2. List three common methods used for mixing quick breads. What is the significance of the type of fat used for each of these mixing methods?
3. What is the most likely explanation for discolored and bitter-tasting biscuits? What is the solution?
4. Describe the resulting product when muffin batter has been overmixed.

ADDITIONAL QUICK BREAD FORMULAS

RECIPE 27.5
CREAM SCONES

Yield: 24 Scones   **Method:** Biscuit

All-purpose flour	1 lb.	450 g
Sugar	1-1/2 oz.	45 g
Baking powder	1 Tbsp.	15 ml
Baking soda	1 tsp.	5 ml
Salt	1 tsp.	5 ml
Unsalted butter, cold	4 oz.	120 g
Egg yolks	2	2
Half-and-half	11 oz.	330 g

1. Combine all ingredients using the biscuit method.
2. Roll out the dough to a thickness of about 1/2 inch (1.25 centimeters). Cut as desired.
3. Bake at 400°F (200°C) for approximately 10 minutes.
4. Brush the tops with butter while hot.

VARIATIONS: One-half cup (125 milliliters) raisins, sultanas or currants may be added to the dry ingredients.

◆◆◆

RECIPE 27.6
SHORTCAKES

Yield: 48 Large Pieces   **Method:** Biscuit

All-purpose flour	4 lb.	1.8 kg
Baking powder	3-3/4 oz.	110 g
Salt	2 tsp.	10 ml
Granulated sugar	13 oz.	390 g
Unsalted butter, cold	1 lb. 12 oz.	840 g
Eggs	7	7
Milk	18 oz.	540 g
Butter, melted	as needed	as needed
Granulated sugar	as needed	as needed

1. Combine all ingredients using the biscuit method.
2. Cut into 3-inch (7.5–centimeter) circles and space 2 inches (5 centimeters) apart on a paper-lined sheet pan.
3. Bake at 400°F (200°C) until lightly browned, approximately 15–18 minutes.
4. Remove from the oven and brush the tops with melted butter, then sprinkle with granulated sugar.

◆◆◆

RECIPE 27.7
BASIC BERRY MUFFINS

STOUFFER STANFORD COURT HOTEL, SAN FRANCISCO, CA
Chef Ercolino Crugnale

Yield: 60 Muffins   **Method:** Muffin

Eggs	8	8
Heavy cream	1 qt.	1 lt
Lemon zest, finely grated	from 2 lemons	from 2 lemons
Nutmeg	1/4 tsp.	1 ml
Granulated sugar	1 lb. 4 oz.	600 g
Baking powder	6 Tbsp.	90 ml
Cake flour	3 lb.	1.3 kg
Kosher salt	1 Tbsp.	15 ml
Berries or nuts*	1 to 1-1/2 qt.	1 to 1.5 lt
Unsalted butter, melted	1 lb.	450 g

1. Whip the eggs, cream and zest together by hand.
2. Sift the dry ingredients together. Add the berries or nuts, tossing to coat them evenly with the flour mixture.
3. Add the dry ingredients to the egg mixture and stir until about two-thirds mixed. Add the melted butter and finish mixing.
4. Portion into greased muffin tins and bake at 375°F (190°C) for approximately 15–18 minutes.

*Blueberries, blackberries, raspberries, chopped pecans or walnuts may be used, as desired.

◆◆◆

RECIPE 27.8
MORNING GLORY MUFFINS

Yield: 18 Muffins   **Method:** Muffin

All-purpose flour	1 lb.	450 g
Granulated sugar	18 oz.	530 g
Baking soda	4 tsp.	20 ml
Cinnamon	4 tsp.	20 ml
Carrots, grated	14 oz.	420 g
Raisins	6 oz.	180 g
Pecan pieces	4 oz.	120 g
Coconut, shredded	4 oz.	120 g
Apple, unpeeled, grated	6 oz.	180 g
Eggs	6	6
Corn oil	12 oz.	360 g
Vanilla extract	4 tsp.	20 ml

1. Sift the dry ingredients together and set aside.
2. Combine the carrots, raisins, pecans, coconut and apple.
3. Combine the eggs, oil and vanilla.
4. Toss the carrot mixture into the dry ingredients. Add the liquid ingredients, stirring just until combined.
5. Bake in well-greased muffin tins at 350°F (170°C) until done, approximately 25 minutes.

◆◆◆

RECIPE 27.9

BASIC BRAN MUFFINS

Yield: 24 Muffins   **Method:** Muffin

Toasted wheat bran	6 oz.	180 g
All-purpose flour	12 oz.	360 g
Sugar	4 oz.	120 g
Baking powder	4 tsp.	20 ml
Salt	1 tsp.	5 ml
Milk	12 oz.	360 g
Honey	3 oz.	90 g
Molasses	3 oz.	90 g
Eggs	2	2
Vanilla	1 tsp.	5 ml
Unsalted butter, melted	4 oz.	120 g

1. Combine all ingredients using the muffin method.
2. Scoop into greased or paper-lined muffin tins. Bake at 350°F (170°C) until lightly brown and firm, approximately 20 minutes.

VARIATIONS: Up to 6 ounces (180 grams) of raisins or chopped nuts may be added to the batter if desired.

◆◆◆

RECIPE 27.10

ZUCCHINI BREAD

Yield: 2 9-in x 5-in (24-cm x 12-cm) Loaves   **Method:** Muffin

Whole eggs	3	3
Corn oil	8 oz.	225 g
Sugar	1 lb. 2 oz.	510 g
Vanilla	1 tsp.	5 ml
Cinnamon	2 tsp.	10 ml
Salt	1 tsp.	5 ml
Baking soda	1 tsp.	5 ml
Baking powder	1/2 tsp.	2 ml
All-purpose flour	14 oz.	420 g
Zucchini, coarsely grated	11 oz.	330 g
Pecans, chopped	4 oz.	120 g

1. Combine all ingredients using the muffin method.
2. Bake in two greased loaf pans at 350°F (170°C), approximately 1 hour.

◆◆◆

RECIPE 27.11

IRISH SODA BREAD

Yield: 1 8-inch-round (20-cm) Loaf   **Method:** Muffin

Currants	2 oz.	60 g
Irish whiskey	1-1/2 oz.	45 g
All-purpose flour, sifted	12 oz.	360 g

Salt	1 tsp.	5 ml
Baking powder	1-1/2 tsp.	7 ml
Baking soda	1 tsp.	5 ml
Brown sugar	1 Tbsp.	15 ml
Lowfat buttermilk	1 pt.	500 ml

1. Soak the currants in the whiskey until plump, at least 1 hour.
2. Sift the dry ingredients together. Stir in the currants and whiskey.
3. Stir in the buttermilk, making a stiff batter.
4. Spread the batter in a greased 8-inch-round cake pan. Bake at 350°F (170°C) until well browned and firm, approximately 45 minutes.

Nutritional values per 1/8 loaf:

Calories	198	Protein	7 g
Calories from fat	4%	Vitamin A	36 IU
Total fat	1 g	Vitamin C	13 mg
Saturated fat	0 g	Sodium	528 mg
Cholesterol	2 mg		

◆◆◆

RECIPE 27.12

BASIC CORN MUFFINS

Yield: 30 Muffins   **Method:** Muffin

Yellow cornmeal	12 oz.	350 g
All-purpose flour	12 oz.	350 g
Sugar	10 oz.	300 g
Baking powder	1 Tbsp.	15 ml
Baking soda	1 tsp.	5 ml
Salt	3/4 tsp.	3 ml
Buttermilk	24 oz.	720 g
Eggs	6	6
Unsalted butter, melted	6 oz.	170 g

1. Combine all ingredients using the muffin method.
2. Portion into greased muffin tins, filling two-thirds full.
3. Bake at 375°F (190°C) for approximately 20–25 minutes.

◆◆◆

RECIPE 27.13

HUSH PUPPIES
(DEEP-FRIED CORNBREAD)

Yield: 60 2-inch (5-cm) Pieces   **Method:** Muffin

Yellow cornmeal	1 lb.	450 g
All-purpose flour	8 oz.	225 g
Baking powder	1 Tbsp.	15 ml
Salt	1 Tbsp.	15 ml
Black pepper	1 Tbsp.	15 ml

Continued

Sugar	2 oz.	60 g
Onion, minced	8 oz.	225 g
Eggs	4	4
Milk	1 pt.	450 ml

1. Combine all ingredients using the muffin method.
2. Drop small scoops (using a #60 or #70 portion scoop) into 375°F (190°C) deep fat. Using the swimming method, deep-fry until golden brown.
3. Remove from the fat and drain. Serve immediately.

◆◆◆

RECIPE 27.14

BLUE CORN MUFFINS

Yield: 60 Muffins   **Method:** Creaming

All-purpose shortening	1 lb.	450 g
Granulated sugar	1 lb. 8 oz.	680 g
Blue cornmeal	1 lb.	450 g
Whole eggs	1 pt.	450 ml
All-purpose flour	2 lb.	900 g
Baking powder	1-1/4 oz.	35 g
Salt	1-1/2 oz.	45 g
Vanilla	1 Tbsp.	15 ml
Honey	12 oz.	340 g
Buttermilk	1 qt.	1 lt

1. Using a mixer fitted with the paddle attachment, cream the shortening, sugar and cornmeal until light and fluffy. Add the eggs. Mix on low speed for 1 minute.
2. Sift the remaining dry ingredients together. Stir the vanilla and honey into the buttermilk.
3. Add the dry ingredients and buttermilk mixture, alternately, to the creamed mixture. Mix on low speed for 2 minutes, scraping down the bowl as necessary.
4. Portion into well-greased muffin pans. Bake at 325°F (160°C) for approximately 15 minutes.

NOTE: Blue cornmeal is derived from variegated Indian corn. Its natural blue-gray color is a result of a high lysine content. Blue corn has a stronger flavor than white or yellow corn and is popular in southwestern cuisine.

◆◆◆

RECIPE 27.15

LEMON TEA BREAD

Yield: 12 Muffins or One Loaf   **Method:** Creaming

Unsalted butter, softened	3 oz.	90 g
Granulated sugar	10 oz.	300 g
Eggs	2	2
Milk	4 oz.	120 g
All-purpose flour	6 oz.	180 g
Baking powder	1 tsp.	5 ml

Salt	1/2 tsp.	2 ml
Lemon zest	1 Tbsp.	15 ml
Lemon juice	4 oz.	120 g

1. Cream the butter with 7 ounces (210 grams) of the sugar. Add the eggs and milk. Mix well.

2. Sift the dry ingredients together and add to the butter mixture. Fold in the lemon zest. Portion into lightly greased pans.

3. Bake at 350° (170°C) until tester comes out clean, approximately 35–40 minutes for a large loaf or 12–15 minutes for muffins. Remove the bread from the pan(s) and place on a cooling rack.

4. Combine 3 ounces (85 grams) of the sugar with the lemon juice. Heat until the sugar dissolves and the mixture is hot. Slowly pour or brush the glaze over the hot bread.

CHAPTER 28
YEAST BREADS

After studying this chapter you will be able to:

◆ select and use yeast
◆ perform the 10 steps involved in yeast bread production
◆ mix yeast doughs using the straight dough method and sponge method
◆ prepare rolled-in doughs

lthough few baked goods intimidate novice bakers as much as yeast breads, few baked goods are actually as forgiving or as comforting to prepare as yeast breads. By mastering a few basic procedures and techniques, you can offer your customers delicious, fresh yeast products.

Yeast breads can be divided into two categories: lean doughs and rich doughs. Lean doughs, such as those used for French and Italian breads, contain little or no sugar or fat. Rich doughs, such as brioche and some multigrain breads, contain significantly more sugar and fat. Rolled-in doughs, so-called because the fat is rolled into the dough in layers, are a type of rich dough used for baked goods such as croissants and sweetened danish.

The study of yeast breads could well occupy this entire text and an entire course. The focus here is narrowed to an understanding of fundamental techniques and procedures for making the most common styles of yeast breads for a small retail shop or restaurant. Most of the formulas in this chapter yield only one or two loaves or a few dozen rolls. Although most of these formulas can be increased successfully if necessary, you can best develop proper judgment skills by first preparing small quantities. We discuss hands-on mixing and make-up techniques, leaving the science of commercial (i.e., mechanical) bread production to others.

YEAST

Yeast is a living organism: a one-celled fungus. Various strains of yeast are present virtually everywhere. Yeast feeds on carbohydrates, converting them to carbon dioxide and alcohol in an organic process known as **fermentation**:

Yeast + Carbohydrates = Alcohol + Carbon Dioxide

Fermentation—*the process by which yeast converts sugar into alcohol and carbon dioxide; it also refers to the time that yeast dough is left to rise— that is, the time it takes for carbon dioxide gas cells to form and become trapped in the gluten network.*

When yeast releases carbon dioxide gas during bread making, the gas becomes trapped in the dough's gluten network. The trapped gas leavens the bread, providing the desired rise and texture. The small amount of alcohol produced by fermentation evaporates during baking.

As with most living things, yeast is very sensitive to temperature. It prefers temperatures between 90°F and 110°F (32–43°C). At temperatures below 34°F (2°C) it becomes dormant; above 138°F (59°C) it dies.

Salt is used in bread making because it conditions gluten, making it stronger and more elastic. Salt also affects yeast fermentation. Because salt inhibits the growth of yeast, it helps control the dough's rise. Too little salt and not only will the bread taste bland, it will rise too rapidly. Too much salt, however, and the yeast will be destroyed. By learning to control the amount of food for the yeast and the temperatures of fermentation, you can learn to control the texture of your yeast-leavened products.

TABLE 28.1   TEMPERATURES FOR YEAST DEVELOPMENT

Temperature		Yeast Development
34°F	2°C	Inactive
60–70°F	16–21°C	Slow action
70–90°F	21–32°C	Best temperature for growth of fresh yeast
105–115°F	41–46°C	Best temperature for growth of dry yeast
125–130°F	52–54°C	Best temperature for activating instant yeast
138°F	59°C	Yeast dies

Types of Yeast

Baker's yeast is available in two forms: compressed and active dry. (You may also encounter a product called brewer's yeast; it is a nutritional supplement with no leavening ability.)

Compressed Yeast

Compressed yeast is a mixture of yeast and starch with a moisture content of approximately 70%. Also referred to as **fresh yeast**, compressed yeast must be kept refrigerated. It should be creamy white and crumbly with a fresh, yeasty smell. Do not use compressed yeast that has developed a sour odor, brown color or slimy film.

Compressed yeast is available in 0.6-ounce (17-gram) cubes and 1-pound (450-gram) blocks. Under proper storage conditions, compressed yeast has a shelf life of 2–3 weeks.

Active Dry Yeast

Active dry yeast differs from compressed yeast in that virtually all of the moisture has been removed by hot air. The absence of moisture renders the organism dormant and allows the yeast to be stored without refrigeration for several months. When preparing doughs, dry yeast is generally rehydrated in a lukewarm (approximately 110°F [43°C]) liquid before being added to the other ingredients.

Dry yeast is available in 1/4-ounce (7-gram) packages and 1- or 2-pound (450-gram or 1-kilogram) vacuum-sealed bags. It should be stored in a cool, dry place and refrigerated after opening.

Instant Yeast

Instant or **quick-rise dry yeast** is also available. It must be blended with the dry ingredients in a bread formula, then activated with hot (approximately 125–130°F [52–54°C]) water. It dramatically speeds the rising process. Instant yeast can be substituted measure for measure for regular dry yeast. Instant yeast is still a living organism and will be destroyed at temperatures above 138°F (59°C).

The flavors of dry and compressed yeasts are virtually indistinguishable, but dry yeast is approximately twice as strong. Because too much yeast can ruin bread, always remember to halve the specified weight of compressed yeast when substituting dry yeast in a formula. Likewise, if a formula specifies dry yeast, double the amount when substituting compressed yeast. All of the formulas in this text requiring yeast use regular active dry yeast.

Sourdough Starter

Prior to commercial yeast production, bakers relied on starters to leaven their breads. Early starters were simple but magical mixtures of flour and liquid (water, potato broth, milk) left to capture wild yeasts from the air and then ferment. Only a portion of the starter was used at a time. The rest was kept for later use, replenished periodically with additional flour and liquid so the magic could continue.

Today, starters are generally fortified with yeast to provide consistency and reliability; they are prized for the unique, sour flavors they impart. Prepared dry cultures are often used commercially to give bread a "sourdough" flavor without requiring the time and space necessary to develop and maintain an active starter.

♦♦♦

RECIPE 28.1

SOURDOUGH STARTER

Sourdough Starter

Yield: 1 qt. (1 lt)

Active dry yeast	1 tsp.	5 ml
Water, warm	4 oz.	120 g
Water, room temperature	14 oz.	400 g
All-purpose flour	2 lb.	1 kg

1. Combine the yeast and warm water. Let stand until foamy, approximately 10 minutes.
2. Stir in the 14 ounces (400 grams) of room-temperature water, then add the flour, 2 ounces (60 grams) at a time.
3. Blend by hand or with the paddle attachment of an electric mixer on low speed for 2 minutes.
4. Place the starter in a warmed bowl and cover with plastic wrap. Let stand at room temperature overnight. The starter should triple in volume but still be wet and sticky. Refrigerate until ready to use.
5. Each time a portion of the starter is used, it must be replenished. To replenish the starter, stir in equal amounts by volume of flour and warm water. Then allow the mixture to ferment at room temperature for several hours or overnight before refrigerating.

NOTE: If liquid rises to the top of the starter it should be stirred back into the mixture. If the starter develops a pink or yellow film it has been contaminated and must be discarded.

PRODUCTION STAGES FOR YEAST BREADS

The production of yeast breads can be divided into 10 stages:

1. scaling ingredients
2. mixing and kneading dough
3. fermenting dough

4. punching down dough
5. portioning dough
6. rounding portions
7. shaping portions
8. proofing products
9. baking products
10. cooling and storing finished products

Stage 1: Scaling Ingredients

As with any other bakeshop product, it is important to scale or measure ingredients accurately when making a yeast bread. Be sure that all necessary ingredients are available and at the proper temperature before starting.

The amount of flour required in a yeast bread may vary depending upon the humidity level, storage conditions of the flour and the accuracy with which other ingredients are measured. The amount of flour stated in most formulas is to be used as a guide; experience teaches when more or less flour is actually needed.

Stage 2: Mixing and Kneading Dough

The way ingredients are combined affects the outcome of the bread. A dough must be mixed properly in order to combine the ingredients uniformly, distribute the yeast and develop the gluten. If the dough is not mixed properly, the bread's texture and shape suffer.

Yeast breads are usually mixed by either the **straight dough method** or the **sponge method**. A third method used for rich, flaky doughs is discussed below in the section on **rolled-in doughs**.

Once ingredients are combined, the dough must be kneaded to develop gluten, the network of proteins that gives a bread its shape and texture. Kneading can be done by hand or by an electric mixer with its dough hook

---

◆◆◆
THE RISE OF YEAST BREADS

How and when the first yeast-leavened bread came into being no one knows. Perhaps some wild yeasts—the world is full of them—drifted into a dough as it awaited baking. Perhaps some ancient baker substituted fermented ale or beer for water one day. In any case, the resulting bread was different, lighter and more appetizing.

Based on models, images and writings found in excavated tombs, we can be fairly certain that the ancient Egyptians saved a bit of fermented dough from one day's baking to add to the next day's. This use of sourdough starter continues today, enjoying widespread popularity.

Other cultures developed their own leavening methods. The Greeks and Romans prepared a wheat porridge with wine, which caused their doughs to ferment. The Gauls and Iberians added the foamy head from ale to their doughs. Both methods resulted in lighter breads that retained their fresh textures longer.

Since ancient times, bread baking has been one of the first household tasks readily turned over to professionals. The first cooks to work outside homes during the Greek and Roman empires were bakers. The bakery trade flourished during the Middle Ages, with a wide variety of breads being produced. Yeast-leavened breads remained the exception, not the norm, until well into the 17th century, however.

The first real collection of bread recipes is found in Nicolas Bonnefon's *Les Délices de la campagne*, published in 1654. Bonnefon's instructions, meant for those dissatisfied with commercial products of the time, included the use of beer yeast. By the end of the 17th century, published works included recipes for breads leavened with sourdough starter and the yeasts used in breweries.

Louis Pasteur finally identified yeast as a living organism in 1857. Soon after, a process for distilling or manufacturing baker's yeast was developed. By 1868, commercial baking yeast was available in stores.

attachment. Dough should be kneaded until it is smooth and moderately elastic. The presence of a few blisterlike air bubbles on the dough's surface also signals that kneading is complete. Because fat and sugar slow gluten development, rich, sweet doughs are generally kneaded longer than lean doughs. Overkneading results in dough that is, at best, difficult to shape and, in extreme cases, sticky and inelastic. Overkneading is rarely a problem, however, except when using a high-speed mixer or food processor.

PROCEDURE FOR KNEADING DOUGH BY HAND

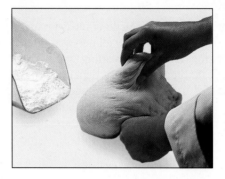

1. First, bring a portion of the dough toward you.

2. Then push the dough away from you with your fist.

3. Repeat until the dough is properly kneaded.

Straight Dough Method

The simplest and most common method for mixing yeast doughs is known as the straight dough method. With this method, all ingredients are simply combined and mixed. The yeast may or may not be combined first with a warm liquid. Be careful that the temperature of the liquid ingredients does not exceed 138°F (59°C) or the yeast will die.

Once the ingredients are combined, the dough is kneaded until it is smooth and elastic. Kneading time varies according to the kneading method used and the type of dough being produced. The straight dough method is illustrated with Recipe 28.2, Soft Yeast Dinner Rolls.

Sponge Method

The sponge method of mixing yeast doughs has two stages. During the first stage the yeast, liquid and approximately one half of the flour are combined to make a thick batter known as a **sponge**. The sponge is allowed to rise until bubbly and doubled in size. During the second stage the fat, salt, sugar and remaining flour are added. The dough is kneaded and allowed to rise again.

These two fermentations give sponge method breads a somewhat different flavor and a lighter texture than breads made with the straight dough method.

Do not confuse sponge method breads with sourdough starters. The sponge method is most often used to improve the texture of heavy doughs such as rye. Unlike a sourdough starter, the first-stage sponge is prepared only for the specific formula and is not reserved for later use. The sponge method is illustrated with Recipe 28.3, Light Rye Bread.

Stage 3: Fermenting Dough

As mentioned earlier, fermentation is the process by which yeast converts sugar into alcohol and carbon dioxide. Fermentation also refers to the time that yeast dough is left to rise—that is, the time it takes for carbon dioxide gas to form and become trapped in the gluten network. Note that **fermentation** refers to the rise given to the entire mass of yeast dough, while **proofing** refers to the rise given to shaped yeast products just prior to baking.

For fermentation, place the kneaded dough into a lightly oiled container large enough to allow the dough to expand. The surface of the dough may be oiled to prevent drying. Cover the dough and place it in a warm place—that is, at temperatures between 75° and 85°F (24–29°C). It is better to allow the dough to rise slowly in a cool place than to rush fermentation.

Fermentation is complete when the dough has approximately doubled in size and no longer springs back when pressed gently with two fingers. The time necessary varies depending on the type of dough, the temperature of the room and the temperature of the dough.

Stage 4: Punching Down Dough

After fermentation, the dough is gently folded down to expel and redistribute the gas pockets with a technique known as **punching down**. Punching down dough also helps even out the dough's temperature and relaxes the gluten.

Stage 5: Portioning Dough

The dough is now ready to be divided into portions. For loaves, the dough is scaled to the desired weight. For individual rolls you can first shape the dough into an even log, then cut off portions with a chef's knife or dough cutter. Weighing the cut dough pieces on a portion scale ensures even-sized portions. When portioning, work quickly and keep the dough covered to prevent it from drying out.

Stage 6: Rounding Portions

The portions of dough must be shaped into smooth, round balls in a technique known as **rounding**. Rounding stretches the outside layer of gluten into a smooth coating. This helps hold in gases and makes it easier to shape the dough. Unrounded rolls rise unevenly and have a rough, lumpy surface.

Stage 7: Shaping Portions

Lean doughs and some rich doughs can be shaped into a variety of forms: large loaves, small loaves, free-form or country-style rounds or individual dinner rolls. Table 28.2 identifies common pan sizes and the approximate weight of the dough used to fill them. Some shaping techniques are diagramed below. Other doughs, particularly brioche, croissant and danish, are usually shaped in very specific ways. Those techniques are discussed and illustrated with their specific formulas.

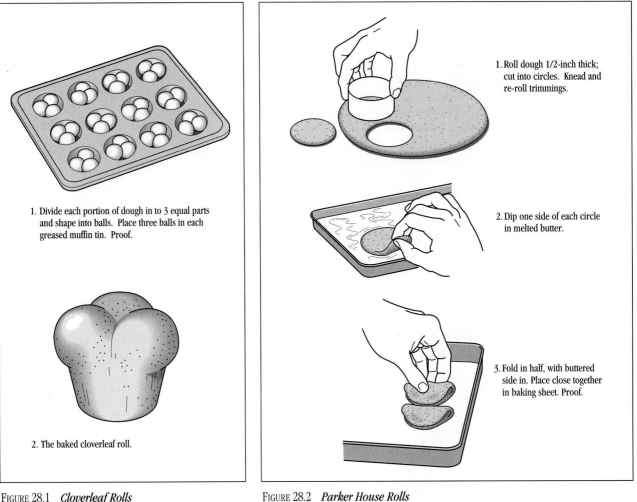

FIGURE 28.1   *Cloverleaf Rolls*

1. Divide each portion of dough in to 3 equal parts and shape into balls. Place three balls in each greased muffin tin. Proof.

2. The baked cloverleaf roll.

FIGURE 28.2   *Parker House Rolls*

1. Roll dough 1/2-inch thick; cut into circles. Knead and re-roll trimmings.

2. Dip one side of each circle in melted butter.

3. Fold in half, with buttered side in. Place close together in baking sheet. Proof.

TABLE 28.2	PAN SIZES	
Pan	Approximate Size	Weight of Dough*
Sandwich Loaf	16 in. × 4 in. × 4-1/2 in.	4 lb.
Pullman	13 in. × 4 in. × 3 in.	3 lb.
Large	9 in. × 5 in. × 3 in.	2 lb.
Medium	8 in. × 4 in. × 2 in.	1 lb. 8 oz.
Small	7 in. × 3 in. × 2 in.	1 lb.
Miniature	5 in. × 3 in. × 2 in.	8 oz.

*Weights given are approximate; variations may occur based on the type of dough used as well as the temperature and time of proofing.

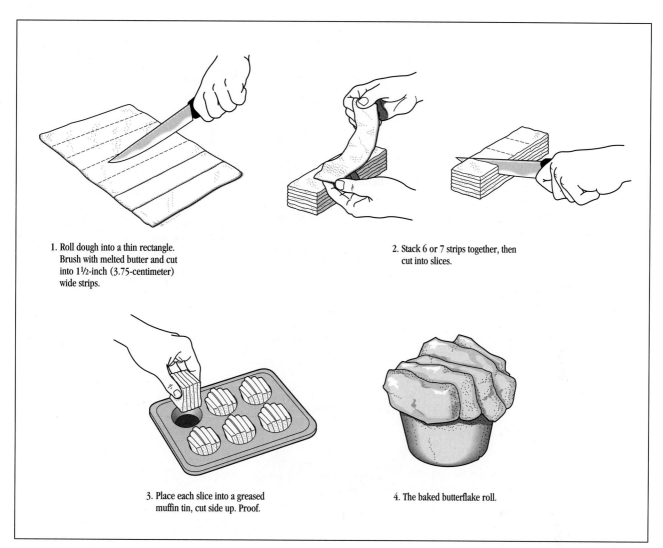

1. Roll dough into a thin rectangle. Brush with melted butter and cut into 1½-inch (3.75-centimeter) wide strips.

2. Stack 6 or 7 strips together, then cut into slices.

3. Place each slice into a greased muffin tin, cut side up. Proof.

4. The baked butterflake roll.

FIGURE 28.3   *Butterflake Rolls*

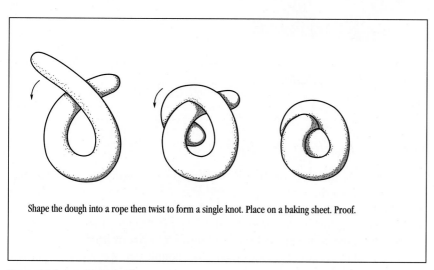

Shape the dough into a rope then twist to form a single knot. Place on a baking sheet. Proof.

FIGURE 28.4   *Bow Knot Rolls*

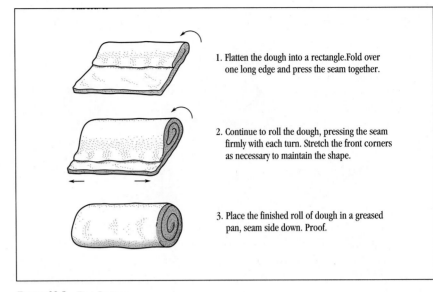

FIGURE 28.5 *Pan Loaves*

1. Flatten the dough into a rectangle. Fold over one long edge and press the seam together.

2. Continue to roll the dough, pressing the seam firmly with each turn. Stretch the front corners as necessary to maintain the shape.

3. Place the finished roll of dough in a greased pan, seam side down. Proof.

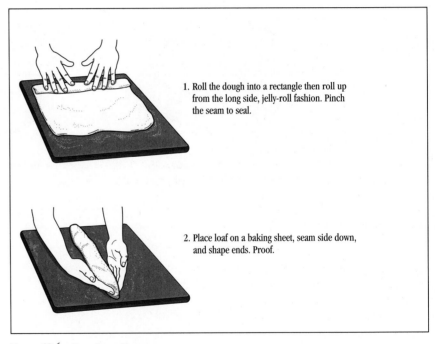

FIGURE 28.6 *Free-Form Loaves*

1. Roll the dough into a rectangle then roll up from the long side, jelly-roll fashion. Pinch the seam to seal.

2. Place loaf on a baking sheet, seam side down, and shape ends. Proof.

Stage 8: Proofing Products

Proofing—*the final rise of shaped yeast products just prior to baking.*

Proofing is the final rise of shaped or panned yeast products before baking. The temperatures should be between 95° and 115°F (35–46°C), slightly higher than the temperatures for fermentation. Some humidity is also desirable to prevent the dough from drying or forming a crust. Temperature and humidity can be controlled with a special cabinet known as a **proof box**.

Proofing should continue until the product doubles in size and springs back slowly when lightly touched. Underproofing results in poor volume and texture. Overproofing results in a sour taste, poor volume and a paler color after baking.

Stage 9: Baking Products

As yeast breads bake, a variety of chemical and physical changes turn the dough into an edible product. These changes are discussed in Chapter 26, Principles of the Bakeshop.

Because of the expansion of gases, yeast products experience a sudden rise when first placed in a hot oven. This rise is known as **oven spring**. As the dough's temperature increases, the yeast dies, the gluten fibers become firm, the starches gelatinize, the moisture evaporates and, finally, the crust forms and turns brown.

Before baking, products can be washed and then, if desired, slashed.

Washes

The appearance of yeast breads can be altered by applying a glaze or **wash** to the dough before baking. The crust is made shiny or matte, hard or soft, darker or lighter by the proper use of washes. Washes are also used to attach seeds, wheat germ, oats or other toppings to the dough's surface.

The most commonly used wash is an egg wash, composed of whole egg and water. Yeast products can also be topped with plain water, a mixture of egg and milk, plain milk or richer glazes containing sugar and flavorings. Even a light dusting of white flour can be used to top dough. (This is commonly seen with potato rolls.)

Avoid using too much wash, as it can burn or cause the product to stick to the pan. Puddles or streaks of egg wash on the dough will cause uneven browning.

Washes may be applied before or after proofing. If applied after proofing, be extremely careful not to deflate the product.

Occasionally a formula will specify that melted butter or oil be brushed on the product after baking. Do not, however, apply egg washes to already baked products, as the egg will remain raw and the desired effect will not be achieved.

TABLE 28.3	WASHES FOR YEAST PRODUCTS
Wash	Use
Whole egg and water	Shine and color
Whole egg and milk	Shine and color with a soft crust
Egg white and water	Shine with a firm crust
Water	Crisp crust
Flour	Texture and contrast
Milk or cream	Color with a soft crust

Slashing

The shape and appearance of some breads can be improved by cutting their tops with a sharp knife or razor just before baking. This is referred to as **slashing** or **docking**. Hard-crusted breads are usually slashed to allow for continued rising and the escape of gases after the crust has formed. Breads that are not properly slashed will burst or break along the sides. Slashing can also be used to make an attractive design on the product's surface.

Steam Injection

The crisp crust desired for certain breads and rolls is achieved by introducing moisture into the oven during baking. Professional bakers' ovens have built-in steam injection jets to provide moisture as needed. To create steam in any oven you can spray or mist the bread with water several times during baking, place ice cubes on the oven floor to melt or keep a pan of hot water on the oven's lowest rack. Rich doughs, which do not form crisp crusts, are baked without steam.

Determining Doneness

Baking time is determined by a variety of factors: the product's size, the oven thermostat's accuracy and the desired crust color. Larger items require a longer baking time than smaller ones. Lean dough products bake faster and at higher temperatures than rich dough products.

Bread loaves can be tested for doneness by tapping them on the bottom and listening for a hollow sound. This indicates that air, not moisture, is present inside the loaf. If the bottom is damp or heavy, the loaf probably needs more baking time. The texture and color of the crust are also a good indication of doneness, particularly with individual rolls. As you bake a variety of yeast products you will develop the experience necessary to determine doneness without strict adherence to elapsed time.

Stage 10: Cooling and Storing Finished Products

The quality of even the finest yeast products suffers if they are cooled or stored improperly. Yeast products should be cooled at room temperature and away from drafts. Yeast breads and rolls should be removed from their pans for cooling. Allow loaves to cool completely before slicing.

Once cool, yeast products should be stored at room temperature or frozen for longer storage. Do not refrigerate baked goods, as refrigeration promotes staling. Do not wrap Italian or French loaves, as this causes crusts to lose the desired crispness.

◆◆◆

RECIPE 28.2
SOFT YEAST DINNER ROLLS

Yield: 75 Rolls   **Method:** Straight Dough

Water, warm	1 lb. 4 oz.	560 g
Active dry yeast	2 oz.	60 g
Bread flour	2 lb. 12 oz.	1.2 kg
Salt	1 oz.	30 g
Sugar	4 oz.	120 g
Dried milk powder	2 oz.	60 g
Shortening	2 oz.	60 g
Unsalted butter, softened	2 oz.	60 g
Eggs, whole	4 oz.	120 g
Egg wash	as needed	as needed

1. Combine the water and yeast in a small bowl. Combine the remaining ingredients (except the egg wash) in the bowl of an electric mixer.
2. Add the water-and-yeast mixture to the remaining ingredients; stir to combine.
3. Knead with a dough hook on second speed for 10 minutes.
4. Transfer the dough to a lightly greased bowl, cover and place in a warm spot. Let rise until doubled, approximately 1 hour.
5. Punch down the dough. Let it rest a few minutes to allow the gluten to relax.
6. Divide the dough into 1-1/4-ounce (35-gram) portions and round. Shape as desired and arrange on paper-lined sheet pans. Proof until doubled in size.
7. Carefully brush the proofed rolls with egg wash. Bake at 400°F (200°C) until medium brown, approximately 12–15 minutes.

1. Mixing the soft yeast dough:

   a) Combining the ingredients in a mixer bowl with the dough hook attached.

   b) Adding the yeast-and-water mixture.

2. Kneading the dough.

3. The dough before rising.

4. Punching down the dough:

   a) Pressing down on the center of the dough with your fist.

   b) Folding the edges of the dough in toward the center.

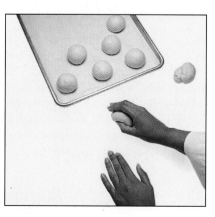

5. Scaling the dough.

6. Rounding the rolls.

7. Egg-washing the rolls.

1. Rye bread starter.

2. Mixing the rye dough.

3. Shaping the rye loaves.

♦♦♦

RECIPE 28.3

LIGHT RYE BREAD

Yield: 2 Large Loaves   **Method:** Sponge

Unbleached wheat flour	1 lb.	450 g
Medium rye flour	8 oz.	225 g
Dark molasses	3 oz.	90 g
Water, warm	1 lb. 4 oz.	600 g
Active dry yeast	1/2 oz.	15 g
Nonfat dry milk	1-1/2 oz.	45 g
Caraway seeds, crushed	2 Tbsp.	30 ml
Kosher salt	1 Tbsp.	15 ml
Unsalted butter, melted	1 Tbsp.	15 ml
Egg wash	as needed	as needed

1. Stir the flours together and set aside.

2. To make the sponge, combine the molasses, water and yeast. Add 8 ounces (225 grams) of the flour mixture. Stir vigorously for 3 minutes. Cover the bowl and set aside to rise until doubled and very bubbly, approximately 1 hour.

3. Stir the milk powder, caraway seeds, salt and butter into the sponge.

4. Gradually add the remaining flour to the sponge. When the dough is too stiff to mix by hand, transfer the dough to a mixer fitted with a dough hook.

5. Continue adding flour until the dough is stiff but slightly tacky. Knead for 5 minutes on low speed.

6. Transfer the dough to a lightly greased bowl, cover and place in a warm place until doubled, approximately 45–60 minutes.

7. Punch down the dough and divide into two pieces. Shape each piece into a round loaf and place on a sheet pan that has been dusted with cornmeal or lightly oiled. Brush the loaves with egg wash and let rise until doubled, approximately 45 minutes.

8. Slash the tops with a razor or knife. Bake at 375°F (190°C) until golden brown and crusty, approximately 25 minutes.

ROLLED-IN DOUGHS

Baked goods made with rolled-in doughs include croissants, Danish pastries and the non-yeast-leavened puff pastry. (Puff pastry is discussed in Chapter 29, Pies, Pastries and Cookies.) The dough is so named because the fat is incorporated through a process of rolling and folding. Products made with a rolled-in dough have a distinctive flaky texture created by the repeated layering of fat and dough. As the dough bakes, moisture is released from the fat in the form of steam. The steam is then trapped between the layers of dough, causing them to rise and separate.

Making Rolled-In Doughs

Rolled-in doughs are made following most of the 10 production stages discussed above. The principal differences are that the butter is incorporated through a turning process after the dough base is fermented and punched down; rolled-in doughs are portioned somewhat differently than other yeast doughs and the portions are then shaped without rounding.

Butter is often used for rolled-in products because of its flavor. Unfortunately, butter is hard to work with because it cracks and breaks when cold and becomes too soft to roll at room temperature. Margarine, shortening or specially formulated high-moisture fats can be used, sometimes in combination with butter, to reduce costs or make the dough easier to work with.

The dough base should not be kneaded too much as gluten will continue to develop during the rolling and folding process. Commercial bakeries, hotels and larger restaurants generally use an electric dough sheeter to roll the dough. This saves time and ensures a more consistent product.

PROCEDURE FOR MAKING ROLLED-IN DOUGHS

1. Mix the dough and allow it to rise.
2. Shape the butter or shortening, then chill it.
3. Roll out the dough evenly, then top with the chilled butter.
4. Fold the dough around the butter, enclosing it completely.
5. Roll out the dough into a rectangle, about 1/2 to 1 inch (1.25 to 2.5 centimeters) thick. Always be sure to roll at right angles; do not roll haphazardly or in a circle as you would pastry doughs.
6. Fold the dough in thirds. Be sure to brush off any excess flour from between the folds. This completes the first turn. Chill the dough for 20 to 30 minutes.
7. Roll out the dough and fold it in the same manner a second and third time, allowing the dough to rest between each turn. After completing the third turn, wrap the dough carefully and allow it to rest for several hours or overnight before shaping and baking.

◆◆◆

RECIPE 28.4

CROISSANTS

Yield: 60 Rolls   Method: Rolled-in

Bread flour	2 lb. 4 oz.	1 kg
Salt	1 oz.	30 g
Sugar	6 oz.	170 g
Milk	1 lb. 6 oz.	625 g
Active dry yeast	1 oz.	30 g
Unsalted butter, soft	1 lb. 8 oz.	680 g
Egg wash	as needed	as needed

1. Stir the flour, salt and sugar together in a mixer bowl fitted with a dough hook.
2. Warm the milk to approximately 90°F (32°C). Stir in the yeast.
3. Add the milk-and-yeast mixture to the dry ingredients. Stir until combined, then knead on second speed for 10 minutes.
4. Place the dough in a large floured bowl, cover and let rise until doubled in size, approximately 1 hour.
5. Prepare the butter while the dough is rising. Place the butter in an even layer between two large pieces of plastic wrap and roll into a flat rectan-

Continued

◆◆◆

THE CULTURED CROISSANT

A croissant brings to mind a Parisian sidewalk café and a steaming cup of café crème. It is, however, a truly international delicacy. Created by bakers in Budapest (Hungary) to celebrate the city's liberation from Turkey in 1686, its shape was derived from the crescent moon of the Turkish flag. The delicacy was soon adopted as a breakfast pastry by both the French and the Italians. The first machine for mass-producing croissants was designed by a Japanese firm and manufactured in Italy. Although croissants became popular in this country only during the last decade or so, Americans now consume millions of croissants each year.

gle, approximately 8 inches × 11 inches (20 centimeters × 27.5 centimeters) and chill.

6. After the dough has risen, punch it down. Roll out the dough into a large rectangle, about 1/2 inch (1.25 centimeters) thick and large enough to enclose the rectangle of butter. Place the unwrapped butter in the center of the dough and fold the dough around the butter, enclosing it completely.

7. Roll out the block of dough into a long rectangle, about 1 inch (2.5 centimeters) thick. Fold the dough in thirds, as if you were folding a letter. This completes the first turn. Wrap the dough in plastic and chill for approximately 20–30 minutes.

8. Repeat the rolling and folding process two more times, chilling the dough between each turn. When finished, wrap the dough well and chill it overnight before shaping and baking.

9. To shape the dough into croissant rolls, cut off one quarter of the block at a time, wrapping and returning the rest to the refrigerator. Roll each quarter of dough into a large rectangle, about 1/4 inch (6 millimeters) thick.

10. Cut the dough into uniform triangles. Starting with the large end, roll each triangle into a crescent and place on a paper-lined sheet pan.

11. Brush lightly with egg wash. Proof until doubled, but do not allow the dough to become so warm that the butter melts.

12. Bake at 375°F (190°C) until golden brown, approximately 12–15 minutes.

1. Rolling out the butter between two sheets of plastic wrap.

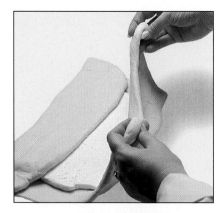

2. After positioning the butter on the rolled-out dough, folding the dough around the butter.

3. Brushing the excess flour from the rolled-out dough.

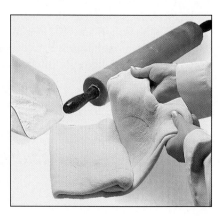

4. Folding the dough in thirds.

5. The finished croissant dough.

6. Cutting the dough into triangles.

7. Baked croissants.

TABLE 28.4   TROUBLESHOOTING CHART

Problem	Cause	Solution
Cannonball of dough	Too much flour forced into the dough	Gradually add water; adjust formula
Crust too pale	Oven temperature too low	Adjust oven
	Dough overproofed	Proof only until almost doubled, then bake immediately
Crust too dark	Oven too hot	Adjust oven
	Too much sugar in dough	Adjust formula or measure sugar carefully
Top crust separates from rest of loaf	Dough improperly shaped	Shape dough carefully
	Crust not slashed properly	Slash dough to a depth of 1/2 in. (1.25 cm)
	Dough dried out during proofing	Cover dough during proofing
Sides of loaf are cracked	Bread expanded after crust had formed	Slash top of loaf before baking
Dense texture	Not enough yeast	Adjust formula or measure yeast carefully
	Not enough fermentation time	Let dough rise until doubled or as directed
	Too much salt	Adjust formula or measure salt carefully
Ropes of undercooked dough running through the product	Insufficient kneading	Knead dough until it is smooth and elastic or as directed
	Insufficient rising time	Allow adequate time for rising
	Oven too hot	Adjust oven
Free-form loaf spreads and flattens	Dough too soft	Add flour
Large holes in bread	Too much yeast	Adjust formula or measure yeast carefully
	Overkneaded	Knead only as directed
	Inadequate punch-down	Punch down properly to knead out excess air before shaping
Blisters on crust	Too much liquid	Measure ingredients carefully
	Improper shaping	Knead out excess air before shaping
	Too much steam in oven	Reduce amount of steam or moisture in oven

CONCLUSION

Fresh yeast breads are a popular and inexpensive addition to any menu and are surprisingly easy to prepare. By understanding and appreciating the importance of each of the ten production stages described above, you will be able to create and adapt formulas to suit your specific operation and needs.

QUESTIONS FOR DISCUSSION

1. Describe the characteristics of lean and rich doughs and give an example of each.

2. Explain the differences between active dry yeast and compressed yeast. Describe the correct procedures for working with these yeasts.

3. Explain the differences between a sponge and a sourdough starter. How are each of these items used?

4. Describe the straight dough mixing method and give two examples of products made with this procedure.

5. Briefly describe the procedure for making a rolled-in dough and give two examples of products made from rolled-in doughs.

6. List the ten production stages for yeast breads. Which of these production stages would also apply to quick bread production? Explain your answer.

ADDITIONAL YEAST BREAD FORMULAS

RECIPE 28.5

BASIC FRENCH BREAD

Yield: 5 lb. (2.2 kg)   **Method:** Straight Dough

Water, warm	1 qt.	1 lt
Active dry yeast	1 oz.	30 g
Bread flour	2 lb. 12 oz.	1.2 kg
Salt	1 oz.	30 g

1. Combine the water and yeast in a mixer bowl. Add the remaining ingredients and mix on low speed with a dough hook until all of the flour is incorporated.

2. Increase to second speed and knead the dough until it is smooth and elastic.

3. Let the dough rise until doubled. Punch down, divide and shape as desired. Let rise again until doubled.

4. Place a pan of water in the oven to generate steam while the dough rises.

5. Bake at 400°F (200°C) until the crust is well developed and golden brown and the bread is baked through, approximately 12 minutes for rolls and 30 minutes for small loaves.

Nutritional values per 1 oz. (30 g) roll:

Calories	56	Protein	2 g
Calories from fat	4%	Vitamin A	0 IU
Total fat	< 1 g	Vitamin C	0 mg
Saturated fat	0 g	Sodium	138 mg
Cholesterol	0 mg		

♦♦♦

RECIPE 28.6

WHITE SANDWICH BREAD

Yield: 2 Large Loaves   **Method:** Straight Dough

Water, warm	12 oz.	340 g
Dry milk	1-1/4 oz.	35 g
Sugar	1 oz.	30 g

Salt	2 tsp.	10 ml
Active dry yeast	1/2 oz.	15 g
Bread flour	1 lb. 8 oz.	680 g
Unsalted butter, soft	1 oz.	30 g
Eggs	2	2

1. Combine the water, milk, sugar, salt, yeast and 12 ounces (340 grams) of flour. Blend well. Add the butter and eggs and beat for 2 minutes.

2. Stir in the remaining flour, 2 ounces (60 grams) at a time. Knead for 8 minutes.

3. Place the dough in a lightly greased bowl, cover and let rise at room temperature until doubled, approximately 1 to 1-1/2 hours.

4. Shape into loaves and let rise until doubled.

5. Bake at 400°F (200°C) if free-form or small loaves; bake at 375°F (190°C) if larger loaves. Bake until brown and hollow sounding, approximately 35 minutes for small loaves and 50 minutes for large loaves.

VARIATION: *Whole wheat*—Substitute up to 12 ounces (340 grams) of whole wheat flour for an equal portion of the bread flour.

◆◆◆

RECIPE 28.7

POTATO CHEDDAR CHEESE BREAD

STOUFFER STANFORD COURT, SAN FRANCISCO, CA
Executive Chef Ercolino Crugnale

Yield: 7 1 lb. 4 oz. (600 g) Loaves   **Method:** Straight Dough

Water, warm (100°F/38°C)	8 oz.	225 g
Active dry yeast	2 oz.	60 g
Bread flour	4 lb. 8 oz.	2.2 kg
Potatoes, boiled, peeled and puréed	2 lb.	1 kg
Kosher salt	1-1/2 oz.	45 g
Cracked pepper	1 oz.	30 g
Unsalted butter, melted	3 oz.	90 g
Cheddar cheese, grated	1 lb.	500 g
Water, room temperature	1 pt.	500 ml

1. Dissolve the yeast in the warm water and set aside.

2. Combine the flour, potatoes, salt, pepper, butter and cheese. Blend on low speed for 2–3 minutes.

3. Slowly add the room temperature water and the yeast mixture. Mix on medium speed for 8–10 minutes.

4. Allow the dough to rise in a warm spot until doubled, approximately 2 hours. Punch down the dough and divide into loaves.

5. Proof until doubled in size, approximately 45 minutes. Bake at 350°F (180°C) until brown, approximately 20–30 minutes.

◆◆◆

RECIPE 28.8

WHOLE WHEAT BREAD

Yield: 2 Large Loaves or 35 Dinner Rolls   **Method:** Straight Dough

Salt	2 tsp.	10 ml
Nonfat dry milk	1-1/4 oz.	35 g
Whole wheat flour	1 lb. 10 oz.	780 g
Water, hot	1 lb. 2 oz.	540 g
Active dry yeast	1/2 oz.	15 g
Honey	3 oz.	90 g
Unsalted butter, soft	1 oz.	30 g

1. In a large mixer bowl, combine the salt and dry milk with 12 ounces (340 grams) of flour.

2. Stir in the hot water, yeast, honey and butter. Beat until combined into a thick batterlike dough.

3. Add the remaining flour 2 ounces (60 grams) at a time. Knead about 8 minutes.

4. Place the dough in a lightly greased bowl and cover. Let rise in a warm place until doubled.

5. Punch down, portion and shape as desired.

6. Let the shaped dough rise until doubled. Bake at 375°F (190°C) until firm and dark brown, approximately 1 hour for loaves and 20 minutes for rolls. Brush the top of the loaves or rolls with melted butter after baking if desired.

◆◆◆

RECIPE 28.9

MULTIGRAIN DATE BREAD

Yield: 2 Small Loaves   **Method:** Straight Dough

Dates, chopped	8 oz.	225 g
Bread flour	1 lb. 8 oz.	680 g
Active dry yeast	1/2 oz.	15 g
Water, warm	1 pt.	450 ml
Honey	4 oz.	120 g
Unsalted butter, melted	2 oz.	60 g
Nonfat dry milk	1-1/4 oz.	35 g
Salt	1 Tbsp.	15 ml
Whole wheat flour	6 oz.	180 g
Rye flour	2 oz.	60 g
Wheat germ	2 oz.	60 g
Bran flakes, toasted	2 oz.	60 g
Sesame seeds	2 Tbsp.	30 ml
Egg wash	as needed	as needed
Poppy or sesame seeds	2 Tbsp.	30 ml

1. In a small bowl, combine the dates with 2 ounces (60 grams) of the bread flour; toss to coat and set aside.

2. In a large mixer bowl, dissolve the yeast in the warm water. Add the honey, butter, milk powder, salt and whole wheat flour. Beat at medium speed for 2 minutes.

3. Stir in the rye flour, wheat germ, bran flakes, sesame seeds and date mixture.

4. Slowly add enough of the remaining bread flour to make a soft dough. Knead until smooth and elastic, approximately 5 minutes.

5. Place the dough in a lightly greased bowl and cover. Allow to rise until doubled, approximately 1-1/2 hours.

6. Punch down the dough and knead for a few seconds.

7. Divide the dough in half. Shape each piece and place in a lightly greased loaf pan. Cover and allow to rise until almost doubled, approximately 45 minutes.

8. Slash the top of the loaves as desired and top with egg wash and poppy or sesame seeds. Bake at 375°F (190°C) until golden brown and firm, approximately 40 minutes. Loaves should be dry and sound hollow when tapped on the bottom. Remove the loaves from the pans to cool.

❖❖❖

RECIPE 28.10

BREADSTICKS

Yield: 24 Breadsticks　　　　　　　**Method:** Straight Dough

Active dry yeast	1/2 oz.	15 g
Water, warm	10 oz.	300 g
Sugar	1 oz.	30 g
Olive oil	4 oz.	120 g
Salt	2 tsp.	10 ml
Bread flour	1 lb. 2 oz.	540 g
Egg wash	as needed	as needed
Sesame seeds	3 Tbsp.	45 ml

1. Stir the yeast, water and sugar together in a mixer bowl.

2. Blend in the oil, salt and 8 ounces (225 grams) of the flour.

3. Gradually add the remaining flour. Knead the dough until it is smooth and cleans the sides of the bowl, approximately 5 minutes.

4. Remove the dough from the bowl and allow it to rest for a few minutes. Roll the dough into a rectangle, about 1/4 inch (6 millimeters) thick.

5. Cut the dough into 24 even pieces. Roll each piece into a rope and twist; bring the ends together, allowing the sides to curl together. Place on a paper-lined sheet pan.

6. Brush with egg wash and top with sesame seeds. Let the sticks rise until doubled, approximately 20 minutes.

7. Bake at 375°F (190°C) until golden brown, approximately 12–15 minutes.

VARIATIONS: *Garlic breadsticks*—Knead 1 ounce (30 grams) grated Parmesan cheese and 2 tablespoons (30 milliliters) minced garlic into the dough.
Herbed breadsticks—Knead 3 tablespoons (45 milliliters) chopped fresh herbs such as basil, parsley, dill and oregano into the dough.

1. Rolling breadstick dough.

2. Twisting breadstick dough.

◆◆◆

RECIPE 28.11

ROMAN FLATBREAD

Yield: 1 Sheet Pan, 12 in. × 18 in.   **Method:** Straight Dough
      (30 cm × 45 cm)

Sugar	1 Tbsp.	15 ml
Active dry yeast	1 Tbsp.	15 ml
Water, lukewarm	12 oz.	340 g
All-purpose flour	1 lb. 2 oz.	540 g
Kosher salt	2 tsp.	10 ml
Onion, chopped fine	3 oz.	90 g
Olive oil	2 tsp.	10 ml
Fresh rosemary, crushed	2 Tbsp.	30 ml

1. Topping the flatbread dough with crushed rosemary.

1. Combine the sugar, yeast and water. Stir to dissolve the yeast. Stir in the flour 4 ounces (120 grams) at a time.

2. Stir in 1-1/2 teaspoons (7 milliliters) of salt and the onion. Mix well, then knead on a lightly floured board until smooth.

3. Place the dough in an oiled bowl, cover and let rise until doubled.

4. Punch down the dough, then flatten it onto an oiled sheet pan. It should be no more than 1 inch (2.5 centimeters) thick. Brush the top of the dough with the olive oil. Let the dough proof until doubled, about 15 minutes.

5. Sprinkle the crushed rosemary and remaining 1/2 teaspoon (2 milliliters) of salt on top of the dough. Bake at 400°F (200°C) until lightly browned, approximately 20 minutes.

◆◆◆

RECIPE 28.12

PIZZA DOUGH

Yield: 1 Large or 8 Individual Pizzas   **Method:** Straight Dough

Water, warm	2 oz.	60 g
Active dry yeast	1 Tbsp.	15 ml
Bread flour	14 oz.	420 g
Water, cool	6 oz.	180 g
Salt	1 tsp.	5 ml
Olive oil	1 oz.	30 g
Honey	1 Tbsp.	15 ml

1. Stir the yeast into the warm water to dissolve. Add the flour.

2. Stir the cool water, salt, olive oil and honey into the flour mixture. Knead with a dough hook or by hand until smooth and elastic, approximately 5 minutes.

3. Place the dough in a lightly greased bowl and cover. Allow the dough to rise in a warm place for 30 minutes. Punch down the dough and divide into portions. The dough may be wrapped and refrigerated for up to two days.

4. On a lightly floured surface, roll the dough into very thin rounds and top as desired. Bake at 400°F (200°C) until crisp and golden brown, approximately 8–12 minutes.

◆◆◆

RECIPE 28.13

BASIC SOURDOUGH BREAD

Yield: 2 Large Loaves   **Method:** Sponge

Active dry yeast	1 Tbsp.	15 ml
Water, warm	12 oz.	340 g
Sourdough starter (Recipe 28.1)	1 cup	225 ml
Honey	1 Tbsp.	15 ml
Bread flour	1 lb. 6 oz.	660 g
Kosher salt	1-1/2 tsp.	7 ml
Distilled vinegar	1 oz.	30 g
Baking soda	1/2 tsp.	2 ml

1. Prepare a sponge by mixing the yeast, water, sourdough starter and honey. Stir in 4 ounces (120 grams) of flour. Beat vigorously by hand or in a mixer on second speed for 3 minutes.

2. Place the sponge in a clean bowl and cover. Set aside until doubled, approximately 1–2 hours.

3. Place the risen sponge into the bowl of a mixer fitted with a dough hook. Add the salt, vinegar and baking soda. Gradually add enough bread flour to make a stiff dough. Knead for 3 minutes on second speed. The dough should clean the bowl, forming a ball around the dough hook.

4. Allow the dough to rest for 5 minutes. Then shape into 2 round or oval loaves and place on a baking sheet that has been dusted with cornmeal.

5. Cover the dough and set aside to proof until doubled, approximately 45 minutes. Slash the top of the loaf with a razor or sharp knife.

6. Bake the bread for 10 minutes in a 450°F (230°C) oven with steam added. Reduce the oven temperature to 375°F (190°C) and continue baking until golden brown and firm, approximately 30–40 minutes.

◆◆◆

RECIPE 28.14

SAN FRANCISCO SOURDOUGH BREAD

STOUFFER STANFORD COURT, SAN FRANCISCO, CA
Executive Chef Ercolino Crugnale

Yield: 1 Loaf   **Method:** Straight Dough

Water, warm (120°F/49°C)	8 oz.	225 g
Active dry yeast	1/2 oz.	15 g
Sourdough starter (recipe follows)	1 cup	225 ml
Bread flour	1 lb.	450 g
Kosher salt	1 Tbsp.	15 ml
Egg white, beaten	1	1

1. Sprinkle the dry yeast over 2 ounces (60 grams) of the warm water and set aside until dissolved and foamy.

2. Combine the sourdough starter and the remaining warm water. Add 6 ounces (180 grams) of bread flour.

Continued

3. Stir until a dough forms then add the yeast mixture. Knead 5 minutes on medium speed.

4. Add the remaining flour and salt. Knead until the dough is smooth and elastic, approximately 10 minutes.

5. Place the dough in a lightly greased bowl and cover with a damp cloth. Let rise in a warm place, about 80–90°F (27–32°C), until doubled.

6. Punch down the dough and shape it into a round loaf. Place the loaf on a greased and cornmeal-dusted sheet pan.

7. Let the loaf rise in a warm place, covered with a damp cloth, until increased to 2-1/2 times its original size.

8. Brush the risen loaf with the beaten egg white and score the top of the loaf with a sharp knife.

9. Bake at 450°F (230°C), with a pan of boiling water underneath the oven rack, for 10 minutes.

10. Reduce the oven temperature to 375°F (190°C), remove the water and continue baking until the loaf is well browned, approximately 35–45 minutes.

SOURDOUGH STARTER

Grapes, off the stem	1 lb.	450 g
Water, warm (100°F/30°C)	as needed	as needed
Bread flour	12 oz.	340 g

1. Mash the grapes thoroughly and place in a covered container. Set aside at room temperature for 48 hours. (Red grapes will give some coloring to the juice; this will be eliminated gradually with continued feeding.)

2. Strain off the fermented juice and discard the pulp. Add enough warm water to the juice to make 1 pint (450 milliliters).

3. Stir in the flour, cover and leave at room temperature overnight.

4. Replenish with 1 pint (450 milliliters) of warm water and 12 ounces (340 grams) of flour daily if starter is kept at room temperature. If kept refrigerated, replenish twice weekly.

◆◆◆

RECIPE 28.15

CHALLAH

Challah is the traditional bread for Jewish Sabbaths and celebrations. Rich with eggs and flavored with honey, it is braided into oval loaves and topped with poppy or sesame seeds. Challah is excellent for toast or sandwiches.

Yield: 2 Large Loaves   **Method:** Straight Dough

Honey	6 oz.	180 g
Salt	1 Tbsp.	15 ml
Bread flour	1 lb. 12 oz.	800 g
Active dry yeast	1/2 oz.	15 g
Water, warm	14 oz.	400 g
Eggs	4	4
Unsalted butter, melted	4 oz.	120 g
Egg wash	as needed	as needed
Sesame or poppy seeds	as needed	as needed

1. Stir together the honey, salt and 8 ounces (225 grams) of flour in a mixer bowl. Add the yeast, water, eggs and butter. Stir until smooth.

2. Using the dough hook, knead the dough on second speed, adding the remaining flour 2 ounces (60 grams) at a time until smooth and elastic, approximately 5 minutes.

3. Place the dough in a lightly greased bowl, cover and let rise until doubled, approximately 1 to 1-1/2 hours.

4. Punch down the dough and divide into six equal portions. Roll each portion into a long strip, about 1 inch (2.5 centimeters) in diameter and 12 inches (30 centimeters) long. Lay three strips side by side and braid. Pinch the ends together and tuck them under the loaf. Place the loaf on a paper-lined sheet pan. Braid the three remaining pieces of dough in the same manner.

5. Brush the loaves with egg wash and sprinkle with sesame or poppy seeds. Proof until doubled, approximately 45 minutes.

6. Bake at 350°F (170°C) until the loaves are golden brown and sound hollow when thumped, approximately 40 minutes.

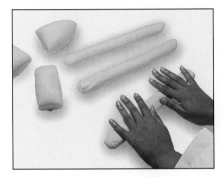
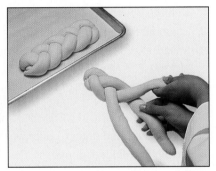

1. Rolling challah dough into ropes.   2. Braiding challah dough.

✦✦✦

RECIPE 28.16

BRIOCHE

Brioche is a rich, tender bread made with an abundance of eggs and butter. The high ratio of fat makes this dough difficult to work with, but the flavor is well worth the extra effort. Brioche is traditionally made in fluted pans and has a cap or topknot of dough; this shape is known as brioche à tête. The dough may also be baked in a loaf pan, making it perfect for toast or canapés.

Yield: 3 Large Loaves or   **Method:** Straight Dough
          60 3-in. (7.5-cm) Rolls

All-purpose flour	4 lb. 7 oz.	2 kg
Eggs	24	24
Salt	1-3/4 oz.	50 g
Sugar	7 oz.	210 g
Active dry yeast	1-3/4 oz.	50 g
Water, warm	7 oz.	210 g
Unsalted butter, room temperature	3 lb.	1.3 kg

Continued

1. Combining the ingredients for brioche.

2. Adding the yeast-and-water mixture to the dough.

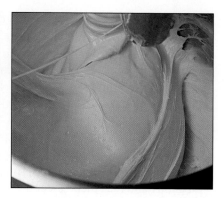

3. Brioche dough after kneading for 20 minutes.

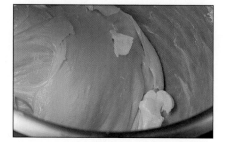

4. Adding the butter to the brioche dough.

1. Place the flour, eggs, salt and sugar into the bowl of a large mixer fitted with the dough hook. Stir the ingredients together.
2. Combine the yeast and water and add to the other ingredients.
3. Knead for 20 minutes on second speed. The dough will be smooth, shiny and moist. It should not form a ball.
4. Slowly add the butter to the dough. Knead only until all the butter is incorporated. Remove the dough from the mixer and place it into a bowl dusted with flour. Cover and let rise at room temperature until doubled.
5. Punch down the dough, cover well and refrigerate overnight.
6. Shape the chilled dough as desired. Place the shaped dough in well-greased pans and proof at room temperature until doubled. Do not proof brioche in a very warm place; the butter may melt out of the dough before proofing is complete.
7. Bake at 375°F (190°C) until the brioche are a dark golden brown and sound hollow. Baking time will vary depending on the temperature of the dough and the size of the rolls or loaves being baked.

VARIATION: *Raisin brioche*—Gently warm 3 ounces (90 milliliters) rum with 6 ounces (180 grams) raisins. Set aside until the raisins are plumped. Drain off the remaining rum and add the raisins to the dough after the butter is incorporated.

5. The finished brioche dough ready for fermentation.

6. Shaping the brioche à tête.

7. Panning the rolls.

8. A finished loaf of brioche baked in a pullman pan.

◆◆◆

RECIPE 28.17
Pecan
Sticky Buns

Yield: 12–15 Buns   **Method:** Straight Dough

Active dry yeast	1 oz.	30 g
Sugar	2 oz.	60 g
Salt	1/2 tsp.	2 ml
Milk	1 Tbsp.	15 ml
Buttermilk	5-1/2 oz.	165 g
Vanilla	1 tsp.	5 ml
Lemon zest, grated	1 Tbsp.	15 ml
Lemon juice	1 tsp.	5 ml
Egg yolks	2	2
All-purpose flour	14 oz.	420 g
Unsalted butter, very soft	8 oz.	225 g
Topping:		
Honey	6 oz.	180 g
Brown sugar	6 oz.	180 g
Pecans, chopped	3 oz.	90 g
Filling:		
Cinnamon	1 tsp.	5 ml
Pecans, chopped	3 oz.	90 g
Brown sugar	4 oz.	120 g
Unsalted butter, melted	3 oz.	90 g

1. Brushing melted butter over the sticky bun dough.

1. Stir the yeast, sugar, salt and milk together in a small bowl. Set aside.

2. Stir the buttermilk, vanilla, lemon zest and lemon juice together and add to the yeast mixture.

3. Add the eggs, flour and softened butter to the liquid mixture. Turn out onto a lightly floured board and knead until the butter is evenly distributed and the dough is smooth. Cover and let rise until doubled.

4. Prepare the topping and filling mixtures while the dough is rising. To make the topping, cream the honey and sugar together. Stir in the nuts. This mixture will be very stiff. To make the filling, stir the cinnamon, pecans and sugar together.

5. Lightly grease muffin cups, then distribute the topping mixture evenly, about 1 tablespoon (15 milliliters) per muffin cup. Set the pans aside at room temperature until the dough is ready.

6. Punch down the dough and let it rest 10 minutes. Roll out the dough into a rectangle about 1/2 inch (1.25 centimeters) thick. Brush with the melted butter and top evenly with the filling mixture.

7. Starting with either long edge, roll up the dough. Cut into slices about 3/4–1 inch (1.8–2.5 centimeters) thick. Place a slice in each muffin cup over the topping.

8. Let the buns proof until doubled, approximately 20 minutes. Bake at 350°F (170°C) until very brown, approximately 25 minutes. Immediately invert the muffin pans onto paper-lined sheet pans to let the buns and their topping slide out.

2. Rolling up the filling in sticky bun dough.

3. Cutting and panning the sticky buns.

◆◆◆

RECIPE 28.18

DANISH PASTRIES

Danish pastry was actually created by a French baker more than 350 years ago. He forgot to knead butter into his bread dough and attempted to cover the mistake by folding in softened butter. This rich, flaky pastry is now popular worldwide for breakfasts, desserts and snacks. The dough may be shaped in a variety of ways and is usually filled with jam, fruit, cream or marzipan.

DOUGH FOR DANISH PASTRIES

Yield: 36 Pastries   **Method:** Rolled-in

Active dry yeast	1/2 oz.	15 g
All-purpose flour	1 lb. 4 oz.	600 g
Sugar	4 oz.	120 g
Water, warm	4 oz.	120 g
Milk, warm	4 oz.	120 g
Eggs, room temperature	2	2
Salt	1 tsp.	5 ml
Vanilla extract	1 tsp.	5 ml
Cinnamon, ground	1/2 tsp.	2 ml
Unsalted butter, melted	1-1/2 oz.	45 g
Unsalted butter, cold	1 lb.	450 g
Egg wash	as needed	as needed

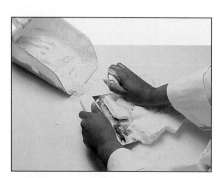

1. Kneading the butter with the flour.

2. Spreading the butter over the rolled-out dough.

3. Folding the dough in thirds to cover the butter.

1. In a large bowl, stir together the yeast and 12 ounces (340 grams) of flour. Add the sugar, water, milk, eggs, salt, vanilla, cinnamon and melted butter. Stir until well combined.

2. Adding the remaining flour gradually, kneading the dough by hand or with a mixer fitted with a dough hook. Knead until the dough is smooth and only slightly tacky to the touch, approximately 2–3 minutes.

3. Place the dough in a bowl that has been lightly dusted with flour. Cover and refrigerate for 1 to 1-1/2 hours.

4. Prepare the remaining butter while the dough is chilling. Start by sprinkling flour over the work surface and placing the cold butter on the flour. Then pound the butter with a rolling pin until the butter softens. Using a pastry scraper or the heel of your hand, knead the butter and flour until the mixture is spreadable. The butter should still be cold. If it begins to melt, refrigerate it until firm. Set the butter aside until the dough is ready.

5. On a lightly floured surface, roll out the dough into a large rectangle about 1/2 inch (1.25 centimeters) thick. Brush away any excess flour.

6. Spread the butter evenly over two thirds of the dough. Fold the unbuttered third over the center, then fold the buttered third over the top. Press the edges together to seal in the butter.

7. Roll the dough into a rectangle about 12 inches × 18 inches (30 centimeters × 45 centimeters). Fold the dough in thirds as before. This rolling and folding (called a turn) must be done a total of six times. Chill the dough between turns as necessary. After the final turn, wrap the dough well and refrigerate for at least 4 hours or overnight.

8. Shape and fill the danish dough as desired. Place the shaped pastries on a paper-lined baking sheet and allow to proof for approximately 15–20 minutes.

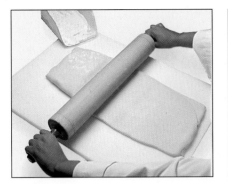

4. Rolling out the dough.

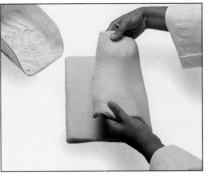

5. Folding the dough in thirds to complete a turn.

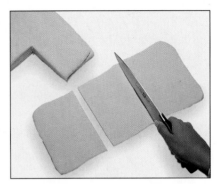

6. Cutting rectangles of danish dough.

9. Brush the pastries with egg wash and sprinkle lightly with sugar if desired. Bake at 400°F (200°C) for 5 minutes. Decrease the oven temperature to 350°F (170°C) and bake until light brown, approximately 12–15 minutes.

FILLINGS FOR DANISH PASTRIES

CREAM CHEESE

Cream cheese	1 lb.	450 g
Sugar	8 oz.	225 g
Salt	1/4 tsp.	1 ml
Vanilla	1 tsp.	5 ml
Flour	2 Tbsp.	30 ml
Egg yolk	1	1
Lemon extract	1 tsp.	5 ml
Lemon zest	2 tsp.	10 ml

7. Piping the cream cheese filling onto the danish dough.

1. Beat the cream cheese until light and fluffy. Stir in the remaining ingredients.

ALMOND CREAM

Almond paste	10 oz.	300 g
Unsalted butter, soft	4 oz.	120 g
Salt	1/4 tsp.	1 ml
Vanilla	1 tsp.	5 ml
Egg whites	2	2

1. Blend the almond paste and butter until smooth. Add the salt and vanilla, then the egg whites. Blend well.

APRICOT

Dried apricots	8 oz.	225 g
Orange juice	1 pt.	450 ml
Sugar	6 oz.	180 g
Salt	1/4 tsp.	1 ml
Unsalted butter	2 oz.	60 g

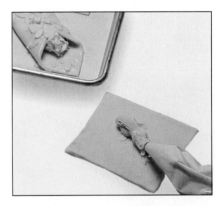

8. Shaping snails from danish dough.

1. Place the apricots and orange juice in a small saucepan. Cover and simmer until the apricots are very tender, approximately 25 minutes. Stir in the sugar and salt. When the sugar is dissolved, add the butter and remove from the heat.

2. Purée the mixture in a blender until smooth. Cool completely before using.

CHAPTER 29 PIES, PASTRIES AND COOKIES

After studying this chapter you will be able to:

+ prepare a variety of pie crusts and fillings
+ prepare a variety of classic pastries
+ prepare a variety of meringues
+ prepare a variety of cookies
+ prepare a variety of dessert and pastry items, incorporating components from other chapters

*M*ention pastry to diners and most conjure up images of buttery dough baked to crisp flaky perfection and filled or layered with rich cream, ripe fruit or smooth custard. Mention pastry to novice chefs and most conjure up images of sophisticated, complex and intimidating work. Although the diners are correct, the novice chefs are not. Pastry making is the art of creating containers for a variety of fillings. Taken one step at a time, most pastries are nothing more than selected building blocks or components assembled in a variety of ways to create traditional or unique desserts.

Perhaps the most important (and versatile) building block is the dough. Pastries can be made with flaky dough, mealy dough, sweet dough, puff pastry, eclair dough or meringue. See Table 29.1. Because pies, tarts and cookies are constructed from some of these same doughs (principally pie dough and sweet dough), they, as well as pie fillings, are discussed in the section on pies and tarts; puff pastry, eclair paste and baked meringue are discussed in the section on classic pastries. The cream, custard and mousse fillings used in some of the recipes at the end of this chapter are discussed in Chapter 31, Custards, Creams, Frozen Desserts and Dessert Sauces. Cakes and frostings are covered in Chapter 30.

PIES AND TARTS

A **pie** is composed of a sweet or savory filling in a baked crust. It can be open-faced (without a top crust) or, more typically, topped with a full or lattice crust. A pie is generally made in a round, slope-sided pan and cut into wedges for service. A **tart** is similar to a pie except it is made in a shallow, straight-sided pan, often with fluted edges. A tart can be almost any shape; round, square, rectangular and petal shapes are the most common. It is usually open-faced and derives much of its beauty from an attractive arrangement of glazed fruit.

TABLE 29.1	CLASSIFICATION OF PASTRY DOUGHS		
Dough	French Name	Characteristics After Baking	Use
Flaky dough	Pâte brisée	Very flaky; not sweet	Prebaked pie shells; pie top crusts
Mealy dough	Pâte brisée	Moderately flaky; not sweet	Custard, cream or fruit pie crusts; quiche crusts
Sweet dough	Pâte sucrée	Very rich; crisp; not flaky	Tart and tartlet shells
Eclair paste	Pâte à choux	Hollow with crisp exterior	Cream puffs; eclairs; savory products
Puff pastry	Pâte feuilletée	Rich but not sweet; hundreds of light, flaky layers	Tart and pastry cases; cookies; layered pastries; savory products
Meringue	Meringue	Sweet; light; crisp or soft depending on preparation	Topping or icing; baked as a shell or component for layered desserts; cookies

Crusts

Pie crusts and tart shells can be made from several types of doughs or crumbs. **Flaky dough, mealy dough** and **crumbs** are best for pie crusts; **sweet dough** is usually used for tart shells. A pie crust or tart shell can be shaped and completely baked before filling (known as **baked blind**) or filled and baked simultaneously with the filling.

Flaky and Mealy Doughs

Flaky and mealy pie doughs are quick, easy and versatile. Flaky dough, sometimes known as pâte brisée, takes its name from its final baked texture. It is best for pie top crusts and lattice coverings and may be used for prebaked shells that will be filled with a cooled filling shortly before service. Mealy dough takes its name from its raw texture. It is used whenever a soggy crust would be a problem (for example, as the bottom crust of a custard or fruit pie) because it resists soaking better than flaky dough. Both flaky and mealy doughs are too delicate for tarts that will be removed from the pan for service. Sweet dough, described below, is better for these types of tarts.

Flaky and mealy doughs contain little or no sugar and can be prepared from the same formula with only a slight variation in mixing method. For both types of dough a cold fat, such as butter or shortening, is cut into the flour. The amount of flakiness in the baked crust depends on the size of the fat particles in the dough. The larger the pieces of fat, the flakier the crust will be. This is because the flakes are actually the sides of fat pockets created during baking by the melting fat and steam. When preparing flaky dough, the fat is left in larger pieces, about the size of peas or peanuts. When preparing mealy dough, the fat is blended in more thoroughly, until the mixture resembles coarse cornmeal. Because the resulting fat pockets are smaller, the crust is less flaky.

The type of fat used affects both the dough's flavor and flakiness. Butter contributes a delicious flavor, but does not produce as flaky a crust as other fats. Butter is also more difficult to work with than other fats because of its lower melting point and its tendency to become brittle when chilled. All-purpose vegetable shortening produces a flaky crust but contributes nothing to its flavor. The flakiest pastry is made with lard. Because some people dislike its flavor for sweet pies, lard is more often used for pâté en croûte or other savory preparations. Some chefs prefer to use a combination of butter with either shortening or lard. Oil is not an appropriate substitute as it disperses too thoroughly through the dough; when baked, the crust will be stiff and crisp.

After the fat is cut into the flour, water or milk is added to form a soft dough. Less water is needed for mealy dough because more flour is already in contact with the fat, reducing its ability to absorb liquid. Cold water is normally used for both flaky and mealy doughs. The water should be well chilled to prevent softening the fat. Milk may be used to increase richness and nutritional value. It will produce a darker, less crisp crust, however. If dry milk powder is used, it should be dissolved in the water first.

Hand mixing is best for small to moderate quantities of dough. You retain better control over the procedure when you can feel the fat being incorporated. It is very difficult to make flaky dough with an electric mixer or food processor, as they tend to cut the fat in too thoroughly. Overmixing develops too much gluten, making the dough elastic and difficult to use. If an electric mixer must be used for large quantities, use the paddle attachment at the lowest speed and be sure the fat is well chilled, even frozen.

Bake blind—*to bake a pie shell before it is filled. The dough is often lined with parchment paper and filled with dried beans or pie weights to prevent the crust from rising.*

◆◆◆

OF TARTS AND TORTES

The names given to desserts can be rather confusing. One country or region calls an item a *torte* while another region calls the same item a *gâteau*. The following definitions are based on classic terms. You will, no doubt, encounter variations depending on your location and the training of those with whom you work.

Cake—In American and British usages, *cake* refers to a broad range of pastries, including layer cakes, coffee cakes and gâteaux. *Cake* may refer to almost everything that is baked, tender, sweet and sometimes frosted. But to the French, *le cake* is a loaf-shaped fruitcake, similar to an American pound cake with the addition of fruit, nuts and rum.

Gâteau—(pl. *gâteaux*) To the French, *gâteau* refers to various pastry items made with puff pastry, eclair paste, short dough or sweet dough. In America, *gâteau* often refers to any cake-type dessert.

Pastry—*Pastry* may refer to a group of doughs made primarily with flour, water and fat. *Pastry* can also refer to foods made with these doughs or to a large variety of fancy baked goods.

Tart—A tart is a pastry shell filled with sweet or savory ingredients. Tarts have straight, shallow sides and are usually prepared open-face. In France and Britain the term **flan** is sometimes used to refer to the same items. A **tartlet** is a small, individual-sized tart.

Torte—In Central and Eastern European countries a *torte* (pl. *torten*) is a rich cake in which all or part of the flour is replaced with finely chopped nuts or bread crumbs. Other cultures refer to any round sweet cake as a torte.

PROCEDURE FOR MAKING FLAKY AND MEALY DOUGHS

1. Sift flour, salt and sugar (if used) together in a large bowl.
2. Cut the fat into the flour.
3. Gradually add cold liquid, mixing gently until the dough holds together. Do not overmix.
4. Cover the dough with plastic wrap and chill thoroughly before using.

✦✦✦

RECIPE 29.1

BASIC PIE DOUGH

Yield: 5 lb. (2.2 kg)

Pastry flour	3 lb.	1300 g
Salt	4 tsp.	20 g
Sugar (optional)	2 oz.	60 g
All-purpose shortening	1 lb. 8 oz.	680 g
Water, cold*	8 oz.	250 ml

1. Sift the flour, salt and sugar together in a large bowl.
2. Cut the shortening into the flour mixture until the desired consistency is reached.
3. Gradually add the cold water, mixing gently until the dough holds together. Do not overmix or add too much water.
4. Cover the dough with plastic wrap and chill thoroughly before using.

*The amount of water needed varies depending upon the manner in which the fat is incorporated. Mealy dough will probably not require the entire 8 ounces (250 milliliters).

1. Cutting the fat into the flour coarsely for flaky dough.

2. Cutting the fat into the flour finely for mealy dough.

3. The finished dough.

Sweet Dough

Sweet dough or **pâte sucrée** is a rich, nonflaky dough used for sweet tart shells. It is sturdier than flaky or mealy dough because it contains egg yolks and the fat is thoroughly blended in. It is also more cookielike than classic pie dough and has the rich flavor of butter. It creates a crisp but tender crust and is excellent for tartlets as well as for straight-sided tarts that will be removed from their pans before service. Sweet dough crusts may be prebaked then filled, or filled and baked simultaneously with the filling. The raw dough may be kept refrigerated up to two weeks or frozen up to three months.

PROCEDURE FOR MAKING SWEET DOUGH

1. Cream softened butter. Add sugar and beat until the mixture is light and fluffy.
2. Slowly add eggs, blending well.
3. Slowly add flour, mixing only until incorporated. Overmixing toughens the dough.
4. Cover the dough with plastic wrap and chill thoroughly before using.

━━━━━━━━━━ ◆◆◆ ━━━━━━━━━━

RECIPE 29.2

SWEET DOUGH

Yield: 7 lb. (3.1 kg)

Unsalted butter, softened	1 lb. 8 oz.	675 g
Powdered sugar	1 lb. 5 oz.	580 g
Egg yolks	1 lb.	450 g
Whole eggs	2	2
All-purpose flour	3 lb. 8 oz.	1600 g

1. Cream the butter and powdered sugar in a large mixer bowl using the paddle attachment.
2. Combine the egg yolks and whole eggs. Slowly add the eggs to the creamed butter. Mix until smooth and free of lumps, scraping down the sides of the bowl as needed.
3. With the mixer on low speed, slowly add the flour to the butter-and-egg mixture. Mix only until incorporated; do not overmix. The dough should be firm, smooth and not sticky.
4. Dust a half-sheet pan with flour. Pack the dough into the pan evenly. Wrap well in plastic wrap and chill until firm.
5. Work with a small portion of the chilled dough when shaping tart shells or other products.

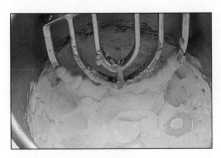

1. Mixing sweet dough.

2. The finished sweet dough.

Shaping Crusts

Crusts are shaped by rolling out the dough to fit into a pie pan or tart shell (mold) or to sit on top of fillings. Mealy, flaky and sweet doughs are all easier to roll out and work with if well chilled, as chilling keeps the fat firm and prevents stickiness. When rolling and shaping the dough, work on a clean, flat surface (wood or marble is best). Lightly dust the work surface, rolling pin and dough with pastry flour before starting to roll the dough. Also, work only with a manageable amount at a time: usually one crust's worth for a pie or standard-sized tart or enough for 10–12 tartlet shells.

Roll out the dough from the center, working toward the edges. Periodically, lift the dough gently and rotate it. This keeps the dough from sticking and helps produce an even thickness. If the dough sticks to the rolling pin or work surface, sprinkle on a bit more flour. Too much flour, however, makes the crust dry and crumbly and causes gray streaks.

PROCEDURE FOR ROLLING AND SHAPING DOUGH FOR A PIE CRUST OR TART SHELL

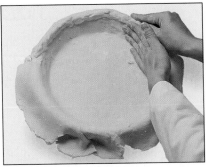

1. A typical pie crust or tart shell should be rolled to a thickness of approximately 1/8 inch (3 millimeters); it should also be at least 2 inches (5 centimeters) larger in diameter than the baking pan.

2. Carefully roll the dough up onto a rolling pin. Position the pin over the pie pan or tart shell and unroll the dough, easing it into the pan or shell. Trim the edges as necessary and flute as desired. Bake or fill as desired.

PROCEDURE FOR ROLLING AND SHAPING DOUGH FOR TARTLET SHELLS

1. A typical crust for tartlets should be approximately 1/4 inch (6 millimeters) thick.
2. Roll the dough out as described above. Then roll the dough up onto the rolling pin.

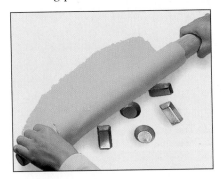

3. Lay out a single layer of tartlet molds. Unroll the dough over the molds, pressing the dough gently into each mold.

4. Roll the rolling pin over the top of the tartlet shells. The edge of the molds will cut the dough. Be sure the dough is pressed against the sides of each mold. Bake or fill as desired.

PROCEDURE FOR ROLLING AND SHAPING DOUGH FOR A TOP CRUST

1. Roll the dough out as before, making the circle large enough to hang over the pan's edge. The dough may be lifted into place by rolling it onto the rolling pin, as with the bottom crust. Slits or designs can be cut from the top crust to allow steam to escape.

2. Seal the top crust to the bottom crust with egg wash or water. Crimp as desired.

PROCEDURE FOR ROLLING AND SHAPING DOUGH FOR A LATTICE CRUST

1. Roll the dough out as described above. Using a ruler as a guide, cut even strips of the desired width, typically 1/2 inch (1.25 centimeters).

2. Using an over-under-over pattern, weave the strips together on top of the filling. Be sure the strips are evenly spaced for an attractive result. Crimp the lattice strips to the bottom crust to seal.

Streusel topping is also used for some pies, particularly fruit pies. A standard recipe is given in Chapter 27, Quick Breads.

Baking Crusts

Pie crusts can be filled and then baked, or baked and then filled. Unfilled baked crusts can be stored at room temperature for two to three days or wrapped in plastic wrap and frozen for as long as three months.

PROCEDURE FOR BAKING UNFILLED (BAKED BLIND) PIE CRUSTS

Dock—*Pricking small holes in an unbaked dough or crust to allow steam to escape and to prevent the dough from rising when baked.*

1. Roll the dough out to the desired thickness and line the pie pan or tart shell. A crimped edge or border can be added.

2. Dock the dough with a fork.

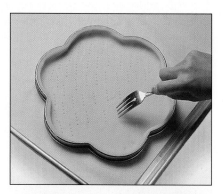

3. Cover the dough with baking parchment or greased aluminum foil. Press the paper or foil against the edge or walls of the shell. Allow a portion of the paper or foil to extend above the pan.

4. Fill the pan with baking weights, dry rice or beans. These will prevent the crust from rising.

5. Bake the weighted crust at 350°F (180°C) for 10–15 minutes.

6. Remove the weights and paper and return the crust to the oven. Bake until golden brown and fully cooked, approximately 10–15 minutes.

7. Allow to cool, then fill as desired or store.

Crumb Crusts

A quick and tasty bottom crust can be made from finely ground crumbs moistened with melted butter. Crumb crusts can be used for unbaked pies such as those with cream or chiffon fillings, or they can be baked with their fillings, as with cheesecakes.

Chocolate cookies, graham crackers, gingersnaps, vanilla wafers and macaroons are popular choices for crumb crusts. Some breakfast cereals such as corn flakes or bran flakes are also used. Ground nuts and spices can be added for flavor. Whatever cookies or other ingredients are used, be sure they are ground to a fine, even crumb. If packaged crumbs are unavailable, a food processor, blender or rolling pin can be used.

The typical ratio for a crumb crust is one part melted butter, two parts sugar and four parts crumbs. For example, 8 ounces (250 grams) graham crackers mixed with 4 ounces (120 grams) sugar and 2 ounces (60 grams) melted butter produce enough crust to line one 9-to-10-inch (22- to 25-centimeter) pan. The amount of sugar may need to be adjusted depending on the type of crumbs used, however; for example, chocolate sandwich cookies need

1. Making a crumb crust.

less sugar than graham crackers. If the mixture is too dry to stick together, gradually add more melted butter. Press the mixture into the bottom of the pan and chill or bake it before filling.

Fillings

Fillings make pies and tarts distinctive and flavorful. Four types of fillings are discussed here: **cream**, **fruit**, **custard** and **chiffon**. There is no one correct presentation or filling-and-crust combination. The apples in an apple pie, for example, may be sliced, seasoned and topped with streusel; caramelized, puréed and blended with cream; chopped and covered with a flaky dough lattice; or poached, arranged over pastry cream and brushed with a shiny glaze. Only an understanding of the fundamental techniques for making fillings—and some imagination—ensures success.

Cream Fillings

A cream filling is really nothing more than a flavored pastry cream. Pastry cream is a type of starch-thickened egg custard discussed in Chapter 31, Custards, Creams, Frozen Desserts and Dessert Sauces. When used as a pie filling, pastry cream should be thickened with cornstarch so that it is firm enough to hold its shape when sliced. Popular flavors are chocolate, banana, coconut and lemon.

A cream filling is fully cooked on the stove top, so a prebaked or crumb crust is needed. The crust can be filled while the filling is still warm, or the filling can be chilled and later placed in the crust. A cream pie is often topped with meringue, which is then browned quickly in an oven or under a broiler.

◆◆◆

RECIPE 29.3

BASIC CREAM PIE

Yield: 3 9-inch (22-cm) Pies

Granulated sugar	1 lb.	500 g
Milk	2 qt.	2 lt
Egg yolks	8	8
Eggs	4	4
Cornstarch	5 oz.	150 g
Unsalted butter	4 oz.	120 g
Vanilla extract	1 oz.	30 g

1. In a heavy saucepan, dissolve 8 ounces (250 grams) of sugar in the milk. Bring just to a boil.

2. Meanwhile, whisk the egg yolks and whole eggs together in a large bowl.

3. Sift the cornstarch and remaining sugar (8 ounces/250 grams) onto the eggs. Whisk until smooth.

4. Temper the egg mixture with approximately one half of the hot milk. Stir the warmed egg mixture back into the remaining milk and return it to a boil, stirring constantly.

5. Stirring constantly and vigorously, allow the cream to boil until thick, approximately 30 seconds. Remove from the heat and stir in the butter and vanilla. Stir until the butter is melted and incorporated.

Continued

6. Pour the cream into prebaked pie crusts.

7. The pies may be topped with meringue while the filling is still warm. The meringue is then lightly browned in a 425°F (210°C) oven. Chill the pies for service.

VARIATIONS: *Chocolate*—Melt 12 ounces (340 grams) bittersweet chocolate. Fold the melted chocolate into the hot cream after adding the butter and vanilla.

Banana—Fold 12 ounces (340 grams) coarsely mashed bananas (about 3 medium bananas) into the warm cream. The juice of one lemon may be added to the bananas to help prevent browning.

Coconut I—Substitute 12 ounces (340 grams) cream of coconut for 12 ounces (340 grams) of milk and 4 ounces (120 grams) of sugar. Top the pie with meringue and shredded coconut.

Coconut II—Stir 8 ounces (250 grams) toasted coconut into the warm cream.

1. Filling a pie shell with chocolate custard.

2. Topping with meringue.

Fruit Fillings

A fruit filling is a mixture of fruit, fruit juice, spices and sugar thickened with starch. Apple, cherry, blueberry and peach are traditional favorites. The fruit can be fresh, frozen or canned. (See Chapter 25, Fruits, for comments on selecting the best fruits for fillings.) The starch can be flour, cornstarch, tapioca or a packaged commercial instant or pregelatinized starch. The ingredients for a fruit filling are most often combined using one of three methods: **cooked fruit**, **cooked juice** or **baked**.

Cooked Fruit Fillings

The cooked fruit filling method is often used when the fruits need to be softened by cooking (for example, apples or rhubarb) or are naturally rather dry. (Poaching fruit, discussed in Chapter 25, Fruits, is a variation of this procedure.) A cooked fruit filling should be combined with a prebaked or crumb crust.

PROCEDURE FOR MAKING COOKED FRUIT FILLINGS

1. Combine the fruit, sugar and some juice or liquid in a heavy, nonreactive saucepan and bring to a boil.

2. Dissolve the starch (usually cornstarch) in cold liquid, then add to the boiling fruit.

3. Stirring constantly, cook the fruit-and-starch mixture until the starch is clear and the mixture is thickened.

4. Add any other flavorings and any acidic ingredients such as lemon juice. Stir to blend.

5. Remove from the heat and cool before filling a prebaked pie or crumb crust.

◆◆◆

RECIPE 29.4

APPLE-CRANBERRY PIE

Yield: 1 9-inch (22-cm) Pie   **Method:** Cooked Fruit Filling

Fresh tart apples such as Granny Smiths, peeled, cored and cut in 1-inch (2.5-centimeter) cubes	1 lb.	450 g
Brown sugar	4 oz.	120 g
Granulated sugar	4 oz.	120 g
Orange zest	1 Tbsp.	15 ml
Ground cinnamon	1 tsp.	5 ml
Salt	1/4 tsp.	1 ml
Cornstarch	2 tsp.	10 ml
Orange juice	3 oz.	90 g
Fresh cranberries, rinsed	1 pt.	500 ml
Partially baked pie shell	1	1
Streusel Topping (Recipe 27.4)	4 oz.	120 g

1. Combine the apples, brown sugar, granulated sugar, orange zest, cinnamon and salt in a large, nonreactive saucepan.

2. Dissolve the cornstarch in the orange juice and add it to the apples.

3. Cover and simmer until the apples begin to soften, stirring occasionally. Add the cranberries, cover and continue simmering until the cranberries begin to soften, approximately 2 minutes.

4. Place the apple-cranberry mixture in the pie shell and cover with the prepared streusel topping. Bake at 400°F (200°C) until the filling is bubbling hot and the topping is lightly browned, approximately 20 minutes.

Variation: *Apple-rhubarb pie*—Substitute cleaned rhubarb, cut into 1-inch (2.5-centimeter) chunks, for the cranberries. Add 1/8 teaspoon (0.5 milliliter) nutmeg.

Cooked Juice Fillings

The cooked juice filling method is used for juicy fruits such as berries, especially when they are canned or frozen. This method is also recommended for delicate fruits that cannot withstand cooking such as strawberries, pineapple or blueberries. Because only the juice is cooked, the fruit retains its shape, color and flavor better. A cooked juice filling should be combined with a prebaked or crumb crust.

PROCEDURE FOR MAKING COOKED JUICE FILLINGS

1. Drain the juice from the fruit. Measure the juice and add water if necessary to create the desired volume.
2. Combine the liquid with sugar in a nonreactive saucepan and bring to a boil.
3. Dissolve the starch in cold water, then add it to the boiling liquid. Cook until the starch is clear and the juice is thickened.
4. Add any other flavoring ingredients.
5. Pour the thickened juice over the fruit and stir gently.
6. Cool the filling before placing it in a precooked pie shell.

═══════════════ ◆◆◆ ═══════════════

RECIPE 29.5

BLUEBERRY PIE FILLING

Yield: 8 lb. (3.6 kg) Filling   **Method:** Cooked Juice Filling

Canned blueberries, unsweetened	1 #10 can	1 #10 can
Sugar	1 lb. 12 oz.	840 g
Cornstarch	4-1/2 oz.	135 g
Water	8 oz.	225 g
Cinnamon	1/2 tsp.	2 ml
Lemon juice	2 Tbsp.	30 ml
Lemon zest, grated fine	1 Tbsp.	15 ml

1. Drain the juice from the canned blueberries, reserving both the fruit and the juice.
2. Measure the juice and, if necessary, add enough water to provide 1 quart (1 liter) of liquid. Bring to a boil, add the sugar and stir until dissolved.
3. Dissolve the cornstarch in 8 ounces (225 grams) of water.
4. Add the cornstarch to the boiling juice and return to a boil. Cook until the mixture thickens and clears. Remove from the heat.
5. Add the cinnamon, lemon juice, lemon zest and reserved blueberries. Stir gently to coat the fruit with the glaze.
6. Allow the filling to cool, then use it to fill prebaked pie shells or other pastry items.

Baked Fruit Fillings

The baked fruit filling method is a traditional technique in which the fruit, sugar, flavorings and starch are combined in an unbaked shell. The dough and filling are then baked simultaneously. Almost any type of fruit and starch can be used. The results are not always consistent, however, because thickening is difficult to control.

PROCEDURE FOR MAKING BAKED FRUIT FILLINGS

1. Combine the starch, spices and sugar.
2. Peel, core, cut or drain the fruit as desired or as directed in the recipe.
3. Toss the fruit with the starch mixture, coating well.
4. Add a portion of juice to moisten the fruit. Small lumps of butter are also often added.

5. Fill an unbaked shell with the fruit mixture. Cover with a top crust, lattice or streusel and bake.

◆◆◆

RECIPE 29.6

CHERRY PIE

Yield: 2 9-inch (22-cm) Pies   **Method:** Baked Fruit Filling

Tapioca	1-1/2 oz.	45 g
Salt	pinch	pinch
Granulated sugar	1 lb.	450 g
Almond extract	1/2 tsp.	2 ml
Canned pitted cherries, drained		
(reserve the liquid)	3 lb.	1.3 kg
Unbaked pie shells	2	2
Unsalted butter	1 oz.	30 g
Egg wash	as needed	as needed
Sanding sugar	as needed	as needed

1. Stir the tapioca, salt and sugar together. Add the almond extract and cherries.

2. Stir in up to 8 ounces (250 grams) of the liquid drained from the cherries, adding enough liquid to moisten the mixture thoroughly.

3. Allow the filling to stand for 30 minutes. Then stir gently and place the filling in an unbaked pie shell.

4. Cut the butter into small pieces. Dot the filling with the butter.

5. Place a top crust or a lattice crust over the filling; seal and flute the edges. Cut several slits in the top crust to allow steam to escape. Brush with an egg wash and sprinkle with sanding sugar.

6. Place on a preheated sheet pan and bake at 400°F (200°C) for 50–60 minutes.

1. Dotting the cherry filling with butter.

Custard Fillings

A custard pie has a soft filling that bakes along with the crust. Popular examples include pumpkin, egg custard and pecan pies. As explained in Chapter 31, Custards, Creams, Frozen Desserts and Dessert Sauces, custards are liquids thickened by coagulated egg proteins. To make a custard pie, an uncooked liquid containing eggs is poured into a pie shell. When baked, the egg proteins coagulate, firming and setting the filling.

The procedure for making custard pies is simple: Combine the ingredients and bake. But there is often a problem: baking the bottom crust completely without overcooking the filling. For the best results, start baking the pie near the bottom of a hot oven at 400°F (200°C). After 10 minutes, reduce the heat to 325–350°F (160–180°C) to finish cooking the filling slowly.

To determine the doneness of a custard pie:

1. Shake the pie gently. It is done if it is no longer liquid. The center should show only a slight movement.
2. Insert a thin knife about 1 inch (2.5 centimeters) from the center. The filling is done if the knife comes out clean.

◆◆◆

RECIPE 29.7

PUMPKIN PIE

Yield: 4 9-inch (22-cm) Pies   **Method:** Baked Custard Filling

Eggs, beaten slightly	4	4
Pumpkin purée	2 lb.	900 g
Granulated sugar	12 oz.	340 g
Salt	1 tsp.	5 ml
Nutmeg, ground	1/2 tsp.	2 ml
Cloves, ground	1/2 tsp.	2 ml
Cinnamon, ground	2 tsp.	10 ml
Ginger, ground	1 tsp.	5 ml
Evaporated milk	24 oz.	700 g
Unbaked pie shells	4	4

1. Combine the eggs and pumpkin. Blend in the sugar.
2. Add the salt and spices, then the evaporated milk. Whisk until completely blended and smooth.
3. Allow the filling to rest for 15–20 minutes before filling the pie shells. This allows the starch in the pumpkin to begin absorbing liquid, making it less likely to separate after baking.
4. Pour the filling into unbaked pie shells. Place in the oven on a preheated sheet pan at 400°F (220°C). Bake for 15 minutes. Lower the oven temperature to 350°F (180°C) and bake until a knife inserted near the center comes out clean, approximately 40–50 minutes.

Chiffon Fillings

A chiffon filling is created by adding gelatin to a stirred custard or a fruit purée. Whipped egg whites are then folded into the mixture. The filling is placed in a prebaked crust and chilled until firm. These preparations are the same as those for chiffons, mousses and Bavarians discussed in Chapter 31, Custards, Creams, Frozen Desserts and Dessert Sauces.

Assembling Pies and Tarts

The various types of pie fillings can be used to fill almost any crust or shell, provided the crust is prebaked as necessary. The filling can then be topped with meringue or whipped cream as desired. Garnishes such as toasted coconut, cookie crumbs and chocolate curls are often added for appearance and flavor.

TABLE 29.2   SUGGESTIONS FOR ASSEMBLING PIES

Filling	Crust	Topping	Garnish
Vanilla or lemon cream	Prebaked flaky dough or crumb	None, meringue or whipped cream	Crumbs from the crust
Chocolate cream	Prebaked flaky dough or crumb	None, meringue or whipped cream	Crumbs from the crust or shaved chocolate
Banana cream	Prebaked flaky dough	Meringue or whipped cream	Dried banana chips
Coconut cream	Prebaked flaky dough	Meringue or whipped cream	Shredded coconut
Fresh fruit	Unbaked mealy dough or sweet dough if shallow tart	Lattice, full crust or streusel	Sanding sugar or cut-out designs if lattice or top crust is used
Canned or frozen fruit	Unbaked mealy dough	Lattice, full crust or streusel	Sanding sugar or cut-out designs if lattice or top crust is used
Chiffon or mousse	Crumb or prebaked, sweetened flaky dough	None or whipped cream	Crumbs, fruit or shaved chocolate
Custard (e.g., pecan or pumpkin)	Unbaked mealy dough	None	Whipped cream
Vanilla pastry cream	Prebaked sweet dough	Fresh fruit	Glaze

Storing Pies and Tarts

Pies and tarts filled with cream or custard must be kept refrigerated to retard bacterial growth. Baked fruit pies may be held at room temperature for service.

Unbaked fruit pies or unbaked pie shells may be frozen for up to two months. Freezing baked fruit pies is not recommended. Custard, cream and meringue-topped pies should not be frozen, as the eggs will separate, making the product runny.

TABLE 29.3   TROUBLESHOOTING CHART FOR PIES

Problem	Cause	Solution
Crust shrinks	Overmixing	Adjust mixing technique
	Overworking dough	Adjust rolling technique
	Not enough fat	Adjust formula
Soggy crust	Wrong dough used	Use mealier dough
	Oven temperature too low	Adjust oven
	Not baked long enough	Adjust baking time
Crumbly crust	Not enough liquid	Adjust formula
	Too much fat	Adjust formula
Tough crust	Not enough fat	Adjust formula
	Overmixing	Adjust mixing technique
Runny filling	Insufficient starch	Adjust formula
	Starch insufficiently cooked	Allow starch to gelatinize completely
Lumpy cream filling	Starch not incorporated properly	Stir filling while cooking
	Filling overcooked	Adjust cooking time
Custard filling weeps or separates	Too many eggs	Reduce egg content or add starch to the filling
	Eggs overcooked	Reduce oven temperature or baking time

CLASSIC PASTRIES

Puff pastry, **éclair paste** and **meringue** are classic components of French pastries; they are used to create a wide variety of dessert and pastry items. Many combinations are traditional. Once you master the skills necessary to produce these products, however, you will be free to experiment with other flavors and assembly techniques.

Puff Pastry

Puff pastry is one of the bakeshop's most elegant and sophisticated products. Also known as **pâte feuilletée**, it is a rich, buttery dough that bakes into hundreds of light, crisp layers.

Puff pastry is used for both sweet and savory preparations. It can be baked and then filled or filled first and then baked. Puff pastry may be used to wrap beef (for beef Wellington), pâté (for pâté en croûte) or almond cream (for an apple tart). It can be shaped into shells or cases known as vol-au-vents or bouchées and filled with shellfish in a cream sauce or berries in a pastry cream. Puff pastry is essential for napoleons, pithiviers and tartes tatin.

Like croissant and danish dough (discussed in Chapter 28, Yeast Breads), puff pastry is a rolled-in dough. But unlike those doughs, puff pastry does not contain any yeast or chemical leavening agents. Fat is rolled into the dough in horizontal layers; when baked, the fat melts, separating the dough into layers. The fat's moisture turns into steam, which causes the dough to rise and the layers to further separate.

Butter is the preferred fat because of its flavor and melt-in-the-mouth quality. But butter is rather difficult to work with as it becomes brittle when cold and melts at a relatively low temperature. Therefore, specially formulated puff pastry shortenings are used to compensate for butter's shortcomings. They do not, however, provide the true flavor of butter.

Raw, frozen, commercially prepared puff pastry is readily available in sheets or precut in a variety of shapes. Some convenience products, especially those made with butter, provide excellent, consistent results. Their expense may be offset by the savings in time and labor. Keep these frozen doughs well wrapped to prevent drying and freezer burn, and prepare according to package directions.

Making Puff Pastry

The procedure described here for making puff pastry is just one of many. Each chef will have his or her own formula and folding method. All methods, however, depend upon the proper layering of fat and dough through a series of turns to give the pastry its characteristic flakiness and rise.

Some chefs prefer to prepare a dough called *blitz* or *quick puff pastry*. It does not require the extensive rolling and folding procedure used for true puff pastry. Blitz puff pastry is less delicate and flaky but may be perfectly acceptable for some uses. A formula for it is given at the end of this chapter.

PROCEDURE FOR MAKING PUFF PASTRY

Detrempe—*a paste made with flour and water during the first stage of preparing a pastry dough, especially rolled-in doughs.*

1. Prepare the dough base (**detrempe**) by combining the flour, water, salt and a small amount of fat. Do not overmix. Overmixing results in greater gluten formation; too much gluten can make the pastry undesirably tough.

2. Wrap the detrempe and chill for several hours or overnight. This allows the gluten to relax and the flour to absorb the liquid.

3. Shape the butter into a rectangle of even thickness; wrap and chill until ready to use.

4. Allow the detrempe and butter to sit at room temperature until slightly softened and of the same consistency.

5. Roll out the detrempe into a rectangle of even thickness.

6. Place the butter in the center of the dough. Fold the dough around the butter, enclosing it completely.

7. Roll out the block of dough and butter into a long, even rectangle. Roll only at right angles so that the layered structure is not destroyed.

8. Fold the dough like a business letter: Fold the bottom third up toward the center so that it covers the center third, then fold the top third down over the bottom and middle thirds. This completes the first turn.

9. Rotate the block of dough one-quarter turn (90 degrees) on the work surface. Roll out again into a long, even rectangle.

10. Fold the dough in thirds again, like a business letter. This completes the second turn. Wrap the dough and chill for approximately 30 minutes. The resting period allows the gluten to relax; the chilling prevents the butter from becoming too soft.

11. Repeat the rolling and folding process, chilling between every one or two turns, until the dough has been turned a total of five times.

12. Wrap well and chill overnight. Raw dough may be refrigerated for a few days or frozen for two to three months.

13. Shape and bake as needed. Baked, unfilled puff pastry can be stored at room temperature for two to three days.

◆◆◆

RECIPE 29.8

PUFF PASTRY

Yield: 2 lb. (1 kg)   **Method:** Rolled-In Dough

All-purpose flour	13 oz.	390 g
Salt	1-1/2 tsp.	7 ml
Unsalted butter, cold	3 oz.	90 g
Water, cold	7 oz.	210 ml
Unsalted butter, softened	10 oz.	300 g

1. To form the detrempe, sift the flour and salt together in a large bowl. Cut the 3 ounces (90 grams) of cold butter into small pieces and then cut the pieces into the flour until the mixture resembles coarse cornmeal.

2. Make a well in the center of the mixture and add all the water at once. Using a rubber spatula or your fingers, gradually draw the flour into the water. Mix until all of the flour is incorporated. Do not knead the dough. The detrempe should be sticky and shaggy-looking.

NOTE: The detrempe can be made in a food processor. To do so, combine the flour, salt and pieces of butter in a food processor bowl fitted with the metal blade. Process until a coarse meal is formed. With the processor running, slowly add the water. Turn the machine off as soon as the dough comes together to form a ball. Proceed with the remainder of the recipe.

Continued

1. Mise en place for puff pastry. The detrempe is shown on the left.

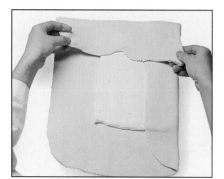

2. Folding the dough around the butter.

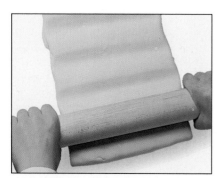

3. Rolling out the dough.

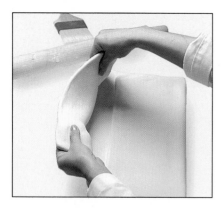

4. Folding the dough in thirds.

3. Turn the detrempe out onto a lightly floured surface. Knead the dough a few times by hand, rounding it into a ball. Wrap the dough tightly in plastic and chill overnight.

4. To roll in the butter, first prepare the 10-ounce (300-gram) piece of butter by placing it between two sheets of plastic wrap. Use a rolling pin to roll the softened butter into a rectangle approximately 5 inches × 8 inches (12.5 centimeters × 20 centimeters). It is important that the detrempe and butter be of almost equal consistency. If necessary, allow the detrempe to sit at room temperature to soften or chill the butter briefly to harden.

5. On a lightly floured board, roll the detrempe into a rectangle approximately 12 inches × 15 inches (30 centimeters × 37.5 centimeters). Lift and rotate the dough as necessary to prevent sticking.

6. Use a dry pastry brush to brush away any flour from the dough's surface. Loose flour can cause gray streaks and can prevent the puff pastry from rising properly when baked.

7. Peel one piece of plastic wrap from the butter. Position the butter in the center of the rectangle and remove the remaining plastic. Fold the four edges of the detrempe over the butter enclosing it completely. Stretch the dough if necessary; it is important that none of the butter be exposed.

8. With the folded side facing up, press the dough several times with a rolling pin. Use a rocking motion to create ridges in the dough. Place the rolling pin in each ridge and slowly roll back and forth to widen the ridge. Repeat until all of the ridges are doubled in size.

9. Using the ridges as a starting point, roll the dough out into a smooth, even rectangle approximately 8 inches × 24 inches (20 centimeters × 60 centimeters). Be careful to keep the corners of the dough as right angles.

10. Use a dry pastry brush to remove any loose flour from the dough's surface. Fold the dough in thirds, like a business letter. If one end is damaged or in worse condition, fold it in first; otherwise start at the bottom. This completes the first turn.

11. Rotate the block of dough 90 degrees, so that the folded edge is on your left and the dough faces you like a book. Roll the dough out again, repeating the ridging technique. Once again, the dough should be in a smooth, even rectangle of approximately 8 inches × 24 inches (20 centimeters × 60 centimeters).

12. Fold the dough in thirds again, completing the second turn. Cover the dough with plastic wrap and chill for at least 30 minutes.

13. Repeat the rolling and folding technique until the dough has had a total of five turns. Do not perform more than two turns without a resting and chilling period. Cover the dough completely and chill overnight before shaping and baking.

NOTE: It is not necessary to work with the entire block of dough when making bouchées, cookies or the like. Cut the block into thirds or quarters and work with one of these portions at a time, keeping the rest chilled until needed.

Shaping Puff Pastry

Once puff pastry dough is prepared, it can be shaped into containers of various sizes and shapes. Classic shapes are bouchées, vol-au-vents and feuilletées. **Bouchées** are small puff pastry shells often used for hors d'oeuvres or appetizers. **Vol-au-vents** are larger, deeper shells, often filled with savory mixtures for a main course. Although they are most often round or square, special vol-au-vent cutters are available in the shape of fish, hearts or petals. **Feuilletées** are square, rectangular or diamond-shaped puff pastry boxes. They can be filled with a sweet or savory mixture.

When making straight cuts in puff pastry, press the tip of your knife into the dough and cut by pressing down on the handle. Do not drag the knife through the dough or you will crush the layers and deform the pastry.

PROCEDURE FOR SHAPING VOL-AU-VENTS AND BOUCHÉES

1. Roll out the puff pastry dough to a thickness of approximately 1/4 inch (6 millimeters).
2. Cut the desired shape and size using a vol-au-vent cutter or rings.

a. A vol-au-vent cutter looks like a double cookie cutter with one cutter about 1 inch (2.5 centimeters) smaller than the other. To cut the pastry, simply position the cutter and press down.

b. To shape with rings, use two rings, one approximately 1 inch (2.5 centimeters) smaller in diameter than the other. The larger ring is used to cut two rounds. One will be the base and is set aside. The smaller ring is then used to cut out an interior circle from the second round, leaving a border ring of dough. (The scrap of dough from the dough ring's center has no further use in making vol-au-vents.)

3. Place the vol-au-vent or bouchée on a paper-lined sheet pan. If you used rings, place the base on the paper-lined sheet pan, brush lightly with water, then top it with the dough ring; score the edge with the back of a paring knife. Chill for 20–30 minutes to allow the dough to relax before baking.
4. Egg-wash if desired and dock the center with a fork.

PROCEDURE FOR SHAPING FEUILLETÉES

1. Roll out the puff pastry dough into an even rectangle approximately 1/8 to 1/4 inch (3 to 6 millimeters) thick.
2. Using a sharp paring knife or chef's knife, cut squares that are about 2 inches (5 centimeters) larger than the desired interior of the finished feuilletée.

3. Fold each square in half diagonally. Cut through two sides of the dough, about 1/2 inch (1.25 centimeters) from the edge. Cut a "V," being careful not to cut through the corners at the center fold.

4. Open the square and lay it flat. Lift opposite sides of the cut border at the cut corners and cross them.

5. Brush water on the edges to seal the dough. Place the feuilletées on a paper-lined sheet pan.

6. Score the edges with the back of a paring knife. Chill for 20 to 30 minutes to allow the dough to relax before baking.

7. Egg-wash if desired and dock the center with a fork.

Puff pastry scraps cannot be rerolled and used for products needing a high rise. The additional rolling destroys the layers. Scraps (known as *rognures*), however, can be used for cookies such as palmiers (Recipe 29.26), turnovers, decorative crescents (fleurons), tart shells, napoleons (Recipe 29.24) or any item for which rise is less important than flavor and flakiness.

Most puff pastry products bake best in a hot oven, about 400–425°F (200–220°C).

Éclair Paste

Éclair paste, also known as **pâte à choux**, bakes up into golden brown, crisp pastries. The inside of these light pastries are mostly air pockets with a bit of moist dough. They can be filled with sweet cream, custard, fruit or even savory mixtures. The dough is most often piped into rounds for **cream puffs**, fingers for **éclairs** or rings for **Paris-Brest**. Éclair paste may also be piped or spooned into specific shapes and deep-fried for doughnut-type products known as **beignets**, **churros** and **crullers**.

Making Éclair Paste

Éclair paste is unique among doughs because it is cooked before baking. The cooking occurs when the flour is added to a boiling mixture of water, milk and butter. This process breaks down the starches in the flour, allowing them to absorb the liquid, speeding gelatinization. Eggs are added to the flour mixture for leavening. The dough produced is batterlike with a smooth, firm texture; it does not have the dry, crumbly texture of other doughs. Without this technique the dough would not puff up and develop the desired large interior air pockets when baked.

Cream Puffs—*baked rounds of éclair paste cut in half and filled with pastry cream, whipped cream, fruit or other filling.*

Profiteroles—*small baked rounds of éclair paste filled with ice cream and topped with chocolate sauce.*

Croquembouche—*a pyramid of small puffs, each filled with pastry cream; a French tradition for Christmas and weddings, it is held together with caramelized sugar and decorated with spun sugar or marzipan flowers.*

Éclairs—*baked fingers of éclair paste filled with pastry cream; the top is then coated with chocolate glaze or fondant.*

Paris-Brest—*rings of baked éclair paste cut in half horizontally and filled with light pastry cream and/or whipped cream; the top is dusted with powdered sugar or drizzled with chocolate glaze.*

Beignets—*squares or strips of éclair paste deep-fried and dusted with powdered sugar.*

Churros—*a Spanish and Mexican pastry in which sticks of eclair paste flavored with cinnamon are deep-fried and rolled in sugar while still hot.*

Crullers—*a Dutch pastry in which a loop or strip of twisted éclair paste is deep-fried.*

PROCEDURE FOR MAKING ÉCLAIR PASTE

1. Combine liquid ingredients and butter and bring to a boil.

2. Add all of the flour to the saucepan as soon as the water-and-butter mixture comes to a boil. If the liquid is allowed to boil, evaporation occurs; this can create an imbalance in the liquid-to-flour ratio.

3. Stir vigorously until the liquid is absorbed. Continue cooking the dough until it forms a ball that comes away from the sides of the pan, leaving only a thin film of dough in the pan.

4. Transfer the dough to a mixing bowl. Add eggs one at a time, beating well after each addition. This may be done in a mixer with the paddle attachment or by hand. The number of eggs used varies depending on the size of each egg and the moisture content of the flour mixture. Stop adding eggs when the dough just begins to fall away from the beaters.

5. The finished dough should be smooth and pliable enough to pipe through a pastry bag; it should not be runny.

6. Pipe the dough as desired and bake immediately. A high oven temperature is necessary at the start of baking; it is then reduced gradually to finish baking and dry the product. Do not open the oven door during the first half of the baking period.

7. Allow the dough to bake until completely dry. If the products are removed from the oven too soon, they will collapse.

8. Baked éclair paste can be stored, unfilled, for several days at room temperature or frozen for several weeks. Once filled, the pastry should be served within two or three hours, as it quickly becomes soggy.

$\diamond\diamond\diamond$

RECIPE 29.9
BASIC ÉCLAIR PASTE

Yield: 2 lb. (1 kg) Dough

Milk*	8 oz.	225 g
Water	8 oz.	225 g
Salt	1-1/2 tsp.	7 ml
Granulated sugar	2 tsp.	10 ml
Butter	7-1/2 oz.	210 g
All-purpose flour	8 oz.	450 g
Eggs	7–9	7–9

1. Preheat the oven to 425°F (220°C). Line a sheet pan with parchment. Have a pastry bag with a large plain tip ready.

2. Place the milk, water, salt, sugar and butter in a saucepan. Bring to a boil. Make sure the butter is fully melted.

3. Remove from the heat and immediately add all the flour. Vigorously beat the dough by hand. Put the pan back on the heat and continue beating the dough until it comes away from the sides of the pan. The dough should look relatively dry.

4. Transfer the dough to a mixing bowl and allow it to cool briefly to a temperature of approximately 130°F (54°C) or lower. Using the mixer's paddle attachment, begin beating in the eggs one at a time.

* For a crisper product, replace the milk with water.

Continued

5. Continue to add the eggs until the mixture is shiny but firm. It may not be necessary to use all nine eggs. The dough should pull away from the sides of the bowl in thick threads; it will not clear the bowl.

6. Put a workable amount of dough into the pastry bag and pipe onto the sheet pan in the desired shapes at once.

7. Bake immediately, beginning at 425°F (220°C) for 10 minutes, then lowering the heat to 375°F (190°C) for another 10 minutes. Continue gradually lowering the oven temperature until the shapes are brown and dry inside. Open the oven door as little as possible to prevent rapid changes in the oven's temperature.

8. Cool completely, then fill as desired. Leftovers can be frozen or stored at room temperature.

1. Heating the butter and milk.

2. Adding the flour to the hot liquid.

3. Stirring the dough to dry it.

4. The finished batter after the eggs are incorporated.

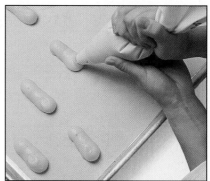

5. Piping éclairs.

Meringues

Meringues are egg whites whipped with sugar. The texture—hard or soft—depends on the ratio of sugar to egg whites.

A low sugar content in comparison with the egg whites creates a **soft meringue**. Soft meringues can be folded into a mousse or Bavarian to lighten it or used in a spongecake or soufflé. Meringues with only a small amount of sugar will always be soft; they will not become crisp no matter how they are used.

TABLE 29.4 MERINGUES

Type	Ratio of Sugar to Egg Whites	Preparation	Use
Common—hard	Twice as much or more	Whip or fold sugar into whipped egg whites	Baked
Common—soft	Equal parts or less	Whip or fold sugar into whipped egg whites	Pie toppings; soufflés; cake ingredient
Swiss	Varies	Warm egg whites with sugar, then whip	Buttercream; pie topping; baked
Italian	Varies	Hot sugar syrup poured into whipped egg whites	Buttercream; frosting; crèmet Chiboust; baked.

Hard meringues are made with egg whites and an equal part or more of sugar. They can be incorporated into a butter cream or pastry cream or used to top a pie or baked Alaska. These toppings are usually placed briefly under a broiler to caramelize the sugar, creating an attractive brown surface.

Hard meringues with twice as much sugar as egg whites can be piped into disks or other shapes and dried in an oven. A low oven temperature evaporates the eggs' moisture, leaving a crisp, sugary, honeycomblike structure. Disks of baked meringue can be used as layers in a torte or cake. Cups or shells of baked meringue can be filled with cream, mousse, ice cream or fruit. Often baked meringues also contain ground nuts (and are then known as *dacquoise*), cocoa powder or other flavorings.

Making Meringues

There are three methods for making meringues: **common**, **Swiss** and **Italian**. Regardless of which preparation method is used, the final product should be smooth, glossy and moist. A meringue should never be dry or spongelike. You should review the procedure for whipping egg whites given in Chapter 8, Eggs and Dairy Products.

Common Meringues

Common meringues are made by first beating egg whites to a soft foam (soft peaks). Granulated sugar is then slowly beaten or folded into the egg whites. The final product may be hard or soft depending on the ratio of sugar to egg whites.

Swiss Meringues

Swiss meringues are made by combining unwhipped egg whites with sugar and warming the mixture over a bain marie to a temperature of approximately 100°F (38°C). The syrupy solution is then whipped until cool and stiff. The final product may be hard or soft depending on the ratio of sugar to egg whites. Swiss meringues are extremely stable but rather difficult to prepare. If the mixture gets too hot it will not whip properly; the result will be syrupy and runny. Swiss meringue is often used as a topping or in buttercream.

Italian Meringues

Italian meringues are made by slowly pouring a hot sugar syrup into whipped egg whites. The heat from the syrup cooks the egg whites, adding stability. Be sure that the sugar syrup reaches the correct temperature and that

TABLE 29.5   TROUBLESHOOTING CHART FOR MERINGUES

Problem	Cause	Solution
Weeps or beads of sugar syrup are released	Old eggs	Use fresher eggs or add starch or stabilizer
	Egg whites overwhipped	Whip only until stiff peaks form
	Not enough sugar	Increase sugar
	Not baked long enough	Increase baking time
	Browning too rapidly	Do not dust with sugar before baking; reduce oven temperature
	Moisture in the air	Do not refrigerate baked meringue
Fails to attain any volume or stiffness	Fat present	Start over with clean bowls and utensils
	Sugar added too soon	Allow egg whites to reach soft peaks before adding sugar
Lumps	Not enough sugar	Add additional sugar gradually or start over
	Overwhipping	Whip only until stiff peaks form
Not shiny	Not enough sugar	Add additional sugar gradually or start over
	Overwhipping	Whip only until stiff peaks form

it is added to the egg whites in a slow, steady stream. Italian meringues are used in buttercream (see Chapter 30, Cakes and Frostings) or folded into pastry cream to produce crème Chiboust. They may be flavored and used as a cake filling and frosting called boiled icing.

COOKIES

Cookies are small, flat pastries usually eaten alone (although not singularly) and rarely used as a component in other desserts. The recent proliferation of cookie shops in malls and office buildings attests to the popularity of freshly baked cookies. They are indeed among the world's best-loved foods.

Part of the pleasure of cookies comes from their versatility. They may be eaten as a midmorning snack or as the elegant end to a formal dinner. Cookies also provide the finishing touch to a serving of ice cream, custard or fruit. Flavors are limited only by the baker's imagination; chocolate, oatmeal, cornmeal, fresh and dried fruit and nuts all find their way into several types of cookies. Several cookie formulas are given at the end of this chapter.

Mixing Methods

Most cookie doughs are mixed by the creaming method used for quick breads and cake batters. (See Chapters 27, Quick Breads, and 30, Cakes and Frostings.) Because cookie dough contains less liquid than these batters, the liquid and flour need not be added alternately, however. Cookies may be leavened with baking soda, baking powder or just air and steam. Most cookies are high in fat, which contributes taste and tenderness and extends shelf life. Overdevelopment of gluten is usually not a problem with cookies because of their high fat and low moisture contents. But careless mixing can cause the dough to become tough and dense instead of tender and flaky.

Procedure for Mixing Cookie Doughs

1. Cream the fat and sugar together to incorporate air and to blend the ingredients completely.
2. Add the eggs gradually, scraping down the bowl as needed.
3. Stir in the liquid ingredients.
4. Stir in the flour, salt, spices and leaveners.
5. Fold in any nuts, chocolate chips or chunky ingredients by hand.

Makeup Methods

Cookie varieties are usually classified by the way in which the individual cookies are prepared. This section describes six preparation or makeup techniques: **drop**, **icebox**, **bar**, **cut-out** or **rolled**, **pressed** and **wafer**. Some doughs can be made up by more than one method. For example, chocolate chip cookie dough can be (a) baked in sheets and cut into bars, (b) dropped in mounds or (c) rolled into logs, chilled and sliced like icebox cookies. Regardless of the makeup method used, uniformity of size and shape is important for appearance and baking time. Cookies should also be evenly spaced on sheet pans for proper air circulation and crust formation.

Drop Cookies

Drop Cookies

Drop cookies are made from a soft dough that is spooned or scooped into mounds for baking. Chunky cookies such as chocolate chip, oatmeal raisin and nut jumbles are common examples. Although a uniform appearance is not as important for drop cookies as for other types, uniform size and placement results in uniform baking time. A portion scoop is recommended for portioning the dough. Drop cookies tend to be thick with a soft or chewy texture.

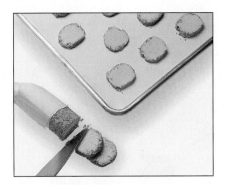

Icebox Cookies

Icebox Cookies

Icebox cookies are made from dough that is shaped into logs or rectangles, chilled thoroughly, then sliced into individual pieces and baked as needed. Icebox cookies can be as simple as a log of chocolate chip dough or as sophisticated as elegant pinwheel and checkerboard cookies assembled with two colors of short dough. This method usually produces uniform, waferlike cookies with a crisp texture.

Bar Cookies

Bar Cookies

Bar cookie dough is pressed or layered in shallow pans and cut into portions after baking, usually squares or rectangles to avoid waste or scraps. This category, also known as sheet cookies, contains a wide variety of layered or fruit-filled products. Brownies, often considered a bar cookie, are discussed in Chapter 30, Cakes and Frostings.

Cut-Out or Rolled Cookies

Cut-out or rolled cookies are made from a firm dough that is rolled out into a sheet and then cut into various shapes before baking. A seemingly infinite selection of cookie cutters is available, or you can use a paring knife or pastry wheel to cut the dough into the desired shapes. Always start cutting cookies from the edge of the dough, working inward. Cut the cookies as close to each other as possible to avoid scraps. Cut-out cookies are usually baked on an ungreased pan to keep the dough from spreading.

Cut-Out or Rolled Cookies

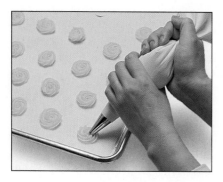

Pressed Cookies

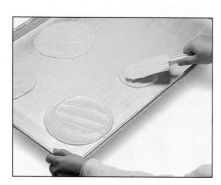

Wafer Cookies

Cut-out cookies are often garnished or decorated with nuts, glaze, fruit or candies. Raw cookies should be decorated as soon as they are placed on the pan. If the dough is allowed to stand, the surface will dry out and the garnish will not adhere properly.

Pressed Cookies

Also referred to as bagged or spritz cookies, these products are made with a soft dough that is forced through a pastry tip or cookie gun. Pressed cookies are usually small, with a distinct, decorative shape. The task of piping out dozens of identical cookies may seem daunting, but the skill can be mastered with practice and an understanding of doughs. Doughs for pressed cookies often include eggs as their only liquid. Eggs, which are a toughener, contribute body and help the cookies retain their shape. Using too much fat or too-soft flour (i.e., one low in protein) can cause the cookies to spread and lose their shape.

Wafer Cookies

Wafer cookies are extremely thin and delicate. They are made with a thin batter that is poured or spread onto a baking sheet and baked. Then, while still hot, the wafer is molded into a variety of shapes. The most popular shapes are the tightly rolled cigarette, the curved tuile and the cup-shaped tulipe. Wafer batter is sweet and buttery and is often flavored with citrus zest or ground nuts. The recipe for the tulipe shown in the photograph that introduces Chapter 31, Custards, Creams, Frozen Desserts and Dessert Sauces, is an example of a wafer cookie used as a pastry container.

Cookie Textures

The textures associated with cookies—crispness, softness, chewiness or spread—are affected by various factors, including the ratio of ingredients in the dough, the oven's temperature and the pan's coating. Understanding these factors allows you to adjust formulas or techniques to achieve the desired results. See Table 29.6.

TABLE 29.6   COOKIE TEXTURES

		Content of				
Desired Texture	Fat	Sugar	Liquid	Flour	Size or Shape	Baking
Crispness	High	High; use granulated sugar	Low	Strong	Thin dough	Well done; cool on baking sheet
Softness	Low	Low; use hydroscopic sugars	High	Weak	Thick dough portion	Use parchment-lined pan; underbake
Chewiness	High	High; use hydroscopic sugars	High	Strong	Not relevant; chilled dough	Underbake; cool on rack
Spread	High	High; use coarse granulated sugar	High; especially from eggs	Weak	Not relevant; room-temperature dough	Use greased pan; low temperature

♦♦♦

THE STORY BEHIND THE CHIP

History was made in 1930 when Ruth Wakefield, innkeeper of the Toll House Inn in Whitman, Massachusetts, cut up a semisweet chocolate bar and added the pieces to cookie dough. She was disappointed, however, that the pieces kept their shape when baked—until her first bite, that is.

Mrs. Wakefield contacted Nestlé Foods Corporation, which published her cookie recipe on the wrapper of their semisweet chocolate bars. The recipe's popularity led Nestlé's to market chocolate chips in 1939.

Under terms of its agreement with the Toll House Inn, Nestlé could not alter the recipe for Original Toll House® Cookies for 40 years. When the agreement expired in 1979, Nestle simplified the recipe. The original Original Toll House® Cookie recipe is no longer published by Nestlé Foods, but is reprinted here for the sake of tradition.

♦♦♦

RECIPE 29.10

ORIGINAL
ORIGINAL TOLL HOUSE® COOKIES

Yield: 50 2-inch Cookies

1 c. + 2 Tbsp.	Sifted cake flour
1/2 tsp.	Baking soda
1/2 tsp.	Salt
1/2 c.	Butter, softened
6 Tbsp.	Granulated sugar
6 Tbsp.	Packed brown sugar
1/2 tsp.	Vanilla extract
1/4 tsp.	Water
1	Egg
1 package (6 oz. or 1 c.)	Nestlé Toll House® Semi-Sweet Chocolate Morsels
1/2 c.	Nuts, chopped coarse

1. Sift the flour, baking soda and salt together and set aside.
2. Combine the butter, sugars, vanilla and water; beat until creamy. Beat in egg. Add the flour mixture; mix well. Stir in Nestlé Toll House® Semi-Sweet Chocolate Morsels and nuts.
3. Drop well-rounded half teaspoons of cookie dough onto greased cookie sheets. Bake at 375°F for 10–12 minutes.

Storing Cookies

Most cookies can be stored for up to one week in an airtight container. Do not store crisp cookies and soft cookies in the same container, however. The crisp cookies will absorb moisture from the soft cookies, ruining the texture of both. Do not store strongly flavored cookies, such as spice, with those that are milder, such as shortbread.

Most cookies freeze well if wrapped airtight to prevent moisture loss or freezer burn. Raw dough can also be frozen, either shaped or unshaped.

CONCLUSION

Pastry making is the backbone of dessert preparation. A wide variety of pastry doughs can be prepared from flour, fat and a liquid. Proper mixing, rolling and shaping techniques are crucial to the success of the finished product. With a selection of properly prepared doughs and fillings, you can prepare an endless variety of endlessly tempting desserts.

QUESTIONS FOR DISCUSSION

1. How does the type of pie filling influence the selection of a pie crust? What type of crust would be best for a fresh uncooked fruit pie? Explain your answer.
2. How does rolling fat into a dough in layers (as with puff pastry) produce a flaky product? Why isn't sweet dough (which contains a high ratio of butter) flaky?
3. Explain the difference between a cream pie filling and a custard pie filling. Give two examples of each type of filling.
4. List and describe three ways of preparing fruit fillings for pies.
5. Why is it said that éclair paste is the only dough that is cooked before it is baked? Why is this step necessary? List three ways for using éclair paste in making classic desserts.
6. Explain the differences and similarities between common, Swiss and Italian meringues.
7. List and describe four makeup methods for cookie doughs.

ADDITIONAL PIE, PASTRY AND COOKIE FORMULAS

Several of the formulas given below are combinations of the pastry items presented in this chapter and the creams, custards and other dessert products covered in other chapters. For example, the Strawberry Napoleon is made with the puff pastry discussed in this chapter, the pastry cream and crème Chantilly discussed in Chapter 31, Custards, Creams, Frozen Desserts and Dessert Sauces, and the fondant glaze discussed in Chapter 30, Cakes and Frostings.

◆◆◆

RECIPE 29.11
GATEAU ST. HONORÉ

NOTE: *This dish appears in the Chapter Opening photograph.*

CITY RESTAURANT, LOS ANGELES, CA
Chef/Owners Susan Feniger and Mary Sue Milliken

Yield: 10 Servings

Puff pastry	1 lb.	450 g
Milk	4 oz.	120 g

Unsalted butter	1-3/4 oz.	50 g
Salt	1/8 tsp.	1/2 ml
All-purpose flour	2-1/2 oz.	75 g
Eggs	2	2
Pastry Cream (recipe follows)	as needed	as needed
Sugar	10 oz.	300 g
Water	4 oz.	120 g
City Chocolate (recipe follows)	as needed	as needed
Heavy cream, cold	1 pt.	450 ml
Semisweet chocolate, melted	3 oz.	90 g

1. Roll out the puff pastry to form a 10-inch (25-centimeter) square; reserve in the refrigerator.

2. Make the cream puff dough by combining the milk, butter and salt in a medium-heavy saucepan. Bring to a boil. Add the flour all at once. Mix quickly with a wooden spoon until a ball forms on the spoon and the flour is evenly moistened. Transfer to a bowl and add the eggs one at a time, beating well after each addition.

3. Fit a piping bag with a large plain tip; fill it with cream puff dough. Line a baking sheet with parchment paper. Pipe dough onto the baking sheet to form small circles about the size of quarters. With a finger dipped in cold water, flatten the point on top of each puff. Drop the pan on the counter to set the puffs.

4. Bake at 450°F (230°C) until uniformly puffed and golden, approximately 10 minutes. Reduce heat to 375°F (190°C) and bake an additional 15–20 minutes. Test for doneness by opening a puff. The inside should be totally dry. Set aside to cool on a rack.

5. Place the puff pastry on a parchment-paper-lined baking sheet and, with a 10-inch (25-centimeter) round cake pan inverted over the dough, trace a circle using a sharp knife. This will be the base for the cake. Prick the circle of puff pastry all over with a fork and set in the refrigerator to rest for 15 minutes.

6. Bake the puff pastry at 425°F (220°C) until puffed and golden, approximately 20 minutes. Reserve at room temperature.

7. Fit a piping bag with a #2 tip; fill it with pastry cream. Make a hole in the bottom of each puff using a small paring knife. Fill each puff with pastry cream and reserve.

8. To make the caramel, combine the sugar and water in a saucepan and cook until golden brown. Immediately remove from heat. Using a fork, dip half of each cream puff into the warm caramel and place on a tray lined with parchment paper. When the caramel has set, turn each puff and dip the uncoated half in the caramel. Immediately arrange the puffs, flat side up, along the edge of the cooled puff pastry to form the wall.

9. Fill the center of the pastry with a even layer of City Chocolate.

10. Whip the cold cream until soft peaks form. Fold half of this cream into the 3 ounces (90 grams) of melted chocolate and set aside.

11. Spoon the remaining whipped cream into a pastry bag fitted with a #8 plain tip. Pipe about five rows of Hershey's Kiss-shaped domes over the chocolate filling, leaving even spaces between the rows. Fill the bag with the chocolate-flavored cream and repeat, filling the spaces between rows. Chill until serving time.

Continued

PASTRY CREAM

Yield: 1-1/4 pt. (600 ml)

Sugar	4 oz.	120 g
Cornstarch	4 Tbsp.	60 ml
Egg yolks	4	4
Milk	1 pt.	450 ml
Vanilla extract	1/2 tsp.	2 ml

1. Mix 2 ounces (60 grams) of sugar and all of the cornstarch in a bowl. Add the egg yolks and mix until a paste is formed. Stir in 4 ounces (120 grams) of milk.
2. Combine the remaining milk and sugar in a saucepan and bring to a boil. Pour the hot milk into the egg yolk mixture, whisking constantly. Then pour the mixture back into the pan.
3. Cook over moderate heat, stirring constantly, until smooth and thick. Remove from the heat and stir for an additional minute. Stir in the vanilla and transfer to a bowl.
4. Cover with buttered parchment paper touching the top and chill a minimum of 2 hours or as long as 2 days.

CITY CHOCOLATE

Yield: 1 lb. 8 oz.

Brandy	1-1/2 Tbsp.	20 ml
Golden raisins	1-1/2 oz.	45 g
Semisweet chocolate	9 oz.	270 g
Unsalted butter	7 oz.	210 g
Eggs, separated	5	5

1. Combine the brandy and raisins in a small saucepan and warm over low heat. Reserve.
2. Chop the chocolate into small pieces and melt with butter over a bain marie. Remove from the heat and stir in the raisins and brandy. Whisk in the yolks until combined.
3. Whisk the egg whites until soft peaks form. Gently fold the whites into chocolate mixture in two stages.

◆◆◆

RECIPE 29.12

CANNOLI ALLA SICILIANA

REX IL RISTORANTE, LOS ANGELES, CA
Executive Chef Odette Fada

Yield: 12 Pieces

Dough:		
All-purpose flour	2 oz.	60 g
Granulated sugar	1/2 oz.	15 g
Cocoa powder	1/2 oz.	15 g
Red Wine	1 Tbsp.	15 ml
Filling:		
Orange zest, candied, chopped	1 oz.	30 g
Chocolate chips	1 oz.	30 g
Pistachio nuts, chopped	1 oz.	30 g
Confectioner's sugar, sifted	1-1/2 oz.	45 g
Fresh ricotta cheese	12 oz.	360 g

1. To make the cannoli, sift the dry ingredients together, then stir in the wine. Add more wine if necessary to produce a stiff dough. Chill the dough for at least 1 hour.

2. Roll the dough very thin and cut it into 2-inch (5-centimeter) squares.

3. Roll each square of dough around a dowel and deep-fry until crisp, approximately 1 minute. Drain on absorbent paper.

4. To make the filling, stir all filling ingredients together and chill until ready to use.

5. To assemble, fit a piping bag with a large plain tip; fill with the filling mixture and pipe it into each of the fried cannoli shells.

6. Serve with a pool of dark chocolate sauce, garnished with candied fruits.

◆◆◆

RECIPE 29.13

LINZER TART

CITY RESTAURANT, Los Angeles, CA

Chef/Owners Susan Feniger and Mary Sue Milliken

Yield: 8–10 Servings

Unsalted butter, softened	8 oz.	225 g
Sugar	8 oz.	225 g
Egg yolks	2	2
Orange zest	2 Tbsp.	30 ml
Lemon zest	1 Tbsp.	15 ml
All-purpose flour	11 oz.	330 g
Hazelnuts, ground fine	6 oz.	180 g
Baking powder	1 tsp.	5 ml
Cinnamon, ground	2 tsp.	10 ml
Cloves, ground	1/2 tsp.	2 ml
Salt	1/4 tsp.	1 ml
Raspberry preserves	6 oz.	180 g

1. To make the dough, cream together the butter and sugar until light and fluffy. Add the egg yolks, lemon and orange zests. Beat until well combined.

2. In another bowl, mix together the remaining ingredients except the preserves. Add the dry mixture all at once to the creamed mixture and mix briefly, until just combined. (This dough looks more like cookie dough than pastry.) Wrap in plastic and chill until firm, about 4 hours or overnight.

3. Divide the dough in half. On a generously floured board, briefly knead one piece of dough and flatten it with the palm of your hand. Gently roll the dough out 1/4 inch (6 millimeters) thick and use it to line a 9- or 10-inch (20–25 centimeter) tart pan with a removable bottom. This rich dough patches easily. Chill about 10 minutes.

4. Roll out the second piece of dough to form a 12-inch- × 4-inch (30 × 10 centimeter) rectangle. Using a sharp knife or pastry wheel, cut lengthwise strips, about 1/3 inch (.8 centimeters) wide.

5. Remove the lined tart shell from the refrigerator and spread the raspberry preserves evenly over it. To create the lattice pattern with the pastry strips, first lay some strips in parallel lines, 1/2 inch (12 millimeters) apart. Then lay a second row of strips at a 45-degree angle to the first. Press the strips to the edge of the crust to seal.

6. Bake at 350°F (180°C) until the crust is golden brown and the filling is bubbly in center, approximately 45 minutes. Set aside to cool.

◆◆◆

RECIPE 29.14
QUICHE DOUGH

Yield: 8 lb. (3.6 kg)

All-purpose flour	4 lb. 7 oz.	2 kg
Salt	1-1/2 oz.	45 g
Unsalted butter, cold	2 lb. 3 oz.	1 kg
Eggs	12	12

1. Combine the flour and salt in a mixer bowl fitted with the paddle attachment. Cut in the butter until the mixture looks like coarse cornmeal.
2. Whisk the eggs together to blend, then add them slowly to the dry ingredients. Blend only until the dough comes together in a ball.
3. Remove from the mixer, cover and chill until ready to use.

◆◆◆

RECIPE 29.15
LEMON MERINGUE PIE

Yield: 2 9-inch (22-cm) Pies

Granulated sugar	1 lb. 4 oz.	600 g
Cornstarch	3 oz.	90 g
Salt	pinch	pinch
Water, cold	24 oz.	750 g
Egg yolks	10	10
Fresh lemon juice	8 oz.	250 g
Lemon zest, grated	2 Tbsp.	60 ml
Prebaked pie shells	2	2
Butter	2 Tbsp.	60 ml
Egg whites	8 oz.	250 g
Granulated sugar	8 oz.	250 g

1. To make the filling, combine the 1 pound 4 ounces (600 grams) of sugar, cornstarch, salt and water in a heavy saucepan. Cook over medium-high heat, stirring constantly, until the mixture becomes thick and almost clear.
2. Remove from the heat and slowly whisk in the egg yolks. Stir until completely blended. Return to the heat and cook, stirring constantly, until thick and smooth.
3. Stir in the lemon juice and zest. When the liquid is completely incorporated, remove the filling from the heat. Add the butter and stir until melted.
4. Set the filling aside to cool briefly. Fill two prebaked pie shells with the lemon filling.
5. To prepare the meringue, whip the egg whites until soft peaks form. Slowly add the 8 ounces (250 grams) of sugar while whisking constantly. The meringue should be stiff and glossy, not dry or spongy looking.
6. Mound the meringue over the filling, creating decorative patterns with a spatula. Be sure to spread the meringue to the edge of the crust, so that all of the filling is covered.
7. Place the pie in a 400°F (200°C) oven until the meringue is golden brown, approximately 5–8 minutes. Let cool at room temperature, then refrigerate. Serve the same day.

VARIATION: *Key lime pie*—Substitute 7 ounces (200 milliliters) key lime juice for the lemon juice and zest. Pour the filling into two prebaked pie shells and chill. Top with whipped cream.

◆◆◆

RECIPE 29.16

FRESH STRAWBERRY PIE

Yield: 2 9-inch (22-cm) Pies

Sugar	1 lb. 7 oz.	700 g
Water	8 oz.	450 g
Cornstarch	2-1/2 oz.	75 g
Water, cold	12 oz.	360 g
Salt	1/2 tsp.	2 ml
Lemon juice	4 Tbsp.	60 ml
Red food coloring	as needed	as needed
Fresh strawberries, rinsed and sliced in half	2 qt.	2 lt
Prebaked pie shells	2	2
Whipped cream	as needed	as needed

1. Bring the sugar and 8 ounces (225 grams) water to a boil.
2. Dissolve the cornstarch in the cold water and add to the boiling liquid. Cook over low heat until clear, approximately 5 minutes.
3. Stir in the salt, lemon juice and enough red food coloring to produce a bright red color.
4. Pour this glaze over the strawberries and toss gently to coat them. Spoon the filling into the prepared pie shells. Chill thoroughly and top with whipped cream for service.

◆◆◆

RECIPE 29.17

BLACKBERRY COBBLER

A cobbler is a home-style baked fruit dessert, usually made with a top crust of flaky pie dough, biscuit dough or streusel topping. The finished product will be slightly runny and is often served warm in a bowl or rimmed dish, accompanied by whipped cream or ice cream.

Yield: 10 Servings

IQF blackberries	2 qt.	2 lt
Sugar	8 oz.	450 g
Tapioca	2 oz.	60 g
Water	10 oz.	300 g
Unsalted butter	2 oz.	60 g
Lemon zest	1 Tbsp.	15 ml

1. Combine all ingredients, tossing the berries gently until well coated with the other ingredients.
2. Transfer to a lightly buttered half-size hotel pan, then set aside for at least 30 minutes before baking.
3. The cobbler can be topped with flaky pie dough (Recipe 29.1), biscuit dough (Recipe 27.1) or streusel topping (Recipe 27.4) before baking.
4. Bake at 350°F (180°C) until the berry mixture bubbles and the crust is appropriately browned, approximately 40–50 minutes.

♦♦♦

RECIPE 29.18
PECAN PIE

Yield: 1 9-inch (22-cm) Pie

Eggs	18	3	3
Sugar	21	3 1/2 oz.	110 g
Corn syrup	48	8 oz.	225 g
Unsulfured molasses	12	2 oz.	60 g
All-purpose flour	6	1 Tbsp.	15 ml
Unsalted butter, melted	12	2 Tbsp.	30 ml
Vanilla extract	6	1 tsp.	5 ml
Salt	1½	1/4 tsp.	2 ml
Pecans, chopped	24	4 oz.	120 g
Unbaked pie shell	6	1	1

1. Whisk the ingredients together in the order listed, stirring in the nuts with a spatula last.

2. Pour the filling into the unbaked pie crust.

3. Place the pie on a preheated sheet pan in a 375°F (190°C) oven. Bake until golden brown and almost set, approximately 40 minutes. Chill completely before slicing.

♦♦♦

RECIPE 29.19
FRENCH APPLE TART

NOTE: The amount of each ingredient needed and the yield will depend on the capacity and number of tart molds used. This procedure may be followed using individual tartlets or with large round, rectangular or daisy-shaped tart pans.

Sweet dough (Recipe 29.2)	as needed
Almond Cream (Recipe 29.23)	as needed
Tart apples, peeled, cored and sliced thin	as needed
Unsalted butter, melted	as needed
Granulated sugar	as needed
Apricot glaze	as needed

1. Line the tart forms with pâte sucrée. Do not prick the dough.

2. Pipe in an even layer of almond cream.

3. Arrange the apples in overlapping rows covering the almond cream completely.

4. Brush the top of the apples with melted butter and sprinkle lightly with granulated sugar.

5. Bake at 375°F (190°C) until the crust is done and the apples are light brown.

6. Allow the tart to cool to room temperature. Brush the top with apricot glaze.

♦♦♦

RECIPE 29.20
FRESH BERRY TART

Yield: 1 9-inch (22-cm) Tart

Sweet dough tart shell, fully baked (Recipe 29.2)	1	1
Pastry cream (Recipe 31.2)	1 pt.	500 ml
Fresh berries such as strawberries, blackberries, blueberries or raspberries	3 pt.	1.5 lt
Apricot glaze	as needed	as needed

1. Fill a cool tart shell with pastry cream.
2. Arrange the berries over the pastry cream in an even layer. Be sure to place the berries so that the pastry cream is covered.
3. Heat the apricot glaze and brush over the fruit to form a smooth coating.

1. Arranging the fruit over the pastry cream.

2. Brushing the apricot glaze over the fruit.

♦♦♦

RECIPE 29.21
QUICK PUFF PASTRY

ADAPTED FROM *NICK MALGIERI'S PERFECT PASTRY*

Yield: 1 lb. 4 oz. (560 g)

Unbleached all-purpose flour	6-1/4 oz.	180 g
Cake flour	1-1/4 oz.	37 g
Unsalted butter	8 oz.	225 g
Salt	1/2 tsp.	2 ml
Water, very cold	4 oz.	120 g

1. To mix the dough, place the all-purpose flour in a 2-quart mixer bowl and sift the cake flour over it. Thoroughly stir the two flours together.
2. Slice 1 ounce (30 grams) of the butter into thin pieces and add to the

Continued

bowl. Rub in the butter by hand, tossing and squeezing in the butter until no visible pieces remain.

3. Cut the remaining butter into 1/2-inch (12-millimeter) cubes. Add the butter cubes to the flour mixture. Toss with a rubber spatula just to separate and distribute the butter. Do not rub the butter into the flour.

4. Dissolve the salt in the water. Make a well in the flour-butter mixture and add the water. Toss gently with the spatula until the dough is evenly moistened. Add drops of water, if necessary, to complete the moistening. Press and squeeze the dough in a bowl to form a rough cylinder.

5. To turn the dough, first lightly flour the work surface and the dough. Using the palm of your hand, press down on the dough three or four times to shape the dough into a rough rectangle.

6. Press and pound the dough with a rolling pin to form an even rectangle about 1/2 inch (12 millimeters) thick. Roll the dough back and forth along its length once or twice until it is an even rectangle about 1/4 inch (6 millimeters) thick. At this stage, pieces of butter are likely to stick to the work surface. If the dough does stick, loosen it with a long spatula or scraper. Clean the surface to minimize further sticking.

7. Fold both ends of the dough in toward the center, then fold them in toward the center again to make four layers. The folded package of dough will resemble a book, with a spine on one side and the cover opening opposite it. Position the package of dough so that the spine is on the left.

8. Lightly flour the work surface and the dough and repeat the pressing as before. Roll the dough along its length as before, then roll several times along its width to form a rectangle approximately 6 inches × 18 inches (15 × 45 centimeters). Fold the dough, both ends in toward the center, then over again as before. Repeat the process once more so that the dough will have three double turns.

9. Wrap the dough well in plastic and chill for at least one hour before using.

10. The dough can be refrigerated for about three days or frozen for up to one month. Defrost frozen dough in the refrigerator over night before using it.

◆◆◆

RECIPE 29.22

APPLE TART WITH VANILLA ICE CREAM

CHRISTOPHER'S AND **CHRISTOPHER'S BISTRO**, PHOENIX, AZ

Chef/Owner Christopher Gross

Yield: 8 Servings

Cake flour	9 oz.	260 g
Salt	1/8 tsp.	.5 ml
Unsalted butter, cut into small pieces	4-1/2 oz.	135 g
Egg	1	1
Water, very cold	2 oz.	60 g
Green apples, peeled, cored and sliced thin	12	12
Unsalted butter, melted	4 oz.	120 g
Granulated sugar	4 oz.	120 g
Caramel sauce	as needed	as needed
Vanilla Ice Cream (recipe follows)	as needed	as needed

1. Combine the flour, salt, pieces of butter and egg in a food processor. Process for a few seconds, until the mixture looks like coarse meal.

2. With the processor running, add the cold water. Stop the machine as soon as the dough comes together, then knead briefly by hand if necessary. Do not overmix the dough. Cover the dough and refrigerate for one hour.

3. Roll the dough out very thin and cut into eight 7-inch (17-centimeter) diameter circles. Place the dough circles on a sheet pan lined with parchment paper.

4. Arrange the apple slices in a fan pattern on top of the tart dough. Brush with melted butter and top each tart with approximately 1 tablespoon (15 milliliters) of sugar.

5. Bake at 350°F (180°C) until brown, approximately 10 minutes. Serve warm with caramel sauce and vanilla ice cream.

VANILLA ICE CREAM

Yield: 2 qt. (2 lt)

Half-and-half	1 pt.	500 ml
Milk	1 pt.	500 ml
Vanilla bean	1	1
Egg yolks	16	16
Granulated sugar	8 oz.	225 g

1. Bring the half and half, milk and vanilla bean to a boil.

2. Whisk the egg yolks and sugar together in a medium bowl. Temper the eggs with a portion of the hot milk mixture.

3. Return the warmed eggs to the hot milk and cook, stirring constantly, until the custard coats the back of a spoon.

4. Strain, chill and process in an ice cream machine according to the manufacturer's directions.

◆◆◆

RECIPE 29.23

FRESH PEACH TART WITH ALMOND CREAM

VINCENT ON CAMELBACK, Phoenix, AZ
Chef Vincent Guerithault

Yield: 8 Servings

Puff pastry	6 oz.	180 g
Almond Cream (recipe follows)	1 lb. 8 oz.	750 g
Fresh peaches, peeled, pitted and sliced	6–8	6–8
Unsalted butter, melted	3 oz.	90 g
Granulated sugar	2 Tbsp.	30 ml
Powdered sugar	as needed	as needed

1. Roll out the puff pastry into a thin strip, approximately 6 inches × 22 inches (the length of a sheet pan) (15 centimeter × 55 centimeter). Lay the dough on a sheet pan lined with parchment paper.

2. Using a large plain tip, pipe four rows of almond cream down the length of the puff pastry. Leave a 3/4-inch (18-millimeter) margin along both long edges of the dough.

Continued

3. Arrange the peach slices over the almond cream, overlapping slightly.

4. Brush the peaches with melted butter and evenly sprinkle the granulated sugar over them.

5. Bake at 400°F (200°C) until the dough is done and the peaches are lightly browned, approximately 20–30 minutes.

6. Serve warm, dusted with powdered sugar and accompanied by vanilla ice cream.

ALMOND CREAM (FRANGIPANE)

Yield: 3 lb. (1.3 kg)

Unsalted butter, softened	8 oz.	225 g
Granulated sugar	1 lb.	450 g
Eggs	8 oz.	225 g
All-purpose flour	5 oz.	150 g
Almonds, ground	12 oz.	360 g

1. Cream the butter and sugar. Slowly add the eggs, scraping down the sides of the bowl as necessary.

2. Stir the flour and ground almonds together, then add to the butter mixture. Blend until no lumps remain.

3. Almond cream may be stored under refrigeration up to three weeks.

◆◆◆

RECIPE 29.24

STRAWBERRY NAPOLEON

Yield: 10 Servings

Puff pastry, cut into 4-inch- × 15-inch (10- × 37-centimeter) strips, docked and baked	3	3
Pastry cream (Recipe 31.2)	1 pt.	500 ml
Fresh strawberries, sliced	1 qt.	1 lt
Crème Chantilly (Recipe 31.6)	1 pt.	500 ml
Sugar Glaze (Recipe 30.12)	as needed	
Dark chocolate, melted	1 oz.	30 g

1. Allow the puff pastry to cool completely before assembling.

2. Place a strip of puff pastry on a cake cardboard for support. Pipe on a layer of pastry cream, leaving a clean margin of almost 1/2 inch (12 millimeters) on all four sides.

3. Top the cream with a layer of berries.

4. Spread on a thin layer of crème Chantilly. Repeat the procedure for the second layer of puff pastry.

5. Chill while you prepare the sugar glaze. When ready to glaze, place the third strip of puff pastry on an icing rack, flat side up. Pour the sugar glaze down the length of the pastry and spread evenly with a metal cake spatula. Allow the excess to drip over the sides.

6. Immediately pipe thin lines of chocolate across the glaze. Use a toothpick to pull a spiderweb pattern in the glaze. Chill to set the glaze, then place the top in position on the napoleon.

RECIPE 29.25
Crème Brûlée Napoleons with Hazelnuts

CITRUS, Los Angeles, CA
Chef Michel Richard

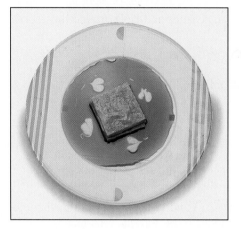

Yield: 8 Servings

Crème Brûlée (recipe follows)		
Caramel Sauce (recipe follows)		
Hazelnuts	6 oz.	180 g
Granulated sugar	6 oz.	180 g
Phyllo dough, defrosted	8 sheets	8 sheets
Unsalted butter, melted	4 oz.	120 g
Powdered sugar	2 oz.	60 g

1. Prepare the crème brulée and caramel sauce up to two days in advance; refrigerate.
2. Place the hazelnuts on a small baking sheet and toast in a 350°F (180°C) oven until brown, approximately 15 minutes. Rub the nuts in a sieve or dry towel to remove their skins.
3. Coarsely grind the nuts with the sugar in a food processor, pulsing on/off.
4. For the pastry, line two large baking sheets with parchment paper. Unroll the phyllo dough and remove one sheet; cover the remaining phyllo with plastic wrap and a damp towel. Brush the sheet with melted butter and sprinkle generously with the hazelnut-sugar mixture. Top with a second sheet of phyllo, pressing to seal. Brush with butter and sprinkle with the nut mixture. Repeat with a third and fourth sheet.
5. Using a ruler as a guide, trim the edges of the phyllo dough with a knife or pastry wheel to form a 12-inch × 16-inch (30-centimeter × 40-centimeter) rectangle. Cut the pastry into three strips lengthwise and four strips crosswise, forming twelve 4-inch (10-centimeter) squares.
6. Transfer the squares to prepared baking sheets in a single layer using a large spatula. Bake until brown, approximately 10 minutes.
7. Make and bake twelve more 4-inch squares using the remaining phyllo, butter and nut mixture.

Continued

8. Place as many phyllo squares as will fit under a broiler at one time on a baking sheet. Sieve powdered sugar generously over the squares. Watching carefully, broil the squares several inches below the heat source until golden brown, approximately 1 minute. Transfer to racks in a single layer. Repeat with the remaining squares.

9. To serve, divide the crème brûlée among the 16 pastry squares, nut side up, spreading evenly. Make eight napoleons by stacking two crème brûlée-filled squares and topping with one unfilled square, nut side up. Place the napoleons in the center of eight large plates.

10. Reheat the caramel sauce and ladle around the napoleons. Serve immediately.

CRÈME BRÛLÉE

Yield: 1 pt. (500 ml)

Milk	4 oz.	120 g
Heavy cream	1 pt.	500 ml
Granulated sugar	4 oz.	120 g
Vanilla beans, slit lengthwise	1 or 2	1 or 2
Egg yolks, blended with a fork	2	2

1. Place the milk, cream and sugar in a heavy medium saucepan. Scrape the seeds from the vanilla beans into the milk mixture. Add the beans and bring to a boil over medium-high heat. Remove from the heat and let the beans steep for at least 1 hour or until the mixture cools to room temperature.

2. To prepare the water bath, place a 9-inch × 13-inch (22-centimeter × 32-centimeter) baking dish in a larger baking pan. Pour enough water into the larger pan to come three quarters of the way up the sides of the baking dish. Remove the baking dish and place the baking pan of water in an oven to preheat.

3. Whisk the egg yolks into the cooled custard mixture. Strain through a fine sieve into the baking dish.

4. Place the baking dish with the custard in the baking pan with the water and bake at 300°F (150°C) until the custard is set and a knife inserted into the center comes out dry, approximately 45 minutes to 1 hour. Remove the baking dish from the water bath. Cool, then cover and refrigerate until 15 minutes before assembling the napoleons.

CARAMEL SAUCE

Yield: 14 oz. (400 g)

Granulated sugar	12 oz.	360 g
Water	as needed	as needed
Heavy cream	10 oz.	300 g

1. Place the sugar in a heavy medium saucepan. Cover with water and cook over low heat until the sugar dissolves, occasionally swirling the pan.

2. Increase the heat and boil until the sugar caramelizes and turns a deep mahogany brown. Watch carefully so that the mixture does not burn.

3. Standing back to avoid splatter, gradually pour in the cream. Simmer the sauce, stirring occasionally, until the caramel dissolves and the sauce is smooth and thick, approximately 3 minutes. Cool and refrigerate.

◆◆◆

RECIPE 29.26
PALMIERS

Puff pastry	as needed
Granulated Sugar	as needed

1. Roll out the puff pastry into a very thin rectangle. The length is not important but the width should be at least 7 inches (17.5 centimeters).
2. Using a rolling pin, gently press the granulated sugar into the dough on both sides.
3. Make a 1-inch (2.5-centimeter) fold along the long edges of the dough toward the center. Sprinkle on additional sugar.
4. Make another 1-inch (2.5-centimeter) fold along the long edges of the dough toward the center. The two folds should almost meet in the center. Sprinkle on additional sugar.
5. Fold one side on top of the other. Press down gently with a rolling pin or your fingers so that the dough adheres. Chill for 1 hour.
6. Cut the log of dough in thin slices. Place the cookies on a paper-lined sheet pan and bake at 400°F (200°C) until the edges are brown, approximately 8–12 minutes.

1. Folding the dough toward the center from both edges.

2. Slicing the log of dough into individual cookies.

◆◆◆

RECIPE 29.27
CHOCOLATE ÉCLAIRS

Yield: 20 Eclairs

Baked Éclair Shells,		
4 inches (10 cm) long, made from		
Éclair Paste (Recipe 29.9)	20	20
Vanilla Pastry Cream (Recipe 31.2)	1 qt.	1 lt
Chocolate glaze:		
Unsweetened chocolate	4 oz.	120 g
Semisweet chocolate	4 oz.	120 g
Unsalted butter	4 oz.	120 g
White corn syrup	4 tsp.	20 ml
White chocolate, melted (optional)	as needed	as needed

1. Use a paring knife or skewer to cut a small hole into the end of each baked, cooled, éclair shell.
2. Pipe the pastry cream into each shell using a piping bag fitted with a small plain tip. Be sure that the cream fills the full length of each shell. Refrigerate the filled éclairs.
3. Prepare the glaze by melting all ingredients together over a bain marie. Remove from the heat and allow to cool until slightly thickened, stirring occasionally.
4. In a single, smooth stroke, drag the top of each filled éclair through the glaze. Only the very top of each pastry should be coated with chocolate.
5. Melted white chocolate may be piped onto the wet glaze, then pulled into patterns using a toothpick. (See sauce-pulling techniques in Chapter 35, Plate Presentation.) Keep finished éclairs refrigerated and serve within 8–12 hours.

1. Filling the éclairs with pastry cream using a piping bag.

2. Dipping the éclairs in chocolate glaze.

✦✦✦

RECIPE 29.28
Baked Meringue

Yield: 6 lb. 8 oz. (3 kg)

Egg whites	2 lb. 3 oz.	1 kg
Sugar	4 lb. 6 oz.	2 kg
Coffee extract (optional)	2-1/2 oz.	75 g

1. Whip the egg whites to soft peaks. With the mixer running at medium speed, slowly add the sugar and continue whipping until very stiff and glossy.

2. Whip in the coffee extract if desired.

3. Spread or pipe the meringue into the desired shapes on parchment-lined sheet pans.

4. Bake at 200°F (120°C) for 5 hours or overnight in a nonconvection oven. The baked meringues should be firm and crisp but not browned.

5. Use in assembling dessert or pastry items.

✦✦✦

RECIPE 29.29
Chocolate Délice

Yield: 1 8-inch (20-cm) Cake

Classic Dacquoise (recipe follows)
Ganache (recipe follows)
Creme Chantilly (recipe follows)
Candied Almonds (recipe follows)

1. Spread an even layer of ganache over two of the dacquoise disks.

2. Top one disk with about 3/4 cup (170-millileters) of crème Chantilly. Place the second disk on top, chocolate side up. Top with another 3/4 cup (170- millileters) of crème Chantilly. Position the third disk on top, flat side up.

3. Spread the remaining crème Chantilly over the top and sides.

4. Sprinkle candied almonds over the top and sides of the cake.

5. Freeze to firm the cream, approximately 1 hour. Remove from freezer and refrigerate for service.

CLASSIC DACQUOISE

Blanched almonds	2 oz.	60 g
Granulated sugar	6 oz.	180 g
Egg whites	3 oz.	90 g

1. Preheat oven to 225°F (110°C). Line a baking sheet with parchment. Draw three 8-inch (20-centimeter) circles on the parchment.

2. Grind the nuts in a food processor. They should be the consistency of cornmeal and as dry as possible. Combine with 2 ounces (60 grams) of the sugar and set aside.

3. Whip the egg whites on medium speed until foamy. Increase the speed and gradually add 1 ounce (30 grams) of the sugar.

4. Continue whipping until the egg whites form soft peaks. Gradually add the remaining sugar.

5. Continue whipping until smooth and glossy, about 2 minutes.

6. Sprinkle the almond-sugar mixture over the meringue and fold together by hand.

7. Using a pastry bag with a plain tip, pipe the meringue into 3 8-inch (20-centimeter) disks.

8. Bake until firm and crisp but not brown, approximately 60–75 minutes. Cool completely.

GANACHE

Semisweet chocolate	4 oz.	120 g
Heavy cream	3 oz.	90 g

1. Chop the chocolate into small pieces and place in a bowl.

2. Heat the cream just to boiling. Pour the cream over the chocolate and stir until the mixture is glossy and smooth. Allow to cool slightly before using.

CRÈME CHANTILLY

Heavy cream	1 qt.	1 lt
Sugar	3 oz.	90 g
Vanilla extract	1 tsp.	5 ml

1. Whip the ingredients together until soft peaks form.

CANDIED ALMONDS

Egg whites	2	2
Granulated sugar	2 oz.	60 g
Sliced almonds	8 oz.	250 g

1. Preheat oven to 325°F (160°C).

2. Whisk the egg whites and sugar together. Add the almonds. Toss with a rubber spatula to coat the nuts completely.

3. Spread the nuts in a thin layer on a lightly greased baking sheet. Bake until lightly toasted and dry, approximately 15–20 minutes. Watch closely to prevent burning.

4. Stir the nuts with a metal spatula every 5–7 minutes during baking.

5. Cool completely. Store in an airtight container for up to 10 days.

◆◆◆

RECIPE 29.30

CHEWY DATE BARS

CITY RESTAURANT, LOS ANGELES, CA
Chef/Owners Susan Feniger and Mary Sue Milliken

Yield: 12 Large Squares		Method: Bar Cookies
Dates, pitted and chopped	1 lb.	450 g
Water	8 oz.	225 g
Granulated sugar	8 oz.	225 g
Lemon juice, fresh	4 oz.	120 g

Continued

Rolled oats	1-1/2 pt.	700 ml
All-purpose flour	10 oz.	300 g
Brown sugar	9 oz.	270 g
Baking soda	3/4 tsp.	4 ml
Salt	3/4 tsp.	4 ml
Unsalted butter, melted	14 oz.	400 g

1. Combine the dates and water in a saucepan. Cook at a low boil until the mixture is as thick as mashed potatoes, approximately 5 minutes. Stir in the granulated sugar and remove from the heat. Add the lemon juice and set aside to cool.

2. In a large bowl, mix together the oats, flour, brown sugar, baking soda and salt. Add the melted butter. Stir to moisten evenly.

3. Spread half of the oat mixture in a well-buttered 9-inch × 12-inch (22-centimeters × 30-centimeters) pan to form an even layer. Cover evenly with all of the date mixture. Spread the remaining oat mixture over the top.

4. Bake at 350°F (180°C) until the top is golden brown and pebbly, approximately 40 minutes. The edges should start caramelizing. Set aside to cool, in the pan on a rack, for about 1 hour. Run a sharp knife along the inside edges to loosen. Invert, trim the edges, and cut into squares. Serve with Caramel Ice Cream, Recipe 31.27.

◆◆◆

RECIPE 29.31

MADELEINES

Yield: 15 Large Cookies

Unsalted butter	4 oz.	120 g
Eggs	2	2
Sugar	3 oz.	90 g
Lemon zest, grated fine	1 tsp.	5 ml
Lemon juice	1/4 tsp.	1 ml
Vanilla extract	1/4 tsp.	1 ml
Baking powder	1/8 tsp.	.5 ml
Cake flour, sifted	3 oz.	90 g

1. Melt the butter over medium heat; continue cooking until the milk solids turn a golden-brown color. Set aside to cool.

2. Whisk the eggs and sugar over a bain marie until warm (98°F/38°C). Remove from the heat and whisk in the lemon zest, lemon juice and vanilla.

3. Sift the baking powder and flour together; stir into the egg mixture. Stir in the melted and cooled butter. Cover the bowl and allow to rest for 1 hour at room temperature.

4. Butter and flour the madeleine shells. Spoon the batter into the shells, filling each three-fourths full.

5. Bake at 450°F (230°C) until the cookies rise in the center and are very light brown on the bottom and edges, approximately 3–4 minutes for 1-1/2-inch (3.7-centimeter) madeleines and 10–12 minutes for 3-inch (7.5- centimeter) madeleines. They should spring back when touched lightly in the center. Remove the madeleines from the oven, invert the pan over a wire cooling rack, and tap lightly to release the cookies from the pan.

◆◆◆

RECIPE 29.32

SUGAR COOKIES

Yield: 3 Dozen   **Method:** Cut-out Cookies

All-purpose flour	12 oz.	360 g
Baking powder	2 tsp.	10 ml
Mace, ground	1/4 tsp.	1 ml
Unsalted butter, softened	4 oz.	120 g
Granulated sugar	8 oz.	250 g
Vanilla extract	1 tsp.	5 ml
Egg	1	1

1. Stir together the flour, baking powder and mace. Set aside.
2. Cream the butter and sugar until light and fluffy. Blend in the vanilla. Add the egg and beat again until fluffy. Gradually add the flour mixture, beating just until well combined.
3. Wrap the dough in plastic wrap and refrigerate until firm, about 1–2 hours.
4. Work with about half the dough at a time, keeping the remainder refrigerated. On a lightly floured board, roll out the dough to a thickness of about 1/8 inch (3 millimeters). Cut as desired with cookie cutters. Carefully transfer the cookies to lightly greased baking sheets.
5. Bake at 325°F (160°C) until golden brown, approximately 10–12 minutes. Let stand for about 1 minute, then transfer to wire racks to cool.

◆◆◆

RECIPE 29.33

GINGERBREAD COOKIES

Yield: 1 Dozen   **Method:** Cut-out Cookies

Unsalted butter, softened	4 oz.	120 g
Brown sugar	4 oz.	120 g
Molasses	6 oz.	180 g
Egg	1	1
All-purpose flour	12 oz.	360 g
Baking soda	1 tsp.	5 ml
Salt	1/2 tsp.	2 ml
Ginger	2 tsp.	10 ml
Cinnamon	1 tsp.	5 ml
Nutmeg	1/2 tsp.	2 ml
Cloves, ground	1/2 tsp.	2 ml

1. Cream the butter and sugar until light and fluffy. Add the molasses and egg and beat to blend well; set aside.
2. Stir together the flour, baking soda, salt, ginger, cinnamon, nutmeg and cloves. Gradually add the flour mixture to the butter mixture, beating until just blended. Gather the dough into a ball and wrap in plastic wrap; refrigerate at least 1 hour.
3. On a lightly floured board, roll out the gingerbread to a thickness of 1/4 inch (6 millimeters). Cut out the cookies with a floured cutter and transfer to greased baking sheets.
4. Bake at 325°F (160°C) until the cookies are lightly browned around the edges and feel barely firm when touched, approximately 10 minutes. Transfer to wire racks to cool. Decorate as desired with Royal Icing (Recipe 30.13).

◆◆◆

RECIPE 29.34

SPRITZ COOKIES

Yield: 7 Dozen   **Method:** Pressed Cookies

Unsalted butter, softened	8 oz.	250 g
Granulated sugar	4 oz.	120 g
Salt	1/4 tsp.	1 ml
Vanilla extract	1 tsp.	5 ml
Egg	1	1
Cake flour, sifted	10 oz.	300 g

1. Cream the butter and sugar until light and fluffy. Add the salt, vanilla and egg; beat well.
2. Gradually add the flour, beating until just blended. The dough should be firm but neither sticky nor stiff.
3. Press or pipe the dough onto an ungreased sheet pan using a cookie press or a piping bag fitted with a large star tip.
4. Bake at 350°F (177°C) until lightly browned around edges, approximately 10 minutes. Transfer to wire racks to cool.

◆◆◆

RECIPE 29.35

SPICED OATMEAL COOKIES

Yield: 3 Dozen   **Method:** Drop Cookies

All-purpose shortening	6 oz.	180 g
Brown sugar	6 oz.	180 g
Granulated sugar	6 oz.	180 g
Eggs	2	2
Orange juice concentrate	2 Tbsp.	30 ml
All-purpose flour	7 oz.	210 g
Baking soda	1 tsp.	5 ml
Baking powder	1 tsp.	5 ml
Salt	1 tsp.	5 ml
Cinnamon	1 tsp.	5 ml
Allspice	1/2 tsp.	2 ml
Nutmeg	1/2 tsp.	2 ml
Regular oats	1 pt.	500 ml
Dark raisins	6 oz.	180 g
Golden raisins	6 oz.	180 g

1. Cream the shortening and sugars until light and fluffy. Add the eggs and orange juice concentrate.
2. Sift the dry ingredients together and add them to the creamed mixture.
3. Blend in the oats and raisins.
4. Portion the dough onto lightly greased sheet pans and bake at 325°F (160°C) until almost firm, approximately 12 minutes.

= ◆◆◆ =

RECIPE 29.36

LACY PECAN COOKIES

Yield: 100 3-inch Cookies   **Method:** Wafer Cookies

Brown sugar	3 lb.	1.3 kg
Unsalted butter	2 lb. 8 oz.	1.1. kg
Dark corn syrup	3 lb. 12 oz.	1.7 kg
All-purpose flour	3 lb.	1.3 kg
Pecans, chopped	2 lb. 8 oz.	1.1 kg

1. Combine the sugar, butter and corn syrup in a large, heavy saucepan. Bring to a full boil.

2. Mix the flour and nuts together.

3. As soon as the sugar mixture comes to a boil, start timing it. Let it boil for a full 3 minutes. Remove from the heat and stir in the flour-nut mixture. Pour into a hotel pan to cool.

4. Let cool completely before baking. Use a small portion scoop to make equal-size balls of dough. Flatten out the balls of dough and place on flat paper-lined sheet pans.

5. Bake at 325°F (160°C) until very dark brown and no longer moist in center, approximately 15–18 minutes. Remove from oven and shape as desired.

CHAPTER 30
CAKES AND FROSTINGS

akes are popular in most bakeshops because a wide variety of finished products can be created from only a few basic cake, filling and frosting formulas. Many of these components can even be made in advance and assembled into finished desserts as needed. Cakes are also popular because of their versatility: They can be served as unadorned sheets in a high-volume cafeteria or as the elaborate centerpiece of a wedding buffet.

Cake making need not be difficult or intimidating, but it does require an understanding of ingredients and mixing methods. This chapter begins by explaining how typical cake ingredients interact. Each of the traditional mixing methods is then explained and illustrated with a recipe. Information on panning batters, baking temperatures, determining doneness and cooling methods follows. The second portion of this chapter presents mixing methods and formulas for a variety of frostings and icings. The third section covers cake assembly and presents some simple and commonly used cake decorating techniques. A selection of popular cake formulas concludes the chapter.

Chapter 29 covers Pies, Pastries and Cookies; Chapter 31 covers Custards, Creams, Frozen Desserts and Dessert Sauces. Some of the desserts presented in those chapters use cake or frosting formulas presented here.

CAKES

Most cakes are created from liquid batters with high fat and sugar contents. The baker's job is to combine all of the ingredients to create a structure that will support these rich ingredients, yet keep the cake as light and delicate as possible. As with other baked goods, it is impossible to taste a cake until it is fully cooked and too late to alter the formula. Therefore, it is extremely important to study any formula before beginning and to follow it with particular care and attention to detail.

Ingredients

Good cakes begin with high-quality ingredients (see Chapter 26, Principles of the Bakeshop). However, even the finest ingredients must be combined in the proper balance. Too much flour and the cake may be dry; too much egg and the cake will be tough and hard. Changing one ingredient may necessitate a change in one or more of the other ingredients.

Each ingredient performs a specific function and has a specific effect on the final product. Cake ingredients can be classified by function as tougheners, tenderizers, moisteners, driers, leaveners and flavorings. Some ingredients fulfill more than one of these functions. For example, eggs contain water, so they are moisteners, and they contain protein, so they are tougheners. By understanding the function of various ingredients you should be able to understand why cakes are made in particular ways and why a preparation sometimes fails. With additional experience, you should be able to recognize and correct flawed formulas and develop your own cake formulas.

Tougheners

Flour, milk and eggs contain protein. Protein provides structure and toughens the cake. Too little protein and the cake may collapse; too much protein and the cake may be tough and coarse-textured.

Tenderizers

Sugar, fats and egg yolks shorten gluten strands, making the cake tender and soft. These ingredients also improve the cake's keeping qualities.

Moisteners

Liquids such as water, milk, juice and eggs bring moisture to the mixture. Moisture is necessary for gluten formation and starch gelatinization, as well as improving a cake's keeping qualities.

Driers

Flour, starches and milk solids absorb moisture, giving body and structure to the cake.

Leaveners

Cakes rise because gases in the batter expand when heated. Cakes are leavened by the air trapped when fat and sugar are creamed together, by carbon dioxide released from baking powder and baking soda and by air trapped in beaten eggs. All cakes rely on natural leaveners—steam and air—to create the proper texture and rise. Because baking soda and baking powder are also used in some cake formulas, you should review the material on chemical leaveners in Chapter 27, Quick Breads.

Flavorings

Flavorings such as extracts, cocoa, chocolate, spices, salt, sugar and butter provide cakes with the desired flavors. Acidic flavoring ingredients such as sour cream, chocolate and fruit also provide the acid necessary to activate baking soda.

Cake ingredients should be at room temperature, approximately 70°F (21°C), before mixing begins. If one ingredient is too cold or too warm it may affect the batter's ability to trap and hold the gases necessary for the cake to rise.

Mixing Methods

Even the finest ingredients will be wasted if the cake batter is not mixed correctly. When mixing any cake batter your goals are to combine the ingredients uniformly, incorporate air cells and develop the proper texture.

All mixing methods can be divided into two categories: *high fat*—those that create a structure that relies primarily on **creamed fat**, and *egg foam*—those that create a structure that relies primarily on **whipped eggs**. Within these broad categories are several mixing methods or types of cakes. Creamed-fat cakes include **butter cakes** (also known as **creaming method cakes**) and **high-ratio cakes**. Whipped-egg cakes include **genoise, spongecakes, angel**

TABLE 30.1 CAKES

Category	Mixing Method/Type of Cake	Key Formula Characteristics	Texture
Creamed Fat (High Fat)	Butter (creaming method)	High-fat formula; chemical leavener used	Fine grain; air cells of uniform size; moist crumb; thin and tender crust
	High-ratio (two-stage)	Emulsified shortening; two-part mixing method	Very fine grain; moist crumb; relatively high rise
Whipped Egg (Egg Foam)	Genoise	Whole eggs are whipped with sugar; no chemical leaveners	Dry and spongy
	Sponge	Egg yolks are mixed with other ingredients, then whipped egg whites are folded in	Moister and more tender than genoise
	Angel food	No fat; large quantity of whipped egg whites; high percentage of sugar	Tall, light and fluffy
	Chiffon	Vegetable oil used; egg yolks mixed with other ingredients, then whipped egg whites folded in; baking powder may be added	Tall, light and fluffy; moister and richer than angel food

food cakes and **chiffon cakes**. See Table 30.1. Although certain general procedures are used to prepare each cake type, there are, of course, variations. Follow specific formula instructions precisely.

Creamed Fat

Creamed-fat cakes include most of the popular American-style cakes: poundcakes, layer cakes, coffeecakes and even brownies. All are based on high-fat formulas containing chemical leaveners. A good high-fat cake has a fine grain, cells of uniform size and a crumb that is moist rather than crumbly. Crusts should be thin and tender.

Creamed-fat cakes can be divided into two classes: butter cakes and high-ratio cakes.

Butter Cakes

Butter cakes, also known as creaming method cakes, begin with softened butter or shortening creamed to incorporate air cells. Because of their high fat content, these cakes usually need the assistance of a chemical leavener to achieve the proper rise.

Modern-day butter cakes—the classic American layer cakes, popular for birthdays and special occasions—are made with the creaming method. These cakes are tender yet sturdy enough to handle rich buttercreams or fillings. High-fat cakes are too soft and delicate, however, to use for roll cakes or to slice into extremely thin layers.

When making butter cakes, the fat should be creamed at low to moderate speeds to prevent raising its temperature. An increased temperature could cause a loss of air cells.

PROCEDURE FOR PREPARING BUTTER (CREAMING METHOD) CAKES

1. Preheat the oven and prepare the pans.
2. Sift the dry ingredients together and set aside.

◆◆◆

POUNDCAKES

Poundcakes are the original high-fat, creaming method cake. They are called poundcakes because early formulas specified one pound each of butter, eggs, flour and sugar. Poundcakes should have a close grain and compact texture but still be very tender. They should be neither heavy nor soggy.

As bakers experimented with poundcake formulas they reduced the amount of eggs and fat, substituting milk instead. These changes led to the development of the modern butter cake.

3. Cream the butter or shortening until it is light and fluffy. Add the sugar and cream until the mixture is fluffy and smooth.

4. Add the eggs slowly, beating well after each addition.

5. Add the dry and liquid ingredients alternately.

6. Divide the batter into prepared pans and bake immediately.

◆◆◆

RECIPE 30.1

CLASSIC POUNDCAKE

Yield: 2 8 × 4 inch (20 × 10 cm) Loaves   **Method:** Creaming

Cake flour	1 lb.	500 g
Baking powder	2 tsp.	10 ml
Salt	1/2 tsp.	2 ml
Unsalted butter, softened	1 lb.	500 g
Granulated sugar	12 oz.	340 g
Eggs	9	9
Vanilla extract	1 tsp.	5 ml
Lemon extract	1 tsp.	5 ml

1. Sift the cake flour, baking powder and salt together; set aside.

2. Cream the butter and sugar until light and fluffy. Add the eggs one at a time, beating well after each addition. Stir in the extracts.

3. Fold in the dry ingredients by hand. Divide the batter into greased loaf pans.

4. Bake at 325°F (160°C) until golden brown and springy to the touch, approximately 1 hour and 10 minutes.

VARIATION: *French-style fruitcake:* Add 6 ounces (180 grams) finely diced nuts, raisins and candied fruit to the batter. Substitute vanilla extract for the lemon extract and add 3 tablespoons (45 milliliters) rum to the batter. After baking, brush the warm cake with additional rum.

1. Creaming the butter.

2. Folding in the flour.

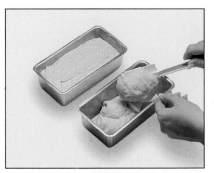

3. Panning the batter.

High-Ratio Cakes

Commercial bakers often use a special two-stage mixing method to prepare large quantities of a very liquid cake batter. These formulas require emulsified shortenings and are known as two-stage cakes because the liquids are added in two stages or portions. If emulsified shortenings are not available, do not substitute all-purpose shortening or butter as they cannot absorb the large amounts of sugar and liquid in the formula.

Because they contain a high ratio of sugar and liquid to flour, these cakes are often known as high-ratio cakes. They have a very fine, moist crumb and relatively high rise. High-ratio cakes are almost indistinguishable from modern butter cakes and may be used interchangeably.

PROCEDURE FOR PREPARING HIGH-RATIO CAKES

1. Preheat the oven and prepare the pans.
2. Place all the dry ingredients and emulsified shortening into a mixer bowl. Blend on low speed for several minutes.
3. Add approximately one half of the liquid and blend.
4. Scrape down the mixer bowl and add the remaining liquid ingredients. Blend into a smooth batter, scraping down the bowl as necessary.
5. Pour the batter into prepared pans using liquid measurements to ensure uniform division.

◆◆◆

RECIPE 30.2

HIGH-RATIO YELLOW CAKE

Yield: 3–4 Sheet Pans   **Method:** High-Ratio

Cake flour	5 lb.	2.2 kg
Granulated sugar	5 lb. 4 oz.	2.3 kg
Emulsified shortening	2 lb. 8 oz.	1.1 kg
Salt	2 oz.	60 g
Baking powder	4 oz.	120 g
Powdered milk	8 oz.	225 g
Light corn syrup	12 oz.	340 g
Water, cold	1 qt.	1 lt
Eggs	2 lb. 8 oz.	1.1 kg
Water, cold	2-1/4 qt.	2.25 lt
Lemon extract	1 oz.	30 g

1. Combine the flour, sugar, shortening, salt, baking powder, powdered milk, corn syrup and 1 quart (1 liter) cold water in a large bowl of a mixer fitted with the paddle attachment. Beat for 5 minutes on low speed.
2. Combine the remaining ingredients in a separate bowl. Add these liquid ingredients to the creamed-fat mixture in three additions. Scrape down the sides of the bowl after each addition.
3. Beat for 2 minutes on low speed.
4. Divide the batter into greased and floured pans. Pans should be filled only halfway. One gallon of batter is sufficient for an 18-inch × 24-inch × 2-inch (45- × 60- × 5- centimeter) sheet pan. Bake at 340°F (170°C) until a cake tester comes out clean and the cake springs back when lightly touched, approximately 12–18 minutes.

Whipped Egg

Cakes based on whipped egg foams include European-style genoise as well as spongecakes, angel food cakes and chiffon cakes. Some formulas contain chemical leaveners, but the air whipped into the eggs (whether whole or separated) is the primary leavening agent. Egg-foam cakes contain little or no fat.

Genoise

Genoise is the classic European-style cake. It is based on whole eggs whipped with sugar until very light and fluffy. Chemical leaveners are not used. A small amount of oil or melted butter is sometimes added for flavor and moisture. Genoise is often baked in a thin sheet and layered with buttercream, puréed fruit, jam or chocolate filling to create multilayered specialty desserts. Because genoise is rather dry, it is usually soaked with a flavored sugar syrup (see Chapter 26, Principles of Baking) or liquor for additional flavor and moisture.

PROCEDURE FOR PREPARING GENOISE

1. Preheat the oven and prepare the pans.
2. Sift the flour with any additional dry ingredients.
3. Combine the whole eggs and sugar in a large bowl and warm over a double boiler to a temperature of 100°F (38°C).
4. Whip the egg-and-sugar mixture until very light and tripled in volume.
5. Fold the sifted flour into the whipped eggs carefully but quickly.
6. Fold in oil or melted butter if desired.
7. Divide into pans and bake immediately.

1. Whipped eggs.

2. Folding in the flour.

◆◆◆

RECIPE 30.3
CLASSIC GENOISE

Yield: 3 Full Sheet Pans **Method:** Whipped Egg

Cake flour	1 lb. 8 oz.	680 g
Eggs	30	30
Granulated sugar	1 lb. 8 oz.	680 g
Unsalted butter, melted (optional)	4 oz.	120 g

1. Sift the flour and set aside.
2. Whisk the eggs and sugar together in a large mixer bowl. Place the bowl over a bain marie and warm the eggs to about 100°F (38°C). Stir frequently to avoid cooking the eggs.
3. When the eggs are warm, remove the bowl from the bain marie and attach to a mixer fitted with a whip attachment. Whip the egg-and-sugar mixture at medium speed until tripled in volume.
4. Quickly fold the flour into the egg mixture by hand. Be careful not to deflate the batter.
5. Pour the melted, cooled butter around the edges of the batter and fold in quickly.
6. Divide the batter immediately into parchment-lined pans. Bake at 350°F (180°C) until light brown and springy to the touch, approximately 8 minutes.

VARIATION: *Chocolate genoise*—Sift 3-1/2 ounces (100 grams) of cocoa powder with the flour.

3. Adding the melted butter.

4. Panning the batter.

Spongecakes

Spongecakes (Fr. *biscuits*) are made with whole separated eggs. A batter is prepared with the egg yolks and other ingredients, then the egg whites are whipped to firm peaks with a portion of the sugar and folded into the batter. Spongecakes are primarily leavened with air, but baking powder may be included in the formula. As with genoise, oil or melted butter may be added if desired.

Spongecakes are extremely versatile. They can be soaked with sugar syrup or a liquor and assembled with buttercream as a traditional layer cake. Or, they can be sliced thinly and layered, like genoise, with jam, custard, chocolate or cream filling.

PROCEDURE FOR PREPARING SPONGECAKES

1. Preheat the oven and prepare the pans.
2. Separate the eggs. Whip the egg whites with a portion of the sugar.
3. Sift the dry ingredients together and combine with liquid ingredients, including the egg yolks, as directed.
4. Carefully fold the whipped egg whites into the batter.
5. Pour the batter into the pans and bake immediately.

◆◆◆

RECIPE 30.4

CLASSIC SPONGECAKE

Yield: 2 9-inch (22-cm) Rounds   **Method:** Whipped Egg

Cake flour, sifted	6 oz.	180 g
Granulated sugar	11 oz.	300 g
Eggs	10	10
Vanilla extract	1-1/2 tsp.	7 ml
Cream of tartar	1-1/2 tsp.	7 ml

1. Line the bottom of two springform pans with parchment. Do not grease the sides of the pans.

2. Sift the flour and 6 ounces (150 grams) of the sugar together and set aside.

3. Separate the eggs, placing the yolks and the whites in separate mixing bowls. Whip the yolks on high speed for 3–5 minutes, until thick, pale and at least doubled in volume. Whip in the vanilla extract. The yolks should be whipped "to ribbon," that is, until they fall from the beater in thick ribbons that slowly disappear into the batter's surface.

4. Place the bowl of egg whites on the mixer and, using a clean whip attachment, beat until foamy. Add the cream of tartar and 2 tablespoons (30 grams) of sugar. Whip at medium speed until the whites are glossy and stiff but not dry.

5. Remove the bowl from the mixer. Pour the egg yolks onto the whipped whites. Quickly fold the two mixtures together by hand. Sprinkle the remaining sugar over the mixture and fold in lightly.

6. Sprinkle one third of the sifted flour over the batter and fold in. Repeat the procedure until all of the flour is incorporated. Do not overmix; fold just until incorporated.

7. Pour the batter into the prepared pans, smoothing the surface as needed. Bake immediately at 375°F (190°C) until the cake is golden brown and spongy, approximately 30 minutes. A toothpick inserted in the center will be completely clean.

8. Allow the cakes to rest in their pans until completely cool, approximately 2 hours.

9. To remove the cakes from their pans, run a thin metal spatula around the edge of each pan. When the cake is completely cool it can be frosted or wrapped in plastic wrap and frozen for 2–3 months.

1. The eggs whipped to ribbon stage.

2. Folding the flour into the batter.

3. Panning the batter.

Angel Food Cakes

Angel food cakes are tall, light cakes made without fat and leavened with a large quantity of whipped egg whites. Angel food cakes are traditionally baked in ungreased tube pans, but large loaf pans can also be used. The pans are left ungreased so that the batter can cling to the sides as it rises. The cakes should be inverted as soon as they are removed from the oven and left in the pan to cool. This technique allows gravity to keep the cakes from collapsing or sinking as they cool.

Although they contain no fat, angel food cakes are not low in calories as they contain a high percentage of sugar. The classic angel food cake is pure white, but flavorings, ground nuts or cocoa powder may be added for variety. Although angel food cakes are rarely frosted, they may be topped with a fruit-flavored or chocolate glaze. They are often served with fresh fruit, a fruit compote or whipped cream.

PROCEDURE FOR PREPARING ANGEL FOOD CAKES

1. Preheat the oven.
2. Sift the dry ingredients together.
3. Whip the egg whites with a portion of the sugar until stiff and glossy.
4. Gently fold the dry ingredients into the egg whites.
5. Spoon the batter into an ungreased pan and bake immediately.
6. Allow the cake to cool inverted in its pan.

◆◆◆

RECIPE 30.5

CHOCOLATE ANGEL FOOD CAKE

Yield: 1 10-inch (25-cm) Tube Cake   **Method:** Whipped Egg

Cocoa powder, alkalized	1 oz.	30 g
Water, warm	2 oz.	60 g
Vanilla extract	2 tsp.	10 ml
Granulated sugar	12 oz.	340 g
Cake flour, sifted	3-1/2 oz.	100 g
Salt	1/4 tsp.	1 g
Egg whites	16	16
Cream of tartar	2 tsp.	10 ml

1. Combine the cocoa powder and water in a bowl. Add the vanilla and set aside.

2. In another bowl, combine 5 ounces (150 grams) of the sugar with the flour and salt.

3. Whip the egg whites until foamy, add the cream of tartar and beat to soft peaks. Gradually beat in the remaining sugar. Continue beating until the egg whites are stiff but not dry.

4. Whisk approximately 1 cup (225 millileters) of the whipped egg whites into the cocoa mixture. Fold this into the remaining egg whites.

5. Sift the dry ingredients over the whites and fold in quickly but gently.

6. Pour the batter into an ungreased tube pan and smooth the top with a spatula. Bake immediately at 350°F (180°C) until the cake springs back when lightly touched and a cake tester comes out clean, approximately 40–50 minutes. The cake's surface will have deep cracks.

7. Remove the cake from the oven and immediately invert the pan onto the neck of a bottle. Allow the cake to rest upside down until completely cool.

8. To remove the cake from the pan, run a thin knife or spatula around the edge of the pan and the edge of the interior tube. If a two-piece tube pan was used, the cake and tube portion are lifted out of the pan. Use a knife or spatula to loosen the bottom of the cake, then invert it onto a cake cardboard or serving platter.

1. Folding the cocoa mixture into the whipped egg whites.

2. Folding in the flour.

3. Cooling the cake upside down in its pan.

4. Removing the cake from the pan.

Chiffon Cakes

Although chiffon cakes are similar to angel food cakes in appearance and texture, the addition of egg yolks and vegetable oil makes them moister and richer. Chiffon cakes are usually leavened with whipped egg whites but may contain baking powder as well. Like angel food cakes, chiffon cakes are baked in an ungreased pan to allow the batter to cling to the pan as it rises. Chiffon cakes can be frosted with a light buttercream or whipped cream or topped with a glaze. Lemon and orange chiffon cakes are the most popular, but formulas containing chocolate, nuts or other flavorings are also common.

PROCEDURE FOR PREPARING CHIFFON CAKES

1. Preheat the oven.
2. Whip the egg whites with a portion of the sugar until almost stiff. Set aside.
3. Sift the dry ingredients together. Add the liquid ingredients, including oil.
4. Fold the whipped egg whites into the batter.
5. Spoon the batter into an ungreased pan and bake immediately.
6. Allow the cake to cool inverted in its pan.

♦♦♦

RECIPE 30.6

ORANGE CHIFFON CAKE

Yield: 1 10-inch (25-cm) Tube Cake   **Method:** Whipped Egg

Cake flour, sifted	8 oz.	225 g
Sugar	12 oz.	340 g
Baking powder	1 Tbsp.	15 ml
Salt	1 tsp.	5 ml
Vegetable oil	4 oz.	120 g
Egg yolks	6	6
Water, cool	2 oz.	60 g
Orange juice	4 oz.	120 g
Orange zest	1 Tbsp.	15 ml
Vanilla extract	1 Tbsp.	15 ml
Egg whites	8 oz.	250 g

1. Sift together the flour, 6 ounces (170 grams) of sugar, the baking powder and salt.
2. In a separate bowl mix the oil, yolks, water, juice, zest and vanilla. Add the liquid mixture to the dry ingredients.
3. In a clean bowl beat the egg whites until foamy. Slowly beat in the remaining 6 ounces (170 grams) of sugar. Continue beating until the egg whites are stiff but not dry.
4. Stir one third of the egg whites into the batter to lighten it. Fold in the remaining egg whites.
5. Pour the batter into an ungreased 10-inch (25-centimeter) tube pan. Bake at 325°F (160°C) until a toothpick comes out clean, approximately 1 hour.
6. Immediately invert the pan over the neck of a wine bottle. Allow the cake to hang upside down until completely cool, then remove from the pan.

Continued

♦♦♦
A BAKER CREATED CHIFFON CAKES

Chiffon cake is one of the few desserts whose history can be traced with absolute certainty. According to Gerry Schremp in her book *Kitchen Culture: Fifty Years of Food Fads*, a new type of cake was invented by Henry Baker, a California insurance salesman, in 1927. Dubbed *chiffon*, it was as light as angel food and as rich as poundcake. For years he kept the formula a secret, earning fame and fortune by selling his cakes to Hollywood restaurants. The cake's secret ingredient—vegetable oil—became public knowledge in 1947 when Baker sold the formula to General Mills, which promoted it on packages of cake flour. Chiffon cakes, in a variety of flavors, became extremely popular nationwide.

ORANGE GLAZE

Powdered sugar	3 oz.	90 g
Orange juice	2 Tbsp.	30 ml
Orange zest	2 tsp.	10 ml

1. Sift the sugar, then stir in the juice and zest.
2. Drizzle the glaze over the top of the cooled cake.

VARIATION: *Lemon chiffon cake*—Substitute 2 ounces (60 grams) fresh lemon juice and 2 ounces water for the orange juice. Substitute lemon zest for the orange zest. Top with Basic Sugar Glaze, Recipe 30.12.

Panning, Baking and Cooling

Preparing Pans

In order to prevent cakes from sticking, most baking pans are coated with fat or a nonstick baking parchment. Pans should be prepared before the batter is mixed, so that they may be filled and the cakes baked as soon as the batter is finished. If the batter stands while the pans are prepared, air cells within the batter will deflate and volume may be lost.

Solid shortening is better than butter for coating pans because it does not contain any water; butter and margarine do contain water and this may cause the cake to stick in places. Solid shortening is also less expensive, tasteless and odorless. Finally, solid shortening does not burn as easily as butter and it holds a dusting of flour better.

Pan release sprays are useful but must be applied carefully and completely. Although relatively expensive, sprays save time and are particularly effective when used with parchment pan liners.

In kitchens where a great deal of baking is done, it may be more convenient to prepare quantities of pan coating to be kept available for use as needed. Pan coating is a mixture of equal-parts oil, shortening and flour that can be applied to cake pans with a pastry brush. It is used whenever pans need to be greased and floured. Pan coating will not leave a white residue on the cake's crust as a dusting of flour often does.

TABLE 30.2   NUTRITIONAL VALUES OF SELECTED CAKES

Per 1/12 Portion of a 9-inch Cake, Unfrosted	Kcal	Protein (g)	Carbohydrates (g)	Total Fat (g)	Saturated Fat (g)	Sodium (mg)
Angel food	130	3	30	0	0	170
Butter cake	260	3	37	11	6	350
Chiffon, lemon	200	4	36	5	mq	200
Devil's food	260	4	35	12	3	450
Sponge (2-in. square)	80	1	11	3	1	125

All cakes are prepared from a typical mix according to package directions.
The Corinne T. Netzer Encyclopedia of Food Values 1992
mq = measurable quantity but data is unavailable

TABLE 30.3 PAN PREPARATIONS

Pan Preparation	Used For
Ungreased	Angel food and chiffon cakes
Ungreased sides; paper on bottom	Genoise layers
Greased and papered	High-fat cakes, sponge sheets
Greased and coated with flour	High-fat cakes, chocolate cakes, anything in a bundt or shaped pan
Greased, floured and lined with paper	Cakes containing melted chocolate, fruit chunks or fruit or vegetable purées

◆◆◆

RECIPE 30.7

PAN COATING

Yield: 1-1/2 qt. (1.5 lt)

Vegetable oil	1 lb.	500 g
All-purpose shortening	1 lb.	500 g
Bread flour	1 lb.	500 g

1. Combine all ingredients in a mixer fitted with the paddle attachment. Blend on low speed for 5 minutes or until smooth.
2. Store in an airtight container at room temperature for up to two months.
3. Apply to baking pans in a thin, even layer using a pastry brush.

Pan coating is not appropriate for all cakes, however. Those containing chocolate, raisins or fruit should still be baked in pans lined with parchment paper to prevent sticking.

Angel food and chiffon cakes are baked in ungreased, unlined pans because these fragile cakes need to cling to the sides of the pan as they rise. Spongecakes and genoise are often baked in pans with a paper liner on the

◆◆◆

BROWNIES

Where do you draw the line between cakes and brownies? The decision must be a matter of texture and personal preference, for the preparation methods are nearly identical. Brownies are generally chewy and fudgy, sweeter and denser than even the richest of butter cakes.

Brownies are a relatively inexpensive and easy way for a food service operation to offer its customers a fresh-baked dessert. Although not as sophisticated as an elaborate gâteau, a well-made brownie can always be served with pride (and a scoop of ice cream).

Brownies are prepared using the same procedures as those for high-fat cakes. Good brownies are achieved with a proper balance of ingredients: A high percentage of butter to flour produces a dense, fudgy brownie; less butter produces a more cakelike brownie. Likewise, the higher the ratio of sugar, the gooier the finished brownie. In some formulas, the fat is creamed to incorporate air, as with butter cakes. In others, the fat is first melted and combined with other liquid ingredients. Brownies are rarely made with whipped egg whites, however, as this makes their texture too light and cakelike.

Each customer and cook has his or her own idea of the quintessential brownie. Some are cloyingly sweet, with a creamy texture and an abundance of chocolate; others are bitter and crisp. Baked brownies can be frozen for 2–3 months if well wrapped.

bottom and ungreased sides. While the ungreased sides give the batter a surface to cling to, the paper liner makes removing the cake from the pan easier.

Filling Pans

Pans should be filled no more than one-half to two-thirds full. This allows the batter to rise during baking without spilling over the edges.

Pans should be filled to uniform depths. High-fat and egg-foam cake batters can be ladled into each pan according to weight. High-ratio cake batter is so liquid that it can be measured by volume and poured into each pan. Filling the pans uniformly prevents both uneven layers and over- or underfilled pans. If you are baking three 8-inch layers to be stacked for one presentation and the amount of batter is different in each pan, the baking times will vary and the final product will suffer.

The cake batter should always be spread evenly in the pan. Use an offset spatula. Do not work the batter too much, however, as this destroys air cells and prevents the cake from rising properly.

Baking

Temperatures

Always preheat the oven before preparing your batter. If the finished batter must wait while the oven reaches the correct temperature, valuable leavening will be lost and the cake will not rise properly.

Most cakes are baked at temperatures between 325° and 375°F (160–190°C). The temperature must be high enough to create steam within the batter and cause that steam and other gases in the batter to expand and rise quickly. If the temperature is too high, however, the cake may rise unevenly and the crust may burn before the interior is completely baked. The temperature must also be low enough that the batter can set completely and evenly without drying out. If the temperature is too low, however, the cake will not rise sufficiently and may dry out before baking completely.

If no temperature is given in a formula or you are altering the dimensions of the baking pan from those specified, use common sense in setting the oven temperature. The larger the surface area, the higher the temperature can usually be. Tall cakes, such as bundt or tube cakes, should be baked at a lower temperature than thin layer or sheet cakes. Tube or loaf cakes take longer to bake than thin sheet cakes; butter cakes, because they contain more liquid, take longer to bake than genoise or spongecake.

Altitude Adjustments

As you learned in Chapter 9, Principles of Cooking, altitude affects the temperatures at which foods cook. The decreased atmospheric pressure at altitudes above 3000 feet affects the creation of steam and the expansion of hot air in cake batters. These factors must be considered when making cakes. Because gases expand more easily at higher altitudes, your cake may rise so much that its structure cannot support it and the cake collapses.

Therefore, the amount of leavening should be decreased at higher altitudes. Chemical leaveners should usually be reduced by one third at 3500 feet and by two thirds at altitudes over 5000 feet. Eggs should be underwhipped to avoid incorporating too much air, which would also create too much rise. In general, oven temperatures should also be increased by 25°F (4°C) at altitudes over 3500 feet to help set the cake's structure rapidly.

Because the boiling point decreases at higher altitudes, more moisture will evaporate from your cake during baking. This may cause dryness and an excessive proportion of sugar, which shows up as white spots on the cake's surface. Correct this by reducing every 8 ounces (225 grams) of sugar by 1/2 ounce (15 grams) at 3000 feet and by 1-1/2 ounces (45 grams) at 7000 feet.

Attempting to adjust typical (i.e., sea level) formulas for high altitudes is somewhat risky, especially in a commercial operation. Try to find and use formulas developed especially for your area or contact the local offices of your state's Department of Agriculture or the Agricultural Extension Service for detailed assistance.

Determining Doneness

In addition to following the baking time suggested in a formula, several simple tests can be used to determine doneness. Whichever test or tests are used, avoid opening the oven door to check the cake's progress. Cold air or a drop in oven temperature can cause the cake to fall. Use a timer to note the minimum suggested baking time. Then, and only then, should you use the following tests to evaluate the cake's doneness:

- ◆ Appearance—The cake's surface should be a light to golden brown. Unless noted otherwise in the formula, the edges should just begin to pull away from the pan. The cake should not jiggle or move beneath its surface.
- ◆ Touch—Touch the cake *lightly* with your finger. It should spring back quickly without feeling soggy or leaving an indentation.
- ◆ Cake tester—If appearance and touch indicate that the cake is done, test the interior by inserting a toothpick, bamboo skewer or metal cake tester into the cake's center. With most cakes, the tester should come out clean. If wet crumbs cling to the tester the cake probably needs to bake a bit longer.

If a formula provides particular doneness guidelines, they should be followed. For example, some flourless cakes are fully baked even though a cake tester will not come out clean.

Cooling

Generally, a cake is allowed to cool for 10–15 minutes in its pan after taking it out of the oven. This helps prevent the cake from cracking or breaking after it is removed from its pan.

To remove the partially cooled cake from its pan, run a thin knife or spatula blade between the pan and the cake to loosen it. Place a wire rack, cake cardboard or sheet pan over the cake and invert. Then remove the pan. The cake can be left upside down to cool completely or inverted again to cool top side up. Wire racks are preferred for cooling cakes because they allow air to circulate, speeding the cooling process and preventing steam from making the cake soggy.

Angel food and chiffon cakes should be turned upside down immediately after they are removed from the oven. They are left to cool completely in their pans to prevent the cake from collapsing or shrinking. The top of the pan should not touch the countertop so that air can circulate under the inverted pan.

All cakes should be left to cool away from drafts or air currents that might cause them to collapse. Cakes should not be refrigerated to speed the cooling process, as rapid cooling can cause cracking. Prolonged refrigeration also causes cakes to dry out.

TABLE 30.4   TROUBLESHOOTING CHART FOR CAKES

Problem	Cause	Solution
Batter curdles during mixing	Ingredients too warm or too cold	Eggs must be room temperature and added slowly
	Incorrect fat used	Use correct ingredients
	Fat inadequately creamed before liquid was added	Add a portion of the flour, then continue adding the liquid
Cake lacks volume	Flour too strong	Use a weaker flour
	Old chemical leavener	Replace with fresh leavener
	Egg foam underwhipped	Use correct mixing method, do not deflate eggs during folding
	Oven too hot	Adjust oven temperature
Crust burst or cracked	Too much flour or too little liquid	Adjust formula
	Oven too hot	Adjust oven temperature
Cake shrinks after baking	Weak internal structure	Adjust formula
	Too much sugar or fat for the batter to support	Adjust formula
	Cake not fully cooked	Test cake for doneness before removing from oven
	Cake cooled too rapidly	Cool away from drafts
Texture is dense or heavy	Too little leavening	Adjust formula
	Too much fat or liquid	Cream fat or whip eggs properly
	Oven too cool	Adjust oven temperature
Texture is coarse with an open grain	Overmixing	Alter mixing method
	Oven too cool	Adjust oven temperature
Poor flavor	Poor ingredients	Check flavor and aroma of all ingredients
	Unclean pans	Do not grease pans with rancid fats
Uneven shape	Butter not incorporated evenly	Incorporate fats completely
	Batter spread unevenly	Spread batter evenly
	Oven rack not level	Adjust oven racks
	Uneven oven temperature	Adjust oven temperature

FROSTINGS

Frosting, also known as **icing**, is a sweet decorative coating used as a filling between the layers or as a coating over the top and sides of a cake. It is used to add flavor and to improve the cake's appearance. Frosting can also extend a cake's shelf life by forming a protective coating.

There are seven general types of frosting: **buttercream**, **foam**, **fudge**, **fondant**, **glaze**, **royal icing** and **ganache**. See Table 30.5. Each type can be produced with a number of formulas and in a range of flavorings.

TABLE 30.5   FROSTINGS

Frosting	Preparation	Texture/Taste
Buttercream	Mixture of sugar and fat (usually butter); can contain egg yolks or egg whites	Rich but light; smooth, fluffy
Foam	Meringue made with hot sugar syrup	Light, fluffy; very sweet
Fudge	Cooked mixture of sugar, butter and water or milk; applied warm	Heavy, rich and candylike
Fondant	Cooked mixture of sugar and water; applied warm	Thick; opaque; sweet
Glaze	Confectioner's sugar with liquid	Thin
Royal icing	Uncooked mixture of confectioner's sugar and egg whites	Hard and brittle when dry
Ganache	Blend of melted chocolate and cream	Rich, smooth, intense flavor

Because frosting is integral to the flavor and appearance of many cakes, it should be made carefully using high-quality ingredients and natural flavors and colors. A good frosting is smooth; it is never grainy or lumpy. It should complement the flavor and texture of the cake without overpowering it.

Buttercream

A buttercream is a light, smooth, fluffy mixture of sugar and fat (butter, margarine or shortening). It may also contain egg yolks for richness or whipped egg whites for lightness. A good buttercream will be sweet, but not cloying; buttery, but not greasy.

Buttercreams are popular and useful for most types of cakes and may be flavored or colored as desired. They may be stored, covered, in the refrigerator for several days but must be softened before use.

Although there are many types of buttercream and many formula variations, we discuss the three most popular styles: **simple**, **Italian** and **French**.

Simple Buttercream

Simple buttercream, sometimes known as **American-style buttercream**, is made by creaming butter and powdered sugar together until the mixture is light and smooth. Cream, eggs (whole, yolks or whites) and flavorings may be added as desired. Simple buttercream requires no cooking and is quick and easy to prepare.

If cost is a consideration, hydrogenated all-purpose shortening can be substituted for a portion of the butter, but the flavor and mouth-feel will be different. Buttercream made with shortening tends to feel greasier and heavier because shortening does not melt on the tongue like butter. It will be more stable than pure butter buttercream, however, and is useful for products that will be on display.

PROCEDURE FOR MAKING SIMPLE BUTTERCREAM

1. Cream softened butter or shortening until the mixture is light and fluffy.
2. Beat in egg, if desired.
3. Beat in sifted powdered sugar, scraping down the sides of the bowl as needed.
4. Beat in the flavoring ingredients.

✦✦✦

RECIPE 30.8

SIMPLE BUTTERCREAM

Yield: 2 lb. (1 kg)

Lightly salted butter, softened	1 lb.	450 g
Egg (optional)	1	1
Powdered sugar, sifted	2 lb.	900 g
Vanilla extract	2 tsp.	10 ml

1. Using a mixer fitted with the paddle attachment, cream the butter until light and fluffy.

2. Beat in the egg if desired. Gradually add the sugar, frequently scraping down the sides of the bowl.

3. Add the vanilla and continue beating until the frosting is smooth and light.

VARIATIONS: *Light chocolate*—Dissolve 1 ounce (30 grams) sifted cocoa powder in 2 ounces (60 grams) cool water. Add to the buttercream along with the vanilla.

Lemon—Decrease the vanilla extract to 1 teaspoon (5 milliliters). Add 1 teaspoon (5 milliliters) lemon extract and the finely grated zest of one lemon.

Italian Buttercream

Italian buttercream, also known as **meringue buttercream**, is based on an Italian meringue, that is, whipped egg whites cooked with hot sugar syrup. (See Chapter 29, Pies, Pastries and Cookies.) Softened butter is then whipped into the cooled meringue and the mixture is flavored as desired. This type of buttercream is extremely soft and light. It can be used on most types of cakes and is particularly popular for multilayered genoise or spongecakes.

PROCEDURE FOR MAKING ITALIAN BUTTERCREAM

1. Whip the egg whites until soft peaks form.
2. Beat granulated sugar into the egg whites and whip until firm and glossy.
3. Meanwhile, combine additional sugar with water and cook to soft ball stage (238°F/115°C).
4. With the mixer on medium speed, pour the sugar syrup into the whipped egg whites. Pour slowly and carefully to avoid splatters.
5. Continue whipping the egg-white-and-sugar mixture until completely cool.
6. Whip softened, but not melted, butter into the cooled egg-white-and-sugar mixture.
7. Add flavoring ingredients as desired.

✦✦✦

RECIPE 30.9

ITALIAN BUTTERCREAM

Yield: 5 lb. (2.2 kg)

Egg whites	14 oz.	400 g
Sugar	1 lb. 11 oz.	750 g
Lightly salted butter, softened but not melted	2 lb. 12 oz.	1250 g

1. All ingredients should be at room temperature before beginning.
2. Place the egg whites in a mixer bowl. Have 9 ounces (250 grams) of sugar nearby.
3. Place 1 pound 2 ounces (500 grams) of sugar in a heavy saucepan with enough water to moisten. Bring to a boil over high heat.
4. As the sugar syrup's temperature approaches a soft ball stage (238°F/115°C), begin whipping the egg whites. Watch the sugar closely so that the temperature does not exceed 238°F (115°C).
5. When soft peaks form in the egg whites, gradually add the 9 ounces (250 grams) of sugar to them. Reduce mixer speed to medium and continue whipping the egg whites to stiff peaks.
6. When the sugar syrup reaches soft ball stage, immediately pour it into the whites while the mixer is running. Pour the syrup in a steady stream between the side of the bowl and the beater. If the syrup hits the beater it will splatter and cause lumps. Continue beating at medium speed until the egg whites are completely cool. At this point the product is known as Italian meringue.
7. Gradually add the softened butter to the Italian meringue. When all of the butter is incorporated, add flavoring ingredients as desired.

VARIATION: *Chocolate:* Add 1 tablespoon (15 milliliters) vanilla extract and 10 ounces (300 grams) melted and cooled bittersweet chocolate.

1. Adding the sugar syrup to the whipped egg whites.

2. Adding the softened butter to the cooled Italian meringue.

3. Finished Italian buttercream.

French Buttercream

French buttercream, also known as **mousseline buttercream**, is similar to Italian buttercream except that the hot sugar syrup is whipped into beaten egg yolks (not egg whites). Softened butter and flavorings are added when the sweetened egg yolks are fluffy and cool. An Italian meringue such as the one created in the above formula is sometimes folded in for additional body and lightness. French buttercream is perhaps the most difficult type of buttercream to master, but it has the richest flavor and smoothest texture. Like a meringue buttercream, mousseline buttercream may be used on almost any type of cake.

PROCEDURE FOR MAKING FRENCH BUTTERCREAM

1. Prepare a sugar syrup and cook to soft ball stage (238°F/115°C).
2. Beat egg yolks to a thin ribbon.

3. Slowly beat the sugar syrup into the egg yolks.
4. Continue beating until the yolks are pale, stiff and completely cool.
5. Gradually add softened butter to the cooled yolks.
6. Fold in Italian meringue.
7. Stir in flavoring ingredients.

◆◆◆

RECIPE 30.10
FRENCH BUTTERCREAM

Yield: 2 qt. (2 lt)

Granulated sugar	1 lb. 10 oz.	800 g
Water	8 oz.	250 g
Egg yolks	16	16
Lightly salted butter, softened		
but not melted	3 lb.	1500 g
Italian Meringue (Recipe 30.9)	1 qt.	1 lt

1. Combine the sugar and water in a small saucepan and bring to a boil. Continue boiling until the syrup reaches 238°F (115°C).

2. Meanwhile, beat the egg yolks in a mixer fitted with a wire whisk on low speed. When the sugar syrup reaches 238°F (115°C), pour it slowly into the egg yolks, gradually increasing the speed at which they are whipped. Continue beating at medium-high speed until the mixture is very pale, stiff and cool.

3. Gradually add the softened butter to the egg mixture, frequently scraping down the sides of the bowl.

4. Fold in the Italian meringue with a spatula. Stir in flavoring extracts as desired.

Foam Frosting

Foam frosting, sometimes known as **boiled icing**, is simply a meringue made with hot sugar syrup. Foam frosting is light and fluffy but very sweet. It may be flavored with extract, liqueur or melted chocolate.

Foam frosting is rather unstable. It should be used immediately and served the day it is prepared. Refrigeration often makes the foam weep beads of sugar. Freezing causes it to separate or melt.

An easy foam frosting can be made by following the formula for Italian Buttercream (Recipe 30.9), but omitting the butter. As soon as the meringue has cooled to room temperature it should be flavored with extract as desired, then used.

Fudge Frosting

A fudge frosting is a warmed mixture of sugar, butter and water or milk. It is heavy, rich and candylike. It is also stable and holds up well. A fudge frosting should be applied warm and allowed to dry on the cake or pastry. When dry, it will have a thin crust and a moist interior. A fudge frosting can be vanilla- or chocolate-based and is used on cupcakes, layer cakes and sheet cakes.

PROCEDURE FOR MAKING FUDGE FROSTING

1. Blend sifted powdered sugar with corn syrup, beating until the sugar is dissolved and the mixture is smooth.
2. Blend in warm melted shortening and/or butter.
3. Blend in hot liquids. Add extracts or flavorings.
4. Use fudge frosting while still warm.

◆◆◆

RECIPE 30.11

BASIC FUDGE FROSTING

Yield: 3 lb. (1500 g)

Powdered sugar, sifted	3 lb.	1500 g
Salt	1/4 tsp.	1 ml
Light corn syrup	2 oz.	60 g
Shortening, melted	4 oz.	120 g
Water, hot (140°F/60°C)	10 oz.	300 g
Vanilla extract	2 Tbsp.	30 ml

1. Blend the sugar, salt and corn syrup. Beat until smooth.
2. Add the melted shortening and blend well.
3. Add the hot water and vanilla and blend well. If the fudge is too stiff it may be thinned with a simple sugar syrup. Use before the icing cools.

VARIATION: *Cocoa fudge frosting:* Sift 4 ounces (120 grams) cocoa powder with the powdered sugar. Add 2 ounces (60 grams) melted unsalted butter with the shortening.

1. Cocoa fudge frosting.

Fondant

Fondant is a thick, opaque sugar paste commonly used for glazing napoleons, petit fours and other pastries as well as some cakes. It is a cooked mixture of sugar and water, with **glucose** or corn syrup added to encourage the correct type of sugar crystallization. Poured onto the surface being coated, fondant quickly dries to a shiny, nonsticky coating. It is naturally pure white and can be tinted with food coloring. Fondant may also be flavored with melted chocolate.

Glucose—*a thick, sweet syrup made from cornstarch, composed primarily of dextrose. Light corn syrup can usually be substituted for it in baked goods or candy making.*

Fondant is rather difficult to make, so it is almost always purchased prepared. To use, thin it with water or simple syrup and carefully warm to 100°F (38°C). Commercially prepared fondant will keep for several months at room temperature in an airtight container. The surface of the fondant should be coated with simple syrup, however, to prevent a crust from forming.

Glaze

A glaze is a thin coating meant to be poured or dripped onto a cake or pastry. A glaze is usually too thin to apply with a knife or spatula. It is used to add moisture and flavor to cakes on which a heavy frosting would be undesirable—for example, a chiffon or angel food cake.

Flat icing is a specific type of glaze used on danish pastries and coffeecakes. It is pure white and dries to a firm gloss.

PROCEDURE FOR MAKING GLAZE

1. Blend sifted powdered sugar with a small amount of liquid and flavorings.
2. Use immediately.

◆◆◆

RECIPE 30.12

BASIC SUGAR GLAZE

Yield: 12 oz. (340 g)

Powdered sugar, sifted	9-1/2 oz.	270 g
Light cream or milk	2 oz.	60 g
Unsalted butter, melted	1 oz.	30 g
Vanilla extract	2 tsp.	10 ml

1. Stir the ingredients together in a small bowl until smooth.
2. Adjust the consistency by adding more cream or milk to thin the glaze if necessary.
3. Adjust the flavor as necessary. (Another extract, such as lemon or almond, may be used if desired.)
4. Use immediately, before the glaze begins to dry.

Royal Icing

Royal icing, also known as **decorator's icing**, is similar to flat icing except it is much stiffer and becomes hard and brittle when dry. It is an uncooked mixture of powdered sugar and egg whites. It may be dyed with food coloring pastes.

Royal icing is used for making decorations, particularly intricate flowers or lace patterns. Prepare royal icing in small quantities and always keep any unused portion covered with a damp towel to prevent hardening.

PROCEDURE FOR MAKING ROYAL ICING

1. Combine egg white and lemon juice, if used.
2. Beat in sifted powdered sugar until the correct consistency is reached.

3. Beat until very smooth and firm enough to hold a stiff peak.
4. Color as desired with paste food colorings.
5. Store covered with a damp cloth and plastic wrap.

RECIPE 30.13
ROYAL ICING

Yield: 6 oz. (180 g)

Powdered sugar	6 oz.	180 g
Egg white, room temperature	1	1
Lemon juice	1/4 tsp.	1 ml

1. Sift the sugar and set aside.
2. Place the egg white and lemon juice in a stainless steel bowl.
3. Add 4 ounces (120 grams) of sugar and beat with an electric mixer or metal spoon until blended. The mixture should fall from a spoon in heavy globs. If it pours, it is too thin and will need the remaining 2 ounces (60 grams) of sugar.
4. Once the consistency is correct, continue beating for 3–4 minutes. The icing should be white, smooth and thick enough to hold a stiff peak. Food coloring paste can be added at this time if desired.
5. Cover the icing with a damp towel and plastic wrap to prevent it from hardening.

Ganache

Ganache is a blend of chocolate and cream. It may also include butter, liquor or other flavorings. Any bittersweet, semisweet or dark chocolate may be used; the choice depends on personal preference and cost considerations.

Depending on its consistency, ganache may be used as a filling, frosting or glaze-type coating on cakes or pastries. The ratio of chocolate to cream determines how thick the cooled ganache will be. Equal parts chocolate and cream generally are best for frostings and fillings. Increasing the percentage of chocolate produces a thicker ganache. Warm ganache can be poured over a cake or pastry and allowed to harden as a thin glaze, or the ganache may be cooled and whipped to create a rich, smooth frosting. If it becomes too firm, ganache can be remelted over a bain marie.

PROCEDURE FOR MAKING GANACHE

1. Melt finely chopped chocolate with cream in a double broiler. Or,
2. Bring cream just to a boil. Then pour it over finely chopped chocolate and allow the cream's heat to gently melt the chocolate.
3. Whichever method is used, cool the cream and chocolate mixture over an ice bath.

Do not attempt to melt chocolate and then add cool cream. This will cause the chocolate to resolidify and lump.

1. Pouring the hot cream over the chopped chocolate.

2. Cool, firm ganache.

◆◆◆

RECIPE 30.14

CHOCOLATE GANACHE

Yield: 2.2 lb. (1 kg)

Bittersweet chocolate	1 lb. 1 oz.	500 g
Heavy cream	1 lb. 1 oz.	500 g
Almond or coffee liqueur	1 oz.	30 g

1. Chop the chocolate into small pieces and place in a large metal bowl.
2. Bring the cream just to a boil, then immediately pour it over the chocolate, whisking to blend. Stir gently until all the chocolate has melted.
3. Stir in the liqueur.
4. Allow to cool, stirring frequently until the desired consistency is achieved. An ice bath may be used to speed the cooling process.

TABLE 30.6   TROUBLESHOOTING CHART FOR FROSTINGS

Problem	Cause	Solution
Frosting breaks or curdles	Fat added too slowly or eggs too hot when fat was added	Add shortening or sifted confectioner's sugar
Frosting is lumpy	Confectioner's sugar not sifted	Sift dry ingredients
	Ingredients not blended	Use softened fat
	Sugar syrup lumps in frosting	Add sugar syrups carefully
Frosting is gritty	Granulated sugar not dissolved	Cook sugar syrups properly; cook fudge frostings as directed
Frosting is too stiff	Not enough liquid	Adjust formula; add small amount of water or milk to thin frosting
	Too cold	Bring frosting to room temperature
Frosting will not adhere to cake	Cake too hot	Cool cake completely
	Frosting too thin	Adjust frosting formula

♦♦♦

CHOCOLATE TRUFFLES

Ganache, a sublime mixture of pure chocolate and cream, is the foundation of one of the world's most sophisticated candies: the chocolate truffle. Truffles take their name from the rough, black, highly prized food they resemble, but there the similarity ends. Chocolate truffles should have a rich, creamy ganache center with a well-balanced, refined flavor.

Chocolate truffles are surprisingly simple to make. Fine chocolate is melted with cream and perhaps butter. The mixture is flavored as desired with liqueur, extracts, fruit or coffee and allowed to harden. Once firm, the ganache is scooped into balls and rolled in cocoa powder, confectioner's sugar or melted chocolate. The classic French truffle is a small, irregularly shaped ball of bittersweet chocolate dusted with cocoa powder. Americans, however, seem to prefer larger candies, coated with melted chocolate and decorated with nuts or additional chocolate. The following recipe can be prepared in either style.

1. Shaping chocolate truffles.

♦♦♦

RECIPE 30.15

DARK CHOCOLATE TRUFFLES

Yield: 150 medium-sized Truffles

Dark chocolate	2 lb.	1 kg
Unsalted butter	1 lb.	500 g
Heavy cream	1 pt.	500 ml
Brandy	4 oz.	120 ml

1. Chop the chocolate and butter into small pieces and place in a large metal bowl.

2. Bring the cream to a boil. Immediately pour the hot cream over the chocolate and butter. Stir until the chocolate and butter are completely melted.

3. Stir in the brandy. Pour the ganache into a flat, shallow, ungreased pan and chill until firm.

4. Shape the ganache into rough balls using a melon ball cutter. Immediately drop each ball into a pan of sifted cocoa powder or confectioner's sugar, rolling it around to coat completely.

5. Truffles can be stored in the refrigerator for 7–10 days. Allow them to soften slightly at room temperature before serving.

ASSEMBLING AND DECORATING CAKES

Much of a cake's initial appeal lies in its appearance. This is true whether the finished cake is a simple sheet cake topped with swirls of buttercream or an elaborate wedding cake with intricate garlands and bouquets of royal icing roses. Any cake assembled and decorated with care and attention to detail is preferable to a carelessly assembled or garishly overdecorated one.

◆◆◆

ADVANCED PATISSERIE

Sugar can be used to create a number of doughs, pastes and syrups used for artistic and decorative work. Mastering even some of these products takes years of experience and practice. Although formulas and preparation methods are beyond the scope of this book, it is important that all pastry cooks be able to recognize and identify certain decorative sugar products.

Blown sugar—a boiled mixture of sucrose, glucose and tartaric acid that is colored and shaped (in a manner very similar to glass blowing) using an air pump. It is used for making pieces of fruit and containers such as bowls and vases.

Gum paste—a smooth dough made of sugar and gelatin; it dries relatively slowly, becoming very firm and hard. The paste can be colored and rolled out, cut and shaped, or molded. It is used for making flowers, leaves and small figures.

Marzipan—a mixture of almond paste and sugar that may be colored and used like modeling clay for sculpting small fruits, flowers or other objects. Marzipan may also be rolled out and cut into various shapes or used to cover cakes or pastries.

Nougat—a candy made of caramelized sugar and almonds that can be molded into shapes or containers. Unlike other sugar decorations, nougat remains deliciously edible.

Pastillage—a paste made with sugar, cornstarch and gelatin. It can be rolled into sheets, then cut into shapes. It dries in a very firm and sturdy form, like plaster. Naturally pure white, it can be painted with cocoa or food colorings. Pastillage is used for showpieces and large decorative items.

Pulled sugar—a doughlike mixture of sucrose, glucose and tartaric acid that is colored, then shaped by hand. Pulled sugar is used for making birds, flowers, leaves, bows and other items.

Spun sugar—made by flicking dark caramelized sugar rapidly over a dowel to create long, fine, hairlike threads. Mounds or wreaths of these threads are used to decorate ice cream desserts, croquembouche and gâteaux.

Thousands of decorating styles or designs are possible, of course. This section describes a few simple options that can be prepared by beginning pastry cooks using a minimum of specialized tools. In planning your cake's design consider the flavor, texture and color of the components used as well as the number of guests or portions that must be served. Consider who will be cutting and eating the cake and how long the dessert must stand before service.

Assembling Cakes

Before a cake can be decorated, it must be assembled and coated with frosting. Most cakes can be assembled in a variety of shapes and sizes: sheet cakes, round layer cakes and rectangular layer cakes are the most common. When assembling any cake, the goal is to fill and stack the cake layers evenly and to apply an even coating of frosting that is smooth and free of crumbs.

Most of the photographs used in this section show the assembly and decoration of a wedding cake. The finished cake is shown in the photograph that introduces this chapter. The complete formula is found in Recipe 30.16.

PROCEDURE FOR ASSEMBLING CAKES

1. Begin by leveling the cake and trimming the edges as needed with a serrated knife.

2. Split the cake horizontally into thin layers if desired. Use cake boards to support each layer as it is removed. Brush away any loose crumbs with a dry pastry brush or your hand.

3. Position the bottom layer on a cake board. Place the layer on a revolving cake stand, if available. Top the layer with a mound of frosting or filling, then use a cake spatula to spread it evenly to the edges.

4. Position the next cake layer over the filling and continue layering and filling the cake as desired.

5. Place a mound of frosting in the center of the cake top. Push it to the edge of the cake with a cake spatula. Do not drag the frosting back and forth or lift the spatula off the frosting, as these actions tend to pick up crumbs.

6. Cover the sides with excess frosting from the top, adding more as necessary. Hold the spatula upright against the side of the cake and, pressing gently, turn the cake stand slowly. This smooths and evens the sides. When the sides and top are smooth, the cake is ready to be decorated as desired.

Simple Decorating Techniques

An extremely simple yet effective way to decorate a frosted cake is with a garnish of chopped nuts, fruit, toasted coconut, shaved chocolate or other foods arranged in patterns or sprinkled over the cake. Be sure to use a garnish that complements the cake and frosting flavors or reflects one of the cake's ingredients. For example, finely chopped pecans would be an appropriate garnish for a carrot cake that contains pecans; shaved chocolate would not.

Side masking is the technique of coating only the sides of a cake with garnish. The top may be left plain or decorated with icing designs or a message. Be sure to apply the garnish while the frosting is still damp enough for it to adhere.

Stencils can be used to apply finely chopped garnishes, confectioner's sugar or cocoa powder to the top of a cake in patterns. A design can be cut from cardboard, or thin plastic forms can be purchased. Even simple strips of parchment paper can be used to create an attractive pattern. If using a stencil on a frosted cake allow the frosting to set somewhat before laying the stencil on top of it. After the garnishes have been sprinkled over the stencil, carefully lift the stencil to avoid spilling the excess garnish and messing the pattern.

Side masking—coating the sides of a carrot cake with chopped pecans.

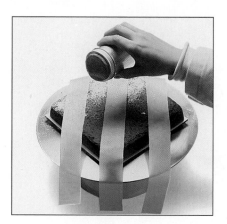

Stencils—creating a design with confectioner's sugar and strips of parchment paper.

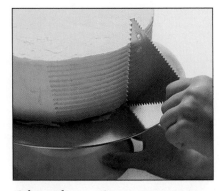

Cake comb—creating a pattern on a frosted cake.

A **cake** or **baker's comb** or serrated knife can be used to create patterns on a cake iced with buttercream, fudge or ganache. Hold the comb against the frosted cake and rotate the cake slowly and evenly to create horizontal lines in the icing.

Piping Techniques

More elaborate and difficult decorations can be produced with the aid of a piping bag and an assortment of pastry tips. With these tools, frosting or royal icing can be used to create borders, flowers and messages. Before applying any decoration, however, plan a design or pattern that is appropriate for the size and shape of the item being decorated.

When used properly, colored frosting can bring cake decorations to life. Buttercream, royal icing and fondant are easily tinted using paste food coloring. Liquid food coloring is not recommended as it may thin the frosting too much. Always add coloring gradually with a toothpick. Frosting colors tend to darken as they sit. It is easy to add more later to darken the color if necessary, but it is difficult to lighten the color if too much is added.

Piping bags made from plastic, nylon or plastic-coated canvas are available in a range of sizes. A disposable piping cone can also be made from parchment paper.

Most decorations and designs are made by using a piping bag fitted with a pastry tip. Pastry tips are available with dozens of different openings and are referred to by standardized numbers. Some commonly used tips are shown below. You can produce a variety of borders and designs by changing the pressure, the angle of the bag and the distance between the tip and the cake surface.

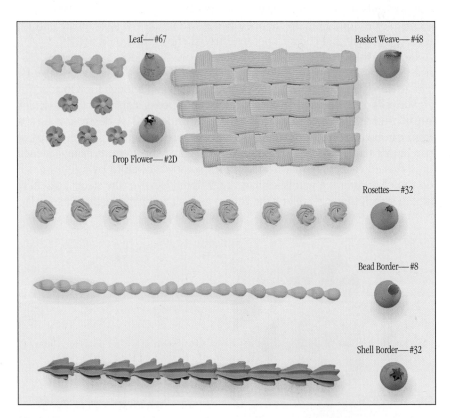

Tip Patterns

♦♦♦
MAKING A PARCHMENT-PAPER CONE

A disposable piping bag or cone is easily made from parchment paper. Begin with an equilateral triangle of uncreased paper. Shape it into a cone as shown, folding the top edges together to hold the shape. The point of the cone can be cut as desired. Paper cones are especially useful for writing messages or piping melted chocolate.

1. Wrapping opposite ends of the parchment triangle.

2. Folding the ends together to seal.

3. Cutting the tip of the filled parchment cone.

PROCEDURE FOR FILLING A PIPING BAG

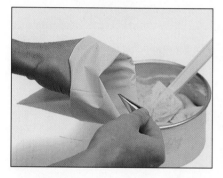

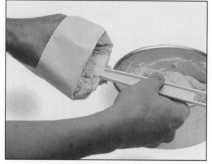

1. Select the proper size piping bag for your task. Insert the desired tip.

2. Fold down the top of the bag, then fill approximately half full with frosting. Do not overfill the bag.

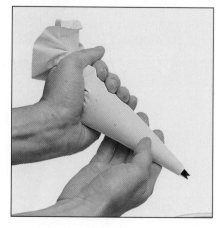

3. Be sure to close the open end tightly before you start piping. Hold the bag firmly in your palm and squeeze from the top. Do not squeeze from the bottom or you may force the contents out the wrong end. Use the fingers of your other hand to guide the bag as you work.

Piped-On Decorating Techniques

Instead of leaving the sides of a frosted cake smooth or coating them with chopped nuts or crumbs, you can pipe on frosting designs and patterns. A simple but elegant design is the basket weave, shown below.

Normally a border pattern will be piped around the base of the cake and along the top edge. Borders should be piped on after nuts or any other garnishes are applied.

Each slice or serving of cake can be marked with its own decoration. For example, a rosette of frosting or a whole nut or piece of fruit could be used as shown below. This makes it easier to portion the cake evenly.

Delicate flowers such as roses can be piped, allowed to harden, then placed on the cake in attractive arrangements. Royal icing is particularly useful for making decorations in advance because it dries very hard and lasts indefinitely.

Applying a basket weave pattern to the sides of the wedding cake.

Applying a shell border to the wedding cake.

Placing royal icing flowers onto cake portions.

PROCEDURE FOR PIPING A BUTTERCREAM ROSE

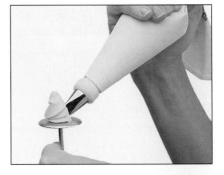

1. Using a #104 tip, pipe a mound of icing onto a rose nail.

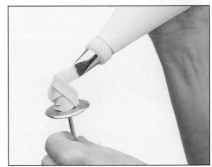

2. Pipe a curve of icing around the mound to create the center of the rose.

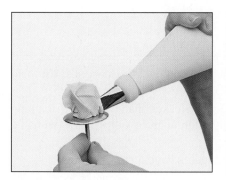

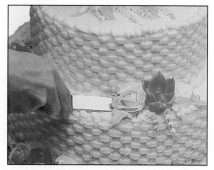

3. Pipe three overlapping petals around the center.

4. Pipe five more overlapping petals around the first three petals.

5. The finished rose is placed on the cake.

The key to success with a piping bag is practice, practice, practice. Use plain all-purpose shortening piped onto parchment paper to practice and experiment with piping techniques. Once you are comfortable using a piping bag, you can apply these newfound skills directly to cakes and pastries.

Storing Cakes

Unfrosted cake layers or sheets can be stored at room temperature for two or three days if well covered. Frosted or filled cakes are usually refrigerated to prevent spoilage. Simple buttercreams or sugar glazes, however, can be left at room temperature for one or two days. Any cake containing custard filling or whipped cream must be refrigerated. Cakes made with foam-type frosting should be eaten the day they are prepared.

Cakes can usually be frozen with great success; this makes them ideal for baking in advance. Unfrosted layers or sheets should be well covered with plastic wrap and frozen at 0°F (-18°C) or lower. High-fat cakes will keep for up to six months; egg foam cakes begin to deteriorate after two or three months.

Frostings and fillings do not freeze particularly well, often losing flavor or changing texture when frozen. Buttercreams made with egg whites or sugar syrups tend to develop crystals and graininess. Foam frostings weep, expelling beads of sugar and becoming sticky. Fondant will absorb moisture and separate from the cake. If you must freeze a filled or frosted cake, it is best to freeze it unwrapped first, until the frosting is firm. The cake can then be covered with plastic wrap without damaging the frosting design. Leave the cake wrapped until completely thawed. It is best to thaw cakes in the refrigerator if time permits. Do not refreeze thawed cakes.

CONCLUSION

The ability to produce good cakes and frostings depends on using the right balance of high-quality ingredients and combining them with the proper techniques. When preparing cakes and frostings, always combine flavors and textures with care; apply frostings, garnishes and decorations with care also. Avoid overly rich, cloyingly sweet or garishly decorated products. With study and practice, you can learn the mixing techniques and assembly skills necessary for producing good cakes. Additional practice will develop the decorating and garnishing skills of a fine pastry chef.

Questions for Discussion

1. Cake ingredients can be classified by function into six categories. List them and give an example of each.
2. What is the primary leavening agent in cakes made with the foaming method? How is this similar to or different from cakes made with the creaming method?
3. What is the difference between a spongecake and a classic genoise?
4. Describe the procedures for making three types of frosting or icing as discussed in this chapter.
5. List the steps employed in assembling and frosting a three-layer cake.

Additional Cake and Frosting Formulas

RECIPE 30.16
Vanilla Raspberry Layer Cake with White Chocolate Buttercream
Note: *This dish appears in the Chapter Opening photograph.*

HYATT REGENCY SCOTTSDALE AT GAINEY RANCH, Scottsdale, AZ
Executive Pastry Chef Judy Doherty

VANILLA CAKES

Yield: 1 8-inch (20-cm), 1 10-inch (25-cm) and 1 14-inch (35-cm) tier for Wedding Cake   **Method:** Two-Stage

Cake flour	1 lb. 14 oz.	850 g
Sugar	2 lb. 8 oz.	1130 g
Baking powder	2-1/2 oz.	70 g
Eggs	28	28
Salt	1 oz.	28 g
Fluid Flex	1 lb. 4 oz.	570 g
Milk	1 pt.	450 ml

1. Prepare pans by spraying with pan release and lining with parchment paper.
2. Combine the flour, sugar, baking powder, eggs and salt in a large mixer bowl. Whip on high speed for 8 minutes.
3. Add Fluid Flex (an emulsifier for spongecakes) and milk. Mix for 8 more minutes at medium speed.
4. Divide the batter between one 8-inch (20-centimeter), one 10-inch (25-centimeter) and one 14-inch (35-centimeter) cake pan. Fill each pan halfway.
5. Bake at 350°F (180°C) for 35–60 minutes, depending upon tier size. The cake is done when it springs back when lightly touched in the center. Allow to cool, then remove from the pans and freeze.

RASPBERRY SYRUP

Water	1 pt.	450 ml
Sugar	1 lb.	450 g
Raspberry liqueur	2 oz.	60 g

1. Bring the sugar and water to a boil, then cool to room temperature. Add the raspberry liqueur.

DIPLOMAT CREAM FILLING

Pastry cream, chilled	1 gal.	4 lt
Raspberry liqueur	4 oz.	120 g
Gelatin	1-1/2 oz.	42 g
Water	6 oz.	170 g
Whipped cream	1 qt.	1 lt

1. Place the pastry cream in a large mixer bowl and whip on high speed until smooth. Add the raspberry liqueur.

2. Soften the gelatin in the water, then place over a low flame and heat to dissolve.

3. Add 1 pint (450 milliliters) of the raspberry flavored pastry cream to the gelatin. Place over a low flame and whip by hand until smooth and the gelatin is incorporated. Add this mixture to the remainder of the pastry cream.

4. Fold in the whipped cream.

WHITE CHOCOLATE BUTTERCREAM

Sugar	5 lb. 8 oz.	2500 g
Water	1 pt. 6 oz.	625 ml
Egg whites	1 lb. 12 oz.	800 g
Unsalted butter, softened	7 lb.	3150 g
White crème de cacao	9 oz.	260 g
White chocolate, melted	1 lb. 8 oz.	680 g

1. Cook the sugar and water to 242°F (117°C), then pour into a measuring container with a handle for easier pouring.

2. Start whipping the egg whites when the sugar reaches 235°F (113°C).

3. When the whites are whipped to firm peaks, add the hot sugar syrup slowly while continuing to whip at low speed. Whip until completely cool.

4. Add the butter and whip until smooth.

5. Add the crème de cacao to the white chocolate. Whip until smooth, then add to the buttercream.

ASSEMBLY: Each cake tier is sliced horizontally into three layers. The layers are brushed with the raspberry syrup, then filled with diplomat cream and fresh raspberries. The top and sides of each tier are coated with the white chocolate buttercream; the sides are coated with a basketweave design; and the tiers are decorated with pulled sugar and royal icing roses. The assembly is illustrated with the photographs appearing throughout this chapter.

◆◆◆

RECIPE 30.17
POPPY SEED CAKE WITH LEMON GLAZE

CITY RESTAURANT, Los Angeles, CA
Chefs Susan Feniger and Mary Sue Milliken

Yield: 8–10 Servings   **Method:** Creaming

Poppy seeds	5 oz.	150 g
Honey	4 oz.	120 g
Water	2 oz.	60 g
Unsalted butter, softened	6 oz.	180 g
Granulated sugar	6 oz.	180 g
Lemon zest, grated	1 Tbsp.	15 ml
Vanilla extract	1 tsp.	5 ml
Eggs	2	2
All-purpose flour	9 oz.	270 g
Baking soda	1 tsp.	5 ml
Baking powder	1 tsp.	5 ml
Salt	1 tsp.	5 ml
Lemon juice, fresh	2-1/2 Tbsp.	35 ml
Sour cream	8 oz.	225 g
Lemon Glaze (recipe follows)	as needed	as needed

1. Combine the poppy seeds, honey and water in a medium saucepan. Cook over moderate heat, stirring frequently, until the water evaporates and the mixture looks like wet sand, approximately 5 minutes. Set aside to cool.
2. Cream the butter and sugar until light and fluffy. Mix in the lemon zest and vanilla. Add the eggs, one at a time, beating well after each addition.
3. In another bowl, combine the flour, baking soda, baking powder and salt. Set aside.
4. When the poppy seed mixture has cooled, stir in the lemon juice. Pour into the creamed-butter mixture and stir until combined.
5. By hand, add the dry ingredients and sour cream to the creamed butter in three stages, alternating liquid and dry, and ending with sour cream.
6. Spoon the batter into a greased and floured 10-inch (25-centimeter) tube pan. Smooth the top with a spatula and tap vigorously on a counter to eliminate air pockets.
7. Bake at 325°F (160°C) until a toothpick inserted near the center comes out clean, approximately 1 hour and 15 minutes. Set aside to cool, in the pan on a rack, about 15 minutes. Invert onto a platter and prepare the Lemon Glaze.
8. Brush the hot Lemon Glaze all over the bottom, top and sides of the cake to flavor it and seal in moisture. Serve with whipped cream.

LEMON GLAZE

Yield: 12 oz. (340 g)

Granulated sugar	8 oz.	225 g
Lemon juice, fresh	4 oz.	120 g

1. Combine the sugar and lemon juice in a small saucepan. Bring to a boil over moderate heat and cook until the sugar is dissolved, approximately 1–2 minutes.

✦✦✦

RECIPE 30.18
CARROT CAKE WITH CREAM CHEESE FROSTING

Yield: 5 Sheet Cakes or 16 10-inch (25-cm) Rounds   **Method:** Creaming

Vegetable oil	3 lb. 8 oz.	1750 g
Granulated sugar	3 lb. 11 oz.	1850 g
Eggs	1 lb. 12 oz.	875 g
Carrots, shredded	5 lb.	2500 g
Crushed pineapple, with juice	3 lb. 4 oz.	1625 g
Baking soda	1-1/2 oz.	45 g
Cinnamon	2 oz.	60 g
Pumpkin pie spice	1-1/2 oz.	45 g
Salt	1-1/2 oz.	45 g
Baking powder	1-1/4 oz.	40 g
Cake flour	4 lb. 10 oz.	2300 g
Coconut, shredded	1 lb.	500 g
Walnut pieces	1 lb.	500 g

1. Blend the oil and sugar in a large mixer bowl fitted with the paddle attachment. Add the eggs, beating to incorporate.
2. Blend in the carrots and pineapple.
3. Sift the dry ingredients together, then add them to the batter. Stir in the coconut and walnuts.
4. Divide the batter into greased and floured pans, scaling at 5 pounds per sheet pan or 1 pound 8 ounces (680 grams) per 10-inch (25-centimeter) round.
5. Bake at 340°F (170°C) until springy to the touch and a cake tester comes out almost clean.

CREAM CHEESE FROSTING

Unsalted butter, softened	12 oz.	350 g
Cream cheese, softened	3 lb.	1500 g
Margarine	12 oz.	350 g
Vanilla extract	1 oz.	30 ml
Powdered sugar, sifted	6 lb.	3000 g

1. Cream the butter and cream cheese until smooth. Add the margarine and beat well.
2. Beat in the vanilla extract. Slowly add the sugar, scraping down the bowl frequently. Beat until smooth.

✦✦✦

RECIPE 30.19
FRESH STRAWBERRY SHORTCAKE

THE FOUR SEASONS, NEW YORK, NY

Yield: 6 Servings   **Method:** Biscuit

Flour	10 oz.	300 g
Salt	1/2 tsp.	2 ml
Sugar	3 Tbsp.	45 ml

Continued

Baking powder	1/2 tsp.	7 ml
Unsalted butter, cold	2-1/2 oz.	75 g
Shortening	2 Tbsp.	30 ml
Zest of one orange		
Milk	2 oz.	60 g
Egg	1	1
Vanilla extract	1 tsp.	5 ml
Heavy cream	1 pt.	450 ml
Confectioner's sugar	3 oz.	90 g
Fresh strawberries, sliced	3 pt.	1350 ml

1. Combine the dry ingredients. Add the butter and shortening and cut in until the mixture looks like cornmeal. Add the orange zest.

2. Combine the milk, egg and vanilla and add to the dry ingredients. Turn out the dough on a board and knead a few times.

3. Divide the dough into six portions. Shape each portion into a circle with your hands. Bake at 450°F (230°C) until lightly browned, about 12–15 minutes. Cool on a rack.

4. Whip the cream with 2 ounces (60 grams) of confectioner's sugar. Split the shortcakes in the middle and fill with the whipped cream and strawberries. Sprinkle confectioner's sugar on top and serve with strawberry sauce.

♦♦♦

RECIPE 30.20

SOUR CREAM COFFEECAKE

Yield: 1 10-inch (25-cm) Tube Cake **Method:** Creaming

Filling:		
Flour	1-1/2 Tbsp.	20 ml
Cinnamon	1 Tbsp.	15 ml
Brown sugar	6 oz.	180 g
Chopped pecans	4 oz.	120 g
Unsalted butter, melted	1 oz.	30 g
Unsalted butter	4 oz.	120 g
Granulated sugar	8 oz.	225 g
Eggs	2	2
Sour cream	8 oz.	225 g
Cake flour, sifted	7 oz.	210 g
Salt	1/4 tsp.	1 ml
Baking powder	1 tsp.	5 ml
Baking soda	1 tsp.	5 ml
Vanilla extract	1 tsp.	5 ml

1. To make the filling, blend all filling ingredients together in a small bowl. Set aside.

2. To make the cake batter, cream the butter and sugar. Add the eggs, one at a time, beating well after each addition. Add the sour cream. Stir until smooth.

3. Sift the presifted flour, salt, baking powder and baking soda together twice. Stir into the batter. Stir in the vanilla extract.

4. Spoon half of the batter into a greased tube pan. Top with half the filling. Cover the filling with the remaining batter and top with the remaining filling. Bake at 350°F (180°C) for 35 minutes.

◆◆◆

RECIPE 30.21

MARBLE SHEET CAKE WITH FUDGE FROSTING

Yield: 1 18- × 24-inch (45- × 60-cm) Sheet Cake   **Method:** Creaming

Cake flour, sifted	1 lb. 11 oz.	1300 g
Baking powder	2-1/2 Tbsp.	35 ml
Salt	1-1/2 tsp.	7 ml
Unsalted butter	12 oz.	360 g
Granulated sugar	1 lb. 11 oz.	1300 g
Milk	24 oz.	720 g
Vanilla extract	1 tsp.	5 ml
Dark chocolate, melted	4-1/2 oz.	135 g
Baking soda	1/4 tsp.	1 ml
Coffee extract	2 tsp.	10 ml
Egg whites	12	12
Cocoa Fudge Frosting (Recipe 30.11)	as needed	as needed

1. Sift the flour, baking powder and salt together; set aside.
2. Cream the butter and sugar until light and fluffy.
3. Combine the milk and vanilla.
4. Add the dry ingredients to the creamed butter alternately with the milk. Stir the batter only until smooth.
5. Separate the batter into two equal portions. Add the melted chocolate, baking soda and coffee extract to half the batter.
6. Whip the egg whites until stiff but not dry. Fold half the whites into the vanilla batter and half into the chocolate batter.
7. Spoon the batter onto a greased sheet pan, alternating the two colors. Pull a paring knife through the batter to swirl the colors together.
8. Bake at 350°F (180°C) until a tester comes out clean, approximately 25 minutes.
9. Allow the cake to cool, then cover the top with Cocoa Fudge Frosting.

◆◆◆

RECIPE 30.22

FRESH COCONUT CAKE

Yield: 1 9-inch (22-cm) Cake   **Method:** Creaming

All-purpose shortening	8 oz.	225 g
Granulated sugar	1 lb.	450 g
Egg yolks	4	4
All-purpose flour	14 oz.	420 g
Salt	1 tsp.	5 ml
Baking powder	4 tsp.	20 ml
Milk	10 oz.	300 g
Vanilla extract	1 tsp.	5 ml
Egg whites	7 oz.	210 g
Coconut milk	4 oz.	120 g

Continued

Frosting (recipe follows)		
Fresh coconut, grated	8 oz.	225 g

1. Cream the shortening and sugar together until light and fluffy. Add the egg yolks one at a time, blending well.
2. Sift the dry ingredients together, then add to the creamed mixture alternately with the milk.
3. Stir in the vanilla.
4. Whip the egg whites until firm peaks form. Fold the whites into the batter. Portion into two 9-inch (22-centimeter) cake pans that have been greased and lined with parchment paper.
5. Bake at 350°F (180°C) until a cake tester comes out clean, approximately 25–30 minutes.
6. Remove the cakes from the oven and prick the top with a toothpick. Brush the coconut milk over the cakes, allowing it to be absorbed completely. Cool on a rack, then remove from the pans.
7. Top one cake layer with frosting, then sprinkle on 2 ounces (60 grams) of the grated coconut. Top with the second cake layer. Coat the top and sides with the remaining frosting, then sprinkle on the remaining coconut.

FROSTING

Granulated sugar	1 lb.	450 g
Light corn syrup	11 oz.	330 g
Egg whites	5	5
Salt	pinch	pinch

1. Bring the sugar and corn syrup to a boil. Cook to 238°F (115°C).
2. Meanwhile, beat the egg whites with the salt until stiff. With the mixer on second speed, add the hot sugar syrup to the whites in a slow, steady stream. Continue whipping until the frosting is cool.

◆◆◆

RECIPE 30.23
SACHER TORTE

Yield: 2 9-inch (22-cm) Cakes

All-purpose flour	10 oz.	280 g
Cocoa powder, alkalized	3 oz.	80 g
Unsalted butter	12-1/2 oz.	360 g
Granulated sugar	18 oz.	520 g
Eggs, separated	14	14
Hazelnuts, toasted and ground	3 oz.	80 g
Apricot jam	18 oz.	520 g
Apricot glaze	as needed	as needed
Chocolate Glaze (Recipe 29.27)	as needed	as needed

1. Grease two 9-inch (22-centimeter) springform pans lightly with butter and line with parchment paper.
2. Sift the flour and cocoa powder together twice; set aside.

3. Cream the butter and 7 ounces (200 grams) of the sugar together until light and fluffy. Gradually add the egg yolks and beat well.

4. Fold in the sifted flour and cocoa and the hazelnuts by hand.

5. Whip the egg whites to soft peaks, then gradually add the remaining sugar and continue whipping until stiff, glossy peaks form.

6. Lighten the batter with about one fourth of the egg whites, then fold in the remaining whites.

7. Pour the batter into the prepared pans and bake at 350°F (180°C) until the cakes are set, approximately 35–45 minutes.

8. Cool the cakes for 5 minutes before removing from the pans.

9. Cool completely, then cut each cake horizontally into three layers. Spread apricot jam on each layer and restack them, creating two 3-layer cakes.

10. Heat the apricot glaze until spreadable. Pour it over the top and sides of each cake.

11. Allow the apricot glaze to cool completely, then pour the chocolate glaze over the top and sides of each cake to create a smooth, glossy coating.

✦✦✦

RECIPE 30.24
Devil's Food Cake

Yield: 5 Sheet Pans or 30 8-inch (20-cm) Rounds   **Method:** High-Ratio

Ingredient	US	Metric
Cake flour	5 lb.	2500 g
Granulated sugar	6 lb.	3000 g
Emulsified shortening	3 lb.	1500 g
Cocoa powder	1 lb.	500 g
Salt	2-1/2 oz.	75 g
Baking powder	3 oz.	90 g
Baking soda	1-1/2 oz.	45 g
Nonfat dry milk powder	9-1/2 oz.	270 g
Vanilla extract	1-1/2 oz.	45 ml
Corn syrup	1 lb.	500 g
Water, cold	2 qt. 8 oz.	2.25 lt
Eggs	4 lb.	2000 g

1. Mix the cake flour, sugar and emulsified shortening in a large mixer bowl on low speed for 5 minutes.

2. Add the cocoa powder, salt, baking powder, baking soda, milk powder, vanilla, corn syrup and 1 quart (1 liter) cold water. Blend well, then scrape down the bowl.

3. Combine the eggs with the remaining 1 quart 8 ounces (1250 milliliters) cold water and add to the batter in three equal parts, blending well and scraping down the bowl after each addition.

4. After all ingredients are incorporated, blend on low speed for 2 minutes.

5. Divide into greased and floured pans, scaling 1 gallon (4 liters) of batter for each sheet pan or 1 pound (450 grams) for each 8-inch (20-centimeter) round layer.

6. Bake at 340°F (170°C) until springy and a toothpick inserted in the center comes out clean.

◆◆◆

RECIPE 30.25

BÛCHE DE NOËL

Yield: 10–12 Servings

Genoise, Recipe 30.3, freshly baked	one-half sheet	one-half sheet
Simple syrup	as needed	as needed
Buttercream—coffee, chocolate		
or vanilla	1 qt.	1 lt

1. Roll up the genoise in a spiral, starting with the long side. Wrap in parchment paper and cool.
2. Carefully unroll the cake. Brush the interior with simple syrup and coat with buttercream, leaving a 1-inch (2.5-centimeter) unfrosted rim around each edge.
3. Reroll the cake tightly and position it with the seam down on a cake cardboard.
4. Cut one end from the cake on a diagonal. Place the cut piece on top of the log, securing with toothpicks.
5. Pipe additional buttercream onto the cake log using a large star tip. Pipe the buttercream onto the ends in a spiral pattern. Decorate as desired with buttercream flowers, baked meringue mushrooms or marzipan figures.

1. Rolling the cake filled with buttercream.

2. Attaching the cut end to the log.

3. Piping on the buttercream.

◆◆◆

RECIPE 30.26

LADYFINGERS

Yield: 80 4-inch (10-cm) Cookies

Cornstarch	3 oz.	90 g
Bread flour	4 oz.	120 g
Eggs, separated	6	6
Granulated sugar	6 oz.	180 g
Lemon juice	1/2 tsp.	2 ml

1. Sift the cornstarch and bread flour together.
2. Whip the egg yolks with 2 ounces (60 grams) of sugar until thick and creamy.
3. Whip the egg whites until foamy. Gradually add 2 ounces (60 grams) of the sugar and the lemon juice. Continue whipping to soft peaks, then add the remaining sugar gradually and whip to stiff peaks.
4. Fold approximately one quarter of the egg whites into the whipped yolks

to lighten them, then gently fold in the remaining whites. Fold in the flour mixture.

5. Place the batter into a pastry bag fitted with a large plain tip. Pipe 4-inch-long (10-centimeter) cookies onto paper-lined sheet pans.

6. Bake immediately at 425°F (220°C) until lightly browned, approximately 8 minutes.

◆◆◆

RECIPE 30.27
GÂTEAU BENOIT

CITY RESTAURANT, Los Angeles, CA
Chefs Susan Feniger and Mary Sue Milliken

Yield: 8 Servings

Semisweet chocolate, chopped	7-1/2 oz.	220 g
Unsalted butter	5-1/2 oz.	165 g
Eggs, separated	4	4
Granulated sugar	4 oz.	120 g
All-purpose flour	2 oz.	60 g
Chocolate Curls (recipe follows)	as needed	as needed
Confectioner's sugar	as needed	as needed

1. Melt the chocolate and butter together over a bain marie. Set aside to cool.

2. Beat the egg yolks until light and fluffy, then slowly add the sugar, beating constantly until pale yellow. Fold in the melted chocolate mixture.

3. Sift the flour over the chocolate mixture and fold just until the flour disappears.

4. Whisk the egg whites to soft peaks. Fold the whites into the chocolate mixture in two parts. Pour the batter into a 10-inch (25-centimeter) cake pan that is buttered, floured and lined with parchment paper. Spread the batter evenly and tap once or twice on a counter to remove air pockets.

5. Bake at 350°F (180°C) until a toothpick inserted in the center comes out with a few flakes clinging to it, approximately 20–25 minutes. Set aside to cool, in the pan on a rack, about 1 hour.

6. To release the cake, run a knife along the inside edge of the pan to loosen. Invert onto a serving platter, peel off parchment, and invert again. Prepare the chocolate curls.

7. Pile the curls on top of the cake in a circular pattern pointing outward from the center. Dust with confectioner's sugar.

CHOCOLATE CURLS

Semisweet chocolate, block	1 lb. or larger	500 g or larger

1. The key to making chocolate curls or cigarettes, is the right temperature. Place the chocolate in an oven with only the pilot light on until it softens slightly, approximately 10–20 minutes. Or place the chocolate in an oven that is off but still warm, until the chocolate just begins to soften. In warm weather, this step may not be necessary.

2. Holding a heavy chef's knife between both hands and applying even pressure, pull the blade across the surface of the block, toward you, at about a 60-degree angle.

3. With some practice you can make either tight cigarette rolls or free-form ruffles. Leftover chocolate can be wrapped in plastic and used again.

◆◆◆

RECIPE 30.28
CHOCOLATE FLOURLESS CAKE

VINCENT ON CAMELBACK, PHOENIX, AZ
Chef Vincent Guerithault

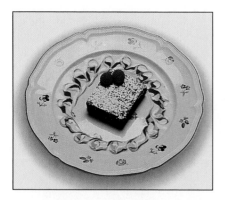

Yield: 21 Servings

Unsalted butter	1 lb.	450 g
Chocolate	27 oz.	800 g
Eggs, separated	20	20
Sugar	7 oz.	200 g
Powdered sugar	as needed	as needed

1. Melt the chocolate and butter over a bain marie.
2. Whisk the yolks into the melted chocolate.
3. Whip the egg whites until shiny. Add the sugar and whip until very stiff. Fold into the chocolate. Pour the batter into a full size hotel pan that is lined with buttered parchment.
4. Bake at 400°F (200°C) for 10 minutes. Reduce oven temperature to 350°F (180°C) and continue baking until done, approximately 40 minutes. A cake tester will not come out clean, even though the cake will be done.
5. Invert the cake onto the back of a sheet pan. Cool completely; then dust with powdered sugar.

◆◆◆

RECIPE 30.29
CONTINENTAL BROWNIES

Yield: 1 Sheet Pan　　　　　　　　　　　　**Method:** Egg Foam

Unsweetened chocolate	2 lb.	1000 g
Unsalted butter	2 lb.	1000 g
Eggs	20	20
Sugar	5 lb. 12 oz.	2.6 kg
Vanilla extract	2 oz.	60 g
All-purpose flour	1 lb. 10 oz.	800 g
Pecan pieces	1 lb.	500 g

1. Melt the chocolate with the butter over a double boiler.
2. While the chocolate is melting, whip the eggs and sugar in a large mixer bowl fitted with the paddle attachment for 10 minutes.
3. Add the melted chocolate and vanilla to the eggs. Stir to blend completely. Stir in the flour and nuts.
4. Spread the batter evenly onto a parchment-lined and buttered sheet pan. The pan will be very full. Bake at 325°F (160°C) for 40 minutes, rotating the pan after the first 20 minutes.
5. Allow to cool completely before cutting. Dust the brownies with confectioner's sugar if desired.

RECIPE 30.30

APPLESAUCE BROWNIES

Yield: 1 Sheet Pan

Unsweetened chocolate	4 oz.	120 g
Cake flour, sifted	1 lb.	450 g
Cocoa powder	9 oz.	270 g
Salt	2 tsp.	10 ml
Egg whites	12	12
Whole eggs	8	8
Granulated sugar	2 lb. 2 oz.	1 kg
Light corn syrup	2 lb.	900 g
Unsweetened applesauce	1-1/2 pt.	670 ml
Canola oil	7 oz.	210 g
Vanilla extract	2 Tbsp.	30 ml

1. Coat a sheet pan with spray pan release.
2. Melt the chocolate over a bain marie and set aside.
3. Sift the flour, cocoa powder and salt together and set aside.
4. Whisk the egg whites and eggs together. Add the sugar, corn syrup, applesauce, oil and vanilla. Whisk in the chocolate.
5. Fold the flour mixture into the egg mixture. Pour into the prepared pan and bake at 350°F (180°C) until a cake tester comes out clean, approximately 25 minutes.

Nutritional value per 2-inch (5-cm) square:

Calories	133	Protein	2 g
Calories from fat	24%	Vitamin A	30 IU
Total fat	3 g	Vitamin C	0
Saturated fat	1 g	Sodium	38 mg
Cholesterol	18 mg		

CHAPTER 31

CUSTARDS, CREAMS, FROZEN DESSERTS AND DESSERT SAUCES

- ◆ prepare a variety of custards and creams
- ◆ prepare a variety of ice creams, sorbets and frozen dessert items
- ◆ prepare a variety of dessert sauces
- ◆ use these products in preparing and serving other pastry and dessert items

◆◆◆

EGGS AND SANITATION

Eggs are high-protein foods that are easily contaminated by bacteria such as salmonella that cause food-borne illnesses. Because custards cannot be heated to temperatures high enough to destroy these bacteria without first curdling the eggs, it is especially important that sanitary guidelines be followed in preparing the egg products discussed in this chapter.

1. Cleanliness is important: Wash your hands thoroughly before beginning; be sure to use clean, sanitized bowls, utensils and storage containers.

2. When breaking or separating eggs, do not allow the exterior of the eggshell to come into contact with the raw egg.

3. Heat the milk to just below a boil before combining it with the eggs. This reduces the final cooking time.

4. Chill the finished product quickly in an ice bath and refrigerate immediately.

5. Do not use your fingers to taste the custard.

6. Do not store any custard mixture, cooked or uncooked, at room temperature.

*T*he bakeshop is responsible for more than just quick breads, yeast breads, pies, pastries, cookies and cakes. It also produces many delightfully sweet concoctions that are not baked and often not even cooked. These include sweet custards, creams, frozen desserts and dessert sauces. Sweet custards are cooked mixtures of eggs, sugar and milk; flour or cornstarch may be added. Sweet custards can be flavored in a variety of ways and eaten hot or cold. Some are served alone as a dessert or used as a filling, topping or accompaniment for pies, pastries or cakes. Creams include whipped cream and mixtures lightened with whipped cream such as Bavarians, chiffons and mousses. Frozen desserts include ice cream and sorbet as well as the still-frozen mousses called semifreddi.

Sauces for these desserts, including fruit purées, caramel sauces and chocolate syrup, are also made in the bakeshop and are discussed in this chapter. Indeed, many of the items presented in this chapter are components, meant to be combined with pastries (Chapter 29) or cakes (Chapter 30) to form complete desserts. Guidelines for assembling desserts are given at this chapter's end.

CUSTARDS

A **custard** is any liquid thickened by the coagulation of egg proteins. A custard's consistency depends on the ratio of eggs to liquid and the type of liquid used. The more eggs used, the thicker and richer the final product will be. The richer the liquid (cream versus milk, for example), the thicker the final product. Most custards, with the notable exception of pastry creams, are not thickened by starch.

A custard can be stirred or baked. A **stirred custard** tends to be soft, rich and creamy. A **baked custard**, typically prepared in a bain marie, is usually firm enough to unmold and slice.

Stirred Custards

A stirred custard is cooked on the stove top either directly in a saucepan or over a double boiler. It must be stirred throughout the cooking process to prevent curdling (overcooking).

A stirred custard can be used as a dessert sauce, incorporated into a complex dessert or eaten alone. The stirred custards most commonly used in food service operations are **vanilla custard sauce** and **pastry cream**. Other popular stirred custards are lemon curd (Recipe 25.16) and **sabayon** (Recipe 31.3).

Vanilla Custard Sauce

A custard sauce is made with egg yolks, sugar and milk or half-and-half. Usually flavored with vanilla bean or pure vanilla extract, a custard sauce can also be flavored with liquor, chocolate, ground nuts or other extracts.

It is prepared on the stove top over direct heat. When making custard sauce, be extremely careful to stir the mixture continually and not allow it to boil, or it will curdle. A properly made custard sauce should be smooth and thick enough to coat the back of a spoon. It should not contain any noticeable bits of cooked egg.

Vanilla custard sauce (Fr. *crème anglaise*) is served with cakes, pastries, fruits and soufflés and is often used for decorating dessert plates. It may be served hot or cold. It is also used as the base for many ice creams.

A very thick version of custard sauce can be made using heavy cream and additional egg yolks. Its consistency is more like a pudding than a sauce. This custard is often served over fruit in a small ramekin or other container and then topped with caramelized sugar for a dessert known as **crème brûlée** (burnt cream). See Recipe 31.15.

Pastry Cream

Pastry cream (Fr. *crème pâtissière*) is a stirred custard made with egg yolks, sugar and milk and thickened with starch (flour, cornstarch or a combination of the two). Because starch protects the egg yolks from curdling, pastry cream can be boiled. In fact, it must be boiled to fully gelatinize the starch and eliminate the taste of raw starch.

Pastry cream can be flavored with chocolate, liquors, extracts or fruits. (Pudding is nothing more than flavored pastry cream.) It is used for filling éclairs, cream puffs, napoleons, fruit tarts and other pastries. Pastry cream thickened with cornstarch is also the filling for cream pies (see Chapter 29, Pies, Pastries and Cookies). Pastry cream is thick enough to hold its shape without making pastry doughs soggy.

Pastry cream can be rather heavy. It can be lightened by folding in whipped cream to produce a **mousseline**, or Italian meringue can be folded in to produce a **crème Chiboust**.

PROCEDURE FOR MAKING VANILLA CUSTARD SAUCE AND PASTRY CREAM

1. Place milk and/or cream in a heavy, nonreactive saucepan; add vanilla bean if desired.
2. In a mixing bowl, whisk together the egg yolks, sugar and starch (if used). Do not use an electric mixer as it incorporates too much air.
3. Bring the liquid just to a boil. **Temper** the egg mixture with approximately one third of the hot liquid.
4. Pour the tempered eggs into the remaining hot liquid and return the mixture to the heat. The stove's temperature can be as hot as you dare: The lower the temperature, the longer the custard will take to thicken; the higher the temperature, the greater the risk of curdling.
5. Cook, stirring constantly, until thickened. Custard sauce should reach a temperature of 185°F (85°C). Pastry cream should be allowed to boil for a few moments.
6. Immediately remove the cooked custard from the hot saucepan to avoid overcooking. Butter or other flavorings can be added at this time.
7. Cool over an ice bath. Store in a clean, shallow container, cover and refrigerate.

Temper—*to heat gently and gradually; refers to the process of slowly adding a hot liquid to eggs to raise their temperature without causing them to curdle.*

PROCEDURE FOR SALVAGING CURDLED VANILLA CUSTARD SAUCE

1. Strain the sauce into a bowl. Place the bowl over an ice bath and whisk vigorously.
2. If this does not smooth out the overcooked sauce, place the sauce in a blender and process for a few moments.

◆◆◆

RECIPE 31.1

VANILLA SAUCE

Yield: 40 oz. (1200 g)

Half-and-half	1 qt.	1 lt
Vanilla bean, split	1	1
Egg yolks	12	12
Granulated sugar	10 oz.	300 g

1. Using a heavy, nonreactive saucepan, bring the half-and-half and vanilla bean just to a boil.
2. Whisk the egg yolks and sugar together in a mixing bowl. Temper the egg mixture with approximately one third of the hot half-and-half, then return the entire mixture to the saucepan with the remaining half-and-half.
3. Cook the sauce over medium heat, stirring constantly, until it is thick enough to coat the back of a spoon. Do not allow the sauce to boil.
4. As soon as the sauce thickens, remove it from the heat and pour it through a fine mesh strainer into a clean bowl. Chill the sauce over an ice bath, then cover and keep refrigerated. The sauce should last 3–4 days.

1. Mise en place for vanilla sauce.

2. Tempering the eggs.

3. The properly cooked sauce.

4. Straining the sauce into a bowl.

◆◆◆

RECIPE 31.2

PASTRY CREAM

Yield: 1 qt. (1 lt)

Cake flour	4 oz.	120 g
Sugar	12 oz.	340 g
Milk	1 qt.	1 lt
Egg yolks	12	12
Vanilla bean	1	1
Unsalted butter	2 oz.	60 g

1. Sift the flour and sugar together.
2. Whisk 8 ounces (225 grams) of the milk into the egg yolks. Then add the flour and sugar and whisk until completely smooth.
3. Heat the remaining milk with the vanilla bean in a heavy, nonreactive

saucepan. As soon as the milk comes to a boil, whisk approximately one third of it into the egg-and-flour mixture and blend completely. Pour the egg mixture into the saucepan.

4. Stir constantly until the custard thickens. As it thickens, the custard will go through a lumpy stage. Although you should not be alarmed, you should increase the speed of your stirring. Continue to stir vigorously and it will smooth out and thicken just before coming to a boil.

5. Allow the pastry cream to boil for approximately 1 minute, stirring constantly.

6. Remove the pastry cream from the heat and immediately pour it into a clean mixing bowl.

7. Fold in the butter until melted. Do not overmix, as this will thin the custard.

8. Cover by placing plastic wrap on the surface of the custard. Chill over an ice bath. Remove the vanilla bean just before using the pastry cream.

1. Stirring the pastry cream as it comes to a boil.

2. Folding butter into the cooked pastry cream.

Sabayon

Sabayon (It. *zabaglione*) is a foamy, stirred custard sauce made by whisking eggs, sugar and wine over low heat. The egg proteins coagulate, thickening the mixture, while the whisking incorporates air to make it light and fluffy. Usually a sweet wine is used; marsala and champagne are the most popular choices.

The mixture can be served warm, or it can be chilled and lightened with whipped cream or whipped egg whites. Sabayon may be served alone or as a sauce or topping with fruit or pastries such as spongecake or ladyfingers.

PROCEDURE FOR MAKING SABAYON

1. Combine egg yolks, sugar and wine in the top of a double boiler.
2. Place the double boiler over low heat and whisk constantly until the sauce is foamy and thick enough to form a ribbon when the whisk is lifted.
3. Remove from the heat and serve immediately, or whisk over an ice bath until cool. If allowed to sit, the hot mixture may separate.
4. Whipped egg whites or whipped cream may be folded into the cooled sabayon.

♦♦♦

RECIPE 31.3

CHAMPAGNE SABAYON

Yield: 1 qt. (1 lt)

Egg yolks	8	8
Granulated sugar	4 oz.	120 g
Salt	1/4 tsp.	1 ml
Marsala wine	2 oz.	60 g
Dry champagne	6 oz.	180 g
Heavy cream (optional)	8 oz.	225 g

1. Combine the egg yolks, sugar and salt in a stainless steel bowl.
2. Add the marsala and champagne to the egg mixture.
3. Place the bowl over a pan of barely simmering water. Whisk vigorously until the sauce is thick and pale yellow, approximately 10 minutes. Serve immediately.
4. To prepare a sabayon mousseline, place the bowl of sabayon over an ice bath and continue whisking until completely cold. Whip the cream to soft peaks and fold it into the cold sabayon.

1. The thickened sabayon.

Baked Custards

A baked custard is based on the same principle as a stirred custard: A liquid thickens by the coagulation of egg proteins. However, with a baked custard, the thickening occurs in an oven. The container of custard is usually placed in a water bath (bain marie) to protect the eggs from curdling. Even though the water bath's temperature will not exceed 212°F (100°C), care must be taken not to bake the custards for too long or at too high a temperature. An over-baked custard will be watery or curdled; a properly baked custard should be smooth-textured and firm enough to slice.

Baked custards include simple mixtures of egg yolks, sugar and milk such as **crème caramel** as well as custard mixtures in which other ingredients are suspended, for example, **cheesecake**, rice pudding, **bread pudding** and quiche.

Crème Caramel

Crème caramel, crème renversée and flan all refer to an egg custard baked over a layer of caramelized sugar and inverted for service. The caramelized sugar produces a golden-brown surface on the inverted custard and a thin caramel sauce.

♦♦♦

RECIPE 31.4

TOFFEE CARAMEL FLAN

Yield: 10-6-ounce (180-ml) Ramekins

Granulated sugar	1 lb. 4 oz.	600 g
Water	8 oz.	250 g
Milk	24 oz.	750 g
Heavy cream	24 oz.	750 g
Cinnamon sticks	2	2

Vanilla bean, split	1	1
Whole eggs	8	8
Egg yolks	4	4
Brown sugar	6 oz.	180 g
Molasses	1 Tbsp.	15 ml
Amaretto liqueur	2 Tbsp.	30 ml

1. Combine the granulated sugar with the water in a small, heavy saucepan; bring to a boil. Cook until the sugar reaches a deep golden brown. Immediately pour about 2 tablespoons (30 milliliters) of the sugar into each of the lightly greased ramekins. Tilt each ramekin to spread the caramel evenly along the bottom. Arrange the ramekins in a 2-inch-deep hotel pan and set aside.

2. Combine the milk, cream, cinnamon sticks and vanilla bean in a large saucepan. Bring just to a boil, cover and remove from the heat. Allow this mixture to **steep** for about 30 minutes.

3. Whisk the eggs, egg yolks, brown sugar, molasses and amaretto together in a large bowl.

4. Uncover the milk mixture and return it to the stove top. Bring just to the boil. Temper the egg-and-sugar mixture with approximately one third of the hot milk. Whisk in the remaining hot milk.

5. Strain the custard through a fine mesh strainer. Pour into the caramel-lined ramekins, filling to just below the rim.

6. Pour enough warm water into the hotel pan to reach halfway up the sides of the ramekins. Bake at 325°F (160°C) for approximately 30–40 minutes. The custards should be almost set, but still slightly soft in the center.

7. Completely chill the baked custards before serving. To unmold, run a small knife around the edge of the custard, invert onto the serving plate and give the ramekin a firm sideways shake. Garnish with fresh fruit or caramelized almonds.

Steep—*to soak food in a hot liquid in order to either extract its flavor or soften its texture.*

1. Filling the ramekins for flans.

Cheesecake

Cheesecakes, which are almost as old as western civilization, have undergone many changes and variations since the ancient Greeks devised the first known recipe. Americans revolutionized the dessert with the development of cream cheese in 1872.

Cheesecake is a baked custard that contains a smooth cheese, usually a soft, fresh cheese such as cream, ricotta, cottage or farmer cheese. A cheesecake may be prepared without a crust or it may have a base or sides of short dough, cookie crumbs, ground nuts or spongecake. The filling can be dense and rich (New York style) or light and fluffy (Italian style). Fruit, nuts and flavorings may also be included in the filling. Cheesecakes are often topped with fruit or sour cream glaze. Recipes for both dense and light cheesecakes are at the end of this chapter.

Some cheesecakes are unbaked and rely on gelatin for thickening; others are frozen. These are not really custards, however, but are more similar to the chiffons or mousses discussed below.

Bread Pudding

Bread pudding is a home-style dessert in which chunks of bread, flavorings and raisins or other fruit are mixed with an egg custard and baked. The result is somewhat of a cross between a cake and a pudding. It is often served with custard sauce, ice cream, whipped cream or a whiskey-flavored butter sauce. Bread pudding is a delicious way to use stale or leftover bread or overripe fruit. A recipe for bread pudding with bourbon sauce appears at the end of this chapter.

Soufflés

A soufflé is made with a custard base that is lightened with whipped egg whites and then baked. The air in the egg whites expands to create a light, fluffy texture and tall rise. A soufflé is not as stable as a cake or other pastry item, however, and will collapse very quickly when removed from the oven.

Soufflés can be prepared in a wide variety of sweet and savory flavors. The flavorings may be incorporated into the custard, as in the following recipe. Alternatively, an unflavored pastry cream can be used as the base; the liqueur, fruit or chocolate are then added to each portion separately.

When making a soufflé, the custard base and egg whites should be at room temperature. First, the egg whites will whip to a better volume, and second, if the base is approximately the same temperature as the egg whites, the two mixtures can be more easily incorporated. The egg whites are whipped to stiff peaks with a portion of the sugar for stability. The whipped egg whites are then gently folded into the base immediately before baking.

A soufflé is baked in a straight-sided mold or individual ramekin. The finished soufflé should be puffy with a lightly browned top. It should rise well above the rim of the baking dish. A soufflé must be served immediately, before it collapses. A warm custard sauce (crème anglaise) is often served as an accompaniment to a sweet soufflé.

A frozen soufflé is not a true soufflé. Rather, it is a creamy custard mixture thickened with gelatin, lightened with whipped egg whites or whipped cream and placed in a soufflé dish wrapped with a tall paper collar. When the paper is removed, the mixture looks as if it has risen above the mold like a hot soufflé.

PROCEDURE FOR MAKING BAKED SOUFFLÉS

1. Butter the mold or ramekins and dust with granulated sugar. Preheat the oven to approximately 425°F (220°C).
2. Prepare the custard base. Add flavorings as desired.
3. Whip the egg whites and sugar to stiff peaks. Fold the whipped egg whites into the base.
4. Pour the mixture into the prepared mold or ramekins and bake immediately.

◆◆◆

RECIPE 31.5

CHOCOLATE SOUFFLÉS

Yield: 8 Servings

Orange juice	1 pt.	500 ml
Eggs, separated	8	8
Sugar	4 oz.	120 g
All-purpose flour	3 oz.	90 g
Bittersweet chocolate, chopped fine	8 oz.	225 g
Orange liqueur	2 oz.	60 g

| Butter, melted | as needed | as needed |
| Granulated sugar | as needed | as needed |

1. To prepare the base, heat the orange juice to lukewarm in a heavy saucepan.

2. Whisk the egg yolks with 3 ounces (90 grams) of the sugar in a large mixing bowl. Whisk in the flour and warm orange juice, then return the mixture to the saucepan.

3. Cook over medium-low heat, stirring constantly, until the custard is thick. Do not allow it to boil. Remove from the heat.

4. Stir in the chocolate until completely melted. Stir in the liqueur. Cover the base mixture with plastic to prevent a skin from forming. Hold for use at room temperature. (Unused base can be keep overnight in the refrigerator; it should be brought to room temperature before mixing with the egg whites.)

5. To prepare the soufflés, brush individual-serving-sized ramekins with melted butter and dust with granulated sugar.

6. Preheat the oven to 425°F (220°C). Place a sheet pan in the oven, onto which you will place the soufflés for baking. (This makes it easier to remove the hot soufflé cups from the oven.)

7. Whip the egg whites to stiff peaks with the remaining 1 ounce (30 grams) of sugar. Fold the whites into the chocolate base and spoon the mixture into the prepared ramekins. The ramekins should be filled to within 1/4 inch (6 millimeters) of the rim. Smooth the top of each soufflé with a spatula and bake immediately.

8. The soufflés are done when well risen, golden brown on top and the edges appear dry. Do not touch a soufflé to test doneness.

9. Sprinkle the soufflés with powdered sugar if desired and serve immediately.

1. Folding the whipped egg whites into the chocolate base.

2. Filling the ramekins.

3. The finished soufflé, ready for service.

CREAMS

Creams (Fr. *crèmes*) include light, fluffy or creamy-textured dessert items made with whipped egg whites or cream. Some, such as **Bavarian creams** and **chiffons**, are thickened with gelatin. Others, such as **mousses** and **crèmes Chantilly**, are softer and lighter. The success of all, however, depends on the proper whipping and incorporation of egg whites or heavy cream.

You should review the material on whipping cream found in Chapter 8, Eggs and Dairy Products. Note that whipping cream has a butterfat content of 30–40 percent. When preparing any whipped cream be sure that the cream, the mixing bowl and all utensils are well chilled and clean. A warm bowl can melt the butterfat, destroying the texture of the cream. Properly whipped cream should increase two to three times in volume.

Crème Chantilly

Crème Chantilly is simply heavy cream whipped to soft peaks and flavored with sugar and vanilla. It can be used for garnishing pastry or dessert items, or it can be folded into cooled custard or pastry cream and used as a component in a pastry.

When making crème Chantilly, the vanilla extract and sugar should be added after the cream begins to thicken. Either granulated or powdered sugar may be used; there are advantages and disadvantages to both. Granulated sugar assists in forming a better foam than powdered sugar, but it may cause the cream to feel gritty. Powdered sugar dissolves more quickly and completely than granulated sugar, but does nothing to assist with foaming. Whichever sugar is used, it should be added just before the whipping is complete to avoid interfering with the cream's volume and stability.

◆◆◆

RECIPE 31.6
CRÈME CHANTILLY (CHANTILLY CREAM)

Yield: 2 to 2-1/2 qt. (2 to 2-1/2 lt)

Heavy cream, chilled	1 qt.	1 lt
Powdered sugar	3 oz.	90 g
Vanilla extract	2 tsp.	10 ml

1. Place the cream in a chilled mixing bowl. Using a balloon whisk, whisk the cream until slightly thickened.
2. Add the sugar and vanilla and continue whisking to the desired consistency. The cream should be smooth and light, not grainy. Do not overwhip.
3. Crème Chantilly may be stored in the refrigerator for several hours. If the cream begins to soften, gently rewhip as necessary.

1. Properly whipped crème Chantilly

Bavarian Cream

A Bavarian cream (Fr. *bavarois*) is prepared by first thickening custard sauce with gelatin, then folding in whipped cream. The final product is poured into a mold and chilled until firm enough to unmold and slice. Although a Bavarian cream can be molded into individual servings, it is most often poured into a round mold lined with spongecake or ladyfingers to create the classic dessert known as a **charlotte**.

Bavarians may be flavored by adding chocolate, puréed fruit, chopped nuts, extracts or liquors to the custard sauce base. Layers of fruit or liquor-soaked spongecake may also be added for flavor and texture.

When thickening a dessert cream with gelatin, it is important to use the correct amount of gelatin. If not enough gelatin is used or it is not incorporated completely, the cream will not become firm enough to unmold. If too much gelatin is used, the cream will be tough and rubbery. The recipes given here use sheet gelatin, although an equal amount by weight of granulated gelatin can be substituted. Refer to Chapter 26, Principles of the Bakeshop, for information on using gelatin.

PROCEDURE FOR MAKING BAVARIAN CREAMS

1. Prepare a custard sauce of the desired flavor.
2. While the custard sauce is still quite warm, stir in softened gelatin. Make sure the gelatin is completely incorporated.

3. Chill the custard until almost thickened, then fold in the whipped cream.

4. Pour the Bavarian into a mold or charlotte form. Chill until set.

=== ◆◆◆ ===

RECIPE 31.7

FRESH FRUIT BAVARIAN

Yield: 1 1-qt. (1-lt) Mold

Fresh fruit such as 2 kiwis, 1 banana
 or 1/2 pint (225 ml) raspberries, blueberries or wild strawberries

Honey	1 Tbsp.	15 ml
Kirsch	2 Tbsp.	30 ml
Egg yolks	4	4
Sugar	4 oz.	120 g
Milk	8 oz.	250 g
Vanilla bean	1/2	1/2
Gelatin, softened	1/2 oz.	14 g
Heavy cream	12 oz.	340 g

1. Lightly spray the bottom of a 1-quart (1-liter) mold with pan release spray. If a smooth mold is being used, line it with a sheet of plastic wrap, allowing the wrap to extend beyond the mold's edges.

2. Peel and thinly slice the fruit if necessary. Mix the honey and kirsch and pour over the fruit. Chill while preparing the Bavarian cream.

3. Prepare a vanilla custard sauce using the yolks, sugar, milk and vanilla. Remove from the saucepan.

4. Add softened gelatin to the hot custard. Chill until thick, but do not allow the custard to set.

5. Whip the cream until stiff and fold it into the chilled and thickened custard. Pour about one third of this mixture (the Bavarian cream) into the mold. Arrange one half of the fruit on top. Pour half of the remaining Bavarian cream on top of the fruit and top with the remaining fruit. Fill with the rest of the Bavarian cream. Chill until completely set, approximately 2 hours.

6. Unmold onto a serving dish. Garnish the top with additional fruit and whipped cream as desired.

NOTE: Gelatin may separate in the freezer, so quick chilling is not recommended. Products made with gelatin keep well for 1–2 days but stiffen with age.

VARIATION: *Charlotte*—Line a 1- to 1-1/2-quart (1- to 1.5-liter) charlotte mold with ladyfingers (Recipe 30.26) before filling with layers of fruit and Bavarian. Invert onto a serving platter when firm and garnish with whipped cream.

=== ◆◆◆ ===

CHARLOTTE, SWEET CHARLOTTE

The original charlotte was created during the 18th century and named for the wife of King George III of England. It consisted of an apple compote baked in a round mold lined with toast slices. A few decades later, the great French chef Carême adopted the name but altered the concept in response to a kitchen disaster. When preparing a grand banquet for King Louis XVIII, he found that his gelatin supply was insufficient for the Bavarian creams he was making, so Carême steadied the sides of his sagging desserts with ladyfingers. The result became known as charlotte russe, probably due to the reigning fad for anything Russian. A fancier version, known as charlotte royale, is made with pinwheels or layers of spongecake and jam instead of ladyfingers. The filling for either should be a classic Bavarian cream.

1. Adding gelatin to the custard base.   *2.* Folding in the whipped egg whites.

Chiffon

A chiffon is similar to a Bavarian except that whipped egg whites instead of whipped cream are folded into the thickened base. The base may be a custard or a fruit mixture thickened with cornstarch. Although a chiffon may be molded like a Bavarian, it is most often used as a pie or tart filling.

PROCEDURE FOR MAKING CHIFFONS

1. Prepare the base, which is usually a custard or a fruit mixture thickened with cornstarch.
2. Add gelatin to the warm base.
3. Fold in whipped egg whites.
4. Pour into a mold or pie shell and chill.

◆◆◆

RECIPE 31.8

LIME CHIFFON

Yield: 1 10-inch (25-cm) Pie or 8 Servings

Granulated gelatin	1/4 oz.	7 g
Water	5 oz.	150 g
Granulated sugar	7 oz.	210 g
Fresh lime juice	3 oz.	90 g
Lime zest	1 Tbsp.	15 ml
Eggs, separated	4	4

1. Soften the gelatin in 1 ounce (30 grams) of the water.
2. Combine 4 ounces (120 grams) of the sugar, the remaining water, lime juice, zest and egg yolks in a bowl over a pan of simmering water.
3. Whisk the egg-and-lime mixture together vigorously until it begins to thicken. Add the softened gelatin and continue whipping until very thick and foamy.
4. Remove from the heat, cover and refrigerate until cool and as thick as whipping cream.
5. Meanwhile, whip the egg whites to soft peaks. Whip in the remaining sugar (3 ounces/90 grams) and continue whipping until stiff but not dry.
6. Fold the whipped egg whites into the egg-and-lime mixture. Pour into a prepared pie crust or serving dishes and chill for several hours, until firm.

VARIATIONS: *Lemon Chiffon*—Substitute lemon juice and lemon zest for the lime juice and zest.

Orange Chiffon—Substitute orange juice for the lime juice and for 4 ounces (120 grams) of the water. Substitute orange zest for the lime zest. Reduce the amount of sugar in the egg yolk mixture to 1 ounce (30 grams).

Mousse

The term *mousse* applies to an assortment of dessert creams not easily classified elsewhere. A mousse is similar to a Bavarian or chiffon in that it is lightened with whipped cream, whipped egg whites or both. A mousse is generally softer than these other products, however, and only occasionally contains a small amount of gelatin. A mousse is generally too soft to mold.

A mousse may be served alone as a dessert or used as a filling in cakes or pastry items. Sweet mousses may be based on a custard sauce, melted chocolate or puréed fruit.

Procedure for Making Mousses

1. Prepare the base, which is usually a custard sauce, melted chocolate or puréed fruit.
2. If gelatin is used, it is softened first, then dissolved in the warm base.
3. Fold in whipped egg whites, if used. If the base is slightly warm when the egg whites are added, their proteins will coagulate making the mousse firmer and more stable.
4. Allow the mixture to cool completely, then fold in whipped cream, if used. Note that the egg whites are folded in before any whipped cream. Although the egg whites may deflate somewhat during folding, if the cream is added first it may become overwhipped when the egg whites are added, creating a grainy or coarse product.

◆◆◆

RECIPE 31.9

Classic Chocolate Mousse

Yield: 1-1/2 to 2 qt. (1.5 to 2 lt)

Bittersweet chocolate	15 oz.	440 g
Unsalted butter	9 oz.	280 g
Egg yolks	7	7
Egg whites	11	11
Granulated sugar	2-1/2 oz.	70 g
Heavy cream	8 oz.	250 g

1. Melt the chocolate and butter in a double boiler over low heat. Stir until no lumps remain.
2. Allow the mixture to cool slightly, then whisk in the egg yolks one at a time.
3. Beat the egg whites until soft peaks form. Slowly beat in the sugar and continue beating until stiff peaks form. Fold the whipped egg whites into the chocolate mixture.
4. Whip the cream to soft peaks. Allow the mousse to cool, then fold in the whipped cream. Make sure no streaks of egg white or cream remain.
5. Spoon the mousse into serving bowls or chill completely and pipe into bowls or baked tartlet shells. The mousse may be used as a cake or pastry filling.

Table 31.1 Cream (Crème) Components

For a:	Begin with a base of:	Thicken with:	Then fold in:
Bavarian	Custard	Gelatin	Whipped cream
Chiffon	Custard or starch-thickened fruit	Gelatin	Whipped egg whites
Mousse	Melted chocolate, puréed fruit or custard	Nothing or gelatin	Whipped cream, whipped egg whites or both

FROZEN DESSERTS

Frozen desserts include **ice cream** and **gelato** and desserts assembled with ice cream such as baked Alaska, bombes and parfaits. Frozen fruit purées, known as **sorbets** and **sherbets**, are also included in this category. Still-frozen desserts, known as **semifreddi**, are made from custards or mousses that are frozen without churning.

When making any frozen mixture, remember that cold dulls flavors. Although perfect at room temperature, flavors seem weaker when the mixture is cold. Thus, it may be necessary to oversweeten or overflavor creams or custards that will be frozen for service. Although liquors and liqueurs are common flavoring ingredients, alcohol drastically lowers a liquid mixture's freezing point. Too much alcohol will prevent the mixture from freezing; thus any liqueurs or liquors must be used in moderation.

Ice Cream and Gelato

Ice cream and gelato are custards that are churned during freezing. They can be flavored with a seemingly endless variety of fruits, nuts, extracts, liqueurs and the like. Gelato is an Italian-style ice cream. It is denser than American-style products because less air is incorporated during churning.

Overrun—*the amount of air churned into an ice cream.*

The USDA requires that products labeled "ice cream" contain not less than 10% milk fat and 20% milk solids, and have no more than 50% **overrun**. "Ice milk" refers to products that do not meet the standards for ice cream. Low-fat products made without cream or egg yolks are also available for the calorie

❖❖❖

ICE CREAM:
FROM ANCIENT CHINA TO DOUBLE FUDGE BROWNIE CHOCOLATE CHIP
WITH COOKIE DOUGH AND TOASTED ALMOND SLIVERS

Despite claims to the contrary, it is impossible to identify any one country as having invented ice cream. More likely, it was invented in several places around the world at various times.

Early ancestors of today's ice creams were flavored water ices, which have been popular in China since prehistoric times. They have also been popular in the Mediterranean and Middle East since the Golden Age of Greece. In fact, Alexander the Great had a penchant for wine-flavored ices, made with ice brought down from the mountains by runners. The Roman Emperor Nero served his guests mixtures of fruit crushed with snow and honey. The Saracens brought their knowledge of making flavored ices with them when they migrated to Sicily in the 9th century. And 12th-century Crusaders returned to western Europe with memories of Middle Eastern sherbets.

The Italians are said to have developed gelato from a recipe brought back from China by Marco Polo in the 13th century. Somehow the dish spread to England by the 15th century, where it was recorded that King Henry V served it at his coronation banquet. Catherine de Medici brought the recipe with her when she married the future king of France in 1533. A different flavor was served during each of the 34 days of their marriage festivities.

Ice cream was first served to the public in Paris during the late 17th century. It was available at fashionable cafés serving another new treat: coffee. French chefs quickly developed many elaborate desserts using ice creams including bombes, coupes and parfaits.

Many of this country's founders—Thomas Jefferson, Alexander Hamilton, James and Dolly Madison—were confirmed ice cream addicts.

George Washington spent over $200, a very princely sum, for ice cream during the summer of 1790.

The mechanized ice cream freezer was invented in 1846, setting the stage for mass production and wide availability. By the late 19th century ice cream parlors were popular gathering places. (Many of today's ice cream parlors take their décor from "Gay Nineties" motifs.)

Despite the disappearance of most ice cream wagons, soda fountains and lunch counters, all of which were popular ice cream purveyors for much of the 20th century, ice cream sales have never waned. Today, over 80% of all ice cream is sold in supermarkets or convenience stores. The public's demand for high-fat, homemade-style "super-premium" ice creams with rich and often-elaborate flavor combinations shows no sign of declining.

conscious. Frozen yogurt uses yogurt as its base. Although touted as a nutritious substitute for ice cream, frozen yogurt may have whole milk or cream added for richness and smoothness.

One hallmark of good ice cream and gelato is smoothness. The ice crystals that would normally form during freezing can be avoided by constant stirring or churning. Churning, usually accomplished mechanically, also incorporates air into the product. The air causes the mixture to expand. Gelato has little incorporated air. Good-quality ice creams and sorbets have enough air to make them light; inferior products often contain overrun. The difference becomes obvious when equal volumes are weighed.

Many food service operations use ice cream makers that have internal freezing units to chill the mixture while churning it. Most commercial machines are suitable for churning either ice cream or sorbet. Follow the manufacturer's directions for using and cleaning any ice cream maker.

PROCEDURE FOR MAKING ICE CREAMS

1. Place the milk and/or cream in a heavy saucepan. If vanilla bean is being used it may be added at this time.
2. Whisk the egg yolks and sugar together in a mixing bowl.
3. Bring the liquid just to a boil. Temper the egg mixture with approximately one third of the hot liquid.
4. Pour the tempered eggs into the remaining hot liquid and return the mixture to the heat.
5. Cook, stirring constantly, until warm.
6. Remove the cooked custard sauce from the hot saucepan immediately. If left in the hot saucepan, it will overcook. Flavorings may be added at this time.
7. Cool the cooked custard sauce over an ice bath. Store covered and refrigerated until ready to process.
8. Process according to the machine manufacturer's directions.

◆◆◆

RECIPE 31.10

ICE CREAM BASE

Yield: 2 qt. (2 lt)

Whole milk	1-1/2 qt.	1500 ml
Heavy cream	1 pt.	500 ml
Vanilla bean, optional	1	1
Egg yolks	16	16
Granulated sugar	20 oz.	600 g

1. Combine the milk and cream in a heavy saucepan and bring to a boil. Add the vanilla bean if desired.
2. Whisk the egg yolks and sugar together in a mixing bowl.
3. Temper the eggs with one third of the hot milk. Return the egg mixture to the saucepan.
4. Cook over medium heat until slightly thickened. Pour through a fine mesh strainer into a clean bowl.
5. Chill the cooked custard sauce completely before processing.

Continued

VARIATIONS: *Chocolate*—Add approximately 9 ounces (250 grams) of finely chopped bittersweet chocolate per quart (liter) of ice cream base. Add the chocolate to the hot mixture after it is strained. Stir until completely melted.

Cappuccino—Steep the hot milk and cream with the vanilla bean and 2–3 cinnamon sticks. After the ice cream base is made, stir in 2 tablespoons (30 milliliters) coffee extract.

Brandied Cherry—Drain the liquid from one 16-ounce (500-gram) can of tart, pitted cherries. Soak the cherries in three tablespoons (45 milliliters) brandy. Prepare the ice cream base as directed, omitting the vanilla bean. Add the brandy-soaked cherries to the cooled custard before processing.

Sherbets and Sorbets

Sherbet and sorbet are frozen mixtures of fruit juice or fruit purée. Sherbet contains milk and/or egg yolks for creaminess; sorbet contains neither.

Sorbet can be prepared in a wide variety of fruit (and even some vegetable) flavors; it is often flavored with an alcoholic beverage. It is served as a first course, a palate refresher between courses or a dessert. Because of its milk content, sherbet tends to be richer than a sorbet, so it is generally reserved for dessert.

Sorbet and sherbet may be made with fresh, frozen or canned fruit. Granulated sugar or sugar syrup is added for flavor and body. The ratio of sugar to fruit purée or juice depends to some extent on the natural sweetness of the specific fruit as well as personal preference. If too much sugar is used, however, the mixture will be soft and syrupy. If too little sugar is used, the sorbet will be very hard and grainy. Egg whites may also be added during churning for body.

◆◆◆

RECIPE 31.11
GRAPEFRUIT SORBET

Yield: 1-1/2 qt. (1.5 lt)

Fresh grapefruit juice	1 qt.	1 lt
Granulated sugar	8 oz.	250 g

1. Combine the juice and sugar.
2. Process in an ice cream maker according to the manufacturer's directions.
3. Pack into a clean container and freeze until firm.

Serving Suggestions for Ice Creams and Sorbets

Ice creams and sorbets are usually served by the scoop, often in cookie cones. Or they can be served as **sundaes**. More formal presentations include **baked Alaska**, **bombes**, **coupes** and **parfaits**.

Still-Frozen Desserts

Still-frozen desserts (It. *semifreddi*) are made with frozen mousse, custard or cream. Layers of spongecake and/or fruit may be added for flavor and texture. Because these mixtures are frozen without churning, air must be incorporated

Sundae—*a great and gooey concoction of ice cream, sauces (hot fudge, marshmallow and caramel, for example), toppings (nuts, candies, and fresh fruit to name a few) and whipped cream.*

Baked Alaska—*ice cream set on a layer of spongecake and encased in meringue, then baked until the meringue is warm and golden.*

Bombe—*two or more flavors of ice cream, or ice cream and sherbet shaped in a spherical mold; each flavor is a separate layer that forms the shell for the next flavor.*

Coupe—*ice cream served with a fruit topping.*

Parfait—*ice cream served in a long, slender glass with alternating layers of topping or sauce.*

by folding in relatively large amounts of whipped cream or meringue. The air helps keep the mixture smooth and prevents it from becoming too hard. Still-frozen desserts develop ice crystals quicker than churned products, so they tend to have a shorter shelf life than ice creams or sorbets.

Still-frozen products include frozen soufflés, **marquis**, mousses and **neapolitans**. The Chocolate Hazelnut Marquis recipe at the end of this chapter (Recipe 31.29) is an example of a still-frozen dessert.

Marquis—*a frozen mousse-like dessert, usually chocolate.*

Neapolitan—*a three-layered loaf or cake of ice cream; each layer is a different flavor and a different color, a typical combination being chocolate, vanilla and strawberry.*

Dessert Sauces

Pastries and desserts are often accompanied by sweet sauces. Dessert sauces provide flavor and texture and enhance plate presentation. Vanilla custard sauce (Recipe 31.1) is the principal dessert sauce. It can be flavored and colored with chocolate, coffee extract, liquor or fruit compound as desired. Other dessert sauces include fruit purées, caramel sauces and chocolate syrups. Techniques for decorating plates with sauces are discussed in Chapter 35, Plate Presentation.

Fruit Purées

Many types of fruit can be puréed for dessert sauces: Strawberries, raspberries, blackberries, apricots, mangoes and papayas are popular choices. They produce thick sauces with strong flavors and colors. Fresh or individually quick frozen (IQF) fruits are recommended.

Puréed fruit sauces, also known as **coulis**, can be cooked or uncooked. Cooking thickens the sauces by reduction and allows any starch thickener to gelatinize. They can also be sweetened with granulated sugar or a sugar syrup. The amount of sweetener will, of course, vary depending upon the fruit's natural sweetness and personal preference.

◆◆◆

RECIPE 31.12
Raspberry Sauce

Yield: 1 qt. (1 lt)

Raspberries, fresh or IQF	2 lb.	1 kg
Granulated sugar	1 lb.	500 g
Lemon juice	1 oz.	30 g

1. Purée the berries and strain through a fine chinois.
2. Stir in the sugar and lemon juice. Adjust the flavor with additional sugar if necessary.

Raspberry sauce.

Caramel Sauce

Caramel sauce is a mixture of caramelized sugar and heavy cream. A liqueur or citrus juice may be used for added flavor. Review the material on caramelizing sugar in Chapter 26, Principles of the Bakeshop, before making caramel sauce.

◆◆◆

RECIPE 31.13
CARAMEL SAUCE

Yield: 4 qt. (4 lt)

Granulated sugar	4 lb. 8 oz.	2 kg
Water	1 pt.	500 g
Lemon juice	2 oz.	60 g
Heavy cream, room temperature	2 qt.	2 lt
Unsalted butter, cut into pieces	5 oz.	150 g

Caramel sauce.

1. Combine the sugar and water in a large, heavy saucepan. Stir to moisten the sugar completely. Place the saucepan on the stove top over high heat and bring to a boil. Brush down the sides of the pan with water to remove any sugar granules.
2. When the sugar comes to a boil, add the lemon juice. Do not stir the sugar, as this may cause lumping. Continue boiling until the sugar caramelizes, turning a dark golden brown and producing a rich aroma.
3. Remove the saucepan from the heat. Gradually add the cream. Be extremely careful, as the hot caramel may splatter. Whisk in the cream to blend.
4. Add the pieces of butter. Stir until the butter melts completely. If necessary, return the sauce to the stove to reheat enough to melt the butter.
5. Strain the sauce and cool completely at room temperature. The sauce may be stored for several weeks under refrigeration. Stir before using.

Chocolate Syrup

Chocolate syrup or sauce can be prepared by adding finely chopped chocolate to warm vanilla custard sauce. A darker syrup can also be made with unsweetened chocolate or cocoa powder. Fudge-type sauces, like the one at the end of this chapter, are really just variations on ganache, discussed in Chapter 30, Cakes and Frostings.

◆◆◆

RECIPE 31.14
DARK CHOCOLATE SYRUP

Yield: 1 pt. (500 ml)

Cocoa powder	2 oz.	60 g
Water	12 oz.	340 g
Granulated sugar	8 oz.	250 g
Unsalted butter	3 oz.	90 g
Heavy cream	1 oz.	30 g

Dark chocolate syrup.

1. Mix the cocoa powder with just enough water to make a smooth paste.
2. Bring the sugar and remaining water to a boil in a small, heavy saucepan. Immediately add the cocoa paste, whisking until smooth.
3. Simmer for 15 minutes, stirring constantly, then remove from the heat.
4. Stir the butter and cream into the warm cocoa mixture. Serve warm or at room temperature.

ASSEMBLING DESSERTS

As noted previously, many pastries and other desserts are assembled from the baked doughs discussed in Chapter 29, Pies, Pastries and Cookies; the cakes, icings and glazes discussed in Chapter 30, Cakes and Frostings; and the creams, custards and other products discussed in this chapter. Many of these desserts are classic presentations requiring the precise arrangement of specific components. Formulas for some of these desserts are found at the end of the chapters in this part. But once you begin to master the basic skills presented in these chapters, you can use your creativity, taste and judgment to combine these components into a wide selection of new, unique and tempting desserts.

Assembled pastries and other desserts generally consist of three principal components: the base, the filling and the garnish. The **base** is the dough, crust or cake product that provides structure and forms the foundation for the final product. The **filling** refers to whatever is used to add flavor, texture and body to the final product. The **garnish** is any glaze, fruit, sauce or accompaniment used to complete the dish.

GUIDELINES FOR ASSEMBLING DESSERTS

1. There should be a proper blend of complementary and contrasting flavors. For example, pears, red wine and blue cheese go well together, as do chocolate and raspberries. Do not combine flavors simply for the sake of originality, however.

2. There should be a proper blend of complementary and contrasting textures. For example, crisp puff pastry, soft pastry cream and tender strawberries are combined for a strawberry napoleon.

3. There should be a proper blend of complementary and contrasting colors. For example, a garnish of red raspberries and green mint looks great.

4. Garnishes should not be overly fussy or garish.

5. The base should be strong enough to hold the filling and garnish without collapsing, yet thin or tender enough to cut easily with a fork.

6. The filling or garnish may cause the base to become soft or even soggy. This may or may not be desirable. If you want a crisp base, assemble the product very close to service. If you want this softening to occur, assemble the product in advance of service.

7. Consider the various storage and keeping qualities of the individual components. It may be best to assemble or finish some products at service time.

8. The final construction should not be so elaborate or fragile that it cannot be portioned or served easily or attractively.

9. Consider whether the product would be better prepared as individual portions or as one large item. This may depend on the desired plate presentation and the ease and speed with which a large product can be cut and portioned for service.

CONCLUSION

If pastry doughs are the backbone of dessert preparations, then custards, creams, mousses and the like are the heart. The skills and techniques presented in this chapter are essential to successful pastry production. Many of these skills, such as whipping cream or preparing custards, will be useful in other areas of the kitchen as well. Once you have mastered these skills as well as those discussed in Chapter 29, Pies, Pastries and Cookies, and Chapter 30, Cakes and Frostings, you will be able to prepare a wide variety of tempting desserts.

*Q*UESTIONS FOR *D*ISCUSSION

1. Eggs and dairy products are susceptible to bacterial contamination. What precautions should be taken to avoid food-borne illnesses when preparing custards?
2. Explain why pastry cream should be boiled and why custard sauce should not be boiled.
3. Identify three desserts that are based on a baked custard.
4. Compare a classically prepared Bavarian, chiffon, mousse and souffle. How are they similar? How are they different?
5. Describe the procedure for making a typical still-frozen dessert. What is the purpose of including whipped cream or whipped egg whites?
6. Explain three ways in which sweet sauces can be used in preparing or presenting a dessert.

*A*DDITIONAL *C*USTARD, *C*REAM, *F*ROZEN *D*ESSERT AND *D*ESSERT *S*AUCE *F*ORMULAS

RECIPE 31.15
*C*RÈME *B*RÛLÉE

NOTE: *This dish appears in the Chapter Opening photograph.*

VINCENT ON CAMELBACK, PHOENIX, AZ
Chef Vincent Guerithault

Yield: 3-1/2 qt. (3.5 lt)

Heavy cream	2 qt.	2 lt
Vanilla beans, split	2	2
Egg yolks	50	50
Granulated sugar	20 oz.	600 g
Fresh berries	as needed	as needed
Tulipe Cookie Cups (recipe follows)		
Granulated sugar	as needed for caramelized topping	

1. Place the cream and the vanilla beans in a large, heavy saucepan. Heat just to a boil.
2. Whisk the egg yolks and sugar together until smooth and well blended.
3. Temper the eggs with one third of the hot cream. Return the egg mixture to the saucepan and cook, stirring constantly, until very thick. Do not allow the custard to boil.
4. Remove from the heat and strain into a clean bowl. Cool over an ice bath, stirring occasionally.

5. To serve, place fresh berries in the bottom of each cookie cup. Top with several spoonfuls of custard.

6. Sprinkle granulated sugar over the top of the custard and caramelize with a propane torch. Serve immediately.

TULIPE COOKIE CUPS

Yield: 4 lb. 8 oz. (2 kg) Batter

Unsalted butter	1 lb.	500 g
Powdered sugar	1 lb.	500 g
All-purpose flour	1 lb.	500 g
Egg whites	1 lb. 8 oz.	750 ml

1. Melt the butter and place in a mixer bowl fitted with the paddle attachment. Add the sugar and blend until almost smooth.

2. Add the flour and blend until smooth. With the mixer running, add the egg whites very slowly. Beat until blended, but do not incorporate air into the batter.

3. Strain the dough through a china cap and set aside to cool completely.

4. Coat several sheet pans with melted butter. Spread the dough into 6-inch (15-centimeter) circles on the pans. Bake at 400°F (200°C) until the edges are brown and the dough is dry, approximately 12–18 minutes.

5. To shape into cups, lift the hot cookies off the sheet pan one at a time with an offset spatula. Immediately place over an inverted glass and top with a ramekin or small bowl. The cookies cool very quickly, becoming firm and crisp.

✦✦✦

RECIPE 31.16

PASTRY CREAM CHIBOUST

Yield: 1 pt. (500 ml)

Gelatin	3 sheets	3 sheets
Milk	6 oz.	180 g
Vanilla bean	1/2	1/2
Egg yolks	3	3
Granulated sugar	3 Tbsp.	45 ml
Cornstarch	2 Tbsp.	30 ml
Granulated sugar	6 oz.	180 g
Water	3 Tbsp.	45 ml
Egg whites	3	3
Cream of tartar	1/8 tsp.	0.5 ml

1. Soak the gelatin in ice water.

2. Prepare a pastry cream by heating the milk and vanilla bean just to a boil. Whisk the egg yolks, 3 tablespoons (45 milliliters) of sugar and the cornstarch together. Temper with one third of the hot milk, then return the mixture to the saucepan and cook over moderate heat until thick. The pastry cream should be allowed to boil briefly to properly gelatinize the starch. Remove the cream from the heat and transfer to a clean bowl.

3. Stir the softened gelatin into the hot cream. Cover and set aside but do not chill or allow the cream to set while preparing the Italian meringue.

4. Prepare an Italian meringue using the remaining ingredients.

5. Quickly and thoroughly incorporate one third of the meringue into the warm pastry cream with a spatula. Gently fold in the remaining meringue.

◆◆◆

RECIPE 31.17

CHOCOLATE POT AU CRÈME

Yield: 8 4-oz. (120-ml) Servings

Milk	1 pt.	500 g
Bittersweet chocolate	8 oz.	225 g
Granulated sugar	7 oz.	210 g
Vanilla extract	1 tsp.	5 ml
Coffee liqueur	2 Tbsp.	30 ml
Egg yolks	7	7

1. Heat the milk just to a simmer. Add the chocolate and sugar. Stir constantly until the chocolate melts; do not allow the mixture to boil. Remove from the heat and add the vanilla and liqueur.
2. Whisk the egg yolks together, then slowly whisk them into the chocolate mixture.
3. Pour the custard into ramekins. Place the ramekins in a hotel pan and add enough hot water to reach halfway up the sides of the ramekins.
4. Bake at 325°F (160°C) until custards are almost set in the center, approximately 30 minutes. Remove from the water bath and refrigerate until thoroughly chilled. Serve garnished with whipped cream and chocolate shavings.

◆◆◆

RECIPE 31.18

PISTACHIO CITRUS CHEESECAKE

Yield: 4 10-inch (25-cm) Cakes

Unsalted butter, melted	as needed	as needed
Pistachios, chopped fine	8 oz.	250 g
Cream cheese, softened	6 lb. 10 oz.	3.7 kg
All-purpose flour	3-1/2 oz.	100 g
Granulated sugar	2 lb. 5 oz.	1 kg
Eggs	18	18
Heavy cream	10 oz.	300 g
Lemon zest, grated fine	4 Tbsp.	60 ml
Orange zest, grated fine	4 Tbsp.	60 ml

1. Brush the sides and bottoms of four cake pans (do not use springform pans) with melted butter. Coat with an even layer of pistachio nuts.
2. Beat the cream cheese until smooth. Add the flour and sugar and beat to incorporate completely.
3. Add the eggs slowly, then stir in the cream. Stir in the zest and pour the batter into prepared pans.
4. Place the cake pans in a water bath and bake at 325°F (160°C) until set, approximately 45 minutes.
5. Cool to room temperature before inverting onto a serving tray or cake cardboard. The nut crust becomes the top of the cakes.

◆◆◆

RECIPE 31.19

New York-Style Cheesecake

Yield: 2 10-inch (25-cm) Cakes

Cream cheese, softened	3 lb. 6 oz.	1.6 kg
Cake flour	2 oz.	60 g
Granulated sugar	18 oz.	540 g
Eggs	8	8
Heavy cream	5 oz.	150 g
Vanilla extract	1 Tbsp.	15 ml

1. Beat the cheese until smooth. Beat in the flour and sugar.
2. Blend in the eggs slowly, then add the cream and vanilla.
3. Pour the batter into well-buttered springform pans. Bake at 300°F (150°C) until set, approximately 1 to 1-1/2 hours.
4. Cool completely before removing the sides of each pan.

◆◆◆

RECIPE 31.20

Bread Pudding with Bourbon Sauce

Yield: 20 Servings

Raisins	8 oz.	250 g
Brandy	4 oz.	120 g
Unsalted butter, melted	2 oz.	60 g
White bread, day-old	24 oz.	720 g
Heavy cream	2 qt.	2 lt
Eggs	6	6
Granulated sugar	1 lb. 10 oz.	800 g
Vanilla extract	2 oz.	60 g
Bourbon Sauce (recipe follows)	as needed	as needed

1. Combine the raisins and brandy in a small saucepan. Heat just to a simmer, cover and set aside.
2. Use a portion of the butter to thoroughly coat a 2-inch-deep (5 centimeter) hotel pan. Reserve the remaining butter.
3. Tear the bread into chunks and place in a large bowl. Pour the cream over the bread and set aside until soft.
4. Beat the eggs and sugar until smooth and thick. Add the remaining ingredients, including the melted butter, raisins and brandy.
5. Toss the egg mixture with the bread gently to blend. Pour into the hotel pan and bake at 350°F (180°C) until browned and almost set, approximately 45 minutes.
6. Serve warm with 2–3 tablespoons (30–45 milliliters) of the Bourbon Sauce.

Continued

BOURBON SAUCE

Unsalted butter	8 oz.	250 g
Granulated sugar	1 lb.	500 g
Eggs	2	2
Bourbon	8 oz.	250 g

1. Melt the butter; stir in the sugar and eggs and simmer to thicken.
2. Add the bourbon and hold in a warm place for service.

♦♦♦

RECIPE 31.21

CHERRY CLAFOUTI

Clafouti—*a country-style French dessert similar to a quiche, in which dark cherries are baked in an egg custard.*

Yield: 1 10-inch (25-cm) Cake

Dark cherries, fresh or canned, pitted	1 lb.	500 g
Eggs	4	4
Milk	12 oz.	340 g
Granulated sugar	2 oz.	60 g
Vanilla extract	1 tsp.	5 ml
All-purpose flour	2 oz.	60 g
Powdered sugar	as needed	as needed

1. Drain the cherries and pat them completely dry with paper towels. Arrange them evenly on the bottom of a buttered 10-inch (25-centimeter) pan. Do not use a springform pan or removable-bottom tartlet pan.
2. Make the custard by whisking the eggs and milk together. Add the sugar, vanilla and flour and continue whisking until all the lumps are removed.
3. Pour the custard over the cherries and bake at 325°F (160°C) for 1 to 1-1/2 hours. The custard should be lightly browned and firm to the touch when done.
4. Dust with powdered sugar and serve the clafouti while still warm.

♦♦♦

RECIPE 31.22

WHITE CHOCOLATE FRANGELICO BAVARIAN

Yield: 4 qt. (4 lt)

Heavy cream	2 qt.	2 lt
White chocolate, chopped	2 lb.	1 kg
Gelatin	8 sheets	8 sheets
Frangelico liqueur	10 oz.	300 g
Vanilla extract	2 tsp.	10 ml

1. Bring 1 quart (1 liter) of cream just to a boil. Immediately pour over the chopped chocolate. Stir until the chocolate melts.
2. Place the gelatin in ice water to soften.
3. Gently heat the liqueur just to a simmer. Remove from the heat and stir in the gelatin, one softened sheet at a time.

4. Add the gelatin mixture to the chocolate. Stir to blend well. Cool over an ice bath, stirring frequently.

5. Whip the remaining 1 quart (1 liter) of cream with the vanilla to stiff peaks.

6. Fold the whipped cream into the chocolate mixture. Chill until ready to use.

◆◆◆

RECIPE 31.23
CHOCOLATE CHIFFON PIE

Yield: 2 9-inch (22-cm) Pies

Gelatin	1/2 oz.	15 g
Milk	20 oz.	600 g
Unsweetened chocolate	4 oz.	120 g
Granulated sugar	6 oz.	180 g
Salt	1/4 tsp.	1 ml
Eggs, separated	6	6
Vanilla extract	2 tsp.	10 ml
Crumb-crust pie shells	2	2

1. Soften the gelatin and set aside.

2. Combine the milk and chocolate in a heavy saucepan and warm over low heat until the chocolate melts.

3. Add 4 ounces (120 grams) of the sugar, the salt and the egg yolks. Continue cooking, stirring constantly, until the mixture thickens.

4. Remove from the heat and add the gelatin, stirring until completely dissolved. Pour the mixture into a bowl and chill until very thick.

5. Whip the egg whites to soft peaks. Add the vanilla and the remaining sugar and whip to stiff peaks. Fold the whites into the chocolate.

6. Mound the chiffon into the pie shells and chill for several hours before serving. Garnish with unsweetened whipped cream and chocolate shavings.

◆◆◆

RECIPE 31.24
WHITE CHOCOLATE MOUSSE CAKE
WITH GRAND MARNIER SAUCE

THE FOUR SEASONS, NEW YORK, NY

Yield: 6 Servings

Mousse:		
White chocolate, cut into small pieces	8 oz.	250 g
Heavy cream	8 oz.	250 g
Unsalted butter	1 oz.	30 g
Rum	1 Tbsp.	15 ml
Egg whites	2	2
Sugar	1 Tbsp.	15 ml
Decoration:		
White chocolate, tempered	10 oz.	300 g
Dark chocolate, melted	2 oz.	60 g

Continued

Sauce:

Orange marmalade	10 oz.	300 g
Grand Marnier liqueur	3 oz.	90 g
Lemon juice	2 Tbsp.	30 ml

1. To make the mousse, melt the chocolate with 3 ounces (90 grams) of the heavy cream and the butter in a double boiler. Remove from the heat and stir until smooth.
2. Stir in the rum and let the mixture cool to room temperature.
3. Whip the remaining cream and chill.
4. Whip the egg whites, adding the sugar gradually until they hold stiff peaks. Gently fold the egg whites into the chocolate mixture, then fold in the whipped cream.
5. Spoon the mousse into six 2-1/2-inch (6.25-centimeter) rings or soufflé molds and chill until firm.
6. To make the decorations, spread thin layers of tempered white chocolate onto a piece of plastic film. Let the chocolate set until firm. With a sharp knife, cut six 2-1/2-inch-diameter (6.25-centimeter) circles and six long strips the same height as the mousse cakes. (Make sure you cut through the plastic film.)
7. Remove the white chocolate mousse cakes from their molds and keep chilled.
8. Warm the white chocolate strips slightly, just enough to bend them, then wrap the side of the cakes, placing the chocolate side against the mousse. Place the circles on top of the cakes. Chill again for 10 minutes and then pull off the plastic wrap.
9. Apply a design of your choice with the melted dark chocolate. Keep the cakes well chilled.
10. To make the sauce, warm the marmalade, liqueur and juice in a saucepan, stirring frequently.
11. Serve the cakes on a pool of the Grand Marnier sauce.

◆◆◆

RECIPE 31.25

RASPBERRY MOUSSE

Yield: 1 qt. (1 lt)

Gelatin	6 sheets	6 sheets
Raspberries, puréed	12 oz.	360 g
Granulated sugar	3 oz.	90 g
Raspberry brandy	2 Tbsp.	30 ml
Heavy cream	8 oz.	250 g

1. Soften the gelatin in ice water and set aside.
2. Place the raspberry purée, sugar and brandy in a nonreactive saucepan and warm just to dissolve the sugar. Remove from the heat and strain through a fine chinois.
3. Add the gelatin, stirring until it is dissolved. Chill the mixture until thick but not set.
4. Whip the cream to soft peaks and fold it into the raspberry mixture.

◆◆◆

RECIPE 31.26

Parnassienne de Mousse au Chocolat (Chocolate Tower)

CHRISTOPHER'S AND CHRISTOPHER'S BISTRO, PHOENIX, AZ
Chef/Owner Christopher Gross

Yield: 8 Servings

Parchment paper molds	8	8
Dark chocolate, chopped	5-1/2 oz.	165 g
Unsalted butter	3 Tbsp.	45 ml
Heavy cream	2 oz.	60 g
Egg whites	10	10
Superfine sugar	4 Tbsp.	60 ml
Dark chocolate, melted	2 oz.	60 g
White chocolate, melted	5 oz.	150 g
Espresso Sauce (recipe follows)	as needed	as needed
Fresh berries	as needed	as needed

1. To make the molds, cut parchment paper into sixteen strips, each 3-1/2 inches (8.75 centimeters) high and 5 inches (12.5 centimeters) long. Roll eight of these strips into tubes and tape closed. Stand these eight tubes upright on a parchment lined sheet pan. Reserve the remaining strips for the tower coating.

2. To make the mousse, melt the 5-1/2 ounces (165 grams) of chocolate and the butter in a medium bowl over a bain marie.

3. Whip the cream to stiff peaks and refrigerate.

4. Whip the egg whites and the superfine sugar to stiff peaks.

5. Fold the egg whites into the melted chocolate, then fold in the whipped cream.

6. Using a large piping bag fitted with a plain tip, pipe the mousse into the eight parchment paper tubes. Freeze until completely solid, several hours or overnight.

7. To make the tower coating, pipe a pattern of melted dark chocolate onto the eight remaining strips of parchment paper. When the dark chocolate hardens, coat the same side of the parchment with the melted white chocolate. Immediately remove a tube of mousse from the freezer. Remove the paper wrapping and wrap the chocolate-coated parchment strip around the frozen mousse, placing the chocolate next to the mousse. Refreeze for 5 minutes, then carefully peel the paper off the tower. The dark and white chocolate coating will remain wrapped around the mousse.

8. Repeat the procedure for wrapping the frozen mousse with chocolate-coated paper for the remaining pieces.

9. For service, ladle espresso sauce onto eight plates, place a mousse tower in the center of each plate and garnish with fresh berries.

ESPRESSO SAUCE

Yield: 1-1/2 pt. (700 ml)

Egg yolks	8	8
Granulated sugar	3-1/2 oz.	100 g

Continued

Half-and-half	1 pt.	450 ml
Espresso beans	3 oz.	90 g
Vanilla bean	1/2	1/2

1. Whisk the egg yolks and sugar together in a medium bowl.
2. Bring the half-and-half, espresso beans and vanilla bean to a simmer in a heavy saucepan.
3. Temper the egg yolks with a portion of the hot half-and-half, then return the mixture to the saucepan. Cook over low heat, stirring constantly, until the sauce is thick enough to coat the back of a spoon. Strain and cool over an ice bath.

◆◆◆

RECIPE 31.27
CARAMEL ICE CREAM

CITY RESTAURANT, Los Angeles, CA
Chef/Owners Susan Feniger and Mary Sue Millikin

Yield: 1-1/2 qt. (1-1/2 lt)

ICE CREAM

Half-and-half	20 oz.	600 g
Heavy cream	12 oz.	360 g
Egg yolks	9	9
Granulated sugar	6 oz.	180 g
Vanilla extract	2 tsp.	10 ml
Sour cream	8 oz.	225 g
Caramel Chunks (recipe follows)	as needed	as needed

1. Combine the half-and-half and cream in a medium-heavy saucepan. Bring to a boil.
2. Whisk together the egg yolks and sugar until thick and pale yellow. Pour in the boiling liquid and stir to combine. Remove from the heat.
3. Add the vanilla and stir. Strain into a large container and chill over an ice bath, stirring occasionally.
4. Stir in the sour cream and pour into an ice cream maker. Process according to the manufacturer's directions.
5. When the ice cream is done, fold in the reserved Caramel Chunks. Store in the freezer for 1–2 days.

CARAMEL CHUNKS

| Granulated sugar | 8 oz. | 225 g |
| Water | 4 oz. | 120 g |

1. Combine the sugar and water in a heavy saucepan. Cook over moderate heat until the color turns deep brown and the aroma is strong, approximately 10–15 minutes.
2. Immediately, and with great care, pour the hot caramel onto a greased sheet pan. Set aside until cool, then crack into 1/2-inch (12-millimeter) pieces.

✦✦✦

RECIPE 31.28

LEMON SORBET

VINCENT ON CAMBELBACK, Phoenix, AZ

Chef Vincent Guerithault

Yield: 1-1/2 qt. (1.5 lt)

Lemon juice	1 pt.	500 ml
Water	1 pt.	500 ml
Granulated sugar	1 lb.	500 g

1. Combine the juice, water and sugar in a large bowl. Stir until the sugar dissolves completely.
2. Pour the lemon mixture into the ice cream/sorbet machine and process according to the manufacturer's directions.
3. The finished sorbet will be rather soft. Pack it into a storage container and freeze at a temperature of 0°F (-18°C) or lower until firm.

✦✦✦

RECIPE 31.29

CHOCOLATE HAZELNUT MARQUIS WITH FRANGELICO SAUCE

Yield: 12 Servings

Dark chocolate	1 lb.	500 g
Unsalted butter	4 oz.	120 g
Hazelnuts, roasted, skinned and chopped coarse	4 oz.	120 g
Eggs, separated	6	6
Frangelico (hazelnut liqueur)	2 oz.	60 g
Salt	pinch	pinch
Frangelico Sauce (Recipe follows)	as needed	as needed
Hazelnuts, roasted and chopped coarse	as needed	as needed
Raspberries	as needed	as needed
Mint	as needed	as needed

1. Line a terrine mold with melted butter and parchment paper.
2. Melt the chocolate and butter over a bain marie. Remove from the heat and stir in the nuts, egg yolks and hazelnut liqueur. Set aside to cool to room temperature but do not use an ice bath as the chocolate will solidify.
3. Whip the egg whites with the salt until stiff but not dry. Fold the whipped whites into the chocolate mixture.
4. Pour the mixture into the pan and freeze overnight.
5. Remove the marquis from the pan and peel off the paper. (Work quickly because this melts quickly.) While still frozen, use a hot knife to slice the loaf into 1/3-inch-thick (8-millimeter) slices. Return the marquis to freeze until just before service.
6. Serve two slices on a pool of frangelico sauce. Garnish with coarsely chopped hazelnuts, fresh raspberries and mint.

FOR THE FRANGELICO SAUCE: Prepare a crème anglaise (Recipe 31.1), omitting the vanilla bean. Stir in 1/2 teaspoon (2 millimeters) vanilla and 2–3 tablespoons (30-45 millimeters) of frangelico, to taste.

✦✦✦

RECIPE 31.30
HOT AND COLD CHOCOLATE

CHRISTOPHER'S AND CHRISTOPHER'S BISTRO, PHOENIX, AZ
Chef/Owner Christopher Gross

Yield: 1 Serving

Chocolate Ice Cream (recipe follows)	1 portion
Chocolate Tart Batter (recipe follows)	1 portion
Espresso Sauce (recipe follows)	as needed
Dark Chocolate Sauce (recipe follows)	as needed

1. Mold the chocolate ice cream in a 3-inch-diameter (7.5-centimeter) ring mold and refreeze.
2. Coat another ring mold with melted butter or pan-release spray and place on a sheet pan lined with parchment paper. Fill this ring with the Chocolate Tart batter to a depth of 1 inch (2.5 centimeters).
3. Bake the tart batter at 375°F (190°C) for 3 minutes. The center should still be liquid.
4. Unmold the circle of ice cream in the center of a chilled plate. Carefully unmold the hot chocolate tart and place it on top of the ice cream. Decorate the plate with Espresso and Dark Chocolate Sauces and serve immediately.

CHOCOLATE ICE CREAM

Yield: 10 Servings

Egg yolks	5	5
Granulated sugar	5 oz.	150 g
Cocoa powder	1-1/2 oz.	45 g
Milk	1 pt.	500 ml
Heavy cream	3 oz.	90 g
Semi-sweet chocolate, chopped	4 oz.	120 g

1. Whisk the egg yolks, sugar and cocoa together.
2. Combine the milk and cream and bring to a boil. Temper the egg mixture

with a portion of the hot milk; return the mixture to the saucepan and continue cooking, stirring constantly, until the custard thickens.

3. Remove from the heat and add the chocolate. Stir until the chocolate melts, then strain and chill.

4. Process the custard in an ice cream maker according to the manufacturer's directions.

CHOCOLATE TART BATTER

Yield: 10 Servings

Eggs	5	5
Granulated sugar	6-1/2 oz.	195 g
Unsalted butter, melted	5 oz.	150 g
Dark chocolate, melted	5 oz.	150 g
Pastry flour	1-1/4 oz.	38 g

1. Whisk the eggs and sugar together until thick. Stir in the melted butter and chocolate then fold in the flour.

2. Allow the batter to rest at room temperature for approximately 1 hour before baking.

ESPRESSO AND DARK CHOCOLATE SAUCES

Yield: 6 oz. (180 g) of Each Sauce

Heavy cream	8 oz.	250 g
Vanilla bean	1/2	1/2
Espresso beans	2 oz.	60 g
Egg yolks	4	4
Dark chocolate, chopped	2 oz.	60 g

1. Combine the cream, vanilla bean and espresso beans in a saucepan and bring to a boil.

2. Whisk the egg yolks together in a mixing bowl and temper with one-third of the hot cream.

3. Return the egg-and-cream mixture to the remaining cream and continue cooking, stirring constantly, until thick. Strain.

4. Divide the espresso sauce in half while still warm. Add the chocolate to one half of the warm sauce and stir until melted.

◆◆◆

RECIPE 31.31

BUTTERSCOTCH SAUCE

Yield: 2 qt. (2 lt)

Granulated sugar	1 lb. 8 oz.	720 g
Light corn syrup	2 lb. 4 oz.	1 kg
Unsalted butter	4 oz.	120 g
Heavy cream	10 oz.	300 g
Scotch	4 oz.	120 g

1. Cook the sugar to a dark brown caramel. Add the corn syrup.

2. Remove the sugar from the heat and slowly add the butter and the cream, stirring until the butter is completely melted.

3. Stir in the scotch and cool.

♦♦♦

RECIPE 31.32

CHOCOLATE FUDGE SAUCE

Yield: 1 gl. (4 lt)

Heavy cream	2 qt.	2 lt
Light corn syrup	6 oz.	180 g
Granulated sugar	8 oz.	225 g
Bittersweet chocolate	4 lb.	2 kg

1. Combine the cream, corn syrup and sugar in a saucepan and bring just to a boil, stirring frequently.
2. Chop the chocolate and place in a large bowl.
3. Pour the hot cream over the chocolate and stir until completely melted.
4. Store well covered and refrigerated. Gently rewarm over a bain marie if desired.

PART FIVE

MEAL SERVICE AND PRESENTATION

Part V begins with a chapter on Breakfast and Brunch and another on Hors d'Oeuvres and Appetizers. In each, we discuss the preparation and presentation of foods typically associated with these categories. This information is designed to synthesize many of the skills presented earlier in the book.

We then present material on several international cuisines. We emphasize each cuisine's distinguishing flavors and cooking procedures; we do not attempt to provide an array of representative recipes.

Part V concludes with a chapter on plate presentation in which we demonstrate simple yet effective techniques for making foods visually appealing.

Chapter 32

Breakfast and Brunch

 *om always said breakfast was the most important meal of the day, and she was probably right. Breakfast (from the expression "to break fast") gives you the energy to get going after a long night's sleep. It should provide at least one fourth of the calories and nutrients consumed during the day.*

Breakfast is often an on-the-go, rushed experience, hence the popularity of breakfast sandwiches, jumbo muffins and disposable coffee cups. Brunch, on the other hand, is a leisurely experience, combining breakfast and lunch into a social occasion. Brunch menus include traditional breakfast foods along with almost anything else. Unlike breakfast, brunch is often accompanied by champagne or other alcoholic beverages and concludes with a pastry or dessert.

Food service operations must offer a variety of breakfast options to appeal to a wide range of consumers. Hotels and resorts may offer a complimentary continental-style breakfast of coffee, juice and simple rolls; a full-service à la carte dining room, a room service menu and a casual snack bar. The grand hotel Sunday and holiday brunch buffet is an American institution for celebrations and special occasions.

Office, retail and commercial complexes are peppered with small shops selling coffee, muffins, bagels and sweet rolls. Coffee houses offering a variety of coffee blends and drinks, pastries, breads and quiche are also popular. Even fast-food facilities have expanded their menus and hours of operation to meet the needs of early-morning diners.

The foods served at breakfast include most of the foods served at other times during the day. A diner's perception of the proper breakfast depends on his cultural, ethnic, economic and geographic background as well as sleep patterns and work schedule.

Breakfast menus typically include:

+ Coffee, tea or other hot beverages
+ Fruits or fruit juices
+ Eggs
+ Breads, including sweet breads
+ Cereals and grains
+ Potatoes
+ Pancakes, waffles and French toast
+ Meats or fish
+ Dairy products, including milk, cheese and yogurt

Although few people could sit down to a breakfast including all of these components even occasionally, most food service operations find it necessary to offer some items from each category in order to meet their customers' expectations.

This chapter discusses cooking methods used for eggs, breakfast meats, pancakes and other griddlecakes and cereals. Other foods typically served at breakfast are noted on the following pages and discussed in more detail elsewhere in this text.

BEVERAGES

Few breakfast menus would be complete without offering coffee, tea or other hot beverages. Whether it's black tea in St. Petersburg or café au lait in Paris, cinnamon-spiced chocolate in Mexico City or a cup of fresh-brewed Colombian in Chicago, people everywhere enjoy starting their day with hot, aromatic, caffeine-laced beverages. Coffees and teas are identified and discussed in Chapter 7, Kitchen Staples. Recipes for a rich hot chocolate and spiced apple cider are at the end of this chapter.

FRUITS

Fruits are popular breakfast foods because they are light and flavorful, require little or no preparation and provide vitamins and natural sugars for energy. Citrus fruits, melons, berries and bananas are breakfast staples. Fruits, whether raw or cooked, fresh, canned, frozen or dried, can be served alone, with a topping of cream or yogurt or as a garnish for cereals, pancakes or French toast. Fresh seasonal fruits can be served at the beginning of the meal, as garnish with the main course, as a light brunch dessert or as juice. Fruits are identified and discussed in Chapter 25, Fruits.

BREADS

Breads, usually rich, sweet and loaded with fruits and nuts, are a staple of many breakfast menus. Sticky pecan buns, glazed cinnamon rolls, fruit-filled muffins, Danish pastries and buttery croissants, which seem too rich later in the day, somehow seem perfect in the morning. Even a humble slice of toast rounds out a breakfast menu, especially if topped with butter and jam. Breakfast breads can be served as an accompaniment to eggs, fruits or other dishes or they can be the complete meal. Chapter 27, Quick Breads; Chapter 28, Yeast Breads; and Chapter 29, Pies, Pastries and Cookies, include several recipes for breakfast breads and pastries.

POTATOES

Potatoes are sometimes served at breakfast and brunch, usually sautéed or pan-fried as hash browns, cottage fries or lyonnaise. Potatoes may be served as a side dish or incorporated into hash or egg casseroles. Unlike breads or fruits, which may be the entire breakfast, potatoes are usually just part of a hearty breakfast, especially one that includes meat and eggs. Potatoes are identified and discussed in Chapter 23, Potatoes, Grains and Pasta.

DAIRY PRODUCTS

Some dairy products are indispensable at breakfast: milk and cream, for example. Other dairy products such as yogurt, crème fraîche and cheese are less commonly served but just as appropriate. Like milk, yogurt and crème fraîche can be used to top cold cereals or fruit. Cheeses are commonly used in omelets and frittatas, blintzes and danish pastries; an assortment of mild cheeses offered with crusty bread and fresh fruit is a delicious breakfast or brunch alternative. Dairy products are identified and discussed in Chapter 8, Eggs and Dairy Products.

EGGS

No other breakfast food is as popular or as versatile as the egg. Eggs can be cooked by almost any method and served with a wide array of seasonings, accompaniments and garnishes. Whatever cooking method is selected, be sure to prepare the eggs carefully: Overcooked eggs and those cooked at too high a temperature will be tough and rubbery. Eggs are described in Chapter 8, Eggs and Dairy Products.

The following cooking methods are those most often used for egg-based breakfast dishes. They include dry-heat cooking methods (baking, sautéing and pan-frying) and moist-heat cooking methods (in-shell cooking and poaching).

Dry-Heat Cooking Methods

Baking

Shirred Eggs

Baked eggs, also referred to as shirred eggs, are normally prepared in individual ramekins or baking dishes. The ramekins can be lined or partially filled with ingredients such as bread, ham, creamed spinach or artichokes. The eggs are often topped with grated cheese, fresh herbs or a sauce. When properly cooked, the egg whites should be set while the yolks are soft and creamy.

PROCEDURE FOR MAKING SHIRRED EGGS

1. Coat each ramekin with melted butter. Add flavoring ingredients as desired.
2. Break one or two eggs into each ramekin. Do not break the yolks. Season with salt and pepper.
3. Bake the eggs until the white is firm, approximately 12–15 minutes. Approximately 3–5 minutes before the eggs are done, add cream or top the eggs with grated cheese, diced ham, fresh herbs or other ingredients as desired.

1. Adding the eggs to the ramekin on top of the ham.

2. The finished shirred eggs with ham.

◆◆◆

RECIPE 32.1

SHIRRED EGGS WITH HAM

Yield: 1 Serving

Whole butter, melted	as needed	as needed
Baked ham, sliced thin	1/2 oz.	15 g
Eggs	2	2
Salt and pepper	TT	TT
Heavy cream, hot	1 Tbsp.	15 ml
Swiss cheese, grated	1 Tbsp.	15 ml

1. Brush the interior of a 6-ounce (180-milliliter) ramekin with melted butter. Line the ramekin with the ham.
2. Break the eggs into a cup and pour them carefully into the ramekin on top of the ham. Season with salt and pepper.
3. Bake at 325°F (160°C) until the eggs begin to set, approximately 8–10 minutes. Remove from the oven, add the cream and grated cheese. Return to the oven until the eggs are cooked and the cheese is melted. Serve immediately.

Quiche

Quiche is a classic breakfast and brunch entree. It consists of an egg custard (eggs, cream or milk and seasonings) and fillings baked in a crust.

The filling usually includes at least one type of cheese, and can also include any number of other ingredients such as cooked, diced meats (for example, sausage, crumbled bacon, ham, fish or shellfish) or blanched vegetables (for example, mushrooms, sautéed onions, asparagus or broccoli). The flavor and texture of these ingredients should complement each other without overpowering the delicate egg custard. Quiche is a good way of using leftovers, but the ingredients should still be fresh and of good quality.

The crust may be made with whole wheat flour, cornmeal or other grains for added flavor and texture. A recipe for quiche dough is given at 29.14.

PROCEDURE FOR MAKING QUICHE

1. Prepare and bake a pie shell.
2. Prepare the garnishes and flavoring ingredients and add them to the pie shell.
3. Prepare a custard and add it to the pie shell. Ratios of eggs to milk or heavy cream vary depending on the specific recipe, but 6–8 eggs to 1 quart (1 liter) of liquid is usually sufficient to bind the custard.
4. Bake the quiche until set; allow it to cool slightly before cutting.

◆◆◆

RECIPE 32.2

QUICHE LORRAINE

Yield: 1 10-in. (25-cm) Quiche

Pie shell, 10-in. (25-cm) diameter, baked	1	1
Bacon, diced and cooked	4 oz.	120 g
Swiss or Gruyère cheese, shredded	2 oz.	60 g
Eggs	4	4
Milk	1 pt.	450 ml
Heavy cream	4 oz.	120 g
Salt and pepper	TT	TT
Nutmeg	TT	TT

1. Place the bacon and shredded cheese in the baked pie shell.
2. To make the custard, combine the eggs, milk and cream and season with salt, pepper and nutmeg.
3. Pour the custard over the bacon and cheese and bake at 350°F (180°C) until the custard is cooked, approximately 1 hour.

Sautéing

Scrambled Eggs

Scrambled eggs are eggs whisked with seasonings and then sautéed. They are stirred nearly constantly during cooking. The finished eggs should be light and fluffy with a tender, creamy texture. A small amount of milk or cream may be added to the eggs to provide a more delicate finished product.

Overcooking or cooking at too high a temperature causes the eggs to become tough and rubbery.

Scrambled eggs are often flavored by sautéing other foods (for example, onions, mushrooms or diced ham) in the pan before adding the eggs or by adding other foods (for example, grated cheeses or herbs) to the eggs just before cooking is complete. Suggested additions include finely diced bell peppers, onions, mushrooms, zucchini or tomatoes; cottage cheese or any variety of shredded firm cheese; crumbled bacon; diced ham, turkey or beef; bits of smoked salmon, cooked shrimp or cooked sausage; and fresh herbs.

PROCEDURE FOR MAKING SCRAMBLED EGGS

1. Break the eggs into a mixing bowl. Season lightly with salt and pepper. Add 1 scant tablespoon (12 milliliters) of milk or cream per egg and whisk everything together.
2. Heat a sauté pan, add clarified butter or oil and heat until the fat begins to sizzle.
3. Sauté any additional ingredients in the hot fat.
4. Pour the eggs into the pan all at once. As the eggs begin to set, slowly stir the mixture with a spatula. Lift cooked portions to allow uncooked egg to flow underneath.
5. Sprinkle on additional ingredients such as cheese or herbs.
6. Cook just until the eggs are set, but still shiny and moist. Remove from the pan and serve immediately.

◆◆◆

RECIPE 32.3

GREEK-STYLE SCRAMBLED EGGS

Yield: 6 6-oz. (180-g) Servings

Eggs	12	12
Heavy cream	2 oz.	60 ml
Salt and pepper	TT	TT
Onion, fine dice	2 oz.	60 g
Clarified butter	3 oz.	90 g
Spinach, chiffonade	2 oz.	60 g
Feta cheese, crumbled	4 oz.	120 g
Greek olives, pitted and chopped	3 Tbsp.	45 ml

1. Combine the eggs, cream, salt and pepper in a mixing bowl. Whisk until well blended.
2. Sauté the onion in the butter until translucent but not brown.
3. Pour the egg mixture into the pan and cook, stirring frequently, until half cooked, approximately 1 minute.
4. Add the spinach to the eggs and continue cooking. Just before the eggs are fully cooked, sprinkle on the cheese.
5. Spoon the cooked egg mixture onto serving plates and garnish with the olives. Serve immediately.

Omelets

Omelets are needlessly intimidating egg creations that begin as scrambled eggs. They are usually prepared as individual servings using two or three eggs. The cooked eggs are then folded around a warm filling.

The filling may contain vegetables, cheeses or meats. Any filling ingredient that needs cooking should be cooked before being added to the omelet. Because the eggs cook relatively quickly, raw fillings would not be properly cooked until the eggs were overcooked.

PROCEDURE FOR MAKING FOLDED OMELETS

1. Fully cook any meats and blanch or otherwise cook any vegetables that will be incorporated into the omelet.
2. Heat an omelet pan over moderately high heat and add clarified butter.
3. Whisk the eggs together in a small bowl. Season with salt and pepper if desired.
4. Pour the eggs into the pan and stir until they begin to set, approximately 10 seconds.
5. Pull cooked egg from the sides of the pan toward the center, allowing raw egg to run underneath. Continue doing so for 20–30 seconds.
6. Spoon any fillings on top of the eggs or add any other garnishes.
7. When cooked as desired, flip one side of the omelet toward the center with a spatula or a shake of the pan. Slide the omelet onto the serving plate so that it lands folded in thirds with the seam underneath.
8. Spoon any sauce or additional filling on top, garnish as desired and serve immediately.

♦♦♦

RECIPE 32.4

SHRIMP AND AVOCADO OMELET

Yield: 1 Serving

Shrimp, peeled, deveined and cut into pieces	3 oz.	90 g
Green onion, sliced	1 Tbsp.	15 ml
Clarified butter	1 oz.	30 g
Eggs	3	3
Salt and pepper	TT	TT
Avocado, peeled and diced	1/4	1/4
Cilantro, chopped	2 tsp.	10 ml

1. Sauté the shrimp and onion in half of the butter for 1 minute. Remove from the heat and set aside.
2. Heat an omelet pan and add the remaining butter.
3. Whisk the eggs together in a small bowl, season with salt and pepper and pour into the omelet pan.
4. Stir the eggs as they cook. Stop when they begin to set. Lift the edges as the omelet cooks to allow the raw eggs to run underneath.
5. When the eggs are nearly set, add the shrimp filling, avocado and cilantro. Fold the front of the eggs over and roll the omelet onto a plate.

1. Lifting the edge of the eggs to allow them to cook evenly.

2. Adding the filling to the eggs.

3. Folding the eggs.

4. Rolling the omelet onto the plate.

Frittatas

Frittatas are essentially open-faced omelets of Spanish-Italian heritage. They may be cooked in small pans as individual portions or in large pans, then cut into wedges for service. A relatively large amount of hearty ingredients are mixed directly into the eggs. The eggs are first cooked on the stove top, then the pan is transferred to an oven or placed under a salamander or broiler to finish cooking.

PROCEDURE FOR MAKING FRITTATAS

1. Fully cook any meats and blanch or otherwise prepare any vegetables that will be incorporated into the frittata.
2. Heat a sauté pan and add clarified butter.
3. Whisk the eggs, flavorings and any other ingredients together; pour into the pan.
4. Stir gently until the eggs start to set. Gently lift the cooked eggs at the edge of the frittata so that the raw eggs can run underneath. Continue cooking until the eggs are almost set.
5. Place the pan in a hot oven or underneath a salamander or broiler to finish cooking and lightly brown the top.
6. Slide the finished frittata out of the pan onto a serving platter.

◆◆◆

RECIPE 32.5

GARDEN FRITTATA

Yield: 1 Serving

Chicken breast, 4 oz. (120 g), boneless, skinless	1	1
Garlic, chopped	1 tsp.	5 ml
Cumin	TT	TT
Salt and pepper	TT	TT
Mushrooms, sliced	2 oz.	60 g
Unsalted butter	3 Tbsp.	45 g
Jalapeño, seeded, minced	1 tsp.	5 ml
Red bell pepper, roasted, seeded, peeled, julienne	2 oz.	60 g
Green onions, sliced	1 oz.	30 g
Cilantro	2 tsp.	10 ml
Eggs, beaten	2	2
Monterey Jack or cheddar cheese	2 oz.	60 g

1. Rub the chicken breast with the garlic, cumin, salt and pepper. Grill or broil the chicken until done. Allow it to rest briefly, then cut into strips.
2. In a well-seasoned 9-inch (23-centimeter) sauté pan, sauté the mushrooms in the butter until tender. Add the jalapeño and sauté for 30 seconds. Add the chicken, roasted pepper, green onions and cilantro and sauté until hot.
3. Add the eggs and season with salt and pepper. Cook the mixture, stirring and lifting the eggs to help them cook evenly, until they begin to set.
4. Sprinkle the cheese over the eggs and place under a salamander or broiler to melt the cheese and finish cooking the eggs. Slide the frittata onto a plate or cut into wedges for smaller portions.

Pan-Frying

Pan-fried eggs are commonly referred to as sunny-side-up or over-easy, over-medium or over-hard. These are visibly different products produced with proper timing and technique. Very fresh eggs are best for pan-frying as the yolk holds its shape better and the white spreads less.

Sunny-side-up eggs are not turned during cooking; their yellow yolks remain visible. They should be cooked over medium-low heat long enough to firm the whites and partially firm the yolks: approximately 4 minutes if cooked on a 250°F (120°C) cooking surface.

For "over" eggs, the egg is partially cooked on one side, then gently flipped and cooked on the other side until done. The egg white should be firm and its edges should not be brown. The yolk should never be broken regardless of the degree of doneness. Not only is a broken yolk unattractive, the spilled yolk will coagulate on contact with the hot pan, making it difficult to serve.

For over-easy eggs, the yolk should remain very runny; on a 250°F (120°C) cooking surface, the egg should cook for about 3 minutes on the first side and 2 minutes on the other. Eggs fried over-medium should be cooked slightly longer, until the yolk is partially set. For over-hard eggs, the yolk should be completely cooked.

PROCEDURE FOR PAN-FRYING EGGS

1. Select a sauté pan just large enough to accommodate the number of eggs being cooked. (An 8-inch-diameter [20-centimeter] pan is appropriate for up to three eggs.)
2. Add a small amount of clarified butter and heat until the fat just begins to sizzle.
3. Carefully break the eggs into the pan.
4. Continue cooking over medium-low heat until the eggs reach the appropriate degree of firmness. Sunny-side-up eggs are not flipped during cooking; "over" eggs are flipped once during cooking.
5. When done, gently flip the "over" eggs once again so that the first side is up, then gently slide the cooked eggs out of the pan onto the serving plate. Serve immediately.

Basted eggs are a variation of sunny-side-up eggs. Basted eggs are cooked over low heat with the hot butter from the pan spooned over them as they cook. Another version of basted eggs is made by adding 1–2 teaspoons (5–10 milliliters) of water to the sauté pan and then covering the pan. The steam cooks the top of the eggs.

Moist-Heat Cooking Methods

In-Shell Cooking (Simmering)

The difference between **soft-cooked eggs** (also called soft-boiled) and **hard-cooked eggs** (also called hard-boiled) is time. Both styles refer to eggs cooked in their shell in hot water. Despite the word "boiled" in their names, eggs cooked in the shell should never be boiled. Boiling toughens eggs and causes discoloration. Instead, eggs should be simmered. Soft-cooked eggs are usually simmered for 3–5 minutes; hard-cooked eggs may be simmered for as long as 12–15 minutes.

Sometimes it is difficult to remove the shell from very fresh eggs. Eggs that are a few days old are better for cooking in the shell.

PROCEDURE FOR MAKING SOFT-COOKED EGGS

1. Fill a saucepan or stockpot with sufficient water to cover the eggs. Bring the water to a simmer.
2. Carefully lower each egg into the simmering water. Simmer uncovered for 3–5 minutes, depending on the firmness desired.
3. Lift each egg out of the water with a slotted spoon or spider. Crack the large end of the shell carefully and serve immediately.

PROCEDURE FOR MAKING HARD-COOKED EGGS

1. Repeat steps 1 and 2 for soft-cooked eggs, simmering the eggs for 12–15 minutes.
2. Lift each egg out of the water with a slotted spoon or spider and place in an ice bath.
3. When the eggs are cool enough to handle, peel them and use as desired or cover and refrigerate for up to 5 days.

Poaching

Eggs that are to be poached should always be very fresh. They should also be kept very cold until used. Cold egg whites stay together better when dropped into hot water. Poached eggs should be soft and moist; the whites should be firm enough to encase the yolk completely, but the yolk should still be runny.

Some chefs add salt to the poaching water for flavor; others feel the salt causes the egg whites to separate. To help the egg whites cling together, add 2 tablespoons (30 milliliters) of white vinegar per quart (liter) of water.

PROCEDURE FOR POACHING EGGS

1. Fill a saucepan or stockpot with at least 3 inches (7.5 centimeters) of water. Add salt and vinegar if desired. Bring the water to a simmer and hold at a temperature of approximately 200°F (90°C).
2. One at a time, crack the eggs into a small ramekin or cup. If a piece of shell falls into the egg, it can be removed; if the yolk breaks, the egg can be set aside for some other use.
3. Gently slide each egg into the simmering water and cook for 3–5 minutes.
4. Lift the poached egg out of the water with a slotted spoon. Trim any ragged edges with a paring knife. Serve immediately.

For quantity service, eggs can be poached in advance and held for up to one day. To do so, cook the eggs as described above. As each egg is removed from the hot water, set it in a hotel pan filled with ice water. This stops the cooking process. The eggs can be stored in the ice water until needed. For banquet-style service, all of the eggs can be reheated at once by placing the entire pan on the stove top. Or, the eggs can be reheated one or two at a time by placing them in a pan of barely simmering water until they are hot.

✦✦✦

RECIPE 32.6

POACHED EGGS

Yield: 1 Serving

Water	as needed	as needed
Salt	1 tsp.	5 ml
Vinegar	2 Tbsp.	30 ml
Eggs	2	2

1. Bring the water to a simmer; add the salt and vinegar.

2. Crack one egg into a cup and carefully add it to the water. Repeat with the other egg.

3. Cook the eggs to the desired doneness, approximately 3–5 minutes. Remove them from the water with a slotted spoon and serve as desired or carefully lower them into ice water and refrigerate for later use.

1. Adding an egg to a pot of simmering water.

2. Lowering the eggs into ice water to cool them for future use.

BREAKFAST MEATS

At other meals, meat is typically the principal food, but at breakfast it is usually an accompaniment. Breakfast meats tend to be spicy or highly flavored. A hearty breakfast menu may include a small beef steak (usually sirloin and often pan-fried) or pork chop. Corned beef, roast beef or roast turkey can be diced or shredded, then sautéed with potatoes and other ingredients for a breakfast hash. Fish, particularly smoked products, are also served at breakfast.

But the most popular breakfast meats are bacon (including Canadian-style bacon), ham and sausages. They are all discussed in Chapter 20, Charcuterie. Bacon can be cooked on a flat griddle, in a heavy skillet or baked on a sheet pan. Regardless of the method used, the cooked bacon should be drained on absorbent paper towels to remove excess fat. Canadian-style bacon is very lean and requires little cooking, although slices are usually sautéed briefly before serving. The round slices may be served like ham and are essential for eggs Benedict. A ham steak is simply a thick slice ideal for breakfast. Fully cooked ham only needs to be heated briefly on a griddle or in a sauté pan before service. The most popular breakfast sausages are made from uncured, uncooked meats. They can be mild to spicy, slightly sweet or strongly seasoned with sage. Recipes for country-style and other sausages are at the end of Chapter 20. Breakfast sausage is available in bulk, links or preformed patties. Link sausage is often steamed, then browned by sautéing at service time. It should be drained on absorbent paper towels to remove excess fat before service.

GRIDDLECAKES AND FRENCH TOAST

Griddlecakes

Pancakes and **waffles** are types of griddlecakes or griddle breads. They are usually leavened with baking soda or baking powder and are quickly cooked on a very hot griddle or waffle iron with very little fat. Griddlecakes should be more than just an excuse for eating butter and maple syrup, however. They should have a rich flavor and a light, tender, moist interior.

Pancake and waffle batters may be flavored with tangy buckwheat flour, fruits, whole grains or nuts. Both pancakes and waffles are usually served with plain or flavored butter and fruit compote or syrup.

Waffles must be cooked in a special waffle iron. This gives the cakes a distinctive gridlike pattern and crisp texture. Electric waffle irons are available with square, round and even heart-shaped molds. The grids should be seasoned well, then never washed. (Follow the manufacturer's directions for seasoning.) Crispy Belgian waffles are made in a waffle iron with extra deep grids. They are served for breakfast or as a dessert, topped with fresh fruit, whipped cream or ice cream.

PROCEDURE FOR MAKING PANCAKES

1. Prepare the batter.
2. Heat a flat griddle or large sauté pan over moderately high heat. Add clarified butter.
3. Portion the pancake batter onto the hot griddle using a portion scoop, ladle or adjustable batter dispenser. Pour the portioned batter in one spot; it should spread into an even circle. Drop the batter so that no two pancakes will touch after the batter spreads.
4. Cook until bubbles appear on the surface and the bottom of the cake is set and golden brown. Flip the pancake using an offset spatula.
5. Cook the pancake until the second side is golden brown. Avoid flipping the pancake more than once as this causes it to deflate.

◆◆◆

RECIPE 32.7

BUTTERMILK PANCAKES

Yield: 24 Pancakes

Flour	1 lb.	450 g
Granulated sugar	2 Tbsp.	30 ml
Baking powder	1 Tbsp.	15 ml
Salt	1-1/2 tsp.	7 ml
Buttermilk	1-1/2 pt.	750 ml
Unsalted butter, melted	2 oz.	60 g
Eggs, beaten	3	3

1. Sift the flour, sugar, baking powder and salt together.
2. Combine the liquid ingredients and add them to the dry ingredients. Mix just until the ingredients are combined.
3. If the griddle is not well seasoned, coat it lightly with clarified butter. Once its temperature reaches 375°F (190°C), drop the batter onto it in 2-ounce (60-gram) portions using a ladle, portion scoop or batter portioner.
4. When bubbles appear on the pancake's surface and the bottom is browned, flip the pancake to finish cooking.

Crepes and Blintzes

Crepes are thin, delicate, unleavened pancakes. They are made with a very liquid batter cooked in a small, very hot sauté pan. Crepe batter can be flavored with buckwheat flour, cornmeal or other grains. Crepes are not eaten as is, but are usually filled and garnished with sautéed fruits, scrambled eggs, cheese or vegetables. Crepes can be prepared in advance, then filled and reheated in the oven.

Blintzes are crepes that are cooked on only one side, then filled with cheese, browned in butter and served with sour cream, fruit compote or preserves. A recipe for cheese blintzes is provided at the end of this chapter.

PROCEDURE FOR MAKING CREPES

1. Prepare the batter.
2. Heat a well-seasoned crepe pan over moderately high heat. Add a small amount of clarified butter.
3. Ladle a small amount of batter into the pan. Tilt the pan so that the batter spreads to coat the bottom evenly.
4. Cook until the crepe is set and the bottom begins to brown, approximately 1 minute. Flip the crepe over with a quick flick of the wrist or by lifting it carefully with a spatula.
5. Cook for an additional 30 seconds. Slide the finished crepe from the pan. Crepes can be stacked between layers of parchment paper for storage.

◆◆◆

RECIPE 32.8
SWEET CREPES

Yield: 30 6-inch (15-cm) Crepes

Whole eggs	6	6
Egg yolks	6	6
Water	12 oz.	350 ml
Milk	18 oz.	550 g
Granulated sugar	6 oz.	180 g
Salt	1 tsp.	5 ml
Flour	14 oz.	420 g
Unsalted butter, melted	5 oz.	150 g
Clarified butter	as needed	as needed

Continued

1. Whisk together all liquid ingredients except the melted butter. Add the sugar, salt and flour; whisk together. Stir in the melted butter. Cover and set aside to rest for at least 1 hour before cooking.
2. Heat a small sauté or crepe pan; brush lightly with clarified butter. Pour in 1 to 1-1/2 ounces (30–45 grams) of batter; swirl to coat the bottom of the pan evenly.
3. Cook the crepe until set and light brown, approximately 30 seconds. Flip it over and cook a few seconds longer. Remove from the pan.
4. Cooked crepes may be used immediately or covered and held briefly in a warm oven. Crepes can also be wrapped well in plastic wrap and refrigerated for 2–3 days or frozen for several weeks.

1. Coating the bottom of the pan evenly with the batter.

2. Flipping the crepe. Notice the proper light brown color.

French Toast

Like a pancake, French toast is sautéed on a griddle and served with butter and syrup. Unlike a pancake, French toast begins with slices of day-old bread. (It is known in France as *pain perdu*, meaning "lost bread," probably because it provided a way to use bread that would otherwise have been discarded.) French bread, sourdough, raisin bread, challah, whole wheat, even stale croissants can be used. The bread is dipped into a batter of eggs, sugar, milk or cream and flavorings, then sautéed in butter. French toast should be served very hot. It may be topped with powdered sugar, fresh fruit, fruit compote or maple syrup as desired.

PROCEDURE FOR MAKING FRENCH TOAST

1. Prepare the batter. Store the batter in a hotel pan that is large enough to accommodate the bread slices. Keep the batter refrigerated until ready to use.
2. Slice the bread as desired. Dip each slice of bread into the batter. Allow the bread to absorb the batter through to the center. Turn the bread so that both sides are coated.
3. Heat a griddle or sauté pan and add clarified butter.
4. Place the batter-dipped bread onto the hot griddle. Cook until the bottom is set and golden brown. The cooking time will be determined by the thickness of the bread.
5. Flip the bread with an offset spatula and cook the toast on the other side. The toast is done when it is not runny in the middle; however, it should not be dry. Remove and serve immediately.

◆◆◆

RECIPE 32.9

CINNAMON FRENCH TOAST

Yield: 6 Servings

Eggs, beaten	10	10
Heavy cream	4 oz.	120 g
Salt	TT	TT
Cinnamon, ground	TT	TT
Thick-sliced bread such as sourdough, cinnamon, banana or brioche	12 slices	12 slices
Unsalted butter	as needed	as needed
Powdered sugar	as needed	as needed

1. Whisk together the eggs, cream, salt and cinnamon.
2. Place the egg mixture in a shallow pan. Place the slices of bread in the egg mixture and let soak for 2–3 minutes, turning them over after the first minute or so.
3. Cook the slices of French toast in a lightly buttered, preheated sauté pan or griddle set at 350°F (180°C) until well browned. Turn the slices and cook on the second side until done.
4. Cut each slice of bread into two triangles.
5. Arrange four triangles on each plate and dust with powdered sugar.

CEREALS AND GRAINS

Oats, rice, corn and wheat are perhaps the most widely eaten breakfast foods. Processed breakfast cereals are ready-to-eat products made from these grains. Most consumers now think of breakfast cereal as a cold food, but not so long ago only hot grains were breakfast staples. Oatmeal, served as a hot porridge

◆◆◆

FROM HEALTH FOOD TO SUGAR SNACK

The century old, multibillion-dollar-a-year American breakfast cereal industry, unlike any other in the world, is rooted in health foods. During the 1890s, Dr. John Harvey Kellogg directed a sanitarium in Battle Creek, Michigan. Among the healthful foods prescribed for his patients was his special mixture of whole grains called "granula." John, along with his brother Will, next created and began marketing wheat flakes as a nutritious breakfast food. They were not an immediate success, however; people found a cold breakfast unappealing. Undeterred, Will continued toying with cold cereals, eventually creating flakes made from toasted corn and malt. Thanks to a massive advertising campaign, the American public finally embraced corn flakes and a financial empire was born.

Charles W. Post was a patient of Dr. Kellogg's Battle Creek Sanitarium in 1891. He adopted the principles of healthful eating espoused by the Kellogg brothers and soon opened his own spa, complete with a factory producing his "Post Toasties" and grape nuts. He promoted them as a cure for appendicitis, consumption and malaria.

Soon Battle Creek became a boomtown, home to more than 40 breakfast cereal companies. Unfortunately for the consumer, not all manufacturers—then and now—were as concerned about health as John, Will and C.W. The addition of sugar, sometimes totaling more than half the cereal's weight, makes some of today's breakfast products more sugary than candy bars. Even some of the granola cereals touted as a healthier alternative to other breakfast cereals and snacks contain 20% or more sugar. But at least they no longer claim to cure malaria.

is still popular, especially with toppings such as cream, brown sugar, fresh or dried fruit or fruit preserves. Grits, made from ground corn, are another grain product served hot at breakfast. Grits may be topped with butter and presented as a starch side dish or served in a bowl as a porridge with cream and brown sugar. Oats and oatmeal, grits and other grains are discussed in Chapter 23, Potatoes, Grains and Pasta.

Ready-to-eat (cold) cereal is usually topped with milk or light cream and sugar. Fresh or dried fruits may be added. Many products are enriched or fortified with vitamins and minerals to compensate for the nutrients lost during processing. Creative cooks can avoid overly sweet, artificially flavored commercial products by making their own ready-to-eat breakfast cereals such as granola, a toasted blend of whole grains, nuts and dried fruits. The results are less expensive, more nutritious and far more interesting.

◆◆◆

RECIPE 32.10
CRUNCHY GRANOLA

Yield: 12 c. (3 lt)

Brown sugar	8 oz.	250 g
Water, hot	4 oz.	120 g
Canola oil	6 oz.	180 g
Old-fashioned oats	18 oz.	500 g
Wheat germ	4 oz.	120 g
Coconut, shredded	2-1/2 oz.	75 g
Salt (optional)	1 Tbsp.	15 ml
Whole wheat flour	2 oz.	60 g
Amaranth flour	2 oz.	60 g
Unbleached all-purpose flour	2 oz.	60 g
Yellow cornmeal	2 oz.	60 g
Pecans, chopped	4 oz.	120 g

1. Dissolve the brown sugar in the hot water. Add the oil.
2. Combine the dry ingredients in a large bowl. Mix thoroughly by hand.
3. Add the brown-sugar-and-oil mixture to the dry ingredients; toss to combine.
4. Spread out the granola in a thin layer on a sheet pan. Bake at 200°F (90°C) until crisp, approximately 1-1/2 to 2 hours. Toss lightly with a metal spatula every 30 minutes.
5. Let the baked granola cool completely at room temperature, then store in an airtight container. Chopped dried fruits, additional nuts or fresh fruits can be added at service time.

NUTRITION

Most nutritionists agree that you and your customers should start the day with a nutritious breakfast. Depending upon what is eaten, a breakfast can supply a good percentage of the day's proteins, carbohydrates, fats, vitamins and minerals.

TABLE 32.1   NUTRITIONAL VALUES OF SELECTED BREAKFAST FOODS

Per portion as noted	Kcal	Protein (g)	Carbohydrates (g)	Total Fat (g)	Saturated Fat (g)	Cholesterol (mg)	Sodium (mg)
Coffee, brewed, 6 oz. (180 ml)	4	0.1	0.8	0	0	0	4
Cream, light, 1 oz. (30 ml)	55	0.8	1	5.5	3.4	19	11
Sugar, granulated, 1 Tbsp. (15 ml)	46	0	11.9	0	0	0	trace
Orange juice, fresh, 6 oz. (180 ml)	83	1.3	19.3	0.4	<0.1	0	2
Egg, hard-cooked, 1 large	77	6.3	0.6	5.3	1.6	213	62
Egg, pan-fried in margarine, 1 large	91	6.2	0.6	6.9	1.9	211	162
Bacon, cooked, 3 slices (20 slices per lb)	109	5.8	0.1	9.4	3.3	16	303
English muffin, 1	130	4.3	25.4	1.3	na	0	206
Corn flakes, 1 oz. (28 g)	100	2	24	0	0	0	250
Milk, 8 oz. (240 ml)	88	7.2	11.2	1.6	0.8	8	240

The Corrine T. Netzer Encyclopedia of Food Values 1992
na = not available

CONCLUSION

Breakfast is an important meal for consumers and food service operations alike. Breakfast menus may offer a variety of items, including fruits, cereals, eggs, pancakes and cured meats, or they can be devoted to one or two specialty items such as coffee and cinnamon rolls. Whatever is served should be prepared and served with care.

QUESTIONS FOR DISCUSSION

1. Explain the differences between a typical breakfast and a typical brunch. Create a sample menu for each of these meals.
2. Explain the difference between an omelet and a frittata.
3. Describe four different types of fried eggs and explain how each is prepared.
4. What is the difference between a soft-cooked egg and a hard-cooked egg? Why are these eggs simmered instead of boiled?
5. List three types of griddlecakes and explain how they are prepared.
6. What problems might be encountered when preparing French toast with very thick slices of bread? How can you avoid these problems?
7. Should meats be fully cooked before being incorporated in egg dishes such as omelettes and quiches? Explain your answer.

$\mathscr{A}$DDITIONAL BREAKFAST RECIPES

RECIPE 32.11

CAMPTON PLACE BAGELS WITH SMOKED TROUT CREAM CHEESE

NOTE: *This dish appears in the Chapter Opening photograph.*

CAMPTON PLACE RESTAURANT, KEMPINSKI HOTELS, SAN FRANCISCO, CA
Chef Jan Birnbaum

Yield: 24 Bagels;
24-oz. (720-g) Spread

Dry yeast	1 Tbsp.	15 ml
Water (95°F/35°C)	8 oz.	250 g
Granulated sugar	3 Tbsp.	45 ml
Malt	3 Tbsp.	45 ml
Flour	1 lb.	450 g
Salt	1 Tbsp.	15 ml
Vegetable oil	2 Tbsp.	30 ml
Egg wash	as needed	as needed
Cream cheese	1 lb.	450 g
Crème fraîche or sour cream	4 oz.	120 g
Pepper, cracked	1/2 tsp.	3 g
Chives, cut	4 Tbsp.	60 ml
Smoked trout	1 lb.	450 g

1. To make the bagels, dissolve the yeast in the water.
2. Thoroughly combine the sugar, malt, flour and salt.
3. Add the oil to the yeast solution, then add the liquid ingredients to the dry ingredients. Mix thoroughly and knead the dough until hands and board come clean. Cover with a moist towel and allow to proof in a warm place (70–85°F/21–29°C) until doubled.
4. Punch down and cut into 1-ounce (30-gram) pieces. Roll into doughnut shapes. Proof the bagels for 15 minutes.
5. Blanch the bagels in simmering water for 4 minutes, turning once. Remove and place on a sheet pan lined with parchment paper.
6. Brush with egg wash and bake at 350°F (180°C) until golden, approximately 20 minutes.
7. To make the cream cheese with smoked trout, whisk the cream cheese in an electric mixer with the paddle attachment for approximately 5 minutes to incorporate air.
8. Add the crème fraîche and whisk for 2–3 minutes.
9. Add the pepper and chives and mix until incorporated, approximately 30 seconds.
10. Fold in 4 ounces (120 grams) of the trout by hand.
11. To assemble, spread 2 ounces (60 grams) of smoked trout on one half of each bagel. Top with two or three thin slices of smoked trout.
12. Place a poached or basted egg on the other half of the bagel.
13. Garnish the plate with fresh tomatoes and baby greens. Serve immediately.

◆◆◆

RECIPE 32.12
HOT CHOCOLATE MOUSSE

Yield: 2 Servings

Milk	8 oz.	250 g
Heavy cream	8 oz.	250 g
Chocolate Fudge Sauce, Recipe 31.32	3 oz.	90 g

1. Heat the milk with 4 ounces (120 grams) of the heavy cream and the fudge sauce over moderate heat, stirring constantly, until almost boiling.
2. Whip the remaining heavy cream to soft peaks.
3. Portion the hot chocolate into warmed cups. Serve the whipped cream on the side.

◆◆◆

RECIPE 32.13
SPICED CIDER

Yield: 2 qt. (2 lt)

Apple cider	1 qt.	1 lt
Orange or cranberry juice	1 qt.	1 lt
Brown sugar	2 oz.	60 g
Cinnamon sticks	2	2
Cloves, whole	5	5
Allspice, whole	5	5

1. Combine all ingredients in a nonreactive saucepan over medium-low heat.
2. Bring the mixture to a simmer, cover and remove from the heat. Let steep for 10–15 minutes. Strain and serve garnished with sliced lemon or a cinnamon stick.

◆◆◆

RECIPE 32.14
ARTICHOKE FRITTATA

THE INN OF THE WHITE SALMON, WHITE SALMON, WA

Yield: 1 9-inch-round (22-cm) frittata

Artichoke hearts, cooked, fresh or canned	8 oz.	250 g
Unsalted butter	1 oz.	30 g
Parmesan cheese, grated	2 oz.	60 g
Eggs	10	10
Half-and-half	6 oz.	180 g
Monterey Jack cheese, grated	4 oz.	120 g

1. Quarter the artichoke hearts.
2. Melt the butter in a sauté pan. Add the artichokes and sauté until heated through but not browned.
3. Distribute the artichokes in an even layer on the bottom of a 9-inch-round

Continued

(22 centimeter) nonstick pan. Sprinkle with 1 ounce (30 grams) of the Parmesan cheese.

4. In a small mixing bowl, whisk the eggs together with the half-and-half. Pour over the artichokes.

5. Sprinkle the Monterey Jack cheese over the entire pan.

6. Bake for 30 minutes at 350°F (180°C). Remove from the oven and sprinkle the remaining 1 ounce (30 grams) of Parmesan cheese over the frittata. Return to the oven until the cheese is melted and light brown, approximately 5 minutes.

◆◆◆

RECIPE 32.15

Lobster Scrambled Eggs with Soft-Shell Crab

CAMPTON PLACE RESTAURANT, KEMPINSKI HOTELS, San Francisco, CA
Executive Chef Jan Birnbaum

Yield: 4 Servings

Fresh soft-shell crabs	2	2
Lobster, 1-1/4 lb. (.5 kg)	1	1
Eggs	10	10
Half-and-half	8 oz.	250 g
Salt and white pepper	TT	TT
New potatoes	1 lb.	500 g
Vegetable oil	5 Tbsp.	75 ml
Onion, medium dice	8 oz.	250 g
Flour, seasoned with salt and white pepper	5 oz.	150 g
Unsalted butter	1 Tbsp.	15 ml

1. Clean the soft-shell crabs. Cut in half and reserve.

2. Cook the lobster in salted water for 3 to 4 minutes and refresh in ice water. Remove the meat from the shells and cut it into 1/2-inch (1.2-centimeter) pieces.

3. In a separate bowl, vigorously whisk together the eggs and half-and-half. Season with salt and white pepper.

4. Wash and dry the potatoes. Toss them in 1 tablespoon (15 milliliters) oil, season with salt and white pepper and roast at 350°F (180°C) for 15 to 25 minutes. They should be undercooked and still very firm. Cut them in half.

5. Sauté the onions in 1 tablespoon (15 milliliters) of oil until soft and translucent. Add 1 tablespoon (15 milliliters) of oil and the potatoes, placing them in the pan with the cut side down. Sauté 1 minute without turning the potatoes. Place in a 300°F (150°C) oven while finishing eggs.

6. Dust the crabs in seasoned flour and sauté them in 2 tablespoons (30 milliliters) of oil. Drain and reserve in warm place.

7. Melt the butter in a nonstick pan. Add the egg mixture and cook over low to medium heat, stirring vigorously and constantly with a rubber spatula. When the eggs begin to set, add the lobster. When the eggs are nearly set, pour them into four 4-inch (10-centimeter) buttered circular rings placed on a nonstick pan. Place in preheated 325°F (160°C) oven and bake for 3 to 4 minutes.

8. Place one ring of eggs in the center of each plate and remove the ring.

9. Place the potatoes around the baked eggs. Stand one crab half on the side of each plate.

♦♦♦

RECIPE 32.16
HOMINY CORNCAKES WITH HAM AND POACHED EGGS IN PIPERADE SAUCE

CAMPTON PLACE RESTAURANT, KEMPINSKI HOTELS, San Francisco, CA
Executive Chef Jan Birnbaum

Yield: 6 Servings

Milk	1 qt.	1 lt
Corn cobs, chopped coarse	2	2
Unsalted butter	2 oz.	60 g
Salt and pepper	TT	TT
Dry grits	1 c.	250 ml
Fresh corn kernels, sautéed	4 oz.	120 g
Chives, cut fine	2 bunches	2 bunches
Red bell peppers, julienne	2	2
Yellow bell peppers, julienne	2	2
Yellow onion, julienne	1	1
Olive oil	2 oz.	60 g
White wine	8 oz.	225 g
Fresh thyme	2 Tbsp.	30 ml
Eggs, poached	12	12
Prosciutto, sliced very thin	12 pieces	12 pieces

1. To make the hominy cakes, bring the milk to a boil with the corn cobs. Remove from the heat and allow to steep for 10 minutes. Strain out the cobs.

2. Return the milk to a boil and add the butter, salt and pepper. As soon as the butter melts, add the grits to the boiling liquid.

3. Cook over low heat, stirring often, for approximately 15–20 minutes. Add the cooked corn kernels and the chives.

4. Spread the mixture out on a lightly greased sheet pan. Cool at least 2 hours in the refrigerator. Cut out 6-inch (15-centimeter) circles of the mixture and cook on a griddle to brown and reheat at time of service.

5. To make the Piperade, sauté the peppers and onion in the olive oil until tender. Deglaze the pan with the wine and allow to reduce. Season with the thyme and salt and pepper.

6. To assemble, place one freshly griddled corncake on a warm plate. Top with the warm Piperade. Arrange two slices of prosciutto and two poached eggs on the plate. Serve immediately.

◆◆◆

RECIPE 32.17

EGGS BENEDICT

Yield: 1 Serving

English muffin, split	1	1
Canadian bacon slices, 1/4 in. (6 mm) thick	2	2
Eggs	2	2
Salt	TT	TT
Vinegar	2 Tbsp.	30 ml
Hollandaise (Recipe 10.14)	4 oz.	120 g
Truffle slices or black olive halves	2	2

1. Toast the English muffin.
2. Sauté or griddle the bacon slices until hot.
3. Bring 1 quart (1 liter) of water to a boil and add the salt and vinegar.
4. Add the eggs and poach until done.
5. Place the muffins on a plate and top with the bacon slices. Place an egg on each slice of bacon and cover with the hollandaise sauce.
6. Garnish each egg with a truffle slice or black olive half and serve.

VARIATIONS: *Poached eggs Sardou*—poached eggs and creamed spinach on an artichoke bottom with hollandaise sauce.

Poached eggs princess style—poached eggs on an English muffin with asparagus tips and hollandaise sauce.

◆◆◆

RECIPE 32.18

APPLE PANCAKES

Yield: 24 Pancakes

Lemon juice	1 oz.	30 g
Apples, peeled, cored and chopped fine	3	3
Flour	5 oz.	150 g
Salt	1/2 tsp.	2 g
Granulated sugar	1 Tbsp.	15 ml
Eggs	4	4
Milk	12 oz.	350 g
Butter, melted	2 oz.	60 g
Powdered sugar	as needed	as needed
Cinnamon, ground	as needed	as needed

1. Sprinkle the lemon juice over the apples to prevent browning, then set aside.
2. Sift the flour, salt and sugar into a bowl. Beat the eggs with the milk.
3. Stir the egg mixture into the flour mixture, blending well. Fold in the apples.
4. Heat the butter in a sauté pan over medium-high heat. Spoon the batter into the pan, in 2-ounce (60-gram) portions. Cook the pancakes, turning once, until golden brown on both sides. Dust with powdered sugar and cinnamon and serve immediately.

◆◆◆

RECIPE 32.19

BUCKWHEAT CREPES
WITH SAUSAGE AND APPLE STUFFING

THE CONYERS HOUSE, SPERRYVILLE, VA

Yield: 8 Servings

All-purpose flour	3 oz.	90 g
Buckwheat flour	1 oz.	30 g
Eggs	2	2
Salt	1/4 tsp.	1 ml
Milk	4 oz.	120 g
Water	6 oz.	180 g
Unsalted butter, melted	1 oz.	30 g
Oil	as needed	as needed
Pork sausage, bulk	1 lb.	450 g
Unsalted butter	2 oz.	60 g
Apples, peeled, cored and diced	6 medium	6 medium
Cinnamon, ground	1 tsp.	5 ml
Apple cider	4 oz.	120 g
Sour cream	8 oz.	250 g
Fresh sage	2 Tbsp.	30 ml

1. To make the crepes, mix the flours together in a medium bowl. Add the eggs and salt. Stir to make a thick batter.
2. Whisk in the milk, then add the water a little at a time. Whisk in the melted butter. Set the batter aside to rest for 20 minutes.
3. Heat a crepe pan and coat it lightly with oil. Pour 1-1/2 ounces (45 grams) of batter into the pan, lifting and tilting to coat the pan evenly.
4. Brown the crepe lightly on one side, cooking until the surface is firm. Remove from the pan and hold in a warm oven until ready to fill and serve.
5. To make the filling, crumble the sausage into a sauté pan; cook over medium-high heat until fully cooked. Remove the sausage from the pan with a slotted spoon and place in a mesh strainer to drain excess fat.
6. Pour off all but 1 tablespoon (15 milliliters) of fat. Add the butter to the pan and melt over medium heat. Add the diced apples and sauté until soft.
7. Sprinkle the cinnamon over the apples and pour in the apple cider. Cook until the cider is reduced by half.
8. Return the drained sausage to the pan. Add the sour cream and sage. Mix well and heat thoroughly.
9. To assemble, spoon a portion of the filling onto each crepe. Roll the crepe around the filling and serve immediately.

◆◆◆

RECIPE 32.20

CHEESE BLINTZES

Yield: 16 Blintzes

Eggs	3	3
Milk	8 oz.	250 g
Vegetable oil	1 oz.	30 g

Continued

Salt	1/2 tsp.	2 ml
Flour	4 oz.	120 g
Clarified butter	as needed	as needed
Ricotta cheese	12 oz.	350 g
Egg yolk	1	1
Salt	1/4 tsp.	1 ml
Lemon juice	1 tsp.	5 ml
Vanilla extract	1 tsp.	5 ml
Butter	2 oz.	60 g

1. To make the batter, whisk together the eggs, milk and oil. Add the salt. Stir in the flour and mix until smooth. Allow the batter to rest for 30 minutes.
2. Heat a crepe pan and add a small amount of clarified butter.
3. Add 1 ounce (30 grams) of the batter to the pan. Tip the pan so the batter coats the entire surface in a thin layer.
4. Cook the pancake until browned on the bottom. Remove it from the pan.
5. To make the filling, drain the cheese in a china cap. Combine the remaining ingredients (except the butter) with the cheese and mix well.
6. To assemble, place a pancake on the work surface with the cooked side down. Place 1 ounce (30 grams) of the filling in the center of the pancake. Fold the opposite ends in and then roll up to form a small package.
7. Sauté each blintz in butter until hot. Serve with sour cream or fruit compote as desired.

◆◆◆

RECIPE 32.21
Banana Brioche French Toast

CAMPTON PLACE RESTAURANT, KEMPINSKI HOTELS, San Francisco, CA
Executive Chef Jan Birnbaum

Yield: 4 Servings

Bananas, sliced	3	3
Lemon juice	2 Tbsp.	30 ml
Zest of two lemons		
Brioche, sliced 1-1/2 inches (3.7 cm) thick	12 slices	12 slices
Eggs	10	10
Heavy cream	11 oz.	330 g
Salt	pinch	pinch
Cinnamon, ground	1/2 tsp.	2 ml
Nutmeg	1/4 tsp.	1 ml
Granulated sugar	3 oz.	90 g
Vanilla extract	1 tsp.	5 ml
Unsalted butter	as needed	as needed
Powdered sugar	as needed	as needed
Mango preserves	as needed	as needed
Macadamia nuts, chopped	as needed	as needed

1. Toss the bananas with the lemon juice and zest.
2. Cut into one side of each slice of bread to create a deep pocket. Stuff the pocket with the banana slices.
3. Whisk together the eggs, cream, salt, cinnamon, nutmeg, sugar and vanilla.

Soak the stuffed bread in this mixture until very soggy. Remove from the egg mixture and drain briefly.

4. Sauté the soaked bread in butter until golden brown on each side. Place in a 375°F (190°C) oven and bake until the bread puffs, approximately 3–4 minutes.

5. Dust with powdered sugar and top with mango preserves and macadamia nuts.

HORS d'OEUVRES AND APPETIZERS

After studying this chapter you will be able to:

◆ prepare and serve a variety of cold and hot hors d'oeuvres
◆ prepare a variety of appetizers
◆ choose hors d'oeuvres and appetizers that are appropriate for the meal or event

*H*ors d'oeuvres, whether hot or cold, are very small portions of foods served before the meal to stimulate the appetite. Hors d'oeuvres can be passed elegantly by waiters or displayed on buffets. Appetizers, whether hot or cold, are generally the first course or introduction to a meal; they are more typically served with dinner than with lunch. Sometimes there is very little difference between an hors d'oeuvre and an appetizer.

Preparing hors d'oeuvres and appetizers uses skills from almost every work station. Because they can consist of meat, poultry, fish, shellfish, vegetables, potatoes, grains, pasta, fruits, baked goods and sauces, they require a detailed knowledge of these foods and how they are prepared.

Although both hors d'oeuvres and appetizers can be divided into hot and cold varieties, it is difficult (and unnecessary) to further categorize them because of the vast variety possible and the absence of any one dominant food type or style.

HORS D'OEUVRES

The French term *hors d'oeuvre* translates as "outside the work." Its usage was correct under the classic kitchen brigade system, for it was the service staff's responsibility to prepare small tidbits for guests to enjoy while the kitchen prepared the meal. Today, however, the kitchen staff prepares the hors d'oeuvres as well as the meals. Cold hors d'oeuvres are usually prepared by the *garde-manger*; hot ones are prepared in the main kitchen.

There are really only two limitations on the type of food and manner of preparation that can be used for hors d'oeuvres: the chef's imagination and the foods at his or her disposal. There are, however, a few guidelines.

UN ARTISTE DE L'HORS D'OEUVRE

"Well may it be said that a good hors d'oeuvre artist is a man to be prized in any kitchen, for, although his duties do not by any means rank first in importance, they nevertheless demand of the chef the possession of such qualities as are rarely found united in one person, reliable and experienced taste, originality, keen artistic sense, and professional knowledge."

AUGUSTE ESCOFFIER,
LE GUIDE CULINAIRE

GUIDELINES FOR PREPARING HORS D'OEUVRES

1. They should be small, one to two bites.
2. They should be flavorful and well seasoned without being overpowering.
3. They should be visually attractive.
4. They should complement the foods to follow without duplicating their flavors.

Cold Hors d'Oeuvres

Cold hors d'oeuvres are divided here into five broad categories based upon preparation method, principal ingredient or presentation style. They are: canapés, caviars, crudités, dips and sushi. These categories may vary somewhat from classical teachings, but they are completely appropriate for modern menus and food service operations.

Canapés

Canapés are tiny, open-faced sandwiches. They are constructed from a base, a spread and one or more garnishes.

The most common **canapé base** is a thin slice of bread cut into an interesting shape and toasted. Although most any variety of bread can be used, spiced, herbed or otherwise flavored breads may be inappropriate for some spreads or garnishes. Melba toasts, crackers or slices of firm vegetables such as cucumbers or zucchini are also popular canapé bases. The base must be strong enough to support the weight of the spread and garnish without falling apart when handled.

The **canapé spread** provides much of the canapé's flavor. Spreads are usually flavored butters, cream cheese or a combination of the two. Several examples of spreads are listed in Table 33.1. Each of the spreads is made by adding the desired amount of the main ingredient (chopped or puréed as appropriate) and seasonings to softened butter or cream cheese and mixing until combined. Quantities and proportions vary according to individual tastes. Other canapé spreads include bound salads (for example, tuna or egg), finely chopped shrimp or liver mousse. Any of a number of ingredients can be combined for spreads, provided the following guidelines are followed.

GUIDELINES FOR MAKING CANAPÉ SPREADS

1. The spread's texture should be smooth enough to produce attractive designs if piped through a pastry bag fitted with a decorative tip.
2. The spread's consistency should be firm enough to hold its shape when piped onto the base, yet soft enough to stick to the base and hold the garnishes in place.
3. The spread's flavor should complement the garnishes and be flavorful enough to stimulate the appetite without being overpowering.

A spread may be a substantial portion of the canapé as well as its distinguishing characteristic. Or it can be applied sparingly and used more as a means of gluing the garnish to the base than as a principal ingredient.

Canapés with bread bases tend to become soggy quickly from both the moisture in the spread and the moisture in the refrigerator where they are stored. Using a spread made with butter will help keep the bread bases crispier, as will buttering the base with a thin coat of softened plain butter before piping on the spread. The best way to ensure a crisp base is to make the canapés as close to service time as possible.

The variety of **canapé garnishes** is vast. The garnish can dominate or complement the spread, or it can be a simple sprig of parsley intended to provide visual appeal but little flavor. Although several ingredients can be used to garnish the same canapé, remember the limitations imposed by the canapé's size and purpose.

PROCEDURE FOR MAKING CANAPÉS

This procedure can be adapted and used with a variety of ingredients to produce a variety of canapés. If the canapé base is a bread crouton, begin with step 1. If some other product is used as the base, prepare that base and begin with step 4.

1. Trim the crust from an unsliced loaf of bread. Slice the bread lengthwise approximately 1/3 inch (8 millimeters) thick.

TABLE 33.1	A SELECTION OF CANAPÉ SPREADS AND SUGGESTED GARNISHES
Spread	Suggested Garnishes
Anchovy butter	Hard-cooked eggs, capers, green or black olive slices
Blue cheese	Grape half, walnuts, roast beef roulade, pear slice, currants, watercress
Caviar butter	Caviar, lemon, egg slice, chives
Deviled ham	Cornichons, mustard butter, sliced radish
Horseradish butter	Smoked salmon, roast beef, smoked trout, marinated herring, capers, parsley
Lemon butter	Shrimp, crab, caviar, salmon, chives, parsley, black olive slices
Liver pâté	Truffle slice, cornichon
Mustard butter	Smoked meats, pâté, dry salami coronet, cornichon
Pimento cream cheese	Smoked oyster, sardine, pimento, parsley
Shrimp butter	Poached bay scallops, shrimp, caviar, parsley
Tuna salad	Capers, cornichons, sliced radish

2. Cut the bread slices into the desired shapes using a serrated bread knife or canapé cutter.
3. Brush the bread shapes with melted butter and bake in a 350°F (180°C) oven until they are toasted and dry. Remove and cool.
4. If desired, spread each base with a thin layer of softened plain butter.
5. Apply the spread to the base. If a thin layer is desired, use a palette knife. If a thicker or more decorative layer is desired, pipe the spread onto the base using a pastry bag and decorative tip.
6. Garnish the canapé as desired.
7. If desired, glaze each canapé with a thin coating of aspic jelly. The aspic jelly can be applied with a small spoon or a spray bottle designated for that purpose.

Barquettes, Tartlets and Profiteroles

Barquettes, tartlets and profiteroles are all adaptations of the basic canapé. A **barquette** is a tiny boat-shaped shell made from a savory dough such as pâte brisée. A **tartlet** is simply a round version of a barquette. A **profiterole** is a small puff made from pâte à choux. These three items can be prepared like canapés by filling them with flavored spreads and garnishing as desired.

Other Types of Canapés

Vegetables such as cherry tomatoes, blanched snow peas, mushroom caps and Belgian endive leaves are sometimes used as canapé bases. They are filled and garnished in the same manner as barquettes, tartlets and profiteroles.

Caviar

Caviar, considered by many to be the ultimate hors d'oeuvre, is the salted roe (eggs) of the sturgeon fish. In the United States, only sturgeon roe can be labeled as simply "caviar." Roe from other fish must be qualified as such on the label (e.g., salmon caviar or lumpfish caviar).

Most of the world's caviar comes from sturgeon harvested in the Caspian Sea and imported from Russia and Iran. Imported sturgeon caviar, classified according to the sturgeon species and the roe's size and color, includes **beluga**, **osetra** and **sevruga** as well as **pressed caviar**. Most of the caviar consumed in this country, however, comes from either domestic sturgeon or other fish and is labeled **American sturgeon caviar**, **golden whitefish caviar**, **lumpfish caviar** or **salmon caviar**.

Purchasing and Storing Caviars

Although all caviar is processed with salt, the best caviar is labeled **malassol**, which means "little salt." Caviar should smell fresh, with no off odors. The eggs should be whole, not broken, and they should be crisp and pop when pressed with the tongue. Excessive oiliness may be caused by a large number of broken eggs. The best way to test caviar's quality is to taste it. Remember, price alone does not necessarily indicate quality.

Most caviar can be purchased fresh or pasteurized in tins or jars ranging from one ounce (28 grams) to over four pounds (2 kilograms). Some caviars are also available frozen. (Frozen caviar should be used only as a garnish and should not be served by itself.) In order to ensure the freshest possible product, always purchase caviar in small quantities as often as possible based on your needs.

Fresh caviar should be stored at 32°F (0°C). Because most refrigerators are considerably warmer than that, store the caviar on ice in the coldest part of the refrigerator and change the ice often. If properly handled, fresh caviar will last one to two weeks before opening and several days after opening. Pasteurized caviar does not require refrigeration until it is opened and will last several days in the refrigerator after opening.

Serving Caviars

Fine caviar should be served in its original container or a nonmetal bowl on a bed of crushed ice, accompanied only by lightly buttered toasts or blinis and sour cream. Connoisseurs prefer china, bone or other nonmetal utensils for serving caviar because metal reacts with the caviar, producing off flavors.

Lesser-quality caviars are often served on ice, accompanied by minced onion, chopped hard-cooked egg whites and yolks (separately), lemon, sour cream and buttered toasts.

Lumpfish and other nonsturgeon caviars are usually not served by themselves. Rather, they are used as ingredients in or garnishes for other dishes.

Crudités

Crudité, a French word meaning "raw thing," generally refers to raw or slightly blanched vegetables served as an hors d'oeuvre. Although almost any vegetable will do, the most commonly used are broccoli, cauliflower, carrots, celery, asparagus and green beans, all of which are often blanched, and cucumbers, zucchini, yellow squash, radishes, green onions, cherry tomatoes, Belgian endive leaves, mushrooms, peppers and jicama, which are served raw.

When preparing crudités, use only the freshest and best-looking produce available. Because they are displayed and eaten raw, blemishes and imperfections cannot be disguised. Vegetables, both blanched and raw, should be cut into attractive shapes. Crudités are usually served with one or more dips.

Dips

Dips can be served hot or cold and as an accompaniment to crudités, crackers, chips, toasts, breads or other foods.

Beluga—*the most expensive caviar, it comes from the largest species (the sturgeon can weigh up to 1750 pounds/800 kilograms); the dark gray and well separated eggs are the largest and most fragile kind.*

Osetra—*considered by some connoisseurs to be the best caviar, the eggs are medium-sized, golden yellow to brown in color and quite oily.*

Sevruga—*harvested from small sturgeon, the eggs are quite small and light to dark gray in color.*

Pressed caviar—*a processed caviar made from osetra and sevruga roes. The eggs are cleaned, packed in linen bags and hung to drain; as salt and moisture drain away, the natural shape of the eggs is destroyed and the eggs are pressed together. Approximately 3 pounds (1.3 kilograms) of roe produce only 1 pound (450 grams) of pressed caviar; pressed caviar has a spreadable, jamlike consistency.*

American sturgeon caviar—*not considered of the same quality as Russian or Iranian caviars, nevertheless, roe from sturgeon harvested in the coastal waters of the American northwest and the Tennessee River is becoming increasingly popular, due in part to its relatively low price.*

Golden Whitefish caviar—*the small and very crisp eggs are a natural golden color and come from whitefish native to the northern Great Lakes.*

Lumpfish caviar—*readily available and reasonably priced, is produced from lumpfish harvested in the North Atlantic. The small and very crisp eggs are dyed black, red or gold; the food coloring is not stable, however, and when used to garnish foods, colored lumpfish caviar has a tendency to bleed.*

Salmon caviar—*the eggs of the chum and silver salmon, a very popular garnish, are large with a good flavor and natural orange color.*

Artful array of crudités and dip.

Cold dips often use mayonnaise, sour cream or cream cheese as a base. The methods for preparing mayonnaise- and sour-cream based dips are identical to those for making mayonnaise-based salad dressings discussed in Chapter 24, Salads and Salad Dressings. The principal difference is that dips are normally thicker than dressings.

To use cream cheese as a base, first soften it by mixing it in an electric mixer with a paddle attachment. Then add the flavoring ingredients such as chopped cooked vegetables, chopped cooked fish or shellfish, herbs, spices, garlic or onions. Adjust the consistency of the dip by adding milk, buttermilk, cream, sour cream or other appropriate liquid.

Some cold dips such as guacamole and hummus use purées of fruits, vegetables or beans as the base.

Hot dips often use a béchamel, cream sauce or cheese sauce as a base and usually contain a dominant flavoring ingredient such as chopped spinach or shellfish. The traditional Italian bagna cauda is an example of a hot, oil-based dip. It is made with olive oil, garlic and anchovies and is kept hot over a small burner while guests dip raw vegetables in it.

Dips can be served in small bowls or hollowed-out cabbages, squash, pumpkins or other vegetables. Hot dips are often served in **chafing dishes**.

The combinations of ingredients and seasonings that can be used to make dips as well as the foods that are dipped in them are limited only by the chef's imagination.

Chafing dish—*a metal dish with a heating unit (flame or electric) used to keep foods warm at tableside or during buffet service.*

◆◆◆

RECIPE 33.1

CLAM DIP

Yield: 3 pt. (1.5 lt)

Cream cheese	1 lb.	450 g
Worcestershire sauce	1 oz.	30 g
Dijon mustard	1 Tbsp.	15 ml
Sour cream	1 lb.	450 g
Canned clams, drained	1 lb.	450 g
Lemon juice	1 oz.	30 g
Salt and pepper	TT	TT
Tabasco sauce	TT	TT
Green onions, sliced	2 oz.	60 g

1. Soften the cream cheese in the bowl of an electric mixer, using the paddle attachment.
2. Add the Worcestershire sauce, Dijon mustard and sour cream; mix until smooth.
3. Add the clams and lemon juice and season with salt, pepper and Tabasco.
4. Add the green onions and mix well.

Sushi

Generally, **sushi** refers to cooked or raw fish and shellfish rolled in or served on seasoned rice. **Sashimi** is raw fish eaten without rice. In Japan, the word sushi (or **zushi**) refers only to the flavored rice. Each combination of rice and another ingredient or ingredients has a specific name. These include: *nigiri zushi* (rice with raw fish), *norimaki zushi* (rice rolled in seaweed), *fukusa* *zushi* (rice wrapped in omelet), *inari zushi* (rice in fried bean curd) and *chi-rashi zushi* (rice with fish, shellfish and vegetables). Although a Japanese sushi master spends years perfecting style and technique, many types of sushi can be produced in any professional kitchen with very little specialized equipment.

Ingredients

Fish—The key to good sushi and sashimi is the freshness of the fish. All fish must be of the highest quality and absolutely fresh, preferably no more than one day out of the water. Ahi and yellowfin tuna, salmon, flounder and sea bass are typically used for sushi. Cooked shrimp and eel are also popular.

Rice—Sushi rice is prepared by adding seasonings such as vinegar, sugar, salt and rice wine (sake or mirin) to steamed short-grain rice. The consistency of the rice is very important. It must be sticky enough to stay together when formed into finger-shaped oblongs, but not too soft.

Seasonings—These include:

- Shoyu—Japanese soy sauce, which is lighter and more delicate than the Chinese variety.
- Wasabi—A strong aromatic root, purchased as a green powder. It is sometimes called green horseradish although it is not actually related to the common horseradish.
- Pickled ginger—fresh ginger pickled in vinegar, which gives it a pink color.
- Nori—a dried seaweed purchased in sheets; it adds flavor and is sometimes used to contain the rolled rice and other ingredients.

◆ ◆ ◆

RECIPE 33.2

ZUSHI
(SUSHI RICE)

Yield: 2 lb. (1 kg)

Short-grain rice	1 lb.	450 g
Water	20 oz.	600 g
Rice vinegar	2 oz.	60 g
Sugar	3 Tbsp.	45 ml
Salt	2-1/2 tsp.	12 ml
Mirin	1 oz.	30 g

1. Wash the rice and allow it to drain for 30 minutes.
2. Combine the rice and water in a saucepan. Bring to a boil, reduce to a simmer, cover and steam for 20 minutes.
3. Combine the rice vinegar, sugar, salt and mirin and add to the rice. Mix well and cool to room temperature.

◆ ◆ ◆

RECIPE 33.3

NIGIRI ZUSHI

Yield: 24 Pieces

Sushi-quality fish fillets such as ahi, salmon, flounder or sea bass	1 lb.	450 g
Wasabi powder	1 oz.	30 g

Continued

Water	1 oz.	30 g
Sushi rice	2 lb.	900 g
Pickled ginger, sliced	2 oz.	60 g
Shoyu	3 oz.	90 g

1. Trim the fish fillets of any skin, bone, imperfections or blemishes. Cut the fillets into 24 thin slices approximately 2 inches long by 1 inch wide (5 centimeters by 2.5 centimeters).
2. Mix the wasabi powder and water to form a paste.
3. With your hands, form a 1-1/2-ounce (50-gram) portion of rice into a finger-shaped mound.
4. Rub a small amount of wasabi on one side of a slice of fish.
5. Holding the rice mound in one hand, press the fish, wasabi side down, onto the rice with the fingers of the other hand.
6. Serve with additional wasabi, pickled ginger and shoyu.

1. Forming a finger-shaped rice mound.

2. Pressing the fish onto the rice.

◆◆◆

RECIPE 33.4

NORIMAKI ZUSHI

Yield: 36 Pieces

Dried shiitake mushrooms	4	4
Shoyu	4 oz.	120 g
Brown sugar	1 Tbsp.	15 ml
Cucumber	1/2	1/2
Sushi-quality fish fillets such as ahi, salmon, flounder or sea bass	5 oz.	150 g
Nori	3 sheets	3 sheets
Sushi rice	18 oz.	500 g
Pickled ginger	2 oz.	60 g
Wasabi paste	2 oz.	60 g

1. Soak the mushrooms in hot water for 20 minutes. Remove the mushrooms and reserve 4 ounces (120 grams) of the liquid. Trim off the mushroom stems.
2. Julienne the mushroom caps. Combine the reserved soaking liquid with 2 tablespoons (30 milliliters) of the shoyu and the brown sugar. Simmer the caps in this liquid and reduce au sec. Remove from the heat and refrigerate.

3. Peel and seed the cucumber; cut it into strips the size of pencils, approximately 6 inches (15 centimeters) long.

4. Trim the fish fillets of any skin, bone, imperfections or blemishes. Cut the fillets into strips the same size as the cucumbers.

5. Cut the sheets of nori in half and place one half sheet on a napkin or bamboo rolling mat. Divide the rice into six equal portions; spread one portion over each half sheet of nori, leaving a half inch (12 millimeter) border of nori exposed.

6. Spread 1 teaspoon (5 milliliters) of wasabi evenly on the rice.

7. Lay one sixth of the mushrooms, cucumber and fish strips in a row down the middle of the rice.

8. Use the napkin or bamboo mat to roll the nori tightly around the rice and garnishes.

9. Slice each roll into six pieces and serve with the remaining shoyu, pickled ginger and wasabi.

1. Preparing the garnishes for the sushi roll.

2. Spreading the rice over the nori.

3. Adding the garnishes in a row down the middle of the rice.

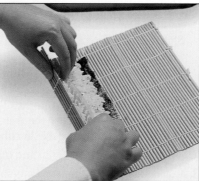

4. Rolling the nori around the rice and garnishes.

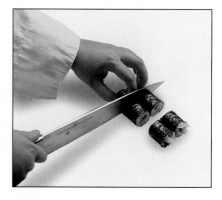

5. Slicing the roll into six pieces.

Hot Hors d'Oeuvres

To provide a comprehensive list of hot hors d'oeuvres would be virtually impossible; therefore we discuss just a few of the more commonly encountered ones that can be easily made in most any kitchen.

Filled Pastry Shells

Because savory (unsweetened) barquettes and tartlets, choux puffs and bouchées can hold a small amount of liquid, they are often baked then filled with warm meat, poultry or fish purées or ragouts, garnished and served hot. They become soggy quickly, however, and must be prepared at the last possible minute before service.

Brochettes

Hors d'oeuvre brochettes are small skewers holding a combination of meat, poultry, game, fish, shellfish or vegetables. They are normally baked, grilled or broiled and are often served with a dipping sauce. Brochettes can be small pieces of boneless chicken breast marinated in white wine and grilled; beef cubes glazed with teriyaki sauce; lamb or chicken satay (saté) with peanut sauce or rabbit and shiitake mushrooms skewered on a sprig of fresh rosemary. (See recipes at the end of this chapter.)

In order to increase visual appeal, the main ingredients should be carefully cut and consistent in size and shape. The ingredients are normally diced, but strips of meat and poultry can also be threaded onto the skewers. Often, ingredients are first marinated.

As hors d'oeuvres, the skewers should be very small, slightly larger than a toothpick. When assembling brochettes, leave enough exposed skewer so diners can pick them up easily. Wooden skewers have a tendency to burn during cooking. Soaking them in water before assembling helps reduce the risk of burning.

♦♦♦

RECIPE 33.5

RABBIT AND SHIITAKE SKEWERS

Yield: 12 Skewers

Rabbit	1	1
Shiitake mushrooms	2 lb.	1 kg
Rosemary sprigs	12	12
Salt and pepper	TT	TT
Olive oil	2 oz.	60 g

1. Bone the rabbit and cut the pieces into 1/2-inch (1.2-centimeter) cubes. One rabbit should produce 36 cubes.
2. Wash the mushrooms. Trim and discard the stems.
3. Cut enough of the mushrooms into 1/2-inch (1.2-centimeter) dice to produce 24 pieces.
4. Skewer three pieces of rabbit and two pieces of mushroom alternately onto each rosemary sprig.
5. Season the skewers and the remaining mushrooms with salt and pepper and brush with olive oil. Grill the skewers and the mushroom caps over medium heat, being careful not to burn the rosemary sprigs.
6. Slice the mushroom caps and arrange a portion of sliced mushrooms and two rabbit skewers on each plate.

Meatballs

Meatballs made from ground beef, veal, pork or poultry and served in a sauce buffet-style are a popular hot hors d'oeuvre. One of the best known is the Swedish meatball. It is made from ground beef, veal and pork bound with eggs and bread crumbs and served in a velouté or cream sauce seasoned with dill. Other sauces that can be used in the same manner are mushroom sauce, red wine sauce or any style of tomato sauce.

◆◆◆

RECIPE 33.6
SWEDISH MEATBALLS

Yield: 4 lb. 8 oz. (2 kg)

Onions, small dice	8 oz.	250 g
Whole butter	2 oz.	60 g
Ground beef	2 lb.	1 kg
Ground pork	2 lb.	1 kg
Bread crumbs, fresh	4 oz.	120 g
Eggs	3	3
Salt	1 Tbsp.	15 ml
Pepper	TT	TT
Nutmeg	TT	TT
Allspice	TT	TT
Lemon zest, grated	1 tsp.	5 ml
Demi-glace, hot	1 qt.	1 lt
Heavy cream, hot	8 oz.	250 g
Fresh dill, chopped	2 Tbsp.	30 ml

1. Sauté the onions in butter without coloring. Remove and cool.
2. Combine the onions with all the ingredients except the demi-glace, cream and dill. Mix well.
3. Portion the meat with a #20 scoop; form into balls with your hands and place on a sheet pan.
4. Bake the meatballs at 400°F (200°C) until firm, approximately 15 minutes. Remove the meatballs from the pan with a slotted spoon, draining well, and place in a hotel pan.
5. Combine the demi-glace, cream and dill; pour over the meatballs.
6. Cover the meatballs and bake at 350°F (180°C) until done, approximately 20 minutes. Skim off the grease from the surface and serve.

Rumaki

Traditionally, rumaki were made by wrapping chicken livers in bacon and broiling or baking them. Today, however, many other foods prepared in the same fashion are called rumaki. For example, blanched bacon can be wrapped around olives, pickled watermelon rind, water chestnuts, pineapple, dates or scallops. These morsels are then broiled, baked or fried and served piping hot.

◆◆◆

RECIPE 33.7

DATE AND CHORIZO RUMAKI

Yield: 32 Pieces

Bacon, thin-cut slices	16	16
Chorizo (Recipe 20.21)	8 oz.	250 g
Cream cheese	4 oz.	120 g
Whole dates, pitted	32	32

1. Partially cook the bacon on a sheet pan in a 350°F (180°C) oven, approximately 5 minutes.
2. Cook the chorizo to render the excess fat. If the chorizo is in links, remove the meat from the casings before cooking.
3. Remove the cooked chorizo from the pan and drain in a mesh strainer or china cap to remove excess fat. Then blend the cream cheese into the meat.
4. Cut the dates open, butterfly style. Stuff each date with a portion of the chorizo mixture.
5. Wrap each date with a half slice of bacon, securing with a toothpick.
6. Arrange the rumaki on a rack placed over a sheet pan. Bake at 350°F (180°C) until the bacon is crisp and the dates are hot, approximately 15–20 minutes.

Stuffed Wonton Skins

Wonton skins are an Asian noodle dough used to produce a wide variety of hors d'oeuvres such as a miniature version of the traditional egg roll or a puff filled with a mixture of seasoned cream cheese and crab. Or they can be stuffed with a wide variety of pork, chicken, shellfish and vegetables before cooking. As hors d'oeuvres, stuffed wonton skins can be steamed, but they are more often pan-fried or deep-fried.

◆◆◆

RECIPE 33.8

STUFFED WONTONS WITH APRICOT SAUCE

Yield: 24 Pieces

Cream cheese	8 oz.	250 g
Crab meat	8 oz.	250 g
Garlic, chopped	1 tsp.	5 ml
Green onion, sliced	1 oz.	30 g
Salt and pepper	TT	TT
Worcestershire sauce	TT	TT
Sesame oil	TT	TT
Wonton skins	24	24
Apricot Sauce (recipe follows)	as needed	as needed

1. Place the cream cheese in the bowl of a mixer and mix until soft.

2. Add the crab, garlic and green onion. Season with salt and pepper, Worcestershire sauce and a drop or two of sesame oil.

3. Place several wonton skins on a work surface. Brush the edges with water. Place 1 tablespoon (15 milliliters) of the cream cheese mixture in the center of each skin. Fold the wonton skin in half to form a triangle; seal the edges.

4. Deep-fry the wontons using the swimming method, at 350°F (180°C) for 10 seconds. Remove the wontons, drain well and refrigerate.

5. At service, deep-fry the wontons at 350°F (180°C) until crisp, approximately 1 minute. Serve with Apricot Sauce.

APRICOT SAUCE

Yield: 8 oz. (250 g)

Apricot preserves	8 oz.	250 g
Fresh ginger, grated	1 Tbsp.	15 ml
Dry mustard	1 tsp.	5 ml
Red wine vinegar	1 Tbsp.	15 ml

1. Combine all ingredients and heat until the preserves melt and the flavors blend.

Other Hot Hors d'Oeuvres

Other types of hot hors d'oeuvres include layers of phyllo dough wrapped around various fillings; vegetables such as mushrooms that are stuffed and baked; tiny red potatoes filled with sour cream and caviar or Roquefort cheese and walnuts; tiny artichoke or clam fritters or any of the hundreds of varieties of chicken wings that are seasoned or marinated, baked, fried, broiled or grilled and served with a cool and soothing or outrageously spicy sauce.

The secret is to let your imagination be your guide, to keep the ingredients harmonious and, if the hors d'oeuvres are to precede dinner, not to allow them to duplicate the foods to be served or overpower them with excessively spicy flavors.

Serving Hors d'Oeuvres

Hors d'oeuvres are not only served as a precursor to dinner. At many events the only food served may be butlered hors d'oeuvres, an hors d'oeuvre buffet or a combination of the two. Whether the hors d'oeuvres are being served before dinner or as dinner, butler style or buffet style, they must always be attractively prepared and displayed.

All events have themes and varying degrees of formality. Long buffets with overflowing baskets of cruditées and sweet potato chips with dips presented in hollowed squashes and cabbages may be appropriate for one event, while elegant silver trays of carefully prepared canapés passed among guests by white-gloved, tuxedoed service staff may be appropriate for another. When preparing and serving hors d'oeuvres, always keep the event's theme in mind and plan accordingly.

When choosing hors d'oeuvres, select an assortment that contrasts flavors, textures and styles. There are no limits to the variety of hors d'oeuvres that can be served, but three to four cold and three to four hot selections are sufficient for most occasions. The following is a small selection of hot and cold hors d'oeuvres that contrast flavors, textures and styles as well as types of food.

Cold:
✦ Canapés of smoked salmon on brioche
✦ Barquettes filled with Roquefort cheese and garnished with grapes
✦ Tiny tortilla cups filled with grilled chicken and spicy tomato salsa

Hot:
✦ Tiny pouches of shrimp wrapped in phyllo dough (Recipe 33.21)
✦ Date and chorizo rumaki (Recipe 33.7)
✦ Rabbit and shiitake mushroom brochettes on rosemary sprigs (Recipe 33.5)
✦ Small chevre tarts (Recipe 33.16)

Butler Service

Butler service hors d'oeuvres or "passed" hors d'oeuvres are presented to guests on trays by the service staff. The hors d'oeuvres can be hot or cold and should be very small to make it easier for the guests to eat them without the aid of a knife or fork. Hot and cold hors d'oeuvres should be passed separately so that they can be kept at the correct temperatures. For a one-hour cocktail reception before a dinner, three to five hors d'oeuvres per person is usually sufficient.

Buffet Service

An hors d'oeuvre buffet should be beautiful and appetizing. It may consist of a single table to serve a small group of people or several huge multilevel displays designed to feed thousands. Colors, flavors and textures must all be taken into account when planning the menu.

Both hot and cold hors d'oeuvres may be served on buffets. Hot hors d'oeuvres are often kept hot by holding them in chafing dishes. Alternatively, hot hors d'oeuvres can be displayed on trays or platters; the trays and platters, however, must be replaced frequently to ensure that the food stays hot. Cold hors d'oeuvres can be displayed on trays, mirrors, platters, baskets, leaves, papers or other serving pieces to create the desired look.

Arranging Buffet Platters

When displaying hors d'oeuvres and other foods on mirrors, trays or platters, the foods should be displayed in a pattern that is pleasing to the eye and flows toward the guest or from one side to the other. An easy and attractive method for accomplishing this is to arrange the items on a mirror or tray with an attractive centerpiece. The food can be placed in parallel diagonal lines, alternating the various styles and shapes. Be careful not to make the tray or mirror too fussy or cluttered, however; often the best approach is to keep it simple. The diagrams in Figure 33.1 may be used as guides for arranging canapés and other foods on trays.

APPETIZERS OR FIRST COURSES

Because eating habits have changed over the years, the types of foods chefs prepare have also changed. Today, even the most elaborate banquets rarely include hors d'oeuvres, an appetizer, soup, salad, entree and dessert, let alone

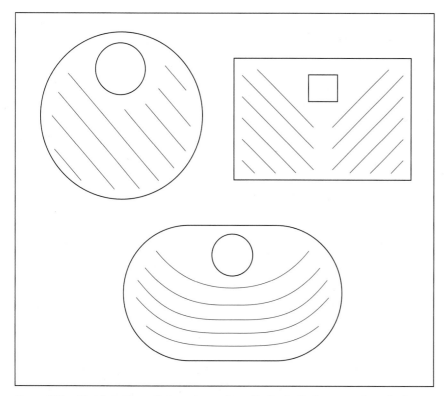

FIGURE 33.1 *Simple patterns that can be used to effectively display canapés and other foods on trays or mirrors.*

separate fish and cheese courses. A more likely progression may be soup (which serves as the appetizer), salad, entree and dessert, or a salad with a small portion of grilled meat or fish that doubles as both appetizer and salad, followed by an entree and dessert. Because of these changes the term **first course** may be more fitting than appetizer.

Generally, appetizers and first courses are small portions of foods intended to whet the appetite in anticipation of more substantial courses to follow. Unlike foods prepared as entrees, appetizers rarely contain the traditional combination of meat or other main item, vegetable and starch. More often, appetizers consist only of the main item accompanied by a sauce and/or garnish. Appetizers do not need to contain any meat, poultry, fish or shellfish, however. Soups, salads, charcuterie items, vegetables, pizzas, pastas and other starch dishes may be served as appetizers. Because they are very rich, some foods such as foie gras and escargots are traditionally served as appetizers. These foods are generally consumed in small amounts and are rarely served as entrees.

Although there are few limitations on what can be served as an appetizer or first course, a few guidelines should be followed to ensure that whatever is served will be well received.

GUIDELINES FOR PREPARING APPETIZERS

1. The first course should be small. Remember, there are other, more substantial courses to follow. As the name implies, an appetizer should stimulate the appetite rather than satisfy it. Remember that rich cream-based sauces tend to satisfy appetites quickly, even when the portions are small. Two to 3 ounces (60–90 grams) of pasta and 2 ounces (60 grams) of sauce is an ample appetizer portion. Many recipes, such as Ahi Tuna Seared with Lavender and Pepper with Whole Grain Mustard Sauce (Recipe 24.24) and Chinese Barbecued Spareribs (Recipe 16.3), can be prepared as an appetizer by simply serving smaller portions.

2. Avoid very spicy foods that may deaden the palate and detract from any more delicate flavors that follow.

3. The first course should be harmonious with the rest of the meal with respect to the types of foods as well as the style. For example, an appetizer of a roasted Anaheim chile stuffed with grilled corn and goat cheese followed by an entree of paupiettes of sole vin blanc would be a poor combination: The strong spices and flavors of the chile would overpower the delicate flavors of the sole; while the chile has strong southwestern ties, the sole is a classic French dish.

4. Avoid duplication of foods within the meal. If fish or shellfish is served as the first course, do not serve fish or shellfish as the main course.

5. For more variety, use several methods of preparation within the meal. If the entree will be grilled or roasted, serve a first course that is poached or sautéed.

6. A first course should always be attractively presented. Remember that often it is the first food the customer sees. It should set the standard for the rest of the meal.

Conclusion

The preparation of hors d'oeuvres and appetizers provides an opportunity for the chef to demonstrate his or her creativity, knowledge of food and skills in presentation and garnishing. Because hors d'oeuvres and appetizers often serve as the guests' introduction to the foods you serve, it is especially important that these foods be properly prepared and of the highest quality.

Questions for Discussion

1. Discuss four guidelines that should be followed when preparing hors d'oeuvres.

2. Identify and describe the three parts of a canapé.

3. Describe the differences between beluga, osetra and sevruga caviars and explain how these foods differ from domestic caviars.

4. Create an hors d'oeuvre menu for a small cocktail party. Include three hot and three cold items and explain the reasons for your selections.

5. List and explain five guidelines that should be followed when preparing appetizers or first courses.

Additional Hors d'Oeuvre and Appetizer Recipes

RECIPE 33.9

Stuffed Squash Blossoms and Buckwheat Blini with Smoked Salmon and Caviar

Yield: 24 Servings

Chevre cheese	8 oz.	250 g
Cream cheese	4 oz.	120 g
Assorted fresh herbs, chopped	2 tsp.	10 ml
Garlic cloves, minced	2	2
Black pepper	TT	TT
Baby squash with blossoms	24	24
Tempura Batter (Recipe 21.4)	24 oz.	700 g
Olive oil	1 Tbsp.	15 ml
Bell peppers, red, yellow and green, julienne	12 oz.	360 g
Salt	TT	TT
Buckwheat Blinis (recipe follows)	24	24
Blackberry preserves	3 oz.	90 g
Smoked salmon, sliced	1 lb.	500 g
Caviar	2 oz.	60 g
Fresh basil sprigs	24	24

1. Blend the chevre cheese and cream cheese in the bowl of an electric mixer until smooth. Fold in the herbs and garlic and season with black pepper.

2. Using a pastry bag fitted with a round tip, fill each of the squash blossoms with the cheese mixture and pinch the flowers shut.

3. Dip each of the squash in tempura batter and deep-fry until lightly browned, approximately 1 minute. Remove and drain well.

4. Sauté the peppers in olive oil until tender. Season with salt and pepper.

5. Carefully split each squash and blossom in half. Arrange two squash halves on each plate and garnish with the julienne peppers.

6. Spread each of the blini with blackberry preserves. Form rosettes out of the salmon slices and place one on each blini.

7. Place the blini on the plate with the squash and peppers and garnish with two dollops of caviar and a sprig of basil.

BUCKWHEAT BLINI

Yield: 24 Blini

Granulated sugar	2 tsp.	10 ml
Dry yeast	1/4 oz.	7 g
Milk, lukewarm	14 oz.	420 g
Buckwheat flour	4 oz.	120 g
All-purpose flour	3 oz.	90 g

Continued

Salt	1/2 tsp.	2 ml
Unsalted butter, melted	3 Tbsp.	45 ml
Vegetable oil	2 Tbsp.	30 ml
Egg yolks	3	3
Egg whites	2	2

1. Stir the sugar and yeast into the warmed milk and let stand until foamy, approximately 5 minutes.
2. Whisk in the flours, salt, butter, oil and egg yolks. Beat until smooth.
3. Cover the batter and allow it to rise in a warm place until doubled, approximately 1 hour.
4. Beat the egg whites to stiff peaks, then fold them into the risen batter.
5. Lightly oil and pre-heat a large sauté pan. Drop 2 tablespoons (30 milliliters) of batter into the sauté pan, spacing the blini at least 1 inch (2.5 centimeters) apart. Cook until the bottom of each blini is golden, approximately 1 minute. Turn the blini and cook an additional 30 seconds. Remove from the pan and keep warm for service.

◆◆◆

RECIPE 33.10

GRAPEFRUIT AND OYSTER HORS D'OEUVRE

Yield: 6 Servings

Grapefruit	1	1
Olive oil	1 oz.	60 g
Fresh ginger, minced	1/4 tsp.	1 ml
Black pepper	TT	TT
Heavy cream	8 oz.	250 g
Horseradish, grated	1 tsp.	5 ml
Salt	TT	TT
Russet potato	1	1
Red tomato	1	1
Yellow tomato	1	1
Oysters	12	12

1. Peel the grapefruit and cut 12 thin segments from it. Squeeze the juice from the remaining grapefruit pulp.
2. Combine the grapefruit juice with the olive oil and ginger and season with black pepper.
3. Whip the cream until stiff and stir in the horseradish. Season with salt and pepper.
4. Peel the potato. Use a mandoline to cut 12 waffle patterned chips. Deep-fry the chips at 350°F (180°C) until crisp. Drain on absorbent paper.
5. Core, blanch and peel the red and yellow tomatoes. Cut each tomato into four wedges. Cut thin strips of flesh from each wedge of tomato to resemble leaves.
6. Shuck the oysters. Place one grapefruit segment on each oyster and spoon 1 teaspoon (5 milliliters) of the grapefruit dressing over each oyster.
7. Arrange two oysters per serving. Garnish with 1 tablespoon (15 milliliters) creamed horseradish, one potato chip, one red tomato leaf, one yellow tomato leaf and a sprig of thyme.

✦✦✦

RECIPE 33.11
SANTA BARBARA PRAWN HORS D'OEUVRE

Yield: 6 Servings

Fresh prawns, head-on	6	6
Sea salt	TT	TT
Pepper	TT	TT
Lime juice	1 oz.	30 g
Ratatouille, chilled (Recipe 22.19)	6 oz.	180 g

1. Arrange the prawns in a hotel pan. Season them with sea salt and pepper and sprinkle with the lime juice.

2. Cover the pan and place in a 400°F (200°C) oven until the prawns are just cooked, approximately 5 minutes. Remove from the oven and cool.

3. Place 1 ounce (30 grams) of ratatouille on each plate and arrange one prawn on top of the ratatouille. Garnish as desired.

✦✦✦

RECIPE 33.12
HUMMUS

Yield: 1 qt. (1 lt)

Chickpeas, cooked	1 lb.	450 g
Tahini paste	8 oz.	225 g
Garlic, chopped	2 tsp.	10 ml
Cumin	1/2 tsp.	2 ml
Lemon juice	4 oz.	120 g
Salt	1 tsp.	5 ml
Cayenne pepper	TT	TT
Olive oil	2 oz.	60 g
Fresh parsley, chopped	2 tsp.	10 ml

Tahini paste—*a paste made from crushed sesame seeds.*

1. Combine the chickpeas, tahini, garlic, cumin and lemon juice in a food processor; process until smooth. Season with salt and cayenne.

2. Spoon the hummus onto a serving platter and smooth the surface. Drizzle the olive oil over the hummus and garnish with the chopped parsley. Serve with warm pita bread that has been cut into quarters.

✦✦✦

RECIPE 33.13
GUACAMOLE

Yield: 1 qt. (1 lt)

Avocados	6	6
Lemon juice	2-1/2 oz.	75 g
Green onion, sliced	4 Tbsp.	60 ml
Cilantro, chopped	3 Tbsp.	45 ml

Continued

Tomatoes, seeded, diced	3 Tbsp.	45 ml
Garlic, chopped	1 tsp.	5 ml
Dried oregano	1/2 tsp.	2 ml
Jalapeños, seeded, chopped	1	1
Salt	TT	TT

1. Cut each avocado in half. Remove the seed and scoop out the pulp.
2. Add the lemon juice to the avocado pulp and mix well, mashing the avocado pulp.
3. Add the remaining ingredients. Season with salt and mix well.

◆◆◆

RECIPE 33.14
SUN-DRIED TOMATO AND BASIL AIOLI

Yield: 1 qt. (1 lt)

Garlic cloves, mashed to a paste	4	4
Egg yolks	4	4
Lemon juice	2 Tbsp.	30 ml
Olive oil	1-1/2 pt.	700 ml
Sun-dried tomatoes, packed in olive oil	4 oz.	120 g
Fresh basil, chopped	4 Tbsp.	60 ml
Salt	1 tsp.	5 ml
Pepper	1/2 tsp.	2 ml

1. Combine the garlic, egg yolks and a few drops of the lemon juice in a bowl and whip until frothy.
2. While whipping the egg yolk mixture, slowly add the olive oil until an emulsion begins to form. Continue adding the oil while whipping until all of the oil is incorporated. A few drops of lemon juice may be added from time to time to thin the sauce.
3. Finely chop the sun-dried tomatoes. Add them, a portion of the olive oil in which they were packed, and the basil to the aioli.
4. Season with salt, pepper and lemon juice.

◆◆◆

RECIPE 33.15
BAGNA CAUDA

Yield: 1 qt. (1 lt)

Anchovy fillets	6 oz.	180 g
Garlic	2 oz.	60 g
Olive oil	24 oz.	700 g
Black pepper	1 tsp.	5 ml

1. Rinse the anchovy fillets under cool water to remove the excess salt. Purée the anchovy fillets and garlic in a food processor.
2. Add the olive oil and season with black pepper.
3. Warm the sauce in a saucepan over low heat.
4. Serve the warm sauce in a fondue pot or casserole accompanied by crudités.

◆◆◆

RECIPE 33.16

CHEVRE TARTS

Yield: 12 Tarts

Tomato concasse	4 oz.	120 g
Pepper	TT	TT
Parmesan cheese, grated	3 oz.	90 g
Puff pastry	8 oz.	250 g
Olive oil	as needed	as needed
Pesto sauce (Recipe 23.27)	2 oz.	60 g
Goat cheese (chevre), Montrachet style	4 oz.	120 g
Zucchini, shredded	1 lb.	450 g

1. Season the tomato with fresh-ground pepper; sprinkle with 1 ounce (30 grams) of the Parmesan cheese.

2. Roll out the puff pastry until it is approximately 1/4 inch (6 millimeters) thick, then cut it into 12 circles approximately 2-1/2 inches (6.25 centimeters) in diameter.

3. Brush a mini-muffin tin with olive oil and line with the puff pastry circles.

4. Add 1 teaspoon (5 milliliters) pesto sauce to each tart.

5. Add 1/3 ounce (10 grams) goat cheese to each tart.

6. Add enough shredded zucchini to each tart to nearly fill it.

7. Top each tart with the tomato and sprinkle with the remaining Parmesan cheese.

8. Bake at 375°F (190°C) until the tarts are brown on top and the dough is cooked, approximately 15–20 minutes.

◆◆◆

RECIPE 33.17

LAMB SATAY WITH PEANUT SAUCE

Yield: 16 Skewers

Lamb leg meat, boned, trimmed	2 lb.	1 kg
Vegetable oil	2 oz.	60 g
Lemon grass, chopped	2 Tbsp.	30 ml
Garlic, chopped	1 Tbsp.	15 ml
Red pepper flakes, crushed	1 tsp.	5 ml
Curry powder	1 Tbsp.	15 ml
Honey	1 Tbsp.	15 ml
Fish sauce	1 Tbsp.	15 ml
Peanut Sauce (recipe follows)	as needed	as needed

1. Cut the lamb into 2-ounce (60-gram) strips approximately 4 inches (10 centimeters) long. Lightly pound the strips with a mallet. Thread the strips onto 6-inch (15-centimeter) bamboo skewers which have been soaked in water.

2. To make the marinade, combine the remaining ingredients in the bowl of a food processor and purée until smooth.

3. Brush the meat with the marinade and allow to marinate for 1 hour.

4. Grill the skewers until done, approximately 2 minutes. Serve with Peanut Sauce.

Continued

PEANUT SAUCE

Yield: 28 oz. (800 g)

Garlic, chopped	1 tsp.	5 ml
Onion, small dice	6 oz.	180 g
Red pepper flakes, crushed	1 tsp.	5 ml
Kaffir lime leaves (optional)	4	4
Curry powder	2 tsp.	10 ml
Lemon grass, minced	1 oz.	30 g
Vegetable oil	1 oz.	30 g
Coconut milk	8 oz.	250 g
Cinnamon sticks	2	2
Bay leaves	4	4
Lime juice	1 oz.	30 g
Rice wine vinegar	4 oz.	120 g
Chicken stock	10 oz.	300 g
Peanut butter	10 oz.	300 g

1. Sauté the garlic, onion, red pepper flakes, lime leaves, curry powder and lemon grass in the vegetable oil for 5 minutes.
2. Add the remaining ingredients and simmer for 30 minutes. Stir often, as the sauce can easily burn. Serve warm.

VARIATIONS: Beef or chicken satay can be made by substituting well-trimmed beef or boneless, skinless chicken meat for the lamb.

◆◆◆

RECIPE 33.18

SPINACH AND ARTICHOKE DIP

Yield: 4 lb. 6 oz. (2 kg)

Onion, medium dice	3 oz.	90 g
Garlic, chopped	2 tsp.	10 ml
Clarified butter	1 oz.	30 g
Frozen chopped spinach, thawed	1 lb. 8 oz.	700 g
Artichoke hearts, canned, chopped coarse	1 lb.	450 g
Cream sauce	1 qt.	1 lt
Worcestershire sauce	2 tsp.	10 ml
Salt and pepper	TT	TT
Tabasco sauce	TT	TT
Parmesan cheese, grated	6 oz.	180 g

1. Sauté the onion and garlic in the butter until tender without coloring.
2. Add the spinach and sauté until hot.
3. Add the artichoke hearts, cream sauce, Worcestershire and 4 ounces (120 grams) of the Parmesan cheese. Mix well.
4. Season with salt, pepper and Tabasco.
5. Transfer the dip to a half hotel pan. Top with the remaining 2 ounces (60 grams) of Parmesan cheese and bake at 350°F (180°C) until hot and browned on top, approximately 20 minutes.

◆◆◆

RECIPE 33.19
KALAMATA OLIVE AND ASIAGO CHEESE CROSTINI

LES GOURMETTES COOKING SCHOOL, PHOENIX, AZ
Barbara Fenzl

Yield: 12 Pieces

French bread	1/2 loaf	1/2 loaf
Basil leaves, chopped	50	50
Tomato concasse	4 oz.	120 g
Garlic, chopped	2 tsp.	10 ml
Kalamata olives, pitted, chopped	15	15
Asiago cheese, grated	2 oz.	60 g

1. Slice the bread 1/4-inch (6-millimeters) thick.
2. Combine the remaining ingredients and mix well.
3. Spread 1/2 tablespoon (8 milliliters) of the mixture on each slice of bread. Place under the broiler or salamander until hot and the cheese is melted, approximately 2 minutes.

◆◆◆

RECIPE 33.20
SPANAKOPITTA

Yield: 90 Triangles

Onion, small dice	4 oz.	120 g
Unsalted butter, melted	6 oz.	180 g
Fresh spinach, cooked and cooled, or frozen spinach, thawed	24 oz.	700 g
Fresh mint, chopped	1 Tbsp.	15 ml
Feta cheese, crumbled	1 lb.	450 g
Eggs, beaten	3	3
Salt and pepper	TT	TT
Phyllo dough	1 lb.	450 g

1. Sauté the onions in 1 tablespoon (15 milliliters) of butter until tender. Remove and cool.
2. Combine the cooled onions, spinach, mint, feta cheese and beaten eggs. Season with salt and pepper and mix well.
3. Spread one sheet of phyllo dough on the work surface; brush with melted butter. Place another sheet of phyllo on top of the first; brush it with butter. Place a third sheet of phyllo on top of the second and brush it with butter as well.
4. Cut the dough into 2-inch-wide (5 centimeter) strips.
5. Place 1 tablespoon (15 milliliters) of the spinach on the end of each strip of phyllo.
6. Starting with the end of the dough strip with the spinach, fold one corner of the dough over the spinach to the opposite side of the strip to form a triangle. Continue folding the dough, keeping it in a triangular shape, like point-folding a flag.
7. Place the phyllo triangles on a sheet pan and brush with melted butter. Bake at 375°F (190°C) until brown and crispy, approximately 20 minutes.

1. Brushing and stacking the layers of phyllo pastry with butter.

2. Placing the filling on the pastry.

3. Folding the pastry and filling into triangles.

◆ ◆ ◆

RECIPE 33.21

SHRIMP CRUMPLE

Yield: 24 Pieces

Rice vinegar	1 Tbsp.	15 ml
Cayenne pepper	TT	TT
Garlic, minced	1 tsp.	5 ml
Ginger, minced	1 tsp.	5 ml
Orange juice	1 Tbsp.	15 ml
Salt and pepper	TT	TT
Fresh thyme	TT	TT
Papaya	1/2	1/2
Shrimp, 16–20 count, peeled and deveined	12	12
Phyllo dough	6 sheets	6 sheets
Whole butter, melted	as needed	as needed

1. To make the marinade, combine the vinegar, cayenne, garlic, ginger and orange juice in a bowl. Stir to combine; season with salt, pepper and thyme.
2. Peel, seed and cut the papaya into medium dice. Place the papaya in a bowl and pour a small amount of marinade over it.
3. Split the shrimp and add them to the marinade.
4. Spread one sheet of phyllo dough on a work surface and brush it with butter. Lay another sheet on top of the first and brush it with butter. Place a third sheet of phyllo on top of the second and brush it with butter as well.
5. Prepare a second stack of phyllo with the three remaining sheets. Cut each stack of phyllo dough into 12 squares.
6. Place one half shrimp in the center of each square of phyllo dough and place several pieces of papaya on each shrimp. Wrap the dough around the shrimp and papaya to form a small pouch.
7. Repeat with remaining shrimp.
8. Bake the phyllo pouches at 350°F (180°C) until the phyllo is browned and the shrimp is cooked, approximately 15–20 minutes.

◆ ◆ ◆

RECIPE 33.22

RED POTATOES
WITH WALNUTS AND GORGONZOLA CHEESE

Yield: 80 Pieces

New red potatoes	40	40
Salt and pepper	TT	TT
Fresh thyme	2 tsp.	10 ml
Olive oil	2 oz.	60 g
Cream cheese	8 oz.	250 g
Gorgonzola cheese	3 oz.	90 g

Bacon, medium dice, cooked	1 oz.	30 g
Sour cream	4 oz.	120 g
Walnuts, chopped coarse	1-1/2 oz.	45 g
Worcestershire sauce	TT	TT
Tabasco sauce	TT	TT
Chives, minced	3 Tbsp.	45 ml

1. Cut the new potatoes in half and scoop out a portion of the inside with a parisienne scoop.
2. Toss the potatoes with the salt, pepper, thyme and olive oil. Arrange the potatoes on a sheet pan with their flat surfaces down and bake at 400°F (200°C) until brown and cooked through, approximately 15 minutes.
3. Soften the cream cheese in the bowl of an electric mixer. Add the Gorgonzola cheese, bacon bits, sour cream and walnuts. Mix until smooth. Season with the Worcestershire and Tabasco sauces.
4. Using a pastry bag and plain tip, fill each hot potato half with the cold cheese mixture and sprinkle with chopped chives.

VARIATION: Fill the cooked potatoes with crème fraîche, top with caviar and sprinkle with sliced chives instead of using the bacon-and-cheese mixture.

◆◆◆

RECIPE 33.23

STUFFED MUSHROOM CAPS

Yield: 48 Pieces

White mushrooms, medium	60	60
Clarified butter	2 oz.	60 g
Onion, minced	4 oz.	120 g
Flour	1 Tbsp.	15 ml
Heavy cream	4 oz.	120 g
Ham, chopped, cooked	4 oz.	120 g
Fresh parsley, chopped	2 Tbsp.	30 ml
Salt and pepper	TT	TT
Swiss cheese, shredded	2 oz.	60 g

1. Wash the mushrooms. Remove and chop the stems and 12 of the caps.
2. Sauté the whole mushroom caps in 1 ounce (30 grams) of clarified butter until partially cooked but still firm. Remove from the pan and reserve.
3. Add the remaining butter to the pan. Sauté the onion and chopped mushrooms until dry.
4. Add the flour and cook 1 minute. Add the cream; bring to a simmer and cook for 2 minutes.
5. Add the ham and parsley, season to taste with salt and pepper; stir to combine. Remove from the pan and cool slightly.
6. Stuff the mushroom caps with the ham mixture and sprinkle with shredded Swiss cheese.
7. Bake the mushrooms at 350°F (180°C) until hot, approximately 10–15 minutes.

◆◆◆

RECIPE 33.24

CROWN ROAST
OF FROG LEGS

CHRISTOPHER'S AND CHRISTOPHER'S BISTRO, PHOENIX, AZ
Chef/Owner Christopher Gross

Yield: 2 Servings

Frog legs	3 pairs	3 pairs
Garlic cloves	20	20
White wine	8 oz.	250 g
Fresh tarragon	6 sprigs	6 sprigs
Heavy cream	approx. 20 oz.	approx. 600 g
Fresh parsley	4 bunches	4 bunches
Chicken stock	8 oz.	250 g
Salt and pepper	TT	TT
Russet potatoes	4	4
Flour	as needed	as needed
Olive oil	1 oz.	30 g
Currant tomatoes	as needed	as needed

1. Separate each set of legs into single legs. Cut the calf meat off the bone and wipe the bones clean. Refrigerate the legs until service.

2. To prepare the sauce, combine five cloves of garlic with the white wine and tarragon and reduce au sec. Add 1 pint (500 milliliters) of heavy cream and reduce until thick. Strain through a chinois and set aside.

3. Blanch the parsley in boiling water for 30 seconds. Remove, drain and refresh. Purée the parsley and chicken stock in a blender. Strain through a chinois and combine with the garlic-cream sauce. Adjust the seasonings and keep warm for service.

4. To prepare the garlic purée, place 15 cloves of garlic in a small saucepan and cover with cold water. Bring the water to a boil. Drain off the water and repeat this process five more times. The garlic will be very soft and cooked. Peel and dice two potatoes. Simmer the potatoes in salted water until very soft. Purée the potatoes with the garlic in a food processor until smooth; pass through a china cap. Warm the potato purée in a small saucepan, adding enough heavy cream to make it the consistency of mashed potatoes. Keep warm for service.

5. To prepare the potato tower, use a Japanese potato spinner to cut two potatoes into long strands. Spray two short lengths of 1-1/2 inch- (3.75-centimeter-) diameter pipe with non-stick coating. Wrap the potato strands evenly around the pipes to create two towers. Deep-fry the potatoes, while still on the pipes, until golden brown.

6. To serve the frog legs, season them with salt and pepper and dredge in flour, leaving the bone clean. Sauté them in 1 ounce (30 grams) of olive oil until done. Place three frog legs inside a potato tower on each plate. Form quenelles from the potato-garlic purée and place two on each plate. Pool the warm sauce on the plate. Garnish with currant tomatoes.

✦✦✦

RECIPE 33.25

GRILLED SHRIMP WITH PROSCIUTTO AND BASIL

Yield: 12 Pieces

Shrimp, 16–20 count, peeled and deveined, tails removed	12	12
Dry white wine	4 oz.	120 g
Rice wine vinegar	2 oz.	60 g
Thyme	2 tsp.	10 ml
Onion, minced	2 oz.	60 g
Cumin, ground	1 Tbsp.	15 ml
Salt and pepper	TT	TT
Vegetable oil	6 oz.	180 g
Dried basil	2 tsp.	10 ml
Garlic cloves, chopped	2	2
Prosciutto slices	3	3
Fresh basil leaves	6	6

1. Combine all of the ingredients except the prosciutto and fresh basil in a stainless steel bowl. Marinate for 30 minutes.

2. Remove the shrimp from the marinade and drain them well.

3. Cut each slice of prosciutto into quarters.

4. Wrap each shrimp first with 1/2 leaf of basil, then a piece of prosciutto; secure with a toothpick.

5. Grill until done, remove the toothpick and serve hot or cold.

✦✦✦

RECIPE 33.26

SMOKED SALMON ROULADE

THE FOUR SEASONS, NEW YORK, NY
Chef Christian Albin

Yield: 4 Servings

Smoked salmon, sliced	10 oz.	300 g
Wasabi powder	1 tsp.	5 ml
Celery root (or celery), small dice	8 oz.	250 g
Sour cream	3 oz.	90 g
Chives, blanched and refreshed	1 bunch	1 bunch
Black caviar	4 oz.	120 g
Radish, cut into strips (placed in ice water to crisp)	4	4
Cucumber, cut in rounds (placed in ice water to crisp)	1/2	1/2

1. Form the slices of smoked salmon into four rectangles. Reserve any salmon trimmings for the stuffing.

2. To make the stuffing, dilute the wasabi powder with 2 teaspoons (10 milliliters) of water. Mix the celery root with the sour cream, diluted wasabi and smoked salmon trimmings.

Continued

3. To make the roulades, place an equal portion of stuffing on each smoked salmon rectangle. Roll up each piece of salmon, neatly locking the stuffing in place.

4. Tie each roulade with a chive "string" at each end. Trim the strings.

5. Place each roulade on a plate. Garnish with caviar, radish strips and cucumber rounds.

◆ ◆ ◆

RECIPE 33.27

ESCARGOT IN GARLIC BUTTER

Yield: 6- 8 piece Servings

Snails, canned	48	48
Butter, softened	1 lb.	450 g
Shallots, minced	2 Tbsp.	30 ml
Garlic, chopped	2 tsp.	10 ml
Parsley, chopped	3 Tbsp.	45 ml
Salt and pepper	TT	TT
Mushroom caps, medium	48	48

1. Drain and rinse the snails.

2. Combine the butter, shallots, garlic, parsley, salt and pepper in a mixer or food processor and mix or process until well blended.

3. Sauté the mushroom caps in a small amount of the butter mixture until cooked but still firm. Remove from the heat and place six caps in each of eight shallow ramekins.

4. Place a snail in each cap and top with a generous amount of the garlic butter.

5. Bake the mushrooms and snails at 450°F (230°C) for 5 to 7 minutes and serve hot.

VARIATIONS:

1. If snail shells are available, place a small amount of the butter in each shell. Push a snail into the buttered shell and add more butter to completely cover the snail. Place the shells in a specially designed escargot dish or a shallow ramekin with 1/2 inch (12 millimeters) of rock salt to hold them in place and cook as above.

2. Prepare 48 small bouchées from puff pastry. Sauté the snails in a generous amount of the garlic butter and place one snail in each bouchée. Drizzle the snail with the garlic butter and serve as an hors d'oeuvre.

◆ ◆ ◆

RECIPE 33.28

TERIYAKI SALMON
WITH PINEAPPLE-PAPAYA SALSA

Yield: 4 Servings

Soy sauce	8 oz.	250 g
Garlic, crushed	1 tsp.	5 ml
Ginger, minced	1 tsp.	5 ml
Brown sugar	2 oz.	60 g
Sake	4 oz.	120 g

Salmon, tranches, 4 oz. (120 g) each	4	4
Vegetable oil	as needed	as needed
Pineapple-Papaya Salsa (Recipe 25.9)	16 oz.	450 g

1. To make the marinade, combine the soy sauce, garlic, ginger, brown sugar and sake.
2. Marinate the salmon tranches in the sauce for 15 minutes.
3. Remove the salmon from the marinade and pat dry. Brush them with vegetable oil and broil or grill until done.
4. Serve the salmon on a bed of warmed Pineapple-Papaya Salsa.

◆◆◆

RECIPE 33.29

Soft Shelled Crab Hors d'Oeuvre

Yield: 12 Servings

Carrots	1 lb.	450 g
Zucchini	2 lb.	1 kg
Soft shelled crabs	12	12
Red tomato	1	1
Yellow tomato	1	1
Assorted fresh herbs, chopped	1 Tbsp.	15 ml
Éclair Paste (Recipe 29.9)	12 oz.	350 g
Olive oil	1 oz.	30 g
Salt and pepper	TT	TT
Flour	as needed	as needed
Beurre Blanc Sauce (Recipe 10.16), infused with 1/2 tsp. (3 ml) saffron threads	4 oz.	120 g
Beurre Blanc Sauce (Recipe 10.16) with the addition of 1 Tbsp. (15 ml) puréed roasted red pepper	4 oz.	120 g

1. Cut the carrots into elongated julienne strips using a mandoline. Cut the unpeeled zucchini in the same fashion.
2. Clean the soft shelled crabs using the following procedure: Lift up the skirt or tail and twist it off, the intestinal tract should remain attached to the tail when you remove it. Cut off the head, including the eyes and antennae. Lift up the top shell on each side where it is pointed and pull out the soft spongy gills.
3. Core, blanch and peel the red and yellow tomatoes. Cut each tomato into four wedges. Cut thin strips of flesh from each tomato wedge to resemble leaves.
4. Stir the chopped fresh herbs into the éclair paste. Pipe the batter through a pastry bag fitted with a small round tip into a 350°F (180°C) fryer in a circular pattern to make garnishes.
5. Sauté the carrots and zucchini in 1 ounce (30 grams) of olive oil until tender, approximately 2 minutes. Season with salt and pepper.
6. Dredge the crabs in flour seasoned with salt and pepper and sauté in 2 ounces (60 grams) of olive oil until done, approximately 4 minutes.
7. Place each crab on a plate. Garnish with the sautéed vegetables, éclair paste and tomato leaves. Decorate the plates with drops of each of the Beurre Blanc Sauces.

◆◆◆

RECIPE 33.30

BLUE CORN AND SHRIMP TAMALES

Yield: 16 Pieces

Fresh blue corn masa	1 lb.	450 g
Baking powder	1/2 tsp.	2 ml
Shortening	4 oz.	120 g
Salt	TT	TT
Onion, small dice	5 oz.	150 g
Red bell pepper, small dice	2 oz.	60 g
Green bell pepper, small dice	2 oz.	60 g
Garlic, chopped	1 tsp.	5 ml
Vegetable oil	1 oz.	30 g
Salt and pepper	TT	TT
Shrimp, 16–20 count, peeled and deveined	16	16
Dried corn husks	as needed	as needed

1. Combine the masa, baking powder and shortening in a bowl of an electric mixer, season with salt and mix until the masa pulls away from the sides of the bowl.

2. Sauté the onion, peppers and garlic in the vegetable oil until tender, season with salt. Remove from the heat and cool.

3. Cut the shrimp in half lengthwise.

4. To assemble the tamales, use a rubber spatula to spread 5 ounces (150 grams) of the masa mixture lengthwise on a 16-inch-by-12-inch (40-centimeter-by-30-centimeter) piece of parchment paper to form a 4-inch-by-12-inch (10-centimeter-by-30-centimeter) band of masa. Spread 1-1/2 ounces (45 grams) of the vegetable mixture in a line lengthwise down the center of the masa.

5. Place eight shrimp halves, end to end, on top of each row of onion-pepper-and-garlic mixture. Roll the mixture in the parchment paper so the masa completely encircles the shrimp and vegetable mixture. Twist the ends of the paper to seal. Repeat three more times to make four rolls. Freeze the rolls.

6. Unwrap each frozen roll and cut into four pieces. Wrap each piece tightly in dry corn husks that have been soaked in water, tying each end with thin strands of husk. Steam the tamales for 30–45 minutes. Allow the steamed tamales to rest 10 minutes after cooking so the masa becomes firm. Serve warm.

◆◆◆

RECIPE 33.31

POTATO RAVIOLI WITH LOBSTER

Yield: 32 Ravioli

Lobster meat	4 oz.	120 g
Salt and pepper	TT	TT
Lemon juice	TT	TT
Baking potatoes, 80 count	2	2
Clarified butter	4 oz.	120 g

1. Dice the lobster and season with salt, pepper and a few drops of lemon juice.

2. Peel the potatoes and slice them very thin (almost translucent) on an electric slicer or mandoline.

3. Place a small piece of lobster between two slices of potato and press the potato slices together with your fingers.

4. Place the ravioli immediately into a hot sauté pan with 1/4 inch (6 millimeters) of clarified butter. Fry until the potato begins to brown. Turn and finish on the other side.

5. Serve the ravioli accompanied by greens or an appropriate sauce such as mushroom sauce.

◆◆◆

RECIPE 33.32

Sautéed Foie Gras on Wild Mushroom Duxelles with Toasted Brioche

ANA WESTIN HOTEL, Washington D.C.
Chef Leland Atkinson

Yield: 4 Servings

Fresh foie gras, A grade	1 lb.	450 g
Wild mushrooms	1 lb.	450 g
Shallots, chopped	2 Tbsp.	30 ml
Garlic, chopped	1 tsp.	5 ml
Butter	1 Tbsp.	15 ml
Tomato paste	1 tsp.	5 ml
Brandy	1 Tbsp.	15 ml
Fresh thyme	1 tsp.	5 ml
Salt and pepper	TT	TT
Madeira sauce (Recipe 10.12)	8 oz.	250 g
Brioche (Recipe 28.16)	8 slices	8 slices

1. Allow the foie gras to come to near room temperature. With a sharp knife, scrape the thin membrane from the outside of the liver. Gently pull the pieces apart. Gently pull out any visible veins. Slice the liver on a slight bias into slices approximately 1 inch (2.5 centimeters) thick. Cover and chill until service.

2. To make the duxelles, clean and chop the wild mushrooms.

3. Sauté the shallots and garlic in the butter.

4. Add the mushrooms and cook until they first release their moisture and then begin to dry, approximately 5 minutes.

5. Add the tomato paste and brandy and cook until dry, stirring often.

6. Add the thyme and adjust the seasonings with salt and pepper. Remove the duxelles from the heat.

7. Quickly sauté the foie gras in a hot dry pan until it is browned on both sides but still bright pink in the middle, approximately 2 minutes.

8. Portion the duxelles onto four warm serving plates. Ladle the Madeira sauce around the duxelles. Blot the foie gras on a dry towel and arrange it over the top of the duxelles. Serve with toasted brioche and fresh thyme garnish.

◆◆◆

RECIPE 33.33
CARPACCIO

Yield: 8 Servings

Beef tenderloin, trimmed of all silverskin and fat	1 lb.	450 g
Mayonnaise, fresh	8 oz.	250 g
Dijon mustard	1 Tbsp.	15 ml
Salt and pepper	TT	TT
Onion	4 oz.	120 g
Capers, chopped	4 tsp.	20 ml
Cracked black pepper	TT	TT
Olive oil	8 tsp.	40 ml

1. Place the tenderloin in the freezer until nearly frozen.
2. Combine the fresh mayonnaise with the mustard. Season with salt and pepper.
3. Peel the onion and cut it in half from the stem to the root end. Slice it very thin.
4. Slice the nearly frozen tenderloin on an electric slicer very thin, almost transparent. On a very cold plate, arrange one slightly overlapping layer of thin slices of beef.
5. Sprinkle each plate of beef with 1/2 teaspoon (2.5 milliliters) of capers, a generous amount of cracked black pepper, salt and 1/2 ounce (15 grams) of shaved onion. Drizzle with 1 teaspoon (5 milliliters) of the olive oil and spoon 1/2 ounce (15 grams) of the mayonnaise in the center of each plate. Serve very cold.

◆◆◆

RECIPE 33.34
EGGPLANT AND SUN-DRIED TOMATO PIZZA

GREENS RESTAURANT, SAN FRANCISCO, CA
Executive Chef Annie Somerville

Yield: 1 15-in. (37-cm) or
2 9-in. (22-cm) Pizzas

Japanese eggplants	2	2
Extra virgin olive oil	2 oz.	60 g
Garlic, chopped	2 tsp.	10 ml
Salt and pepper	TT	TT
Pizza dough (Recipe 28.12)	1 lb.	450 g
Sun-dried tomatoes, packed in oil	5	5
Provolone cheese, grated	4 oz.	120 g
Mozzarella cheese, grated	2 oz.	60 g
Parmesan cheese, grated	1/2 oz.	15 g
Fresh basil, chiffonade	12 leaves	12 leaves

1. Slice the eggplant diagonally into 1/2-inch (1.2-centimeter) slices.
2. Toss the eggplant with 1 ounce (30 grams) of olive oil and the garlic; season with salt and pepper.

3. Place the eggplant slices on a baking sheet and roast at 375°F (190°C) until soft in the center, approximately 15–20 minutes. Cool and slice into strips.

4. Preheat the oven to 500°F (260°C). Roll out the dough and place it on a lightly oiled pizza pan or well-floured wooden peel; brush it lightly with the remaining olive oil. Lay the eggplant and sun-dried tomatoes on top. Toss the provolone and mozzarella cheeses together and sprinkle on the pizza.

5. Bake the pizza until the crust is golden and crisp, approximately 8–12 minutes. Remove from the oven and sprinkle with the Parmesan cheese and basil.

◆◆◆

RECIPE 33.35

SPRING ROLLS

Yield: 36 Rolls

Peanut oil	2 oz.	60 g
Sesame oil	3 Tbsp.	45 ml
Onions, julienne	12 oz.	350 g
Red bell peppers, julienne	12 oz.	350 g
Snow peas, julienne	12 oz.	350 g
Fresh ginger, grated	1 Tbsp.	15 ml
Garlic, chopped	1 Tbsp.	15 ml
Napa cabbage, julienne	8 oz.	250 g
Bean sprouts	1 lb.	450 g
Cashews, unsalted, crushed	1 lb.	450 g
Cayenne pepper	1 tsp.	5 ml
Salt and pepper	TT	TT
Rice paper wrappers	36	36

1. Heat the oils and sauté the onions and peppers for 30 seconds.

2. Add the snow peas, ginger and garlic; sauté for 15 seconds.

3. Add the cabbage, bean sprouts, cashews, cayenne, salt and pepper. Cook for 15 seconds more.

4. Remove from the heat, cool and refrigerate.

5. Soak the rice paper wrappers in water for a few seconds to soften them. Place 2 ounces (60 grams) of filling in each wrapper, fold the sides over toward the middle and roll up into a cigar shape. Brush the edge with water and press to seal.

6. Deep-fry the spring rolls at 350°F (180°C) until hot and crispy, approximately 45 seconds.

CHAPTER 34

INTERNATIONAL FLAVOR PRINCIPLES

After studying this chapter you will be able to:

◆ understand the flavor principles of several cuisines

◆ prepare chicken and starch dishes incorporating the flavor principles and representative cooking methods of each of these cuisines

eople worldwide share a love of food. But the ingredients, flavorings, seasonings and cooking methods they use are not the same. Whether defined by geography, history, ethnicity, politics or religion, various societies eat different foods seasoned and prepared in distinctive manners. These differences shape and define their particular cuisine.

Because this book is a guide to understanding the hows and whys of cooking and is not simply a collection of recipes, we will not explore here all of the world's cuisines nor provide a comprehensive selection of recipes illustrating the cuisines discussed. Instead, we delve into the flavor principles that distinguish several important cuisines from European and American traditions.

Once you understand these principles, you should be able to prepare a variety of dishes that reflect a particular cuisine's flavor principles and cooking methods. To illustrate this point, and because most societies eat chicken, we include a chicken and starch recipe from each of the cuisines discussed.

Cookery—*the art, practice or work of cooking.*

Cuisine—*the ingredients, seasonings, cooking procedures and styles and eating habits attributable to a particular group of people; the group can be defined by geography, history, ethnicity, culture or religion.*

National cuisine—*the characteristic cuisine of a nation.*

Regional cuisine—*a set of recipes based upon local ingredients, traditions and practices; within a larger geographical, political, cultural or social unit, regional cuisines are often variations of each other that blend together to create a national cuisine.*

Ethnic cuisine—*the cuisine of a group of people having a common cultural heritage as opposed to the cuisine of a group of people bound together by geography or political factors.*

Professional cooking—*a system of cooking based upon a knowledge of ingredients and procedures.*

♦♦♦
RECIPES FOR
ETHNIC CUISINES

In *Ethnic Cuisine: The Flavor Principle Cookbook*, Elisabeth Rozin writes: "Every culture tends to combine a small number of flavoring ingredients so frequently and so consistently that they become definitive of that particular cuisine" (p. xiv). She calls these defining flavors "flavor principles" and notes that they are "designed to abstract what is absolutely fundamental about a cuisine and, thus, to serve as a guide in cooking and developing new recipes" (p. xvii). She identifies the following flavor principles for European cuisines:

Greek:
tomato, cinnamon *or* olive oil, lemon, oregano

Italian:
generally—olive oil, garlic, basil
Northern Italy—wine vinegar, garlic
Southern Italy—olive oil, garlic, parsley and/or anchovy plus tomato as a variation

French:
generally—olive oil, garlic, basil *or* wine, herb *or* butter and/or cream and/or cheese plus wine and/or stock
Southern France—olive oil, garlic, parsley and/or anchovy plus tomato as a variation
Provence—olive oil, thyme, rosemary, marjoram, sage plus tomato as a variation
Normandy—apple, cider, Calvados

Spanish:
olive oil, garlic, nut *or* olive oil, onion, pepper, tomato

Hungarian:
onion, lard, paprika

Eastern European Jewish:
onion, chicken fat

Eastern and Northern European:
sour cream, dill *or* paprika *or* allspice or caraway

CHINESE CUISINES

China, a large, geographically diverse country, nurtures several distinctive regional cuisines, the most prominent of which are called here Northern, Southern, Western and Eastern. All Chinese cuisines emphasize a sophisticated contrast and harmony of flavors (sweet, sour, bitter, spicy and salty) and textures (crisp, crunchy, chunky, chewy, smooth and liquid) and rely on the quick cooking of attractively cut, bite-sized pieces of food. Reducing all foods to bite-sized pieces promotes the quick infusion of flavorings. Most cooking is done in a wok that can be used for stir-frying, deep-frying and steaming. Anthropologists suggest that the reliance on quick cooking methods was the result of chronic fuel shortages. Although these quick cooking methods can produce fully cooked foods in minutes, the careful cutting and preparation techniques often require far more time.

Staples include several varieties of rice, noodles (made from rice, beans and wheat) and soy beans (eaten as seeds, beans, sprouts and curd, and used for oil and sauce). Pork, poultry (particularly chicken and duck), fish (particularly pike, carp and bass) and shellfish are regularly consumed, as are a large assortment of vegetables (including varieties of mushrooms, several cabbages, bamboo shoots, water chestnuts and snow peas) and fruits (including litchi, pears, plums and various citrus fruits).

Common spices are star anise, cinnamon, cloves, fennel and Szechuan peppercorns (these are sometimes blended for five spice powder), lemon balm, tangerine peel, coriander, sesame seeds and oil, lotus nut paste, lotus root and hot chiles (a New World import). Commonly used sauces include plum, oyster, hoisin and both light and dark soy.

Chinese - (clockwise from top left) chicken in black bean sauce, white rice, rolls of moo shu chicken, plum sauce, moo shu chicken

Northern China

Northern China includes Beijing, the capital. Some consider this region's cuisine to be the most aristocratic of the regional cuisines; indeed, it is sometimes referred to as Mandarin cuisine, named for the centuries-old Chinese aristocratic and bureaucratic classes.

Northern Chinese dishes are generally lightly spiced and contain little residual oil. Because northern China is relatively dry, rice is not a regional staple, as rice needs an abundance of water to grow. Instead, wheat and millet, eaten as noodles, dumplings and pancakes, are popular. *Chao mian* is a dish of thin wheat noodles stir-fried with other ingredients. Freshwater fish are regularly consumed, as is lamb, a meat rarely eaten elsewhere in china. Meats and poultry are most often roasted or barbecued; Peking duck is a well-known example. Mongol influence still exists in the form of the Mongolian hot pot: a simmering broth into which each diner submerges bits of meat, poultry, vegetables or bean curd.

A classic Northern Chinese dish is Moo Shu Chicken: The wood ears (mushrooms) and bamboo shoots provide contrasting textures, the duck sauce (also known as plum sauce) is a delicate condiment and the pancakes are classically Mandarin. The dish is best enjoyed by spreading 1/2 teaspoon (3 milliliters) of the duck sauce on each pancake, then topping with green onions and 2–3 tablespoons (30–45 milliliters) of the moo shu. The pancake is then rolled up with the ends folded in.

◆◆◆

RECIPE 34.1

MOO SHU CHICKEN

Yield: 4 Servings

Chicken breast, boneless, skinless	8 oz.	250 g
Marinade:		
Chinese rice wine	1 tsp.	5 ml
Salt	TT	TT
Egg white, beaten	1	1
Soy sauce	1/2 tsp.	3 ml
Wood ear mushrooms, dried	5	5
Eggs	3	3
Vegetable oil	4 oz.	120 g
Garlic, chopped	1 tsp.	5 ml
Hoisin sauce	2 oz.	60 g
Bamboo shoots, shredded	3 oz.	90 g
Bok choy, shredded	3 oz.	90 g
Carrot, shredded	3 oz.	90 g
Salt	1 tsp.	5 ml
Chicken stock	2 oz.	60 g
Green onions, shredded	1 oz.	30 g

1. Slice the chicken into thin strips, approximately 1-1/2 inches by 1/4 inch (4 centimeters by .6 centimeters), and marinate in the rice wine, salt, egg white and soy sauce for 15 minutes.

2. Soak the wood ears in hot water until soft. Break off the hard stems and shred the mushrooms.

3. Beat the eggs. Heat 1 tablespoon (15 milliliters) of the oil in a wok and cook the eggs. Do not let them brown. Remove the eggs, shred and set aside.

4. Stir-fry the garlic in 2 ounces (60 grams) of oil until golden. Add the chicken and stir-fry until the chicken is very lightly browned. Remove the chicken, drain and set aside.

5. Add the hoisin sauce and 2 tablespoons (30 milliliters) of oil to the wok; quickly stir-fry the sauce. Add the bamboo shoots, bok choy, carrots and shredded mushrooms and cook for 5 minutes.

6. Add the chicken, salt, chicken stock and shredded eggs. Stir-fry over high heat for 1 minute.

7. Serve hot, garnished with green onions.

◆◆◆

RECIPE 34.2

DUCK SAUCE

Yield: 4 oz. (110 g)

Sweet bean sauce	3 Tbsp.	45 ml
Hoisin sauce	3 Tbsp.	45 ml
Sugar	1 tsp.	5 ml
Sesame oil	1 Tbsp.	15 ml

1. Combine and stir all the ingredients until smooth. Serve at room temperature.

◆◆◆

RECIPE 34.3

MANDARIN PANCAKES

Yield: 16 5-inch (12.5-centimeter) Pancakes

All-purpose flour	8 oz.	250 g
Sesame oil	1 Tbsp.	15 ml
Salt	pinch	pinch
Boiling water	6 oz.	180 g

1. Place the flour, 1/2 teaspoon (2 milliliters) of sesame oil and a pinch of salt in a bowl. Add the boiling water and gradually mix by hand to make a soft dough.

2. On a lightly floured surface, gently knead the dough until smooth. Cover with a damp cloth and let rest for 15 minutes.

3. Shape the dough into a cylinder about 1 inch (2.5 centimeters) in diameter, adding more flour if necessary. Slice the log into 16 equal pieces; roll each piece into a ball and then flatten each to make a disk.

4. Brush the tops of eight disks with the remaining sesame oil. Then place an unoiled disk on top of each oiled disk. Using a rolling pin, flatten each pair of disks into a 5-inch (12.5-centimeter) circle. Cover the pancakes with a dry towel.

5. Heat an ungreased 8-inch (20-centimeter) skillet over high heat for 30 seconds to 1 minute. Reduce the heat to medium.

6. Place one pancake pair into the skillet. When it puffs and bubbles appear on its surface, turn it over and cook the other side until it is speckled brown, approximately 1 minute. Then turn the pancake and cook the first side until it too is speckled brown, approximately 30 seconds. Remove the pancake and wrap it in a clean, dry towel.

Continued

7. Repeat until each pancake pair is cooked.

8. Just before service, separate each pancake pair by gently pulling apart at the edges. Serve warm.

Southern China

Southern Chinese cuisine is centered in and around Canton, a fertile area rich with rice paddies, vegetable farms and fruit orchards. All these ingredients are found in the cuisine, along with an abundance of saltwater and freshwater fish and shellfish as well as more exotic ingredients such as abalone, sea urchin, snake, shark fins, turtle, snails and eel. Both rice and wheat noodle dishes are very popular.

Southern Chinese cuisine emphasizes the freshness of its local ingredients; therefore stir-frying is a popular cooking method. When stir-frying, most of the spices and nonliquid flavoring ingredients are added at the start. Their flavors are released by quickly sautéing them in hot oil. The liquid flavoring ingredients are usually mixed with a thickening agent (often cornstarch) and added toward the end of cooking. This mixture then boils and thickens, coating the foods with the flavoring sauce.

◆◆◆

RECIPE 34.4

CHICKEN AND SNOW PEAS IN BLACK BEAN SAUCE

Yield: 4 Servings

Chicken breasts, boneless, skinless	2 lb.	1 kg
Egg white	1	1
Chinese rice wine	6 oz.	180 g
Cornstarch	2 Tbsp.	30 ml
Soy sauce	2 oz.	60 g
Granulated sugar	2 tsp.	10 ml
Onions, small	2	2
Peanut oil	4 oz.	120 ml
Garlic, minced	1 Tbsp.	15 ml
Fresh ginger, minced	2 tsp.	10 ml
Fermented black beans, mashed	3 Tbsp.	45 ml
Snow peas, fresh	4 oz.	120 g

1. Slice the chicken into thin strips, approximately 1-1/2 inches by 1/4 inch (4 centimeters by .6 centimeters).

2. Combine the egg white, one third of the wine and 1 tablespoon (15 milliliters) of the cornstarch. Add the chicken and refrigerate for 2 hours.

3. For the sauce, mix the soy sauce, sugar and the remaining wine and cornstarch.

4. Quarter the onions and separate the layers.

5. Stir-fry the chicken in 3 ounces (90 grams) of oil. Remove and set aside.

6. If necessary, add all the remaining oil and stir-fry the garlic and ginger for 30 seconds. Add the onions and mashed beans and stir-fry for 30 seconds. Add the snow peas and cook for 1 minute.

7. Return the chicken to the wok, add the sauce mixture and stir-fry until hot and the sauce has thickened.

8. Serve immediately with short-grain white rice.

VARIATION: Add 2 ounces (60 grams) sliced mushrooms and reduce the amount of snow peas by half.

Western China

Encompassing the cookery of both Szechuan and Hunan provinces, Western Chinese cuisine is distinguished by its spiciness. Favorite seasonings include ginger, vinegar, garlic, sesame oil, green onions and hot chiles. Szechuan recipes usually incorporate chiles in paste form, while Hunan dishes use fresh chiles. Hunan cuisine is typically more sweet and sour than Szechuan cuisine. Both, however, include countless dishes that offer diners several competing spices. After the first fiery sensation passes, these multiple flavors should be recognizable and savored.

Both rice and wheat are grown in western China. Fresh and dried freshwater fish, pork, beef and poultry are common ingredients, as are several types of mushrooms. Often the meats are subjected to several preparations for one dish.

◆◆◆

RECIPE 34.5

JAR GAI
(SZECHUAN-STYLE FRIED CHICKEN)

Yield: 4 Servings

Chicken breasts, boneless, skinless	1 lb.	500 g
Cornstarch	5 Tbsp.	75 ml
Salt	1 tsp.	5 ml
Five spice powder	3/4 tsp.	4 ml
Chicken stock	8 oz.	250 g
Granulated sugar	2 tsp.	10 ml
Light soy sauce	1 Tbsp.	15 ml
Sesame oil	1/2 tsp.	3 ml
Rice wine vinegar	1 tsp.	5 ml
Chinese rice wine	2 tsp.	10 ml
Black pepper, ground	1/4 tsp.	2 ml
Cold water	1 Tbsp.	15 ml
Canola or corn oil	4 oz.	120 g
Red chiles, dried and seeded	15	15
Garlic, chopped fine	2 tsp.	10 ml
Fresh ginger, peeled and chopped fine	2 tsp.	10 ml
Green onions, trimmed and cut into 2-in. (5-cm) lengths	4	4

1. Slice the chicken into thin strips, approximately 1-1/2 inches by 1/4 inch (4 centimeters by .6 centimeters).

2. Combine 4 tablespoons (60 milliliters) of the cornstarch, the salt and 1/2

Continued

In traditional Chinese culture, little separates philosophy, religion and food, and certain rituals are associated with all meals. Meals are also full of symbolism: Braised turtle, for instance, signifies long life; round foods are consumed on holidays dedicated to the full moon.

Just as each dish should provide contrasting flavors and textures, an entire meal should be composed of several complementary and contrasting dishes. A festive Chinese dinner often starts with a cold dish, followed by several hot dishes, then a light soup, usually clear with a few uncooked or undercooked garnishes. Normally, no one hot dish is meant as the main course, and each should offer a different dominant flavor or texture. Rice, noodles or pancakes are served as an accompaniment; tea is the principal beverage and fresh or crystallized fruit constitutes dessert.

American and European eating habits have given rise to a first course of small, usually hot appetizers such as steamed or fried pork dumplings (*chiao-tzu*), steamed yeast-risen wheat buns with various fillings (*bao*) or spring rolls. (Traditionally, all manner of stuffed dumplings and other small dishes, known collectively as *dim sum*—Cantonese for "heart's delight"—are served as a mid-morning meal.) The appetizers are then followed by soup. Fortune cookies are an American invention; moon cakes (*yue bing*), pastries with various sweet fillings made of bean pastes, nuts or fruits surrounding a piece of salted duck egg yolk, are a more traditional sweet served as dessert.

Although the Chinese knew of forks for centuries, they viewed their use at the table as barbaric, preferring the more delicate chopsticks.

teaspoon (3 milliliters) of the five spice powder. Toss the chicken pieces in the mixture; dust off any excess cornstarch.

3. Mix 4 ounces (120 grams) of the stock with the sugar, soy sauce, sesame oil, vinegar, wine, pepper and the remaining five spice powder.

4. In a separate bowl, mix the water and remaining cornstarch.

5. Heat the oil and stir-fry the chicken in small batches.

6. Degrease the pan, reserving 2 tablespoons (30 milliliters) of the oil. Add the chiles, garlic and ginger; stir-fry until the garlic and ginger are golden and the chiles turn dark.

7. Add the green onions and toss for a few seconds. Add the stock mixture and bring to a boil.

8. Thicken the sauce with the remaining cornstarch-and-water mixture.

9. Return the chicken to the pan and toss to heat thoroughly.

10. Serve immediately with short-grain white rice.

Eastern China

Shanghai, a large city on China's east coast, has been the principal point of contact between foreigners and Chinese since the 19th century. Its cuisine reflects this contact. For example, dairy products, which rarely appear in Chinese cuisine, are sometimes used in Eastern Chinese recipes. Similarly, meats are often subjected to slow cooking methods more typical of Europe, such as red-cooking, a form of simmering named for the rich, red-brown sauce that results from cooking the meat in soy sauce. Wine, soy sauces, vinegars (especially an aged vinegar known as Chinkiang) and sugar are the predominant flavorings.

Eastern Chinese cuisine also reflects the fertile area's year-round growing season, many rivers and long shoreline. While most other regional Chinese cuisines incorporate only one or two vegetables in a dish, Shanghai chefs will blend six or more, often cutting them into different shapes.

◆◆◆

RECIPE 34.6

SEE YO GAI (RED-COOKED CHICKEN)

Yield: 4 Servings

Roasting chicken, 3–4 lb. (1.3–1.8 kg)	1	1
Cold water	12 oz.	350 g
Dark soy sauce	12 oz.	350 g
Chinese rice wine	2 oz.	60 g
Fresh ginger, peeled and sliced thin	2 oz.	60 g
Garlic, chopped	1 tsp.	5 ml
Star anise	10	10
Granulated sugar	1-1/2 Tbsp.	23 ml
Sesame oil	2 tsp.	10 ml

1. Place the washed chicken, breast side down, in a lidded saucepan small enough so that the liquid ingredients will cover it completely.

2. Add all other ingredients except the sesame oil and slowly bring to a boil. Reduce the heat and simmer for 15 minutes. Turn the chicken and simmer for 20 minutes, basting the bird every 5 minutes.

3. Remove the pot from the heat and leave covered until cool.*

4. Remove the chicken and brush it with the sesame oil. The chicken can be carved in joints or, in the traditional Chinese manner, split lengthwise and chopped into strips 1-1/2 inches (4 centimeters) wide.

5. Serve the chicken at room temperature* with the leftover sauce for dipping and a noodle dish as an accompaniment.

*Allowing cooked chicken to cool in this manner and then serving it at room temperature is not consistent with sound food-handling procedures; it is, however, an authentic practice.

Japanese Cuisine

As with their arts, the Japanese strive for a cuisine that reflects *sappari*: clarity, lightness, simplicity and order. Small portions of subtly combined ingredients, flavors and textures beautifully presented on dishes that complement the food are its hallmarks.

Rice, both sweet and savory, is the staple of the Japanese diet; indeed, *gohan*, a Japanese word for rice, also refers to a meal. Rice is served steamed, pressed into cakes or made into noodles. Other staples are soybean products

Japanese - (clockwise from top left) sake, white rice, chicken yakitori with dipping sauce, ebi sushi

❖❖❖
A JAPANESE MEAL

The aesthetics of a Japanese meal are of great importance. The aesthetic considerations relate to both the beauty of the food as well as to its presentation. Great care is often taken to cut, carve and form foods into delightful shapes: a carrot slice can be cut like a blossom for spring and a maple leaf in the autumn; a nigiri zushi can be tied with a bow of green onion; a choice morsel of raw fish can be formed into the shape of a rose. Lacquered and porcelain trays, dishes and covered bowls are commonly used for service, and care is taken to make sure the shape, material, size, color and pattern complement the food.

Traditional dinners cooked by highly trained chefs known as *kappo* consist of at least four different courses. They combine liquid, crisp and simmered foods, some spicy and others bland. Alternating consistencies and tastes is a golden rule of Japanese cuisine. Generally tofu and invariably rice are served. Bites of rice are often eaten along with the other foods. Tea and sake are common dinner drinks.

including bean curd (tofu), bean paste (miso), sprouts, seeds and sauce. Japanese cuisine also relies on a variety of noodles, including ones made from wheat (the thin ramen, the thicker somen and the very thick udon), buckwheat (soba) and mung beans.

Fish and shellfish play important roles in Japanese cuisine for two reasons. First, Japan is a nation of mountainous islands that depends on the sea as the source for much of its protein. And, second, until the 19th century much of the Japanese population followed Buddhist teachings that prescribed a vegetarian diet supplemented with fish and shellfish. During this century, however, there has been a marked increase in the consumption of meat (especially beef) and poultry (especially chicken).

Typical seasonings—used, for the most part, quite judiciously—include rice wine vinegar, wasabi (a pungent green root erroneously called green horseradish), daikon (a white radish), pepper, sesame oil and seeds, ginger, soy sauce (known as *shoyu*, generally lighter and more delicate than Chinese soy sauce), rice wine (mirin, which is light and sweet and used only for cooking, and sake, a finer product used for cooking and drinking), tamari sauce, seaweed and pressed algae products (from the delicate to the very fishy), dried fish and shellfish and a variety of pickled foods (collectively known as *zuke*) as well as fresh herbs. Many dishes are marinated before cooking.

Yakitori, a classic Japanese flavoring combination of soy sauce, rice wine and sugar, is often used for broiled or grilled dishes.

❖❖❖
RECIPE 34.7
CHICKEN YAKITORI

Yield: 8 Servings

Soy sauce	8 oz.	250 g
Sake	8 oz.	250 g
Granulated sugar	2 oz.	60 g
Chicken breasts, boneless	2 lb.	1 kg
Cornstarch	1 Tbsp.	15 ml
Sesame seeds	1 Tbsp.	15 ml

1. Combine the soy sauce, sake and sugar. Reserve 8 ounces (250 grams) of the mixture.

2. Brush the chicken with a portion of the reserved soy sauce mixture and grill over hot charcoal until done, basting regularly.

3. To make the sauce, combine 2 ounces (60 grams) of the soy sauce mixture with the cornstarch. Bring the remainder to a boil in a small saucepan and stir in the cornstarch slurry. Stirring constantly, continue boiling until the sauce thickens. Simmer 1 minute.

4. Serve with short-grain white rice and garnish with sesame seeds.

Japanese cooking generally relies on quick cooking of bite-sized pieces of food. Foods can be grilled (called *yakimono;* if done tableside, as is typical, they are referred to as *nabemon*), steamed (*mushimono*), simmered in an aromatic broth (these liquid-based dishes often start with *dashi,* a fish-flavored stock made from kelp and bonito; the cooking process is referred to as *nimono*) or deep-fried (*agemono*). The deep-frying technique and batter

◆◆◆

ASIAN FLAVORS
IN AN AMERICAN KITCHEN

Asian flavors now play an increasingly important role in Western food preparations. Whether called "East-West," "Pan-Asian," or "Pacific Style" food, this type of cooking ranges from ideas as simple as swirling butter into a classic Chinese black-bean sauce for a more velvet texture to drizzling an Asian sauce across the top of barbecued salmon to brushing butter infused with ginger, garlic, and cilantro on sourdough baguettes.

Several trends have led to this merging of cuisines. During the late 1960s the environmental movement and the rising popularity of health foods caused many Americans to reevaluate their diet and move away from meals based heavily on fats, sugar, and starches. Within a few years, starting in the 1970s, the growing interest in a healthier diet resulted in a new type of French cooking, *nouvelle cuisine*, which included experimentation with Asian seasonings. At about the same time, Richard Nixon's 1972 trip to China caused an enormous surge in the popularity of Chinese food in America. Chinese and other Asian seasonings became commonplace in supermarkets.

While many of us were traveling through Asia, fascinated with these new flavors, a huge Asian emigration to America began. Thai, Vietnamese, Korean, Japanese, and Filipino restaurants now proliferate. The new dishes offered in these restaurants, the "exotic" condiments and fresh herbs available in local Asian markets, and a flood of Asian cookbooks reinforce this ongoing trend. Examples of Asian and Pacific Style food appear on the menus of many of America's top young chefs. The fresh tastes of the Pacific are becoming a common part of contemporary cuisine.

—*from CHOPSTIX by* HUGH CARPENTER

known as tempura are actually derived from cooking techniques and recipes Portuguese Jesuits introduced to the Japanese during the late 16th century.

Japanese cuisine also offers a variety of raw foods, collectively known as *namamono*. Sashimi, small slices of fresh fish served with a soy sauce spiked with mustard and wasabi, is popular; as are *nigiri zushi* (small balls of sushi—vinegar-flavored rice—topped with a slice of raw fish or shellfish) and *maki zushi* (raw fish or shellfish rolled in sushi and crisp seaweed). Recipes and techniques for these are given in Chapter 33, Hors d'Oeuvres and Appetizers.

INDIAN CUISINES

Indian cuisine offers more than curry. The Indian subcontinent is home to many peoples, including Hindus, Buddhists and Muslims; each has a distinctive cuisine, and each cuisine has influenced the others, giving rise to several regional cuisines. Kasmir in the far north is famous for its meat and chickpeas, while the northern areas of Delhi and Bengal are famous for their tandoori and intensely sweet desserts, respectively. The western seaport of Bombay is known for its pork and vinegar, while vegetarian dishes made with tamarind, semolina and coconut are popular in the southern seaport of Madras.

The heart of Indian cookery is the masala, the combination of spices that gives each dish its distinctive taste. A masala's preparation, subtlety and sophistication are the tests by which chefs are often judged. The timing of its incorporation into the dish is critical. Common spices for masalas are turmeric, cumin seeds, coriander seeds, fenugreek, saffron, fennel seeds, mace, nutmeg, cardamom, clove, cinnamon, mustard seeds, sesame seeds, and black, red and white peppercorns. Garlic, onions and chiles are also popular flavorings, as are several herbs including coriander leaves, mint leaves and sweet basil. Souring agents include vinegar, lemon juice and imli (water with extract of tamarind). Curry powder is really nothing more than a commercial masala typically containing fenugreek, coriander, cumin, turmeric, ginger, celery seeds,

◆◆◆

When discussing foreign—that is, not French—foods, Escoffier opined that "if only for the sake of novelty or variety, it is occasionally permissible to poach upon the preserves of foreign nations."

Indian - (clockwise from top) naan, chicken tandoor, mango chutney, saffron rice

mace and pepper. The word *curry* is probably derived from the Tamil word *kari*, meaning sauce or combination of seasonings; the product is considered an inferior British invention never used in true Indian cooking.

◆◆◆

RECIPE 34.8

MASALA

Yield: 3 oz. (90 g)

Coriander seeds	4 Tbsp.	60 ml
Cumin seeds	2 Tbsp.	30 ml
Black peppercorns, whole	1 Tbsp.	15 ml
Cardamom seeds (measure after removing pods)	2 tsp.	10 ml
Cinnamon sticks, 3 in. (7.5 cm) long	4	4
Cloves, whole	1 tsp.	5 ml
Nutmeg, whole	1	1

1. In a small saucepan, separately dry-roast the coriander seeds, cumin seeds, peppercorns, cardamom seeds, cinnamon and cloves. As each begins to smell fragrant, remove from the pan to cool. After dry-roasting the cardamom, peel it, remove the seeds and discard the pods.
2. With a mortar and pestle or spice grinder, blend all the roasted spices to a fine powder.
3. Finely grate the nutmeg and mix it in with the other spices.
4. Store tightly covered and away from light.

The staples of Indian cuisine are rice, dals and bread. The rice is usually long-grain and served steamed and mixed with flavorings and garnishes. For special occasions, aromatic rices such as basmati are eaten. Dals are pulses such as lentils, beans and peas; nearly 60 varieties of protein-rich pulses are used in Indian cookery. These include the small, sweet yellow *chana dal, moong dal* (mung beans) and the salmon-colored split pea called *masoor dal.* Breads, called *roti,* include *capitis* (flat, unleavened rounds made of whole wheat flour), *naan* (one of the few leavened breads), *paratha* (a flaky bread fried on a pan called a *tava*) and *poori* (a deep-fried puffy bread). Many pan-fried breads are stuffed with savory mixtures or dusted with flavorings. Rice and lentil flours are also used for breads.

Devout Muslims do not eat pork; devout Hindus do not eat beef and devout Buddhists do not eat any meat, poultry, fish, shellfish or dairy product.

For those who do eat meat and poultry, the most commonly eaten are mutton and chicken, prepared in a variety of ways: stewed with spices; marinated and grilled; braised in yogurt or cream (called *kormas*); sautéed and baked (called *bhoona*) or formed into meatballs (called *koftas*). A wide variety of freshwater and saltwater fish and shellfish are also consumed. Dairy products include a mild white fresh cheese known as *paneer.*

The long tradition of vegetarianism and the variety of vegetables and spices available have made for a vegetarian cuisine rich in flavors and textures. Vegetables are usually fried with spices and served without any sauce. These pungent dishes are known as *foogath* in the South and *bhujia* in the North. Vegetables can be puréed and delicately spiced (called *bharta*); or mashed, shaped into balls and fried.

Chutneys are relishes made from fruits, vegetables and herbs. Sometimes their flavors are tempered by marinating or cooking, although most fresh chutneys are nothing more than a mixture of raw foods, ground or finely cut and blended with seasonings. Chutneys are used to add contrast to the highly spiced dishes that dominate Indian cuisines.

Clarified butter made from water buffalo milk, known as *ghee*, is an important cooking medium, although ghee's expense has made a hydrogenated vegetable fat called *vanaspati* more popular. Usually, only meat is cooked in ghee; vegetable oils are used for vegetables.

The *degchi* is a commonly used cooking vessel. Traditionally made of brass but now also made of aluminum, it is a tall, straight-sided, flat-rimmed pot used for boiling, stewing, braising or steaming. When lidded, it can be used as an oven by placing coals below the pot as well as on the lid.

Northern India

The cuisine of Northern India reflects the strong Muslim presence found in northern and central India since the 16th-century Mogul invasions. This presence has given rise to a regional cuisine using meat. The area's geography favors wheat, not rice, so capitis is a dietary staple. Generally, Northern Indian cuisine produces dryer foods with thick sauces. A typical Northern masala calls for cumin, fenugreek, ginger and garlic. After the spices are ground and mixed, they are added to the dish without further preparation.

One of the best-known Northern Indian dishes is tandoori chicken. The tandoor is a jar-shaped clay oven usually buried in the earth and heated by placing hot coals inside. The meat or poultry is threaded on skewers and placed inside the oven to cook. The finished product has a wonderfully dry, crusty surface. Although it is difficult to reproduce the surface in a conventional oven, it is possible to reproduce the flavors.

♦♦♦

RECIPE 34.9

TANDOORI MURGH (CHICKEN TANDOOR)

Yield: 4 Servings

Roasting chicken, 3 lb. (1.3 kg)	1	1
Saffron strands	1/2 tsp.	3 ml
Boiling water	1 Tbsp.	15 ml
Garlic, chopped	2 Tbsp.	30 ml
Fresh ginger, peeled and minced	1 Tbsp.	15 ml
Lemon juice	2 Tbsp.	30 ml
Chilli powder	1 tsp.	5 ml
Paprika	1-1/2 tsp.	8 ml
Masala (Recipe 34.8)	2 tsp.	10 ml
Salt	1 tsp.	5 ml
Ghee (or clarified butter or canola oil)	3 Tbsp.	45 ml
Lemons, wedged	2	2

1. Quarter and skin the chicken, making slits in the drumsticks, thighs and breasts to allow the spices to penetrate.
2. Steep the saffron in boiling water for 10 minutes. Then combine it with the garlic, ginger, lemon juice, chilli powder, paprika, masala and salt; blend until smooth.
3. Season the chicken with the spice mixture, covering the entire surface, especially the slits. Cover and marinate, under refrigeration, for at least two hours or overnight.
4. Roast the chicken on a rack at 350°F (180°C), basting periodically with ghee, until done, approximately 45 minutes.
5. Serve hot, garnished with lemon wedges and accompanied by naan.

Southern India

The cuisine of Southern India is heavily influenced by Hindus. It offers a wide range of meatless dishes with rich, spicy sauces. Rice is the principal crop and it is eaten with almost every meal, as plain or flavored rice or as rice-flour breads such as *idli* and *dosa*. Southern Indian cuisine uses more fresh herbs than Northern Indian cuisine and its masalas are wet; that is, the ground spices are mixed into a paste with vinegar, water or coconut milk. (Wet masalas must be used immediately.) Typical spices used in Southern Indian masalas include mustard seed, tamarind and asafetida (a fennel-like resin). Chiles are more popular in the south than in the north, as is garlic.

♦♦♦

RECIPE 34.10

MURGHI KARI (CHICKEN CURRY)

Yield: 4 Servings

Onions, small dice	8 oz.	250 g
Garlic, crushed	2 tsp.	10 ml

Ghee (or clarified butter)	2 Tbsp.	30 ml
Fresh ginger, fine dice	2 oz.	60 g
Turmeric	1-1/2 tsp.	8 ml
Coriander seeds, ground	1-1/2 tsp.	8 ml
Cumin seeds, ground	1 tsp.	5 ml
Cayenne pepper	1 tsp.	5 ml
Fenugreek, ground	1/2 tsp.	3 ml
Coconut milk	20 oz.	575 g
Roasting chicken, 3 lb.		
(1.3 kg), cut into 8 pieces	1	1
Salt	1 tsp.	5 ml
Green chiles, slit lengthwise	3	3
Lemon juice	1 oz.	30 ml

1. Stir-fry the onions and garlic in the ghee until the onions are golden brown.
2. To make the wet masala, mix the ginger, turmeric, coriander, cumin, cayenne pepper and fenugreek; add just enough of the coconut milk to form a paste.
3. Add the wet masala to the onions and stir-fry for 8 minutes.
4. Add the chicken pieces and cook, turning them frequently, for 6–8 minutes.
5. Add the remaining coconut milk, salt and chiles. Bring to a boil, cover and reduce to a simmer. Cook until the chicken is done, approximately 45 minutes.
6. Just before service, stir in the lemon juice and adjust the seasonings. Serve with saffron rice and a chutney.

◆◆◆

RECIPE 34.11

KESAR CHAVAL (SAFFRON RICE)

Yield: 6 Servings

Basmati rice	1 pt.	450 ml
Saffron threads	1 tsp.	5 ml
Boiling water	1 qt.	900 ml
Ghee (or clarified butter)	3 oz.	90 g
Cinnamon sticks, 2 in. (5 cm) long	1	1
Cloves, whole	4	4
Onion, fine dice	5 oz.	150 g
Dark brown sugar	1 Tbsp.	15 ml
Salt	2 tsp.	10 ml
Cardamom seeds	1/4 tsp.	2 ml

1. Wash the rice and drain thoroughly.
2. Steep the saffron in 2 ounces (60 grams) of the boiling water.
3. In a saucepan, heat the ghee, add the cinnamon and cloves. Add the onions and stir-fry until they are soft and slightly brown.
4. Add the rice and stir until it is well coated with the ghee and the grains are a light golden color.

Continued

5. Stirring constantly, add the remaining boiling water, brown sugar, salt and cardamom seeds. Bring to a boil and reduce to a simmer.

6. Gently stir in the saffron and its water, cover and simmer until the rice has absorbed all the liquid.

7. Fluff with a fork and serve at once.

Throughout India, many foods are eaten in the form of savory snacks (collectively known as *chat*) which are served as appetizers or at teatime. Examples include *chanachur* (made from split peas, peanuts, lemon, peppers and lentil flour, all the ingredients being fried separately), *samosas* (deep-fried tidbits like turnovers, stuffed with meat, potatoes or vegetables), *pakoras* (vegetables or other foods dipped in chickpea flour and deep-fried), spiced fish balls and eggplant fritters served with chutney.

Sweet snacks (collectively known as *meethai*) are also an integral part of Indian cuisines. Many are made from milk that is condensed into a thick mass called *mawa*. *Mawa* is then cooked with sugar and flavorings such as coconut, almond, pistachio or kewra (a perfumed flower essence). *Jelebis* are pretzel-like sweets made from a batter of wheat and chickpea flour, oil and curds that is deep-fried and then dipped into a sugar syrup.

NORTH AFRICAN AND MIDDLE EASTERN CUISINES

Stretching from Morocco at the northwest tip of Africa, along the southern and eastern portions of the Mediterranean Sea and north to Lebanon, is a land primarily populated by Arabs. It is rich in religious and culinary traditions and offers a range of national cuisines. These various cuisines can be divided into two main groups: North African and Middle Eastern.

All of the cuisines, however, share certain staples, seasonings and a fondness for sweets. Wheat in various forms is eaten throughout the area. Legumes, including lentils, beans and peas, provide starch. Pork is virtually nonexistent for religious reasons; lamb is the principal meat, chicken the principal poultry. Fish from the Mediterranean is also popular. Garlic, onions, peppers, tomatoes and citrus are commonly used flavoring ingredients. Spices include cumin, ginger and peppercorns; herbs include mint, coriander and parsley. Eggplants, cucumbers, squash, okra, tomatoes, quinces, dates, figs, melons, pomegranates, mangoes and bananas are popular. A consistent theme among the various cuisines is a combination of fruits and nuts cooked with savory meat dishes.

North African

The cuisines of North Africa include those of Morocco, Algeria and Tunisia as well as those of the more nomadic Bedouin tribes. This area, often referred to as the Maghreb, was once the granary for Imperial Rome. More recently, France was the dominant foreign influence. North African cuisine is based on cereals, vegetables, dried fruits and grilled meats. The national cuisines differ to a degree: Foods are more highly seasoned in Algeria and Tunisia and more subtly spiced in Morocco.

A principal spice mixture (known as *ras al hanout* in Morocco) consists of cinnamon, cumin, coriander, ginger and turmeric. Other North African season-

Middle Eastern - (clockwise from top left) baklava, medjool dates, pita bread, harissa, Tangier couscous

ings and flavoring ingredients include garlic, onions, tomatoes, olives, fresh coriander leaves, fresh mint leaves, parsley and dried limes or lemons.

Many North African meat dishes include fruit or other sweet foods. For example, *tajine*, a type of slow-cooked ragout, may be made with mutton or rabbit with prunes and accompanied by fennel with lemon; chicken is cooked with cinnamon, kumquats and onions, and mutton is cooked with quinces and honey. Meats, often reduced to bite-sized chunks or ground balls, are often grilled or spit-roasted as kebabs. Fish can be grilled or fried. Vegetables are cooked in a sauce and frequently served with scrambled eggs, marinated and served in a salad or stuffed with sweet and savory foods. Soups are always highly aromatic and often associated with religious festivities. The soups often combine dried vegetables or cereals (lentils, beans, chickpeas, unripe wheat) with meat (diced mutton or chicken) or fish.

Wheat is the principal grain and it is used to make one of the better-known North African dishes: couscous. Couscous refers to both the starch and the completed dish. The starch is made of semolina flour produced from hard durum wheat. It is steamed over a watery stew of lamb, chicken, beef (usually in the form of meatballs), fish or tripe and vegetables in a couscousier. A couscousier consists of two bulbous pots. The bottom one sits on the heat and holds the watery stew. The second sits on top of the first; it has a perforated bottom and holds the couscous. As the stew simmers, steam rising from it gently cooks the couscous and infuses flavors. The dish can be flavored with saffron (Morocco), tomato purée (Algeria) or ginger and pepper (Tunisia). Traditionally mixed with smeun fat, a sort of rancid butter, the couscous and stew are more typically served with harissa, a hot and pungent

◆◆◆
A MOROCCAN MEAL

A classic Moroccan meal starts with a *b'stilla* (a semolina dough pie stuffed with layers of ground pigeon meat, spices and sugar and then deep-fried) followed by a couscous. Dessert would be a sweet pudding such as one made with raisins, almonds and currants cooked in milk and thickened with semolina, *rghaifs* (pancakes fried in butter and topped with honey or stuffed with almonds) or *criouch* (cakes covered with honey and sesame seeds). Minted tea (which is far more mint than tea) is a typical beverage.

sauce (see Recipe 11.14). Couscous is eaten by taking a small amount of the couscous along with a morsel of meat or vegetable, rolling it into a ball and popping it into the mouth. This entire action should be accomplished with only the first three fingers of the right hand.

◆◆◆

RECIPE 34.12
SEKSU TANJAOUI (TANGIER COUSCOUS)

Yield: 4 Servings

Roaster chicken, quartered with giblets, 3–4 lb. (1.3–1.8 kg)	1	1
Salt	2 tsp.	10 ml
Pepper	1 Tbsp.	15 ml
Ginger, ground	2-1/2 tsp.	12 ml
Saffron, pulverized and mixed with turmeric	1/2 tsp.	3 ml
Cayenne pepper	pinch	pinch
Onions, medium, quartered	3	3
Bouquet garni:		
Fresh coriander	4 sprigs	4 sprigs
Fresh parsley	4 sprigs	4 sprigs
Whole butter	8 oz.	250 g
Water	5 pt.	2.5 lt
Couscous	1 lb. 8 oz.	700 g
Onion, large, julienne	1	1
Raisins	3 oz.	90 g
Chicken stock	as needed	as needed

1. Place the chicken, salt, pepper, ginger, saffron, cayenne, onion quarters, bouquet garni and half the butter in the bottom of the couscousier. Melt the butter and stir the ingredients to coat them with the melted butter. Add 5 pints (2.5 liters) of water; bring to a boil, reduce to a simmer and cook 1 hour.

2. Combine the couscous with 3 quarts (3 liters) cold water; mix and drain. Gently break apart any lumps.

3. After the stew has simmered for 1 hour, place the couscous in the top pot or a metal colander suspended over the pot, lower the heat and steam for 20 minutes. Do not cover the couscous while it steams.

4. Remove the colander and add the sliced onions and raisins to the stew; adjust its consistency with water or chicken stock if necessary. Replace the colander and steam for 15 minutes. Dot the couscous with the remaining butter and steam for 5 minutes. Fluff the couscous with a fork to distribute the melted butter.

5. Serve the couscous with the stew and Harissa, Recipe 11.14.

Middle Eastern

The cuisines of the Middle East include those of Egypt, Jordan, Syria and Lebanon. This is the southern portion of the Levant, an area that stretches from Egypt through Israel, north to Turkey and east through Greece. Now predominantly Arab, the area has been ruled by the Egyptians, Romans, Turks, British and French, to name a few. Each nationality has left its mark.

Generally, rice and wheat (wheat for bread flour and bulgur) are the principal staples, as are legumes, especially chickpeas. Chickpeas are used in many dishes, most notably *hummus*, in which they are mashed with sesame seed paste, and *ful medames*, an ancient Egyptian dish in which the beans are flavored with garlic and dressed with lemon juice and oil. Important spices include cinnamon, cumin, ginger, coriander, allspice and hot peppers, as well as some more unusual spices such as *mahlab* (ground black-cherry pits, which gives food a slightly fruity flavor), *zatar* (a variety of thyme that tastes like a cross between thyme and oregano) and *sumac* (which gives meats a woody taste). Dried whole limes and verjuice are also used for flavorings.

Yogurt is used as a beverage, pudding and flavoring ingredient. Olive oil is a typical cooking medium as well as a dressing and a basic ingredient in many of the vegetable dishes called *yakhni*. Sesame seed oil is also used, especially in Lebanese dishes. Tahini is a popular paste made from crushed sesame seeds. Produce of importance includes garlic, okra, cucumbers, eggplants and lemons as well as tomatoes and peppers (New World imports).

Several varieties of freshwater and saltwater fish are enjoyed grilled, baked or poached. Little beef is consumed, although camel is eaten (hump meat is the choicest). Lamb, however, dominates Middle Eastern cuisine. It can be grilled, roasted, braised, stewed with vegetables or made into a variety of meatballs (called *kofta*) and kebabs. It is also the basic ingredient in the Lebanese and Syrian dish known as *kibbeh*. For kibbeh, ground lamb is mixed with onion-flavored bulgur, parsley and pine nuts. It is then shaped into cakes and grilled, deep-fried or baked, or stuffed with savory ingredients and deep-fried. Chicken is also popular, whether spit-roasted, marinated in oil and citrus or stuffed with rice and pine nuts and baked in an earthenware casserole.

◆◆◆

RECIPE 34.13

DAJAJ MAHSHY
(CHICKEN STUFFED WITH RICE, CURRANTS AND PINE NUTS)

Yield: 4 Servings

Long-grain white rice	1 c.	250 ml
Whole butter	4 oz.	120 g
Onions, fine dice	3 oz.	90 g
Pine nuts	3 Tbsp.	45 ml
Water	1 pt.	500 ml
Dried currants	2 Tbsp.	30 ml
Salt	2 Tbsp.	30 ml
Pepper	TT	TT
Fryer chicken, 3 to 3-1/2 lb. (1.3 to 1.5 kg), including coarsely chopped giblets	1	1
Yogurt	2 oz.	60 g

1. Wash the rice and set aside.
2. Sauté the onions in the butter until transparent.
3. Add the coarsely chopped giblets and pine nuts and sauté until the pine nuts are browned.

Continued

4. Stir in the rice and cook until the grains are coated with butter.
5. Add the water, currants, 1 tablespoon (15 milliliters) of the salt and pepper to taste; cover and cook until the rice is done.
6. Remove from the heat and mix in the remaining butter.
7. Stuff the chicken's cavity with the rice mixture and truss.
8. Season the yogurt with the remaining salt and pepper. Brush half of the mixture over the chicken. Roast the chicken at 350°F (180°C), basting periodically with the yogurt mixture until done, approximately 1 hour.
9. Carve the chicken and serve it with the rice.

Middle Eastern sweets are very sweet; they include *ataif* (pancakes drenched with syrup and topped with chopped nuts and thick clotted cream), *muhallabia* (a milk pudding flavored with orange flower water) and *ma'amoul* (pastries stuffed with dates or nuts and coated with powdered sugar or served in cream) as well as the more familiar halva, candied dates, baklava and Turkish delight.

MEXICAN CUISINE

Mexican cuisine is rooted in its pre-Columbian past and nurtured by centuries of Spanish influence. For thousands of years before Columbus's arrival, the people of Mexico lived on a diet of squash, corn (maize) and beans supplemented with fresh vegetables (avocados, peppers, tomatoes), fruit (manioc and bananas) and occasionally fish, shellfish, game and wild poultry. The population relied on steaming and slow cooking methods such as wrapping meats, poultry and fish in leaves and slow-roasting them over hot embers or stewing foods with little liquid in tightly lidded earthenware pots.

In the wake of Hernan Cortes's conquest of Mexico in 1521 came pigs, cattle and dairy products, chicken, wheat, rice, sesame seeds, citrus and almonds. The Spanish also brought with them a new manner of cooking: rendering fat from meat and using the rendered fat and vegetable oils to fry foods. All of these foods, to one degree or another, were soon integrated into the local cuisines; sautéing and pan-frying became standard cooking methods. (Although the people of Mexico quickly adopted European foods and cooking methods, Europeans waited centuries before adopting Mexican foods and appreciating Mexican cuisine.)

Mexico has given rise to several regional cuisines of note. Unfortunately, many consumers in this country erroneously believe that Mexican cuisine starts and ends with tacos and refried beans.

The most characteristic feature of Mexican cookery is the widespread use of chiles. There are about 100 varieties, many of which have a hot, pungent taste. (Unlike English, Mexican Spanish differentiates between the word *hot* as applied to a food's temperature—*caliente*—and *hot* as applied to its degree of spiciness—*chiloso*.) Fresh chiles can be served raw; stuffed and baked; stewed; chopped with tomatoes, herbs and oil for a salsa; or minced and used as a seasoning. Or they can be dried and used whole or ground as a seasoning. Other seasonings include garlic, cinnamon, cumin, oregano, onion, achiote seeds, basil, peppercorns, cilantro and other fresh herbs.

Fresh vegetable salsas accompany many dishes. Guacamole, for example, is an ancient dish made from avocados and flavorings such as onions and tomatoes. The numerous fresh salsas are usually categorized as either red or green. Red salsa, called *salsa roja*, is made from chiles (usually dried), onions

Mexican - (clockwise from top left) poblano rice, poblano chili, coconut candies, chicken mole on corn tortillas, hybiscus water

and tomato. Green salsa, called *salsa verde*, is made from chiles (usually fresh), onions and tomatillos.

Corn flour is used to make a dough called *masa*. Popular throughout Mexico, smooth masa is pressed (traditionally by hand) into flat rounds and quickly cooked on a griddle to make tortillas. Tortillas are eaten like bread, filled with savory mixtures for burritos, fried crisp and topped for tostadas, folded around savory mixtures and fried for tacos, or used for turnovers (quesadillas, empanadas and enchiladas). Tamales are made from a coarser masa dough that is stuffed with a savory mixture of beans, meats or poultry, encased in corn husks and steamed. Many of these masa-based dishes are considered snack foods known as *antojitos*, the traditional portable snacks of the Mexican marketplace.

Wheat flour is also used for tortillas (especially in north Mexico) as well as for a variety of leavened breads. Rice, although not indigenous, is also a staple of Mexican diets.

As they were during pre-Columbian times, beans are still a staple. They are usually dried, then reconstituted in water and served in a soupy fashion, or mashed and fried in lard or oil to make a smooth paste called *frijoles refritos* (refried beans).

Chicken is popular throughout the country. Meat is used somewhat sparingly in most Mexican regional cuisines. Beef and dairy products are more widely consumed in the north, while goat and goat cheese are more typical of the country's central regions. Fish and shellfish are eaten along both coasts.

The ancient manner of slow cooking is still used for meats, poultry and fish; there is a great variety of stews and soups. The ancient cooking method known as *pibil*, in which meats were wrapped in maguey or banana leaves and cooked in a pit lined with hot coals, is often replaced today by steaming banana-leaf wrapped meats. Some meats and vegetables are also grilled (called *al carbon*) or seared and roasted. A popular meat marinade known as *adobado* combines chiles, garlic and herbs.

Sauce making is very different from European traditions and includes a step known as "frying the sauce." Most sauces start with dried peppers that are soaked, seeded and ground to a paste and then mixed with herbs, spices and vegetables. The mixture, sometimes thickened with ground toasted pumpkin seeds or nuts, is then puréed and fried in oil or lard. This sauce is added to partially cooked and drained meat or poultry and the dish is then simmered to blend the flavors.

Moles are dishes made with a classic cooking method that incorporates this sauce-making technique. The meat or poultry is cooked and then steeped or simmered in a sauce made from chiles and other ingredients.

♦♦♦

RECIPE 34.14
MOLE ROJO CON POLLO
(RICH RED MOLE WITH CHICKEN)

Yield: 4 Servings

Chiles, dried, stemmed, seeded and deveined:		
Chiles anchos	2 oz.	60 g
Chiles mulatos	1 oz.	30 g
Chiles pasilla	1/3 oz.	10 g
Vegetable oil	3 oz.	90 g
Tomato, medium, roasted, cored, peeled and diced	1	1
Medium tomatillos, husked, washed and simmered until tender	3	3
Mexican chocolate, chopped	1 oz.	30 g
Oregano, dried	1/2 tsp.	3 ml
Thyme, dried	1/4 tsp.	2 ml
Bay leaf	1	1
Peppercorns	8	8
Cloves	3	3
Cinnamon stick	1 in.	2.5 cm
Sesame seeds	2 Tbsp.	30 ml
Raisins	2 Tbsp.	30 ml
Garlic, chopped	1 tsp.	5 ml
Onion, thickly sliced	2 oz.	60 g
Peanuts	1 oz.	30 g
Plantain, small, peeled and diced (optional)	4 oz.	120 g
Corn tortilla, stale	1/2	1/2
White bread slice, stale	1	1
Chicken stock	1 qt.	900 ml
Chicken, 3-1/2 lb. (1.6 kg), quartered	1	1
Salt	1 tsp.	5 ml
Granulated sugar	1 Tbsp.	15 ml

1. Sauté the chiles in 3 tablespoons (45 milliliters) of oil until nutty brown.

Remove, reserving the oil. Cover the chiles with boiling water and soak for 1 hour. Drain and set aside.

2. Combine the tomatoes, tomatillos, chocolate, oregano and thyme in a large bowl. Pulverize the bay leaf, peppercorns, cloves and cinnamon and combine with the tomato mixture.

3. Toast the sesame seeds and add them to the tomato mixture.

4. Sauté the raisins in the reserved chili oil until they puff; add them to the tomato mixture.

5. In the same oil, sauté the garlic, onion and peanuts until they are well browned; add to the tomato mixture.

6. Sauté the plantain until golden brown; add to the tomato mixture.

7. Sauté the tortilla until brown; shred it and add to the tomato mixture.

8. Lay the bread in the pan and quickly flip it to coat both sides with the fat; then brown it on both sides. Tear it into pieces and add to the tomato mixture.

9. Stir the tomato mixture well. Purée it with 6 ounces (180 grams) of chicken stock and strain through a china cap.

10. Purée the reconstituted chiles with 2 ounces (60 grams) of chicken stock; strain through a china cap in a separate bowl and set aside.

11. Sauté the chicken in oil. Remove and degrease the pan. In the same pan, sauté the chile purée until it is thick and dark. Add the tomato purée and cook until thick.

12. Add 1-1/2 pints (700 milliliters) of chicken stock. Simmer the sauce 45 minutes. Season with salt and sugar. If the sauce is thicker than heavy cream, dilute it with additional chicken stock.

13. Add the chicken to the pan and braise until done.

14. Degrease the sauce. Garnish the chicken with sesame seeds and serve with the sauce and Arroz a la Poblana.

❖❖❖

RECIPE 34.15

ARROZ A LA POBLANA
(RICE WITH POBLANO CHILES)

Yield: 4 Servings

Vegetable oil	1-1/2 Tbsp.	23 ml
Onion, small dice	5 oz.	150 g
Long- or medium-grain rice	1 c.	250 ml
Chicken stock, hot	14 oz.	400 g
Salt	TT	TT
Chiles poblanos, fresh, roasted and peeled, seeded, julienne	3	3
Fresh corn kernels	6 oz.	180 g
Mexican queso fresco (or feta or farmers cheese), crumbled	5 oz.	150 g
Parsley or cilantro sprigs	as needed	as needed

1. Sauté the onion in oil until translucent. Add the rice and sauté without coloring.

Continued

A MEXICAN MEAL

A typical Mexican meal may start with a hearty soup such as *pozole rojo* (pork and hominy soup with red chile and fresh garnishes) followed by a meat-and-sauce dish served with beans, rice and tortillas. Dessert would be flan. Popular beverages include *horchata* (cinnamon-infused milk with ground rice), *agua de jamaica* (usually served before a meal; a sweetened, hibiscus-flower-infused water), *agua de tamarindo* (a sweetened, tamarind-infused water) and *cerveza* (beer).

2. Add the hot stock, salt, chiles and corn to the rice mixture; bring to a boil, reduce to a simmer, cover and cook until all liquid has evaporated.

3. Add the crumbled cheese to the rice and toss to combine.

4. Serve as a side dish garnished with parsley or cilantro sprigs.

Sweets, especially candies, candied fruits and hard cookies or cakes, are popular throughout Mexico. The more commonly encountered deserts such as flans and caramels are derived from the Spanish tradition.

Mexico is a country rich in regional cuisines. A few observations about them follow.

Central (Mexico City)

Blended with tomatoes, the fiery hot *guajillos* or smoky *chipotles* are the principal chiles used for sauces. Also popular are the common black chile and the *pasilla*. A great variety of beans are used, but the purplish *flor de mayo* and the tan *bayo* are the most popular. Cooking methods include mole. A typical meat dish would be lamb wrapped in maguey or banana leaves cooked in brick pits and served with a sauce of fermented maguey juice and pasilla.

West Central (Guadalajara)

The defining sauce is made with a purée of the very hot *de arbol* chiles, sometimes thickened with tomatillos. De arbol also come bottled, pickled with vinegar. A great variety of beans are used, but as with Central Mexican cuisine, flor de mayo and bayo are the most popular. A typical meat dish would be kid (young goat) marinated in chiles and slow-cooked in a sealed container. From the west coast also comes seviche, a dish of finely chopped fish and shellfish marinated in lime juice, cilantro, tomato chunks and herbs.

Central East Coast (Veracruz)

Although still used in abundance, chiles play a less prominent role. Herbs (especially cilantro, basil, bay leaves, parsley and oregano) and spices (peppercorns and cinnamon) are a vital part of the cuisine. The area is known for its fish and shellfish cooked in a chunky broth of olives, herbs and chiles (usually jalapeños). The basic bean is black and usually cooked with a sprig of epazote.

Northern (Sonora, Chihuahua)

As in West Central Mexico, the defining sauce is made with a purée of the very hot de arbol chiles, sometimes thickened with tomatillos. This region is known for its wheat and beef, which is sometimes dried and called *carne seca*. A typical pork dish is the simmered *carne con chile colorado*. Popular beans are pintos and the yellowish-tan *piruano*.

Southeastern (Yucatan)

This regional cuisine is unique, using achiote seeds as the principal seasoning. Fresh chiles are usually ground with salt and lime or purchased in a bottled form. A vinegary orange-red and a green sauce made with the local *habañero* chiles are especially popular. Seasonings are added to most dishes in the form of a paste that can be brick red (made from achiote seeds ground with oregano, black pepper, cloves and cumin mixed with garlic and vinegar), olive-amber (a mild blend of garlic, allspice, cinnamon and other spices) or coal black (made from burnt chiles, achiote, spices and garlic). A typical pork dish is flavored with achiote and wrapped in banana leaves, then slowly steamed or roasted. The most commonly used bean is black and usually cooked with a sprig of epazote.

Southern (Oaxaca)

A wide range of dried peppers are used in many different stews and sauces, some of which combine sweeter spices such as cloves and cinnamon with savory foods. A typical meat or poultry dish would be kid or chicken marinated in chiles, then wrapped in avocado leaves and steamed. Some consider this region to produce the finest *chorizo*, a pork sausage made with herbs, spices, a touch of vinegar and deep red chiles. The basic black bean is also regularly used throughout the south.

CONCLUSION

Although the foods and flavorings may differ from the cuisine of one culture to the cuisine of another, the fundamentals of cookery do not: Quality ingredients need to be prepared, seasoned and cooked, then presented in an attractive and appropriate manner. With a good purveyor, a little practice and an understanding of the principles discussed throughout this book, a world of great cooking and eating is available to you and your customers.

QUESTIONS FOR DISCUSSION

1. Which of the cuisines discussed rely on slow-cooking methods for meats? Which rely on quick-cooking methods?
2. Identify the flavor principle for each of the cuisines discussed.
3. Which New World product plays an important role in some Asian cuisines?
4. Compare and contrast the cuisines of Japan and North Africa.
5. Compare and contrast one of the cuisines of India and one of the cuisines of China.
6. Explain why there may be several cuisines within a single country.

CHAPTER 35
PLATE PRESENTATION

After studying this chapter you will be able to:

◆ understand the basic principles of plate presentation
◆ use a variety of techniques to add visual appeal to plated foods

hile food preparation is very much a science, food presentation is an art. Good plate presentation results from careful attention to the colors, shapes, textures and arrangements of the foods. Great plate presentation requires experience and style.

In this chapter we describe several methods of presenting foods. We realize that for every guideline we suggest, there are exceptions. Nor are our examples meant to take the place of more traditional techniques. They are intended only to spark your imagination. As you gain experience, you will undoubtedly develop your own style.

The final step in food preparation is to justify the hours of hard work spent cooking the food by serving and presenting it properly.

Service is the process of delivering the selected foods to diners in the proper fashion. Hot foods should be served very hot and on heated plates; cold foods should be served very cold and on chilled plates. Foods should be cooked to the proper degree of doneness: A roast rack of lamb ordered medium rare should be medium rare—not medium, not rare. Pasta should be served al dente—slightly chewy, not mushy. Bread should be fresh, not stale. Portion sizes should be appropriate. First courses and appetizers should be small enough so that the diner can still appreciate the courses that follow. Rich foods should be served in smaller portions than other foods.

Presentation is the process of offering the selected foods to diners in a fashion that is visually pleasing. When presenting foods, always bear in mind that diners eat first with their eyes and then with their mouths. The foods must be pleasantly and appropriately colored, cut or molded. And the colors, textures, shapes and arrangements of all foods must work together to form a pleasing composition on the plate. Any decorative touches such as the manipulation of sauces or the addition of garnishes should be done thoughtfully and well. Most importantly, plates should be neat and clean. Inspect all plates before they leave the kitchen; wipe drops of sauce or specks of food from their rims with a clean towel.

Presentation techniques are divided here into two broad categories: Those applied to specific foods and those applied to the plate as a whole. The techniques described here use foods or recipes that appear elsewhere in the text.

THE FOOD

The most attractive foods will always be the ones that are properly prepared, but they can be made even more attractive by cutting or molding them into various shapes. Both of these techniques preserve the integrity of the food; that is, neither changes the food itself, they only change the way the food is presented.

◆◆◆

GARNISHES
(AN ADMITTEDLY CRANKY ADMONITION)

I am a strong believer in the simple, edible garnish that has a close flavor kinship to the dish. In my world, dyed daikon flamingos, writhing carrot dragons, and blinking Christmas lights in the empty eye sockets of a stir-fried lobster—all garnishes of the Hong Kong sort—are out. So, too, are radish flowers, tomato rosettes, and vegetable pellets sculpted to look like suppositories. I find all of this loathsome.

In my own rather minimalist style, the fanciest I get is an occasional scallion brush. Otherwise, a leggy piece of coriander or a flourish of scallion rings are all that our already colorful dishes require, Or, if the dish is green, a confetti of finely diced red bell pepper will do the job.

The issue is a visible one, but it needs to make sense on your tongue. A garnish is primarily designed to tickle the eye, but it also should meld seamlessly with the other flavors on the plate or contrast with them in a meaningful way.

Garnishing the rims of plates—a current feature of trendy restaurants in the 90s—is something I find very peculiar. I spill and splatter my own food quite nicely, thank you, and don't want the kitchen to do it for me.

Ditto the rage for a whole chive aloft each appetizer or a cage of spun sugar looming above a dessert. It is admittedly wonderful to give a little height to a dish: One can arrange cold shrimp, for example, in a lively tumble with just a touch or two. But the unrelated vertical garnish is often absurd, a bit of Dr. Seuss on the plate.

I sound cranky, and perhaps I am! Restaurant cooks frequently spend too much time decorating their food, and too little time paying attention to its taste. This, I think, is sad.

—from CHINA MOON COOKBOOK
by BARBARA TROPP

Preparing Foods Properly

Foods look best when prepared properly. A sirloin steak grilled medium rare should be pink inside; its surface should glisten and be branded with well-defined and neatly executed hatch marks. When serving asparagus with hollandaise the stalks should be bright green and crisp looking; the hollandaise sauce should be smooth and shiny, not grainy and dingy. A lemon meringue pie should be attractively browned on top; the filling should be a true lemony yellow and the crust golden brown and without cracks.

Whether a recipe calls for browning foods under a salamander before service, poaching a galantine of chicken wrapped in cheesecloth to maintain its shape or adding vinegar when braising red cabbage, proper cooking procedures can enhance the texture, shape and color of many cooked foods. Throughout this text we have discussed the proper cooking procedures for many, many foods. Use them.

Cutting Foods

The careful cutting of foods often increases their visual appeal and reflects the chef's attention to detail. Here we distinguish between cutting foods to decorate the plate and cutting the foods to be consumed. Decorative garnishes such as tomato and radish roses, frizzed scallions, watermelon boats and the like fall within the former category. Cutting foods into beautiful garnishes is an art unto itself, requiring skill and practice. While beyond the scope of this text, books on creating food garnishes are listed in the Bibliography.

The latter category includes the meats, poultry, fish, vegetables and starches that are the meal. Each should be carefully cut. Vegetables can be cut into uniform shapes and sizes such as julienne, batonnet or tourné. If serving sliced meats or poultry, the slices should be of even thickness; fish can be cut into tranches. Individual stew ingredients and soup or salad garnishes should be of uniform sizes. All of these techniques are simple, fundamental and effective.

Some foods take the shape of the pan in which they are cooked. Polenta and gratin or escalloped potatoes, for example, can be presented attractively when baked in and removed from individual casseroles, or they can be baked in a hotel pan and then cut into various shapes.

PROCEDURE FOR CUTTING POLENTA

1. Cook the polenta according to the recipe. When it is done, pour it onto a well-oiled or buttered half sheet pan. Then chill it in the refrigerator until firm.
2. Once the polenta is firm, flip the pan over onto a work table. Lift off the pan; the polenta will come out easily. Using a chef's knife or circular cutters, cut the polenta into the desired shape. The polenta can be sautéed or grilled for service.

Cutting polenta into various shapes.

PROCEDURE FOR CUTTING GRATIN OR ESCALLOPED POTATOES

1. Select a recipe that produces a firm finished product so that the finished dish will hold its shape after cutting.
2. Bake the potatoes in a well-greased hotel pan and refrigerate until cold and firm. Then cut the potatoes into various shapes with a chef's knife or circular cutters and remove them to a clean pan with a spatula.
3. For service, reheat the potatoes in a 325°F (160°C) oven until hot.

Cutting potatoes with a circular cutter.

Molding Foods

Some foods, particularly grains or vegetables bound by sauces, can be molded into attractive, hard-edged shapes by using metal rings, circular cutters or other forms. These molded forms create height and keep the plate neat and clean.

PROCEDURE FOR MOLDING GRAINS

1. Fill a timbale, soup cup or other mold of the appropriate size and shape with the hot grains, firmly pressing them together.

2. For à la carte service, immediately unmold the grains onto the serving plate by placing the mold upside down on the plate and tapping its rim.

3. For banquet service, place the filled molds in a hotel pan and refrigerate until needed. Shortly before service, fill the hotel pan with hot water to a point about two thirds up the side of the molds. Be careful not to splash any water onto the grains. Cover the pan with foil and place in the oven. Heat until the grains are hot, then plate as desired.

Unmolding a timbale of rice.

PROCEDURE FOR MOLDING VEGETABLES

1. Position a ring mold on the plate and fill it with the vegetables. Press the foods into the ring to help them hold the shape. Level the top.

2. Carefully lift off the ring.

THE PLATE

Properly cooked, carefully cut and appropriately molded foods should not be haphazardly slapped onto a plate. Rather, you should choose and position the foods carefully to achieve a plate presentation with a balanced, harmonious composition.

The composition can be further enhanced by decorating the plate with garnishes, crumbs or sauces. Some of these techniques (for example, decorating the plate with powdered sugar) do not substantially affect the flavors of the foods, they only make the completed presentation more attractive. Other techniques (for example, garnishing a dessert with finely chopped nuts or painting a plate with two sauces) add flavor and texture to the finished dish.

Composition—*a completed plate's structure of colors, textures, shapes and arrangements.*

Choosing Plates

Restaurant china is available in many different shapes, sizes, colors and patterns. It is often the chef's responsibility to choose the appropriate piece of china for a particular dish.

Sizes and Shapes

Most plates are round, but oval plates, often referred to as platters, are becoming more common. Plates are available in a variety of sizes from a small 4-inch (10-centimeter) bread plate to a huge 14-inch (35-centimeter) charger or base plate. Plates are typically concave; their depths vary within a limited range of about 1 inch (2.5 centimeters). Most plates have rims; rim diameters also vary. Soup bowls can be rimmed or rimless. Soup plates are usually larger and shallower than soup bowls and have wide rims. Soup cups are also available. There are also dozens of plate designs intended for a specific purpose, such as plates with small indentations for holding escargots, or long, rectangular plates with grooves for holding asparagus.

Choose plates large enough to hold the food comfortably without overcrowding or spilling. Oversized, rimmed soup plates are becoming quite popular for serving any food with a sauce. Be careful when using oversized plates, however, as the food may look sparse, creating poor value perception.

Regardless of whether you choose a round, oval or less-conventionally-shaped plate, be sure to choose one with a size and shape that best highlights the food and supports the composition. For example, in the photo to the left, the rectangular dish with round corners and raised rim accentuates the geometrically simple yet effective composition of the square date bar and spherical scoop of ice cream.

Chewy Date Bars with Caramel Ice Cream (Recipes 29.30 and 31.27)

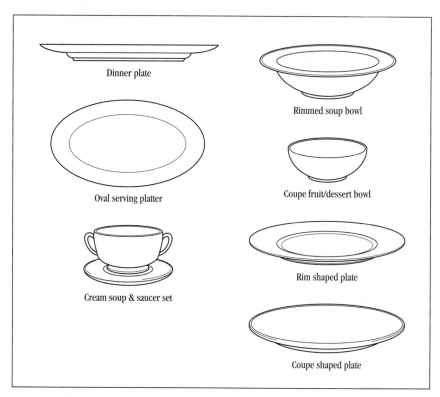

Dinner plate

Rimmed soup bowl

Oval serving platter

Coupe fruit/dessert bowl

Cream soup & saucer set

Rim shaped plate

Coupe shaped plate

FIGURE 35.1   *Common Restaurant China*

Colors and Patterns

White and cream are by far the most common colors for restaurant china. Almost any food looks good on these neutral colors.

Colored and patterned plates can be used quite effectively to accent food, however. The obvious choice is to contrast dark plates with bright- or light-colored foods and light plates with dark-colored foods.

The food should always be the focal point of any plate. Be careful in selecting restaurant china with intricate designs and brightly colored patterns that can conflict or compete with the colors, shapes and arrangements of the foods. The colors and shapes in the pattern should blend well and harmonize with the foods served. The swirling patterns of blues, grays, pinks and yellows along the plate rim shown to the right, for example, harmonize well with the colors of the salmon blini and its accompaniments.

Salmon Blini with Stuffed Squash Blossoms (Recipe 33.9)

Arranging Foods on Plates

You should strive for a well-balanced plate composition. This can be achieved by carefully considering colors, textures, shapes and arrangements.

Colors

Foods come in a rainbow of colors and to the extent appropriate, foods of different colors should be presented together. Generally, the colors should provide balance and contrast. But no matter how well prepared or planned, some dishes simply have dull, boring or similar colors. If so, try adding another ingredient or garnish for a splash of color. The vivid red lobster claws and the shiny black mussel shells shown here add striking color notes to a paella dish that would otherwise be dominated by yellow rice, tan chicken, brown sausages and gray clam shells.

Paella (Recipe 19.29)

Textures

Visual texture refers to how smooth or rough, coarse or fine a food looks. Mashed potatoes and carrot purée both look smooth and soft. Salmon mousseline and spinach soufflé both have slightly grainy surfaces. Rösti potatoes and meatloaf both appear coarse. The flavors of each food in these pairs differ; their visual textures do not.

Typically, foods with similar textures look boring together; foods with different textures look more exciting. Serve carrots cut julienne with the mashed potatoes to achieve a balance of hard and soft textures; steamed leaf spinach with the salmon mousseline for a combination of smooth and grainy textures; and a baked potato with the meatloaf for pairing fluffy and coarse textures. These pairs generally maintain the same range of flavors as the first set of pairs while providing different visual textures.

The cassoulet shown to the right harmoniously combines several textures in one dish: the pebbly beans, the slices of smooth slab bacon and coarse sausage and the bumpy skin of the duck leg. Indeed, the variation in textures is so dramatic and appealing that many diners may not even notice that all the principal ingredients are essentially the same color.

Cassoulet (Recipe 16.10)

Shapes

For a more dramatic presentation, combine foods with different shapes on one plate. The plate shown on the next page is an excellent example of simple shapes artfully combined: ovals of evenly sliced lamb loin with cleanly cut

Lamb Loin with Rösti Potatoes (Recipe 15.10)

triangles of crisp potatoes and long, thin spears of asparagus. The three very different shapes lend contrast and character to the dish.

Arrangements

Having decided on the colors, textures and shapes of the foods that will go on the plate, you must next decide where to place each individual item to achieve a balanced and unified composition. Mostly this takes judgment and style, but there are a few general guidelines.

GUIDELINES FOR ARRANGING FOODS ON A PLATE

1. Strike a balance between overcrowding the plate and leaving large gaps of space. Foods should not touch the plate rim nor necessarily be confined to the very center.

2. Choose a focal point for the plate—that is, the point to which the eye is drawn. This is usually the highest point on the plate. Design the plate with the highest point to the rear or center. Avoid placing foods of equal heights around the edge of the plate leaving a hole in the center—the eye will naturally be drawn to that gap.

3. The plate's composition should flow naturally. For example, make the highest point the back of the plate and have the rest of the food become gradually shorter toward the front of the plate. Slicing and fanning foods can attract the eye and help establish a flow.

The grilled duck with roasted vegetables shown below elegantly illustrates these principles. Height is established by a structure composed of the duck leg and thigh, sliced turnips and baby carrots. The structure sits toward the back of the plate. Its height, placement and striking appearance make it the focal point. The neatly sliced duck breast is then fanned across the plate in front of this focal point, drawing the viewer into the plate.

Grilled Duck with Roasted Vegetables

Decorating Plates

The colors, textures, shapes and arrangements of foods on a plate can be improved or highlighted by decorating a plate with herbs, spices and other garnishes, baked hippen masse dough and sauces. If any of these are to be applied after the principal food is placed on the plate, be prepared to do so quickly so that the food is served at its proper temperature.

Plate Dusting

An attractive method for decorating dessert plates is to cover the entire plate with a dusting of powdered sugar, cocoa powder or both before placing the dessert on the plate. Use sugar on dark-colored plates and cocoa on light-colored plates. These items can be dusted onto the plate with a shaker can or sifter in a free-form fashion or into any desired pattern by using a template. The template can be a doily or a stencil placed over the plate before it is dusted.

PROCEDURE FOR DUSTING DESSERT PLATES

1. Place a template over the plate. Dust the sugar or cocoa over the template.

2. Carefully remove the template.

Provided they complement the food, very finely chopped nuts can also be used to decorate plates for sweet or savory foods. See, for example, the plate of French toast garnished with chopped macadamia nuts shown here. Plates for savory foods can be decorated in a similar fashion by sprinkling them with finely chopped herbs such as thyme or minced vegetables such as a combination of brightly colored peppers.

Garnishing Plates with Herbs

Using fresh herbs is one of the easiest ways to add color, texture and flow to a plate. Whether the herb is an ingredient in the dish or merely a decoration, it should always complement the foods and be consistent with their seasonings. A sprig of fresh rosemary garnishing a beautifully roasted rack of lamb, or tiny leaves of chervil garnishing delicately poached fillets of sole are natural combinations. Sprigs of fresh green mint (often with a fresh berry or two or a strawberry cut in a fan) are often the perfect decoration for a dessert plate.

Banana Brioche French Toast (Recipe 32.21)

Using herbs to garnish a plate.

Garnishing Plate Rims with Herbs or Spices

Finely chopped herbs or nuts or whole or ground spices can be used to decorate plate rims. Whatever garnishing items are used, they should complement the main foods and be consistent with their seasonings.

PROCEDURE FOR GARNISHING PLATE RIMS

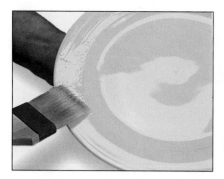

1. Apply a light coating of oil or softened butter to the plate rim with a pastry brush. Be careful to apply the oil or butter only where you want the herbs, spices or other garnishes to stick.

2. Sprinkle the desired amount of garnish over the oiled or buttered area. Then tip the plate to let the excess garnish fall away.

3. Alternatively, a small portion of the plate can be brushed and decorated.

Garnishing Plates with Hippen Masse

An increasingly popular presentation technique is to pipe batters into intricate designs and then bake them to form crisp, rigid, cookielike garnishes. These garnishes are then used to create height and add texture.

◆◆◆

RECIPE 35.1
SAVORY HIPPEN MASSE

ARIZONA BILTMORE, PHOENIX, AZ

Yield: 1 lb. (450 g)

Egg whites, room temperature	8 oz.	250 g
Wondra flour	4 oz.	120 g
Heavy cream	3 oz.	90 g
Granulated sugar	1 oz.	30 g
Salt and white pepper	TT	TT
Dried thyme, crushed	1 tsp.	5 ml

1. Stir the egg whites together to blend. Stir in all of the flour at once.
2. Blend in the heavy cream, then add the remaining ingredients.
3. Strain the batter through a china cap and allow to rest for 30 minutes.
4. Lightly oil the back of a very flat sheet pan. Pipe the hippen masse onto the pan using a plastic squeeze bottle. Pipe the batter into decorative patterns appropriate for the desired plate presentation.
5. Bake at 375°F (190°C) until set and lightly browned. Remove from the oven, then remove the decorations from the sheet pan while still slightly warm.

1. Piping the batter onto an oiled sheet pan.

2. Using the baked batter as a component when composing a plate. Carousel of Sonoma Lamb (Recipe 15.11)

Decorating Plates with Sauces

The sauce is an integral part of most any dish: It adds flavor and moisture; it also adds color, texture and flow to the plate. A rich, glossy bordelaise or Madeira sauce pooled beneath sautéed tournedos of beef is a classic example. A chunky salsa of tomatoes, papaya and pineapple beneath a juicy piece of grilled salmon is a more contemporary approach.

Sauces are also used in other, less traditional ways to add visual appeal. For example, if using a vinaigrette dressing for grilled foods, let the oil and vinegar separate and pool on the plate, creating the interesting effect illustrated here.

One or more colored sauces can also be used to paint plates. One technique is simply to drizzle or splatter the sauce onto the plate. In the photo below, the sauce boldly splattered across the plate is the same rich magenta beet vinaigrette as that pooled beneath the sea bass; the plate's drama is heightened by the contrasting tomato ovals and potato spikes.

Grilled Quail with Balsamic Raspberries (Recipe 18.15)

Pan-seared Sea Bass with Beet Vinaigrette (Recipe 19.22)

Alternatively, one or more colored sauces can be applied to a plate using squirt bottles to create abstract patterns or representational designs. Painting plates with different-colored sauces also facilitates flow and adds color. Although this technique can be used with hot sauces, it is more often used with cold sauces (such as vanilla, caramel, chocolate and fruit-flavored ones) for dessert presentations. The sauces must be thick enough to hold the pattern once it is created and they should all be of the same viscosity.

PROCEDURE FOR PAINTING A DESIGN WITH SAUCES

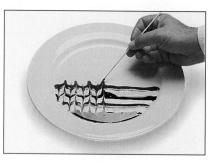

1. Apply the sauces to the plate in parallel lines of alternating colors.

2. Carefully pull a toothpick through the sauces, perpendicular to the parallel lines in the sauces.

PROCEDURE FOR PAINTING A SPIDER WEB DESIGN

1. Pool one sauce evenly across the entire base of the plate, then apply a contrasting sauce onto the base sauce in a spiral.

2. Draw a thin-bladed knife or a toothpick through the sauces from the center point toward the edge. Then, leaving a half inch (1.2 centimeter) space along the edge, draw a knife blade or toothpick from the edge to the center.

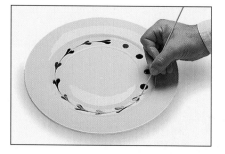

Other patterns can be produced by squirting the sauces onto the plate in different patterns or by pulling the knife or toothpick through the sauces in different directions. As shown to the left, a circle of chocolate-sauce dots in a pool of vanilla sauce is pulled to create a leaf wreath.

CONCLUSION

Although the techniques described in this chapter—as well as many other ones—can be used to create a variety of effects, often the most elegant plates are those with the simplest designs. Thoughtful presentation improves the appeal and appearance of any food as well as the completed plate, but it cannot mask poor-quality, poorly prepared or bland-tasting foods.

$\mathcal{Q}$UESTIONS FOR DISCUSSION

1. Explain why proper service and presentation are important in food service operations.

2. Distinguish between cutting and molding foods for visual appeal and creating garnishes out of foods.

3. How can the selection of service ware such as bowls and platters affect the visual appeal of the foods served?

4. List and describe four techniques for garnishing plates.

5. Describe how color, texture, shape and arrangement can be used to create a well-balanced plate composition.

Twenty Suggested Menus

The following menus are designed for beginning students. They use basic skills and techniques that students should master before progressing to more difficult items.

Beginning Menu 1:

RECIPE 24.4 **MESCLUN SALAD WITH RASPBERRY VINAIGRETTE**
RECIPE 13.9 **PEPPER STEAK**
RECIPE 22.6 **BROCCOLI ALMONDINE**
RECIPE 27.1 **COUNTRY BISCUITS**
RECIPE 31.17 **CHOCOLATE POT AU CRÈME**

Beginning Menu 2:

RECIPE 24.7 **TOMATO AND ASPARAGUS SALAD WITH FRESH MOZZARELLA**
RECIPE 19.1 **BROILED BLACK SEA BASS WITH HERB BUTTER AND SAUTÉED LEEKS**
RECIPE 23.5 **BASIC SIMMERED RICE**
RECIPE 25.4 **PEARS POACHED IN RED WINE**

Beginning Menu 3:

RECIPE 11.2 **HEARTY VEGETABLE BEEF SOUP**
Tossed salad with
  RECIPE 24.17 **ROQUEFORT DRESSING** and
  RECIPE 24.20 **GARLIC CROUTONS**
RECIPE 17.23 **TURKEY SCALLOPINE**
RECIPE 23.17 **BROWN RICE PILAF WITH PINENUTS**
RECIPE 31.9 **CLASSIC CHOCOLATE MOUSSE**

Beginning Menu 4:

RECIPE 11.18 **CHEDDAR AND LEEK SOUP**
RECIPE 19.6 **RED SNAPPER EN PAPILLOTE WITH JULIENNE VEGETABLES AND BASIL BUTTER**

RECIPE 23.4 **DUCHESSE POTATOES**
RECIPE 31.21 **CHERRY CLAFOUTI**

Beginning Menu 5:

RECIPE 11.15 **FRENCH ONION SOUP**
RECIPE 12.1 **GRILLED LAMB CHOPS WITH HERB BUTTER**
RECIPE 23.15 **POLENTA**
RECIPE 22.14 **STIR-FRIED SNOW PEAS**
RECIPE 25.11 **GRATIN OF FRESH BERRIES WITH CRÈME FRAÎCHE**

Beginning Menu 6:

RECIPE 11.4 **CREAM OF BROCCOLI SOUP**
RECIPE 13.1 **T-BONE STEAK**
RECIPE 23.14 **STEAK FRIES**
RECIPE 22.11 **BROILED TOMATO**
RECIPE 28.2 **SOFT YEAST DINNER ROLLS**
RECIPE 31.18 **PISTACHIO CITRUS CHEESECAKE**

Beginning Menu 7:

RECIPE 11.23 **FRESH PEACH AND YOGURT SOUP**
RECIPE 17.19 **DUCK BREAST SALAD WITH HAZELNUTS**
RECIPE 28.10 **BREADSTICKS**
RECIPE 29.29 **CHOCOLATE DÉLICE**

Beginning Menu 8:

Tossed salad with
  RECIPE 24.3 **EMULSIFIED VINAIGRETTE DRESSING**
RECIPE 12.2 **ROAST PRIME RIB OF BEEF AU JUS**
RECIPE 23.1 **BAKED POTATOES**
RECIPE 22.17 **MAPLE GLAZED CARROTS**
RECIPE 28.5 **BASIC FRENCH BREAD**
RECIPE 29.6 **CHERRY PIE**

BEGINNING MENU 9:

RECIPE 12.5   *NEW ENGLAND BOILED DINNER*
RECIPE 28.8   *WHOLE WHEAT BREAD*
RECIPE 25.2   *BAKED APPLES*

BEGINNING MENU 10:

RECIPE 11.5   *PURÉE OF SPLIT PEA SOUP*
RECIPE 13.4   *HOMESTYLE MEATLOAF* with mushroom sauce
RECIPE 22.2   *BAKED BUTTERNUT SQUASH*
RECIPE 23.3   *LYONNAISE POTATOES*
RECIPE 31.10   *CHOCOLATE ICE CREAM*
RECIPE 29.32   *SUGAR COOKIES*

The following menus are designed for intermediate-level students. They include dishes that integrate multiple techniques in order to build upon skills previously learned.

INTERMEDIATE MENU 1:

RECIPE 19.33   *FRIED OYSTERS WITH HERBED CRÈME FRAÎCHE*
RECIPE 24.28   *WARM LAMB SALAD WITH BOURBON VINAIGRETTE*
RECIPE 28.4   *CROISSANTS*
RECIPE 31.29   *CHOCOLATE HAZELNUT MARQUIS*

INTERMEDIATE MENU 2:

RECIPE 20.18   *RABBIT PÂTÉ EN CROÛTE*
RECIPE 11.8   *VICHYSSOISE*
RECIPE 18.12   *BRAISED PARTRIDGE WITH RED CABBAGE*
RECIPE 23.35   *SPAETZLE*
RECIPE 29.4   *APPLE CRANBERRY PIE* with
    RECIPE 31.27   *CARAMEL ICE CREAM*

INTERMEDIATE MENU 3:

RECIPE 20.8   *VEGETABLE TERRINE IN BRIOCHE*
RECIPE 19.27   *PAUPIETTES OF SOLE WITH MOUSSELINE OF SHRIMP*
RECIPE 23.13   *RÖSTI POTATOES*
Salad of baby greens with shaved parmesan cheese and
    RECIPE 24.11   *THREE PEPPERCORN CRANBERRY VINAIGRETTE*
RECIPE 29.27   *CHOCOLATE ÉCLAIRS*

INTERMEDIATE MENU 4:

RECIPE 11.3   *BEEF CONSOMMÉ*
RECIPE 23.22   *GOAT'S CHEESE RAVIOLI IN HERBED CREAM SAUCE*
RECIPE 19.5   *STEAMED SALMON WITH LEMON AND OLIVE OIL*
RECIPE 22.3   *STIR-FRIED ASPARAGUS WITH SHIITAKE MUSHROOMS*
RECIPE 23.7   *BULGAR PILAF*
RECIPE 29.24   *STRAWBERRY NAPOLEON*

INTERMEDIATE MENU 5:

Tossed green salad with
    RECIPE 24.1   *BASIC VINAIGRETTE DRESSING* and
    RECIPE 20.14   *RED PEPPER MOUSSE*
RECIPE 16.10   *CASSOULET*
RECIPE 28.14   *SAN FRANCISCO SOURDOUGH BREAD*
RECIPE 31.22   *WHITE CHOCOLATE FRANGELICO BAVARIAN* served with
    RECIPE 29.36   *LACY PECAN COOKIES*

INTERMEDIATE MENU 6:

RECIPE 19.36   *SQUID STUFFED WITH GRILLED EGGPLANT*
RECIPE 11.16   *MINESTRONE*
RECIPE 17.15   *FREE RANGE CHICKEN*
RECIPE 29.12   *CANNOLI ALLA SICILIANA*

INTERMEDIATE MENU 7:

RECIPE 19.4   *BLUE CRAB CAKES WITH FRESH SALSA*
Romaine lettuce with
    RECIPE 24.12   *RED ONION VINAIGRETTE*
RECIPE 17.14   *CHICKEN STUFFED WITH SPINACH IN SAFFRON SAUCE*
RECIPE 23.2   *GRATIN DAUPHINOISE*
RECIPE 31.7   *FRESH FRUIT BAVARIAN CHARLOTTE* made with
    RECIPE 30.26   *LADYFINGERS*

INTERMEDIATE MENU 8: BRUNCH BUFFET

RECIPE 24.25   *VINE-RIPENED TOMATO SALAD*
RECIPE 32.3   *GREEK-STYLE SCRAMBLED EGGS*
RECIPE 32.5   *GARDEN FRITTATA*
RECIPE 23.16   *GRITS AND CHEESE SOUFFLÉ*
RECIPE 27.2   *BLUEBERRY MUFFINS*
RECIPE 28.18   *DANISH PASTRIES*
RECIPE 30.20   *SOUR CREAM COFFEECAKE*
RECIPE 25.8   *FIGS WITH BERRIES AND HONEY MOUSSE*
RECIPE 32.12   *HOT CHOCOLATE MOUSSE*

INTERMEDIATE MENU 9:

RECIPE 24.21   *WILTED SPINACH SALAD WITH ROASTED PEPPERS*
RECIPE 11.13   *CHICKEN SOUP WITH MATZO BALLS*
RECIPE 12.6   *AUNT RUTHIE'S POT ROAST*
RECIPE 22.4   *BRUSSELS SPROUTS IN PECAN BUTTER*
RECIPE 28.15   *CHALLAH*
RECIPE 30.22   *FRESH COCONUT CAKE*

INTERMEDIATE MENU 10:

RECIPE 24.22   *WHITE ASPARAGUS MOUSSE WITH GARDEN FRESH LETTUCES*
RECIPE 11.17   *SEAFOOD BOUILLABAISSE*
RECIPE 28.11   *ROMAN FLATBREAD*
RECIPE 29.23   *FRESH PEACH TART WITH ALMOND CREAM*

Appendix II

Measurement and Conversion Charts

Measurement Conversion Chart

Formulas for Exact Measures	When you know:	Multiply by:	To find:	Rounded Measures for Quick Reference		
Mass	ounces	28.35	grams	1 oz.		= 30 g
(Weight)	pounds	0.45	kilograms	4 oz.		= 120 g
	grams	0.035	ounces	8 oz.		= 225 g
	kilograms	2.2	pounds	16 oz.	= 1 lb.	= 450 g
				32 oz.	= 2 lb.	= 900 g
				36 oz.	= 2 1/4 lb.	= 1000 g (1 kg)
Volume	teaspoons	5.0	milliliters	1/4 tsp.	= 1/24 oz.	= 1 ml
(Capacity)	tablespoons	15.0	milliliters	1/2 tsp.	= 1/12 oz.	= 2 ml
	fluid ounces	29.57	milliliters	1 tsp.	= 1/6 oz.	= 5 ml
	cups	0.24	liters	1 Tbsp.	= 1/2 oz.	= 15 ml
	pints	0.47	liters	1 c.	= 8 oz.	= 250 ml
	quarts	0.95	liters	2 c. (1 pt.)	= 16 oz.	= 500 ml
	gallons	3.785	liters	4 c. (1 qt.)	= 32 oz.	= 1 lt
	milliliters	0.034	fluid ounces	4 qt. (1 gal.)	= 128 oz.	= 3 3/4 lt
Temperature	Fahrenheit	5/9 (after subtracting 32)	Celsius	32°F	= 0°C	
	Celsius	9/5 (then add 32)	Fahrenheit	122°F	= 50°C	
				212°F	= 100°C	

CONVERSION GUIDELINES

1 gallon	=	4 quarts
		8 pints
		16 cups (8 ounces)
		128 ounces
1 fifth bottle	=	approximately 1 1/2 pints or exactly 26.5 ounces
1 measuring cup	=	8 ounces (a coffee cup is generally 6 ounces)
1 large egg white	=	1 ounce (average)
1 lemon	=	1 to 1 1/4 ounces of juice
1 orange	=	3 to 3 1/2 ounces of juice

SCOOP SIZES

Scoop Measure	Level Measure
6	2/3 cup
8	1/2 cup
10	2/5 cup
12	1/3 cup
16	1/4 cup
20	3 1/5 tablespoons
24	2 2/3 tablespoons
30	2 1/5 tablespoons
40	1 3/5 tablespoons

The number scoop determines the number of servings in each quart of a mixture, for example, with a No. 16 scoop, one quart of mixture will yield 16 servings.

LADLE SIZES

Size	Portion of a Cup	Number per Quart	Number per Liter
1 oz.	1/8	32	34
2 oz.	1/4	16	17
2 2/3 oz.	1/3	12	13
4 oz.	1/2	8	8.6
6 oz.	3/4	5 1/3	5.7

CANNED GOOD SIZES

Size	No. of Cans per Case	Average Weight	Average No. Cups per Can
No. 1/2	8	8 oz.	1
No. 1 tall (also known as 303)	2 & 4 doz.	16 oz.	2
No. 2	2 doz.	20 oz.	2 1/2
No. 2 1/2	2 doz.	28 oz.	3 1/2
No. 3	2 doz.	33 oz.	4
No. 3 cylinder	1 doz.	46 oz.	5 2/3
No. 5	1 doz.	3 lb. 8 oz.	5 1/2
No. 10	6	6 lb. 10 oz.	13

BIBLIOGRAPHY AND RECOMMENDED READING

GENERAL INTEREST

Bickel, Walter, ed. and trans. *Hering's Dictionary of Classical and Modern Cookery*. 12th Eng. ed. London: Virtue & Company Limited, 1991.

Culinary Institute of America. *The New Professional Chef*. 5th ed. New York: Van Nostrand Reinhold, 1991.

Dawson, Hannelore. *Great Food for Great Numbers*. New York: Van Nostrand Reinhold, 1991.

Escoffier, Auguste. *Le Guide culinaire*. (Translation entitled *The Escoffier Cookbook and Guide to the Fine Art of Cookery for Connoisseurs, Chefs, Epicures*). New York: Crown Publishers, 1969.

Gisslen, Wayne. *Professional Baking*. New York: John Wiley & Sons, Inc., 1985.

———. *Professional Cooking*. 2nd ed. New York: John Wiley & Sons, Inc., 1989.

The Grand Masters of the French Cuisine. Selected and adapted by Celine Vence and Robert Courtine. New York: G.P. Putnam & Sons, 1978.

Haines, Robert G. *Food Preparation*. Homewood, Ill.: American Technical Publishers, Inc., 1988.

Lang, Jennifer Harvey, ed. *Larousse Gastronomique*. American ed. New York: Crown Publishers, Inc., 1988.

Leith, Prue. *The Cook's Handbook*. New York: A & W Publishers, Inc., 1981.

Pauli, Eugen, *Classical Cooking the Modern Way*. 2nd ed. New York: Van Nostrand Reinhold, 1989.

Pepin, Jacques. *The Art of Cooking*. New York: Alfred A. Knopf, 1987.

———. *La Technique*. New York: Wallaby/Pocket Books, 1976.

Rombauer, Irma von Starkloff and Marion Rombauer Becker. *Joy of Cooking*. New York: The Bobbs-Merrill Co., Inc., Macmillan, 1975.

Shugart, Grace and Mary Molt. *Food for Fifty*. 9th ed. New York: Macmillan, 1993.

Willan, Anne. *La Varenne Pratique*. New York: Crown Publishers, 1989.

FOOD HISTORY

Clair, Colin. *Kitchen & Table: A Bedside History of Eating in the Western World*. New York: Abelard-Schuman Limited, 1965.

Fussell, Betty. *The Story of Corn*. New York: Borzoi Books, Alfred A. Knopf, Inc., 1992.

Hale, William Harlan, and The Editors of Horizon Magazine. *The Horizon Cookbook and Illustrated History of Eating and Drinking Through the Ages*. New York: American Heritage Publishing Co., Inc., 1968.

Mintz, Sidney W. *Sweetness and Power: The Place of Sugar in Modern History*. New York: Penguin Books, 1985.

Norman, Barbara. *Tales of the Table: A History of Western Cuisine*. Englewood Cliffs, N.J.: Prentice-Hall, 1972.

Revel, Jean-François. *Culture and Cuisine*. (Trans. of *Un Festin en paroles*.) New York: Da Capo Press, Inc., 1982.

Rupp, Rececca. *Blue Corn and Square Tomatoes*. Pownal, Vt.: Garden Way Publishing, 1987.

Schremp, Gerry. *Kitchen Culture: Fifty Years of Food Fads*. New York: Pharos Books, A Scripps Howard Co., 1991.

Shapiro, Laura. *Perfection Salad: Women and Cooking at the Turn of the Century*. New York: Farrar, Straus and Giroux, 1986.

Tannahill, Reay. *Food in History*. New York: Crown Publishers, Inc., 1988.

Toussaint-Samat, Maguelonne. *A History of Food*. Translated by Anthea Bell. Cambridge, Mass.: Blackwell Publishers, 1992.

Wheaton, Barbara Ketcham. *Savoring the Past*. Philadelphia: The University of Pennsylvania Press, 1983.

Willan, Anne. *Great Cooks and Their Recipes: From Taillevent to Escoffier*. Boston: Little, Brown and Co., A Bulfinch Press Book, 1992.

SANITATION AND SAFETY

The Educational Foundation of the National Restaurant Association. *Applied Foodservice Sanitation: A Foundation Textbook*. 4th ed. John Wiley & Sons, Inc., 1992.

Guthrie, Rufus K. *Food Sanitation*. 3d ed. New York: Van Nostrand Reinhold, 1988.

National Assessment Institute. *Handbook for Safe Food Service Management*. Englewood Cliffs, N.J.: Regents/Prentice Hall, 1994.

NUTRITION

Brody, Jane E. *Jane Brody's Nutrition Book*. New York: Bantam Books, Inc., 1982.

Freyberg, Nicholas, and Willis A. Gortner. *The Food Additives Book*. New York: Bantam Books, Inc., 1982.

Hamilton, Eva Mae Nunnelley, Eleanor Noss Whitney, and Frances Sienkiewicz Sizer. *Nutrition: Concepts and Controversies*. 4th ed. St. Paul, Minn.: West Publishing Co., 1988.

Netzer, Corinne T. *The Corinne T. Netzer Encyclopedia of Food Values*. New York: Dell Publishing, 1992.

Spiller, Gene. *The Super Pyramid Eating Program: Introducing the Revolutionary Five New Food Groups*. New York: Times Books, Random House, Inc., 1993.

FOOD COSTING AND MENU PRICING

Coltman, Michael M. *Financial Control for Your Foodservice Operation*. New York: Van Nostrand Reinhold, 1991.

Keister, Douglas C. *Food and Beverage Control*. 2nd ed. Englewood Cliffs, N.J.: Prentice Hall, 1990.

McVety, Paul J., and Bradley J. Ware. *Fundamentals of Menu Planning*. New York: Van Nostrand Reinhold, 1989.

Miller, Jack E. *Menu Pricing and Strategy*. 2nd ed. New York: Van Nostrand Reinhold, 1987.

Schmidt, Arno. *Chef's Book of Formulas, Yields, and Sizes*. New York: Van Nostrand Reinhold, 1990.

TOOLS

Bridge, Fred, and Jean F. Tibbetts. *The Well-Tooled Kitchen*. New York: William Morrow and Co., 1991.

GENERAL INGREDIENTS

DeMers, John. *The Community Kitchens Complete Guide to Gourmet Coffee*. New York: Simon & Schuster, 1986.

Dowell, Philip, and Adrian Bailey. *Cook's Ingredients*. New York: William Morrow and Co., 1980.

Jordan, Michele Anna. *The Good Cook's Book of Oil & Vinegar*. Reading, Mass.: Addison-Wesley, 1992.

Norman, Jill. *The Complete Book of Spices*. American ed. New York: Viking Studio Books, 1991.

Ortiz, Elisabeth Lambert. *The Encyclopedia of Herbs, Spices and Flavorings*. 1st American ed. New York: Dorling Kindersley, Inc., 1992.

Schapira, Joel, and Karl Schapira. *The Book of Coffee and Tea*. New York: St. Martin's Press, 1975.

Schuler, Stanley, ed. *Simon & Schuster's Guide to Herbs and Spices*. New York: Fireside and Simon & Schuster, 1990.

Stobart, Tom. *Herbs, Spices and Flavorings*. Woodstock, N.Y.: The Overland Press, 1982.

EGGS, DAIRY AND CHEESE

Eggcyclopedia. 2nd ed. Park Ridge, Ill.: American Egg Board, revised 1989.

Jones, Evan. *The World of Cheese*. New York: Alfred A. Knopf, 1984.

Marquis, Vivienne, and Patricia Haskell. *The Cheese Book*. New York: Simon & Schuster, 1985.

FOOD SCIENCE

Freeland-Graves, H., and Gladys C. Peckham. *Foundations of Food Preparation*. 5th ed. New York: Macmillan, 1987.

McGee, Harold. *On Food and Cooking*. New York: Charles Scribner's Sons, 1984.

McWilliams, Margaret. *Food Fundamentals*. 4th ed. New York: Macmillan, 1985.

Potter, Norman N. *Food Science*. 4th ed. Westport, Conn.: The AVI Publishing Co. Inc., 1986.

STOCKS, SAUCES AND SOUPS

Clayton, Bernard. *The Complete Book of Soups and Stews*. New York: Simon & Schuster, 1984.

Davis, Deidre. *A Fresh Look at Saucing Foods*. Reading, Mass.: Addison-Wesley, 1993.

Larousse, David Paul. *The Sauce Bible: Guide to the Saucier's Craft*. New York: John Wiley & Sons, Inc., 1993.

Peterson, James. *Sauces: Classical and Contemporary Sauce Making*. New York: Van Nostrand Reinhold, 1991.

Sokolov, Raymond A. *The Saucier's Apprentice*. New York: Alfred A. Knopf, 1976.

MEAT

Libby, James A. *Meat Hygiene*. Philadelphia: Lea & Febiger, 1975.

The Meat Buyers Guide. Reston, Va.: National Association of Meat Purveyors, 1990.

Thomas, John R., and P. Thomas Ziegler. *The Meat We Eat*. Danville, Ill.: Interstate Printers & Publishers, Inc., 1985.

The Editors of Time-Life Books. *The Good Cook: Lamb*. London: Time Life International (Nederland) B.V., 1981.

The Editors of Time-Life Books. *The Good Cook: Beef and Veal*. London: Time Life International (Nederland) B.V., 1978.

POULTRY

The Editors of Time-Life Books. *The Good Cook: Poultry*. London: Time Life International (Nederland) B.V., 1978.

GAME

Cameron, Angus, and Judith Jones. *The L.L. Bean Game and Fish Cookbook*. New York: Random House, 1983.

Little, Carolyn. *The Game Cookbook*. Wiltshire, England: The Crowood Press, 1988.

Marrone, Teresa. *Dressing and Cooking Wild Game*. New York: Prentice Hall Press, 1987.

FISH AND SHELLFISH

Cronin, Isaac, Jay Harlow, and Paul Johnson. *The California Seafood Cookbook*. Berkeley, Calif.: Harris Publishing Co., Inc. (Aris Books), 1983.

The Fish List: FDA Guide to Acceptable Market Names for Food Fish Sold in Interstate Commerce. Washington, D.C.: U.S. Government Printing Office, 1988.

Howarth, A. Jan. *The Complete Fish Cookbook*. New York: St. Martin's Press, 1983.

King, Shirley. *Fish, The Basics.* New York: Simon & Schuster, 1990.

———. *Saucing the Fish.* New York: Simon & Schuster, 1976.

Loomis, Susan Herrmann. *The Great American Seafood Cookbook.* New York: Workman Publishing, 1988.

McClane, A. J. *The Encyclopedia of Fish Cookery.* New York: Holt, Rinehart and Winston, 1977.

The Seafood Handbook: Seafood Standards. Rockland, Maine: Seafood Business Magazine, 1991.

CHARCUTERIE

Ehlert, Friedrich W., et al. *Pâtés and Terrines.* Reprint. London: Hearst Books, 1990.

Grigson, Jane. *The Art of Charcuterie.* Reprint. New York: The Echo Press, 1991.

The Editors of Time-Life Books. *The Good Cook: Terrines, Pâtés and Galantines.* London: Time Life International (Nederland) B.V., 1981.

VEGETABLES AND FRUITS

Andrews, Jean. *Peppers: The Domesticated Capsicums.* Austin, Tex.: University of Texas Press, 1984.

Bauer, Cathy, and Juel Andersen. *The Tofu Cookbook.* Emmaus, Pa.: Rodale Press, 1979.

Beck, Bruce. *Produce: A Fruit and Vegetable Lovers' Guide.* New York: Friendly Press, 1984.

Brennan, Georgeanne, Isaac Cronin, and Charlotte Glenn. *The New American Vegetable Cookbook.* Berkeley, Calif.: Harris Publishing Co., 1985.

Brown, Marlene. *International Produce Cookbook and Guide.* Los Angeles: HP Books, 1989.

Davidson, Alan. *Fruit: A Connoisseur's Guide and Cookbook.* New York: Simon & Schuster, 1991.

DeWitt, Dave, and Nancy Gerlach. *The Whole Chile Pepper Book.* Boston: Little, Brown and Co., 1990.

Holthaus, Fusako. *Tofu Cookery.* Tokyo: Kodansha International, 1992.

Miller, Mark, with John Harrisson. *The Great Chile Book.* Berkeley, Calif.: Ten Speed Press, 1991.

Murdich, Jack. *Buying Produce.* New York: William Morrow and Co., 1986.

Payne, Rolce Redard, and Dorrit Speyer Senior. *Cooking With Fruit.* New York: Crown Publishers, Inc., 1992.

Schmidt, Jimmy. *Cooking For All Seasons.* New York: Macmillan, 1991.

Schneider, Elizabeth. *Uncommon Fruits and Vegetables: A Commonsense Guide.* New York: Harper & Row, 1986.

GRAINS AND PASTA

Bugialli, Giuliano. *On Pasta.* New York: Simon & Schuster, 1988.

Della Croce, Julia. *Pasta Classica.* San Francisco: Chronicle Books, 1987.

Gelles, Carol. *The Complete Whole Grain Cookbook.* New York: Donald I. Fine, Inc., 1989.

Greene, Bert. *The Grains Cookbook.* New York: Workman Publishing, 1988.

Kummer, Corby. "Pasta." *The Atlantic,* 258, no. 1 (July 1986): 35–47.

Leblang, Bonnie Tandy, and Joanne Lamb Hayes. *Rice.* New York: Harmony Books, 1991.

Scott, Marisa Luisa, and Jack Denton Scott. *Rice.* New York: Times Books, 1985.

Spier, Carol. *Food Essentials: Grains and Pasta.* New York: Crescent Books, 1993.

SALADS AND SALAD DRESSINGS

Blair, Eulalia. C. *Salads for Foodservice Menu Planning.* New York: Van Nostrand Reinhold, 1988.

Idone, Christopher. *Christopher Idone's Salad Days.* New York: Random House, 1989.

Muller, Veronika. *Salads.* New York: Van Nostrand Reinhold, 1989.

Nathan, Amy. *Salad.* San Francisco: Chronicle Books, 1985.

BREADS

Albright, Barbara, and Leslie Weiner. *Mostly Muffins.* New York: St. Martin's Press, 1984.

Alston, Elizabeth. *Biscuits and Scones.* New York: Clarkson N. Potter, Inc., 1988.

Amendola, Joseph. *The Bakers' Manual.* 4th ed. New York: Van Nostrand Reinhold, 1993.

Clayton, Bernard. *Bernard Clayton's New Complete Book of Breads.* Rev. ed. New York: Simon & Schuster, 1987.

Cunningham, Marion. *The Fannie Farmer Baking Book.* New York: Alfred A. Knopf, 1984.

David, Elizabeth. *English Bread and Yeast Cookery.* Notes by Karen Hess. American ed. New York: The Viking Press, 1980.

Jones, Judith, and Evan Jones. *The Book of Bread.* New York: Harper & Row, 1982.

Ortiz, Joe. *The Village Baker: Classic Regional Breads from Europe and America.* Berkeley, Calif.: Ten Speed Press, 1993.

Weiner, Leslie, and Barbara Albright. *Simply Scones.* New York: St. Martin's Press, 1988.

PASTRIES AND DESSERTS

Bernachon, Maurice, and Jean-Jacques Bernachon. *A Passion for Chocolate.* Translated and adapted for the American kitchen by Rose Levy Beranbaum. New York: William Morrow and Co., Inc., 1989.

Braker, Flo. *The Simple Art of Perfect Baking.* Shelburne, Vt.: Chapters Publishing, Ltd., 1992.

Fletcher, Helen S. *The New Pastry Cook.* New York: William Morrow and Co., Inc., 1986.

Friberg, Bo. *The Professional Pastry Chef.* 2nd ed. New York: Van Nostrand Reinhold, 1990.

Healy, Bruce, and Paul Bugat. *Mastering the Art of French Pastry.* Woodbury, N.Y.: Barron's, 1984.

Hyman, Philip, and Mary Hyman, trans. *The Best of Gaston Lenotre's Desserts.* Woodbury, N.Y.: Barron's, 1983.

London, Sheryl, and Mel London. *Fresh Fruit Desserts: Classic and Contemporary.* New York: Prentice Hall Press, 1990.

Purdy, Susan G. *A Piece of Cake.* New York: Macmillan, 1989.

Roux, Michel, and Albert Roux. *The Roux Brothers on Pâtisserie.* New York: Prentice Hall Press, 1986.

Silverton, Nancy. *Desserts by Nancy Silverton.* New York: Harper & Row, 1986.

Sultan, William J. *The Pastry Chef.* New York: Van Nostrand Reinhold, 1983.

Sultan, William J. *Practical Baking.* 5th ed. New York: Van Nostrand Reinhold, 1990.

MEAL SERVICE

Alston, Elizabeth. *Breakfast with Friends: Seasonal Menus to Celebrate the Morning.* New York: McGraw-Hill, 1989.

Bristow, Linda Kay. *Bread and Breakfast*. San Ramon, Calif.: 101 Productions, 1985.

Janericco, Terence. *The Book of Great Hors d'Oeuvre*. New York: Van Nostrand Reinhold, 1990.

Kolpas, Norman. *Breakfast and Brunch Book*. Los Angeles: HP Books, 1988.

Kotschevar, Lendal H. *Short Order Cooking*. New York: Van Nostrand Reinhold, 1990.

INTERNATIONAL CUISINES

Bayless, Rick, with Deann Groen Bayless. *Authentic Mexican: Regional Cooking from the Heart of Mexico*. New York: William Morrow and Co., Inc., 1987.

Bugialli, Giuliano. *The Fine Art of Italian Cooking*. New York: Random House, 1990.

Casas, Penelope. *The Foods and Wines of Spain*. New York: Alfred A. Knopf, 1991.

Curnonsky [Maurice Edmond Sailland]. *Traditional French Cooking*. Translation of *Cuisine et vins de France*, English ed. Jeni Wright. New York: Doubleday, 1989.

Devi, Yamuna. *The Art of Indian Vegetarian Cooking*. New York: E.P. Dutton, 1987.

Downer, Lesley. *At the Japanese Table*. San Francisco: Chronicle Books, 1993.

Efrain, Martinez. *Classic Spanish Cooking with Chef Ef.* Los Angeles: Lowell House, 1993.

Field, Carol. *Celebrating Italy*. New York: William Morrow & Co., Inc., 1990.

Gin, Maggie. *Regional Cooking of China*. San Francisco: 101 Productions, 1984.

Grigson, Jane. *Jane Grigson's Book of European Cookery*. New York: Atheneum, 1983.

Hazan, Marcella. *Essentials of Classic Italian Cooking*. New York: Alfred A. Knopf, 1993.

Jaffrey, Madhur. *An Invitation to Indian Cooking*. New York: Vintage Books, 1973.

———. *A Taste of India*. New York: Atheneum, 1986.

Kasper, Lynn Rossetto. *The Splendid Table: Recipes from Emilia-Romagna the Heartland of Northern Italian Food*. New York: William Morrow & Co., Inc., 1992.

Kennedy, Diana. *The Cuisines of Mexico*. Rev. ed. New York: Harper & Row, 1986.

Lo, Kenneth. *The Encyclopedia of Chinese Cooking*. New York: Bristol Books, 1979.

McDermott, Nancie. *Real Thai: The Best of Thailand's Regional Cooking*. San Francisco: Chronicle Books, 1992.

Olaore, Ola. *Traditional African Cooking*. London: Foulsham & Company Ltd., 1990.

Randelman, Mary Urrutia, and Joan Schwartz. *Memories of a Cuban Kitchen*. New York: Macmillan, 1992.

Richie, Donald. *A Taste of Japan*. New York: Kodansha, 1985.

Roden, Claudia. *A Book of Middle Eastern Food*. New York: Vintage Books, 1972.

Rojas-Lombardi, Felipe. *The Art of South American Cooking*. New York: HarperCollins, 1991.

Rose, Evelyn. *The New Complete International Jewish Cookbook*. New York: Carroll & Graf Publishers, Inc., 1992.

Routhier, Nicole. *The Foods of Vietnam*. New York: Stewart, Tabori & Chang, 1989.

Rozin, Elisabeth. *Ethnic Cuisine: The Flavor-Principle Cookbook*. Lexington, Mass.: S. Green Press, 1983. Reprint. New York: Penguin Books USA Inc., Viking Penguin, 1992.

Sandler, Bea. *The African Cookbook*. New York: World Publishing, 1970.

Scharfenberg, Horst. *The Cuisines of Germany: Regional Specialties and Traditional Home Cooking*. New York: Poseidon Press, 1980.

Solomon, Charmaine. *The Complete Asian Cookbook*. New York: McGraw-Hill, 1976.

———. *Charmaine Solomon's Thai Cookbook*. Rutland, Vt.: Charles E. Tuttle Co., 1991.

Toomre, Joyce. *Classic Russian Cooking: Elena Molokhovets' A Gift to Young Housewives*. Translated, introduced, and annotated by Joyce Toomre. Bloomington, Ind.: Indiana University Press, 1992.

Volokh, Anne, with Mavis Manus. *The Art of Russian Cuisine*. New York: Collier Books, 1983.

Von Bremzen, Anya, and John Welchman. *Please To The Table: The Russian Cookbook*. New York: Workman Publishing Co., 1990.

Wolfert, Paula. *Couscous and Other Good Food from Morocco*. New York: Harper & Row, 1973.

PRESENTATION AND GARNISHING

Budgen, June. *The Book of Garnishes*. Los Angeles: HP Books, 1986.

Grotz, Peter. *Successful Cold Buffets*. New York: Van Nostrand Reinhold, 1990.

Haydock, Robert, and Yukiko Haydock. *Japanese Garnishes*. New York: Holt, Rinehart and Winston, 1980.

Larousse, David Paul. *Edible Art: Forty-Eight Garnishes for the Professional*. New York: Van Nostrand Reinhold, 1987.

Lynch, Francis Talyn. *Garnishing: A Feast for Your Eyes*. Los Angeles: HP Books, 1987.

BOOKS BY CONTRIBUTING CHEFS

Ash, John, and Sid Goldstein. *American Game Cooking*. Reading, Mass.: Addison-Wesley (Aris Books), 1991.

Beranbaum, Rose Levy. *The Cake Bible*. New York: William Morrow and Co., Inc., 1988.

Carpenter, Hugh, and Teri Sandison. *Chopstix: Quick Cooking with Pacific Flavors*. New York: Stewart, Tabori & Chang, 1990.

Golden, Harris. *Golden's Kitchen: The Artistry of Cooking and Dining on the Light Side*. Rev. 2nd ed. Phoenix, Ariz.: Quail Run Books, 1989.

Kerr, Graham. *Graham Kerr's Minimax Cookbook*. New York: Doubleday, 1992.

Malgieri, Nick. *Nick Malgieri's Perfect Pastry*. New York: Macmillan, 1989.

Medrich, Alice. *Cocolat*. New York: Warner Books, 1990.

Milliken, Mary Sue, and Susan Feniger. *City Cuisine*. New York: William Morris and Co., Inc., 1989.

Miller, Mark. *Coyote Cafe*. Berkeley, Calif.: Ten Speed Press, 1989.

Puck, Wolfgang. *Adventures in the Kitchen: 175 New Recipes from Spago, Chinois on Main, Postrio and Eureka*. New York: Random House, 1991.

———. *The Wolfgang Puck Cookbook*. New York: Random House, 1986.

Richard, Michel. *Michel Richard's Home Cooking with a French Accent*. New York: William Morrow and Co., Inc., 1993.

Roberts, Michael. *Secret Ingredients*. New York: Bantam Books, 1988.

Somerville, Annie. *Fields of Greens: New Vegetarian Recipes from the Celebrated Greens Restaurant*. New York: Bantam Books, 1993.

Tropp, Barbara. *China Moon Cookbook*. New York: Workman Publishing Co., 1992.

GLOSSARY

Acid—foods such as citrus juice, vinegar and wine that have a sour or sharp flavor (most foods are slightly acidic); acids have a pH of less than 7.

Acidulation—the browning of cut fruit caused by the reaction of an enzyme (polyphenoloxidase) with the phenolic compounds present in these fruits; this browning is often mistakenly attributed to exposure to oxygen.

Additives—substances added to foods to prevent spoilage or to improve appearance, texture, taste or nutritional value.

Aerobic bacteria—those that thrive on oxygen.

Aging—(1) the period of time during which freshly killed meat is allowed to rest so that the effects of rigor mortis dissipate; (2) the period during which freshly milled flour is allowed to rest so that it will whiten and produce less sticky doughs; the aging of flour can be chemically accelerated.

Airline breast—a boneless chicken breast with the first wing bone attached.

À la carte—(1) a menu on which each food and beverage is listed and priced separately; (2) foods cooked to order as opposed to foods cooked in advance and held for later service.

Albumen—the principal protein found in egg whites.

Al dente—(ahl den-tay) cooked foods (usually vegetables and pasta) that are prepared firm to the bite, not soft or mushy.

Alkali—also known as a base, any substance with a pH higher than 7; baking soda is one of the few alkaline foods.

Alkaloid—a number of bitter organic substances with alkaline properties; found most often in plants and sometimes used in drugs.

Allemande—(ah-luh-mahnd) a sauce made by adding lemon juice and a liaison to a velouté made from veal or chicken stock; used to make several small sauces of the velouté family.

Allumette—(al-u-met) (1) a matchstick cut of 1/8 inch × 1/8 inch × 1–2 inches (3 millimeters × 3 millimeters × 2.5–5 centimeters) usually used for potatoes; (2) a strip of puff pastry with a sweet or savory filling.

American service—restaurant service where the waiter takes the orders and brings the food to the table; the food is placed on dishes (plated) in the kitchen, making it a relatively fast method for seated service.

Amino acid—the basic molecular component of proteins; each of the approximately two dozen amino acids contain oxygen, hydrogen, carbon and nitrogen atoms.

Anaerobic bacteria—those that are able to live and grow without the presence of oxygen.

Animal husbandry—the business, science and practice of raising domesticated animals.

Anterior—at or toward the front of an object or place; opposite of posterior.

Appetizers—also known as first courses, usually small portions of hot or cold foods intended to whet the appetite in anticipation of the more substantial courses to follow.

Aquafarming—also known as aquaculture, the business, science and practice of raising large quantities of fish and shellfish in tanks, ponds or ocean pens.

Aromatic—a food added to a preparation to enhance the flavor and aroma; includes herbs and spices as well as some vegetables.

Aspic or **aspic jelly**—a clear jelly usually made from a clarified stock thickened with gelatin; used to coat foods, especially charcuterie items, and for garnish.

As-purchased (A.P.)—the condition or cost of an item as it is purchased or received from the supplier.

As-served (A.S.)—the weight or size of a food product as sold or served after processing or cooking.

Au gratin—(ah graw-ton) foods with a browned or crusted top; often made by browning a food with a bread crumb, cheese, and/or sauce topping under a broiler or salamander.

Au jus—(ah zhew) roasted meats, poultry or game served with their natural, unthickened juices.

Au sec—(ah sec) cooked until nearly dry.

Bacteria—single-celled microorganisms, some of which can cause diseases, including food-borne diseases.

Bain marie—(bane mah-ree) (1) a hot water bath used to gently cook food or keep cooked food hot; (2) a container for holding food in a hot water bath.

Baking—a dry-heat cooking method in which foods are surrounded by hot, dry air in a closed environment; similar to roasting, the term baking is usually applied to breads, pastries, vegetables and fish.

Baking powder—a mixture of sodium bicarbonate and one or more acids, generally cream of tartar and/or sodium aluminum sulfate, used to leaven baked goods; it releases carbon dioxide gas if moisture is present in a formula. Single-acting baking powder releases carbon dioxide gas in the presence of moisture only; double-acting baking powder releases some carbon dioxide gas upon contact with moisture, more gas is released when heat is applied.

Baking soda—the chemical sodium bicarbonate, an alkaline compound that releases carbon dioxide gas when combined with an acid and moisture; used to leaven baked goods.

Ballotine—(bahl-lo-teen) similar to a galantine, it is usually made by stuffing a deboned poultry leg with forcemeat; it is then poached or braised and normally served hot.

Barbecue—(1) to cook foods over dry heat created by the burning of hardwood or hardwood charcoals; (2) a tangy tomato- or vinegar-based sauce used for grilled foods; (3) foods cooked by this method and/or with this sauce.

Barding—tying thin slices of fat, such as bacon or pork fatback, over meats or poultry that have little to no natural fat covering in order to protect and moisten them during roasting.

Basting—moistening foods during cooking (usually roasting, broiling or grilling) with melted fat, pan drippings, sauce or other liquids to prevent drying and to add flavor.

Batonnet—(bah-toh-nah) foods cut into matchstick shapes of 1/4 inch × 1/4 inch × 2–2 1/2 inches (6 millimeters × 6 millimeters × 5–6 centimeters).

Batter—(1) a semiliquid mixture containing flour or other starch used to make cakes and breads. The gluten development is minimized and the liquid forms the continuous medium in which other ingredients are disbursed; generally contains more fat, sugar and liquids than a dough; (2) a semiliquid mixture of liquid and starch used to coat foods for deep-frying.

Baumé scale—(boh-may) see **Hydrometer**.

Bavarian cream—a sweet dessert mixture made by thickening custard sauce with gelatin and then folding in whipped cream; the final product is poured into a mold and chilled until firm.

Beard—a clump of dark threads found on a mussel.

Béarnaise—(bare-naze) a sauce made of butter and egg yolks and flavored with a reduction of vinegar, shallots, tarragon and peppercorns.

Beating—a mixing method in which foods are vigorously agitated to incorporate air or develop gluten; a spoon or electric mixer with its paddle attachment is used.

Béchamel—(bay-shah-mell) a leading sauce made by thickening milk with a white roux and adding seasonings.

Beef—the meat of domesticated cattle.

Beefalo—the product of crossbreeding a bison (American buffalo) and a domestic beef animal.

Berry—(1) the kernel of certain grains such as wheat; (2) small, juicy fruits that grow on vines and bushes.

Beurre blanc—(burr blanhk) (Fr. for white butter) an emulsified butter sauce made from shallots, white wine and butter.

Beurre composé—(burr kom-poz-a) see **Compound butter**.

Beurre manié—(burr man-yay) a combination of equal amounts by weight of flour and soft, whole butter; it is whisked into a simmering sauce at the end of the cooking process for quick thickening and added sheen and flavor.

Beurre noir—(burr nwar) (Fr. for black butter) whole butter heated until dark brown; sometimes flavored with vinegar.

Beurre noisette—(burr nwah-zett) whole butter heated until it turns light brown, giving off a nutty aroma.

Beurre rouge—(burr rooge) (Fr. for red butter) an emulsified butter sauce made from shallots, red wine and butter.

Bilateral—symmetrical halves arranged along a central axis.

Biscuit method—a mixing method used to make biscuits, scones and flaky doughs; it involves cutting cold fat into the flour and other dry ingredients before any liquid is added.

Bisque—(bisk) a soup made from shellfish; classic versions are thickened with rice.

Bivalves—mollusks such as clams, oysters and mussels that have two bilateral shells attached at a central hinge.

Blanching—very briefly and partially cooking a food in boiling water or hot fat; usually used to assist preparation (for example, to loosen peels from vegetables), as part of a combination cooking method, to remove undesirable flavors or to prepare a food for freezing.

Blanquette—(blang-kett) a white stew made of a white sauce and meat or poultry that is simmered without first browning.

Blending—a mixing method in which two or more ingredients are combined just until they are evenly distributed; a spoon, rubber spatula, whisk or electric mixer with its paddle attachment is used.

Bloom—(1) a white, powdery layer that sometimes appears on chocolate if the cocoa butter separates; (2) a measure of gelatin's strength.

Blown sugar—a boiled mixture of sucrose, glucose and tartaric acid colored and shaped using an air pump; used to make fruits and containers.

Boiling—a moist-heat cooking method that uses convection to transfer heat from a hot (approximately 212°F [100°C]) liquid to the food submerged in it; the turbulent waters and higher temperatures cook foods more quickly than do poaching or simmering.

Bordelaise—(bor-da-lays) a brown sauce flavored with a reduction of red wine, shallots, pepper and herbs and garnished with marrow.

Bouchées—(boo-shays) small puff pastry shells often filled with a savory mixture and used for hors d'oeuvres.

Bound salad—a salad composed of cooked meats, poultry, fish, shellfish, pasta or potatoes combined with a dressing.

Bouquet garni—(boo-kay gar-nee) fresh herbs and vegetables tied into a bundle with twine and used to flavor stocks, sauces, soups and stews.

Bouquetiere—(buk-a-tyer) a garnish (bouquet) of carefully cut and arranged fresh vegetables.

Braising—a combination cooking method in which foods are first browned in hot fat, then covered and slowly cooked in a small amount of liquid over low heat; braising uses a combination of simmering and steaming to transfer heat from the liquid (conduction) and the air (convection) to the foods.

Bran—the tough outer layer of a cereal grain and the part highest in fiber.

Brandy—an alcoholic beverage made by distilling the fermented mash of grapes or other fruits.

Brawn—also called an aspic terrine, made from simmered meats packed into a terrine and covered with aspic.

Brazier or **brasier**—a pan designed for braising; usually round with two handles and a tight-fitting lid.

Breading—(1) a coating of bread or cracker crumbs, cornmeal or other dry meal applied to foods that will typically be deep-fried or pan-fried; (2) the process of applying this coating.

Brigade—also known as the kitchen brigade, a system of staffing a kitchen so that each worker is assigned a set of specific tasks; these tasks are often related by cooking method, equipment or the type of foods being produced.

Brine—a mixture of salt, water and seasonings used to preserve foods.

Brioche—(bree-yohsh) a rich yeast bread containing large amounts of eggs and butter.

Brochettes—(bro-shetts) skewers, either small hors d'oeuvre or large entree size, threaded with meat, poultry, fish, shellfish and/or vegetables and grilled, broiled or baked; sometimes served with a dipping sauce.

Broiling—a dry-heat cooking method in which foods are cooked by heat radiating from an overhead source.

Broth—a flavorful liquid obtained from the long simmering of meats and/or vegetables.

Browning—see **Caramelization**.

Brown sauce—see **Espagnole**.

Brown stew—a stew in which the meat is first browned in hot fat.

Brown stock—a richly colored stock made of chicken, veal, beef or game bones and vegetables, all of which are caramelized before they are simmered in water with seasonings.

Brunch—a late morning to early afternoon meal that takes the place of both breakfast and lunch; a brunch menu often offers breakfast foods as well as almost anything else.

Brunoise—(broo-nwah) (1) foods cut into cubes of 1/8 inch × 1/8 inch × 1/8 inch (3 millimeters × 3 millimeters × 3 millimeters); (2) foods garnished with vegetables cut in this manner.

Buffet service—diners generally serve themselves foods arranged on a counter or table or are served by workers assigned to specific areas of the buffet. Usually buffet-service-style restaurants charge by the meal; restaurants offering buffet service that charge by the dish are known as cafeterias.

Butcher—(1) to slaughter and dress or fabricate animals for consumption; (2) the person who slaughters and fabricates animals.

Butler service—the use of servers to pass foods (typically hors d'oeuvres) or drinks arranged on trays.

Buttercream—a light, smooth, fluffy frosting of sugar, fat and flavorings; egg yolks or whipped egg whites are sometimes added. There are three principal kinds: simple, Italian and French.

Butterflying—slicing boneless meat, fish or shrimp nearly in half lengthwise so that they spread open like a book; used to increase surface area and speed cooking.

Cafeteria—see **Buffet service**.

Caffeine—an alkaloid found in coffee beans, tea leaves and cocoa beans that acts as a stimulant.

Cake—in American usage, refers to a broad range of pastries including layer cakes, coffeecakes and gâteaux; can refer to almost anything that is baked, tender, sweet and sometimes frosted.

Calf—(1) a young cow or bull; (2) the meat of calves slaughtered when they are older than five months.

Calorie—the unit of energy measured by the amount of heat required to raise 1000 grams of water one degree Celsius; it is also written as *kilocalorie* or *kcal* and is used as a measure of food energy.

Canapé—(kahn-ah-pay) tiny open-faced sandwich served as an hors d'oeuvre; usually composed of a small piece of bread or toast topped with a savory spread and garnish.

Canning—a preservation method in which the food is sealed in a glass or metal container and subjected to high temperatures for a specific period of time in order to destroy microorganisms that cause spoilage; the sealed environment eliminates oxidation and retards decomposition.

Capon—(kay-pahn) the class of surgically castrated male chickens; they have well-flavored meat and soft, smooth skin.

Capsaicin—(kap-say-ih-sin) an alkaloid found in a chile pepper's placental ribs that provides the pepper's heat.

Caramelization—the process of cooking sugars; the browning of sugar enhances the flavor and appearance of foods.

Carbohydrates—a group of compounds composed of oxygen, hydrogen and carbon that supply the body with energy (4 calories per gram); carbohydrates are classified as simple (including certain sugars) and complex (including starches and fiber).

Carotenoid—a naturally occurring pigment that predominates in red and yellow vegetables such as carrots and red peppers.

Carryover cooking—the cooking that occurs after a food is removed from a heat source; it is accomplished by the residual heat remaining in the food.

Cartilage—also known as gristle, a tough, whitish elastic connective tissue that helps give structure to an animal's body.

Carve—to cut cooked meat or poultry into portions.

Casings—membranes used to hold forcemeat for sausages; they can be natural animal intestines or manufactured from collagen extracted from cattle hides.

Casserole—(1) a heavy dish, usually ceramic, for baking foods; (2) foods baked in a casserole dish.

Caul fat—a fatty membrane from pig or sheep intestines; it resembles fine netting and is used to bard roasts and pâtés and to encase forcemeat for sausages.

Cellulose—a complex carbohydrate found in the cell wall of plants; it is edible but indigestible by humans.

Cephalopods—mollusks with a single, thin internal shell called a pen or cuttlebone, well-developed eyes, a number of arms that attach to the head and a saclike fin-bearing mantle; include squid and octopus.

Chafing dish—a metal dish with a heating unit (flame or electric) used to keep foods warm at tableside or during buffet service.

Chalazae cords—thick, twisted strands of egg white that anchor the yolk in place.

Charcuterie—the production of pâtés, terrines, galantines, sausages and similar foods.

Cheesecloth—a light, fine mesh gauze used to strain liquids and make sachets.

Chef de partie—also known as station chef, produces the menu items under the direct supervision of the chef or sous-chef.

Chef du cuisine—also known simply as chef, the person responsible for all kitchen operations, developing menu items and setting the kitchen's tone and tempo.

Chef's knife—an all-purpose knife used for chopping, slicing and mincing; its tapering blade is 8–14 inches long.

Chemical hazards—a danger to the safety of food caused by chemical substances, especially cleaning agents, pesticides and toxic metals.

Chemical leavening agents—see **Baking powder** and **Baking soda**; through chemical reactions between acids and bases, these products release gases used to leaven baked goods.

Chevre—(shev-ruh) (Fr. for goat) generally refers to a cheese made from goat's milk.

Chiffonade—(cheh-fon-nahd) (1) to finely slice or shred leafy vegetables or herbs; (2) the finely cut leafy vegetables or herbs often used as a garnish or bedding.

Chile—a member of the capsicum plant family.

Chili—the stewlike dish containing chiles.

Chilled—a food that has been refrigerated.

Chilli—a commercial spice powder containing a blend of seasonings.

China cap—a cone-shaped strainer made of perforated metal.

Chinoise—(shen-wasz) a conical strainer made of fine mesh, used for straining and puréeing foods.

Chlorophyll—a naturally occurring pigment that predominates in green vegetables such as cabbage.

Cholesterol—a fatty substance found in foods derived from animal products and in the human body; it has been linked to heart disease.

Chop—(1) a cut of meat including part of the rib; (2) to cut an item into small pieces where uniformity of size and shape is neither feasible nor necessary.

Chowder—a hearty soup made from fish, shellfish and/or vegetables, usually containing milk and potatoes and often thickened with roux.

Chutney—a sweet-and-sour condiment made of fruits and/or vegetables cooked in vinegar with sugar and spices; some chutneys are reduced to a purée, while others retain recognizable pieces of their ingredients.

Cider—mildly fermented apple juice; nonalcoholic apple juice may also be labeled cider.

Citrus—fruits characterized by a thick rind, most of which is a bitter white pith (albedo) with a thin exterior layer of colored skin (zest); their flesh is segmented, juicy and varies from bitter to tart to sweet.

Clarification—(1) the process of transforming a broth into a clear consommé by trapping impurities with a clearmeat consisting of the egg white protein albumen, ground meat, an acidic product, mirepoix and other ingredients; (2) the clearmeat used to clarify a broth.

Clarified butter—purified butterfat; the butter is melted and the water and milk solids are removed.

Classes—the subdivisions of poultry kinds based on the bird's age and tenderness.

Classic cuisine—a late 19th- and early 20th-century refinement and simplification of French grande cuisine. Classic (or classical) cuisine relies upon the thorough exploration of culinary principles and techniques and emphasizes the refined preparation and presentation of superb ingredients.

Clean—to remove visible dirt and soil.

Clearmeat—see **Clarification**.

Clear soups—unthickened soups including broths, consommés and broth-based soups.

Coagulation—the irreversible transformation of proteins from a liquid or semi-liquid state to a drier, solid state; usually accomplished through the application of heat.

Cocoa butter—the fat found in cocoa beans and used in fine chocolates.

Colander—a perforated bowl, with or without a base or legs, used to strain foods.

Collagen—a protein found in nearly all connective tissues; it dissolves when cooked with moisture.

Combination cooking methods—cooking methods, principally braising and stewing, that employ both dry-heat and moist-heat procedures.

Composed salad—a salad prepared by arranging each of the ingredients (the base, body, garnish and dressing) on individual plates in an artistic fashion.

Compound butter—also known as a beurre composé, a mixture of softened whole butter and flavorings used as a sauce or to flavor and color other sauces.

Compound sauces—see **Small sauces**.

Concasse—(kon-kaas say) peeled, seeded and diced tomatoes.

Concasser—(kon-kaas-say) to pound or chop coarsely; usually used for tomatoes or parsley.

Condiment—traditionally, any item added to a dish for flavor, including herbs, spices and vinegars; now also refers to cooked or prepared flavorings such as prepared mustards, relishes, bottled sauces or pickles.

Conduction—the transfer of heat from one item to another through direct contact.

Confit—meat or poultry (often lightly salt-cured) slowly cooked and preserved in its own fat and served hot.

Connective tissues—tissues found throughout an animal's body that hold together and support other tissues such as muscles.

Consommé—a rich stock or broth that has been clarified with clearmeat to remove impurities.

Contaminants—biological, chemical or physical substances that can be harmful when consumed in sufficient quantities.

Contamination—the presence, generally unintentional, of harmful organisms or substances.

Convection—the transfer of heat caused by the natural movement of molecules in a fluid (whether air, water or fat) from a warmer area to a cooler one. Mechanical convection is the movement of molecules caused by stirring.

Cookery—the art, practice or work of cooking.

Cookies—small, sweet, flat pastries; usually classified by preparation or makeup techniques as drop, icebox, bar, cutout, pressed and wafer.

Cooking—the transfer of energy from a heat source to a food; this energy alters the food's molecular structure, changing its texture, flavor, aroma and appearance.

Cooking medium—the air, fat, water or steam in which a food is cooked.

Coring—the process of removing the seeds or pit from a fruit or fruit-vegetable.

Cost of goods sold—the total cost of food items sold during a given period; calculated as beginning inventory plus purchases minus ending inventory.

Cost per portion—the cost of one serving; calculated as the total recipe cost divided by the number of portions produced from that recipe.

Coulis—(koo-lees) a sauce made from a purée of vegetables or fruit; may be hot or cold.

Count—the number of individual items in a given measure of weight or volume.

Court bouillon—(cort boo-yon) water simmered with vegetables, seasonings and an acidic product such as vinegar or wine; used for simmering or poaching fish, shellfish or vegetables.

Couscoussier—two bulbous pots, the top one has a perforated bottom and sits snugly on the bottom pot; used to cook couscous.

Cows—female cattle after their first calving, principally raised for milk and calf production.

Cream filling—a pie filling made of flavored pastry cream thickened with cornstarch.

Creaming—a mixing method in which softened fat and sugar are vigorously combined to incorporate air; used for making some quick breads, cookies and high-fat cakes.

Creams—also known as crèmes, include light, fluffy or creamy-textured dessert foods made with whipped cream or whipped egg whites, such as Bavarian creams, chiffons, mousses and crème Chantilly.

Cream soup—a soup made from vegetables cooked in a liquid that is thickened with a starch and puréed; cream is then incorporated to add richness and flavor.

Crème Anglaise—(crem ahn-glas) or crème a l'anglaise; see **Vanilla custard sauce**.

Crème caramel—(crem cah-rah-mel) like crème renversée and flan, a custard baked over a layer of caramelized sugar and inverted for service.

Crème Chantilly—(crem shan-tee) heavy cream whipped to soft peaks and flavored with sugar and vanilla; used to garnish pastries or desserts or folded into cooled custard or pastry cream for fillings.

Crème Chiboust—(crem chee-boos) a pastry cream lightened by folding in Italian meringue.

Crème patissière—(crem pah-tees-syehr) see **Pastry cream**.

Crepe—(krayp) a thin, delicate unleavened griddlecake made with a very thin egg batter cooked in a very hot sauté pan; used in sweet and savory preparations.

Critical control point—under the HACCP system, it is any step during the processing of a food when a mistake can result in the transmission, growth or survival of pathogenic bacteria.

Croissant—(krwah-san) a crescent-shaped roll made from a rich, rolled-in yeast dough.

Croquette—(crow-kett) a food that has been puréed or bound with a thick sauce (usually béchamel or velouté), made into small shapes, then breaded and deep-fried.

Cross-contamination—the transfer of bacteria or other contaminants from one food, work surface or equipment to another.

Croute, en—(awn croot) a food encased in a bread or pastry crust.

Crouton—a bread or pastry garnish, usually toasted or sautéed until crisp.

Crudités—(croo-dee-tays) generally refers to raw or blanched vegetables served as an hors d'oeuvre and often accompanied by a dip.

Crustaceans—shellfish characterized by a hard outer skeleton or shell and jointed appendages; include lobsters, crabs and shrimp.

Cuisine—the ingredients, seasonings, cooking procedures and styles attributable to a particular group of people; the group can be defined by geography, history, ethnicity, politics, culture or religion.

Cuisson—(kwee-zon) the liquid used for shallow poaching.

Curdle—the separation of milk or egg mixtures into solid and liquid components; caused by overcooking, high heat or the presence of acids.

Curing salt—a mixture of salt and sodium nitrite that inhibits bacterial growth; used as a preservative, often for charcuterie items.

Custard—any liquid thickened by the coagulation of egg proteins; its consistency depends on the ratio of eggs to liquid and the type of liquid used. Custards can be baked in the oven or cooked in a bain marie or on the stove top.

Cutlet—a relatively thick boneless slice of meat.

Cutting—(1) reducing a food to smaller pieces; (2) a mixing method in which solid fat is incorporated into dry ingredients until only lumps of the desired size remain.

Cutting loss—the unavoidable and unrecoverable loss of food during fabrication; the loss is usually the result of food particles sticking to the cutting board or the evaporation of liquids.

Cuttlebone—also known as the pen, the single, thin internal shell of cephalopods.

Cycle menu—a menu that changes every day for a certain period and then repeats the same daily items in the same order (e.g., on a seven-day cycle, the same menu is used every Monday).

Dairy products—include cow's milk and foods produced from cow's milk such as butter, yogurt, sour cream and cheese.

Decline phase—a period during which bacteria die at an accelerated rate, also known as the negative growth phase.

Decoction—(1) boiling a food until its flavor is removed; (2) a procedure used for brewing coffee.

Decorator's icing—see **Royal icing**.

Deep-frying—a dry-heat cooking method using convection to transfer heat to a food submerged in hot fat; foods to be deep-fried are usually first coated in batter or breading.

Deglaze—to swirl or stir a liquid (usually wine or stock) in a sauté pan or other pan to dissolve cooked food particles remaining on the bottom; the resulting mixture often becomes the base for a sauce.

Degrease—to skim the fat from the top of a liquid such as a sauce or stock.

Demi-glace—(deh-me glass) (Fr. for half-glaze) a mixture of half brown stock and half brown sauce reduced by half.

Detrempe—(day-trup-eh) a paste made with flour and water during the first stage of preparing a pastry dough, especially rolled-in doughs.

Deveining—the process of removing a shrimp's digestive tract.

Deviled—meat, poultry or other food seasoned with mustard, vinegar and other spicy seasonings.

Diagonals—elongated or oval-shaped slices of cylindrical vegetables or fruits.

Dice—(1) to cut foods into cubes: 1/4 inch (6 millimeters) for small, 3/8 inch (9 millimeters) for medium and 5/8 (1.5 centimeters) for large; (2) the cubes of cut food.

Dietary fiber—see **Fiber**.

Dip—a thick, creamy sauce, served hot or cold, to accompany crudités, crackers, chips or other foods, especially as an hors d'oeuvre; dips are often based on sour cream, mayonnaise or cream cheese.

Direct contamination—the contamination of raw foods in their natural setting or habitat.

Docking—pricking small holes in an unbaked dough or crust to allow steam to escape and prevent the dough from rising when baked.

Dough—a mixture of flour and other ingredients used in baking; has a low moisture content and gluten forms the continuous medium into which other ingredients are embedded; it is often stiff enough to cut into shapes.

Drawn—a market form for fish in which the viscera is removed.

Dredging—coating a food with flour or finely ground crumbs; usually done prior to sautéing or frying or as the first step of the standardized breading procedure.

Dressed—(1) an animal carcass trimmed or otherwise prepared for consumption; (2) a market form for fish in which the viscera, gills, fins and scales are removed.

Drupes—see **Stone fruits**.

Dry-heat cooking methods—cooking methods, principally broiling, grilling, roasting and baking, sautéing, pan-frying and deep-frying, that use air or fat to transfer heat through conduction and convection; dry-heat cooking methods allow surface sugars to caramelize.

Drying—a preservation method in which the food's moisture content is dramatically reduced; drying changes the food's texture, flavor and appearance.

Duchesse potatoes—(duh-shees) a purée of cooked potatoes, butter and egg yolks, seasoned with salt, pepper and nutmeg; can be eaten as is or used to prepare several classic potato dishes.

Dumpling—any of a variety of small starchy products made from doughs or batters that are simmered or steamed; can be plain or filled.

Durum—a type of hard wheat milled into semolina flour which is used for making pasta.

Duxelles—(duke-sell) a coarse paste made of finely chopped mushrooms sautéed with shallots in butter.

Éclair paste—(ay-clahr) also known as pâte à choux, a soft dough that produces hollow baked products with crisp exteriors; used for making éclairs, cream puffs and savory products.

Edible portion (E.P.)—the amount of a food available for consumption after trimming or fabrication.

Egg wash—a mixture of beaten eggs (whole eggs, yolks or whites) and a liquid, usually milk or water, used to coat doughs before baking to add sheen.

Elastin—a protein found in connective tissues, particularly ligaments and tendons, it often appears as the white or silver covering on meats known as silverskin; elastin does not dissolve when cooked.

Émincé—(eh-manss) a small, thin boneless piece of meat.

Emulsification—the process by which generally unmixable liquids, such as oil and water, are forced into a uniform distribution.

Emulsion—(1) a uniform mixture of two unmixable liquids; (2) flavoring oils such as orange and lemon, mixed into water with the aid of emulsifiers.

Endosperm—the largest part of a cereal grain and a source of protein and carbohydrates (starch); it is the part used primarily in milled products.

Entree—(ahn-tray) the main dish of an American meal, usually meat, poultry, fish or shellfish accompanied by a vegetable and starch; in France, the first course, served before the fish and meat courses.

Enzymatic browning—see **Acidulation**.

Enzyme—proteins that aid specific chemical reactions in plants and animals.

Escalope—(ess-cal-lop) see **Scallop**.

Espagnole—(ess-spah-nyol) also known as brown sauce, a leading sauce made of brown stock, mirepoix and tomatoes thickened with brown roux; often used to produce demi-glace.

Essential nutrients—nutrients that must be provided by food because the body cannot or does not produce them in sufficient quantities.

Ethnic cuisine—generally, the cuisine of a group of people having a common cultural heritage, as opposed to the cuisine of a group of people bound together by geography or political factors.

Ethylene gas—a colorless, odorless hydrocarbon gas naturally emitted from fruits and fruit-vegetables that encourages ripening.

Evaporation—the process by which heated water molecules move faster and faster until the water turns to a gas (steam) and vaporizes; evaporation is responsible for the drying of foods during cooking.

Extracts—concentrated mixtures of ethyl alcohol and flavoring oils such as vanilla, almond and lemon.

Extrusion—the process of forcing pasta dough through perforated plates to create various shapes; pasta dough that is not extruded must be rolled and cut.

Fabricate—to cut a large item into smaller portions; often refers to the butchering of fish or shellfish.

Fabricated cuts—individual portions of meat cut from a subprimal.

Facultative bacteria—those that can adapt and will survive with or without oxygen.

Fancy—(1) fish that has been previously frozen; (2) a quality grade for fruits, especially canned or frozen.

Fatback—fresh pork fat from the back of the pig, used primarily for barding.

Fats—(1) a group of compounds composed of oxygen, hydrogen and carbon atoms that supply the body with energy (9 calories per gram); fats are classified as saturated, monounsaturated or polyunsaturated; (2) the general term for butter, lard, shortening, oil and margarine used as cooking media or ingredients.

Fermentation—(1) the process by which yeast converts sugar into alcohol and carbon dioxide; (2) the period of time that yeast bread dough is left to rise.

Feuillettes—(fuh-yuh-lyeth) square, rectangular or diamond-shaped puff pastry boxes that can be filled with a sweet or savory mixture.

Fiber—also known as dietary fiber, indigestible carbohydrates found in grains, fruits, and vegetables; fiber aids digestion.

FIFO (First In, First Out)—an inventory storage and utilization process in which the oldest product is always used first.

Filé—(fee-lay) a seasoning and thickening agent made from dried, ground sassafras leaves.

Filet, Fillet—(fee-lay) (1) filet: the boneless tenderloin of meat; (2) fillet: the side of a fish removed intact, boneless or semiboneless, with or without skin; (3) to cut such a piece.

Fish scaler—an inflexible, rasplike tool used to remove scales from fish.

Fish velouté—a velouté sauce made from fish stock.

Flambé—(flahm-bay) food served flaming; produced by igniting brandy, rum or other liquor.

Flash-frozen—food that has been frozen very rapidly using metal plates, extremely low temperatures or chemical solutions.

Flatfish—fish with asymmetrical, compressed bodies that swim in a horizontal position and have both eyes on the top of the head; include sole, flounder and halibut.

Flat icing—a white, glossy glaze used on danish pastries.

Flavonoid—a naturally occurring pigment that predominates in red, purple and white vegetables such as cauliflower, red cabbage and beets.

Flavoring—an item that adds a new taste to a food and alters its natural flavors; flavorings include herbs, spices, vinegars and condiments.

Fleuron—(floor-ahn) a crescent-shaped piece of puff pastry used as a garnish.

Flour—a powdery substance of varying degrees of fineness made by milling grains such as wheat, corn or rye.

Foie gras—(fwah grah) liver of specially fattened geese.

Fold—a measurement of the strength of vanilla extract.

Folding—a mixing method used to gently incorporate light, airy products into heavier ingredients (for example, mixing dry ingredients with whipped eggs).

Fond—(fahn) (1) Fr. for stock; (2) Fr. for bottom; the concentrated juices, drippings and bits of food left in pans after foods are roasted or sautéed; used to flavor sauces made directly in the pans in which the foods were cooked.

Fondant—(fahn-dant) a sweet, thick opaque sugar paste commonly used for glazing pastries such as napoleons or making candies.

Fond lié—(fahn lee-ay) See **Jus lié**.

Food cost—the cost of the materials that go directly into the production of menu items.

Food cost percentage—the ratio of the cost of foods served to the food sales dollars during a given period.

Food danger zone—the temperature range of 40–140°F (5–60°C) which is most favorable for bacterial growth.

Food Pyramid—a dietary guide that prioritizes and proportions food choices among six general food groups.

Forcemeat—a preparation made from uncooked ground meats, poultry, fish or shellfish, seasoned, and emulsified with fat; commonly prepared as country-style, basic and mousseline and used for pâtés, sausages and other charcuterie items.

Formula—a recipe; the term is most often used in the bakeshop.

Frangipane—(fran-juh-pahn) a sweet almond and egg filling cooked inside pastry.

Free-range chickens—chickens allowed to move freely and forage for food; as opposed to chickens raised in coops.

Free-range veal—the meat of calves that are allowed to roam freely and eat grasses and other natural foods; this meat is pinker and more strongly flavored than that of milk-fed calves.

Freezer burn—the surface dehydration and discoloration of food that results from moisture loss at below-freezing temperatures.

French service—restaurant service where one waiter (a captain) takes the order, does the tableside cooking and brings the drinks and food, the secondary or back waiter serves bread and water, clears each course, crumbs the table and serves the coffee.

Fresh—a food that is not and has never been frozen.

Fresh-frozen—a food that has been frozen while still fresh.

Fricassee—(frick-a-see) a white stew in which the meat is cooked in fat without browning before the liquid is added.

Frittata—(free-tah-ta) an open-faced omelet of Spanish-Italian heritage.

Frosting—also known as icing, a sweet decorative coating used as a filling

between the layers or as a coating over the top and sides of a cake.

Fruit—refers to the edible organ that develops from the ovary of a flowering plant and contains one or more seeds (pips or pits).

Fruit-vegetables—foods such as avocados, eggplants, chile peppers and tomatoes that are botanically fruits but are most often prepared and served like vegetables.

Frying—a dry-heat cooking method in which foods are cooked in hot fat; includes sautéing and stir-frying, pan-frying and deep-frying.

Fumet—(foo-may) a stock made from fish bones or shellfish shells and vegetables simmered in a liquid with flavorings.

Fungi—a large group of plants ranging from single-celled organisms to giant mushrooms; the most common are molds and yeasts.

Galantine—similar to a ballottine, it is a charcuterie item made from a forcemeat of poultry, game or suckling pig usually wrapped in the skin of the bird or animal and poached in an appropriate stock; often served cold, usually in aspic.

Game—birds and animals hunted for sport or food; many game birds and animals are now ranch-raised and commercially available.

Game hen—the class of young or immature progeny of Cornish chickens or of a Cornish chicken and White Rock chicken; they are small and very flavorful.

Ganache—(ga-nosh) a rich blend of chocolate and heavy cream and, optionally, flavorings, used as a pastry or candy filling or frosting.

Garde-manger—(gar mawn-zhay) (1) also known as the pantry chef, the cook in charge of cold food production, including salads and salad dressings, charcuterie items, cold appetizers and buffet items; (2) the work area where these foods are prepared.

Garnish—(1) food used as an attractive decoration; (2) a subsidiary food used to add flavor or character to the main ingredient in a dish (for example, noodles in chicken noodle soup).

Gastronomy—the art and science of eating well.

Gâteau—(ga-toe) (1) in American usage, refers to any cake-type dessert; (2) in

French usage, refers to various pastry items made with puff pastry, éclair paste, short dough or sweet dough.

Gelatin—a tasteless and odorless mixture of proteins (especially collagen) extracted from bones, connective tissues and other animal parts; when dissolved in a hot liquid and then cooled, it forms a jellylike substance; used as a thickener and stabilizer.

Gelatinization—the process by which starch granules are cooked. They absorb moisture when placed in a liquid and heated; as the moisture is absorbed, the product swells, softens and clarifies slightly.

Gelato—(jah-laht-to) an Italian-style ice cream that is denser than American-style ice cream.

Genoise—(zhen-waahz) (1) a form of whipped-egg cake that uses whole eggs whipped with sugar; (2) a French sponge cake.

Germ—the smallest portion of a cereal grain and the only part that contains fat.

Giblets—the collective term for edible poultry viscera including gizzards, hearts, livers and necks.

Gizzard—a bird's second stomach.

Glace de poisson—(glahss duh pwah-sawng) a syrupy glaze made by reducing a fish stock.

Glace de viande—(glahss duh vee-awnd) a dark, syrupy meat glaze made by reducing a brown stock.

Glace de volaille—(glahss duh vo-lahy) a light brown, syrupy glaze made by reducing a chicken stock.

Glaze—(1) any shiny coating applied to food or created by browning; (2) the dramatic reduction and concentration of a stock; (3) a thin, flavored coating poured or dripped onto a cake or pastry.

Gliaden—see **Gluten**.

Glucose—an important energy source for the body; also known as blood sugar.

Gluten—a tough elastic substance created when flour is moistened and mixed; it gives structure and strength to baked goods and is responsible for their volume, texture and appearance. The proteins necessary for gluten formation are glutenin and gliaden.

Glutenin—see **Gluten**.

Grading—a series of voluntary programs offered by the United States Department of Agriculture to designate a food's overall quality.

Grains—(1) grasses that bear edible seeds, including corn, rice and wheat; (2) the fruit (i.e., seed or kernel) of such grasses.

Gram—the basic unit of weight in the metric system; equal to approximately one-thirtieth of an ounce.

Grande Cuisine—the rich, intricate and elaborate cuisine of the 18th- and 19th-century French aristocracy and upper classes. It is based upon the rational identification, development and adoption of strict culinary principles.

Grate—to cut a food into small, thin shreds by rubbing it against a serrated metal plate known as a grater.

Green meats—freshly slaughtered meats that have not had sufficient time to age and develop tenderness and flavor.

Gremolada—(greh-moa-lah-dah) an aromatic garnish of chopped parsley, garlic and lemon zest used for osso buco.

Grilling—a dry-heat cooking method in which foods are cooked by heat radiating from a source located below the cooking surface; the heat can be generated by electricity or by burning gas, hardwood or hardwood charcoals.

Grind—to pulverize or reduce food to small particles using a mechanical grinder or food processor.

Grinding—a milling process in which grains are reduced to a powder; the powder can be of differing degrees of fineness or coarseness.

Gristle—see **Cartilage**.

Gross profit—or gross margin, the difference between the cost of goods sold and sales during a given period of time.

Gum paste—a smooth dough of sugar and gelatin that can be colored and used to make decorations, especially for pastries.

HACCP—see **Hazard Analysis Critical Control Points**.

Hanging—the practice of allowing eviscerated (drawn or gutted) game to age in a dry, well-ventilated place; hanging helps tenderize the flesh and strengthen its flavor.

Hazard Analysis Critical Control Points (HACCP)—a rigorous system of self-inspection used to manage and maintain sanitary conditions in all types of food service operations; it focuses on the flow of food through the food service facility to identify any point or step in preparation (known as a critical control point) where some action must be taken to prevent or minimize a risk or hazard.

Heifers—young cows; cows before their first calving.

Heimlich maneuver—the first aid procedure for choking victims in which sudden upward pressure is applied to the upper abdomen in order to force any foreign object from the windpipe.

Herbs—any of a large group of aromatic plants whose leaves, stems or flowers are used to add flavors to other foods.

High-ratio cakes—a form of creamed-fat cake that uses emulsified shortening and has a two-stage mixing method.

Hollandaise—(holl-uhn-daze) an emulsified sauce made of butter, egg yolks and flavorings (especially lemon juice).

Homogenization—the process by which milk fat is prevented from separating out of milk products.

Hors d'oeuvres—(ohr durvs) very small portions of hot or cold foods served before the meal to stimulate the appetite.

Hotel pan—a rectangular, stainless steel pan with a lip allowing it to rest in a storage shelf or steam table; available in several standard sizes.

Hull—also known as the husk, the outer covering of a fruit, seed or grain.

Hybrid—the result of crossbreeding different species that are genetically unalike; it is often a unique product.

Hybrid menu—a menu combining features of a static menu with a cycle menu or a market menu of specials.

Hydrogenation—the process used to harden oils: Hydrogen atoms are added to unsaturated fat molecules, making them partially or completely saturated and thus solid at room temperature.

Hydrometer—a device used to measure specific gravity; it shows degrees of concentration on the Baumé scale.

Hygroscopic—the characteristic of a food to readily absorb moisture from the air.

Icing—see **Frosting**.

IMPS/NAMP—see **NAMP/IMPS**.

Induction cooking—a cooking method that uses a special coil placed below the stove top's surface in combination with specially designed cookware to generate heat rapidly with an alternating magnetic field.

Infection—in the food safety context, a disease caused by the ingestion of live pathogenic bacteria that continue their life processes in the consumer's intestinal tract.

Infrared cooking—a heating method that uses an electric or ceramic element heated to such a high temperature that it gives off waves of radiant heat that cook the food.

Infusion—(1) the extraction of flavors from a food at a temperature below boiling; (2) a group of coffee brewing techniques including steeping, filtering and dripping; (3) the liquid resulting from this process.

Instant-read thermometer—a thermometer used to measure the internal temperature of foods; the stem is inserted in the food, producing an instant temperature readout.

Intoxication—in the food safety context, a disease caused by the toxins that bacteria produce during their life processes.

Inventory—the listing and counting of all foods in the kitchen, storerooms and refrigerators.

IQF (Individually Quick Frozen)—the technique of rapidly freezing each individual item of food such as slices of fruit, berries or pieces of fish before packaging; IQF foods are not packaged with syrup or sauce.

Irradiation—a preservation method used for certain fruits, vegetables and grains in which ionizing radiation sterilizes the food, slows ripening and prevents sprouting; irradiation has little effect on the food's texture, flavor or appearance.

Jam—a fruit gel made from fruit pulp and sugar.

Jelly—a fruit gel made from fruit juice and sugar.

Juice—the liquid extracted from any fruit or vegetable.

Julienne—(ju-lee-en) (1) to cut foods into stick-shaped pieces, approximately 1/8 inch × 1/8 inch × 1–2 inches (3 millimeters × 3 millimeters × 2.5–5 centimeters); (2) the stick-shaped pieces of cut food.

Jus lié—(zhew lee-ay) also known as fond lié, a sauce made by thickening brown stock with cornstarch or similar starch; often used like a demi-glace, especially to produce small sauces.

Kinds—the categories of poultry recognized by the United States Department of Agriculture: chickens, ducks, geese, guineas, pigeons and turkeys

Kitchen brigade—see **Brigade**.

Kneading—working a dough to develop gluten.

Kosher—Prepared in accordance with Jewish dietary laws.

Lag phase—a period, usually following transfer from one place to another, during which bacteria do not experience much growth.

Lamb—the meat of sheep slaughtered under the age of one year.

Lard—the rendered fat of hogs.

Larding—inserting thin slices of fat, such as pork fatback, into low-fat meats in order to add moisture.

Leading sauces—also known as mother sauces, the foundation for the entire classic repertoire of hot sauces; the five leading sauces (béchamel, velouté, espagnole [also known as brown], tomato and hollandaise) are distinguished by the liquids and thickeners used to make them. They can be seasoned and garnished to create a wide variety of small or compound sauces.

Lean doughs—yeast doughs that contain little or no sugar or fat; used for French or Italian breads.

Leavener—an ingredient or process that produces or incorporates gases in a baked product in order to increase volume, provide structure and give texture.

Lecithin—a natural emulsifier found in egg yolks.

Legumes—(lay-gyooms) (1) Fr. for vegetables; (2) a large group of vegetables with double-seamed seed pods; depending upon the variety, the seeds, pod and seeds together, or the dried seeds are eaten.

Liaison—(lee-yeh-zon) a mixture of egg yolks and heavy cream used to thicken and enrich sauces.

Liqueur—a strong, sweet, syrupy alcoholic beverage made by mixing or redistilling neutral spirits with fruits, flowers, herbs, spices or other flavorings; also known as a cordial.

Liquor—an alcoholic beverage made by distilling grains, vegetables or other foods; includes rum, whiskey and vodka.

Liter—the basic unit of volume in the metric system, equal to slightly more than a quart.

Log phase—a period of accelerated growth for bacteria.

Macaroni—(1) any dried pasta made with wheat flour and water; (2) in American usage, an elbow-shaped pasta tube.

Macerate—to soak foods in a liquid, usually alcoholic, to soften them.

Macronutrients—the nutrients needed in large quantities: carbohydrates, proteins, fats and water.

Madeira—a Portuguese fortified wine heated during aging to give it a distinctive flavor and brown color.

Maître d'hotel (maître d')—(may-tr dohtel) (1) the leader of the dining room brigade, also known as the dining room manager, he oversees the dining room or "front of the house" staff; (2) a compound butter flavored with chopped parsley and lemon juice.

Mandoline—a stainless steel, hand-operated slicing device with adjustable blades.

Marbling—Whitish streaks of inter- and intramuscular fat.

Marinade—the liquid used to marinate foods; it generally contains herbs, spices and other flavoring ingredients as well as an acidic product such as wine, vinegar or lemon juice.

Marinate—to soak a food in a seasoned liquid in order to tenderize the food and add flavor to it.

Market menu—a menu based upon product availability during a specific time period; it is written to use foods when they are in peak season or readily available.

Marmalade—a citrus jelly that also contains unpeeled slices of citrus fruit.

Marsala—a flavorful fortified sweet-to-semidry Sicilian wine.

Marzipan—a paste of ground almonds, sugar and egg whites used to fill and decorate pastries.

Matzo—thin, crisp unleavened bread made only with flour and water; can be ground into meal that is used for matzo balls and pancakes.

Mayonnaise—a thick, creamy sauce consisting of oil and vinegar emulsified with egg yolks, usually used as a salad dressing.

Mealy potatoes—also known as starchy potatoes, those with a high starch content and thick skin; they are best for baking.

Medallion—a small, round piece of meat or fish.

Melt—the process by which certain foods, especially those high in fat, gradually soften then liquefy when heated.

Menu—a list of foods and beverages available for purchase.

Meringue—(muh-reng) a foam made of beaten egg whites and sugar.

Metabolism—all of the chemical reactions and physical processes that occur continuously in living cells and organisms.

Meter—the basic unit of length in the metric system, equal to slightly more than one yard.

Mezzaluna—a two-handled knife with one or more thick, crescent-shaped blades used to chopped and mince herbs and vegetables.

Micronutrients—the nutrients needed only in small amounts: vitamins and minerals.

Microorganisms—single-celled organisms as well as tiny plants and animals that can be seen only through a microscope.

Microwave cooking—a heating method that uses radiation generated by a special oven to penetrate the food. It agitates water molecules, creating friction and heat; this energy then spreads throughout the food by conduction (and by convection in liquids).

Mignonette— a small cut or medallion of meat.

Milk-fed veal—also known as formula-fed veal, it is the meat of calves fed only a nutrient-rich liquid and kept tethered in pens; this meat is whiter and more mildly flavored than that of free-range calves.

Milling—the process by which grain is ground into flour or meal.

Mince—to cut a food item into very small pieces.

Mineral—inorganic micronutrients necessary for regulating body functions and proper bone and teeth structures.

Mirepoix—(meer-pwa) a mixture of coarsely chopped onions, carrots and celery used to flavor stocks, stews and other foods; generally, a mixture of 50% onions, 25% carrots and 25% celery, by weight, is used.

Mise en place—(meez on plahs) (Fr. for putting in place) refers to the preparation and assembly of all necessary ingredients and equipment.

Mix—to combine ingredients in such a way that they are evenly dispersed throughout the mixture.

Moist-heat cooking methods—cooking methods, principally simmering, poaching, boiling and steaming, that use water or steam to transfer heat through convection; moist-heat cooking methods are used to emphasize the natural flavors of foods.

Molding—the process of shaping foods, particularly grains and vegetables bound by sauces, into attractive, hard-edged shapes by using metal rings, circular cutters or other forms.

Molds—(1) algaelike fungi that form long filaments or strands; for the most part, molds affect only food appearance and taste; (2) containers used for shaping foods.

Mollusks—shellfish characterized by a soft, unsegmented body, no internal skeleton and a hard outer shell.

Monounsaturated fats—see **Unsaturated fats**.

Monter au beurre—(mohn-tay ah burr) to finish a sauce by swirling or whisking in butter (raw or compound) until it is melted; used to give sauces shine, flavor and richness.

Mortar and pestle—a hard bowl (the mortar) in which foods such as spices are ground or pounded into a powder with a club-shaped tool (the pestle).

Mother sauces—(Fr. *sauce mère*), see **Leading sauces**.

Mousse—(moose) a soft, creamy food, either sweet or savory, lightened by adding whipped cream, beaten egg whites or both.

Mousseline—(moose-uh-leen) (1) a delicately flavored forcemeat based on white meat, fish or shellfish lightened with cream and egg whites; (2) a sauce or cream lightened by folding in whipped cream.

Muffin method—a mixing method used to make quick bread batters; it involves combining liquid fat with other liquid ingredients before adding them to the dry ingredients.

Muscles—animal tissues consisting of bundles of cells or fibers that can contract and expand; they are the portions of a carcass usually consumed.

Mushrooms—members of a broad category of plants known as fungi; they are often used and served like vegetables.

Mutton—the meat of sheep slaughtered after they reach the age of one year.

NAMP/IMPS—the Institutional Meat Purchasing Specifications (IMPS) published by the United States Department of Agriculture; the IMPS are illustrated and described in *The Meat Buyer's Guide* published by the National Association of Meat Purveyors (NAMP).

Nappe—(nap) (1) the consistency of a liquid, usually a sauce, that will coat the back of a spoon; (2) to coat a food with sauce.

National cuisine—the characteristic cuisine of a nation.

Nectar—the diluted, sweetened juice of peaches, apricots, guavas, black currants or other fruits, the juice of which would be too thick or too tart to drink straight.

Net cost—a food's total cost after subtracting the value of the trim and cutting loss.

Noisette—(nwah-zet) (1) a small, usually round, portion of meat cut from the rib or loin; (2) Fr. for hazelnut.

Noodles—flat strips of pasta-type dough that contains eggs; may be fresh or dried.

Nouvelle cuisine—(Fr. for new cooking) a mid-20th-century movement away from many classic cuisine principles and toward a lighter cuisine based on natural flavors, shortened cooking times and innovative combinations.

Nut—(1) the edible single-seed kernel of a fruit surrounded by a hard shell; (2) generally refers to any seed or fruit with an edible kernel in a hard shell.

Nutrients—the chemical substances found in food that nourish the body by promoting growth, facilitating body functions and providing energy; there are six categories of nutrients: proteins, carbohydrates, fats, water, minerals and vitamins.

Nutrition—the science that studies nutrients.

Oblique cuts—also known as roll cuts, small pieces of food, usually vegetables, with two angle-cut sides.

Offal—also called variety meats, edible entrails (for example, the heart, kidneys, liver, sweetbreads and tongue) and extremities (for example, oxtail and pig's feet) of an animal.

Oignon brûlée—(ohn-nawng brew-lay) (Fr. for burnt onion) charred onion halves; used to flavor and color stocks and sauces.

Oignon piqué—(ohn-nawng pee-kay) (Fr. for pricked onion) a bay leaf tacked with a clove to a peeled onion; used to flavor sauces and soups.

Oil—a type of fat that remains liquid at room temperature.

Organic farming—a method of farming that does not rely on synthetic pesticides, fungicides, herbicides or fertilizers.

Oven spring—the rapid rise of yeast goods in a hot oven, resulting from the production and expansion of trapped gases.

Paillarde—(pahy-lahrd) a scallop of meat pounded until thin; it is usually grilled.

Panada or **panade**—(1) something other than fat added to a forcemeat to enhance smoothness, aid emulsification or both; it is often béchamel, rice or crustless white bread soaked in milk; (2) a mixture for binding stuffings and dumplings, notably quenelles, often choux pastry, bread crumbs, frangipane, puréed potatoes or rice.

Pan-broiling—a dry-heat cooking method that uses conduction to transfer heat to a food resting directly on a cooking surface; no fat is used and the food remains uncovered.

Pan-dressed—a market form for fish in which the viscera, gills and scales are removed and the fins and tail are trimmed.

Pan-frying—a dry-heat cooking method in which food is placed in a moderate amount of hot fat.

Pan gravy—a sauce made by deglazing pan drippings from roast meat or poultry

and combining them with a roux or other starch and stock.

Papillote, en—(awn poppy-yote) a cooking method in which food is wrapped in paper or foil and then heated so that the food steams in its own moisture.

Parboiling—partially cooking a food in a boiling or simmering liquid; similar to blanching but the cooking time is longer.

Parchment (paper)—heat-resistant paper used throughout the kitchen for tasks such as lining baking pans, wrapping foods to be cooked en papillote and covering foods during shallow poaching.

Parcooking—partially cooking a food by any cooking method.

Paring knife—a short knife used for detail work, especially cutting fruits and vegetables; it has a rigid blade approximately 2–4 inches long.

Parstock or par—the amount of stock necessary to cover operating needs between deliveries.

Pasta—(1) an unleavened paste or dough made from wheat flour (often semolina), water and eggs; the dough can be colored and flavored with a wide variety of herbs, spices or other ingredients and cut or extruded into a wide variety of shapes and sizes; it can be fresh or dried and is boiled for service; (2) general term for any macaroni product or egg noodle.

Pasteurization—the process of heating a liquid to a prescribed temperature for a specific period of time in order to destroy pathogenic bacteria.

Pastillage—a paste made of sugar, cornstarch and gelatin; it may be cut or molded into decorative shapes.

Pastry cream—also known as crème patissière, a stirred custard made with egg yolks, sugar and milk and thickened with starch; used for pastry and pie fillings.

Pâte—(paht) Fr. for dough.

Pâté—(pah-tay) traditionally, a fine savory meat filling wrapped in pastry, baked and served hot or cold as opposed to a terrine, which was a coarsely ground and highly seasoned meat mixture baked in an earthenware mold and served cold; today the words *pâté* and *terrine* are generally used interchangeably.

Pâte à choux—(paht ah shoe) see **Éclair paste**.

Pâte au pâté—(paht ah pah-tay) a specially formulated pastry dough used for wrapping pâté when making pâté en croûte.

Pâte brisée—(paht bree-zay) a dough that produces a very flaky baked product containing little or no sugar; flaky dough is used for prebaked pie shells or pie top crusts; mealy dough is a less flaky product used for custard, cream or fruit pie crusts.

Pâté en croute—(pah-tay awn croot) a pâté baked in pastry dough such as pâte au pâté.

Pâte feuilletée—(paht fuh-yuh-tay) also known as puff pastry, it is a rolled-in dough used for pastries, cookies and savory products, it produces a rich and buttery but not sweet baked product with hundreds of light, flaky layers.

Pâte sucrée—(paht sew-kra) a dough containing sugar that produces a very rich, crisp (not flaky) baked product; also known as sweet dough, it is used for tart shells.

Pathogen—any organism that causes disease; usually refers to bacteria.

Patissier—(pah-tees-sir-yair) a pastry chef, the person responsible for all baked items, including breads, pastries and desserts.

Paupiette—(po-pee-et) thin slices of meat, poultry or fish spread with a savory stuffing and rolled, then braised or poached.

Paysanne—(pahy-sahn) foods cut into flat squares of 1/2 inch × 1/2 inch × 1/4 inch (1.2 centimeters × 1.2 centimeters × 6 millimeters).

Pearling—a milling process in which all or part of the hull, bran and germ are removed from the grain.

Pectin—a gelatinlike carbohydrate obtained from certain fruits, used to thicken jams and jellies.

Persillade—(payr-se-yad) (1) a food served with or containing parsley; (2) a mixture of bread crumbs, parsley and garlic used to coat meats, usually lamb.

pH—a symbol for the level of acidity or alkalinity of a solution; expressed on a scale of 0 to 14.0; 7.0 is considered neutral or balanced acid/alkaline. The lower the pH value, the more acidic the substance.

Phyllo—(fee-low) pastry dough made

with very thin sheets of a flour and water mixture; several sheets are often layered with melted butter and used in sweet or savory preparations.

Physical hazards—a danger to the safety of food caused by particles such as chips, metal shavings, bits of wood or other foreign matter.

Picked—refers to the crab or lobster meat removed from the shell with a fine, needle-like tool called a pick.

Pigment—any substance that gives color to an item.

Pilaf—a cooking method for grains in which the grains are lightly sautéed in hot fat and then a hot liquid is added; the mixture is simmered without stirring until the liquid is absorbed.

Poaching—a moist-heat cooking method that uses convection to transfer heat from a hot (approximately 160–180°F [71–82°C]) liquid to the food submerged in it.

Polyunsaturated fats—See **Unsaturated fats**.

Pomes—members of the Rosaceae family, they are tree fruits with a thin skin and firm flesh surrounding a central core containing many small seeds (called pips or carpels); include apples, pears and quince.

Pork—the meat of hogs usually slaughtered under the age of one year.

Posterior—at or toward the rear of an object or place; opposite of anterior.

Potentially hazardous foods—foods on which bacteria thrive.

Poultry—the collective term for domesticated birds bred for eating; they include chickens, ducks, geese, guineas, pigeons and turkeys.

Preserve—(1) a fruit gel that contains large pieces or whole fruits; (2) to extend the shelf life of a food by subjecting it to a process such as irradiation, canning, vacuum-packing, drying or freezing and/or by adding preservatives.

Primal cuts—the primary divisions of muscle, bone and connective tissue produced by the initial butchering of the carcass; primals are further broken down into smaller, more manageable cuts.

Prime cost—the combination of food costs and direct labor.

Prix fixe—(pree feks) (Fr. for fixed price) refers to a menu offering a complete meal for a set price, also known as table d'hôte.

Professional cooking—a system of cooking based upon a knowledge of and appreciation for ingredients and procedures.

Profiterole—(pro-feet-uh-roll) small round pastry made from éclair paste filled with a savory filling and served as an hors d'oeuvre or filled with ice cream and served as a dessert.

Proofing—the rise given shaped yeast products just prior to baking.

Proteins—a group of compounds composed of oxygen, hydrogen, carbon and nitrogen atoms necessary for manufacturing, maintaining and repairing body tissues and as an alternative source of energy (4 calories per gram); protein chains are constructed of various combinations of amino acids.

Puff pastry—see **Pâte feuilletée**.

Pulled sugar—a doughlike mixture of sucrose, glucose and tartaric acid that can be colored and shaped by hand.

Pulses—dried seeds from a variety of legumes.

Pumpernickel—(1) coarsely ground rye flour; (2) bread made with this flour.

Purée—(pur-ray) (1) to process food to achieve a smooth pulp; (2) food that is processed by mashing, straining or fine chopping to achieve a smooth pulp.

Purée soup—a soup usually made from starchy vegetables or legumes; after the main ingredient is simmered in a liquid, the mixture, or a portion of it, is puréed.

Putrefactives—bacteria that spoil food without rendering it unfit for human consumption.

Quenelle—(cuh-nell) a small, dumpling-shaped portion of a mousseline forcemeat poached in an appropriately flavored stock; it is shaped by using two spoons.

Quiche—a savory tart or pie consisting of a custard baked in a pastry shell with a variety of flavorings and garnishes.

Quick bread—a bread, including loaves and muffins, leavened by chemical leaveners or steam rather than yeast.

Radiation cooking—a heating process that does not require physical contact between the heat source and the food being cooked; instead, energy is transferred by waves of heat or light striking the food. Two kinds of radiant heat used in the kitchen are infrared and microwave.

Raft—formed during the clarification process from the clearmeat and impurities from the stock; it rises to the top of the simmering stock and releases additional flavors.

Ragout—(rah-goo) (1) traditionally, a well-seasoned, rich stew containing meat, vegetables and wine; (2) any stewed mixture.

Ramekin—a small, ovenproof dish, usually ceramic.

Rancidity—a chemical change in fats caused by exposure to air, light or heat that results in objectionable flavors and odors.

Recipe—a set of written instructions for producing a specific food or beverage; also known as a formula.

Recommended Dietary Allowance (RDA)—a standard for the daily intake of various nutrients established by the National Food and Nutrition Board.

Recovery time—the length of time it takes hot fat to return to the desired cooking temperature after food is submerged in it.

Reduce—to cook a liquid mixture, often a sauce, until its quantity decreases because of evaporation; typically done to concentrate flavors and thicken liquids.

Refreshing—submerging a food in cold water to quickly cool it and prevent further cooking, also known as shocking; usually used for vegetables.

Regional cuisine—a set of recipes based on local ingredients, traditions and practices; within a larger geographical, political, cultural or social unit, regional cuisines are often variations of each other that blend together to create a national cuisine.

Relishes—cooked or pickled sauces usually made with vegetables or fruits and often used as a condiment.

Remouillage—(Fr. for rewetting) a stock produced by reusing the bones from another stock.

Render—(1) to melt and clarify fat; (2) to cook meats in order to remove the fat.

Ricer—a sieve-like utensil with small holes through which soft food is forced; it produces particles about the size of a grain of rice.

Rich doughs—yeast doughs such as those used for brioche and some multi-grain breads that contain a significant amount of sugar and fat.

Rillette—(ree-yet) meat or poultry slowly cooked, mashed and preserved in its own fat and served cold and usually spread on toast.

Ripe—(1) fully grown and developed fruit; the fruit's flavor, texture and appearance are at their peak and the fruit is ready to eat; (2) an unpleasant odor indicating that a food, especially meat, poultry, fish or shellfish, may be past its prime.

Risotto—(re-zot-toe) (1) a cooking method for grains in which the grains are lightly sautéed in butter and then a liquid is gradually added; the mixture is simmered with near-constant stirring until the still-firm grains merge with the cooking liquid; (2) a Northern Italian rice dish prepared this way.

Roasting—a dry-heat cooking method that heats food by surrounding it with hot, dry air in a closed environment or on a spit over an open fire; similar to baking, the term roasting is usually applied to meats, poultry, game and vegetables.

Roe—(roh) fish eggs.

Roll cuts—see **Oblique cuts**.

Rolled-in dough—a dough in which a fat is incorporated in many layers by using a rolling and folding procedure; it is used for flaky baked goods such as croissants, puff pastry and danish.

Rondeau—(ron-doe) a shallow, wide, straight-sided pot with two loop handles.

Rondelles—(ron-dells) or rounds, disk-shaped slices of cylindrical vegetables or fruits.

Rotisserie—cooking equipment that slowly rotates meat or other foods in front of a heating element.

Roulade—(roo-lahd) (1) a slice of meat, poultry or fish rolled around a stuffing; (2) a filled and rolled spongecake.

Round fish—fish with round, oval or compressed bodies that swim in a vertical position and have eyes on both sides of their heads; includes salmon, swordfish and cod.

Rounding—the process of shaping dough into smooth, round balls; used to stretch the outside layer of gluten into a smooth coating.

Roux—(roo) a cooked mixture of equal parts flour and fat, by weight, used as a thickener for sauces and other dishes; cooking the flour in fat coats the starch granules with the fat and prevents them from lumping together or forming lumps when introduced into a liquid.

Royal icing—also known as decorator's icing, an uncooked mixture of confectioner's sugar and egg whites that becomes hard and brittle when dry; used for making intricate cake decorations.

Russian service—restaurant service in which the entree, vegetables and starches are served from a platter onto the diner's plate by a waiter.

Sabayon—(sa-by-on) also known as zabaglione, a foamy, stirred custard sauce made by whisking eggs, sugar and wine over low heat.

Sachet d'épices or **sachet**—(sah-shay day-pea-say) (Fr. for bag of spices) aromatic ingredients tied in a cheesecloth bag and used to flavor stocks and other foods; a standard sachet contains parsley stems, cracked peppercorns, dried thyme, bay leaf, cloves and, optionally, garlic.

Salad—a single food or a mix of different foods accompanied or bound by a dressing.

Salad dressing—a sauce for a salad; most are based on a vinaigrette, mayonnaise or other emulsified product.

Salad greens—a variety of leafy vegetables that are usually eaten raw.

Salamander—a small broiler used primarily for browning or glazing the tops of foods.

Salsa—(sahl-sah) (Sp. for sauce) (1) generally, a cold chunky mixture of fresh herbs, spices, fruits and/or vegetables used as a sauce for meat, poultry, fish or shellfish; (2) in Italian usage, a general term for pasta sauces.

Salt curing—the process of surrounding a food with salt or a mixture of salt, sugar, nitrite-based curing salt, herbs and spices; salt curing dehydrates the food, inhibits bacterial growth and adds flavor.

Sanitation—the creation and maintenance of conditions that will prevent food contamination or food-borne illness.

Sanitize—to reduce pathogenic organisms to safe levels, usually with heat or chemical disinfectants.

Sashimi—(sah-shee-mee) raw fish eaten without rice; usually served as the first course of a Japanese meal.

Saturated fats—fats found mainly in animal products and tropical oils; they are usually solid at room temperature. The body has more difficulty breaking down saturated fats than either monounsaturated or polyunsaturated fats.

Sauce—generally, a thickened liquid used to flavor and enhance other foods.

Sausage—a seasoned forcemeat usually stuffed into a casing; a sausage can be fresh, smoked and cooked, dried or hard.

Sautéing—(saw-tay-ing) a dry-heat cooking method that uses conduction to transfer heat from a hot pan to food with the aid of a small amount of hot fat; cooking is usually done quickly over high temperatures.

Sauteuse—(saw-toose) the basic sauté pan with sloping sides and a single long handle.

Sautoir—(saw-twahr) a sauté pan with straight sides and a single long handle.

Savory—(1) spiced or seasoned, as opposed to sweet, foods; (2) (savoury) a highly seasoned last course of a traditional English dinner.

Scald—to heat a liquid, usually milk, to just below the boiling point.

Scallop—(Fr. escalope) a thin, boneless slice of meat.

Score—to cut shallow gashes across the surface of a food before cooking.

Scoville Heat Units—a subjective rating for measuring a chile's heat; the sweet bell pepper usually rates 0, the tabasco rates from 30,000 to 50,000 and the habañera rates from 100,000 to 300,000 units.

Seafood—an inconsistently used term encompassing some or all of the following: saltwater fish, freshwater fish, saltwater shellfish, freshwater shellfish, other edible marine life.

Sear—to brown food quickly over high heat; usually done as a preparatory step for combination cooking methods.

Season—(1) traditionally, to enhance flavor by adding salt; (2) more commonly, to enhance flavor by adding salt and/or pepper as well as herbs and spices; (3) to mature and bring a food (usually beef or game) to a proper condition by aging or special preparation; (4) to prepare a pot, pan or other cooking surface to prevent sticking.

Seasoning—traditionally, an item added to enhance the natural flavors of a food without dramatically changing its taste; salt is the most common seasoning although all herbs and spices are often referred to as seasonings.

Semi à la carte—a menu on which some foods (usually appetizers and desserts) and beverages are priced and ordered separately, while the entree is accompanied by and priced to include other dishes such as a salad, starch or vegetable.

Semifreddi—(seh-mee-frayd-dee) also known as still-frozen desserts, made with frozen mousse, custard or cream into which large amounts of whipped cream or meringue are folded in order to incorporate air; layers of spongecake and/or fruits may be added for flavor and texture; they include frozen soufflés, marquis, mousses and neapolitans.

Semolina—see **Durum**.

Sfoglia—(sfo-glee-ah) a thin, flat sheet of pasta dough that can be cut into ribbons, circles, squares or other shapes.

Shallow poaching—a moist-heat cooking method that combines poaching and steaming; the food (usually fish) is placed on a vegetable bed and partially covered with a liquid (cuisson) and simmered.

Shellfish—aquatic invertebrates with shells or carapaces.

Sherbet—a frozen mixture of fruit juice or fruit purée that contains milk and/or egg yolks for creaminess.

Shocking—see **Refreshing**.

Shortening—(1) a white, tasteless, solid fat formulated for baking or deep-frying; (2) any fat used in baking to tenderize the product by shortening gluten strands.

Shred—to cut into thin but irregular strips.

Shuck—(1) a shell, pod or husk; (2) to remove the edible portion of a food (e.g., clam meat, pea and ear of corn) from its shell, pod or husk.

Side Masking—the technique of coating only the sides of a cake with garnish.

Sift—(1) to shake a dry, powdered substance through a sieve or sifter to remove lumps and incorporate air; (2) to mix together powdery substances by sifting.

Silverskin—the tough connective tissue that surrounds certain muscles; see **Elastin**.

Simmering—(1) a moist-heat cooking method that uses convection to transfer heat from a hot (approximately 185–205°F [85–96°C]) liquid to the food submerged in it; (2) maintaining the temperature of a liquid just below the boiling point.

Skim—to remove fat and impurities from the surface of a liquid during cooking.

Slice—to cut an item into relatively broad, thin pieces.

Slurry—a mixture of raw starch and cold liquid used for thickening.

Small sauces—also known as compound sauces, made by adding one or more ingredients to a leading sauce; they are grouped together into families based on their leading sauce. Some small sauces have a variety of uses; others are traditional accompaniments for specific foods.

Smoke point—the temperature at which a fat begins to break down and emit smoke.

Smoking—any of several methods for preserving and flavoring foods by exposing them to smoke, includes cold smoking (in which the foods are not fully cooked) and hot smoking (in which the foods are cooked).

Solid pack—canned fruits or vegetables with little or no water added.

Sorbet—(sore-bay) a frozen mixture of fruit juice or fruit purée; similar to sherbet but without milk products.

Soufflé—(soo-flay) either a sweet or savory fluffy dish made with a custard base lightened with whipped egg whites and then baked; the whipped egg whites cause the dish to puff when baked.

Sous-chef—(soo-shef) a cook who supervises food production and who reports to the executive chef; he is second in command of a kitchen.

Specifications or **specs**—standard requirements to be followed in procuring items from suppliers.

Spices—any of a group of strongly flavored or aromatic portions of plants (other than leaves) used as flavorings, condiments or aromatics.

Springform pan—a circular baking pan with a separate bottom and a side wall held together with a clamp which is released to free the baked product.

Spring lamb—the meat of sheep slaughtered before they have fed on grass or grains.

Spun sugar—a decoration made by flicking dark caramelized sugar rapidly over a dowel to create long, fine, hairlike threads.

Squab—the class of young pigeon used in food service operations.

Staling—also known as starch retrogradation, a change in the distribution and location of water molecules within baked products; stale products are firmer, drier and more crumbly than fresh baked goods.

Standard breading procedure—the procedure for coating foods with crumbs or meal by passing the food through flour, then an egg wash and then the crumbs; it gives foods a relatively thick, crisp coating when deep-fried or pan-fried.

Standardized recipe—a recipe producing a known quality and quantity of food for a specific operation.

Staples—(1) certain foods regularly used throughout the kitchen; (2) certain foods, usually starches, that help form the basis for a regional or national cuisine and are principal components in the diet.

Starch—(1) complex carbohydrates from plants that are edible and either digestible or indigestible (fiber); (2) a rice, grain, pasta or potato accompaniment to a meal.

Starch retrogradation—see **Staling**.

Starchy potatoes—see **Mealy potatoes**.

Static menu—a menu offering patrons the same foods every day.

Station chef—the cook in charge of a particular department in a kitchen.

Steak—(1) a cross-section slice of a round fish with a small section of the bone attached; (2) a cut of meat, either with or without the bone.

Steamer—(1) a set of stacked pots with perforations in the bottom of each pot, they fit over a larger pot filled with boiling or simmering water and are used to steam foods; (2) a perforated insert made of metal or bamboo placed in a pot and used to steam foods; (3) a type of soft-shell clam from the East Coast; (4) a piece of gas or electric equipment in which foods are steamed in a sealed chamber.

Steaming—a moist-heat cooking method in which heat is transferred from steam to the food being cooked by direct contact; the food to be steamed is placed in a basket or rack above a boiling liquid in a covered pan.

Steel—a tool, usually made of steel, used to hone or straighten knife blades.

Steep—to soak a food in a hot liquid in order to extract its flavor or impurities or to soften its texture.

Steers—male cattle castrated prior to maturity and principally raised for beef.

Sterilize—to destroy all living microorganisms.

Stewing—a combination cooking method similar to braising but generally involving smaller pieces of meat that are first blanched or browned, then cooked in a small amount of liquid which is served as a sauce.

Stir-frying—a dry-heat cooking method similar to sautéing in which foods are cooked over very high heat using little fat while stirring constantly and briskly; often done in a wok.

Stirring—a mixing method in which ingredients are gently mixed until blended using a spoon, whisk or rubber spatula.

Stock—(Fr. fond) a clear, unthickened liquid flavored by soluble substances extracted from meat, poultry or fish and their bones as well as from a mirepoix, other vegetables and seasonings.

Stone fruits—members of the genus Prunus and also known as drupes, they are tree or shrub fruits with a thin skin, soft flesh and one woody stone or pit; include apricots, cherries, nectarines, peaches and plums.

Straight dough method—a mixing method for yeast breads in which all ingredients are simply combined and mixed.

Strain—to pour foods through a sieve, mesh strainer or cheesecloth to separate or remove the liquid component.

Streusel—(stroo-zel) a crumbly mixture of fat, flour, sugar and sometimes nuts and spices; used to top baked goods.

Subcutaneous fat—also known as exterior fat; the fat layer between the hide and muscles.

Submersion poaching—a poaching method in which the food is completely covered with the poaching liquid.

Subprimal cuts—the basic cuts produced from each primal.

Sucrose—the chemical name for refined or table sugar, it is refined from the raw sugars found in the large tropical grass called sugar cane and the root of the sugar beet; it is available as white or brown granules, molasses or powdered sugar.

Sugar—a carbohydrate that provides the body with energy and gives a sweet taste to foods.

Sugar syrups—either simple syrups (thin mixtures of sugar and water) or cooked syrups (melted sugar cooked until it reaches a specific temperature).

Suprême—(su-prem) (1) a sauce made by adding cream to a velouté made from chicken stock; it is used to make several compound sauces of the velouté family; (2) a boneless, skinless chicken breast with the first wing segment attached.

Sushi—(szu-she) cooked or raw fish or shellfish rolled in or served on seasoned rice.

Sweating—cooking a food (typically vegetables) in a small amount of fat, usually covered, over low heat without browning until the food softens and releases moisture; sweating allows the food to release its flavor more quickly when cooked with other foods.

Sweetbreads—the thymus glands of a calf or lamb.

Sweet dough—see **Pâte sucrée**.

Syrup—sugar that is dissolved in liquid, usually water, and often flavored with spices or citrus zest.

Syrup pack—cans of fruits with a light, medium or heavy syrup added.

Table d'hôte—(tab-bluh dote) see **Prix fixe**.

Tang—the portion of a knife's blade that extends inside the handle.

Taproots—more commonly referred to as roots, includes edible single roots that extend deep into the ground to provide the above-ground plant with nutrients.

Tart—a sweet or savory filling in a baked crust made in a shallow, straight-sided pan without a top crust.

Tartlet—a small, single-serving tart.

Temperature danger zone—the broad range of temperatures between 40° and 140°F (4–60°C) at which bacteria multiply rapidly.

Tempering—(1) heating gently and gradually; (2) refers to the process of

slowly adding a hot liquid to eggs or other foods to raise their temperature without causing them to curdle; (3) refers to a process for melting chocolate.

Terrine—(1) traditionally, a loaf of coarse forcemeat cooked in a covered earthenware mold and without a crust; today, the word is used interchangeably with pâté; (2) the mold used to cook such items, usually a rectangle or oval shape and made of ceramic.

Thickening agents—ingredients used to thicken sauces, include starches (flour, cornstarch and arrowroot), gelatin and liaisons.

Timbale—(tim-bull) (1) a small pail-shaped mold used to shape foods; (2) a preparation made in such a mold.

Tisanes—(teh-zahns) beverages made from herbal infusions that do not contain any tea.

Tomato sauce—a leading sauce made from tomatoes, vegetables, seasonings and white stock; it may or may not be thickened with roux.

Toque—(toke) the tall white hat worn by chefs.

Torte—in Central and Eastern European usage, refers to a rich cake in which all or part of the flour is replaced with finely chopped nuts or bread crumbs.

Tossed salad—a salad prepared by placing the greens, garnishes and salad dressing is a large bowl and tossing to combine.

Tourner—(toor-nay) (Fr. for to turn), to cut foods, usually vegetables, into football-shaped pieces with seven equal sides and blunt ends.

Toxins—byproducts of living bacteria that can cause illness if consumed in sufficient quantities.

Tranche—(tranch) an angled slice cut from fish fillets.

Trim loss—the amount of a food item removed when preparing it for consumption.

Tripe—the edible lining of a cow's stomach.

Truffles—(1) flavorful tubers that grow near the roots of oak or beech trees; (2) rich chocolate candies made with ganache.

Truss—to tie poultry with butcher's twine into a compact shape for cooking.

Tube pan—a deep round baking pan with a hollow tube in the center.

Tuber—the fleshy root, stem or rhizome of a plant from which a new plant will grow; some, such as potatoes, are eaten as vegetables.

Tunneling—the holes that may form in baked goods as the result of overmixing.

Unit cost or **price**—the price paid to acquire one specified unit.

Univalves—single-shelled mollusks with a single muscular foot, such as abalone.

Unsaturated fat—fats that are normally liquid (oils) at room temperature; they may be monounsaturated (from plants such as olives and avocados) or polyunsaturated (from grains and seeds such as corn, soybeans and safflower as well as from fish).

Vanilla custard sauce—also known as crème anglaise, a stirred custard made with egg yolks, sugar and milk or half-and-half and flavored with vanilla; served with or used in dessert preparations.

Vanillin—(1) whitish crystals of vanilla flavor that often develop on vanilla beans during storage; (2) synthetic vanilla flavoring.

Variety—the result of breeding plants of the same species that have different qualities or characteristics; the new plant often combines features from both parents.

Variety meats—see **Offal**.

Veal—the meat of calves under the age of nine months.

Vegetable—refers to any herbaceous plant (one with little or no woody tissue) that can be partially or wholly eaten; vegetables can be classified as cabbages, fruit-vegetables, gourds and squashes, greens, mushrooms and truffles, onions, pods and seeds, roots and tubers, and stalks.

Velouté—(veh-loo-tay) a leading sauce made by thickening a white stock (either fish, veal or chicken) with roux.

Venison—meat from any member of the deer family including elk, moose, reindeer, red-tailed deer, white-tailed deer and mule deer; it is typically a lean, dark red meat with a mild aroma.

Vent—(1) to allow circulation or escape of a liquid or gas; (2) to cool a pot of hot liquid by setting the pot on blocks in a cold water bath and allowing cold water to circulate around it.

Vinaigrette—(vin-nay-greht) a temporary emulsion of oil and vinegar (usually three parts oil to one part vinegar) seasoned with herbs, salt and pepper; used as a salad dressing or sauce.

Vinegar—a thin, sour liquid used as a preservative, cooking ingredient and cleaning solution.

Viruses—the smallest known form of life; they invade the living cells of a host and take over those cells' genetic material, causing the cells to produce more viruses; some viruses can enter a host through the ingestion of food contaminated with those viruses.

Viscera—internal organs.

Vitamins—compounds present in foods in very small quantities; they do not provide energy but are essential for regulating body functions.

Vol-au-vent—(vul-oh-van) a large, deep puff pastry shell often filled with a savory mixture for a main course.

Volume—the space occupied by a substance; volume measurements are commonly expressed as liters, teaspoons, tablespoons, cups, pints and gallons.

Wash—a glaze applied to dough before baking; a commonly used wash is made with whole egg and water.

Water bath—see **Bain marie**.

Water pack—canned fruits with water or fruit juice added.

Waxy potatoes—those with a low starch content and thin skin; they are best for boiling.

Weight—the mass or heaviness of a substance; weight measurements are commonly expressed as grams, ounces and pounds.

Wheel—(1) a large boneless piece of fish (such as swordfish or tuna) from which steaks are cut, also known as a center cut; (2) a cylindrical-shaped cheese.

Whetstone—a dense, grained stone used to sharpen or hone a knife blade.

Whipping—a mixing method in which foods are vigorously beaten in order to incorporate air; a whisk or an electric mixer with its whip attachment is used.

White stew—see **Fricassee** and **Blanquette**.

White stock—a light-colored stock made from chicken, veal, beef or fish bones simmered in water with vegetables and seasonings.

Whitewash—a thin mixture or slurry of flour and cold water used like cornstarch for thickening.

Wine—an alcoholic beverage made from the fermented juice of grapes; may be sparkling (effervescent) or still (noneffervescent) or fortified with additional alcohol.

Work section—see **Work station**.

Work station—a work area in the kitchen dedicated to a particular task, such as broiling or salad making; work stations using the same or similar equipment for related tasks are grouped together into work sections.

Yeasts—microscopic fungi whose metabolic processes are responsible for fermentation; they are used for leavening bread and in cheese, beer, and wine making.

Yield—(1) the total amount of a food item created or remaining after trimming or fabrication; (2) the total amount of a product made from a specific recipe.

Yield factor or **percentage**—the ratio of the edible portion to the amount purchased.

Yield grades—a grading program for meat that measures the amount of usable meat on a carcass.

Zest—the thin, colored part of a citrus peel.

Zushi—(zhoo-she) the seasoned rice used for sushi.

RECIPE INDEX

Ahi tuna, seared with lavender and pepper with whole-grain mustard sauce, salad of, 690
Albufera Sauce, 208
Allemande Sauce, 207
Almond Cream (Frangipane), 807, 846
Almonds, candied, 851
Angel food cake, chocolate, 866
Antelope, braised, in sour cream, 425–26
Apple-Cranberry Pie, 819
Apple Fritters, 558–59
Apple Horseradish Sauce, 226
Apple(s):
    apple sauce, 734
    baked, 707–8
    pancakes, 956
✦ Applesauce Brownies, 899
Apple tart:
    French, 842
    with vanilla ice cream, 844–45
Apricot Filling for Danish Pastry, 807
Apricot Sauce, 972–73
Artichoke(s):
    fennel ratatouille, 341
    frittata, 953–54
    and spinach dip, 982
    stuffed with Italian sausage, 610
    wedges, 435
✦ Asian Chicken Salad, 693
Asparagus:
    stir-fried, with shiitake mushrooms, 595
    and tomato salad, with fresh mozzarella, 680
Aspic-Jelly-Coated Chilled Mousse, 522
Aunt Ruthie's Pot Roast, 283
Aurora Sauce, 208
Avocado, and shrimp omelet, 941

Bagna Cauda, 980
Baked Apples, 707–8
Baked Beans, 611
Baked Butternut Squash, 594

Baked Meringue, 850
Baked Potatoes, 622
Baked Ziti with Fresh Tomato Sauce, 656
Banana Brioche French Toast, 958–59
Banana Fritters, 732–33
Bananas Foster, 732
Barbecue Sauce, 225
Basic Cream Pie, 817–18
Basil Butter, 218
Basil Vinaigrette, 646
Beans, baked, 611
Bean salad, tricolor, 534–35
Béarnaise Sauce, 215–16
Béchamel, 205
    small sauces, 205–6
Beef:
    Bourguignon, 304
    broth, 232
    Chateaubriand, 299
    Chili con Carne, 304–5
    consommé, 235
    Entrecôtes Bordelaise, 301
    Hearty Vegetable Beef Soup, 233
    Hungarian Goulash, 303
    London broil, marinated, 298
    meatloaf, home-style, 299
    Minute Steak Dijonaise, 300
    New England Boiled Dinner, 280
    Oxtail Ragout, 305
    Pepper Steak, 301–2
    short ribs of, braised, 303
    Stroganoff, 300–301
    Swiss Steak, 302
    T-Bone Steak, 298
    Tournedos Rossini, 300
Beef Bourguignon, 304
Beef Stroganoff, 300–301
Beer-Battered Onion Rings, 557
Beets, Harvard, 608
Bercy Sauce, 207
Berries, fresh, gratin of, with creme fraiche, 730–31
Berry Compote, 734
Berry tart, fresh, 843
Beurre blanc, 217
Chipotle, 503

citrus, 493
soy, 488
Biscuits, country, 767
Black bass:
    broiled, with herb butter and sautéed leeks, 466–67
    steamed, with Sansho pepper, 492
✦ Black bean soup, southwestern style, 255
Blackberry Cobbler, 841
Blanquette of Lamb, 345–46
Blintzes, 947–49
    cheese, 957–58
Blueberry Muffins, 768–69
Blueberry Pie Filling, 820
✦ Blue cheese dressing, low-fat, 686–87
Blue corn:
    muffins, 776
    and shrimp tamales, 990
Blue Crab Cakes with Fresh Salsa, 471–72
Boar, mustard-roasted loin of, with pan gravy, 431
Boiled Lobster, 479
Bolognese sauce, 653
    spinach and ricotta lasagna with, 657
Bordelaise Sauce, 210–11
Bouillabaisse, seafood, 252–53
Bourbon Baked Ham, 361
Bourbon Sauce, 924
Braised Antelope in Sour Cream, 425–26
Braised Celery with Basil, 601–2
Braised Chicken with Apple Cider and Cashew Butter, 409
Braised Cipolline Onions, 645
Braised Eel with Raisins, 490
Braised Rabbit with Cavatelli Pasta, 430–31
Braised Red Cabbage with Apples and Wine, 613
Braised Rhubarb, 733
Braised Romaine Lettuce, 614
Braised Short Ribs of Beef, 303
Bran muffins, basic, 774
Breaded Veal Cutlets, 278

Bread Pudding with Bourbon Sauce, 923–24
Breads, *See* Yeast breads; Quick breads
Breadsticks, 799
Brioche, 803–4
    raisin, 804
    vegetable terrine in, 535–36
Broccoli:
    almondine, 600
    cream of, soup, 237
Broiled Grapefruit, 722
Broiled Tomato, 606
Broth(s):
    beef, 232
    cappelletti in, 654–55
    celery, thyme-scented, 645
    chicken, 248–49
    soba noodles in, 655
Brownies:
    ✦ applesauce, 899
    continental, 898
    fudge:
        with ingredient substitutes, 47
        traditional, 47
Brown Rice Pilaf with Pine Nuts, 649
Brussels Sprouts in Pecan Butter, 597–98
Bûche de Noël, 896
Buckwheat Blini, 977–78
Buckwheat Crepes with Sausage and Apple Stuffing, 957
✦ Buffalo steak, grilled, 432
Bulgur Pilaf, 634–35
Buttermilk Pancakes, 946–47
Butternut squash, baked, 594
Butterscotch Sauce, 931

Caesar Dressing, 684–85
Cakes:
    brownies, applesauce, 899
    brownies, continental, 898
    Bûche de Noël, 896
    Carrot Cake with Cream Cheese Frosting, 891
    Chocolate Angel Food Cake, 866
    Chocolate Flourless Cake, 898
    coconut cake, fresh, 893–94

✦ *indicates a healthful recipe.*

SUBJECT INDEX